Israel's Scriptures in Early Christian Writings

Israel's Scriptures
in Early Christian Writings

The Use of the Old Testament in the New

Edited by

Matthias Henze *and* David Lincicum

William B. Eerdmans Publishing Company
Grand Rapids, Michigan

Wm. B. Eerdmans Publishing Co.
4035 Park East Court SE, Grand Rapids, Michigan 49546
www.eerdmans.com

© 2023 Matthias Henze and David Lincicum
All rights reserved
Published 2023
Printed in the United States of America

29 28 27 26 25 24 23   1 2 3 4 5 6 7

ISBN 978-0-8028-7444-3

Library of Congress Cataloging-in-Publication Data

A catalog record for this book is available from the Library of Congress.

Contents

	Acknowledgments	xi
	List of Abbreviations	xiii
	Introduction *Matthias Henze and David Lincicum*	1

PART 1: CONTEXTS — 21

1. What Were the "Scriptures" in the Time of Jesus? — 23
   Edmon L. Gallagher

2. Israel's Scriptures in the Hebrew Bible — 47
   Marc Zvi Brettler

3. Israel's Greek Scriptures and Their Collection in the Septuagint — 81
   Martin Karrer

4. Israel's Scriptures in Early Jewish Literature — 109
   Grant Macaskill

5. Israel's Scriptures in the Dead Sea Scrolls — 138
   Susan Docherty

CONTENTS

6. Israel's Scriptures in Philo and the Alexandrian Jewish Tradition — 162
   Michael B. Cover

7. Israel's Scriptures in Josephus — 188
   Michael Avioz

PART 2: ISRAEL'S SCRIPTURES IN THE NEW TESTAMENT — 207

A. THE GOSPELS AND ACTS — 209

8. Israel's Scriptures in Matthew — 209
   Matthias Konradt

9. Israel's Scriptures in Mark — 236
   Elizabeth Evans Shively

10. Israel's Scriptures in Luke — 263
    Martin Bauspiess

11. Israel's Scriptures in John — 285
    Jaime Clark-Soles

12. Israel's Scriptures in Acts — 315
    Dietrich Rusam

B. THE APOSTLE PAUL — 337

13. Israel's Scriptures in Romans — 337
    Jens Schröter

14. Israel's Scriptures in 1 and 2 Corinthians — 363
    Katja Kujanpää

15. Israel's Scriptures in Galatians — 388
    A. Andrew Das

Contents

16.	Israel's Scriptures in Ephesians and Colossians Paul Foster	407
17.	Israel's Scriptures in Philippians and Philemon Angela Standhartinger	429
18.	Israel's Scriptures in 1 and 2 Thessalonians Todd D. Still	441
19.	Israel's Scriptures in the Pastoral Epistles Gerd Häfner	453
	C. Hebrews and the Catholic Letters	467
20.	Israel's Scriptures in Hebrews Gabriella Gelardini	467
21.	Israel's Scriptures in James Karl-Wilhelm Niebuhr	500
22.	Israel's Scriptures in 1 Peter, Jude, and 2 Peter Jörg Frey	523
23.	Israel's Scriptures in the Johannine Letters George Parsenios	544
	D. The Book of Revelation	555
24.	Israel's Scriptures in the Revelation of John Ian K. Boxall	555

PART 3: THEMES AND TOPICS FROM ISRAEL'S SCRIPTURES IN THE NEW TESTAMENT — 577

25.	God Archie T. Wright	579

CONTENTS

26.	Messiah *J. Thomas Hewitt*	598
27.	Holy Spirit *John R. Levison*	622
28.	Covenant *Richard J. Bautch*	645
29.	Law *Claudia Setzer*	674
30.	Wisdom *Benjamin Wold*	699
31.	Liturgy and Prayer *Rodney A. Werline*	721
32.	Eschatology *Garrick V. Allen*	743

PART 4: TRACING ISRAEL'S SCRIPTURES — 765

33.	Deuteronomy in the New Testament *Gert J. Steyn*	767
34.	Isaiah in the New Testament *Benjamin E. Reynolds*	795
35.	The Psalms in the New Testament *Matthias Henze*	816
36.	Daniel in the New Testament *Alexandria Frisch and Jennie Grillo*	860

37.	Figures of Ancient Israel in the New Testament *Valérie Nicolet*	880

PART 5: ISRAEL'S SCRIPTURES IN EARLY CHRISTIANITY OUTSIDE THE NEW TESTAMENT — 929

38.	Israel's Scriptures in the Apocryphal Gospels *Tobias Nicklas*	931
39.	Israel's Scriptures in the Apocryphal Apocalypses *Michael Karl-Heinz Sommer*	952
40.	Israel's Scriptures in the *Adversus Judaeos* Literature *David Lincicum*	977
41.	Israel's Scriptures in Marcion and the Critical Tradition *Dieter T. Roth*	1000
42.	Israel's Scriptures in Early Christian Pictorial Art *Robin M. Jensen*	1023
	List of Contributors	1055
	Index of Modern Authors	1059
	Index of Subjects	1072
	Index of Scripture and Other Ancient Sources	1083

Acknowledgments

In February 2016, as the idea for this book gradually took shape, a group of friends and colleagues met for a workshop at Rice University to discuss the project. The workshop participants were M. Eugene Boring of Brite Divinity School, James D. Ernest of Eerdmans Publishing, J. Ross Wagner of Duke Divinity School, Jason Ford, graduate student at Rice (now graduated), and the two editors. We would like to thank our colleagues for sharing their considerable expertise with us. The keen editorial suggestions they made, and our productive discussions at the Rice workshop, have made this a better volume.

We are especially indebted to M. Eugene Boring. Gene was instrumental in conceiving of and developing this project in its early stages. He pushed us to think big and to approach Israel's Scriptures in the New Testament from more than one angle. This volume is one more record of the generosity of Gene's spirit and the depth of his knowledge of New Testament scholarship.

Matthias Henze wishes to thank Rice's School of Humanities and Dean Kathleen Canning for the sabbatical during the academic year 2021–2022 that allowed him to devote large periods of time to do his part in bringing the book manuscript over the finish line. During the spring semester 2022 he was the Martin Hengel Fellow at the University of Tübingen, Germany. Matthias is most grateful to the Philipp-Melanchthon-Stiftung, and to Volker Henning Drecoll in particular, for providing such a wonderful environment in the Tübinger Stift.

David Lincicum expresses warm thanks to Mike Rea and the Center for the Philosophy of Religion for a fellowship in the academic year 2020–2021 that enabled some of the work on this volume to be completed; to Tim Matovina, the Department of Theology, and the College of Arts and Letters at Notre Dame for supporting the leave; to the Provost's Office for a Rapid Recovery and Resilience Grant that helped to fund editorial assistance by the excellent Jen Guo, who undertook the work with intelligent precision and care; and to Julia, Naomi, Edie, Margaret, and Theo for their support, forbearance, and distraction.

The essays in this volume were written during the COVID-19 pandemic, when contributors had only sporadic access to their libraries. We owe all of them a warm thanks for their contributions under trying circumstances.

Special thanks are due to Michael Thomson, formerly acquisitions and development editor at Eerdmans, who discussed this book with us when it was only an idea. Many thanks to James Spinti, our copyeditor. Raleigh Heth kindly undertook the prodigious work of creating the indexes with his customary insight. We are especially grateful to the editorial team at Eerdmans, who saw this project through with characteristic professionalism: James Ernest, a big supporter of this project from its very beginning; Trevor Thompson, our trusted point person over the years; Amy Kent, who helped with the logistics; Kristine Nelson, who designed the cover; and Jenny Hoffman, our senior project editor. We are most grateful.

Matthias Henze
David Lincicum

Abbreviations

AB	Anchor (Yale) Bible
ABIG	Arbeiten zur Bibel und ihrer Geschichte
Abr.	Ambrose, *De Abraham*; Philo, *De Abrahamo*
ABR	*Australian Biblical Review*
ABRL	Anchor (Yale) Bible Reference Library
AcBib	Academia Biblica
Adv. Jud.	Tertullian, *Adversus Judaeos*
Ag. Ap.	Josephus, *Against Apion*
AGJU	Arbeiten zur Geschichte des antiken Judentums und des Urchristentums/Ancient Judaism and Early Christianity
AIL	Ancient Israel and Its Literature
AJSR	*Association for Jewish Studies Review*
AKG	Arbeiten zur Kirchengeschichte
Akh.	Akhmim Codex
ALD	Aramaic Levi Document
Alex.	Lucian, *Alexander* (*Pseudomantis*)
ALGHJ	Arbeiten zur Literatur und Geschichte des hellenistischen Judentums
AnBib	Analecta Biblica
AncSoc	*Ancient Society*
ANF	*The Ante-Nicene Fathers: Translations of the Writings of the Fathers Down to A.D. 325*. Edited by Alexander Roberts and James Donaldson. 10 vols. 1885–1887.
ANRW	*Aufstieg und Niedergang der römischen Welt: Geschichte und Kultur Roms im Spiegel der neueren Forschung*. Part 2, *Principat*. Edited by Hildegard Temporini and Wolfgang Haase. Berlin: de Gruyter, 1972–.

ABBREVIATIONS

Ant.	Josephus, *Jewish Antiquities*
ANTF	Arbeiten zur neutestamentlichen Textforschung
AOAT	Alter Orient und Altes Testament
aor.	aorist
APF	*Archiv für Papyrusforschung*
Apoc. Ab.	Apocalypse of Abraham
Apoc. Dan.	Apocalypse of Daniel
Apoc. Pet.	Apocalypse of Peter
Apoc. Sedr.	Apocalypse of Sedrach
Apoc. Zeph.	Apocalypse of Zephaniah
Apol.	Aristides, *Apologia*; Justin, *Apologia*; Plato, *Apologia*; Tertullian, *Apologeticus*
Apos. Con.	Apostolic Constitutions and Canons
AS	*Aramaic Studies*
Ascen. Isa.	Ascension of Isaiah
ASEs	*Annali di storia dell'esegesi*
ASNU	Acta Seminarii Neotestamentici Upsaliensis
ATANT	Abhandlungen zur Theologie des Alten und Neuen Testaments
Aug	*Augustinianum*
AUSS	*Andrews University Seminary Studies*
Autol.	Theophilus of Antioch, *Apologia ad Autolycum*
b.	Babylonian
B. Bat.	Baba Batra
B. Meṣ.	Baba Meṣiʿa
B. Qam.	Baba Qamma
Bapt.	Basil of Caesarea, *De baptismo*; Tertullian, *De baptismo*
BARIS	British Archaeological Reports International Series
Barn.	Barnabas
BASP	*Bulletin of the American Society of Papyrologists*
BBB	Bonner biblische Beiträge
BBR	*Bulletin for Biblical Research*
BCR	Biblioteca di cultura religiosa
BEATAJ	Beiträge zur Erforschung des Alten Testaments und des antiken Judentums
BECNT	Baker Exegetical Commentary on the New Testament
Ber.	Berakot
BETL	Bibliotheca Ephemeridum Theologicarum Lovaniensium
BEvT	Beiträge zur evangelischen Theologie
BHQ	Biblia Hebraica Quinta
BHT	Beiträge zur historischen Theologie

Abbreviations

Bib	*Biblica*
Bib. hist.	Diodorus Siculus, *Bibliotheca historica*
BibInt	*Biblical Interpretation*
BibInt	Biblical Interpretation Series
BibSem	The Biblical Seminar
BJS	Brown Judaic Studies
BKAT	Biblischer Kommentar, Altes Testament
BMSEC	Baylor-Mohr Siebeck Studies in Early Christianity
BN.B	Biblische Notizen Beiheft
BNTC	Black's New Testament Commentaries
BPat	Biblioteca Patristica
BR	*Biblical Research*
BSac	*Biblia Sacra*
BThSt	Biblisch-theologische Studien
BTS	Biblical Tools and Studies
BWANT	Beitrage zur Wissenschaft vom Alten und Neuen Testament
ByzF	*Byzantinische Forschungen*
BZ	*Biblische Zeitschrift*
BZABR	Beihefte zur Zeitschrift für altorientalische und biblische Rechtsgeschichte
BZAW	Beihefte zur Zeitschrift für die alttestamentliche Wissenschaft
BZNW	Beihefte zur Zeitschrift für die neutestamentliche Wissenschaft
c.	century
Carm.	Paulinus of Nola, *Carmina*
Carn. Chr.	Tertullian, *De carne Christi*
Catech.	Augustine, *De cathechizandis rudibus*
CBET	Contributions to Biblical Exegesis and Theology
CBiPa	Cahiers de Biblia Patristica
CBQ	*Catholic Biblical Quarterly*
CBQMS	Catholic Biblical Quarterly Monograph Series
CBR	*Currents in Biblical Research*
CCSC	Catholic Commentary on Sacred Scripture
CCSL	Corpus Christianorum: Series Latina
CEAug	Collection des études Augustiniennes, Série antiquité
Cels.	Origen, *Against Celsus*
CEJL	Commentaries on Early Jewish Literature
ch(s).	chapter(s)
Cher.	Philo, *De cherubim*
CIJ	*Corpus Inscriptionum Judaicarum*. Edited by Jean-Baptiste Frey. 2 vols. Rome: Pontifical Biblical Institute, 1936–1952.

ABBREVIATIONS

Civ.	Augustine, *De civitate Dei*
CJT	*Canadian Journal of Theology*
Comm. Dan.	Hippolytus, *Commentarium in Danielem*
Comm. Matt.	Origen, *Commentarium in evangelium Matthaei*
ConBNT	Coniectanea Neotestamentica or Coniectanea Biblica: New Testament Series
ConC	Concordia Commentary
Conf.	Philo, *De confusione linguarum*
Congr.	Philo, *De congressu eruditionis gratia*
Contempl.	Philo, *De vita contemplativa*
CRINT	Compendia Rerum Iudaicarum ad Novum Testamentum
CrStHB	Critical Studies in the Hebrew Bible
CSHJ	Chicago Studies in the History of Judaism
CTB	Calwer Taschenbibliothek
DCLS	Deuterocanonical and Cognate Literature Studies
Decal.	Philo, *De decalogo*
Decr.	Athanasius, *De decretis*
Dem.	Irenaeus, *Demonstration of the Apostolic Preaching*
Dem. ev.	Eusebius, *Demonstratio evangelica*
Det.	Philo, *Quod deterius potiori insidari soleat*
Deus	Philo, *Quod Deus sit immutabilis*
Dial.	Justin, *Dialogus cum Tryphone*
Diem lum.	Gregory of Nyssa, *Diem luminum*
Did.	Didache
Diog.	Diognetus
DJD	Discoveries in the Judaean Desert
DOP	*Dumbarton Oak Papers*
DSD	*Dead Sea Discoveries*
DSI	De Septuaginta Investigationes
DSS	Dead Sea Scrolls
Ebib	*Etudes bibliques*
Ebr.	Philo, *De ebrietate*
EBR	*Encyclopedia of the Bible and Its Reception*. Edited by Constance M. Furey et al. Berlin: de Gruyter, 2009–.
EC	*Early Christianity*
ECDSS	Eerdmans Commentaries on the Dead Sea Scrolls
ECF	Early Church Fathers
ECL	Early Christianity and Its Literature
ECM	Editio Critica Maior
EHLL	Khan, Geoffrey, ed. *Encyclopedia of Hebrew Language and Linguistics*. 4 vols. Leiden: Brill, 2013.

Abbreviations

EHS.T	Europäische Hochschulschriften Reihe 23, Theologie
EJL	Early Judaism and Its Literature
EJT	*European Journal of Theology*
EKKNT	Evangelisch-Katholischer Kommentar zum Neuen Testament
Eleem.	Cyprian, *De opere et eleemosynis*
Enarrat. Ps.	Augustine, *Enarrationes in P*salmos
EncJud	*Encyclopedia Judaica*. Edited by Michael Berenbaum and Fred Skolnik. 2nd ed. 22 vols. Detroit: Macmillan Reference USA, 2007.
Ep.	Augustine, *Epistulae*; Cyprian, *Epistulae*; Seneca, *Epistulae morales*
Epist.	Jerome, *Epistulae*
ET	English translation
EuroJTh	*European Journal of Theology*
EvQ	*Evangelical Quarterly*
EWNT	*Exegetisches Wörterbuch zum Neuen Testament*. Edited by Horst Robert Balz et al. 3 vols. Stuttgart: Kohlhammer, 1978–1983.
FAT	Forschungen zum Alten Testament
FB	Forschung zur Bibel
FC	Fathers of the Church
fem.	feminine
FHJA	Holladay, Carl R. *Fragments from Hellenistic Jewish Authors*. 4 vols. SBLTT 20, 30, 39, 40. Pseudepigrapha 10, 12, 13, 14. Chico, CA: Scholars Press, 1983–1996.
FJTC	Flavius Josephus: Translation and Commentary
frag(s).	fragment(s)
FRLANT	Forschungen zur Religion und Literatur des Alten und Neuen Testaments
FTS	Frankfurter theologische Studien
Fug.	Philo, *De fuga et inventione*
GCS	Die griechischen christlichen Schriftsteller der ersten [drei] Jahrhunderte
Gig.	Philo, *De gigantibus*
Giṭṭ.	Giṭṭin
Gk. Apoc. Ezra	Greek Apocalypse of Ezra
GLAE	Greek Life of Adam and Eve
Gos. Heb.	Gospel of the Hebrews
Gos. Pet.	Gospel of Peter
Gos. Thom.	Gospel of Thomas
GSTR	Giessener Schriften zur Theologie und Religionspädagogik
Haer.	Hippolytus, *Refutatio omnium haeresium* (*Philosophoumena*); Irenaeus, *Adversus haereses* (*Elenchos*)
HAT	Handbuch zum Alten Testament

HBS	History of Biblical Studies
HBT	*Horizons in Biblical Theology*
HCS	Hellenistic Culture and Society
HdO	Handbuch der Orientalistik
HDR	Harvard Dissertations in Religion
Heb.	Hebrew
HeBAI	*Hebrew Bible and Ancient Israel*
Hen	*Henoch*
Her.	Philo, *Quis rerum divinarum heres sit*
Herm. Mand.	Shepherd of Hermas, Mandate(s)
Hipp.	Euripides, *Hippolytus*
Hist.	Herodotus, *Histories*
Hist. eccl.	Eusebius, *Historia ecclesiastica*
HNT	Handbuch zum Neuen Testament
HSM	Harvard Semitic Monographs
HTB	Histoire due texte biblique. Lausanne, 1996–
HThKAT	Herders Theologischer Kommentar zum Alten Testament
HThKNT	Herders Theologischer Kommentar zum Neuen Testament
HTR	*Harvard Theological Review*
HTS	Harvard Theological Studies
HUCM	Monographs of the Hebrew Union College
HvTS	*Hervormde teologiese studies*
IBS	*Irish Biblical Studies*
ICC	International Critical Commentary
Idol.	Tertullian, *De idololatria*
IECOT	International Exegetical Commentary on the Old Testament
Ign. *Eph.*	Ignatius, *To the Ephesians*
IJO	Ameling, Walter, David Noy, Alexander Panayotov, and Hanswulf Bloedhorn, eds. *Inscriptiones Judaicae Orientis*. 3 vols. TSAJ 99, 101–102. Tübingen: Mohr Siebeck, 2004.
Il.	Homer, *Iliad*
inscr.	inscription
Int	*Interpretation*
ISBL	Indiana Studies in Biblical Literature
JAJSup	Journal of Ancient Judaism Supplements
JAOS	*Journal of the American Oriental Society*
JBL	*Journal of Biblical Literature*
JBR	*Journal of Bible and Religion*
JCPS	Jewish and Christian Perspectives Series
JECS	*Journal of Early Christians Studies*

Abbreviations

JETS	*Journal of the Evangelical Theological Society*
JGRChJ	*Journal of Greco-Roman Christianity and Judaism*
JJMJS	*Journal of the Jesus Movement in Its Jewish Setting*
JJS	*Journal of Jewish Studies*
JMT	*Journal of Moral Theology*
Jo. Hier.	Jerome, *Adversus Joannem Hierosolymitanum liber*
Jos. Asen.	Joseph and Aseneth
JPTSup	Journal of Pentecostal Theology Supplement
JQR	*Jewish Quarterly Review*
JQRSup	Jewish Quarterly Review Supplement
JRASup	Journal of Roman Archaeology Supplement
JRS	*Journal of Roman Studies*
JSHJ	*Journal for the Study of the Historical Jesus*
JSHRZ	Jüdische Schriften aus hellenistisch-römischer Zeit
JSJ	*Journal for the Study of Judaism in the Persian, Hellenistic, and Roman Periods*
JSJSup	Supplements to the Journal for the Study of Judaism
JSNT	*Journal for the Study of the New Testament*
JSNTSup	Journal for the Study of the New Testament Supplement Series
JSP	*Journal for the Study of the Pseudepigrapha*
JSPL	*Journal for the Study of Paul and His Letters*
JSPSup	Journal for the Study of the Pseudepigrapha Supplement Series
JSS	*Journal of Semitic Studies*
JSSSup	Journal of Semitic Studies Supplement Series
JTI	*Journal of Theological Interpretation*
JTISup	Journal of Theological Interpretation Supplement Series
JTS	*Journal of Theological Studies*
J.W.	Josephus, *Jewish War*
KAV	Kommentar zu den Apostolischen Vätern
KD	Kerygma und Dogma
KEK	Kritisch-exegetischer Kommentar über das Neue Testament (Meyer-Kommentar)
KJV	King James Version
LAB	Pseudo-Philo, Liber Antiquitatum Biblicarum
Lad. Jac.	Ladder of Jacob
LAE	Life of Adam and Eve
Lam. Rab.	Lamentations Rabbah
Laps.	Cyprian, *De lapsis*
Laz.	John Chrysostom, *De Lazaro*
LCL	Loeb Classical Library

ABBREVIATIONS

LEC	Library of Early Christianity
Leg.	Philo, *Legum allegoriae*
Let. Aris.	Letter of Aristeas
LHBOTS	Library of Hebrew Bible/Old Testament Studies
Lib. ed.	Plutarch, *De liberis educandis*
Life	Josephus, *The Life*
Liv. Pro.	Lives of the Prophets
LNTS	Library of New Testament Studies
LSJ	Liddell, Henry George, Robert Scott, and Henry Stuart Jones. *A Greek-English Lexicon*. 9th ed. with revised supplement. Oxford: Clarendon, 1996.
LSTS	The Library of Second Temple Studies
LThPM	Louvain Theological and Pastoral Monographs
LTQ	*Lexington Theological Quarterly*
LXX	Septuagint
LXX^{Gö}	Göttingen Septuagint
LXX^{OG}	Old Greek
LXX^{Ra}	Rahlfs, Alfred, ed., *Septuaginta: Id est Vetus Testamentum Graece Iuxta LXX Interpretes*. Stuttgart: Privilegierte Württembergische Bibelanstalt, 1935.
LXX$^{Ra\text{-}Ha}$	Rahlfs, Alfred, and Robert Hanhart, eds. *Septuaginta: Id est Vetus Testmentum graece iuxta LXX interpretes*. 4th ed. Stuttgart: Deutsches Bibelgesellschaft, 2006.
m.	Mishnah
Mak.	Makkot
Marc.	Tertullian, *Adversus Marcionem*
Mart. Ascen. Isa.	Martyrdom and Ascension of Isaiah
MdB	*Le Monde de la Bible*
MEAH	*Miscelánea de estudios arabes y hebraicos*
Meg.	Megillah
Mek.	Mekilta
MEOL	Mededelingen en Verhandelingen van het Vooraziatisch Egyptisch Genootschap Ex oriente lux
Migr.	Philo, *De migration Abrahami*
MJSt	Münsteraner judaistische Studien
MJTh	Marburger Jahrbuch Theologie
MNTC	Moffatt New Testament Commentary
Mos.	Philo, *De vita Mosis*
MS(S)	manuscript(s)
MSJ	*The Master's Seminary Journal*

Abbreviations

MT	Masoretic Text
Mut.	Philo, *De mutatione nominum*
Myst.	Ambrose, *De mysteriis*; Cyril of Jerusalem, *Mystagogic Catecheses*
NA²⁸	Aland, Barbara, Kurt Aland, J. Karavidopoulos, Carlo M. Martini, Bruce M. Metzger, and Holger Strutwolf. *Novum Testamentum Graece*. 28th rev. ed. Stuttgart: Deutsche Bibelgesellschaft, 2012.
NASB	New American Standard Bible
Nat.	Pliny the Elder, *Naturalis historia*
NCBC	New Cambridge Bible Commentary
Neot	*Neotestamentica*
NETS	*A New English Translation of the Septuagint: And the Other Greek Translations Traditionally Included under That Title*. Edited by Albert Pietersma and Benjamin G. Wright. New York: Oxford University Press, 2007.
NHC	Nag Hammadi Codices
NHS	Nag Hammadi Studies
NICNT	New International Commentary on the New Testament
NIDB	Sakenfeld, Katharine Doob, ed. *New Interpreter's Dictionary of the Bible*. 5 vols. Nashville: Abingdon, 2006–2009.
NIGTC	New International Greek Text Commentary
NovT	*Novum Testamentum*
NovTSup	Supplements to Novum Testamentum
NS	new series
NSBT	New Studies in Biblical Theology
NTD	Das Neue Testament Deutsch
NTL	New Testament Library
NTOA	Novum Testamentum et Orbis Antiquus
NTS	*New Testament Studies*
NTSI	New Testament and the Scriptures of Israel
NTTS	New Testament Tools and Studies
NTTSD	New Testament Tools, Studies, and Documents
OBO	Orbis Biblicus et Orientalis
OBS	Oxford Bible Series
OCD	*Oxford Classical Dictionary*. Edited by Simon Hornblower and Antony Spawforth. 3rd ed. Oxford: Clarendon, 1996.
Oct.	Minucius Felix, *Octavius*
OG	Old Greek version of the Hebrew Bible
OIP	Oriental Institute Publications
OLA	Orientalia Lovaniensia Analecta
Opif.	Philo, *De opificio mundi*

ÖTK	Ökumenischer Taschenbuchkommentar
OTL	Old Testament Library
OTP	*Old Testament Pseudepigrapha*. Edited by James H. Charlesworth. 2 vols. New York: Doubleday, 1983, 1985.
OTS	Old Testament Studies
P.Bodm.	Bodmer papyri
P.Oxy.	Oxyrhynchus papyri
P.Ryl.	Rylands papyri
Pan.	Epiphanius of Salamis, *Panarion*
PAPM	Les oeuvres de Philon d'Alexandrie
par.	parallel(s)
Parad.	Ambrose, *De paradiso*
Pasc.	Melito of Sardis, *Peri pascha*
Pat.	Tertullian, *De patientia*
PatMS	Patristic Monograph Series
PBTM	Paternoster Biblical and Theological Monographs
Pelag.	Jerome, *Adversus Pelagionos dialogi III*
per.	person
Pers	*Perspectives*
Pesaḥ.	Pesaḥim
Pesiq. Rab.	Pesiqta Rabbati
pf.	perfect
PFES	Publications of the Finnish Exegetical Society
Phil.	Polycarp, *Epistle to the Philippians*
pl.	plural
PL	Migne, Jacques-Paul, ed. Patrologia Latina. 217 vols. Paris, 1844–1855.
Plant.	Philo, *De plantatione*
PNTC	Pillar New Testament Commentary
Pol.	Aristotle, *Politica*
Post.	Philo, *De posteritate Caini*
Pr. Man.	Prayer of Manasseh
Praem.	Philo, *De praemiis et poenis*
Praep. ev.	Eusebius, *Praeparatio evangelica*
Praes.	Tertullian, *De praescriptione haereticorum*
Prax.	Tertullian, *Adversus Praxean*
pres.	present
Princ.	Origen, *De principiis (Peri archōn)*
Prom.	Aeschylus, *Prometheus vinctus*
Prot. Jas.	Protevangelium of James
Protep.	Clement of Alexandria, *Protepticus*

Abbreviations

PRSt	*Perspectives in Religious Studies*
PTA	Papyrologische Texte und Abhandlungen
PTS	Patristische Texte und Studien
PTSDSSP	Princeton Theological Seminary Dead Sea Scrolls Project
QG	Philo, *Quaestiones et solutiones in Genesin*
Qidd.	Qiddušin
Qu. hebr. Gen.	Jerome, *Questionum hebraicarum liber in Genesim*
Ques. Ezra	Questions of Ezra
Rab.	Rabbah (biblical book + Rabbah)
RB	*Revue biblique*
RBS	Resources for Biblical Study
rec(s).	recension(s)
Res.	Tertullian, *De resurrectione carnis*
ResQ	*Restoration Quarterly*
RevQ	*Revue de Qumrân*
RGRW	Religions in the Graeco-Roman World
RHPR	*Revue d'Histoire et de Philosophie Religieuses*
RHT	*Revue d'Histoire des Textes*
RTP	*Revue de théologie et de philosophie*
Šabb.	Šabbat
Sacr.	Ambrose, *De sacramentis*
Sanh.	Sanhedrin
SANT	Studien zum Alten und Neuen Testament
SAPERE	Scripta Antiquitatis Posterioris ad Ethicam REligionemque pertinentia
SBLMS	Society of Biblical Literature Monograph Series
SBLSBS	Society of Biblical Literature Sources for Biblical Studies
SBLStBL	Society of Biblical Literature Studies in Biblical Literature
SBLTT	Society of Biblical Literature Texts and Translations
SC	Sources chrétiennes
SCS	Septuagint and Cognate Studies
SDSS	Studies in the Dead Sea Scrolls and Related Literature
SECA	Studies in Early Christian Apocrypha
Serm.	Augustine, *Sermones*
sg.	singular
SHAW	Sitzungsberichte der Heidelberger Akademie der Wissenschaften
SHBC	Smyth & Helwys Bible Commentary
SHR	Studies in the History of Religions (supplements to *Numen*)
Sib. Or.	Sibylline Oracles
SJ	Studia Judaica
SJLA	Studies in Judaism in Late Antiquity

SJT	*Scottish Journal of Theology*
SKI	Studien zu Kirche und Israel
SKKNT	Stuttgarter kleiner Kommentar, Neues Testament
SMRT	Studies in Medieval and Reformation Traditions
Smyrn.	Ignatius of Antioch, *To the Smyrnaeans*
SNT	Studien zum Neuen Testament
SNTSMS	Society for New Testament Studies Monograph Series
SNTSU	*Studien zum Neuen Testament und seiner Umwelt*
Somn.	Philo, *De somniis*
SP	Samaritan Pentateuch
Spec.	Philo, *De specialibus legibus*
SPhilo	*Studia Philonica*
SPhiloA	*Studia Philonica Annual*
SPhiloM	Studia Philonica Monograph Series
Spir. Sanc.	Basil of Caesarea, *De Spiritu Sancto*
StBibLit	Studies in Biblical Literature (Lang)
STDJ	Studies on the Texts of the Desert of Judah
StPB	Studia Post-biblica
Strom.	Clement of Alexandria, *Stromata*
SubBi	Subsidia Biblica
Sukk.	Sukkah
Sull.	Plutarch, *Sulla*
SUNT	Studien zur Umwelt des Neuen Testaments
SVTG	Septuaginta: Vetus Testamentum Graecum Auctoritate Academiae Scientiarum Gottingensis editum
SVTP	Studia in Veteris Testamenti Pseudepigraphica
SymS	Symposium Series
Syr.	Syriac
T. Ab.	Testament of Abraham
T. Adam	Testament of Adam
T. Ash.	Testament of Asher
T. Benj.	Testament of Benjamin
T. Dan.	Testament of Dan
T. Gad	Testament of Gad
T. Iss.	Testament of Issachar
T. Job	Testament of Job
T. Jos.	Testament of Joseph
T. Jud.	Testament of Judah
T. Lev.	Testament of Levi
T. Mos.	Testament of Moses

Abbreviations

T. Naph.	Testament of Naphtali
T. Reub.	Testament of Reuben
T. Sim.	Testament of Simeon
T. Sol.	Testament of Solomon
T. Zeb.	Testament of Zebulun
Tanḥ.	Tanḥuna
TANZ	Texte und Arbeiten zum neutestamentlichen Zeitalter
TBN	Themes in Biblical Narrative
TCSt	Text-Critical Studies
TENTS	Texts and Editions for New Testament Study
Test.	Ps.-Gregory of Nyssa, *Testimonies against the Jews*
Text	*Textus*
Tg. Isa.	Targum Isaiah
Tg. Neb.	Targum of the Prophets
Tg. Neof.	Targum Neofiti
Tg. Ps.-J.	Targum Pseudo-Jonathan
Tg. Yer. I	Targum Yerušalmi I
THB	Textual History of the Bible
THBSup	Supplements to the Textual History of the Bible
Thf	*Theoforum*
THKNT	Theologischer Handkommentar zum Neuen Testament
TJ	*Trinity Journal* NS
Trall.	Ignatius, *To the Trallians*
TranseuSup	Supplements to Transeuphratène
TS	*Theological Studies*
TSAJ	Texte und Studien zum antiken Judentum/Texts and Studies in Ancient Judaism
TSMJ	Texts and Studies in Medieval and Early Modern Judaism
TUGAL	Texte und Untersuchungen zur Geschichte der altchristlichen Literatur
TynBul	*Tyndale Bulletin*
Unit. eccl.	Cyprian, *De catholicae ecclesiae unitate*
v(v).	verse(s)
Val.	Tertullian, *Adversus Valentinianos*
VC	*Vigiliae Christianae*
VCSup	Supplements to Vigiliae Christianae
VF	*Verkündigung und Forschung*
VIEG.B	Veröffentlichungen des Instituts für europäische Geschichte Mainz Beiheft
Vir. ill.	Jerome, *De viris illustribus*

ABBREVIATIONS

Virt.	Philo, *De virtutibus*
Vis. Paul	Vision of Paul
v.l.	variant reading(s)
VT	*Vetus Testamentum*
VTSup	Supplements to Vetus Testamentum
WBC	Word Biblical Commentary
WGRW	Writings of the Greco-Roman World
WMANT	Wissenschaftliche Monographien zum Alten und Neuen Testament
y.	Jerusalem
Yad.	Yadayim
ZABR	*Zeitschrift für Altorientalische und Biblische Rechtsgeschichte*
ZAC	*Zeitschrift für Antikes Christentum/Journal of Ancient Christianity*
ZNW	*Zeitschrift für die neutestamentliche Wissenschaft*
ZTK	*Zeitschrift für Theologie und Kirche*

Introduction

MATTHIAS HENZE AND DAVID LINCICUM

The Scriptures of Israel permeate nearly every page of the New Testament. The narratives, theological convictions, ethical instructions, liturgical responses, and hopes of those Scriptures together form the cultural encyclopedia necessary to understand what Jesus and his earliest followers did and thought. The books of Moses and the Prophets are the great predecessor texts that supply the fundamental orientation for many authors of the Second Temple period, including the adherents to the Jesus movement. We might even say that the authors of the New Testament are aware of their belatedness or their posteriority in regard to God's great salvific actions in the past, and so their writings bear a retrospective and, at times, recapitulative character. This is not to claim that there is nothing novel or surprising in the New Testament nor to deny the way in which its authors are thorough participants in Greco-Roman culture. But the Scriptures of Israel served as a crucial lens through which both that novelty and the surrounding culture were interpreted and engaged.

This book takes as the subject of its investigation the productive interaction of what later Christians will come to call the Old and New Testaments.[1] It is born of the conviction that those who penned the writings that came to compose the New Testament inherited strategies of scriptural interpretation from their Jewish predecessors and negotiated the lively discourses of contemporary

---

1. This language is clearly anachronistic for the first and most of the second century CE. The first unambiguous use of "Old Testament" and "New Testament" as titles of book collections comes in Clement of Alexandria (*Strom.* 1.44.3; 3.71.3; 4.134.4, etc.) and Tertullian (*Marc.* 4.1.1; *Prax.* 15.1, 31.1, etc.), though note also Melito *apud* Eusebius, *Hist. eccl.* 4.26.13–14; see Wolfram Kinzig, "Καινὴ διαθήκη: The Title of the New Testament in the Second and Third Centuries," *JTS* 45, no. 2 (1994): 519–44.

readers in the formation of their own approach. The study of Israel's Scriptures in the New Testament and closely related literature has received a great deal of attention over the past few decades, and we believe the time is ripe for a focused volume representing the *status quaestionis* while pressing the field toward new avenues of scholarship.

This collection gathers an impressive international cohort of authors, each a specialist in their field, to consider afresh old questions and to pose new ones. The New Testament's engagement with scriptural traditions has been intensively studied, and it is our hope that this book serves as an up-to-date, authoritative survey of both the phenomena of the primary sources and the state of scholarship about those sources. In this introductory chapter, we set the present volume in the context of other scholarly approaches to the field, underline the importance of Jewish scriptural interpretation for understanding what we see in the New Testament, specify our terminology for categorizing discrete engagements with Scripture, and offer a brief overview of the plan of the book.

Previous Study of Israel's Scriptures in the New Testament

Since at least the sixteenth century, scholars have devoted intense attention to the study and elucidation of the way in which the writers of the New Testament drew on the Jewish Scriptures, though the roots of such concern stretch back to at least the second century CE.[2] It was early recognized that many of the citations in the New Testament did not neatly align with the transmitted Hebrew text or with the standard Septuagintal text, and one pole of scholarly concern centered on the question of the accuracy of such citations. Another stream of inquiry took up comparative questions and asked about the extent to which the New Testament authors' interpretations could be paralleled in roughly contemporary Jewish literature. And a third major focus concerned the legitimacy of the

---

2. For significant early work, see, e.g., Joannes Drusius, *Τὰ Ἱερὰ Παράλληλα: Parallela Sacra, hoc est, locorum veteris Testamenti cum ijs, quae in novo citantur coniuncta commemoratio, Ebraice et Graece* (Franeker: Radaeud, 1588); Franciscus Junius, *Sacrorum Parallelorum libri tres*, 3rd ed. (London: Bishop, 1591); Louis Cappellus, *Critica Sacra, sive de variis quae in sacris veteris testamenti libris occurrunt lectionibus libri sex* (Paris: Cramoisy, 1650); Willem Surenhusius, ספר המשוה *sive Βίβλος καταλλαγῆς in quo secundum veterum Theologorum Hebraeorum Formulas allegandi, & Modos interpretandi conciliantur loca ex V. in N. T. allegate* (Amsterdam: Boom, 1713); Johann Gottlob Carpzov, *A Defence of the Hebrew Bible in Answer to the Charge of Corruption Brought against It by Mr. Whiston, in His "Essay towards Restoring the True Text of the Old Testament, &c." Wherein Mr. Whiston's Pretences Are Particularly Examined and Confuted*, trans. M. Marcus (London: Lintot, 1729); Henry Owen, *The Modes of Quotation Used by the Evangelical Writers Explained and Vindicated* (London: Nichols, 1789).

Introduction

interpretations: Were the authors of the New Testament drawing on the original intention of the scriptural authors or twisting the texts to their own ends?[3] These questions continued to be prosecuted in the nineteenth and early twentieth centuries.[4] Apologetic defenses of the New Testament authors' citation practices were mounted, but research increasingly turned toward textual and com-

---

3. For the framing of the history of research in terms of these questions, see David Lincicum, "Paul's Engagement with Deuteronomy: Snapshots and Signposts," *CBR* 7, no. 1 (2008): 37-67.

4. A selection of the most important works in the nineteenth and early twentieth centuries includes the following: Johann C. C. Döpke, *Hermeneutik der neutestamentlichen Schriftsteller* (Leipzig: Vogel, 1829); Samuel Davidson, *Sacred Hermeneutics Developed and Applied: Including a History of Biblical Interpretation from the Earliest of the Fathers to the Reformation* (Edinburgh: Clark, 1843), 334-515; F. August G. Tholuck, "The Use Made of the Old Testament in the New, and Especially in the Epistle to the Hebrews," in *A Commentary on the Epistle to the Hebrews*, trans. James Hamilton and J. E. Ryland, 2 vols. (Edinburgh: Clark, 1842), 2:181-245; Tholuck, "Citations of the Old Testament in the New," *BSac* 11 (1854): 568-616; Edward W. Grinfield, *Novum Testamentum Graecum, editio Hellenistica*, 2 vols. (London: Pickering, 1843), 2:1447-93; Grinfield, *Scholia Hellenistica in Novum Testamentum: Philone et Josepho patribus apostolicis aliisq. ecclesiæ antiquæ scriptoribus necnon libris apocryphis maxime deprompta* (London: Pickering, 1848), 859-944; Grinfield, *An Apology for the Septuagint, in Which Its Claims to Biblical and Canonical Authority Are Briefly Stated and Vindicated* (London: Pickering, 1850); Henry Gough, *The New Testament Quotations, Collated with the Scriptures of the Old Testament, in the Original Hebrew and the Version of the LXX; and with the Other Writings, Apocryphal, Talmudic, and Classical, Cited or Alleged So to Be; With Notes, and a Complete Index* (London: Walton & Maberly, 1855); Thomas H. Horne, *An Introduction to the Criticism of the Old Testament and to Biblical Interpretation; With an Analysis of the Books of the Old Testament and Apocrypha*, rev. and ed. John Ayre (London: Longman, Green, Longman, & Roberts, 1860), 113-208; David M. Turpie, *The Old Testament in the New: A Contribution to Biblical Criticism and Interpretation* (London: Williams & Norgate, 1868); Turpie, *The New Testament View of the Old: A Contribution to Biblical Introduction and Exegesis* (London: Hodder & Stoughton, 1872); Emil Friedrich Kautzsch, *De veteris testamenti locis a Paulo Apostolo allegatis* (Leipzig: Metzger & Wittig, 1869); Helen MacLachlan, *Notes on References and Quotations in the New Testament Scriptures from the Old Testament* (London: Blackwood, 1872); Eduard Böhl, *Forschungen nach einer Volksbibel zur Zeit Jesu und deren Zusammenhang mit der Septuaginta-Übersetzung* (Vienna: Braumüller, 1873); Böhl, *Die alttestamentlichen Citate im Neuen Testament* (Vienna: Braumüller, 1878); Crawford Howell Toy, *Quotations in the New Testament* (New York: Scribner's Sons, 1884); August Clemen, *Der Gebrauch des Alten Testamentes in den Neutestamentlichen Schriften* (Gütersloh: Bertelsmann, 1895); Hans A. Vollmer, *Die alttestamentlichen Citate bei Paulus: Textkritisch und biblisch-theologisch gewürdigt nebst einem Anhang ueber das Verhältnis des Apostels zu Philo* (Freiburg im Breisgau: Mohr, 1895); Franklin Johnson, *The Quotations of the New Testament from the Old Considered in the Light of General Literature* (Philadelphia: American Baptist Publication Society, 1896); Otto Michel, *Paulus und seine Bibel* (Gütersloh: Bertelsmann, 1929); Louis Venard, "Citations de l'Ancien Testament dans le Nouveau Testament," in *Supplément au Dictionnaire de la Bible*, ed. Louis Pirot (Paris: Letouzey et Ané, 1934), 2:23-51; Joseph Bonsirven, *Exégèse rabbinique et exégèse paulinienne* (Paris: Beauchesne et ses Fils, 1939).

parative study.⁵ Already there had been vast erudition employed to investigate the proximity of the New Testament's citations to the text of the Hebrew Bible, the Samaritan Pentateuch, the targumim, the rabbinic tradition, contemporary Hellenistic Jewish authors, or the Septuagintal pandects that were just coming to European attention in the seventeenth and eighteenth centuries. In the nineteenth century, the European colonial powers facilitated cultural expropriation of manuscripts or financed archaeological expeditions that led to further advances, such as Constantine Tischendorf's "discovery" of Codex Sinaiticus.⁶ Such gains led to the work of creating a critical edition of the various books of the Septuagint in the early twentieth century, the necessary precursor to close consideration of the textual character of the New Testament citations: the "Larger Cambridge Septuagint" by Alan England Brooke, Norman McLean, and Henry St. John Thackeray (1906–1940), and the Göttingen critical edition of the Septuagint (1931–). At the turn of the century, we also find efforts to comprehensively set forth the citations of Scripture in the New Testament in an analytical form.⁷

At the same time, scholarship made important strides in the study of early Jewish literature, with many texts of the so-called Pseudepigrapha edited and translated for the first time. Following on from the pioneering efforts of the bibliophile Johann Albert Fabricius and his *Codex Pseudepigraphus Veteris Testamenti* (1713–1714), scholarship, particularly in the latter half of the nineteenth century, intensified the publication and study of early Jewish texts.⁸ This research came to an important fruition in the major German and English collections: Emil Kautzsch's *Die Apokryphen und Pseudepigraphen des Alten Testaments* (1900) and R. H. Charles, *The Apocrypha and Pseudepigrapha of the Old Testament* (1913).⁹ These materials

---

5. E.g., Davidson, *Sacred Hermeneutics*; Turpie, *Old Testament in the New*; MacLachlan, *Notes on References and Quotations in the New Testament*.

6. On Tischendorf and Sinaiticus, see Christfried Böttrich, "Neue Dokumente zur Geschichte der 'Codex Sinaiticus,'" *EC* 1, no. 4 (2010): 605–19; Böttrich, *Der Jahrhundertfund: Entdeckung und Geschichte des Codex Sinaiticus* (Leipzig: Evangelische Verlagsanstalt, 2011); Böttrich, "Supplements to the Rediscovery of *Codex Sinaiticus* in the Nineteenth Century," *EC* 8, no. 3 (2017): 395–406.

7. Wilhelm Dittmar, *Vetus Testamentum in Novo: Die alttestamentlichen Parallelen des Neuen Testaments im Wortlaut der Urtexte und der Septuaginta zusammengestellt*, 2 vols. (Göttingen: Vandenhoeck & Ruprecht, 1899–1903) (this was partially redone by Hans Hübner in an unfinished project of the same name); Eugen Hühn, *Die alttestamentlichen Citate und Reminiscenzen im Neuen Testamente* (Freiburg im Breisgau: Mohr, 1900).

8. Fabricius, *Codex Pseudepigraphus Veteris Testamenti* (Hamburg: Felginer, 1713–1714).

9. Kautzsch, *Die Apokryphen und Pseudepigraphen des Alten Testaments*, 2 vols. (Tübingen: Mohr, 1900); Charles, *The Apocrypha and Pseudepigrapha of the Old Testament*, 2 vols. (Oxford: Clarendon, 1913). For details, see James Charlesworth, "A History of Pseudepigrapha Research: The Re-emerging Importance of the Pseudepigrapha," *ANRW* 19.1:56–88, esp. 56–60.

Introduction

supplied further impetus for the tasks of comparing the citation techniques and hermeneutics of the New Testament authors with their Jewish contemporaries.[10]

Developments in scholarship during the second half of the twentieth century fundamentally transformed each of these poles of inquiry. The discovery and publication of the Dead Sea Scrolls demonstrated more textual diversity than scholars had previously supposed as variant Hebrew texts of some portions of the Bible became known. Moreover, scholarship had long known of the phenomenon of later revisers of the Septuagint and the Greek versions associated with Aquila, Symmachus, and Theodotion that Origen had assembled in his Hexapla, but these had largely been thought to be second-century phenomena, too late to influence the textual basis, or *Vorlage*, of the New Testament authors.[11] With the discovery of the Greek Minor Prophets Scroll from Naḥal Ḥever (8ḤevXIIgr = Rahlfs 943), scholars now had a Hebraizing revision of the Septuagint—that is, the product of a reviser who has changed the Septuagintal text to make it more closely approximate the Hebrew—from the period contemporaneous with the earliest years of the Jesus movement.[12] A sense of the complicated state of the Hebrew and Greek texts of the Scriptures emerged, and scholars began to examine the New Testament's scriptural citations once again in light of this newfound awareness of textual plurality.[13]

The Dead Sea Scrolls also shed light on the types of reading strategies we witness in the New Testament texts. The discovery of the scrolls spurred a flurry of comparative studies and offered a window into another eschatologically oriented

---

10. Representative comparative studies include Döpke, *Hermeneutik der neutestamentlichen Schriftsteller*; Henry St. John Thackeray, *The Relation of St. Paul to Contemporary Jewish Thought* (New York: Macmillan, 1900); and Bonsirven, *Exégèse rabbinique et exégèse paulinienne*.

11. In addition to the so-called Quinta, Sexta, and Septima that were sometimes included; on the Hexapla, see Alison Salvesen, ed., *Origen's Hexapla and Fragments: Papers Presented at the Rich Seminar on the Hexapla, Oxford Centre for Hebrew and Jewish Studies, 25th July–3rd August, 1994*, TSAJ 58 (Tübingen: Mohr Siebeck, 1998); and Peter J. Gentry, "Origen's Hexapla," in *The Oxford Handbook of the Septuagint*, ed. Alison Salvesen and Timothy M. Law (Oxford: Oxford University Press, 2021), 553–71. For the versions generally, see Armin Lange and Emanuel Tov, eds., *The Hebrew Bible*, THB 1 (Leiden: Brill, 2016–2017).

12. Dominique Barthélemy, *Les devanciers d'Aquila*, VTSup 10 (Leiden: Brill, 1963); Emanuel Tov, Robert Kraft, and P. J. Parsons, *The Greek Minor Prophets Scroll from Naḥal Ḥever (8ḤevXIIgr)*, DJD 8 (Oxford: Clarendon, 1990).

13. For representative, excellent studies of the *Vorlagen* of New Testament quotations, see Dietrich-Alex Koch, *Die Schrift als Zeuge des Evangeliums: Untersuchungen zur Verwendung und zum Verständnis der Schrift bei Paulus*, BHT 69 (Tübingen: Mohr Siebeck, 1986); Maarten J. J. Menken, *Old Testament Quotations in the Fourth Gospel: Studies in Textual Form*, CBET 15 (Kampen: Kok Pharos, 1996); Menken, *Matthew's Bible: The Old Testament Text of the Evangelist*, BETL 173 (Leuven: Peeters, 2004); cf. also Timothy H. Lim, "Qumran Scholarship and the Study of the Old Testament in the New," *JSNT* 38, no. 1 (2015): 68–80.

movement intensely focused on scriptural activity. Krister Stendahl's *The School of St. Matthew* was one of the first studies to take advantage of the just-published material, but many others followed in its wake.[14] Some studies in the early years after the Qumran discoveries drew connections that seem, in retrospect, sensationalist or unlikely. But the succeeding decades have resulted in a broad renewal of the study of Second Temple Judaism in its own right and for its own sake, and this efflorescence of scholarship has resulted in a deeper understanding of the contours of the Jewish movements in which the early Jesus followers came of age. We have learned that the authors of the New Testament writings did not approach their ancestral Scriptures as virginal readers, but rather that they stood downstream in a long tradition of interpretation and counterinterpretation.

The impulse to attempt to grasp the use of the Scriptures on the authors' own terms, rather than imposing a modern standard of evaluation by which one might assess the validity of their stances, was fueled by the incisive study of Richard B. Hays, *Echoes of Scripture in the Letters of Paul*.[15] Hays was largely responsible for introducing New Testament scholarship to the analytic of intertextuality and so to the benefits of a more subtle emphasis on the productive quality of "echoes" or "allusions" to Scripture for understanding Paul's letters. In the aftermath of Hays's book, intertextual studies on the New Testament have proliferated.[16] While such studies have sometimes tended to be ahistorical in nature to a problematic degree, the general interest in engagements with Scripture that extend beyond explicit citation has proven salutary.

This is not to say that the concern to vindicate the rectitude of the New Testament writers' hermeneutical stance toward Scripture has disappeared. Debates surrounding this topic have often taken place under the question, Do the writers of the New Testament respect the original context of their citations? Closely allied with this has been the further question, Are modern methods of interpretation, including a concern for authorial intention, congruent with what we see in the New Testament invocations of Scripture? These debates seem at

---

14. Krister Stendahl, *The School of St. Matthew, and Its Use of the Old Testament*, ASNU 20 (Lund: Gleerup, 1954; 2nd ed., 1968).

15. Hays, *Echoes of Scripture in the Letters of Paul* (New Haven: Yale University Press, 1989); cf. also now his *Echoes of Scripture in the Gospels* (Waco, TX: Baylor University Press, 2016).

16. The reception and critique of Hays's concept of intertextuality has been regularly explored; see, e.g., Samuel Emadi, "Intertextuality in New Testament Scholarship: Significance, Criteria, and the Art of Intertextual Reading," *CBR* 14, no. 1 (2015): 8–23; David A. Shaw, "Converted Imaginations? The Reception of Richard Hays's Intertextual Method," *CBR* 11, no. 2 (2013): 234–45; David I. Yoon, "The Ideological Inception of Intertextuality and Its Dissonance in Current Biblical Studies," *CBR* 12, no. 1 (2013): 58–76. Note also part 3 in David Allen and Steve Smith, eds., *Methodology in the Use of the Old Testament in the New: Context and Criteria*, LNTS 579 (London: T&T Clark, 2019).

Introduction

times to be fueled by theological anxieties about what it might mean for a New Testament idea to be founded on shaky hermeneutical ground.[17] Unsurprisingly, much depends on what one means by disputed terms like "context."[18]

The past few decades have also seen progress in understanding a number of issues raised by the citation practices reflected in the New Testament. We have seen enlightening studies on the techniques of citation, including ways of abridging, modifying, or adapting source texts to a setting in the quoting composition.[19] Other scholarship has called attention to phenomena like composite citations, or "generic citations" in which an introductory formula is not followed by a particular source text.[20] Yet other studies have drawn on discussions of the rhetoric of quotation to analyze the rhetorical effects of the citations in the New Testament.[21]

Two major synthetic projects are also worth mentioning. Steve Moyise and Maarten J. J. Menken edited a series of volumes on Israel's Scriptures in the New Testament, in which they assembled contributors to examine, in turn, Psalms (2004), Isaiah (2005), Deuteronomy (2007), Minor Prophets (2009), and Genesis (2012) in the New Testament.[22] Each volume begins with an introductory survey of the respective book in Second Temple Judaism before proceeding to a corpus-by-corpus examination of the scriptural book's reception. A second project, G. K. Beale and D. A. Carson's edited volume, *Commentary on the New Testament Use of the Old Testament*, surveys, book by book, the New Testament authors' engagement with Israel's Scriptures in a running commentary.[23] The

---

17. Note the framing in G. K. Beale, ed., *The Right Doctrine from the Wrong Texts? Essays on the Use of the Old Testament in the New* (Grand Rapids: Baker, 1994).

18. See Arthur Keefer, "The Meaning and Place of Old Testament Context in OT/NT Methodology," in Allen and Smith, *Methodology in the Use of the Old Testament in the New*, 73–85.

19. See esp. Christopher D. Stanley, *Paul and the Language of Scripture: Citation Technique in the Pauline Epistles and Contemporary Literature*, SNTSMS 74 (Cambridge: Cambridge University Press, 1992), esp. 3–184.

20. For composite citations, see Sean A. Adams and Seth M. Ehorn, "What Is a Composite Citation?," in *Composite Citations in Antiquity*, vol. 1, *Jewish, Graeco-Roman and Early Christian Uses*, ed. Sean A. Adams and Seth M. Ehorn, LNTS 525 (London: Bloomsbury, 2016), 1–16. For generic citations, see Gregory R. Lanier, "'As It Is Written' . . . Where? Examining Generic Citations of Scripture in the New Testament," *JSNT* 43, no. 4 (2021): 570–604.

21. E.g., Meir Sternberg, "Proteus in Quotation-Land: Mimesis and the Forms of Reported Discourse," *Poetics Today* 3, no. 2 (1982): 107–56; Herbert Clark and Richard Gerrig, "Quotations as Demonstrations," *Language* 66, no. 4 (1990): 764–805; Christopher D. Stanley, *Arguing with Scripture: The Rhetoric of Quotations in the Letters of Paul* (London: T&T Clark, 2004), 1–97; Katja Kujanpää, "From Eloquence to Evading Responsibility: The Rhetorical Functions of Quotations in Paul's Argumentation," *JBL* 136, no. 1 (2017): 185–202.

22. The volumes appeared in the Library of New Testament Studies (London: T&T Clark, 2004–2012).

23. Beale and Carson, *Commentary on the New Testament Use of the Old Testament* (Grand

present volume attempts to combine the merits of both source-text and citing-text orientations while remaining thoroughly committed to a historical consideration of these scriptural engagements that roots them firmly in the context of Second Temple Judaism.

Early Christian Interpretation and Early Jewish Interpretation

Early Judaism forms the crucial milieu in which early Christian scriptural interpretation is forged.[24] The New Testament participates in and emerges from the interpretative discourse of contemporary Judaism. At one time it was customary for studies of "the Old Testament in the New" to thematize the putative differences between the New Testament and contemporary Jewish interpreters, often to the disadvantage of the latter, which were characterized as alternately fanciful, atomistic, allegorical, or otherwise implausible. But we have witnessed a flourishing in the study of Second Temple scriptural practices over the past few decades, fueled in part by the Qumran discoveries mentioned above, and this has helped us to rethink the nature of New Testament interpretation as well.[25]

This is a point the present volume labors to make at length, and in this introductory chapter we can do no more than mention a few examples. Many of the same books that are prominent in Second Temple interpretation are also important in the New Testament (e.g., Genesis, Deuteronomy, Psalms, and Isa-

---

Rapids: Baker Academic, 2007). For the strengths and limitations of the project, see the review by Maarten J. J. Menken in *NovT* 52, no. 2 (2010): 189-91.

24. Of course, the term "Christian" is anachronistic for the earliest communities (Paul never uses the term), but it usefully specifies the type of Judaism that comes to expression in the New Testament.

25. For a few major treatments of early Jewish interpretation with further bibliography, see, e.g., Matthias Henze, ed., *A Companion to Biblical Interpretation in Early Judaism* (Grand Rapids: Eerdmans, 2012); Henze, ed., *Biblical Interpretation at Qumran* (Grand Rapids: Eerdmans, 2005); Daniel K. Falk, *The Parabiblical Texts: Strategies for Extending the Scriptures among the Dead Sea Scrolls*, LSTS 63 (London: Bloomsbury, 2007); Louis H. Feldman, *Josephus's Interpretation of the Bible*, HCS 27 (Berkeley: University of California Press, 1998); Feldman, *Studies in Josephus' Rewritten Bible*, JSJSup 58 (Leiden: Brill, 1998); Adam Kamesar, "Biblical Interpretation in Philo," in *The Cambridge Companion to Philo*, ed. Adam Kamesar, Cambridge Companions to Philosophy (Cambridge: Cambridge University Press, 2009), 65-92; Peder Borgen, *Philo of Alexandria: An Exegete for His Time*, NovTSup 86 (Leiden: Brill, 1997); Valentin Nikiprowetzky, *Le commentaire de l'Écriture chez Philon de'Alexandrie: Son caractère et sa portée; Observations philologiques*, ALGHJ 11 (Leiden: Brill, 1977); Maren R. Niehoff, *Jewish Exegesis and Homeric Scholarship in Alexandria* (Cambridge: Cambridge University Press, 2011).

Introduction

iah).²⁶ The pesharim from Qumran (e.g., 1QpHab; 4Q163; 4Q169; 4Q171) present a sort of lemmatized commentary with a distinctly actualizing impulse by which the interpretation of the ancient text is coordinated with events in the interpreting community's recent past. Although lacking the running character of the pesharim, broadly similar, "presentifying" impulses mark certain scriptural interpretations in the New Testament that might be called, in Timothy Lim's apt phrase, "pesheresque."²⁷ Or again, attention to the ways in which Philo, Josephus, the Ps.-Philonic Liber Antiquitatum Biblicarum, or any number of other compositions retell and rewrite the scriptural texts has helped to contextualize and make sense of the broad retellings of Israel's history we find in places such as Acts 7:2–53; 13:6–41; and Heb 11. Finally, fresh attention to the subtle dynamics at play in the Alexandrian tradition of allegorical interpretation, seen in, for example, Aristobulus, the Letter of Aristeas, or Philo of Alexandria, has helped to call into question the tendentious refusal to consider Paul's interpretation as sometimes allegorical in character even though he uses the term ἀλληγορούμενα ("speaking allegorically").

These are merely illustrative examples that signal how thoroughly authors of the New Testament participated in the hermeneutical practices of contemporary Judaism. This should not be surprising to us given the ways in which the so-called parting of the ways between Christianity and Judaism has been problematized over the past few decades. If all of the authors of the New Testament can be characterized as either Jewish or Judeophiles of one sort or another, then we should expect a close consonance between their interpretative stances and those of the surrounding Jewish culture. This is not to say that all of the scriptural interpretations in the New Testament can be easily paralleled in non-Christian early Judaism nor to claim that the concrete conclusions of early Christian interpretation were uncontested by their contemporaries. But the same could be said about Philo's, Josephus's, or the Qumran community's interpretations. Judaism from the Greco-Roman period was home to a capacious and diverse set of scriptural convictions.

Analyzing the "Uses" of Scripture

Among scholars who have analyzed the reception of Jewish Scripture in the New Testament, there has been a dizzying array of terms used to describe discrete tex-

---

26. See Armin Lange and Matthias Weingold, *Biblical Quotations and Allusions in Second Temple Jewish Literature*, JAJSup 5 (Göttingen: Vandenhoeck & Ruprecht, 2011).

27. See Timothy H. Lim, *Holy Scripture in the Qumran Commentaries and Pauline Letters* (Oxford: Clarendon, 1997).

tual engagements. Should one speak of marked and unmarked citations, explicit and implicit quotations, formal and informal references? Of echoes, allusions, reminiscences, paraphrases, or invocations? And how might one determine the presence of a textual engagement and draw distinctions among these various types of engagement?[28]

The adoption of any set of nomenclature will involve some arbitrariness, and rather than suggest that our categories are definitive or incontestable, we simply present them as those terms we have recommended to the contributors in this volume as a means of obtaining continuity across chapters. By and large these are the four categories you will find in this book, with a handful of exceptions.

Marked Citation

By "marked citation" we understand an explicit citation of a discrete text that is marked for the reader in some way. This marking is most usually accomplished by an introductory formula of some kind ("As it is written" or "Isaiah says"). But this can also be marked for the reader in other ways, including by the presence of an interpretative gloss (e.g., 1 Cor 15:27: "For 'God has put all things in subjection under his feet' [cf. Ps 8:6]. But when it says, 'All things are put in subjection,' it is plain that this does not include the one who put all things in subjection under him"), a syntactical dissonance (e.g., Gal 3:12: "But the law does not rest on faith; on the contrary, 'Whoever does the works of the law will live by them' [Lev 18:5]"), or something similar.[29]

---

28. Stanley E. Porter has written more on these various categories than anyone else. See his essays: "The Use of the Old Testament in the New Testament: A Brief Comment on Method and Terminology," in *Early Christian Interpretation of the Scriptures of Israel: Investigations and Proposals*, ed. Craig A. Evans and James A. Sanders, JSNTSup 148 (Sheffield: Sheffield Academic, 1997), 79–96; Porter, "Further Comments on the Use of the Old Testament in the New Testament," in *The Intertextuality of the Epistles: Explorations of Theory and Practice*, ed. Thomas L. Brodie, Dennis R. MacDonald, and Stanley E. Porter, New Testament Monographs 16 (Sheffield: Sheffield Phoenix, 2006), 98–110; Porter, "Allusions and Echoes," in *As It Is Written: Studying Paul's Use of Scripture*, ed. Stanley E. Porter and Christopher D. Stanley, SymS 50 (Atlanta: Society of Biblical Literature, 2008), 125–55; Porter, "Pauline Techniques of Interweaving Scripture into His Letters," in *Paulinische Schriftrezeption: Grundlagen – Ausprägungen – Wirkungen – Wertungen*, ed. Florian Wilk and Markus Öhler, FRLANT 268 (Göttingen: Vandenhoeck & Ruprecht, 2017), 23–55.

29. There is useful discussion of marked citations in Koch, *Die Schrift als Zeuge*, 11–23; Stanley, *Paul and the Language of Scripture*, ch. 2. Unless otherwise noted, all biblical quotations are from the NRSV.

Introduction

Unmarked Citation

An "unmarked citation" might have a verbatim agreement with a scriptural predecessor text but is not marked as such for the reader in any way, and so a gentile with little exposure to Scripture might have no indication that a foreign text is being cited. See, for example, 1 Cor 5:13: "God will judge those outside. 'Drive out the wicked person from among you.'" Paul cites a refrain that recurs several times in Deuteronomy (17:7; 19:19; 21:21; 22:21, 24; 24:7), but by leaving it unmarked Paul allows the reader to simply hear this as a direct imperative.

Verbal Allusion

A verbal allusion is a reference to a specific word or string of words without an explicit marker. We do not distinguish between allusion and echo, which some might see as a matter of authorial intention, but we group these more subtle engagements together. We have also not specified, as Hays famously did, a set of criteria to detect the presence of a meaningful echo.[30] Examples here might include John 1:1 as an allusion to Gen 1:1: "In the beginning was the Word, and the Word was with God, and the Word was God." Or again, the vision of Rev 13:1 of a beast with ten horns rising out of the sea seems to be a clear allusion to Dan 7:2–14 (esp. vv. 2 and 7).

Conceptual Allusion

A conceptual allusion is a reference to a theme or topic that is not tied to a specific text in Scripture but nonetheless may be plausibly seen to derive from it. For example, Rom 9:4–5 offers a catalogue of the benefits Israel has enjoyed: "They are Israelites, and to them belong the adoption, the glory, the covenants, the giving of the law, the worship, and the promises; to them belong the patriarchs, and from them, according to the flesh, comes the Messiah." It would be possible to adduce a whole string of scriptural texts that refer to, say, glory or covenant, but the allusion is to the broader concept rather than to a particular text.

We must immediately point out that the boundaries between these categories are evidently fuzzy, and that it is not important to draw hard lines between them. An unmarked citation can easily shade into a verbal allusion, and one can imagine a spirited debate attempting to argue for one rather than another designation in any given case. Similarly, one might discuss where to draw the boundary

---

30. See Hays, *Echoes of Scripture in the Letters of Paul*, 29–33.

between verbal and conceptual allusions. We intend these categories as useful heuristics rather than airtight boxes, but this does not diminish their value. It may be difficult to pinpoint where violet shades into purple, or art into smut, and one cannot deny the subjective nature of such judgments, but that does not evacuate the labels of their utility.

On another matter of terminology, we have asked our contributors to attempt to avoid anachronisms as far as possible and so to speak of "Israel's Scriptures" rather than the "Old Testament" and to avoid terms such as "Bible" or "canon" unless there is a good reason to do so in individual cases. It would be problematic to convey the impression that the evangelists, for example, each had before them a complete and identical copy of their respective Bibles, including in one hefty volume all the books from Genesis to Malachi (or Genesis to 2 Chronicles or Ezra or 2 Maccabees as the case may be). The book technology to create pandects would not exist for several centuries after the New Testament was written, and not every author will have had access to each scroll that in time came to compose the Christian Old Testament or Jewish Tanak. Moreover, although the Christian Old Testament and the Jewish Tanak today exist irrevocably as collections, those are collections forged in reception during the centuries following the composition of the earliest Christian writings.

The Plan of This Book

This book proceeds in five major sections. The first section, "Contexts," supplies necessary information about the Jewish settings in which New Testament interpretation came to be. These are not comprehensive articles on Scripture and scriptural interpretation in each of the subject areas. Instead, the purpose of these chapters is more specific: to make sure the reader is cognizant of the various modes of scriptural interpretation that were possible in early Judaism and that were available to New Testament authors. In other words, these chapters illustrate the very nature of "Scripture" in early Judaism by describing various aspects that we would necessarily miss if all we were reading were the Jewish Scriptures and the New Testament.

We are keenly aware of the danger of treating early Jewish literature merely as background to the New Testament. This is emphatically not our intention. Our reading is not teleological; obviously, the value of early Jewish literature cannot be reduced to the light it sheds on the New Testament. It would be equally wrong, however, to treat Israel's Scriptures in the New Testament and in early Christian literature without giving due consideration to the world of early Judaism. These chapters chart a middle ground, surveying and analyzing the role of Scripture

Introduction

and scriptural interpretation in early Judaism and pointing to the significance this has for our modern reading of Israel's Scripture in the New Testament without making specious claims that such phenomena necessarily led to the formation of early Christianity.

The second section, "Israel's Scriptures in the New Testament," the longest section in the book, provides a book-by-book analysis of the writings of the New Testament and their engagement with the Scriptures. How pronounced is scriptural exegesis in a given book or author? Which books are cited, which books are ignored? Is the use of Scripture a dominant or important theme?

These chapters provide state-of-the-art treatments of these and other questions. The authors analyze the citation techniques that introduce Scripture, such as introductory formulas, together with the form of the engagement—marked or unmarked citations, verbal or conceptual allusions. They also consider the major purposes for which an author invokes Scripture, paying particular attention to how contemporary Jewish authors interpreted similar texts. They also treat the question of the nature of the scriptural texts, including the textual *Vorlage* an author presupposes and its proximity to Hebrew or Greek traditions.

The third section, "Themes and Topics from Israel's Scriptures in the New Testament," considers major themes that cut across the corpora that make up the New Testament: God, Messiah, Holy Spirit, covenant, law, wisdom, liturgy and prayer, eschatology. Again, these are not exhaustive surveys of the topics, but focused analyses of the way in which the Scriptures of Israel function for the authors of the New Testament as determinative resources in conceptualizing a given theme. To underscore again the early Jewish context of the Jesus movement, these chapters consider not simply their respective subjects in the scriptural texts themselves but also as they are received and debated in early Jewish literature before coming to the ways in which the authors of the New Testament negotiate the lively tradition of interpretation and counterinterpretation. By considering one theme across the writings of the New Testament, these chapters illuminate both the commonalities and distinctives among the ways in which these various authors understand and actualize their scriptural heritage.

The fourth section, "Tracing Israel's Scriptures," takes up the influence of scriptural texts in the New Testament from a related but distinctive angle: How were individual books or figures received by the New Testament authors? Like the chapters in the third section, these chapters also cut across the various corpora and authors that make up the New Testament. But they take their scope from a specific book of Scripture—Deuteronomy, Isaiah, Psalms, Daniel—or in the case of the final chapter in the section, consider the reception of individual figures from Scripture in the New Testament. These chapters shed light on the sorts of hermeneutical trajectories that accompany their respective books or figures in early Judaism and on what is common and what is distinctive in the ways in which individual authors of the New Testament negotiate that heritage.

The final section of the book, "Israel's Scriptures in Early Christianity Outside the New Testament," offers one of the most distinctive features of this collection. Spurred by the growing emphasis on reception in biblical studies, the chapters in this section investigate the early impact of the New Testament authors' use of Scripture. It would be impossible to be exhaustive given the broad scope of early Christian interpretative activity.[31] But these chapters are illustrative probes that consider specifically how several sets of texts or media—apocryphal gospels, apocryphal apocalypses, the *adversus Judaeos* tradition, the critical tradition associated with Marcion and his heirs, and early Christian pictorial art—take up and interpret the Scriptures of Israel, with one eye on how the authors of the New Testament supplied a hermeneutical precedent for them or, conversely, how they might have ignored the precedent set by the New Testament in order to strike out on their own.

Together we hope these five sections yield significant new insights by posing questions of ancient Jewish and Christian scriptural interpretation from a variety of angles. Serious readers will want to make ample use of the index since certain topics or texts recur in chapters across the volume. We have not imposed an artificial uniformity on the conclusions drawn by the various contributors. Consequently, this book contains a lively dialogue that promises fresh appreciation of a perennial set of concerns.

Conclusion

As this volume attests, the study of the reception of Israel's Scriptures in the New Testament is lively and variegated. Together with the contributors, we offer these chapters as a further word in an ongoing conversation that holds interest for historians, biblical specialists, and theologians concerned to grapple with the full breadth of what comes to be the Christian canon. The rich variety and sheer intensity of the early Jesus followers' investigations of Scripture ensure that the conversation will continue for many years hence. Certainly, there are questions about these investigations that we have not thematized in this volume. For example, we have not tried to intervene in debates about more theoretical matters, including the propriety of using intertextuality as a method (rather than

---

31. See the excellent recent collection, Paul M. Blowers and Peter W. Martens, eds., *The Oxford Handbook of Early Christian Biblical Interpretation* (Oxford: Oxford University Press, 2019).

Introduction

a theory of language) or whether a Gadamerian *Wirkungsgeschichte* might be as productive a lens through which to view the turn to Scripture as the model of intertextuality.[32] In the end, this volume hopes to extend a dialogue, not to preempt one, and we will be gratified if the chapters in this collection give the occasion for fresh thought, intellectual engagement, and ultimately, new vistas.

Bibliography

Adams, Sean, and Seth Ehorn. "What Is a Composite Citation? An Introduction." Pages 1–16 in *Composite Citations in Antiquity*. Vol. 1, *Jewish, Graeco-Roman and Early Christian Uses*. Edited by Sean A. Adams and Seth M. Ehorn. LNTS 525. London: Bloomsbury, 2016.

Allen, David, and Steve Smith, eds. *Methodology in the Use of the Old Testament in the New: Context and Criteria*. LNTS 579. London: T&T Clark, 2019.

Barthélemy, Dominique. *Les devanciers d'Aquila*. VTSup 10. Leiden: Brill, 1963.

Barton, John. "Déjà Lu: Intertextuality, Method or Theory?" Pages 1–16 in *Reading Job Intertextually*. Edited by Katherine J. Dell and William L. Kynes. LHBOTS 574. London: T&T Clark, 2013.

Beale, G. K., ed. *The Right Doctrine from the Wrong Texts? Essays on the Use of the Old Testament in the New*. Grand Rapids: Baker, 1994.

Beale, G. K., and D. A. Carson, eds. *Commentary on the New Testament Use of the Old Testament*. Grand Rapids: Baker Academic, 2007.

Blowers, Paul M., and Peter W. Martens, eds. *The Oxford Handbook of Early Christian Biblical Interpretation*. Oxford: Oxford University Press, 2019.

Böhl, Eduard. *Die alttestamentlichen Citate im Neuen Testament*. Vienna: Braumüller, 1878.

———. *Forschungen nach einer Volksbibel zur Zeit Jesu und deren Zusammenhang mit der Septuaginta-Übersetzung*. Vienna: Braumüller, 1873.

Bonsirven, Joseph. *Exégèse rabbinique et exégèse paulinienne*. Paris: Beauchesne et ses Fils, 1939.

Borgen, Peder. *Philo of Alexandria: An Exegete for His Time*. NovTSup 86. Leiden: Brill, 1997.

---

32. Steve Moyise, "Intertextuality and Historical Approaches to the Use of Scripture in the New Testament," in *Reading the Bible Intertextually*, ed. Stefan Alkier, Richard B. Hays, and Leroy Huizenga (Waco, TX: Baylor University Press, 2009), 23–33; John Barton, "Déjà Lu: Intertextuality, Method or Theory?," in *Reading Job Intertextually*, ed. Katherine J. Dell and William L. Kynes, LHBOTS 574 (London: T&T Clark, 2013), 1–16; Hans-Georg Gadamer, *Truth and Method*, trans. Joel Weinsheimer and Donald G. Marshall, 2nd ed. (London: Continuum, 1989), esp. part 2.2.

Böttrich, Christfried. *Der Jahrhundertfund: Entdeckung und Geschichte des Codex Sinaiticus*. Leipzig: Evangelische Verlagsanstalt, 2011.

———. "Neue Dokumente zur Geschichte der 'Codex Sinaiticus.'" *EC* 1, no. 4 (2010): 605–19.

———. "Supplements to the Rediscovery of *Codex Sinaiticus* in the Nineteenth Century." *EC* 8, no. 3 (2017): 395–406.

Cappellus, Louis. *Critica Sacra, sive de variis quae in sacris veteris testamenti libris occurrunt lectionibus libri sex*. Paris: Cramoisy, 1650.

Carpzov, Johann Gottlob. *A Defence of the Hebrew Bible in Answer to the Charge of Corruption Brought against It by Mr. Whiston, in His "Essay towards Restoring the True Text of the Old Testament, &c." Wherein Mr. Whiston's Pretences Are Particularly Examined and Confuted*. Translated by M. Marcus. London: Lintot, 1729.

Charles, R. H. *The Apocrypha and Pseudepigrapha of the Old Testament*. 2 vols. Oxford: Clarendon, 1913.

Charlesworth, James. "A History of Pseudepigrapha Research: The Re-emerging Importance of the Pseudepigrapha." *ANRW* 19.1: 54–88.

Clark, Herbert, and Richard Gerrig, "Quotations as Demonstrations." *Language* 66, no. 4 (1990): 764–805.

Clemen, August. *Der Gebrauch des Alten Testamentes in den Neutestamentlichen Schriften*. Gütersloh: Bertelsmann, 1895.

Davidson, Samuel. *Sacred Hermeneutics Developed and Applied: Including a History of Biblical Interpretation from the Earliest of the Fathers to the Reformation*. Edinburgh: Clark, 1843.

Dittmar, Wilhelm. *Vetus Testamentum in Novo: Die alttestamentlichen Parallelen des Neuen Testaments im Wortlaut der Urtexte und der Septuaginta zusammengestellt*. 2 vols. Göttingen: Vandenhoeck & Ruprecht, 1899–1903.

Döpke, Johann C. C. *Hermeneutik der neutestamentlichen Schriftsteller*. Leipzig: Vogel, 1829.

Drusius, Joannes. *Τὰ Ἱερὰ Παράλληλα: Parallela Sacra, hoc est, locorum veteris Testamenti cum ijs, quae in novo citantur coniuncta commemoratio, Ebraice et Graece*. Franeker: Radaeud, 1588.

Emadi, Samuel. "Intertextuality in New Testament Scholarship: Significance, Criteria, and the Art of Intertextual Reading." *CBR* 14, no. 1 (2015): 8–23.

Fabricius, Johann Albert. *Codex Pseudepigraphus Veteris Testamenti*. Hamburg: Felginer, 1713–1714.

Falk, Daniel K. *The Parabiblical Texts: Strategies for Extending the Scriptures among the Dead Sea Scrolls*. LSTS 63. London: Bloomsbury, 2007.

Feldman, Louis H. *Josephus's Interpretation of the Bible*. HCS 27. Berkeley: University of California Press, 1998.

Introduction

———. *Studies in Josephus' Rewritten Bible*. JSJSup 58. Leiden: Brill, 1998.

Gadamer, Hans-Georg. *Truth and Method*. Translated by Joel Weinsheimer and Donald G. Marshall. 2nd ed. London: Continuum, 1989.

Gentry, Peter J. "Origen's Hexapla." Pages 553–71 in *The Oxford Handbook of the Septuagint*. Edited by Alison Salvesen and Timothy M. Law. Oxford: Oxford University Press, 2021.

Gough, Henry. *The New Testament Quotations, Collated with the Scriptures of the Old Testament, in the Original Hebrew and the Version of the LXX; and with the Other Writings, Apocryphal, Talmudic, and Classical, Cited or Alleged So to Be; With Notes, and a Complete Index*. London: Walton & Maberly, 1855.

Grinfield, Edward W. *An Apology for the Septuagint, in Which Its Claims to Biblical and Canonical Authority Are Briefly Stated and Vindicated*. London: Pickering, 1850.

———. *Novum Testamentum Graecum, editio Hellenistica*. 2 vols. London: Pickering, 1843.

———. *Scholia Hellenistica in Novum Testamentum: Philone et Josepho patribus apostolicis aliisq. ecclesiæ antiquæ scriptoribus necnon libris apocryphis maxime depromta*. London: Pickering, 1848.

Hays, Richard B. *Echoes of Scripture in the Gospels*. Waco, TX: Baylor University Press, 2016.

———. *Echoes of Scripture in the Letters of Paul*. New Haven: Yale University Press, 1989.

Henze, Matthias, ed. *Biblical Interpretation at Qumran*. Grand Rapids: Eerdmans, 2005.

———, ed. *A Companion to Biblical Interpretation in Early Judaism*. Grand Rapids: Eerdmans, 2012.

Horne, Thomas H. *An Introduction to the Criticism of the Old Testament and to Biblical Interpretation; With an Analysis of the Books of the Old Testament and Apocrypha*. Revised and edited by John Ayre. London: Longman, Green, Longman, & Roberts, 1860.

Hühn, Eugen. *Die alttestamentlichen Citate und Reminiscenzen im Neuen Testamente*. Freiburg im Breisgau: Mohr, 1900.

Johnson, Franklin. *The Quotations of the New Testament from the Old Considered in the Light of General Literature*. Philadelphia: American Baptist Publication Society, 1896.

Junius, Franciscus. *Sacrorum Parallelorum libri tres*. 3rd ed. London: Bishop, 1591.

Kamesar, Adam. "Biblical Interpretation in Philo." Pages 65–92 in *The Cambridge Companion to Philo*. Edited by Adam Kamesar. Cambridge Companions to Philosophy. Cambridge: Cambridge University Press, 2009.

Kautzsch, Emil Friedrich. *De veteris testamenti locis a Paulo Apostolo allegatis*. Leipzig: Metzger & Wittig, 1869.

———. *Die Apokryphen und Pseudepigraphen des Alten Testaments*. 2 vols. Tübingen: Mohr, 1900.

Keefer, Arthur. "The Meaning and Place of Old Testament Context in OT/NT Methodology." Pages 73–85 in *Methodology in the Use of the Old Testament in the New: Context and Criteria*. Edited by David Allen and Steve Smith. LNTS 579. London: T&T Clark, 2019.

Kinzig, Wolfram. "Καινὴ διαθήκη: The Title of the New Testament in the Second and Third Centuries." *JTS* 45, no. 2 (1994): 519–44.

Koch, Dietrich-Alex. *Die Schrift als Zeuge des Evangeliums: Untersuchungen zur Verwendung und zum Verständnis der Schrift bei Paulus*. BHT 69. Tübingen: Mohr Siebeck, 1986.

Kujanpää, Katja. "From Eloquence to Evading Responsibility: The Rhetorical Functions of Quotations in Paul's Argumentation." *JBL* 136, no. 1 (2017): 185–202.

Lange, Armin, and Emanuel Tov, eds. *The Hebrew Bible*. THB 1. Leiden: Brill, 2016–2017.

Lange, Armin, and Matthias Weingold. *Biblical Quotations and Allusions in Second Temple Jewish Literature*. JAJSup 5. Göttingen: Vandenhoeck & Ruprecht, 2011.

Lanier, Greg. "'As It Is Written'... Where? Examining Generic Citations of Scripture in the New Testament." *JSNT* 43, no. 4 (2021): 570–604.

Lim, Timothy H. *Holy Scripture in the Qumran Commentaries and Pauline Letters*. Oxford: Clarendon, 1997.

———. "Qumran Scholarship and the Study of the Old Testament in the New." *JSNT* 38, no. 1 (2015): 68–80.

Lincicum, David. "Paul's Engagement with Deuteronomy: Snapshots and Signposts." *CBR* 7, no. 1 (2008): 37–67.

MacLachlan, Helen. *Notes on References and Quotations in the New Testament Scriptures from the Old Testament*. London: Blackwood, 1872.

Menken, Maarten J. J. *Matthew's Bible: The Old Testament Text of the Evangelist*. BETL 173. Leuven: Peeters, 2004.

———. *Old Testament Quotations in the Fourth Gospel: Studies in Textual Form*. CBET 15. Kampen: Kok Pharos, 1996.

———. Review of *Commentary on the New Testament Use of the Old Testament*, edited by G. K. Beale and D. A. Carson. *NovT* 52, no. 2 (2010): 189–91.

Michel, Otto. *Paulus und seine Bibel*. Gütersloh: Bertelsmann, 1929.

Moyise, Steve. "Intertextuality and Historical Approaches to the Use of Scripture in the New Testament." Pages 23–32 in *Reading the Bible Intertextually*. Edited by Stefan Alkier, Richard B. Hays, and Leroy Huizenga. Waco, TX: Baylor University Press, 2009.

Moyise, Steve, and Maarten J. J. Menken, eds. *Deuteronomy in the New Testament: The New Testament and the Scriptures of Israel*. LNTS 358. London: T&T Clark, 2007.

———, eds. *Genesis in the New Testament*. LNTS 466. London: T&T Clark, 2012.
———, eds. *Isaiah in the New Testament*. NTSI. London: T&T Clark, 2005.
———, eds. *The Minor Prophets in the New Testament*. LNTS 377. London: T&T Clark, 2009.
———, eds. *Psalms in the New Testament*. NTSI. London: T&T Clark, 2004.
Niehoff, Maren R. *Jewish Exegesis and Homeric Scholarship in Alexandria*. Cambridge: Cambridge University Press, 2011.
Nikiprowetzky, Valentin. *Le commentaire de l'Écriture chez Philon de'Alexandrie: Son caractère et sa portée; Observations philologiques*. ALGHJ 11. Leiden: Brill, 1977.
Owen, Henry. *The Modes of Quotation Used by the Evangelical Writers Explained and Vindicated*. London: Nichols, 1789.
Porter, Stanley E. "Allusions and Echoes." Pages 29–40 in *As It Is Written: Studying Paul's Use of Scripture*. Edited by Stanley E. Porter and Christopher D. Stanley. SymS 50. Atlanta: Society of Biblical Literature, 2008.
———. "Further Comments on the Use of the Old Testament in the New Testament." Pages 98–110 in *The Intertextuality of the Epistles: Explorations of Theory and Practice*. Edited by Thomas L. Brodie, Dennis R. MacDonald, and Stanley E. Porter. New Testament Monographs 16. Sheffield: Sheffield Phoenix, 2006.
———. "Pauline Techniques of Interweaving Scripture into His Letters." Pages 23–55 in *Paulinische Schriftrezeption: Grundlagen – Ausprägungen – Wirkungen – Wertungen*. Edited by Florian Wilk and Markus Öhler. FRLANT 268. Göttingen: Vandenhoeck & Ruprecht, 2017.
———. "The Use of the Old Testament in the New Testament: A Brief Comment on Method and Terminology." Pages 79–96 in *Early Christian Interpretation of the Scriptures of Israel: Investigations and Proposals*. Edited by Craig A. Evans and James A. Sanders. JSNTSup 148. Sheffield: Sheffield Academic, 1997.
Salvesen, Alison, ed. *Origen's Hexapla and Fragments: Papers Presented at the Rich Seminar on the Hexapla, Oxford Centre for Hebrew and Jewish Studies, 25th July–3rd August, 1994*. TSAJ 58. Tübingen: Mohr Siebeck, 1998.
Shaw, David A. "Converted Imaginations? The Reception of Richard Hays's Intertextual Method." *CBR* 11, no. 2 (2013): 234–45.
Stanley, Christopher D. *Arguing with Scripture: The Rhetoric of Quotations in the Letters of Paul*. London: T&T Clark, 2004.
———. *Paul and the Language of Scripture: Citation Technique in the Pauline Epistles and Contemporary Literature*. SNTSMS 74. Cambridge: Cambridge University Press, 1992.
Stendahl, Krister. *The School of St. Matthew, and Its Use of the Old Testament*. ASNU 20. Lund: Gleerup, 1954. 2nd ed., 1968.
Sternberg, Meir. "Proteus in Quotation-Land: Mimesis and the Forms of Reported Discourse." *Poetics Today* 3, no. 2 (1982): 107–56.

Surenhusius, Willem. ספר המשוה *sive Βιβλος καταλλαγης in quo secundum veterum Theologorum Hebraeorum Formulas allegandi, & Modos interpretandi conciliantur loca ex V. in N. T. allegate*. Amsterdam: Boom, 1713.

Thackeray, Henry St. John. *The Relation of St. Paul to Contemporary Jewish Thought*. New York: Macmillan, 1900.

Tholuck, F. August G. "Citations of the Old Testament in the New." *BSac* 11 (1854): 568–616.

———. "The Use Made of the Old Testament in the New, and Especially in the Epistle to the Hebrews." Pages 181–245 in vol. 2 of *A Commentary on the Epistle to the Hebrews*. Translated by James Hamilton and J. E. Ryland. 2 vols. Edinburgh: Clark, 1842.

Tov, Emanuel, Robert A. Kraft, and P. J. Parsons. *The Greek Minor Prophets Scroll from Naḥal Ḥever (8ḤevXIIgr)*. DJD 8. Oxford: Clarendon, 1990.

Toy, Crawford Howell. *Quotations in the New Testament*. New York: Scribner's Sons, 1884.

Turpie, David M. *The New Testament View of the Old: A Contribution to Biblical Introduction and Exegesis*. London: Hodder & Stoughton, 1872.

———. *The Old Testament in the New: A Contribution to Biblical Criticism and Interpretation*. London: Williams & Norgate, 1868.

Venard, Louis. "Citations de l'Ancien Testament dans le Nouveau Testament." Pages 23–51 in vol. 2 of *Supplément au Dictionnaire de la Bible*. Edited by Louis Pirot. Paris: Letouzey et Ané, 1934.

Vollmer, Hans A. *Die alttestamentlichen Citate bei Paulus: Textkritisch und biblisch-theologisch gewürdigt nebst einem Anhang Ueber das Verhältnis des Apostels zu Philo*. Freiburg im Breisgau: Mohr, 1895.

Yoon, David I. "The Ideological Inception of Intertextuality and Its Dissonance in Current Biblical Studies." *CBR* 12, no. 1 (2013): 58–76.

PART 1

CONTEXTS

The authors of the New Testament were not the first readers of Israel's Scriptures, nor were they the only ones. They were active participants in a rich and variegated tradition of scriptural engagement that began in the Hebrew Bible itself and developed significantly during Second Temple times. Before we turn our attention to the use of Israel's Scriptures in the New Testament, therefore, we need to be cognizant of the Jewish settings in which New Testament interpretation came to be.

The first section, "Contexts," supplies this necessary information. It addresses two principal questions. First, when we speak of Israel's Scriptures at the time of the New Testament, what exactly do we mean, and what is our evidence? Two chapters specifically address these issues, one on the Scriptures at the time of Jesus, the other on Israel's Greek Scriptures. And second, who were the first interpreters of Israel's Scriptures, and what do we know about the interpreters who came before and are contemporary with the New Testament authors? The volume includes five chapters on the beginnings and early development of Jewish scriptural interpretation. We begin with a chapter on the interpretation of Scripture within Scripture itself. The next chapters deal with early Jewish literature (the chapter includes a discussion of Israel's writings that never became part of the Hebrew Bible but were nonetheless considered Scripture by some during the Second Temple period), the Dead Sea Scrolls, Philo, and Josephus.

It is important to note that these are not comprehensive articles on Scripture and scriptural interpretation in each of the subject areas. Instead, the purpose of these chapters is more specific: to make sure the reader is mindful of the various modes of scriptural interpretation that were possible in early Judaism and that may help us better understand the engagement with Scripture in the New Testament. In other words, these chapters illustrate the very nature of "Scripture" in early Judaism by describing various aspects that we would necessarily miss if all we read were the Jewish Scriptures and the New Testament.

We are keenly aware of the danger of treating early Jewish literature merely as background to the New Testament. This is emphatically *not* our intention. Our reading is not teleological. Obviously, the value of early Jewish literature cannot be reduced to the light it sheds on the New Testament. It would be equally wrong, however, to treat Israel's Scriptures in the New Testament and in early Christian literature without giving due consideration to the world of early Judaism. These chapters chart a middle ground, surveying and analyzing the role of Scripture and scriptural interpretation in early Judaism and pointing to the significance this has for our modern reading of Israel's Scripture in the New Testament without making specious claims that such phenomena necessarily led to the formation of early Christianity.

∼

1

What Were the "Scriptures" in the Time of Jesus?

EDMON L. GALLAGHER

According to the Gospels in the New Testament, Jesus frequently engaged with other Jews on the interpretation of Israel's Scriptures. He often thought his interlocutors mistaken on a doctrinal point because they had failed to consider the relevant passage of Scripture. He accused the Sadducees of knowing "neither the Scriptures [τὰς γράφας] nor the power of God" (Mark 12:24) because they failed to understand that God's self-identification at the burning bush (Exod 3:6) had implications for the doctrine of the resurrection of the dead. In regard to divorce, the Pharisees' undue focus on Deut 24:1–4 blinded them to the more immediate relevance of Gen 2:24 to the question (Mark 10:3–9). The prevailing notions of the Messiah as the son of David prevented the scribes from understanding the true significance of Ps 110:1 (Mark 12:35–37). These debates concern biblical interpretation and, in that way, resemble discussions in rabbinic literature—or many other forms of religious discourse, ancient and modern. At no point does the conversation turn toward the identity of the Scriptures of Israel. Jesus never cited a passage of Scripture that the Pharisees declared noncanonical the way that Martin Luther did at the Leipzig Debate in the summer of 1519 when John Eck defended the doctrine of purgatory by citing 2 Macc 12:43–45.[1] Judging from the Gospels, there was no disagreement among Jews as to which were their authentic Scriptures.

I offer my thanks to John D. Meade and Matthew J. Thomas for their comments on this chapter.

1. See Ian Christopher Levy, "The Leipzig Disputation: Masters of the Sacred Page and the Authority of Scripture," in *Luther at Leipzig: Martin Luther, the Leipzig Debate, and the Sixteenth-Century Reformations*, ed. Mickey L. Mattox, Richard J. Serina Jr., and Jonathan Mumme, SMRT 218 (Leiden: Brill, 2019), 115–44, esp. 137–38.

But, of course, the question cannot be resolved that easily. The Gospels do not actually say that all Jews agreed on the identity of the Scriptures. The first person to make such a claim was Josephus (*Ag. Ap.* 1.37–43, quoted below), writing at the end of the first century, around the time many scholars would date the last of the four New Testament Gospels. Scholars debate the extent to which Josephus can speak for Jews in his own day, much less Jews of previous generations. Given that his is the first explicit statement about the existence of a widely recognized and delimited set of Scriptures, earlier evidence will necessarily present more ambiguities and thus be subject to varying interpretations. Nevertheless, scholars have often made the attempt to trace the process of collecting Israel's Scriptures into a defined group, which would come to be known in later Christian circles as the biblical—or, more specifically, Old Testament—canon.

This chapter will, again, survey the relevant evidence in Second Temple Jewish literature, rabbinic literature, and early Christian literature. We will see that while all Jews of whom we have record accepted the Torah as authoritative Scripture and at least a great many Jews so regarded certain other writings (e.g., some prophetic books, some form of the Psalter), we cannot be certain about the status enjoyed by a number of books that eventually did find a place in the Hebrew Bible and/or in those Christian Old Testaments more expansive than the Hebrew Bible. Our uncertainty about the status of these books two millennia ago, based on ambiguous evidence, probably in some cases reflects uncertainty or disagreement among ancient Jewish groups or even individual Jews. The following categorization will be helpful to keep in mind as we survey the evidence.

- Writings universally (or widely) recognized as Scripture (e.g., Torah)
- Writings about which some ancient Jews were not certain as to whether they should be considered Scripture (e.g., Esther, Tobit, Jubilees)
- Writings about which ancient Jews disagreed as to whether they should be considered Scripture (e.g., Esther, Tobit, Jubilees)
- Writings universally recognized as not Scripture (e.g., Qumran's Community Rule, Philo's tractates)

There may be significant overlap between the second and third categories; the difference is that some writings may not have provoked strong feelings one way or the other among Jews (second category), while other writings (or some of the same writings?) may have occasioned disagreement. A writing such as Esther, for instance, may have belonged to both categories: Perhaps the Qumran community firmly rejected Esther while other Jews firmly accepted it as Scripture and still other Jews were not at all certain what to make of the book. Then again, perhaps the Qumran community was not certain what to make of the book while other

What Were the "Scriptures" in the Time of Jesus?

Jews firmly accepted it as Scripture, or maybe even the Qumran community regarded Esther as Scripture. All of these positions have been maintained in modern scholarship. The ancient evidence does not allow for easy answers.

Terminology

We use the term "canon" in a variety of ways today, often in reference to literature: the canon of classical authors, the Shakespeare canon, or even the Harry Potter canon or the Star Wars canon. Apparently, such usage is relatively modern: In 1768, David Ruhnken applied the term "canon" to the lists of classical authors developed by the Hellenistic grammarians, such as Aristophanes and Aristarchus.[2] Ruhnken derived this usage of the term from the biblical tradition, where the word had long been used to denote the select list of authoritative writings. We can trace this meaning back to the mid-fourth century CE, when Athanasius, bishop of Alexandria, mentioned that the Shepherd of Hermas was "not in the canon" (μὴ ὂν ἐκ τοῦ κανόνος).[3] Before Athanasius, the term "canon" had been used in a variety of meanings—and within Christian circles, in regard to the "rule [κανών] of faith" or the canon tables of Eusebius in reference to the Gospels or the canons of ecclesiastical councils—but not in reference to a list of literary works or authors.[4] Today scholars debate more than ever the significance of the term "canon" as applied to the Jewish and Christian Scriptures, the precise definition of the term "canon" in this context, and how to date the development of the canon in relation to the various definitions proposed by scholars.[5] To oversimplify, the debate has to do with whether we consider the term "canon" to apply to a list of authoritative books or an authoritative list of books, as Metzger put it some decades ago.[6] Ancient Jews did not use the term "canon,"[7] and to many modern scholars the term connotes a level of solidity that did not charac-

---

2. David Ruhnken, "Historia critica oratorum Graecorum," in *P. Rutilii Lupi: De Figuris Sententiarum et Elocutionis Duo Libri* (Lyons: Luchtmans, 1768), xcv. See Rudolf Pfeiffer, *History of Classical Scholarship: From the Beginning to the End of the Hellenistic Age* (Oxford: Oxford University Press, 1968), 203–7.

3. Athanasius, *Decr.* 18.3, *Athanasius Werke*, ed. Hans-Georg Opitz, 4 vols. (Berlin: de Gruyter, 1935–1941), 2:15.

4. See Bruce M. Metzger, *The Canon of the New Testament: Its Origin, Development, and Significance* (Oxford: Oxford University Press, 1987), 289–93, on the early history of the term.

5. See Tomas Bokedal, *The Formation and Significance of the Christian Biblical Canon: A Study in Text, Ritual, and Interpretation* (London: Bloomsbury, 2014), 39–80.

6. Metzger, *Canon*, 282–87.

7. Gilles Dorival, *The Septuagint from Alexandria to Constantinople: Canon, New Testament, Church Fathers, Catenae* (Oxford: Oxford University Press, 2021), 3–7.

terize the (collection of) Scriptures during the time of Jesus. Nevertheless, the term is used so often in modern scholarship, even intentionally about the time of Jesus—either because these scholars think the collection of Scriptures had achieved significant stabilization or they think the term should not be limited to such a narrow definition—that we cannot avoid it in this discussion even if we wanted to.[8] As Tomas Bokedal says, "the vibrant ecclesial notion of canon predates the application of the term 'canon' to the two-testament Bible."[9]

As to what terms ancient Jews actually used, we have seen that the Greek term γραφαί, "Scriptures," is common. Josephus habitually uses a version of the term "holy books/writings" (usually ἱεραὶ βίβλοι or ἱερὰ γράμματα).[10] Other Greek-speaking Jews (later?) likely used the term ἐνδιάθηκος, "encovenanted" or "testamentary."[11] The rabbis used the term ספרים חצונים ("external books") to designate books external to their conception of the Scriptures.[12]

Types of Evidence

In the absence of an explicit statement about which books count as Scripture and which books do not, how can we tell whether an ancient book was received as Scripture? In an essay on the development of the Jewish Bible, John Barton has listed nine clues for making such an evaluation.[13] These clues are the prevalence of manuscripts of the book, citations and commentary, translations, exemplifi-

---

8. Scholars who believe in an early stabilization of the contours of the biblical canon will be named below. Scholars advocating a definition of canon not equivalent to a closed list but with emphasis on the normative authority of the writings include most prominently Brevard S. Childs, e.g., in his *An Introduction to the Old Testament as Scripture* (Philadelphia: Fortress, 1979); see also James A. Sanders, *Torah and Canon* (Philadelphia: Fortress, 1972); Stephen B. Chapman, "The Canon Debate: What It Is and Why It Matters," *JTI* 4, no. 4 (2010): 273–94.

9. Bokedal, *Formation and Significance*, 39; see also Dorival, *Septuagint from Alexandria to Constantinople*, 5: "even if the word 'canon' is lacking, the reality of the canon did exist in these ancient Jewish milieus: that is, a list of books understood as being in some sense normative."

10. For ἱεραὶ βίβλοι see *Ant.* 1.82, 139; 2.347; 3.81, 105; 9.28, 46; 12.113; *J.W.* 3.352; *Ag. Ap.* 1.1, 91, 217; for ἱερὰ γράμματα, see *Ant.* 10.210; 13.167; *Ag. Ap.* 1.54, 127. Josephus also uses ἱερὰ βιβλία (*Life* 418) and ἱεραὶ γραφαί (*Ag. Ap.* 2.45). He twice uses the term κανών in the sense of "prototype" (*Ant.* 10.49) or "rule" (*Ag. Ap.* 2.174).

11. Éric Junod, "La formation et la composition de l'Ancien Testament dans l'Église grecque des quatre premiers siècles," in *Le Canon de l'Ancien Testament: Sa formation et son histoire*, ed. Jean-Daniel Kaestli and Otto Wermelinger, MdB (Geneva: Labor et Fides, 1984), 120–23.

12. Sid Z. Leiman, *The Canonization of Hebrew Scripture: The Talmudic and Midrashic Evidence* (Hamden, CT: Archon, 1976) 86–92; Philip S. Alexander, "The Formation of the Biblical Canon in Rabbinic Judaism," in *The Canon of Scripture in Jewish and Christian Tradition*, ed. Philip S. Alexander and Jean-Daniel Kaestli (Prahins: Éditions du Zèbre, 2007), 71–72.

13. John Barton, "The Old Testament Canons," in *From the Beginnings to 600*, vol. 1 of *The*

What Were the "Scriptures" in the Time of Jesus?

cation, consistency (or, let us say, the felt need to explain away apparent contradictions), truth ("it may be said that texts treated allegorically can normally be taken to have a high status"), overinterpretation, nontriviality, and contemporary relevance. Most of these points have to do with interpretation, so we might simplify Barton's list in the manner of James VanderKam, who proposes two main types of evidence: the prevalence of manuscripts and the use (or function) of the book in other literature.[14] The issue about manuscripts has to do especially with Qumran and whether many manuscripts of the book were found there or only a few (or none), and secondarily we could think about manuscripts elsewhere, such as the later Septuagint codices and which books were included. The issue about use or function has to do with how the book is cited or used by other literature. Do they attribute its words to God or otherwise signal that they conceive of its contents as inspired or authoritative? The significance of the number of ancient manuscripts for our question of identifying Scripture will occupy us below. The second point, on use, we can explore briefly here.

Ancient Jewish and Christian literature contains many quotations, so this category provides a great deal of evidence difficult to interpret.[15] Often such quotations indicate that the person quoting the text regards the text as sacred Scripture and this person also assumes his or her audience will share that opinion. Sometimes an introductory formula will provide a surer indication for this high regard. When Acts represents the apostle Paul preaching in the synagogue at Pisidian Antioch, the sermon features these lines:

> [32]And we bring you the good news that what God promised to our ancestors [33]he has fulfilled for us, their children, by raising Jesus; as also it is written [γέγραπται] in the second psalm, "You are my Son; today I have begotten you" [Ps 2:7]. [34]As to his raising him from the dead, no more to return to corruption, he has spoken in this way, "I will give you the holy promises made to David" [Isa 55:3]. (Acts 13:32–34 NRSV)[16]

Here it is clear that Ps 2:7 is quoted as the speech of God, as is Isa 55:3. Within the narrative of Acts, there are occasions when Paul disputes with Jews about

---

New Cambridge History of the Bible, ed. James Carleton Paget and Joachim Schaper (Cambridge: Cambridge University Press, 2013), 152–58.

14. James C. VanderKam, *The Dead Sea Scrolls and the Bible* (Grand Rapids: Eerdmans, 2012), 66.

15. For an index to these quotations, see Armin Lange and Matthias Weigold, *Biblical Quotations and Allusions in Second Temple Jewish Literature*, JAJSup 5 (Göttingen: Vandenhoeck & Ruprecht, 2011). The standard editions of the Greek New Testament contain a helpful index of such quotations; see NA[28], 836–78.

16. Unless otherwise noted, all translations are by the author.

the meaning of such passages (see 13:45; 17:2–3), but they do not question the authority of these passages or their divine origin.

Then again, quotations do not always indicate this same level of attributed authority. When Paul quotes the Greek poets Epimenides and Aratus in Acts 17:28, the author of Acts probably does not intend his readers to imagine that Paul considered these writings authoritative or on par with Jewish Scripture. Earlier we saw that Athanasius in the fourth century CE first used the term "canon" in reference to the collection of Scriptures in a passage in which he excludes from the canon the Shepherd of Hermas (*Decret.* 18.3). In that very passage, Athanasius quoted the Shepherd (introducing the quotation with γέγραπται) in order to make a theological point.[17] When there is not an explicit quotation but some more general use (an allusion or similar), such as Paul's apparent reuse of ideas from the Wisdom of Solomon in Romans,[18] what evidence does such use provide for the identity of Jewish Scripture?

In the absence of an explicit statement (or even with such a statement!), scholars will disagree. Here we will attempt to survey the all-too-limited evidence and the most prominent positions taken by scholars on the basis of that evidence. We start with what is perhaps still the most prominent idea on the development of the Jewish Bible in antiquity.

The Canonical Sections: A Clue to the Development of the Canon?

The Jewish Bible today is sometimes called the Tanak, an acronym referring to its three sections: Torah, Neviim (Prophets), and Ketuvim (Writings). These same three sections are explicitly attested in sources as early as late antiquity (Jerome, the Talmud), at which point they had achieved standardization in terms of contents (but not internal sequence).[19] The well-known talmudic list is the earliest Jewish source that explicitly names each of the canonical books. The earlier Jewish account in Josephus provides tantalizing details (to be studied below) but fails to name the books. In truth, even the talmudic list does not name all of the books, as it assumes its readers will have no trouble knowing the five books of

---

17. For discussion, see Edmon L. Gallagher, "Origen on the Shepherd of Hermas," *EC* 10, no. 2 (2019): 201–15, esp. 211–12.

18. See Timothy H. Lim, *The Formation of the Jewish Canon*, ABRL (New Haven: Yale University Press, 2013), 169–72.

19. See Jerome, *Preface to Samuel and Kings*; and b. B. Bat. 14b; both in Edmon L. Gallagher and John D. Meade, *The Biblical Canon Lists from Early Christianity: Texts and Analysis* (Oxford: Oxford University Press, 2017), 65–69 (talmudic list), 198–203 (Jerome).

What Were the "Scriptures" in the Time of Jesus?

the Torah. The Talmud lists the books in the following sequence (if we may be permitted to add the omitted Torah).

Torah: Genesis, Exodus, Leviticus, Numbers, Deuteronomy
Neviim: Joshua, Judges, Samuel, Kings, Jeremiah, Ezekiel, Isaiah, the Twelve (Minor Prophets)
Ketuvim: Ruth, Psalms, Job, Proverbs, Ecclesiastes, Song of Songs, Lamentations, Daniel, Esther, Ezra(-Nehemiah), Chronicles

This list as presented in the Talmud is a *baraita*, an earlier (Tannaitic) tradition omitted from previous compilations (Mishnah, Tosefta) and now incorporated into this later rabbinic compilation.[20] Usually such *baraitot* are dated to the second century CE or earlier, so scholars often assume that this list of books, too, should be dated to that period rather than to the time of the compilation of the Talmud centuries later (perhaps sixth century).[21] As mentioned, the late fourth-century list of Jerome includes the same books in the same categories (using the titles Law, Prophets, Hagiographa), but the sequence of books within the second and third categories differs between Jerome and the Talmud.[22] Certainly by the fourth century CE, and probably by the second century CE or earlier, at least one prominent form of the Jewish Bible had settled into its now familiar tripartite structure.

Why a tripartite structure? The most prominent twentieth-century view on the development of the Jewish Bible takes this structure as a clue to the growth of the canon: the Torah was canonized first, then the Prophets, then the Writings. This three-stage model became popular at the end of the nineteenth century and, according to one recent estimate, "still has some claim to being a majority view within scholarship."[23] The traditional formulation of this view attributes the canonization of the Torah to the period of Ezra, the canonization of the Prophets to around 200 BCE, and the canonization of the Writings to the late first century CE at a meeting of rabbis called the Council of Yavneh.[24] If this theory be

---

20. On *baraitot* in the Babylonian Talmud, see H. L. Strack and Günter Stemberger, *Introduction to the Talmud and Midrash*, trans. Markus Bockmuehl (Minneapolis: Fortress, 1992), 198–99. See also p. 177 on *baraitot* in the Palestinian Talmud and p. 104 on the language of *baraitot*.

21. On the date, see Gallagher and Meade, *Biblical Canon Lists*, 66.

22. Jerome actually has two slightly different enumerations of the Old Testament: the first numbers twenty-two books, with Ruth considered a part of Judges and Lamentations considered a part of Jeremiah (thus, in the Prophets section); the second numbers twenty-four books, with Ruth and Lamentations counted independently within the Writings. Jerome's second list corresponds more closely (but still not identically) with the talmudic list.

23. Stephen B. Chapman, "Collections, Canons, and Communities," in *The Cambridge Companion to the Hebrew Bible/Old Testament*, ed. Stephen B. Chapman and Marvin A. Sweeney, Cambridge Companions to Religion (Cambridge: Cambridge University Press, 2016), 34.

24. One of the classic presentations of this theory is Herbert Edward Ryle, *The Canon of*

granted, the Scriptures at the time of Jesus would consist of (1) a settled collection of Torah in five books, (2) a settled collection of Prophets in eight books, (3) and a variety of other writings (lowercase) that would within a century solidify into the Writings (capitalized) in eleven books.

There is some evidence for this three-stage theory of canonization. A common phrase to refer to Scripture in the late Second Temple period is "the law and the prophets" or similar (see, e.g., Matt 7:12; 22:40), and this phrase may in fact reflect the first two sections of the Tanak, that is, the Law (five books) and the Prophets (eight books), both already canonized, while the Writings were still in flux.[25] There are also some tripartite formulations in this same period, the most well-known examples being in the Gospel of Luke (24:44, Law, Prophets, Psalms) and the preface to the Greek translation of Sirach (second century BCE), which three times says something along the lines of "law, prophets, and the remaining books."[26] Scholars have often thought that such tripartite formulations reflect closed sections of the Torah and Prophets, whereas the loose and inconsistent way in which the books outside the Torah and Prophets are labeled suggests that other Scriptures also circulated without yet forming a settled collection. As opposed to such loose tripartite formulations, Josephus at the end of the first century attests a definite and closed collection of Scripture consisting of twenty-two books.[27] By the time of Josephus, one might imagine, the Council of Yavneh had already settled the matter of the canon, as rabbinic sources reveal (m. Yad. 3:5). At the opposite end of the process, the Torah would have been canonized, but not the Prophets, before the separation between Jews and Samaritans (since the Samaritans took with them their version of the Torah but no version of the Prophets). The Prophets category must have been canonized before the writing of Ben Sira in the early second century BCE, since Ben Sira refers to the prophetic literature,[28]

---

the Old Testament: An Essay on the Gradual Growth and Formation of the Hebrew Canon of Scripture (London: Macmillan, 1892). For more recent examinations with negative evaluations of the theory, see Armin Lange, "Canonical History of the Hebrew Bible," in *The Hebrew Bible: Overview Articles*, ed. Armin Lange and Emanuel Tov, THB 1A (Leiden: Brill, 2016), 35–48 (§1.1.2.1.2); Dorival, *Septuagint from Alexandria to Constantinople*, 7–31.

25. The phrase is common in the New Testament and in Jewish literature outside the New Testament; see John Barton, *Oracles of God: Perceptions of Ancient Prophecy in Israel after the Exile* (Oxford: Oxford University Press, 1986), 44–55. This is the way the phrase was understood by Albert C. Sundberg, *The Old Testament of the Early Church*, HTS 20 (Cambridge: Harvard University Press, 1964).

26. For discussion of these formulations, see Gallagher and Meade, *Biblical Canon Lists*, 9–13; Roger T. Beckwith, "A Modern Theory of the Old Testament Canon," *VT* 41, no. 4 (1991): 385–95.

27. Josephus, *Ag. Ap.* 1.37–42, in Gallagher and Meade, *Biblical Canon Lists*, 57–65.

28. On the attestation of Scripture in Ben Sira's Praise of Famous Men (chs. 44–50), see Lim, *Formation of the Jewish Canon*, 102–6, with appendix 5, pp. 208–12.

What Were the "Scriptures" in the Time of Jesus?

and before the writing of Daniel in the second century BCE, otherwise Daniel would have featured in the Prophets section, whereas it is in the Ketuvim.

Though this model of canonization may still be prominent, it has received attacks from all sides over the past few decades. These attacks essentially amount to demonstrations of the tenuous nature of the evidence used in support of this model. For example, the idea that a Council of Yavneh at the end of the first century settled the biblical canon by codifying the Writings is based on the barest of evidence. After the destruction of Jerusalem by the Romans in 70 CE, some Jewish leaders assembled in the coastal town of Yavneh, and they discussed a variety of topics as reported in rabbinic literature. Among their discussions there arose the question as to whether Qoheleth (Ecclesiastes) and Song of Songs "defile the hands" (m. Yad. 3.5), a phrase indicating the holiness of an object.[29] From such meager evidence (and slightly more) there developed the idea of a Council of Yavneh that canonized the Ketuvim.[30] Most scholars have now abandoned this idea, though Yavneh (without the council) is sometimes still cited as the place where the Jewish canon took its definitive form.[31]

If we cannot point to a Council of Yavneh as canonizing the Ketuvim, should we date the determination of the third division earlier or later? Scholars have gone in both directions. Some scholars have seen the tripartite references to Scripture mentioned earlier (Luke 24:44; prologue to Greek Sirach) as evidence for a collection of Ketuvim (the third section of the Tanak) not loosely defined but stable and determined, and some of these scholars thus trace the present form of the Tanak to the second century BCE.[32] In this case, the Scriptures at the time of Jesus would be essentially the current Jewish Bible, the Tanak. This view has some plausibility since the Judean troubles in the early second century BCE associated with Antiochus IV Epiphanes and the Maccabees resulted in a Hasmonean dynasty ruling over an independent Jewish state for several decades. Some scholars associate the Hasmoneans with the effort to promote a defined collection of Scripture, especially in light of a passage in 2 Maccabees attributing to Judah the Maccabee a collection of books (2 Macc 2:13–14).[33] On

---

29. Timothy H. Lim, "Defilement of Hands as a Principle Determining the Holiness of Scriptures," *JTS* 61, no. 2 (2010): 501–15.

30. For the traditions relating to Yavneh with a focus on the books of Scripture, see Leiman, *Canonization of Hebrew Scripture*, 120–24.

31. The initial blow against a council at Yavneh was struck by Jack P. Lewis, "What Do We Mean by Jabneh?," *JBR* 32, no. 2 (1964): 125–32. For the idea that the biblical canon solidified at Yavneh but without a council, see Lim, *Formation of the Jewish Canon*.

32. Extensively argued in Roger T. Beckwith, *The Old Testament Canon of the New Testament Church and Its Background in Early Judaism* (Grand Rapids: Eerdmans, 1985).

33. Karel van der Toorn, *Scribal Culture and the Making of the Hebrew Bible* (Cambridge: Harvard University Press, 2007), 233–64; David M. Carr, *The Formation of the Hebrew Bible: A New Reconstruction* (Oxford: Oxford University Press, 2011), ch. 5. However, these scholars

the other hand, all of this evidence is rather vague, and it might be the case that the Jewish biblical canon was undetermined until the second or third centuries CE (or later?).³⁴ Evidence for this view would be, on the one hand, a lack of evidence from the time of Jesus for clear boundaries separating the books now considered canonical from all other books and, on the other hand, the clear evidence—especially at Qumran but even in the New Testament—that writings later deemed noncanonical enjoyed widespread popularity and authority in this period. (We will look at this evidence later, the interpretation of which is disputed.) But there is also evidence against such a late date for the closed canon, particularly Josephus, who declares that at the end of the first century there did exist a limited set of Jewish Scriptures numbering twenty-two volumes and that this matter had been settled for many years.

The old consensus that the Prophets section of the Tanak was established around 200 BC is also no longer secure. It was especially Barton in 1986 who put forth an argument, compelling to many scholars, that the term "prophets" in the common ancient phrase "the law and the prophets" did not refer to the second section of the Tanak but to all Scripture outside the Torah.³⁵ Scholars often now understand this phrase to refer to "the law and other inspired literature" without reference to the canonical divisions of the Tanak.³⁶ Evidence for this view includes the frequent attribution of the label "prophet" to those writings now inhabiting the Ketuvim, such as the Psalms or the books of Solomon or Daniel.³⁷ During the period when the old consensus still dominated, Albert Sundberg famously described the Scriptures at the time of Jesus as consisting of "closed collections of Law and Prophets as well as other religious writings that belonged to no fixed collection."³⁸ But if the new consensus is right, then the Prophets section itself was not closed, but there existed alongside the Torah an unbounded collection of other Scriptures with the label "prophets." Then again, we might also have to reckon with a contemporary conception of the Jewish Scriptures with somewhat more structure in order to account for those few tripartite formulations (especially the prologue to Sirach and Luke 24:44).³⁹

---

do not think the canon was as sharply defined during the Maccabean era as Beckwith (previous note) does.

34. Lee Martin McDonald, *The Formation of the Biblical Canon*, 2 vols. (London: Bloomsbury, 2017), 1:415–18; Eva Mroczek, *The Literary Imagination in Jewish Antiquity* (Oxford: Oxford University Press, 2016), 156–83.

35. Barton, *Oracles of God*.

36. Julius Steinberg and Timothy J. Stone, "The Historical Formation of the Writings in Antiquity," in *The Shape of the Writings*, Siphrut 16 (Winona Lake, IN: Eisenbrauns, 2015), 10; this is also how Beckwith takes the phrase in his "Modern Theory."

37. See Matt 24:15 (Daniel); 11Q5 (11QPsª) XXVII, 3–11 (David); b. Soṭah 48b (Solomon).

38. Sundberg, *Old Testament of the Early Church*, 129.

39. See again Steinberg and Stone, "Historical Formation."

What Were the "Scriptures" in the Time of Jesus?

The identity of the Torah could also be questioned, since not only do the individual books of the Pentateuch exist in variant editions at Qumran but also rewritten Torahs (e.g., the Temple Scroll, Jubilees, texts formerly known as "Reworked Pentateuch") circulated in the Second Temple period. When people in antiquity claimed to accept the Torah of Moses as their Scripture, did they have a particular form of the Torah in mind, or would any of the above do?[40]

Stephen Chapman has shown how unlikely the three-stage view is from the other side.[41] The common formula "the law and the prophets" corresponds well to the evidence in the Bible that the Torah never existed independently of an equally authoritative corpus of prophetic literature. For instance, "They made their hearts adamant in order not to hear the Torah and the words that YHWH of hosts had sent by his spirit through the former prophets" (Zech 7:12). Such verses along with redactional evidence within Scripture (e.g., Deut 34:10–12; Mal 3:22–24 [4:4–6 ET]) suggest that the Torah was always accompanied by other literature equally authoritative so that there would not have been a closing of the Torah section without a collection of prophetic texts.

Assessing the Evidence for Scripture at the Time of Jesus

The three-stage theory, whether it still be the predominant theory or not, faces such significant difficulties that we must seek another model. In what follows we will look at some of the most prominent bits of evidence available to help us understand what someone in the time of Jesus might have considered Scripture. We will look first at Qumran, then the New Testament, and finally Josephus.

Qumran

The Dead Sea Scrolls yielded something like 900 manuscripts, around 220 of which are copies of books now in the Tanak. Every book of the modern Jewish

---

40. Such questions are raised by Barton, "Old Testament Canons," 150. But note the comment of John J. Collins, *The Dead Sea Scrolls: A Biography* (Princeton: Princeton University Press, 2013), 195: "In fact, however, citations of the Torah in the Scrolls generally conform to the traditional text, not to the Temple Scroll. If the authors of the Temple Scroll wanted it to be accepted as the official Torah, they failed."

41. Stephen B. Chapman, *The Law and the Prophets: A Study in Old Testament Canon Formation*, FAT 27 (Tübingen: Mohr Siebeck, 2010); Chapman, "Second Temple Jewish Hermeneutics: How Canon Is Not an Anachronism," in *Invention, Rewriting, Usurpation: Discursive Fights over Religious Traditions in Antiquity*, ed. Jörg Ulrich, Anders-Christian Jacobsen, and David Brakke, Early Christianity in the Context of Antiquity 11 (New York: Lang, 2011), 281–96, esp. 287–94.

Bible is preserved at Qumran in at least one (sometimes very tiny, fragmentary) copy except for the book of Esther. Some books in the deuterocanon (books in the Catholic Bible but absent from the Protestant Bible) were also found: Ben Sira (= Ecclesiasticus), Tobit, and the Epistle of Jeremiah. Also, a version of Ps 151 was found there, which is a part of the Psalter in Eastern churches (such as the Greek Orthodox Church). The Qumran caves also yielded documents usually labeled pseudepigrapha, such as Jubilees and various booklets associated with Enoch, which, grouped together, comprise 1 Enoch. Both Jubilees and 1 Enoch form part of the Ethiopian Bible.

It is difficult to know what the presence of these scrolls at Qumran means for our question. If the Qumran group owned a copy of a writing, does that mean they attributed divine authority to that writing? Did they regard it as scriptural, biblical, canonical? No one would say that the mere presence of a copy of a text at Qumran would indicate such a judgment. After all, many copies of the group's own compositions were discovered, but no one argues that the Qumran group regarded their own compositions as on par with the Scriptures (even if they regarded their Teacher of Righteousness to be inspired in some sense). VanderKam suggests (as noted earlier) that an indication for scriptural authority might derive not from the mere presence of a copy but the presence of many copies of the same work. He also points to function: "Does the work function authoritatively?" That is, does other literature cite the relevant book as authoritative?[42] Such a line of reasoning leads many scholars to the conclusion that most of the books in the modern Jewish Bible would have been viewed as Scripture with the possible exceptions of Esther, Chronicles, Ezra, and Nehemiah since each of these latter books are preserved in either a single scroll or not at all at Qumran, and they are not cited by other literature.[43] Possibly additional books were considered scriptural as well. The most frequent nominees in this regard are Jubilees (preserved in fourteen scrolls), the Enoch booklets (collectively preserved in eleven scrolls), and perhaps Tobit (five scrolls). Aside from the sheer number of scrolls, it is clear that the Enoch booklets were important at Qumran, judging from the calendar texts in the scrolls.[44] The book of Jubilees was cited as authoritative in the Damascus Document (CD XVI, 1–3) and in 4Q228.[45]

---

42. VanderKam, *Dead Sea Scrolls*, 66.

43. VanderKam, *Dead Sea Scrolls*, 67; Eugene Ulrich, "Our Sharper Focus on the Bible and Theology Thanks to the Dead Sea Scrolls," *CBQ* 66, no. 1 (2004): 9. Ulrich adds Qoheleth to this poorly attested group (preserved in two scrolls).

44. See Sacha Stern, "Qumran Calendars and Sectarianism," in *The Oxford Handbook of the Dead Sea Scrolls*, ed. Timothy H. Lim and John J. Collins (Oxford: Oxford University Press, 2010), 232–53; Lim, *Formation of the Jewish Canon*, 143–44.

45. Lim, *Formation of the Jewish Canon*, 131–35, doubts whether such evidence indicates that Jubilees was considered on par with Scripture.

What Were the "Scriptures" in the Time of Jesus?

What were the Scriptures at Qumran? According to scholarly consensus, the Torah was considered Scripture, though there might be some doubt as to the form of the authoritative Torah or the extent to which such an issue mattered to the community. To the Torah, we can add the books in the Prophets section of the Tanak and at least some of the books in the Ketuvim, especially Daniel and (some version of) the Psalter. But probably not Esther because not only has no scroll turned up but also Purim does not feature among the holidays observed at Qumran, though the scroll of Esther demands such observance. Other writings besides those in the modern Jewish Bible were also very important at Qumran, perhaps even scriptural. Barton well summarizes the evidence: "We can certainly say, however, that *at least* the books now in the Hebrew canon were regarded as highly important by the community, though we cannot know that it was these books *at most*."[46]

New Testament

There is a remarkable similarity between the books popular at Qumran (judging by number of scrolls) and those most frequently quoted in the New Testament. In both cases, the three most popular books are Deuteronomy, Isaiah, and the Psalter.[47] The New Testament quotes the Scripture hundreds of times, and there are quotations of, or strong allusions to, all the books of the modern Jewish Bible except for Esther, Ecclesiastes, and Song of Songs.[48] Some books outside the Tanak also exerted an influence on the New Testament writers. The connections between the New Testament, particularly Paul, and the Wisdom of Solomon have long intrigued scholars.[49] The Epistle of Jude (vv. 14–15) explicitly quotes from The Book of Watchers (= 1 En. 1:9). This quotation in Jude influenced the

---

46. Barton, "Old Testament Canons," 153 (emphasis original).

47. On the number of Scrolls at Qumran, see James C. VanderKam and Peter Flint, *The Meaning of the Dead Sea Scrolls: Their Significance for Understanding the Bible, Judaism, Jesus, and Christianity* (San Francisco: HarperSanFrancisco, 2002), 150, who also note that if non-Qumran scrolls from the Judean Desert are added, Genesis jumps ahead of Isaiah into the third position. In any case, the top five from the Judean Desert and from the New Testament would still be the same, including Genesis and Exodus with the above-mentioned three books. For further comparison of the Dead Sea Scrolls with the New Testament in this regard, see George J. Brooke, *The Dead Sea Scrolls and the New Testament* (Minneapolis: Fortress, 2005), 27–51.

48. But on Esther, cf. Mark 6:23 with Esth 5:3, 6; 7:2. On Ecclesiastes, cf. Rom 8:20 with Eccl 1:2. I am assuming that the Minor Prophets constitute a single book; there are no quotations of, or very strong allusions to, Obadiah, Nahum, and Zephaniah, but presumably they were included within the Book of the Twelve.

49. Folker Blischke, "Die *Sapientia Salomonis* und Paulus," in *Sapientia Salomonis (Weisheit Salomos)*, ed. Karl-Wilhelm Niebuhr, SAPERE 27 (Tübingen: Mohr Siebeck, 2015), 273–92; Lim, *Formation of the Jewish Canon*, 169–72; Edmon L. Gallagher, *Translation of the Seventy: History, Reception, and Contemporary Use of the Septuagint* (Abilene, TX: ACU Press, 2021), 70–75.

way both Jude and the Enochic writings were subsequently received, with some (e.g., Tertullian) thinking that Jude conferred scriptural authority on Enoch, and others thinking the quotation of Enoch casts doubt on the scriptural status of Jude.[50] The New Testament leaves us with the same sorts of questions as the Qumran evidence. There seems to be a general stability about the writings considered Scripture, and this stability especially concerns those writings making up the modern Jewish Bible, but we cannot say with certainty whether all of the books of the Tanak would have been granted scriptural status. The other writings that were certainly influential and would eventually be received into the canon of some Christian groups (e.g., Wisdom, Enoch) might also have been considered Scripture by the New Testament writers.

Josephus

What we have lacked in earlier sources we find in Josephus: an explicit statement about which books count as Jewish Scripture. Unfortunately, Josephus was not quite as explicit as we would wish (and as later sources often are). At the end of the first century CE—so, roughly six or seven decades after the crucifixion of Jesus—Josephus wrote a polemical work called *Against Apion*. The point of the work was to argue that Judaism was a noble religion in part because its legislation was delivered in distant antiquity and because there was a limited and internally consistent set of volumes by inspired prophets that both preserved this legislation and narrated the history of the Jewish people from the creation of the world until a few centuries prior to the time of Josephus.

> (1.37) Naturally, then, or rather necessarily—see that it is not open to anyone to write of their own accord, nor is there any disagreement present in what is written, but the prophets alone learned, by inspiration of God [κατὰ τὴν ἐπίπνοιαν τὴν ἀπὸ τοῦ θεοῦ], what had happened in the distant and most ancient past and recorded plainly events in their own time just as they occurred—(38) among us there are not thousands of books in disagreement and conflict with each other, but only twenty-two books, containing the record of all time, which are rightly trusted. (39) Five of these are the books of Moses, which contain both the laws and the tradition from the birth of humanity up to his death; this is a period of a little less than 3,000 years. (40) From the death of Moses until Artaxerxes, king of the Persians after Xerxes, the prophets after Moses wrote the history of what took place in their own times in thir-

---

50. Nicholas J. Moore, "Is Enoch Also among the Prophets? The Impact of Jude's Citation of *1 Enoch* on the Reception of Both Texts in the Early Church," *JTS* 64, no. 2 (2013): 498–515.

teen books; the remaining four books contain hymns to God and instructions for people on life. (41) From Artaxerxes up to our own time every event has been recorded, but this is not judged worthy of the same trust, since the exact line of succession of the prophets did not continue [διὰ τὸ μὴ γενέσθαι τὴν τῶν προφητῶν ἀκριβῆ διαδοχήν]. (42) It is clear in practice how we approach our own writings. Although such a long time has now passed, no-one has dared to add, to take away, or to alter anything; and it is innate in every Judean, right from birth, to regard them as decrees of God [θεοῦ δόγματα], to remain faithful to them and, if necessary, gladly to die on their behalf. (43) Thus, to date many have been seen, on many occasions, as prisoners of war suffering torture and all kinds of deaths in theaters for not letting slip a single word in contravention of the laws and the records associated with them [παρὰ τοὺς νόμους καὶ τὰς μετὰ τούτων ἀναγραφάς].[51]

Josephus intended by this passage to contrast the few ancient Jewish books with the innumerable books among the Greeks that are riddled with errors and that have not attained the same revered status as have the twenty-two books among the Jews. Despite the claim at §38, the Jews do possess more books than just the twenty-two, as Josephus himself acknowledged later in this passage (§41). But these twenty-two merited special status as the "decrees of God" (§42) because they were all produced by prophets who received "inspiration from God" (§37).[52] This unique standing did not apply to the books written after the time of the Persian king Artaxerxes (465–424 BCE) because of the failure of the "exact line of succession of the prophets" (§41).[53] Josephus did not explain what he meant by this last remark; he did not think the gift of prophecy was unknown in Israel after Artaxerxes, for he considered the late second-century BCE high priest John Hyrcanus to be a prophet (*J.W.* 1.68–69; *Ant.* 13.299). Apparently Josephus envisioned a "line of prophets" stretching unbroken from Moses to the time of Artaxerxes, after which the line was broken, though a prophet may have still occasionally arisen.[54] Somehow this failure of the "exact line of succession of the prophets" diminished the authority of the literature written after Artaxerxes, so

---

51. Translation by John Barclay, *Against Apion*, FJTC 10 (Leiden: Brill, 2007), 28–32.

52. Peter Höffken, "Zum Kanonsbewusstsein des Josephus Flavius in *Contra Apionem* und in den *Antiquitates*," *JSJ* 32, no. 2 (2001): 161, points out that ἐπίπνοια appears only here in Josephus.

53. Oliver Gussmann, "Flavius Josephus und die Entstehung des Kanons Heiliger Schriften," in *Kanon in Konstruktion und Dekonstruktion*, ed. Eve-Marie Becker and Stefan Scholz (Berlin: de Gruyter, 2012), 350–52. Gussmann (351) points out that Artaxerxes does not elsewhere in Josephus serve as a pivotal dividing line.

54. Höffken, "Zum Kanonsbewusstsein," 162–63, also points out that a theme of unbroken prophets is not found in the *Antiquities* (162 n. 11). On the idea of the cessation of prophecy,

that, apparently, it was not considered a record of the "decrees of God" and was not thought to be a product of "inspiration from God."

Josephus did not explicitly identify all of the twenty-two books considered authentic records of the "decrees of God." Besides the five books making up the Law of Moses (§39), there are thirteen books written by prophets who recorded the events contemporary with themselves (τὰ κατ' αὐτοὺς πραχθέντα) and four books containing not history but hymns and instructions for life (§40). These descriptions, along with what we have already seen from Qumran, the New Testament, and elsewhere, provide sufficient hints to suggest that Josephus's collection of Scripture resembled very closely the twenty-four-book Tanak (in content, if not in structure). His third category of hymns and instructions no doubt contained the Psalter and Proverbs, and probably also Ecclesiastes and Song of Songs.[55] These are the types of books that could not easily be labeled "history." As for the thirteen historical books composed by prophets, possibly they constituted the rest of the Jewish canon in this way: Joshua, Judges + Ruth (cf. *Ant.* 5.318–337), Samuel, Kings, Chronicles, Ezra-Nehemiah (or 1 Esdras), Esther, Isaiah, Jeremiah + Lamentations (cf. *Ant.* 10.78), Ezekiel, the Twelve Minor Prophets (counted as one book), Daniel, and Job.[56] At least, this accords with the guesses of many scholars and with the reckoning of some early Christians.[57]

Remaining Ambiguity

We have seen that, according to most scholars, the majority of the books now making up the Tanak already functioned as normative authority—and thus as canon in the definition of some scholars—for most Jews at the time of Jesus.[58] We do not know that Jews at this time had a clearly determined collection of Scriptures; neither do we know that they did not. The earliest certain evidence for such a conception is in Josephus, at the end of the first century CE, and he attributes this conception to all Jews for long ages past. With all due allowance

---

see Juan Carlos Ossandón Widow, *The Origins of the Canon of the Hebrew Bible: An Analysis of Josephus and 4 Ezra*, JSJSup 186 (Leiden: Brill, 2018), 46–54.

55. Jean-Daniel Kaestli regards the identification of this grouping rather obvious; "La formation et la structure du canon biblique: Que peut apporter l'étude de la Septante?," in Alexander and Kaestli, *Canon of Scripture in Jewish and Christian Tradition*, 109.

56. Josephus used 1 Esdras at *Ant.* 11.1–158; and Nehemiah at *Ant.* 11.159–183. Josephus also knew a version of Esther with more material than in the Hebrew text (cf. *Ant.* 11.184–296); see Ossandón Widow, *Origins of the Canon*, ch. 6.

57. For references, see Barclay, *Against Apion*, 30 n. 165. For the early Christian lists, see Gallagher and Meade, *Biblical Canon Lists*.

58. Bokedal, *Formation and Significance*, 73–79.

for probable exaggeration on the part of Josephus, his statement indicates at least that Josephus himself was familiar with both the concept and the reality (not the terminology) of a closed canon even if not all Jews would have accepted his definition of the canon.

Several points of ambiguity remain as we try to understand the identity of the Scriptures at the time of Jesus. Even in late antiquity, not all questions about the status of the books of the Tanak were definitively settled among Jews. The rabbis continued to raise concerns (with tongue in cheek?) about Esther, Ezekiel, Ecclesiastes, and Song of Songs.[59] The book of Ben Sira continued to be cited in rabbinic literature.[60] As for the first century and earlier, despite assurances from Josephus, we cannot be sure that all Jews accepted the collection of Scriptures he promoted. Various theories have suggested otherwise.

Alexandrian Canon

One idea that was popular in the early twentieth century and has recently made something of a comeback is the Alexandrian canon theory. The theory was designed to explain how Christians ended up with more books (i.e., the deuterocanon) in their Old Testament than what are in the Jewish Bible. Since Christians used the Greek translation of Scripture, the Septuagint, and since the Septuagint is most strongly associated with Alexandria, Egypt, the home of a vibrant Jewish population in antiquity, some scholars suggested that Christians inherited the canon of Alexandrian Jews, which was broader, more inclusive, than the canon of Palestinian Jews. While for decades scholars have cited Sunderg's 1964 monograph as demolishing the idea—based essentially on a lack of evidence for what the canon of Alexandrian Jews might have been or, rather, that they even had a concept of a closed canon in the pre-Christian era—recently several prominent scholars have rehabilitated some version of the theory.[61] One problem with the Alexandrian canon idea is that our major representative of Alexandrian Judaism, Philo—a contemporary of Jesus—cites the Pentateuch constantly, occasionally cites several other books now in the Tanak, but he never cites Jewish Scripture that did not find a place in the Tanak. Patristic authors who explicitly reflect on the relationship of their canon to that of the Jews did not think that they received a canon from Jews inclusive of the deuterocanonical books; often the biblical canon promoted by patristic authors excluded these books, and those

---

59. See the collection of sources in Leiman, *Canonization of Hebrew Scripture*, 72–86.

60. Jenny R. Labendz, "The Book of Ben Sira in Rabbinic Literature," *AJSR* 30, no. 2 (2006): 347–92.

61. Sundberg, *Old Testament of the Early Church*. See the discussion and references in Lange, "Canonical History," 39–40 (§1.1.2.1.2).

authors who included the deuterocanonical books within the canon did so in full knowledge that they were expanding the canon beyond what Jews accepted.[62]

Samaritans and Sadducees

The Samaritans consider themselves the heirs of the northern Israelite tribes who adhere to the Mosaic Torah in its authentic form, as distinct from Jews. Scholars debate the timing of the permanent schism between Jews and Samaritans, with a second-century BCE date now holding sway.[63] The Samaritans accept only the Torah as Scripture, a position that can be traced back at least to the third century CE since Origen is our earliest certain evidence for it (*Cels.* 1.49).[64] In the same passage, Origen also claims that Sadducees accept only the Torah as Scripture, a claim made also by later patristic authors.[65] It is not clear whether Origen could have had first-hand knowledge of Sadducees since the common scholarly assumption is that they ceased to exist as an independent party shortly after the destruction of the temple.[66] It may be that Origen misinterpreted information such as that in Josephus (e.g., *Ant.* 13.297) that attributes to the Sadducees an adherence only to the written Torah as opposed to the oral Torah. Or he might have confused Sadducees and Samaritans. Or perhaps Sadducees provide evidence for a biblical canon quite at variance from that proposed by Josephus.[67]

---

62. For the biblical canons promoted by patristic authors, see Gallagher and Meade, *Biblical Canon Lists*. For a discussion of Christians promoting a canon explicitly wider than the Jewish canon, see Edmon L. Gallagher, *Hebrew Scripture in Patristic Biblical Theory: Canon, Language, Text*, VCSup 114 (Leiden: Brill, 2012), 53–60. Of course, we may doubt whether these patristic authors understood the historical process leading to their own biblical canon.

63. Gary N. Knoppers, *Jews and Samaritans: The Origins of Their Early Relations* (Oxford: Oxford University Press, 2013); Reinhard Pummer, *The Samaritans: A Profile* (Grand Rapids: Eerdmans, 2016).

64. Chapman, "Collections, Canons, and Communities," 48 n. 22, wonders whether the Samaritans before the third century CE might have accepted more Scripture, a question also entertained by Armin Lange, "From Literature to Scripture: The Unity and Plurality of the Hebrew Scriptures in Light of the Qumran Library," in *One Scripture or Many? Canon from Biblical, Theological, and Philosophical Perspectives*, ed. Christine Helmer and Christof Landmesser (Oxford: Oxford University Press, 2004), 61.

65. For sources, see Emil Schürer, *The History of the Jewish People in the Age of Jesus Christ (175 BC–AD 135)*, rev. Geza Vermes and Fergus Millar, 3 vols. in 4 (Edinburgh: T&T Clark, 1973–1987), 2:408 n. 24.

66. See, however, Martin Goodman, "Sadducees and Essenes after 70 CE," in *Crossing the Boundaries: Essays in Biblical Interpretation in Honour of Michael D. Goulder*, ed. Stanley E. Porter, Paul Joyce, and David E. Orton, BibInt 8 (Leiden: Brill, 1994), 347–56.

67. See the discussion with further references in Gallagher and Meade, *Biblical Canon Lists*, 19–20. Possibly other statements in Josephus (e.g., *Ant.* 18.16) could more easily be interpreted in

What Were the "Scriptures" in the Time of Jesus?

Jewish Pluralism and Scriptural Collections

The possibilities of an Alexandrian canon and a Sadducean Torah-only canon alongside a canon more closely agreeing with the one promoted by Josephus suggest that maybe different Jewish groups maintained different collections of Scripture. Such a proposal is defended by Timothy Lim, who further argues that in the days of Jesus, it was the Pharisaic party who adhered to the canon promoted by Josephus and that later became the biblical canon of the rabbis (who saw themselves as descended from the Pharisees).[68] During the days of Jesus, there would have been no standard collection of Scripture uniting all Jewish parties, though the Torah would have been universally accepted. Such an idea remains a possibility, but we lack clear evidence substantiating the diversity of scriptural collections before the end of the first century CE, nor do we have evidence for overt disagreements on the identity of Scripture during the Second Temple period.[69]

Variant Literary Editions

A variety of textual forms for some of the biblical books circulated in antiquity, as evident from a comparison of the traditional Hebrew (Masoretic) text with the Dead Sea Scrolls, the various Greek translations and their revisions, and the Samaritan Pentateuch. Aside from the Pentateuch (briefly mentioned earlier), there were variant literary editions at least for Jeremiah and the Psalter, as well as in the case of large passages of Joshua and Samuel.[70] For some books (e.g., Job, Proverbs), the Septuagint presents a version substantially different from the Masoretic Text. Perhaps, then, even when ancient Jews affirmed the scriptural status of the Psalms—certainly the case for the Qumran group, the early Christians, and Josephus—they might not have agreed on the authoritative version of the Psalter.[71] On the other hand, Emanuel Tov has proposed that the temple may have kept a deposit of authoritative versions of the biblical books, a proposal

---

reference to a Sadducean Torah-only canon, though Josephus may be susceptible of other interpretations, as well. Does Jesus cite Exod 3:6 to establish the doctrine of the resurrection (rather than, say, Dan 12:2) because his Sadducean interlocutors accept only the Torah (Mark 12:26)?

68. Lim, *Formation of the Jewish Canon*. On the relationship of the rabbis to the Pharisees, see the standard work by Strack and Stemberger, *Introduction to the Talmud and Midrash*, 1–7. Josephus is often connected to the Pharisees, based on his own statement (*Life* 12), but see Steve Mason's commentary on this passage in *Life of Josephus*, FJTC 9 (Leiden: Brill, 2003), 21 n. 91.

69. See Lange, "Canonical History," 38–39.

70. See the essays collected in the first section of Eugene Ulrich, *The Dead Sea Scrolls and the Origins of the Bible*, SDSS (Grand Rapids: Eerdmans, 1999).

71. See Mroczek, *Literary Imagination*, ch. 1.

that he himself has labeled "hypothetical" and that has engendered resistance from some scholars but remains a strong possibility.[72] In the first century CE, there does seem to have been a desire in certain quarters for Hebrew and Greek copies of Scripture to correspond to the textual tradition now familiar in the Masoretic Text, as evidenced by extant revisions of the Greek translations toward a proto-Masoretic tradition and by Hebrew manuscript discoveries in the Judean Desert outside the Qumran caves.[73] The textual pluriformity in the late Second Temple period is preserved to some extent in the quotations of Scripture in the New Testament, which often conform to the traditional Septuagint text, even in its departures from the Masoretic Text, but can also depart from the Septuagint, whether toward the Masoretic Text or in a different direction.[74]

Conclusions

Since our earliest list of books constituting the Jewish Bible is dated to the late first century CE (Josephus), and it does not even name all of the books included in the collection, we are forced into speculation for the time period of Jesus. The evidence can be read in all kinds of ways as scholars continue to prove. Judging from the lack of overt disagreement among ancient Jews regarding such questions, it seems safe to conclude (1) that most Jews had a good idea about which books were widely regarded as Scripture and (2) that these books were essentially the same as those in the collection of Josephus. At the same time, there was probably room for doubt about some books, and these possibly doubted books would probably correspond to those books poorly attested at Qumran and not quoted in the New Testament (e.g., Esther, Ecclesiastes, Tobit, Sirach, Wisdom of Solomon). As I mentioned at the beginning of this chapter, alongside books that were clearly Scripture and other books that were clearly not Scripture, there seem to have been some books that were not clearly (or clearly not!) in either category. Nevertheless, the Scriptures enjoyed enough generally recognized definition that when Jesus accused the Sadducees of not knowing the Scriptures (Mark 12:24; see also v. 10), the Sadducees did not need to ask Jesus which ones he meant.

---

72. Emanuel Tov, "The Text of the Hebrew/Aramaic and Greek Bible Used in the Ancient Synagogues," in *Hebrew Bible, Greek Bible, and Qumran: Collected Essays*, TSAJ 121 (Tübingen: Mohr Siebeck, 2008), 171–88. For an evaluation as to how Tov's idea might play into discussions of the Jewish canon, see Edmon L. Gallagher, "The Jerusalem Temple Library and Its Implications for the Canon of Scripture," *ResQ* 57 (2015): 39–52.

73. For a brief summary of this evidence with references to other literature, see Gallagher and Meade, *Biblical Canon Lists*, 23–24.

74. Gallagher, *Translation of the Seventy*, ch. 6.

What Were the "Scriptures" in the Time of Jesus?

BIBLIOGRAPHY

Alexander, Philip S. "The Formation of the Biblical Canon in Rabbinic Judaism." Pages 57–80 in *The Canon of Scripture in Jewish and Christian Tradition*. Edited by Philip S. Alexander and Jean-Daniel Kaestli. Prahins: Éditions du Zèbre, 2007.

Athanasius. *Athanasius Werke*. Edited by Hans-Georg Opitz. 4 vols. Berlin: de Gruyter, 1935–1941.

Barclay, John. *Against Apion*. FJTC 10. Leiden: Brill, 2007.

Barton, John. "The Old Testament Canons." Pages 145–64 in *From the Beginnings to 600*. Vol. 1 of *The New Cambridge History of the Bible*. Edited by James Carleton Paget and Joachim Schaper. Cambridge: Cambridge University Press, 2013.

———. *Oracles of God: Perceptions of Ancient Prophecy in Israel after the Exile*. Oxford: Oxford University Press, 1986.

Beckwith, Roger T. "A Modern Theory of the Old Testament Canon." VT 41, no. 4 (1991): 385–95.

———. *The Old Testament Canon of the New Testament Church and Its Background in Early Judaism*. Grand Rapids: Eerdmans, 1985.

Blischke, Folker. "Die *Sapientia Salomonis* und Paulus." Pages 273–92 in *Sapientia Salomonis (Weisheit Salomos)*. Edited by Karl-Wilhelm Niebuhr. SAPERE 27. Tübingen: Mohr Siebeck, 2015.

Bokedal, Tomas. *The Formation and Significance of the Christian Biblical Canon: A Study in Text, Ritual, and Interpretation*. London: Bloomsbury, 2014.

Brooke, George J. *The Dead Sea Scrolls and the New Testament*. Minneapolis: Fortress, 2005.

Carr, David M. *The Formation of the Hebrew Bible: A New Reconstruction*. Oxford: Oxford University Press, 2011.

Chapman, Stephen B. "The Canon Debate: What It Is and Why It Matters," *JTI* 4, no. 4 (2010): 273–94.

———. "Collections, Canons, and Communities." Pages 28–54 in *The Cambridge Companion to the Hebrew Bible/Old Testament*. Edited by Stephen B. Chapman and Marvin A. Sweeney. Cambridge Companions to Religion. Cambridge: Cambridge University Press, 2016.

———. *The Law and the Prophets: A Study in Old Testament Canon Formation*. FAT 27. Tübingen: Mohr Siebeck, 2010.

———. "Second Temple Jewish Hermeneutics: How Canon Is Not an Anachronism." Pages 281–96 in *Invention, Rewriting, Usurpation: Discursive Fights over Religious Traditions in Antiquity*. Edited by Jörg Ulrich, Anders-Christian Jacobsen, and David Brakke. Early Christianity in the Context of Antiquity 11. New York: Lang, 2011.

Childs, Brevard S. *An Introduction to the Old Testament as Scripture*. Philadelphia: Fortress, 1979.
Collins, John J. *The Dead Sea Scrolls: A Biography*. Princeton: Princeton University Press, 2013.
Dorival, Gilles. *The Septuagint from Alexandria To Constantinople: Canon, New Testament, Church Fathers, Catenae*. Oxford: Oxford University Press, 2021.
Gallagher, Edmon L. *Hebrew Scripture in Patristic Biblical Theory: Canon, Language, Text*. VCSup 114. Leiden: Brill, 2012.
———. "The Jerusalem Temple Library and Its Implications for the Canon of Scripture." *ResQ* 57 (2015): 39–52.
———. "Origen on the Shepherd of Hermas." *EC* 10, no. 2 (2019): 201–15.
———. *Translation of the Seventy: History, Reception, and Contemporary Use of the Septuagint*. Abilene, TX: ACU Press, 2021.
Gallagher, Edmon L., and John D. Meade. *The Biblical Canon Lists from Early Christianity: Texts and Analysis*. Oxford: Oxford University Press, 2017.
Goodman, Martin. "Sadducees and Essenes after 70 CE." Pages 347–56 in *Crossing the Boundaries: Essays in Biblical Interpretation in Honour of Michael D. Goulder*. Edited by Stanley E. Porter, Paul Joyce, and David E. Orton. BibInt 8. Leiden: Brill, 1994.
Gussmann, Oliver. "Flavius Josephus und die Entstehung des Kanons Heiliger Schriften." Pages 345–62 in *Kanon in Konstruktion und Dekonstruktion*. Edited by Eve-Marie Becker and Stefan Scholz. Berlin: de Gruyter, 2012.
Höffken, Peter. "Zum Kanonsbewusstsein des Josephus Flavius in *Contra Apionem* und in den *Antiquitates*." *JSJ* 32, no. 2 (2001): 159–77.
Junod, Éric. "La formation et la composition de l'Ancient Testament dans l'Église grecque des quatre premiers siècles." Pages 105–34 in *Le Canon de l'Ancien Testament: Sa formation et son histoire*. Edited by Jean-Daniel Kaestli and Otto Wermelinger. MdB. Geneva: Labor et Fides, 1984.
Kaestli, Jean-Daniel. "La formation et la structure du canon biblique: Que peut apporter l'étude de la Septante?" Pages 99–113 in *The Canon of Scripture in Jewish and Christian Tradition*. Edited by Philip S. Alexander and Jean-Daniel Kaestli. Prahins: Éditions du Zèbre, 2007.
Knoppers, Gary N. *Jews and Samaritans: The Origins of Their Early Relations*. Oxford: Oxford University Press, 2013.
Labendz, Jenny R. "The Book of Ben Sira in Rabbinic Literature." *AJSR* 30, no. 2 (2006): 347–92.
Lange, Armin. "The Canonical Histories of the Jewish Bible and the Christian Old Testament with Special Attention to the Deuterocanonical Books—A Synthesis." Pages 5–112 in *The Deuterocanonical Books: Overview Articles*. Edited by Matthias Henze and Frank Feder. THB 2A. Leiden: Brill, 2020.
———. "Canonical History of the Hebrew Bible." Pages 35–81 in *The Hebrew Bible:

Overview Articles. Edited by Armin Lange and Emanuel Tov. THB 1A. Leiden: Brill, 2016.

———. "From Literature to Scripture: The Unity and Plurality of the Hebrew Scriptures in Light of the Qumran Library." Pages 51–107 in *One Scripture or Many? Canon from Biblical, Theological, and Philosophical Perspectives*. Edited by Christine Helmer and Christof Landmesser. Oxford: Oxford University Press, 2004.

Lange, Armin, and Matthias Weingold. *Biblical Quotations and Allusions in Second Temple Jewish Literature*. JAJSup 5. Göttingen: Vandenhoeck & Ruprecht, 2011.

Leiman, Sid Z. *The Canonization of Hebrew Scripture: The Talmudic and Midrashic Evidence*. Hamden, CT: Archon, 1976.

Levy, Ian Christopher. "The Leipzig Disputation: Masters of the Sacred Page and the Authority of Scripture." Pages 115–44 in *Luther at Leipzig: Martin Luther, the Leipzig Debate, and the Sixteenth-Century Reformations*. Edited by Mickey L. Mattox, Richard J. Serina Jr., and Jonathan Mumme. SMRT 218. Leiden: Brill, 2019.

Lewis, Jack P. "What Do We Mean by Jabneh?" *JBR* 32, no. 2 (1964): 125–32.

Lim, Timothy H. "Defilement of Hands as a Principle Determining the Holiness of Scriptures." *JTS* 61, no. 2 (2010): 501–15.

———. *The Formation of the Jewish Canon*. ABRL. New Haven: Yale University Press, 2013.

Mason, Steve. *Life of Josephus*. FJTC 9. Leiden: Brill, 2003.

McDonald, Lee Martin. *The Formation of the Biblical Canon*. 2 volumes. London: Bloomsbury T&T Clark, 2017.

Metzger, Bruce M. *The Canon of the New Testament: Its Origin, Development, and Significance*. Oxford: Oxford University Press, 1987.

Moore, Nicholas J. "Is Enoch Also among the Prophets? The Impact of Jude's Citation of *1 Enoch* on the Reception of Both Texts in the Early Church." *JTS* 64, no. 2 (2013): 498–515.

Mroczek, Eva. *The Literary Imagination in Jewish Antiquity*. Oxford: Oxford University Press, 2016.

Ossandón Widow, Juan Carlos. *The Origins of the Canon of the Hebrew Bible: An Analysis of Josephus and 4 Ezra*. JSJSup 186. Leiden: Brill, 2018.

Pfeiffer, Rudolf. *History of Classical Scholarship: From the Beginning to the End of the Hellenistic Age*. Oxford: Oxford University Press, 1968.

Pummer, Reinhard. *The Samaritans: A Profile*. Grand Rapids: Eerdmans, 2016.

Ruhnken, David. "Historia critica oratorum Graecorum." Pages xxxiii–c in *P. Rutilii Lupi: De Figuris Sententiarum et Elocutionis Duo Libri*. Lyons: Luchtmans, 1768.

Ryle, Herbert Edward. *The Canon of the Old Testament: An Essay on the Gradual Growth and Formation of the Hebrew Canon of Scripture*. London: Macmillan, 1892.

Sanders, James A. *Torah and Canon*. Philadelphia: Fortress, 1972.

Schürer, Emil. *The History of the Jewish People in the Age of Jesus Christ (175 BC–AD*

135). Revised by Geza Vermes and Fergus Millar. 3 vols. in 4. Edinburgh: T&T Clark, 1973–1987.

Steinberg, Julius, and Timothy J. Stone. "The Historical Formation of the Writings in Antiquity." Pages 1–58 in *The Shape of the Writings*. Siphrut 16. Winona Lake, IN: Eisenbrauns, 2015.

Stern, Sacha. "Qumran Calendars and Sectarianism." Pages 232–53 in *The Oxford Handbook of the Dead Sea Scrolls*. Edited by Timothy H. Lim and John J. Collins. Oxford: Oxford University Press, 2010.

Strack, H. L., and Günter Stemberger. *Introduction to the Talmud and Midrash*. Translated by Markus Bockmuehl. Minneapolis: Fortress, 1992.

Sundberg, Albert C. *The Old Testament of the Early Church*. HTS 20. Cambridge: Harvard University Press, 1964.

Toorn, Karel van der. *Scribal Culture and the Making of the Hebrew Bible*. Cambridge: Harvard University Press, 2007.

Tov, Emanuel. "The Text of the Hebrew/Aramaic and Greek Bible Used in the Ancient Synagogues." Pages 171–88 in *Hebrew Bible, Greek Bible, and Qumran: Collected Essays*. TSAJ 121. Tübingen: Mohr Siebeck, 2008.

Ulrich, Eugene. *The Dead Sea Scrolls and the Origins of the Bible*. SDSS. Grand Rapids: Eerdmans, 1999.

———. "Our Sharper Focus on the Bible and Theology Thanks to the Dead Sea Scrolls." *CBQ* 66, no. 1 (2004): 1–24.

VanderKam, James C. *The Dead Sea Scrolls and the Bible*. Grand Rapids: Eerdmans, 2012.

VanderKam, James C., and Peter Flint. *The Meaning of the Dead Sea Scrolls: Their Significance for Understanding the Bible, Judaism, Jesus, and Christianity*. San Francisco: HarperSanFrancisco, 2002.

2

Israel's Scriptures in the Hebrew Bible

MARC ZVI BRETTLER

In discussing allusions to Moses in early Jewish and Christian sources, Dale Allison notes that the author of Matthew had no "anxiety of influence": he freely reused earlier sources, often without acknowledgment, because he believed that "imitation was not an act of inferior repetition but an inspired act of fresh interpretation."[1] Matthew is typical of many ancient texts, including those now incorporated into the Hebrew Bible. The anonymous exilic and postexilic prophet or prophets of Isa 40–66, for example, frequently reused earlier texts (for examples, see below, pp. 65–74). In so doing, he announces that he is "a reader, a traditionalist, a recycler. He wants his audience to know that he invests the great labor necessary to inherit a tradition. In so doing, he emphasizes at once his dependence and his originality: he shows that he knows and reveres older texts—and that he differs from them in specific and identifiable ways."[2]

This point about both dependence and originality is key for understanding citations and allusions in Hebrew Bible and New Testament texts. I am not suggesting that these later texts were specifically influenced by Isaiah, though some were, but rather that the types of allusion found in Isa 40–66 are part of

---

I would like to thank Jonathan Homrighausen and Matthew Arakaky for their assistance with this chapter, alongside the following scholars who were kind enough to comment on an earlier draft: Mark Goodacre, Richard Hays, Amy-Jill Levine, and Ross Wagner.

1. Dale C. Allison Jr., *The New Moses: A Matthean Typology* (Edinburgh: T&T Clark, 1993), 272.
2. Benjamin D. Sommer, *A Prophet Reads Scripture: Allusion in Isaiah 40–66*, Contraversions (Stanford: Stanford University Press, 1998), 166.

a tradition that continued in the New Testament and beyond.³ Some may have been influenced directly by a variety of scriptural texts, while others stand in continuity with the Hebrew Bible, mediated by texts that chronologically bridge the Hebrew Bible and the New Testament.

My main point is that early Jewish readers who encountered the New Testament—the group that is the focus of this chapter—would not have been surprised by the New Testament's many allusions to the Jewish Scriptures and the over 225 marked citations of the Jewish Scriptures, averaging almost one per chapter.⁴ However, some of the particular uses to which these allusions were put may have seemed strange and unfamiliar.

Despite various criteria that New Testament scholars have developed to determine allusions or even partial citations, these are often contested. Scholars of the Hebrew Bible, often integrating the work of New Testament scholars, have also struggled to develop criteria for determining allusions within the Hebrew Bible.⁵ I do not have the space in this chapter to defend each text I cite as allusive or to explain the details of why I believe a particular alluded text is later than the text it may be alluding to. I instead try to use consensus cases, to the extent that they exist, and will use multiple examples, so even if one is uncertain, the main argument may stand. To make matters simpler, most of my examples are from texts universally considered late, such as Daniel, Chronicles, and Ezra-Nehemiah.

I now turn to specific texts from the Hebrew Bible, using the four categories suggested in this volume's introduction. These categories form a continuum, expressed in the following chart:⁶

---

3. See Marc Zvi Brettler and Amy-Jill Levine, "Isaiah's Suffering Servant: Before and After Christianity," *Int* 73, no. 2 (2019): 158–73. For that prophet's broader influence, esp. on Mark, see Joel Marcus, *The Way of the Lord: Christological Exegesis of the Old Testament in the Gospel of Mark* (Edinburgh: T&T Clark, 1992).

4. Dale C. Allison Jr., "The Old Testament in the New Testament," in *From the Beginnings to 600*, vol. 1 of *The New Cambridge History of the Bible*, ed. James Carleton Paget and Joachim Schaper (Cambridge: Cambridge University Press, 2013), 479.

5. For the New Testament, see esp. Richard B. Hays, *Echoes of Scripture in the Letters of Paul* (New Haven: Yale University Press, 1989), 29–33, and his fuller, more recent formulation in his *The Conversion of the Imagination: Paul as Interpreter of Israel's Scripture* (Grand Rapids: Eerdmans, 2005), 25–50 ("'Who Has Believed Our Message?' Paul's Reading of Isaiah"). For the Hebrew Bible, see esp. Sommer, *Prophet Reads Scripture*; Ziony Zevit, ed., *Subtle Citation, Allusion, and Translation in the Hebrew Bible* (Sheffield: Equinox, 2017).

6. See, similarly, Stanley E. Porter, "Pauline Techniques in Interweaving Scripture into His Letters," in *Paulinische Schriftrezeption: Grundlagen – Ausprägungen – Wirkungen – Wertungen*, ed. Florian Wilk and Markus Öhler, FRLANT 268 (Göttingen: Vandenhoeck & Ruprecht, 2017), 23–55, esp. 55.

Table 2.1. Degrees of Connection between Texts

closest connection   **weakest connection**
Explicit citation→   implicit citation→   verbal allusion→   conceptual allusion

It is sometimes unclear exactly where each case fits best, and thus the four categories are somewhat ambiguous. All of these categories are explored by Michael Fishbane in his magisterial *Biblical Interpretation in Ancient Israel*, which is the starting point for discussing most of the topics in this chapter.[7] Building upon his insights, it is possible to see how each category shows significant continuity between how the New Testament uses the Old and how the Hebrew Bible uses the Scriptures of Israel.

Marked Citations

Quotation is fundamental to most Jewish literature.[8] Given that quotation marks were invented in the Renaissance, biblical quotations are marked by a variety of introductory phrases or other grammatical indications.[9] To complicate matters further, it was acceptable in antiquity both to quote without acknowledging the source and to quote imprecisely.

More specifically, this first category of marked citations consists of cases where the Hebrew text explicitly indicates that it is citing an earlier work. Isolating these cases in the Hebrew Bible is not totally straightforward since Hebrew terms such as לאמר and ככתוב, typically translated as "saying," and "as is written," which can be used to mark such citations, have other functions as well, and often introduce paraphrases rather than exact quotations.

Quotations that are marked by introductory formulas are much less prominent in the Hebrew Bible than they are in the New Testament, and they are distributed in a skewed fashion: While the New Testament writers generally considered what we more or less know now as the Greek Scriptures to be quote worthy, only books composed in the later period of biblical Israel had the opportunity to quote from books now found in Scripture; by definition, the earlier books

---

7. Michael Fishbane, *Biblical Interpretation in Ancient Israel* (Oxford: Clarendon, 1985).
8. Michael Marmur, "Why Jews Quote," *Oral Tradition* 29, no. 1 (2014): 5–46.
9. For the invention of quotation marks, see Ruth Finnegan, *Why Do We Quote? The Culture and History of Quotation* (Cambridge: Open Book, 2013), 79–94. For introduction to biblical quotations, see esp. Seidel's law, discussed in Bernard M. Levinson, *Deuteronomy and the Hermeneutics of Legal Innovation* (New York: Oxford University Press, 1997), 19.

that now form Scripture did not have (what are now) scriptural books to quote from. The quotation of earlier (Hebrew) Scripture in later (Hebrew) Scripture is often discussed (anachronistically) as reflecting a "canon within a canon"—later biblical books quote "those writings or books, or parts of them, which a community considered especially important for one reason or another."[10] I avoid the problematic terms "canonical" or "authoritative," preferring "quote worthy."

The Citation Formulas "Saying" and "As Is Written"

The Hebrew word לאמר ("to say," "saying") sometimes introduces a quotation, but clauses introduced by לאמר may also "be retold, iterative, hypothetical, fabricated, or semi-direct" citations.[11] In other words, לאמר on occasion introduces an indirect quote or paraphrase, and should be rendered as "said that," which need not introduce a quotation.[12]

None of the texts using לאמר introduces a precise quotation. This phenomenon of inexact quotation should not be considered in isolation. When the Bible quotes or repeats itself, it often shortens, lengthens, or paraphrases the original quotation.[13] Whether the change is significant is typically a judgment call, "assessed only in light of the context in which the quotation is placed," and small changes "may take on a significance far beyond their size."[14] Overreading these changes is as problematic as underreading.

Nor are texts that use ככתוב more straightforward. Modern norms would lead us to expect ככתוב, "as is written," to introduce an exact quotation, but in many places this is not so. In postexilic texts, this formula is sometimes used to exegete earlier texts, to explain what the earlier text "really" means from the later author's perspective.[15]

---

10. On the broader concept, see George J. Brooke, "'The Canon within the Canon,' at Qumran and in the New Testament," in *The Scrolls and the Scriptures: Qumran Fifty Years After*, ed. Stanley E. Porter and Craig A. Evans, JSPSup 26 (Sheffield: Sheffield Academic, 1997), 242–66, quotation from p. 266.

11. Cynthia L. Miller-Naudé, "Direct and Indirect Speech: Biblical Hebrew," *EHLL* 1:742.

12. Cynthia L. Miller, *The Representation of Speech in Biblical Hebrew Narrative: A Linguistic Analysis*, HSM 55 (Atlanta: Scholars Press, 1996); Samuel A. Meier, *Speaking of Speaking: Marking Direct Discourse in the Hebrew Bible*, VTSup 46 (Leiden: Brill, 1992), 94. I thank Dr. Tania Notarius for calling the former work to my attention.

13. George W. Savran, *Telling and Retelling: Quotation in Biblical Narrative*, ISBL (Bloomington: Indiana University Press, 1988), esp. 29–36.

14. Savran, *Telling and Retelling*, 36, 109.

15. Kevin L. Spawn, *"As It Is Written" and Other Citation Formulae in the Old Testament: Their Use, Development, Syntax, and Significance*, BZAW 311 (Berlin: de Gruyter, 2002), 258

Two Early Examples:
Variation between the Later Text and the Text It Quotes

Two of the earliest quotations of earlier texts in the Hebrew Bible are found in a late stratum of the multilayered book of Kings.[16] These citations illustrate two key issues related to quotations of the scriptural texts in the New Testament. The first shows that later texts may rephrase earlier ones in small ways, and the second, that later texts may significantly revise their source.

Second Kings 14:6 explains why King Amaziah of Judah killed only those who killed his father, Joash, but did not kill the assassins' descendants:

וְאֶת־בְּנֵי הַמַּכִּים לֹא הֵמִית כַּכָּתוּב בְּסֵפֶר תּוֹרַת־מֹשֶׁה אֲשֶׁר־צִוָּה יְהוָה לֵאמֹר לֹא־יוּמְתוּ אָבוֹת עַל־בָּנִים וּבָנִים לֹא־יוּמְתוּ עַל־אָבוֹת כִּי אִם־אִישׁ בְּחֶטְאוֹ יָמוּת [יוּמָת:]

But he did not put to death the children of the assassins, in accordance with what is written [כַּכָּתוּב] in the Book of the Teaching of Moses [בְּסֵפֶר תּוֹרַת־מֹשֶׁה], where the LORD commanded [לֵאמֹר], "Parents shall not be put to death for children, nor children be put to death for parents; a person shall be put to death only for his own crime."[17]

The citation is marked as explicit in several ways. It is immediately preceded by לאמר, which may function to introduce direct discourse. The notation of the source, "the Book of the Teaching of Moses," which here refers to (an early form of) Deuteronomy, indicates firmly that it is meant as a quotation.[18] The text quoted is Deut 24:16:

לֹא־יוּמְתוּ אָבוֹת עַל־בָּנִים וּבָנִים לֹא־יוּמְתוּ עַל־אָבוֹת אִישׁ בְּחֶטְאוֹ יוּמָתוּ׃

Parents shall not be put to death for children, nor children be put to death for parents: a person shall be put to death only for his own crime.

---

and passim. See also the comment on כתוב in Sara Japhet, *Ezra-Nehemia*, Mikra Leyisra'el (Tel Aviv: Am Oved, 2019), 364 [Hebrew].

16. On the layers of Kings, see Anthony F. Campbell and Mark A. O'Brien, *Unfolding the Deuteronomistic History: Origins, Upgrades, Present Text* (Minneapolis: Fortress, 2000); Thomas Römer, *The So-Called Deuteronomistic History: A Sociological, Historical and Literary Introduction* (London: T&T Clark, 2005).

17. The biblical translations follow NJPS, sometimes with minor adjustments.

18. See, e.g., John Gray, *I and II Kings: A Commentary*, 2nd rev. ed., OTL (London: SCM, 1970), 604.

This is part of a miscellany of laws in Deuteronomy, applied by this Deuteronomist to King Amaziah.

The Hebrew of Kings is not quite identical to Deuteronomy. While the NJPS translation in both cases uses a semicolon to introduce the clause "a person shall be put to death only," in Deuteronomy this semicolon is unmarked, as contrasts often are in Biblical Hebrew, while in Kings it is more explicit through the use of the כי אם, "rather," which introduces exceptive clauses.[19] The final word in Kings is written (ketiv) יָמוּת, "(he) will die," but according to tradition is read (qere) as יוּמָת, "(he) shall be killed," while Deuteronomy reads differently than both of these: the plural יוּמָתוּ, "(they) shall be killed." An author of Kings may have quoted a non-MT form of the verse or may be citing loosely from memory.[20] Alternately, the author of Kings may have had a loose idea of what it means to quote, as noted above. In any case, these slight differences have no impact on meaning.

This segment of Kings quotes Deuteronomy because it clearly explains why Amaziah did not kill anyone beyond the conspirators: he followed "the Book of the Teaching of Moses, where the LORD commanded. . . ."[21] The author thus quotes to illustrate the point one of Kings' earlier editors made in the introduction to Amaziah's reign: "He did what was pleasing to the LORD" (2 Kgs 14:3). For this late redactor, "pleasing" behavior is reflected in following the divine law as laid out in the lawbook, an early form of Deuteronomy (see 2 Kgs 22–23).

The form introducing the quotation, ככתוב ב ("written in"), may sound familiar to New Testament readers. It is reflected in Mark 1:2: καθὼς γέγραπται ἐν. Joel Marcus notes: "Only here and in Rom 9:25 does a New Testament author cite an Old Testament passage with the word 'in' plus the name of the author."[22] In contrast, ככתוב ב appears ten more times in the Hebrew Bible, also followed by a reference to Torah.[23] Most of these references are from the late books, Ezra-Nehemiah and Chronicles, which anchor practices specifically in the Torah.[24]

---

19. Paul Joüon, *A Grammar of Biblical Hebrew*, trans. and rev. by T. Muraoka, 2 vols., SubBi 27 (Rome: Pontifical Biblical Institute, 2006), §173.

20. See the variants recorded in Carmel McCarthy, *Deuteronomy*, BHQ 5 (Stuttgart: Deutsche Bibelgesellschaft, 2007), 70, and the note on 118*; and cf. the slightly different 2 Chr 25:4. On variations in the biblical text in this early period, see Emanuel Tov, *Textual Criticism of the Hebrew Bible*, 3rd ed. (Minneapolis: Fortress, 2012), 161–90.

21. For evidence that this Kings reference is later than Deut 24:6 and thus is likely quoting it, see Campbell and O'Brien, *Unfolding the Deuteronomistic History*, 435 n. 44; Römer, *So-Called Deuteronomistic History*, 157–58, esp. 158 n. 115.

22. Joel Marcus, *Mark 1–8: A New Translation with Introduction and Commentary*, AB 27 (New York: Doubleday, 1999), 142.

23. Josh 8:31; 1 Kgs 2:3; Ezra 3:2; Neh 10:35, 37; 2 Chr 23:18; 25:4; 31:3; 35:12, 26. Some of these reflect parallel passages.

24. The Joshua and Kings texts are from a late layer of the DtrH.

The New Testament authors were less Torah-centric and generally anchored their citations more broadly and vaguely in the wider Scriptures of Israel. This difference—looking back specifically to the Torah or to broader parts of the Scriptures of Israel—is an important reminder to look for differences within similarities when we compare the use of the scriptural texts in the New Testament to the use of older scriptural texts in the Hebrew Bible.

First Kings 2:3 also uses the formula "as is written in the *Torah* of Moses," and (the MT of) 1 Kgs 2:4 uses the quotation word לֵאמֹר twice, and it is rendered in the NJPS translation through punctuation rather than words:[25]

לְמַעַן֩ יָקִ֨ים יְהוָ֜ה אֶת־דְּבָר֗וֹ אֲשֶׁ֨ר דִּבֶּ֣ר עָלַי֮ לֵאמֹר֒ אִם־יִשְׁמְר֨וּ בָנֶ֜יךָ אֶת־דַּרְכָּ֗ם לָלֶ֤כֶת לְפָנַי֙ בֶּאֱמֶ֔ת בְּכָל־לְבָבָ֖ם וּבְכָל־נַפְשָׁ֑ם לֵאמֹ֔ר לֹֽא־יִכָּרֵ֤ת לְךָ֙ אִ֔ישׁ מֵעַ֖ל כִּסֵּ֥א יִשְׂרָאֵֽל׃

> Then the LORD will fulfill the promise that He made concerning me [לֵאמֹר]: "If your descendants are scrupulous in their conduct, and walk before Me faithfully, with all their heart and soul, [לֵאמֹר] your line on the throne of Israel shall never end!"

"The promise" (literally, "word" or "utterance") refers to God's promise to David of a continuous dynasty, found in 2 Sam 7:12–16:

> [12]When your days are done and you lie with your fathers, I will raise up your offspring after you, one of your own issue, and I will establish his kingship. [13]He shall build a house for My name, and I will establish his royal throne forever [עַד עוֹלָם]. [14]I will be a father to him, and he shall be a son to Me. When he does wrong, I will chastise him with the rod of men and the affliction of mortals; [15]but I will never withdraw My favor from him as I withdrew it from Saul, whom I removed to make room for you. [16]Your house and your kingship shall ever [עַד עוֹלָם] be secure before you; your throne shall be established forever [עַד עוֹלָם].

In contrast to the previous case concerning intergenerational punishment, the citation in 1 Kgs 2 hardly overlaps with the vocabulary of the promise and uses many phrases absent from it.

---

25. The second לֵאמֹר is awkward, and not reflected in some LXX manuscripts and the Vulgate. C. F. Burney, *Notes on the Hebrew Text of the Books of Kings* (Oxford: Clarendon, 1903), 14, retains both, but Meier, *Speaking of Speaking*, 96, with good reason excises the second לֵאמֹר. BHS suggests that it should possibly be deleted ("dl?").

The lack of substantial verbal overlap is the least of the problems in this citation. Kings significantly reworks the ideas of 2 Samuel. In Samuel, individual kings are punished, but 2 Sam 7 unequivocally promises an eternal dynasty: the Hebrew עַד עוֹלָם, "forever," as noted above, is found in 2 Samuel verses 13 and 16 (twice), as well as several times later in the chapter. Yet the promise for dynastic continuity in 1 Kings is introduced with אִם, "if," making it conditional.

This change from an unconditional to a conditional promise is used by many scholars in determining the layering of Kings: an early stage of the dynastic promise, preceding the Babylonian exile of 586 BCE, offered an unconditional promise for an eternal dynasty while exilic and later authors, who experienced the rupture of this dynasty, turned this divine promise into a conditional pledge.[26] First Kings 2:4 thus drastically revises the text it purports to quote while presenting that revision as a citation.[27]

These two examples reflect a range of differences: Second Kings 14:6 quotes closely the text it claims to be quoting, and the slight differences do not change the meaning of the original. Almost all of the words of the original appear in the later text. First Kings 2:4, like several cases in Chronicles, changes both the words and the meaning of the earlier text.[28] These texts can be placed on opposite sides of a continuum—a continuum that would look very similar to the variations found when New Testament texts quote the Hebrew Scriptures.

Additional Parallels to New Testament Citation Formulas

Some of the formulas popular for New Testament citations of scriptural texts have Hebrew equivalents in later texts of the Scriptures of Israel. Most of these Greek formulas introduce citations with verbs of speaking (BDAG, s.v. "λέγω"), writing (BDAG, s.v. "γράφω"), or especially in Matthew, claim that certain verses

---

26. The classic American exposition is Frank Moore Cross, *Canaanite Myth and Hebrew Epic: Essays in the History of the Religion of Israel* (Cambridge: Harvard University Press, 1973), 274–89, esp. 287. For refinements and variations, see Campbell and O'Brien, *Unfolding the Deuteronomisitc History*; Römer, *So-Called Deuteronomistic History*. Specifically, on the changes to the dynastic promise, see William M. Schniedewind, *Society and the Promise to David: The Reception History of 2 Samuel 7:1–17* (New York: Oxford University Press, 1999); on 1 Kgs 2:4, see 162. Campbell and O'Brien, *Unfolding the Deuteronomistic History*, 332, esp. n. 3; and Römer, *So-Called Deuteronomistic History*, 145–46, see 1 Kgs 2:4 as a late element in Kings. Some (mostly European) scholars dispute this chronological explanation between the different forms of the oracles; see, e.g., Jan Rückl, *A Sure House: Studies in the Dynastic Promise to David in the Books of Samuel and Kings*, OBO 281 (Fribourg: Academic Press; Göttingen: Vandenhoeck & Ruprecht, 2016).

27. Whether this infinitive construct is used twice (e.g., MT) or once (e.g., in the Lucianic branch of the LXX) is immaterial for this point; see above, n. 25.

28. See Spawn, *"As It Is Written."*

Israel's Scriptures in the Hebrew Bible

are fulfilled (BDAG, s.v. "πληρόω") through Jesus. Though each of these verbs appear in citations found in the Scriptures of Israel, they are not used to the same extent nor in the same proportions as in the New Testament. Further, as the following example illustrates, it is not certain that each is used specifically to cite what might be considered "Scripture."

A Greek verb for speaking, λέγω, would be reflected in Hebrew אמר or דבר. The verb אמר, for example, is used in Joel in a manner that looks like it introduces a scriptural citation:

> But everyone who invokes the name of the LORD shall escape; for there shall be a remnant on Mount Zion and in Jerusalem, as the LORD promised [אמר]. Anyone who invokes the LORD will be among the survivors. (Joel 3:5 [2:32 ET])

Although this looks like a quotation of a well-known text, no such text is found in the Hebrew Bible, and none of the suggestions of which text it is quoting is compelling.[29] Similarly, the verb דבר, "to speak," which is semantically close to אמר, is never used to cite Scripture. Although the formula כדבר יהוה אשר דבר, "in accordance with the word that the LORD had spoken," appears frequently in what Gerhard von Rad called the "prophecy-fulfillment pattern" (e.g., 1 Kgs 15:29),[30] these all cite general situations rather than something explicitly said.[31] Given the use of דבר in this formula, its absence in cases where Scripture is cited, alongside the absence of the verb אמר in suggesting a citation, is remarkable. The lack of these two words for speaking, דבר and אמר, likely suggests that Scripture was cited not as something read, but as something written—and that this transition transpired late in the Second Temple period. It is unsurprising that a written text would quote a written text. This contrasts sharply with the many citations using λέγω in the New Testament, reflecting what Jesus *said* when citing a written text.

Late Hebrew Bible texts use the verb כתב and its passive participle כָּתוּב, the main Hebrew verb for writing corresponding to the Greek γράφω, and its perfect passive γέγραπται, in a variety of ways and forms for citing Scripture.[32] Indeed, the Septuagint renders many of the Hebrew Bible's ככתוב citation formulas as καθὼς γέγραπται or other forms of γράφω. In the above example, where Kings

---

29. Spawn, *"As It Is Written,"* 230–31.
30. Gerhard von Rad, "The Deuteronomic Theology of History in *I and II Kings*," in *The Problem of the Hexateuch and Other Essays* (London: SCM, 1984), 205–21.
31. See, e.g., 1 Kgs 15:29: וַיְהִי כְמָלְכוֹ הִכָּה אֶת־כָּל־בֵּית יָרָבְעָם לֹא־הִשְׁאִיר כָּל־נְשָׁמָה לְיָרָבְעָם עַד־הִשְׁמִדוֹ "As soon as he [King Baasha] became king, he struck down all the House of Jeroboam; he did not spare a single soul belonging to Jeroboam until he destroyed it—in accordance with the word that the LORD had spoken through His servant, the prophet Ahijah the Shilonite [כִּדְבַר יְהוָה אֲשֶׁר דִּבֶּר בְּיַד־עַבְדּוֹ אֲחִיָּה הַשִּׁילֹנִי]."
32. Note the title of Spawn, *"As It Is Written."*

notes that a king followed what was written in Deuteronomy (2 Kgs 14:6), the Septuagint's citation formula foreshadows Mark's:

> But he did not put to death the children of the assassins, in accordance with what is written [כַּכָּתוּב/καθὼς γέγραπται] in the Book of the Teaching of Moses [בְּסֵפֶר תּוֹרַת־מֹשֶׁה/ἐν βιβλίῳ νόμων Μωυσῆ], where the Lord commanded [אֲשֶׁר־צִוָּה יְהוָה לֵאמֹר/ὡς ἐνετείλατο κύριος λέγων]. . . .

The Septuagint translators' choice of citation formulas provides the template followed by Mark and other New Testament authors. Most often ככתוב is rendered καθὼς γέγραπται. Other times they use another form of the same verb, as in 2 Chr 31:3: "also the king's portion, from his property, for the burnt offerings—the morning and evening burnt offering, and the burnt offerings for sabbaths, and new moons, and festivals, as prescribed in the Teaching of the Lord [כַּכָּתוּב בְּתוֹרַת יְהוָה/τὰς γεγραμμένας ἐν τῷ νόμῳ κυρίου]."

Although 2 Kgs 14:6 is not an entirely exact citation of Deut 24:16, it is far more precise than other texts using כתב in citation formulas that significantly revise or extend the meaning of the cited texts.[33] The parade example is Neh 8:15b, which commands:

> צְאוּ הָהָר וְהָבִיאוּ עֲלֵי־זַיִת וַעֲלֵי־עֵץ שֶׁמֶן וַעֲלֵי הֲדַס וַעֲלֵי תְמָרִים וַעֲלֵי עֵץ עָבֹת לַעֲשֹׂת סֻכֹּת כַּכָּתוּב׃

> Go out to the mountains and bring leafy branches of olive trees, pine trees, myrtles, palms and [other] leafy trees to make booths, as it is written [כַּכָּתוּב].

Most scholars think that this verse refers to Lev 23:40–42:

> וּלְקַחְתֶּם לָכֶם בַּיּוֹם הָרִאשׁוֹן פְּרִי עֵץ הָדָר כַּפֹּת תְּמָרִים וַעֲנַף עֵץ־עָבֹת וְעַרְבֵי־נָחַל וּשְׂמַחְתֶּם לִפְנֵי יְהוָה אֱלֹהֵיכֶם שִׁבְעַת יָמִים׃ וְחַגֹּתֶם אֹתוֹ חַג לַיהוָה שִׁבְעַת יָמִים בַּשָּׁנָה חֻקַּת עוֹלָם לְדֹרֹתֵיכֶם בַּחֹדֶשׁ הַשְּׁבִיעִי תָּחֹגּוּ אֹתוֹ׃ בַּסֻּכֹּת תֵּשְׁבוּ שִׁבְעַת יָמִים כָּל־הָאֶזְרָח בְּיִשְׂרָאֵל יֵשְׁבוּ בַּסֻּכֹּת׃

> On the first day you shall take the product of hadar trees, branches of palm trees, boughs of leafy trees, and willows of the brook, and you shall rejoice before the Lord your God seven days. You shall observe it as a festival of the Lord for seven days in the year; you shall observe it in the seventh month as

---

33. See also the citation of Deut 27:5–6 in Josh 8:30–31a.

a law for all time, throughout the ages. You shall live in booths seven days; all citizens in Israel shall live in booths.[34]

Nehemiah 8 has different, or perhaps more specific vegetation than Leviticus mandates. It commands that this vegetation must be used to build booths, which may be suggested by the juxtaposition of Lev 23:40 and 42, but is not explicit.[35]

Given von Rad's observation that a major structuring device of the Deuteronomistic History (DtrH), the books of Deuteronomy–Kings, is that God's word is fulfilled,[36] we would expect the root מלא, "to fulfill," to be frequent when the Scripture of Israel cites earlier texts. But within the Deuteronomistic History, only 1 Kgs 2:27 uses the word מלא, the Hebrew equivalent of the πληρόω used in the New Testament fulfillment texts: "So Solomon dismissed Abiathar from his office of priest of the Lord—thus fulfilling [לְמַלֵּא/πληρωθῆναι LXX] what the Lord had spoken at Shiloh regarding the house of Eli." This verse refers back to the episode narrated in 1 Sam 2:27–36. Unlike the New Testament references, rather than quoting the earlier text, it refers to the fulfillment of an idea expressed in the earlier text.

The Scriptures of Israel provide only two examples that parallel the use best-known from Matthew. One example, 2 Chr 36:21, describes the destruction of the temple (noted in the previous verses), followed by the return under Cyrus (the following verses) as happening

in fulfillment [לְמַלֹּאות/τοῦ πληρωθῆναι LXX] of the word of the Lord [דְּבַר־יְהוָה] spoken by Jeremiah, until the land paid back its sabbaths; as long as it lay desolate it kept sabbath, till seventy years were completed.

But the phase that immediately follows "Jeremiah" is actually from Leviticus:

אָז תִּרְצֶה הָאָרֶץ אֶת־שַׁבְּתֹתֶיהָ כֹּל יְמֵי הֳשַׁמָּה . . . כָּל־יְמֵי הָשַׁמָּה תִּשְׁבֹּת

Then shall the land make up for its sabbath years throughout the time that it is desolate. . . . Throughout the time that it is desolate, it shall observe the rest (Lev 26:34a, 35a).

---

34. See most recently Japhet, *Ezra-Nehemia*, 364–65.

35. See discussion in Spawn, *"As Is Written,"* 101–4; and the earlier remarks of Fishbane, *Biblical Interpretation*, 109–13, who credits Yehezkel Kaufmann with the observation that Nehemiah is a type of midrash on the last verses of Lev 23.

36. Von Rad, "The Deuteronomic Theology of History," 208–9, 220–21.

This citation in 2 Chr 36:21 is a mashup of Leviticus and Jeremiah; Leviticus is underlined, and Jeremiah is underlined in bold:

לְמַלֹּאות דְּבַר־יְהוָה בְּפִי יִרְמְיָהוּ <u>עַד־רָצְתָה הָאָרֶץ אֶת־שַׁבְּתוֹתֶיהָ כָּל־יְמֵי הָשַׁמָּה שָׁבָתָה</u> **לְמַלֹּאות שִׁבְעִים שָׁנָה**׃

> in fulfillment of the word of the LORD spoken by Jeremiah, <u>until the land paid back its sabbaths; as long as it lay desolate it kept sabbath,</u> **till seventy years were completed.**

The Jeremiah citation refers to several passages where the Babylonians will dominate the world for seventy years—the exact phrase used in Chronicles—after which Israel will be restored (Jer 25:11, 12; and esp. 29:10; cf. Zech 1:12; Dan 9:2). Even though most of the quotation is (somewhat loosely) from Leviticus, the Chronicler attributed it only to Jeremiah, perhaps because he was a prophet, and the point of the verse is that a prophetic oracle has been fulfilled. The fulfillment of prophetic oracles typifies the formula's use in the New Testament.

Such citational mashups are found in the New Testament as well; for example, Mark 1:2 attributes a quote to Isaiah, but before citing some version of Isa 40:3 in 1:3, Mark 1:2 cites Mal 3:1a (combined with Exod 23:20a).[37] In both cases, an author signals an explicit citation or quotation from a particular book but quotes a different book before returning to the book signaled. While the Chronicler attributes this quote to a specific prophet, this pattern is less usual in the New Testament, which typically describes fulfillment of Scripture more generally. Finally, Chronicles does not speak of fulfillment alone but connects it to the word "spoken by Jeremiah." This establishes a pattern followed by most New Testament fulfillment references: combining fulfillment with another verb, such as speaking.[38]

The other occurrence that parallels Matthew's fulfillment formula is Dan 9:2:

בִּשְׁנַת אַחַת לְמָלְכוֹ אֲנִי דָּנִיֵּאל בִּינֹתִי בַּסְּפָרִים מִסְפַּר הַשָּׁנִים אֲשֶׁר הָיָה דְבַר־יְהוָה אֶל־יִרְמִיָה הַנָּבִיא לְמַלֹּאות לְחָרְבוֹת יְרוּשָׁלַםִ שִׁבְעִים שָׁנָה׃

> In the first year of his [Darius son of Ahasuerus] reign, I, Daniel, consulted the books concerning the number of years that, according to the word of the

---

37. Both Matthew and Luke fix this by omitting the quotation from Malachi; see Mark Goodacre, "The Evangelists' Use of the Old Testament and the Synoptic Problem," in *New Studies in the Synoptic Problem: Oxford Conference, April 2008; Essays in Honour of Christopher M. Tuckett*, ed. Paul Foster et al., BETL 239 (Leuven: Peeters, 2011), 281–89, esp. 284–89. See the similar mashup in Matt 27:9–10.

38. In some cases, the New Testament passage continues with a reference to a specific text.

Lord that had come to Jeremiah the prophet, were to be the term of [lit. "to fulfill"; Heb. לְמַלֹּאות] Jerusalem's desolation—seventy years.

Through a very creative word-play between the two words "seventy" (*shivi'im*) and "weeks" (*shuvu'im*), which would have been written identically though pronounced with different vowels, the author of this chapter, helped by the angel Gabriel, interprets the prophet's seventy as *shavu'im shivi'im,* "seventy weeks of years," namely 70 × 70 = 490 years (9:24).[39] This move helps keep an ancient, problematic prophecy alive through radical reinterpretation and thus provides a helpful model for understanding many of the fulfillment citations in Matthew.

The Purposes of Citations

The citation of the Scriptures of Israel in the New Testament, like those in the Hebrew Bible, conveys authority and creates cultural memory and identity.[40] Citations in the New Testament center around Jesus's mission, life, death, and resurrection. Typically, scriptural verses are interpreted in reference to him, though sometimes also in relation to him and his community, what Richard Hays has called "ecclesiocentric."[41] These citations read earlier Scripture eschatologically, or to use David Lincicum's phrase, they read "the scriptures of Israel as directed to the eschatological present."[42]

This is very different than how the newer portions of the Scriptures of Israel use the older portions. They lack a single focus, and they are not directed toward an individual. This is not surprising: the Hebrew Bible lacks the focus or center that the New Testament has—it is a much more diverse collection, despite attempts to find its theological *Mitte*.[43] As explored above, it cites earlier Scripture for several reasons: to show that the prophetic word is still true (2 Chr 37:21;

---

39. The literature on this passage is immense; see the clear and helpful summary in Carol A. Newsom with Brennan W. Breed, *Daniel: A Commentary*, OTL (Louisville: Westminster John Knox, 2014), 299–300; see esp. the discussion in Fishbane, *Biblical Interpretation*, 482–83.

40. For authority, see Allison, "Old Testament in the New Testament," 484. For cultural memory and identity, see Jeremy Punt, "Identity, Memory, and Scriptural Warrant: Arguing Paul's Case," in *Paul and Scripture: Extending the Conversation*, ed. Christopher D. Stanley, ECL 9 (Atlanta: Society of Biblical Literature, 2012), 25–53.

41. See, e.g., 1 Pet 2:7–8, and Hays, *Echoes of Scripture in the Letters of Paul*, esp. 84–87.

42. David Lincicum, "How Did Paul Read Scripture?," in *The New Cambridge Companion to St. Paul*, ed. Bruce W. Longenecker, Cambridge Companions to Religion (Cambridge: Cambridge University Press, 2020), 237.

43. See Marc Zvi Brettler, "Jewish Theology of the Psalms," in *The Oxford Handbook of the Psalms*, ed. William P. Brown (New York: Oxford University Press, 2014), 487–94, whose comments are relevant to the Bible as a whole.

Dan 9); to aid in the characterization of a king (2 Kgs 2:4); to sanction the later interpretation, and perhaps observance, of particular laws (Neh 8:15).[44] The New Testament shares some of these reasons, but it does so in a completely Christocentric or ecclesiocentric fashion.

Finally, the New Testament contains many more explicit (and implicit) citations than are found in the (later books of the) Hebrew Bible. This is because Scripture became increasingly important in the very late Second Temple period, after the latest books incorporated in the Hebrew Bible were written, and thus books from this late period, around and soon after the destruction of the Second Temple, quote Scripture and treat it differently than do earlier books.[45] In addition, relative to the Hebrew Bible, more theological debates are in the background of the New Testament, and citations are excellent tools to resolve those debates, especially when Scripture can be quoted to foster interpretations that "did not match Jewish expectations."[46]

Unmarked Citations

In everyday life, we often reuse phrases that originate with others, but without acknowledging them as borrowings. In some cases, we may repeat or lightly paraphrase a well-known saying, song snippet, or literary work; sometimes this reuse saves us the effort of finding a new way of expressing something, while in other cases we mean to call specific attention to the earlier source we are quoting—perhaps to make ourselves sound clever or to pick up on the meaning or context of that source. Some of these reuses may be short, comprising a phrase or two, while others are much more substantial. Unmarked citations, namely cases where a later writer borrows significant phrases from an earlier one, are used in ancient literature for a similar variety of reasons. Sometimes, knowingly or not, these sources combine distinct earlier texts or phrases, just as we might do today.

But by their nature as "unmarked," isolating implicit citations in the Hebrew Bible is more subjective than finding explicit citations introduced with citation formulas. Thinking about the citations raises some very broad issues: For example, should Chronicles, which reworks much of Samuel-Kings (as well as some

---

44. For more examples, see Spawn, *"As It Is Written."* He concludes: "This analysis has sought to demonstrate that certain postexilic citation bases were developed exegetical devices used to improve the interpretation and observance of the law after its vindication in the events of the sixth century B. C. E." (258). He makes a good case concerning the interpretation of law, but his arguments concerning observance of the law are less compelling.

45. See, e.g., the entries in this volume by Grant Macaskill, "Israel's Scriptures in Early Jewish Literature" (§5); and Susan Docherty, "Israel's Scriptures in the Dead Sea Scrolls" (§6).

46. Allison, "Old Testament in the New Testament," 484.

other scriptural works) be considered one long citation? What of Deuteronomy, which reworks much of the Covenant Collection in Exodus and portions of the Torah's (E?) narrative?[47] Do sections of the Holiness Collection that rework Deuteronomy count as unmarked citations?[48] Complicating the process, how do we know that a later text is quoting a specific, extant, earlier one, and not a lost text that both depend on?[49] Finally, as in the previous section, how can we know if differences between the earlier and later texts reflect different norms of citation, or if the changes were intended by the later author, or if this author had a different version of the earlier text than now appears in the MT or other extant versions?[50] Given these issues, the examples below must be viewed with caution—but even if individual cases are open to dispute, as a group they illustrate that unmarked citations are frequent in the Scriptures of Israel.[51]

The book of Chronicles, most likely from the late fourth century BCE, is replete with citations, so much so that Jerome called it "an epitome."[52] It cites large sections of Samuel and Kings and smaller parts from each book of the Torah, Joshua (but not Judges), Isaiah, Jeremiah, Ezekiel, Psalms, Ezra-Nehemiah, and possibly Zechariah.[53] The large extent to which it cites earlier Scripture may be seen visually in various works that present Chronicles and its sources in parallel columns.[54] In many cases, these citations are verbatim or close to it. Changes range from spelling differences and use of synonyms to major "changes by the Chronicler, who rewrote . . . to suit his purpose."[55]

One example of a subtle reworking of earlier texts is 1 Chr 16:8–36. Here newly appointed Levitical singers present a devotional song comprising three psalms: 16:8–22 from Pss 105:1–15; 16:23–33 from Ps 96:1b–13; and 16:34–36 from Ps 106:1, 47–48. The Chronicler not only combines three psalms, he quotes from them

---

47. Levinson, *Deuteronomy and the Hermeneutics of Legal Innovation*; many of his later works refine and extend his initial argument.

48. Jeffrey Stackert, *Rewriting the Torah: Literary Revision in Deuteronomy and the Holiness Legislation*, FAT 52 (Tübingen: Mohr Siebeck, 2007).

49. Commentaries on the beginning of Isa 2 and Micah 4 neatly illustrate this problem; they debate which prophet or book is copying from whom or if both texts depend on an earlier text that has been lost.

50. Concerning Chronicles, see Gary N. Knoppers, *I Chronicles 1–9: A New Translation with Introduction and Commentary*, AB 12 (New York: Doubleday, 2003), 70.

51. Michael Fishbane makes this case very securely in his *Biblical Interpretation in Ancient Israel*.

52. Cited in Knoppers, *I Chronicles 1–9*, 68. For the dating of Chronicles, see Sara Japhet, *I & II Chronicles: A Commentary*, OTL (London: SCM, 1993), 28.

53. Knoppers, *I Chronicles 1–9*, 68; Japhet, *I & II Chronicles*, 14–18.

54. See, e.g., Abba Bendavid, *The Twice-Told Tale: Parallels in the Bible* (Jerusalem: Carta, 2017).

55. Adele Berlin, "Psalms in the Book of Chronicles," in *Shai le-Sara Japhet: Studies in the Bible, Its Exegesis and Its Language*, ed. Moshe Bar-Asher et al. (Jerusalem: Bialik, 2007), 34*.

selectively—exactly as the New Testament does with its sources. Sometimes he quotes exactly (e.g., 1 Chr 16:10–11 = Ps 105:3–4); elsewhere the words are the same but spelled slightly differently (1 Chr 16:8–9 = Ps 105:1–2) or with slightly different grammatical forms (פיו vs. פיהו for "his mouth" in 1 Chr 16:12 = Ps 105:5). Some changes are more significant: for example, the change from "offspring of Abraham" (Ps 105:6) to "offspring of Israel" (1 Chr 16:13) likely reflects an adjustment to suit his ideology.[56]

A more elaborate case indicating that the Chronicler purposefully tinkered with his texts appears in the section concerning Solomon's dedication of the temple.[57] First Kings 8:65–66 (partially emended with the LXX) reads:

וַיַּעַשׂ שְׁלֹמֹה בָעֵת־הַהִיא ׀ אֶת־הֶחָג וְכָל־יִשְׂרָאֵל עִמּוֹ קָהָל גָּדוֹל מִלְּבוֹא חֲמָת ׀
עַד־נַחַל מִצְרַיִם לִפְנֵי יְהוָה אֱלֹהֵינוּ שִׁבְעַת יָמִים
: [the remainder of the MT verse is omitted, following LXX]
בַּיּוֹם הַשְּׁמִינִי שִׁלַּח אֶת־הָעָם וַיְבָרֲכוּ אֶת־הַמֶּלֶךְ וַיֵּלְכוּ לְאָהֳלֵיהֶם שְׂמֵחִים וְטוֹבֵי
לֵב עַל כָּל־הַטּוֹבָה אֲשֶׁר עָשָׂה יְהוָה לְדָוִד עַבְדּוֹ וּלְיִשְׂרָאֵל עַמּוֹ׃

So Solomon and all Israel with him—a great assemblage, [coming] from Lebo-hamath to the Wadi of Egypt—observed the Feast at that time before the LORD our God, seven days. On the eighth day he let the people go. They bade the king good-bye and went to their homes, joyful and glad of heart over all the goodness that the LORD had shown to His servant David and His people Israel.

As expected, Kings follows the legislation of Deut 16:13, 15, where the feast of Sukkot is a seven-day festival, and thus the people can leave Jerusalem on the following, eighth day. The Priestly legislation, which Deuteronomy did not know (or at least did not recognize), however, has appended an additional eighth day to the festival, עֲצֶרֶת, "a solemn gathering," in which all work was prohibited. The Chronicler integrated this addition into his description of Solomon's temple consecration (2 Chr 7:8–10):

---

56. Japhet, *I & II Chronicles*, 318; see also Howard N. Wallace, "What Chronicles Has to Say About Psalms," in *The Chronicler as Author: Studies in Text and Texture*, ed. M. Patrick Graham and Steven L. McKenzie, JSOTSup 263 (Sheffield: Sheffield Academic, 1999), 287–88; Louis Jonker, "The Chronicler Singing Psalms: Revisiting the Chronicler's Psalm in 1 Chronicles 16," in *"My Spirit at Rest in the North Country" (Zechariah 6.8): Collected Communications to the XXth Congress of the International Organization for the Study of the Old Testament, Helsinki 2010*, ed. Hermann Michael Niemann and Matthias Augustin, BEATAJ 57 (Frankfurt am Main: Lang, 2011), 115–30.

57. On these texts, see David Bar-Cohn, "Shemini Atzeret: Redacting a Missing Festival into Solomon's Temple Dedication," *TheTorah.Com*, October 20, 2019, https://www.thetorah.com/article/shemini-atzeret-redacting-a-missing-festival-into-solomons-temple-dedication.

Israel's Scriptures in the Hebrew Bible

וַיַּ֣עַשׂ שְׁלֹמֹ֣ה אֶת־הֶחָ֣ג בָּעֵ֣ת הַהִ֡יא שִׁבְעַ֣ת יָמִים֩ וְכָל־יִשְׂרָאֵ֨ל עִמּ֜וֹ קָהָ֧ל גָּד֣וֹל מְאֹ֗ד מִלְּב֥וֹא חֲמָ֖ת עַד־נַ֣חַל מִצְרָ֑יִם: וַיַּעֲשׂ֣וּ בַיּ֣וֹם הַשְּׁמִינִ֔י עֲצָ֖רֶת כִּ֣י | חֲנֻכַּ֣ת הַמִּזְבֵּ֗חַ עָשׂוּ֙ שִׁבְעַ֣ת יָמִ֔ים וְהֶחָ֖ג שִׁבְעַ֥ת יָמִֽים: וּבְי֣וֹם עֶשְׂרִ֣ים וּשְׁלֹשָׁה֩ לַחֹ֨דֶשׁ הַשְּׁבִיעִ֜י שִׁלַּ֣ח אֶת־הָעָ֣ם לְאָהֳלֵיהֶ֗ם שְׂמֵחִים֙ וְט֣וֹבֵי לֵ֔ב עַל־הַטּוֹבָ֗ה אֲשֶׁ֨ר עָשָׂ֧ה יְהוָ֛ה לְדָוִ֥יד וְלִשְׁלֹמֹ֖ה וּלְיִשְׂרָאֵ֥ל עַמּֽוֹ:

> At that time Solomon kept the Feast for seven days—all Israel with him—a great assemblage from Lebo-hamath to the Wadi of Egypt. On the eighth day they held a solemn gathering; they observed the dedication of the altar seven days, and the Feast seven days. On the twenty-third day of the seventh month he dismissed the people to their homes, rejoicing and in good spirits over the goodness that the Lord had shown to David and Solomon and His people Israel.

While citing his main text of Kings, the Chronicler inserts the legislation of Leviticus, creating the type of mash-up we saw above (p. 58), as in some citations found in both the Hebrew Bible and the New Testament. From his perspective, David surely knew and followed the laws of Leviticus; the Chronicler therefore adjusts the chronology so that all went home on the twenty-third, not the twenty-second, of the seventh month. This is one of many examples in Chronicles where the base text is "corrected" or revised in light of other scriptural, especially Torah, texts.[58] In discussing Paul, Ross Wagner speaks of "Reading Hosea through Isaiah-Colored Glasses"; here, in a comparable way, Chronicles reads Kings through Torah-colored glasses.[59] And this can happen because Samuel–Kings at that point was seen as somewhat fluid and malleable.

Not only historical texts cite and revise earlier texts; this phenomenon is also well-attested in legal texts. One of Fishbane's students, Bernard M. Levinson, further developed his methods to show how many of the laws in the Deuteronomic Law Collection revise laws in the Covenant Collection (Exod 19:22–23:33).[60] Deuteronomy often accomplishes this by quoting snippets of the earlier law and then changing several words or adding and deleting material. For example, in the revision of the Hebrew slave law of Exod 21:2–11 in Deut 15:12–18, the Deuteronomist sometimes adheres to his source quite closely: Exodus 21:2 reads, כִּ֤י תִקְנֶה֙ עֶ֣בֶד עִבְרִ֔י שֵׁ֥שׁ שָׁנִ֖ים יַעֲבֹ֑ד וּבַ֨שְּׁבִעִ֔ת יֵצֵ֥א לַֽחָפְשִׁ֖י חִנָּֽם:, "If you buy a Hebrew servant, for six years he shall be subject to you. But in the seventh year he shall go away a free person without obligation." Deut 15:12 revises it to read:

---

58. Fishbane, *Biblical Interpretation in Ancient Israel*, brings other cases, especially in Chronicles and Ezra-Nehemiah. Each is slightly different, but together they illustrate the malleability of the cited text.

59. J. Ross Wagner, *Heralds of the Good News: Isaiah and Paul "in Concert" in the Letter to the Romans*, NovTSup 101 (Leiden: Brill, 2002), 89.

60. See n. 61.

כִּי־יִמָּכֵר לְךָ אָחִיךָ הָעִבְרִי אוֹ הָעִבְרִיָּה וַעֲבָדְךָ שֵׁשׁ שָׁנִים וּבַשָּׁנָה הַשְּׁבִיעִת תְּשַׁלְּחֶנּוּ חָפְשִׁי מֵעִמָּךְ, "But if your brother is sold to you, whether a Hebrew man or a Hebrew woman, he shall be subject to you six years, and in the seventh year you shall send him out a free person from you." These verses overlap by more than 50 percent. Yet, within 15:12–18, Deuteronomy offers significant changes by insisting through added words, contrary to Exod 21:7–11, that male and female slaves must be treated equally. Deuteronomy 15:13–15 also adds to Exodus that the master should give the slave significant gifts at the end of the sixth year and that this legislation commemorates the exodus. These substantial differences are incorporated into the larger law.[61] A similar phenomenon is illustrated by Jeffrey Stackert, who has shown how the Holiness Legislation in the second half of Leviticus has revised laws in Deuteronomy, though the citations in Leviticus are not as lengthy or prominent as Deuteronomy's citation from the Exodus Covenant Collection.[62]

The New Testament predominantly cites material that it takes as prophetic, especially from Torah, Prophets, and Psalms. This is narrower than the unmarked citations in the Scriptures of Israel, which are not predominantly prophetic. For example, Jer 3:1 cites a Torah text from Deut 24 to illustrate that the relationship between Israel and YHWH is broken. Jeremiah 3:1 opens by citing Deut 24:1–4's law that if a divorced woman remarries and her second husband dies or divorces her, she may not return to her first husband. Not only are these passages thematically similar, but Jer 3:1's יְשַׁלַּח אִישׁ אֶת־אִשְׁתּוֹ וְהָלְכָה מֵאִתּוֹ וְהָיְתָה לְאִישׁ־אַחֵר ("a man divorces his wife, and she leaves him and marries another man") is a slightly reworked citation of Deut 24:1(end)–2: וְשִׁלְּחָהּ מִבֵּיתוֹ: וְיָצְאָה מִבֵּיתוֹ וְהָלְכָה וְהָיְתָה לְאִישׁ־אַחֵר:, "and sends her away from his house; she leaves his household and becomes the wife of another man." The slight differences between Jeremiah and Deuteronomy, as I have noted, are typical of most cases when the Hebrew Bible or the New Testament quote the earlier Scriptures of Israel.[63] Also, just as Jer 3:1–5 allegorizes the interhuman law of Deut 24:1–4 to the relationship of God and Israel, so New Testament texts such as 1 Cor 9:9–11 allegorize Hebrew Bible verses that have no hint of original allegorical intent. But it is noteworthy that Jeremiah, in contrast to most cases where the New Testament uses earlier texts, is not implying that Deuteronomy is in some sense prophetic.

---

61. The Priestly law in Lev 25:39–46 further revises the law in Deuteronomy, though it rarely cites it. See Bernard M. Levinson, "The Manumission of Hermeneutics: The Slave Laws of the Pentateuch as a Challenge to Contemporary Pentateuchal Theory," in *Congress Volume Leiden 2004*, ed. André Lemaire, VTSup 109 (Leiden: Brill, 2006), 281–324.

62. Stackert, *Rewriting the Torah*.

63. On variation in Hebrew Bible quotations of the Hebrew Bible, see Juha Pakkala, "The Quotations and References of the Pentateuchal Laws in Ezra-Nehemiah," in *Changes in Scripture: Rewriting and Interpreting Authoritative Traditions in the Second Temple Period*, ed. Hanne von Weissenberg, Juha Pakkala, and Karko Marttila, BZAW 419 (Berlin: de Gruyter, 2011), 193–221.

But the Hebrew Bible certainly contains many cases of prophetic texts that are cited in later texts in addition to prophetic texts that cite nonprophetic sources, much like Jer 3. Benjamin D. Sommer, another student of Fishbane, brings many such examples in *A Prophet Reads Scripture: Allusion in Isaiah 40–66*.[64] A few texts that Sommers considers to be allusions share enough vocabulary in the same order that they may be considered implicit citations. For example, Isa 60:21a, וְעַמֵּךְ כֻּלָּם צַדִּיקִים לְעוֹלָם יִירְשׁוּ אָרֶץ, "And your people, all of them righteous, shall possess the land for all time" is a (slightly reworked) citation of Ps 37:29a, צַדִּיקִים יִירְשׁוּ־אָרֶץ, "The righteous shall inherit the land"—three shared words, in the same order, secure this as a citation. This citation may suggest that the prophet understood Psalms as a prophetic work and involves a change in genre: "a hymn has given rise to prophecy."[65] This approach shows significant continuity with how the Dead Sea Scrolls read the Psalter as prophecy; as is often the case, the Scrolls offer important intermediate evidence, anticipating the New Testament.[66]

A final example illustrates how a later text may rework an earlier one to such an extent that it fully reverses the text's original or contextual meaning. Psalm 8:5 [8:4 ET] asks: מָה־אֱנוֹשׁ כִּי־תִזְכְּרֶנּוּ וּבֶן־אָדָם כִּי תִפְקְדֶנּוּ, "what is man [better: a human] that You have been mindful of him, mortal man that You have taken note of him?" The continuation of the psalm offers a clear answer—humans are indeed great, just a bit less than divine (8:6 [8:5]), and thus God gives them dominion over the natural world (8:7–9 [8:6–8]). Job concludes his second speech by citing this psalm: מָה־אֱנוֹשׁ כִּי תְגַדְּלֶנּוּ וְכִי־תָשִׁית אֵלָיו לִבֶּךָ׃ וַתִּפְקְדֶנּוּ, "What is man, that You make much of him, That You fix Your attention upon him? You inspect him" (Job 7:17–18a). Job employs the same words—that is what secures this example as a citation—but with the opposite meaning, perhaps even a parody: in relation to God, humans are insignificant, not worthy of and unable to withstand divine scrutiny.[67] And as we will see in the next section, sometimes allusions in Isa 40–66 also overturn the text to which they allude.

---

64. Sommer, *Prophet Reads Scripture*.

65. Sommer, 112; see 111–12 for demonstrating that Isaiah is citing this psalm.

66. 11Q5 (11QPsª) XXVII, 11, כול אלה דבר בנבואה אשר נתן לו מלפני העליון, "all these he composed through prophecy given him by the Most High," suggests that Psalms was revealed to David through prophecy although it does not suggest that the psalms are prophetic texts *about the future*, an idea reflected in the pesharim to Psalms.

67. See Michael Fishbane, "The Book of Job and Inner-Biblical Discourse," in *The Voice from the Whirlwind: Interpreting the Book of Job*, ed. Leo G. Perdue and W. Clark Gilprin (Nashville: Abingdon, 1991), 87–89; for a somewhat contrasting view see Raymond C. Van Leeuwen, "Psalm 8.5 and Job 7.17–18: A Mistaken Scholarly Commonplace?," in *The World of the Aramaeans I: Biblical Studies in Honour of Paul-Eugene Dion*, ed. P. M. Michele Daviau, John William Wevers, and Michael Weigl, JSOTSup 324 (Sheffield: Sheffield Academic, 2001), 205–15. On Job's use of inner-biblical allusion more broadly, see Katharine Dell and Will Kynes, eds., *Reading Job Intertextually*, LHBOTS 574 (London: T&T Clark, 2013).

The Scriptures of Israel contain many more implicit than explicit citations—as does the New Testament. Although most of the implicit citations are from the latest works in the Hebrew Bible, especially Chronicles and Ezra-Nehemiah, such citations are also found in earlier books from the exilic period (sections of Isa 40–66) and even the late preexilic period (parts of Deuteronomy). Like New Testament citations of Israel's Scriptures, these citations at times read nonallegorical material in an allegorical fashion or read Psalms prophetically. But in most other ways, these implicit citations parallel the explicit ones: they treat their source material with significant freedom and vary greatly in the topics they treat instead of being focused on a single theme or individual.

Conceptual Allusion

We often look at the present through the past and thus allude to it in a variety of ways. Sometimes we hint at an earlier situation in general, sometimes with, but often without using such explicit markers as "this reminds me of . . ." Such allusions generally serve the same purposes as citations, noted above. In the Bible, as opposed to everyday speech, such allusions frequently help to create typologies.

Isolating allusions is at least as difficult within the Hebrew Bible as is finding allusions to the Old in the New.[68] I distinguish between verbal and conceptual allusion, and I will treat conceptual allusion first. Both conceptual and verbal allusions may create typologies, a topic I treat below under verbal allusions.

As this volume's editors note, a conceptual allusion refers to "a reference to a theme or topic that is not tied to a specific text in Scripture," as in Rom 9:4–5, which refers to topics or themes such as covenants, giving of the law, promises,

---

68. I do not distinguish between allusion and echo, as some have; see, e.g., Sommer, *A Prophet Reads Scripture*, 15, 30–31; Steven Moyise, "Intertextuality and the Study of the Old Testament in the New Testament," in *The Old Testament in the New Testament: Essays in Honour of J. L. North*, ed. Steve Moyise, JSNTSup 189 (Sheffield: Sheffield Academic, 2000), 14–41. See esp. the attempt of Stanley E. Porter to distinguish carefully between various terms in "Further Comments on the Use of the Old Testament in the New Testament," in *The Intertextuality of the Epistles: Explorations of Theory and Practice*, ed. Thomas L. Brodie, Dennis R. MacDonald, and Stanley E. Porter, New Testament Monographs 16 (Sheffield: Sheffield Phoenix, 2007), 98–110. The best discussions of how to isolate allusions in the Hebrew Bible are Sommer, *A Prophet Reads Scripture*; Zevit, *Subtle Citation, Allusion, and Translation*. My interest here is specifically in allusion, not in intertextuality that includes cases where texts are related in some way other than an earlier text influencing, to a smaller or greater extent, a later one. See Geoffrey D. Miller, "Intertextuality in Old Testament Research," *CBR* 9, no. 3 (2011): 283–309; and concerning the New Testament, Samuel Emedi, "Intertextuality in New Testament Scholarship: Significance, Criteria, and the Art of Intertextual Reading," *CBR* 14, no. 1 (2015): 8–23. For a defense of the term "intertextuality," see Porter, "Pauline Techniques in Interweaving Scripture," 23–55.

patriarchs, and the messiah. These two verses, along with their surrounding context, do not suggest that Paul is referring to specific passages in the Hebrew Bible—thus this is a conceptual rather than a verbal allusion.

Transposing this idea to the Scriptures of Israel, a conceptual allusion would be a text that refers to people or concepts found in earlier traditions but in a vague enough sense that it is unlikely that a specific text or texts lie in the background. By this understanding, the Hebrew Bible contains many conceptual allusions—but with one serious complication.

In the case of the New Testament, we are quite sure that its authors knew, more or less, some form(s) of what now constitutes the Hebrew Bible, though likely only in Greek. But we cannot know what books of the Hebrew Bible each biblical author knew. I will illustrate this with one example: What texts that became Torah texts, if any, did Amos, living in the eighth century in the Northern Kingdom, know? And given that Amos did not write everything in the book attributed to him, what books did his later editors know? Thus, when the book of Amos refers to the destruction of Sodom and Gomorrah in 4:11, is he alluding to Gen (18–)19 or to some well-known tradition?[69] If the latter is the case, this would not be a conceptual allusion to the Scriptures of Israel at all.

Concerning conceptual allusions, it is safer to refer to literature recognized as exilic or later whose content overlaps with the Torah to some extent. This corpus would include Isa 40–66, and especially Pss 105, 106, 114, 135, and 136, and Neh 9, all of which reprise traditions that are known in the Torah, the central fount of allusion. Some of these verses refer to events such as the exodus, the giving of the Torah, and the conquest of the land. The possibility that some of these late texts contain conceptual allusions to texts (or ideas) that otherwise did not make it into, or are hardly represented in, the canon must also be considered.[70]

Given all of these problems, I will not broadly explore conceptual allusions in the Scriptures of Israel. I ask a different question related to this book's project instead: What late texts in the Scriptures of Israel allude to the items that Paul recalls in Rom 9:4–5? These include adoption, glory, covenants, law, worship, promises, patriarchs, the messiah—ideas central to Paul and other early followers of Jesus. These later texts from the Scriptures of Israel allude to seven of the eight, and thus Paul is strongly continuous with the biblical tradition.[71]

---

69. On the dating of the unit containing Amos 4:11, see, e.g., Hans Walter Wolff, *Joel and Amos: A Commentary on the Books of the Prophets Joel and Amos*, Hermeneia (Philadelphia: Fortress, 1977), 217–18.

70. Psalm 114, e.g., is often read as comporting with the Torah but contains several references that disagree with it and likely reflect alternate ancient traditions (see esp. 114:2, 4, and 8). See Marc Zvi Brettler, "A Jewish Historical-Critical Commentary on Psalms: Psalm 114 as an Example," *HeBAI* 5, no. 4 (2016): 401–34.

71. I will offer just one example of each: adoption (Isa 63:8, indirectly, by calling Israel

Significantly, the missing item is the messiah, namely the future, ideal king.⁷² This gap is unsurprising. Isaiah 55:1–5 describes how the promise of an unbroken dynasty to David has been democratized to all Israel—in the words of Brevard Childs, "the covenant of David, which has been sustained by the eternal loyalty of God, was seen as continuing in the new people of Israel."⁷³ Further, John Collins has shown the unimportance of messianism in the Persian period; indeed, Lamentations, commemorating the destruction of the First Temple, expresses no desire for a messiah or messianic age.⁷⁴ Messianic stirrings became stronger in the late Hellenistic period, as reflected in some Dead Sea Scrolls where the term משיח, "anointed," is used for the ideal, Davidic king. The New Testament's use of Χρίστος for this king is taking up an idea found mostly in pre-Persian period texts, where this figure is never called משיח.

Verbal Allusion

In an afterword to the essays he collected on allusion in the Hebrew Bible, Ziony Zevit laments the lack of a "shared protocol" for isolating biblical allusions, particularly verbal allusion. All of the verbal allusions I include here, then, may be disputed—though I try to use examples that fulfill the criteria that scholars have developed in Zevit's book.⁷⁵ As in my discussion of citation, rather than attempting a broad survey, I highlight examples that serve as an appropriate background for allusions in the New Testament, and I note both similarities and differences between how the Hebrew Bible alludes to itself and how the New Testament alludes to the scriptural tradition.

As noted earlier, Sommer adduces many verbal allusions in Isa 40–66 in his *A Prophet Reads Scripture*, where he shows how the corpus uses allusion frequently

---

YHWH's sons); glory (Isa 60:1–2, and often in Isa 40–66); covenants (Ps 105:10); law (Neh 9:13); worship (Ezra 3:12, if the reference in Paul is to the temple); promises (Ps 105:9–11, 42); and patriarchs (Ezek 33:24; Pss 105:9; 135:4).

72. It is prudent to avoid the term "messiah" when referring to this individual in the Hebrew Bible. Its use is anachronistic there since the only place in the Hebrew Bible where משיח may refer to the future, ideal Davidic king is Dan 9:25–26, but see John J. Collins, *Daniel: A Commentary on the Book of Daniel*, Hermeneia (Minneapolis: Fortress, 1993), 354–56.

73. Childs, *Isaiah: A Commentary*, OTL (Louisville: Westminster John Knox, 2001); and the classic article by Otto Eissfeldt, "The Promises of Grace to David in Isaiah 55,1–5," in *Israel's Prophetic Heritage: Essays in Honor of James Muilenburg*, ed. Bernhard W. Anderson and Walter J. Harrelson (New York: Harper & Row, 1962), 196–207.

74. John J. Collins, *The Scepter and the Star: The Messiahs of the Dead Sea Scrolls and Other Ancient Literature*, ABRL (New York: Doubleday, 1995), 34–41. For a different view, see Matthew V. Novenson, *The Grammar of Messianism: An Ancient Jewish Political Idiom and Its Users* (New York: Oxford University Press, 2017), 116–60.

75. Zevit, *Subtle Citation, Allusion, and Translation*, 243.

because of the intimate relationship it tries to create with earlier material, as he "sees himself as prophet and disciple."[76] Sometimes he confirms his sources, other times he reverses or even polemicizes against what they say—as we saw above that Job 7 reverses Ps 8.[77] Most New Testament authors shared this complex attitude.

Typologies

Verbal allusions in the Hebrew Bible, and some conceptual allusions as well, sometimes cluster to create a typology, a trope "which sees in persons, events, or places the prototype, pattern, or figure of historical persons, events, or places that follow it in time."[78] Although the term "typology" is classical in origin and often associated with the New Testament and early Christianity, typologies abound in the Scriptures of Israel, and in many ways the typological readings in the New Testament are in continuity with them.[79]

Comparison is the fundamental element of typology, and comparison, both explicit and implicit, is fundamental to the Scriptures of Israel. For example, in Josh 1:5b, YHWH says to Joshua, כַּאֲשֶׁר הָיִיתִי עִם־מֹשֶׁה אֶהְיֶה עִמָּךְ, "As I was with Moses, so I will be with you"; this כַּאֲשֶׁר, "(just) as" is one element that creates a Joshua-Moses typology (see more below). Similarly, throughout, Kings compares in very general terms northern kings to the first northern king, Jeroboam son of Nebat (see, negatively, e.g., 1 Kgs 15:34; 2 Kgs 15:28), while it compares southern, Judean kings to their ancestor David (see positively, Hezekiah and Josiah in 2 Kgs 18:3 and 22:2; negatively, e.g., Ahaz, in 2 Kgs 16:2; and in-between, e.g., Amaziah in 2 Kgs 14:3–4). Such explicit comparisons legitimize the search in the Hebrew Bible for additional comparisons that are expressed through verbal allusions.

Moses is especially subject to typologies in the Hebrew Bible, as noted in Allison's *The New Moses: A Matthean Typology*.[80] I comment briefly on three of his suggestions—the ones I find most compelling because of their verbal allusions: Joshua, Elijah, and Josiah.

---

76. Sommer, *Prophet Reads Scripture*, 179.
77. See esp. Sommer, 144, on Isa 40:28 and the beginning of Gen 2.
78. Fishbane, *Biblical Interpretation*, 350.
79. Jonathan Kaplan, *My Perfect One: Typology and Early Rabbinic Interpretation of Song of Songs* (New York: Oxford University Press, 2015), 21–26. To the best of my knowledge, no systematic study of typology in the Hebrew Bible has been written. For now, see Fishbane, *Biblical Interpretation*, 350–79; and Marc Zvi Brettler, *The Creation of History in Ancient Israel* (London: Routledge, 1995), 48–61. Many of the following examples are taken from these sources. Yet, it is important to invoke typology carefully so as not to engage in what Allison, *New Moses*, 18, calls "Typologicalmania."
80. Allison, *New Moses*, 11–95.

As noted above, Josh 1:5 suggests a Joshua-Moses typology. As Allison summarizes, Joshua's life-story is patterned after that of Moses: they both send spies, cross water, celebrate a significant Passover, deliver valedictory speeches, and more.[81] These thematic similarities are enhanced by verbal similarities; for example, the similar instructions they receive: וַיֹּאמֶר אַל־תִּקְרַב הֲלֹם שַׁל־נְעָלֶיךָ מֵעַל רַגְלֶיךָ כִּי הַמָּקוֹם אֲשֶׁר אַתָּה עוֹמֵד עָלָיו אַדְמַת־קֹדֶשׁ הוּא, "And He said, 'Do not come closer. Remove your sandals from your feet, for the place on which you stand is holy ground'" (Exod 3:5), and וַיֹּאמֶר שַׂר־צְבָא יְהוָה אֶל־יְהוֹשֻׁעַ שַׁל־נַעַלְךָ מֵעַל רַגְלֶךָ כִּי הַמָּקוֹם אֲשֶׁר אַתָּה עֹמֵד עָלָיו קֹדֶשׁ הוּא וַיַּעַשׂ יְהוֹשֻׁעַ כֵּן, "The captain of the Lord's host answered Joshua, 'Remove your sandals from your feet, for the place where you stand is holy.' And Joshua did so" (Josh 5:15). The text makes clear the purpose of this typology: Joshua will continue the battles that Moses started for the conquest of the land (see esp. Deut 1:38; 3:21, 28; Josh 1:2) and is given the same authority as Moses (see Num 27:20; Deut 34:9). The book of Joshua explicitly notes that Joshua is Moses's legitimate successor, and the verbal similarities create a typology that reinforces his continuity and legitimacy.

Second, it is widely accepted that Kings presents Elijah as a second Moses.[82] The thematic similarities between the figures are numerous, and as above, with Joshua, are anchored by verbal allusions. First Kings 19:18 states that Elijah "arose and ate and drank; and with the strength from that meal he walked forty days and forty nights as far as the mountain of God at Horeb [הַר הָאֱלֹהִים חֹרֵב]." This verse alludes to Moses's not eating for forty days and nights in Deut 9:9 (cf. Exod 34:28); the term הַר הָאֱלֹהִים חֹרֵב is found only here and in Exod 3:1, of Moses at the burning bush. This passage in 1 Kgs 19 is the only case of a new theophany at Sinai/Horeb—the revelation of the laws is replaced by a קוֹל דְּמָמָה דַקָּה, "a soft murmuring sound" or "a still, small voice" (19:12).[83] Patterning Elijah after Moses legitimates Elijah as a proper successor to Moses—though of lower status, as 1 Kgs 19 suggests: "Moses is unique, and Elijah is a distant second."[84] The Moses-Horeb (Sinai) typology thus functions differently from most of the New Testament's depictions of Jesus as a new Moses, where Jesus is of Moses's stature or greater. Furthermore, this is the only time the Scriptures of Israel use Horeb-Sinai in a typology; in the Scriptures of Israel, nothing replaces Sinai. In the New Testament this typology, with Jesus offering (a) new (interpretation of the) law, is much more prominent. Three examples immediately come to mind: Jesus's initial sermon in Matthew, which he delivers from a mount (Matt 5:1–

---

81. Allison, *New Moses*, 25–26.
82. Allison, *New Moses*, 39–45.
83. George W. Savran, *Encountering the Divine: Theophany in Biblical Narrative*, JSOTSup 420 (London: T&T Clark, 2005), 207–29.
84. Allison, *New Moses*, 45. Quotation from Savran, *Encountering the Divine*, 227.

7:29 // Luke 6:17–7:1); the transfiguration, which again takes place on a mountain and specifically parallels Jesus and Moses (Matt 17:1–8 // Luke 9:28–34 // Mark 9:2–8); and Paul's contrast between Jesus's teaching and the Mosaic covenant (2 Cor 3:12–18) in which Jesus's followers have a fuller vision of God.[85]

Third, Richard Elliott Friedman has assembled an impressive number of parallels between Moses and King Josiah, the great reforming king described in 2 Kgs 22–23.[86] The author of (an early edition of) Kings copies phrases from Deuteronomy to show Josiah's full compliance with the Mosaic Torah, namely Deuteronomy. For example, Deut 6:5 mandates וְאָ֣הַבְתָּ֔ אֵ֖ת יְהוָ֣ה אֱלֹהֶ֑יךָ בְּכָל־לְבָבְךָ֥ וּבְכָל־נַפְשְׁךָ֖ וּבְכָל־מְאֹדֶֽךָ׃, "You shall love the LORD your God with all your heart and with all your soul and with all your might." This commandment is fulfilled only by Josiah in 2 Kgs 23:25:

וְכָמֹ֩הוּ֩ לֹֽא־הָיָ֨ה לְפָנָ֜יו מֶ֗לֶךְ אֲשֶׁר־שָׁ֤ב אֶל־יְהוָה֙ בְּכָל־לְבָב֤וֹ וּבְכָל־נַפְשׁוֹ֙ וּבְכָל־מְאֹד֔וֹ כְּכֹ֖ל תּוֹרַ֣ת מֹשֶׁ֑ה וְאַחֲרָ֖יו לֹֽא־קָ֥ם כָּמֹֽהוּ׃

> There was no king like him before who turned back to the LORD with all his heart and soul and might, in full accord with the Teaching of Moses; nor did any like him arise after him.

This typology of Josiah as a new Moses shows how great Josiah was—he is the hero of this edition of the Deuteronomic History, restoring the Mosaic Torah. The typology also has a literary function of framing this edition of the Deuteronomistic History, which concluded with Josiah, a Moses-like figure. Moses becomes even more of a central typological figure in the New Testament and in other Second Temple and later Jewish literature.[87]

Events rather than people can also stand at the center of a typology. The exodus from Egypt is especially subject to typology—it is both reenacted and preenacted.[88] The idea that the exodus will be reenacted is explicit in Jer 23:7–8:

---

85. For specific allusions in these passages, see the annotations in Amy-Jill Levine and Marc Zvi Brettler, *The Jewish Annotated New Testament*, 2nd ed. (Oxford: Oxford University Press, 2017), esp. Alan J. Avery-Peck's sidebars on 2 Cor 3:12–18 on pp. 353–54.

86. See Allison, *New Moses*, 46–50, esp. 46–47. Richard Elliott Friedman, "From Egypt to Egypt: Dtr¹ and Dtr²," in *Traditions in Transformation: Turning Points in Biblical Faith* (Winona Lake, IN: Eisenbrauns, 1981), 172–73, further discusses this connection.

87. See the examples collected in Allison, *New Moses*. Chronicles revises Kings here, using verbal allusions to depict Hezekiah as a second Moses. See Robb Andrew Young, *Hezekiah in History and Tradition*, VTSup 155 (Leiden: Brill, 2012), 257–58, and esp. the examples in 258 n. 4.

88. See Yair Zakovitch, *"And You Shall Tell Your Son...": The Concept of the Exodus in the Bible* (Jerusalem: Magnes, 1991), esp. 46–98.

Assuredly, a time is coming—declares the Lord—when it shall no more be said, "As the Lord lives, who brought the Israelites out of the land of Egypt," but rather, "As the Lord lives, who brought out and led the offspring of the House of Israel from the northland and from all the lands to which I have banished them." And they shall dwell upon their own soil.

It is found often in Isa 40–55, which imagines the return from Babylon as a new exodus; the return itself in Ezra 1 also picks up specific words from Exodus.[89] Genesis 12:10–20, describing Abram and Sarai's descent to Egypt, preenacts the exodus and uses terms to guide the reader to that preenactment, such as נגע, "plague" (Gen 12:17; Exod 11:1).[90] This exodus typology helps fulfill the Deuteronomic injunction to "remember that you were slaves in the land of Egypt" (e.g., Deut 5:15) and stresses that God who saved once can save again. The exodus becomes a paradigmatic event reflecting God's power to save Israel from its enemies (see Judg 6:13). Additional material in the ancestral stories can be read as a prequel, and preenactment to create a typology is likely at work in the concubine of Gibeah story at the end of Judges: the bad Benjaminites prefigure the bad King Saul.[91]

Just as the New Testament employs antitypes—most famously in Rom 5 and 1 Cor 15, depicting Jesus and Adam as opposites—so later biblical texts engage in antitypology with earlier traditions.[92] Sometimes this is accomplished without strong literary connections, as when Saul is depicted as the antithesis of David in 1 Samuel, or through the general statement that a Davidic king did not follow that path of his ancestor (e.g., 1 Kgs 15:3, of Abijam).[93]

Other times antitypes are demonstrated through allusion. For example, Jonah is depicted as a negative figure in the Hebrew Bible: he flees his mission and whines excessively. In 4:3, after Nineveh repents and has been forgiven, he asks God to kill him, stating: וְעַתָּה יְהוָה קַח־נָא אֶת־נַפְשִׁי מִמֶּנִּי כִּי טוֹב מוֹתִי מֵחַיָּי, "Please, Lord,

---

89. Zakovitch, *"And You Shall Tell Your Son,"* 57; Japhet, *Ezra-Nehemiah*, 19–20, 58–59; on Deutero-Isaiah, see the classic article, Bernhard W. Anderson, "Exodus Typology in Second Isaiah," in Anderson and Harrelson, *Israel's Prophetic Heritage*, 177–95.

90. Brettler, *Creation of History*, 51–55; and Christoph Levin, "Abraham and Sarah in Egypt: A Story Composed to Prefigure the Exodus," *TheTorah.Com*, October 28, 2020, https://www.thetorah.com/article/abraham-and-sarah-in-egypt-a-story-composed-to-prefigure-the-exodus.

91. For ancestral stories as prequel, see Megan Warner, "Back to the Future: Reading the Abraham Narratives as Prequel," *BibInt* 25 (2017): 479–96. For the end of Judges, see Cynthia Edenburg, *Dismembering the Whole: Composition and Purpose of Judges 19–21*, AIL 24 (Atlanta: SBL Press, 2016), 221–26.

92. Here and elsewhere in this chapter, I am using "antitype" in its sense of "a person or thing that represents the opposite of someone or something else"; see https://www.lexico.com/en/definition/antitype.

93. For Saul as the antithesis of David, see Brettler, *Creation of History*, 103.

take my life, for I would rather die than live." This verse recollects Elijah, who, (legitimately) fleeing from Jezebel after the defeat of Baal's prophets on Mount Carmel, prays: | וַיָּבֹא וַיֵּשֶׁב תַּחַת רֹתֶם אַחַת [אֶחָד] וַיִּשְׁאַל אֶת־נַפְשׁוֹ לָמוּת וַיֹּאמֶר רַב עַתָּה יְהוָה קַח נַפְשִׁי כִּי־לֹא־טוֹב אָנֹכִי מֵאֲבֹתָי׃, "He came to a broom bush and sat down under it, and prayed that he might die. 'Enough!' he cried. 'Now, O LORD, take my life, for I am no better than my fathers'" (1 Kgs 19:4b). The depiction in Jonah 4:6 of the prophet sitting under a plant that provided shade, like Elijah in 1 Kgs 19:4, secures this allusion, suggesting that Jonah is the antitype of Elijah.[94]

From the perspective of the later New Testament, it is noteworthy that no Hebrew Bible text uses Adam in its typology. Aside from his appearance in Genesis and in the first word of Chronicles, he appears at most once more, in Job 31:33, though scholars debate whether אדם there is a common or a proper noun.[95] Adam does, however, become more significant in late Second Temple literature. In creating their Adam-Jesus relationship, the New Testament authors use the broad categories of type and antitype known from the Scriptures of Israel but insert new figures into it.[96]

The later the biblical book, the more ability it has to allude to earlier works. As noted above, much of Chronicles may be seen as one long unmarked citation, and Ezra-Nehemiah has many citations and allusions. But that does not mean that all late biblical books are allusive: The late book of Ecclesiastes, for example, is not allusive. But Esther, another late book, contains many literary citations in both the Hebrew and Greek editions; it alludes most clearly to the Joseph story and to the story of Saul and Amalek in 1 Sam 15.[97] Jonathan Grossman suggests that it employs "dynamic analogies" to many other earlier biblical works, including Genesis, Joshua, and Kings.[98] But Esther contains no obvious citations and

---

94. Uriel Simon, *Jonah: The Traditional Hebrew Text with the New JPS Translation*, JPS Bible Commentary (Philadelphia: Jewish Publication Society, 1999), 38.

95. Most modern scholars agree that "Adam" in Hos 6:7 is a place name rather than a personal name; see, e.g., Francis I. Andersen and David Noel Freedman, *Hosea: A New Translation with Inroduction and Commentary*, AB 24 (Garden City, NY: Doubleday, 1980), 439, who note that "it is surprising that so little use is made of this tradition [concerning the person Adam found in Gen 2–3] in the Hebrew Bible."

96. Silviu N. Bunta, "Adam (Person) II. Judaism A. Second Temple and Hellenistic Judaism," *EBR* 1:300–303; for New Testament references, mostly Pauline, see James D. G. Dunn and Silviu N. Bunta, "Adam (Person) III. New Testament," *EBR* 1:306–11.

97. Adele Berlin, *Esther: The Traditional Hebrew Text with the New JPS Translation*, JPS Bible Commentary (Philadelphia: Jewish Publication Society, 2001), xxxvi–xli.

98. Jonathan Grossman, *Esther: The Outer Narrative and the Hidden Reading*, Siphrut 6 (Winona Lake, IN: Eisenbrauns, 2011), 218–33. One of his more convincing examples is Esth 8:6 // Gen 44:34.

certainly no marked citations; in that way it is similar to Revelation, which is highly allusive but lacks marked citations.

Typologies in the Hebrew Bible have a variety of functions. Comparing people to Moses, for example, generates meaning: it shows that the later individual has some of Moses's characteristics or partakes in his greatness. Other typologies highlight YHWH's greatness—he provided an exodus for the Israelites not once, but several times. And typologies show connection to earlier texts or times and thus continuity between the present and the past. This broad function is shared between many late biblical authors and many New Testament writers, where this last purpose of highlighting continuity, that the New is not New but is a continuation of the Old, is especially significant. The main New Testament prooftext for this—"do not think that I have come to abolish the law or the prophets; I have come not to abolish but to fulfill" (Matt 5:17)—is found in the Sermon on the Mount, discussed above as an example of Jesus-Moses typology with its allusions to Sinai/Horeb.

This section on literal allusions adduces only a fraction of the evidence—that Sommer could write a book-length treatment on only twenty-seven chapters of Isaiah offers some sense of how extensive this phenomenon is. We might debate individual occurrences of allusions, but not their broad use. They are much more frequent than citations since they are much less intrusive literarily. In the New Testament, Jesus is a new Moses just as Joshua, Josiah, and others are a new Moses—it is as if some New Testament authors, aware of these typological applications of Moses, do not want Jesus to be left out of this figuration. Similarly, they extend the exodus typology found in the Scriptures of Israel to Jesus.[99] But some of the New Testament's typologies are absent in the Hebrew Bible, such as the use of Adam as an antitype. In the Scriptures of Israel, apart from 1 Kgs 19:12, Sinai is not frequently or importantly typologized, while it is in the new law emphasized in the New Testament.[100] In both cases, the lack or near lack of a crucial New Testament typology in the Hebrew Bible teaches us much about the different emphases, and the essence, of each text.

Conclusions

Each of the categories so crucial to the New Testament—explicit citations, implicit citations, conceptual allusions, literal allusions—is well-attested in the later books from the Hebrew Bible. Citations are less prominent than in the New Testament, while allusions are as common. Having citations requires a well-established, quote-

---

99. Marcus, *Way of the Lord*, 24–26.
100. See, e.g., the Sermon on the Mount in Matt 5, and Allison, *New Moses*, 172–207.

worthy scroll, book, or sets of books to be cited; this was just beginning to happen in the late period of the Hebrew Bible but was much more established when the writings eventually incorporated into the New Testament were written. (What a difference a few centuries make!)[101] In some cases, we find continuity when both the Hebrew Bible and the New Testament pick up the same texts or figures, as in the appeal to Moses typology. We even find that the use of allegorical typologies has some basis in the Scriptures of Israel (see above, on Jer 3:1–5 and Deut 24:1–4).

Many of the citation formulas and reasons for allusion are shared between the late Hebrew Bible texts and the New Testament—there is significant continuity between these corpora, and as the articles in the first section of this book illustrate, the literature of Qumran and other compositions from that period help trace that continuity more precisely. But there are significant differences as well. None of these is surprising in retrospect. Citations and allusions in the New Testament focus on Jesus or the early church, showing "that Jesus was indeed the telos of Israel's history"; those in the Scriptures of Israel lack such a single, clear focus.[102] And the formula of Jesus fulfilling a verse from the Scriptures of Israel that is so significant in the New Testament, especially in Matthew, is barely present in the Hebrew Bible. There is not much new in the New Testament in terms of the issues that this chapter explores.[103] Much of its newness is reflected in its rebalancing of what is found in the Hebrew Bible, often taking an element or passage that is peripheral or not especially significant (e.g., Jer 31:31 or the fulfillment formula) and making it much more prominent.

Bibliography

Allison, Dale C., Jr. *The New Moses: A Matthean Typology*. Edinburgh: T&T Clark, 1993.

———. "The Old Testament in the New Testament." Pages 479–502 in *From the Beginnings to 600*. Vol. 1 of *The New Cambridge History of the Bible*. Edited by

---

101. Citations and allusions to the Hebrew Bible in so-called intertestamental literature is a major discussion, treated by other essays in this volume. For a sense of the primary data, see Armin Lange and Matthias Weigold, *Biblical Quotations and Allusions in Second Temple Jewish Literature*, JAJSup 5 (Göttingen: Vandenhoeck & Ruprecht, 2011).

102. Allison, "Old Testament in the New Testament," 485. For a different formulation, see C. F. D. Moule, "Fulfillment-Words in the New Testament: Use and Abuse," *NTS* 14, no. 3 (1968): 301, "Thus, to a unique degree, Jesus is seen as the goal, the convergence-point, of God's plan for Israel, his covenant-promise."

103. See, e.g., Craig A. Evans, "From Prophecy to Testament: An Introduction," in *From Prophecy to Testament: The Function of the Old Testament in the New*, ed. Craig A. Evans (Peabody, MA: Hendrickson, 2004), 1–2.

James Carlton Paget and Joachim Schaper. Cambridge: Cambridge University Press, 2013.

Andersen, Francis I., and David Noel Freedman. *Hosea: A New Translation with Inroduction and Commentary*. AB 24. Garden City, NY: Doubleday, 1980.

Anderson, Bernhard W. "Exodus Typology in Second Isaiah." Pages 177–95 in *Israel's Prophetic Heritage: Essays in Honor of James Muilenburg*. Edited by Bernhard W. Anderson and Walter J. Harrelson. New York: Harper, 1962.

Bar-Cohn, David. "Shemini Atzeret: Redacting a Missing Festival into Solomon's Temple Dedication." *TheTorah.Com*. October 20, 2019. https://www.thetorah.com/article/shemini-atzeret-redacting-a-missing-festival-into-solomons-temple-dedication.

Bendavid, Abba. *The Twice-Told Tale: Parallels in the Bible*. Jerusalem: Carta, 2017.

Berlin, Adele. *Esther: The Traditional Hebrew Text with the New JPS Translation*. JPS Bible Commentary. Philadelphia: Jewish Publication Society, 2001.

———. "Psalms in the Book of Chronicles." Pages 21*–36* in *Shai le-Sara Japhet: Studies in the Bible, Its Exegesis and Its Language*. Edited by Moshe Bar-Asher, Dalit Rom-Shiloni, Emanuel Tov, and Nili Wazana. Jerusalem: Bialik, 2007.

Brettler, Marc Zvi. *The Creation of History in Ancient Israel*. London: Routledge, 1995.

———. "A Jewish Historical-Critical Commentary on Psalms: Psalm 114 as an Example." *HeBAI* 5, no. 4 (2016): 401–34.

———. "Jewish Theology of the Psalms." Pages 485–98 in *The Oxford Handbook of the Psalms*. Edited by William P. Brown. New York: Oxford University Press, 2014.

Brettler, Marc, and Amy-Jill Levine. "Isaiah's Suffering Servant: Before and After Christianity." *Int* 73, no. 2 (2019): 158–73.

Brooke, George J. "'The Canon within the Canon,' at Qumran and in the New Testament." Pages 242–66 in *The Scrolls and the Scriptures: Qumran Fifty Years After*. Edited by Stanley E. Porter and Craig A. Evans. JSPSup 26. Sheffield: Sheffield Academic, 1997.

Bunta, Silviu N. "Adam (Person) II. Judaism A. Second Temple and Hellenistic Judaism." *EBR* 1:300–303.

Burney, C. F. *Notes on the Hebrew Text of the Books of Kings*. Oxford: Clarendon, 1903.

Campbell, Anthony F., and Mark A. O'Brien. *Unfolding the Deuteronomistic History: Origins, Upgrades, Present Text*. Minneapolis: Fortress, 2000.

Childs, Brevard. *Isaiah: A Commentary*. OTL. Louisville: Westminster John Knox, 2001.

Collins, John J. *Daniel: A Commentary on the Book of Daniel*. Hermeneia. Minneapolis: Fortress, 1993.

———. *The Scepter and the Star: The Messiahs of the Dead Sea Scrolls and Other Ancient Literature*. ABRL. New York: Doubleday, 1995.

Cross, Frank Moore. *Canaanite Myth and Hebrew Epic: Essays in the History of the Religion of Israel*. Cambridge: Harvard University Press, 1973.

Dell, Katharine, and Will Kynes, eds. *Reading Job Intertextually*. LHBOTS 574. London: T&T Clark, 2013.

Dunn, James D. G., and Silviu N. Bunta. "Adam (Person) III. New Testament." *EBR* 1:306–11.

Edenburg, Cynthia. *Dismembering the Whole: Composition and Purpose of Judges 19–21*. AIL 24. Atlanta: SBL Press, 2016.

Eissfeldt, Otto. "The Promises of Grace to David in Isaiah 55,1–5." Pages 196–207 in *Israel's Prophetic Heritage: Essays in Honor of James Muilenburg*. Edited by Bernhard W. Anderson and Walter J. Harrelson. New York: Harper, 1962.

Emedi, Samuel. "Intertextuality in New Testament Scholarship: Significance, Criteria, and the Art of Intertextual Reading." *CBR* 14, no. 1 (2015): 8–23.

Evans, Craig A. "From Prophecy to Testament: An Introduction." Pages 1–22 in *From Prophecy to Testament: The Function of the Old Testament in the New*. Edited by Craig A. Evans. Peabody, MA: Hendrickson, 2004.

Finnegan, Ruth. *Why Do We Quote? The Culture and History of Quotation*. Cambridge: Open Book, 2013.

Fishbane, Michael. *Biblical Interpretation in Ancient Israel*. Oxford: Clarendon, 1985.

———. "The Book of Job and Inner-Biblical Discourse." Pages 86–98 in *The Voice from the Whirlwind: Interpreting the Book of Job*. Edited by Leo G. Perdue and W. Clark Gilprin. Nashville: Abingdon, 1991.

Friedman, Richard Elliott. "From Egypt to Egypt: Dtr^1 and Dtr^2." Pages 167–92 in *Traditions in Transformation: Turning Points in Biblical Faith*. Winona Lake, IN: Eisenbrauns, 1981.

Goodacre, Mark. "The Evangelists' Use of the Old Testament and the Synoptic Problem." Pages 281–98 in *New Studies in the Synoptic Problem: Oxford Conference, April 2008; Essays in Honour of Christopher M. Tuckett*. Edited by Paul Foster, Andrew Gregory, John S. Kloppenborg, and Jozef Verheyden. BETL 239. Leuven: Peeters, 2011.

Gray, John. *I and II Kings: A Commentary*. 2nd rev. ed. OTL. London: SCM, 1970.

Grossman, Jonathan. *Esther: The Outer Narrative and the Hidden Reading*. Siphrut 6. Winona Lake, IN: Eisenbrauns, 2011.

Hays, Richard B. *The Conversion of the Imagination: Paul as Interpreter of Israel's Scripture*. Grand Rapids: Eerdmans, 2005.

———. *Echoes of Scripture in the Letters of Paul*. New Haven: Yale University Press, 1989.

Japhet, Sara. *I & II Chronicles: A Commentary*. OTL. London: SCM, 1993.

———. *Ezra-Nehemia*. Mikra Leyisra'el. Tel Aviv: Am Oved, 2019. [Hebrew]

Jonker, Louis. "The Chronicler Singing Psalms: Revisiting the Chronicler's Psalm in 1 Chronicles 16." Pages 115–30 in *"My Spirit at Rest in the North Country" (Zechariah 6.8): Collected Communications to the XXth Congress of the International Organization for the Study of the Old Testament, Helsinki 2010*. Edited by Hermann Michael Niemann and Matthias Augustin. BEATAJ 57. Frankfurt am Main: Lang, 2011.

Joüon, Paul. *A Grammar of Biblical Hebrew*. Translated and revised by T. Muraoka. 2 vols. SubBi 27. Rome: Pontifical Biblical Institute, 2006.

Kaplan, Jonathan. *My Perfect One: Typology and Early Rabbinic Interpretation of Song of Songs*. New York: Oxford University Press, 2015.

Knoppers, Gary N. *I Chronicles 1–9: A New Translation with Introduction and Commentary*. AB 12. New York: Doubleday, 2003.

Lange, Armin, and Matthias Weingold. *Biblical Quotations and Allusions in Second Temple Jewish Literature*. JAJSup 5. Göttingen: Vandenhoeck & Ruprecht, 2011.

Levin, Christoph. "Abraham and Sarah in Egypt: A Story Composed to Prefigure the Exodus." *TheTorah.Com*, October 28, 2020. https://www.thetorah.com/article/abraham-and-sarah-in-egypt-a-story-composed-to-prefigure-the-exodus.

Levine, Amy-Jill, and Marc Zvi Brettler. *The Bible with and without Jesus*. New York: HarperOne, 2020.

———. *The Jewish Annotated New Testament*. 2nd ed. Oxford: Oxford University Press, 2017.

Levinson, Bernard M. *Deuteronomy and the Hermeneutics of Legal Innovation*. New York: Oxford University Press, 1997.

———. "The Manumission of Hermeneutics: The Slave Laws of the Pentateuch as a Challenge to Contemporary Pentateuchal Theory." Pages 281–324 in *Congress Volume Leiden 2004*. Edited by André Lemaire. VTSup 109. Leiden: Brill, 2006.

Lincicum, David. "How Did Paul Read Scripture?" Pages 225–38 in *The New Cambridge Companion to St. Paul*. Edited by Bruce W. Longenecker. Cambridge Companions to Religion. Cambridge: Cambridge University Press, 2020.

Marcus, Joel. *Mark 1–8: A New Translation with Introduction and Commentary*. AB 27. New York: Doubleday, 1999.

———. *The Way of the Lord: Christological Exegesis of the Old Testament in the Gospel of Mark*. Edinburgh: T&T Clark, 1992.

Marmur, Michael. "Why Jews Quote." *Oral Tradition* 29, no. 1 (2014): 5–46.

McCarthy, Carmel. *Deuteronomy*. BHQ 5. Stuttgart: Deutsche Bibelgesellschaft, 2007.

Meier, Samuel A. *Speaking of Speaking: Marking Direct Discourse in the Hebrew Bible*. VTSup 46. Leiden: Brill, 1992.

Miller, Cynthia L. *The Representation of Speech in Biblical Hebrew Narrative: A Linguistic Analysis*. HSM 55. Atlanta: Scholars Press, 1996.

Miller, Geoffrey D. "Intertextuality in Old Testament Research." *CBR* 9, no. 3 (2011): 283–309.

Miller-Naudé, Cynthia L. "Direct and Indirect Speech: Biblical Hebrew." *EHLL* 1:739–44.

Moule, C. F. D. "Fulfillment-Words in the New Testament: Use and Abuse." *NTS* 14, no. 3 (1968): 293–320.

Moyise, Steve. "Intertextuality and the Study of the Old Testament in the New Testament."

Pages 14–41 in *The Old Testament in the New Testament: Essays in Honour of J. L. North*. Edited by Steve Moyise. JSNTSup 189. Sheffield: Sheffield Academic, 2000.

Newsom, Carol A., with Brennan W. Breed. *Daniel: A Commentary*. OTL. Louisville: Westminster John Knox, 2014.

Novenson, Matthew V. *The Grammar of Messianism: An Ancient Jewish Political Idiom and Its Users*. New York: Oxford University Press, 2017.

Pakkala, Juha. "The Quotations and References of the Pentateuchal Laws in Ezra-Nehemiah." Pages 193–221 in *Changes in Scripture: Rewriting and Interpreting Authoritative Traditions in the Second Temple Period*. Edited by Hanne von Weissenberg, Juha Pakkala, and Karko Marttila. BZAW 419. Berlin: de Gruyter, 2011.

Porter, Stanley E. "Further Comments on the Use of the Old Testament in the New Testament." Pages 98–110 in *The Intertextuality of the Epistles: Explorations of Theory and Practice*. Edited by Thomas L. Brodie, Dennis R. MacDonald, and Stanley E. Porter. New Testament Monographs 16. Sheffield: Sheffield Phoenix, 2006

———. "Pauline Techniques of Interweaving Scripture into His Letters." Pages 23–55 in *Paulinische Schriftrezeption: Grundlagen – Ausprägungen – Wirkungen – Wertungen*. Edited by Florian Wilk and Markus Öhler. FRLANT 268. Göttingen: Vandenhoeck & Ruprecht, 2017.

Punt, Jeremy. "Identity, Memory, and Scriptural Warrant: Arguing Paul's Case." Pages 25–53 in *Paul and Scripture: Extending the Conversation*. Edited by Christopher D. Stanley. ECL 9. Atlanta: Society of Biblical Literature, 2012.

Römer, Thomas. *The So-Called Deuteronomistic History: A Sociological, Historical and Literary Introduction*. London: T&T Clark, 2005.

Rückl, Jan. *A Sure House: Studies in the Dynastic Promise to David in the Books of Samuel and Kings*. OBO 281. Fribourg: Academic Press; Göttingen: Vandenhoeck & Ruprecht, 2016.

Savran, George W. *Encountering the Divine: Theophany in Biblical Narrative*. JSOTSup 420. London: T&T Clark, 2005.

———. *Telling and Retelling: Quotation in Biblical Narrative*. ISBL. Bloomington: Indiana University Press, 1988.

Schniedewind, William M. *Society and the Promise to David: The Reception History of 2 Samuel 7:1–17*. New York: Oxford University Press, 1999.

Simon, Uriel. *Jonah: The Traditional Hebrew Text with the New JPS Translation*. JPS Bible Commentary. Philadelphia: Jewish Publication Society, 1999.

Sommer, Benjamin D. *A Prophet Reads Scripture: Allusion in Isaiah 40–66*. Contraversions. Stanford: Stanford University Press, 1998.

Spawn, Kevin L. *"As It Is Written" and Other Citation Formulae in the Old Testament: Their Use, Development, Syntax, and Significance*. BZAW 311. Berlin: de Gruyter, 2002.

Stackert, Jeffrey. *Rewriting the Torah: Literary Revision in Deuteronomy and the Holiness Legislation*. FAT 52. Tübingen: Mohr Siebeck, 2007.

Tov, Emanuel. *Textual Criticism of the Hebrew Bible*. 3rd ed. Minneapolis: Fortress, 2012.

Van Leeuwen, Raymond C. "Psalm 8.5 and Job 7.17–18: A Mistaken Scholarly Commonplace?" Pages 205–15 in *The World of the Aramaeans I: Biblical Studies in Honour of Paul-Eugene Dion*. Edited by P. M. Michele Daviau, John William Wevers, and Michael Weigl. JSOTSup 324. Sheffield: Sheffield Academic, 2001.

Von Rad, Gerhard. "The Deuteronomic Theology of History in *I* and *II Kings*." Pages 205–21 in *The Problem of the Hexateuch and Other Essays*. London: SCM, 1984.

Wagner, J. Ross. *Heralds of the Good News: Isaiah and Paul "in Concert" in the Letter to the Romans*. NovTSup 101. Leiden: Brill, 2002.

Wallace, Howard N. "What Chronicles Has to Say about Psalms." Pages 267–91 in *The Chronicler as Author: Studies in Text and Texture*. Edited by M. Patrick Graham and Steven L. McKenzie. JSOTSup 263. Sheffield: Sheffield Academic, 1999.

Warner, Megan. "Back to the Future: Reading the Abraham Narratives as Prequel." *BibInt* 25 (2017): 479–96.

Wolff, Hans Walter. *Joel and Amos: A Commentary on the Books of the Prophets Joel and Amos*. Hermeneia. Philadelphia: Fortress, 1977.

Young, Robb Andrew. *Hezekiah in History and Tradition*. VTSup 155. Leiden: Brill, 2012.

Zakovitch, Yair. *"And You Shall Tell Your Son . . .": The Concept of the Exodus in the Bible*. Jerusalem: Magnes, 1991.

Zevit, Ziony, ed. *Subtle Citation, Allusion, and Translation in the Hebrew Bible*. Sheffield: Equinox, 2017.

3

Israel's Greek Scriptures and Their Collection in the Septuagint

MARTIN KARRER

All of the writings of the New Testament were written in Greek and all of them cite the Scriptures of Israel in Greek. This is also true for the Christian writings of the second century that did not enter the New Testament canon (Did., 1 Clem., Ign., Barn., Justin).

To be sure, some early Christian authors knew Hebrew; this is suspected particularly regarding the authors of Matthew and the Apocalypse. However, these authors did not demand the knowledge of Hebrew or Aramaic from their readers. They quoted Israel's Scriptures as all the other Christian authors who wrote in Greek did. A Greek translation was added very early even to the only transmitted Aramaic quotation in the New Testament, Jesus's statement from the cross (Matt 27:46 // Mark 15:34).[1]

Sometimes Jesus's followers translated a word from the Hebrew Scriptures themselves; but that was the exception.[2] Normally they relied on Greek versions that already existed. The overwhelming majority of their citations and allusions used Israel's Scriptures according to the translation that is known as the "Septuagint" (LXX) today.

I thank David Herbison for his help in the English translation and Benjamin Blum for help in preparing the chapter for print.

1. Mark 15:34 transliterates an Aramaic version of Ps 22 (21 LXX).

2. Again, Mark 15:34 // Matt 27:46 is most important. Both Greek renderings differ from the Greek Psalter (LXX Ps 21:2); evidently, Ps 22:2 was translated on a case-by-case basis.

That term arose in Hellenistic Judaism and early Christianity (see below) but did not become conventional before the late second century CE.[3] From Augustine onward, the Latin loanword "Septuaginta" described the large collection of Israel's Scriptures as received in Christianity.[4] Yet, the borders of the collection were not firmly fixed even up to modern times. Since the hand edition of Alfred Rahlfs (1935), the Septuagint covers the Torah (Nomos), historical and prophetical books, Psalms, wisdom books, and younger narratives (sometimes in two textual forms). The critical Göttingen edition quotes the so-called younger translations in a second apparatus, an indication of the long and complex history of the text and its transmission.

Indeed, that translation which started in the third century BCE turned out to be the grandest translation project of antiquity. Accidental variants emerged in the time of transmission. A tendency for revision arose in the first century BCE (called "kaige"). The so-called new translations appeared on the horizon in New Testament times (Aquila, Theodotion, Symmachus). Therefore, the New Testament quotations and allusions are influenced by the oldest form of the Septuagint translation (which is often named "Old Greek") and by these developments.[5]

The history of the Greek translation and collection of Israel's Greek Scriptures is long and complex, as indicated. Yet the momentum of the Greek language was so strong among the followers of Jesus that it delayed the translation of Israel's Greek and Hebrew Scriptures into Latin for more than a century.[6] Hence, an overview on the Greek Scriptures of Israel gives not only insight into the self-understanding of Israel in the Hellenistic and early Roman times; it points to a prominent presupposition and context of early Christian thought.

The Triumph of Hellenism and the Translation of the Torah (and Hexateuch) in Alexandria

1. In 333 BCE, Alexander the Great defeated the Persians at the Battle of Issus. The regions in which the Jewish and Jewish-Samarian population lived—Judea, Samaria, and Egypt in the south, as well as former Babylon in the east—came under the rule of Alexander and his successors, the Diadochi. The Greek language spread quickly, promoted by Hellenistic settlement policies and economic

---

3. Around 200 CE, the term served to indicate the translation of Israel's Scriptures with an open scope (cf. Irenaeus, *Haer.* 3.21.2).

4. Cf. Augustine, *Civ.* 18.42–44.

5. A database of the New Testament citations and their sources can be found at https://projekte.isbtf.de/lxx-nt/index.php.

6. The Old Latin translation (*Vetus Latina*) first began in the late second c. CE.

exchange. Jews settled in many newly founded municipalities.[7] The Jewish quarter of Alexandria, the capital of the Ptolemaic kingdom in the southern Mediterranean, became the greatest and most famous of such resettlements and the starting place for the Septuagint.

A translation of holy Scriptures, however, was not self-evident. Two hundred years of Persian rule had passed without generating sustained efforts to translate the older Hebrew writings into the Persian (Imperial Aramaic) linguistic superstratum. But the linguistic difference between Greek and Hebrew was stronger, and the Greek inculturation of Judaism occurred quickly. It took less than two generations before the most important of Israel's writings needed to be translated into Greek.

2. A contemporary account of the translation process is lacking, though it can be deduced from later witnesses that the Torah was translated in Alexandria during the reign of Ptolemy II Philadelphus, beginning about 270/260 BCE.[8] The work proceeded well; the translation of the "law of Moses" (as was said in Greek) was perhaps already completed by the time Ptolemy died (246 BCE).[9] Different translators were responsible for the five books from Genesis to Deuteronomy.[10] Nevertheless, a uniform linguistic tone developed, more obliged to the language of daily life than to Classical Greek and, yet, erudite.[11] The common tone presupposes that the foundations for the Greek linguistic competence of the translators had been laid before 270.[12] The hellenization of Judaism was accomplished already before the translation of Genesis.

The Letter of Aristeas (late second c. BCE) ascribes the initiative for the translation to the Ptolemaic dynasty and the administrator of the Alexandrian library (esp. Let. Aris. 9–11 and 301–311). However, the author of the Letter of Aristeas did not use reliable information. Seen sociohistorically, the Jewish settlers had

---

7. That is evinced by inscriptions (see, e.g., *IJO* 2 for Lydia and Phrygia).

8. See Felix Albrecht, "Die alexandrinische Bibelübersetzung: Einsichten zur Entstehungs-, Überlieferungs- und Wirkungsgeschichte der Septuaginta," in *Alexandria*, ed. Tobias Georges, Felix Albrecht, and Reinhard Feldmeier, Civitatum Orbis Mediterranei Studia 1 (Tübingen: Mohr Siebeck, 2013), 209–43.

9. Cf. Martin Rösel, "From the Tora to *Nomos*: Perspectives of Research on the Greek Pentateuch," in *Introduction to the Septuagint*, ed. Siegfried Kreuzer (Waco, TX: Baylor University Press, 2019), 65–73. For the term "law of Moses," see Josh 9:2 etc.

10. Thus the majority of research; Theo A. W. van der Louw, "The Unity of LXX Genesis and Exodus," *VT* 69, no. 2 (2019): 270–84, sees the translator of Genesis working on Exodus, too.

11. See esp. John A. L. Lee, *The Greek of the Pentateuch: Grinfield Lectures on the Septuagint 2011–2012* (Oxford: Oxford University Press, 2018).

12. Anneli Aejmelaeus, "The Septuagint and Oral Translation," in *XIV Congress of the IOSCS, Helsinki, 2010*, ed. Melvin K. H. Peters, SCS 59 (Atlanta: Society of Biblical Literature, 2013), 5–13.

their own interest in the Greek availability of their Scripture; a political commission may only have been thought of additionally. The challenges from the cultural and political milieu of Alexandria (including that of the Museion) and the inner-Jewish interests came together as the impetus for the translation.[13]

3. That the translation began with Genesis fitted into the situation: Joseph was buried in Egypt, as the last verse of the book wrote (ἔθαψαν αὐτὸν καὶ ἔθηκαν ἐν τῇ σορῷ ἐν Αἰγύπτῳ, Gen 50:26). Exodus 1:7 could be added; the descendants of Jacob and Joseph had increased "tremendously" in Egypt already in old times as the translator maintained there.[14] Thus, the narrative was apt for legitimating the present life in Alexandria and along the banks of the Nile.

Nevertheless, the memory of the fathers included a strong conflict. A king came to power who did not know Joseph, as is told in Exod 1:8. The version emphasized that the conflict (causing the exodus of Israel) resulted from the king's ignorance (οὐκ ᾔδει, Exod 1:8 LXX). That meant implicitly: if acquaintance was established, as occurred in the translation, optimism was permitted that the terrors of the story would not reoccur. That way, it became possible to read the books from Exodus to Numbers in a Greek and Egyptian context despite the conflict story.[15]

Leviticus, Numbers, and Deuteronomy were either translated according to their present order after Exodus, or the self-contained law code of Deuteronomy was first taken up.[16] In both cases, the regulations for the life of the Jewish population dominated. The term "Judeans" (Ιουδαῖοι) was missing in the narrated world (the time of the fathers and Moses). But Judah was praised as one of the fathers (Gen 49:8–12). The translation of the Torah established a foundation for the life of the social group of "Judeans" in Egypt, Judea, and elsewhere.

13. Cf. Siegfried Kreuzer, "The Origins and Transmission of the Septuagint," in Kreuzer, *Introduction*, 3–56, esp. 4–20; and Benjamin G. Wright, *The Letter of Aristeas: "Aristeas to Philocrates" or "On the Translation of the Law of the Jews,"* CEJL (Berlin: de Gruyter, 2015), 6–15.

14. The translation of Exod 1:7 does not understand תמלא as *niphal*, but rather active. The effect suits the situation of the early third c. well: the prospering land "multiplied" the Jewish population.

15. Some details in LXX Exodus can be read as more "Egypt friendly" than the MT, beginning with Exod 2:5–10 LXX; see Helmut Utzschneider, "Die LXX als 'Erzählerin': Beobachtungen an der LXX-Fassung der Geburts- und Kindheitsgeschichte des Mose (Ex 2,1–10)," in *Die Septuaginta: Texte, Theologien, Einflüsse; 2. Internationale Fachtagung veranstaltet von Septuaginta Deutsch (LXX. D), Wuppertal 23.–27.7.2008*, ed. Wolfgang Kraus, Martin Karrer, and Martin Meiser, WUNT 252 (Tübingen: Mohr Siebeck, 2010), 462–77, esp. 472–73.

16. The majority of research holds to the canonical order, e.g., Carsten Ziegert, *Diaspora als Wüstenzeit: Übersetzungswissenschaftliche und theologische Aspekte des griechischen Numeribuches*, BZAW 480 (Berlin: de Gruyter, 2015), 309–10. The priority of the translation of Deuteronomy is advocated by Cornelis G. den Hertog, "Erwägungen zur relativen Chronologie der Bücher Levitikus und Deuteronomium innerhalb der Pentateuchübersetzung," in vol. 2 of *Im Brennpunkt: die Septuaginta*, ed. Siegfried Kreuzer and Jürgen Peter Lesch, BWANT 161 (Stuttgart: Kohlhammer, 2004), 216–28.

The translation of the Torah (Genesis–Deuteronomy) was very successful. It spread widely and was less reworked later on than the younger parts of the Septuagint ("kaige" did not become relevant in Genesis–Deuteronomy).

4. The translation work went on soon since the narrative of the fathers did not end with Deuteronomy. The book of Joshua reported the way of Israel from Egypt into the territory of the twelve tribes (Judea-Galilee). Until 200 BCE this area was under Ptolemaic rule; then only after heavy conflict did it belong to the Seleucids. It seems reasonable to situate the translation of Joshua still within the era of Ptolemaic dominance (or, at the latest, within the context of the conflicts at the beginning of the second c.).[17]

Hence, the expansion of the translation from the Torah to the Hexateuch (Genesis–Joshua) explained that the "Judeans" living in Egypt had social and religious roots in Judea. After the end of Ptolemaic dominance, the transmission of the Hexateuch outside of Egypt permitted respect for Egypt as well as distance. Some of the following translations and receptions show that ambivalence (cf., e.g., Hos 11:1–5).

Translation, Inculturation, and Identity

1. In Alexandria and Ptolemaic Egypt, the Jewish settlers were treated analogously to the demographic groups that settled there from Greek cities. All these groups brought their traditions with them and cultivated the memory of their provenance. It is for this reason that the rendering of Ἰουδαῖοι with the sociohistorical term "Judeans" (settlers, having ties to Judea) is more adequate to the Hellenistic sources than a rendering with the religious description "Jews."[18] Seen in the Ptolemaic context, the Jewish settlers ("Judeans") were one of the self-conscious and competing groups living in Alexandria and in the Ptolemaic kingdom.

2. The substantive implementation of "Jewish" laws was limited by the legislation of the respective state's power. The praxis of the laws written in Exodus–Deuteronomy therefore concentrated on familial contexts. In the greater public, such an implementation hardly took place.[19] Nevertheless, the Letter of

---

17. Michaël N. van der Meer, "Provenance, Profile, and Purpose of the Greek Joshua," in *XII Congress of the International Organization for Septuagint and Cognate Studies (Leiden 2004)*, ed. Melvin K. H. Peters, SCS 54 (Atlanta: Society of Biblical Literature, 2006), 55–80.

18. For the social history, see the research of Sylvie Honigman (e.g., "Politeumata and Ethnicity in Ptolemaic Egypt," *AncSoc* 33 [2003]: 61–102) and Patrick Sänger, *Die ptolemäische Organisationsform politeuma: Ein Herrschaftsinstrument zugunsten jüdischer und anderer hellenischer Gemeinschaften*, TSAJ 178 (Tübingen: Mohr Siebeck, 2019).

19. See James M. S. Cowey and Klaus Maresch, "An die Archonten wegen Auflösung einer Verlobung," in *Urkunden des Politeuma der Juden von Herakleopolis (144/3–133/2 v. Chr.) (P. Polit. Iud.)*, ed. James M. S. Cowey and Klaus Maresch (Wiesbaden: Westdeutscher, 2001), 56–71.

Aristeas referred to the Greek Pentateuch simply as the "Laws" of the Jews (τῶν Ἰουδαίων νόμιμα, Let. Aris. 10).[20] The idea of the law was not bounded by the circumstances.

In terms of legal and cultural history, this is comparable to the Greek settlers' remembrance of the great lawgivers of their regions.[21] The Greek lawgivers—Solon, Lycurgus, or Plato—had safeguarded the distinction of the Greek groups. According to Deuteronomy, the law of Israel possessed a corresponding or even greater distinction. Moses himself imparted, according to Deut 4:5–8, that the foreign people will hear the laws done by the children of Israel since these laws possess a preeminent wisdom and understanding (σοφία καὶ σύνεσις, 4:6).[22]

The Hebrew text of Deut 4 had already shaped the conviction that Israel had the best and wisest law. Now the point became discernable in the Greek world via the translation. Anyone speaking Greek could and should read: the law of Israel possesses a high level of intellectual authority and power; it is given by God and understandable all over the world.

The idea of God's legislation (νομοθεσία) ensured the relevance of Israel's law throughout the era of the Diadochi and up to the early Roman Empire.[23] It therefore radiated into the period of Philo and the New Testament.[24]

3. A peculiarity of the Septuagint made life among foreign cults easier: the Hebrew text of the Torah frequently employs the term "Elohim" for God, a word that is actually plural; the one God is, so to speak, the sum of the gods. The translator of Exod 22:28 took the plural suffix "-im" (ים) literally. He wrote θεοὺς οὐ κακολογήσεις "you shall not revile gods" (22:27 LXX[Ra]; 22:28 LXX[Gö]). This opened the possibility for an unpolemical cooperation of religions; the foreign

---

20. In the first centuries BCE and CE, this collection was also called "the legislation" (νομοθεσία, 2 Macc 6:23; Rom 9:4).

21. The translation of תּוֹרָה ("instruction") with νόμος ("law") was not compulsory. The word νόμος is missing in Genesis, and only once in Genesis does one encounter the term τὰ νόμιμα (in Gen 26:5). The word νόμος becomes the guiding concept beginning in the translation of Exod 12:43, 49 and throughout Deuteronomy.

22. Cf. Adrian Schenker, "Was führte zur Übersetzung der Tora ins Griechische? Dtn 4,2–8 und Platon (Brief VII,326a–b)," in Kraus, Karrer, and Meiser, Die Septuaginta, 23–35.

23. One first encounters the term νομοθεσία in Aristobulus in the middle of the second c. BCE (frag. 3.1 = Eusebius, Praep. ev. 13.12.1). Aristobulus was of the persuasion that the Jewish law was made available to non-Jews long before; therefore, he created the anachronism that even Plato should have followed the Jewish law. For our purposes it is more interesting that Aristobulus saw the law as rooted in the writings of Israel from the exodus to the taking of the land (κράτησις τῆς χώρας). This means that Joshua was closely connected to the books of the Law in his time.

24. Philo, the prominent Alexandrian contemporary of Paul, developed the idea of νομοθεσία with the help of the legends regarding the translation of the Torah: the translation was carried out by Ptolemaic commission, he writes, because the good laws of God should not remain concealed from the Greek (non-Jewish) half of humanity (Philo, Mos. 2.27–44).

gods were not accepted, but it was forbidden to blaspheme them. The Judaism of the first century imparted that idea to early Christianity.[25]

4. At the same time, the inculturation required an awareness of their own identity. The Hebrew *Vorlage* of the Greek translation delineated decisive identity markers: the veneration of the one God, circumcision, Sabbath, feasts, and dietary restrictions.[26] The Greek translation transferred the verbal articulation into the context of the nations and influenced the language. For example, a special metaphor distinguished circumcision (περιτομή) from being uncircumcised (Gen 17:11–14, etc.). The newly coined word ἀκροβυστία expressed a specific view of the foreskin:[27] to the gentiles, the "end" (ἀκρο . . .) was "filled," so to speak (βυστία derived from βύω).[28] Early Christianity inherited this metaphoric perspective.[29]

The linguistic development soon concerned the demographic terminology: ἔθνος ("people/nation") designated groups of cognate origin in Greek tradition. However, the Hebrew word גוי ("ethnicity") had taken on a connotation of distance before the Greek translation was begun.[30] Thus starting with Exod 1:9 the word ἔθνος occurs for "the others." Jewish identity, by contrast, was preferably expressed by the terms γένος (1:9; "family-group") and λαός (1:20). The distinction between ἔθνος/ἔθνη ("gentiles") and λαός ("people of the one God") established itself and prevailed up to the time of the New Testament.[31]

5. These idioms and a number of other *termini* permit us to speak of a Jewish sociolect (going on in part to Jewish Christianity).[32] For example, the translators of the Torah avoided describing the sanctuary of God with the foreign term for a temple and its cella (ναός); they always wrote "tent," σκηνή.[33] They discarded

25. Exodus 22:28 will be expanded in some manuscripts up to the Byzantine period by one word that clarifies the point: "you shall not revile foreign [ἀλλοτρίους!] gods." Cf. the apparatus in *Exodus*, ed. John William Wevers, SVTG 2.1 (Göttingen: Vandenhoeck & Ruprecht, 1991), 265 *ad loc.*; and cf. Martin Karrer, "Begegnung und Widerspruch: Der eine Gott und die Religionen in der frühchristlichen Mission," *Religionen unterwegs* 13, no. 4 (2007): 10.

26. For the decisive veneration of the "one God," see Deut 6:4–5, quoted in Mark 12:29–30 par.

27. It took the place of (ἀκρο)ποσθία, as the "foreskin" was typically called in Greek.

28. This derivation is not certain, though folk-etymologically probable; cf. Gilles Dorival, "La lexicographie de la Septante," in *Die Sprache der Septuaginta/The Language of the Septuagint*, ed. Eberhard Bons and Jan Joosten, vol. 3 of *Handbuch zur Septuaginta*, ed. Martin Karrer, Wolfgang Kraus, and Siegfried Kreuzer (Gütersloh: Gütersloher Verlagshaus, 2016), 291–92.

29. Paul will grapple with it: see περιτομή/ἀκροβυστία in Gal 5:6 and elsewhere.

30. This is demonstrated by Adi Ophir and Ishay Rosen-Zvi, *Goy: Israel's Multiple Others and the Birth of the Gentile*, Oxford Studies in the Abrahamic Religions (Oxford: Oxford University Press, 2018), 114, based on the book of Sirach (esp. the Hebrew fragments).

31. The followers of Jesus will take it up and try to overcome it: cf., e.g., the composite citation in 1 Pet 2:9–10.

32. Cf. contributions in Bons and Joosten, ed., *Sprache* (n. 29), e.g., 246–56.

33. The temple in Jerusalem, however, was a solid building. The translators of the Historical

the image of a god, which is not to be worshiped, in calling it εἴδωλον, "idol" (Exod 20:4; Deut 29:16, etc.). They termed Israel's altar θυσιαστήριον (Exod 17:15, etc.) in contrast to the altar of the gentiles (βωμός, Exod 34:13, etc.). They rejected an initiation into mysteries and other related ideas.[34] All of these categories remained standard into the New Testament period.[35]

Nonetheless, the bulk of the vocabulary in the Greek Pentateuch accorded with the common Greek of the time.[36] The use of language did not break from Greek syntax and morphology.[37] Thus the Judaism of the Greek diaspora attracted little attention on a day-to-day basis due to its language—and this will also set the course for early Christianity. The difference of religion and inner life in the ethnicity did not destroy communal life with the "others."

The Progress of the Translations in the Second Century BCE

Originally, the name "Septuagint" referred to the translation of the Pentateuch that was done by seventy-two translators (six from each tribe of Israel) according to the legend (Let. Aris. 39.46–50).[38] But the process of translation did not stop with the law or hexateuch; it broadened in the second century BCE:

1. Around 200 BCE the Ptolemaic dominance over Judea and Galilee ended. The Seleucids achieved supremacy. The knowledge of the Greek language advanced in the Jewish centers of their empire quickly. From 180/170 BCE at the latest there was sufficient linguistic competence in Jerusalem and its surroundings

---

Books will therefore use the term ναός; but they will emphasize the peculiarity of Israel's holy of holies by the Hebrew loanword δαβιρ (1 Kgs = 3 Kgdms 6:5).

34. For the mysteries, cf. the addition in Deut 23:18(17)b LXX (τελεσφόρος, τελισκόμενος). Cf. Martin Rösel, "Vorlage oder Interpretation? Zur Übersetzung von Gottesaussagen in der Septuaginta des Deuteronomiums," in *Ein Freund des Wortes*, ed. Sebastian Grätz, Axel Graupner, and Jörg Lanckau (Göttingen: Vandenhoeck & Ruprecht, 2019), 255–56. Many details could be added; see the overview regarding language by Folker Siegert, *Zwischen Hebräischer Bibel und Altem Testament: Eine Einführung in die Septuaginta*, MJSt 9 (Münster: LIT, 2001), 121–286.

35. See σκηνή in Acts 7:44; σκηνή and sacrificial terminology from Exodus-Leviticus-Numbers in Heb 9; θυσιαστήριον in Matt 5:23–24, etc.; βωμός in Act 17:23.

36. See John A. L. Lee, *A Lexical Study of the Septuagint Version of the Pentateuch*, SCS 14 (Chico, CA: Scholars Press, 1983); and Lee, *Greek*; as well as the lexicons to the Septuagint; regarding epigraphy, see also James K. Aitken, *No Stone Unturned: Greek Inscriptions and Septuagint Vocabulary*, CrStHB 5 (Winona Lake, IN: Eisenbrauns, 2014).

37. Koine forms are often found alongside Attic forms in the textual transmission.

38. It is not known when the term "Seventy-Two" condensed to "Seventy" ("Septuagint"); the latter number recalls the seventy elders endorsing Moses (Num 11:24–29).

for translational works.[39] Therefore, the localization of translations (or biblical texts written in Greek) is difficult from the second century onward.[40]

The hellenization of Jerusalem rapidly entered into a conflict. Greek remained the "lingua franca." The ancestral temple priesthood, however, left Jerusalem and went to Egypt; between 167 and 164 BCE, the temple of Leontopolis was established, which was in existence until 73/74 CE.[41] Hence, potential translators are to be found under the new emigrants as well.

2. In that situation prophetic books were translated. The translation of the Dodekapropheton, which seems to have been done first, introduced the idiom of the "almighty" God into Greek Judaism (παντοκράτωρ for צבאות, Hos 12:6; Amos 4:13, etc.).[42]

Greek Isaiah can be dated between 170 and 150 BCE and esteems Egypt in a remarkable way. Were the translators emigrants from Jerusalem/Palestine, or had they lived in Egypt already before the crisis of Jerusalem? Anyway, they created a new kind of actualizing translation. They understood the book of Isaiah as a unity showing God in his ability to heal (cf. ἰάσομαι, Isa 7:4; 57:19; etc.) and his creating and universal might (Isa 65:17–18; 66:18–21). Their free and contemporary rendering made an impact within and outside of the Egyptian region (esp. Isa 19:18–20, 24–25) and marked a high point of translational competence.[43]

---

39. While extant Greek inscriptions from the Ptolemaic period are still rare in Judaea, they are multiplying under the Seleucids; cf. Werner Eck, "Nebeneinander oder miteinander? Die Aussagekraft der verschiedenen Sprachen auf Inschriften in Iudaea-Palaestina," in *Sprachen-Schriftkulturen-Identitäten der Antike: Beiträge des XV. Internationalen Kongresses für Griechische und Lateinische Epigraphik*, ed. Petra Amann et al., Tyche Supplementband 10 (Vienna: Holzhausen, 2019), 51–54.

40. Not even the Mesopotamian center of the Seleucid Empire can be left out of consideration: a Babylonian provenance of the Epistle of Jeremiah cannot be ruled out even if an origin in the surroundings of Jerusalem is more probable (Benjamin G. Wright, "Epistole Jeremiu/Epistula Ieremiae/Epistle of Jeremiah," in Kreuzer, *Introduction*, 563).

41. Josephus, *J.W.* 7.426–429. Cf. Meron M. Piotrkowski, *Priests in Exile: The History of the Temple of Onias and Its Community in the Hellenistic Period*, SJ 106 (Berlin: de Gruyter, 2019).

42. For the date and characteristics of the Dodekapropheton, see Cécile Dogniez and Philippe Le Moigne, eds., *Les Douze Prophètes dans la LXX: Protocoles et procédures dans la traduction grecque; Stylistique, poétique et histoire*, VTSup 180 (Leiden: Brill, 2019). For the idiom of "almighty," see Evangelia G. Dafni, "ΠΑΝΤΟΚΡΑΤΩΡ in Septuaginta-Amos 4,13: Zur Theologie der Sprache der Septuaginta," in *The Septuagint and Messianism*, ed. Michael A. Knibb, BETL 195 (Leuven: Peeters, 2006), 443–54; and Hermann Spieckermann and Reinhard Feldmeier, *Der Gott der Lebendigen: Eine biblische Gotteslehre*, Topics of Biblical Theology 1 (Tübingen: Mohr Siebeck, 2011), 149–202.

43. For the discussion, see Isaac Leo Seeligmann, *The Septuagint Version of Isaiah: A Discussion of Its Problems*, MEOL 9 (Leiden: Brill, 1984); the studies of Arie van der Kooij (e.g., "Esaias/Isaias/Jesaja," in Kreuzer, *Introduction*, 515–27); Michaël van der Meer, ed., *Isaiah in Context: Studies in Honour of Arie van der Kooij on the Occasion of His Sixty-Fifth Birthday*, VTSup 138 (Leiden: Brill, 2010); Ronald L. Troxel, *LXX-Isaiah as Translation and In-*

The Dodekapropheton and the Greek Isaiah were widely received (esp. in early Christianity).[44]

3. Both the Dodekapropheton and Isaiah articulated the universal relevance of the one God intriguingly but differently (παντοκράτωρ is missing in Isaiah). Evidently the time of the Diadochi provoked an interest in defining Jewish monotheistic identity against a world-wide horizon. Interestingly, an insertion into Exod 23:22 highlighted the universal claim of the one God in a polysemous tension:[45] The longer text of the verse articulates "mine [= God's] is the whole land/the entire earth" (ἐμὴ γάρ ἐστιν πᾶσα ἡ γῆ); one may read a praise of the land of Israel (γῆ in narrow sense) as well as of God's universal presence (γῆ in a wide sense).[46]

4. Under Jonathan (160–143 BCE), a Hasmonean state was established that existed for about a century. The expansion of the Hasmoneans, however, led to a Judean-Samaritan conflict.

The Old Greek of the Torah was translated before that Judean-Samaritan clash. An old stratum of the text spoke of Gerizim in Deut 27:4 perhaps (which is assumed already for the Hebrew *Vorlage*). But now the Samaritan tradition was depreciated by the Hasmoneans. As a consequence, the relevance of Gerizim was lost in the Septuagint. The main text of the Septuagint, which entered Christendom, follows the "Judean" tradition though the relevance of Gerizim is recognizable in the secondary tradition of the *Vetus Latina* (Deut 27:4).[47]

The Samaritans kept their old text in distance from the younger growth of the Septuagint collection. They concentrated on the Torah (the heart of the Septuagint). As a consequence, the larger collection of the Septuagint that is read today (Genesis to Maccabees) stays in the tradition of "Judean" theology. Nevertheless

---

terpretation: *The Strategies of the Translator of the Septuagint of Isaiah*, JSJSup 124 (Leiden: Brill, 2008); Keunjoo Kim, "Theology and Identity of the Egyptian Jewish Diaspora in Septuagint of Isaiah" (PhD diss., University of Oxford, 2009), https://ora.ox.ac.uk/objects/uuid:3a0507b0-32ad-419d-8a94-84cd2b76e856/download_file?safe_filename=Thesis.pdf&file_format=application%2Fpdf&type_of_work=Thesis.

44. Esp. well known is Isa 7:14 LXX (cf. Matt 1:23); see Martin Rösel, "Die Jungfrauengeburt des endzeitlichen Immanuel: Jesaja 7 in der Übersetzung der Septuaginta," in *Tradition and Innovation: English and German Studies on the Septuagint*, ed. Martin Rösel, SCS 70 (Atlanta: SBL Press, 2018), 197–219.

45. The reading is considered secondary conventionally (as in LXX^{Gö} against LXX^{Ra}); if so, then it probably belongs to the second c. BCE.

46. J. Cornelis de Vos, "Das Land Israel in der Sicht der Septuaginta: Beispiele aus Exodus, Josua und Jesaja," in *Die Septuaginta und das frühe Christentum*, ed. Thomas S. Caulley and Hermann Lichtenberger, WUNT 277 (Tübingen: Mohr Siebeck, 2011), 91–92, considers the insertion to be the *Ausgangstext* (against Wevers). According to him, the line implies, "dass das Volk Israel heilig sein kann auf der ganzen Erde, also auch in Ägypten" (92) [ET: "that the people of Israel can be holy on all the earth, including in Egypt"].

47. See Stefan Schorch, "Der Samaritanische Pentateuch in der Geschichte des hebräischen Bibeltextes," *VF* 60, no. 1 (2015): 24–26.

parts of the Psalms, Prophets, and wisdom books may have been used by the Samaritans in Greek. Research on the Samaritan participation in the textual development would be welcome.

5. The translations went on. At the same time, the text of Israel's Hebrew Scriptures was not yet fully stabilized in the second century. Some peculiarities must be seen against this background:

- First Esdras looks like a rewriting of 2 Chron 35–36, the Hebrew book Ezra, and Neh 8. Did the translator use a Hebrew rewriting of the narrative, or was he rendering freely a Hebrew text that was only slightly variated against today's Hebrew text?[48]
- The Old Greek book of Jeremiah is considerably shorter than the MT. Either LXX Jeremiah preserves an older Hebrew *Vorlage* (as preferred by the majority of scholarship) or the Greek translator considered large abridgments justified.[49] Conceptually, the translator strengthened the criticism in Jer 38:32 (LXX sees, against Jer 31:32 MT, the covenant with the patriarchs as destroyed) and the mercy of God (see, e.g., 27:20 beside MT 50:20).[50]
- The most important Greek manuscript of the book of Ezekiel, papyrus 967 Ra., orders chapters 36–39 differently than does MT (ch. 37 is found after 39).[51]

In many cases the text developed up to New Testament time. That way, the early Christians could use different strata of translation. The Greek Jeremiah, e.g., will be extensively reworked.[52] This is recognizable in the so-called Theodotianic text (// MT) and may be occasionally posited in the New Testament.[53]

48. See Kristin De Troyer, "The Septuagint," in *From the Beginnings to 600*, vol. 1 of *The New Cambridge History of the Bible*, ed. James Carlton Paget and Joachim Schaper (Cambridge: Cambridge University Press, 2013), 277.

49. For the controversy about the introductory questions, see the commentaries, esp. Hermann-Josef Stipp, *Jeremia 25–52*, HAT 12.2 (Tübingen: Mohr Siebeck, 2019), 3–6.

50. For LXX Jer 38:31–34, see Adrian Schenker, *Das Neue am neuen Bund und das Alte am alten: Jer 31 in der hebräischen und griechischen Bibel*, FRLANT 212 (Göttingen: Vandenhoeck & Ruprecht, 2006).

51. See Ingrid E. Lilly, *Two Books of Ezekiel: Papyrus 967 and the Masoretic Text as Variant Literary Editions*, VTSup 150 (Leiden: Brill, 2012); Michael Konkel, "Die Ezechiel-Septuaginta, Papyrus 967 und die Redaktionsgeschichte des Ezechielbuches: Probleme und Perspektiven am Beispiel von Ez 34," in *Das Buch Ezechiel: Komposition, Redaktion und Rezeption*, ed. Jan Christian Gertz, Corinna Körting, and Markus Witte, BZAW 516 (Berlin: de Gruyter, 2020), 43–62.

52. The most important scholarly propositions come from Henry St. John Thackeray, "Notes and Studies: The Greek Translators of Jeremiah," *JTS* 4, no. 14 (1903): 245–66; and Emanuel Tov, *The Septuagint Translation of Jeremiah and Baruch*, HSM 8 (Missoula, MT: Scholars Press, 1976), a correction to Thackeray.

53. Cf. the reception of Jer 10:7 in Rev 15:3–4; Juan Hernández, "Recensional Activity and the Transmission of the Septuagint in John's Apocalypse," in *Die Johannesoffenbarung: Ihr Text*

6. The translation of the divine name, which had started in the third century (Exod 3:14), remained of interest. Maybe, the choice of the participle ὁ ὤν ("The One Who Is") in LXX Exod 3:14 had happened accidentally. But it introduced an ontological dimension into the understanding of God unintentionally (which was not present in the Hebrew relative clause אהיה אשר אהיה).

The Greek phrase was taken up by the translator of Jeremiah according to the Göttingen edition (ὁ ὤν, Jer 1:6 LXX[Ziegler]; diff. LXX[Ra]). Later on, it was corrected in some Jeremiah passages in order to bring the text closer to the Hebrew. That can be seen in reading the text of Jer 4:10; 14:13; 39[32]:17 LXX together with the *variae lectiones* (or in LXX[Ra] beside LXX[Gö]).

Receptions of Exod 3:14 LXX went on in writings up to the first cent. CE (Wis 13:1; Philo, *Somn*. 1.230–231; *Mut*. 7ff.; 11; 14). Thus, the Christian carrying on the idea that is attested starting with Rev 1:8 is embedded into a broader stream of Greek Jewish thought.[54]

7. By about 130/120 BCE, most of the historical and prophetic books, the core of the Psalms, and the first parts of the wisdom books were translated.[55] The complex history of the second century makes it difficult to imagine a common milieu for these ongoing translations. Nevertheless, four aspects are of general interest:

First, the wide-ranging scribal scholarship of the translators can be supposed.[56] Moreover, all of them knew the Alexandrian writings of the law (Genesis–Deuteronomy) and oriented themselves verbally to a certain degree accordingly.

Second, the term γραφή, "writing/Scripture," became established gradually. The citation formula "it is written" was, originally, used in a relatively free manner; it referenced the law (cf., e.g., "as it is written in the law of Moses," καθὰ γέγραπται ἐν τῷ νόμῳ Μωυσῆ, Josh 9:2 LXX) as well as other writings of Israel (LXX 3 Kgdm 11:41; 20:11; 22:39, etc.). In the translation of the books of Chronicles (dated before 158 BCE), then, the term γραφή was solidified in the sense of

---

und ihre Auslegung, ed. Martin Karrer and Michael Labahn, ABIG 38 (Leipzig: Evangelische Verlagsanstalt, 2012), 83–98, esp. 96–98.

54. See Martin Karrer, "Septuaginta und antike Philosophie," in *Die Septuaginta: Orte und Intentionen; 5. internationale Fachtagung veranstaltet von Septuaginta Deutsch (LXX.D), Wuppertal, 24.–27. Juli 2014*, ed. S. Kreuzer, Martin Meiser, and Marcus Sigismund, WUNT 361 (Tübingen: Mohr Siebeck, 2016), 26–30.

55. Dating the translation of the wisdom books is particularly difficult. According to the majority of scholars, at least Proverbs was translated prior to 130/120 (though sometimes it is dated to around 100; consult the introductions to the Septuagint).

56. See Arie van der Kooij, "Perspectives on the Study of the Septuagint: Who Are the Translators?," in *Perspectives in the Study of the Old Testament and Early Judaism*, ed. Florentino García Martínez and Adam S. van der Woude, VTSup 73 (Leiden: Brill, 1998), 214–29.

"Scripture" (1 Chr 15:15, etc.).⁵⁷ The trajectory had begun that would result in the expression "holy Scriptures" (a term used by Paul in Rom 1:2).

Third, the great scope of the translations called for a taxonomy of part-collections. The prologue of the Greek Sirach (117 BCE at the latest) mentioned the law (ὁ νόμος), the prophecies (αἱ προφητεῖαι), and the remaining scrolls (τὰ λοιπὰ τῶν βιβλίων; Prol. 1.8–10.24–25).⁵⁸ The Historical Books were implicitly included in the prophecies.⁵⁹ Thus the later arrangement of the Bible started to become apparent.

Fourth, the author of Greek Sirach wished to include the work of his grandfather (Prol. 7) into the wide radius of honored Scriptures. He was partially successful. The Hebrew version of Sirach, with the exception of fragments, will be lost later on. But the Greek text and daughter translations will circulate broadly. In respect to Sirach, the attribute "Scripture" can be given first to a Greek instead of a Hebrew text.⁶⁰

Thus, at the end of the second century we come across a new complexity. The Greek translations are spreading widely, while a different tier of Hebrew writings comes to the horizon.

Dynamics around the New Testament Period

Hebrew and Greek Scriptures of Israel remained related but could, nevertheless, develop separately from the first century BCE onward. Therefore, not only were the last translations completed, but Scriptures written originally in Greek were valued highly (they became part of the Septuagint later on). At the same time, dynamics of revision evolved and significantly affected the transmission of the earlier translated texts:

---

57. For dating Greek Chronicles, it is important that Eupolemos (cited by Eusebius, *Praep. ev.* 9. 34, 11) knew 2 Chr 4:13 LXX.

58. See Markus Witte, "Der 'Kanon' heiliger Schriften des antiken Judentums," in *Texte und Kontexte des Sirachbuchs: Gesammelte Studien zu Ben Sira und zur frühjüdischen Weisheit*, FAT 98 (Tübingen: Mohr Siebeck, 2015), 39–58; and Francis Borchardt, "Prologue of Sirach (Ben Sira) and the Question of Canon," in *Sacra Scriptura: How "Non-Canonical" Texts Functioned in Early Judaism and Early Christianity*, ed. James H. Charlesworth, Lee Martin McDonald, and Blake A. Jurgens, Jewish and Christian Texts in Contexts and Related Studies 20 (London: Bloomsbury, 2014), 64–71.

59. First through Fourth Kingdoms mention Elijah, Nathan, and other prophets. The current names of the books 1–2 Samuel/1–2 Kings are younger.

60. For the research on Sirach, see Gerhard Karner, Frank Ueberschaer, and Burkhard M. Zapff, eds., *Texts and Contexts of the Book of Sirach = Texte und Kontexte des Sirachbuchs*, SCS 66 (Atlanta: SBL Press, 2017).

1. The Hebrew Scriptures of the Tanak that were still unavailable in Greek were translated between the first century BCE and the early second century CE. The dating and localization of the single texts is, admittedly, difficult. A broad consensus nevertheless persists that Esther (LXX first c. BCE), Ruth, Lamentations, and the Song of Solomon belong to the late translations; they are preferably localized to Jerusalem or its surroundings.[61] Second Esdras (Hebrew-Aramaic Ezra-Nehemiah) stands at the end; scholarship dates this work to the end of the first or even the early second century CE.[62] This means that the era of the Septuagint extends to the end of the New Testament period.

Moreover, the work of translation was not limited to the Scriptures that we know today through the Tanak (the Hebrew Bible). The Enoch literature and the book of Jubilees were also included (and translated perhaps already in the second century BCE).[63] The early followers of Jesus were particularly influenced by the Enoch literature, with the result that many allusions to 1 Enoch can be found in the New Testament.

2. Several wisdom texts and narratives written between the second century BCE and second century CE are more deeply embedded into the Greek linguistic context. Some of those writings used Hebrew and Aramaic stories and rewrote them (Tobit, 1 Maccabees), integrated Hebrew (or Aramaic) letters in translation (2 Maccabees) or revived a motif of a Hebrew-Aramaic tale (Judith). Others were written in Greek from the beginning (Wisdom; 3 Maccabees). These texts spread in Greek widely; the youngest such writing (4 Maccabees) again belongs to the end of the time of the New Testament and may have originated in southern Asia Minor.[64] This confirms an observation already made: the range of the Septuagint

---

61. For Esther, see the colophon Est F 11 = 10:3; and Beate Ego, *Ester*, BKAT 21 (Göttingen: Vandenhoeck & Ruprecht, 2017), 5–6, 55–56, 73, 428–29. For Ruth, see Eberhard Bons, "Die Septuaginta-Version des Buches Ruth," in *Textkritik und Textgeschichte: Studien zur Septuaginta und zum hebräischen Alten Testament*, FAT 93 (Tübingen: Mohr Siebeck, 2014), 217–39. For the other books, consult the introductions; for current projects on Esther (Kristin De Troyer) see https://uni-salzburg.elsevierpure.com/de/projects/vetus-latina-und-josephusversion-des-eiterbuches and https://uni-salzburg.elsevierpure.com/de/projects/die-tochter%C3%BCbersetzungen-des-estherbuches-teil-1-und-2.

62. Evidence for the first c. CE is offered by Dieter Böhler, "Esdras II/2 Esdras/Ezra-Nehemiah," in Kreuzer, *Introduction*, 231; the second c. is preferred by R. Glenn Wooden, "2 Esdras," in *The T&T Clark Companion to the Septuagint*, ed. James K. Aitken (London: Bloomsbury T&T Clark, 2015), 196–97.

63. These works did not, however, persist in the Greek-speaking world long-term; therefore, only fragments remain. For Jubilees, see Frank Feder and Matthias Henze, *The Deuterocanonical Scriptures*, THB 2C (Leiden: Brill, 2019), 22–26.

64. The edition by R. Hiebert will appear soon. Jan Willem van Henten, "A Jewish Epitaph in a Literary Text: 4 Macc. 17.8–10," in *Studies in Early Jewish Epigraphy*, ed. Jan Willem van

writings reaches (in its present scope) until the end of the New Testament period, and its originating locale overlaps with that of the New Testament.

3. The large number of writings induced the question: How can the religiously decisive Greek-Jewish literature be listed and delimited? The term "canon" was not used in the centuries under consideration here. Nevertheless, a promising criterion was at hand. The Hebrew tradition allowed for orientation in remembering the basis of the translational process. Therefore the idea evolved that the Greek writings of highest value are the ones correlated to the Hebrew Scriptures (and the Hebrew Scriptures were thought of as old).

That concentration was reflected in the late first century in Josephus (*Ag. Ap.* 1.37–41 = I 8) and in 4 Ezra (14:44–46).[65] Both sources speak of recognized Scriptures in general without listing them individually. The preeminent position of the Law was universally recognized (the references refer to it as "the Book of the Law," "the Law of Moses," or "the Book of Moses").[66] The other collections of the Hebrew Bible and the Septuagint, the Prophets (= historical books and Prophets), Psalms, and wisdom literature (Ketuvim) were accepted as well but varied in detail (for the more skeptical position of the Samaritans, see above).

An important portion of early Christian authors participated in the tendency to limit the Scriptures (but none of the New Testament Scriptures accepted the Torah exclusively as the Samaritans did).[67] The Letter to the Hebrews, for example, oriented its argumentation strictly on citations from the Law, Prophets, Psalms, and the undisputed core of the wisdom literature (Proverbs). The anonymous Christian author ignored Scriptures only delivered in Greek and even the book of Esther, the Hebrew of which attracted little attention for a long time.[68]

Henten and P. W. van der Horst (Leiden: Brill, 1994), 44–69, proposed that 4 Maccabees was composed in Cilicia or its environs.

65. See, e.g., Jean-Marie Auwers and Henk Jan de Jonge, eds., *The Biblical Canons*, BETL 163 (Leuven: Peeters, 2003), e.g., 28–31; Erich Bosshard-Nepustil, *Schriftwerdung der Hebräischen Bibel: Thematisierungen der Schriftlichkeit biblischer Texte im Rahmen ihrer Liturgiegeschichte*, ATANT 106 (Zurich: TVZ, 2015), 240–44, and elsewhere.

66. One encounters these designations, e.g., in 2 Chr. 35:12 (βιβλίον Μωυσῆ), 1 Esdr 8:3 (Μωυσέως νόμος), 1 Esdr 9:45 (βιβλίον τοῦ νόμου), Ezra (2 Esdr) 7:6 (νόμος Μωυσῆ). In the New Testament, one may compare, e.g., Acts 28:23 (ὁ νόμος Μωϋσέως).

67. The early Christian relation to the Samaritans is complex. John 4:22 ("salvation is from the Judeans/Jews") is localized in Sychar near Samaria and can be read as a legitimation of Judean priority.

68. Beyond the New Testament, I draw attention to 1 Clement: that work uses the Law, Prophets (esp. Isaiah), Psalms, and select wisdom books (esp. Proverbs and Job); see Horacio E. Lona, "Septuagintazitate des Neuen Testaments im Ersten Clemensbrief," in *Textual History and the Reception of Scripture in Early Christianity: Textgeschichte und Schriftrezeption im*

4. Many Greek translations were two or three centuries old when Christianity spread. Therefore, the Greek language developed its own dynamic.

A striking example is the translation of קום with ἀνίστημι. Originally this word meant "stand up" in a literal sense (e.g., standing in court, Ps 1:5). However, in Greek ἀνίστημι could also include the nuance of rising from the dead (i.e., resurrection). The inner-Greek linguistic development helped develop the notion of the resurrection. This found expression in an early growth of the book of Job; Job 42:17a LXX (the Greek text belonging to about the New Testament period) speaks of the resurrection of Job (differently, MT).[69]

A second example is the translation of ברית ("covenant"). The translators of the Torah (Gen 17:4, etc.) introduced the rendering διαθήκη, bringing along a distinct accent: the term does not describe an agreement between equal partners, but rather a decree of God (cf. the phrase διατίθεμαι τὴν διαθήκην, Deut 29:13). The decree was formulated exclusively in the singular in Hebrew (a plural for ברית is lacking). The Greek plural (taken up first in Sir 44:18) allowed the semantic tendency to strengthen. That point will be picked up by Paul; according to Rom 9:4, God bound himself to Israel through the διαθῆκαι.[70]

5. A great number of the transmitters of the Greek Scriptures modified the ideal of translation from the first century BCE onward. The Hebrew text had formed the standard for the Greek translation from the beginning.[71] But the previous translations often had looked for an equilibrium to the target language and sometimes preferred a free Greek narrative. Now the proximity to the source language gained priority. The translation technique introduced strong Greek isomorphs to the Hebrew language (cf. the scroll of the Dodekaporopheton from Naḥal Ḥever). Ultimately, the reproduction of the Hebrew was pursued to such an extent that even violations of Greek syntax were tolerated. Second Esdras wrote, for example, names in Greek indeclinably as in Hebrew despite the fact that Greek would demand a declination.

The unusual Greek rendition of וגם ("and also") with καί γε gave the long-standing tendency the name "kaige." The variety of linguistic appearances pro-

---

frühen Christentum, ed. Martin Karrer and Johannes de Vries, SCS 60 (Atlanta: Society of Biblical Literature, 2013), 279–93.

69. An overview of the development of eschatology in the Septuagint writings is provided by Holger Gzella, "Verheißung: Die Zukunft angesichts Gottes," in *Die Theologie der Septuaginta/The Theology of the Septuagint*, ed. Hans Ausloos and Bénédicte Lemmelijn, vol. 5 of *Handbuch zur Septuaginta*, ed. Martin Karrer, Wolfgang Kraus, and Siegfried Kreuzer (Gütersloh: Gütersloher Verlagshaus, 2020), 503–53.

70. The current state of research is summarized by Christian Eberhart et al., eds., *Berit – Diatheke – Foedus – Covenant – Bund* (Tübingen: Mohr Siebeck, forthcoming).

71. That is already reflected in Let. Aris. 32.301–311.

hibits one from speaking of a deliberate and unified redaction. The rendition of the texts rather changed gradually in the manuscripts.[72] Moreover, the most prominent reworking, Daniel Θ, attracted the name of Theodotion. Therefore, the relation between kaige and the so-called younger translation attributed to the figure of Theodotion (mostly ascribed to the second c. CE) needs clarification.[73]

The followers of Jesus occasionally used manuscripts with the kaige tendency; the eponymous καί γε is found in the citation of Joel 3:2 in Acts 2:18 (against the simple καί in the Old Greek of Joel 3:2). The famous Son of Man phrase from Dan 7:13 was probably even received in both of the existing versions; the older Septuagint text (LXX[Ra] and Papyrus 967) identified the Son of Man and the Ancient of Days (cf. Rev 1:13–14) whereas the Theodotionic text did not make this identification (cf. Rev 1:7).

6. That was, however, not the only tendency of textual renewal. Motifs of the so-called younger translations of Aquila and Symmachus were prepared in the first century CE as well. This left traces likewise in the New Testament (Matt 2:15, e.g., quotes Hos 11:1 in a textual form similar to Aquila; Rom 12:19 and Heb 10:30 recall the Symmachus text of Deut 32:35/Ode 2:35).[74]

7. One may deliberate whether kaige and the new translations were coupled with a certain skepticism against the theological dignity of the Greek language. Indeed, the divine name was reproduced in Hebrew script in the Septuagint manuscripts for a time.[75] The early Jewish literature occasionally expressed the conviction that just Hebrew was the "holy language" (T. Naph. 8:6 [Heb.]) and the language of creation (Jub. 12:25–27).[76] Yet, the skepticism against the Greek language achieved no great significance. No rejection of the Greek language penetrated into the writings of the Septuagint; even the Tetragrammaton did not continue in the transmission (the Christian manuscripts prefer the Greek word κύριος, "Lord").

---

72. The discussion was begun by Dominique Barthélemy, *Les devanciers d'Aquila*, VTSup 10 (Leiden: Brill, 1963); an overview of more recent discussion is provided by Anneli Aejmelaeus and Tuukka Kauhanen, eds., *The Legacy of Barthélemy: 50 Years after "Les devanciers d'Aquila,"* DSI 9 (Göttingen: Vandenhoeck & Ruprecht, 2013); and the introductions to the LXX.

73. See De Troyer, "Septuagint," 280–82. Theodotion is sometimes considered the consummation of kaige; see Natalio Fernández Marcos, *The Septuagint in Context: Introduction to the Greek Version of the Bible* (Leiden: Brill, 2000), esp. 152–53.

74. Sometimes, a long development can be detected. E.g., a first trace of Hab 2:3–4 Aquila may be found in 2 Pet 3:9–10 (βραδύνει); in the end, Eusebius, *Dem. ev.* 6.14 will use both, Aquila and Septuagint. An additional influence of (proto-) Symmachus may be found in Rev 2:23 (ἐραυνῶν νεφροὺς καὶ καρδίας); cf. Jer 11:20 Symmachus.

75. See Papyrus Fouad 266 (second/first c. BCE), 8ḤevXIIgr, etc.

76. For the contexts, see Alexis Léonas, *L'aube des traducteurs: De l'hébreu au grec; Traducteurs et lecteurs de la Bible des Septante (IIIe s. av. J.-C.–IVe s. apr. J.-C.)*, Initiations bibliques (Paris: Cerf, 2007), chs. 2–5.

8. Was there something like a median in the diverging textual forms? Jerome mentioned the relevance of a Lucianic or "common" text (*Epist.* 106, §2.2). Critical scholarship classified that textual form (also referred to as the Antiochene text) as a revision of late antiquity (around 300) for a long time. Many of its features, however, look like a free Greek translation and fit the Old Greek. The great significance of the so-called Antiochene text in the historical books (ed. Fernández Marcos and Busto Saiz) is acknowledged, and it seems that the textual form must be upgraded in other parts of the Septuagint.[77]

New Testament quotations are of relevance here. The Antiochene text of 3 Kgdms (1 Kgs) 19:18 is used in Rom 11:4 (Βάαλ fem.), and Heb 1 includes two variants of the so-called Antiochene text of the Psalms (cf. πυρὸς φλόγα, Heb 1:7 next to Ps 103[104]:4; and ἑλίξεις, Heb 1:12 next to Ps 101[102]:27). That proves that Antiochene variants were widespread in New Testament times.

9. A new edition of the Psalms is in preparation (LXX Gottingensis). Two aspects must be mentioned:

First, the collection of the Psalms was fluid until the first century (cf. 11Q5 [11QPs^a] for the Hebrew transmission). The main text of the Septuagint Psalter (the text of the critical editions) shows a significant order. It begins in a diptych; Pss 1–2 praise the law and criticize foreign nations (2:1–3). Correspondingly the Psalter of the Septuagint ends with a reminiscence of David's victory over Goliath (Ps 151 LXX). The text abstracts from Goliath; the defeat of the "foreigner" (ἀλλόφυλος, 151:6) is decisive. The Masoretic Text (today's Hebrew Psalter), however, lacks Ps 151, and early Christianity never cites it (Goliath is not mentioned in the New Testament at all). It appears as if the majority of Judaism, and with it the group of Jesus's followers, did not share the critical view of foreigners that—perhaps prior to the Jewish revolt—made its way into the Septuagint Psalter.

Second, Rahlfs's verdict against Lucianic variants in the Psalter is open to question. Therefore, it will be of interest how the edition will rate the long text of Ps 13(14) (the textual form used by Paul in Rom 3:10–17), the rendition σῶμα (Heb 10:5) in Ps 39(40):7 ("body" instead of "ears") and other variants.[78] In every case, the different forms of the text and the reception are relevant for the edition.

---

77. For the different positions in the scholarly discussion, see De Troyer, "Septuagint," 282–86; Siegfried Kreuzer and Marcus Sigismund, eds., *Der antiochenische Text der Septuaginta in seiner Bezeugung und seiner Bedeutung*, DSI 4 (Göttingen: Vandenhoeck & Ruprecht, 2013); and contributions by S. Kreuzer, F. Albrecht, et al. in Siegfried Kreuzer and Martin Karrer, eds., *Trifaria varietas? Entstehung, Entwicklung und Problematik des Konzepts von Rezensionen des biblischen Textes*, BN.B 184 (Freiburg im Breisgau: Herder, 2020).

78. See Martin Karrer, Ulrich Schmid, and Marcus Sigismund, "Textgeschichtliche Beobachtungen zu den Zusätzen in den Septuaginta-Psalmen," in Kraus, Karrer, and Meiser, *Septuaginta*, 140–61.

Israel's Greek Scriptures and Their Collection in the Septuagint

Outlook

In sum, "Septuagint" meant the translation of the Torah/nomos initially. But the Greek translation grew up. All the writings of the Tanak were translated up to the New Testament time. New texts were written in Greek from the second or first century BCE and integrated into the collection successively. Some of the extant Scriptures were reworked from the first century BCE onward, and new translations followed. Sometimes, therefore, two versions of a book took root in the collection (e.g., Dan).[79] Hence, the radius of the Septuagint was becoming larger and larger. On the other hand, criteria for a delimitation loomed ahead (esp. in comparison to the Hebrew Scriptures). What will become the focal tendency?

1. Rabbinic Judaism concentrated on the Hebrew Scriptures more and more. The Greek-speaking followers of Jesus, on the other hand, preferred the greater radius of the Greek Scriptures. Previous investigations assessed that differing tendency as an indication of a harsh and early parting of the ways. Current examinations show the contrary: Judaism did not completely abandon and refuse the Septuagint in Byzantine times.[80] And, what is more, the Greek Scriptures continually remind Christianity of its Jewish roots.

Indeed, the selection of the Greek Scriptures that became part of the Septuagint beyond the Tanak is done within Israel. The books of Sirach and Wisdom highlight the quality of Israel's wisdom thoughts. The narratives (Judith, Tobit, 1–4 Maccabees) present ethical examples out of the tribes of Israel. The young writings praise the fathers (Sir 44–50 and Wis 10) and the sanctuary in Jerusalem (Tob 13) no less than the old ones. Scriptures written originally in Greek reject foreign gods (Bel and the Dragon, Baruch), praise Solomon, and outline true wisdom (Wisdom). They speak of Jewish identity in a foreign environment (Tobit, Judith) and are continually mindful of dietary and purity regulations.[81] This all becomes part of the Christian Greek Bible despite the narratives of halakhic change told in New Testament writings.[82]

2. The addition of the Psalms of Solomon, which happened very late, can be seen in that perspective, too. The psalms were, according to recent scholarship,

---

79. The interest in Israel's Scriptures will go on in Christianity after the New Testament times: see the Hexapla of Origen as an example.

80. See Jonas Leipziger, *Lesepraktiken im antiken Judentum: Rezeptionsakte, Materialität und Schriftgebrauch*, Materiale Textkulturen 34 (Berlin and Boston: de Gruyter, 2021), esp. 222–29.

81. The great female figures of the Jewish stories are of special interest; see Beate Ego, "Frauengestalten und ihre Religion im Wandel: Von den Überlieferungen der Hebräischen Bibel zu den Apokryphen," in *Frauen im antiken Judentum und frühen Christentum*, ed. Jörg Frey and Nicole Rupschus, WUNT 2/489 (Tübingen: Mohr Siebeck, 2019), 11–30.

82. Cf., e.g., Acts 10:9–16 concerning the dietary regulations.

written in Greek around the turn of the era and connected with the name of Solomon.[83] They were too young to be appended to the larger Psalter, but they are an important witness for the Jewish interest in wisdom, justice, and a good king.

Nowadays, linguistic insight makes an old conjecture unnecessary; Pss. Sol. 17:32 includes the phrase χριστὸς κύριος ("an anointed Lord") in the *Ausgangstext*, an idiom that Luke seized upon for the Christmas story (Luke 2:11).[84] Nevertheless, the ancient church respected the circumscribed distribution of the Psalms of Solomon in Judaism. The psalms were added only as an appendix to the biblical texts in the Codex Alexandrinus; the other Greek pandects (full Bibles) from the fourth to sixth (and the younger pandects up to the fifteenth) centuries excluded them.[85]

3. Seen from the perspective of the Septuagint's history, the early Christian writings and the Greek-Jewish literature are next-door neighbors. Hence one becomes mindful of more points of Jewish-Christian contact. For example, the names of the books of the Septuagint arose in Judaism.[86] Nevertheless, many of them are reported first by the Christian Melito of Sardis after a visit in Jewish communities (cf. Eusebius, *Hist. eccl.* 4.26). Or the Christians lost many manuscripts with Septuagint writings in the persecutions; and yet, they could retrieve the lost data easily. The exchange of manuscripts between Jews and Christians must have been quite active (and the exchange presupposes that Greek Scriptures were widespread in Judaism with regard to the Septuagint as well as to younger translations).

4. The Odes, the youngest part in the present critical edition of the Septuagint (LXX$^{\text{Ra-Ha}}$), needs special attention in that respect. The starting point of this small collection of psalms was a set of Jewish songs that had not been included in the Psalter (Exod 15:1–19, etc.). This core of the Odes was generated in Greek-speaking communities of the early and high Roman Empire (Odes 1–9, or 10 in the numbering of Codex Alexandrinus). New Testament songs and an early

---

83. Consult contributions in Eberhard Bons and Patrick Pouchelle, eds., *The Psalms of Solomon: Language, History, Theology*, EJL 40 (Atlanta: SBL Press, 2015); and Felix Albrecht, *Psalmi Salomonis*, SVTG 12.3 (Göttingen: Vandenhoeck & Ruprecht, 2018), 34.

84. Albrecht, *Psalmi Salomonis*, 356, places χριστὸς κύριος in the main text and thus corrects the older editions that conjectured χριστὸς κυρίου.

85. See Martin Karrer, "Septuagint and New Testament in Papyri and Pandects: Texts, Intertextuality and Criteria of Edition," in *New Avenues in the Exegesis of the Bible in the Light of the LXX*, ed. Leonardo Pessoa and Daniela Scialabba, The Septuagint in Its Ancient Context (Brepols: Turnhout, forthcoming), §III.1.

86. Some names developed through the centuries. E.g., the designation "exagoge" ("leading out" of the Hebrews from Egypt; Aristobulus according to Eusebius, *Praep. ev.* 13.12.1) is older than "exodos"; see Anna Mambelli, "Le prime attestazioni di Ἔξοδος come titolo del secundo libro del Pentateuco," in *Exodos: Storia di un vocabolo*, ed. Eberhard Bons, Anna Mambelli, and Daniela Scialabba (Bologna: Società Editrice Il Mulino, 2019), 167–77.

ecclesial liturgical text were attached to this collection afterward (Odes 11–14 of Alexandrinus). This expanded text did not become a constituent part of the Septuagint before the fifth century.[87]

Younger copies and editions mingled the Jewish psalms and the New Testament songs. As a consequence, Rahlfs's edition altered the sequence and overshadowed the Jewish basis of the textual history (Luke 1:46–55, 68–79 is his Ode 9 against the Codex Alexandrinus). If a future edition would return to the order of the Codex Alexandrinus, the Jewish sound of the Magnificat, Benedictus, and Nunc dimittis (the songs in Luke 1–2), included among the Odes, would become better visible.

5. Modern hermeneutics can react to these observations in two ways. On the one hand, one may question the expansion of the Septuagint Scriptures. In this case, the translation of the Hebrew Tanak determines the bounds of the Septuagint. The old heart of the Septuagint, the nomos (Torah) is revaluated. Writings of the current edition of the Septuagint (Rahlfs/Rahlfs-Hanhart) that do not have an equivalent in the Hebrew Bible turn out to be "deuterocanonical."[88] The Psalms of Solomon and Odes become marginal writings.

On the other hand, one may recognize an important *proprium* in the breadth and growth of the Septuagint.[89] Then, precisely the wide range of Scriptures in the Greek tradition and the variety of texts in the Septuagint makes for continuity between the history and theology of early Judaism and early Christianity. Christianity and Judaism are unified not only in a high valuation of the Torah (nomos) and of the Greek writings with Hebrew equivalents (historical books, Prophets, Psalms, and wisdom literature); Christianity and Judaism are further connected by the great number of younger and additional writings that entered the Septuagint.[90]

I conclude with an observation regarding the so-called full Bibles of the fourth century: The current division of the biblical books into the Septuagint and New Testament is foreign to these codices. Neither Sinaiticus nor Vaticanus separate the two scriptural collections with a blank leaf or an intervening title.

---

87. The oldest witnesses are Codex Alexandrinus (A), Codex Veronensis (R), and Codex Turicensis (T) from the fifth through seventh c.; Sinaiticus and Vaticanus (fourth c.) did not include the Odes.

88. This assessment is reflected in, e.g., the recently published series Textual History of the Bible. It dedicates volumes 2A-C to the "Deuterocanonical Scriptures."

89. Historically speaking, the Septuagint collection was even more flexible than is apparent from the current Greek editions: The Coptic and Ethiopic daughter versions presuppose an even greater scope of the collection in late antiquity.

90. More information concerning the reception of the Septuagint is given in Martin Meiser and Florian Wilk, eds., *Die Wirkungs- und Rezeptionsgeschichte der Septuaginta; The History of the Septuagint's Impact and Reception*, Handbuch zur Septuaginta 6 (Gütersloh: Gütersloher Verlagshaus, 2022).

To the contrary, Matthew in each case begins directly after the previous writing of the Septuagint. What we observed in particular with the Odes is thus valid in general. What we call today the New Testament is, in the context of the growth of the Septuagint, a continuation of Israel's Greek literature. If we take this seriously, the Septuagint helps us recognize the obligation of Christianity to Judaism.

Bibliography

Aejmelaeus, Anneli. "The Septuagint and Oral Translation." Pages 5–13 in *XIV Congress of the IOSCS, Helsinki, 2010*. Edited by Melvin K. H. Peters. SCS 59. Atlanta: Society of Biblical Literature, 2013.

Aejmelaeus, Anneli, and Tuukka Kauhanen, eds. *The Legacy of Barthélemy: 50 Years after "Les devanciers d'Aquila."* DSI 9. Göttingen: Vandenhoeck & Ruprecht, 2013.

Aitken, James K. *No Stone Unturned: Greek Inscriptions and Septuagint Vocabulary.* CrStHB 5. Winona Lake, IN: Eisenbrauns, 2014.

Albrecht, Felix. "Die alexandrinische Bibelübersetzung: Einsichten zur Entstehungs-, Überlieferungs- und Wirkungsgeschichte der Septuaginta." Pages 209–43 in *Alexandria*. Edited by Tobias Georges, Felix Albrecht, and Reinhard Feldmeier. Civitatum Orbis Mediterranei Studia 1. Tübingen: Mohr Siebeck, 2013.

———. *Psalmi Salomonis*. SVTG 12.3. Göttingen: Vandenhoeck & Ruprecht, 2018.

Ausloos, Hans, and Bénédicte Lemmelijn, eds. *Die Theologie der Septuaginta / The Theology of the Septuagint*. Handbuch zur Septuaginta 5. Gütersloh: Gütersloher Verlagshaus, 2020.

Auwers, Jean-Marie, and Henk Jan de Jonge, eds. *The Biblical Canons*. BETL 163. Leuven: Peeters, 2003.

Barthélemy, Dominique. *Les devanciers d'Aquila*. VTSup 10. Leiden: Brill, 1963.

Böhler, Dieter. "Esdras II/2 Esdras/Ezra-Nehemiah." Pages 229–32 in *Introduction to the Septuagint*. Edited by Siegfried Kreuzer. Waco, TX: Baylor University Press, 2019.

Bons, Eberhard. "Die Septuaginta-Version des Buches Ruth." Pages 217–39 in *Textkritik und Textgeschichte: Studien zur Septuaginta und zum hebräischen Alten Testament*. FAT 93. Tübingen: Mohr Siebeck, 2014.

Bons, Eberhard, et al., eds. *Die Sprache der Septuaginta/The Language of the Septuagint*. Handbuch zur Septuaginta 3. Gütersloh: Gütersloher Verlagshaus, 2016.

Bons, Eberhard, and Patrick Pouchelle, eds. *The Psalms of Solomon: Language, History, Theology*. EJL 40. Atlanta: SBL Press, 2015.

Borchardt, Francis. "Prologue of Sirach (Ben Sira) and the Question of Canon." Pages 64–71 in *Sacra Scriptura: How "Non-Canonical" Texts Functioned in Early Judaism and Early Christianity*. Edited by James H. Charlesworth, Lee Martin

McDonald, and Blake A. Jurgens. Jewish and Christian Texts in Contexts and Related Studies 20. London: Bloomsbury, 2014.

Bosshard-Nepustil, Erich. *Schriftwerdung der Hebräischen Bibel: Thematisierungen der Schriftlichkeit biblischer Texte im Rahmen ihrer Lituraturgeschichte.* ATANT 106. Zurich: TVZ, 2015.

Cowey, James M. S., and Klaus Maresch. "An die Archonten wegen Auflösung einer Verlobung." Pages 56–71 in *Urkunden des Politeuma der Juden von Herakleopolis (144/3–133/2 v. Chr.) (P. Polit. Iud.): Papyri aus den Sammlungen von Heidelberg, Köln, München und Wien.* Edited by James M. S. Cowey and Klaus Maresch. Wiesbaden: Westdeutscher, 2001.

Dafni, Evangelia G. "ΠΑΝΤΟΚΡΑΤΩΡ in Septuaginta-Amos 4,13: Zur Theologie der Sprache der Septuaginta." Pages 443–54 in *The Septuagint and Messianism.* Edited by Michael A. Knibb. BETL 195. Leuven: Peeters, 2006.

De Troyer, Kristin. "The Septuagint." Pages 267–88 in *From the Beginnings to 600.* Vol. 1 of *The New Cambridge History of the Bible.* Edited by James Carlton Paget and Joachim Schaper. Cambridge: Cambridge University Press, 2013.

Dogniez, Cécile, and Philippe Le Moigne, eds. *Les Douze Prophètes dans la LXX: Protocoles et procédures dans la traduction grecque; Stylistique, poétique et histoire.* VTSup 180. Leiden: Brill, 2019.

Dorival, Gilles. "La lexicographie de la Septante." Pages 271–305 in *Die Sprache der Septuaginta/The Language of the Septuagint.* Edited by Eberhard Bons and Jan Joosten. Vol. 3 of *Handbuch zur Septuaginta.* Edited by Martin Karrer, Wolfgang Kraus, and Siegfried Kreuzer. Gütersloh: Gütersloher Verlagshaus, 2016.

Eberhart, Christian, et al., eds. *Berit – Diatheke – Foedus – Covenant – Bund.* Tübingen: Mohr Siebeck, forthcoming.

Eck, Werner. "Nebeneinander oder miteinander? Die Aussagekraft der verschiedenen Sprachen auf Inschriften in Iudaea-Palaestina." Pages 43–58 in *Sprachen-Schriftkulturen-Identitäten der Antike: Beiträge des XV. Internationalen Kongresses für Griechische und Lateinische Epigraphik.* Edited by Petra Amann, Thomas Corste, Fritz Mitthof, and Hans Taeuber. Tyche Supplementband 10. Vienna: Holzhausen, 2019.

Ego, Beate. *Ester.* BKAT 21. Göttingen: Vandenhoeck & Ruprecht, 2017.

———. "Frauengestalten und ihre Religion im Wandel: Von den Überlieferungen der Hebräischen Bibel zu den Apokryphen." Pages 11–30 in *Frauen im antiken Judentum und frühen Christentum.* Edited by Jörg Frey and Nicole Rupschus. WUNT 2/489. Tübingen: Mohr Siebeck, 2019.

Feder, Frank, and Matthias Henze. *The Deuterocanonical Scriptures.* THB 2C. Leiden: Brill, 2019.

Fernández Marcos, Natalio. *The Septuagint in Context: Introduction to the Greek Version of the Bible.* Leiden: Brill, 2000.

Gzella, Holger. "Verheißung: Die Zukunft angesichts Gottes." Pages 503–53 in *Die Theologie der Septuaginta/The Theology of the Septuagint*. Edited by Hans Ausloos and Bénédicte Lemmelijn. Vol. 5 of *Handbuch zur Septuaginta*. Edited by Martin Karrer, Wolfgang Kraus, and Siegfried Kreuzer. Gütersloh: Gütersloher Verlagshaus, 2020.

Henten, Jan Willem van. "A Jewish Epitaph in a Literary Text: 4 Macc. 17.8–10." Pages 44–69 in *Studies in Early Jewish Epigraphy*. Edited by Jan Willem van Henten and Pieter Willem van der Horst. AGJU 21. Leiden: Brill, 1994.

Hernández, Juan. "Recensional Activity and the Transmission of the Septuagint in John's Apocalypse." Pages 83–98 in *Die Johannesoffenbarung: Ihr Text und ihre Auslegung*. Edited by Martin Karrer and Michael Labahn. ABIG 38. Leipzig: Evangelische Verlagsanstalt, 2012.

Hertog, Cornelis G. den. "Erwägungen zur relativen Chronologie der Bücher Levitikus und Deuteronomium innerhalb der Pentateuchübersetzung." Pages 216–28 in vol. 2 of *Im Brennpunkt: Die Septuaginta*. Edited by Siegfried Kreuzer and Jürgen Peter Lesch. BWANT 161. Stuttgart: Kohlhammer, 2004.

Honigman, Sylvie. "Politeumata and Ethnicity in Ptolemaic Egypt." *AncSoc* 33 (2003): 61–102.

Jobes, Karen H., and Moisés Silva. *Invitation to the Septuagint*. Grand Rapids: Baker Academic, 2015.

Karner, Gerhard, Frank Ueberschaer, and Burkhard M. Zapff, eds. *Texts and Contexts of the Book of Sirach = Texte und Kontexte des Sirachbuchs*. SCS 66. Atlanta: SBL Press, 2017.

Karrer, Martin. "Begegnung und Widerspruch: Der eine Gott und die Religionen in der frühchristlichen Mission." *Religionen unterwegs* 13, no. 4 (2007): 9–15.

———. "Septuagint and New Testament in Papyri and Pandects: Texts, Intertextuality and Criteria of Edition." In *New Avenues in the Exegesis of the Bible in the Light of the LXX*. Edited by Leonardo Pessoa and Daniela Scialabba. The Septuagint in Its Ancient Context. Brepols: Turnhout, forthcoming.

———. "Septuaginta und antike Philosophie." Pages 3–35 in *Die Septuaginta: Orte und Intentionen; 5. internationale Fachtagung veranstaltet von Septuaginta Deutsch (LXX.D), Wuppertal, 24.–27. Juli 2014*. Edited by Siegfried Kreuzer, Martin Meiser, and Marcus Sigismund. WUNT 361. Tübingen: Mohr Siebeck, 2016.

Karrer, Martin, Ulrich Schmid, and Marcus Sigismund. "Textgeschichtliche Beobachtungen zu den Zusätzen in den Septuaginta-Psalmen." Pages 140–61 in *Die Septuaginta: Texte, Theologien, Einflüsse; 2. Internationale Fachtagung veranstaltet von Septuaginta Deutsch (LXX. D), Wuppertal 23.–27.7.2008*. Edited by Wolfgang Kraus, Martin Karrer, and Martin Meiser. WUNT 252. Tübingen: Mohr Siebeck, 2010.

Kim, Keunjoo. "Theology and Identity of the Egyptian Jewish Diaspora in Septuagint of Isaiah." PhD diss., University of Oxford, 2009. https://ora.ox.ac.uk/objects/uuid:3a0507b0-32ad-419d-8a94-84cd2b76e856/download_file?safe_filename=Thesis.pdf&file_format=application%2Fpdf&type_of_work=Thesis.

Konkel, Michael. "Die Ezechiel-Septuaginta, Papyrus 967 und die Redaktionsgeschichte des Ezechielbuches: Probleme und Perspektiven am Beispiel von Ez 34." Pages 43–62 in *Das Buch Ezechiel: Komposition, Redaktion und Rezeption*. Edited by Jan Christian Gertz, Corinna Körting, and Markus Witte. BZAW 516. Berlin: de Gruyter, 2020.

Kooij, Arie van der. "Esaias/Isaias/Jesaja." Pages 515–27 in *Introduction to the Septuagint*. Edited by Siegfried Kreuzer. Waco, TX: Baylor University Press, 2019.

———. "Perspectives on the Study of the Septuagint: Who Are the Translators?" Pages 214–29 in *Perspectives in the Study of the Old Testament and Early Judaism*. Edited by Florentino García Martínez and Adam S. van der Woude. VTSup 73. Leiden: Brill, 1998.

Kreuzer, Siegfried, ed. *Introduction to the Septuagint*. Waco, TX: Baylor University Press, 2019 (German 2016 as vol. 1 of the Handbuch zur Septuaginta).

———. "The Origins and Transmission of the Septuagint." Pages 3–56 in *Introduction to the Septuagint*. Edited by Siegfried Kreuzer. Waco, TX: Baylor University Press, 2019.

Kreuzer, Siegfried, and Marcus Sigismund, eds. *Der antiochenische Text der Septuaginta in seiner Bezeugung und seiner Bedeutung*. DSI 4. Göttingen: Vandenhoeck & Ruprecht, 2013.

Kreuzer, Siegfried, and Martin Karrer, eds. *Trifaria varietas? Entstehung, Entwicklung und Problematik des Konzepts von Rezensionen des biblischen Textes*. BN.B 184. Freiburg im Breisgau: Herder 2020.

Lee, John A. L. *The Greek of the Pentateuch: Grinfield Lectures on the Septuagint 2011–2012*. Oxford: Oxford University Press, 2018.

———. *A Lexical Study of the Septuagint Version of the Pentateuch*. SCS 14. Chico, CA: Scholars Press, 1983.

Leipziger, Jonas. *Lesepraktiken im antiken Judentum: Rezeptionsakte, Materialität und Schriftgebrauch*. Materiale Textkulturen 34. Berlin: de Gruyter, 2021.

Léonas, Alexis. *L' aube des traducteurs: De l'hébreu au grec; Traducteurs et lecteurs de la Bible des Septante (IIIe s. av. J.-C.–IVe s. apr. J.-C.)*. Initiations bibliques. Paris: Cerf, 2007.

Lilly, Ingrid E. *Two Books of Ezekiel: Papyrus 967 and the Masoretic Text as Variant Literary Editions*. VTSup 150. Leiden: Brill, 2012.

Lona, Horacio E. "Septuagintazitate des Neuen Testaments im Ersten Clemensbrief." Pages 279–93 in *Textual History and the Reception of Scripture in Early Chris-*

tianity: Textgeschichte und Schriftrezeption im frühen Christentum. Edited by Martin Karrer and Johannes de Vries. SCS 60. Atlanta: Society of Biblical Literature, 2013.

Louw, Theo A. W. van der. "The Unity of LXX Genesis and Exodus." *VT* 69, no. 2 (2019): 270–84.

Mambelli, Anna. "Le prime attestazioni di Ἔξοδος come titolo del secundo libro del Pentateuco." Pages 167–77 in *Exodos: Storia di un vocabolo*. Edited by Eberhard Bons, Anna Mambelli, and Daniela Scialabba. Bologna: Società Editrice Il Mulino, 2019.

Meer, Michaël van der, ed. *Isaiah in Context: Studies in Honour of Arie van der Kooij on the Occassion of His Sixty-Fifth Birthday*. VTSup 138. Leiden: Brill, 2010.

———. "Provenance, Profile, and Purpose of the Greek Joshua." Pages 55–80 in *XII Congress of the International Organization for Septuagint and Cognate Studies (Leiden 2004)*. Edited by Melvin K. H. Peters. SCS 54. Atlanta: Society of Biblical Literature, 2006.

Meiser, Martin, and Florian Wilk, eds. *Die Wirkungs- und Rezeptionsgeschichte der Septuaginta. The History of the Septuagint's Impact and Reception*. Handbuch zur Septuaginta 6. Gütersloh: Gütersloher Verlagshaus, 2022

Ophir, Adi, and Ishay Rosen-Zvi. *Goy: Israel's Multiple Others and the Birth of the Gentile*. Oxford Studies in the Abrahamic Religions. Oxford: Oxford University Press, 2018.

Piotrkowski, Meron M. *Priests in Exile: The History of the Temple of Onias and Its Community in the Hellenistic Period*. SJ 106. Berlin: de Gruyter, 2019.

Rösel, Martin. "Die Jungfrauengeburt des endzeitlichen Immanuel: Jesaja 7 in der Übersetzung der Septuaginta." Pages 197–219 in *Tradition and Innovation: English and German Studies on the Septuagint*. Edited by Martin Rösel. SCS 70. Atlanta: SBL Press, 2018.

———. "From the Tora to *Nomos*: Perspectives of Research on the Greek Pentateuch." Pages 65–73 in *Introduction to the Septuagint*. Edited by Siegfried Kreuzer. Waco, TX: Baylor University Press, 2019.

———. "Vorlage oder Interpretation? Zur Übersetzung von Gottesaussagen in der Septuaginta des Deuteronomiums." Pages 250–62 in *Ein Freund des Wortes*. Edited by Sebastian Grätz, Axel Graupner, and Jörg Lanckau. Göttingen: Vandenhoeck & Ruprecht, 2019.

Sänger, Partick. *Die ptolemäische Organisationsform politeuma: Ein Herrschaftsinstrument zugunsten jüdischer und anderer hellenischer Gemeinschaften*. TSAJ 178. Tübingen: Mohr Siebeck, 2019.

Schenker, Adrian. *Das Neue am neuen Bund und das Alte am alten: Jer 31 in der hebräischen und griechischen Bibel*. FRLANT 212. Göttingen: Vandenhoeck & Ruprecht, 2006.

———. "Was führte zur Übersetzung der Tora ins Griechische? Dtn 4,2–8 und Platon (Brief VII,326a-b)." Pages 23–35 in *Die Septuaginta: Texte, Theologien, Einflüsse; 2. Internationale Fachtagung veranstaltet von Septuaginta Deutsch (LXX. D), Wuppertal 23.–27.7.2008*. Edited by Wolfgang Kraus, Martin Karrer, and Martin Meiser. WUNT 252. Tübingen: Mohr Siebeck, 2010.

Seeligmann, Isaac Leo. *The Septuagint Version of Isaiah: A Discussion of Its Problems*. MEOL 9. Leiden: Brill, 1984.

Schorch, Stefan. "Der Samaritanische Pentateuch in der Geschichte des hebräischen Bibeltextes." VF 60, no. 1 (2015): 18–28.

Siegert, Folker. *Zwischen Hebräischer Bibel und Altem Testament: Eine Einführung in die Septuaginta*. MJSt 9. Münster: LIT, 2001.

Spieckermann, Hermann, and Reinhard Feldmeier. *Der Gott der Lebendigen: Eine biblische Gotteslehre*. Topics of Biblical Theology 1. Tübingen: Mohr Siebeck, 2011.

Stipp, Hermann-Josef. *Jeremia 25–52*. HAT 12.2. Tübingen: Mohr Siebeck, 2019.

Thackeray, Henry St. John. "Notes and Studies: The Greek Translators of Jeremiah." JTS 4, no. 14 (1903): 245–66.

Tilly, Michael. *Einführung in die Septuaginta*. Darmstadt: WBG, 2010.

Tov, Emanuel. *The Septuagint Translation of Jeremiah and Baruch*. HSM 8. Missoula, MT: Scholars Press, 1976.

Troxel, Ronald L. *LXX-Isaiah as Translation and Interpretation: The Strategies of the Translator of the Septuagint of Isaiah*. JSJSup 124. Leiden: Brill, 2008.

Utzschneider, Helmut. "Die LXX als 'Erzählerin': Beobachtungen an der LXX-Fassung der Geburts- und Kindheitsgeschichte des Mose (Ex 2,1–10)." Pages 462–77 in *Die Septuaginta: Texte, Theologien, Einflüsse; 2. Internationale Fachtagung veranstaltet von Septuaginta Deutsch (LXX. D), Wuppertal 23.–27.7.2008*. Edited by Wolfgang Kraus, Martin Karrer, and Martin Meiser. WUNT 252. Tübingen: Mohr Siebeck, 2010.

Vos, J. Cornelis de. "Das Land Israel in der Sicht der Septuaginta: Beispiele aus Exodus, Josua und Jesaja." Pages 87–105 in *Die Septuaginta und das frühe Christentum*. Edited by Thomas S. Caulley and Hermann Lichtenberger. WUNT 277. Tübingen: Mohr Siebeck, 2011.

Wevers, John William, ed. *Exodus*. SVTG 2.1. Göttingen: Vandenhoeck & Ruprecht, 1991.

Witte, Markus. "Der 'Kanon' heiliger Schriften des antiken Judentums." Pages 39–58 in *Texte und Kontexte des Sirachbuchs: Gesammelte Studien zu Ben Sira und zur frühjüdischen Weisheit*. FAT 98. Tübingen: Mohr Siebeck, 2015.

Wooden, R. Glenn. "2 Esdras." Pages 195–202 in *The T&T Clark Companion to the Septuagint*. Edited by James K. Aitken. London: Bloomsbury T&T Clark, 2015.

Wright, Benjamin G. "Epistole Jeremiu/Epistula Ieremiae/Epistle of Jeremiah." Pages

559–64 in *Introduction to the Septuagint*. Edited by Siegfried Kreuzer. Waco, TX: Baylor University Press, 2019.

———. *The Letter of Aristeas: "Aristeas to Philocrates" or "On the Translation of the Law of the Jews."* CEJL. Berlin: de Gruyter, 2015.

Ziegert, Carsten. *Diaspora als Wüstenzeit: Übersetzungswissenschaftliche und theologische Aspekte des griechischen Numeribuches*. BZAW 480. Berlin: de Gruyter, 2015.

4

Israel's Scriptures in Early Jewish Literature

GRANT MACASKILL

My contribution to this volume is focused on what is here labeled as "early Jewish literature." This designation invites some comment that will at once set some bounds on this chapter—within the context of this book and in relation to other contributions—and open some of the distinctive questions that need to be considered within this particular chapter.

The "early" part of the label is generally defined by the time period that stretched from the end of the Babylonian exile (593 BCE) through to the fall of Jerusalem in 70 CE, although these points are indicative rather than decisive for what tends to be included; in practice, scholars usually categorize writings from the third century BCE to the second century CE as belonging to early Judaism, reflecting the incorporation of the earliest material from the period into the Bible.[1] The "Jewish" part of the label, meanwhile, points to the cultural matrix

1. The word "early" thus points to the period in which the culture in question *began* to establish its recognizable qualities. Obviously, these qualities can be traced back into the preexilic period. For this reason, Gabriele Boccaccini has argued for the use of "middle Judaism" as a label (*Middle Judaism: Jewish Thought, 300 B.C.E. to 200 C.E.* [Minneapolis: Fortress, 1991]). The term "early Judaism," however, acknowledges that a distinctively new set of conditions obtained after the exile, both through the cultural interference generated by the exile itself and the absence of the Northern Kingdom as a neighboring religio-cultural center. The contrastive term *Spätjudentum* ("late Judaism") was popular in the late nineteenth and early twentieth centuries but was essentially pejorative in its overtones: as a backdrop to the emergence of Christianity, it considered the Judaism of the intertestamental period to be legalistic and lifeless, marked by a decline from "biblical" religion. Its employment of "late" was also fundamentally neglectful of the subsequent developments in Jewish thought and culture, over the following

associated with postexilic Judea and its distinctive tribal, cultural, religious, and ideological values, even as these extended into the geographical territories outside Judea itself.

In other contexts, we might apply the label "early Jewish literature" to a wide range of works that can broadly (and often tentatively) be dated to the Second Temple period, including the Dead Sea Scrolls, Philo, Josephus, and much of the biblical material itself.[2] Indeed, in its earliest stages, Christianity emerged as a distinctive group within early Judaism rather than an initially separate movement, and much (if not all) of the New Testament can be categorized as early Jewish literature.[3] Within this volume, those identifiable corpora, each of which has a particular set of associations and circumstances that demarcate it *within* early Judaism, will be dealt with in their own dedicated chapters. This leaves us here to consider a miscellany of "not otherwise categorized" material that exists outside of these collections yet is still widely considered to be early and Jewish. Most of this represents the literature that we tend to label as "apocrypha and pseudepigrapha," terms that are recognized to be problematic but that continue to be the accepted scholarly categories for the diverse works in question.[4] These umbrella terms cover a wide range of specific genres and subgenres, but it is noteworthy that a large proportion of the material is narrative in some sense: it comprises stories, often incorporating forms associated with apocalyptic, sapiential, or prophetic literature, and these stories involve distinctive receptions of the narratives found in Israel's Scriptures. Some overlap only minimally with the biblical material, while others are effectively retellings of the stories, sometimes labeled as "rewritten Bible."[5]

This chapter will focus on five issues that are particularly important to our evaluation of the significance of the early Jewish writings in relation to the central themes of this volume. First, we will begin with some discussion of the material

---

two millennia. It has largely been dropped from scholarly usage, but echoes of its values are maintained in some popular discourse around Judaism in the time of Jesus.

2. See, e.g., the collection of essays in Matthias Henze, ed., *A Companion to Biblical Interpretation in Early Judaism* (Grand Rapids: Eerdmans, 2012).

3. In recent years there has been something of a shift in the study of books often regarded as late and hence further removed from the Jewish character of earliest Christianity, particularly as a result of developments in the study of early Jewish apocalyptic and mysticism. This has had particular significance for the study of John's Gospel and Ephesians. See, e.g., Benjamin E. Reynolds and Loren T. Stuckenbruck, eds., *The Jewish Apocalyptic Tradition and the Shaping of New Testament Thought* (Minneapolis: Fortress, 2017).

4. For these problems and a helpful reflection on the terminology, see Michael E. Stone, "Categorization and Classification of the Apocrypha and Pseudepigrapha," in *Apocrypha, Pseudepigrapha and Armenian Studies: Collected Essays*, vol. 1, O2LA 144 (Leuven: Peeters, 2006), 3–14.

5. See Matthias Henze, "Preface," in Henze, *Companion to Biblical Interpretation*, viii–x.

witnesses to the early Jewish writings, that is, the actual manuscript evidence and the contexts in which it has been preserved. This will be relevant, point by point, to each of the issues that we will subsequently consider throughout this chapter and is all too often neglected by New Testament scholars when they make use of the early Jewish writings as "background." Second, we will consider the influence that these writings may have exerted upon the New Testament and the possibility that some of them were regarded (at least in some circles) as Scriptures in their own right. Third, we will consider what relevance the early Jewish writings may have for our understanding of the status and function of the Mosaic Torah within the diversity of the early Judaism from which Christianity emerged. Fourth, recognizing the distinctively narrative character of many apocryphal and pseudepigraphical writings, we will consider the ways in which the early Jewish writings complicate the story world of early Judaism. Fifth, we will analyze the generative dynamics visible in the emergence of the novel stories in the early Jewish writings, the factors that gave rise to these new stories and their particular features. The first four of these sections effectively concern how the early Jewish writings might function as background to the New Testament, providing resources that might have influenced early Christian writings. The final section is more concerned with how they provide context, exemplifying interpretative dynamics that may be paralleled within the New Testament corpus.

The Early Jewish Writings: Material Contexts, Provenance, and Transmission

Some readers might be surprised by the fact that the largest proportion of the works we generally categorize as "early Jewish writings" have been preserved only in Christian contexts. In fact, prior to the discovery of the Dead Sea Scrolls in the mid-twentieth century, the arguments for these works being of early Jewish origin were based almost entirely on internal evidence, that is, on elements of their content that were best explained as products of Jewish thought. Scholars had access to later collections of Jewish works, such as those found in the Cairo Genizah, and they could trace parallels between the pseudepigrapha and the traditions preserved in rabbinic literature, but there remained much uncertainty about the origins of the material preserved in these. The scroll remains found near Qumran provided external evidence for both the antiquity and the Jewishness of some of our writings.

The presence of pseudepigraphical and apocryphal works among the scrolls complicates discussions about the status of particular works as "scriptural" within early Judaism. The fact that some of these works are represented in multiple copies and appear to exercise influence over the interpretation of biblical material suggests that they enjoyed the status of Scripture at Qumran, as they do in some particular streams of later Christianity, notably the Ethiopian and Eritrean one. Conversely, the fact that they are not widely preserved in their own right elsewhere within Judaism (although many of their *elements* can be found in later traditions), suggests that the status of these works was contested. This variegation may well be reflected in the New Testament, with some authors more obviously influenced by specific pseudepigrapha and apocrypha than others.

As important as the scrolls have been to the study of the early Jewish writings, they provide evidence relevant to only some of the works in view. There are still large sections of the literature that we can access only through later Christian manuscripts and that we still believe to be Jewish. For these, we continue to be heavily reliant on matters of content to provide clues as to their origins and pathways of transmission and to help us distinguish works of early Jewish origin from works of Christian composition. This, inevitably, involves the weighing of various points of detail, such as allusions to historical events, the presence of cultic or halakic elements, or linguistic evidence that the work in question was translated from a Hebrew or Aramaic original (which is a strong indicator of Jewish authorship, but one that must be balanced by the recognition that Jewish authors were also happy to use Greek).[6] The absence of obvious Christian features is also generally considered an important factor.

The problem, of course, is that a range of explanations can usually be offered for the evidence on display in any given work. Christian features may be present, but it is often difficult to know whether such features are original or redactional and whether they reflect authorship or transmission. Conversely, it is dangerous to assume that all Christian works will exhibit obvious markers of Christian beliefs: the shared commitment to the biblical traditions of Judaism might generate works with no obviously Christian features that display impressive scriptural erudition. The growing evidence for continued entanglement of Jewish and Christian communities in the early centuries of the Common Era points to an awareness of the detail of Jewish cultic traditions in Christian circles and highlights the possibility that Christian writers might generate works that would be effectively indistinguishable from Jewish compositions.[7] In addition,

---

6. On the evidence relevant to identifying the provenance of a given pseudepigraphon, and how this should be evaluated, see James R. Davila, *The Provenance of the Pseudepigrapha: Jewish, Christian or Other*, JSJSup 105 (Leiden: Brill, 2005), esp. 3–9, 10–73. Davila's important study represents a minority position that is less confident in our ability to demonstrate the early Jewish provenance of many of the pseudepigrapha than most.

7. For the continued entanglement, see, e.g., the collection of essays in Adam H. Becker and

there is a much wider spectrum of possibilities for authorship than the simple "Jewish or Christian" options that are often utilized: as well as the variegation visible within both early Judaism and early Christianity, there might be groups that occupy the fringes or borderlands of each.

The study of the literature often categorized as early Jewish writings is, then, fraught with problems, but this does not mean that we should avoid them. Instead, we should treat them with more care than is often visible in New Testament scholarship, where they are frequently cited without adequate discussion of the challenges. This requires scholars to be attentive to the contexts of transmission and their linguistic and cultural characteristics and not to isolate individual works from these.

Interestingly, when we pay this kind of attention to transmissional contexts, we begin to notice that certain geographical centers are particularly influential in the pathways of early development and transmission, particularly in the post-70 CE period. Notable among these are Egypt and Roman Syria, and specifically the cities of Alexandria and Antioch. In both cases, there were strong Jewish communities in the first century with traceable pathways of transmission linking them to Palestine. In both cases, too, the local forms of Christian tradition exhibit a demonstrable uptake of Jewish literary tradition beyond what we would today categorize as biblical, with some evidence of particular entanglement with the interpretative culture embodied at Qumran.[8] Alexandria and Antioch were also hugely influential within the wider literary culture of early Christianity. Recognizing this is important as it allows some geographically specific granularity to be introduced to our discussions of Jewish influence: Christian works

---

Annette Yoshiko Reed, eds., *The Ways That Never Parted: Jews and Christians in Late Antiquity and the Early Middle Ages*, TSAJ 95 (Tübingen: Mohr Siebeck, 2003); and Michal Bar-Asher Siegel, *Early Christian Monastic Literature and the Babylonian Talmud* (Cambridge: Cambridge University Press, 2013). For the difficulties in distinguishing Christian and Jewish writings, see Davila, *Provenance of the Pseudepigrapha*, 74–119.

8. There are, e.g., distinctive parallels between the psalms preserved in the Syriac tradition and those in 11Q5 (11QPs^a), both of which contain additional works not preserved in other contexts. George J. Brooke has recently traced some of the differences between approaches to exegesis at Qumran, and in the wider movement with which it was associated, and in official circles in Jerusalem. See Brooke, "Hot at Qumran, Cold in Jerusalem: A Reconsideration of Some Late Second Temple Period Attitudes to the Scriptures and Their Interpretation," in *Ha-'ish Moshe: Studies in Scriptural Interpretation in the Dead Sea Scrolls and Related Literature in Honor of Moshe J. Bernstein*, ed. Binyamin Y. Goldstein, Michael Segal, and George J. Brooke, STDJ 122 (Leiden: Brill, 2017), 64–77. The significance of this for Matthew is noted in his essay, "Inspecting the School of St. Matthew," in *Krister among the Jews and Gentiles: Essays in Appreciation of the Life and Work of Krister Stendahl*, ed. Paula Fredriksen and Jesper Svartvik, Studies in Judaism and Christianity (Mahwah, NJ: Paulist, 2018), 101–21.

that emerged, for example, in Syria, in a community known to be influenced by that cultural center, might be more likely to exhibit entanglement with particular Jewish pseudepigrapha than those that emerged elsewhere. Arguably, as we will see, this is visible within the New Testament itself, with works often regarded as of Syrian origin—such as Matthew's Gospel and possibly the Epistle of Jude—exhibiting the most explicit traces of pseudepigraphical influence.

The Early Jewish Writings as Israel's Scripture: The Influence of "Nonbiblical" Writings on the New Testament

Now that we have discussed the issues of provenance and context that locate our texts in relation to the New Testament, we can begin to consider the influence that some may have had upon specific authors or thinkers within the emergent Christian movement.

In some cases, the influence of these writings suggests that they were treated as Scriptures, functioning alongside those we would now label as biblical texts and contributing to their interpretation. In other cases, it is unclear whether the early Jewish writings were treated as Scripture or simply contributed to the cultural stock of the communities in which they circulated. This, of course, need not mean that they were any less influential in practice. We can trace an analogy within modern faith communities (e.g., evangelicalism), for which the "noncanonical" works of respected contemporary teachers can often determine how Scripture is interpreted within the subculture that they inhabit.

Without separating categories too sharply, it is helpful to differentiate instances where there is evidence for the direct textual influence of specific early Jewish writings upon the New Testament from those where the writings might bear witness to a literary and cultural background that resources more broadly the ideas and language encountered in early Christian writings. It is also possible that early Jewish and early Christian writings might bear independent witness to a common culture or to shared patterns of thought (e.g., that of the period following the fall of Jerusalem) so that they provide mutual context more than background. Direct textual influence is often suspected where there are distinctive parallel forms of expression; broader influence as background is considered where one work is generally considered to be older and where there seem to be parallels that are less obviously manifest in specific linguistic correspondence; mutual context can be considered where works come from a similar time period and share distinctive ideas or imagery but articulate these using quite different lexical and syntactical resources. Of course, we cannot firewall these categories from each other as if relationships will fall strictly into one and not the others. The dating of works is often imprecise (so identifying the direction of influence can be difficult), works may be preserved in different languages (so linguistic parallels are not always straightforward), and certain ideas might become associated with a particular vocabulary or idiom, even within the oral component of a culture (so that the parallel presence of such linguistic elements in two texts may simply reflect their shared indebtedness to a culture in which both participate, perhaps to varying degrees). So, the different categories are heuristically useful but need to be applied somewhat tentatively.

There are multiple points in the New Testament where the evidence indicates that nonbiblical Jewish writings directly influence the authors in question. The most explicit of these is in the Epistle of Jude, which directly quotes from the book of Enoch (specifically, from the opening section of the Book of Watchers, 1 En. 1:9) and attributes the words to Enoch as authentic prophecy: "It was also about these that Enoch, in the seventh generation from Adam, prophesied, saying, 'See, the Lord is coming with ten thousands of his holy ones, to execute judgment on all, and to convict everyone of all the deeds of ungodliness that they have committed in such an ungodly way, and of all the harsh things that ungodly sinners have spoken against him'" (Jude 14–15 NRSV).

The closeness of the quotation to the preserved text of 1 En. 1:9, along with the attribution, indicates direct textual influence. The quotation functions quite comfortably alongside elements drawn from the biblical Scriptures (e.g., the references to Cain, Balaam, and Korah in v. 11) and apostolic traditions (cited in 1:17–18). While it may be possible to explain the citation and its placement in ways that do not require the author of the epistle to have regarded Enoch's writings as "scriptural"—that is, by introducing alternative categories of authoritative or prophetic writings—the simplest explanation is that the author did indeed ascribe the status of Scripture to the Book of the Watchers. Given that the manuscript evidence from Qumran points to the embedding of this book within a bigger Enochic collection, the quotation in the Epistle of Jude should probably be taken as evidence that this wider Enochic "testament" functioned as Scripture for the author.[9] Jude also cites a tradition for which no early sources have been preserved, concerning Michael's rebuke of Satan over the body of

---

9. "Testament" is the category advanced by George Nickelsburg for the form of the Enochic material preserved at Qumran, e.g., in Nickelsburg, *1 Enoch 1: A Commentary on the Book of 1 Enoch Chapters 1–36, 81–108*, Hermeneia (Minneapolis: Fortress, 2001), 21–26. It is likely that the Enochic testament also informs 1 Pet 3:19 and the reference to the imprisoned spirits.

Moses, which further expands the range of nonbiblical material that the work treats as authoritative.[10]

A more subtle example is found in Matt 25:31–46, the famous passage in which the Son of Man sits in judgment upon the nations with individuals separated as sheep and goats. This account opens with the words, "when the Son of Man comes in his glory, and all the angels with him, then he will sit on the throne of his glory" (Matt 25:31 NRSV). The term "throne of his glory" corresponds very closely to language encountered in the Parables of Enoch, especially 1 En. 62:3–5. The occurrence there of "the throne of his glory" is part of a scheme of references to the glorious throne that is developed systematically through the book. What is particularly important is just how distinctive the qualifier "his" is within the phrase, regardless of whether it technically qualifies "throne" or "glory." While the imagery in the Matthean and Enochic texts is obviously shaped by the representation of the Son of Man in Dan 7, fused with elements from the various servant passages in Isaiah, its identification of the glorious throne with the Son of Man himself is a distinctive development.[11] Richard Bauckham, in fact, sees the Enochic text as the only place in non-Christian Jewish writings of this era where a figure other than God is seated upon this throne, and while his claims can be contested, they reflect the highly distinctive correspondence of Matthew and Enoch at this point.[12] The degree of lexical similarity—taking into account the different languages in which Matthew and the Parables of Enoch have been preserved—suggests a textual relationship rather than merely a common association with an underlying culture. A host of further points of contact between Matthew and the Parables have been noted, which reinforce the conclusion that the evangelist has been influenced by the Enochic work, a view in line with the broad drift toward seeing the Parables as an early Jewish work.[13] Interestingly, there are also a number of partial correspondences with 2 Enoch, particularly in the moral-instructional material that is unique to Matthew, but the striking similarities emerge with equally striking divergences that might problematize

---

10. For a recent treatment of the problem, including reviews of previous explanations, see Ryan E. Stokes, "Not over Moses' Dead Body: Jude 9, 22–24 and the Assumption of Moses in Their Early Jewish Context," *JSNT* 40, no. 2 (2017): 192–213.

11. For a discussion of this, and further bibliography, see Grant Macaskill, "Matthew and the Parables of Enoch," in *Parables of Enoch: A Paradigm Shift*, ed. James H. Charlesworth and Darrell Bock, Jewish and Christian Texts in Contexts and Related Studies 11 (London: Bloomsbury T&T Clark, 2013), 218–30.

12. See Bauckham, *God Crucified: Monotheism and Christology in the New Testament* (Carlisle: Paternoster, 1998), 20.

13. Macaskill, "Matthew and the Parables of Enoch," 227–29. That the Parables are an early Jewish work is reflected in the introductory discussion of George Nickelsburg and James C. VanderKam, *1 Enoch 2: A Commentary on the Book of 1 Enoch Chapters 37–82*, Hermeneia (Minneapolis: Fortress, 2012).

any theory of direct textual relationship and might instead point to a common culture within which particular forms and tropes circulated.[14]

The distinctive similarities between Matthew's Gospel and the Parables of Enoch might open the way for nuanced evaluation of whether the Son of Man title functions differently in this gospel to the others and whether this might be connected to particular geographical and cultural factors in its development. The majority of Matthew scholars believe that the work emerged in Syrian Antioch in the late first century, and this, as we have already noted, is one of the transmissional hotspots for the pseudepigraphical texts. It is possible, then, that Matthew's version of the gospel is quite distinctively influenced by the Enochic material. Such discussions need to be placed within a broader conversation about where the developed representation of the Son of Man in the Parables of Enoch, or in the traditions that this work attests, might be located in relation to the emergence and development of early Christianity.

Importantly, the points of detail that we have discussed to this point are linked to specific interpretative "events" within the pseudepigrapha that involve distinctive combinations of prior Scriptures. The recombination of Danielic and Isaianic elements in the Parables of Enoch creates a new image of the enthroned Son and his relationship to justice that Matthew then invokes: the evangelist does not simply *happen* to parallel the combination of texts seen in the Parables through a shared reading strategy but appears to receive and develop this recombinant event. First Enoch 1:9, likewise, combines a number of antecedent scriptural texts that utilize theophanic imagery (the details of which we will consider further below), and it is this later recombinant iteration of the trope that Jude chooses to cite. The likely influence of the story of the Watchers on 1 Pet 3:19, similarly, reflects a particular reading of Gen 6–9, which is now determinative for that author's own theological construction. We will consider some of the generative factors involved in these interpretations below, but at this point we note simply that the reception of these pseudepigraphical works apparently as Scripture also entails the reception and transmission of particular *interpretations* of prior Scriptures.

As well as such specific points of correspondence with the early Jewish writings, there are also some parallels of thought that are of a broader kind yet within which particular nonbiblical writings appear to be especially important or influential for the New Testament authors. The Wisdom of Solomon provides some helpful illustrations of this.

The date and place of Wisdom's composition has been a matter of some debate, but the balance of opinion favors the view that it was written during the early

---

14. The common elements include the development of the beatitude form (2 En. 42; Matt 5:3–12), teaching on the avoidance of oath-taking (2 En. 49; Matt 5:33–37), teaching on almsgiving (2 En. 51, Matt 6:2–4), and teaching on nonretaliation and vengeance (2 En. 50; Matt 5:38–42).

Roman period, some time before the New Testament works began to appear.[15] The work is most commonly considered to be of Alexandrian provenance: it exhibits numerous similarities with Philo's works and appears disproportionately interested in the stories about Israel and Egypt. As with Philo's work, it reflects the incorporation of Greek philosophical thought into the sapiential traditions of Judaism, but we need be careful in our use of the terms "hellenization" to describe this:[16] Wisdom draws somewhat eclectically from Greek philosophical thought, but the ideas that it appropriates are transformed by their new context within Judaism even as they introduce new elements into Jewish tradition. Moreover, the eclecticism visible in Wisdom's assimilation of Greek material extends also to Jewish influence, with nonbiblical mystical elements also detectable in its imagery.[17] With such an eclectic work, we need to work hard to identify the controlling concepts and what these say about the determining beliefs of the author.

For the study of the New Testament in general, Wisdom is especially important as a witness to watershed developments in belief about death and the immortality of the soul and the implications of these for both theodicy and eschatology.[18] Importantly, these developments draw upon the resources of Israel's Scriptures—including the linguistic elements of individual verses and the narratives of Israel—but reconceive the significance of these as a result of the incorporation of Greek philosophical reflection, particularly those of middle Platonism. This is to observe that the evolution of ideas about the immortality of the soul and postmortem judgment visible within early Judaism is not (as sometimes argued) a straightforward development of biblical traditions or a flowering of their inner germ, but the result of conceptual recombination, as biblical and Greek materials transform each other in mutual encounter.

One radical—but easily overlooked—element within this is the representation of death as something alien, something that cannot be credited to divine purpose (e.g., Wis 1:14–16; 2:24). Because the imagery of Gen 3 provides some of the building blocks for discourse about death within Judaism, it can mistakenly be assumed that the alienness of death is a concept traceable back to the opening chapters of the Bible; in reality, the segregation of death from the will of God is a

---

15. See David Winston, *The Wisdom of Solomon: A New Translation with Introduction and Commentary*, AB 43 (New York: Doubleday, 1979), 3.

16. John J. Collins, *Jewish Wisdom in the Hellenistic Age* (Edinburgh: T&T Clark, 1998), 173–95.

17. See, e.g., Stefan Schorch, "Jacob's Ladder and Aaron's Vestments: Traces of Mystical and Magical Traditions in the Book of Wisdom," in *Studies in the Book of Wisdom*, ed. Geza G. Xeravits and Joszef Zsengeller, JSJSup 142 (Leiden: Brill, 2010), 183–95.

18. See Collins, *Jewish Wisdom*, 173–95.

dramatic development in the Hellenistic period, reflected in Wisdom but absent from many other works of this period.

Wisdom also creatively develops Jewish reflection on cosmic order and morality, particularly in relation to justice and idolatry and to the operation of the divine Spirit. Many of the raw materials are drawn from biblical resources, notably the personification of Wisdom that is found in Prov 8, which grows further here into something more thoroughly hypostatic as Wisdom (and the divine Spirit) are represented in increasingly personal and self-subsistent terms. The functioning of these biblical resources is shaped not only by the influence of Greek thought but also by what we might call "existential challenges" to the logic of divine purpose: the world seems unjust and unhappy, and the fate of Israel seems to be at odds with what would be expected for those living in alignment with divine Wisdom. The work is driven by the pressure to account for this experience and its fusion of biblical and Greek elements provides novel purchase on some of the issues: the vindication of Wisdom will only be comprehended by the righteous, who have been enabled by God's spirit, the agent of Wisdom, to see the truth of an eternity that stretches beyond death.

These ideas illuminate multiple elements encountered across the New Testament. They are often cited in relation to traces of a putative early "Wisdom Christology" and to the developing association of Christ with the ordering of the cosmos (as in Col 1:25–23), and they are considered relevant to the developing ideas of immortality and afterlife within early Christianity visible across the New Testament.[19]

Within this, there is a particular density of correspondences with Paul's writings that has been noted and explored in a number of recent studies.[20] The parallels are not of the kind that suggest direct textual dependency, yet they are so many and so striking that Wisdom must be considered to represent either a window onto an interpretative culture shared with Paul or (more likely) a text that was programmatic for the interpretative culture within which he was formed. The fact that Paul does not quote Wisdom suggests that he did not accord it the status of Scripture, and it is

---

19. For a discussion of these, see Ben Witherington III, *Jesus the Sage: The Pilgrimage of Wisdom* (Edinburgh: T&T Clark, 1994). I offer some critical comments on Witherington in Macaskill, *Revealed Wisdom and Inaugurated Eschatology in Ancient Judaism and Early Christianity*, JSJSup 115 (Leiden: Brill, 2007), esp. 253–56, but acknowledge the broad trajectory in the hypostasization of Wisdom.

20. E.g., Jonathan A. Linebaugh, *God, Grace, and Righteousness in Wisdom of Solomon and Paul's Letter to the Romans: Texts in Conversation*, NovTSup 152 (Leiden: Brill, 2013); Joseph R. Dodson, *The "Powers" of Personification: Rhetorical Purpose in the "Book of Wisdom" and the Letter to the Romans*, BZNW 161 (Berlin: de Gruyter, 2008). These works provide detailed reviews of previous discussions of the similarities.

noteworthy that the recent studies comparing Paul and Wisdom have highlighted and sought to explain their "broad continuity and deep discontinuity," often seeing Paul as reading a common body of Scripture in "dialogue" with Wisdom.[21]

In addition to Paul's programmatic identification of idolatry as the defining manifestation of sin, multiple details in his writings mirror the watershed developments in Jewish thought that are encountered in Wisdom. Death is an alien power that has "entered" the world through the idolatrous sin of one man (Rom 5:12, cf. Wis 1:16); only those enlightened to wisdom by the Spirit of God will comprehend this (e.g., 1 Cor 2:10–14), but the true vindication of God's wisdom will not be visible within the circles of this life—it will be seen only in the eschaton, as the perishable is raised incorruptible (1 Cor 15:42–54; 2 Cor 3–5; cf. Wis 2:23). Paul also offers an extended and surprising review of the place of Israel in God's purposes, in Rom 9–11, that can be compared to a parallel review in Wis 10–19. As with the other early Jewish examples we have considered, what is striking is that Wisdom mediates not just novel ideas, but novel *interpretations*, readings of Scripture that are associated with particular tropes: the entry of death, the incorruptibility of spirit, and other related ideas.

In broad terms, these examples highlight the influence of the nonbiblical early Jewish writings on the New Testament writings. Such influences might vary in character from author to author and work to work, with the variation possibly reflecting geographical and cultural factors. In the case of Matthew and Jude, works often understood to have been composed in Syrian Antioch, early Jewish writings not incorporated into later biblical collections seem to be directly influential and, indeed, to be treated as Scriptures. In the case of Paul's writings—the work of a Pharisee who enjoyed an advanced Roman education—there are multiple contact points with the Wisdom of Solomon present in a greater density than could be explained by mere coincidence but not of a sort that suggest Wisdom was regarded as Scripture for Paul.

The early Jewish writings, then, complicate our understanding of "scriptural" interpretation in the New Testament period, problematizing assumptions about the limits of an accepted canon and highlighting the influence of noncanonical writings. These complications play out in the next two areas to be considered in this chapter: the status of the Mosaic Torah within early Judaism and the "story world" that might have shaped early Christin identity.

---

21. Linebaugh, *God, Grace and Righteousness*, 19.

Israel's Scriptures in Early Jewish Literature

The Status of the Torah in the Early Jewish Writings

While Moses is not the only figure associated with the revelation of God and his will, the accounts of the exodus and the giving of law, embedded as they are within narratives that stretch back to creation, overshadow and influence the content of Israel's Scriptures more widely. Scholars of early Judaism, however, have asked whether this status is genuinely ubiquitous within the literature of the period or whether it might reflect the eventual dominance of one particular stream of early Jewish thought within the wider culture, assimilating—but never eliminating—other iterations of Judaism. The debate around this has centered on demonstrably early Jewish writings that are considered to be at least uninterested in the Mosaic Torah and perhaps even hostile to its status.

The most developed recent form of the argument was offered by Gabriele Boccaccini in his 1998 study, *Beyond the Essene Hypothesis*, though the approach is represented quite diffusely in discussions of the primary literature.[22] Boccaccini argues that the primary Enoch literature, attested in fragmentary form at Qumran, originally constituted an alternative body of instruction associated not with the culture hero of Moses but with that of Enoch and containing an alternative account of the origin of evil, in which this is traced to the descent of the Watchers (angels), who marry human women and reveal heavenly secrets. Boccaccini detects a polemical silence in the Enochic literature about the giving of the law through Moses and a conspicuous emphasis on the role of Enoch as the one who receives authoritative instruction from God. He sees this as reflecting a fundamental fault line between two radically different kinds of Judaism: Zadokite Judaism, which venerated Moses and generated the Zadokite priesthood, and Enochic Judaism. The book of Jubilees, which appears to venerate *both* the Enochic and the Zadokite texts is, in his account, the product of a deliberate attempt to hybridize or synthesize the two, and it plays a key role in the development of the Essene strand within Judaism and, within this, the Qumran sect. The eventual affirmation of both sets of literature distinguishes the Qumran group and wider Essenism from more narrowly Zadokite forms of Judaism (as preserved among the Sadducees) and generates some distinctive theological elements that can be traced into the New Testament.[23] For Boccaccini, then, one

---

22. Boccaccini, *Beyond the Essene Hypothesis: The Parting of the Ways between Qumran and Enochic Judaism* (Grand Rapids: Eerdmans, 1998). See also his previous study *Middle Judaism*. Forerunners of the ideas developed in these works are found in Paolo Sacchi's study of it (*L'apocalittica giudaica e la sua Storia*, BCR 55 [Brescia: Paideia, 1990]; translated as *Jewish Apocalyptic and Its History*, trans. William J. Short, JSPSup 20 [Sheffield: Sheffield Academic, 1996]).

23. For a useful set of essays considering the issues, see Gabriele Boccaccini and John J.

of the key problems with New Testament scholarship is that it has failed to recognize how the texts in question can be mapped onto the inner diversity of early Judaism, operating instead with flatter accounts that are governed too narrowly by the forms of Judaism that he labels as Zadokite.

In the space that we have available here, it would be neither feasible nor desirable to attempt a full evaluation of this thesis. Already a significant body of scholarly literature has grown around it, and we could hardly do justice to the breadth or the granularity of this in the space of a few paragraphs. Instead, we will highlight some points that have emerged from the debate and that bear very specifically upon the study of the New Testament.

Most importantly, the debate must be properly located in relation to the emergence of the New Testament writings within early Judaism. The more radical elements of Boccaccini's thesis concern *originary* polemics that, by the early Common Era, have already given way to a functional mutuality, within which the Enochic and Zadokite texts are read together, but only within certain streams of Judaism. This functional mutuality of Enochic and Zadokite thought is reflected in Jubilees and in many of the Qumran texts, even if some of the earlier writings attested at Qumran might preserve traces of hostility toward the Torah.[24] There is, in other words, a common core of Scripture that seems within this period to be accepted by all Jewish groups and other writings that were considered authoritative only by some.

At the same time, however, the soteriological ultimacy of the core writings contained in the Torah is clearly modified or relativized by its coordination with these other writings: the mysteries revealed through Enoch and other figures become decisive for salvation and right living, making possible an opening of eyes that the Torah by itself could not accomplish. It is worth noting that a parallel phenomenon is visible in the Wisdom of Solomon, where the Spirit of divine Wisdom becomes the decisive factor in salvation: here, too, Torah remains important, but only relative to the operation of Wisdom.

As we have now noted repeatedly, the outworking of these dynamics within the New Testament might be shaped by geographical and social factors. An author working in Antioch and clearly influenced by Enochic traditions, such as Matthew, might straightforwardly transfer ideas about Enochic revelation onto

---

Collins, eds., *The Early Enoch Literature*, JSJSup 121 (Leiden: Brill, 2007).

24. E.g., Benjamin Wold has argued that a similarly negative (or, at least, ambivalent) attitude toward Torah is seen in the protosectarian work 4QInstruction (4Q415–418a), within which a body of revealed wisdom—the *raz nihyeh*—serves as the basis for moral instruction and final judgment, effectively displacing Torah from its place of primacy in moral regulation. See Wold, *4QInstruction: Divisions and Hierarchies*, STDJ 123 (Leiden: Brill, 2018), esp. 146–71. Wold's reading acknowledges that 4QInstruction contributes to a range of perspectives on the Torah visible in the Qumran material.

the person and teaching of Jesus, affirming the Torah while also subordinating its soteriological significance.[25] Paul, meanwhile, as a product of a different social background within Judaism, might draw on different resources to articulate parallel convictions. In his case, Wisdom's representation of the divine Spirit might be the key soteriological resource, but one that is transformed by his distinctive convictions about Jesus.

The Early Jewish Writings and the Complicated Stories of Israel

Just as the early Jewish writings complicate the status of Torah in ways that might help to cast light on its complicated functioning within the New Testament writings, so they complicate the story world of Israel and her Scriptures. Whether or not specific early Jewish writings were themselves considered scriptural by individual authors or communities, they attest the pluriformity of the narratives associated with Israel. This is important because much current New Testament scholarship is heavily preoccupied with "narrative dynamics" and the question of how "storied worldviews" might inform the range of New Testament writings.[26]

The interest in narrative within New Testament scholarship is closely entangled with the question of how prior Scriptures are read by—or exert an influence upon—the authors of the New Testament, though the two issues are not identical: the way that a perceived or reconstructed storyline that runs *through* Israel's Scriptures might shape the thinking of a New Testament writer is a distinct matter from the way that a specific text *in* those Scriptures might be interpreted. Nevertheless, the two issues are entangled in what is sometimes rather imprecisely referred to as "intertextuality."[27] The use of narrative categories varies be-

---

25. This is broadly the point that I made in *Revealed Wisdom*.

26. See the essays in Bruce Longenecker, ed., *Narrative Dynamics in Paul: A Critical Assessment* (Louisville: Westminster John Knox, 2002). N. T. Wright has extended the idea of narrative dynamics in a way that governs his core findings. See, e.g., "The Plot, the Plan and the Storied Worldview," in vol. 1 of *Paul and the Faithfulness of God*, 2 vols. (London: SPCK, 2013), 457–537.

27. From its original use as a label within semiotics for the emergence of meaning in the reader's interaction with networks of texts, coined by Julia Kristeva (*Desire in Language: A Semiotic Approach to Literature and Art*, ed. Leon S. Roudiez, trans. Thomas Gora, Alice Jardine, and Leon S. Roudiez [New York: Columbia University Press, 1980]), the term has come to be used in biblical studies as something of an umbrella term for the use and influence of prior Scriptures; in many cases, the awareness of both the creative role of the reader and the multiplicity of texts and signs being combined visibly in the early use of the term is absent. As

tween different families of scholarship, but there are significant points of overlap, particularly in the tendency to think of a singular story of Israel, a metanarrative that is either developed or disrupted by the story of Jesus.

N. T. Wright, for example, identifies a coherent "storied worldview" within Second Temple Judaism. While allowing for some variation (notably, in a range of texts that retell the story to deal with a perceived failure to reach fulfillment), he writes that "we can and must say that most Jews of Paul's day perceived themselves, at a deep, worldview level, as *living in a story in search of an ending.*"[28] The key point to isolate from this statement is that Wright speaks of "a story," that is, a singular (if internally complex) narrative that functions at a "deep" level.[29] In his reading of the New Testament material, he sees multiple points of allusion to this grand narrative, most famously to the motif of exile and return but also to the figure of Adam, whose position at the beginning of the story arc gives him a certain programmatic significance. It is important to note that, in Wright's approach, the allusions to earlier parts of the storyline are often of a somewhat impressionistic sort: they operate through broad similarity recognizable to Jewish readers familiar with the story of their Scriptures rather than precise points of lexical correspondence.

One of the factors that has contributed to the popularity of Wright's approach is that it parallels some of the emphases in the legacy of the biblical theology movement. This approach continues to be programmatic in some circles, notably those of Anglophone evangelicalism but with some prominent German advocates, too.[30] While the term "biblical theology" functions quite flexibly, it has come to be used in a very determined way of a movement characterized by a commitment to the singularity of meaning of any given Scripture, identified with the author's intent and controlled by the unfolding story of salvation history. Hence, good exegesis is concerned to locate author and text correctly within this story arc and to identify connections between the parts. Any suggestion that the

---

William Tooman notes, "Attempts to resignify 'intertextuality' in biblical studies run the risk of, at best, disorienting readers and, at worst, diluting the value and utility of our scholarly technical vocabulary." *Gog of Magog: Reuse of Scripture and Compositional Technique in Ezekiel 38–39*, FAT 2/52 (Tübingen: Mohr Siebeck, 2011), 11–12.

28. Wright, *Paul and the Faithfulness of God*, 109 (emphasis original).

29. In his more recent works, Wright has acknowledged the need to allow the narrative to have an inner complexity, likening this to the form of *A Midsummer Night's Dream*. See "Plot, the Plan and the Storied Worldview," 457–537.

30. The work of Gregory K. Beale, e.g., *The Temple and the Church's Mission: A Biblical Theology of the Dwelling Place of God*, NSBT 17 (Downers Grove, IL: IVP Academic, 2004) is a good exemplar of Anglophone biblical theology. Peter Stuhlmacher, *Biblische Theologie des Neuen Testaments*, 2 vols. (Göttingen: Vandenhoek & Ruprecht, 1999), is perhaps the best exemplar of recent German scholarship.

meaning of a text might be decoupled from the author's intention and might be arrived at by bringing an interpretative key *back* to the scriptural text in question is treated with distrust.

An apparently contrastive approach to the role of story is taken by Richard Hays and is paralleled to some extent by the "apocalyptic school" of Pauline scholarship. Unlike Wright and the biblical theology movement, Hays does not consider the unfolding or developing story of the biblical narrative—seen in broadly linear terms—to determine the significance of the Christ event; rather the story of Jesus becomes the controlling element by which Israel's Scriptures are reread by the New Testament authors. In the same way, the authorial intent associated with the original Scriptures has less programmatic significance for Paul (and now, too, the evangelists) than the narrative dynamics at work in their wider contexts as these are engaged by the reader.[31]

This looks quite different from the approach taken by Wright and by those of the biblical theology movement, but Hays also claims that his approach to Paul's reading of Scripture is an attempt to make sense of the apostle as "a first-century Jewish Christian, seeking to come to terms hermeneutically with his Jewish heritage."[32] The "story" of Israel—repeatedly referenced in the singular—is the key element in Paul's usage of Israel's Scriptures; narrative dynamics, rather than interpretative rules, are the characteristic factor in the apostle's use of Scripture, with his categories of allusion and echo always invoking the story of God's dealing with Israel.

It is noteworthy, though, that in making his claims about narrative, Hays distances Paul's interpretation of Scripture from the regulated interpretative practices seen in Qumran and in Philo and from the practice and thought of rabbinic midrash.[33] That is, having claimed as the warrant for his own approach that it takes seriously Paul's identity as a first-century Jew, he then represents Paul's approach as quite different from the principal witnesses to early Jewish exegesis. In particular, what this means is that Hays tends to emphasize individual texts within Scripture and the narrative dynamics at work in their wider context as more influential than combinations of texts or their constituent elements, which might function in a nonnarratival or symbolic fashion.

When viewed within their material contexts, rather than read in isolation from these, what is particularly striking about the early Jewish stories is that

---

31. See Richard B. Hays, *Echoes of Scripture in the Gospels* (Waco, TX: Baylor University Press, 2016); Hays, *Echoes of Scripture in the Letters of Paul* (New Haven: Yale University Press, 1989), 156.

32. Hays, *Echoes of Scripture in the Letters of Paul*, xii.

33. For Qumran and Philo, see Hays, *Echoes of Scripture in the Letters of Paul*, 155; for rabbinic midrash, 168–73.

multiple tellings exist side by side. The stories about the patriarchs and Israel narrated in 1 Enoch are found alongside those in the Mosaic Torah; the pseudepigraphical traditions about Noah or Melchizedek are found alongside the ones contained in the Genesis accounts; the Epistle of Jeremiah is found alongside the book of Jeremiah that we would recognize from our Bibles.

This is true not just of the stories concerning individual characters but of the history/histories of Israel itself. We can find multiple examples of historical review within the writings that effectively rehearse the biblical history but with a striking level of variation within the detail. The events narrated (often symbolically) in these texts are recognizable from the biblical narratives—and the ability of the reader to recognize the allusions to these is basic to their function—but they often recast the detail or significance of these events in ways that differ both from the biblical stories and from each other. In 1 Enoch, for example, there are two symbolically charged reviews, which run from creation to the coming end times: the "Animal Apocalypse," 1 En. 85–90, and the "Apocalypse of Weeks," 1 En. 91:11–17; 93:1–10.[34] There are enough points of contact with the biblical material to allow readers to identify the figures represented in the symbolism of these two apocalypses, but the details of the stories differ, particularly in terms of the evaluation or valorizing of certain events or characters.

Those events, moreover, comprise pivotal points in the narratives. In the Animal Apocalypse, much is made of the theophany at Sinai (1 En. 89:29–35), yet there is no explicit mention of the giving of the law to Moses; hence the soteriological or covenantal significance of the Mosaic Torah is effectively neglected and the emphasis shifts to the theophanic revelation. Where the material in the biblical books of Ezra and Nehemiah indicates that the genuine repentance of those in exile—in line with the requirements of Torah—leads to restoration, the Animal Apocalypse refuses to apply its redemptive motif of "opened eyes" to this period: the return from exile and the building of the Second Temple continues to exemplify the works of spiritual blindness. Instead, the critical repentance takes place later, in the recent past of the Hellenistic era, among those who have embraced the teaching now documented in the writings of Enoch. The Apocalypse of Weeks contains a number of parallels to this but follows a different schema that divides history into ten periods, a pattern found in other ancient works but with massive variation between the details.[35] It is silent on the building of the

---

34. The ordering of the material appears to have been disrupted: the content of 93:1–10 actually contains the first seven weeks. See the discussion in Nickelsburg, *1 Enoch 1*, 414–16, 438.

35. See the discussion in John J. Collins, *The Apocalyptic Imagination: An Introduction to the Jewish Apocalyptic Literature*, 2nd ed., Biblical Resource Series (Grand Rapids: Eerdmans, 1998).

Second Temple and effectively dismisses the entirety of the Second Temple period (up to its own time, at least) as filled with the acts of a "perverse generation," reversed only with the electing of the chosen to be recipients of wisdom and revelation in the eschaton.[36] So, while we might see the broad historical review as equivalent to the story of Israel's salvation found in the Bible, there are significant differences of valorization associated with pivotal points in the narrative.

Such is the scale of these differences that they effectively constitute different versions of the story. Hence, the early Jewish authors of the New Testament would not necessarily have seen themselves as belonging to "the story of Israel" but rather as living in the world represented by a whole host of stories, coherent but not uniform. Faced with new experiences, they had a range of stories and versions of stories upon which to draw and belonged to a culture that accommodated the emergence of new interpretative works.

Creative and Interpretative Dynamics in the Early Jewish Writings

Now that we have described the functional pluriformity of the stories of Israel in the early Jewish literature and the relation of this to the status of Israel and her Scriptures, we can consider in this final section the factors that are visible in the generation of new writings and their relevance for our understanding of early Jewish interpretation. Why did the new stories (or versions) emerge in the first place, and what factors contributed to their character? The phenomena that we see to be at work in the early Jewish writings provide context for our analysis of the phenomena visible within the New Testament.

Some of the elements in early Jewish writings clearly reflect responses to circumstances; as we have noted, the identification of historical allusions is often an important element of attempts to trace provenance. While a fairly late example (and one involving complex textual and redactional issues), 4 Ezra contains material that seeks to make sense of the apparent victory of foreign powers over the Jewish people after the Jewish War, grappling with issues of theodicy and covenant in obvious conversation with scriptural material. Coming from an earlier period and further removed from particular experiences within Palestine,

---

36. Note the similarities in language with 1 En. 99:2, where woe is pronounced on those "who alter the true words and pervert the eternal covenant" (trans. Nickelsburg, *1 Enoch 1*, 481). This might reinforce the point made above, that a standard of righteousness appears to be assumed—the eternal covenant and its true words—even if a new way of understanding this appears now to be normative.

Wisdom of Solomon grapples with similar issues. Less obviously, some of the violent imagery about the giants in the Book of the Watchers has been understood to be colored by the wars of the Diadochoi.[37]

It is a conspicuous feature of this activity that it venerates the scriptural material, not merely looking to it for answers but also presuming that there must be a way to read it that can accommodate these current or recent events. Hence, the interpretation of Israel's Scriptures is colored by a commitment to both their providential and existential significance as the word of God. Interestingly, this commitment is reflected not just by the tendency to allude to Scripture but by the willingness to modify or recast it in new and relevant terms. Functioning together, these two points of commitment generate fresh retroactive readings of Scriptures that allow their meaning to be existential, and not merely historical. In doing so, of course, they often generate new writings that are associated by pseudepigraphy with biblical figures. It is worth noting that there are parallels to this process within the biblical material itself, with plenty of examples of older Scriptures being creatively reread in the light of recent circumstances and generating new prophetic material.[38]

Some of the circumstances to which these writings respond may be constituted by ideological or political struggles faced not *by* but *within* early Judaism, reflecting the diversity of embodiments that existed within this culture. We can find plenty of evidence within these novel texts of conflicts or disagreements, which are sometimes focused upon the status of other Jewish writings. There is some evidence, for example, that Ben Sira is anxious about the kind of apocalyptic thought represented in the Enochic material and that he sought to assert a more *obviously* Torah-centered piety.[39] At the same time, much of the Enochic material (particularly in the Epistle of Enoch, 1 En. 92–105; and in the Parables of Enoch, 37–71) condemns unacceptable teaching that perverts and transgresses "the eternal law" (1 En. 99:2). Clearly, then, the authors are disturbed by other embodiments of Judaism and articulate their concerns through the generation of new works.

The raw materials from which these polemical elements emerge are often the Scriptures of Israel themselves, with disagreements revolving around what it means to live faithfully in the light of these, but often the mode of pursuing this disagreement is one that involves a new act of storytelling rather than more obviously halakic debate. This storytelling is often rather casually labeled by New

---

37. Nickelsburg, *1 Enoch 1*, 170.
38. See Eibert J. C. Tigchelaar, *Prophets of Old and the Day of the End: Zechariah, the Book of Watchers and Apocalyptic*, OTS 35 (Leiden: Brill, 1995).
39. See, e.g., Randall A. Argall, *1 Enoch and Sirach: A Comparative Literary and Conceptual Analysis of the Themes of Revelation, Creation and Judgment*, EJL 8 (Atlanta: Scholars Press, 1995).

Testament scholars as "midrash." While this word usefully highlights the possibility that the principles visible in later rabbinic midrashim may be at work in these Second Temple texts—principles that bear little resemblance to most modern exegesis—the category of writing that it invokes is too broad and elastic for the term to be of much formal heuristic value for the New Testament scholar.[40]

A further element that contributes to the generation of the early Jewish writings is the influence of ambient cultures and their own philosophical and mythological literature. I avoid using the word "hellenization" here: while that term, carefully understood, can helpfully label the cultural dynamic in which much of the early Jewish material emerged, it can also be conceived too narrowly. In reality, the kind of globalization associated with Alexander's legacy was one that allowed the diversity of local cultures to interfere with each other under the umbrella of a collective superculture.

It takes little time with the early Jewish material to find examples of mythological elements traceable to ambient cultures. The sharing of secret skills by the various angelic figures listed in 1 En. 8 is generally seen to reflect the Prometheus myth; the novel story of Abram inventing the seed-plow in Jub. 11 is seen to reflect the story of Enlil, from Mesopotamian myth. Other examples can be traced to Egyptian mythologies, such as the mentioning of the phoenix in relation to the movement of the sun in 2 En. 12. Along with these mythical elements, there is an explicit uptake of Greek philosophical traditions in works like the Wisdom of Solomon, as we have seen, but traces of philosophical discourse can also be found more diffusely through the early Jewish writings.

Of course, there are countless examples of this within the biblical material itself, and here, as there, it is important to recognize that the uptake of such elements was not necessarily the result of unwitting assimilation. Rather, elements are typically (if not invariably) transformed by their combination with the traditions and values of Israel's scriptural heritage. There is, for example, a certain subversion entailed by remapping the stories of Enlil onto the figure of Abram in the context of a narrative concerned with covenant fidelity (Jub. 11). Despite this, anxieties about the incorporation of mythological elements into Jewish writings may have contributed to the concerns about apocalyptic that we have noted in, for example, Sirach. There are possible parallels to this anxiety in the New Testament, notably in the warnings about preoccupation with myths in 1 Timothy (1:4; 4:7) and Titus (1:14). Nevertheless, the widespread evidence of ambient cultural influence on the composition of the new stories challenges any notion of an isolable world of Hebrew thought and culture.

---

40. Hays disagrees that the principles visible in later rabbinic midrashim are already at work in Second Temple texts; see Hays, *Echoes of Scripture in the Letters of Paul*, 10–14, 154–56.

Importantly, one of the results of this influence is the development of tropes, themes, forms, and even genres within the Jewish writings that are proportionately more significant in the pseudepigraphical and apocryphal writings than in the biblical material. Such elements have been prominent in the discussion of apocalyptic, in particular, and at the heart of debates about how apocalyptic should be characterized and analyzed.[41] Tropes such as heavenly ascent or descriptions of the divine throne, themes and motifs like the revealing of wisdom, and the use of forms or genres such as the testament are not unique to these writings, but they are *proportionately* more common than they are in the biblical material as a consequence of contextual cultural influence. For the interpretation of the New Testament, the point of note is that elements and concepts that may seem to be of limited significance within the biblical material, and seemingly of less relevance, may have been much more important in the scriptural world of the earliest Christians. And, to repeat our observation, those elements might be encountered more frequently in some geographical areas than others: certain forms, symbols, or themes might be present in greater density in works that originated or passed through Antioch than in those that arose in Jerusalem.

This problematizes some of the approaches to biblical theology that seek to demarcate sharply "Hebrew thought" from that of surrounding cultures. It has been a defining feature of certain models of biblical theology, paralleled in some theological scholarship, that the controlling conceptualities of, and within, Israel's Scriptures are those of Hebrew language and the distinctive thought associated with it, with the Masoretic Text constituting the authoritative text form.[42] But the early Jewish writings bear witness to a Judaism marked by a complex of attitudes to the Hellenistic world, and even those strands most concerned to maintain boundaries exhibit a level of conceptual influence from the surrounding world.[43]

---

41. The approach taken by John Collins, e.g., in his seminal study in *Semeia* 14, sought to distill an essential definition of apocalypse in which all exemplars participate, while Klaus Koch famously listed the characteristic features of apocalyptic, itemizing the relevant elements that are variously present. See Collins, "Introduction: Towards the Morphology of a Genre," *Semeia* 14 (1979): 1–20; and Koch, *Ratlos vor der Apokalyptik: Eine Streitschrift über ein vernachlässigtes Gebiet der Bibelwissenschaft, und die schädlichen Auswirkungen auf Theologie und Philosophie* (Gütersloh: Mohn, 1970).

42. This was visible in some of the interactions between T. F. Torrance and James Barr, reflected in the latter's *The Semantics of Biblical Language* (Oxford: Oxford University Press, 1961), e.g., 5–6. For a fuller discussion, see Daniel Driver, *Brevard Childs, Biblical Theologian: For the Church's One Bible*, FAT 2/46 (Tübingen: Mohr Siebeck, 2010), 88–89.

43. Lutz Doering has recently highlighted that 4QMMT, a text characterized by a concern to maintain boundaries, shows numerous points of entanglement with Hellenistic thought and writing. See Doering, "4QMMT and/as Hellenistic Literature," in *Interpreting and Living*

While all of these generative factors might have been important, however, we should not overlook the extent to which the emergence of new writings might have resulted simply from the ongoing vitality of the interpretative tradition itself. Israel's Scriptures were read and reread, and those who read them told new stories and wrote new works that drew upon them. As James Kugel notes: "It would be wrong to imply that interpreters were *always* motivated by ideology or some outside interest, that they were always seeking to import some extrabiblical doctrine or political stand into the world of the Bible. Very often their primary or sole motivation appears to be making sense out of the biblical text—but making sense out of *all* of it, its little details, chance juxtapositions, everything."[44]

Kugel's words here begin to highlight the fact that we need to be careful not to assume that the interpretative values or practices of early Jews were equivalent to those of modern exegesis. Because of their commitment to the divine origin of the Scriptures and their providential care, early Jewish readers seem much more interested in the collective functioning of the Scriptures—that is, how they are to be read *together*—than in the isolation of one author's thought or theology. In fact, one of the most striking features of the use of Scripture within the early Jewish writings is the degree of recombination that is visible.

As an example of this, we might consider the opening of the Book of the Watchers, one of the subsections of 1 Enoch. The book opens with a superscription (1:1) that describes Enoch blessing the righteous chosen; this appears to derive its language primarily from Deut 33:1, where Moses blesses the children of Israel. The superscription is followed by an introduction that describes Enoch taking up his "discourse" about his vision of the Holy One, as one whose eyes have been opened by God (1:2). George Nickelsburg highlights multiple points of correspondence between this line and the language used in the Balaam oracle in Num 24:15–17, but with key terms modified to accommodate the preferred language of the Enochic authors; hence, for example, "Almighty" becomes "Holy One."[45] This introduces a theophany (1:4–9) that is set on Sinai and that draws further upon the imagery of Deut 33:1–3, combining this with elements from other texts that also utilize theophanic imagery, notably Jer 25:30 and Micah 1:3–4, and Isa 24:16 and 26:21.[46] The fusion of elements generates a novel theoph-

---

God's Law at Qumran: Miqṣat Maʿaśe Ha-Torah, Some of the Works of the Torah (4QMMT), ed. Reinhard G. Kratz, SAPERE 37 (Tübingen: Mohr Siebeck, 2020), 179–98.

44. James L. Kugel, *Traditions of the Bible: A Guide to the Bible as It Was at the Start of the Common Era* (Cambridge: Harvard University Press, 1998), 21 (emphasis original).

45. Nickelsburg, *1 Enoch 1*, 138.

46. For detailed analysis of the passage and its use of biblical texts, see Lars Hartman, *Asking for a Meaning: A Study of 1 Enoch 1–5*, ConBNT 12 (Lund: Gleerup, 1979).

anic narrative that is—for all its newness—recognizably informed by recurrent tropes within Israel's Scriptures.

Another example exemplifies this kind of creative recombination, but in a way that is particularly relevant to our concern with stories. Jubilees 11 elaborates the biblical story of Abram with an entirely novel account of how, having turned away from idols to God in his youth and having prayed for deliverance from the errors of humanity, he successfully drives away the ravens sent by Mastema (10:10) from his newly planted seed. His name becomes great throughout the land and multitudes are delivered from hunger because of his skill; after this, he invents the seed plow machine and, thereafter, all people till the land "as Abram commanded them" (10:23).

While obviously located within the Abraham cycle of stories, Andrew Teeter notes multiple lexical points of contact between this account in Jub. 11 and the Gideon narrative in Judg 7–8: among other details, he notes that both involve the sowing of seed (Jub. 11:11; Judg 7:3), which is then attacked so as to "destroy the land" or "destroy the produce of the land" (Jub. 11:11; Judg 7:4, 5), as a result of which God's people are "reduced to poverty" (Jub. 11:12; Judg 7:6).[47] Teeter also notes a play on the identification of men and birds in Judg 7:3 and 7:25, which facilitates the figural interplay with the story of Abram in Gen 15 and helps to explain why the Gideon story seems to resource so extensively this new tale about Abram. Any one of these links, taken by itself, might be dismissed as coincidental, and any conclusions drawn from them considered to embody a kind of parallelomania, but the collective force is more impressive. As he writes, "Viewing them together, some kind of connection between the story of Gideon in Judges 6–8 and the Abram/Ravens tale in Jubilees 11 would seem quite evident."[48] The figuration at work in the text seems to extend beyond the alignment of Abram and Gideon, however. The depiction of "all within the land" coming to Abram to be delivered from the conditions of grain shortage brought about by the ravens has obvious thematic and verbal parallels with the Joseph story in Gen 41 and 47. So, if this new story is told in a way that seems to render Abram in ways shaped by other scriptural stories through some form of figuration, it is striking that the figuration is complex, not simple. This involves narrative connections, to be sure, but the narrative is not operating at an overarching level; rather, the author of Jubilees appears to have detected similarities and correspondences that allow stories and their characters from different parts of Scripture, and different times in Israel's past, to be overlaid.

---

47. D. Andrew Teeter, "On 'Exegetical Function' in Rewritten Scripture: Inner-Biblical Exegesis and the Abram/Ravens Narrative in Jubilees," *HTR* 106, no. 4 (2013): 373–402.

48. Teeter, "On 'Exegetical Function,'" 386.

Conclusions

Any New Testament scholars who seek to make use of works typically categorized as "early Jewish writings" need to disabuse themselves of naïveté around the provenance of these works. It is too easy to cite texts without adequate awareness of where they might be located—temporally, geographically, and transmissionally—and to reinforce scholarly myths and generalizations about early Judaism and its thought. When we approach the writings more carefully, we can begin to identify factors relevant at a granular level to the study of the New Testament in relation to Israel's Scriptures. The New Testament reflects both the cohesion and the diversity of early Judaism in ways shaped by cultural and geographical influences.

The early Jewish writings complicate our understanding of the "Scriptures" and the "story world" of early Judaism, and these complications are profoundly significant for our approaches to biblical theology. While we might consider the issues to be concentric—in the sense that there is a core of material that is common to the various streams of Judaism but that is read and expanded in different ways by different communities—we cannot assume that references or allusions to biblical characters, stories, or texts in the New Testament are shaped only or primarily by the contextualizing narrative (or narrative dynamics) in the biblical material. Neither can we assume that authors placed themselves within a singular "story of Israel" since multiple iterations and valorizations of the history of God's dealings with Israel can be found. The complex representations of Israel and the Torah in the New Testament need to be framed against the complex picture of early Judaism.

Within this complex picture, one of the most striking characteristics of the interpretation of Israel's Scriptures is its level of recombinance. Elements from across Israel's Scriptures are combined with each other and with elements drawn from surrounding cultures and their mythologies. The recombinant works that result from this—borrowing the language of genetics to label the emergence of new composite material from multiple sources—might serve as the background to specific texts within the New Testament, but they also demonstrate the kind of phenomenal dynamics that we should expect to be visible there as literature that emerges within early Judaism. As such, the tendency among New Testament scholars to look for the appropriation of *individual* texts and their narrative contexts, rather than *combinations* of texts, reflects a misleading set of assumptions that has the capacity to seriously distort our interpretation of the evidence.

A final point can now be made on the place of canon in biblical interpretation to guard against this chapter being seen as a thoroughgoing rejection of canonical interpretative methodologies. While there is some evidence for a kind of "canon consciousness" at work within the development of the biblical material itself, a full-orbed canonical approach—whether a Jewish approach concerned with Tanak or a Christian one concerned with "Old Testament"—is properly retroactive in character and no less valid for this.[49] It brings a set of decisions about the limits of the canon back to the texts in order to frame their interpretation and allows these to dialogue with the features of the texts observed through close exegesis. I have argued elsewhere for the necessity of such an approach to proper theological exegesis since canonical identification is part of theological method, historically speaking.[50] Theological interpretation of Scripture involves such *construction*. What I challenge here is not this kind of careful implementation of the categories of canon, which might actually accommodate and then replicate the phenomena of recombinance—the interpretative combinations of writings from different parts of the canon, governed by linguistic and figural correspondences and not narrative dynamics—quite easily. Rather, what I challenge is the careless confusion of such categories, and the decisions they rest upon, with the historical identifications of early Judaism.

Bibliography

Argall, Randall A. *1 Enoch and Sirach: A Comparative Literary and Conceptual Analysis of the Themes of Revelation, Creation and Judgment*. EJL 8. Atlanta: Scholars Press, 1995.

Barr, James. *The Semantics of Biblical Language*. Oxford: Oxford University Press, 1961.

Bauckham, Richard. *God Crucified: Monotheism and Christology in the New Testament*. Carlisle: Paternoster, 1998.

Beale, Gregory K. *The Temple and the Church's Mission: A Biblical Theology of the Dwelling Place of God*. NSBT 17. Downers Grove, IL: InterVarsity Press, 2004.

Becker, Adam H., and Annette Yoshiko Reed, eds. *The Ways That Never Parted: Jews and Christians in Late Antiquity and the Early Middle Ages*. TSAJ 95. Tubingen: Mohr Siebeck, 2003.

Boccaccini, Gabriele. *Beyond the Essene Hypothesis: The Parting of the Ways between Qumran and Enochic Judaism*. Grand Rapids: Eerdmans, 1998.

---

49. Canon consciousness was famously claimed by James Sanders, *Torah and Canon* (Philadelphia: Fortress, 1972).

50. See Macaskill, "Identifications, Articulations and Proportions in Practical Theological Interpretation," *JTI* 14, no. 1 (2020): 3–15.

———. *Middle Judaism: Jewish Thought, 300 B.C.E. to 200 C.E.* Minneapolis: Fortress, 1991.

Boccaccini, Gabriele, and John J. Collins, eds. *The Early Enoch Literature.* JSJSup 121. Leiden: Brill, 2007.

Brooke, George J. "Hot at Qumran, Cold in Jerusalem: A Reconsideration of Some Late Second Temple Period Attitudes to the Scriptures and Their Interpretation." Pages 64–77 in *Ha-'ish Moshe: Studies in Scriptural Interpretation in the Dead Sea Scrolls and Related Literature in Honor of Moshe J. Bernstein.* Edited by Binyamin Y. Goldstein, Michael Segal, and George J. Brooke. STDJ 122. Leiden: Brill, 2017.

———. "Inspecting the School of St. Matthew." Pages 101–21 in *Krister among the Jews and Gentiles: Essays in Appreciation of the Life and Work of Krister Stendahl.* Edited by Paula Fredriksen and Jesper Svartvik. Studies in Judaism and Christianity. Mahwah, NJ: Paulist, 2018.

Collins, John J. *The Apocalyptic Imagination: An Introduction to the Jewish Apocalyptic Literature.* 2nd ed. Biblical Resource Series. Grand Rapids: Eerdmans, 1998.

———. "Introduction: Towards the Morphology of a Genre." *Semeia* 14 (1979): 1–20.

———. *Jewish Wisdom in the Hellenistic Age.* Edinburgh: T&T Clark, 1998.

Davila, James R. *The Provenance of the Pseudepigrapha: Jewish, Christian or Other.* JSJSup 105. Leiden: Brill, 2005.

Dodson, Joseph R. *The "Powers" of Personification: Rhetorical Purpose in the "Book of Wisdom" and the Letter to the Romans.* BZNW 161. Berlin: de Gruyter, 2008.

Doering, Lutz. "4QMMT and/as Hellenistic Literature." Pages 179–98 in *Interpreting and Living God's Law at Qumran: Miqṣat Ma'aśe Ha-Torah, Some of the Works of the Torah (4QMMT).* Edited by Reinhard G. Kratz. SAPERE 37. Tübingen: Mohr Siebeck, 2020.

Driver, Daniel. *Brevard Childs, Biblical Theologian: For the Church's One Bible.* FAT 2/46. Tübingen: Mohr Siebeck, 2010.

Hartman, Lars. *Asking for a Meaning: A Study of 1 Enoch 1–5.* ConBNT 12. Lund: Gleerup, 1979.

Hays, Richard B. *Echoes of Scripture in the Gospels.* Waco, TX: Baylor University Press, 2016.

———. *Echoes of Scripture in the Letters of Paul.* New Haven: Yale University Press, 1989.

Henze, Matthias, ed. *A Companion to Biblical Interpretation in Early Judaism.* Grand Rapids: Eerdmans, 2012.

———. "Preface." Pages viii–x in *A Companion to Biblical Interpretation in Early Judaism.* Edited by Matthias Henze. Grand Rapids: Eerdmans, 2012.

Koch, Klaus. *Ratlos vor der Apokalyptik: Eine Streitschrift über ein vernachlässigtes*

Gebiet der Bibelwissenschaft, und die schädlichen Auswirkungen auf Theologie und Philosophie. Gütersloh: Mohn, 1970.

Kristeva, Julia. *Desire in Language: A Semiotic Approach to Literature and Art*. Edited by Leon S. Roudiez. Translated by Thomas Gora, Alice Jardine, and Leon S. Roudiez. New York: Columbia University Press, 1980.

Kugel, James L. *Traditions of the Bible: A Guide to the Bible as It Was at the Start of the Common Era*. Cambridge: Harvard University Press, 1998.

Linebaugh, Jonathan A. *God, Grace, and Righteousness in Wisdom of Solomon and Paul's Letter to the Romans: Texts in Conversation*. NovTSup 152. Leiden: Brill, 2013.

Longenecker, Bruce, ed. *Narrative Dynamics in Paul: A Critical Assessment*. Louisville: Westminster John Knox, 2002.

Macaskill, Grant. "Identifications, Articulations and Proportions in Practical Theological Interpretation." *JTI* 14, no. 1 (2020): 3–15.

———. "Matthew and the Parables of Enoch." Pages 218–30 in *Parables of Enoch: A Paradigm Shift*. Edited by James H. Charlesworth and Darrell Bock. Jewish and Christian Texts in Contexts and Related Studies 11. London: Bloomsbury T&T Clark, 2013.

———. *Revealed Wisdom and Inaugurated Eschatology in Ancient Judaism and Early Christianity*. JSJSup 115. Leiden: Brill, 2007.

Nickelsburg, George. *1 Enoch 1: A Commentary on the Book of 1 Enoch Chapters 1–36, 81–108*. Hermeneia. Minneapolis: Fortress, 2001.

Nickelsburg, George, and James C. VanderKam. *1 Enoch 2: A Commentary on the Book of 1 Enoch Chapters 37–82*. Hermeneia. Minneapolis: Fortress, 2012.

Reynolds, Benjamin E., and Loren T. Stuckenbruck, eds. *The Jewish Apocalyptic Tradition and the Shaping of New Testament Thought*. Minneapolis: Fortress, 2017.

Sacchi, Paolo. *Jewish Apocalyptic and Its History*. Translated by William J. Short. JSPSup 20. Sheffield: Sheffield Academic, 1996.

———. *L'apocalittica giudaica e la sua Storia*. BCR 55. Brescia: Paideia, 1990.

Sanders, James. *Torah and Canon*. Philadelphia: Fortress, 1972.

Schorch, Stefan. "Jacob's Ladder and Aaron's Vestments: Traces of Mystical and Magical Traditions in the Book of Wisdom." Pages 183–95 in *Studies in the Book of Wisdom*. Edited by Geza G. Xeravits and Joszef Zsengeller. JSJSup 142. Leiden: Brill, 2010.

Siegel, Michal Bar-Asher. *Early Christian Monastic Literature and the Babylonian Talmud*. Cambridge: Cambridge University Press, 2013.

Stokes, Ryan E. "Not over Moses' Dead Body: Jude 9, 22–24 and the Assumption of Moses in Their Early Jewish Context." *JSNT* 40, no. 2 (2017): 192–213.

Stone, Michael E. "Categorization and Classification of the Apocrypha and Pseudepigrapha." Pages 3–14 in *Apocrypha, Pseudepigrapha and Armenian Studies: Collected Essays*. Vol. 1. OLA 144. Leuven: Peeters, 2006.

Stuhlmacher, Peter. *Biblische Theologie des Neuen Testaments*. 2 vols. Göttingen: Vandenhoek & Ruprecht, 1999.

Teeter, D. Andrew. "On 'Exegetical Function' in Rewritten Scripture: Inner-Biblical Exegesis and the Abram/Ravens Narrative in Jubilees." *HTR* 106, no. 4 (2013): 373–402.

Tigchelaar, Eibert J. C. *Prophets of Old and the Day of the End: Zechariah, the Book of Watchers and Apocalyptic*. OTS 35. Leiden: Brill, 1995.

Tooman, William A. *Gog of Magog: Reuse of Scripture and Compositional Technique in Ezekiel 38–39*. FAT 2/52. Tübingen: Mohr Siebeck, 2011.

Winston, David. *The Wisdom of Solomon: A New Translation with Introduction and Commentary*. AB 43. New York: Doubleday, 1979.

Witherington, Ben, III. *Jesus the Sage: The Pilgrimage of Wisdom*. Edinburgh: T&T Clark, 1994.

Wold, Benjamin. *4QInstruction: Divisions and Hierarchies*. STDJ 123. Leiden: Brill, 2018.

Wright, N. T. *Paul and the Faithfulness of God*. 2 vols. London: SPCK, 2013.

———. "The Plot, the Plan and the Storied Worldview." Pages 457–537 in vol. 1 of *Paul and the Faithfulness of God*. 2 vols. London: SPCK, 2013.

5

Israel's Scriptures in the Dead Sea Scrolls

SUSAN DOCHERTY

The story of the chance discovery by a young Bedouin shepherd in 1947 of the first of the Qumran caves with its hidden cache of ancient scrolls has been widely rehearsed.[1] Excavations of the area over the following decade uncovered over nine hundred fragmentary manuscripts in eleven caves on the northwestern slopes above the Dead Sea. A twelfth cave was discovered as late as 2017, although it contained only pieces of broken storage jars and other material fragments. Many of the Qumran scrolls are partial copies of the writings that would come to form the Jewish Bible, as well as of other works that were already recognized as having influence among some early Jewish groups (e.g., 1 Enoch, Jubilees). A considerable quantity of previously unknown compositions also came to light, including exegetical works of various kinds, community rules, liturgical texts, legal treatises, and wisdom instructions. These documents date from the third century BCE to the first century CE, and archaeological evidence indicates that the site itself was occupied in two major phases between approximately 130 BCE and 68 CE.[2]

---

1. For a summary, see James C. VanderKam and Peter W. Flint, *The Meaning of the Dead Sea Scrolls: Their Significance for Understanding the Bible, Judaism, Jesus and Christianity* (San Francisco: Harper, 2002), 3–36.
2. On the archaeology of the site, see Katharina Galor, Humbert Jean-Baptiste, and Jürgen K. Zangenberg, eds., *Qumran: The Site of the Dead Sea Scrolls; Archaeological Interpretations and Debates*, STDJ 57 (Leiden: Brill, 2004); Robert Cargill, *Qumran through Real Time: A Virtual Reconstruction of Qumran and the Dead Sea Scrolls*, Bible in Technology 1 (Piscataway, NJ: Gorgias, 2009); and Jodi Magness, "Qumran," in *The Eerdmans Dictionary of Early Judaism*, ed. John J. Collins and Daniel C. Harlow (Grand Rapids: Eerdmans, 2010), 1126–31.

Israel's Scriptures in the Dead Sea Scrolls

The Dead Sea discoveries are an immensely significant source of first-hand information about numerous aspects of belief and practice in the late Second Temple period, particularly the development and reception of Israel's Scriptures. Not only did the caves contain the oldest extant manuscripts of the texts now regarded by both Jews and Christians as biblical, but they also offered up new forms of engagement with them, including the distinctive genre of pesher commentary. This chapter will explore the multiple ways in which the Scriptures are used and interpreted across this literature, highlighting throughout the implications of this evidence for reading the near-contemporary writings that make up the New Testament.[3] The first section will address the question of the status and authority ascribed to the Scriptures within the scrolls and the variety of forms in which they were accessed. The second will consider the range of genres and methods through which these texts were redeployed and exegeted. Three overarching questions frame this survey: (1) Was there such a thing as "Scripture" at Qumran, and, if so, what did it look like? (2) How were the writings that are now termed "scriptural" interpreted at Qumran? (3) How do the scrolls contribute to a fuller understanding of the reuse of the Scriptures within the New Testament?

Defining Scripture in the Dead Sea Scrolls

As has been emphasized throughout this volume, no such entity as a definitive Bible, with a stable text and a fixed list of contents, existed during the Second Temple period. The Dead Sea discoveries corroborate this picture of ongoing fluidity but also illustrate the gradual emergence of an authoritative collection of Scriptures.

Scripture at Qumran: Authority and Canon

Approximately one quarter of the texts found in the Qumran caves, around 220, are copies of books that are now included within the Jewish Bible.[4] The majority of these were written in the first century BCE or early decades of the first century CE so predate by hundreds of years the other primary witnesses to the Scriptures

---

3. This chapter is concerned specifically with the texts found at Qumran and will not directly consider the subsequent discoveries of a small number of scriptural manuscripts at other locations in the vicinity of the Dead Sea, such as Wadi Muraba'at and Naḥal Ḥever.

4. Around 930 items are included in the major inventories, but numerous fragments remain unidentified; for an assessment of the Qumran biblical manuscripts, see Eibert J. C. Tigchelaar, "The Dead Sea Scrolls," in Collins and Harlow, *Eerdmans Dictionary of Early Judaism*, 164.

in both their Masoretic (MT) and Septuagint (LXX) forms.[5] They are all in Hebrew with the exception of five Greek manuscripts of the Pentateuch (Exodus, Leviticus [two], Numbers, and Deuteronomy) and three Aramaic targumim (to Leviticus and Job [two]). They have survived in various states of preservation, from the almost complete Isaiah Scroll (1QIsa[a]) through to tiny scraps containing only a couple of legible letters.

The number of extant copies of a text is one measure of its authority at Qumran, albeit an imperfect one, given both the complexities involved in classifying often very fragmentary documents and the element of chance inherent in their survival. On that basis, the greatest importance was attached to the Psalms (at least thirty-six manuscripts), Deuteronomy (thirty-one or thirty-two), Isaiah (twenty-one), and Genesis (nineteen or twenty), followed by Exodus (seventeen), Leviticus (fifteen), Numbers (eight), the Minor Prophets (eight or nine), Daniel (eight), Jeremiah (six), and Ezekiel (six).[6] The former prophets and wisdom writings are distinctly less well-represented among the scrolls, with only two to four copies each found of Joshua, Judges, Samuel, Kings, Ruth, Job, Proverbs, Song of Solomon, Qohelet, and Lamentations. No more than a few snippets of Chronicles and Ezra can be identified, and only one possible manuscript of Esther (4Q550), while Nehemiah is not definitely attested.[7] Some books that are included in the Greek but not Hebrew Bible are present, such as Tobit (five manuscripts), Sirach (two), and possibly the Letter of Jeremiah (7Q2 [pap7QepJer]). There is evidence also of a high regard for other texts that would not ultimately be received into the Jewish canon: approximately fifteen manuscripts of the book of Jubilees have been recovered, for example, and at least twelve of 1 Enoch.

---

5. For further detail on the dating of the scrolls, see Brian Webster, "Chronological Index of the Texts from the Judaean Desert," in *The Texts from the Judaean Desert: Indices and an Introduction to the Discoveries in the Judaean Desert Series*, ed. Emanuel Tov, DJD 39 (Oxford: Clarendon, 2002), 351–446.

6. The figures are slightly fluid, as fragments continue to be identified and reclassified. For a summary of the numbers of copies, see James C. VanderKam, *The Dead Sea Scrolls and the Bible* (Grand Rapids: Eerdmans, 2012), 3. Fuller lists, based on the manuscripts published at that time, can be found in Emanuel Tov, "A Categorized List of All the 'Biblical Texts' Found in the Judaean Desert," *DSD* 8, no. 1 (2001): 67–84; and Armin Lange, "Annotated List of the Texts from the Judaean Desert Classified by Content and Genre," in Tov, *Texts From the Judaean Desert*, 115–64. For Deuteronomy, see the discussion in Eibert J. C. Tigchelaar, "A Forgotten Qumran Cave 4 *Deuteronomy* Fragment (4Q38D = 4QDEUTu)," *RevQ* 23, no. 4 (2008): 525–28. All the Hebrew biblical manuscripts for each now-scriptural book have also been collected and published together in Eugene Ulrich, *The Biblical Qumran Scrolls: Transcriptions and Textual Variants*, VTSup 134 (Leiden: Brill, 2010).

7. The identification of the Esther fragment is uncertain, but a knowledge of Esther is demonstrated by other forms of appeal to it within the scrolls; see Shemaryahu Talmon, "Was the Book of Esther Known at Qumran?," *DSD* 2, no. 2 (1995): 249–67.

Israel's Scriptures in the Dead Sea Scrolls

A second significant indicator of the status that a now-scriptural work enjoyed is the frequency with which it is directly quoted or implicitly reused within other writings. A tradition of communal study and interpretation at Qumran of the Psalms, Isaiah, and the Minor Prophets, for instance, is demonstrated in the pesharim, a series of explicit commentaries on these particular texts. A marked interest in the Pentateuchal books, especially Genesis and Deuteronomy, is also evident from the number of manuscripts in which they are either reworked (e.g., 4Q158; 4Q364–367; 11Q19) or expanded in order to create new narratives centering on the flood and the patriarchal era (e.g., 1Q19; 1Q23; 1Q24; 2Q26; 4Q180–181; 4Q370; 4Q530–533; 6Q8).[8] Deuteronomy is also clearly fundamental to the movement's self-understanding as a renewed covenant community governed by law (e.g., CD III, 10–20), and the passages excerpted for inclusion in extract collections (e.g., 4Q174; 4Q175; 4Q176; 11Q13) likewise confirm the significance of both Deuteronomy and Isaiah. The Minor Prophets and Isaiah figure prominently in citations and allusions within major sectarian works like the Community Rule (1QS), the War Scroll (1QM), and the Damascus Document (CD).[9] These compositions also reflect an emphasis on the Pentateuchal books, especially Genesis and Deuteronomy, and include considerable reference to Numbers, Leviticus, Ezekiel, and Jubilees, too. Although direct citations from the Psalms are not frequent, they clearly serve as the primary inspiration, both in content and form, for the Hodayot or Thanksgiving Hymns (1QH). Ezekiel exerts a similarly implicit influence on other liturgical works like the Songs of the Sabbath Sacrifice (4Q400–407; 11Q17).[10]

These preferences for the Pentateuch, the prophetic literature, and the Psalms are dictated partly by the specific concerns of the Dead Sea community with

---

8. See further Sidnie White Crawford, "Reading Deuteronomy in the Second Temple Period," in *Reading the Present in the Qumran Library: The Perception of the Contemporary by Means of Scriptural Interpretations*, ed. Kristin De Troyer and Armin Lange, SymS 30 (Atlanta: Society of Biblical Literature, 2005), 127–40; and Crawford, "Genesis in the Dead Sea Scrolls," in *The Book of Genesis: Composition, Reception and Interpretation*, ed. Craig A. Evans, Joel N. Lohr, and David L. Petersen, VTSup 152 (Leiden: Brill, 2012), 353–73.

9. In an early study, Joseph Fitzmyer identifies forty-three quotations within 1QS, 1QM, CD, and 4Q174, including eleven from the Minor Prophets, nine from Deuteronomy, seven from Isaiah, and five from Numbers (Fitzmyer, "The Use of Explicit Old Testament Quotations in Qumran Literature and in the New Testament," *NTS* 7, no. 4 [1961]: 297–333). For other general investigations of the scriptural quotations in the major sectarian works, see Geza Vermes, "Biblical Proof-Texts in Qumran Literature," *JSS* 34, no. 2 (1989): 493–508; and Jonathan G. Campbell, *The Exegetical Texts*, Companion to the Qumran Scrolls 4 (London: T&T Clark, 2004). For a recent study of the reuse of Scripture in the Damascus Document specifically, see Jonathan D. H. Norton, "Composite Quotations in the Damascus Document," in *Composite Citations in Antiquity*, vol. 1, *Jewish, Graeco-Roman and Early Christian Uses*, ed. Sean A. Adams and Seth M. Ehorn, LNTS 525 (London: Bloomsbury, 2016), 92–118.

10. On the reuse of Ezekiel within the Dead Sea Scrolls, see D. Nathan Phinney, "Ezekiel, Book of," in Collins and Harlow, *Eerdmans Dictionary of Early Judaism*, 619–20.

eschatology, liturgy, law, and with the meaning of their own history.[11] However, they also illustrate the emerging authority of a small group of received writings, the normativity of which is implied by the injunction in the scrolls to "understand the book of Moses [and] the book[s of the pr]ophets and Davi[d]" (4Q397 IV, 9–10; cf. 1QS I, 2–3).[12] These texts do appear to have attained a status at Qumran that could be called "scriptural," but no fixed collection or "canon" had yet been determined. This central core of authoritative writings was surrounded by a larger, more fluid, and less clearly defined wider circle of other significant works, not all of which (e.g., 1 Enoch, Jubilees) would ultimately become canonical in Judaism.

Implications: Scripture and Its Authority in the New Testament

Second Temple Jewish literature beyond the scrolls likewise attests to the early preeminence of the Pentateuch, the Prophets, and the Psalms, and this provides the context for New Testament appeals to these same normative writings. Thus the first Christians, like the members of the Dead Sea sect, expended considerable time and effort in communal study of them and perceived an analogous need to explain Jesus's life and death and their own practices as according with them: "everything written about me in the law of Moses, the prophets, and the psalms must be fulfilled" (Luke 24:44; cf., e.g., Acts 3:18; Rom 3:28–31; 9:6–33; Gal 3:6–9; Heb 7:15–22; 8:6–13).[13] The fact that an inner core of "scriptural" texts had attained a particular authority at this time—Genesis, Deuteronomy, Psalms, Isaiah, and the Minor Prophets—means that the distribution of quotations in the New Testament overlaps markedly with the pattern of the scrolls.[14] Other writings that were influential at Qumran are also reflected in the New Testament, although not nearly to the same extent. Parallels between the Enochic literature and the Gospel of Matthew are frequently highlighted, for example, and 1 Enoch is also quoted as an authoritative source in Jude 14–15 (cf. 1 En. 1:9).[15]

---

11. For a fuller discussion of the reasons for the strong appeal of certain sections of Scripture at Qumran, see George J. Brooke, "'The Canon within the Canon' at Qumran and in the New Testament," in *The Scrolls and the Scriptures: Qumran Fifty Years After*, ed. Stanley E. Porter and Craig A. Evans, JSPSup 26 (Sheffield: Sheffield Academic, 1997), 250–58.

12. The English translation used throughout for quotations from the Qumran literature is Florentino García Martínez and Eibert J. C. Tigchelaar, *The Dead Sea Scrolls Study Edition*, 2 vols. (Grand Rapids: Eerdmans, 1997–1998).

13. All scriptural quotations follow the NRSV.

14. See esp. Brooke, "Canon within the Canon," 250–60; and Craig A. Evans, "Why Did the New Testament Writers Appeal to the Old Testament?," *JSNT* 38, no. 1 (2015): 36–37.

15. On the possible connections between Matthew's Gospel and the Enochic literature, see Amy E. Richter, *Enoch and the Gospel of Matthew*, PTMS 183 (Eugene, OR: Pickwick, 2012).

Scripture at Qumran: *Text Form and Variety*

The Dead Sea discoveries highlight the great variety of forms in which Jews in the late Second Temple era were likely to encounter these emerging scriptural writings, both materially and textually. In addition to whole books or combinations of books (e.g., 4Q17 [4QExod-Lev^f]; 4Q23 [4QLev-Num^a]), numerous excerpts of different kinds were made, including short texts for inclusion in phylacteries (e.g., 4Q128–148); copies of single psalms, perhaps for use in personal or communal prayer (e.g., Ps 119 is reproduced in 5Q5; cf. possibly the Prayer of Daniel [Dan 9:4b–19] in 4Q116 [4QDan^e]); and thematic anthologies of passages extracted from several different scriptural locations (4Q174; 4Q175; 11Q13; cf. the words of consolation from Isa 40–55 in 4Q176). There are also examples of rewritings of large sections of the Pentateuch, like the Temple Scroll (11Q19; 11Q20; cf. 4Q365a) and the Reworked Pentateuch (4Q158; 4Q364–367), which combine and reorder this traditional material. It is not clear whether these documents were regarded at Qumran as scriptural copies or interpretative texts.[16]

In addition to these varied physical forms, the Scriptures were also available in a plurality of versions. All three of the major text types (MT, SP, LXX) are preserved among the scrolls. The Masoretic or proto-Masoretic form is well represented in copies of most of the now-scriptural books, but other manuscripts offer expansionist readings parallel to those that characterize the Samaritan Pentateuch (e.g., 4Q17; 4Q22 [4QpaleoExod^m]; 4Q27 [4QNum^b]; 4Q41 [4QDeut^n]) or provide a Hebrew text close to that from which the Septuagint was apparently translated (e.g., 4Q13 [4QExod^b]; 4Q44 [4QDeut^q]; 4Q51 [4QSam^a]).[17] Thus both the shorter version of Jeremiah found in the Greek Bible (e.g., 4Q71 [4QJer^b]; 4Q72a [4QJer^d]) and the longer form preserved in Hebrew (e.g., 4Q70 [4QJer^a]; 4Q72 [4QJer^c]) are attested. Other works were also evidently still circulating in more than one literary edition: the best preserved Psalms scroll found at Qumran, 11Q5 (11QPs^a), for instance, differs from the Masoretic collection in its contents and order, so that apparently new psalms are included alongside those that would become canonical.[18] The fluidity of the scriptural text in this

---

16. See the treatment of this question in Sidnie White Crawford, *Rewriting Scripture in Second Temple Times*, SDSS (Grand Rapids: Eerdmans, 2008), 39–59.

17. For the view that proto-Masoretic texts predominated at Qumran, see esp. Emmauel Tov, *Textual Criticism of the Hebrew Bible*, 3rd ed. (Minneapolis: Fortress, 2012), 26–37, 108. However, this conclusion may overstate the often-fragmentary manuscript evidence since all the major text types agree in many places; for further discussion of the text form of the scriptural citations in the pesharim, see Timothy H. Lim, *Holy Scripture in the Qumran Commentaries and Pauline Letters* (Oxford: Clarendon Press, 1997), 69–94.

18. See esp. Peter W. Flint, *The Dead Sea Psalms Scrolls and the Book of Psalms*, STDJ 17

period is further confirmed by the evidence of the many copies that exhibit divergences, both slight and more substantial, from all three of the extant major forms, and that are, therefore, often termed nonaligned (e.g., 4Q10 [4QGen^k]; 4Q47 [4QJosh^a]).[19] A variety of textual types can even be employed within the same work (e.g., 4Q175), which implies that no one tradition was preferred within the sect.[20] Since these copies were made by different scribal hands, and some at least were brought to the site from elsewhere, they exemplify the general state of scriptural pluriformity that persisted until the late first century CE.[21]

Scribal Exegesis

It is almost certain that many of the minor variant readings attested in the scrolls did not originate as copying errors but were deliberately introduced by scribes in order to clarify a perceived difficulty in the text. The addition in 4Q7 (4QGen^g) of an extra letter מ at the end of the first occurrence of the Hebrew word for "day" in Gen 1:5 (יומם for MT יום) in order to distinguish between the two uses of this term ("daytime," as opposed to night, and a whole twenty-four-hour period of a "day") is one example of this kind of exegetical amendment.[22] The boundaries between Scripture and its interpretation in this era were rather more permeable than is sometimes acknowledged—and the early scribes evidently did not understand their role in handing on the tradition as an entirely passive one.[23] This process of

---

(Leiden: Brill, 1997); see also Flint, "Psalms Scrolls," in Collins and Harlow, *Eerdmans Dictionary of Early Judaism*, 1107–10.

19. For further detail, see VanderKam and Flint, *Meaning of the Dead Sea Scrolls*, 149–200; Emanuel Tov, "The Biblical Texts from the Judaean Desert: An Overview and Analysis," in *The Bible as Book: The Hebrew Bible and the Judean Desert Discoveries*, ed. Edward D. Herbert and Emanuel Tov (New Castle: Oak Knoll, 2002), 139–66; Eugene Ulrich, *The Dead Sea Scrolls and the Origins of the Bible*, SDSS (Grand Rapids: Eerdmans, 1999), 23–33; and George J. Brooke, "Scripture and Scriptural Tradition in Transmission: Light from the Dead Sea Scrolls," in *The Scrolls and Biblical Traditions: Proceedings of the Seventh Meeting of the IOQS in Helsinki*, ed. George J. Brooke et al., STDJ 103 (Leiden: Brill, 2012), 1–17.

20. See further Timothy H. Lim, "Authoritative Scriptures and the Dead Sea Scrolls," in *The Oxford Handbook of the Dead Sea Scrolls*, ed. Timothy H. Lim and John J. Collins (Oxford: Oxford University Press, 2007), 311.

21. For a summary of the contribution of the Qumran material to scholarly understanding of the history of the biblical text, see Emanuel Tov, "Understanding the Text of the Bible 65 Years after the Discovery of the Dead Sea Scrolls," *Open Theology* 1 (2014): 89–96.

22. See further George J. Brooke, "The Qumran Scrolls and the Demise of the Distinction between Higher and Lower Criticism," in *New Directions in Qumran Studies: Proceedings of the Bristol Colloquium on the Dead Sea Scrolls, 8–10 September 2003*, ed. Jonathan G. Campbell, William John Lyons, and Lloyd K. Pietersen, LSTS 52 (London: T&T Clark, 2005), 29–30.

23. See, e.g., Ulrich, *Dead Sea Scrolls and Origins of the Bible*, 8–12, 23–24.

actively shaping the scriptural texts can also be observed in the quotations within sectarian compositions, which sometimes differ from all other known versions and incorporate exegetical alterations. The replacement in the Habakkuk pesher of the usual word "their nakedness" (מעוריהם) with the otherwise unattested "their feasts" (מועדיהם) in the citation of Hab 2:15 is probably such an interpretative move, involving the alteration of only a single letter (the graphically similar ד for ר), which enables this verse to be applied in the ensuing commentary to the subject of the proper dating of festivals, a matter of dispute between the community and other streams of contemporary Judaism (1QpHab XI, 2–8).[24]

It is also clear that the Qumran exegetes were aware of the coexistence of multiple text forms and could consciously exploit this variety. Two versions of Hab 2:16 are appealed to in 1QpHab XI, 9–13, for example, through the references to the verbs "stagger" (הרעל in the quotation; cf. LXX) and "be uncircumcised" (הערל in the commentary; cf. MT), which differ only in the order of the middle two consonants. This implies a view of Scripture as intentionally plural and polyvalent so that textual variants were regarded as clues to the full meaning of the divine revelation. A purposeful selection could on occasion be made, therefore, from among the available forms of the one that best supported the argument. The citation of Hab 1:17 in the pesher, for instance, has "his sword" (חרבו) where the MT has "his net" (חרמו), a minor consonantal difference that facilitates the direct application of this verse to the Romans: "the Kittim who will cause many to die by the edge of the sword" (1QpHab VI, 8–10). This reading is reflected also in the Greek translation of the Minor Prophets scroll from Naḥal Ḥever so is more likely to represent an exegetical choice than an adaptation of the text.

Implications of Textual Pluriformity: Citation Practice in the New Testament

Appreciating the extent of textual pluriformity in the late Second Temple period is essential for a proper understanding of the scriptural quotations in the New Testament. Since the publication of the scrolls, it has become much more widely accepted that the early Christian authors may be faithfully reproducing the text available to them, even where this differs from the majority of surviving witnesses to it.[25] A Hebrew version of Amos 9:11 (the fallen booth of David) similar to the Greek text cited in Acts 15:16 appears in two Qumran manuscripts

---

24. See the fuller discussion of these verses in Timothy H. Lim, *Pesharim*, Companion to the Qumran Scrolls 3 (London: Sheffield Academic, 2002), 54–63.

25. See, e.g., Gert J. Steyn, *A Quest for the Assumed Septuagint Vorlage of the Explicit Quotations in Hebrews*, FRLANT 235 (Göttingen: Vandenhoeck & Ruprecht, 2011).

(4Q174 I, 12; CD VII, 16), for example, and the longstanding puzzle about the source of the fulfillment quotation in Matt 2:23 ("He will be called a Nazorean") may have been solved by the discovery in 4Q51 of a previously unknown textual plus referring to Samuel as a נזיר (1 Sam 1:22).[26] The discovery of extract collections dating from the early centuries BCE also supports the theory that the first followers of Jesus, too, may have accessed the Scriptures through such excerpted forms, like anthologies of key messianic passages, or liturgical compilations. This would help to explain unusual text forms and other features of New Testament citation practice, such as inaccurate attribution (e.g., Matt 27:9), composite quotation, and the use of catenae, or chains of supporting passages (e.g., Acts 3:22–25; Rom 3:10–18; 4:3–8; 9:25–33; 15:8–12; 2 Cor 6:16–18; Heb 1:5–13).[27]

Conversely, however, Qumran scribal conventions clearly included the alteration of scriptural forms, both when copying and quoting them, together with the exploitation of textual variety for exegetical purposes. This raises the possibility that similar methods are also employed in the New Testament. The citations in Matthew's Gospel, for instance, especially the distinctive group of ten fulfillment quotations, do not consistently follow extant versions of either the LXX or MT (see, e.g., Isa 9:1–2 at Matt 4:15–16; Isa 42:1–4 at Matt 12:18–21).[28] They are often understood, therefore, as resulting from the same kind of sustained editorial and exegetical work on the part of the evangelist and his circle as is evidenced in the scrolls.[29] It is also quite feasible that early Christian interpreters sometimes made an intentional choice of a particular text form for theological reasons. Two main Greek renderings of a difficult Hebrew phrase in Ps 40:6 (39:7 LXX) occur in the ancient manuscripts, for example, "ears [ὠτία] you have

---

26. For an early notice of the Acts 15:16 parallel, see Jan de Waard, *A Comparative Study of the Old Testament Text in the Dead Sea Scrolls and in the New Testament*, STDJ 4 (Leiden: Brill, 1965), 24–26. For Matt 2:23, see Timothy H. Lim, "Qumran Scholarship and the Study of the Old Testament in the New Testament," *JSNT* 38, no. 1 (2015): 70–71.

27. For the most recent full treatment of the phenomenon of composite quotation within the New Testament, see Sean A. Adams and Seth M. Ehorn, eds., *Composite Citations in Antiquity*, vol. 2, *New Testament Uses*, LNTS 593 (London: Bloomsbury, 2018). For catenae, see esp. Martin C. Albl, *"And Scripture Cannot Be Broken": The Form and Function of the Early Christian Testimonia Collections*, NovTSup 96 (Leiden: Brill, 1999).

28. For further detail, see Maarten J. J. Menken, *Matthew's Bible: The Old Testament Text of the Evangelist*, BETL 173 (Leuven: Peeters, 2004), 15–33, 67–88.

29. Krister Stendahl was the first to suggest that the text form of the quotations in Matthew was due to the work of a "school" akin to the Dead Sea sect; see Stendahl, *The School of St Matthew and Its Use of the Old Testament*, ANSU 20 (Lund: Gleerup, 1954). See also Philip S. Alexander, "The Bible in Qumran and Early Judaism," in *Texts in Context: Essays by Members of the Society for Old Testament Study*, ed. A. D. H. Mayes (Oxford: Oxford University Press, 2000), 35–62.

dug," and "a body [σῶμα] you have prepared." The latter reading is employed in Hebrews and is obviously key to the epistle's claim that Jesus's death replaces the sacrifices required by the Mosaic law (Heb 10:5–10; cf. the convenient translation "virgin," παρθένος, for the Hebrew "young woman" in Matt 1:23 [Isa 7:14]).[30]

Interpreting Scripture in the Dead Sea Scrolls

This commitment of the members of the Dead Sea movement to constant study of the Scriptures (e.g., 1QS VI, 6–8) is reflected throughout their literature, in the multiple and creative ways in which these authoritative texts are copied, rewritten, expanded, imitated, quoted, and commented on. This section will explore the major forms of scriptural interpretation and methods of exegesis employed within the scrolls and consider the implications of this for an understanding of New Testament practice.

Forms of Scriptural Interpretation: The Pesharim and Prophetic Interpretation

The exegetical form most widely associated with Qumran is the pesher, in which a short scriptural text is first cited and then explained. The comment is prefaced by the introductory formula *pishro*, or "its interpretation is . . . ," and generally involves restating phrases from within the quotation and relating them directly to some aspect of the community's history or future expectation. A wide range of exegetical techniques are employed to produce this new meaning, all of which involve an intense focus on individual scriptural words. Their consonants may be rearranged, for example, as when the term "temple" (היכל) in Hab 2:20 is read as "he will destroy" (יכלה; 1QpHab XII, 16–XIII, 3; cf. the comment on Hab 1:12 at 1QpHab V, 1, 6). Plays on words with similar sounds or appearances are equally common, as in the pun on the noun משל ("saying" or "taunt") and the verb משל ("to rule," 1QpHab VIII, 6–9; cf. Hab 2:6).[31] Specific terms within the lemma are also often identified with figures associated with the sect or with their opponents, using semicryptic designations, such as the Teacher of Righteousness (assumed to be the group's founder and first leader), the Wicked Priest (one or more of Israel's

---

30. For further examples, see Jonathan D. H. Norton, *Contours in the Text: Textual Variation in the Writings of Josephus, Paul and the Yahad*, LNTS 430 (London: Bloomsbury, 2011), 39–56.

31. For further detail and examples, see Maurya P. Horgan, *Pesharim: Qumran Interpretations of Biblical Books*, CBQMS 8 (Washington, DC: Catholic Biblical Association of America, 1979), 245–47.

high priests), and the Kittim (the Romans). This contemporizing and eschatological approach to exegesis is well illustrated by this example from the commentary on Habakkuk: "And what it says: 'Since you pillaged many peoples all the rest of the nations will pillage you.' Its interpretation concerns the last priests of Jerusalem, who will accumulate riches and loot from plundering the nations. However, in the last days their riches and their loot will be given into the hands of the army of the Kittim" (1QpHab IX, 2–7; cf. Hab 2:8a; cf. e.g., 1QpHab XI, 3–4).[32]

Continuous pesharim, covering large sections of a scriptural work in sequence, survive in approximately eighteen manuscripts, most of which date from the first century BCE: six on Isaiah; three on Psalms; two each on Hosea, Micah, and Zephaniah; and one on Nahum, Habakkuk, and Malachi. Several of these are extremely fragmentary, however, so that their classification is uncertain (esp. 3Q4; 4Q168; 5Q10). This form of commentary appears to have been applied particularly to the writings of the prophets, including the Psalms, as their presumed author, David, was widely regarded as a prophet in this period (e.g., 11Q5 XXVII, 11; *Ant.* 8.109–119; Acts 2:30). In addition, some of the anthologies of excerpts found among the scrolls (e.g., 4Q174; 4Q177; 11Q13) apparently represent a different kind of pesher exegesis. These are often labeled "thematic pesharim," as they bring together passages from several scriptural locations to illuminate a common topic.[33] In these texts, too, interpretations are introduced as a pesher (e.g., 4Q174 I, 19; 4Q177 I, 8; II, 9; III, 6; 11Q13 II, 12, 17), and the Scriptures are read eschatologically and as referring directly to the movement's leaders or opponents (e.g., 4Q174 I, 7–9, 10–12, 15–17; IV, 2–5; 4Q177 I, 2–3, 8–9; II, 3–7, 9–10, 11–13; III, 13–14, 16; 11Q13 II, 12, 24). Pesher is also sometimes used by scholars in a more general sense of an exegetical method, as well as a literary genre, since isolated instances of the operation are found within the Qumran literature more widely, although the technical term is not always attached to them. Pentateuchal as well as prophetic texts can be interpreted in this way. In the Damascus Document, for example, the "well" of Num 21:8 is equated with the law (CD VI, 3–11) and the "scepter" of Num 24:13 with the expected messiah (CD VII, 19–21; cf. e.g., CD IV, 13–19 [Isa 24:17]; CD VII, 14–19 [Amos 5:26–27]; CD XIX, 5–13 [Zech 13:7]; 1QS VIII, 13–15 [Isa 40:3]; 4Q177 III, 13–14 [Hos 5:8]; 4Q252 IV, 3–6 [Gen 49:3–4]; 4Q464 III, 7 [Gen 15:3]).[34]

---

32. The interpretations do not always completely ignore the original context of the scriptural lemma in applying it to a contemporary situation (e.g., 1QpHab XII, 6–9); see esp. George J. Brooke, "Reading the Plain Meaning of Scripture in the Dead Sea Scrolls," in *Jewish Ways of Reading the Bible*, ed. George J. Brooke, JSSSup 11 (Oxford: Oxford University Press, 2000), 67–90.

33. This description was coined by Jean Carmignac in his "Le document de Qumrân sur Melkisédeq," *RevQ* 7, no. 3 (1970): 343–78.

34. For further discussion of whether these passages all qualify as examples of pesher,

The choice of the introductory formula *pishro* is a very revealing indicator of the Dead Sea community's distinctive understanding of both Scripture and its exegesis. Its roots lie in the Aramaic verb פשר, which is used in the book of Daniel of the interpretation of dreams and other mysterious visions, such as the writing on the wall (Dan 2:4-7; 4:6-9, 19; 5:12-16, 26; 7:16). The related Hebrew word פתר occurs in the accounts of Joseph's ability to explain dreams in Egypt (Gen 40:8-19; 41:8-16).[35] This term implies, then, that Scripture was regarded at Qumran as something like a code, which divinely inspired interpreters like the Teacher of Righteousness and his followers were able to decipher. Since the sectaries supposed that they were living on the brink of the final eschaton, they read the entire Scriptures as a treasury of prophecies that either had been realized in their own history and experiences or were about to be enacted. Furthermore, their tradition of scriptural exegesis was seen as itself forming part of the gradual process of divine revelation: "And God told Habakkuk to write what was going to happen to the last generation, but he did not let him know the consummation of the era.... And as for what he says: 'So that may run the one who reads it.' Its interpretation concerns the Teacher of Righteousness, to whom God has made known all the mysteries of the words of his servants the prophets" (1QpHab VII, 1-5; cf. Hab 2:5-10; cf. 1QpHab VII, 8; 1QS VIII, 11-12).

There are marked affinities between the underlying hermeneutical assumptions of the pesharim and sections of the New Testament, although the term "pesher" is never used in early Christian interpretation, so the two cannot simply be equated. Nevertheless, the first followers of Jesus also read the Scriptures through an eschatological lens (e.g., Acts 1:17; 3:18-26; 1 Cor 10:11; Heb 1:1-2; cf. 1 Pet 4:7; Rev 1:3), as a source of concrete predictions of contemporary events and their own experiences (e.g., Matt 1:23; 2:15; 4:12-17; 8:14-17; John 2:14-22; 12:36-43; Acts 1:15-26; 2:22-36), and as fully comprehensible only through the insights of a uniquely authoritative interpreter, Jesus (e.g., John 2:22; 6:45-59; Rom 16:25-26; 1 Cor 4:1; Heb 1:1-2). The treatment of scriptural citations by some New Testament authors also strongly resembles the methods characteristic of the Qumran commentaries: phrases are stressed in turn, repeated, and related directly to Jesus and his followers both by Paul (Rom 10:6-10; cf. Deut 30:11-14)

---

see Devorah Dimant, "Qumran Sectarian Literature," in *Jewish Writings of the Second Temple Period: Apocrypha, Pseudepigrapha, Qumran Sectarian Writings, Philo, Josephus*, ed. Michael E. Stone, CRINT 2 (Assen: Van Gorcum; Philadelphia: Fortress, 1984), 490-505; Lim, *Pesharim*, 47-48; and George J. Brooke, "Shared Exegetical Traditions between the Scrolls and the New Testament," in Lim and Collins, *Oxford Handbook of the Dead Sea Scrolls*, 577.

35. For a fuller overview of the term's etymology and range of meaning, see Horgan, *Pesharim*, 230-59; and Shani Berrin, "Qumran Pesharim," in *Biblical Interpretation at Qumran*, ed. Matthias Henze, SDSS (Grand Rapids: Eerdmans, 2005), 110-33.

and in Hebrews (Heb 3:12–4:10; cf. Ps 95:7-11), for instance, in a way that has been characterized by Timothy Lim as "pesheresque."[36]

Beyond Pesher—Other Forms of Interpretation

Since the pesher on Habakkuk was among the first of the scrolls to be discovered, scholarly attention was initially focused largely on this novel genre. The publication over time of all the other manuscripts from the caves, though, has since underscored the breadth and diversity of ways in which the Qumran sectaries engaged with Scripture. Several attempts have been made to classify this wealth of exegetical literature on the basis of criteria such as content (distinguishing between halakic and haggadic interpretation, for instance) or the methods employed in it (whether or not it is an example of pesher exegesis or whether implicit allusions are preferred to direct citations).[37] These divisions have proved artificial, however, or else too restrictive to capture the full range of material, but a more comprehensive and helpful taxonomy has now been developed by George Brooke. He identifies five forms of scriptural reuse that are prominent across the entire Dead Sea corpus: legal, narrative, exhortatory, poetic, and prophetic interpretation.[38] The prophetic exegesis characteristic of the pesharim has been discussed above, so an outline of the four remaining categories and their potential relevance for the New Testament will follow.

Legal Interpretation

There has been a pronounced shift in scholarship over the last two decades toward a far greater appreciation of the centrality of legal interpretation within the scrolls.[39] This fundamental concern for the law and its correct application is apparent, first, in the number of texts that treat legal matters, especially purity

---

36. See Lim, *Holy Scripture*, 134.

37. For an overview of the history of research into Qumran exegetical literature, see George J. Brooke, "From Bible to Midrash: Approaches to Biblical Interpretation in the Dead Sea Scrolls by Modern Interpreters," in *Northern Lights on the Dead Sea Scrolls: Proceedings of the Nordic Qumran Network 2003–2006*, ed. Anders Klostergard Petersen et al., STDJ 80 (Leiden: Brill, 2009), 1–19.

38. See esp. Brooke, "Shared Exegetical Traditions," 571–78; cf. Brooke, "Biblical Interpretation at Qumran," in *The Bible and the Dead Sea Scrolls*, vol. 1, *Scripture and the Scrolls; The Second Princeton Symposium on the Dead Sea Scrolls*, ed. James H. Charlesworth (Waco, TX: Baylor University Press, 2006), 304–14. James VanderKam similarly identifies three main types of interpretation within the Qumran literature: legal, narrative, and prophetic; see Vanderkam and Flint, *Meaning of the Dead Sea Scrolls*, 293–308.

39. See, e.g., Lawrence H. Schiffman, "Halakah and Sectarianism in the Dead Sea Scrolls,"

regulations (e.g., 4Q274; 4Q276–278; 4Q284). The Temple Scroll (11Q19–21) is a particularly important halakic work, in which legal material from across the Scriptures is harmonized and reorganized according to its subject. Leviticus 19:28 is combined with Deut 14:1–2 (11Q19 XLVIII, 7–10), for example, because both passages forbid the Israelites from cutting or physically marking their bodies in memory of the dead.[40] 4QMMT (4Q394–399), whatever its original purpose, also sets out the sectaries' position on various legal matters about which there was internal disagreement within early Judaism, such as the conduct of sacrificial worship.[41] Second, several compositions take the form of rules (1QS; 1QSa; 1QM; cf. CD IX–XVI), indicating a determination to pattern all aspects of community life and organization after the law. Finally, in various exegetical texts, including in the pesharim, scriptural verses from narrative and prophetic contexts are read as referring to the proper observance of the Torah (e.g., 1QpHab VIII, 1 [Hab 2:4]; 4Q174 I, 11–12 [Amos 9:11]; CD VI, 3–7 [Num 21:18]).

At the same time, New Testament commentators are increasingly coming to recognize the extent to which Jesus and his first followers engaged with contemporary legal debates, often addressing the very issues that surface in the scrolls, including divorce, the Sabbath, purity rules, and the place of the temple (e.g., Mark 2:23–28; 7:1–14; 10:1–10; 12:28–34; Acts 10:9–35; 1 Cor 7:10–16). Sometimes there is even a direct correlation between the proof texts cited in the scrolls and the New Testament.[42] That early Christian use of Scripture was not always innovative is suggested, for example, by the appeal within the Damascus Document to the principle of creation ("male and female he created them," Gen 1:27) to support the prohibition on taking a second wife (CD IV, 19–V, 2; cf. Matt 19:3–9; Mark 10:2–12).[43]

---

in *The Dead Sea Scrolls in Their Historical Context*, ed. Timothy H. Lim (Edinburgh: T&T Clark, 2000), 123–42.

40. For a fuller discussion of this text, see Moshe J. Bernstein and Shlomo A. Koyfman, "The Interpretation of Biblical Law in the Dead Sea Scrolls: Forms and Methods," in Henze, *Biblical Interpretation at Qumran*, 61–87.

41. There is ongoing debate about whether or not 4QMMT is a letter to the sect's opponents in Jerusalem; see Steven D. Fraade, "To Whom It May Concern: 4QMMT and Its Addressee(s)," *RevQ* 19, no. 4 (2000): 507–26.

42. Examples of studies engaging with the significance of the Jewish law within the New Testament include Thomas Kazen, *Jesus and Purity Halakhah: Was Jesus Indifferent to Impurity?*, ConBNT 38 (Stockholm: Almqvist & Wiksell, 2002); and James G. Crossley, "Halakah and Mark 7.4 '. . . and Beds,'" *JSNT* 25, no. 4 (2003): 433–47.

43. For a detailed study of this possible parallel, see Lutz Doering, "Marriage and Creation in Mark 10 and CD 4–5," in *Echoes from the Caves: Qumran and the New Testament*, ed. Florentino García Martínez, STDJ 85 (Leiden: Brill, 2009), 133–64; cf. Serge Ruzer, *Mapping*

Narrative Interpretation

This more implicit form of exegesis involves rewriting scriptural narratives but with exegetical alterations, such as additions, omissions, and rearrangements.[44] The book of Jubilees, a large-scale supplemented retelling of Genesis and the early chapters of Exodus, for example, was evidently well received at Qumran.[45] Several previously unknown shorter compositions of this type, relating in various ways to popular figures and episodes from Israel's history, were also discovered in the caves. These include the single fragmentary copy of the Genesis Apocryphon, an expansive account of the lives of the early patriarchs Noah and Abraham, and the apocrypha of Joseph (4Q371–373) and Joshua (4Q378; 4Q379). In these works, an interpreter is able to shape the scriptural material to fit a particular theological agenda and to introduce new teaching that becomes infused with the authority of the original. The Dead Sea movement's dualistic and apocalyptic views are reinforced in the Visions of Amram (4Q543–548), for instance, through the attribution to the father of Aaron and Moses of warnings about the evil angelic watcher Melki-resha', who rules over the sons of darkness.

Stephen's speech in Acts (Acts 7:2–53; cf. 2:14–36; Heb 11:4–38) offers a New Testament parallel to this form of exegesis. Here, Israel's history is retold selectively in order to support the claim that in persecuting Jesus and his disciples, the audience are repeating a long-established pattern of rejection of God's will (Acts 7:51–53). Scriptural narratives also provide frameworks or models for the presentation of Jesus's life within the Gospels, so that he is depicted as a new Moses (e.g., Matt 2:12–20; 5:1–7:29), for example, or a second Elijah (e.g., Luke 4:24–27; 7:11–17; 9:59–62).

Exhortatory Interpretation

Exhortation to faithfulness to the law and to certain kinds of behavior is widespread in the Qumran literature and is frequently grounded in the actions of individual scriptural figures or in the larger narratives of God's dealings with

---

the New Testament: Early Christian Writings as Witness for Jewish Biblical Exegesis, JCPS 13 (Leiden: Brill, 2007), 131–47.

44. There is extensive literature discussing this genre, which is often—but rather contentiously—termed "rewritten Scripture"; see Moshe Bernstein, "'Rewritten Bible': A Generic Category Which Has Outlived Its Usefulness?," *Text* 22 (2005): 169–96; White Crawford, *Rewriting Scripture*; and Molly M. Zahn, *Genres of Rewriting in Second Temple Judaism: Scribal Transmission and Composition* (Cambridge: Cambridge University Press, 2020).

45. On Jubilees, see esp. James C. VanderKam, *Jubilees: A Commentary in Two Volumes*, Hermeneia (Minneapolis: Fortress, 2018).

Israel in history (e.g., 4Q369; 4Q375). Episodes like the flood (e.g., 4Q370) or the actions of wicked kings (e.g., 4Q398) can also be recalled to underline the dangerous consequences of sin. A section of the Damascus Document, for instance, contrasts the many Israelites who have abandoned God's commandments with Abraham, who remained obedient to them and so was reckoned as God's friend (CD II, 14–III, 12). This passage is obviously comparable to the treatment of the exemplars of faith in Hebrews (Heb 11:4-38). Scripture is likewise deployed in a paraenetic way elsewhere in the New Testament, either to advocate the imitation of scriptural characters (e.g., Jas 2:18-26; 5:7-11, 13-18) or to caution against repeating their mistakes (e.g., Matt 24:37-44; Luke 17:26-36; Heb 3:7–4:10; 12:15-17).

Poetic Interpretation

Finally, scriptural genres, motifs, and vocabulary are drawn on implicitly in order to create new sectarian compositions. This pastiche-like style is particularly common in prayers and wisdom texts and is clearly exemplified in the Hodayot (1QH; cf. 1Q28b V, 23-27; 4Q184; 4Q185), a set of hymns inspired by the scriptural Psalms but deeply influenced also by the language and thought of the prophets and wisdom literature.[46] The hymnic passages in the New Testament weave together allusions from a range of scriptural locations in a very similar way. The Song of Mary (Luke 1:46-55; cf. 1:68-79; 2:29-35), for instance, is modeled on the prayer of Hannah (1 Sam 2:1-10) but consists of a mosaic of references to other texts, including the Pentateuchal covenant narratives, the Psalms, and Isaiah.[47]

Major Exegetical Techniques

The forms of interpretation discussed above all employ a wide range of specific exegetical techniques, two of which are particularly prominent across the entire Qumran corpus and appear to underpin the reading of Scripture within the sect: segmentation or atomization and textual juxtaposition. This section will briefly highlight these methods since they are equally fundamental to other strands of early Jewish hermeneutics, as well as to the later rabbinic midrashim, so are particularly relevant for understanding the reuse of Scripture in the New Testament.

---

46. For a detailed study of the reuse of Scripture in this text, see Julie A. Hughes, *Scriptural Allusions and Exegesis in the Hodayot*, STDJ 59 (Leiden: Brill, 2006).

47. See Stephen Farris, *The Hymns of Luke's Infancy Narratives: Their Origin, Meaning and Significance*, JSNTSup 9 (Sheffield: JSOT Press, 1985); and Kenneth D. Litwak, *Echoes of Scripture in Luke-Acts: Telling the History of God's People Intertextually*, LNTS 282 (London: T&T Clark, 2005), 66-115.

Segmentation

Segmentation involves the breaking down of a scriptural lemma into smaller units that are then explained in turn. As has already been demonstrated, this atomizing approach is especially characteristic of the pesharim, in which key words or phrases from a quotation are isolated, repeated, and given a precise new meaning. A similar exegetical stress on key scriptural terms is a feature of New Testament interpretation also. In the debate between Jesus and the Sadducees about resurrection, for instance, the present tense verb ("I *am* the God of Abraham") serves as the basis for the argument that the patriarchs are still alive (Matt 22:23–33; Mark 12:18–27; Luke 20:27–40; cf. Exod 3:6), and the precise referent of the key word "Lord" in Ps 110:1 is at issue on another occasion (Matt 22:41–45; Mark 12:35–37; Luke 20:41–44). The technique of segmentation is especially visible in Hebrews, where the author's interpretation of Ps 95:7–11 depends on a specific focus on selected terms, like "rest" and "today" (Heb 3:7–4:10; cf. the stress on "old" in Heb 8:13; cf. Jer 31:31–34). It is also employed by Paul in his Letter to the Galatians, where the singular form of the noun σπέρμα ("seed" or "offspring") is decisive for his argument that Christ is the one in whom the promises made to Abraham are fulfilled (Gal 3:16; cf. Gen 12:7; 22:17–18).[48] Similar axioms about the relevance and significance of every single scriptural word therefore appear to underlie exegetical practice within both the Dead Sea community and early Christianity.

Juxtaposition of Scriptural Texts

Equally constitutive of all forms of Qumran scriptural interpretation is the association of texts on the basis of either a common motif (e.g., reasons for trusting in God in battle in 1QM X, 1–8; cf. Num 10:9; Deut 7:21; 20:2–5) or a shared word (e.g., "king" and "star" in CD VII, 9–21; cf. Num 24:17; Isa 7:17; Amos 5:25; 9:11), in a manner reminiscent of the later rabbinic technique of *gezerah shawa*.[49] This technique is the basis for the formation of extract collections like 4Q174; 4Q175; and 11Q13 and also enables the creation of pastiche-like compositions such as the Hodayot. The importance for sectarian legal interpretation, too, of bringing texts together has been illustrated above in the discussion of the Temple Scroll. An

---

48. See also the discussion of this passage in Moisés Silva, "Galatians," in *Commentary on the New Testament Use of the Old Testament*, ed. G. K. Beale and D. A. Carson (Grand Rapids: Baker Academic, 2007), 807.

49. For further discussion of the centrality of this technique within early Jewish exegesis, see Moshe J. Bernstein, "Interpretation of Scriptures," in vol. 1 of *Encyclopedia of the Dead Sea Scrolls*, ed. Lawrence H. Schiffman and James C. VanderKam (New York: Oxford University Press, 2000), 376–83.

innovative understanding of the law can sometimes be justified by this means, as in the use of Deut 5:12 and Isa 58:13 in the Damascus Document to argue that Sabbath observance requires people to refrain even from talking about work on that day (CD X, 14-19).[50]

Textual association is an equally essential component of early Christian interpretation of Scripture. Connections are forged in a variety of ways, from appeals to two supporting texts in the legal debates in the gospels (e.g., Matt 12:1-8 [1 Sam 21:1-6 and Hos 6:6]), through collections of verses sharing a common word (e.g., "stone," Luke 20:17-18; 1 Pet 2:6-8), to more developed cases of exegetical interplay between scriptural passages (e.g., Heb 2:12-13 [Ps 22:22 and Isa 8:17-18]; 3:7-4:10 [Gen 2:2 and Ps 95:7-11]; 7:1-3 [Gen 14:17-20 and Ps 110:4]). Some identical textual combinations even occur in both the scrolls and the New Testament, such as the linking of Lev 26:12 and Ezek 37:27 by Paul to ground his injunction against idolatry in the identity of believers as God's holy people (11Q19 XXIX, 7-8; cf. 2 Cor 6:16-7:1; cf. the appeal to 2 Sam 7 and Ps 2 in 4Q174 and Heb 1:5).

QUMRAN AND THE NEW TESTAMENT: COMMON INTERPRETATIVE TRADITIONS

The final area in which the Dead Sea discoveries illuminate the New Testament is in the interpretation of some specific scriptural texts. A number of common traditions of legal argument and thematic association have been highlighted above, and there are some further significant parallels, especially in wisdom and apocalyptic writings.[51] A series of beatitudes has been discovered at Qumran with intriguing correspondences to those found in Matthew, for example, including a blessing on the person of "pure heart" (4Q525 II, 1; cf. Matt 5:8), and a closing reference to a time of persecution or opposition (4Q525 II, 5-6; cf. Matt 5:10-12; Luke 7:22-23). It is also evident that the book of Revelation draws on a wider tradition of early Jewish exegesis of Isaiah and Ezekiel in its descriptions of the heavenly throne chariot (Rev 4:1-11; cf. 4Q385) and the new Jerusalem (Rev 21:1-22:5; cf. 2Q24; 4Q554; 4Q544ª; 5Q15; 11Q18).[52]

---

50. This difference—at least in theory—from rabbinic halakah, which preferred to rely only on the Pentateuch and not on supporting texts from the prophets or wisdom writings, is observed by Bernstein and Koyfman, "Interpretation of Biblical Law," 73-74.

51. For further detail on the examples presented here and others, see Brooke, "Shared Exegetical Traditions," 582-86; and VanderKam, *Dead Sea Scrolls*, 118-66.

52. See Philip S. Alexander, *The Mystical Texts*, LSTS 61 (Edinburgh: T&T Clark, 2006), 138-42; and Håkan Ulfgard, "The Songs of the Sabbath Sacrifice and the Heavenly Scene of the Book of Revelation," in Petersen, *Northern Lights on the Dead Sea Scrolls*, 251-66.

The scrolls also demonstrate a prior history of eschatological reading of some of the sections of Scripture that were applied by the early Christians to Jesus as Messiah, such as the sonship of the Davidic king (2 Sam 7:14; cf. 4Q174 I, 10–11; Heb 1:5) or the striking of the shepherd and scattering of the flock (Zech 13:7; cf. CD XIX, 7–10; Matt 26:31; Mark 14:27; John 16:32). Similarly, the messianic age is characterized as one of healing and liberation in both 4Q521 and the Gospels of Matthew and Luke through allusions to identical verses of Isaiah (Isa 35:5–6; 61:1) supplemented with nonscriptural references, such as the expectation of the raising of the dead (4Q521 II, 1–13; Matt 11:2–6; Luke 7:18–22; cf. Luke 4:18–21).

The interpretation of other texts cited in the New Testament can also now be placed more firmly in a wider exegetical context since the Qumran literature reveals how another early Jewish group applied to itself scripturally derived designations, like the people of the new covenant (Jer 31:31–34; e.g., CD III, 10–20; XIX, 33–34; cf. Luke 22:20; 2 Cor 3:6; Heb 8:7–10:10), the precious cornerstone (Isa 28:16; 1QS VIII, 7; cf. 1 Pet 2:4–6), or the voice crying in the wilderness (Isa 40:3; 1QS VIII, 13–16; cf. Matt 3:3; Mark 1:2–4; Luke 3:2–7; John 1:23).[53] The meaning of these passages was clearly subject to debate and contestation in this period, and the followers of Jesus often understood them in a very different way from the Dead Sea sectaries.[54] The "righteous [who] lives by faith" (Hab 2:4b), for instance, is related by Paul to the "faith" in Christ that makes even gentiles righteous apart from the law (Rom 1:17; Gal 3:11; cf. Heb 10:37–39), whereas for the Qumran commentators, it refers to those who remain faithful to the law and to their community's founder: "Its interpretation concerns all observing the Law in the House of Judah, whom God will free from the house of judgement on account of their toil and of their loyalty to the Teacher of Righteousness" (1QpHab VIII, 1–3). These often-contrasting readings notwithstanding, the Dead Sea discoveries highlight the extent to which both the selection and the interpretation of Scripture within the early Jesus movement is indebted to a long and broad Jewish exegetical heritage.

Conclusions

Almost every manuscript composed or preserved at Qumran is intrinsically related to the still-fluid but unquestionably authoritative collection of Israel's Scriptures. The scrolls illustrate the wide range of techniques that could be ap-

---

53. See further Ruzer, *Mapping the New Testament*, 215–37.
54. On this point, see esp. Timothy H. Lim, "Studying the Qumran Scrolls and Paul in Their Historical Context," in *The Dead Sea Scrolls as Background to Postbiblical Judaism and Early Christianity: Papers from an International Conference at St. Andrews in 2001*, ed. James R. Davila, STDJ 46 (Leiden: Brill, 2003), 135–56.

plied within late Second Temple Judaism to interpret them, together with the array of creative ways in which they could be deployed in new compositions. The early followers of Jesus utilized many of the same exegetical tools to engage with these normative texts, although often reaching different conclusions about their meaning. Above all, they shared with the members of the Qumran movement the underpinning assumptions that these Scriptures are to be read eschatologically, under the influence of an inspired teacher, and as relating directly to their own history and experiences. New Testament interpretation of Scripture is, then, fully understood only when placed in its early Jewish exegetical context, to which the Dead Sea discoveries offer a uniquely valuable witness.

Bibliography

Adams, Sean A., and Seth M. Ehorn, eds. *Composite Citations in Antiquity*. Vol. 2, *New Testament Uses*. LNTS 593. London: Bloomsbury, 2018.

Albl, Martin C. *"And Scripture Cannot Be Broken": The Form and Function of the Early Christian Testimonia Collections*. NovTSup 96. Leiden: Brill, 1999.

Alexander, Philip S. "The Bible in Qumran and Early Judaism." Pages 35–62 in *Texts in Context: Essays by Members of the Society for Old Testament Study*. Edited by A. D. H. Mayes. Oxford: Oxford University Press, 2000.

———. *The Mystical Texts*. LSTS 61. Edinburgh: T&T Clark, 2006.

Bernstein, Moshe J. "Interpretation of Scriptures." Pages 376–83 in vol. 1 of *Encyclopedia of the Dead Sea Scrolls*. Edited by Lawrence H. Schiffman and James C. VanderKam. New York: Oxford University Press, 2000.

———. "'Rewritten Bible': A Generic Category Which Has Outlived Its Usefulness?" *Text* 22 (2005): 169–96.

Bernstein, Moshe J., and Shlomo A. Koyfman. "The Interpretation of Biblical Law in the Dead Sea Scrolls: Forms and Methods." Pages 61–87 in *Biblical Interpretation at Qumran*. Edited by Matthias Henze. Grand Rapids, Eerdmans: 2005.

Berrin, Shani. "Qumran Pesharim." Pages 110–33 in *Biblical Interpretation at Qumran*. Edited by Matthias Henze. SDSS. Grand Rapids: Eerdmans, 2005.

Brooke, George J. "Biblical Interpretation at Qumran." Pages 287–319 in *The Bible and the Dead Sea Scrolls*. Vol. 1, *Scripture and the Scrolls; The Second Princeton Symposium on the Dead Sea Scrolls*. Edited by James H. Charlesworth. Waco, TX: Baylor University Press, 2006.

———. "'The Canon within the Canon,' at Qumran and in the New Testament." Pages 242–66 in *The Scrolls and the Scriptures: Qumran Fifty Years After*. Edited by Stanley E. Porter and Craig A. Evans. JSPSup 26. Sheffield: Sheffield Academic, 1997.

———. "From Bible to Midrash: Approaches to Biblical Interpretation in the Dead Sea Scrolls by Modern Interpreters." Pages 1–19 in *Northern Lights on the Dead*

Sea Scrolls: Proceedings of the Nordic Qumran Network 2003-2006. Edited by Anders Klostergard Petersen, Torleif Elgvin, Cecilia Wassén, Hanne von Weissenberg, and Mikael Winninge. STDJ 80. Leiden: Brill, 2009.

———. "The Qumran Scrolls and the Demise of the Distinction between Higher and Lower Criticism." Pages 26-42 in *New Directions in Qumran Studies: Proceedings of the Bristol Colloquium on the Dead Sea Scrolls, 8-10 September 2003*. Edited by Jonathan G. Campbell, William John Lyons, and Lloyd K. Pietersen. LSTS 52. London: T&T Clark, 2005.

———. "Reading the Plain Meaning of Scripture in the Dead Sea Scrolls." Pages 67-90 in *Jewish Ways of Reading the Bible*. Edited by George J. Brooke. JSSSup 11. Oxford: Oxford University Press, 2000.

———. "Scripture and Scriptural Tradition in Transmission: Light from the Dead Sea Scrolls." Pages 1-17 in *The Scrolls and Biblical Traditions: Proceedings of the Seventh Meeting of the IOQS in Helsinki*. Edited by George J. Brooke, Daniel K. Falk, Eibert J. C. Tigchelaar, and Molly M. Zahn. STDJ 103. Leiden: Brill, 2012.

———. "Shared Exegetical Traditions between the Scrolls and the New Testament." Pages 565-91 in *The Oxford Handbook of the Dead Sea Scrolls*. Edited by Timothy H. Lim and John J. Collins. Oxford: Oxford University Press, 2010.

Campbell, Jonathan G. *The Exegetical Texts*. Companion to the Qumran Scrolls 4. London: T&T Clark, 2004.

Cargill, Robert. *Qumran through Real Time: A Virtual Reconstruction of Qumran and the Dead Sea Scrolls*. Bible in Technology 1. Piscataway, NJ: Gorgias, 2009.

Carmignac, Jean. "Le document de Qumrân sur Melkisédeq." *RevQ* 7, no. 3 (1970): 343-78.

Crawford, Sidnie White. "Genesis in the Dead Sea Scrolls." Pages 353-73 in *The Book of Genesis: Composition, Reception and Interpretation*. Edited by Craig A. Evans, Joel N. Lohr, and David L. Petersen. VTSup 152. Leiden: Brill, 2012.

———. "Reading Deuteronomy in the Second Temple Period." Pages 127-40 in *Reading the Present in the Qumran Library: The Perception of the Contemporary by Means of Scriptural Interpretations*. Edited by Kristin De Troyer and Armin Lange. SymS 30. Atlanta: Society of Biblical Literature, 2005.

———. *Rewriting Scripture in Second Temple Times*. SDSS. Grand Rapids: Eerdmans, 2008.

Crossley, James G. "Halakah and Mark 7.4 '. . . and Beds.'" *JSNT* 25, no. 4 (2003): 433-47.

Dimant, Devorah. "Qumran Sectarian Literature." Pages 483-550 in *Jewish Writings of the Second Temple Period: Apocrypha, Pseudepigrapha, Qumran Sectarian Writings, Philo, Josephus*. Edited by Michael E. Stone. CRINT 2. Assen: Van Gorcum; Philadelphia: Fortress, 1984.

Doering, Lutz. "Marriage and Creation in Mark 10 and CD 4-5." Pages 133-64 in

Echoes from the Caves: Qumran and the New Testament. Edited by Florentino García Martínez, STDJ 85. Leiden: Brill, 2009.

Evans, Craig A. "Why Did the New Testament Writers Appeal to the Old Testament?" JSNT 38, no. 1 (2015): 36–48.

Farris, Stephen. The Hymns of Luke's Infancy Narratives: Their Origin, Meaning and Significance. JSNTSup 9. Sheffield: JSOT Press, 1985.

Fitzmyer, Joseph A. "The Use of Explicit Old Testament Quotations in Qumran Literature and in the New Testament." NTS 7, no. 4 (1961): 297–333.

Flint, Peter W. The Dead Sea Psalms Scrolls and the Book of Psalms. STDJ 17. Leiden: Brill, 1997.

———. "Psalms Scrolls." Pages 1107–10 in The Eerdmans Dictionary of Early Judaism. Edited by John J. Collins and Daniel C. Harlow. Grand Rapids: Eerdmans, 2010.

Fraade, Steven D. "To Whom It May Concern: 4QMMT and Its Addressee(s)." RevQ 19, no. 4 (2000): 507–26.

Galor, Katharina, Humbert Jean-Baptiste, and Jürgen K. Zangenberg, eds. Qumran: The Site of the Dead Sea Scrolls; Archaeological Interpretations and Debates. STDJ 57. Leiden: Brill, 2004.

Horgan, Maurya P. Pesharim: Qumran Interpretations of Biblical Books. CBQMS 8. Washington, DC: Catholic Biblical Association of America, 1979.

Hughes, Julie A. Scriptural Allusions and Exegesis in the Hodayot. STDJ 59. Leiden: Brill, 2006.

Kazen, Thomas. Jesus and Purity Halakhah: Was Jesus Indifferent to Impurity? ConBNT 38. Stockholm: Almqvist & Wiksell, 2002.

Lange, Armin. "Annotated List of the Texts from the Judaean Desert Classified by Content and Genre." Pages 115–64 in The Texts from the Judaean Desert: Indices and an Introduction to the Discoveries in the Judaean Desert Series. Edited by Emanuel Tov. DJD 39. Oxford: Clarendon, 2002.

Lim, Timothy H. "Authoritative Scriptures and the Dead Sea Scrolls." Pages 303–22 in The Oxford Handbook of the Dead Sea Scrolls. Edited by Timothy H. Lim and John J. Collins. Oxford: Oxford University Press, 2007.

———. Holy Scripture in the Qumran Commentaries and Pauline Letters. Oxford: Clarendon, 1997.

———. Pesharim. Companion to the Qumran Scrolls 3. London: Sheffield Academic, 2002.

———. "Qumran Scholarship and the Study of the Old Testament in the New." JSNT 38, no. 1 (2015): 68–80.

———. "Studying the Qumran Scrolls and Paul in Their Historical Context." Pages 135–56 in The Dead Sea Scrolls as Background to Postbiblical Judaism and Early

Christianity: Papers from an International Conference at St. Andrews in 2001. Edited by James R. Davila. STDJ 46. Leiden: Brill, 2003.

Litwak, Kenneth D. *Echoes of Scripture in Luke-Acts: Telling the History of God's People Intertextually.* LNTS 282. London: T&T Clark, 2005.

Magness, Jodi. "Qumran." Pages 1126–31 in *The Eerdmans Dictionary of Early Judaism.* Edited by John J. Collins and Daniel C. Harlow. Grand Rapids: Eerdmans, 2010.

Menken, Maarten J. J. *Matthew's Bible: The Old Testament Text of the Evangelist.* BETL 173. Leuven: Peeters, 2004.

Norton, Jonathan D. H. "Composite Quotations in the Damascus Document." Pages 92–118 in *Composite Citations in Antiquity.* Vol. 1, *Jewish, Graeco-Roman and Early Christian Uses.* Edited by Sean A. Adams and Seth M. Ehorn. LNTS 525. London: Bloomsbury, 2016.

———. *Contours in the Text: Textual Variation in the Writings of Josephus, Paul and the Yahad.* LNTS 430. London: Bloomsbury, 2011.

Phinney, D. Nathan. "Ezekiel, Book of." Pages 619–20 in *The Eerdmans Dictionary of Early Judaism.* Edited by John J. Collins and Daniel C. Harlow. Grand Rapids: Eerdmans, 2010.

Richter, Amy E. *Enoch and the Gospel of Matthew.* PTMS 183. Eugene, OR: Pickwick, 2012.

Ruzer, Serge. *Mapping the New Testament: Early Christian Writings as Witness for Jewish Biblical Exegesis.* JCPS 13. Leiden: Brill, 2007.

Schiffman, Lawrence H. "Halakah and Sectarianism in the Dead Sea Scrolls." Pages 123–42 in *The Dead Sea Scrolls in Their Historical Context.* Edited by Timothy H. Lim. Edinburgh: T&T Clark, 2000.

Silva, Moisés. "Galatians." Pages 785–812 in *Commentary on the New Testament Use of the Old Testament.* Edited by G. K. Beale and D. A. Carson. Grand Rapids: Baker Academic, 2007.

Stendahl, Krister. *The School of St. Matthew, and Its Use of the Old Testament.* ASNU 20. Lund: Gleerup, 1954.

Steyn, Gert J. *A Quest for the Assumed Septuagint Vorlage of the Explicit Quotations in Hebrews.* FRLANT 235. Göttingen: Vandenhoeck & Ruprecht, 2011.

Talmon, Shemaryahu. "Was the Book of Esther Known at Qumran?" *DSD* 2, no. 3 (1995): 249–67.

Tigchelaar, Eibert J. C. "The Dead Sea Scrolls." Pages 163–80 in *The Eerdmans Dictionary of Early Judaism.* Edited by John J. Collins and Daniel C. Harlow. Grand Rapids: Eerdmans, 2010.

———. "A Forgotten Qumran Cave 4 *Deuteronomy* Fragment (4Q38D = 4QDEUTu)." *RevQ* 23, no. 4 (2008): 525–28.

Tov, Emanuel. "The Biblical Texts from the Judaean Desert: An Overview and Analysis." Pages 139–66 in *The Bible as Book: The Hebrew Bible and the Judean Desert Discoveries*. Edited by Edward D. Herbert and Emanuel Tov. New Castle: Oak Knoll, 2002.

———. "A Categorized List of All the 'Biblical Texts' Found in the Judaean Desert." *DSD* 8, no. 1 (2001): 67–84.

———. *Textual Criticism of the Hebrew Bible*. 3rd ed. Minneapolis: Fortress, 2012.

———. "Understanding the Text of the Bible 65 Years after the Discovery of the Dead Sea Scrolls." *Open Theology* 1 (2014): 89–96.

Ulfgard, Håkan. "The Songs of the Sabbath Sacrifice and the Heavenly Scene of the Book of Revelation." Pages 251–66 in *Northern Lights on the Dead Sea Scrolls: Proceedings of the Nordic Qumran Network 2003–2006*. Edited by Anders Klostergard Petersen, Torleif Elgvin, Cecilia Wassén, Hanne von Weissenberg, and Mikael Winninge. STDJ 80. Leiden: Brill, 2009.

Ulrich, Eugene. *The Biblical Qumran Scrolls: Transcriptions and Textual Variants*. VTSup 134. Leiden: Brill, 2010.

———. *The Dead Sea Scrolls and the Origins of the Bible*. SDSS. Grand Rapids: Eerdmans, 1999.

VanderKam, James C. *The Dead Sea Scrolls and the Bible*. Grand Rapids: Eerdmans, 2012.

———. *Jubilees: A Commentary in Two Volumes*. Hermeneia. Minneapolis: Fortress, 2018.

VanderKam, James C., and Peter W. Flint. *The Meaning of the Dead Sea Scrolls: Their Significance for Understanding the Bible, Judaism, Jesus and Christianity*. San Francisco: Harper, 2002.

Vermes, Geza. "Biblical Proof-Texts in Qumran Literature." *JSS* 34, no. 2 (1989): 493–508.

Waard, Jan de. *A Comparative Study of the Old Testament Text in the Dead Sea Scrolls and in the New Testament*. STDJ 4. Leiden: Brill, 1965.

Webster, Brian. "Chronological Index of the Texts from the Judaean Desert." Pages 351–446 in *The Texts from the Judaean Desert: Indices and an Introduction to the Discoveries in the Judaean Desert Series*. Edited by Emanuel Tov. DJD 39. Oxford: Clarendon, 2002.

Zahn, Molly M. *Genres of Rewriting in Second Temple Judaism: Scribal Transmission and Composition*. Cambridge: Cambridge University Press, 2020.

6

Israel's Scriptures in Philo and the Alexandrian Jewish Tradition

MICHAEL B. COVER

In the preface to his 1828 Leipzig edition of Philo's works, the German Lutheran theologian and liberal statesman Karl Ernst Richter commended the writings of the Alexandrian Jewish exegete to novice readers with a studied enthusiasm,

> so that they might peruse Philo, before all others, with highest diligence. For in the books of this Jewish philosopher are contained not a few things which are useful to stir up and nourish a sense of piety, the love of virtue, and the study of rational philosophy. From these books, moreover, the true student of theology, if he should carefully compare them [i.e., Philo's works] with the books of the New Testament and the writings of the fathers, will learn what is the truer font of our *dogmatic theology*, as well as the reason why this latter differs in so many respects from that most simple *religion*, which we owe Jesus and his disciples.[1]

---

1. Karl Ernst Richter, *Philonis Judaei opera omnia* (Leipzig: Schwickert, 1828–1830), 1:vii: "enixe hortamur, ut Philonem praeter ceteros omnes summa diligentia manibus volutent. In huius enim philosophi Iudaei libris haud pauca continentur, quae ad pietatis sensum, virtutis amorem, et philosophiae rationalis studium excitandum et alendum magnopere conferant; ex his quoque quivis theologiae vere studiosus, si accurate eos cum libris N. T. et scriptis Patrum contulerit, discet, quis verior sit *theologiae* nostrae *dogmaticae* fons, et qua de causa haec a simplicissima illa *religione*, quam Jesu eiusque discipulis debemus, in multis differat" (emphasis original). Unless otherwise noted, all translations are by the author.

Israel's Scriptures in Philo and the Alexandrian Jewish Tradition

Although a significant number of modern scholars now consider Philo a Middle-Platonizing scriptural *exegete* rather than a Middle Platonist *philosopher*, and not all feel so great a rift between the New Testament and Nicaea, Richter's exhortation to attend to Philo "before all others" has indisputably proved fruitful.[2] Philo (ca. 20 BCE–50 CE), a rough contemporary of Jesus and Paul the apostle, has provided one of the largest witnesses to Jewish thought in the Roman diaspora. The majority of his writings are Greek scriptural commentaries, but they also include philosophical dialogues and apologetic and historiographical treatises. Like the great Nile Delta, on whose western banks Alexandria was situated, Philo's works are enriched by variegated sediments from a number of scholarly tributaries and rivulets, including the text- and literary-critical insights of the Homeric scholiasts, the Platonic commentaries in the school of Eudorus, and the rich tapestry of Hellenistic Jewish literature that preceded him. Philo's decision to anthologize and architectonically systematize the deposits of these various currents make his corpus a veritable genizah of tradition and insight, a crowning achievement of the same Alexandrian Judaism, which a little upstream chronologically had produced the Septuagint.

Richter saw Philo's usefulness in his ability to provide a point of differentiation from both the primitive Christian kerygma and later patristic writings. Most recent scholars—with a few notable exceptions—would agree that no author of a New Testament work knew Philo's writings directly. Far from diminishing his importance, this ignorance of Philo by the earliest Christians, alongside the clear linguistic and religious similarities they share with his corpus, makes the Alexandrian an indispensable bank of contemporaneous comparative material. What scholar of the New Testament can read Philo's allegorical interpretations of Abraham and Sarah without hearing echoes of Paul's epistle to the Galatians? The similarities are as striking as the unmistakable differences such that the apocalyptic exegesis of the apostle from Tarsus receives clearer delineation in juxtaposition with his bright, Platonizing Alexandrian shadow (although there is also some Platonism in Paul). Something similar might be said of Philo's illuminative relationship to a theologian like Origen. Although Origen's exegesis—unlike that of his New Testament forebears—clearly owes a debt and has a genetic relationship to Philo's allegorical commentaries, there can be no missing the fact that Origen's christological readings of the Septuagint range wider through those Scriptures and are focalized through a messianism not espoused by his

---

2. For Philo as an exegete, see Valentin Nikiprowetzky, *Le commentaire de l'Écriture chez Philon d'Alexandrie: Son caractère et sa portée; Observations philologiques*, ALGHJ 11 (Leiden: Brill, 1977). For the question of whether Philo was a "Middle Platonist," see David T. Runia, "Was Philo a Middle Platonist? A Difficult Question Revisited," *SPhiloA* 5 (1993): 112–40.

Alexandrian predecessor.[3] Due to considerations of space and scope, I will limit this chapter primarily to Richter's first "conferendum"—comparing Philo and his Alexandrian Jewish exegetical tradition with the interpretation of "Israel's Scriptures" in the New Testament.

The Interpretation of Israel's Scriptures in Alexandrian Judaism: Philo and His Predecessors

One of the achievements of Philonic scholarship, beginning at least as early as the 1970s, was to recognize that far from being an individual genius, Philo is the heir of a long Alexandrian Jewish literary and philosophical tradition.[4] To better understand Philo's place within this tradition, it is important briefly to chart a diachronic picture of the ways that the Alexandrian Jews received the Scriptures of Israel over the course of the centuries from the death of Alexander the Great to the principates of Gaius and Claudius. For the purpose of summary, these interpretive types can be grouped according to seven headings: translation, extension, rewriting, poeticization, dramatization, homily, and commentary.

Translation

The primary way, both chronologically and in terms of subsequent influence, that Alexandrian Judaism shaped the interpretation of Israel's Scriptures in the New Testament was in the translation of the Jewish Hebrew and Aramaic writings into Hellenistic Greek. This process, which according to legend was carried out at the request of Ptolemy II Philadelphus (d. 246 BCE), is retold with slightly different nuances by Aristobulus, the Letter to Aristeas, and Philo of Alexandria's *De vita Mosis*.[5] According to the Letter of Aristeas, Ptolemy wished to have a translation of the Jewish Scriptures for the great library of Alexandria (Let. Aris. 30). Seventy-two Jewish scholars gathered on the island of Pharos and worked together to complete the translation in seventy-two days—an auspicious coincidence (Let. Aris. 47–50, 307). Philo tells a similar

---

3. Michael B. Cover, "Origen," in *The Reception of Philo of Alexandria*, ed. Courtney Friesen, David Lincicum, and David Runia (Oxford: Oxford University Press, forthcoming).

4. For evidence of Hellenistic Jewish sources or traditions anthologized in Philo's writings, see Robert G. Hamerton-Kelly, "Sources and Traditions in Philo Judaeus: Prolegomena to an Analysis of His Writings," *SPhilo* 1 (1972): 3–26.

5. See Benjamin G. Wright III, "Translation as Scripture: The Septuagint in Aristeas and Philo," in *Septuagint Research: Issues and Challenges in the Study of the Greek Jewish Scriptures*, ed. Wolfgang Kraus and R. Glenn Wooden, SCS 53 (Atlanta: Society of Biblical Literature, 2006), 50.

story, with several developments. Most importantly, the Jewish scholars make independent translations only to discover that by a miracle all their versions were identical (Philo, *Mos.* 2.25–44, esp. 37). Philo adds the judgment that anyone who peruses both the Hebrew and Greek texts would find that they are so alike as to be "sisters"—even "one and the same in both contents and words" (Philo, *Mos.* 2.40). In addition to translating the Hebrew/Aramaic books that would become the Scriptures of the rabbis, Alexandrian Jews also produced translations of Hebrew works like 1 Enoch and Sirach, the former of which is cited in Jude (vv. 14–15), and the latter of which (Ben Sira) has an intriguing hermeneutical prologue on the difficulties of translation.[6] Apparently not all Jewish authors shared Philo's optimism about the Greek Scriptures (Sir, Prologue, 22–26)!

The production of the Septuagint—undoubtedly a more piecemeal and protracted process than the narratives allege—was a massive cultural achievement, and one that did more than render the Scriptures of Israel accessible to Greek readers. It also infused those Scriptures with new Greek cultural and philosophical idioms, which would open the door to novel historiographical and theological modes of interpretation, allegoresis, and theology. Its influence for Hellenophone Jewish and Christian thought is not unlike that of the 1611 Authorized Version of the Bible for the English-speaking world. As Benjamin Wright III claims, the translation of the seventy *was* in a sense Scripture.[7] Although resonances of Hebrew versions of scriptural books are sometimes detectable in the New Testament, in the majority of cases, the Septuagint *is* the Scripture of Israel cited or alluded to by early Christian authors. In addition, as Dietrich-Alex Koch has shown, Paul's citations of Septuagint Isaiah (and to a slightly lesser degree, of the Pentateuch) agree most closely, among the majuscules, with the Codex Alexandrinus—a fact bespeaking the ongoing significance of the Alexandrian textual tradition in Christian scriptural interpretation.[8]

Extension

The second way that Alexandrian Judaism shaped the reading of the Scriptures of Israel in the New Testament was by extending them. Extension is the writing of new works in a scriptural key, composed originally in Greek, that imitate

---

6. First Maccabees, 4 Ezra, and 2 Baruch are also notable members of this category.

7. Wright, "Translation as Scripture," 61.

8. Dietrich-Alex Koch, *Die Schrift als Zeuge des Evangeliums: Untersuchungen zur Verwendung und zum Verständnis der Schrift bei Paulus*, BHT 69 (Tübingen: Mohr Siebeck, 1986), 48–53. Some doubts have been raised about the Alexandrian provenance of this codex. See W. Andrew Smith, *A Study of the Gospels in Codex Alexandrinus: Codicology, Palaeography, and Scribal Hands*, NTTSD 48 (Leiden: Brill, 2014), 250.

or extend models present in the translated works. Some but not all of these would become the Scriptures of Israel from the vantage point of early Christians. Key examples include Wisdom of Solomon and 2–4 Maccabees.[9] These works echo Hebrew predecessors, such as Proverbs or 1 Maccabees, the latter of which imitates or extends (with some generic transformation) in its own right the Deuteronomistic History and the historiographical tales of Daniel. In cases of extension, the infusion of Greek cultural and philosophical idioms is deeper and more pervasive than in the translated works that enabled them.

Rewriting

Other Alexandrian Jews, rather than writing a form of continuous history with Israel's past, provided a more direct form of mediation by rewriting the scriptural books themselves.[10] Chief among these Alexandrian or Egyptian authors were the Jewish historians Demetrius (mid- to late third century BCE) and Artapanus (early to mid-second century BCE).[11] What sets these writings apart from the previous group is their conscious adoption of Greco-Roman historiographical genres and their recasting of scriptural history, with the supplementation of extrascriptural material, in new narrative modes.

Poeticization

In addition to imitating pagan prose genres, some Alexandrian Jews offered interpretations of Israel's Scriptures set in poetic meter. A number of anony-

---

9. The precise provenance of these works (other than 3 Maccabees) is sometimes disputed, and there is no reason to consider all culturally refined Greek Jewish writings as stemming from Alexandria. The case must be argued independently for each work. Second Maccabees, for instance, has some explicit Egyptian connection and concern with Egyptian celebration of Jerusalem festivities and shares a more-refined Greek historiographical style than 1 Maccabees, which was originally written in Hebrew; Wisdom of Solomon partakes in the philosophical thought world of Alexandrian Middle Platonism; 4 Maccabees in certain ways also echoes both Philo and Wisdom of Solomon, although the case is often made for an Antiochene provenance.

10. For complications arising from categorizing the Alexandrian Jewish historians within the nongeneric framework of "rewritten Bible," see Erich Gruen, *Fragmentary Jewish Historians and Biblical History*, Kieler Felix-Jacoby-Vorlesungen 3 (Göttingen: Vandenhoeck & Ruprecht, 2019), 15–16.

11. Demetrius's Alexandrian provenance seems likely on the basis of his reference to Ptolemaic dating in frag. 6, although whether he wrote under Ptolemy III or IV remains a matter of dispute (see *FHJA* 1:51 and 1:55 n. 3). Artapanus is clearly writing from Egypt, although some imagine his popular style points to an area outside Alexandria, such as Memphis (*FHJA* 1:190) or Leontopolis; see Gregory E. Sterling, *Historiography and Self-Definition: Josephos, Luke-Acts and Apologetic Historiography*, NovTSup 64 (Leiden: Brill, 1992), 169.

mous Jewish fragments imitate the meter of Homer.¹² More successful, and more widely received, was a Jewish pseudepigraphon called the *Sentences* of Ps.-Phocylides, a hexameter work of wisdom poetry modeled after the style and even the metrical proclivities of the sixth-century poet Phocylides of Miletus.¹³ This strategy of Jewish hexameter poets may be called "camouflage," as the anonymous author aimed to enculturate Jewish thought by giving it a home within the educational commonplaces of his day.¹⁴

Dramatization

Equally poetic, but more forthcoming about its Jewish origins, is the strategy of the Alexandrian tragedian Ezekiel (second century BCE), who has bequeathed to posterity the most complete example of a Hellenistic dramatic work, pagan or otherwise.¹⁵ In his *Exagoge*, Ezekiel retells the story of Moses and the exodus, interweaving traditions known both from Israel's Scriptures and the Hellenistic Jewish historians of Alexandria. Although fragmentary and difficult to reconstruct in its entirety, Ezekiel's dramatization of the Moses narrative seems to draw on elements of both historiographical and apocalyptic Judaism and represents a major development in the Jewish Alexandrian interpretation of Israel's Scriptures, setting them on the "main stage" of Hellenistic culture and competition.

Homily

Two final modes of Alexandrian Jewish interpretation of Israel's Scriptures fall into more straightforward interpretive genres insofar as they depend upon the explicit exegesis of textual lemmas. The first of these is the Jewish synagogue homily. We are fortunate to possess, in the Armenian translations of Philo's

---

12. Harold W. Attridge, "Fragments of the Pseudo-Greek Poets," OTP 2:821–30.

13. Michael Cover, "Jewish Wisdom in the Contest of Hellenistic Philosophy and Culture: Pseudo-Phocylides and Philo of Alexandria," in the *Wiley Blackwell Companion to Wisdom Literature*, ed. Samuel L. Adams and Matthew Goff, Wiley Blackwell Companions to Religion (Hoboken, NJ: Wiley Blackwell, 2020), 236. Cf. Jonathan Klawans, "The Pseudo-Jewishness of Pseudo-Phocylides," *JSP* 26, no. 3 (2017): 201–33.

14. Walter Wilson, *The Sentences of Pseudo-Phocylides*, CEJL (Berlin: de Gruyter, 2005), 6. Although the provenance of Pseudo-Phocylides is disputed, some scholars link it to Alexandria on the basis of medical terminology. The fact that the *gnomologion* of Pseudo-Homeric fragments are found in the corpus of Aristobulus (see below) confirms that poeticization was one of the Alexandrian Jewish tactics.

15. FHJA 2:311–13. An Alexandrian provenance seems likely but is still disputed. See Pierluigi Lanfranchi, *L'Exagoge d'Ezéchiel le Tragique: Introduction, texte, traduction et commentaire*, SVTP 21 (Leiden: Brill, 2006); and Howard Jacobson, *The Exagoge of Ezekiel* (Cambridge: Cambridge University Press, 1983).

works edited by Johann Baptist Aucher (1826), two early specimens of this genre, *De Jona* and *De Sampsone*.¹⁶ These are pseudonymously ascribed to Philo, but exegetical and theological differences suggest that they stem from one or more anonymous Jewish homilists. Folker Siegert has dated these homilies to first- or early second-century CE Alexandria, noting that their rhetoric and style of expression would be suitable to the diplostoon synagogue.¹⁷ Both homilies exemplify a similar interpretive pattern, which involves a renarration of the scriptural story and moral exhortation. The homily *De Jona*, which Siegert suggests might have been given on the Day of Atonement, is primarily deliberative and has as its theme "repentance" (μετάνοια). *De Sampsone*, by contrast, which purports to have been written down by a stenographer while it was being delivered extemporaneously, is partially apologetic or forensic in nature and aims to defend Samson as a paradigm of wisdom despite certain narratives that point to the contrary.¹⁸ In terms of the style and pacing of their scriptural interpretation, both homilies share similarities with the speeches/homilies of Acts and certain interpretive sections of Hebrews.

Commentary

In addition to preaching homilies, Alexandrian Jews offered scholastic interpretations of Israel's Scriptures—primarily for use in private schools, though also perhaps for public presentation—in the form of lemmatic "commentaries" (ὑπομνήματα). Although Philo offers the most extensive and elaborate examples of this mode of interpretation, he was by no means the first, having a number of predecessors and contemporary colleagues, both Jewish and non-Jewish.¹⁹

The practice of writing commentaries is a scribal and pedagogical practice that transcends any single culture or language group—as such, it may be thought

---

16. Pseudo-Philo, "*On Jonah* and *On Samson*," trans. Gohar Muradyan and Aram Topchyan, in *Outside the Bible: Ancient Jewish Writings Related to Scripture*, ed. Louis H. Feldman, James L. Kugel, and Lawrence H. Schiffman, 3 vols. (Lincoln: University of Nebraska Press, 2013) 1:750–803, 807–81; Johann Baptist Aucher, *Philonis Iudaei paralipomena armena* (Venice: Lazari, 1826).

17. Folker Siegert, *Drei hellenistisch-jüdische Predigten, Bd II, Ps.-Philon, "Über Jona," "Über Jona" (Fragment), und "Über Simson*," WUNT 1/61 (Tübingen, Mohr Siebeck, 1992), 11, 49–51. For this title for the Alexandrian "double stoa" synagogue, see y. Sukk. 55b.

18. For further analysis of the patterns of exegesis in these two homilies, see Michael Cover, *Lifting the Veil: 2 Corinthians 3:7–18 in Light of Jewish Homiletic and Commentary Traditions*, BZNW 210 (Berlin: de Gruyter, 2015), 195–212.

19. On Philo's anonymous colleagues, see, e.g., David Hay, "Philo's References to Other Allegorists," *SPhilo* 6 (1979–1980): 41–75; Maren Niehoff, *Jewish Exegesis and Homeric Scholarship in Alexandria* (Cambridge: Cambridge University Press, 2011).

of as a near-universal human literary phenomenon.[20] Although only fragments remain, textual commentaries in the Greek tradition likely begin with explanations of Homer, the culture's pedagogically most central author.[21] Commentaries often take up issues as simple as parsing archaic forms or dealing with narrative inconsistencies[22]—a special preoccupation of the Hellenistic Alexandrian scholiasts such as Aristarchus and Zenodotus, who emended or athetized texts they found in error.[23] As early as the sixth century BCE, however, in the writings of Theagenes of Rhegium, we find evidence that scholars offered allegorical readings of venerated authors in an attempt to reveal deeper scientific or theological meanings embedded within mythological expressions (D-K frag. 2).[24] In Alexandrian Jewish tradition, this strategy was adopted by Philo's predecessor, Aristobulus "the Peripatetic" (second century BCE), who suggested that Moses was composing mythological allegory when he used phrases such as "the right hand of God."[25] Later philosophical commentators in the school of the Alexandrian Platonist Eudorus would make significant generic and theological advances on this method, adducing secondary lemmas from the same "inspired" author (Plato) in order to resolve questions of doctrinal unity across various treatises.[26]

Philo

Philo was the heir to this rich and variegated commentary tradition in Roman Alexandria. He composed three different commentaries or commentary series on the Pentateuch: the *Quaestiones et Solutiones in Genesin et Exodum*, the Allegorical Commentary, and the Exposition of the Law.[27] Although all three series are fairly designated as species of commentary, the latter two represent creative

---

20. See, e.g., the practice of literary commentary by Akkadian scribes as charted by Uri Gabbay, "Akkadian Commentaries from Ancient Mesopotamia and Their Relation to Early Hebrew Exegesis," *DSD* 19, no. 3 (2012): 267–312.

21. Francesca Schironi, "Greek Commentaries," *DSD* 19, no. 3 (2012): 405–6. The oldest extant commentary on a Greek text is the Derveni papyrus, which contains a copy of a fifth-century BCE Macedonian commentary on an Orphic hexameter poem.

22. So, e.g., P.Oxy. 8.1086, ii 51–54, on Homer, *Il.* 2.784; for text, translation, and analysis, see Schironi, "Greek Commentaries," 414.

23. Niehoff, *Jewish Exegesis and Homeric Scholarship in Alexandria*, 112–29.

24. Schironi, "Greek Commentaries," 433.

25. Clement, *Strom.* 1.15.4. According to Holladay, *FHJA* 3:73, this designation is "inappropriate" *stricto sensu*, but correctly indicates the general philosophical orientation of Aristobulus's exegesis. The quotation is from Aristobulus, frag. 2 (*FHJA* 3:138–39).

26. For the *Anonymous Theaetetus Commentary* and its interpretive patterns, see Cover, *Lifting the Veil*, 134–44.

27. See James R. Royse, "The Works of Philo," in *The Cambridge Companion to Philo*, ed.

redeployments of this form, which blend it with other genres, including homily and biography.

Quaestiones et Solutiones in Genesin et Exodum

Philo's first series—although the relative sequence remains disputed—is ostensibly the least creative from a generic point of view. As Homeric commentators before him had done with Greece's first poet, Philo asks in a series of "questions" (ζητήματα) about textual lemmas culled in sequence from LXX Genesis and Exodus.[28] He then offers a series of "answers" (λύσεις) to these, proceeding first literally and then (sometimes) allegorically. The *Sitz im Leben* for this commentary is often taken to be a private Jewish philosophical school run by Philo, perhaps in a house or apartment financed by his wealthy brother Alexander the Alabarch.[29] The series, as it survives in its fullest (Armenian) version, covers texts of Gen 2:4–28:9 and portions of Exod 12:2–28:34.[30]

The Allegorical Commentary

Philo's second commentary series, which has long been hailed as his *magnum opus* on account of its exegetical and theological richness, is known as the Allegorical Commentary. It consists of eighteen extant treatises, each of which offers a sequential lemmatic commentary on one or more primary texts from Genesis.[31] Although the treatises in this series best match the classical commentary form, there is no denying that Philo has made significant transformations to the genre by giving each treatise at least a titular thematic focus. From this perspective, the treatises of the Allegorical Commentary blend elements of commentary, philosophical treatise, and homily.[32]

Adam Kamesar, Cambridge Companions to Philosophy (Cambridge: Cambridge University Press, 2009), 32–64.

28. For Homeric commentators, see Schironi, "Greek Commentaries," 419.

29. For the hypothesis of Philo's private school, see Gregory Sterling, "'The School of Sacred Laws': The Social Setting of Philo's Treatises," *VC* 53, no. 2 (1999): 148–64.

30. As the Greek fragments suggest, the series likely covered more pentateuchal material than is extant in Armenian. See Françoise Petit, *Quaestiones in Genesim et in Exodum: Fragmenta Graeca*, PAPM 33 (Paris: Cerf, 1978). For a new fragment of Philo, potentially stemming from the *QE*, which interprets Exod 3:3, see Michael B. Cover, "A New Fragment of Philo's *Quaestiones in Exodum* in Origen's Newly Discovered Homilies on the Psalms? A Preliminary Note," *SPhiloA* 30 (2018): 15–29.

31. Some of these, like *De gigantibus* and *Quod Deus sit immutabilis* are half-treatises, and several other treatises, such as *De testamentis*, are lost. See Royse, "Works of Philo," 38–45.

32. Philo refers to the unitive subject of a treatise or series of treatises as a πραγματεία (see

Perhaps the greatest advance of the Allegorical Commentary, from a generic point of view, is Philo's development of the interpretation of "secondary lemmas." A "lemma" is a snippet of text cited by a commentator prior to the transcription of his or her explanatory notes. A "secondary lemma" is a text drawn from beyond the immediate context of the primary lemma being commented upon. The secondary lemma may be taken from a different work by the same author or from another writing deemed authoritative by the commentator. In more rudimentary Alexandrian philosophical commentaries, like the *Anonymous Theaetetus Commentary*, secondary lemmas are introduced to solve problems presented by the primary lemma but generally receive no sustained development of their own. Philo's innovation is to allow the interpretation of these secondary lemmas to develop in their own right—often in such a way that they entail a longer and richer allegoresis than Philo's main text. The concatenation of such secondary-level interpretations and their hierarchical arrangement in relationship to Philo's interpretations of primary texts means that the Allegorical Commentary offers not merely a compilation or anthology of allegorical exegeses but a new architectonic allegory of the soul, which is greater than the sum of its individual, traditional parts.[33]

The Exposition of the Law

Philo's third series—and, by the nearly undisputed consensus of modern scholars, his last—differs from the previous two in terms of its generic blend and intended audience. Philo penned this series after his failed leadership efforts in the embassy to the Roman emperor Gaius Caligula, during which a delegation of Alexandrian Jews sailed to Rome and pleaded for imperial protection from local Egyptian violence and for a reestablishment of their special legal status and other privileges.[34] Having met with ridicule and misunderstanding from the imperial entourage, as well as from the rival Alexandrian delegation, Philo conceived during and after his months in Rome the need for a more exoteric kind of commentary, one that conformed more readily to the expectations of the Roman literary public and was less difficult in its philosophical and exegetical content.[35]

Contempl. 1; *Congr.* 147). Other authors (such as Polybius, *Hist.* 1.1.4) will use the term to refer to a systematic or historical treatise.

33. For Philo as a maker of allegory, as well as an author of allegoresis, see Mikolaj Domaradzki, "The Value and Variety of Allegory: A Glance at Philo's *De gigantibus*," SPhiloA 31 (2019): 13–28.

34. Philo, *Spec.* 3.1, offers a brief autobiographical glimpse into the pressures of the embassy and its resulting literary productions.

35. For Philo's attention to Roman historiographical conventions in his defense speech

The Exposition of the Law was his resulting commentary. It begins with the two-volume *De vita Mosis*—a philosophical biography in the manner of Porphyry's *Vita Plotini*, aimed at introducing the author and his teachings.[36] Rather than working in a linear fashion, the "Life" (βίος) follows the pattern of what would later be called by Fredrich Leo the "Suetonian type" of biography, focusing on Moses's exemplarity in a number of areas: king, philosopher, lawgiver, prophet, and priest (*Mos.* 2.1).[37] The Exposition itself, by contrast, proceeds sequentially through the Pentateuch, offering Philo's most panoptic vision of the whole Mosaic achievement: beginning with creation (*De opificio mundi*), Philo then offers commentary on the patriarchal "living laws" (*De Abrahamo, De Iosepho*) and at last turns to the written laws of the Pentateuch (*De decalogo, De specialibus legibus* 1–4, and *De praemiis et poenis*).

Focusing specifically on the patriarchal section of the Exposition of the Law—the one which has most direct parallel in the Allegorical Commentary—one can see that these treatises do not belong to the same species of commentary: they do not cite lemmas, followed by interpretive comments. As a result, these patriarchal treatises are sometimes thought to belong to the nongeneric category of "rewritten Bible."[38] Other scholars, including Maren Niehoff and Sean Adams, have recently argued that these texts are Greco-Roman philosophical biographies.[39] This would surprise, given that Philo's *De vita Mosis*, which clearly belongs to this genre, follows a different pattern. The patriarchal narratives of the Exposition, moreover, form an integral unity with the legal exegesis that is to follow (Philo, *Abr.* 1–6). And clenching the matter, the structure of *De Abrahamo* follows a clear interchange of rewritten narrative and allegorical exposition, in the manner of a commentary with a paraphrastic lemma.[40] We are, of course,

---

before Gaius, see Michael Cover, "Reconceptualizing Conquest: Colonial Narratives and Philo's Roman Accuser in the *Hypothetica*," *SPhiloA* 22 (2010): 183–207.

36. See Gregory E. Sterling, "Philo of Alexandria's *Life of Moses*: An Introduction to the Exposition of the Law," *SPhiloA* 30 (2018): 34, for the argument that the *Vita* introduces just the Exposition, not the entire corpus.

37. See Adela Yarbro Collins, *Is Mark's Gospel a Life of Jesus? The Question of Genre*, Père Marquette Lecture in Theology (Milwaukee: Marquette University Press, 1990), 26: "The Suetonian type of biography [according Fredrich Leo's 1901 study] . . . combines a tale in chronological order with a systematic characterization of an individual and his achievements." See Friedrich Leo, *Die griechisch-römische Biographie nach ihrer literarischen Form* (Leipzig: Teubner, 1901).

38. Peder Borgen, "Philo: An Interpreter of the Laws of Moses," in *Reading Philo: A Handbook to Philo of Alexandria*, ed. Torrey Seland (Grand Rapids: Eerdmans, 2014), 76.

39. Maren R. Niehoff, *Philo of Alexandria: An Intellectual Biography*, ABRL (New Haven: Yale University Press, 2018), 109; Sean A. Adams, *Greek Genres and Jewish Authors: Negotiating Literary Culture in the Greco-Roman Era* (Waco, TX: Baylor University Press, 2020).

40. See Cover, *Lifting the Veil*, 121–22.

hindered in our assessment of the nature of these treatises on account of our missing the critical lives of Isaac and Jacob. But *De Abrahamo*'s programmatic role in the sequence suggests that Philo's patriarchal treatises in the Exposition are better classified not as philosophical biography or serial biography but as biographical commentary.

Convergences: Israel's Scriptures in Philo and the New Testament

It is perhaps misleading to speak in a synonymous way of Philo and the New Testament authors interpreting the "Scriptures of Israel," as though each were focused on the same body of texts or had identical understandings of scriptural inspiration. Most authors of the New Testament share a relatively equal and balanced interest in all three emergent divisions of Tanakh—the Law of Moses, the Prophets/Psalms, and the Writings.[41] Pleromatic scriptural proof is established by concatenating texts from two or three *different divisions of Scripture*, as it is in the thematic pesharim or the Amoraic *petiḥot*.[42] This practice of interpreting the Scriptures suggests a relatively democratic, pneumatological understanding of inspiration, such as that articulated in 2 Tim 3:16: that "*all* scripture is God-breathed and useful for teaching, for reproof, for correction, for education in righteousness, so that God's human being may be perfect, equipped for every good work."

Philo is similarly interested in the moral perfection of "God's human being" (*Mut.* 24, 125); his Scriptures, however, are most especially the Scriptures of Moses and his "school" (among which are included many of the psalms).[43] Other authors from the prophets and the writings, such as Jeremiah and Hosea, have to be introduced to Philo's scriptural constellations by way of claims to inspiration.[44] The "Law" (νόμος) of Moses constitutes for Philo the Scripture within the Scriptures, the center point of the concentric circles of Scripture, which is surrounded by the prophets of Israel and then, in a further satellite orbit, the writings of the divine Plato and Homer, which occupy a third order of ambiguous authority.[45] Pleromatic

---

41. For these divisions at least *in nuce*, see Sir Prologue 1:1; Sir 38:24–39:3; Luke 24:27, 44.

42. So Gal 4:21–31 (Gen 21; Isa 54); Heb 7:1–21 (Gen 14; Ps 109 [110] LXX).

43. For the psalmist as a student of Moses, see Philo, *Conf.* 39; *Plant.* 39; *Somn.* 2.245.

44. For Moses and Jeremiah as representatives of different prophetic schools, see Philo, *Cher.* 49. For a similar presentation of Hosea, see Philo, *Mut.* 139.

45. For Plato and Homer in Philo's works, see Gert Roskam, "Nutritious Milk from Hagar's School: Philo's Reception of Homer," *SPhiloA* 29 (2017): 1–32; Michael Cover, "Philo's Poetics of Association: The Use of Secondary and Tertiary Lemmas in *On the Cherubim*" (paper presented at the Society of Biblical Literature Annual Meeting, Boston, MA, November 19, 2017): "Recognizing the formal interchangeability of biblical and classical texts in Philo's com-

scriptural proof for Philo is established principally by drawing texts from two or three *different Mosaic books*—for example, from Genesis and Leviticus—interpreting Moses by Moses.[46] Secondary or tertiary proofs from the Prophets and Writings, while not absent, are comparatively rare. By way of overgeneralization, one might say that if the interpretive principles of the New Testament authors are democratic, pneumatological, and focused on all three divisions of Tanakh, Philo's exegesis is hierarchical, logocentric, and (in keeping with the Alexandrian critical preference) devoted to the genius of a single author: Moses and his school.

For Philo, the "Scriptures of Israel" are especially and most properly so in a subjective sense: While they remain the books authored by Moses for the particular people of Israel, they are also the Scriptures as read by the Israel soul—a more universal subject. The Israel soul, according to Philo's etymological allegoresis, is the one who "sees God." The interpretation of the Scriptures, especially in the Allegorical Commentary, involves a vision of the unified purpose of Moses and of the Logos, who inspires and unifies his works. That this unity involves reading the Torah through Platonizing spectacles and with an eye to the psychological allegory is thus in complete keeping both with Philo's attention to the "Scripture within the Scriptures" and his historical preference for the Mosaic school.

A comprehensive picture of the uses of Philo in New Testament scholarship goes beyond the scope of this chapter. There are too many contributions to this field to map. What follows here instead is a series of examples illustrating the importance of Philo for the interpretation of Israel's *Scriptures* in the New Testament, with a special focus on formal and thematic dimensions of exegetical theology. These can be divided into two categories: narrative and legal exegesis.

Narrative Exegesis

Paul

Philo's exegesis of Israel's Scriptures has proved illuminating as a comparandum in the field of Pauline studies. In addition to his being a close contemporary of Philo from the Jewish Greek diaspora with an openness to the Roman world, Paul offers some of the longest and most developed allegorical exegeses of a wide variety of pentateuchal texts in the New Testament—albeit in epistolary form. This suggests that Paul, in the course of his advanced Jewish education,

---

mentaries does not mean that they possess an equal degree of theological authority or innate literary congruence with pentateuchal and other scriptural texts."

46. See, e.g., Philo, *Mut.* 2–10, which concatenates Gen 17:1; Exod 20; and Exod 33 to develop an account of theological vision.

had acquired some familiarity with both the themes and forms of the Hellenistic pentateuchal commentary tradition. Whether this included Homeric and Platonist commentaries or was restricted to the commentaries known in his Jewish circles in Tarsus, Antioch, and Jerusalem remains a matter of debate.

In looking for examples from Paul's epistolary exegesis that appear "Philonic," one might intuitively reach first for the famous allegory of the sons of Sarah and Hagar in Gal 4:21–31.[47] Despite the common use of the verb "speak allegorically" (ἀλληγορεῖσθαι), which is *not* the Alexandrian's favored terminology for Moses's process of composition, Philo's allegoresis of these two mothers in *De congress eruditionis gratia* as the "wisdom" and "the preliminary studies," respectively—with its humanistic and pedagogical focus—is so far removed from Paul's apocalyptic and dualistic division of earthly and heavenly churches as cosmic polarities as to suggest either the apostle's ignorance of Philonic tradition or his reimagination of it in a new polemical context.[48] Thinking along these lines, Jürgen Becker suggests that the Galatians allegory stems from Antiochene (rather than Alexandrian) tradition.[49] Paul's exegetical amplification of his interpretation of Gen 21:9–10 with Isa 54:1 LXX follows the more typical pattern of common Judaism, seeking pleromatic scriptural proof in the synergy of law and prophets.[50] Elements of Paul's Galatians' allegory that find some analogy in Philo include (1) the interpretation of a paraphrastic primary lemma (as is usual in the Exposition of the Law and sometimes in the Allegorical Commentary), rather than a direct quotation; (2) the introduction of a longer secondary lemma from the Prophets to amplify a relatively shorter primary lemma from the Pentateuch; and, on the thematic plane, (3) the propaedeutic role of what Hagar symbolizes—be it the preliminary studies in Philo's case (*Congr.* 11–12) or the full Jewish law for gentile believers in Paul's (Gal 3:24).

The influence of Philonic interpretive tradition (though not necessarily of Philo himself) is felt more readily in Paul's Corinthian correspondence.[51] It is not

---

47. See Cover, *Lifting the Veil*, 31–48.

48. Michael Cover, "'Now and Above; Then and Now' (Gal 4:21–31): Platonizing and Apocalyptic Polarities in Paul's Eschatology," in *Galatians and Christian Theology: Justification, the Gospel, and Ethics in Paul's Letter*, ed. Mark W. Elliott et al. (Grand Rapids: Baker Academic, 2014), 220–29.

49. Jürgen Becker, "Der Brief an die Galater," in *Die Briefe an die Galater, Epheser und Kolosser*, ed. Jürgen Becker and Ulrich Luz, NTD 8.1 (Göttingen: Vandenhoeck & Ruprecht, 1998), 70–74.

50. For the special connection between Moses and Isaiah in Philo's thought, see QG 2.43. On Philo's non-pentateuchal citations more generally, see Naomi G. Cohen, *Philo's Scriptures: Citations from the Prophets and Writings; Evidence for a Haftarah Cycle in Second Temple Judaism*, JSJSup 123 (Leiden: Brill, 2007).

51. *Pace* Gudrun Holtz, "Von Alexandrien nach Jerusalem: Überlegungen zur Vermittlung philonisch-alexandrinischer Tradition an Paulus," *ZNW* 105, no. 2 (2014): 228–63.

surprising that as Paul's geographical horizon expanded westward, his exegetical perspective broadened as well.⁵² In the Corinthian correspondence, we find evidence that Paul worked with (and against) the Alexandrian exegete-apostle Apollos (1 Cor 1:12). In light of such connections, it is most likely that Paul encountered the Alexandrian pentateuchal commentary tradition most directly not in Jerusalem, nor in Antioch or Tarsus, but during his numerous stays in Corinth and through his apostolic dialogue with Apollos, the "man skillful with words" (ἀνὴρ λόγιος, Acts 18:24) from late antiquity's "Second City."

The *locus classicus* illustrating the probable influence of Alexandrian commentary tradition on the Corinthian correspondence comes in 1 Cor 15, particularly 1 Cor 15:45–49. Here, in a discussion of the resurrection body, Paul makes a complex argument about the first and last (or the first and second) Adam in three movements:

> ⁴⁵So also it has been written: *The first human being Adam became a living soul* [Gen 2:7c], while the last Adam became *a life-making spirit* [cf. Gen 2:7b]. ⁴⁶The spiritual does not come first, but the psychic; then the spiritual [comes after]. ⁴⁷The first human being is from the earth, of clay [Gen 2:7]; the second human being is from heaven [cf. Gen 1:27]. ⁴⁸What sort [of character] the human being of clay possesses, such is also [the character of] people of clay; but what sort [of character] the heavenly human being possesses, such is also [the character of] heavenly people. ⁴⁹And just as we bore the image [Gen 1:27] of the [human being] of clay, we will also bear the image of the heavenly [human being].

Space does not allow for a full explication of this fascinating passage.⁵³ Here, we shall have to content ourselves with a description of Paul's exegetical pattern. At the beginning of this passage Paul paraphrases and interprets Gen 2:7. He then amplifies this interpretation by introducing a two-fold interpretation of Gen 1:27. In formal terms, we may say that in 1 Cor 15:45–46 Paul cites and interprets a

---

52. Cover, *Lifting the Veil*, 25. This comment is not meant to entail a judgment on the relative chronology of Paul's letters, esp. that Paul wrote Galatians before 1 Corinthians. Although I find this traditional sequence plausible, Paul could clearly contextualize his rhetoric and exegesis to fit the customs of his addressees and opponents. Thus, even if he had some familiarity with the Alexandrian Jewish commentary tradition when he wrote Galatians, he might have chosen to engage or reproduce other exegetical modes when addressing the crisis in the Galatian churches in hopes that these would be more effective than exegesis from abroad.

53. See Gregory E. Sterling, "'Wisdom among the Perfect': Creation Traditions in Alexandrian Judaism and Corinthian Christianity," *NovT* 37 (1995): 355–84.

Israel's Scriptures in Philo and the Alexandrian Jewish Tradition

primary pentateuchal lemma (Gen 2:7), which he then clarifies and expands in 1 Cor 15:47–49 by relating (without lemmatic citation) the interpretation of a secondary pentateuchal text (Gen 1:27). Paul's transition between Gen 2:7 and Gen 1:27 is signaled by his shift from the apocalyptic polarity "first and last Adam" (1 Cor 15:45), which focuses on Gen 2:7, to the protological, philosophical polarity "first and second human being" (1 Cor 15:47), which puts Gen 2:7 and Gen 1:27 in creative interpretive dialogue.

The three-fold exegetical pattern seen in the Pauline pericope echoes that found in the first extant treatise of Philo's Allegorical Commentary (*Leg.* 1.31):

And God molded the human being, taking clay from the earth, and he breathed into his face breath of life, and the human being became a living soul [Gen 2:7]. There are two [δίττα] kinds of human beings: the first [ὁ μέν] is a heavenly human being [Gen 1:27], the second [ὁ δέ] is earthly [Gen 2:7]. *The first [human being] is heavenly, because it has come to be according to the image of God* [Gen 1:27] *and has no share in perishable and entirely earthlike substance, whereas the earthly [human being] was established out of disconnected matter, which [Moses] calls "clay."*

These first few lines of the Allegorical Commentary mirror very closely, in both form and content, Paul's argumentation in 1 Cor 15:45, 47–49.[54] Philo first, like Paul, (1) cites Gen 2:7. He then suggests that (2) Gen 1:27 and Gen 2:7 speak of two different types of human being, the heavenly and the earthly (modified by "clay" language).[55] The secondary lemma, Gen 1:27, is not cited but alluded to, as in 1 Corinthians. Philo concludes, like Paul, by arguing (3) that the difference between the heavenly and earthly human beings has to do with the former being created "according to the image" of God (Gen 1:27). The structural similarities are set out in table 6.1:

---

54. First Corinthians 15:46 belongs to a different interpretive tradition, which sees a two-human schema within Gen 2:7. On this, see Sterling, "Wisdom among the Perfect," 359.

55. Berndt Schaller ("Adam und Christus bei Paulus; Oder, über Brauch und Fehlbrauch von Philo in der neutestamentlichen Forschung," in *Philo und das Neue Testament: Wechselseitige Wahrnehmungen; 1. Internationales Symposium zum Corpus Judaeo-Hellenisticum, 1.–4. Mai 2003, Eisenach/Jena*, ed. Roland Deines and Karl-Wilhelm Niebuhr, WUNT 1/172 [Tübingen: Mohr Siebeck, 2004], 143–53) points out that Philo does not speak of a "first and second Adam" in *Leg.* 1.31; neither, however, does Paul in 1 Cor 14:47–49. Both pericopes are concerned with protological-anthropological traditions; in Paul's texts, this common tradition is further coordinated with the eschatological Adam tradition (1 Cor 15:45b–46), which is absent from Philo.

Table 6.1. Two Human Beings Commentary Tradition in Paul and Philo

	Paul	Philo
1. Citation of Gen 2:7 (primary lemma)	1 Cor 15:45	*Leg.* 1.31a
2. Two humans tradition, with allusion to Gen 1:27 (secondary lemma)	1 Cor 15:47	*Leg.* 1.31b
3. Identification of the heavenly human being with the image of God (Gen 1:27)	1 Cor 15:48–49	*Leg.* 1.31c

Paul and Philo are thus clearly echoing the same commentary tradition. Of course, Paul's understanding of the first and second human beings differs from Philo's. For Philo, the first human is heavenly; the second is earthly and clay-like. One begins as the first, heavenly type (Gen 1:27), perfect according to the image (in one's mind); upon becoming embodied and embroiled with somatic needs and emotions, one becomes more earth-like, the human being of clay (Gen 2:7). For Paul, by contrast, the first human being—Adam—is from earth and subject to sin and death (Gen 2:7); the second human being—Christ, or the "second Adam"—is the heavenly human being (Gen 1:27). Whereas Philo's first-second sequence follows the sequence of Genesis, as well as the Platonist, protological order of soul before body, Paul's interpretation radically inverts this scriptural order, turning the "second human being" of Scripture (Gen 2:7) into the "first human being" in accordance with the apostle's "apocalyptic start-up software."[56] One only becomes conformed to the "image of God" (Gen 1:27)—now construed as the "second human being"—through participation in the resurrection of the last Adam, Christ, who helps the human being return to his or her full human potential.

Unlike the rival Philonic and Pauline interpretations of Sarah and Hagar, which seem to bear only tangential relationship to one another, the first and second human being sequence in *Leg.* 1.31 and 1 Cor 15:45, 47–49 are too closely related, in this author's view, not to stem from a common tradition. In 1 Cor 15, Paul intentionally engages and reinterprets a well-known Jewish "two human beings" exegetical tradition, which was apparently in circulation in Corinth. Perhaps, like Philo, Apollos at some point wondered whether in the final state, bodies were necessary at all. Becoming again like the first man in the image of God would not require this. No doubt, the exegetical sophistication of this interpretation of Israel's Scriptures could have appealed to well-educated Jews and Godfearers in Corinth. Paul, too, apparently found the exegesis helpful,

---

56. I take this phrase from Margaret M. Mitchell, *Paul, the Corinthians, and the Birth of Christian Hermeneutics* (Cambridge: Cambridge University Press, 2010), 11.

especially insofar as it relates the image of God (Gen 1:27) to Jesus, the man from heaven and the unique son of God. Where Paul disagrees with Philo is in his eschatology: to become fashioned after the image of God, the first human being, does not mean to become bodiless but to attain a real and spiritual body (1 Cor 15:44), one that no longer cleaves to the clay of earth but to the image of God within.

Philo's Allegorical Commentary sheds light on another important exegetical passage in the Corinthian correspondence, which is one of the most complicated in the New Testament: 2 Cor 3:7–18. Here, Paul's context and his pattern of exegesis are different. Writing again to the Corinthians in what may be a sequence of two, five, or even more letters, Paul addresses a number of new challenges to the community. We may differentiate Paul's interpretation of Israel's Scriptures in these two passages as follows. In 1 Cor 15:45, 47–49, Paul echoes very closely, in both pattern and content, the scriptural interpretation of *Leg.* 1.31. This involves the interpretation of both a primary (Gen 2:7) and a secondary (Gen 1:27) lemma. In 2 Cor 3:7–18, by contrast, Paul offers an extended interpretation of a single pentateuchal lemma, Exod 34:29–35, moving sequentially through the verses:

> ⁷Now if the ministry of death, chiseled in letters on stone tablets [cf. Exod 34:1, 4], came in glory [cf. Exod 34:10], so that the people of Israel could not gaze at Moses's face because of the glory of his face [Exod 34:30], a glory now set aside, ⁸how much more will the ministry of the Spirit come in glory? ⁹For if there was glory in the ministry of condemnation, much more does the ministry of justification abound in glory! ¹⁰Indeed, it is *has* not *been glorified—that which has been glorified* [Exod 34:29–30]⁵⁷—because of the greater glory; ¹¹for if what was set aside came through glory, much more has the permanent come in glory!
>
> ¹²Since, then, we have such a hope, we act with great boldness, ¹³not like Moses, who put a veil over his face to keep the people of Israel from gazing at the end of the glory that was being set aside [Exod 34:33]. ¹⁴But their minds were hardened. Indeed, to this very day, when they hear the reading of the old covenant, that same veil is still there, since only in Christ is it set aside. ¹⁵Indeed, to this very day whenever Moses is read, a veil lies over their minds; ¹⁶but *when one turns to the Lord, the veil is removed* [Exod 34:34]. ¹⁷Now the Lord is the Spirit, and where the Spirit of the Lord is, there is freedom. ¹⁸And all of us, with unveiled faces, seeing the glory of the Lord as though reflected

---

57. Paul's phrase, οὐ δεδόξασται τὸ δεδοξασμένον, cleverly cites and subverts the identical perfect verb δεδόξασται ἡ ὄψις (Exod 34:29) and perfect participle δεδοξασμένη ἡ ὄψις (Exod 34:30) in scriptural sequence.

in a mirror, are being transformed into the same image from one degree of glory to another; for this comes from the Lord, the Spirit. (NRSV, modified in 2 Cor 3:10)

In this passage, although no citation formula is used, Paul offers a sequential commentary on Exod 34, focusing principally on Exod 34:29–30; 34:33; and 34:34. In each of the two halves of the exegesis (2 Cor 3:7–11; 3:12–18), Paul comments first on a paraphrase of a verse (2 Cor 3:7; 3:13) and then proceeds to an allegorical reading of a particular text of Exodus via modified citation (2 Cor 3:10; 3:16). The pattern of exegesis is thus both rhetorically organized and traditionally rich. Particularly in 2 Cor 3:16, Paul echoes (and transforms) an allegorical tradition that reads Moses as a type of the soul, which upon entering the tabernacle (moving within the veil), beholds the glory of the Lord and receives thereby spiritual transformation.

In length and depth of the interpretation, this Pauline passage looks most like one of Philo's extended exegeses of a secondary lemma in the Allegorical Commentary.[58] Philo provides a very intriguing parallel, in both theme and structure, in *Mut.* 134–136. There, the Alexandrian presents a sequential exegesis of Gen 38:15, 25–26 as a secondary lemma, amplifying his interpretation of Sarah's divine pregnancy in Gen 17:16. Intriguingly, Exod 3:6 // 34:33–35 is invoked as a tertiary lemma:

> §134. Tamar also became pregnant from divine seeds. And although she did not see the One who sowed them—for at that time, it is written that *her face was veiled* [Gen 38:15] just as Moses [was], when he turned aside, intent on seeing God [Exod 3:6; cf. Exod 34:33–35]—she nevertheless inspected the symbols and tokens [left behind]. And judging within herself that a mortal does not *give* these, she cried out, *To Whomsoever these things belong, by Him I have conceived* [Gen 38:25a]. §135. Whose is the *ring*, the proof, the seal of the universe, the archetypal form/idea, by which all things, being without form and symbolized without quality, were impressed [into matter]? Whose also is the *little necklace*, Fate, the necessary sequence and analogy, which possesses the uninterrupted chain of all things? And whose is the *staff*, the mainstay, the unshaken, the unturned, establishment of mind, temperance, and instruction? The scepter, the kingdom, whose [are these]? Do they not belong to God alone?" [Gen 38:25b] §136. Therefore the thankful manner, that is, Judah, delighted by her steadfast and godly [reasoning], speaks frankly and

---

58. For another formal parallel, see Philo, *Deus* 87–90; Cover, *Lifting the Veil*, 126–28.

boldly: *She is justified, for I gave her to no mortal* [Gen 38:26], thinking that it would be impious to pollute divine things with profane ones.

Philo's exegesis of Tamar's interpretation of the signs given by her divine husband creatively misreads the text such that God rather than Judah is the true father of her psychic offspring. The pattern of exegesis and allegorical themes are quite similar to those found in 2 Cor 3:7–18. Of course, one cannot miss the critical difference: whereas Philo's Tamar behaves "as Moses" (ὡς Μωϋσῆς), reading the scriptural signs and symbols while wearing the veil (2 Cor 3:14!), Paul insists that his ideal Christian reader needs to remove the veil and read the Scriptures of Israel "*not* as Moses" (οὐ καθάπερ Μωϋσῆς). This difference only highlights the sense that Paul is drawing on Alexandrian commentary tradition in his Corinthian correspondence and redeploying it in competition with other Christian exegetes and apostles. As Richter argued, Philonic exegesis proves illuminating for the New Testament exegete both in its similarities and its differences from the early Christian writings.

John and Hebrews

Space does not permit an exhaustive survey of all the ways in which Philo's exegesis in the Allegorical Commentary might illuminate the New Testament and early Christian writings. Continuing with the theme of sequential exegesis and the association of multiple lemmatic proofs, I want to turn briefly to two other *loci classici* in the demonstration of Philo's value for the New Testament scholar: John 6 and Heb 3–4.[59] Each of these texts involves an extended sequential exegesis of Israel's Scriptures similar to that found elsewhere in the Philonic corpus. In John 6:31–58, Jesus sequentially interprets, word for word, a modified citation of Ps 77:24 LXX; in Heb 3:7–4:13, the anonymous author offers a sequential interpretation of Ps 94:7–11 LXX. Both texts are homiletic in nature and offer an allegorical exposition of a psalm.

Several observations from a Philonic perspective are warranted. First, the appearance of homiletic patterns of exegesis in Philo's commentaries suggests that the latter incorporated popular material despite their scholastic *Sitz im Leben*. Like the later Amoraic collections, which belong both to the synagogue and the *beth midrash*, Philo's "commentaries" (ὑπομνήματα) straddle several different

---

59. For John 6 and Philonic exegesis, see Peder Borgen, *Bread from Heaven: An Exegetical Study of the Concept of Manna in the Gospel of John and the Writings of Philo*, NovTSup 10 (Leiden: Brill, 1965).

genres and were a product of both the Alexandrian "prayer houses" (προσευχαί) and the private Jewish philosophical school.

Second, both John 6 and Heb 3–4 offer a reading of a psalm that corresponds to a pentateuchal text: in John's case, Exod 16:4, 15; and in the case of Hebrews, Num 12:7 (Heb 3:5).[60] Without speciously positing form-critical identity, one can still note that the coordination of pentateuchal and non-pentateuchal texts in the New Testament writings gains something by comparison with Philo's linking of primary and secondary lemmas in his Allegorical Commentary—a process that I have elsewhere called Philo's "poetics of association."[61] As has been well-established since the exegetical turn in Philonic scholarship in the 1970s, Philo links scriptural texts—either two Mosaic texts or texts from different authors or divisions—by one of two kinds of affinity: the lexical (verbal) or the thematic.[62] In several seminal studies of the Allegorical Commentary, David Runia has offered extended analyses of Philo's exegetical poetics with special attention to Philo's "modes of transition."

Articulated in the language of Runia's analysis, the coordination of Exod 16:4, 15 and Ps 77:24 LXX in John 6 is achieved through both lexical and thematic connections. In addition to narrating the same story, exact or near lexical equivalents for "bread," "heaven," "gave," and "to eat" (ἄρτος/ἄρτοι, οὐρανοῦ, ἔδωκεν, φαγεῖν) are present in each text. The poetics associating Num 12:7 and Ps 94:7–11 LXX in Hebrews, to the contrary, are less readily apparent. There is no direct lexical equivalence between the lemmas as quoted by the homilist. In addition, the shift of thematic focus from Moses to the wilderness people might also suggest that the anonymous homilist has shifted rhetorical, scriptural, and thematic focus.

How then does the anonymous homilist of Hebrews coordinate Num 12 and Ps 94 LXX? In this case, attending to Philo's lexical and thematic modes of transition in the Allegorical Commentary provides a way through the seeming impasse. First, one must recall that Ps 94:7–11 LXX retells a narrative of Israel's rebellion found also in Num 14:1–25. Whereas in Heb 3:1–6 the homilist comments on Moses's faithful tabernacle service in Num 12, in Heb 3:7–4 (where Ps 94 LXX is cited) he turns to Israel's grumbling in the wilderness—a theme also found in Num 14. Beneath the surface, there is a sequential narrative principle at work. Although nowhere stated by the homilist, Ps 94:11 LXX (Heb 3:11) and Num 14:23

60. The psalm citation is inflected with a phrase from Exod 16:4, ἐκ τοῦ οὐρανοῦ. Other elements of Exod 16:4, 15 appear throughout the interpretation of the psalm.

61. Cover, "Poetics of Association."

62. For the exegetical turn in Philonic scholarship, see Nikiprowetzky, *Le commentaire de l'Écriture*; David T. Runia, "The Structure of Philo's Allegorical Treatises: A Review of Two Recent Studies and Some Additional Comments," *VC* 38, no. 3 (1984): 209–56; Runia, "Further Observations on the Structure of Philo's Allegorical Treatises," *VC* 41, no. 2 (1987): 105–38.

also share a lexeme, "I swore" (ὤμοσα, albeit the nature of God's oath is different in these passages). A fuller study of Heb 3–4 in light of Philo's interpretation of texts of Numbers would thus seem warranted.

Second, thematic correspondences between Num 12:7 and Ps 94:11 LXX emerge when one considers the latter (Ps 94 LXX) in terms of the priestly reading of the former (Num 12) by the author of Hebrews. In Heb 3:1–6, Moses's faithful service in the "house" is understood by the homilist to suggest his priesthood—foreshadowing his assertion of the christological priesthood (Heb 4:14) and his references to Melchizedek (Heb 7) and the heavenly tabernacle (Heb 9–10) later in the homily. Viewed from this angle, the verb of "entrance" in Ps 94:11b LXX (Heb 3:11; 4:3: εἰσελεύσονται) acquires a new priestly overtone, which resonates with the metaphor of priestly entrance later in other portions of the homily (see, e.g., Heb 4:14, 16; 10:5, 22). Again, more research into the allegorical and tropological import of the homilist's rhetoric of "entrance" in light of the Philonic corpus is a desideratum.[63]

Legal Exegesis

Philo contributes not only to our understanding of New Testament exegesis of Israel's narrative Scriptures but also of Israel's legal Scriptures. Due to limitations of space, one brief example will have to suffice. In Rom 13:9, we find a curious citation of the tenth commandment: "you shall not desire" (οὐκ ἐπιθυμήσεις). The negative verb is followed in LXX Exodus and Deuteronomy by a string of direct objects: "your neighbor's wife, your neighbor's house, your neighbor's field," and more. Especially in Greek, however, it is possible to simplify this command to read "you shall not desire," thereby bringing it into closer parallelism with the other four two-word commands of the second table of the Decalogue.

Is this modification on Paul's part simply stylistic or for the sake of abbreviation? Possibly; however, as Hans Svebakken has recently demonstrated, the practice of shortening the tenth commandment might also be done out of philosophical consideration, giving to the originally casuistic law a universal, philosophical meaning.[64] In many Hellenistic philosophical schools, "desire" (ἐπιθυμία) is accounted one of the principal passions of the soul, which interrupts it acting rightly. Philo himself cites and interprets the same shortened version of the tenth commandment in *Spec.* 4.78—a point that suggests that Paul

---

63. On the theme of entrance in Philo and Hebrews, see Scott D. Mackie, *Eschatology and Exhortation in the Epistle to the Hebrews*, WUNT 2.223 (Tübingen: Mohr Siebeck, 2007).

64. Hans Svebakken, *Philo of Alexandria's Exposition on the Tenth Commandment*, SPhiloM 6 (Atlanta: Society of Biblical Literature, 2012).

knows this exegetical tradition and adopts it in his philosophical development of a Jewish "flesh" hamartiology, interweaving it with the negative passion of "desire" (Rom 13:14) drawn from philosophical ethics.[65]

These examples of light shed by Philo on the interpretation of Israel's narrative and legal Scriptures in the New Testament only scratch the surface of the Alexandrian's enormous potential to assist the contemporary New Testament exegete. It is hoped that the reader will have found sufficient material here to whet her interest in Philo as a useful tool for understanding Israel's Scriptures and their reception in early Christianity.

Bibliography

Adams, Sean A. *Greek Genres and Jewish Authors: Negotiating Literary Culture in the Greco-Roman Era*. Waco, TX: Baylor University Press, 2020.
Attridge, Harold W. "Fragments of Pseudo-Greek Poets." *OTP* 2:821–30.
Aucher, Johann Baptist. *Philonis Iudaei paralipomena armena*. Venice: Lazari, 1826.
Barclay, John M. G. "Paul and Philo on Circumcision: Romans 2.25–9 in Social and Cultural Context." *NTS* 44, no. 4 (1998): 536–56.
Becker, Jürgen. "Der Brief an die Galater." Pages 9–103 in *Die Briefe an die Galater, Epheser und Kolosser*. Edited by Jürgen Becker and Ulrich Luz. NTD 8.1. Göttingen: Vandenhoeck & Ruprecht, 1998.
Borgen, Peder. *Bread from Heaven: An Exegetical Study of the Concept of Manna in the Gospel of John and the Writings of Philo*. NovTSup 10. Leiden: Brill, 1965.
———. "Philo: An Interpreter of the Laws of Moses." Pages 75–101 in *Reading Philo: A Handbook to Philo of Alexandria*. Edited by Torrey Seland. Grand Rapids: Eerdmans, 2014.
Cohen, Naomi G. *Philo's Scriptures: Citations from the Prophets and Writings; Evidence for a Haftarah Cycle in Second Temple Judaism*. JSJSup 123. Leiden: Brill, 2007.
Collins, Adela Yarbro. *Is Mark's Gospel a Life of Jesus? The Question of Genre*. Père Marquette Lecture in Theology. Milwaukee: Marquette University Press, 1990.
Collins, John J. "Love of Neighbor in Hellenistic-Era Judaism." *SPhiloA* 32 (2020): 97–111.
Cover, Michael. "Jewish Wisdom in the Contest of Hellenistic Philosophy and Cul-

---

65. Numerous other contributions to legal exegesis in the New Testament, which draw upon Philo, have been made. For two additional topics, see John J. Collins, "Love of Neighbor in Hellenistic-Era Judaism," *SPhiloA* 32 (2020): 97–111; John M. G. Barclay, "Paul and Philo on Circumcision: Romans 2.25–9 in Social and Cultural Context," *NTS* 44 (1998): 536–56.

ture: Pseudo-Phocylides and Philo of Alexandria." Pages 229–47 in the *Wiley Blackwell Companion to Wisdom Literature*. Edited by Samuel L. Adams and Matthew Goff. Wiley Blackwell Companions to Religion. Hoboken, NJ: Wiley Blackwell, 2020.

———. *Lifting the Veil: 2 Corinthians 3:7–18 in Light of Jewish Homiletic and Commentary Traditions*. BZNW 210. Berlin: de Gruyter, 2015.

———. "A New Fragment of Philo's *Quaestiones in Exodum* in Origen's Newly Discovered Homilies on the Psalms? A Preliminary Note." *SPhiloA* 30 (2018): 15–29.

———. "'Now and Above; Then and Now' (Gal 4:21–31): Platonizing and Apocalyptic Polarities in Paul's Eschatology." Pages 220–29 in *Galatians and Christian Theology: Justification, the Gospel, and Ethics in Paul's Letter*. Edited by Mark W. Elliott, Scott J. Hafemann, N. T. Wright, and John Frederick. Grand Rapids: Baker Academic, 2014.

———. "Origen of Alexandria." In *The Reception of Philo of Alexandria*. Edited by Courtney Friesen, David Lincicum, and David Runia. Oxford: Oxford University Press, forthcoming.

———. "Philo's Poetics of Association: The Use of Secondary and Tertiary Lemmas in *On the Cherubim*." Paper presented at the Society of Biblical Literature Annual Meeting, Boston, MA, November 19, 2017.

———. "Reconceptualizing Conquest: Colonial Narratives and Philo's Roman Accuser in the *Hypothetica*." *SPhiloA* 22 (2010): 183–207.

Domaradzki, Mikolaj. "The Value and Variety of Allegory: A Glance at Philo's *De gigantibus*." *SPhiloA* 31 (2019): 13–28.

Gabbay, Uri. "Akkadian Commentaries from Ancient Mesopotamia and Their Relation to Early Hebrew Exegesis." *DSD* 19, no. 3 (2012): 267–312.

Gruen, Erich. *Fragmentary Jewish Historians and Biblical History*. Kieler Felix-Jacoby-Vorlesungen 3. Göttingen: Vandenhoeck & Ruprecht, 2019.

Hamerton-Kelly, Robert G. "Sources and Traditions in Philo Judaeus: Prolegomena to an Analysis of His Writings." *SPhilo* 1 (1972): 3–26.

Hay, David. "Philo's References to Other Allegorists." *SPhilo* 6 (1979–1980): 41–75.

Holtz, Gudrun. "Von Alexandrien nach Jerusalem: Überlegungen zur Vermittlung philonisch-alexandrinischer Tradition an Paulus." *ZNW* 105, no. 2 (2014): 228–63.

Jacobson, Howard. *The Exagoge of Ezekiel*. Cambridge: Cambridge University Press, 1983.

Klawans, Jonathan. "The Pseudo-Jewishness of Pseudo-Phocylides." *JSP* 26, no. 3 (2017): 201–33.

Koch, Dietrich-Alex. *Die Schrift als Zeuge des Evangeliums: Untersuchungen zur Verwendung und zum Verständnis der Schrift bei Paulus*. BHT 69. Tübingen: Mohr Siebeck, 1986.

Lanfranchi, Pierluigi. *L'Exagoge d'Ezéchiel le Tragique: Introduction, texte, traduction et commentaire*. SVTP 21. Leiden: Brill, 2006.

Leo, Friedrich. *Die griechisch-römische Biographie nach ihrer literarischen Form*. Leipzig: Teubner, 1901.

Mackie, Scott D. *Eschatology and Exhortation in the Epistle to the Hebrews*. WUNT 2.223. Tübingen: Mohr Siebeck, 2007.

Mitchell, Margaret M. *Paul, the Corinthians, and the Birth of Christian Hermeneutics*. Cambridge: Cambridge University Press, 2010.

Niehoff, Maren R. *Jewish Exegesis and Homeric Scholarship in Alexandria*. Cambridge: Cambridge University Press, 2011.

———. *Philo of Alexandria: An Intellectual Biography*. ABRL. New Haven: Yale University Press, 2018.

Nikiprowetzky, Valentin. *Le commentaire de l'Écriture chez Philon d'Alexandrie: Son caractère et sa portée; Observations philologiques*. ALGHJ 11. Leiden: Brill, 1977.

Petit, Françoise. *Quaestiones in Genesim et in Exodum: Fragmenta Graeca*. PAPM 33. Paris: du Cerf, 1978.

Pseudo-Philo. "*On Jonah* and *On Samson*." Pages 1:750–881 in *Outside the Bible: Ancient Jewish Writings Related to Scripture*. Edited by Louis H. Feldman, James L. Kugel, and Lawrence H. Schiffman. Translated by Gohar Muradyan and Aram Topchyan. 3 vols. Lincoln: University of Nebraska Press, 2013.

Richter, Karl Ernst. *Philonis Judaei opera omnia*. 8 vols. Leipzig: Schwickert, 1828–1830.

Roskam, Gert. "Nutritious Milk from Hagar's School: Philo's Reception of Homer." *SPhiloA* 29 (2017): 1–32.

Royse, James R. "The Works of Philo." Pages 32–64 in *The Cambridge Companion to Philo*. Edited by Adam Kamesar. Cambridge Companions to Philosophy. Cambridge: Cambridge University Press, 2009.

Runia, David T. "Further Observations on the Structure of Philo's Allegorical Treatises." *VC* 41, no. 2 (1987): 105–38.

———. "The Structure of Philo's Allegorical Treatises: A Review of Two Recent Studies and Some Additional Comments." *VC* 38, no. 3 (1984): 209–56.

———. "Was Philo a Middle Platonist? A Difficult Question Revisited." *SPhiloA* 5 (1993): 112–40.

Schaller, Berndt. "Adam und Christus bei Paulus; Oder, über Brauch und Fehlbrauch von Philo in der neutestamentlichen Forschung." Pages 143–53 in *Philo und das Neue Testament: Wechselseitige Wahrnehmungen; 1. Internationales Symposium zum Corpus Judaeo-Hellenisticum, 1.–4. Mai 2003, Eisenach/Jena*. Edited by Roland Deines and Karl-Wilhelm Niebuhr. WUNT 1/172. Tübingen: Mohr Siebeck, 2004.

Schironi, Francesca. "Greek Commentaries." *DSD* 19, no. 3 (2012): 399–441.

Siegert, Folker. *Drei hellenistisch-jüdische Predigten: Bd. II, Ps.-Philon, "Über Jona," "Über Jona" (Fragment), und "Über Simson."* WUNT 1/61. Tübingen: Mohr Siebeck, 1992.

Smith, W. Andrew. *A Study of the Gospels in Codex Alexandrinus: Codicology, Palaeography, and Scribal Hands.* NTTSD 48. Leiden: Brill, 2014.

Sterling, Gregory E. *Historiography and Self-Definition: Josephos, Luke-Acts and Apologetic Historiography.* NovTSup 64. Leiden: Brill, 1992.

———. "Philo of Alexandria's *Life of Moses*: An Introduction to the Exposition of the Law." *SPhiloA* 30 (2018): 31–46.

———. "'The School of Sacred Laws': The Social Setting of Philo's Treatises." *VC* 53, no. 2 (1999): 148–64.

———. "'Wisdom among the Perfect': Creation Traditions in Alexandrian Judaism and Corinthian Christianity." *NovT* 37, no. 4 (1995): 355–84.

Svebakken, *Philo of Alexandria's Exposition on the Tenth Commandment.* SPhiloM 6. Atlanta: Society of Biblical Literature, 2012.

Wilson, Walter. *The Sentences of Pseudo-Phocylides.* CEJL. Berlin: de Gruyter, 2005.

Wright, Benjamin G., III. "Translation as Scripture: The Septuagint in Aristeas and Philo." Pages 47–61 in *Septuagint Research: Issues and Challenges in the Study of the Greek Jewish Scriptures.* Edited by Wolfgang Kraus and R. Glenn Wooden. SCS 53. Atlanta: Society of Biblical Literature, 2006.

7

Israel's Scriptures in Josephus

MICHAEL AVIOZ

Flavius Josephus is generally known as a historian, less as an exegete.[1] However, recent years have seen a paradigm shift, and a growing number of scholars now view Josephus as an interpreter of Scripture.[2]

When dealing with the relationship between the New Testament and Josephus, scholars have usually turned to historical study.[3] Dean Pinter compared Paul and Josephus's view of the Romans, exploring "how Paul and Josephus perceive, interpret and respond to divine and imperial power."[4] George Carras

---

1. Unless otherwise stated, translations of Josephus follow the Brill Josephus Project: Steve Mason, ed., Flavius Josephus: Translation and Commentary (Leiden: Brill, 2000–). On Josephus as a historian, see Tessa Rajak, *Josephus: The Historian and His Society*, 2nd ed. (London: Duckworth, 2002); Martin Goodman, *Judaism in the Roman World: Collected Essays*, AGJU 66 (Leiden: Brill, 2007); and Martin Friis, *Image and Imitation: Josephus' Antiquities 1–11 and Greco-Roman Historiography*, WUNT 2/472 (Tübingen: Mohr Siebeck, 2018).

2. Louis H. Feldman, *Josephus's Interpretation of the Bible* (Berkeley: University of California Press, 1998); Sarah J. K. Pearce, "Josephus as Interpreter of Biblical Law: The Representation of the High Court of Deut. 17:8–12 according to *Jewish Antiquities* 4.218," *JJS* 46, no. 1 (1998): 30–42; James L. Kugel, *Traditions of the Bible: A Guide to the Bible as It Was at the Start of the Common Era* (Cambridge: Harvard University Press, 1998); Herbert W. Basser, "Josephus as Exegete," *JAOS* 107, no. 1 (1987): 21–30; Michael Avioz, *Josephus' Interpretation of the Books of Samuel*, LSTS 86 (London: T&T Clark, 2015).

3. Steve Mason, "The Writings of Josephus: Their Significance for New Testament Study," in *Handbook for the Study of the Historical Jesus*, vol. 2, *The Study of Jesus*, ed. Tom Holmén and Stanley E. Porter, 4 vols. (Leiden: Brill, 2011), 1639–86; Joseph Sievers and Gaia Lembi, eds., *Josephus and Jewish History in Flavian Rome and Beyond*, JSJSup 104 (Leiden: Brill, 2005).

4. Pinter, "Divine and Imperial Power: A Comparative Analysis of Paul and Josephus" (PhD diss., Durham University, 2009), 22.

pointed out several similarities between Paul and Josephus.[5] He analyzed *Ag. Ap.* 2.190–219, which offers a summary of the law and may be among the "earliest and oldest theological précis compiled by a contemporary of the NT writers."[6] He tried to show shared Jewish ideas in both.

Timothy Lim writes that "Josephus was neither a philosopher nor an exegete like Philo."[7] How, then, should we define him? Lim defines him as a "historian of the Jewish people." However, as I will argue below, Josephus is not only a historian. Josephus not only "systematizes and reassembles passages" but also deals with difficulties inherent in the biblical laws and stories and tries to make the biblical record clearer.[8]

According to James Kugel, ancient interpreters "assumed that the Bible was fundamentally a cryptic text: that is, when it said A, often it might really mean B."[9] The biblical exegete's tasks are, among others, to translate the biblical text into a language familiar to its readers; to explain and clarify complicated halakic issues (issues of Jewish law), to reconcile contradictions in the Hebrew Bible, to address problematic ethical issues that arise in the biblical narrative, and to emphasize the relevance of the Hebrew Bible for the contemporary reader.[10] In the following, I will emphasize the benefits of Josephan scholarship for the study of the New Testament, focusing on his biblical interpretation.

Methods

Like many ancient interpreters, Josephus used additions, omissions, rearrangements, harmonizations, conflation, unification, homogenization, and paraphrase

---

5. Carras, "Paul, Josephus and Judaism: The Shared Judaism of Paul and Josephus" (PhD diss., University of Oxford, 1989); Carras, "Jewish Sensibilities and the Search for the Jewish Paul—The Lukan Paul Viewed through Josephan Judaism: Interplay with *Apion* 2:190–219," in *The Early Reception of Paul the Second Temple Jew: Text, Narrative and Reception History*, ed. Isaac W. Oliver, Gabriele Boccaccini, and J. Barton Scott, LSTS 92 (London: T&T Clark, 2018), 167–78.

6. Geza Vermes, "A Summary of the Law by Flavius Josephus," *NovT* 23, no. 4 (1982): 301 n. 50.

7. Lim, "Deuteronomy in the Judaism of the Second Temple Period," in *Deuteronomy in the New Testament*, ed. Maarten J. J. Menken and Steve Moyise, LNTS 358 (London: T&T Clark, 2007), 6–26.

8. Quotation from Lim, "Deuteronomy," 26.

9. Kugel, *How to Read the Bible: A Guide to Scripture, Then and Now* (New York: Free Press, 2007), 14.

10. James L. Kugel, "Early Interpretation: The Common Background of Late Forms of Biblical Exegesis," in *Early Biblical Interpretation*, ed. James L. Kugel and Rowan A. Greer, LEC 3 (Philadelphia: Westminster, 1986), 9–106.

when dealing with Israel's Scripture.[11] Interpreters attempted to solve difficulties, clarify ambiguities, and fill in gaps. What Howard Jacobson writes about Pseudo-Philo can be easily applied to Josephus as well:

> L. A. B. [Liber Antiquitatum Biblicarum], like much other midrash, is interpretive, is problem-solving, and is literarily creative. It fills gaps, clarifies ambiguities, resolves difficulties and contradictions, provides connections, responds to the readers' curiosity, expands or subtracts for tendentious purposes, makes changes to enhance the reputation of a biblical hero or worsen that of a villain, and answers questions that are implicitly raised by the Bible's narrative.[12]

In my recent book on Josephus, I have tried to highlight Josephus's exegetical traits in his rewriting of the narratives in the books of Samuel.[13] Josephus mediates between the Hebrew Bible and his readers, and he might be viewed as a cornerstone of ancient biblical interpretation. Josephus makes efforts to connect the narratives in a reasonable way. He compares characters and is aware of analogies within the book itself. He fills gaps and expands upon brief descriptions. He provides details, motives, and messages. He explains difficult words, settles contradictions, and identifies biblical sites.

Motives

What were Josephus's motives when adding, omitting, or changing Israel's Scripture? While Louis Feldman pointed mainly to the apologetic motives, other scholars have argued that his main motive was interpretation.[14] It is not always easy to dis-

---

11. John Screnock, "Translation and Rewriting in the Genesis Apocryphon," in *Reading the Bible in Ancient Traditions and Modern Editions: Studies in Memory of Peter W. Flint*, ed. Andrew B. Perrin, Kyung S. Baek, and Daniel K. Falk, EJL 47 (Atlanta: SBL Press, 2017), 453–81; Amram Tropper, *Rewriting Ancient Jewish History: The History of the Jews in Roman Times and the New Historical Method*, Routledge Studies in Ancient History 10 (London: Routledge, 2016), 69, writes that Josephus "interpreted, conflated, rearranged, omitted, invented, fleshed out, condensed, embellished, simplified, dramatized, romanticized, harmonized, Hellenized, Romanized, eroticized, psychologized, naturalized, philosophized, apologized, whitewashed, moralized, theologized, systematized, exaggerated, enhanced, and more."

12. Howard Jacobson, "Biblical interpretation in Pseudo-Philo's 'Liber Antiquitatum Biblicarum,'" in *A Companion to Biblical Interpretation in Early Judaism*, ed. Matthias Henze (Grand Rapids: Eerdmans, 2012), 180.

13. Avioz, *Josephus' Interpretation of the Books of Samuel*.

14. See in Feldman's many publications noted in n. 46 below.

tinguish between these two, apology and interpretation, and one should be mindful of the following considerations: Are there real exegetical difficulties in the biblical record? Are there additional, similar rewritten narratives where Josephus adds or omits certain elements? Can we locate similar changes in the biblical text in other Second Temple sources? When Josephus deviates from the biblical record, does it mean that he had a different *Vorlage* at his disposal? Let us start with omissions.

Omissions

Omissions may be the result of several factors. Shaye Cohen writes:

> Josephus freely omits whatever he does not need: long lists of Semitic names, incidents embarrassing (Reuben and Bilhah; Judah and Tamar; the golden calf; the complaint of Aaron and Miriam against Moses' wife) or difficult (the mention of Goliath in 2 Samuel 21.19) . . . and miracles. Some passages he just forgot (the pestilence of the Ten Plagues [Exod. 7–12]; the reign of Tola [Judg. 10:1–2]). He condenses technical material (the laws and rituals of the Pentateuch) and uninteresting details (the complications of the apportionment of Canaan among the tribes).[15]

However, Cohen adds that Josephus is not consistent since he does not always omit this kind of material. We may distinguish between intentional and unintentional omissions. Intentional and unintentional may be related to the following:

1. Textual reasons: Josephus may preserve a divergent version, different from the MT, the LXX, or both. Regarding the height of David's brothers, for example, 1 Sam 16:7 MT has "But the Lord said to Samuel: 'Do not look on his appearance or on the height of his stature.'" The LXX follows the MT: "Do not look on his appearance or on the posture of his size." However, Josephus follows neither the MT or the LXX. His version alters both texts: "Seeing that none of these were inferior to the eldest in appearance" (*Ant.* 6.162).
2. Apologetic concerns: the most famous omission by Josephus is the golden calf (Exod 32), a narrative that presents Aaron in a problematic light and portrays Israel as idolatrous, right after the Decalogue and the theophany at Sinai.[16] Also relevant here is the omission of circumcision from several places.

---

15. Cohen, *Josephus in Galilee and Rome: His* Vita *and Development as a Historian*, Columbia Studies in the Classical Tradition 8 (Leiden: Brill, 1979), 37.

16. See Gregory E. Sterling, "When Silence Is Golden: The Omission of the Golden Calf

Here we may include personal, national, theological, and ideological reasons for omissions.[17]

3. Complexity: the source may be too obscure and complicated for Josephus, and omitting it may solve the problem. An example is the David and Goliath story in 1 Sam 17.
4. Irrelevance: Josephus did not find the whole Bible relevant for his aim of reconstructing the history of Israel. Josephus himself states in *Ant.* 9.242: "This prophet prophesied many other things about Ninue in addition to these that I did not think it necessary to speak of, but have passed over in order not to seem tiresome to my readers." He also avoids mentioning lists of names, as in *Ant.* 2.176; 7.369; 11.152 (on Ezra). Finally, Josephus omits direct speeches and the poetic literature of Israel's Scripture: Gen 49; Exod 15; Deut 34; Judg 5; 1 Sam 2; 2 Sam 22; a large part of the Latter Prophets, Ecclesiastes, Proverbs, and Psalms. Probably, this genre contained very difficult language and did not contain historiography.

Generally speaking, Jason von Ehrenkrook advises the following with regard to omitting the prohibition of images by Pseudo-Phocylides, which applies to Josephus as well: "In the end, it is difficult to know what to make of this omission, and we should be cautious not to read too much into the silence . . . any attempt to answer such questions enters the realm of speculation."[18]

Additions

As is the case with omissions, the matter of additions is complex, too. There are additions in Josephus's retelling that may be motivated by apologetic concerns, while other additions have various motives.

When Josephus adds that Abraham meant to sacrifice his son on Mount Moriah in Jerusalem (Gen 22; *Ant.* 1.224), this is an exegetical addition trying to fill in a gap in the biblical narrative where one cannot tell where exactly Abraham was going. This exegetical tradition is shared by other Second Temple sources as well.[19]

Story in Josephus," in *Golden Calf Traditions in Early Judaism, Christianity, and Islam*, ed. Eric Mason and Edmondo F. Lupieri, TBN 23 (Leiden: Brill, 2019), 87–96.

17. See Paul Spilsbury, "*Contra Apionem* and *Antiquitates Judaicae*: Points of Contact," in *Josephus' "Contra Apionem": Studies in Its Character and Context with a Latin Concordance to the Portion Missing in Greek*, ed. Louis H. Feldman and John R. Levison, AGJU 34 (Leiden: Brill, 1996), 348–68.

18. Jason von Ehrenkrook, *Sculpting Idolatry in Flavian Rome: (An)Iconic Rhetoric in the Writings of Flavius Josephus*, EJL 33 (Atlanta: Society of Biblical Literature, 2011), 83.

19. See Feldman, *Josephus's Interpretation*, 257; Michael Avioz, "Abraham in Josephus' Writ-

Josephus's exegetical additions may be intended to explain difficult words as well.

1. Josephus translates the name "Calebite" (1 Sam 25:3) as "man who conformed his manner of life to Cynic practice" (*Ant.* 6.296). Josephus does not entertain the possibility that he may be a descendant of Caleb, but his exegesis is possible as well.
2. Elijah tells Israel that they are פסחים על שתי הסעפים (1 Kgs 18:21).[20] It is a difficult and disputed phrase. Josephus explained that Elijah told them that they are "divided in mind and opinions" (*Ant.* 8.337). Josephus had no dictionary that could help him understand this difficult phrase, but he handled it with his exegetical intuition.
3. Josephus guessed correctly the meaning of a *hapax legomenon*, explaining the word ילקוט in 1 Sam 17:40 as a "pouch" (*Ant.* 6.189).

Josephus's extrabiblical additions are intended to solve ambiguities in the biblical text: Why was Lot saved out of Sodom (Gen 19)? How old was Isaac during the Akedah (Gen 22)? Where should we locate Salem in Gen 14? What was the sin of Sodom and Gomorrah (Gen 18–19)? How should we understand Isaac's words to Jacob in Gen 27, as a blessing, a prophecy, or a prayer?[21]

Let us expand on the Akedah. The Hebrew Bible does not indicate what Isaac's age was when he was bound by his father (Gen 22). Josephus (*Ant.* 1.227) is the only source who gives the age of twenty-five for Isaac. The rabbis speak of thirty-seven (Lam. Rab. 24; Tanḥ. Vayera 23, 42, etc.). Yet, when it comes to the testimony of Seder Olam Rabbah 1, it might be that the correct version is twenty-six.[22] In this case, one can suppose that Josephus knew this tradition and perhaps preferred the number twenty-five. It can hardly be deemed a coincidence. Chaim Milikowsky argues that Josephus used some form of Seder Olam.

Apologetic concerns may have motivated Josephus's retelling of the narrative of Abram and Sarai in Egypt (Gen 12; *Ant.* 1.157). Josephus adds that Abram went to Egypt to learn about the Egyptians and to teach them astronomy. In this

---

ings," in *Abraham in Jewish and Early Christian Literature*, ed. Sean A. Adams and Zanne Domoney-Lyttle, LSTS 93 (London: T&T Clark, 2019), 93–108.

20. NRSV translates "limping with two different opinions"; NJPS has "hopping between two opinions."

21. On Josephus's retelling of these narratives, see Kugel, *Traditions of the Bible*; Feldman, *Josephus's Interpretation*; Feldman, *Studies in Josephus' Rewritten Bible*, JSJSup 58 (Leiden: Brill, 1998). The problem with Feldman's approach is that the exegetical point of view of Josephus has not been emphasized.

22. Chaim Milikowsky, *Seder Olam: Critical Edition, Commentary and Introduction*, 2 vols. (Jerusalem: Yad Ben-Zvi, 2013), I.60 [Hebrew].

case, this addition may be apologetic since this is part of his attempt to show his audience that the Jews also contributed to world culture.[23]

And yet, there is an addition that can be categorized as stemming neither from apologetic nor exegetical reasons: when Josephus presents the long story of Moses in Egypt (*Ant.* 2.238–253), prior to his initial encounter with pharaoh, he includes a tradition known to us from later sources.[24] Similarly, Josephus adds that the sons of Jacob were buried in Hebron, a detail not mentioned in the Bible (*Ant.* 2.199; cf. Jub. 46:9).

Josephus's additions in his rewriting of the biblical narratives help him emphasize their positive characterizations. Feldman mentions the following cases, among others: Gideon's father is described as one of the foremost among the tribe of Manasseh (*Ant.* 5.213); Jephthah is a mighty man by reason of the valor of his ancestors (*Ant.* 5.257); and Samson's father is one of the foremost among the Danaites (*Ant.* 5.276).[25]

All the omissions and additions do not accord with Josephus's promise that he will proceed by "neither adding nor omitting anything" (*Ant.* 1.17). Scholars have tried to explain the gap in various ways.[26]

Josephus psychologized and rationalized the biblical story and added both drama and human emotions.[27] When comparing the speech of Judah in Gen 44 to the rewriting of Josephus, one can easily discern Greco-Roman adaptation since in Josephus's account Judah uses reason and logic to convince Joseph.[28]

Repetitions

Israel's Scripture is filled with repetitions in all genres: poetry and prose, laws and narratives, prophecy and psalmody. Scholars have dealt with these phenomena

---

23. See Annette Yoshiko Reed, "Abraham as Chaldean Scientist and Father of the Jews: Josephus, *Ant.* 1.154–168, and the Greco-Roman Discourse about Astronomy/Astrology," *JSJ* 35, no. 2 (2004): 119–58.

24. See, most recently, Robert A. Kraft, "Moses and Ethiopia: Old Scripturesque Traditions behind Josephus, *Ant.* 2.238–253," in *The Embroidered Bible: Studies in Biblical Apocrypha and Pseudepigrapha in Honour of Michael E. Stone*, ed. Lorenzo DiTommaso, Matthias Henze, and William Adler, SVTP 26 (Leiden: Brill, 2018), 602–16.

25. Feldman, *Josephus's Interpretation*, 87.

26. Cf. *Ant.* 2.347; 4.196; 9.208, 214; 10.218. See Sabina S. Inowlocki, "'Neither Adding nor Omitting Anything': Josephus' Promise Not to Modify the Scriptures in Greek and Latin Context," *JJS* 56, no. 1 (2005): 48–65.

27. See Françoise Mirguet, *An Early History of Compassion: Emotion and Imagination in Hellenistic Judaism* (New York: Cambridge University Press, 2017), 38.

28. Abraham Schalit, *Josephus Flavius, Jewish Antiquities*, 3 vols. (Jerusalem: Bialik 1967), 1:lxii [Hebrew].

in various ways.²⁹ Many commentators through the ages have tried to explain the presence of such repetitions. One form of these repetitions are doublets, the seeming repetition of a certain law, narrative, or prophecy twice or more often.

Josephus treats doublets in the Pentateuch in various ways:

1. Synthesizing the various versions into one version: Josephus tries to reconcile the numbers 40 and 150, which both mark the duration of the flood narrative (Gen 7:12, 24; *Ant.* 1.89–90).
2. Omitting one of the repeated stories: in this case, Josephus chooses which one to omit in order to avoid the repetition. In the wife-sister stories that appear in both Genesis 12 and 20, he omits the first (*Ant.* 1.162–164). In Josephus's retelling of the book of Numbers, he omits the story in Num 20:1–13 (*Ant.* 4.76–78), as it seemed to him to repeat a similar story in Exod 17:1–7 (*Ant.* 3.33–38). In both accounts, the people complain of a lack of water in the desert. Moses consults God and the problem is solved by God through his messenger, Moses.
3. Considering the stories as separate and different: in his retelling of the Hagar stories in Gen 16 and 21, Josephus presents both stories (*Ant.* 1.186–190, 215–219), presumably because they are sufficiently different. For example, in Gen 16 the motivation for running to the desert comes from Hagar, while in Gen 21 it is Sarah who demands that Hagar be expelled.³⁰

What Can Josephus Contribute to New Testament Scholarship?

What can Josephus contribute to New Testament scholarship with regard to the modes of interpretation? One of the ways in which we can understand a text is to categorize it by its proper genre. This is accomplished through a comparison of a given text with similar texts written at that time. This is true for both the New Testament and Josephus. Many scholars define Josephus's *Ant.* 1–11 as "rewritten Bible" or "rewritten Scripture."³¹ The definition, scope,

---

29. See the review of Aulikki Nahkola, *Double Narratives in the Old Testament: The Foundations of Method in Biblical Criticism*, BZAW 290 (Berlin: de Gruyter, 2001). On repetition in Israel's Scripture, see Susan Zeelander, *Closure in Biblical Narrative*, BibInt 111 (Leiden: Brill, 2012), with bibliography.

30. See Avioz, *Josephus' Interpretation of the Books of Samuel.*

31. Cf. Geza Vermes, *Scripture and Tradition in Judaism: Haggadic Studies*, 2nd ed., StPB 4 (Leiden: Brill, 1973), 75–95. See also Paul Spilsbury, *The Image of the Jew in Flavius Josephus' Paraphrase of the Bible*, TSAJ 69 (Tübingen: Mohr Siebeck, 1998), 15–16; Gregory Sterling, *Historiography and Self-Definition: Josephos, Luke-Acts, and Apologetic Historiography*, NovTSup 64 (Leiden: Brill, 1992), 257–58; Molly M. Zahn, "Genre and Rewritten Scripture: A Reassessment," *JBL* 131,

and elements of this genre are still debated.[32] Jonathan Campbell claimed that the New Testament Gospels should also be included in the category of rewritten Scriptures.[33] Bruce Fisk argued that Paul is retelling the story of Elijah (1 Kgs 19) in Rom 11:2–5.[34] He compares Paul and early Jewish biblical interpretation regarding their use of catchword linkage, strategic omission, and creative embellishment. Omission can be a hermeneutical tool to avoid embarrassment from the commentator's audience, thus building an ideal picture of individuals or groups.

Paul refers to Elijah's complaint (1 Kgs 19:10, 14; Rom 11:3) and part of God's reply (1 Kgs 19:18; Rom 11:4), but he omits several elements from it. Fisk concludes, "All of this suggests that the omission is intentional and not without significance: the charge that Israel had violated the covenant is precisely what Paul did not wish to emphasize."[35] He finds these points in Josephus's retelling of the same story.

Susan Docherty compares the exegetical methods applied to the Scriptures in the New Testament with the Jewish texts termed rewritten Bible. She compares Liber Antiquitatum Biblicarum to the New Testament, specifically the treatment of citations containing direct speech and "using scriptural allusions in narrative transitions and the shared technique of repeating key texts."[36] The similarities in the depiction of Isaac, Moses, and Samson between Liber Antiquitatum Biblicarum and the New Testament illustrate the rootedness of New Testament scriptural interpretation in an early Jewish context. She deals with Josephus only in passing, but her insights are valuable for Josephus as well.

---

no. 2 (2012): 271–88; Zuleika Rodgers, "Josephus's Biblical Interpretation," in Henze, *Companion to Biblical Interpretation*, 436–64; Avioz, *Josephus' Interpretation of the Books of Samuel*.

32. Other compositions included in this category are Jubilees, the Genesis Apocryphon, and Pseudo-Philo's Liber Antiquitatum Biblicarum.

33. Jonathan G. Campbell, "'Rewritten Bible' and 'Parabiblical Texts': A Terminological and Ideological Critique," in *New Directions in Qumran Studies: Proceedings of a Bristol Colloquium on the Dead Sea Scrolls, 8–10 September 2003*, ed. Jonathan G. Campbell, William John Lyons, and Lloyd K. Pietersen, LSTS 52 (London: T&T Clark, 2005), 43–68. See also Craig A. Evans, "Luke and the Rewritten Bible: Aspects of Lukan Hagiography," in *The Pseudepigrapha and Early Biblical Interpretation*, ed. James H. Charlesworth and Craig A. Evans, JSPSup 14 (Sheffield: JSOT Press, 1993), 170–201.

34. Bruce N. Fisk, "Paul among the Storytellers: Reading Romans 11 in the Context of Rewritten Bible," in *Paul and Scripture: Extending the Conversation*, ed. Christopher D. Stanley, ECL 9 (Atlanta: Society of Biblical Literature, 2012), 55–94.

35. Fisk, "Paul among the Storytellers," 82.

36. Susan E. Docherty, "Exegetical Methods in the New Testament and 'Rewritten Bible': A Comparative Analysis," in *Ancient Readers and Their Scriptures: Engaging the Hebrew Bible in Early Judaism and Christianity*, ed. Garrick Allen and John Anthony Dunne, AGJU 107 (Leiden: Brill, 2018), 97.

In the conclusion of his paper, Garrick Allen writes: "the gospel tradition adopted a number of compositional proclivities from early Judaism. The gospels should feature more fully in discussions about the dynamics of transmission, exegesis, literary growth and rewriting in early Jewish texts."[37]

As for repetitions, there are several studies that explored the functions of repetitions in the New Testament. Janice Capel Anderson pointed to seven functions of repetition in Matthew: (1) to highlight or draw attention; (2) to establish or fix in the mind of the reader; (3) to emphasize the importance of something; (4) to create expectations, increasing predictability and assent (anticipation); (5) to cause review and reassessment (retrospection); (6) to unify disparate elements, sometimes creating a background pattern against which other elements can be understood; and (7) to build patterns of association or draw contrasts.[38]

The sixth category is of interest to Josephus studies since it accords with Josephus's habit of assembling various laws dealing with similar issues in one place. Thus, Sukkot is mentioned in four books (Exod 23:13; Lev 23:33–43; Num 29:12–38; Deut 16:13–16). Josephus discusses the particulars of the halakic laws in *Ant.* 3.244-247. Laws of the cities of refuge appear in Exod 21:12–14; Num 35; Deut 4:4–41; 19:1–12. Josephus deals with them only in *Ant.* 4.172–173.

In her treatment of Josephus and the New Testament, Helen Bond focuses mainly on historical inquiry, yet in one paragraph she writes:[39]

> Both Josephus and the NT authors were heirs to the Jewish scriptures, and Josephus's lengthy retelling of the tradition in the first half of Jewish Antiquities (part of a larger contemporary interest in rewriting the Bible) gives an indication of how some of the stories were interpreted in the late first century.... The NT authors tend to use their sacred writings differently—quoting, alluding, or spinning stories around particular passages—but questions over which texts they used (the Septuagint? another early Greek version? a form of the Masoretic text?) are common to both.

What Bond refers to only in passing should be elaborated more fully in future research. The differences between the New Testament and Josephus are apparent, but more research is needed on the similarities between them.

---

37. Garrick V. Allen, "Rewriting and the Gospels," *JSNT* 41, no. 1 (2018): 68.

38. Janice Capel Anderson, *Matthew's Narrative Web: Over, and Over, and Over Again*, JSNTSup 91 (Sheffield: JSOT Press, 1994), 44. See also Diana Jill Kirby, "Repetition in the Book of Revelation" (PhD diss., Catholic University of America, 2009).

39. Helen Bond, "Josephus and the New Testament," in *A Companion to Josephus*, ed. Honora Howell Chapman and Zuleika Rodgers, Blackwell Companions to the Ancient World (Oxford: Wiley-Blackwell, 2016), 155.

Josephus's *Vorlage* and Audience

One of the vexing problems in analyzing Josephus and the Jewish Scriptures relates to the text he had at his disposal. Was it similar to the MT or to the LXX? This topic is still debated among scholars since Josephus is quite tricky. In some cases, his text is similar to the MT; in others, to the LXX; and in still others, to none. Therefore, no unequivocal conclusions can be drawn when comparing Josephus to other witnesses.[40]

A similar issue has been evoked in Pauline studies.[41] According to Moisés Silva, of Paul's 107 scriptural quotations, 42 agree with both the LXX and the MT, 31 do not follow either the LXX or the MT, 17 agree with the LXX against the MT, and 7 agree with the MT against the LXX.[42] There are scholars who argue that Paul knew Hebrew, had studied his Hebrew Bible, and had sections of it memorized.[43] Christopher Beetham concludes that "Paul had possessed a competent knowledge of the proto-LXX text-form that had been available to him."[44]

One may mention in this regard the question of Josephus's audience. Scholars have debated whether his intended audience was gentile, Jewish, or both.[45] Determining the audience is very important in order to explore the message that the authors wished to convey to their readers.

Current State of Research on Josephus's Interpretation of Scripture

The study of Josephus's retelling of Israel's Scripture relies heavily on Feldman's works, going back to the early sixties of the twentieth century. Feldman has assembled many of his essays in four volumes.[46]

---

40. See Michael Avioz, "The Septuagint in Josephus's Writings," in *Wirkungsgeschichte*, ed. Martin Meiser and Florian Wilk, vol. 6 of *Handbuch zur Septuaginta/Handbook of the Septuagint*, ed. Martin Karrer, Wolfgang Kraus, and Siegfried Kreuzer (Gütersloh: Gütersloher Verlagshaus, forthcoming), with earlier bibliography.

41. Christopher A. Beetham, *Echoes of Scripture in the Letter of Paul to the Colossians*, BibInt 96 (Leiden: Brill, 2008).

42. Silva, "Old Testament in Paul," in *Dictionary of Paul and His Letters*, ed. Gerald F. Hawthorne and Ralph P. Martin (Downers Grove, IL: InterVarsity Press, 1993), 631.

43. Beetham, *Echoes of Scripture*, 258–60.

44. Beetham, 37 n. 86.

45. See the literature in Avioz, *Josephus' Interpretation of the Books of Samuel*, 191–95. Most scholars recognize that Paul's audience in Rome was predominantly gentile. See, e.g., Mark D. Nanos, *The Mystery of Romans: The Jewish Context of Paul's Letter* (Minneapolis: Fortress, 1996), 77–84; Robert Jewett, *Romans: A Commentary*, Hermeneia (Minneapolis: Fortress, 2007), 70.

46. Louis H. Feldman, *Studies in Hellenistic Judaism*, AGSU 30 (Leiden: Brill, 1996); Feld-

In every Josephan rewritten biblical story, Feldman examines a fixed set of virtues of the biblical characters: genealogy, courage, wisdom, piety, morality, handsomeness, humility, compassion, and more. Feldman consistently compares Josephus with the rabbinic literature and with the Greco-Roman writers. These comparisons undoubtedly enrich both readers and scholars.

However, acquaintance with the art of biblical narrative may help us reach more accurate conclusions with regard to Josephus's interpretation of the Hebrew Bible. In fact, the title of Feldman's 1998 monumental book, *Studies in Josephus' Rewritten Bible*, is misleading since it deals only in part with what we may call "interpretation." Most of the book is devoted to the characterization mostly of male characters, but interpretation means much more than that: the scholar must first learn the biblical story itself, mark the main difficulties arising from it, and only then approach Josephus. Otherwise, the analysis becomes atomistic, disregarding its immediate context.

In addition, as Mark Roncace has shown, Feldman focuses on the differences between Josephus and the Hebrew Bible while ignoring the many similarities that are present between the two sources.[47]

Another renowned scholar is Christopher Begg.[48] He is mainly interested in the question of Josephus's version of the biblical text. In addition, he deals with other questions, such as, What are the techniques that Josephus used in order to make the biblical story readable? What did he omit, add, or change in the biblical text? What were his motives? Did Josephus use the Hebrew, Greek, and/or Latin or Aramaic versions of the sources? Who is Josephus's intended audience? However, since he analyzes each story separately, he misses the similarities between sets of narratives in the same book or in the whole of Josephus's interpretation of the Hebrew Bible.

---

man, *Studies in Josephus' Rewritten Bible*; Feldman, *Josephus's Interpretation*; and Feldman, *Judaism and Hellenism Reconsidered*, JSJSup 107 (Leiden: Brill, 2006).

47. Roncace, "Josephus' (Real) Portraits of Deborah and Gideon: A Reading of *Antiquities* 5.198–232," *JSJ* 31 (2000): 247–74; Roncace, "Another Portrait of Josephus' Portrait of Samson," *JSJ* 35, no. 2 (2004): 185–207.

48. Christopher T. Begg, *Josephus' Account of the Early Divided Monarchy (AJ 8, 212–420): Rewriting the Bible*, BETL 108 (Leuven: Leuven University Press, 1993); Begg, *Josephus' Story of the Later Monarchy (AJ 9,1–10, 185)*, BETL 145 (Leuven: Leuven University Press, 2000). Begg was part of the Brill Josephus Project, where he translated and interpreted books 5–10; Begg, *Judean Antiquities 5–7*; Begg and Spilsbury, *Judean Antiquities 8–10*. RAMBI (index of articles on Jewish studies) lists about one hundred articles written by Begg on Josephus.

CONTEXTS

Josephus, the Midrash, and the New Testament

Scholars have pointed out the affinities between Josephus's *Antiquities* and the rabbinic midrashim.[49] Ninety years ago, Salomon Rappaport published his important book *Agada und Exegese bei Flavius Josephus*.[50] In this book Rappaport tried to show that Josephus did not invent haggadic materials but rather followed Second Temple traditions, which he borrowed from the Aramaic targum. Rappaport cites hundreds of instances where Josephus parallels midrashic traditions. In fact, no similar book has appeared since, and further inquiry is needed. Rappaport's work is the only one that systematically attempts to note Josephus's divergences from the entire Bible. He assumed that Josephus's additions always parallel rabbinic tradition, even though he must admit that there are some additions not found in rabbinic or apocryphal literature, and he acknowledges that there are places where Josephus definitely shows his independence of rabbinic exegesis.

Josephus's *Antiquities* may seem to belong to the genre of midrash in that it retells the biblical narrative by arranging and supplementing it, explaining difficult passages, and defending the Jews against charges that had been made against them on the basis of the biblical text.

If, however, we accept the definition of Gary Porton, then in midrash the original verse is explicitly cited or clearly alluded to.[51] Josephus, although he may be explaining the verses as does the midrash, does not cite the original verse as such. Moreover, midrashim are not, or at least originally were not created to be, a running commentary.[52] Rabbinic midrashim present more than one comment or interpretation of a given incident, whereas Josephus merely paraphrases the text in his own way and only occasionally presents alternate versions and explanations.

Interestingly, Philip Long summarized the views that consider the New Testament a midrash and rejects them.[53] Jesus did not create a coherent commentary

---

49. Feldman, *Josephus's Interpretation*, 16, 65–73; and Feldman, *Judaism and Hellenism*, 322–23.
50. Rappaport, *Agada und Exegese bei Flavius Josephus* (Vienna: Kohut-Stiftung, 1930).
51. Gary Porton, "Midrash: Palestinian Jews and the Hebrew Bible in the Greco-Roman Period," *ANRW* 19.2:112.
52. Feldman, *Josephus's Interpretation*, 16–17.
53. Phillip J. Long, *Jesus the Bridegroom: The Origin of the Eschatological Feast as a Wedding Banquet in the Synoptic Gospels* (Eugene, OR: Pickwick, 2013), 35–42. Those who accept the New Testament as midrash include, e.g., E. Earle Ellis, ed., *The Gospel of Luke* (London: Nelson, 1966); J. Duncan M. Derrett, "The Parable of the Great Supper," in *Law in the New Testament* (London: Darton, Longman & Todd, 1970), 126–55; Michael D. Goulder, *Midrash and Lection in Matthew: The Speaker's Lectures in Biblical Studies, 1969–71* (London: SPCK,

on Scripture or seek to explain textual difficulties or legal problems by means of midrash.

Summary

Josephus's writings have much to contribute to New Testament studies, not only when historical inquiry is concerned but also with regard to the history of interpretation and to the ways in which we should evaluate their retelling of Israel's Scriptures. Both Josephus scholars and New Testament scholars share similar problems of *Vorlage* and intended audiences. These compositions belong together to the category of rewritten Scripture. Scholars dealing with the interpretation of the New Testament can benefit from Josephan scholars in their explorations of rewriting techniques. The opposite is true as well: the results of New Testament scholarship bear on Josephus studies.

Bibliography

Allen, Garrick V. "Rewriting and the Gospels." *JSNT* 41, no. 1 (2018): 58–69.
Anderson, Janice Capel. *Matthew's Narrative Web: Over, and Over, and Over Again.* JSNTSup 91. Sheffield: JSOT Press, 1994.
Avioz, Michael. "Abraham in Josephus' Writings." Pages 93–108 in *Abraham in Jewish and Early Christian Literature*. Edited by Sean A. Adams and Zanne Domoney-Lyttle. LSTS 93. London: T&T Clark, 2019.
———. *Josephus' Interpretation of the Books of Samuel.* LSTS 86. London: Bloomsbury T&T Clark, 2015.
———. "The Septuagint in Josephus's Writings." Pages 475–80 in *Wirkungsgeschichte*. Edited by Martin Meiser and Florian Wilk. Vol. 6 of *Handbuch zur Septuaginta/Handbook of the Septuagint*. Edited by Martin Karrer, Wolfgang Kraus, and Siegfried Kreuzer. Gütersloh: Gütersloher Verlagshaus, 2022.
Barclay, John. *Against Apion.* FJTC 10. Leiden: Brill, 2007.
Basser, Herbert W. "Josephus as Exegete." *JAOS* 107, no. 1 (1987): 21–30.

1974); John Drury, *Tradition and Design in Luke's Gospel: A Study in Early Christian Historiography* (Atlanta: John Knox, 1976); Dale Miller and Patricia Miller, *The Gospel of Mark as Midrash on Earlier Jewish and New Testament Literature*, Studies in Bible and Early Christianity (Lewiston: Mellen, 1990).

Beetham, Christopher A. *Echoes of Scripture in the Letter of Paul to the Colossians*. BibInt 96. Leiden: Brill, 2008.

Begg, Christopher T. *Josephus' Account of the Early Divided Monarchy (AJ 8, 212–420): Rewriting the Bible*. BETL 108. Leuven: Leuven University Press, 1993.

———. *Josephus' Story of the Later Monarchy (AJ 9,1–10, 185)*. BETL 145. Leuven: Leuven University Press, 2000.

———. *Judean Antiquities 5–7*. FJTC 4. Leiden: Brill, 2005.

Begg, Christopher T., and Paul Spilsbury. *Judean Antiquities 8–10*. FJTC 5. Leiden: Brill, 2005.

Bond, Helen. "Josephus and the New Testament." Pages 147–58 in *A Companion to Josephus*. Edited by Honora Howell Chapman and Zuleika Rodgers. Blackwell Companions to the Ancient World. Oxford: Wiley-Blackwell, 2016.

Campbell, Jonathan G. "'Rewritten Bible' and 'Parabiblical Texts': A Terminological and Ideological Critique." Pages 43–68 in *New Directions in Qumran Studies: Proceedings of a Bristol Colloquium on the Dead Sea Scrolls, 8–10 September 2003*. Edited by Jonathan G. Campbell, William John Lyons, and Lloyd K. Pietersen. LSTS 52. London: T&T Clark, 2005.

Carras, George P. "Jewish Sensibilities and the Search for the Jewish Paul—The Lukan Paul Viewed through Josephan Judaism: Interplay with *Apion* 2:190–219." Pages 167–78 in *The Early Reception of Paul the Second Temple Jew: Text, Narrative and Reception History*. Edited by Isaac W. Oliver, Gabriele Boccaccini, and J. Barton Scott. LSTS 92. London: T&T Clark, 2018.

———. "Paul, Josephus and Judaism: The Shared Judaism of Paul and Josephus." PhD diss., University of Oxford, 1990.

Cohen, Shaye J. D. *From the Maccabees to the Mishnah*. 2nd ed. Louisville: Westminster John Knox, 2006.

———. *Josephus in Galilee and Rome: His* Vita *and Development as a Historian*. Columbia Studies in the Classical Tradition 8. Leiden: Brill, 1979.

Derrett, J. Duncan M. "The Parable of the Great Supper." Pages 126–55 in *Law in the New Testament*. London: Darton, Longman & Todd, 1970.

Docherty, Susan E. "Exegetical Methods in the New Testament and 'Rewritten Bible': A Comparative Analysis." Pages 77–97 in *Ancient Readers and Their Scriptures: Engaging the Hebrew Bible in Early Judaism and Christianity*. Edited by Garrick Allen and John Anthony Dunne. AGJU 107. Leiden: Brill, 2018.

Drury, John. *Tradition and Design in Luke's Gospel: A Study in Early Christian Historiography*. Atlanta: John Knox, 1976.

Ehrenkrook, Jason von. *Sculpting Idolatry in Flavian Rome: (An)Iconic Rhetoric in the Writings of Flavius Josephus*. EJL 33. Atlanta: Society of Biblical Literature, 2011.

Ellis, E. Earle, ed. *The Gospel of Luke*. London: Nelson, 1966.

Evans, Craig A. "Luke and the Rewritten Bible: Aspects of Lukan Hagiography."

Pages 170–201 in *The Pseudepigrapha and Early Biblical Interpretation*. Edited by James H. Charlesworth and Craig A. Evans. JSPSup 14. Sheffield: JSOT Press, 1993.

Feldman, Louis H. *Antiquities 1–4*. FJTC 3. Leiden: Brill, 2000.

———. *Josephus's Interpretation of the Bible*. HCS 27. Berkeley: University of California Press, 1998.

———. *Judaism and Hellenism Reconsidered*. JSJSup 107. Leiden: Brill, 2006.

———. *Studies in Hellenistic Judaism*. AGSU 30. Leiden: Brill, 1996.

———. *Studies in Josephus' Rewritten Bible*. JSJSup 58. Leiden: Brill, 1998.

Fisk, Bruce N. "Paul among the Storytellers: Reading Romans 11 in the Context of Rewritten Bible." Pages 55–94 in *Paul and Scripture: Extending the Conversation*. Edited by Christopher D. Stanley. ECL 9. Atlanta: Society of Biblical Literature, 2012.

Friis, Martin. *Image and Imitation: Josephus' Antiquities 1–11 and Greco-Roman Historiography*. WUNT 2/472. Tübingen: Mohr Siebeck, 2018.

Goodman, Martin. *Judaism in the Roman World: Collected Essays*. AGJU 66. Leiden: Brill, 2007.

Goulder, Michael D. *Midrash and Lection in Matthew: The Speaker's Lectures in Biblical Studies, 1969–71*. London: SPCK, 1974.

Henten, Jan Willem van. *Judean Antiquities 15*. FJTC 7b. Leiden: Brill, 2014.

Inowlocki, Sabina S. "'Neither Adding nor Omitting Anything': Josephus' Promise Not to Modify the Scriptures in Greek and Latin Context." *JJS* 56, no. 1 (2005): 48–65.

Jacobson, Howard. "Biblical interpretation in Pseudo-Philo's 'Liber Antiquitatum Biblicarum.'" Pages 180–99 in *A Companion to Biblical Interpretation in Early Judaism*. Edited by Matthias Henze. Grand Rapids: Eerdmans, 2012.

Jewett, Robert. *Romans: A Commentary*. Hermeneia. Minneapolis: Fortress, 2007.

Kirby, Diana Jill. "Repetition in the Book of Revelation." PhD diss., Catholic University of America, 2009.

Kraft, Robert A. "Moses and Ethiopia: Old Scripturesque Traditions behind Josephus, *Ant*. 2.238–253." Pages 602–16 in *The Embroidered Bible: Studies in Biblical Apocrypha and Pseudepigrapha in Honour of Michael E. Stone*. Edited by Lorenzo DiTommaso, Matthias Henze, and William Adler. SVTP 26. Leiden: Brill, 2018.

Kugel, James L. "Early Interpretation: The Common Background of Late Forms of Biblical Exegesis." Pages 9–106 in *Early Biblical Interpretation*. James L. Kugel and Rowan A. Greer. LEC 3. Philadelphia: Westminster, 1986.

———. *How to Read the Bible: A Guide to Scripture, Then and Now*. New York: Free Press, 2007.

———. *Traditions of the Bible: A Guide to the Bible as It Was at the Start of the Common Era*. Cambridge: Harvard University Press, 1998.

Lim, Timothy H. "Deuteronomy in the Judaism of the Second Temple Period." Pages

6–26 in *Deuteronomy in the New Testament*. Edited by Maarten J. J. Menken and Steve Moyise. LNTS 358. London: T&T Clark, 2007.

Long, Phillip J. *Jesus the Bridegroom: The Origin of the Eschatological Feast as a Wedding Banquet in the Synoptic Gospels*. Eugene, OR: Pickwick, 2013.

Mason, Steve. *Judean War 2*. FJTC 1B. Leiden: Brill, 2008.

———. *Life of Josephus*. FJTC 9. Leiden: Brill, 2001.

———. "The Writings of Josephus: Their Significance for New Testament Study." Pages 1639–86 in *Handbook for the Study of the Historical Jesus*. Vol. 2, *The Study of Jesus*. Edited by Tom Holmén and Stanley E. Porter. 4 vols. Leiden: Brill, 2011.

Milikowsky, Chaim. *Seder Olam: Critical Edition, Commentary and Introduction*. 2 vols. Jerusalem: Yad Ben-Zvi, 2013. [Hebrew]

Miller, Dale, and Patricia Miller. *The Gospel of Mark as Midrash on Earlier Jewish and New Testament Literature*. Studies in Bible and Early Christianity. Lewiston: Mellen, 1990.

Mirguet, Françoise. *An Early History of Compassion: Emotion and Imagination in Hellenistic Judaism*. New York: Cambridge University Press, 2017.

Nahkola, Aulikki. *Double Narratives in the Old Testament: The Foundations of Method in Biblical Criticism*. BZAW 290. Berlin: de Gruyter, 2001.

Nanos, Mark D. *The Mystery of Romans: The Jewish Context of Paul's Letter*. Minneapolis: Fortress, 1996.

Pearce, Sarah J. K. "Josephus as Interpreter of Biblical Law: The Representation of the High Court of Deut. 17:8–12 according to *Jewish Antiquities* 4.218." *JJS* 46, no. 1 (1998): 30–42.

Pinter, Dean L. "Divine and Imperial Power: A Comparative Analysis of Paul and Josephus." PhD diss., Durham University, 2009.

Porton, Gary. "Midrash: Palestinian Jews and the Hebrew Bible in the Greco-Roman Period." *ANRW* 19.2:103–38.

Rajak, Tessa. *Josephus: The Historian and His Society*. 2nd ed. London: Duckworth, 2002.

Rappaport, Solomon. *Agada und Exegese bei Flavius Josephus*. Vienna: Kohut-Stiftung, 1930.

Reed, Annette Yoshiko. "Abraham as Chaldean Scientist and Father of the Jews: Josephus, *Ant.* 1.154–168, and the Greco-Roman Discourse about Astronomy/Astrology." *JSJ* 35, no. 2 (2004): 119–58.

Rodgers, Zuleika. "Another Portrait of Josephus' Portrait of Samson." *JSJ* 35, no. 2 (2004): 185–207.

———. "Josephus's Biblical Interpretation." Pages 436–64 in *A Companion to Biblical Interpretation in Early Judaism*. Edited by Matthias Henze. Grand Rapids: Eerdmans, 2012.

Roncace, Mark. "Josephus' (Real) Portraits of Deborah and Gideon: A Reading of *Antiquities* 5.198–232." *JSJ* 31 (2000): 247–74.

Schalit, Abraham. *Josephus Flavius, Jewish Antiquities*. 3 vols. Jerusalem: Bialik 1967. [Hebrew]

Screnock, John. "Translation and Rewriting in the Genesis Apocryphon." Pages 453–81 in *Reading the Bible in Ancient Traditions and Modern Editions: Studies in Memory of Peter W. Flint*. Edited by Andrew B. Perrin, Kyung S. Baek, and Daniel K. Falk. EJL 47. Atlanta: SBL Press, 2017.

Sievers, Joseph, and Gaia Lembi. *Josephus and Jewish History in Flavian Rome and Beyond*. JSJSup 104. Leiden: Brill, 2005.

Silva, Moisés. "Old Testament in Paul." Pages 630–42 in *Dictionary of Paul and His Letters*. Edited by Gerald F. Hawthorne and Ralph P. Martin. Downers Grove, IL: InterVarsity Press, 1993.

Spilsbury, Paul. "Contra *Apionem* and *Antiquitates Judaicae*: Points of Contact." Pages 348–68 in *Josephus' "Contra Apionem": Studies in Its Character and Context with a Latin Concordance to the Portion Missing in Greek*. Edited by Louis H. Feldman and John R. Levison. AGJU 34. Leiden: Brill, 1996.

———. *The Image of the Jew in Flavius Josephus' Paraphrase of the Bible*. TSAJ 69. Tübingen: Mohr Siebeck, 1998.

Spilsbury, Paul, and Chris Seeman. *Judean Antiquities 11*. FJTC 6a. Leiden: Brill, 2018.

Sterling, Gregory E. *Historiography and Self-Definition: Josephos, Luke-Acts and Apologetic Historiography*. NovTSup 64. Leiden: Brill, 1992.

———. "When Silence Is Golden: The Omission of the Golden Calf Story in Josephus." Pages 87–96 in *Golden Calf Traditions in Early Judaism, Christianity, and Islam*. Edited by Eric Mason and Edmondo F. Lupieri. TBN 23. Leiden: Brill, 2019.

Tropper, Amram. *Rewriting Ancient Jewish History: The History of the Jews in Roman Times and the New Historical Method*. Routledge Studies in Ancient History 10. London: Routledge, 2016.

Vermes, Geza. *Scripture and Tradition in Judaism: Haggadic Studies*. 2nd ed. StPB 4. Leiden: Brill, 1973.

———. "A Summary of the Law by Flavius Josephus." *NovT* 24, no. 4 (1982): 289–303.

Zahn, Molly. "Genre and Rewritten Scripture: A Reassessment." *JBL* 131, no. 2 (2012): 271–88.

Zeelander, Susan. *Closure in Biblical Narrative*. BibInt 111. Leiden: Brill, 2012.

PART 2

Israel's Scriptures in the New Testament

The second section, "Israel's Scriptures in the New Testament," the longest section in our volume, provides a book-by-book analysis of the writings of the New Testament and their diverse forms of engagement with the Jewish Scriptures. New Testament writers display a considerable diversity in their use of Scripture: some did not refer to Scripture at all, while for others Israel's authoritative writings were foundational, providing them with language and motifs, theological concepts or a particular framework, or simply scriptural authority for their own thinking and writing. The chapters in this section address some of these foundational questions: How pronounced is scriptural interpretation in a given book or author? Is the use of Scripture a dominant or minor theme? Which books are cited and to what end, and which books are ignored?

These chapters provide state-of-the-art treatments of these and other questions. The contributors were asked to analyze the citation techniques that introduce Scripture, such as introductory formulas, together with the form of the engagement—marked or unmarked citations, verbal or conceptual allusions. They consider the major purposes for which an author invokes Scripture, paying particular attention to how contemporary Jewish authors interpreted similar texts. And they treat the question of the nature of the scriptural texts, including the textual *Vorlage* an author presupposes and its proximity to the Hebrew or Greek textual traditions.

Understanding the art of scriptural interpretation in the New Testament is a form of interpretation in itself. The boundaries between the four categories we employ are not always firm, and modern interpreters will at times disagree on whether a particular reference in the New Testament to a scriptural precursor text should be labeled as, for example, an unmarked citation or verbal allusion. It should not surprise, then, that there are occasional disagreements among the contributors to this volume on specific texts. Often, these disagreements reflect long-standing exegetical debates. We have refrained from imposing a unified view across the volume and have opted, instead, for the debate to continue in these pages.

∽

A. THE GOSPELS AND ACTS

8

Israel's Scriptures in Matthew

MATTHIAS KONRADT

Matthew narrates his Jesus story with constant reference to Israel's Scriptures, from the opening words "book of the origin/history [βίβλος γενέσεως]" in 1:1, which take up a phrase encountered in Gen 2:4 and 5:1, to the motif that God is with his people in Jesus's last words, which bring the Gospel to an end in 28:20 (see Gen 26:24; 28:15; Exod 3:12; Josh 1:5; Isa 41:10, etc.; for the wording see esp. Hag 1:13; 2:4; Jer 49:11). The Gospel of Matthew contains a large number of marked citations, of which the fulfillment citations—which are found inserted into Markan material (4:15–16; 8:17; 12:18–21; 13:35; 21:5) and also occur in the special material (1:23; 2:15, 18, 23; 27:9–10)—constitute just one detail that is characteristic of Matthew.[1] Alongside this there are numerous unmarked citations and verbal as well as conceptual allusions. The density of the citations and allusions corresponds with the fact that significant portions of Israel's Scriptures were taken up in Matthew. In addition to the Torah (especially Deuteronomy), the book of Isaiah and the Psalms are of central significance, but Jeremiah, Ezekiel, Hosea, Micah, Zechariah, and Daniel are also important.[2]

---

1. Cf. Donald Senior, "The Lure of the Formula Quotations: Re-assessing Matthew's Use of the Old Testament with the Passion Narrative as Test Case," in *The Scriptures in the Gospels*, ed. Christopher M. Tuckett, BETL 131 (Leuven: Leuven University Press, 1997), 89–115, esp. 103–14. Unless otherwise noted, all translations are by the author.

2. Cf. the table of citations and allusions in Brandon D. Crowe, *The Obedient Son: Deuteronomy and Christology in the Gospel of Matthew*, BZNW 188 (Berlin: de Gruyter, 2012), 27. On Isaiah see the overview in Richard Beaton, "Isaiah in Matthew's Gospel," in *Isaiah in the*

Thematically, within the Matthean story of Jesus, Israel's Scriptures are relevant not only to positioning Jesus's ministry in the horizon of the history of Israel attested in the Scriptures and of the theological traditions that characterize the people of God and to demonstrating that this ministry is in accordance with Scripture, but the contrast between Jesus and the Jewish authorities is also illuminated from the perspective of Scripture. In this connection, within the Matthean special material, one can even observe the phenomenon—which extends beyond the interspersing of individual motifs (such as Pilate's washing of hands in Matt 27:24; cf. Deut 21:6–8; Pss 26:6; 73:13)—that in two passages (Matt 2 and 27:3–10) the scriptural reception may well have made a creative contribution to the genesis of the texts (cf. below, "Christology" and "The Configuration of Characters in the Matthean Jesus Story"). In composing his work, the evangelist has in view an audience or readership that is meant to think about the Jesus story in the horizon of Scripture: the Matthean Jesus story echoes in the resonant space of Scripture and it acquires greater timbre when it is heard within this space. This is not a matter of mere proof texting. Rather, it is central to the narrative that references to scriptural passages often also evoke their contexts and the overarching nexuses in which they are embedded, and thus the intertextual dimension of Matthew's text contributes to the creation of its meaning.

Israel's Scripture in the Gospel of Matthew

Introducing Scripture

The Matthean forms of introducing a scriptural citation are varied. They reveal a deliberate construction insofar as the introductions in many cases indicate groups of related quotations. Among the most striking phenomena of Matthean scriptural reception are the so-called formula quotations, which are characterized by the stereotypical introductory phrase, with the basic elements (1) ἵνα/ὅπως πληρωθῇ or (2) τότε ἐπληρώθη + τὸ ῥηθέν + διὰ τοῦ προφήτου λέγοντος.

New Testament, ed. Steve Moyise and Maarten J. J. Menken (London: T&T Clark, 2005), 63–78 (with a focus on the quotations). On Jeremiah, see Michael Knowles, *Jeremiah in Matthew's Gospel: The Rejected Prophet Motif in Matthaean Redaction*, JSNTSup 68 (Sheffield: Sheffield Academic, 1993). On Zechariah, see Charlene McAfee Moss, *The Zechariah Tradition and the Gospel of Matthew*, BZNW 156 (Berlin: de Gruyter, 2008); Clay Alan Ham, *The Coming King and the Rejected Shepherd: Matthew's Reading of Zechariah's Messianic Hope*, New Testament Monographs 4 (Sheffield: Sheffield Phoenix, 2005); and Paul Foster, "The Use of Zechariah in Matthew's Gospel," in *The Book of Zechariah and Its Influence*, ed. Christopher M. Tuckett (Burlington, VT: Ashgate, 2003), 65–85.

More specifically, there are subvariants or expansions with which Matthew constructs subgroups (the insertion of ὑπὸ κυρίου in 1:22; 2:15; the explicit identification of Isaiah in 4:14; 8:17; 12:17,³ of Jeremiah in 2:17 and 27:9, connected with the opening of the introduction with τότε ἐπληρώθη); the phrase consists of just the basic elements in the variant (1) only in 13:35 and 21:4 (on the deviations in 2:23, see "Christology"). The concept of fulfillment also echoes in the redactional introduction to the quotation of Isa 6:9 in Matt 13:14–15: "with them is fulfilled the prophecy of Isaiah that says [ἀναπληροῦται αὐτοῖς ἡ προφητεία Ἡσαΐου ἡ λέγουσα]". The prophetic character of the quoted text is further highlighted in the introduction to Isa 29:13 in Matt 15:7 (cf. also 11:13).

With the insertion of ὑπὸ κυρίου in 1:22 and 2:15, the words of the prophet are explicitly identified as the speech of God. Here it is also worth pointing out the introduction to God's self-presentation in Exod 3:6 with "that which was spoken to you by God, saying" (τὸ ῥηθὲν ὑμῖν ὑπὸ τοῦ θεοῦ λέγοντος) in Matt 22:31 (in contrast to Mark 12:26). Matthew has also introduced other quotations, always redactionally, as God's speech, namely the commandment to honor one's parents from Exod 20:12; Deut 5:16 (+ Exod 21:17 [21:16 LXX]) in Matt 15:4 ("God said", in contrast to Mark 7:10: "Moses said") and Gen 2:24 in Matt 19:4–5 (ὁ κτίσας ... εἶπεν). In the direct speech of Jesus's Sadducee opponents in 22:24, Μωϋσῆς εἶπεν is used to introduce the free paraphrase of Deut 25:5–6, which is clearly influenced by Gen 38:8 (cf. also Matt 19:7–8). The quotation of Ps 110:1 in Matt 22:44 is presented in the introduction as having been spoken by David *in the Spirit* (v. 43 // Mark 12:36).

In addition to 22:31 (see above), the element of the introduction to the fulfillment quotations τὸ ῥηθέν ("what was spoken"), which refers to the *spoken* word and is characteristic of Matthew within the New Testament, also occurs in the redactional identification of the "abomination of desolation" (Dan 9:27; 11:31; 12:11) as "which was spoken of by the prophet Daniel" in Matt 24:15. There is also a counterpart to this in 3:3 (see below). Finally, we can point to ἐρρέθη ("it was spoken") in the introduction to the theses in the series of antitheses (5:21, 27, 31, 33, 38, 43).

Alongside this, Matthew refers to the *written* word with γέγραπται (4:4, 6, 7, 10; 11:10; 21:13; 26:31), expanded by διὰ τοῦ προφήτου in 2:5 (see further the general reference to the scriptural testimony in 26:24). The reference to what has been *written* corresponds with the fact that in Jesus's conflict with his opponents,

---

3. As a *varia lectio* this also occurs in Matt 13:35, but this reading is secondary. Contra, e.g., Maarten J. J. Menken, *Matthew's Bible: The Old Testament Text of the Evangelist*, BETL 173 (Leuven: Peeters, 2004), 90–92.

scriptural references are repeatedly introduced with the phrase "have you never/not read [οὐδέποτε/οὐκ ἀνέγνωτε]" (19:4; 21:16, 42; 22:31; cf. 12:3, 5).

The two introductions to the quotation of Hos 6:6 in Matt 9:13 and 12:7 are correlated, and the knowledge that this is scriptural is presupposed: the injunction to the Pharisees to learn what it means (μάθετε τί ἐστιν) is followed by a contrary-to-fact conditional clause referring to their failure to recognize its meaning (εἰ δὲ ἐγνώκειτε τί ἐστιν).

Quotations of scriptural references concerning the interpretation of the role of John the Baptist as predecessor and forerunner are characteristically introduced by the identification formula οὗτός ἐστιν. This is adopted from Q in Matt 11:10 with the continuation περὶ οὗ γέγραπται ("of whom it is written"; cf. Luke 7:27). Matthew 3:3 is redactionally adapted to this: οὗτος γάρ ἐστιν ὁ ῥηθεὶς διὰ Ἡσαΐου τοῦ προφήτου λέγοντος ("This is the one of whom it was spoken by the prophet Isaiah, who said") replaces the Markan introduction καθὼς γέγραπται ἐν τῷ Ἡσαΐᾳ τῷ προφήτῃ ("as it is written in Isaiah the prophet") in Mark 1:2. The notion of fulfillment is absent from the quotations related to the Baptist. It is exclusively connected with Jesus's ministry and with the opposition to Jesus.

With the quotations of some Decalogue commandments, the love command in Matt 19:18–19, and the double commandment of love in 22:37–39, it is apparent from the preceding dialogue that Torah commandments are being cited. Matthew 19:18 employs only the singular neuter article τό to identify the quotation (differently Mark 10:19).

Matthew never speaks of Scripture in the singular, but instead always uses the plural (21:42; 22:29; 26:54, 56), even where he found a singular in Mark and introduces a specific passage (cf. Matt 21:42 with Mark 12:10).[4]

Using Scripture

Christology

It is self-evident that a large portion of scriptural references in a Gospel serves to illuminate the role of Jesus as the protagonist and to interpret his ministry. In Matthew this occurs in so many different ways that the following discussion can only present a few main aspects of the substantial contribution that citations and verbal and conceptual allusions to Israel's Scriptures make to the presentation of Jesus as the Messiah. Six main points follow.

---

4. On this see already Wilhelm Rothfuchs, *Die Erfüllungszitate des Matthäus-Evangeliums: Eine biblisch-theologische Untersuchung*, BWANT 88 (Stuttgart: Kohlhammer, 1969), 113.

Israel's Scriptures in Matthew

1. Beyond the opening of the Gospel with "book of the origin" (see above), scriptural references already define the superscription of Matthew in 1:1, as the appositional identification of Jesus Christ as the son of David *and* the son of Abraham connects one, if not *the*, central theological concern of the evangelist with God's history with Israel witnessed in Israel's Scriptures. Christologically, Matthew connects Jesus's attention to Israel during his earthly ministry emphasized in the Matthean Jesus story with Jesus's Davidic messiahship.[5] The Abrahamic sonship not only strengthens the connection with Israel through the significance of Abraham as the patriarch of God's people; it also brings into play the promise of universal salvation of the nations (Gen 12:3; 18:18; 22:18; 26:4). In short: through conceptual allusions, the genealogical information in 1:1 evokes motifs from Israel's Scriptures that function as guiding themes of the Matthean Jesus story.

Moreover, scriptural references run like a common thread through the prologue in 1:2–4:16. This section serves the function within the narrative as a whole of introducing Jesus's messianic identity, which is fundamentally defined by his Davidic and divine sonship. In this, both aspects are not only illuminated individually from the perspective of Scripture, such as, for example, in the appeal to Ps 2:7 and Isa 42:1 as central textual references at the proclamation of Jesus as the Son of God by the voice from heaven in Matt 3:17.[6] Rather, in terms of a conceptual allusion, the connection between Davidic and divine sonship also acquires contours in light of the occasional occurrences of the motif of the divine sonship of the (Davidic) king in Israel's Scriptures (2 Sam 7:14; Pss 2:7; 89:27–28) as an inversion of the relation between the two aspects emerges:[7] It is not the Davidic ruler who is accepted by God as his son, but rather the Son of God—begotten by the Holy Spirit—who is positioned among the descendants of David by way of "Joseph, son of David" (1:20). This inversion corresponds with the fact that Jesus's divine sonship appears as *the* central christological predicate in Matthew as a whole.[8] The relationship introduced in Matt 1 is deepened in the Matthean

---

5. See in detail Matthias Konradt, *Israel, Church, and the Gentiles in the Gospel of Matthew*, BMSEC 2 (Waco, TX: Baylor University Press, 2014), 18–49. Cf. further H. Daniel Zacharias, *Matthew's Presentation of the Son of David: Davidic Tradition and Typology in the Gospel of Matthew* (London: T&T Clark, 2017).

6. Leroy A. Huizenga, *The New Isaac: Tradition and Intertextuality in the Gospel of Matthew*, NovTSup 131 (Leiden: Brill, 2009), 153–87, has made a different suggestion, invoking Gen 22 as the central reference text.

7. For a messianic interpretation of 2 Sam 7:11–14 see 4Q174 frag. 1 I+21+2 [3,]10–13.

8. On Matthew's christological concept, see Matthias Konradt, "Gospel of Matthew," in *From Paul to Josephus: Literary Receptions of Jesus in the First Century CE*, ed. Helen Bond, vol. 1 of *The Reception of Jesus in the First Three Centuries* (London: T&T Clark, 2020), 107–38, esp. 113–22.

revision of Mark 12:35-37 in Matt 22:41-46 on the basis of a messianic interpretation of Ps 110:1. It is indeed correct to regard the Messiah as a son of David, as the Pharisees do (22:42), but this is only one side of the coin. When David—as the speaker of the Psalms—speaks of his messianic son as "lord," this is due to the fact that the Messiah is simultaneously the Son of God begotten of the Holy Spirit and as such is superior to David. In short, the core of Matthew's christological conception is illuminated by references to the Scriptures of Israel.

This characteristic feature of the Matthean Jesus story is reinforced by the genealogy in 1:2-17, the entrance to the prologue. In that the Matthean genealogy of Jesus—in contrast to Luke 3:23-38—is drawn by way of the kings of Judah (cf. 1 Chr 3:10-16), it presents itself beyond the genealogy from Abraham to David as a condensed presentation of the history of Israel, which according to 1:17 progresses purposefully in three sets of fourteen generations toward Jesus, with whom the vacancy on the throne of David that has existed since the Babylonian captivity (1:11, 17)—and thus the exile itself—comes to an end.[9] At the same time, the number of generations from Abraham (1:2) to Joseph (1:16) comes to exactly forty, a symbolically charged number within the biblical narrative world (to maintain three times fourteen generations up to Jesus, David must be counted twice as the end of the first segment and beginning of the second, which accords with 1:17). In this way Matthew signals that the period of the history of promise has reached its completion. Further, the three epochs marked in 1:17 are linked with central conceptual christological aspects: the first epoch, from Abraham to David, is associated with the central promises of salvation; the line of kings corresponds with the royal coloration of Matthean Christology; finally, in the third segment the concentration of names that are connected with priesthood and the temple can be read as a reference to Jesus's priestly function, which becomes explicit in 1:21—by means of another allusion to Ps 130:8: Jesus "will save his people from their sins."[10]

While the genealogy serves to programmatically link Jesus's emergence with the history of Israel, his journey as depicted in Matt 2-4 appears as a sort of successful recapitulation of Israel's history.[11] Matthew 2 reveals a series of allusions to the narrative of the danger to and rescue of Moses as a child (Exod 2) and its early Jewish elaboration (see above all Josephus, *Ant.* 2.205-237); Matt 2:20 even

---

9. On this see Nicholas G. Piotrowski, *Matthew's New David at the End of Exile: A Sociorhetorical Study of Scriptural Allusions*, NovTSup 170 (Leiden: Brill, 2016), 34-37 and passim.

10. Cf. Karl-Heinrich Ostmeyer, "Der Stammbaum des Verheißenen: Theologische Implikationen der Namen und Zahlen in Mt 1.1-17," *NTS* 46, no. 2 (2000): 175-92, esp. 182-85.

11. On this, see in detail Joel Kennedy, *The Recapitulation of Israel: Use of Israel's History in Matthew 1:1-4:11*, WUNT 2/257 (Tübingen: Mohr Siebeck, 2008).

contains a citation-like allusion to Exod 4:19 LXX.[12] The typological references to the Moses narrative are connected with contrasting motifs since Egypt mutates into Jesus's place of refuge, while the danger to the savior comes from the Jerusalem authorities. Christologically, these references to the Moses narrative reinforce the idea that Jesus's story is guided by God. Beyond this, through the quotation of Hos 11:1 in Matt 2:15, Jesus as a child is typologically associated with the people of Israel in its early period: just as God called his son Israel out of Egypt *when the people were young* (Hos 11:1), so too did God call Jesus. At this point it becomes clear that πληροῦσθαι ("be fulfilled") in the phrase introducing the formula quotations is not always to be understood in the sense of prediction and realization but can also be meant in the sense of a typological correspondence. Once again there is also a contrasting motif: unlike Israel—the son of God (Exod 4:22)—following the exodus, in the temptations of Jesus by the devil following his forty-day sojourn in the desert, which repeats Israel's forty years in the desert in compact form (Exod 16:35; Num 14:33–34; Deut 8:2–4, and elsewhere), Jesus proves his divine sonship through obedience to the will of the Father (Matt 4:1–11). In all three episodes Jesus responds to the temptation with a quotation from Deuteronomy: in 4:4 with Deut 8:3, in 4:7 with Deut 6:16, and in 4:10 with Deut 6:13; 10:20.[13] As the obedient Son of God, he can be the light that rises upon the people who sit in darkness (4:16), as is then unfolded in the narrative of his public ministry that begins in 4:17. With regard to the genesis of the legendary narrative in Matt 2, the significance of the scriptural quotations and allusions is hardly just a matter of fleshing out a preexisting framework. It should rather be assumed that the reflection on Hos 11 and the Moses narrative were a fundamental source of inspiration for the composition of Matt 2.

2. The fundamental significance of scriptural references for Matthew's presentation of Jesus as the Messiah is further reinforced in the prologue by the fact that of the ten fulfillment quotations with which Matthew seeks to demonstrate the scriptural nature of Jesus's journey and ministry, and which he thereby also comments upon and interprets, five occur in 1:2–4:16. As Matthew shows with the identical introductory formula, the quotation of Hos 11:1 in 2:15 stands in tandem with the quotation of Isa 7:14 in 1:22–23. The insertion of "by the Lord [ὑπὸ κυρίου]," which occurs only here, lends a special weight to the content of the quotations: this is a matter of the fundamental determination of Jesus's identity

---

12. Various other allusions in addition to this occur in the rest of the Gospel, such that Matthew's Jesus story is provided with a couple of Mosaic "overtones." See above all Dale C. Allison, *The New Moses: A Matthean Typology* (Edinburgh: T&T Clark, 1993).

13. Cf. Richard B. Hays, *Echoes of Scripture in the Gospels* (Waco, TX: Baylor University Press, 2016), 117–20. On the significance of Deuteronomy for Matthew's portrayal of Jesus as the obedient Son of God, see Crowe, *Son*.

as Immanuel and the Son of God. By connecting the two quotations, Matthew signals that the two aspects reciprocally interpret one another: In his Son, God is present with humanity, and Jesus can be Immanuel because he is God's Son begotten by the Holy Spirit. From the contextual embedding of the quotation of Isa 7:14 in 1:22–23, it follows that the prophetic word does not speak of the future (natural) pregnancy of a virgin, but rather refers to the *existing* pregnancy of a virgin, whereby the quotation is linked with the motif of divine sonship. Matthew has also altered the wording; in contrast to MT and LXX, in the last sentence he uses the third-person plural καλέσουσιν ("they will call"). Matthew thus looks ahead to the later confession of the disciples:[14] in Jesus they experience the salvific presence of God; for them he is therefore the Immanuel.

The fulfillment quotation in 2:23, which shows Jesus's home in Nazareth to be scriptural, presents a special case. As the indefinite plural διὰ τῶν προφητῶν ("through the prophets") indicates, Matthew was aware of the fact that the words "he will be called a Nazorean" are not found in Israel's Scriptures. The "quotation" should apparently be read such that it concerns an aspect witnessed by (various) prophets. It is most plausible to hear an echo here of the Hebrew word נצר (*nēṣer*), which occurs in the "messianic" prophecy of Isa 11:1.[15] This can be seen alongside further texts, including Jer 23:5; 33:15; Zech 3:8; 6:12, which employ the equivalent Hebrew term צמח (*ṣemaḥ*), thus making sense of the general reference to the prophets (cf. 26:56) in the introduction to the quotation. Far beyond the superficial aspect of showing that Jesus's upbringing in the insignificant town of Nazareth is compatible with Scripture, the quotation serves to draw attention once again to the fact that in Jesus the hopes of Israel which rest upon the *Davidic* Messiah have been fulfilled (cf. previously 2:6!).

With 4:14–16 begins a series of three successive fulfillment quotations in which Isaiah is explicitly identified as the source. All three quotations relate to Jesus's ministry and his salvific significance. The quotation from Isa 8:23–9:1 in Matt 4:15–16, which brings the prologue to a close, has a programmatic character:

---

14. Cf. Richard Beaton, *Isaiah's Christ in Matthew's Gospel*, SNTSMS 123 (Cambridge: Cambridge University Press, 2002), 90. By contrast, Menken, *Matthew's Bible*, 127–31, postulates that Matthew found the third-per. pl. in the revised version of the LXX he used (cf. the third-per. masc. sg. pf. *qal* or *pual* in 1QIsaᵃ).

15. Cf., e.g., Krister Stendahl, *The School of St. Matthew and Its Use of the Old Testament*, ASNU 20 (Lund: Gleerup, 1954), 103–4, 198–99; Robert H. Gundry, *The Use of the Old Testament in St. Matthew's Gospel with Special Reference to the Messianic Hope*, NovTSup 18 (Leiden: Brill, 1967), 103–4; McAffee Moss, *Zechariah Tradition*, 38–40; Piotrowski, *David*, 158–69. The main alternative is the assumption of an allusion to the nazirite or specifically to Judg 13:5, 7 (so, e.g., Menken, *Matthew's Bible*, 161–77). This is poorly suited to the "glutton and drunkard" (Matt 11:19) Jesus.

Israel's Scriptures in Matthew

with it Matthew not only demonstrates that Capernaum (and the surrounding region) being the center of the Messiah's ministry (cf. 8:5; 9:1; 11:23; 17:24) is in agreement with Scripture but at the same time, with the phrase "Galilee of the gentiles," foreshadows the end of the Gospel: the command given in Galilee to missionize *all peoples* (28:16–20). In the quotation, however, this is connected with the reference to Jesus's earthly ministry to Israel and his salvific significance for the people of God: Jesus is identified as the light that rises upon Israel, God's people, which sits in the darkness.[16] That Matthew here, in contrast to the actual wording of the quotation, speaks of the *rising* of the light is reminiscent of 2:2, 9 and thereby of Num 24:17 LXX: "A star will rise from Jacob."

With the quotation from Isa 53:4 in 8:17, Matthew then positions Jesus's therapeutic ministry in the horizon of Scripture in order to demonstrate that the Messiah promised in the Scriptures is a healing Messiah. This is a decisive point for Matthew. Although the absence of illness appears occasionally in early Jewish texts as a sign of the messianic age (see, e.g., 2 Bar. 73:2 and above all 4Q521, where, however, the messiah does not himself appear as a healer), Matthew's focus on the *healing* son of David (9:27; 12:23; 15:22; 20:30–31; 21:[9,]15) sets a unique accent within the context of early Jewish messianology. Matthew must have thus been all the more anxious to demonstrate his conception on the basis of Israel's Scriptures. In this connection, alongside the fulfillment quotation in 8:17, above all Jesus's response to John the Baptist's question in 11:4–6 is significant. Here, Jesus's reference to his ministry contains clear allusions to the promises from Isaiah (Isa 26:19; 29:18–19; 35:5–6; 61:1), according to which the relief of physical infirmities represents an essential characteristic of the salvific age promised to Israel. According to Matthew, anyone who knows Scripture can recognize from Jesus's ministry that he is the promised Messiah (in 11:2 Matthew explicitly speaks of the "works of the Messiah"). This concept also includes the fulfillment quotation from Zech 9:9 in Matt 21:5, which Matthew introduced into the narrative of Jesus's entry into Jerusalem. The beginning of the quotation from Zech 9:9 ("rejoice greatly, daughter Zion") is modified by the words from Isa 62:11 ("say to daughter Zion") in order to bring the quotation into agreement with the event described in Matt 21:9–11. The concentration on gentleness (cf. Matt 11:29) among the attributes that characterize the king in Zech 9:9 corresponds with the presentation of Jesus outlined above as a healing Messiah and at the same time deliberately depicts an alternative to militarily tinged messianic expectations (cf., e.g., Pss. Sol. 17:21–25; 1QSb V, 24–29; 4Q161 frags. 8–10, 23, 25–26; 4Q285 frag. 5,

---

16. According to Isa 9:1, the people *walk* in darkness (LXX: ὁ πορευόμενος; MT: ההלכים). Matthew could have been influenced here by Isa 42:7 and/or Ps 107:10 (cf. Menken, *Matthew's Bible*, 24).

3-4), which were discredited by the results of the revolt against Rome (66-70 CE). Against this background, Matthew seeks to emphasize that anyone who correctly understands Israel's Scriptures recognizes that Jesus's appearance precisely as a gentle king and healer corresponds with the promises of the prophets.

The third fulfillment quotation explicitly attributed to Isaiah, from Isa 42:1-4 in Matt 12:18-21, is the most extensive quotation in all of Matthew. Significant aspects of Jesus's ministry are reflected here and positioned within the horizon of the fulfillment of Scripture.[17] The reference to the servant as ὁ ἀγαπητός μου εἰς ὃν εὐδόκησεν ἡ ψυχή μου ("my beloved, in whom my soul is well pleased") as well as the reference to the Spirit recall 3:16-17 and incorporate the quotation into the evangelist's Christology of divine sonship; the text does not form the basis for a Christology of a divine *servant*, which can be conceptually differentiated from the Son of God Christology. For 12:19, the Matthean context suggests a reference to the conflict between Jesus and the Pharisees and his withdrawal (12:15; cf. 15:21). The metaphor of the bruised reed and smoldering wick in 12:20ab—in itself applicable in various ways—resonates in the Matthean context with the desolate state of the crowds (9:36; 10:6); that is, 12:20ab reflects Jesus's attention to the "languishing, lost sheep," which are spoken of in 12:15 in the form of Jesus's healing ministry. The temporal clause that closes 12:20 combines Isa 42:3c (LXX: εἰς ἀλήθειαν ἐξοίσει κρίσιν/"he will bring forth justice for truth") with 42:4b (LXX: ἕως ἂν θῇ ἐπὶ τῆς γῆς κρίσιν/"until he has established justice on earth"), and also replaces εἰς ἀλήθειαν/לאמת ("for truth") with εἰς νῖκος ("to victory"). Isaiah 42:4a was left out because the statement is incompatible with Jesus's passion.[18] In Matt 12:20, the temporal clause includes the event of Jesus's death and resurrection since he does not succumb to his enemies through his death, but rather carries the "victory" in his exaltation to universal Lord, which establishes the reason that as the exalted Lord he leads justice to victory. With regard to the placement of the quotation of Isa 42:1-4 within the Matthean Jesus narrative, it has to be noted with regard to 12:20 that Matthew used the first indication of Jesus's death in connection with the conflict with the Jewish authorities (12:14) in order to introduce a quotation that he could read within his christological perspective in relation to this conflict and its salvific, "victorious" outcome. More specifically, Jesus's "victory" of Easter is connected with the notion that the hope of the nations will be fulfilled, which in the Matthean version of the quotation—with the LXX—refers concretely to his "name" (MT: ולתורתו). In the larger context, this recalls the interpretation of the name Jesus in 1:21 and the immanuel motif in 1:23; in addition, there is a connection between 12:21 and the phrase "in

---

17. On the contextual references of the quotation see Menken, *Matthew's Bible*, 57-63.
18. Cf. the exemplary discussion in Menken, *Matthew's Bible*, 68.

the name ... of the Son" in the baptism command of 28:19. Within the quotation itself, 12:21 connects with 12:18d. Accordingly, Matthew will have understood the proclamation of justice in line with 28:19–20 (see also 24:14). The scriptural anchoring of the universal dimension of the Christ event, which already echoed in 4:15–16 (on this see further below, "The Justification of the Universality of Salvation"), is concretized here by the statement in 12:20c with regard to the significance of Jesus's death and resurrection for the universality of salvation. In short, with the quotation of Isa 42:1–4, Matthew illuminates essential aspects of his theological conception.[19]

Finally, it is a specific Matthean feature that in 13:35 Jesus's speech in parables is also categorized as the fulfillment of Scripture by means of the prophetically understood words of the Psalms from Ps 78:2:[20] Jesus's way of speaking to the people in parables is intended by God. Within the parable speech, the quotation is to be considered together with the marked citation of Isa 6:9–10 in Matt 13:14–15. Matthew found only an unmarked and abbreviated free rendering of Isa 6:9–10 in Mark 4:12. Matthew identified this quotation-like allusion and—after his own brief summary of what the quotation says in 13:13—offers a full quotation of Isa 6:9–10 LXX. On the basis of the LXX wording, the hardening of the heart, deafness, and closed eyes in Matthew are presented not as a fate caused by God, but rather as culpable failure (cf. by contrast in MT "make the heart of this people hard"). Analogously to the quotation of Hos 11:1 in Matt 2:15, this is not about the realization of a promise, but rather a typological correlation (in this vein, cf. also the application of Isa 29:13 to the scribes and Pharisees in Matt 15:7–9), whereby an aspect of "filling up the measure" might resonate in the use of the prefix ἀνα-: What is said of the people in Isa 6:9–10 is now taking place in the crowds and, moreover, reaches the full measure here. By drawing on Isa 6:9–10, Matthew makes it clear that the deficient reaction of the crowds is no reason for the disciples to be disconcerted, but is in fact precisely in full agreement with the testimony of Scripture.

3. Matthew further drew the shepherd metaphor, which is of great significance in the Matthean Jesus story, from Israel's Scriptures.[21] This metaphor is intro-

---

19. Cf. also the analysis in Beaton, *Isaiah's Christ*, 148–73.

20. On Asaph as prophet see 2 Chr 29:30, cf. also 1 Chr 25:2. On the insertion of "Isaiah" see n. 4.

21. The intertextual dimension of the Matthean shepherd motif has been given much attention in recent research. See among others John Paul Heil, "Ezekiel 34 and the Narrative Strategy of the Shepherd and the Sheep Metaphor in Matthew," *CBQ* 55, no. 2 (1993): 698–708; Young S. Chae, *Jesus as the Eschatological Davidic Shepherd: Studies in the Old Testament, Second Temple Judaism, and in the Gospel of Matthew*, WUNT 2/216 (Tübingen: Mohr Siebeck, 2006); Joel Willitts, *Matthew's Messianic Shepherd-King: In Search of "The Lost Sheep of the*

duced programmatically with the marked citation in 2:6, in which Matthew has added a few words from 2 Sam 5:2 to the quotation from Mic 5:1. These words refer to David's rule over Israel in 2 Samuel and now serve to define the role of the *Davidic* Messiah as the messianic shepherd of his people. The elaboration of the motif in the following narrative by means of further scriptural references is not only relevant to the interpretation of Jesus's ministry in a narrower sense but also to the configuration of characters in the narrative as a whole (on this see below, "The Configuration of Characters in the Matthean Jesus Story"). The shepherd metaphor is further interpreted in connection with a scriptural reference in terms of Jesus's relation to his disciples in the passion narrative. In the quotation from Zech 13:7 in Matt 26:31, τὰ πρόβατα is supplemented by τῆς ποίμνης ("the sheep *of the flock*"), which is hardly influenced by another version of the text (LXX A, which also contains τῆς ποίμνης, could be influenced by Matt 26:31), but rather stems from the pen of the evangelist himself. With this addition, Matthew indicates that the disciples, as the portion of the lost sheep that has already been gathered, are Jesus's flock in the narrower sense, a flock which will now be scattered (for a while).[22]

4. Finally, scriptural references are of central christological relevance in the interpretation of the passion of Jesus. Following Mark (Mark 14:27), in the first line of the quotation in Matt 26:31, the imperative of the scriptural text (sg. in MT, pl. in LXX) is changed to a first-person singular such that it is God himself who strikes the shepherd. Through the—revised—scriptural quotation, Jesus's death is interpreted as God's action. In the narrative of Jesus's arrest in Gethsemane, Matthew expanded the motif of the fulfillment of Scripture found in Mark 14:49. The wording of the narrator's comment in Matt 26:56 (// Mark 14:49) is strongly reminiscent of the introduction to the formula quotations and especially, due to the redactional phrase τοῦτο δὲ ὅλον γέγονεν ("but all this has taken place") at the beginning, of 1:22 and 21:4 (without ὅλον/"all").[23] This comment is preceded in the passage Matthew added in 26:52–54 by Jesus's own comment on the necessity of the event illuminated by a reference to the Scriptures: "How then would the Scriptures be fulfilled, that it must happen this way?" (26:54).

The lack of specificity of this general reference to the Scriptures invites the reader to think comprehensively of the scriptural allusions and quotations in the passion and its broader context. Thus alongside the marked citations in 26:31

House of Israel," BZNW 147 (Berlin: de Gruyter, 2007); Wayne Baxter, *Israel's Only Shepherd: Matthew's Shepherd Motif and His Social Setting*, LNTS 457 (London: T&T Clark, 2012).

22. Cf. Menken, *Matthew's Bible*, 222.

23. See Graham N. Stanton, "Matthew's Use of the Old Testament," in *A Gospel for a New People: Studies in Matthew* (Edinburgh: T&T Clark, 1992), here 356.

and 27:9–10, there are conceptual allusions to, for example, the tradition of the violent fate of prophets (Jer 2:30; 2 Chr 36:15–16; Neh 9:26, and elsewhere), which was introduced in the preceding context by 21:11; 23:37, or the motif of the suffering of the righteous (e.g., Ps 37:32; Wis 2:10–20). That the authorities seek false testimony from the beginning in the trial against Jesus is reminiscent of the motif of the appearance of false witnesses that occurs repeatedly in the presentation of the suffering righteous person in the psalter (Pss 27:12; 35:11–12; 109:2–3). The interpretation in 20:28; 26:28 that Jesus's death occurs for the salvation *for many* allows an association with language of God's servant who has borne the sins of many (Isa 53:11–12) in the servant song of Isa 52:13–53:12. With regard to the universal dimension of the salvation grounded in Jesus's death, the quotation from Isa 42:1–4 in Matt 12:18–21 should also be noted. Furthermore, Jesus's silence in 26:63 is reminiscent of the silence of the servant in Isa 53:7, and the fact that in the mockery of Jesus he is spat upon in the face and struck by the members of the high council in 26:67–68 and by the soldiers in 27:30 recalls the fate of God's servant in Isa 50:6. In addition, there are several references to Ps 22 in the passion narrative (27:35, 39, 46; on 27:43 see "The Configuration of Characters in the Matthean Jesus Story") and to Ps 69:22 (27:34, 48).[24] Given the great importance that Matthew ascribes to Jesus's Davidic sonship, it is hardly insignificant in this connection that the messianic son of David dies with words from a psalm of David (27:46). Another characteristic feature of Matthew is the motif of innocent blood (27:4, 24–25), with which Matthew takes up a phrase widely used in Israel's Scriptures (cf. 1 Sam 19:5; 1 Kgs 2:5; Jer 7:6; 19:4, and elsewhere) in the interpretation of Jesus's death.[25] Finally, in comparison to the Markan note about the tearing of the temple curtain (Mark 15:38), Matthew's broadly expanded presentation of the events following Jesus's death in Matt 27:51–53 is strongly characterized by scriptural references (Ezek 37:7, 12–13 LXX: earthquake, opening of tombs; Zech 14:4–5: splitting [of the Mount of Olives], earthquake, coming of the holy ones).

5. While the preceding discussion has made it clear that the entire Matthean presentation of Jesus's ministry and his passion are characterized by continual

---

24. On the significance of Ps 22 in the Matthean Passion narrative, see, e.g., Zacharias, *Presentation*, 171–86, and especially Alida C. Euler, *Psalmenrezeption in der Passionsgeschichte des Matthäusevangeliums: Eine intertextuelle Studie zur Verwendung, theologischen Relevanz und strukturgebenden Funktion der Psalmen in Mt 26–27 im Lichte frühjüdischer Psalmenrekurse*, WUNT 2/571 (Tübingen: Mohr Siebeck, 2022).

25. On this see Catherine Sider Hamilton, *The Death of Jesus in Matthew: Innocent Blood and the End of Exile*, SNTSMS 167 (Cambridge: Cambridge University Press, 2017); and Johannes Vortisch, *Das unschuldige Blut im Matthäusevangelium: Zur geschichtstheologischen Deutung des Todes Jesu* (forthcoming), with different emphases.

references to Israel's Scriptures, the status of the resurrected Christ as the universal Lord exalted to God is also reinforced by scriptural quotations. In this the renewed reference—after 22:43-44—to Ps 110:1 in Matt 26:64 as well as to Dan 7:13-14 in Matt 24:30; 26:64; and 28:18 is of key significance. While 24:30 and 26:64 refer to the parousia, the adoption of Dan 7:14a in Matt 28:18b is concerned with the present lordship of the exalted one. That the Son of Man is given authority is associated in Dan 7:14 with the fact that all peoples serve him. In Matt 28 this element is transformed in line with the universal mission of the disciples, through whom (people from) all nations are to become disciples, who orient their lives around what Jesus commanded and thus "serve" the exalted Lord.[26]

6. With regard to the importance of Israel's Scriptures in the Matthean presentation of Jesus, we must finally point to the fact that not only do many marked citations occur in Jesus's direct speech (Matt 4:4, 7, 10 → Deut 8:3; 6:16, 13; 10:20; Matt 9:13; 12:7 → Hos 6:6; Matt 11:10 → Mal 3:1; Matt 13:14-15 → Isa 6:9-10; Matt 15:8-9 → Isa 29:13; Matt 19:4-5 → Gen 1:27; 2:24; Matt 19:18-19 → Exod 20:12-16; Lev 19:18; Matt 21:13 → Isa 56:7; Matt 21:16 → Ps 8:3; Matt 21:42 → Ps 118:22-23; Matt 22:32 → Exod 3:6; Matt 22:37-39 → Deut 6:5; Lev 19:18; Matt 22:44 → Ps 110:1; Matt 26:31 → Zech 13:7), but so do unmarked citations and citation-like allusions (e.g., Matt 5:34-35 → Isa 66:1 + Ps 48:3; Matt 7:23 → Ps 6:9; Matt 10:35-36 → Mic 7:6; Matt 11:23 → Isa 14:11, 13, 15; Matt 11:29 → Jer 6:16; Matt 12:40 → Jonah 2:1; Matt 13:42a, 50a → Dan 3:6; Matt 16:27b → Ps 62:13 // Prov 24:12; Matt 18:16 → Deut 19:15; Matt 21:13 → Jer 7:11; Matt 21:33 → Isa 5:1-2; Matt 23:39 → Ps 118:26 [as the words of Jerusalem]; Matt 24:29 → Isa 13:10 + 34:4; Matt 24:30 → Dan 7:13; Matt 26:38 → Pss 42:6, 12; 43:5; Matt 26:54 → Dan 2:28, 29, 45; Matt 26:64 → Ps 110:1; Dan 7:13; Matt 27:46 → Ps 22:2; Matt 28:18 → Dan 7:14). The density of these scriptural references contributes significantly to underscoring the continuity between the Scriptures of Israel and the proclamation of Jesus.

The Configuration of Characters in the Matthean Jesus Story

The presentation of Jesus as the messianic shepherd of God's people Israel corresponds with references to the crowds, using phrases drawn from Israel's Scriptures, as "sheep without a shepherd" (9:36, cf. Num 27:17; 1 Kgs 22:17 // 2 Chr 18:16; Jdt 11:19, and elsewhere) and as the "lost sheep of the house of Israel" (Matt 10:6; 15:24; cf. Jer 27:6 LXX/50:6 MT; and Ezek 34:4, 16). This is not just a matter of identifying individual reference texts. Rather, conceptually it is fundamental for

---

26. Cf. Hays, *Echoes of Scripture in the Gospels*, 184-85.

Matthew that the configuration of the main characters of the narrative—namely, Jesus's and his disciples' conflict with the authorities and the situation of the people—is prefigured in Scripture. Of particular significance here in terms of conceptual allusions are Jer 23:1–6 and Ezek 34. Both texts take the past shepherds harshly to task and connect the accusation of the old shepherds with the proclamation that God himself takes care of the rest of his sheep and provides them with new shepherds, or a successor of David (Jer 23:5–6; Ezek 34:23, cf. also 37:24). This same constellation also defines the Matthean Jesus narrative: the bad shepherds are replaced by the Davidic Messiah (and his disciples).

The characterization of the authorities as bad shepherds incorporated through these scriptural references goes hand in hand with the fact that Herod and the Jewish authorities assisting him in Matt 2 reflect the role of the pharaoh who is inimical to Israel in the Moses narrative. In the passion narrative Matthew has expanded the mockery of Jesus by the high priests, scribes, and elders from Mark 15:31–32 in Matt 27:43 by placing the words of the godless mockers from Ps 22:9 on their lips so that the authorities themselves slip into the role of the wicked: like a ravening and roaring lion they have opened their maws against the righteous (Ps 22:14). In light of the reference to Jesus's divine sonship at the end of the mocking speech in 27:43, an allusion to Wis 2 (see above all vv. 13, 16, 18) might also resonate here. With regard to the horizon of meaning that this allusion opens up, it can be noted in particular that Wis 2–3 also contain the motif of the confirmation of the Son of God through what happens after his death, which is also key for the interpretation of Jesus's fate (see also Wis 4:7–5:16). This aspect was already illuminated through a scriptural quotation in the interpretation of the parable of the wicked tenants, which addresses the ongoing resistance of the authorities in Israel against God's messengers and ultimately God's son (Matt 21:33–46). Here the failure of the tenants' endeavor to dispense with the son as the heir of the vineyard by killing him in order to take possession of the vineyard (= Israel) themselves is illuminated by a reference to Ps 118:22–23, where the tenants (= the authorities in Israel) reappear as the builders and the statement that the stone they have rejected has become the cornerstone brings into view the resurrection of the Son of God, which dooms their plan to failure.

The references of the shepherd/sheep metaphor to Ezekiel and Jeremiah incorporate the aspect that the role of the authorities in the basic configuration of the Matthean Jesus story corresponds with the testimony of Israel's Scriptures, and thus the resistance brought by the Pharisees against the message of Christ in the environment of the Matthean communities is no reason for confusion or doubt. This same aspect is emphatically reinforced by the two fulfillment quotations in 2:17–18 and 27:9–10. Instead of "so that . . . might be fulfilled [ἵνα/ ὅπως πληρωθῇ]," both quotations are introduced with "then was fulfilled [τότε ἐπληρώθη]." The actions of Jesus's opponents—specifically, the murder of the children of Bethlehem (Matt 2:16) and the high priests' and elders' course of action against Jesus as well as their dealings with Judas and his regretted betrayal—are indeed foreseen in the Scriptures, according to Matthew, but of course neither planned nor willed by God. In the introductions to both of the quotations, Matthew explicitly refers to the prophet Jeremiah, who functions here as a prophet of doom. Unlike in the LXX version of the words of Jeremiah, the quotation in 2:18 does not speak of weeping for the *sons*, which would have fit the context well, but rather of weeping for the *children*. In this way Matthew creates a cross-reference to 27:25 ("His blood be on us *and our children*") and thus interweaves Matt 2 and the passion with one another.[27] The actions of the authorities against Jesus—in various ways—brings doom upon the people. The quotation in 27:9–10, which takes up the motif of blood money and the purchase of the field from the preceding narrative of Judas's regret, is also ascribed to Jeremiah. In fact, it is a mixed quotation that connects a very free rendering of the primary reference text Zech 11:13 with allusions to the potter and the field in Jer 18:1–12; 19:1–13; and 32; the final clause agrees with Exod 9:12 LXX. While in Zech 11:13 the first-person singular is used with reference to actions of the repudiated shepherd, Matthew has connected these actions with the behavior of the authorities through the third-person plural (the connecting factor is the ambiguity of the Greek verb form ἔλαβον = "I took" or "they took"). The ascription of the quotation to Jeremiah instead of Zechariah is no mistake, but should rather be understood as an appellative signal to the addressees that they ought to consider the events depicted in Matt 27:3–8 in light of Jeremiah. Jeremiah 19 must have been of particular importance to Matthew in terms of conceptual allusions: first, the elders of the people and the elders of the priests are addressed in Jer 19 (v. 1, cf. the constellation of characters in Matt 27:3); second, Jer 19 announces the destruction of Jerusalem, which, third, is justified by the spilling of innocent blood (19:4; cf. Matt 27:4, 25). Fourth, in Jer 19:11, in the context of the destruction of the city symbolized by the breaking of the potter's vessel, there is an explicit reference to the judgment of her inhabitants (cf. 19:12 and already 19:3), who are identified in 19:11 as "this people (τὸν λαὸν τοῦτον)" (cf. again Matt 27:25). In Israel's Scriptures and early Jewish tradition, Jeremiah is the prophet most closely associated with the destruction of the temple (in addition to Jeremiah itself, see, e.g., 2 Chr 36:19–21; Sir 49:6–7). It is therefore not surprising that a broad reception of Jeremiah or the figure of Jeremiah is found in the context of the confrontation with the destruction of the Second Temple following 70 CE

---

27. By contrast, Menken, *Matthew's Bible*, 157–58, postulates that Matthew found "children [τέκνα]" in his version of the LXX.

(2 Bar.; 4 Bar.; Josephus, *Ant.* 10.79–80, 89–96, 112–130, 156–158, 176–180, and elsewhere). The reception of Jeremiah encountered in Matthew is to be situated within this context (alongside 2:17–18 and 27:9–10; cf. 21:13 [quoting Jer 7:11]; 23:35 [the phrase "righteous blood" is likely influenced by Lam 4:13], as well as the mention of Jeremiah in Matt 16:14). More specifically, Matthew's attempt to illuminate the wrongdoing of Jesus's opponents through allusions to Jeremiah goes hand in hand with his consideration that the destruction of the Second Temple is punishment for the enemies of Jesus and his followers.[28] The parallels with Judas's fate in Acts 1:16–20 show that Matt 27:3–10 is not the evangelist's own free creation; however, the common basis of tradition is limited to the connection of Judas's payment with the purchase of a field and the elucidation of the event with a scriptural reference, which is carried out very differently in Acts 1:18 with Ps 69:26 than it is in Matt 27. With regard to the genesis of Matt 27:3–10, the numerous scriptural references suggest that the text is the result of a creative process of interpretation in which the tradition about Judas was further developed in light of the reading of Scripture, primarily the books of Jeremiah and Zechariah, such that the evidence here is analogous to Matt 2.

Torah

Israel's Scriptures also play a major role in Matthean ethics. Jesus's ethical instruction, whose central significance in Matthean theology is exemplified by the words of the resurrected Christ in 28:18–20, is not limited to an explication of the Torah, but Jesus's interpretation of Torah constitutes a fundamental and indispensable point of reference for the disciples' way of life. In the Sermon on the Mount, Matthew has framed the body of the discourse with two statements on the Torah and the Prophets (5:17[–20]; 7:12) and, in so doing, connects Jesus's teaching explicitly with the Scriptures of Israel. Here the meaning of God's will, as it is set down in the Torah and the Prophets, is ultimately and authoritatively laid out for the crowds representing all Israel, who according to 4:25–5:1; 7:28–29 constitute the outer circle of the audience. The statement that programmatically opens the body of the Sermon on the Mount in 5:17—that Jesus has not come to abolish the Torah and the Prophets, but to fulfill them—is explicated by the series of antitheses in 5:21–48. The wording of the theses, each of which is contrasted with Jesus's instruction, only agrees (almost) verbatim with the Torah in 5:27 (cf.

---

28. In detail on this see Matthias Konradt, "Die Deutung der Zerstörung Jerusalems und des Tempels im Matthäusevangelium," in *Studien zum Matthäusevangelium*, WUNT 358 (Tübingen: Mohr Siebeck, 2016), 219–57, esp. 241–57.

Exod 20:14; Deut 5:18) and 5:38 (cf. Exod 21:24–25; Lev 24:19–20; Deut 19:21). In 5:21, the commandment "you shall not commit murder" (Exod 20:13; Deut 5:17) is supplemented with a punitive provision for which one can adduce Old Testament commandments as reference texts (cf. Exod 21:12; Lev 24:17), but which is not found in this form in the Torah. The third thesis (5:31) is not even a Torah commandment but is based on material from the Torah with Deut 24:1–4. Likewise, the fourth thesis (5:33) is not found in this form anywhere in the Torah, but once again there are commandments that can be invoked as context (Lev 19:12; Zech 8:17, as well as Num 30:3; Deut 23:22). Finally, in 5:43, the commandment of love in Lev 19:18 is quoted in part ("as yourself" is missing); instead, there is once again an addendum: "and hate your enemy." The other—complete (!)—quotations of the love commandment in 19:19 and 22:39 clearly show that, first, Matthew by no means criticizes the commandment of neighborly love itself, and he therefore, second, cannot have seen 5:43 as an adequate paraphrase of the Torah. The fact that this cannot be a critique of the commandments themselves also applies with the same clarity to the Decalogue commandments in 5:21, 27 in view of 15:19; 19:18. The mixed evidence on the wording of the theses suggests that Matthew did not simply want to reproduce Torah commandments with these theses, but rather sought to convey a certain understanding of the Torah that either interprets the commandments literally or limits their meaning or scope through interpretation. This assumption is reinforced by the opening of the introduction to the theses with "you have heard" (the absence of this element in 5:31 can be explained by the immediate continuation of the preceding antithesis): "It was said" is parallel to the introduction to the fulfillment quotations (cf., e.g., 1:22) and thus points to the authority of God that stands behind the Torah (the Decalogue commandments in Exod 20 are God's direct speech); the "ancients" are accordingly the Sinai generation. But "you have heard" points to the (synagogal) process of transmitting the Torah commandments. According to the statement in Matt 5:20, which functions as the major premise of the antitheses, the theses more specifically represent what Matthew views as the insufficient Torah understanding of the scribes and Pharisees. The antitheses thus belong in the context of the conflict between Jesus and the Jewish authorities over the correct understanding of the will of God, which pervades the entire Gospel (9:9–13; 12:1–14; 15:1–20; 19:3–9; 22:34–40; 23:16–26). In this, Jesus is presented as the one and only teacher (23:8–10) who has brought to light in his instruction the full meaning of the commandments and their deeper intention and thus enables a "better righteousness" that allows access to the kingdom of heaven to the people who follow him (5:20).

Matthew's Torah hermeneutic is centrally characterized by the fact that social commandments are categorically superordinate to ritual commandments (15:19;

19:16–22; 22:34–40; 23:23). That Matthew invariably speaks of "Torah *and Prophets*" in 5:17; 7:12; and 22:40 can be understood in this context.²⁹ For Matthew, the prophetic testimony serves to justify this superordination. The repeated quotation of Hos 6:6 in Matt 9:13 and 12:7, with which Matthew justifies the central position of mercy as an ethical guideline, is of programmatic significance. In addition, we can point to 23:23, where the emphasis on justice, mercy, and faith/faithfulness as "the weightier matters of the law" is inspired by Mic 6:8. The consequence of this "prophetic" interpretation of the Torah is significant for the Matthean presentation of Jesus's ministry: when Jesus turns his attention to sinners, according to 9:13 this is not a lived criticism of the Torah but, on the contrary, a manifestation of the fulfillment of the Torah and Prophets through Jesus.

The Pharisees, by contrast, manifest their misunderstanding of the will of God in 9:9–13 and 12:1–8. The evangelist also repeatedly expresses the authorities' insufficient knowledge of Scripture by using the phrase "have you not/never read [οὐκ/οὐδέποτε ἀνέγνωτε]" to introduce Jesus's scriptural references in the conflict with his opponents, though this not only applies to their understanding of God's will but also includes other areas of Jesus's ministry (12:3 [// Mark 2:25]; 12:5; 19:4; 21:16; 21:42 [// Mark 12:10]; 22:31 [// Mark 12:26]). As the historical context of this clearly strengthened element of the narrative, compared with Mark, the conflict with the Pharisees that characterizes the situation of the Matthean community should be taken into account. In this conflict, Matthew is concerned with demonstrating on the basis of Scripture that the Christ-believing ecclesia is the legitimate custodian of Israel's theological traditions.

The Justification of the Universality of Salvation

It is not only with regard to Jesus's ministry in Israel that references to Israel's Scriptures generate a resonant space in which the Matthean narrative acquires a deeper timbre; rather, they also serve an important function in the justification of the universality of salvation connected with Jesus's appearance. Matthew seeks to make clear that the inclusion of gentiles in salvation does not signify a fundamental break from the theological foundation of God's people Israel; on the contrary, this brings to fulfillment exactly what God's history with Israel as attested in the Scriptures was always concerned with. The universal dimension of

---

29. This must be clearly differentiated from the phrase in Matt 11:13, where Matthew speaks conversely of "Prophets and Law." Here the concern is with the prophetic function of Scripture, with the promises, while the phrase "law and prophets" always refers to the legal will of God as it is expressed in Scripture.

the reference to Abraham in the superscription of the Gospel in 1:1 was already pointed out in "Christology." The further references to Abraham in 3:9 and 8:11 confirm this aspect: with the mission to the gentiles, new children of Abraham are actually raised up (3:9), and among the many that will eat with Abraham, Isaac, and Jacob (8:11) there are also people from the gentiles—it should be noted here that the motif of the eschatological feast that resonates in 8:11 also occurs in Isa 25:6–8 with a universalistic orientation.[30] Matthew's claim that the history of election that began with Abraham finds its true continuation in the communities of Christ-believers that are open to gentiles is then reflected in the striking integration of four non-Jewish women (Tamar, Rahab, Ruth, and the wife of Uriah) in the genealogy of Jesus in 1:2–16. In this way Matthew makes it clear that Israel had always been open for people from the gentiles who join in the worship of the one God.[31] The coming of the magi to the infant Jesus in 2:1–12 then brings into play the motif of the pilgrimage of the nations (Isa 2:2–5; 60; 66:18; Mic 4:1–5, and elsewhere; more specifically, in the triad of gifts in 2:11, the first two, gold and incense, are reminiscent of Isa 60:6), which is simultaneously transformed messianically since the "pilgrimage" of the magi does not end at Zion, but at Jesus, the Immanuel, in order to pay homage to the king of the Jews (2:2, 11; but on this cf. Ps 72:10–11 and Pss. Sol. 17:31a). In short, the motif of the pilgrimage of the nations is decoupled from Zion theology.[32] In Matt 15:21–28, Matthew has introduced a biblical atmosphere to the narrative by identifying the gentile asking for help for her daughter as a Canaanite (15:22) and supplementing Tyre (Mark 7:24) with Sidon (Matt 15:21; on this pair cf. 11:21) so that the narrative comes to be seen against the background of the classic opposition between Israel and Canaan/foreign nations, and the ultimate granting of her request anticipates the post-Easter triumph over this opposition. We have already pointed to the universality of salvation in the two fulfillment quotations from Isa 8:23–9:1 and 42:1–4 in Matt 4:15f and 12:18–21 in "Christology."[33]

---

30. On Abraham cf. Carolin Ziethe, *Auf seinen Namen werden die Völker hoffen: Die matthäische Rezeption der Schriften Israels zur Begründung des universalen Heils*, BZNW 233 (Berlin: de Gruyter, 2018), 107–55.

31. Consult for many Hays, *Echoes of Scripture in the Gospels*, 112.

32. See Ziethe, *Namen*, 162–64.

33. For a comprehensive analysis of the significance of appeals to Israel's Scriptures in the framework of the Matthean justification of the universal dimension of salvation, see Ziethe, *Namen*.

Israel's Scriptures in Matthew

Further Allusions and the Biblical Coloration of the Narrative

Beyond what has already been said, Matthew contains numerous allusions to narratives, motifs, or legal regulations from Israel's Scriptures, familiarity with which Matthew presupposes among his addressees. The meaning of the Matthean text is also often produced or deepened by these allusions. A few examples will have to suffice. Matthew adopted some from his sources, but others are found only in Matthew (italicized in the following): the thirty pieces of silver that the authorities pay Judas as traitor's wages in *Matt 26:15* are adopted from Zech 11:12 and at the same time echo Exod 21:32, where thirty pieces of silver are identified as compensation for the owner of a slave who has been killed by a bull, such that the authorities' contempt for Jesus is expressed—in stark contrast to the anointing with expensive oil that precedes this passage (Matt 26:6–13). Matthew 12:4 and *12:5* presuppose that the addressees are familiar with the regulations regarding the bread of the presence in Lev 24:5–9 and the commandment regarding the offerings to be brought on the Sabbath (Num 28:9–10). The payment of the workers in the vineyard in *Matt 20:8* accords with the commandment in Lev 19:13; Deut 24:14–15. Matthew 12:3–4 presupposes familiarity with 1 Sam 21:1–7; Matt 12:41–42, with Jonah 3 and 1 Kgs 10:1–13 // 2 Chr 9:1–12; Matt 23:35, with Gen 4 and 2 Chr 24:20–22; and Matt 24:37–39, with the Noah narrative in Gen 6–8. Jesus's instruction on the infinite willingness to forgive in *Matt 18:22* acquires clearer contours from the Lamech song in Gen 4:24: limitless forgiveness replaces strict retribution. The healing of the blind and the lame in the temple in *Matt 21:14* is seen more clearly through the contrast with David's actions in 2 Sam 5:8. Matthew's account of the death of Judas, the betrayer of the messianic son of David, in *Matt 21:5* as suicide by hanging is inspired by the suicide of Ahithophel, David's disloyal advisor, in 2 Sam 17:23. The scene Matthew has introduced into the transfiguration narrative in 17:6–7 is reminiscent of Dan 8:16–18, where the archangel Gabriel touches Daniel, who lay with his face to the ground before the angel, and sets him on his feet. The redactional identification of the event of Matt 17:3–5 as a "vision" (ὅραμα) in 17:9 strengthens the connection with Daniel, as the occurrences of "vision" (ὅραμα) in the LXX are strikingly concentrated in Daniel. Matthew may have been particularly inspired here by Dan 7:13, 15 LXX, and so by the same context that is not only received in 24:30; 26:64 but is also alluded to in 28:18–20 such that the character of Matt 17:1–9 as an anticipation of the reality of the resurrection is further underscored by the allusions to Daniel.

Alongside this, there are various places in Matthew where we can observe the phenomenon that scriptural allusions serve less to broaden or deepen the meaning of the text than as a literary device that lends a biblical coloration to the text. This applies, for example, to Matt 4:2, where unlike Mark 1:13 and Luke 4:2, the evangelist has Jesus fast for forty days *and nights*, which recalls Moses on Sinai (Exod 34:28; Deut 9:9, 18; cf. further Elijah in 1 Kgs 19:8), but this does not provide a key for the interpretation of the text. To cite just one further example, a similar case is found in the echoes of the Sinai tradition that can be seen in Matt 17:1–9, in addition to the allusions to Daniel already mentioned. Moses also climbs a mountain with three companions (and seventy elders), namely Mount Sinai (Exod 24:9, 12–15), which is covered by a cloud from which God calls out to Moses (24:15–16). As Moses returns after climbing the mountain again, his face is radiant (Exod 34:29–35; cf. 2 Cor 3:7; LAB 12:1). In addition, the command to "listen to him" (Matt 17:5) has a counterpart in the announcement of a prophet like Moses in Deut 18:15. The differences in the relations among the motifs and their configuration make it clear that the transfiguration narrative is not simply modeled on the Moses narrative. However, the echoes of the divine revelation on Sinai do help to envelop the vision of the transfiguration of Jesus, which has been granted to the three disciples, with a biblical aura and to position it in the context of the foundational salvation-historical narrative of Israel.

The Nature of the Scriptural Text

With regard to the question of the version of text that Matthew used, we can exclude the quotations that Matthew adopted verbatim from the *Vorlage* of Mark and Q, or in which minor differences do not allow for plausible conclusions to be drawn, as is consistently the case for differences between Matthew and Mark in quotations adopted from Mark.[34] Differences between Matthew and Luke in Q material raise the problem of the reconstruction of Q. Nevertheless, it can be concluded with sufficient plausibility that Matthew has expanded quotations in two cases (Matt 4:4: Deut 8:3; Matt 10:35–36: Mic 7:6), but only Matt 4:4 offers significant evidence.

The numerous quotations that still remain after these exclusions do not present a unified picture. The evidence is complex and can only be presented here with a few examples and in its basic features. On the one hand, there is evidence that the LXX was used. Thus, for example, the expansion of the quotation from Deut 8:3 compared to Q/Luke 4:4 in Matt 4:4 agrees with the LXX against the MT, likewise for the quotation of Deut 19:15 in Matt 18:16, as well as the quotations of Isa 6:9–10 in Matt 13:14–15 and of Ps 8:3 in Matt 21:16.[35] On the other hand, the opposite is the case, for example, for the quotation of Hos 11:1 in Matt

---

34. Cf. the discussion of the quotations in Menken, *Matthew's Bible*, 205–25.
35. Cf. Menken, *Matthew's Bible*, 230 (on Matt 13:14–15), 240–41 (on Matt 4:4), 271–72 (on Matt 18:16), 274 (on Matt 21:16). As a few others, Menken regards the quotation of Isa 6:9–10 in

2:15 and for Isa 53:4 in Matt 8:17. If, in Hos 6:6, LXX B (ἔλεος θέλω ἢ θυσίαν) is the original reading and the LXX A reading, which agrees with Matt 9:13; 12:7, is hexaplaric, then Matthew also agrees with the MT against the LXX here.³⁶ There is a whole series of quotations that agree in part with the LXX but in part with the MT against the LXX, thus for example Jer 31(38):15 in Matt 2:18; Isa 8:23–9:1 in Matt 4:15–16; Isa 42:1–4 in Matt 12:18–21; Zech 9:9 in Matt 21:5; or Jer 6:16 in Matt 11:29.³⁷ In Matt 13:35, in the first line of the quotation from Ps 78:2, Matthew reproduces the LXX text verbatim (Ps 77:2a LXX), while the second line presents a free rendering that does not agree with any known version of the text.

One possible explanation of this evidence is that Matthew had a hebraizing LXX recension.³⁸ This hypothesis has the disadvantage of operating on the basis of an unknown text, but the existence of such a recension is plausible from a text-historical perspective in view of the plurality of textual forms in the first century CE and in particularly in light of the Greek version corrected toward the MT in the Greek Minor Prophets Scroll found at Naḥal Ḥever (8HevXIIgr).³⁹ However, a further aspect must also be considered: If Matt 2:23 alludes to the word נֵצֶר (nēṣer) in Isa 11:1, this presupposes an awareness of the Hebrew text (if the subdivision of the genealogy in three times fourteen generations is based on the Hebrew numerical value of David [4 = ד + 6 = ו + 4 = ד], this also indicates a bilingual milieu). Accordingly, for Hos 6:6; 11:1; and Isa 53:4, for example, Matthew's own translation of the Hebrew text⁴⁰ can be at play, while Isa 8:23–9:1; 42:1–4; Jer 31(38):15, and other quotations can derive from an independent translation of the Hebrew text that is influenced by the LXX.⁴¹

Matt 13:14-15 as a later interpolation (230-31) and ascribes Ps 8:3 in Matt 21:16 to pre-Matthean tradition (274-78).

36. According to, e.g., Gundry, *Use*, 111; Menken, *Matthew's Bible*, 229, LXX A is hexaplaric.

37. For Matt 2:18, consult the analyses by Christine Ritter, *Rachels Klage im antiken Judentum und frühen Christentum: Eine auslegungsgeschichtliche Studie*, AGJU 52 (Leiden: Brill, 2003), 118-19; Menken, *Matthew's Bible*, 148-55. For Matt 4:15-16, see Stendahl, *School of St. Matthew*, 104-6; Gundry, *Use*, 105-8; Beaton, *Isaiah's Christ*, 97-102; Menken, *Matthew's Bible*, 22-27. For Matt 12:18-21, cf. the discussions in Stendahl, *School of St. Matthew*, 107-15; Gundry, *Use*, 110-16; Beaton, *Isaiah's Christ*, 123-41; Menken, *Matthew's Bible*, 67-88. For Matt 21:5, see Gundry, *Use*, 120-21; Menken, *Matthew's Bible*, 111-15. For Matt 11:29, see W. D. Davies and Dale C. Allison Jr., *A Critical and Exegetical Commentary on the Gospel according to Saint Matthew*, 3 vols., ICC (Edinburgh: T&T Clark, 1988-1997), 2:291.

38. Thus the general thesis of Menken, *Matthew's Bible*, passim.

39. See Emanuel Tov, Robert A. Kraft, and P. J. Parsons, *The Greek Minor Prophets Scroll from Naḥal Ḥever (8HevXIIgr)*, DJD 8 (Oxford: Clarendon, 1990). On this cf. Menken, *Matthew's Bible*, 7-9.

40. See, e.g., Gundry, *Use*, 93, 109, 111; Jean Miler, *Les citations d'accomplissement dans l'Évangile de Matthieu: Quand Dieu se rend présent en toute humanité*, AnBib 140 (Rome: Editrice Pontificio Istituto Biblico, 1999), 47, 112 (on Hos 11:1 and Isa 53:4), on Isa 53:4 further, e.g., Stendahl, *School*, 106-7; Beaton, *Isaiah's Christ*, 111-14.

41. Cf. Stendahl, *School of St. Matthew*, 102-3, 106, 115; Gundry, *Use*, 94-97, 105-8, 110-16;

Matthew appears to have been bilingual and apparently had access to both Hebrew and Greek versions of the texts.[42] In the series of Decalogue commandments in Matt 15:19; 19:18, he follows the MT.

The answer to the question of the form of the text that was available to Matthew is also made more difficult because Matthew shows that he deals freely with the wording of quotations, as is not only made clear by the multiple deliberate mixed quotations (e.g., Matt 2:6: Mic 5:1 + Sam 5:2; Matt 21:5: Zech 9:9 with an introduction from Isa 62:11; Matt 27:9–10: Zech 11:13 + Exod 9:12) but is also documented in redactional interventions. To cite just one further example alongside what has already been mentioned (see, e.g., "Christology" on Isa 7:14 and 42:1–4 in Matt 1:23; 12:18–21; and "The Configuration of Characters in the Matthean Jesus Story" on Jer 31:15 in Matt 2:18): in Matt 2:6, "(house of) Ephratha" in Mic 5:1 is replaced by "land of Judah" in order to allude to Judah as the patriarch of the royal family (cf. Matt 1:2–3); further, the statement about Bethlehem's status is inverted by the insertion of "by no means [οὐδαμῶς]", probably in order to indicate that the significance of the city has been fundamentally altered by the birth of the Messiah.[43]

Conclusion

The exceedingly numerous and varied appeals to the Scriptures of Israel in Matthew emerge as an extremely important part of the evangelist's communicative strategy: In the community's conflict with the Pharisee-dominated synagogue, they serve to reassure the addressees that the Christ-believing ecclesia is the true custodian of the theological traditions of Israel. On the basis of Israel's Scriptures, Jesus is identified in detail as the promised Messiah, and his ethical instruction brings to light the full significance and deeper intention of the proclamation of God's will in the Torah and the Prophets; the Scriptures serve to situate the opposition of the authorities within the ongoing resistance of the ruling classes to God's messengers, and at the same time they are delegitimized by the demonstration of their ignorance of the Scriptures and their misguided understanding of the Torah; by contrast, the ecclesia that confesses Jesus as the Messiah stands fully upon the foundation of the Scriptures of Israel.

If one asks how the exceedingly numerous references to the Scriptures of Israel in the Matthean Jesus story can be explained in terms of the formation of Matthew, it can be presupposed that the final form of the Gospel is the result

---

on Jer 31(38):15 also Knowles, *Jeremiah*, 36–38, as well as above all the comprehensive presentation of quotations and allusions in Davies and Allison, *Matthew*, 1:29–58.

42. Cf., e.g., Davies and Allison, *Matthew*, 1:33, 44–45.

43. Cf. exemplarily Stanton, "Use," 360–61.

of a long process of reflection by a Jewish-Christian group centered around or in any case with the evangelist—a group that, on the one hand, articulated in their gatherings the Jesus tradition that had been passed down to them (already containing scriptural quotations and allusions) and, on the other, intensively and independently read and reflected upon the Scriptures. In such a setting it would in any case make sense to closely connect the two entities and to allow each to interpret the other. It should also be considered, as has been suggested for the examples of Matt 2 and 27:3–10, that the reflection on Scripture in the elaboration of the Jesus tradition developed an eminently creative potential.

Bibliography

Allison, Dale C. *The New Moses: A Matthean Typology*. Edinburgh: T&T Clark, 1993.

Baxter, Wayne. *Israel's Only Shepherd: Matthew's Shepherd Motif and His Social Setting*. LNTS 457. London: T&T Clark, 2012.

Beaton, Richard. "Isaiah in Matthew's Gospel." Pages 63–78 in *Isaiah in the New Testament*. Edited by Steve Moyise and Maarten J. J. Menken. London: T&T Clark, 2005.

———. *Isaiah's Christ in Matthew's Gospel*. SNTSMS 123. Cambridge: Cambridge University Press, 2002.

Blomberg, Craig L. "Matthew." Pages 1–109 in *Commentary on the New Testament Use of the Old Testament*. Edited by G. K. Beale and D. A. Carson. Grand Rapids: Baker Academic, 2007.

Chae, Young S. *Jesus as the Eschatological Davidic Shepherd: Studies in the Old Testament, Second Temple Judaism, and in the Gospel of Matthew*. WUNT 2/216. Tübingen: Mohr Siebeck, 2006.

Crowe, Brandon D. *The Obedient Son: Deuteronomy and Christology in the Gospel of Matthew*. BZNW 188. Berlin: de Gruyter, 2012.

Davies, W. D., and Dale C. Allison Jr. *A Critical and Exegetical Commentary on the Gospel according to Saint Matthew*. 3 vols. ICC. Edinburgh: T&T Clark, 1988–1997.

Euler, Alida C. *Psalmenrezeption in der Passionsgeschichte des Matthäusevangeliums: Eine intertextuelle Studie zur Verwendung, theologischen Relevanz und strukturgebenden Funktion der Psalmen in Mt 26–27 im Lichte frühjüdischer Psalmenrekurse*. WUNT 2/571. Tübingen: Mohr Siebeck, 2022.

Foster, Paul. "The Use of Zechariah in Matthew's Gospel." Pages 65–85 in *The Book of Zechariah and Its Influence*. Edited by Christopher M. Tuckett. Burlington, VT: Ashgate, 2003.

Gundry, Robert H. *The Use of the Old Testament in St. Matthew's Gospel with Special Reference to the Messianic Hope*. NovTSup 18. Leiden: Brill, 1967.

Ham, Clay Alan. *The Coming King and the Rejected Shepherd: Matthew's Reading of Zechariah's Messianic Hope*. New Testament Monographs 4. Sheffield: Sheffield Phoenix, 2005.

Hamilton, Catherine Sider. *The Death of Jesus in Matthew: Innocent Blood and the End of Exile*. SNTSMS 167. Cambridge: Cambridge University Press, 2017.

Hatina, Thomas, ed. *Biblical Interpretation in Early Christian Gospels*. Vol. 2, *The Gospel of Matthew*. LNTS 310. London: T&T Clark, 2008.

Hays, Richard B. *Echoes of Scripture in the Gospels*. Waco, TX: Baylor University Press, 2016.

Heil, John Paul. "Ezekiel 34 and the Narrative Strategy of the Shepherd and the Sheep Metaphor in Matthew." *CBQ* 55, no. 4 (1993): 698–708.

Huizenga, Leroy A. *The New Isaac: Tradition and Intertextuality in the Gospel of Matthew*. NovTSup 131. Leiden: Brill, 2009.

Kennedy, Joel. *The Recapitulation of Israel: Use of Israel's History in Matthew 1:1–4:11*. WUNT 2/257. Tübingen: Mohr Siebeck, 2008.

Knowles, Michael. *Jeremiah in Matthew's Gospel: The Rejected Prophet Motif in Matthaean Redaction*. JSNTSup 68. Sheffield: Sheffield Academic, 1993.

Konradt, Matthias. "Die Deutung der Zerstörung Jerusalems und des Tempels im Matthäusevangelium." Pages 219–57 in *Studien zum Matthäusevangelium*. WUNT 358. Tübingen: Mohr Siebeck, 2016.

———. "Gospel of Matthew." Pages 107–38 in *From Paul to Josephus: Literary Receptions of Jesus in the First Century CE*. Edited by Helen Bond. Vol. 1 of *The Reception of Jesus in the First Three Centuries*. London: T&T Clark, 2020.

———. *Israel, Church, and the Gentiles in the Gospel of Matthew*. BMSEC 2. Waco, TX: Baylor University Press, 2014.

Menken, Maarten J. J. *Matthew's Bible: The Old Testament Text of the Evangelist*. BETL 173. Leuven: Peeters, 2004.

———. "A Source of Its Own: Matthew Citing Scripture." Pages 45–66 in *An Early Reader of Mark and Q*. Edited by Jozef Verheyden and Gilbert van Belle. BTS 21. Leuven: Peeters, 2016.

Miler, Jean: *Les citations d'accomplissement dans l'Évangile de Matthieu: Quand Dieu se rend présent en toute humanité*. AnBib 140. Rome: Pontifical Biblical Institute, 1999.

Moffitt, David M. "Righteous Bloodshed, Matthew's Passion Narrative, and the Temple's Destruction: Lamentations as a Matthean Intertext." *JBL* 125, no. 2 (2006): 299–320.

Moss, Charlene McAfee. *The Zechariah Tradition and the Gospel of Matthew*. BZNW 156. Berlin: de Gruyter, 2008.

Ostmeyer, Karl-Heinrich, "Der Stammbaum des Verheißenen: Theologische Implikationen der Namen und Zahlen in Mt 1.1–17," *NTS* 46, no. 2 (2000): 175–92.

Piotrowski, Nicholas G. *Matthew's New David at the End of Exile: A Socio-rhetorical Study of Scriptural Allusions*. NovTSup 170. Leiden: Brill, 2016.

Ritter, Christine. *Rachels Klage im antiken Judentum und frühen Christentum: Eine auslegungsgeschichtliche Studie*. AGJU 52. Leiden: Brill, 2003.

Rothfuchs, Wilhelm. *Die Erfüllungszitate des Matthäus-Evangeliums: Eine biblisch-theologische Untersuchung*. BWANT 88. Stuttgart: Kohlhammer, 1969.

Segbroeck, Frans van. "Les citations d'accomplissement dans l'Évangile selon saint Matthieu d'après trois ouvrages récents." Pages 107–30 in *L'Évangile selon Matthieu: Rédaction et théologie*. Edited by M. Didier. BETL 29. Gembloux: Duculot, 1971.

Senior, Donald. "The Lure of the Formula Quotations: Re-assessing Matthew's Use of the Old Testament with the Passion Narrative as Test Case." Pages 89–115 in *The Scriptures in the Gospels*. Edited by Christopher M. Tuckett. BETL 131. Leuven: Leuven University Press, 1997.

Sider Hamilton, Catherine. *The Death of Jesus in Matthew: Innocent Blood and the End of Exile*. SNTSMS 167. Cambridge: Cambridge University Press, 2017.

Soares Prabhu, George M. *The Formula Quotations in the Infancy Narratives of Matthew*. AnBib 53. Rome: Pontifical Biblical Institute, 1976.

Stanton, Graham N. "Matthew's Use of the Old Testament." Pages 346–63 in *A Gospel for a New People: Studies in Matthew*. Edinburgh: T&T Clark, 1992.

Stendahl, Krister. *The School of St. Matthew and Its Use of the Old Testament*. ASNU 20. Lund: Gleerup, 1954.

Tov, Emanuel, Robert A. Kraft, and P. J. Parsons. *The Greek Minor Prophets Scroll from Naḥal Ḥever (8ḤevXIIgr)*. DJD 8. Oxford: Clarendon, 1990.

Vortisch, Johannes. *Das unschuldige Blut im Matthäusevangelium: Zur geschichtstheologischen Deutung des Todes Jesu*. Forthcoming.

Willitts, Joel. *Matthew's Messianic Shepherd-King: In Search of "The Lost Sheep of the House of Israel."* BZNW 147. Berlin: de Gruyter, 2007.

Zacharias, H. Daniel. *Matthew's Presentation of the Son of David: Davidic Tradition and Typology in the Gospel of Matthew*. London: T&T Clark, 2017.

Ziethe, Carolin. *Auf seinen Namen werden die Völker hoffen: Die matthäische Rezeption der Schriften Israels zur Begründung des universalen Heils*. BZNW 233. Berlin: de Gruyter, 2018.

9

Israel's Scriptures in Mark

ELIZABETH EVANS SHIVELY

New Testament writers commonly use a variation of the phrase "the law (of Moses) and the prophets" to refer to the entirety of Israel's Scriptures.[1] Mark never uses this synecdoche, but he nevertheless builds the narrative of the gospel upon "all the Scriptures" by employing texts from the Law, the Prophets, and the Psalms.[2] Mark's use of Israel's Scriptures is, therefore, quite comprehensive.

In another sense, however, Mark's use of Israel's Scriptures is rather selective. At the beginning, Mark names Isaiah as the hermeneutical key to both prologue and narrative (1:2–3). In chapters 1–10, other prophets and commandments dominate, as Mark ties God's current activity in Jesus to God's prior activity in Israel to make a case for Jesus's authority. In chapters 11–13, Mark incorporates Pss 110 and 118 to depict Jesus's entry into Jerusalem as Messiah and eschatologically driven prophetic texts to explain the events flanking Jesus's death. Finally, in chapters 14–16, Mark incorporates Zechariah and psalms of lament (esp. Pss 22, 42–43, 68) to tell the story of Jesus's passion and resurrection.

In still another sense, Mark's use of Israel's Scriptures is complex and pervasive in the deployment of scriptural language, motifs, and models to construct a particular narrative.[3] Whereas Matthew and Luke more often present their use

---

1. E.g., Matt 5:17; 7:12; 11:13; 22:40; Luke 16:16; 24:27, 44; Acts 13:15; 24:14; 28:23.
2. I use "Mark" to refer to the evangelist without making judgment about the actual author's identity.
3. Scholars who recognize that Mark's use of Scriptures is joined to his narrative strategy include Richard B. Hays, *Echoes of Scripture in the Gospels* (Waco, TX: Baylor University Press, 2016), esp. 98; Thomas Hatina, *In Search of a Context: The Function of Scripture in Mark's Nar-*

of Scripture in a straightforward prophecy-fulfillment sort of way, Mark's use of Scripture "form[s] part of the story stuff."[4] In this regard, Mark recruits an argument structure or "plot" from the book of Isaiah, into which he incorporates many other Scriptures that cohere with and elaborate it, to tell of how God is breaking into the world to redeem his people and establish his reign through his Messiah, Jesus.[5]

Isaiah as Mark's Hermeneutical Key

Morna Hooker left a methodological gash in Markan scholarship, generating the scholarly impulse to evaluate Mark's use of Scripture discretely, atomistically, and according to a criterion of verbal correspondence alone.[6] Against this trend, Richard Hays demonstrates Mark's technique of figural reading, an intertextual reading strategy that places the implied contexts of scriptural citations, allusions, and echoes in dialogue with the story of Jesus. Hays insists that Mark—like the other evangelists—thereby engages in the "revolutionary" practice of "reading [Israel's Scriptures] backwards in light of new revelatory events."[7] Hays's work would be all the more strengthened with the recognition that Israelite scribal practices and Jewish exegetical traditions already exhibit the very sorts of strategies he expounds.[8] Dialogical reading strategies abound within Israel's Scriptures and in Second Temple and rabbinic writings, through the use and interpretation

---

rative, JSNTSup 232 (Sheffield: Sheffield Academic, 2002); W. S. Vorster, "The Production of the Gospel of Mark: An Essay on Intertextuality," *HvTS* 49, no. 3 (1993): 385–96.

4. Vorster, "Production," 391. Vorster takes Mark's use of Scriptures noncontextually, while I take the opposite approach.

5. I assume that Mark and his earliest readers read the book of Isaiah as a unified work by a single prophet.

6. Hooker adopts Henry J. Cadbury's atomistic approach to the Hebrew Bible in her *Jesus and the Servant: The Influence of the Servant Concept of Deutero-Isaiah in the New Testament* (London: SPCK, 1959), 21–22. Kelli O'Brien, e.g., explicitly takes forward Hooker's program in *The Use of Scripture in the Markan Passion Narrative*, LNTS 384 (London: T&T Clark, 2010).

7. Hays, *Echoes of Scripture in the Gospels*, 11.

8. For discussions of the reuse of texts in Israel's Scriptures and Second Temple literature, see Michael Fishbane's programmatic work, *Biblical Interpretation in Ancient Israel* (Oxford: Clarendon, 1985); and recent methodological developments in Molly M. Zahn, *Genres of Rewriting in Second Temple Judaism: Scribal Composition and Transmission* (Cambridge: Cambridge University Press, 2020); William A. Tooman, *Gog of Magog: Reuse of Scripture and Compositional Technique in Ezekiel 38–39*, FAT 2/52 (Tübingen: Mohr Siebeck, 2011); Tooman, "Scriptural Reuse in Ancient Jewish Literature: Comments and Reflections on the State of the Art," in *Methodology in the Use of the Old Testament in the New: Context and Criteria*, ed. David Allen and Steve Smith, LNTS 597 (London: T&T Clark, 2019), 23–39.

of prior texts, scriptural motifs, larger argument structures, and organizational patterns in new situations.[9] In these cases, as William Tooman comments, "it is the [shared] *pattern of content* . . . that establishes the connection between the texts. Under these conditions, the writers do not have to provide much in the way of explicit allusions to confirm the connection . . . by this technique whole series of stories can be intertextually aligned."[10] Such "intertextual alignment" provides a cultural touchstone for a writer to explain and a community of readers to understand their present situation according to their Scriptures.

Consider the reuse of texts and motifs about Isaiah's servant (Isa 40–53). Early Jewish writers and redactors—beginning with the book of Isaiah itself—regularly reimagined their own suffering and hope for divine vindication and exaltation in light of the experience of Isaiah's servant in Isa 50; 52–53. First, the postexilic writer of Isa 54–66 applied what was said in Isa 40–55 to an unnamed individual of his own time and to a group of "offspring" or "servants" (promised to the "servant" of Isa 40–53 in 53:10–11), who were to extend the servant's mission in the face of opposition as they waited for God's coming (e.g., Isa 61–66). Then, Isa 54–66 generated an "interpretive revolution," as later scribal communities followed this exegetical lead.[11] The suffering servant provided a pattern for describing the suffering of righteous individuals and groups, seeking to explain experiences of trauma despite their covenant obedience, for example, in Zech 12:9–13:1, 7–9; Pss 22; 69; 102; Daniel (11:32–33; 12:1–2); the Wisdom of Solomon (Wis 3:1–9); 2 Macc 7; and the Dead Sea Scrolls (1QH^a XII, 23; 1QH^a XV, 5–6; XVI, 26–27; 4Q427 7 II, 7–9; 4Q451).[12] Isaiah's servant thus proved to be a powerful and lasting image for

---

9. Tooman, "Scriptural Reuse," 32. See also the numerous scriptural examples discussed in Michael B. Shepherd, *The Text in the Middle*, StBibLit 162 (New York: Lang, 2014). For Qumran, see Jonathan G. Campbell, *The Exegetical Texts*, Companion to the Qumran Scrolls 4 (London: T&T Clark, 2004).

10. Tooman, "Scriptural Reuse," 34 (emphasis added).

11. Jacob Stromberg, "Isaiah's Interpretive Revolution: How Isaiah's Formation Influenced Early Jewish and Christian Interpretation," in *The Book of Isaiah: Enduring Questions Answered Anew; Essays Honoring Joseph Blenkinsopp and His Contribution to the Study of Isaiah*, ed. Richard J. Bautch and J. Todd Hibbard (Grand Rapids: Eerdmans, 2015), 214–32. Reading and writing were social and communal activities in the Second Temple period. See Zahn, *Genres of Rewriting*, 29–34.

12. For Zechariah, see Martin Hengel, "The Effective History of Isaiah 53 in the Pre-Christian Period," in *The Suffering Servant: Isaiah 53 in Jewish and Christian Sources*, ed. Bernd Janowski and Peter Stuhlmacher (Grand Rapids: Eerdmans, 2004), 85–90. Scholars have long recognized that Ps 22 is composed or edited in light of Isa 50 and 53, due to verbal, conceptual, thematic, and logical parallels; see Michael A. Lyons, "The Servants in Psalms 22, 69, and 102," in *Isaiah's Servants in Early Judaism and Christianity: The Isaian Servant and the Exegetical Formation of Community Identity*, ed. Michael A. Lyons and Jacob Stromberg, WUNT 2/554 (Tübingen: Mohr Siebeck, 2021), 45–64. For Daniel, see Hengel, "Effective History," 91–98;

God's people, who sought to root their experiences in their Scriptures. Just as the servant suffered for doing right, so would they; and just as the suffering servant was vindicated and exalted, so would the suffering righteous be.[13]

Mark also follows this exegetical lead, in multiple directions. First, Mark takes up the servant motif of Isa 40–55 to portray Jesus after the pattern but also as the fulfillment of Isaiah's servant.[14] Second, he takes up and extends the servant's mission to the community of suffering servants—Jesus's disciples and subsequent followers—who are to continue his activity after he is gone, as they await his return (see Isa 54; 55–66).[15] Third, Mark incorporates into the Isaian framework some of the very texts that reuse Isa 53 (see above), that is, Daniel, Zech 13, and Pss 22, 69, perhaps because he recognizes their coherent pattern of content and shared motifs. Thus, for example, when readers encounter new Scriptures in Mark's narrative, like Pss 22 and 69 in chapter 15, these do not now offer replacement motifs; rather, they *add* to Mark's progressive, blended profile of Jesus.[16] In this way, Mark constructs a whole narrative that tells the good news of God's redemptive activity for his people through his authoritative, suffering, and exalted Messiah according to the Scriptures (Mark 9:12; 14:21, 29).[17]

Mark's Presentation of Scripture

I group Mark's presentation of Scripture into the following categories according to the approach of this volume: marked and unmarked citation, verbal allusion, and conceptual allusion. Nevertheless, it is immediately clear that a hard distinction between citation and allusion is sometimes difficult to maintain because

---

John J. Collins, *Daniel: A Commentary on the Book of Daniel*, Hermeneia (Minneapolis: Fortress, 1993), 385–93. For 2 Maccabees, see Hengel, "Effective History," 96. For the Dead Sea Scrolls, see John J. Collins, "The Dead Sea Scrolls and the New Testament: The Case of the Suffering Servant," in *Method and Meaning: Essays on New Testament Interpretation in Honor of Harold W. Attridge*, ed. Andrew B. McGowan and Kent H. Richards, RBS 67 (Atlanta: Society of Biblical Literature, 2012), 279–95.

13. See the essays in Lyons and Stromberg, *Isaiah's Servants in Early Judaism and Christianity*.

14. See also Isa 53:3 in Matt 8:17; Isa 53:1 in John 12:38 and Rom 10:16–17; Isa 53:12 in Luke 22:37; Isa 53:7–8 in Acts 8:32–35; Isa 53:4–6, 9 in 1 Pet 2:21–25; Isa 52–53 in Phil 2:5–11.

15. I develop this argument in Elizabeth E. Shively, "The Servant(s) in the Gospel of Mark and the Textual Formation of Early Christian Identity," in Lyons and Stromberg, *Isaiah's Servants in Early Judaism and Christianity*, 143–88.

16. Contra Hays, *Echoes of Scripture in the Gospels*, 87; and O'Brien, *Use of Scripture*, 76–87, who argue that Isaiah's servant is not in view in the passion narrative.

17. Zahn discusses reuse of Scripture as a type of interpretation and a means of reinforcing authority in *Genres of Rewriting*, 133–34.

Mark uses near verbatim, conflated, adapted, and implied scriptural sources, both with and without explicit markers.[18]

Marked and Unmarked Citations

By my count, Mark cites Scripture thirty-five times: Torah (eleven times), Prophets (thirteen times), and Psalms (eleven times).[19] Citations may be marked or unmarked. Some citations appear alone, while others are combined with one or more citations or verbal allusions.[20] Table 9.1 summarizes this data. Brackets indicate verbal allusions conflated with citations.

Table 9.1. Marked and Unmarked Citations

Marker	Markan text	Source text(s)[21]
It is written in the prophet Isaiah[22]	1:2–3	Exod 23:20; Mal 3:1; Isa 40:3
	1:11	Ps 2:7 [Isa 42:1]
	4:12	Isa 6:9–10
Isaiah prophesied rightly about you . . . as it is written	7:6–7	Isa 29:13
Moses said	7:10	Exod 20:12/Deut 5:16; Exod 21:17
	8:18	Jer 5:21; Ezek 12:2 [Isa 6:9–10]
	9:48	Isa 66:24
	10:6–8	Deut 24:1–4; Gen 1:27/5:2; Gen 2:24
You know the commandments	10:19	Exod 20:12–16/Deut 5:16–20
	11:9–10	Ps 118:25–26

---

18. This practice appears in Israel's Scriptures and Jewish tradition. See Tooman, *Gog and Magog*, 5; Jonathan G. Campbell, *Use of Scripture in the Damascus Document 1–8, 19–20*, BZAW 228 (Berlin: de Gruyter, 1995), 88–109.

19. For alternative summary counts, see Rikk E. Watts, "Mark," in *Commentary on the New Testament Use of the Old Testament*, ed. G. K. Beale and D. A. Carson (Grand Rapids: Baker Academic, 2007), 111; Sharyn E. Dowd, "Reading Mark Reading Isaiah," *LTQ* 30 (1995): 142 n. 5; and Robert G. Bratcher, ed., *Old Testament Quotations in the New Testament*, rev. ed., Helps for Translators 3 (London: United Bible Societies, 1967), 11–16.

20. See further Steven Moyise, "Composite Citations in the Gospel of Mark," in *Composite Citations in Antiquity*, vol. 2, *New Testament Uses*, ed. Sean A. Adams and Seth M. Ehorn, LNTS 593 (London: Bloomsbury T&T Clark, 2016), 16–33.

21. Allusions are indicated in brackets. For more detailed discussions of the *Vorlagen* than I can offer in this chapter, see the entries in Watts, "Mark."

22. Unless otherwise noted, all translations are by the author.

Is it not written	11:17	Isa 56:7 [Jer 7:11]
Have you not read this Scripture?	12:10–11	Ps 118:22–23
Moses wrote	12:19	Deut 25:5
Have you not read in the book of Moses	12:26	Exod 3:6
The first (commandment) . . . the second (commandment)	12:29, 31	Deut 6:4–5; Lev 19:18b
David himself, by the Holy Spirit, declared	12:36	Ps 110:1
	13:24–25	Dan 12:11; Isa 13:10; Isa 34:4
It is written	14:27	Zech 13:7 [Isa 53:10]
	14:34	Ps 42:6; 42:12; 43:5
	14:62	Ps 110:1 [Dan 7:13]
	15:19	Ps 22:18
	15:24	Ps 22:19
	15:34	Ps 22:2

Mark may or may not choose to mark citations (and/or allusions) with introductory formulas. Thus, the presence of an introductory formula (a marker) does not make any instance of scriptural use a citation but instead functions to heighten the rhetorical effect of the citation it introduces.[23] For instance, Mark's Jesus names Moses or David as the author of Scripture in contexts where it is imperative to establish Jesus's authoritative interpretation of the law. In these cases, Mark employs introductory formulas to appeal directly to Israel's sacred texts and/or their authoritative writers. Conversely, the absence of an introductory formula (i.e., an unmarked citation) does not make an instance of scriptural use insignificant; rather, it suggests that the author assumes a shared a body of scriptural knowledge. Additionally, Mark has a penchant for combining Scripture with Scripture by conflating two or more citations, two or more allusions, or citations and allusions.

Verbal Allusions

Mark's Gospel is shot through with verbal allusions, displayed in table 9.2, below. Like citations, verbal allusions may appear in Mark's Gospel alone or in com-

---

23. Jonathan D. H. Norton discusses this phenomenon in Qumran texts in "Composite Quotations in the Damascus Document," in *Composite Citations in Antiquity*, vol. 1, *Jewish, Graeco-Roman, and Early Christian Uses*, ed. Sean A. Adams and Seth M. Ehorn, LNTS 525 (London: Bloomsbury, 2016), 114.

bination with one or more allusion or citation. To be comprehensive, I include allusions mixed with citations. In these entries, citations are bracketed.

Table 9.2. Verbal Allusions

Markan text	Source text(s)
1:10	Isa 64:1
1:11	[Ps 2:7] Isa 42:1
3:27	Isa 42:22; 49:24; 53:12
4:32	Dan 4:14
6:34	Num 27:17; Ezek 34:5–6; Zech 10:2; Isa 40:11; 44:28
8:18	[Jer 5:21; Ezek 12:2] Isa 6:9–10
8:31	Dan 7:13; Ps 118:22; Hos 6:2
8:27, etc.[24]	Isa 42:16; 59:10
8:37	Ps 49:8
9:7	Exod 40:34; Deut 18:15; Isa 50:4
9:11–12	Mal 4:6
9:31	Dan 7:13; Isa 53:6b, 12; Hos 6:2
10:3–4	Deut 24:1–4
10:33–34	Dan 7:13; Isa 50:6; Isa 53:6b, 12; Hos 6:2
10:45	Isa 53:10–12; Dan 7:13
11:17	[Isa 56:7] Jer 7:11
13:12	Mic 7:6
13:19	Dan 12:1
13:26–27	Dan 7:13; Zech 2:10; Deut 30:4
14:18	Ps 41:10
14:24	Exod 24:8; Zech 9:11; Isa 53
14:34	Pss 42:5, 11; 43:5
14:56	Ps 27:12; 35:11
14:61	Isa 53:7
14:62	[Ps 110:1] Dan 7:13
14:65	Isa 50:6
15:23	Ps 68:21
15:29–30	Ps 22:8
15:36	Ps 69:22

Verbal allusions are recognizable by verbal and thematic correspondences to source texts, reinforced by coherence with the narrative trajectory of the gospel.

24. Also Mark 9:33; 10:17, 32, 52.

Consider the parable of the strong man (Mark 3:27) and its correspondences with Isa 42:22; 49:24–25; 53:12 LXX.

But no one is able to enter the house of <u>the strong man [τοῦ ἰσχυροῦ]</u> to <u>plunder his goods [διαρπάσαι τὰ σκεύη]</u> unless he first binds <u>the strong man [τὸν ἰσχυρόν]</u>. Then he may plunder [διαρπάσει] his house (Mark 3:27)	The people were spoiled and <u>plundered [διηρπασμένος]</u> (Isa 42:22) Will anyone take <u>the spoils from a giant [παρὰ γίγαντος σκῦλα]</u>? ... If one should take a giant captive he will take <u>spoils [σκῦλα]</u>, and by taking them <u>from a strong man [παρὰ ἰσχύοντος]</u>, he will be saved. (Isa 49:24–25) He shall inherit many and shall distribute the <u>spoils [σκῦλα] of the strong [ἰσχυρῶν]</u>, because his soul was handed over to death. (Isa 53:12)

These verbal and thematic correspondences suggest that Mark interprets Jesus's exorcisms in view of a broad theme in Isaiah. According to this theme, Israel's exile necessitates the greater power and authority of the Lord as the one who comes with strength to subjugate the oppressor of God's people (Mark 1:7; cf. Isa 40:10 LXX).

Conceptual Allusions

We have yet to grasp the range and function of Mark's literary borrowing because of the tendency to overvalue citations and explicit verbal allusions as measuring rods of the extent to which Mark uses Scripture. Consider the following list of conceptual allusions (table 9.3).

Table 9.3. Conceptual Allusions

Marker	Markan text	Source text(s)
	1:4–8	1 Kings, Joshua, Exodus
	1:12–13	Exodus
What Moses commanded	1:44	Lev 13 and 14
	2:7	Isa 43:25
What is not lawful on the sabbath	2:24	Exod 20:9–11; Deut 23:25

Have you never read what David did	2:25–26	1 Sam 21:1–7
Is it lawful... on the sabbath	3:4	Deut 30:15
	5:21–24, 35–43	2 Kgs 4:17–37
	6:23	Esther 5:3, 6; 7:2
	6:41	Ps 23:1; Exodus
	6:48	Job 9:8; Exod 33:19–33; 34:6
	7:24–30	1 Kgs 17–24
	9:2–8	Exod 24:1, 9, 13, 15; Mal 4:5–6; Exod 40:34; Deut 18:15
How is it written	9:12	Dan 7:13; Isa 53:3; Pss 22:7; 118:22
As it is written	9:13	1 Kgs 19:2, 10, 14; Mal 4:5–6
	10:45	Dan 7:13; Isa 53:10–12
	12:1–9	Isa 5:1–4; Ps 80:8, 9
	13:3–4	Zech 14:4
	13:14	Dan 9:27; 11:31; 12:11
As it is written	14:21	Dan 7:13; Isa 53:3; Pss 22:7; 118:22
	14:41	Dan 7:13
Let the Scriptures be fulfilled	14:49	Isa 53:12[25]

In these cases, Mark employs Scripture conceptually by evoking broader scriptural texts, motifs, and narrative patterns other than what is explicitly stated. Conceptual allusions are common and recognizable by correspondences in recurring motifs, contextual lines of reasoning, and broad organizational patterns.[26] Notice that in several instances, Mark employs introductory formulas to mark conceptual allusions. For example, when Jesus heals the man with scale disease, he says, "See that you say nothing to anyone; but go, show yourself to the priest, and offer for your cleansing *what Moses commanded*, as a testimony to them" (1:44). The phrase "what Moses commanded" assumes a shared body of cultural knowledge between Jesus and the man on one level and between Mark and his readers on another.[27] This marker enables informed readers to recognize Lev 13–14 and fill in gaps to understand what the restored man is expected to do.

---

25. Cf. Luke 22:37, one of Mark's earliest interpreters.
26. I rely on Tooman's principles for recognizing verbal and conceptual allusions, based on his observations of exegetical practices in Israel's Scriptures and Jewish tradition: *uniqueness* (uniqueness to a particular source), *distinctiveness* (distinctive but not exclusive to a particular source), *multiplicity* (several elements of source in close proximity), *thematic correspondence* (similar subject, theme, or argument); Tooman, *Gog and Magog*, 27.
27. I acknowledge the complex media situation of the ancient world and use "reader(s)"

Israel's Scriptures in Mark

Mark's Use of Scripture

Mark 1–10

Mark's exegetical strategy is exemplary in the prologue (1:1–13), so my discussion of this section is singularly extensive. Mark proclaims the "good news of Jesus, Messiah, Son of God" (1:1) and explains the line with a mixed citation of Exod 23:20; Mal 3:1; and Isa 40:2–3.[28] Mark responds to and develops an argument structure already at work in these very texts, since Mal 3:1 combines Exod 23:20 with the royal procession theme of Isa 40:3 (also in 57:14; 62:10).[29] Malachi writes in a postexilic context to affirm continuity between the Sinai covenant and the hoped-for restoration to which he points. According to the prophet, the new covenant will be established not through a return to the land, but through God's purifying presence. Mark travels in this stream of exegetical tradition, rewriting the combined Scriptures as that which is "written in the prophet Isaiah" (1:2). This marker both appeals directly to Israel's sacred writings and alerts informed readers to incorporate Exod 23:20 and Mal 3:1 into Isaiah's "text" in a new situation, that of the eschatological fulfillment of God's redemptive promises.[30] By using Exodus, Mark portrays the Lord speaking to Jesus about sending "*my* messenger [John] before *you*" (instead of "before *me*" as in Mal 3:1). This usage signals Jesus's identity and authority by placing him into the divine counsel and into Israel's climactic history ahead of his coming from Nazareth to the Jordan River (Mark 1:9). By using

---

for the sake of convenience. Umberto Eco calls this the "cultural encyclopedia," the "regulative hypothesis that allows both speakers to figure out the 'local' dictionary they need in order to ensure the good standing of their communicative interaction," in *Semiotics and the Philosophy of Language* (London: Macmillan, 1984), 80.

28. The addition of υἱοῦ τοῦ θεοῦ ("Son of God") is a textual change to the ECM of Mark, which will also appear in the main text of the NA29. For recent arguments in favor of the longer reading, which includes "Son of God," see Max Botner, "The Role of Transcriptional Probability in the Text-Critical Debate on Mark 1:1," *CBQ* 77, no. 3 (2015): 467–80; Tommy Wasserman, "The 'Son of God' Was in the Beginning (Mark 1:1)," *JTS* 62, no. 1 (2011): 20–50.

29. Contra Jocelyn McWhirter, who argues that Mark joins and interprets these texts as messianic prophecies based on shared vocabulary, in "Messianic Exegesis in Mark 1:2–3," in *"What Does the Scripture Say?" Studies in the Function of Scripture in Early Judaism and Christianity*, vol. 1, *The Synoptic Gospels*, ed. Craig A. Evans and H. Daniel Zacharias, LNTS 469 (London: T&T Clark, 2012), 158–78. The combination of the *piel* stem of the verb פנה + the object דרך ("prepare/clear the way") appears only in Mal 3:1 and the Isaiah texts. The targum of Isaiah retains the textual connection between Mal 3:1 and the Isaiah texts, which suggests that Malachi is moving in this exegetical stream of tradition.

30. I discuss the nature of the text below. Watts identifies a structure in which 1:1a (the attribution to Isaiah) and 1:2b (the quotation of Isa 40:3) function as a frame for vv. 1b–2a (the quotation of Exod 23:20 and Mal 3:1); Rikk E. Watts, *Isaiah's New Exodus in Mark*, Biblical Studies Library (Grand Rapids: Baker Academic, 2000), 86.

Mal 3:1, Mark reinterprets the unnamed voice of Isa 40:3 as Malachi's preparatory, eschatological covenant messenger (see Mal 4:5–6 [3:22–23 LXX]).

In 1:4–13, Mark elaborates the themes of the opening citation through narration and the incorporation of corresponding Scriptures. First, the conceptual use of Scripture helps to concretize the activity of the "messenger" and the "voice" in John's ministry (1:4–8). John's role as Malachi's covenant messenger is developed in a setting that recalls Elijah, who also once appeared in the wilderness, at the Jordan River (1 Kgs 17:3; 19:3–18; 2 Kgs 2:4–11), and in the same clothes (2 Kgs 1:8). Later, Mark reinforces John-as-Elijah through the conceptual use of Scripture in his narration of John's opposition to Herod (6:14–29; 1 Kgs 18–19; 21) and of Jesus's discussion about Elijah's preparatory appearance and suffering (9:9–13; Mal 4:5–6). Here in the prologue, John announces Jesus's coming as the "stronger one" (1:7), a correlation with God who comes as a strong one gently to rule his people (Isa 40:10).

Second, a conceptual allusion to the wider context of Isaiah signals that God is indeed breaking into the world to establish that kingly reign: when Jesus rises from the water of his baptism and "the heavens are torn apart" (1:10), the divine presence descends audibly and visibly into Jesus, suggesting a theophany and the fulfillment of Isa 63:19 (64:1 ET). Third, a mixed citation of Ps 2:7 and Isa 42:1 in Mark 1:11 confirms that Jesus is the locus of God's kingly activity.[31] Psalm 2 portrays clashing kingdoms and the extension of God's kingly rule through his Davidic son; and Isa 42 has God present Israel as his chosen servant in whom he places his Spirit for a mission to the world. Mark portrays Jesus as Isaian servant and Davidic king from the start, offering a blended character frame through which readers may filter all subsequent data. Finally, Mark elaborates the themes of the opening citation in the temptation account (1:12–13). Mark recontextualizes the scriptural narration with apocalyptic themes to portray the Spirit-filled Jesus's mission, fundamentally, in terms of a conflict of kingdoms—God's and Satan's.[32] Mark offers a new vision of a new exodus as the Spirit-filled Jesus enters the wilderness to overcome the enemy and then enters the land to announce the arrival of God's reign (1:14–15).

In the first ten chapters, Mark builds a case for Jesus's messianic identity and authority upon the prologue's scriptural framework. At the start of a series of conflicts (2:1–3:6), a mix of conceptual and verbal allusions signals how Jesus and his opponents use Scripture to ground their understanding about forgiveness of sins, table fellowship, and the interpretation of Sabbath law. For example, the scribes' question, "Who can forgive sins but God alone?" (2:7) points to a

---

31. For discussion of the language, see Shively, "Servant(s)," 161–62.
32. Elizabeth E. Shively, *Apocalyptic Imagination in the Gospel of Mark: The Literary and Theological Role of Mark 3:22–30*, BZNW 189 (Berlin: de Gruyter, 2012).

shared belief that the "one God" of Israel has authority to forgive sins (Deut 6:4; Isa 43:25). In response, Jesus demonstrates the coherence of his activity with that of the one God by extending forgiveness and healing as the self-designated Son of Man (Mark 2:10). This verbal allusion to Dan 7:13–14, where one like a son of man receives authority and power from the Ancient of Days, implies that Mark's Jesus similarly receives divine authority to forgive sins on the earth and later, as lord over the Sabbath, to provide and to heal (Mark 2:10, 28; cf. 3:2–4).

Jesus begins to involve his disciples in his authoritative activity and authorizes the Twelve with his very own mission to preach and exorcise demons (3:14–15; cf. 1:14–15, 38–39). Just afterward, Jesus's family and a group of scribes disrupt that mission (3:20–21). Scribes from Jerusalem seek to discredit Jesus's growing authority—no doubt to restore their own (cf. 1:21–28)—by circulating a rumor that he casts out demons as one empowered by Satan (3:22, 30). Jesus refutes the rumor with a series of parables, culminating in the parable of the strong man (3:27). Mark's use of Isaiah (see the discussion above) develops Jesus's power and authority as the stronger one (Mark 1:7): by the Spirit's power, he rescues the enemy's "spoils"—those whom Satan oppresses—to establish them as a new family that does God's will (3:31–35).

The parables of the kingdom (ch. 4) further explain the scribes' response to Jesus and his to them. Jesus uses Isa 6:9–10 to explain his statement that "those outside" receive everything in parables "so that they may not turn again and be forgiven" (ἀφεθῇ αὐτοῖς), rather than "I will heal them" (ἰάσομαι αὐτούς in the OG; רפא in the MT). The use of "forgiveness" language recalls the immediately preceding unforgivable-sin saying (3:28). Then, the Markan Jesus expresses a parabolic judgment against the scribes for misnaming the Spirit's power to which his exorcisms testify. Now, Jesus explains that judgment using Isa 6:9–10. Like Isaiah, Jesus teaches in parables to confirm "outsiders" in their spiritual blindness and self-condemnation. Mark's narrative use of Isa 6:9–10 thus affords readers the opportunity to recognize coherence between the authority and kingship of the one Lord God and the Lord Jesus, and the responses of God's past and present people (cf. Isa 5; Mark 12:1–9).

The two episodes following the parables of the kingdom further facilitate this coherence. First, when Jesus calms a storm, his disciples are unable to recognize his identity or authority over nature and so reply, "Who is this, that even the wind and the sea obey him?" (4:41).[33] Second (and by contrast), when the healed Gerasene

---

33. For a discussion of a verbal allusion to Jonah 1:5–16 in Mark 4:38–41 and its narrative function, see Elizabeth Struthers Malbon, "Jonah, Jesus, Gentiles, and the Sea: Markan Narrative Intersections," in *Reading the Gospel of Mark in the Twenty-First Century*, ed. Geert Van Oyen, BETL 301 (Leuven: Peeters, 2019), 251–95.

man asks Jesus "that he might be with him" (ἵνα μετ' αὐτοῦ ᾖ, 5:18; cf. 3:14), Jesus instead sends him home to tell "how much the Lord has done for you" (5:19), after which the man perceptively proclaims how much *Jesus* has done for him (5:20).

Subsequently, Jesus extends God's reign throughout Galilee as he preaches and casts out demons and sends his disciples out to do the same (6:1–12; cf. 1:14–15; 3:14–15). Mark draws conceptual allusions from stories of past prophets for the telling of Jesus's ministry. For example, the exodus narrative provides patterns of content for the events in the wilderness at the opening of the gospel, for the two feedings (6:30–44; 8:1–10), and for the transfiguration (9:2–8).[34] Furthermore, the Elijah-Elisha narrative in 1 Kgs 16:29–2 Kgs 13 provides patterns of content for several of Jesus's healings (2 Kgs 4:17–37 in 5:21–24, 35–43; 1 Kgs 17:17–24 in 7:24–30; 2 Kgs 4:31–37 in 9:14–29).[35] The coherence of content between these past narratives and Mark's present one communicates the coherence of divine activity across time and establishes Jesus's authority as God's agent.

Jesus feeds the five thousand, walks on the sea (6:32–52), and extends the purity of God's kingdom to any sick who touch his garments (6:53–56). Yet scribes from Jerusalem (cf. 3:22) join the Pharisees to show more concern with the ritual impurity Jesus's disciples might incur from touching food with unwashed hands (7:1). Their challenge recapitulates and extends prior moments of opposition to Jesus (2:1–3:6; 3:22–30). Earlier, Jesus had spoken to his opponents enigmatically, in parables (3:27; 4:10–12); now he speaks plainly, citing Isa 29:13 as a judgment against them. Jesus also contrasts the authority on which he himself stands (what "Moses said," 7:10) with the authority on which the Pharisees stand ("but you say . . . ," v. 11). But then, significantly, Jesus does exactly what he had accused the religious leaders of doing. Turning again to parables, he stands on his own authority to offer teaching-as-doctrine about what truly defiles a person (7:14–16), that is, the evils that pervade the heart (7:21–23). So that the reader does not miss the point, Mark adds the parenthetical comment to Jesus's postparabolic teaching, "thus he declared all foods clean" (7:19). Put quite simply, Mark reinforces Jesus's authority as divine lawgiver and, even more, as divine purifier.[36] The religious leaders' repeated challenges exhibit their lack of perception on these points.

Jesus's disciples exhibit the same lack of perception when they fail to recognize Jesus in the wake of the second feeding miracle, as he walks on the sea (6:52). Their

---

34. William M. Swartley, *Israel's Scripture Traditions and the Synoptic Gospels: Story Shaping Story* (Peabody, MA: Hendrickson, 1994).

35. Adam Winn, *Mark and the Elijah-Elisha Narrative: Considering the Practice of Greco-Roman Imitation in the Search for Markan Source Material* (Eugene, OR: Pickwick, 2010); Thomas L. Brodie, *The Crucial Bridge: The Elijah-Elisha Narrative as an Interpretive Synthesis of Genesis-Kings and a Literary Model for the Gospels* (Collegeville, MN: Liturgical Press, 2000).

36. See further Elizabeth E. Shively, "Purification of the Body and the Reign of God in the Gospel of Mark," *JTS* 71 (2020): 62–89.

Israel's Scriptures in Mark

downward spiral of imperception converges with that of the religious leaders when they are on a boat with Jesus for a third time. Jesus warns them against the leaven of the Pharisees, that human-centered misunderstanding that pervades and defiles the heart (cf. 7:6, 21–23). Jesus cites Jer 5:21 and possibly alludes to Ezek 12:2–5, both of which allude to Isa 6:9–10, to explain his disciples' lackluster response to his feeding miracle. An intratextual allusion to Mark 4:12 is unmistakable since Jesus's own disciples have now joined the cast of outsiders who look without perceiving, who hear without understanding, and whose hearts are hard.

The central section of the gospel features Jesus's instruction to his unperceiving disciples (Mark 8:22–10:52). Throughout, Mark uses the word "way" (ὁδός, 8:27; 9:33; 10:17, 32, 46, 52).[37] This language alludes intratextually to Mark's opening citation ("way," ὁδός in 1:2, 3; see Mal 3:1; Isa 40:3) and alludes to texts in Isaiah in which God's people fumble "on the way," like the blind (59:10; cf. CD VIII–X), and in which the blind are healed "on the way" (42:16; cf. 35:5–7). Mark calls attention to the conceptual allusion by framing 8:22–10:52 with miracle stories in which Jesus provides physical sight to blind men, signaling the spiritual perception his disciples need "on the way" (8.22–26; 10:46–52).

"On the way" (8:27), Peter confesses that Jesus is the "Messiah" (v. 29). Jesus responds by explaining what "Messiah" means, predicting that he must become the exalted Son of Man, paradoxically, as the *suffering* servant and royal son. Three times, Mark's Jesus predicts his passion (8:31; 9:31; 10:32–34), each time using verbal allusions that cohere with and elaborate his prior portrait. In what follows, I join the three predictions to indicate the verbal parallels, delineating three parts: the Son of Man must *suffer*, *be killed*, and *rise*. The language of the second and third parts is consistent, while the language of the first part develops the theme of Jesus's suffering through repetition and variation.

Table 9.4. Scriptural Use in the Passion Predictions

The Son of Man (τὸν υἱὸν τοῦ ἀνθρώπου)	... as it were a son of man [ὡς υἱὸς ἀνθρώπου] was coming upon the clouds of heaven ... and authority was given to him ... (Dan 7:13–14)
First part 8:31: must [δεῖ] suffer many things and be rejected [ἀποδοκιμασθῆναι] by the elders, the chief priests, and the scribes,	The stone which the builders rejected [ἀπεδοκίμασαν], this one became the chief cornerstone (Ps 118:22 [117:22 LXX])

---

37. See also Watts, *New Exodus*, 170–73, 239–52; Joel Marcus, *The Way of the Lord: Christological Exegesis of the Old Testament in the Gospel of Mark* (Louisville: Westminster John Knox, 1992), 29.

9:31: is to be handed over [παραδίδοται] into human hands,

The Lord handed him over [παρέδωκεν] for our sins (Isa 53:6b)

10:33–34: will be handed over [παραδοθήσεται] to the chief priests and the scribes and they will condemn him to death [θανάτῳ];

his soul was handed over to death [παρεδόθη εἰς θάνατον ἡ ψυχὴ αὐτοῦ] (Isa 53:12)

then they will hand him over [παραδώσουσιν] to the gentiles. They will mock him [ἐμπαίξουσιν], and spit upon [ἐμπτύσουσιν] him, and flog [μαστιγώσουσιν] him,

I have given my back to flogging [μάστιγας] . . . but I did not turn away my face from the shame of spitting [ἐμπτυσμάτων] (Isa 50:6)

Second part
8:31: and be killed [ἀποκτανθῆναι],

9:31: and they will kill him [ἀποκτενοῦσιν αὐτόν]

10:34: and kill [ἀποκτενοῦσιν] him.

Third part
8:31: and after three days rise [μετὰ τρεῖς ἡμέρας ἀναστῆναι].

On the third day we will rise up [ἐν τῇ ἡμέρᾳ τῇ τρίτῃ ἀναστηούμεθα] that we may live before him. (Hos 6:2)

9:31: And three days after being killed, he will rise [μετὰ τρεῖς ἡμέρας ἀναστήσεται]

10:34: And after three days he will rise [μετὰ τρεῖς ἡμέρας ἀναστήσεται]

By combining the Son of Man title with an allusion to Ps 118:22, Mark highlights the rejection of God's messianic king Jesus and the kingdom he has come to bring for God's people. The context of Ps 118:22 combines Scriptures already joined in Israel's tradition, Scriptures important to Mark and extended in the passion predictions. Psalm 118:14 cites Isa 12:2, which uses Exod 15:2 (the Song of Moses) to extol the salvation of the messianic king (the "stone") through a new exodus.[38] The "stone" enters the city gates (Ps 118:19), but the very builders of the gates reject him (118:22). Mark's use of these texts in combination with language from Isa 50, 53 to describe Jesus's passion conveys the suffering through which the messianic king accomplishes salvation. By incorporating an allusion to Hos 6:2, Mark predicts the Son of Man's exaltation. Hosea addresses a sick and incurable Israel that returns to the Lord to "rise" from the dead (like Ezekiel's dry bones). Mark, though, changes the first-person plural ("we") to third-person singular ("he"), so that the allusion not only coheres grammatically with Mark's narrative but also thematically with Isaiah's account of the suffering one who is exalted to receive many offspring (cf. Isa 52:13; 53:10b). Mark's use of these texts in combination conveys the entanglement of divine and human agency in the workings of salvation as the Son of Man/king is exalted after suffering and dying.

The transfiguration follows on the heels of the first passion prediction to confirm Jesus's teaching. Initially, Jesus appears with Moses and Elijah, God's prophets and miracle workers. An allusion to Exod 40:34 in Mark 9:7 suggests that Mark interprets the presence of the cloud in light of the revelation of God's glory to Moses on Mount Sinai. When the two prophets disappear, heaven affirms that Jesus "is my beloved son," as at the baptism, now adding, "listen to him" (ἀκούετε αὐτοῦ, 9:7). The language corresponds to Deut 18:15, which predicts that God will raise up a prophet like Moses, and "you shall listen to him" (αὐτοῦ ἀκούσεσθε). Crucially, Moses and Elijah are also God's servants.[39] Moses is the first servant, through whom God speaks and works (Deut 34:5; Exod 14:31; Josh 1:13). Isaiah's servant is built on the pattern of the Mosaic servant, teacher, and prophet, for like Moses, God gives Isaiah's servant words to speak to Israel (Isa 50:4), and those who fear the Lord are called to "listen to the voice of my servant" (ἀκουσάτω τῆς φωνῆς παιδὸς αὐτοῦ, 50:10). The divine instruction, "listen to him" suggests then that Jesus is the servant and prophet like—though greater than—Moses, who speaks with God's own authority; yet what makes him greater is his suffering and death (8:31; cf. 10:45).

After each prediction, however, Jesus's disciples misconstrue the nature of his mission (8:32–33; 9:32; 10:35–41). And each time, Jesus responds with corrective teaching about the nature of the disciples' mission, effectively binding theirs to his (8:34–37; 9:33–37; 10:42–45). Finally, Jesus uses his own example of service, explicitly, to impress upon them that to become great is to be a servant (διάκονος, δοῦλος, 10:43, 44).[40]

---

38. See further Shepherd, *Text in the Middle*, 139.

39. Moses is God's servant in Exod 14:31; Deut 34:5; Num 12:7; Josh 1:1, 7, 12, 15; 9:24; 11:15; 22:4, 5; 1 Kgs 8:56; 2 Kgs 18:12; 21:8; 2 Chr 1:3; 24:9; Neh 1:7; 9:14; 10:29; Ps 105:26; Mal 4:4; Bar 1:20; 2:28. Elijah is God's servant in 2 Kgs 9:36; 10:10.

40. Mark uses the Greek terms for "serve" (διακονηθῆναι, διακονῆσαι) in 10:45 after using διάκονος ("servant") and δοῦλος ("servant") synonymously in vv. 43 and 44.

This example combines a conceptual allusion to Dan 7:13–14 with a verbal allusion to Isa 53:12, texts already used in the second and third passion predictions, and in the Beelzebul discourse:

For even the Son of Man did not come to be served [διακονηθῆναι], but to serve [διακονῆσαι] and to give his life [τὴν ψυχὴν αὐτοῦ] as a ransom for many [λύτρον ἀντὶ πολλῶν] (Mark 10:45)	. . . to justify a righteous one who serves many well [δικαιῶσαι δίκαιον εὖ δουλεύοντα πολλοῖς], and he himself shall bear their sins. Therefore he shall inherit many [πολλούς] and shall distribute the spoils of the strong [ἰσχυρῶν], because his soul [ψυχὴ αὐτοῦ] was handed over to death (Isa 53:10–12)

Once more, the combined images of Daniel's glorious one-like-a-son-of-man with Isaiah's suffering servant highlight the purpose of Jesus's coming for imperceptive disciples. In contrasting statements ("not," οὐκ, 10:45a . . . "but," ἀλλά, 45b), Jesus addresses his disciples' lording-it-over-others attitude, for if *even the Son of Man* has come to serve, then how can his disciples think they are above their master by refusing to do so?

Yet the Son of Man's service is more than exemplary; it is unique. This uniqueness is underscored by the combination of "ransom" (λύτρον), which evokes the image of a slave price, and "on behalf of many" (ἀντὶ πολλῶν), which indicates submission to a vicarious death on behalf of others. The word λύτρον does not correspond to a specific term in Isa 53.[41] It is a conceptual allusion corresponding to a broader theme that appears throughout Isa 40–55, the Lord's activity as redeemer (ὁ λυτρούμενος) to liberate Israel (the "spoils" and "plunder") from captivity and sin. In this regard, while the noun λυτρόν occurs once in Isaiah, the cognate verb λυτρόω occurs throughout (eleven times).[42] God is "your redeemer" (σου ὁ λυτρούμενός, Isa 41:14; 43:14; 44:24); his action is *to redeem*, and Israel is called

---

41. λύτρον is absent from Isa 53:10 LXX, and the Hebrew אָשָׁם ("guilt offering") is never translated by λύτρον in the LXX. It appears in the New Testament only in Mark 10:45 and its parallel in Matt 20:28. Related words appear elsewhere in the New Testament: λύτρωσις ("redemption/ransoming"; Luke 1:68; 2:38; Heb 9:12); λυτρώτης ("redeemer/ransomer"; Acts 7:35); λυτρόω ("redeem/ransom"; Luke 24:21; Titus 2:14; 1 Pet 1:18). For a list of the various interpretations offered for this tricky term, see Shively, "Servant(s)," 175–78.

42. "Redeem" (λυτρόν) appears only twenty times in the Jewish Greek Scriptures with a range of meaning; but the cognate verb λυτρόω appears over one hundred times, and nearly half of the appearances render either גאל or פדה in contexts that remember the Lord's redemption of his people from Egypt or that look ahead to a new exodus.

"the *redeemed* of the Lord" (51:10; 44:22, 23; 51:10; 52:3; 62:12; 63:9). In chapter 53, the writer describes *how* the Redeemer (ὁ λυτρούμενος) will accomplish redemption, climactically, through the servant's death, which God accepts as a vicarious offering for the peoples' sins (Isa 53:12). Thus, the term λύτρον in Mark 10:45, set within Mark's foundational Isaian hermeneutical framework, evokes a larger block of scriptural material that culminates in the description of the servant's death as the ransom by which he liberates the spoils of the strong (Isa 52:12; cf. Mark 1:7; 3:28) so that he may inherit "many," that is, the community that does God's will.

Mark 11–13

As Jesus enters Jerusalem, crowds welcome him as messianic king, shouting "Hosanna!" ("Save now!"; Mark 11:9–10). This verbal allusion to Ps 118:25–26 [117:25–26 LXX] sets the stage for the fulfillment of Jesus's first passion prediction. The "stone" is greeted at the city gates before he is rejected at the temple, where no one welcomes him at all (11:11).

Jesus returns to the temple the next day to perform a prophetic act of judgment (11:15–19), using Scripture to identify a contradiction between the temple's divine purpose ("to become a house of prayer for all nations," 11:17; Isa 56:7) and its current activity (it has become "a den of robbers," Jer 7:11). The withering of the fig tree that frames the episode functions as a living parable that interprets Jesus's judgment: like the fig tree's leaves, the temple's bustling activity gives the appearance of fruitfulness, but within it is barren.

Jesus's subsequent temple teaching recapitulates and accelerates the earlier cycle of conflicts (2:1–3:6). Again, the religious leaders are concerned with Jesus's authority to do and say what he does. He responds to their challenges by telling the parable of the vineyard, which alludes to Isa 5:1–7 (Mark 12:1–9). The man of the parable sends a series of servants, of whom his son is the climactic servant and heir: the phrase "he still had one" (ἔτι ἕνα εἶχεν) in 12:6 intimates that the man *still had one servant*, that is (climactically), his beloved son (cf. 1:10–11; Ps 2:7; Isa 42:1). The tenants recognize that this son is the heir (κληρονόμος) of the vineyard/Israel and plot to kill him for his inheritance (ἡ κληρονομία, 12:7). Yet instead, by being killed (ἀποκτείνω, 12:5, 7–8), as Jesus predicted three times (ἀποκτείνω in 8:31; 9:31; 10:34), the servant-son gives the inheritance to "others." In light of the intratextual references to the passion prediction and Mark's prior use of Isa 53:12, informed readers may detect a verbal allusion to Isa 53:12 LXX, "he will inherit many [κληρονομήσει πολλούς] . . . because his soul was delivered to death." Mark uses Ps 118 again, adding it to the scriptural blend to convey that the rejected king will become the cornerstone of a new temple given to others through his death and resurrection (12:10–11).

After gleaning that Jesus has told the parable against them, groups of religious leaders attempt to entrap Jesus with their questions until a lone scribe asks him about the first, or greatest, commandment (Mark 12:28). Jesus gives him two: love God (Deut 6:4–5) and love your neighbor (Lev 19:18). The scribe agrees; however, Jesus replies that he is "not far" from the kingdom of God. Mark's earlier uses of the Shema shed light on this comment. First, it appeared on the lips of the scribes who knew that the "one God" has authority to forgive sins (2:7). Second, the Shema appeared on the lips of Jesus, who, when a rich young man called him a good teacher, protested that only the "one God" is good (10:18). In both cases, Jesus's interlocutors did not recognize the authority and goodness of the "one God" manifest in Jesus. Similarly, in 12:28–34, the scribe seems content to keep the law without recognizing that the confession that Israel's God is *one* involves *two* Lords (cf. Mark 5:19–20), and so, he is "not far." This is underscored by the juxtaposition of Jesus's question about the scribes' teaching, in which he compares the two Lords of Ps 110:1 (12:35–37). The point is that the reign of the one Lord God is manifest in a *second* Lord, the Messiah, who is not only David's son but also God's.[43]

Finally, Jesus leaves for the Mount of Olives, where he sits opposite the temple to pronounce its fate.[44] Throughout most of the speech, Jesus focuses on his followers, who, he warns, after he is gone must endure steadfastly to the end through suffering and tribulation for his sake and the gospel's. The destruction of the temple may be a harbinger, preceded by the desolating sacrilege (Mark 13:14; see Dan 9:27; 11:31; 12:11); but it is not the end of all things, as these disciples appear to believe. The end will come only after Jesus's followers endure the kind of suffering that the disciples have resisted so far in the narrative. A series of imperatives throughout 13:5–23 marks Jesus's instruction to his followers about living in light of the worldly upheaval.

The speech recalls Jesus's earlier teaching, just after the first passion prediction, in which he calls his followers to serve as self-sacrificial witnesses "for my sake" (8:35; see 13:9) and the "gospel's" (8:35; see 13:10). He warns that those who are ashamed of him and his words amid a hostile environment, the Son of Man will likewise be ashamed of when he comes "in the glory of his Father" with the holy angels (8:38; see 13:24–27, cf. Isa 65:13c). In 13:9–13 Jesus uses scriptural language to predict that they will continue his ministry in the Spirit's power, for "it is necessary to proclaim the gospel" (δεῖ κηρυχθῆναι τὸ εὐαγγέλιον, 13:10; cf. 1:14) to all nations. Language from Isa 53:6b, 12, which Jesus recently used

---

43. See also Marcus, *Way of the Lord*, 139–45; Max Botner, *Jesus Christ as the Son of David in the Gospel of Mark*, SNTSMS 174 (Cambridge: Cambridge University Press, 2019).

44. For a discussion of Mark's use of Zechariah in ch. 13 and throughout the Gospel, see Paul T. Sloan, *Mark 13 and the Return of the Shepherd: The Narrative Logic of Zechariah in Mark*, LNTS 604 (London: T&T Clark, 2019).

to predict his own suffering and death, describes how they will imitate him in being "handed over" (παραδίδωμι, 9:31; 10:33; cf. 8:31; παραδώσουσιν ὑμας, 13:9; παραδιδόντες, v. 11; παραδώσει εἰς θάνατον, v. 12) to affliction. This scriptural use looks beyond the current moment of incomprehension to when Jesus's Spirit-filled followers continue his mission faithfully after his death.

Then 13:24–27 shifts from commands to cosmic upheaval, with an allusion to Dan 7:13 that depicts the coming of the Son of Man in the role of the Ancient of Days. Earlier, Jesus had taken up the authority of the one God to forgive sins on the earth; now he takes up the authority of the one God to judge. A conflated citation from Isa 13:10; 34:4; Joel 2:10–11 enables Jesus to portray apocalyptic armies as divine instruments of judgment that overwhelm the entire cosmos. The outcome and climax of the Son of Man's judgment is the conquest of hostile powers to gather an eschatological community, the goal of Jesus's mission since the outset of the narrative (3:14–15, 28, 31–35; 10:28–31).

The final parable pictures the Son of Man/Jesus as a man gone on a "journey" (ἀπόδημος, 13:34), similar to the parable of the vineyard, in which God is as a man who "goes on a journey" (ἀποδημέω, 12:1). But in this parable, the man does not lease his property to tenants, to whom he sends his servants; instead, he leaves his property in the charge of his "servants" (δούλοις, 13:34). Readers might imagine these "servants" to be those Jesus has rescued from one house so that they might do God's will in another (3:31–35), by witnessing, suffering, and even dying for his sake and the gospel's (13:9–13; cf. 8:34–9:1).

Mark 14–16

With the start of the passion narrative, Mark continues to apply a contextual interpretation of Isaiah, blending other coherent Scriptures into the narration.[45] Jesus shares the Passover meal with those who will betray and abandon him (14:22–25). He interprets his blood as the blood of the covenant, "poured out for many" (τὸ ἐκχυννόμενον ὑπὲρ πολλῶν), an allusion to Exod 24:8, which describes the initiation of the Sinai covenant. Moses "pours out" (ἐγκέω) the blood of sacrificial animals on the altar (24:6) and sprinkles it on the people, saying, "behold, the blood of the covenant which the Lord has made with you" (24:8). Jesus will soon ratify a new covenant by pouring out his blood, effecting the

---

45. Scholars who see the suffering servant motif in the passion narrative include Watts, *New Exodus*; Rikk E. Watts, "Jesus' Death, Isaiah 53, and Mark 10:45: A Crux Revisited," in *Jesus and the Suffering Servant: Isaiah 53 and Christian Origins*, ed. William H. Bellinger Jr. and William R. Farmer (Harrisburg, PA: Trinity Press International, 1998), 125–51; Marcus, *Way of the Lord*, esp. 1–2, 17–21; Adela Yarbro Collins, "Mark's Interpretation of the Death of Jesus," *JBL* 128, no. 3 (2009): 545–54; Collins, "The Significance of Mark 10:45 among Gentile Christians," *HTR* 90, no. 4 (1997): 371–82.

cleansing and forgiveness to which John the Baptist's preparation had pointed (cf. Jer 31:31; Ezek 34:25; 37:26). Yet Mark reads the allusion to Exod 24:8 through the locution of Isa 53:11–12, in which the servant "pours out [הֶעֱרָה] himself to death" (MT) and "bore the sin of many" (רַבִּים, MT; πολλῶν, LXX).[46] By combining an allusion to Isa 53:11–12, Mark reads this Passover sacrifice through the locution of the servant's vicarious suffering and death. Verbal and thematic correspondence with Mark 10:45 indicate narrative development, intimating that redemption (λύτρον) from sin, death, and satanic power is effected by Jesus's death (14:24). After Jesus reinterprets the Passover meal to explain his death, he interprets the messianic banquet to explain his subsequent life. The interpretation of the second meal suggests the servant's exaltation (Mark 14:25; Isa 52:12).

Just after the meal, Jesus employs a marked citation of Zech 13:7 as the ground for his prediction that the Twelve will all abandon him, or "all stumble" (πάντες σκανδαλισθήσεσθε, 14:27). Mark adapts the grammar to the current context so that the command in Zechariah that the sword "strike the shepherds [pl.]" (Zechariah) becomes the first-person expression, "*I* will strike the *shepherd* [sg.]." This adaptation enhances a coherence between Zechariah and Isaiah, who presents God as the one who "strikes" or "wounds" the servant (Isa 53:4, 6, 10; cf. 8:31). The language of "stumbling," however, also involves the disciples as agents of their own abandonment. They will become "little ones" who stumble (σκανδαλίζω, 9:42, 43, 45, 47; cf. Isa 66:24; cf. 4:17) because they have not removed what destroys their faith (by watching and praying, 14:32–42). Nevertheless, the term ἀλλά ("but") creates a logical relationship between verses 14:27b and 28, proposing the resolution to the scattering in Jesus's resurrection.

A plot twist comes when Jesus goes to the place called Gethsemane to pray. So far, Jesus has spoken confidently about the divine necessity of his suffering and death; now, distressed and agitated, he asks God to remove the cup of his wrath (14:36, a conceptual allusion to Isa 51:17 and Ps 69:15; cf. 10:38). Jesus's words, "I am deeply grieved" (14:34) allude to Pss 42:5, 11; 43:5, tracing the psalmist's movement from agonizing pleas to confident trust in God's deliverance. Jesus's use of these psalms of lament unites him with the praying and suffering David and enables him to display the same transformative movement from anguish to trust.[47] Strengthened by prayer, he emerges to meet his accusers and go with them willingly, declaring, "let the Scriptures be fulfilled" (14:49).

---

46. E.g., Adela Yarbro Collins, *Mark: A Commentary*, Hermeneia (Minneapolis: Fortress, 2007), 657; Douglas J. Moo, *The Old Testament in the Gospel Passion Narratives* (Sheffield: Almond Press, 1983), 130–32.

47. See Jen Gilbertson, "Jesus Laments: The Significance of the Allusion to Psalms 42–43 in Mark 14:34" (paper presented at the Virtual Annual Meeting of the Society of Biblical Literature, November 10, 2020); Joel Marcus, *Mark 8–16: A New Translation with Introduction and Commentary*, AB 27A (New Haven: Yale University Press, 2009), 983–84.

At Jesus's trial before the high priest, he "was silent [ἐσιώπα] and did not answer" (οὐκ ἀπεκρίνατο οὐδέν; Mark 14:61). This allusion to Isa 53:7, "like a sheep that before its shearers is silent,"[48] develops Jesus's portrait as suffering servant. But, immediately juxtaposed to 14:61, Jesus breaks "character" by breaking his silence to the high priest, "you shall see the Son of Man seated at the right hand of power and coming with the clouds of heaven" (v. 62), a composite verbal allusion to Dan 7:13 and Ps 110:1 that integrates the image of the Danielic Son of Man with Davidic king.[49] On the heels of the previous verse, the effect is to blend these figures in the portrait of Jesus, suffering servant (14:61) and messianic king who will judge as Son of Man (v. 62).

After Jesus's trial before Pilate, Mark tells how the soldiers mistreat him, with a verbal allusion, such that they "spit" (ἐμπτύειν) on him, cover his "face" (πρόσωπον), and "beat" (ῥαπίσμασιν) him (Mark 14:65; see "beatings," ῥαπίσματα; "spitting," ἐμπτυσμάτων; "face," πρόσωπόν in Isa 50:6 LXX). This same verbal allusion appears in the second passion prediction about gentile mistreatment (Mark 10:34) so that its use here underscores the fulfillment of Jesus's words.

Mark returns to the psalms of lament, particularly Ps 22, to narrate Jesus's crucifixion. The soldiers cast lots to divide up Jesus's clothes (Mark 15:24; see Ps 22:19 [21:19 LXX]); those who pass by the cross "shake their heads" at him (κινοῦντες τὰς κεφαλάς, 15:29; ἐκίνησαν κεφαλήν, Ps 21:8 LXX); his opponents mock him ("save yourself," σῶσον σεαυτόν, 15:30; σωσάτω αὐτόν, Ps 21:9 LXX); those crucified along with him reproach him ("he saved others," ἄλλους ἔσωσεν, 15:31b; Ps 21:9 LXX; and "they reviled him," ὠνείδιζον, 15:32b; ὄνειδος, Ps 21:7 LXX). Finally, Jesus cries out using the language of Ps 22:2 (21:2 LXX; Mark 14:34).

In using Ps 22, Mark augments the portrait of Jesus as Isaiah's suffering servant by developing the image of the suffering, Davidic Messiah. Significantly, Ps 22 coheres with the "plot" of Isa 40–66 in its vocabulary and motifs:

1. A righteous figure suffers and is despised by others (Ps 22:6–7, 12–19; Isa 49:7; 53:3, 7);
2. The suffering figure is vindicated/exalted by YHWH (Ps 22:22b–26; Isa 49:8; 50:7–9; 52:13; 53:10–12);
3. The whole earth acknowledges Israel's God (Ps 22:28–30; Isa 42:10–13; 45:22–24; 49:6–7; 51:5), who reigns as king (Ps 22:29; Isa 52:7);
4. YHWH's salvific acts are proclaimed (Ps 22:31–32; Isa 48:20; 52:10).[50]

---

48. LXX ἄφωνος; MT אלם; LXX translates אלם with σιωπάω elsewhere.
49. Recall 8:31; 9:12, 31; 10:33, 35; 14:21, 41.
50. Culled from Michael A. Lyons, "Psalm 22 and the 'Servants' of Isaiah 54; 56–65," *CBQ* 77, no. 4 (2015): 643.

In the wake of Mark's development of suffering and vindication of the righteous using Ps 118 and Zech 13, such scriptural integration affords the expectation that this "plot" should accompany Jesus's suffering and death, and, in fact, it does.[51] Mark narrates the suffering of the righteous/servant (chs. 14–15), his divine vindication/exaltation (15:38–39; 16:6–7), the "whole earth" acknowledging Israel's God (15:39), and the proclamation of God's saving acts (16:1–8 with 13:9–13).

The scene at the empty tomb recalls Jesus's promise that he will meet his disgraced disciples in Galilee (16:6–7). There is no explicit scriptural use, but the intratextual allusion to 14:27–28 carries forward the conceptual allusion to Zechariah's restoration hope, confirming its fulfillment in Jesus's resurrection. The conceptual allusion emphasizes the promise of restoration to the remnant and enhances the Isaian motif of the exalted servant who receives an offspring. One might even imagine the risen Jesus baptizing disciples with the Spirit to equip them to serve (1:8; 13:11).

The Nature of Mark's Scriptural Text

Mark's citations and verbal allusions appear to follow a Greek *Vorlage* that itself closely follows the MT. Yet it is sometimes difficult to discern whether Mark uses a Greek source or translates (or paraphrases) a Hebrew source into Greek. In some cases, Mark's text may resemble a Greek manuscript, which may in turn bear witness to a Hebrew *Vorlage*. For example, the citation of Zech 13:7 in Mark 14:27 closely matches Codex Marchalianis (Q), and the citation of Isa 42:1 in Mark 1:11 (ἐν σοὶ εὐδόκησα, "in you I am well pleased") closely matches Theodotion and Symmachus (εἰς ὅν εὐδόκησεν; cf. Isa 42:1 in Matt 12:18, which has εἰς ὅν εὐδόκησεν).

Mark exercises considerable freedom with textual forms for contextual, or theological, or pragmatic reasons. Mark may change grammar or word order, or may substitute or omit words (see, e.g., Exod 23:20; Mal 3:1; and Isa 40:3 in 1:2–3; Ps 2:7 and Isa 42:1 in Mark 1:11; Isa 6:9–10 in Mark 4:11; Jer 5:21 and Ezek 12:2 in Mark 8:18; Exod 20:12–17 // Deut 5:16–21 in Mark 10:19; Deut 6:4–5 and Lev 19:18b in Mark 12:29, 31; and Zech 13:7 in Mark 14:27).

---

51. Contra Stephen P. Ahearne-Kroll, who argues that Jesus's cry from the cross does not invoke the larger context of Ps 22 and so does not envision resurrection. Ahearne-Kroll, *The Psalms of Lament in Mark's Passion: Jesus' Davidic Suffering*, SNTSMS 142 (Cambridge: Cambridge University Press, 2007). Holly J. Carey demonstrates that Mark's use of Ps 22 does envision the whole psalm, without considering Mark's use of Isaiah. Holly J. Carey, *Jesus' Cry from the Cross: Towards a First-Century Understanding of the Intertextual Relationship between Ps 22 and the Narrative of Mark's Gospel*, LNTS 398 (Edinburgh: T&T Clark, 2009).

Conclusion

I have argued that Mark recruits an argument structure or "plot" from Isaiah, recognizable by a shared pattern of content: God's redemptive intervention for Israel and the nations, Israel's rejection of God/prophets/Jesus resulting in spiritual blindness and hardening, the suffering and vindication of the righteous servant(s), and the anticipation of God's/Jesus's universal reign. Mark "intertextually aligns" and augments this plot with corresponding texts and motifs from the exodus, the Deuteronomic History, Psalms, and Prophets.[52]

The recognition of this contextual and integrated use of Scripture suggests three implications about God, Jesus, and his followers. First, Mark is about God and Jesus. Mark's use of Scripture affords the recognition that the one God's presence, words, and actions are manifest in the presence, words, and actions of Jesus. It is not merely that Jesus is divine, but that he is the very expression of divinity. Second, Mark is about Jesus as the servant, David, and Son of Man. Mark's use of Scripture generates a blended portrait of Jesus as God's servant and royal son (David) who, because he suffers according to the divine will, is exalted to deliver a kingdom to God's people. Third, Mark is about messiahship and discipleship. Mark's use of Scripture affords possibilities for servant-followers to respond steadfastly, imitating Jesus in their own righteous suffering.

Finally, Mark's use of Scripture is not only profoundly contextual and integrative; if understood within Second Temple practices of writing and reading, it is also profoundly social. Mark was likely the first to narrativize the tradition about Jesus, that is, to tell it as a story in written form. In so doing, Mark also narrativized Isaiah's announcement of the "good news," transforming this mode of proclamation into a geographical-narrative framework to address a new reading community. Mark's scriptural-narrative imagination thus lends coherence among the past, present, and future of God's activity and his people's experience, generating a lens through which readers might maintain their identity as his servant-followers.

Bibliography

Ahearne-Kroll, Stephen P. *The Psalms of Lament in Mark's Passion: Jesus' Davidic Suffering*. SNTSMS 142. Cambridge: Cambridge University Press, 2007.

Botner, Max. *Jesus Christ as the Son of David in the Gospel of Mark*. SNTSMS 174. Cambridge: Cambridge University Press, 2019.

---

52. Quotation from Tooman, "Scriptural Reuse," 34.

———. "The Role of Transcriptional Probability in the Text-Critical Debate on Mark 1:1." *CBQ* 77, no. 3 (2015): 467–80.
Bratcher, Robert G., ed. *Old Testament Quotations in the New Testament*. Rev. ed. Helps for Translators 3. London: United Bible Societies, 1967.
Brodie, Thomas L. *The Crucial Bridge: The Elijah-Elisha Narrative as an Interpretive Synthesis of Genesis–Kings and a Literary Model for the Gospels*. Collegeville, MN: Liturgical Press, 2000.
Campbell, Jonathan G. *The Exegetical Texts*. Companion to the Qumran Scrolls 4. London: T&T Clark, 2004.
———. *Use of Scripture in the Damascus Document 1–8, 19–20*. BZAW 228. Berlin: de Gruyter, 1995.
Carey, Holly J. *Jesus' Cry from the Cross: Towards a First-Century Understanding of the Intertextual Relationship between Psalm 22 and the Narrative of Mark's Gospel*. LNTS 398. Edinburgh: T&T Clark, 2009.
Collins, Adela Yarbro. *Mark: A Commentary*. Hermeneia. Minneapolis: Fortress, 2007.
———. "Mark's Interpretation of the Death of Jesus." *JBL* 128, no. 3 (2009): 545–54.
———. "The Significance of Mark 10:45 among Gentile Christians." *HTR* 90, no. 4 (1997): 371–82.
Collins, John J. *Daniel: A Commentary on the Book of Daniel*. Hermeneia. Minneapolis: Fortress, 1993.
———. "The Dead Sea Scrolls and the New Testament: The Case of the Suffering Servant." Pages 279–95 in *Method and Meaning: Essays on New Testament Interpretation in Honor of Harold W. Attridge*. Edited by Andrew B. McGowan and Kent H. Richards. RBS 67. Atlanta: Society of Biblical Literature, 2012.
Dowd, Sharyn E. "Reading Mark Reading Isaiah." *LTQ* 30 (1995): 133–43.
Eco, Umberto. *Semiotics and the Philosophy of Language*. London: Macmillan, 1984.
Fishbane, Michael. *Biblical Interpretation in Ancient Israel*. Oxford: Clarendon, 1985.
Gilbertson, Jen. "Jesus Laments: The Significance of the Allusion to Pss 42–43 in Mark 14:34." Paper presented at the Virtual Annual Meeting of the Society of Biblical Literature. November 10, 2020.
Hatina, Thomas. *In Search of a Context: The Function of Scripture in Mark's Narrative*. JSNTSup 232. Sheffield: Sheffield Academic, 2002.
Hays, Richard B. *Echoes of Scripture in the Gospels*. Waco, TX: Baylor University Press, 2016.
Hengel, Martin. "The Effective History of Isaiah 53 in the Pre-Christian Period." Pages 75–146 in *The Suffering Servant: Isaiah 53 in Jewish and Christian Sources*. Edited by Bernd Janowski and Peter Stuhlmacher. Grand Rapids: Eerdmans, 2004.
Hooker, Morna. *Jesus and the Servant: The Influence of the Servant Concept of Deutero-Isaiah in the New Testament*. London: SPCK, 1959.

Lyons, Michael A. "Psalm 22 and the 'Servants' of Isaiah 54; 56–65." *CBQ* 77, no. 4 (2015): 640–56.

———. "The Servants in Psalms 22, 69, and 102." Pages 45–64 in *Isaiah's Servants in Early Judaism and Christianity: The Isaian Servant and the Exegetical Formation of Community Identity*. Edited by Michael A. Lyons and Jacob Stromberg. WUNT 2/554. Mohr Siebeck, 2021.

Lyons, Michael A., and Jacob Stromberg, eds., *Isaiah's Servants in Early Judaism and Christianity: The Isaian Servant and the Exegetical Formation of Community Identity*. WUNT 2/554. Tübingen: Mohr Siebeck, 2021.

Malbon, Elizabeth Struthers. "Jonah, Jesus, Gentiles, and the Sea: Markan Narrative Intersections." Pages 251–95 in *Reading the Gospel of Mark in the Twenty-First Century*. Edited by Geert Van Oyen. BETL 301. Leuven: Peeters, 2019.

Marcus, Joel. *Mark 8–16: A New Translation with Introduction and Commentary*. AB 27A. New Haven: Yale University Press, 2009.

———. *The Way of the Lord: Christological Exegesis of the Old Testament in the Gospel of Mark*. Louisville: Westminster John Knox, 1992.

McWhirter, Jocelyn. "Messianic Exegesis in Mark 1:2–3." Pages 158–78 in *"What Does the Scripture Say?" The Function of Scripture in Early Judaism and Christianity*. Vol. 1, *The Synoptic Gospels*. Edited by Craig A. Evans and H. Danny Zacharias. LNTS 469. London: T&T Clark, 2012.

Moo, Douglas J. *The Old Testament in the Gospel Passion Narratives*. Sheffield: Almond Press, 1983.

Moyise, S. "Composite Citations in the Gospel of Mark." Pages 16–33 in *Composite Citations in Antiquity*. Vol. 2, *New Testament Uses*. Edited by Sean A. Adams and Seth M. Ehorn. LNTS 593. London: Bloomsbury, 2016.

Norton, Jonathan D. H. "Composite Quotations in the Damascus Document." Pages 92–118 in *Composite Citations in Antiquity*. Vol. 1, *Jewish, Graeco-Roman, and Early Christian Uses*. Edited by Sean A. Adams and Seth M. Ehorn. LNTS 525. London: Bloomsbury, 2016.

O'Brien, Kelli. *The Use of Scripture in the Markan Passion Narrative*. LNTS 384. London: T&T Clark, 2010.

Shepherd, Michael B. *The Text in the Middle*. StBibLit 162. New York: Lang, 2014.

Shively, Elizabeth E. *Apocalyptic Imagination in the Gospel of Mark: The Literary and Theological Role of Mark 3:22–30*. BZNW 189. Berlin: de Gruyter, 2012.

———. "Purification of the Body and the Reign of God in the Gospel of Mark." *JTS* 71 (2020): 62–89.

———. "The Servant(s) in the Gospel of Mark and the Textual Formation of Early Christian Identity." Pages 143–88 in *Isaiah's Servants in Early Judaism and Christianity: The Isaian Servant and the Exegetical Formation of Community Identity*. Edited by Michael J. Lyons and Jacob Stromberg. WUNT 2/554. Tübingen: Mohr Siebeck, 2021.

Sloan, Paul T. *Mark 13 and the Return of the Shepherd: The Narrative Logic of Zechariah in Mark*. LNTS 604. London: T&T Clark, 2019.
Stromberg, Jacob. "Isaiah's Interpretive Revolution: How Isaiah's Formation Influenced Early Jewish and Christian Interpretation." Pages 214–32 in *The Book of Isaiah: Enduring Questions Answered Anew; Essays Honoring Joseph Blenkinsopp and His Contribution to the Study of Isaiah*. Edited by Richard J. Bautch and J. Todd Hibbard. Grand Rapids: Eerdmans, 2015.
Swartley, William M. *Israel's Scripture Traditions and the Synoptic Gospels: Story Shaping Story*. Peabody, MA: Hendrickson, 1994.
Tooman, William A. *Gog and Magog: Reuse of Scripture and Compositional Technique in Ezekiel 38–39*. FAT 2/52. Tübingen: Mohr Siebeck, 2011.
———. "Scriptural Reuse in Ancient Jewish Literature: Comments and Reflections on the State of the Art." Pages 23–39 in *Methodology in the Use of the Old Testament in the New: Context and Criteria*. Edited by David Allen and Steve Smith. LNTS 597. London: T&T Clark, 2019.
Vorster, W. S. "The Production of the Gospel of Mark: An Essay on Intertextuality." *HvTS* 49, no. 3 (1993): 385–96.
Wasserman, Tommy. "The 'Son of God' Was in the Beginning (Mark 1:1)." *JTS* 62, no. 1 (2011): 20–50.
Watts, Rikk E. *Isaiah's New Exodus in Mark*. Biblical Studies Library. Grand Rapids: Baker, 2000.
———. "Jesus' Death, Isaiah 53, and Mark 10:45: A Crux Revisited." Pages 125–51 in *Jesus and the Suffering Servant: Isaiah 53 and Christian Origins*. Edited by William H. Bellinger Jr. and William R. Farmer. Harrisburg, PA: Trinity Press International, 1998.
———. "Mark." Pages 111–250 in *Commentary on the New Testament Use of the Old Testament*. Edited by G. K. Beale and D. A. Carson. Grand Rapids: Baker Academic, 2007.
Winn, Adam. *Mark and the Elijah-Elisha Narrative: Considering the Practice of Greco-Roman Imitation in the Search for Markan Source Material*. Eugene, OR: Pickwick, 2010.
Zahn, Molly M. *Genres of Rewriting in Second Temple Judaism: Scribal Composition and Transmission*. Cambridge: Cambridge University Press, 2020.

10

Israel's Scriptures in Luke

MARTIN BAUSPIESS

In Luke, as in the other Gospels, Israel's Scriptures play an important role. Luke cites from the Scriptures, he alludes to them, and he takes up certain concepts and ideas, which he integrates in his own narrative. But beyond the Gospels of Mark and Matthew, Luke not only deals *materialiter* with the Scriptures but also depicts Jesus explicitly as an interpreter of Scripture at the beginning (Luke 4:14–30) and at the end of his work (24:25–27, 44–49).[1] Therefore, if we want to ask for Luke's view on the Scriptures, we must have in view both aspects: the concept of Scripture Luke depicts in a narrative way, and the way he deals concretely with Scripture. In conclusion, we will have to ask whether there is a consistent understanding of the Scriptures, which leads to what we know today as the "Old" and the "New Testament."

Luke cites more often from the Scriptures than Mark (thirteen times), but not as often as Matthew (thirty-eight times) does. If we take as a "marked citation" a sentence with a formula of introduction (e.g., "it has been written," γέγραπται), we can identify seventeen direct quotations, which refer to twenty-one texts from the Scriptures.[2] Most of them derive from the Pentateuch (six from Deuteronomy,

---

1. See Christfried Böttrich, "Das Alte im Herzen des Neuen," in *Ex oriente Lux: Studien zur Theologie des Alten Testaments; Festschrift für Rüdiger Lux zum 65. Geburtstag*, ed. Angelika Berlejung and Raik Heckl, ABIG 39 (Leipzig: Evangelische Verlagsanstalt, 2012), 627. To go further, one would have to ask how the interpretation of the Scriptures by *Jesus* is connected with the interpretations given by the apostles, e.g., Peter or Philip, in Acts.

2. Following Dietrich Rusam, *Das Alte Testament bei Lukas*, BZNW 112 (Berlin: de Gruyter, 2003), 4. Fitzmyer names twenty-three direct quotations and twenty-five passages from the

three from Exodus, and two from Leviticus), followed by quotes of Isaiah (five), three from the Psalms, and one of Malachi.[3] Nevertheless, these quotations are just a small part of Luke's reception of the Scriptures. In fact, we can find more than four hundred allusions to the Scriptures that are not direct quotations.[4]

In addition, one has to be aware of the fact that Luke does not have a completed "canon" of "the Scripture"; there is not yet an "Old Testament" from which derives a "New Testament."[5] Generally, there is no completed "Old Testament" before the "New Testament." Both parts of the Christian Bible come to their completion *together*.[6] In fact, in the discussion about a hermeneutic of the canon, this thesis has been criticized, but it finds its confirmation, as we will see, on the basis of the text of Luke's Gospel.[7]

Luke does not speak of "the Scripture." He has other expressions to describe his reference to the texts of ancient Judaism. Only in one place in Luke's Gospel does the word "Scripture" (γραφή) appear in the singular (Luke 4:21, also in Acts 1:16; 8:32, 35), but it does not mean the Scripture as a whole corpus. Rather, it refers to a specific passage of Scripture that he quotes in context (Isa 61:1–2). In other cases, Luke speaks of the "Scriptures" in the plural (αἱ γραφαί, Luke 24:27, 32, 45; also in Acts 17:2, 11; 18:24, 28). He can use the term ὁ νόμος ("the law") with the meaning of the (written) Torah (Luke 2:27; 10:26; 16:17; cf. Matt 5:18) or describe it as the "law of Moses" (ὁ νόμος Μωϋσέως, Luke 2:22) or "the law of the Lord" (ὁ νόμος κυρίου, Luke 2:23, 24, 39).[8] He can name "Moses" (Luke 5:14; 20:28) or "the prophets" (Luke 18:31) as the subject of scriptural statements. Above all, it is striking that Luke uses the phrase "the law and the prophets"

Scriptures (Joseph A. Fitzmyer, "The Use of the Old Testament in Luke-Acts," in *To Advance the Gospel: New Testament Studies*, 2nd ed., Biblical Resource Series [Grand Rapids: Eerdmans, 1998], 297 with 311 n. 5). Böttrich, "Das Alte im Herzen des Neuen," 627–28 follows the counting of Rusam.

3. Luke 2:23 (Exod 13:2, 15); 2:24 (Lev 12:6–8; 5:11); 3:4–6 (Isa 40:3–5); 4:4 (Deut 8:3); 4:8 (Deut 6:13); 4:10–11 (Ps 90:11–12 LXX); 4:12 (Deut 6:16); 4:18–19 (Isa 61:1–2; 58:6); 7:27 (Mal 3:1); 10:27 (Deut 6:5; Lev 19:18); 18:20 (Exod 20:12–16/Deut 5:16–20); 19:46 (Is 56:7); 20:17 (Ps 117:22 LXX); 20:28 (Deut 25:5–6; Gen 38:8); 20:37 (Exod 3:6); 20:42–3 (Ps 109:1 LXX); see Rusam, *Das Alte Testament bei Lukas*, 2–3.

4. Böttrich, "Das Alte im Herzen des Neuen," 628.

5. For the lack of a canon, see Rusam, *Das Alte Testament bei Lukas*, 26–27. Against Fitzmyer, "Use of the Old Testament in Luke-Acts," 295.

6. Hartmut Gese, "Das biblische Schriftverständnis," in *Zur biblischen Theologie: Alttestamentliche Vorträge*, 3rd ed. (Tübingen: Mohr Siebeck, 1989), 11.

7. Notger Slenczka, "Die Kirche und das Alte Testament," in *Das Alte Testament in der Theologie*, ed. Elisabeth Gräb-Schmidt, MJTh 25 (Leipzig: Evangelische Verlagsanstalt, 2013), 104. Slenczka argues against Brevard Childs as well as against the position of Hartmut Gese.

8. This is in addition to numerous passages in Acts that I have not specifically listed here.

(ὁ νόμος καὶ οἱ προφῆται, Luke 16:16; Matt 5:17; 7:12; 11:13; 22:40; cf. John 1:45), and, in a single instance "the law and the prophets and the psalms" (Luke 24:44). Similar formulations are found in 2 and 4 Maccabees, in the Prologue of Sirach, and, suggestively, in Qumran (see 2 Macc 15:9; 4 Macc 18:10; 1QS I, 3; 4Q397).[9] Since the first two parts of the later Masoretic canon are mentioned with "Law" and "Prophets," not a few commentators see here an indication that, at the time of Luke, its first parts were already fixed, while the part of the "Writings," to which the Psalms also belong, was still unfinished.[10] Nevertheless, we can see that, for Luke, the reference to the *written* word has an important meaning.

Finally, for an investigation of Luke's understanding of the Scriptures, it is important to be aware of the fact that the Gospel of Luke is not a uniformly conceived text but is created in the process of absorbing and processing source material. The author himself mentions "many" (πολλοί) who have already written a narrative (διήγησις), as he himself does, and that he takes up their writings (Luke 1:1).[11] Therefore, we can assume that Luke knew more than one other gospel, the Gospel of Mark and another writing. Because of his technique of dealing with the Markan material, some commentators developed the hypothesis of a "Proto-Luke," in which the Lukan *Sondergut* was already connected with material from Q.[12] Although it is not possible to prove this thesis, it is important

---

9. See Konrad Schmid and Jens Schröter, *Die Entstehung der christlichen Bibel: Von den ersten Texten zu den heiligen Schriften* (Munich: Beck, 2019), 200–201, 241, 357–58.

10. Schmid and Schröter, *Die Entstehung der Bibel*, 358, cf. 241. According to Schmid and Schröter, in Luke 24:44 the Psalms are not mentioned as a text from the third part of the "Tanak," but as one of the prophetic texts. They can point to the observation that, for Luke, the Psalms are prophetic texts, as one sees in Acts 2:30.

11. When Luke is writing that he has "followed all of them from the beginning," he does not mean that he wrote his gospel on the grounds of historical investigation. He means that he follows the sources he had and that he created a narrative from these that can show the true meaning of Jesus's story and therefore strengthen the Christian faith of his readers. See Martin Bauspiess, *Geschichte und Erkenntnis im lukanischen Doppelwerk: Eine exegetische Untersuchung zu einer christlichen Perspektive auf Geschichte*, ABIG 42 (Leipzig: Evangelische Verlagsanstalt, 2012), 210–13.

12. See from the older discussion B. H. Streeter, *The Four Gospels: A Study of Their Origins*, 9th ed. (London: Macmillan, 1956); Joachim Jeremias, *Neutestamentliche Theologie*, vol. 1, *Die Verkündigung Jesu* (Berlin: Evangelische Verlagsanstalt, 1973), 48–49; from the newer discussion Thomas Brodie, *Proto-Luke: The Oldest Gospel Account; A Christ-Centered Synthesis of Old Testament History Modelled Especially on the Elijah-Elisha Narrative* (Limerick: Dominican Biblical Institute, 2006); Kim Paffenroth, *The Story of Jesus according to L*, JSNTSup 147 (Sheffield: Sheffield Academic, 1997). Critical of this thesis is Michael Wolter, *Das Lukasevangelium*, HNT 5 (Tübingen: Mohr Siebeck, 2008), 15. For Jeremias, the hypothesis gains plausibility from the fact that Luke uses a "Blocktechnik" in dealing with the Markan material, which can also be assumed for his dealing with his other sources.

to realize that the assumption of a written source Q is also purely hypothetical. What we can see is that Luke refers to sources in which scriptural references were already included. As a consequence, we cannot simply assume that Luke independently introduces scriptural quotations when they appear in his work in the perspective of the narrator, as is the case in Luke 2:23, 24; and in Luke 4:4–6.[13] The Lukan reception of the Scriptures is to be understood as a process of tradition and interpretation, which we will investigate exemplarily in different parts of the Third Gospel. In addition, we must take into account that Luke writes his gospel as the first part of a two-part work, "Luke-Acts." We will see that this fact is also important for Luke's reception of the Scriptures since Luke-Acts comes to an end with the quotation of Isa 6:9–10 in Acts 28:26–27.

In many cases, Luke refers to the Greek text of the Septuagint, but there are also instances where the Hebrew text could be in the background.[14] Of course, the question of the *Vorlage* is connected with the question of the sources of the Gospel of Luke. Dietrich Rusam states that the hypothesis of a "collection of testimonies" is entirely speculative.[15] If there are changes in comparison to the Septuagint, one can ask if this can be explained by recourse to Luke's editorial intervention. However, where this does not prove probable, we can assume that Luke had an alternative Greek version at hand.[16]

Israel's Scriptures in the Gospel of Luke

The Origins of Jesus (Luke 1:5–2:52)

The Lukan birth narrative is an example of the fact that direct quotations are just a small part of the reception of the Scriptures in his work. Although there are only two direct quotations in this part of the gospel (Luke 2:23, 24), it becomes clear that the whole narration is told on the basis of the story of Israel.[17] It is especially

---

13. Suggested by Rusam, *Das Alte Testament bei Lukas*, 4.
14. Otfried Hofius, "Alttestamentliche Motive im Gleichnis vom verlorenen Sohn," in *Neutestamentliche Studien*, WUNT 132 (Tübingen: Mohr Siebeck, 2000), 151, comes to the conclusion that the parable of the lost son refers to the Hebrew text. This fact could be explained with the thesis that Luke is not the author of this parable but that it derives from the proclamation of Jesus (153).
15. Rusam, *Das Alte Testament bei Lukas*, 28.
16. Cf. Rusam, *Das Alte Testament bei Lukas*, 26. He quotes the result of the studies of Dietrich-Alex Koch, who states that there was a tendency to correct the text of the Septuagint based on a Hebrew *Vorlage* at the time of the first century.
17. See Fitzmyer, "Use of the Old Testament in Luke-Acts," 203.

the motif of an unexpected or miraculous birth, which recalls the stories of Sara and Isaac (Gen 18:1–15) or of Samuel and Hannah (1 Sam 1:1–2:11). The Magnificat (Luke 1:46–55) is obviously an allusion to the song of Hannah (1 Sam 2:1–10), but the question is how this motif is interpreted in the context of the Lukan birth narrative.[18] The commonality between the song of Hannah and the song of Mary is that both speak of the exaltation of the poor and lowly (1 Sam 2:8; Luke 1:52–53). But beyond Hannah, Mary sings of a complete reversal of power relations, in which not only are the lowly placed "among the mighty of the nations" (1 Sam 2:8) but also "the rulers are cast down from their thrones" (Luke 1:52). This corresponds to the way in which the motif of the miraculous birth is outperformed in the story of Jesus's birth. While with Hannah a barren woman (1 Sam 1:5–6) has a child (1:19–20), with Mary a *virgin* (Luke 1:27) is promised a son.[19] Here we can also observe a characteristic difference between the Gospel of Luke and the Gospel of Matthew: while Matthew quotes Isa 7:14 LXX at the corresponding passage (Matt 1:23), Luke does not quote Isaiah, but he explicitly addresses the fact that Mary had not yet had sexual intercourse (Luke 1:34).[20] While Matthew is concerned with proving that "the Scriptures" foretold the birth of Jesus, Luke emphasizes the theological meaning of the virgin birth and thus the fact that it is due to the work of the Holy Spirit and that Jesus therefore is the Son of God (Luke 1:35). This tendency can also be observed in other passages in the comparison between Luke and Matthew: while Matthew wants to prove individual aspects of Jesus's life as "proven" by the Scripture with the so-called formula quotations, Luke calls upon Scripture as a whole as the horizon in which he tells the Jesus story.[21] Especially in Acts, he seems to imitate the style of the narratives of the Septuagint.[22] Therefore, it seems reasonable to search for conceptual allusions in Luke's work, for instance from the Elijah-Elisha narrative or the motif of Jesus as

---

18. Ulrike Mittmann-Richert, *Magnifikat und Benediktus: Die ältesten Zeugnisse der judenchristlichen Tradition von der Geburt des Messias*, WUNT 2/90 (Tübingen: Mohr Siebeck, 1996), 17–21. She underlines that there are several other allusions to texts of Israel's Scriptures, especially from the Psalms and the prophets (see 21). For the Magnificat's interpretation in Luke, see Helmer Ringgren, "Luke's Use of the Old Testament," *HTR* 79, no. 1/3 (1986): 227–35, esp. 230–32. Ringgren shows that "there are allusion to several other OT texts" (230), which are held together "by the antithesis motif centered around ταπεινός/ὑψοῦν, exemplified without the exact wording by 1 Samuel 2" (231).

19. Bauspiess, *Geschichte und Erkenntnis*, 317–19. Unless otherwise noted, all translations are by the author.

20. Cf. Darrell L. Bock, *Luke*, BECNT 3 (Grand Rapids: Baker, 1994), 1:108.

21. For Matthew's tendency, see Matt 1:22–23; 2:15, 17–18, 23; 4:14–16; 8:17; 12:17–21; 13:35; 21:4–5; 27:9–10. For more on this topic, see ch. 8 by Matthias Konradt in this volume. For Luke's outlook, see Rusam, *Das Alte Testament bei Lukas*, 6.

22. Eckart Plümacher, *Lukas als hellenistischer Schriftsteller: Studien zur Apostelgeschichte*,

a "prophet," the figure of God's servant or the exodus tradition.[23] The Lukan birth narrative shows exemplarily how Luke refers to the horizon of the Scriptures and gives an interpretation of them from the perspective of belief in Jesus Christ. The Scriptures give him the language that enables him to express what happened in the story of Jesus. However, his view also becomes clear in such instances where he quotes directly. A particularly significant example of this is found at the beginning of the main body of his gospel.

The Story of Jesus as the Epiphany of God's Salvation

The Opening of the Body (Luke 3:4–6)

For an understanding of Luke's reception of the Scriptures, the opening of the body of his gospel is illuminating. In Luke 3:1-2 Luke formulates one of the two famous "world-historical reminiscences" (the other being at the beginning of the Christmas story in Luke 2:1-2). In fact, many exegetes consider these "reminiscences" as proof for Luke's self-understanding as a "historian" and of Luke-Acts as historiography.[24] But it is interesting that this dating of the beginning of Jesus's coming to his public work is connected in Luke 3:4-6 with an extensive direct quotation of Isa 40:3-5, which is obviously given according to the version of the Septuagint (table 10.1).

Table 10.1. Isaiah 40:3–5 and Luke 3:4–6

Isa 40:3–5 LXX	Luke 3:4–6
	⁴ὡς γέγραπται
	ἐν βίβλῳ λόγων Ἠσαΐου τοῦ προφήτου·

SUNT 9 (Göttingen: Vandenhoeck & Ruprecht, 1972), 38–72; cf. Böttrich, "Das Alte im Herzen des Neuen," 616 n. 17; Fitzmyer, " Use of the Old Testament in Luke-Acts," 296.

23. For Elijah-Elisha, see John S. Kloppenborg and Joseph Verheyden, eds., *The Elijah-Elisha Narrative in the Composition of Luke*, LNTS 493 (London: T&T Clark, 2014). For Jesus as prophet, see Böttrich, "Das Alte im Herzen des Neuen," 630–31. For God's servant, see Ulrike Mittmann-Richert, *Der Sühnetod des Gottesknechts: Jesaja 53 im Lukasevangelium*, WUNT 220 (Tübingen: Mohr Siebeck, 2008). For the exodus tradition, see Kerstin Schiffner, *Lukas liest Exodus: Eine Untersuchung zur Aufnahme ersttestamentlicher Befreiungsgeschichte im lukanischen Werk als Schrift-Lektüre*, BWANT 172 (Stuttgart: Kohlhammer, 2008).

24. See, e.g., Rainer Riesner, "Das lukanische Doppelwerk und die antike Biographie," in *Lebensgeschichte und Religion*, ed. Detlev Dormeyer, Herbert Mölle, and Thomas Ruster, Religion und Biographie 1 (Münster: LIT, 2000), 139. For Wolter, *Das Lukasevangelium*, 156, the quite precise dating in Luke 3:1-2 (compared to 1:5 and 2:1) reveals the intention to determine the story of Jesus as a part of world history and of the history of Israel.

³φωνὴ βοῶντος ἐν τῇ ἐρήμῳ· Ἑτοιμάσατε τὴν ὁδὸν κυρίου, εὐθείας ποιεῖτε τὰς τρίβους τοῦ θεοῦ ἡμῶν· ⁴πᾶσα φάραγξ πληρωθήσεται καὶ πᾶν ὄρος καὶ βουνὸς ταπεινωθήσεται, καὶ ἔσται πάντα τὰ σκολιὰ εἰς εὐθεῖα καὶ ἡ τραχεῖα εἰς πεδία· ⁵καὶ ὀφθήσεται ἡ δόξα κυρίου, καὶ ὄψεται πᾶσα σὰρξ τὸ σωτήριον τοῦ θεοῦ· ὅτι κύριος ἐλάλησεν.	φωνὴ βοῶντος ἐν τῇ ἐρήμῳ· ἑτοιμάσατε τὴν ὁδὸν κυρίου, εὐθείας ποιεῖτε τὰς τρίβους αὐτοῦ· ⁵πᾶσα φάραγξ πληρωθήσεται καὶ πᾶν ὄρος καὶ βουνὸς ταπεινωθήσεται, καὶ ἔσται τὰ σκολιὰ εἰς εὐθείαν καὶ αἱ τραχεῖαι εἰς ὁδοὺς λείας· ⁶καὶ ὄψεται πᾶσα σὰρξ
³the voice of one crying in the desert Prepare the way of the Lord, make straight the paths of our God ⁴Every valley shall be filled and every mountain and hill shall be made low, and all the crooked shall become straight and the rough places a plain ⁵and the glory of the Lord shall be revealed and all flesh will see the salvation of God. For the Lord has spoken.	⁴As it is written in the book of the word of Isaiah the prophet: the voice of one crying in the desert: prepare the way of the Lord, make his paths straight. ⁵Every valley shall be filled and every mountain and hill shall be made low, and the crooked shall become straight and the rough places shall become level ways ⁶And all flesh will see the salvation of God.

The quotation in Luke 3:4–6 corresponds relatively literally to the Septuagint. The modification of τὰς τρίβους τοῦ θεοῦ ἡμῶν ("the paths of our God") in Isa 40:3b to τὰς τρίβους αὐτοῦ ("his paths") in Luke 3:4b does not change the meaning of the verse. Minor variations in wording are found in Isa 40:4 in comparison with Luke 3:5. Luke omits the revelation of the δόξα κυρίου ("the glory of the Lord") announced in Isa 40:5a LXX, but quotes the following phrase literally: καὶ ὄψεται πᾶσα σὰρξ τὸ σωτήριον τοῦ θεοῦ ("and all of the flesh will see the salvation of God"). While the Septuagint emphasizes that the κύριος himself spoke in these words (Isa 40:5b LXX), Luke introduces the quotation as "written in the book of the words of the prophet Isaiah" (Luke 3:4a; cf. Mark 1:2a, without hint of the "book" of Isaiah). This introduction is characteristic: Luke refers to the prophetic message in the form of a "book," as written prophecy.

The exact dating of the appearance of the Baptist in the fifteenth year of the reign of Caesar Tiberius, the time of Pontius Pilatus, and the rest in Luke 3:1 is characteristically connected with the reference to the fact that "the word of the Lord came to John the son of Zechariah" (Luke 3:2b).[25] This connection of dating and word-revelation has its parallel in the beginning of prophetic books (Jer 1:1-3; Mic 1:1; Hos 1:1).[26] Therefore, the "synchronisms" are not an expression of the historical character of Luke's work. They are rather an expression of the fact that Luke tells the story of Jesus in the horizon of Israel's story with its God because for him the story of Jesus is *God's* story. John the Baptist is introduced in this context—taking up what was said in the birth narrative—as the conclusion of the prophecy of the Scriptures. This corresponds to the verse often quoted to describe the Lukan understanding of the Baptist, Luke 16:16, which says: "The law and the prophets go up to John, from then on the reign of God is proclaimed" (ὁ νόμος καὶ οἱ προφῆται μέχρι Ἰωάννου· ἀπὸ τότε ἡ βασιλεία τοῦ θεοῦ εὐαγγελίζεται).[27]

It is difficult to say which model the evangelist Luke had for the beginning of the body of his Gospel. However, we can safely assume that Luke at least knew the beginning of the Gospel of Mark. It is therefore not quite correct when Rusam states that the author of the Third Gospel in Luke 3:4-6 formulates his text independently from Mark's Gospel.[28] For Luke already knew from the beginning of the Gospel of Mark the connection between the appearance of the Baptist with the quotation from the "prophet Isaiah" (Mark 1:2a), which, however, turns out on closer examination to be a mixed quotation from Isa 40:3; Exod 23:20; and Mal 3:1 (Mark 1:2b-3). Already in the Gospel of Mark, Isa 40:3 is connected with the appearance of the Baptist and his announcement of the beginning of the story of Jesus. Luke "corrects" Mark 1:2-3 in that he quotes only from the book of Isaiah in Luke 3:4-6. The observation made above gains importance, that Isa 40:5b LXX points out that the announcement made is a word of the κύριος ("Lord"). Luke does not quote this reference and instead opens the quotation

---

25. The fact that Zechariah is mentioned in this connection also recalls what is said about John the Baptist to and by his father in the birth narrative. What is narrated in Luke 3:1-6 is the fulfillment of what was announced in Luke 1:13-17, 76-79 (Heinz Schürmann, *Das Lukasevangelium*, HThKNT 3.1-2 [Freiburg im Breisgau: Herder, 1969], 1:152).

26. Bauspiess, *Geschichte und Erkenntnis*, 326-27, cf. François Bovon, *Das Evangelium nach Lukas*, EKKNT 3.1-4 (Neukirchen-Vluyn: Neukirchener Verlag, 1989), 1:169; Schürmann, *Lukasevangelium*, 1:149.

27. For the discussion of this text see Wolter, *Das Lukasevangelium*, 554-56.

28. Rusam, *Das Alte Testament bei Lukas*, 4.

Israel's Scriptures in Luke

with a reference to the book of Isaiah. The word of God that Isaiah delivers is available to Luke "in the book of the words of the prophet Isaiah." Accordingly, he makes explicit reference to the prophetic proclamation in the form of a Scripture. It is obvious, however, that the "extension" of the Isaiah quotation by verses 4 and 5 is not only done for the sake of literary accuracy, but rather, the evangelist gains an important motif from the word in Isaiah. The quotation amounts to the words καὶ ὄψεται πᾶσα σὰρξ τὸ σωτήριον τοῦ θεοῦ ("and all flesh will see the salvation of God," Luke 3:6 = Isa 40:5 LXX). Luke sees announced by Isaiah in a special way that in the coming of Jesus "the salvation of God" enters visibly into history. Luke especially underlines repeatedly the visibility of Jesus's story.[29] In any case, the keyword τὸ σωτήριον τοῦ θεοῦ ("the salvation of God") is found not only at the beginning but also at the end of Luke-Acts, in Acts 28:28.[30] There it immediately follows the "hardening motif" of Isa 6:9-10 (Acts 28:26-27) and serves to draw the conclusion from this quotation from Isaiah: "Let it be known to you, then, that this salvation of God is sent to the gentiles also; and they will hear" (γνωστὸν οὖν ἔστω ὑμῖν ὅτι τοῖς ἔθνεσιν ἀπεστάλη τοῦτο τὸ σωτήριον τοῦ θεοῦ· αὐτοὶ καὶ ἀκούσονται). By the "salvation of God" Luke evidently understands the "reign of God" (Acts 28:31), which in turn is indissolubly linked to the person of Jesus.[31] In this sense, the keyword τὸ σωτήριον τοῦ θεοῦ already occurs in the birth story. When old Simeon sees the baby Jesus, he says to God: "My eyes have seen your salvation" (εἶδον οἱ ὀφθαλμοί μου τὸ σωτήριόν σου, Luke 2:30). Here we can go further and say: the "salvation of God" is the person of Jesus himself. Therefore, we can conclude that Luke quotes Isa 40:5 in Luke 3:6 because he sees the coming of Jesus announced here.

This makes two things clear. First, the texts of Israel's Scripture are read from the point of view of fulfillment in the Christ story, that is, from the perspective of faith in Jesus Christ. By referring to the "Scriptures," Luke emphasizes that the Christian community has its roots in the history of Israel's hope, which finds expression in Israel's Scripture. This understanding of Scripture can be observed in other passages as well. Instead of going into further individual examples, however, I would like to point out another fact that is significant for the Lukan understanding of the Scriptures. Second, the author not only engages in exegesis of Scripture from this perspective himself, but he also presents the process of scriptural interpretation narratively. This observation underlines that Luke makes the reception of the Scriptures the object of reflection.

---

29. See Bauspiess, *Geschichte und Erkenntnis*, 334-37.
30. Cf. Rusam, *Das Alte Testament bei Lukas*, 160. The hint of the "knowledge of salvation" (γνῶσις σωτηρίας) in Luke 1:76 could also be mentioned.
31. On the motif of the βασιλεία τοῦ θεοῦ in Luke-Acts, see Alexander Prieur, *Die Verkündigung der Gottesherrschaft: Exegetische Studien zum lukanischen Verständnis der βασιλεία τοῦ θεοῦ*, WUNT 2/89 (Tübingen: Mohr Siebeck, 1996).

Jesus as Interpreter of Scripture

It is striking that the author of the Third Gospel deliberately frames his Jesus narrative with the motif of "Jesus as interpreter of Scripture." It stands at the beginning of Jesus's public activity, which the narrator opens with the so-called inaugural sermon of Jesus in Nazareth (Luke 4:14-30). And it appears twice at the end of the gospel, in Luke's Easter chapter: in the account of the two disciples on the road to Emmaus (Luke 24:13-35, vv. 25-27; cf. v. 32), and in the subsequent appearance of the risen Jesus to the disciples (Luke 24:36-49, vv. 44-48).[32] It is plausible to suggest that the author inserted the motif editorially.[33] In all three places mentioned, what we have already observed in the course of the reception of Scripture is confirmed.

During the "inaugural sermon" in Nazareth, Luke has Jesus quote the prophet Isaiah again (Luke 4:18-19). The quotation is from Isa 61:1-2 and again follows the Septuagint, but it is changed compared to the original context (table 10.2).

Table 10.2. Isaiah 61:1-2 and Luke 4:19-20

Isa 61:1-2 LXX	Luke 4:19-20
πνεῦμα κυρίου ἐπ' ἐμέ,	πνεῦμα κυρίου ἐπ' ἐμὲ
οὗ εἵνεκεν ἔχρισέν με·	οὗ εἵνεκεν ἔχρισέν με
εὐαγγελίσασθαι πτωχοῖς ἀπέσταλκέν με, ἰάσασθαι τοὺς συντετριμμένους τῇ καρδίᾳ, κηρύξαι αἰχμαλώτοις ἄφεσιν καὶ τυφλοῖς ἀνάβλεψιν,	εὐαγγελίσασθαι πτωχοῖς, ἀπέσταλκέν με, κηρύξαι αἰχμαλώτοις ἄφεσιν καὶ τυφλοῖς ἀνάβλεψιν, <u>ἀποστεῖλαι τεθραυσμένους ἐν ἀφέσει,</u>
καλέσαι ἐνιαυτὸν κυρίου δεκτὸν <u>καὶ ἡμέραν ἀνταποδόσεως.</u>	κηρύξαι ἐνιαυτὸν κυρίου δεκτόν.
The spirit of the Lord is upon me, because he has anointed me to bring good news to the poor he has sent me, to bind up the broken hearted, to proclaim liberty to the captives and recovery of sight to the blind to call the year of the Lord's favor <u>and a day of vengeance.</u>	The spirit of the Lord is upon me, because he has anointed me to bring good news to the poor he has sent me, to proclaim liberty to the captives and recovery of sight to the blind <u>to set the oppressed free,</u> to proclaim the year of the Lord's favor.

---

32. In Luke 24:44 Jesus recalls the pre-Easter announcement of the passion. The same reference is found in the first scene of the appearance of the risen Lord in Luke 24:6b-8. On Luke 18:31-33 see below.

33. Bauspiess, *Geschichte und Erkenntnis*, 296-98.

Two things can be noted with regard to the reception of the quotation from Isaiah. First, a clause is inserted that is taken from Isa 58:6 LXX (ἀπόστελλε τεθραυσμένους ἐν ἀφέσει, "Set the oppressed free!") and has been adapted to the structure of the sentence. Luke sees Jesus's efficacy in word and deed announced by Isaiah, and he also sees announced in it that it is God himself who works in Jesus. Second, Luke 4:20 lets the quotation end with the announcement of the time of salvation. He deletes the announcement of judgment that follows this announcement in Isaiah. The history of Jesus is for Luke a time of salvation, which becomes visible in the healings of Jesus but above all in the fact that in him the reign of God is present and proclaimed (Luke 16:16). As a consequence, Luke focuses on the story of Jesus as a story of God's salvation (cf. Luke 5:26; 7:16).

A special accent is now set by the fact that Jesus quotes this announcement from the Scriptures. Here, too, a look at the Gospel of Mark is instructive, taking into account the author's dependence on sources, which is difficult to determine. In Mark's Gospel, the scene of Jesus's appearance in Nazareth is told as well (Mark 6:1–6). Common to both scenes is the saying about the prophet not being welcome in his hometown (Mark 6:4; Luke 4:24) and the reaction of those present (Mark 6:3; Luke 4:22). For an understanding of Luke 4:16–30, it is important to note that the reaction related in 4:22 is, as it is in Mark, a reaction of *irritation*:[34] The people who hear Jesus's interpretation of Isa 61:1–2 in Luke 4:21 ("today, this Scripture passage is fulfilled in your ears") cannot understand what he is saying. A comparison between Mark 6:3 and Luke 4:22 shows how Luke understands the scene: while in Mark those present ask, "Is not this the carpenter, the son of Mary?," in Luke they ask, "Is not this the son of Joseph?" In this context, Luke deliberately recalls Jesus's "sonship of Joseph," which was already a theme in the birth narrative (Luke 2:1–20) and in the family tree of Jesus (Luke 3:23–38) that leads the narrative of Jesus's baptism (Luke 3:21–22) to what follows. The family tree is commented on in Luke 3:23 with the words about Jesus: "He was, *as it was thought*, the son of Joseph" (ὢν υἱός, ὡς ἐνομίζετο, Ἰωσήφ). According to this hint, Jesus is placed in the family story of Joseph. What becomes clear is this: according to Luke, Jesus is not "adopted" by God in the baptism. Rather, an "adoption" *by Joseph* takes place, with which Jesus enters into the story of humankind. The naming of Joseph had the same resonance in the story of the birth in Luke 2:4. By the reference

---

34. Both verbs, θαυμάζειν and μαρτυρεῖν are used with a negative connotation: the people in Nazareth are irritated about the statement of Jesus and they "give testimony against him" (Bauspiess, *Geschichte und Erkenntnis*, 332–33; against Schürmann, *Das Lukasevangelium*, 234; cf. Bovon, *Das Evangelium nach Lukas*, 1:213). Wolter, *Das Lukasevangelium*, 194, sees an open reaction that is not already completed as consent or rejection.

that Joseph comes "from the city of David"—namely Bethlehem—the promise from Mic 5:1 is recalled, according to which the Messiah comes from Bethlehem. If Luke had previously made it clear in the announcement of the birth (Luke 1:26–38)—as we have seen—that Jesus is the Son of God, he now makes it clear that he enters the story of Israel's hope through Joseph. The people in Nazareth, however, try to understand Jesus from his "earthly" origin: as the "son of Joseph." According to Luke, one cannot understand Jesus in this way: he can only be understood from God and from the beginning, which God has set in Bethlehem (Luke 2:11–12, 16–20). From here, however, light is also shed on the speech of Jesus as a "prophet" (see below). The saying about the prophet who is not welcome in his hometown gains a deep meaning for Luke: with reference to Jesus, one cannot understand him if he is not understood with regard to his relation to God. This, according to Luke, has to be understood based on the Scriptures.

This understanding is confirmed in the narrative of the two disciples on the road to Emmaus in Luke's Easter chapter (Luke 24:13–35). Here, too, Jesus interprets the Scriptures for the disciples (Luke 24:25–27). A tension can be observed in the overall narrative: while according to Luke 24:31 the disciples' eyes are opened when Jesus breaks bread with them, which is recalled again in 24:35b, the opening of knowledge according to 24:35a occurs through the exposition of Scripture. The narrative is originally—from 24:16 onward—entirely based on the revelation of Jesus in the Lord's Supper. However, it is supplemented by Luke with the motif of interpreting Scripture. At this point it is also crucial how Luke describes the process of knowledge. Luke 24:25–27 states:

ὦ ἀνόητοι καὶ βραδεῖς τῇ καρδίᾳ	Oh, unintelligent and slow of heart
τοῦ πιστεύειν ἐπὶ πᾶσιν	to believe in everything
οἷς ἐλάλησαν οἱ προφῆται·	that the prophets have said:
οὐχὶ ταῦτα ἔδει	Did not the
παθεῖν τὸν χριστὸν	the Messiah have to suffer
καὶ εἰσελθεῖν εἰς τὴν δόξαν αὐτοῦ;	and enter into his glory?
καὶ ἀρξάμενος ἀπὸ Μωϋσέως	And beginning with Moses
καὶ ἀπὸ πάντων τῶν προφητῶν	and with all the prophets
διερμήνευσεν αὐτοῖς	he interpreted to them
ἐν πάσαις ταῖς γραφαῖς	in all the Scriptures the things
τὰ περὶ ἑαυτοῦ	concerning him.

In my opinion, this scene is often interpreted in a distorting sense: Here it is *not* said that the Emmaus disciples overcome their hopelessness and sadness (cf.

Luke 24:17) by reading the Scriptures themselves and "come to terms" with it.[35] What is said is that *Jesus opens* their eyes to himself and that knowledge comes only in the encounter with the Risen One. Two hints are given in this context: First, it is important for the interpretation of the passage that ὁ χριστός in Luke 24:26 is to be written in lower case and does not mean the name ("Christ") but the title ("the Messiah"). What Jesus reveals to the disciples is that the Messiah must suffer, die, and rise again, precisely what the announcement of suffering in Luke 18:31–33 had described as announced "through the prophets" (18:31; cf. Luke 24:25; cf. the reference back to the announcement of suffering in Luke 24:6–8!). Second, he interprets for them "out of all the prophets," where again the prophetic *books* are probably meant, τὰ περὶ ἑαυτοῦ, that which is written about himself in Scripture. From Jesus himself, then, it becomes clear what "the Messiah" must experience in order for God's will to be fulfilled in him: he must suffer, die, and rise again and thus take up his reign, which had been announced in the birth announcement (Luke 1:32–33; cf. Acts 2:30–31). Once again it becomes clear how Luke understands "the Scriptures": they are only understood when they are read from the encounter with Jesus—this is the enormous claim that the author of Luke's Gospel makes.

This is confirmed in the narrative that follows the Emmaus narrative in Luke 24:36–49. Jesus tells the disciples "that all things must be fulfilled that are written in the Law of Moses, and in the Prophets, and in the Psalms concerning me" (δεῖ πληρωθῆναι πάντα τὰ γεγραμμένα ἐν τῷ νόμῳ Μωϋσέως καὶ τοῖς προφήταις καὶ ψαλμοῖς περὶ ἐμοῦ; Luke 24:44), again with a preceding reference to the passion announcement (24:44a). When the following verse says that Jesus "opens their mind to understand the Scriptures" (τότε διήνοιξεν αὐτῶν τὸν νοῦν τοῦ συνιέναι τὰς γραφάς), it can be asked whether Jesus here opens the "mind" of the disciples or the mind of the Scriptures. In my opinion, it is more reasonable to think that the narrator here speaks of the "opening" of the sense of the disciples, whereby however the true sense of the Scripture is also opened.[36] Jesus changes the perspective of the disciples so that they can read the Scripture now from the perspective of Jesus. From here, according to Luke's claim, the "true" sense of the Scripture opens up. When Luke depicts Jesus as an interpreter of the Scriptures, he not only remembers the exegesis of the earthly Jesus, but he also presents in a narrative way how he understands the hermeneutic of the Scriptures.[37]

---

35. Exemplarily in this sense is the interpretation of Böttrich, "Das Alte im Herzen des Neuen," 629.

36. See Joshua L. Mann, "What Is Opened in Luke 24:45, the Mind or the Scriptures?," *JBL* 135, no. 4 (2016): 799–806 and his conclusion on 806.

37. In this sense Rusam, *Das Alte Testament bei Lukas,* 494, cf. Böttrich, "Das Alte im Herzen des Neuen," 627. He speaks of "situations of reception" that were depicted by Luke.

Jesus as a "Prophet"

Indeed, this suggestion finds its affirmation in the motif of Jesus as a "prophet," which is often declared as one of the most important motifs in Luke-Acts. The importance of conceptual allusions to the Elijah-Elisha stories in the telling of the story of Jesus has been repeatedly emphasized in Luke research.[38] Especially in the healing miracles of Jesus there are allusions to motifs, but also in the feeding of the five thousand and the "ascension" (Luke 24:51; Acts 1:9–11; cf. 2 Kgs 2:11–14).[39] The motif already appears in Jesus's inaugural sermon in Nazareth, in which Jesus explicitly refers to the story of Elijah (Luke 4:25–26; 1 Kgs 17:7–16) and Elisha (Luke 4:27; 2 Kgs 5:1–14). Those listening react angrily (Luke 4:28) and decide to kill Jesus (Luke 4:29). This reaction parallels the end of Stephen's speech in Acts (Acts 7:58).[40] In this speech, Stephen says to the Jewish crowd: "Which of the prophets did your fathers not persecute? And they killed those who proclaimed the coming of the Righteous One before, whose betrayers and murderers you have now become" (Acts 7:52). This refers to the death of Jesus, who in Luke 23:47—deviating from the Markan text—is called δίκαιος. According to this, in his fate of death he joins the fate of the prophets. But this thesis is obviously polemical because it is claimed that the Jewish listeners are acting against their own God.[41] Thus, the labeling of Jesus as a "prophet" is to be understood in an ambivalent sense from the very beginning.

The meaning of this topic becomes clear in the two places where Jesus is explicitly referred to as προφήτης ("prophet"): at the end of the narrative of the raising of the young man in Nain (Luke 7:11–17) in Luke 7:16 and in the Emmaus narrative in Luke 24:19.

The story of the raising of the young man in Nain (Luke 7:11–17) is the first story of the resurrection of a dead person that Luke tells. Here, too, a parallelism between the Gospel of Luke and the Acts of the Apostles can be seen because in both parts of Luke-Acts two raisings of the dead are told, two by Jesus and one each in which Peter and Paul are the actors.[42] While the narrative of the raising

---

38. According to Böttrich, "Das Alte im Herzen des Neuen," 636, they even represent "a kind of substructure or subtext of the Lukan Jesus story." Brodie, *Proto-Luke* also sees in the Elijah-Elisha narratives a "literary model" according to which the story of Jesus is told (Böttrich, "Das Alte im Herzen des Neuen," 637). See also the anthology by Kloppenborg and Verheyden, *Elijah-Elisha Narrative*; Rusam, *Das Alte Testament bei Lukas*, 216–18.

39. Böttrich, "Das Alte im Herzen des Neuen," 636.

40. Rusam, *Das Alte Testament bei Lukas*, 214–15.

41. This is very much in line with what is said in the "scheme of contrast" in the missionary speeches of the Acts of the Apostles: "You killed him—but God raised him up."

42. Luke 7:11–17 (the boy in Nain); Luke 8:40–42.49–56 (the daughter of Jairus); Acts 9:36–

of Jairus's daughter (Luke 8:40–42, 49–56) has a parallel in Mark and in Matthew (Mark 5:21–24, 35–43; Matt 9:18–19, 23–26), the narrative about the young man of Nain belongs to the Lukan *Sondergut*.

As already mentioned, the narratives of the raising of a dead person are also preformed in the Elijah-Elisha tradition (1 Kgs 17:17–24 = 3 Kgdms 17:17–24 LXX; 2 Kgs 4:31–37 = 4 Kgdms 4:31–37 LXX). Luke 7:15b is a direct quote from 1 Kgs 17:24.[43] The Elijah narratives have a place in the Jesus tradition even before Luke. Luke, however, obviously deepened the tradition consciously.[44] The advance made over the raising of the dead narrative of Elijah is unmistakable. Thus, in 3 Kgdms 17:18a, Elijah is introduced as a "man of God" (ἄνθρωπος τοῦ θεοῦ). The narrative concludes with the mother of the resurrected son acknowledging Elijah as ἄνθρωπος τοῦ θεοῦ and confessing that "the word of the Lord in your mouth is true" (17:24). In keeping with this, Elijah calls upon the κύριος— God—before the healing (17:20–21), asking him to heal the boy. The raising of the son (17:22) can only be understood as the granting of this request from God, by which God confirms that Elijah is acting on his behalf. This observation is confirmed by a look at the parallel Elisha narrative in 2 Kgs 4:31–37 = 4 Kgdms 4:31–37 LXX: Elisha also prays to the κύριος before healing the boy (4:33). Elisha finally brings the dead boy back to life through an "act of synanachrosis" (4:34).[45] Such a gesture of resurrection (which admittedly is not narrated of Elijah either) is missing in the narration Luke 7:11–17, as is a prayer of Jesus to the κύριος in which Jesus asks him for the resurrection of the boy. Rather, in Luke 7:13 Jesus *himself* is referred to as ὁ κύριος.[46] He himself "has mercy" on the boy (7:13) and awakens him by his own word (7:14: νεανίσκε, σοὶ λέγω, ἐγέρθητι. "Young man, I say to you, rise!"). The reaction of those present accordingly goes beyond that narrated in view of Elijah, but at the same time establishes a connection to the prophetic tradition: Jesus is called προφήτης μέγας ("a great prophet," 7:16a), which can possibly be understood as an allusion to the eschatologically under-

---

42 (Peter and Tabitha in Joppa); Acts 20:7–12 (Paul and Eutychus in Troas); for Acts 20:7–12, see Martin Bauspiess, "Ein tröstlicher Zwischenfall (Eutychus in Troas)—Apg 20,7–12," in *Die Wunder der Apostel*, vol. 2 of *Kompendium der frühchristlichen Wundererzählungen*, ed. Ruben Zimmermann (Gütersloh: Gütersloher Verlagshaus, 2017), 268–79.

43. Wolter, *Das Lukasevangelium*, 274; cf. Thomas L. Brodie, "Towards Unravelling Luke's Use of the Old Testament: Luke 7.11–17 as an *Imitatio* of 1 Kings 17.17–24," *NTS* 32, no. 2 (1986): 247–67.

44. Bovon, *Das Evangelium nach Lukas*, 1:358.

45. See Bauspiess, "Ein tröstlicher Zwischenfall," 274.

46. The phenomenon of Jesus being referred to as ὁ κύριος on the narrative level in the Lukan narrative is found in several places (Luke 7:13, 19; 10:1, 39, 41; 11:39; 12:42a; 13:15; 17:5, 6; 18:6; 19:8a, 31, 34; 22:61a, b; cf. Luke 1:43, 76; 2:11; see Joseph A. Fitzmyer, "κύριος," *EWNT* 2:818).

stood promise of a "prophet like Moses" in Deut 18:15 (cf. Acts 3:23-24; 7:37).[47] But this designation is explained in 18:16b by a statement that contains a clear allusion to the Benedictus spoken by Zacharias (Luke 1:68, 78).[48] A closer look at the Benedictus reveals further allusions in Luke 7:16:

> Luke 7:16b
> προφήτης μέγας ἠγέρθη ἐν ἡμῖν
> καὶ ὅτι ἐπεσκέψατο ὁ θεὸς τὸν λαὸν αὐτοῦ.
> A great prophet has risen among us,
> and God has visited his people.

> Luke 1:68-69
> Εὐλογητὸς κύριος ὁ θεὸς τοῦ Ἰσραήλ,
> ὅτι ἐπεσκέψατο καὶ ἐποίησεν λύτρωσιν τῷ λαῷ αὐτοῦ,
> καὶ ἤγειρεν κέρας σωτηρίας ἡμῖν
> ἐν οἴκῳ Δαυὶδ παιδὸς αὐτοῦ
> Blessed be the Lord, God of Israel,
> for he has visited and brought redemption to his people.
> He has raised up a horn for our salvation
> in the house of his servant David.

The reaction of those present is characterized in Luke 7:16a as praise to God—a response to God's saving action. In this motif, too, there is a connection with the Benedictus. Thus, we see that Jesus's act of raising the boy from death is a "visitation" of God himself, in which he turns to his people. It is probably no coincidence that after Luke 7:11-17 John the Baptist appears (Luke 7:18-28), whose role finds its description in the Benedictus:

> Luke 1:76-79
> Καὶ σὺ δέ, παιδίον, προφήτης ὑψίστου κληθήσῃ·
> προπορεύσῃ γὰρ ἐνώπιον κυρίου ἑτοιμάσαι ὁδοὺς αὐτοῦ,
> τοῦ δοῦναι γνῶσιν σωτηρίας τῷ λαῷ αὐτοῦ
> ἐν ἀφέσει ἁμαρτιῶν αὐτῶν,
> διὰ σπλάγχνα ἐλέους θεοῦ ἡμῶν,
> ἐν οἷς ἐπισκέψεται ἡμᾶς ἀνατολὴ ἐξ ὕψους,

---

47. Bovon, *Das Evangelium nach Lukas*, 1:364-65; Wolfgang Kraus, "Die Bedeutung von Dtn 18,15-18 für das Verständnis Jesu als Prophet," *ZNW* 90, no. 3/4 (1999): 165-66, emphasizes the distinction between the motif of Jesus as a "prophet" and as "a prophet like Moses."
48. Wolter, *Das Lukasevangelium*, 276.

ἐπιφᾶναι τοῖς ἐν σκότει καὶ σκιᾷ θανάτου καθημένοις,
τοῦ κατευθῦναι τοὺς πόδας ἡμῶν εἰς ὁδὸν εἰρήνης.
And you, child, will be called the prophet of the Most High;
for you will go before the Lord to prepare his ways,
to give knowledge of salvation to his people
by the forgiveness of their sins.
By the tender mercy of our God,
by which the daybreak from on high will visit us
to shine on those who sit in darkness and in the shadow of death,
to guide our feet into the path of peace.

On the one hand, it is noticeable that in Luke 1:76, Isa 40:3 is alluded to (cf. Luke 3:4, see above); on the other hand, the one whom the Baptist precedes is called κύριος. In the context of Luke's Gospel, however, this now refers to Jesus. There are also close references to the narrative of Luke 7:11–17: the σπλάγχνα ἐλέους θεοῦ ἡμῶν ("the tender mercy of our God," Luke 1:78) finds a narrative illustration in Luke 7:13: καὶ ἰδὼν ὁ κύριος ἐσπλαγχνίσθη ἐπ᾽ αὐτῇ ("When the Lord saw her, he had mercy on her").[49] Attention has already been drawn to the connection between Luke 1:77 (τοῦ δοῦναι γνῶσιν σωτηρίας τῷ λαῷ αὐτοῦ) and Luke 3:6. At the inquiry of the Baptist's disciples to Jesus (ὁ κύριος, 7:19), he refers them to his acts of healing and raising from the dead (7:22). These actions speak for themselves, and they make clear what was said in 4:21: The announcement that God comes to his people with salvation is fulfilled in Jesus. But those present cannot fully grasp this. Luke lets them "express themselves with a still incomplete confession of faith."[50] Thus, on the one hand, the connection to the prophetic tradition is an expression of the fact that Luke sees the story of Jesus as a part of Israel's history of hope. On the other hand, he reinterprets this tradition.

After the narration of the raising of the young man in Nain, the question of Jesus's identity is raised (Luke 7:18–23).[51] In Luke 7:26 it is said that even John the Baptist is "more than a prophet" (cf. Luke 16:16, see below). Elijah appears on the mountain of transfiguration (Luke 9:28–36) together with Moses (9:30). Moses and Elijah—as representatives of the law and the prophets (cf. Mal 3:22–23)—are "speaking of his [i.e., Jesus's] departure, which he was about to accomplish in Jerusalem" (ἔλεγον τὴν ἔξοδον αὐτοῦ, ἣν ἤμελλεν πληροῦν ἐν Ἰερουσαλήμ, 9:31).

---

49. The verb appears twice again in Luke's Gospel, in Luke 10:33 and 15:20, in both cases in a parable narration. Esp. in Luke 15:20 it is a picture of God's love to a person who comes back to him, cf. Hofius, "Alttestamentliche Motive," 151.
50. Bovon, *Das Lukasevangelium nach Lukas*, 1:364.
51. Wolter, *Das Lukasevangelium*, 277.

But at the end of the scene, Jesus is proclaimed the son of God (9:35) and stands alone (v. 36). Law and prophets give testimony to Jesus's way. Therefore, Luke finds this way preformed in the Scriptures. As in the Elijah narratives, God's presence is experienced in Jesus. Nevertheless, Jesus is different from, and more than, a prophet.

The same can be said with regard to the Emmaus narrative: when the disciples, encountered by the risen Christ, tell him about the "things concerning Jesus of Nazareth" and depict him as "a prophet mighty in deed and word before God and all the people" (ἀνὴρ προφήτης δυνατὸς ἐν ἔργῳ καὶ λόγῳ ἐναντίον τοῦ θεοῦ καὶ παντὸς τοῦ λαοῦ, Luke 24:19), this does not describe in the full sense what the story of Jesus means for Luke. Hence, this knowledge is not able to give hope to the disciples (24:21). Not even the reports of the women of the empty tomb (Luke 24:22–24) can do that. Only the scriptural interpretation that the risen Lord himself gives them (24:25–27) and only the fact that they recognize him (24:31 in contrast to v. 24b: "but him they did not see," αὐτὸν δὲ οὐκ εἶδον) allow them to truly comprehend the announcement of the prophets (24:25). The evangelist Luke is thus aware that faith in Christ transcends what Israel's Scriptures are saying about the expected "prophet" (Deut 18:15) and about God's saving action toward his people, and he fills it anew from the history of Jesus. Therefore, it is just one side of the coin when Christfried Böttrich states that Luke gives Jesus "the features of a prophet" and intends to present him as "the prophet like Moses."[52] Nevertheless, this does not mean that the "prophetic Christology" is only an "auxiliary construction," as Böttrich suspects.[53] In fact, we can see that the Lukan reception of motifs from Israel's Scripture is always standing in context with a new interpretation from the perspective of faith in Jesus Christ. Therefore, there is no reason to refuse the thesis that there is an "outbidding" (*Überbietung*) of the tradition of Elijah and Elisa in Luke, as Böttrich does.[54] In the same way, we can understand the motifs of Jesus as a "martyr" or the "Isaian servant of God."[55] Luke underlines the motifs to make clear that one has to understand the story of Jesus in the context of Israel's story with God. This assertion, however, is only understandable from the perspective of faith in the resurrected Jesus, as the Emmaus story impressively shows.

---

52. Böttrich, "Das Alte im Herzen des Neuen," 630, 631.
53. Böttrich, "Das Alte im Herzen des Neuen," 631.
54. Böttrich, "Das Alte im Herzen des Neuen," 638. Correctly seen by Bovon, *Das Evangelium nach Lukas*, 1:358.
55. Cf. Böttrich, "Das Alte im Herzen des Neuen," 630.

The Claim of Israel's Scriptures

The positive claim Luke makes for Israel's writings becomes clear in the context of a speech of Jesus addressed to the Pharisees (Luke 16:14–31), in which the story of the rich man and the poor Lazarus (Luke 16:19–31) is told. Here we find the famous phrase in 16:16: "the law and the prophets go until John (the Baptist)." In Luke 16:17 Luke emphasizes—as does Matt 5:18—that Jesus's proclamation of the reign of God does not abolish the law in a general sense.[56] In the law, for Luke, the will of God for humanity finds expression. Once again, it becomes clear that Luke reflects on the possibility of *understanding* the "Scriptures." In the narrative of the rich man, the man sees from Hades the poor Lazarus, who is in Abraham's bosom (16:23). With the mention of "resting in Abraham's bosom," an early Jewish motif is taken up (Jub. 22:26–23:2).[57] When the man asks Abraham for help, Abraham gives the answer: "they have Moses and the prophets, they should hear them" (ἔχουσιν Μωϋσέα καὶ τοὺς προφήτας· ἀκουσάτωσαν αὐτῶν). It is remarkable how the rich man reacts to this claim: "No, father Abraham, but if one went to them from the dead, they will repent" (οὐχί, πάτερ Ἀβραάμ, ἀλλ' ἐάν τις ἀπὸ νεκρῶν πορευθῇ πρὸς αὐτοὺς μετανοήσουσιν, 16:30). Abraham's answer, "If they do not listen to Moses and the prophets, they will not be persuaded even if one rose from the dead" (εἰ Μωϋσέως καὶ τῶν προφητῶν οὐκ ἀκούουσιν, οὐδ' ἐάν τις ἐκ νεκρῶν ἀναστῇ πεισθήσονται, v. 31), is a hint to the experience of the post-Easter Christian missionary proclamation.[58] Luke makes it clear that those who are not convinced of the resurrection of Jesus ultimately do not understand the meaning contained in "Moses and the Prophets." The understanding of Scripture, however, has ethical consequences for Luke.[59] In making this claim, he speaks in a very fundamental way that does not refer to the discussion of individual ethical questions, but to the contention that is made to the Pharisees that in the preaching of Jesus, as in the post-Easter Christian preaching, the will of God as articulated in the Scriptures is actually expressed.

Especially significant in this context is the third announcement of the passion in Luke 18:31–33. Luke 18:31 underlines (contrast Mark 10:33) that on the way of Jesus to Jerusalem—the way to the cross—"everything is fulfilled that was written through the prophets about the Son of Man." Here, as in Luke 9:30–31

---

56. Wolter, *Das Lukasevangelium*, 556.
57. Wolter, *Das Lukasevangelium*, 559–60.
58. Bovon, *Das Evangelium nach Lukas*, 3:126; Wolter argues explicitly against this interpretation, *Das Lukasevangelium*, 563.
59. Cf. Rusam, *Das Alte Testament bei Lukas*, 493 (with regard to Luke 10:27 and 18:20).

(see above), Luke underlines that the story of Jesus, which leads to the cross and the resurrection, is announced in the Scriptures. Of course, this is only recognizable if one already knows about the "outcome" of this story. This "prophetic" understanding of the Scriptures is the point of divergence between Judaism and emerging Christianity, which at the time of Luke is already a firmly established factor.[60] This fact leads to the central intention of Luke in his reception of Israel's Scriptures.

Conclusion

The fact that the author of Luke's Gospel places a second work alongside his narration of the Jesus story already shows what he is concerned with in his portrayal: Luke reflects from a later standpoint, in which the church is in its majority influenced by gentile Christianity, on the beginnings of the story about Jesus Christ. In his time, the movement that had started with Jesus has already become a fixed group with a visible identity (cf. Acts 11:26). When Luke tells the story of Jesus again with the story of the developing of the church, he wants to make clear that the "church" has its foundation in Israel's hope (cf. Acts 28:20). Therefore, he reflects on the reception of the Scriptures. In Luke-Acts, we can see a development that leads to the two-part canon of the Bible including the "Old" and the "New Testament." Unlike Matthew, Luke introduces fewer scriptural references into his text. Rather, he expands on the existing scriptural references and reflects on the perspective from which they take on their meaning for those who believe in Christ. The fact that the author explicitly reflects on the understanding of the tradition before him finds evidence in Luke 1:1-4. This reflection also determines his reception of the Scriptures.

He reflects on the reception of the Scriptures by narrating their interpretation by Jesus. This will be continued in Acts when, for example, the text of the prophet Isaiah (Isa 53:7-8) is the starting point for giving testimony about Jesus (Acts 8:35). And it is then certainly no coincidence that there is also a quotation from the Scriptures at the end of Acts (Acts 28:26-27). At the end of his narrative, Luke makes clear that the understanding of the Scriptures evokes a division within Judaism (Acts 28:24-25) that leads to Christianity as its own religious community. What we can see here is that the hermeneutic of the Scriptures developed by Luke corresponds exactly to what we can observe in the concrete reception of several texts or concepts from Israel's Scriptures: they describe the place of origin and the roots of the movement of the Christ-believing community. Therefore,

---

60. Rusam, *Das Alte Testament bei Lukas*, 494.

faith in Jesus Christ cannot be proclaimed without Israel's Scriptures, nor the Christian hope without the hope of Israel.

Bibliography

Bauspiess, Martin. "Ein tröstlicher Zwischenfall (Eutychus in Troas)." Pages 268–79 in *Kompendium der frühchristlichen Wundererzählungen*. Vol. 2 of *Die Wunder der Apostel*. Edited by Ruben Zimmermann. Gütersloh: Gütersloher Verlagshaus, 2017.

———. *Geschichte und Erkenntnis im lukanischen Doppelwerk: Eine exegetische Untersuchung zu einer christlichen Perspektive auf Geschichte*. ABIG 42. Leipzig: Evangelische Verlagsanstalt, 2012.

Bock, Darrell L. *Luke*. 2 vols. BECNT 3. Grand Rapids: Baker, 1994, 1996.

Böttrich, Christfried. "Das Alte im Herzen des Neuen: Beobachtungen zur Einheit beider Testamente am Beispiel des Evangelisten Lukas." Pages 623–46 in *Ex oriente Lux: Studien zur Theologie des Alten Testaments; Festschrift für Rüdiger Lux zum 65. Geburtstag*. Edited by Angelika Berlejung and Raik Heckl. ABIG 39. Leipzig: Evangelische Verlagsanstalt, 2012.

Bovon, François. *Das Evangelium nach Lukas*. EKKNT 3.1–4. Neukirchen-Vluyn: Neukirchener Verlag, 1989–2009.

Brodie, Thomas L. *Proto-Luke: The Oldest Gospel Account; A Christ-Centered Synthesis of Old Testament History Modelled Especially on the Elijah-Elisha Narrative*. Limerick: Dominican Biblical Institute, 2006.

———. "Towards Unravelling Luke's Use of the Old Testament: Luke 7.11–17 as an Imitatio of 1 Kings 17.17–24." *NTS* 32, no. 2 (1986): 247–67.

Fitzmyer, Joseph A. "κύριος." *EWNT* 2:811–20.

———. "The Use of the Old Testament in Luke-Acts." Pages 295–313 in *To Advance the Gospel: New Testament Studies*. 2nd ed. Grand Rapids: Eerdmans, 1998.

Gadenz, Pablo T. *The Gospel of Luke*. CCSC. Grand Rapids: Baker Academic, 2018.

Gese, Hartmut. "Das biblische Schriftverständnis." Pages 9–30 in *Zur biblischen Theologie: Alttestamentliche Vorträge*. 3rd ed. Tübingen: Mohr Siebeck, 1989.

Green, Joel B. *The Gospel of Luke*. NICNT. Grand Rapids: Eerdmans, 1997.

Hatina, Thomas, ed. *Biblical Interpretation in Early Christian Gospels*. Vol. 3, *The Gospel of Luke*. LNTS 376. London: T&T Clark, 2010.

Hofius, Otfried. "Alttestamentliche Motive im Gleichnis vom verlorenen Sohn." Pages 145–153 in *Neutestamentliche Studien*. WUNT 132. Tübingen: Mohr Siebeck, 2000.

Jeremias, Joachim. *Neutestamentliche Theologie*. Vol. 1, *Die Verkündigung Jesu*. Berlin: Evangelische Verlagsanstalt, 1973.

Kloppenborg, John S., and Joseph Verheyden, eds. *The Elijah-Elisha Narrative in the Composition of Luke*. LNTS 493. London: T&T Clark, 2014.
Kraus, Wolfgang. "Die Bedeutung von Dtn 18,15–18 für das Verständnis Jesu als Prophet." *ZNW* 90, no. 3/4 (1999): 153–76.
Levine, Amy-Jill, and Ben Witherington III. *The Gospel of Luke*. NCBC. Cambridge: Cambridge University Press, 2018.
Mann, Joshua L. "What Is Opened in Luke 24:45, the Mind or the Scriptures?" *JBL* 135, no. 4 (2016): 799–806.
Mittmann-Richert, Ulrike. *Der Sühnetod des Gottesknechts: Jesaja 53 im Lukasevangelium*. WUNT 220. Tübingen: Mohr Siebeck, 2008.
———. *Magnifikat und Benediktus: Die ältesten Zeugnisse der judenchristlichen Tradition von der Geburt des Messias*. WUNT 2/90. Tübingen: Mohr Siebeck, 1996.
Paffenroth, Kim. *The Story of Jesus according to L*. JSNTSup 147. Sheffield: Sheffield Academic, 1997.
Plümacher, Eckart. *Lukas als hellenistischer Schriftsteller: Studien zur Apostelgeschichte*. SUNT 9. Göttingen: Vandenhoeck & Ruprecht, 1972.
Prieur, Alexander. *Die Verkündigung der Gottesherrschaft: Exegetische Studien zum lukanischen Verständnis der βασιλεία τοῦ θεοῦ*. WUNT 2/89. Tübingen: Mohr Siebeck, 1996.
Riesner, Rainer. "Das lukanische Doppelwerk und die antike Biographie." Pages 131–44 in *Lebensgeschichte und Religion*. Edited by Detlev Dormeyer, Herbert Mölle, and Thomas Ruster. Religion und Biographie 1. Münster: LIT, 2000.
Ringgren, Helmer. "Luke's Use of the Old Testament." *HTR* 79, no. 1/3 (1986): 227–35.
Rusam, Dietrich. *Das Alte Testament bei Lukas*. BZNW 112. Berlin: de Gruyter, 2003.
Schiffner, Kerstin. *Lukas liest Exodus: Eine Untersuchung zur Aufnahme ersttestamentlicher Befreiungsgeschichte im lukanischen Werk als Schrift-Lektüre*. BWANT 172. Stuttgart: Kohlhammer, 2008.
Schmid, Konrad, and Jens Schröter. *Die Entstehung der christlichen Bibel: Von den ersten Texten zu den heiligen Schriften*. Munich: Beck, 2019.
Schürmann, Heinz. *Das Lukasevangelium*. HThKNT 3.1–2. Freiburg im Breisgau: Herder, 1969–1993.
Slenczka, Notger. "Die Kirche und das Alte Testament." Pages 83–119 in *Das Alte Testament in der Theologie*. Edited by Elisabeth Gräb-Schmidt. MJTh 25. Leipzig: Evangelische Verlagsanstalt, 2013.
Streeter, B. H. *The Four Gospels: A Study of Their Origins*. 9th ed. London: Macmillan, 1956.
Wolter, Michael. *Das Lukasevangelium*. HNT 5. Tübingen: Mohr Siebeck, 2008.

11

Israel's Scriptures in John

JAIME CLARK-SOLES

John uses Israel's Scriptures to achieve multiple ends.[1] In this chapter, I address both the forms of the Scriptures' appearances in John and their functions. In the "Israel's Scriptures in John" section, I discuss how Israel's Scriptures appear as marked and unmarked citations and verbal and conceptual allusions (their forms). I then pay specific attention to some examples from the text that highlight how John uses Scripture. As for their functions, I focus on three overlapping categories: making christological claims (theological function), communal formation and maintenance (sociological function), and using narrative rhetoric to affect the audience(s) in a particular way (rhetorical function). The categories are not distinct because a single use of Scripture serves more than one purpose. The theological function, the development of a Christology in the text, serves as the overarching structure of this section because John is making theological claims that are rhetorically embedded in a story for the benefit of a community, but

---

I am grateful for the help of April Simpson, New Testament PhD graduate from Southern Methodist University and now assistant professor of religion at Georgetown College, and Kelsey Spinnato, Hebrew Bible/Old Testament PhD candidate at Southern Methodist University, in preparing this chapter.

1. The authorship of the Gospel of John is unknown. Although various suggestions have been made over the centuries regarding the author's identity, the Gospel never names the author, who may be any gender. In this chapter, I use "John" and "he" to refer to the unknown author simply for ease of reference. Consult Sandra S. Schneiders, *Written That You May Believe: Encountering Jesus in the Fourth Gospel*, 2nd ed. (New York: Crossroad, 2003), esp. 231–54, "A Feminist Reexamination of the Authorship of the Fourth Gospel."

the sociological function is discussed alongside the theological one.² In "What Scripture Does John Use?" I present the many options scholars have posited for the *Vorlage* of John and conclude that more emphasis needs to be placed on orality in the first century.

Israel's Scriptures in John

Marked and Unmarked Citations: An Overview

John contains a number of scriptural citations. In some cases, though not all, the author supplies a comment signaling to the audience that he is drawing from scriptural tradition (these are called marked citations). Though scholarly lists vary, the following are included in this presentation (those with an asterisk appear least often on lists):³

Table 11.1. Marked Citations in John

John	Hebrew Bible/ Old Testament	Citation Marker
1:23	Isa 40:3	καθὼς εἶπεν Ἠσαΐας ὁ προφήτης, "as the prophet Isaiah said"
2:17	Ps 68:10 LXX	ὅτι γεγραμμένον ἐστίν, "that it was written"
6:31	Ps 77:24 LXX; Exod 16:4, 15	καθὼς ἐστιν γεγραμμένον, "as it is written"
6:45	Isa 54:13	ἔστιν γεγραμμένον ἐν τοῖς προφήταις, "It is written in the prophets"
7:38*	Joel 3:18; Zech 14:8	καθὼς εἶπεν ἡ γραφή, "As the scripture has said"

---

2. For this chapter, I deal with the final form of the text while recognizing that the text and the community with which it is associated have longer histories.

3. I have consulted several lists, including Andreas Köstenberger, "John," in *Commentary on the New Testament Use of the Old Testament*, ed. G. K. Beale and D. A. Carson (Grand Rapids: Baker Academic, 2007), 415–512; Bruce G. Schuchard, "Form Versus Function: Citation Technique and Authorial Intention in the Gospel of John," in *Abiding Words: The Use of Scripture in the Gospel of John*, ed. Alicia D. Myers and Bruce G. Schuchard, RBS 81 (Atlanta: SBL Press, 2015), 23–46; and the notes in Adele Reinhartz, "The Gospel according to John," in *The Jewish Annotated New Testament*, ed. Amy-Jill Levine and Marc Zvi Brettler, 2nd ed. (Oxford: Oxford University Press, 2017), 168–218. All translations and versifications are from the NRSV unless otherwise noted.

7:42*	2 Sam 7:12; Jer 23:5; Mic 5:2	οὐχ ἡ γραφὴ εἶπεν, "Has not the scripture said"
8:17*	Deut 17:6; 19:15	καὶ ἐν τῷ νόμῳ δὲ τῷ ὑμετέρῳ γέγραπται, "In your [pl.] law it is written"
10:34	Ps 81:6 LXX; cf. Exod 7:1	οὐκ ἔστιν γεγραμμένον ἐν τῷ νόμῳ ὑμῶν, "Is it not written in your law"
12:14–15	Zech 9:9	καθώς ἐστιν γεγραμμένον, "as it is written"
12:38	Isa 53:1 LXX	ἵνα ὁ λόγος Ἠσαΐου τοῦ προφήτου πληρωθῇ ὃν εἶπεν, "This was to fulfill the word spoken by the prophet Isaiah"
12:39–40	Isa 6:10	ὅτι πάλιν εἶπεν Ἠσαΐας, "because Isaiah also said"
13:18	Ps 41:9	ἵνα ἡ γραφὴ πληρωθῇ, "But it is to fulfill the scripture"
15:25	Pss 34:19 LXX; 68:5 LXX; cf. Pss. Sol. 7:1	ἵνα πληρωθῇ ὁ λόγος ὁ ἐν τῷ νόμῳ αὐτῶν γεγραμμένος, "It was to fulfill the word that is written in their law"
17:12*	Isa 57:4 LXX; Zech 10:10 LXX; Ps 41:9; Prov 24:22a LXX	ἵνα ἡ γραφὴ πληρωθῇ, "so that the scripture might be fulfilled"
19:24	Ps 22:18	ἵνα ἡ γραφὴ πληρωθῇ ἡ λέγουσα, "This was to fulfill what the scripture says"
19:28	Ps 68:22 LXX	ἵνα τελειωθῇ ἡ γραφή, "in order to fulfill the scripture"
19:36	Exod 12:10, 46 LXX	ἵνα ἡ γραφὴ πληρωθῇ, "so that the scripture might be fulfilled"
19:37	Zech 12:10	καὶ πάλιν ἑτέρα γραφὴ λέγει, "And again another passage of scripture says"

Additionally, the author of John cites Scripture *without* signaling that he is doing so (called unmarked citations).

Table 11.2. Unmarked Citations in John

John	Hebrew Bible/Old Testament
1:51	Gen 28:12
12:13	Ps 117:26 LXX; cf. Zeph 3:15 LXX
12:27	Ps 6:4

There are also myriad scriptural allusions present throughout John, which are too many to list here. In order of preponderance, the Fourth Gospel quotes Psalms the most, then Isaiah, then Zechariah, and then the Pentateuch. Expanding to allusions, Genesis figures prominently.

John's scriptural citations are usually unique to John among the Four Gospels. For example, while all of the gospels quote part of Ps 22, only John quotes Ps 22:18. Even where John shares material with other gospels, there are differences. For example, all of the gospels cite Isa 40:3, but only the Fourth Gospel has John the Baptist speak the words, identifying himself as the one crying out, rather than having the words spoken about him by the narrator (John 1:23). Also significant is what John does *not* cite that is cited elsewhere in the New Testament, especially the Synoptics. While Mark and Matthew depict Jesus as voicing Ps 21:2 LXX (22:2 MT) on the cross, John patently does not since such a proclamation would be antithetical to John's own Christology in which Jesus is God. Notably, in contrast to Matthew, Mark, Luke, Revelation, Paul (Gal 5:14), and James, John does *not* cite Lev 19:18 ("but you shall love your neighbor as yourself"), even though he uses love language more than any other New Testament author. Furthermore, John does not cite Deut 6:5: "You shall love the LORD your God with all your heart, and with all your soul, and with all your might," though all of the Synoptics do. As such, John's uniqueness is highlighted.

Scripture in John

In dealing with the use of Scripture in John, one quickly recognizes the difficulty of categorizing the material since scholarly lists, even of direct citations, do not exactly agree. What to include in which category depends partially on how one defines marked citation, unmarked citation, verbal allusion, and conceptual allusion. We will consider each of these categories in turn.

One complicating factor in identifying which Scriptures are used by the author is that John contains composite citations in which "literary borrowing occurs in a manner that includes two or more passages (from the same or different authors) fused together and conveyed as though they are only one."[4] Catrin Williams identifies eight such cases in John: 6:31; 7:38; 12:13; 12:15; 12:40; 13:18; 19:36; and 19:37.[5]

---

4. Sean A. Adams and Seth M. Ehorn, "What Is a Composite Citation? An Introduction," in *Composite Citations in Antiquity*, vol. 1, *Jewish, Graeco-Roman, and Early Christian Uses*, ed. Sean A. Adams and Seth M. Ehorn, LNTS 525 (London: Bloomsbury, 2016), 4.

5. Catrin H. Williams, "Composite Citations in the Gospel of John," in *Composite Citations in Antiquity*, vol. 2, *New Testament Uses*, ed. Sean. A. Adams and Seth M. Ehorn, LNTS 593 (London: Bloomsbury, 2018), 96.

Additionally, there are numerous instances in which the citation does not exactly match the LXX or MT or it conflates the versions.[6] For example, consider John 6:45: "It is written in the prophets, 'And they shall all be taught by God' [καὶ ἔσονται πάντες διδακτοὶ θεοῦ]. Everyone who has heard and learned from the Father comes to me." This is probably a citation of Isa 54:13, but it does not exactly match either the Greek (καὶ πάντας τοὺς υἱούς σου διδακτοὺς θεοῦ) or the MT (וכל־בניך למדו יהוה).

Marked Citations

There is no single or specific citation "formula" used by the author to indicate that he is intentionally drawing upon Israel's Scriptures. In fact, there is variety, though four verbs dominate: "write" (γράφω); "fulfill" (πληρόω or τελέω); and "say" (λέγω). The language of "written" appears in the passive, usually as a periphrastic participle but once as a finite verb (John 8:17). It appears sometimes by itself—"it is written"—and sometimes with more specificity as to where: in "the prophets" (John 6:45), in "your [pl.] law" (John 8:17; 10:34), and once with a note "about him" (i.e., Jesus, at 12:16). Fulfillment language (usually πληρόω; once [19:28] τελέω) always appears in the passive. What gets fulfilled? Isaiah's spoken word (e.g., 12:38), Scripture (always in the singular; e.g., 13:18), and the word written in "their law" (e.g., 15:25). Speaking language occurs as well (usually λέγω; once [12:41] λαλέω): Isaiah said (1:23; 12:38, 39, 41); Scripture said (7:38). Sometimes one finds "Isaiah said" followed by a scriptural quotation. In other cases, we encounter an oblique reference, such as the summary in 12:41: "Isaiah said these things." This verse is especially fascinating because the author uses two different words for speaking, λέγω and λαλέω. He doubles up on speech language and does not use writing language. This matters for understanding ancient attitudes about speech and writing that, in fact, differ from the modern almost-exclusive preoccupation with Scripture in written rather than spoken form. I attend to that topic in more detail below.

In most of the instances noted above we find an express acknowledgment *that* Scripture is being cited along with the ability to discern *which* material is being cited. Only in four instances (John 1:23; 12:38, 39, 41), however, does John name which specific author or book is being cited. In each case it is Isaiah, once at the beginning of Jesus's public ministry, and the other three times at the conclusion of his public ministry. Two of those four occurrences specifically identify Isaiah

---

6. Technically, the LXX refers only to the translation of the first five books (the Torah) into Greek. However, I will use LXX as shorthand for the full Greek translation of Israel's Scriptures.

as a prophet. The preponderance of Isaiah citations and their placement at key places in John indicate that Isaiah is of special importance to John.

However, there are instances where the author explicitly indicates that he is citing Scripture, but we do not seem to be able to locate a particular matching Scripture. For example, John 7:38 says: "As the scripture [ἡ γραφή] has said, 'Out of the womb [κοιλία] of him shall flow rivers of living water'" (my trans.). Clearly the author signals a citation, but because scholars have been unable to determine the exact source, most relegate it to an allusion rather than a citation.

Some would include John 19:28 in this category, where Jesus says, "I thirst" (which he says only in John). Despairing that no identical, identifiable scriptural text is available, scholars relegate it to the category of allusion. I find this a bit puzzling for at least three reasons. First, the whole "quotation" is one word in Greek: διψῶ, which is not much to go on. It is true that our standard LXX does not contain the first-person singular of the verb, though in other forms it appears in numerous scriptural texts. Most notably, over half of the occurrences of the word appear in Isaiah, the one author the Fourth Gospel overtly names, repeatedly. Second, certainly there are a number of places where John changes a word, especially a verb tense (e.g., John 2:17), and it is still considered a citation. Third, the author identifies it as a quotation like the others by use of the expression "in order to fulfill the scripture," as he does in numerous other places in the passion narrative. It seems odd to exclude this one. Whether it gets counted as a citation or an allusion, Ps 68:22 LXX (69:22 MT) is usually adduced here.

It is also noteworthy that most scholars exclude John 8:17 as a citation even though it is introduced with the same language as John 10:34, which everyone includes. The NRSV, for instance, translates John 8:17 this way, which is problematic on several counts: "In your law it is written that the testimony of two witnesses is valid" (καὶ ἐν τῷ νόμῳ δὲ τῷ ὑμετέρῳ γέγραπται ὅτι δύο ἀνθρώπων ἡ μαρτυρία ἀληθής ἐστιν). Is there any reason not to translate it thus: "Even in your [pl.] own law it is written: 'The testimony of two people is valid'" (my trans.) and find Deut 17:6 and 19:15 as the source?

Lastly, it is appropriate to note where the author invokes or appeals to Scripture more broadly but still uses explicit language that refers to Scripture qua Scripture. We see this in material such as John 12:41, which provides a kind of conclusion to the passage beginning with 12:36: "Isaiah said this because he saw his glory and spoke about him." Notice that John both summarizes what has preceded and simultaneously provides an allusion to Isa 6, where Isaiah sees the glory of the Lord. Thus, the narrator is indicating that Isaiah recognized the preexistent divine Jesus.

Unmarked Citations

There are also three places where the author does not flag that he is quoting tradition but is likely referring to particular instances of Scripture (John 1:51; 12:13; 12:27). For example, in John 1:51 Jesus says, "Very truly, I tell you, you will see heaven opened and the angels of God ascending and descending upon the Son of Man." This might be a citation from Gen 28:12, which refers to Jacob's ladder and "the angels of God were ascending and descending on it."

Allusions

In addition to marked and unmarked citations, the Fourth Gospel contains many scriptural allusions. By definition, allusions contain no introductory formula. Rather, hearing them depends upon an interpreter's familiarity with Scripture and, even then, is a more subjective enterprise. There are two main problems when addressing allusions in the Fourth Gospel. First, how do we determine whether or not the author is alluding to Scripture? In addition to the categories of citation and allusion, Richard Hays also mentions echoes, which are even softer than allusions and may only be "subliminally recalled" by the author without creating a "semantic link between the earlier text and the later."[7] In John it is not always possible to determine if the author is making an intentional allusion.

The second problem is the sheer volume of allusions in the Fourth Gospel. No essay or chart could contain them. NA[28] finds allusions to more than 230 scriptural texts. While it has almost certainly omitted some and probably included some that do not belong, the fact of volume still remains. And that number does not even include levels of allusion such as the generic structure of a text (e.g., John 6 as homiletical midrash or the Farewell Discourse as testamentary literature). Scholars devote articles, even entire monographs, to a single allusion or cluster of allusions in John.[8]

The present volume distinguishes between verbal allusions and conceptual allusions. Examples of verbal allusions would include the absolute "I AM" state-

---

7. Richard B. Hays, *Echoes of Scripture in the Letters of Paul* (New Haven: Yale University Press, 1989), 24.

8. E.g., Peder Borgen treats material from John 6:31–58 as midrash (Borgen, *Bread from Heaven: An Exegetical Study of the Concept of Manna in the Gospel of John and the Writings of Philo*, rev. ed., NovTSup 10 [Leiden: Brill, 1981]). Nils Dahl contends that John 8:44 alludes to Gen 4 (Dahl, "Der Erstgeborene Satans und der Vater des Teufels (Polyk. 7,1 und Joh 8,44)," in *Apophoreta: Festschrift für Ernst Haenchen zu seinem 70. Geburtstag am 10. Dezember 1964*, ed. Walther Eltester and Franz Heinrich Kettler, BZNW 30 [Berlin: Töpelmann, 1964], 70–84).

ments (John 4:26; 6:20; 8:24, 28, 58; 13:19; 18:5, 6, 8), allusions to Jesus as the paschal lamb (e.g., John 1:29), and the opening of John as alluding to Gen 1:1. Conceptual allusions would include the "I am" statements with the predicate nominative (e.g., John 6:35; 8:12; 10:9, 11, 14; 15:1); Jesus as the prophet like Moses and king of Israel (e.g., John 1:41, 45); Jesus as the good shepherd (e.g., John 10:1–18), the suffering servant (e.g., John 1:29), the antitype of Moses (e.g., John 7:22), David (e.g., John 10:11), and Jacob (e.g., John 1:47); and various Jewish feasts and festivals (e.g., John 7:2). The conceptual allusions to these Jewish feasts and festivals actually help set narrative time in the Gospel. For example, the story of Jesus cleansing the temple in John 2:13–25 begins and ends with reference to Passover.

While we cannot address all of the allusions in John, one of the most important groups of allusions in John comes from Genesis. Starting with Gen 1:1, "In the beginning," and ending in a garden with a man and a woman and *the* gardener, and at many points in between, Genesis shapes John.[9]

John's Use of Scripture

John states his purpose near the end of the Gospel (John 20:30–31): "Now Jesus did many other signs in the presence of his disciples, which are not written in this book [τῷ βιβλίῳ]. But these are written so that you may come to believe [πιστεύ[σ]ητε] that Jesus is the Messiah, the Son of God, and that through believing you may have life in his name." Everything in John, not only Scripture, serves this purpose.

Let me make a few introductory comments: First, the author informs the reader that he has intentionally chosen what to include and exclude; thus, there's nothing essential "missing," and the reader should not waste time trying to supplement (perhaps from material she knows from other gospels) but rather carefully pore over what is there and trust that it is sufficient for deciding to believe in Jesus. Second, the Gospel is aimed at a community—"so that you [pl.] may come to believe." The author does not imagine lone-ranger Christians apart from a community—no feeding a merely individualistic piety. Third, the textual tradition contains both the present tense, "so that you may continue to believe," which would indicate that the Gospel is written for those who *already* believe but who need encouragement to continue to do so, and the aorist tense, "so that you might come to believe," which would indicate that that the Gospel is directed to those who do *not yet* believe. Both readings have equally excellent early and

---

9. Jaime Clark-Soles, *Reading John for Dear Life: A Spiritual Walk through the Fourth Gospel* (Louisville: Westminster John Knox, 2016), 12–13, 137–39.

strong support in the manuscript tradition, which is why NA[28] chooses to print both in the body of the text, enclosing the *sigma* in brackets. Finally, the telos of believing and belonging is Life (ζωή), as Jesus declares: "I am the way, and the truth, and the life" (John 14:6). Thus, the end takes us back to the beginning in two ways. First, the reader recalls the beginning of the Gospel, which takes us back to the beginning of time: "In the beginning was the Word.... What has come into being in it was Life [ζωή], and the life was the light of human beings" (John 1:1, 4; my trans.). Second, John 1:1 takes us all the way back to the beginning of Gen 1:1 ("In the beginning") and the creation story, including the creation of the first human beings. In the LXX the woman is named Zoe (Life) because she is the mother of "all living things" (πάντων τῶν ζώντων, Gen 3:20). From start to finish, John is steeped in Israel's Scriptures and uses them for the purposes of Christology, community, and holy story. In what follows I provide examples of the uses of direct citations and allusions as they relate to these functions of the Scriptures, but first I present a quick walk through the Gospel, selectively highlighting various citations and allusions of importance along the way, with special attention paid to their (dis)similarity to the LXX and MT.

The Use of Scripture in John

The first marked citation is in John 1:23. John quotes Isa 40:3, probably the LXX, though replacing the verb ἑτοιμάζω with εὐθύνω, which is the verb used in the unquoted parallel half of the Isaiah verse. Isaiah 40:3–5 appears in all Four Gospels, but only in John does John the Baptist speak it himself, making him the only character in the Gospel of John other than Jesus to apply Scripture in self-description. In fact, John himself may even be understood to say the words: "as the prophet Isaiah said" (recall that our oldest manuscripts have no punctuation).

The first unmarked citation occurs at John 1:51. Although some scholars consider this an allusion, it does appear that John is quoting from Gen 28:12.[10] Here Jesus is telling Nathanael that he will "see heaven opened and the angels of God ascending and descending upon the Son of Man." Genesis doesn't mention heaven being opened, but the language about "angels of God ascending and descending" matches the MT (the LXX uses finite verbs where John and the MT use participles). In Genesis, Jacob sees these angels upon a ladder, not the Son of Man, so John transfers that idea onto Jesus, who bridges heaven and earth.

Although not specifying that the quotation is from the Psalms, John nevertheless marks John 2:17 as a citation ("it was written"). Unlike in the previous

---

10. For an example of a scholar who calls this an allusion, consult Reinhartz, note to John 1:51, in "Gospel according to John," 177.

two citations, which are spoken aloud by John the Baptist and Jesus respectively, this one is "remembered" by Jesus's disciples during Jesus's "temple tantrum." Interestingly, the previous verse (John 2:16) contains a conceptual allusion when Jesus declares, "Take these things out of here! Stop making my Father's house a marketplace," which parallels the Synoptic citation of Isa 56:7 and Jer 7:11 (cf. Mark 11:17 and par.). The Synoptics announce that this is a scriptural quotation, but John has Jesus speak it; instead of "my house" he speaks of "my Father's house." In John 2:17, however, John marks his unique (among the gospels) citation of Ps 69:9. John changes the verb from the past tense, as it appears in Ps 68:10 LXX (69:10 MT) to the future that appears in John 2:17. As will be explored later, this citation is one example of the way John presents Jesus as an authoritative leader.

Another Psalms quotation occurs at John 6:31, in the midst of the Bread from Heaven Discourse (John 6:22–59), which also includes a second marked citation and as a whole is a conceptual allusion to the manna given during Israel's wilderness wandering (Exod 16:4–15; a similar story appears in Num 11:8 without the phrase "bread from heaven"). The citation at John 6:31, quoted by Jesus's opponents, comes from Ps 77:24 LXX (78:24 MT). The second line of the verse (LXX) says, "and bread [grain, in MT] of heaven he gave to them." John quotes this, adding ἐκ τοῦ between "bread" and "heaven," and φαγεῖν, "to eat," at the end, which is drawn from the psalm's parallel half-verse (thus the quotation does not exactly match either the LXX or MT, which are more similar to one another than to the quotation in John). John 6 as a whole is immensely important for the topic at hand and demonstrates the multifaceted nature of our question about the use of Scripture in the New Testament. Peder Borgen has provided a sustained treatment of how John 6 draws upon midrashic techniques employed by Jewish interpreters in this period. In his intricate, strategic hermeneutic, a rhetorical juggernaut, John employs Jewish exegetical techniques regnant in the first century.[11]

John's next marked citation, in John 6:45, is part of Jesus's response to "the Jews" who are complaining that Jesus claimed to "have come down from heaven" (6:42, quoting 6:38). Jesus's response includes a probable quotation of Isa 54:13, though the exact source is not named ("it is written in the prophets"). Again, this quotation does not exactly match either the LXX or the MT. Both the LXX and MT specify that those being taught are "your sons," which is omitted in John. John uses the nominative where the LXX uses the accusative, but both texts use θεοῦ where one would expect κυρίου as the translation of MT's יְהוָה.

The last line of Jesus's speech during the Festival of Booths in John 7:24 can be considered a verbal allusion to several texts. Jesus tells "the Jews" not to "judge

---

11. Borgen, *Bread from Heaven*.

by appearances, but judge with right judgment." The idea of not judging by appearances is related to Isa 11:3–4, in which the shoot of Jesse is described as using righteousness to judge instead of "what his eyes see" or "what his ears hear." The same idea is related to 1 Sam 16:7, another text associated with Jesse: when sent to the sons of Jesse to anoint a new king, Samuel is also told not to judge by appearances. Noting additional scriptural passages often adduced as allusions (including Lev 19:15; Deut 16:18–19; Isa 16:5; Jer 21:12; Ezek 44:24), Adam Kubiś argues that Zech 7:9 and 8:16 are the most likely texts behind John 7:24. Among his reasons for this claim, Kubiś demonstrates that "the lexical affinity between Zech 7:9 and John 7:24 is very close."[12]

John 7:38, mentioned briefly earlier, is an interesting case. It is very clearly a marked citation and as such is included in my list of citations, but it is unclear what text is being quoted. The possible allusions though, especially to the idea of living water (e.g., Zech 14:8) or flowing water (e.g., Joel 3:18), are many. John 7:42 ("Has not the scripture said that the Messiah is descended from David and comes from Bethlehem, the village where David lived?") is similar. Again, it is a marked citation without a discernable direct quotation. It is more likely a conglomeration of scriptural ideas about the origins of the Messiah. These ideas can be traced to such texts as 2 Sam 7:12 and Jer 23:5 (the promise of a kingdom for David's offspring) and Mic 5:2 (5:1 MT; a king from Bethlehem).

John 10:34 is another Psalms citation from Ps 81:6 LXX (82:6 MT). Although the quotation is introduced with "Is it not written in your law," "law" is taken broadly here to refer to Scripture and not just Torah. The MT and LXX of Ps 82:6 match one another, and the Greek is identical to that in John. This citation might also allude to Exod 7:1 (God making Moses like a god to pharaoh). Like John 2:17, 10:34 showcases how John presents Jesus as an authoritative leader.

The second of John's three unmarked citations occurs at John 12:13. Like 1:51, the verse contains no citation formula. This is one of Williams's "composite citations" because John seems to be combining more than one quotation from Scripture. Both John 12:13 and Ps 117:26 LXX (Ps 118:26 MT) have the following line: "Blessed is the one who comes in the name of the Lord." Trying to account for the source of the apposition of "the King of Israel" to "the Lord," some have posited Zeph 3:15. If not a composite citation, then the additional line can be said to be a Johannine addition.

Two different psalms could serve as the base text for John 15:25. Psalm 34:19 LXX (35:19 MT) and Ps 68:5 LXX (69:5 MT) include the phrase "those who hate me without cause" in both the LXX and MT. John uses this phrase, but the verb he uses is finite instead of a participle ("they hated me").

---

12. Adam Kubiś, *The Book of Zechariah in the Gospel of John*, Ebib 64 (Pendé: Gabalda, 2012), 434.

John 21:16, in which the resurrected Jesus tells Simon Peter to "tend my sheep," is one of several conceptual allusions to shepherds in Israel's Scriptures, especially David, who was shepherd and king. Though David was known as a literal shepherd, in 2 Sam 5:2 and Ps 78:70–72 David is called the shepherd, not of sheep, but of Israel, which is probably the idea John is alluding to here.

The Function of Scripture in John

Scripture in John functions in multiple ways but especially theologically and sociologically, with rhetoric undergirding those. Theologically, John uses Scripture to create a high Christology (relative to the Synoptics) by highlighting Jesus as an authoritative leader, by giving him various titles, by describing him with metaphors, by associating him with other biblical figures, and by explaining the events of the cross as the fulfillment of Scripture.

However, theologies have no meaning apart from the communities who use them. They are created by communities for communities, so one could argue that while the formation of Christology is ostensibly the main purpose of Scripture, in actuality the formation and maintenance of certain kinds of communities is more primary. In an effort to convince his audience to believe in the Johannine Jesus and join the Johannine community, John presents some characters to emulate and some not to. The reader is supposed to feel sympathetic toward certain characters and less so toward others. For instance, Ruth Sheridan has written at length about the way John's use of Scripture in chapters 1–12 functions to characterize "the Jews" in the narrative negatively, as increasingly "obdurate."[13]

Elsewhere, Sheridan analyzes how John 8:17 ("In your law it is written that the testimony of two witnesses is valid") fits into the rhetoric of the larger literary unit of John 7:1–8:59, where Jesus and his opponents wrangle.[14] Though the exact phrase "the testimony of two witnesses is valid" does not appear in

---

13. Sheridan, *Retelling Scripture: "The Jews" and the Scriptural Citations in John 1:19–12:15*, BibInt 110 (Leiden: Brill, 2012). She also addresses the history of the ensuing Christian anti-Semitism that has resulted. Ethical interpretation requires noting that the translation "the Jews" for *hoi Ioudaioi* may contribute to anti-Semitism. Jesus is a Jew, as are the vast majority of early Christians, so the term does not mean ethnic Jews per se but rather a literary character in the narrative. For a fuller treatment, consult Clark-Soles, "'The Jews' in the Fourth Gospel," in *Reading John for Dear Life*, 155–62. Consult also Adele Reinhartz, *Cast Out of the Covenant: Jews and Anti-Judaism in the Gospel of John* (Lanham, MD: Lexington Books/Fortress Academic, 2018).

14. Ruth Sheridan, "The Testimony of Two Witnesses: John 8:17," in Myers and Schuchard, *Abiding Words*, 161–84.

the LXX, scholars variously suggest Deut 17:6; 19:15; and Num 35:30 as possible sources. Drawing on Hays's work on intertextuality, Sheridan studies each of the three scriptural texts in their original literary contexts and then shows how John (ironically) recontextualizes them to accuse "the Jews" who have contested and accused Jesus on the basis of Scripture. The forensic tone and features injected by the appeal to Scriptures concerning idolatry, blasphemy, and bearing false witness shape the narrative to characterize Jesus as legitimate and "the Jews" in the narrative unit as acquiring "blood guilt" in the process.[15]

Given some kind of perceived conflict with the parent tradition alluded to, it is reasonable to assume that the Johannine community, which likely started out as a group entirely within Judaism, eventually became separate. What we witness in this gospel is part of that process. The Gospel may exhibit a point in the group's history where it is separating from the parent tradition and forming a new group and working hard at separate group identity formation and maintenance.[16]

To speak of Christology in John is to begin with John 1:1 and go all the way through the second ending at John 21:25. As noted, the thesis statement of John 20:30–31 names Messiah and Son of God as two crucial features of Jesus. He is presented as a multitude of other things as well. Most explicitly among the canonical gospels, Jesus is God (e.g., John 20:28). In addition, he is referred to as the Word (λογός; e.g., 1:14) and "the one coming into the world" (11:27). His identity is presented using metaphors (e.g., good shepherd [10:11], true vine [15:1]), many of which are connected to Jewish feasts and festivals—such as bread from heaven (6:31; tied to the wilderness wanderings) and light of the world (8:12; tied to Hanukkah). His body is the true temple (2:21) and tabernacle (1:14).

To illustrate John's Christology, I provide examples of how John uses citations and allusions to present Jesus as an authoritative leader and the hermeneutical lens through which Scripture should be interpreted, metaphors and titles for Jesus, ways that Scripture (and specific figures) serve as a christological witness, and ways in which the passion fulfills Scripture. Interspersed throughout these examples are comments about how John constructs this theology for the benefit of his community.

---

15. This verdict has continued to fuel Christian anti-Semitism ever since. Attention to intertextuality reminds us that texts have lives and afterlives as they continue to be received by communities who are in turn shaped by them down to the present day. Communities who considered these texts sacred have an ethical responsibility for the ramifications of their interpretive choices.

16. For a summary of the scholarly discussion on this matter, consult Jaime Clark-Soles, *Scripture Cannot Be Broken: The Social Function of the Use of Scripture in the Fourth Gospel* (Leiden: Brill, 2003), ch. 2.

Jesus as Authoritative Leader

In John, Scripture is employed in various ways to demonstrate Jesus as an authoritative leader (e.g., John 2:17; 10:34; 12:37–41; 13:18; 15:25).[17] Here we attend to four of these verses.

In the midst of Jesus's "temple tantrum" (John 2:13–25) his disciples collectively recall Ps 69:9 (Ps 68:10 LXX; 69:10 MT). In John 2:17, John signifies that he is citing Scripture and then cites Ps 69:9. The citation serves to show that Scripture witnessed to Christ; John subtly accomplishes this by, as noted earlier, changing the verb from the past tense as it appears in the psalm to the future tense, thus pointing to Jesus centuries later. Moreover, John 2:17 implies that Ps 69:9 was written with Jesus in mind, so that one finds the community assuming that it is the telos of Scripture.

During the controversy with the opponents who want to stone him (John 10:31–39), Jesus invokes part of Ps 82:6 (Ps 81:6 LXX) with reference to his identity as "God's Son" (John 10:36). As in John 2:17, the citation indicates that Scripture itself corroborates Jesus's special identity as "the one whom the Father has sanctified and sent into the world" (John 10:36). It also claims that the opponents are unjustly persecuting him. He and his opponents both ostensibly consider Scripture authoritative (since the opponents claim to be honoring Scripture by stoning Jesus for blasphemy, but John implies that they, in fact, do not honor Scripture, while Jesus does). In addition, as the one sent by the Father, Jesus is shown to have special insight. He is the hermeneutical key and locus of authority for valid interpretation of Scripture.

In John 12:37–41, John uses Isa 53:1 and 6:10 to insist that Jesus warrants fidelity and belief. Isaiah makes a connection between healing and being saved from unbelief. At John 12:34 the crowd initiates a conversation on Jesus's messiahship. He responds by exhorting them to "believe" (12:36). Some do not believe, however, and the author accounts for some being able to resist Jesus by citing Scripture. If the Johannine community at its early layer is conceived of as a sectarian group in tension with the parent tradition, as posited above, one could understand how the citation of Isa 53:1 and 6:10 in John 12:37–41 functions for John's audience in multiple ways. First, it shows that Scripture, which is shared with the parent tradition, is also authoritative for the sect. In other words, they do *not* make the Marcionite move of abandoning Scripture, leaving it to Judaism and the lesser demiurge god and declaring a clean break between Judaism and Christianity. Second, John uses Scripture to indicate that Isaiah was speaking

---

17. For the ways in which Jesus is depicted as an authoritative leader, consult Clark-Soles, *Scripture Cannot Be Broken*, ch. 5, "The Community of the Fourth Gospel."

specifically about Jesus and the experience of the Johannine community. Once again, John indicates that Scripture finds its telos in this Johannine Jesus. Third, Scripture functions to degrade outsiders who do not join the sect and to affirm those who "get it" and participate in the Johannine community.

In John 15:25, which is part of the Farewell Discourse (chs. 14–17), Jesus is preparing the disciples in the narrative and, presumably, the late first-century audience of the Gospel, for the same kind of rejection, persecution, and derision that he himself encountered. The narrator intensifies Jesus's word by declaring: "It was to fulfill the word that is written in their law, 'They hated me without a cause,'" citing Pss 35:19 (Ps 34:19 LXX) and 69:4 (Ps 69:5 MT; 68:5 LXX). Notice that "law" here clearly extends beyond the Pentateuch to encompass Scripture more broadly since the citations are from the Psalms.[18] When one attends to how communities are formed and shaped, it is reasonable to suggest that such a citation could serve multiple purposes. Here I name three by way of illustration. First, the citation establishes insiders and outsiders. There are those who hate and those who love; the former are the outsiders, the opponents, and the latter the insiders, those in the community. Second, the citation demonstrates that Jesus, their founder, had special insight regarding Scripture, such that he could adduce it and appropriately apply it to his and their situation (by showing how they are hated in the present). Third, it prepares the community to endure persecution without apostatizing—they should expect to be hated since Jesus, their founder, was hated.

Metaphors/Titles

John uses Scripture extensively regarding metaphors and titles applied to Jesus. I present examples here related to the "I am" statements and Woman Wisdom. John houses two kinds of "I am" statements. One includes a predicate nominative. For example, in John 10:11, 14 Jesus declares, "I am the good shepherd." Readers familiar with Scripture will recall other good shepherds, such as Moses (Exod 3:1), David (2 Sam 5:2), and God (Ps 23).

The second category contains the absolute "I AM" statements, which refer to the places where Jesus uses the phrase ἐγώ εἰμι ("I AM"), God's own self-designation in Scripture, with no predicate. These instances reveal Jesus's divine identity. In the exodus narrative, God tells Moses to confront pharaoh. When Moses asks who he can say sent him, God replies, "I AM WHO I AM . . . Thus you shall say to the Israelites, 'I AM has sent me to you'" (Exod 3:14). Allusions to Exod 3:14

---

18. Consult Jonathan Klawans, "The Law," in Levine and Brettler, *Jewish Annotated New Testament*, 655–58.

occur through the use of absolute "I AM" statements in John 4:26; 6:20; 8:24, 28, 58; 13:19; 17:24; 18:5, 6, 8, though often the phrase is diluted in the English translation to the flaccid "I am he" instead of the more powerful and proper "I AM." In addition to the absolute "I AM" statements that point to Jesus's divinity, we find other allusions to God/Jesus as creator, as in John 9:11, where Jesus re-creates the man with the visual impairment by drawing from the dirt of earth.[19]

Woman Wisdom is powerfully alluded to in John. Read the prologue (John 1:1–18) alongside Prov 8:22–31; Sir 24:1–9; and Prov 1:20–33, and John casts Jesus in the mold of Woman Wisdom. Woman Wisdom (חָכְמָה in Hebrew, σοφία in Greek) is God's partner: she helps to create the world (e.g., Prov 8:22–31), she delights in the human race, and she continually tries to help humans get knowledge and eschew ignorance (e.g., Prov 8:32–36). She cries aloud incessantly (e.g., Prov 1:20–21). Unfortunately, Scripture indicates that she is often rejected because fools hate knowledge and, more often than not, humans would rather wallow in ignorance (e.g., Prov 1:29–31). The theme of Jesus's rejection in John becomes more poignant when one understands that John draws upon both Isaiah (overtly) and Woman Wisdom (allusively).

John also depicts Jesus as the physical and symbolic replacement of many special spaces that heretofore marked the unique locus of God. His body replaces the temple. Stunningly, John 1:14 declares: "And the Word became flesh and tabernacled [ἐσκήνωσεν] among us, and we have seen his glory, the glory as of a father's only son, full of grace and truth" (my trans.). English translations obscure the allusion by using the words "lived" or "dwelt" instead of "tabernacled," which John intends (cf. Exod 25:8).

Many of the examples in this section are verbal and conceptual allusions, so it is important to recognize the power of allusive language. First, allusions signify the author's own view of Scripture as the mold into which contemporary experiences somehow fit. Second, the use of allusions presumes more sophisticated knowledge on the part of the audience than do citations. Third, by allusions the author teaches the audience to understand their world in scriptural terms; in sociological terms, this falls under the idea of the production of worldview. Allusion serves the same social function as all insider language—it creates a bond among the community members and between the community(ies) and the author. Speaking in such terms teaches the community that they are part of the unfolding drama between God and humanity that began ages ago. The community becomes part of something larger than itself; the mundane and seemingly insignificant details of its own situation are transcended and given significance by association with the scriptural story.

19. For a fuller discussion, consult Clark-Soles, *Reading John*, 47–58.

Scripture and Biblical Figures as Christological Witnesses to Jesus and Elements of Social Memory

John relies on Scripture from Isaiah and draws upon figures such as Moses and Jacob to convey some of his christological convictions.[20] Sometimes John connects these figures to direct citations, but usually he does so in a verbally allusive or even typological (i.e., conceptually allusive) manner. These sorts of allusions are only possible because they are part of the community's social memory. Social memory theory acknowledges that a group's identity is tied closely to its collective memory, defined as "a fluid, variable, and selective phenomenon related closely to the identity of a group; it entails the construction of a shared past that is continuous with the present, and at the same time, serves to unite the group."[21] Foundational figures—such as Moses, Isaiah, and the ancestors, specifically Abraham and Jacob—belong to the past but also serve to "embody the normative values that distinguish the group in the present."[22] These figures serve as a bridge insofar as the ancient figures testify to Jesus, upon whom this new community is founded.

Social memory analysis draws upon a broader conversation about ancient literacy and orality and performance of texts. While modern readers are fixated on the notion of a stable, original text, the ancients had a broader view of the matter. There was attention to and a respect for "what is written," but simultaneously there was respect for the oral nature of shared texts that are performed, such that when John refers to scriptural figures, John likely "is drawing on the collective memory of these foundational characters and evoking wider commemorative frameworks associated with them" than merely specific quotations.[23]

Moses. Moses functions both as a christological witness and typologically, in part because he belongs to the community's collective social memory. In fact, John makes seven distinct references to Moses (John 1:17, 45; 3:14; 5:45–47; 6:32; 7:19–23; 9:28–29). As a christological witness, for instance, already in John 1:45 Philip deploys Scripture to entice Nathanael, saying: "We have found him about whom Moses in the law and also the prophets wrote, Jesus son of Joseph from Nazareth."

Again, in John 5:46 we learn that Moses "wrote about" Jesus. In John 5:18, "the Jews" accuse Jesus of blasphemy for "making himself equal to God." Jesus defends himself, drawing upon the scriptural tradition he shares with his opponents.

---

20. Sanghee M. Ahn, *The Christological Witness Function of the Old Testament Characters in the Gospel of John*, Paternoster Biblical Monographs (Milton-Keynes: Paternoster, 2014).

21. Catrin Williams, "Patriarchs and Prophets Remembered: Framing Israel's Past in the Gospel of John," in Myers and Schuchard, *Abiding Words*, 190.

22. Williams, "Patriarchs and Prophets Remembered," 192.

23. Williams, "Patriarchs and Prophets Remembered," 188–89.

They try to use Scripture *against* him, and he seeks to show that, on the contrary, Scripture testifies and corroborates his identity. John depicts Jesus as incisively getting to the root of the disagreement: "You search the scriptures because you think that in them you have eternal life; and it is they that testify on my behalf" (John 5:39). They all agree that Scripture is authoritative and revelatory. They disagree about how it applies to Jesus. Jesus then gets more specific, naming Moses as an author of Scripture: "Do not think that I will accuse you before the Father; your accuser is Moses, on whom you have set your hope. If you believed Moses, you would believe me, for he wrote about me. But if you do not believe what he wrote, how will you believe what I say?" (John 5:45–47). No specific verse is cited, but the conceptual allusion is prominent. Because Moses is part of the collective memory of the Johannine community, John can re-present Moses in a way that certifies that contemporary Johannine Christians (and all that follow) are in continuity with Scripture when they choose to follow Jesus, even if other Jewish interpreters of the same Scriptures at that time might disagree. Given that Moses is such a central figure in the parent Jewish tradition, the battle over Moses in the narrative is not so surprising.

Moses functions typologically as well. In Deut 18:15–18 Moses promises his people that God will raise up a prophet like him. John alludes to this in John 1:25 when the Pharisees send "priests and Levites from Jerusalem" (1:19) to ask John the Baptist if he is the Messiah, Elijah, or *the* prophet. "The prophet" is a reference to Moses, and John demonstrates amply that Jesus is not only the prophet *like* Moses but also the prophet *superior to* Moses.[24] Consult, for instance, the Bread from Heaven Discourse in John 6:22–59. First, John insists that God, not Moses, provided the bread. Second, the Moses event was a one-time event, denoted by the past tense verb "gave," whereas what God has provided in Jesus is ongoing, denoted by the presence of the present tense "gives" (6:31–32). Furthermore, though Moses provides bread to the multitudes miraculously (cf. Exod 16), Jesus is superior to Moses in that he himself *is* the bread.

Isaiah. The citation of Isa 40:3 in John 1:23 is an example of John's dependence on Greek rhetorical tactics for the construction of his gospel.[25] When John the Baptist speaks Isa 40:3 in the first person, says Alicia Myers, "John figuratively takes on Isaiah's prophetic mantle, initiating the Gospel's blending of their voices into one: a voice whose divine origins reach across time to support Jesus' identity as God's Son and persists in the confession of the Gospel community."[26]

---

24. Consult Wayne Meeks, *The Prophet-King: Moses Traditions and the Johannine Christology*, NovTSup 14 (Leiden: Brill, 1967).

25. Consult, e.g., Alicia D. Myers, *Characterizing Jesus: A Rhetorical Analysis of the Use of Scripture in the Fourth Gospel's Presentation*, LNTS 458 (London: T&T Clark, 2012).

26. Alicia D. Myers, "A Voice in the Wilderness: Classical Rhetoric and the Testimony of John (the Baptist) in John 1:19–34," in Myers and Schuchard, *Abiding Words*, 121–22.

John explicitly claims in John 12:41 that Isaiah personally witnessed Jesus in some form; that is, Isaiah saw Jesus's glory. As Williams notes, "The scriptural setting for this remark is undoubtedly Isaiah's call-vision (Isaiah 6:1–13), which forms the wider context of the immediately preceding quotation from Isa 6:10 (John 12:40), while the reference to the Prophet having 'seen his glory' relates specifically to Jewish interpretative renderings of his encounter with the enthroned 'Lord' as a vision of the divine [*doxa*] (LXX Isa 6:1; cf. T. Isa. 6:1)."[27] If one traces the language of "seeing" Jesus and Jesus's glory, one finds that Isaiah's vision serves a larger social memory purpose for the Johannine Christians. They are the ones who, like Isaiah (thus, in concert with Scripture as a broader category), recognize Jesus's glory and believe; on the contrary, the opponents, who "loved human glory [δόξαν] more than the glory that comes from God" (John 12:43), could not believe in Jesus, according to Isaiah. Isaiah, then, serves the Johannine collective memory.

Abraham. If the proper memory of Moses is contested between John's community and the Jewish opponents in the narrative, so also is Abraham's. Not surprisingly, Abraham appears voluminously in ancient Jewish interpretation, including various books of the New Testament. He was touted for hospitality and rejection of idolatry and was the one in whom all nations would be blessed. In John, his function is primarily related to origins and a paternal identity brawl: In John 8 a battle over who rightly owns and understands and extends the line of Abraham takes place. John 8 contains such vitriol that it can be difficult to read. The "Jews" who appear as the opponents here claim ethnic, physical descent from Abraham; they rest on the memory of Abraham as their father. In a profoundly stunning move, John transfers the terms to spiritual and ethical descent, that is, how one *performs* Abrahamic identity. John contests their Abrahamic claim, assigns their paternity to the devil, and claims that the real "spiritual bloodline" to God comes through Jesus. In the immediate narrative context, the opponents seek to kill Jesus. Abraham is presented as one who, instead, *received* God's messengers.[28] As such, John claims, Abraham belongs to the collective memory of the Johannine Christians, not the opponents.

Furthermore, not only does a proper understanding of Abraham lead one to faith in Jesus, but Jesus also becomes superior to Abraham (as he is also superior to Moses): "Before Abraham was, I am" (John 8:58). Abraham becomes a christological witness and a forerunner to Jesus; Jesus, however, is everything good that Abraham was and then some—both preexistent and divine. Just as the Samaritan woman asks, "Are you greater than our ancestor Jacob?" (John 4:12), so the opponents in chapter 8 ask, "Are you greater than our father Abraham?"

---

27. Williams, "Patriarchs and Prophets Remembered," 208.
28. Williams, "Patriarchs and Prophets Remembered," 202–3.

(John 8:53). In both cases, the answer is yes. Canonical and noncanonical Jewish traditions about Abraham rejoicing and seeing Jesus's "day" likely lie behind this passage.[29]

Jacob. For the purposes of this chapter, Jacob's appearances fall mostly under verbal and conceptual allusions, but in John 1:51 ("Very truly, I tell you, you will see heaven opened and the angels of God ascending and descending upon the Son of Man"), John cites Gen 28:12, Jacob's vision of a ladder with angels ascending and descending. Recall that during that dream God promises Jacob that "all the families of the earth shall be blessed" in him and his offspring (28:14). Jacob awakes and builds a shrine marking his encountering and calling the place Beth-El, "house of God" (Gen 28:17). John draws upon this Jacob narrative but presents Jesus as superior to Jacob insofar as Jesus *becomes* the ladder connecting earth and heaven, just as in John 6 he outdoes Moses's manna moment because he *becomes* the bread from heaven.

Jacob is central to the gripping exchange between Jesus and the Samaritan woman in John 4. Conceptual allusion is at play with the well scene, which Scripture depicts as a typical locale of betrothal (e.g., Gen 24; Exod 2), including for Jacob and Rachel (Gen 29). The Samaritan woman's question makes John's point when she asks: "Are you greater than our ancestor Jacob, who gave us the well, and with his sons and his flocks drank from it?" (John 4:12). Jesus is like Jacob, insofar as he represents Israel, the bridegroom, "wooing" Samaria, of which the woman is a representative, but he is also superior to Jacob, in fact, because the water Jacob drew for Rachel was temporary and Jesus's is eternal (John 4:13–14).[30]

The Cross: Fulfillment and Allusion

John presents Jesus as a fulfillment of Scripture broadly. We encountered this in John 12:41, where John expressly states that it was Jesus's glory Isaiah saw. There are particular instances, however, where John uses the verb "to fulfill," as we saw in John 12:38. This fulfillment language is concentrated at the scene of the cross, with four direct citations regarding Jesus's clothes, his thirst, his unbroken bones, and his side being pierced, respectively (John 19:24, 28, 36, and 37).

All of the Evangelists record the dividing of Jesus's garments, but John's rendition (John 19:24) is peculiar. First, he gives more detail; he indicates the exact number of soldiers involved and the exact number of pieces into

---

29. Williams, "Patriarchs and Prophets Remembered," 205–6.
30. For "wooing" Samaria, consult Schneiders, *Written That You May Believe.*

which the garments are divided. He also mentions a seamless tunic, which is the particular piece of clothing over which lots were cast among the soldiers. Also, John allows the soldiers themselves to speak in first person rather than reporting on them in third person. The structure of the material about dividing Jesus's garments is chiastic in a way that serves to focus attention on the scriptural citation itself. Having set up the scene depicting the soldiers' actions in detail, the author then turns to a citation taken from Ps 22:18 (22:19 MT; 21:19 LXX) and concludes by once again commenting on the actions of the soldiers. While all of the Evangelists refer to this psalm, only John indicates that he is quoting from Scripture and quotes the Greek exactly. His narrative concerning the division of garments differs from the Synoptics because its details are dictated by the scriptural quotation itself. This holds true even in permitting the soldiers to speak in first person since the psalm itself uses first-person language. John's reading of the psalm's parallelism leads him to posit two garments rather than one.

As noted earlier, the first-person singular of the verb "to thirst" (διψάω) does not appear in the LXX, so it is unclear which specific Scripture John cites at 19:28, if any. Psalm 69:21 ("They gave me poison for food, and for my thirst they gave me vinegar to drink" [68:22 LXX; 69:22 MT]) or Ps 63:1 ("O God, you are my God, I seek you, my soul thirsts for you" [62:2 LXX; 63:2 MT]) is usually suggested. True to John's depiction of Jesus throughout the Gospel, Jesus is eminently in control of himself on the cross. John depicts Jesus not as suffering from thirst but as making perfunctory mention of it on his way to completing his list of personal tasks. It may be that the author is either combating docetic tendencies (by indicating Jesus's thirst) or inventing them (by depicting Jesus not as actually needing any physical relief but simply aligning himself with Scripture).

John 19:33 mentions that the soldiers did not break Jesus's legs, and in John 19:36 we are told, "These things occurred so that the scripture might be fulfilled, 'None of his bones shall be broken.'" In citing Exod 12:46 and Ps 34:20 (33:21 LXX; 34:21 MT), the author depicts Jesus as the Passover lamb of Exodus, that great story of the deliverance of God's people and a return "home. In fact, John uses scriptural allusions to accomplish this as well, as is evident in John the Baptist's double announcement of Jesus as the Lamb of God (John 1:29, 36). When John depicts Jesus as the Passover lamb, he emphasizes Jesus as liberator (not as an atoning sacrifice as construed in penal substitutionary atonement theories). John also addresses this theme in chapter 8, where Jesus says, "You will know the truth, and the truth will make you free" (v. 32), that truth, of course, being Jesus himself ("I am the way, and the truth, and the life," John 14:6), who, unlike in the Synoptics, dies on a different day such that he is slaughtered at the time when the Passover lamb would be slaughtered.[31]

Immediately, John (19:37) invokes another citation (most likely to Zech 12:10): "And again another passage of scripture [ἑτέρα γραφή] says, 'They will look on the one whom they have pierced.'" Of all of the gospels, only John specifically indicates that he is citing Scripture *as fulfillment of Scripture* with respect to the crucifixion. Showing Jesus's death as a fulfillment of Scripture serves an apologetic christological function. As we find in other New Testament texts, a crucified messiah presents a problem of sorts, as it is unexpected and shameful on the face of it. It is easy to imagine those opposed to John's Christianity enthusiastically and facilely "proving" to the Johannine Christians that a crucified messiah was not in accordance with Scripture, as Deut 21:23 clearly expresses. That a crucified messiah could cause some embarrassment is indicated elsewhere in the New Testament (Heb 12:2; Gal 3:13; 1 Cor 1:23). The author of the Fourth Gospel, by adducing Scripture in relating the story of the crucifixion, provides his community with a defense against scripturally knowledgeable detractors by showing that, in fact, Scripture *does* corroborate Christian christological claims. Furthermore, Jesus is shown to have special insight regarding Scripture when he cites Scripture in a perfectly timed manner, having understood at which part of the unfolding drama he presently found himself.

Conclusion

John's use of Scripture is polyvalent. To understand it thoroughly requires recognizing that he uses Scripture at the level of marked and unmarked citations as well as verbal and conceptual allusions. He uses it (1) to convey his theology (particularly his Christology), (2) to establish and maintain a particular kind of community that behaves in a certain way in its host culture, and (3) to shape his narrative in a way that invites his audience to believe (or to continue to believe) in the Johannine Jesus and participate in the Johannine community.

The text was produced and performed for potential and actual Johannine Christians. As noted earlier, the thesis statement (John 20:30–31) can be interpreted either as "so that you may come to believe" or "so that you might continue to believe." John is clearly interested in both. It is reasonable to assume that different audiences, ancient and modern alike, would have different levels of familiarity with Scripture. Given that John's usage ranges from marked citations to allusions to "echoes," there is an entry point for everyone. The more one knows

---

31. For an excellent, concise discussion of Jesus as the Paschal Lamb in John, consult Craig Koester, *The Word of Life: A Theology of John's Gospel* (Grand Rapids: Eerdmans, 2008), 112–17.

Scripture, the more she will recognize it throughout John and experience the text as more and more layered over time.

The intertextuality on display in John is multifaceted. The most basic, rudimentary use of Scripture is proof texting, the use of a scriptural quotation to make a theological point without much regard for the quotation's original context. Some scholars have argued that John draws upon *testimonia*, an early collection of Christian proof texts.[32] Certainly, other ancient Jews employed this technique as well, as evidenced by the Qumran pesharim. In this technique, the author draws a clear line between the scriptural text and the current setting while showing that the former finds its fullest meaning in the latter.

John is capable of leaving more space for scriptural connections as well. We find an example of this in Borgen's treatment of the Bread Discourse in John 6 as Jewish midrash.[33] Myers has us contemplate the ways John draws on intertextual techniques from classical rhetoric.[34] All of this raises several important questions about the ancient and contemporary readers, three of which deserve special mention.

First, how does interpretation proceed in light of the context of scriptural citations? So, for instance, if John's ancient readership was primarily Jewish and consequently familiar with Scripture, when they heard the array of scriptural citations and allusions, would they think only of the immediate citation or context or did the mention of it bring to mind a much larger context for them? This prompts a subgroup of related questions. How does it change the meaning of John's use of Scripture in a particular place for the reader to know the larger context? Should a contemporary reader consult the original context? Does the original context matter, or is the meaning solely located in the way John has recontextualized it in his narrative?

Second, John's audience contained non-Jewish readers. How would the deployment of Scripture work upon them? Presumably, the repeated performance/reading of John trains readers up in the knowledge of Scripture while providing particular ways of interpreting it (namely with Jesus as the hermeneutical lens). Additionally, Myers has compellingly argued that John is heavily influenced by Greco-Roman rhetoric, theater, philosophy, and culture.[35] Certainly, non-Jewish audiences were familiar with and able to recognize intertextuality since it was

---

32. E.g., J. Rendel Harris, *Testimonies*, 2 vols. (Cambridge: Cambridge University Press, 1916–1920); C. H. Dodd, *According to the Scriptures: The Sub-structure of New Testament Theology* (New York: Scribner's Sons, 1953), 23–60.

33. Borgen, *Bread from Heaven*.

34. Myers, *Characterizing Jesus*; Myers, "Voice in the Wilderness."

35. Myers, *Characterizing Jesus*; Myers, "Voice in the Wilderness."

always at play in the culture, from literature to theater performances to political speeches, where the past masters were used for rhetorical force.

Finally, current literary methodologies, such as reader-response criticism, have taught us that meaning derived from a text is not limited to the original author's intent. Readers themselves come to the text not as blank slates but with their own backgrounds and their interpretive practices having been shaped by the reading communities in which they were raised. Thus, the power of intertextuality includes not only intended effects but even unintended ones. This is why, for example, if you consult scholarly charts on allusions in John, they will not agree, since how one defines the parameters of marked citation, unmarked citation, verbal allusion, and conceptual allusion may differ, and each interpreter may recognize different resonances in the text. This is not a cause for despair, but quite the opposite. This is as it should be. The text will not be contained; it spills over; it is more than the sum of its parts.

What Scripture Does John Use?

Whence John sources his scriptural citations is debated. As noted earlier, scholars do not agree exactly on how many citations there are in John.[36] No matter how many one includes, however, the majority of the citations do not agree exactly with any known version of Scripture in any language, as is illustrated in the parsed examples given earlier in the chapter. This raises a number of questions. Are we to imagine that the author is referring to a fixed written text? Would the author feel free to modify the text? If so, what might motivate him to do so, and is there a discernible method of modification? What views were held by other ancient Jewish communities regarding Written and Oral Torah, and how might that inform this conversation? Does the conviction about authorship influence the scholar's understanding of the issue (i.e., if the author is considered an eyewitness)? Here I summarize different ways scholars address the topic of John's scriptural source(s). I find the first three arguments unconvincing, but the fourth, having to do with orality and fluidity, seems to fit better with ancient understandings of text, composition, and authority.

First, some posit that the author is drawing upon *testimonia*, an early collection of Christian proof texts.[37] This would explain why there are some shared verses among various ancient authors.

---

36. E.g., Köstenberger finds fourteen ("John," 415), and Schuchard finds thirteen ("Form Versus Function," 28).

37. See note 33 above; cf. the broader argument of Martin C. Albl, *"And Scripture Cannot*

Second, some scholars assume that there was a fixed, stable text, represented by LXX or MT and where there are differences between John and those sources (e.g., John 2:17, where the Greek of Ps 68:10 [69:9 ET; 69:10 MT] has κατέφαγεν, the aorist—corresponding to the Hebrew perfect—but John has καταφάγεταί, the future), they are due to John's faulty memory.[38] Those who hold this view posit the author as an eyewitness to Jesus's ministry (presumed to be John, son of Zebedee, though the Gospel itself never explicitly names its author or "the beloved disciple").

Third, some scholars assume that there was a fixed, stable text, represented by LXX or MT, and where there are differences between John and his source, they are due not to a deficiency on the author's part, but quite the opposite—the Evangelist was a creative genius and differences are due to poetic license and creativity. Bruce Schuchard argues that "the evangelist's Old Testament was a Greek Bible."[39] He considers the evangelist to be "an eyewitness to Jesus who consciously composed his Gospel with the intention to persuade, with the expectation that the result of his work would be Scripture."[40] Schuchard counts thirteen marked citations, three of which he considers verbatim from the Greek (John 10:34; 12:38; 19:24), seven of which are close with some intentional modifications, such as abbreviating texts (e.g., John 1:23; 6:31; 19:37), and three of which present an exceptional challenge since their "significantly redacted shape and form do not exhibit close agreement with the Greek" (John 12:15, 40; 13:18).[41] Noting that some scholars argue for a Hebrew source for some citations (esp. 19:37), Schuchard suggests that John was likely a Palestinian Jew who *knew* Hebrew but chose to use only the Greek text since his audience was Greek speaking. While everyone agrees that John used Greek Scripture, there is debate about whether and how often he might have used Hebrew. Unlike Schuchard, other scholars argue for direct dependence on a Hebrew Bible by John (such as Maarten Menken and Andreas Köstenberger).[42] The subject becomes even more complicated when trying to posit original Greek or Hebrew texts, prototexts, and "corrected" versions of those texts. In some cita-

---

Be Broken": The Form and Function of the Early Christian Testimonia *Collections*, NovTSup 96 (Leiden: Brill, 1999).

38. For one scholar who makes this argument, consult Charles Goodwin, "How Did John Treat His Sources?," *JBL* 73, no. 2 (1954): 61–75.

39. Schuchard, "Form Versus Function," 34. Schuchard has addressed this subject across his career, first in his monograph *Scripture within Scripture: The Interrelationship of Form and Function in the Explicit Old Testament Citations in the Gospel of John*, SBLDS 133 (Atlanta: Scholars Press, 1992).

40. Schuchard, "Form Versus Function," 26–27.

41. Schuchard, "Form Versus Function," 32.

42. Maarten J. J. Menken, *Old Testament Quotations in the Fourth Gospel: Studies in Textual Form*, CBET 15 (Kampen: Kok Pharos, 1996); Köstenberger, "John," 415–512.

tions (e.g., John 12:38; 19:24), the LXX and MT appear to agree with one another (understanding that one is comparing across languages), thus taking the conversation into the relationship between the LXX and MT and how one would decide which one John is adducing where they agree. It is not surprising then, that it is difficult to draw any solid conclusions on the matter.

Fourth, more recent discussions of the use of Israel's Scriptures in the New Testament have considered seriously the fact that in a fundamentally oral culture, the fixation solely on a codified, stable text typical of post-Enlightenment sensibilities does not really apply. Instead, we are invited to understand that the text was primarily experienced as orally performed. Ancient media and culture, social memory theory, and other more recent methodologies have injected new life into the exploration of the topic, and it has mushroomed in a variety of productive directions relevant to our discussion.[43] I mention a few here to show the possibilities for advancing the conversation.

Scholars have long recognized the two-fold Torah, Written and Oral, as scriptural for ancient Jews: "Jews too supplemented the Pentateuch with oral traditions and exegetical explanations, such that the Written Torah finds its completion in the Oral Torah preserved in the Mishnah, Talmud, and other rabbinic writings."[44] In addition, Israel's Scripture was likely not "closed" until the late first century CE (and even then some aspects were still in flux), and the "final" form of John's Gospel is dated to the late first century CE (though, of course, changes and variants in the textual tradition continue to appear for centuries, so I use the word loosely). Thus, there is ample fluidity. Add to that about sixty years between Jesus's death and the "final" form of the Gospel of John, a period during which the Gospel was related orally, and further add that just because the Gospel appeared in a written form does not mean that oral performances ceased, and one begins to see how many moving parts there are. Rather than lament that it is impossible to certify the number of citations, the various ways of using Scripture (marked and unmarked citations and verbal and conceptual allusions), and the *Vorlage*, we should recognize that conceiving of Scripture in the first century more broadly enriches our view and honors the fact that living communities are organic creatures. In this way, we are equipped to paint a more accurate, if far more complex and layered, picture of how John's employment of Scripture played in the communities who experienced and were shaped by his gospel.

The formation of the Jewish and Christian canons was a lengthy, somewhat winding process, but certainly the New Testament authors knew (some form of) the LXX, which includes all the material that Protestant Christians call "the

---

43. Consult, e.g., Anthony Le Donne and Tom Thatcher, eds., *The Fourth Gospel in First-Century Media Culture*, LNTS 426 (London: T&T Clark, 2011).

44. Klawans, "Law," 658.

Apocrypha." This means that when we refer to "Israel's Scriptures" in this chapter, we are in danger of being anachronistic (since there was no final closed canon by John's time) and excluding material that John himself considered scriptural but many modern Christian interpreters do not. For instance, John arguably alludes to such apocryphal books as the Wisdom of Solomon and Sirach and so-called Old Testament pseudepigrapha, such as Psalms of Solomon (at John 15:25, citing Pss. Sol. 7:1), which have not been included in this chapter.

Annette Yoshiko Reed and Eva Mroczek are two scholars doing some of the most compelling and exciting work in Jewish antiquity on the interplay of the written and the oral (John certainly highlights language of both writing and speech), intertextuality, and social memory. If space permitted, applying Reed's insights on Jewish testamentary literature to the Farewell Discourse in John (chs. 14–17) would be worthwhile since the Farewell Discourse falls into that genre (even while Reed's work complexifies our generic taxonomies). The Testaments of the Twelve Patriarchs certainly, like John, draw upon Israel's Scriptures and also display the intricate relationship between the ancient text and the author's current community and the commitment to importance of both the written and the oral. As Reed writes: "Writing was only one of the many technologies of memory, even in Jewish literary circles."[45]

Mroczek's stunning book helps us think about ancient Jewish literature beyond the categories of "Bible" and "books," since neither applies to the ways sacred literature was regarded.[46] As she discusses the ways ancient Jewish literature, such as the Qumran literature, relates to texts that predate it (some of which ends up in the canon and some of which does not), many of her insights apply to John's employment of texts that he considered sacred. She carefully avoids forcing texts into rigid categories and, instead, follows their lead to see what the authors themselves considered sacred and how their own work might relate to it. Many of our assumptions about how these authors regarded sacred texts are unduly influenced by the way modern people view texts and sacred texts. For instance, scholars use the category "rewritten Bible" for texts like Jubilees, but Mroczek contests such a notion since "Bible" is anachronistic (a category determined by scholars who define "Bible" as including very particular texts and excluding others, the contents of which would not match Jubilees' list).

Mroczek's work expands our horizon and bears upon the question of *Vorlage*. While we may be curious to see how John interacts with texts he considers sacred, we need not assume that the "meaning" depends upon identifying which version

---

45. Annette Yoshiko Reed, "Textuality between Death and Memory: The Prehistory and Formation of the Parabiblical Testament," *JQR* 104, no. 3 (2014): 411.

46. Eva Mroczek, *The Literary Imagination in Jewish Antiquity* (New York: Oxford University Press, 2016).

of which Greek or Hebrew (or other) text he cites. Rather, we can follow John as he takes us on a journey of meaning that includes reference to sacred texts.

Conclusion

John's use of Israel's Scriptures is thoroughgoing. From the very first words, "in the beginning," John tells a story whose structure and content depend upon Scripture as it has been written, spoken, digested, and lived by scriptural ancestors and followers of Jesus. John is influenced by and employs interpretive strategies and tactics used by other ancient authors, including citations, allusions, midrash, pesher, and *exempla*. The more the reader is familiar with Scripture, the more resonances she will hear and the more layers she will uncover.

John uses Scripture to accomplish myriad ends: to convey theology, to shape a community, and to craft a narrative that invites readers to believe (or continue to believe) in Jesus and participate in an abundant life. The second ending of John reads: "But there are also many other things that Jesus did; if every one of them were written down, I suppose that the world itself could not contain the books that would be written" (John 21:25). Likewise, were we to consider every way that John uses Israel's Scriptures, surely the world itself could not contain the books that would be written.

Bibliography

Adams, Sean A., and Seth M. Ehorn. "What Is a Composite Citation? An Introduction." Pages 1–16 in *Jewish, Graeco-Roman, and Early Christian Uses*. Edited by Sean A. Adams and Seth M. Ehorn. Vol. 1 of *Composite Citations in Antiquity*. LNTS 525. London: Bloomsbury, 2016.

Ahn, Sanghee M. *The Christological Witness Function of the Old Testament Characters in the Gospel of John*. Paternoster Biblical Monographs. Milton Keynes: Paternoster, 2014.

Albl, Martin C. *"And Scripture Cannot Be Broken": The Form and Function of the Early Christian* Testimonia *Collections*. NovTSup 96. Leiden: Brill, 1999.

Borgen, Peder. *Bread from Heaven: An Exegetical Study of the Concept of Manna in the Gospel of John and the Writings of Philo*. Rev. ed. NovTSup 10. Leiden: Brill, 1981.

Clark-Soles, Jaime. *Reading John for Dear Life: A Spiritual Walk through the Fourth Gospel*. Louisville: Westminster John Knox, 2016.

———. *Scripture Cannot Be Broken: The Social Function of the Use of Scripture in the Fourth Gospel.* Leiden: Brill, 2003.

Dahl, Nils. "Der Erstgeborene Satans und der Vater des Teufels (Polyk. 7,1 und Joh 8,44)." Pages 70–84 in *Apophoreta: Festschrift für Ernst Haenchen zu seinem 70. Geburtstag am 10. Dezember 1964.* Edited by Walther Eltester and Franz Heinrich Kettler. BZNW 30. Berlin: Töpelmann, 1964.

Dodd, C. H. *According to the Scriptures: The Sub-structure of New Testament Theology.* New York: Scribner's Sons, 1953.

Goodwin, Charles. "How Did John Treat His Sources?" *JBL* 73, no. 2 (1954): 61–75.

Harris, J. Rendel. *Testimonies.* 2 vols. Cambridge: Cambridge University Press, 1916–1920.

Hays, Richard B. *Echoes of Scripture in the Letters of Paul.* New Haven: Yale University Press, 1989.

Klawans, Jonathan. "The Law." Pages 655–58 in *The Jewish Annotated New Testament.* Edited by Amy-Jill Levine and Marc Zvi Brettler. 2nd ed. Oxford: Oxford University Press, 2017.

Koester, Craig. *The Word of Life: A Theology of John's Gospel.* Grand Rapids: Eerdmans, 2008.

Köstenberger, Andreas J. "John." Pages 415–512 in *Commentary on the New Testament Use of the Old Testament.* Edited by G. K. Beale and D. A. Carson. Grand Rapids: Baker Academic, 2007.

Kubiś, Adam. *The Book of Zechariah in the Gospel of John.* EBib 64. Pendé: Gabalda, 2012.

Le Donne, Anthony, and Tom Thatcher, eds. *The Fourth Gospel in First-Century Media Culture.* LNTS 426. London: T&T Clark, 2011.

Meeks, Wayne A. *The Prophet-King: Moses Traditions and the Johannine Christology.* NovTSup 14. Leiden: Brill, 1967.

Menken, Maarten J. J. *Old Testament Quotations in the Fourth Gospel: Studies in Textual Form.* CBET 15. Kampen: Kok Pharos, 1996.

Mroczek, Eva. *The Literary Imagination in Jewish Antiquity.* New York: Oxford University Press, 2016.

Myers, Alicia D. *Characterizing Jesus: A Rhetorical Analysis of the Use of Scripture in the Fourth Gospel's Presentation.* LNTS 458. London: T&T Clark, 2012.

———. "A Voice in the Wilderness: Classical Rhetoric and the Testimony of John (the Baptist) in John 1:19–34." Pages 119–40 in *Abiding Words: The Use of Scripture in the Gospel of John.* Edited by Alicia D. Myers and Bruce G. Schuchard. RBS 81. Atlanta: SBL Press, 2015.

Myers, Alicia D., and Bruce G. Schuchard, eds. *Abiding Words: The Use of Scripture in the Gospel of John.* RBS 81. Atlanta: SBL Press, 2015.

Reed, Annette Yoshiko. "Textuality between Death and Memory: The Prehistory and Formation of the Parabiblical Testament." *JQR* 104, no. 3 (2014): 381–412.

Reinhartz, Adele. *Cast Out of the Covenant: Jews and Anti-Judaism in the Gospel of John*. Lanham, MD: Lexington Books/Fortress Academic, 2018.

———. "The Gospel according to John." Pages 168–218 in *The Jewish Annotated New Testament*. Edited by Amy-Jill Levine and Marc Zvi Brettler. 2nd ed. Oxford: Oxford University Press, 2017.

Schneiders, Sandra S. *Written That You May Believe: Encountering Jesus in the Fourth Gospel*. 2nd ed. New York: Crossroad, 2003.

Schuchard, Bruce G. "Form Versus Function: Citation Technique and Authorial Intention in the Gospel of John." Pages 23–46 in *Abiding Words: The Use of Scripture in the Gospel of John*. Edited by Alicia D. Myers and Bruce G. Schuchard. RBS 81. Atlanta: SBL Press, 2015.

———. *Scripture within Scripture: The Interrelationship of Form and Function in the Explicit Old Testament Citations in the Gospel of John*. SBLDS 133. Atlanta: Scholars Press, 1992.

Sheridan, Ruth. *Retelling Scripture: "The Jews" and the Scriptural Citations in John 1:19–12:15*. BibInt 110. Leiden: Brill, 2012.

———. "The Testimony of Two Witnesses: John 8:17." Pages 161–84 in *Abiding Words: The Use of Scripture in the Gospel of John*. Edited by Alicia D. Myers and Bruce G. Schuchard. RBS 81. Atlanta: SBL Press, 2015.

Williams, Catrin H. "Composite Citations in John." Pages 94–127 in *New Testament Uses*. Edited by Sean A. Adams and Seth M. Ehorn. Vol. 2 of *Composite Citations in Antiquity*. LNTS 593. London: Bloomsbury, 2018.

———. "Patriarchs and Prophets Remembered: Framing Israel's Past in the Gospel of John." Pages 187–212 in *Abiding Words: The Use of Scripture in the Gospel of John*. Edited by Alicia D. Myers and Bruce G. Schuchard. RBS 81. Atlanta: SBL Press, 2015.

12

Israel's Scriptures in Acts

DIETRICH RUSAM

The Acts of the Apostles is the continuation of Luke's Gospel. This work, following the destiny of Jesus and the resurrection, deals with the spreading of the Christian message. Only secondarily does the fate of individual persons play a role here. Acts begins with a detailed account of the ascension of the Risen One (Acts 1:4-11). This marks the beginning of the Christian mission described in the book. These are the last words of the Risen One to his disciples: "But you will receive power when the Holy Spirit has come upon you; and you will be my witnesses in Jerusalem, in all Judea and Samaria, and to the ends of the earth" (Acts 1:8).[1] The stages of the inception of the mission are Jerusalem, Judaea, Samaria, and the whole pagan world.

From now on the core of the Christ confessors is on their own (Acts 1:13-14). The feast of Pentecost (2:1-41) with its "preparations" (1:15-26) has as its consequence the first Christian community (1:42-47). The following chapters deal with Jerusalem and depict, with Peter and John as the protagonists, later joined by Stephen, the fate of the growing church. For the author of Acts, the stoning of Stephen is basically the opportunity to introduce the protagonist of the second part of Acts, Saul (Paul; Acts 8:1), and an important example of the incipient persecution of the Jerusalem community (cf. 12:1), so that a scattering of the church members first begins in Judea and Samaria (8:1-3).

The Christian missionary history in these two parts of the Roman province of Syria is presented up to 11:18. At this stage, the call of Saul (Paul) occurs, together

---

1. Unless otherwise noted, all translations are from the NRSV.

with the theoretical justification of the mission to the gentiles by the visions of Peter (10:1–48).

The worldwide mission to the gentiles starts with Acts 11:18, a verse that as well as 8:1 alludes to Acts 1:8. The name χριστιανοί ("Christians") appears here for the first time for the congregation in Antioch (Acts 11:26). Thus, for Luke, the new community has detached itself from Judaism locally and organizationally and has established itself as an independent entity. In this phase, the three missionary journeys of Paul, the meeting in Jerusalem with James and Peter (and probably also with John), and the imprisonment and trial of Paul, which ends with his transfer to Rome, are told. Here Paul preaches the kingdom of God for two years and teaches about Jesus Christ with all boldness "unhindered" (or "no one forbidding him"); this is also the last word of Acts in the Greek text.

The open ending of Acts has often been discussed. There are two reasons in particular for the author's intention to have deliberately designed the conclusion in this way. First, the death of Paul, which appears to be presupposed in Acts 20:24 and 21:13, would mark a conclusion that is not intended to be so. And second, the plan of salvation drawn up by the Risen One at his ascension in Acts 1:8 of the disciples witnessing to the ends of the earth was not reached with the arrival of the message in Rome, the center of the world. The commission of the Risen One in Acts 1:8 extends to the present day. Thus, the readers become a part of the history of the proclamation of the gospel. The open ending is thus a literary move on the part of Luke.

In Acts we often find a detailed or suggestive engagement with the Jewish Scriptures. In addition to marked and unmarked quotations, Luke also uses verbal allusions to a concrete written word, as well as references to a theme of Jewish Scripture. As in Luke, it is always the narrative figures who argue with Scripture, never the narrator himself. Thus, the figures become "reliable characters" for the reader.[2] The quotations are frequently found at the beginning (Acts 1–5), when the first apostles—especially Peter—appear, and in the middle (Acts 13, in the first Pauline speech) of Acts. After the ascension of Jesus (Acts 1:1–14), the disciples and the first community have to make sure that what has happened and what they will do in the future is in accordance with Scripture.

---

2. Wayne C. Booth, *The Rhetoric of Fiction*, 2nd ed. (Chicago: University of Chicago Press, 1983), 211–15, introduced this terminology into literary studies; cf. Robert C. Tannehill, *The Narrative Unity of Luke-Acts: A Literary Interpretation*, 2 vols. (Philadelphia: Fortress, 1986–1990), 1:8: "When the views of a character do mirror those of the implied author, we have 'reliable commentary.'"

Here Peter plays a prominent role. Thus, in the first five chapters of Acts, a scriptural word is quoted no less than fifteen times (marked or unmarked). Then there is another scriptural quotation in the story of the baptism of the Ethiopian eunuch in Acts 8:32–33, before Paul refers several times to Scripture in his first sermon in Acts 13. At the Jerusalem council, James, the brother of Jesus, pronounces the common decision (Acts 15:16–18) with the help of Scripture, and at the end of the book of Acts, it is once again Paul who looks back on his experiences on the basis of Isa 6:9–10 (Acts 28:26–27).

For Luke, the whole Scripture is to be understood prophetically. In Acts 3:22 and 7:37 Moses is called a "prophet" explicitly. Since he is regarded as the author of the Torah (cf. Luke 24:26, 44), the Torah is to be interpreted accordingly. The following Torah passages are quoted or alluded to in Acts: Gen 1; 22:18; Exod 3:6, 15; 20:11; Lev 23:29; Deut 18:15, 19; 21:22. According to early Jewish understanding, 1 and 2 Samuel and 1 and 2 Kings belong to the "former prophets." Accordingly, Luke's Paul also calls Samuel a "prophet" (Acts 13:20; cf. 3:24). First Samuel 13:14 in Acts 13:22 is to be interpreted accordingly. In addition, the actual scriptural prophets are a treasure trove for scriptural passages that are to be interpreted as the history of Jesus and of mission. The passages Isa 11:1; 44:28; 53:7–8; 55:3; Amos 6:9–10; 9:11–12; Joel 3:1–5; Hab 1:5 are all quoted or alluded to in Acts. However, the Lukan characters prefer the Psalms. Thus, we find the following passages in Acts: Pss 2:1–2, 7; 16:8–11; 69:26; 89:21; 109:8; 110:1; 118:22; 146:6.[3] Here it is striking that Ps 16:8–11 is used both by Peter in his sermon on Pentecost (Acts 2:25–28) and, in abbreviated form, by Paul in his "inaugural sermon" (Acts 13:23). According to Luke, Peter and Paul therefore agree theologically. The broad use of the Psalms is possible for Luke because in his opinion the author of the Psalms, David, can be called a prophet (Acts 2:16), too.[4] Luke shares the common view that the Psalms are to be understood prophetically.[5] When Peter refers in Acts 3:18, 24 to "all prophets" and in Acts 3:21 to "God's holy prophets," Luke means the entire Jewish Scripture, which is to be understood prophetically. This is also made clear by the fact that precisely the three groups of Scriptures in Acts play an outstanding role that according to Luke 24:44 bear witness to Jesus: the Torah of Moses, the Prophets, and the Psalms.

---

3. Even though Luke undoubtedly uses the Septuagint, this chapter is based on the numbering of the Hebrew.

4. Cf. b. Pesaḥ. 117a; see Notker Füglister, "Die Verwendung und das Verständnis der Psalmen und des Psalters um die Zeitenwende," in *Beiträge zur Psalmenforschung: Psalm 2 und 22*, ed. Josef Schreiner, FB 60 (Würzburg: Echter, 1988), 367.

5. See Füglister, "Die Verwendung und das Verständnis der Psalmen," 368.

Israel's Scripture in the Book of Acts

Peter as a "Reliable Character"

The Election of Matthias (Acts 1)

Scripture twice attests a person taken up into heaven, and Acts 1:4-12 consciously recalls the ascension of Enoch (Gen 5:24) or Elijah (2 Kgs 2:11-12). However, there are no direct verbal allusions.

The first quotation from the Scriptures in Acts is fundamental: in Acts 1:20 Peter quotes Pss 69:26 and 109:8[1] in the context of the election of the twelfth apostle.[6] Shortly before, Peter describes the fate of the traitor Judas. This is of interest to him only because it shows the correctness of his argumentation: Judas had bought a field with the money he had received and had burst out in the middle and his bowels gushed out there.

Characteristic for the death of an enemy of God in antiquity is the "gushing of the guts."[7] Peter then expressly mentions that it had become known to all Jerusalemites that this field was therefore called the "field of blood." Thus Ps 69:26 was "fulfilled": "May his camp become desolate, and let there be no one to dwell in it." This quotation, which refers to an event that has already taken place, demonstrates to the reader the reliability of the use of Scriptures in Luke and the reliability of Peter. With the introduction "It had to be 'fulfilled'" it becomes clear: for Luke, the events related to Jesus and the apostolic mission are the "fulfillment" of the Scriptures of Israel.[8] After this retrospect, in the same breath (Acts 1:20), Peter quotes Ps 109:8 as an instruction for action.[9] Because Ps 69:26 has been fulfilled, Ps 109:8 must now also be fulfilled: "Let another take his office." If one compares the Septuagint version of the psalm, it becomes clear that the original form of the Septuagint (λάβοι) has been converted by the Lukan Peter to an

---

6. Cf. Tannehill, *Narrative Unity of Luke-Acts*, 2:21: "What Peter does through his speech in Acts 1:16-22 may seem a rather small thing.... Nevertheless, it can be understood as an important step in strengthening the community in the faith."

7. Cf. Herodotus, *Hist.* 4.205; Pausanias 9.36.2-3; Lucian, *Alex.* 59; Diodorus Siculus, *Bib. hist.* 13.2-3; Plutarch, *Sull.* 36.2; Apollodorus, *Bibliotheca* 3.5.1-2.

8. Cf. Luke 1:1; 4:27; 21:22; 24:44; Acts 3:18.

9. Similar to Luke 24:26, 44; and 22:37, δεῖ is found here in connection with the fulfillment of Scripture (cf. Tannehill, *Narrative Unity of Luke-Acts*, 2:20). Each time it is about the necessity of the suffering of Jesus. Cf. Robert L. Brawley, *Text to Text Pours Forth Speech: Voices of Scripture in Luke-Acts*, ISBL (Bloomington: Indiana University Press, 1995), 64: "Understanding the demise of Judas is still a part of understanding the passion of Jesus."

imperative (λάβετο) in order to make the instruction clear: "Let his position be taken by another!" In other words: now a new apostle is to be elected![10]

The Sermon at Pentecost (Acts 2)

The Pentecost event is patterned on an occurrence that had already happened in reverse in Jewish Scripture (cf. Gen 11:1–9). After being filled with the Holy Spirit in Acts 2, the hearers of the disciples ask themselves, "And how is it that we hear, each of us, in our own native language?" The fact that they understood Peter's sermon, in contrast to Gen 11:7, shows its success (Acts 2:41). For Luke the events of Pentecost, in narrative allusion to the result of Gen 11, are the abolition of language differences within the Christian community.

Peter interprets what had happened at Pentecost in a detailed sermon with the help of a quotation from Joel 3:1–5a. Here we find the longest quotation in Luke-Acts. Furthermore, the book of Joel is also named as the place where the quotation was found. For Luke the Pentecost event was predicted in Joel 3. Peter refers only briefly to the coming of the Spirit (2:33). But the last sentence of the citation gives Peter the opportunity to explain in four steps that the "Lord" is Jesus.[11]

The brief reference to the earthly work of Jesus (2:22; first step) is a conceptual allusion: The term "signs and miracles" is prepared by Acts 2:19 (Joel 3:3 has been altered here), and so it is very easily recognizable by the reader. At the same time, it alludes to the "signs and miracles" that God worked when Israel left Egypt (Exod 7:3; Deut 6:22; 7:19; 26:8; 28:46; 34:11; Neh 9:10; Ps 139:5), even though in the present context of verse 22 these terms describe the ministry of Jesus. The following verse mentions the crucifixion of Jesus—still without written proof (2:23; second step).[12] In the third step (2:24–32) we find a double scriptural proof for the resurrection of Jesus. At first, Peter quotes Ps 16:8–11, but in the following argument he uses only one verse from it (Ps 16:10). The other verses are quoted to emphasize Jesus's closeness to God.[13] The reference following the quotation from the Scriptures to the tomb of David in Jerusalem (cf. 1 Kgs 2:10),

---

10. According to Charles H. Cosgrove ("The Divine Δεῖ in Luke-Acts: Investigations into the Lukan Understanding of God's Providence," *NovT* 26, no. 2 [1984]: 183), Peter is (after Jesus) the second of the "initiators and strategists of the divine purpose."

11. See Gerhard Schneider, "Gott und Christus als KYRIOS nach der Apostelgeschichte," in *Lukas: Theologie der Heilsgeschichte. Aufsätze zum lukanischen Doppelwerk*, BBB 59 (Königstein: Hanstein, 1985), 213–26, esp. 225.

12. It is interesting that in verse 23, in addition to the presupposed divine "must" of Jesus's passion, the human question of guilt is addressed. This can later justify the call to repentance (v. 38; cf. Acts 3:13–19).

13. Acts 2:25–26 refer to the earthly life of Jesus.

which still exists "at present," is intended to show that David cannot have spoken of himself in Ps 16:8–11.[14]

The following verse, 2:30, contains a conceptual allusion to the promise of Nathan (2 Sam 7:12–13; cf. 1 Kgs 9:5; Ps 89:4–5). A verbal allusion to Ps 132:11 could also be suspected because only there is the promise of the descendant of David on Israel's throne described as an "oath of God."[15] Luke ensures that the reader is able to recognize the allusion by emphasizing it in the Gospel: Jesus is David's descendant (Ps 110:1 in Luke 20:41–44; cf. Luke 1:32–33). This makes it clear to Peter that in Ps 16:8–11 David spoke of Jesus as a prophet. Subsequently, Ps 16:10 is taken up again in 2:31, although in comparison with the quotation in verse 27 the tense is changed: while 2:27 was about prophecy (ἐγκαταλείψεις, future), it is now about fulfillment: Jesus actually did not see corruption (ἐγκατελείφθη, effective aorist).

In the fourth step (2:33–36) Peter uses Scripture to justify the ascension as a precondition for Jesus being the "Lord" (Acts 2:21). For this purpose, he puts the proof of Scripture aside and brings the train of thought to an end, which he had begun with the quotation of Joel: "The exalted one has received the promise of the Holy Spirit from the Father and has poured it out" (cf. Luke 24:49; Acts 1:4, 8). In fact, Peter invokes some of what the Risen One had claimed in Luke 24:46–49: the Scriptural conformity of the resurrection, the ascension, and the outpouring of the Spirit. Therefore, he takes over a word of Jesus (Mark 12:35–37; cf. Luke 20:41–44). This again shows the reliability of Peter. The use of Ps 110:1, which follows the wording of the Septuagint, shows that the throne of David (2:30; cf. Luke 1:32–33) does not mean the throne over Israel but dominion over all humankind. The exaltation of Jesus at the right hand of God is thus a messianic enthronement.[16] When Peter speaks in 2:35 of the enemies of the Messiah (Ps 110:1b), in the present context this is a call for his audience to repent. Acts 2:36 therefore expressly reminds them that they were responsible for the crucifixion. That is why Peter also calls them—similar to the Lukan Jesus (Luke 5:32 and 15:7, 10)—to conversion in 2:38.

All in all, Peter's speech has the function of proving Jesus to be the one who, as the messianic "Lord" seated at the right hand of God, poured out the Spirit on the

---

14. Josephus, *Ant.* 7.392–394; 13.249; and *J.W.* 1.61 tells us that the tomb of David in Jerusalem was known. Cf. Mark L. Strauss, *The Davidic Messiah in Luke-Acts: The Promise and Its Fulfillment in Lukan Christology*, JSNTSup 110 (Sheffield: Sheffield Academic, 1995), 138: "The unexpressed implication is that since David's tomb remains undisturbed, his body *did* undergo decay, so he cannot have fulfilled the prophecy spoken in Psalm 16."

15. Possibly also 2 Chr 6:9–10 and Pss. Sol. 17:4 are alluded to (cf. Martin Rese, *Alttestamentliche Motive in der Christologie des Lukas*, SNT 1 [Gütersloh: Mohn, 1969], 108).

16. See Jürgen Roloff, *Die Apostelgeschichte*, NTD 5 (Göttingen: Vandenhoeck & Ruprecht, 1981), 60.

disciples. For Luke the earthly Jesus is the "Lord" (Luke 1:43; 2:11; 5:8; 6:46; 7:6; 11:1; 22:61; 23:42), but it is Peter who brings the scriptural proof for this in Acts 2.

There is an unmarked quotation in Peter's answer (2:39) to the question of the audience. Joel 3:5b is, however, easily recognizable because Joel 3:1–5a was already cited in Acts 2:17–21. Here is the continuation of the Joel citation: "everyone whom the Lord our God calls to himself." The Lukan addition of "our God" is meant to underline that God himself is the subject of the election.

The Healing of the Paralytic (Acts 3)

In the context of the subsequent healing of the paralytic in Acts 3:1–9, there is a conceptual allusion to Scripture through the formulation that the affected person has been paralyzed "from the womb" (Judg 13:5; 16:17; Job 1:21; 38:8; Pss 22:11; 71:6; Jer 1:5; cf. also Wis 7:1).[17] This is the earliest possible time at which the bond with God begins. We see that Luke imitates the language of the Septuagint. The fact that Peter and John appear together here is probably due to the fact that according to Deut 19:15 two witnesses are necessary in case of doubt. For Luke, the healing of the paralyzed man is a prime example of the salvation that people can experience "by believing in the name of Jesus" (cf. Acts 2:21) and happens in continuation and imitation of Jesus's own healing ministry (cf. Luke 5:17–26; 7:22). The ability to produce "signs" is justified by Joel 3:3 (quoted in Acts 2:19). And Peter's speech after the healing also begins with a conceptual allusion: "The God of Abraham and Isaac and Jacob" introduces him with the same formulation toward Moses at the burning bush (Exod 3:6). Moses is to say to the Israelites: "The God of our fathers, the God of Abraham and the God of Isaac and the God of Jacob" has sent me to you (Exod 3:15). With the help of the apposition "the God of our fathers," Peter joins his listeners together. This identification with God is intended to evoke several associations at once.[18] The same formulation in Luke 20:37 shows that this God is a God of the living, who can very well raise the dead. And, in fact, the following passage also deals with the raising of the dead. The note that God glorified his "servant Jesus" is immediately followed by a verbal allusion to the servant of the Servant Song in Isa 52:13–53:12. There it is said that God's "servant will be exalted and very glorified." This hidden reference to Scripture is recognized by the reader after the quotation of Isa 52:12 in Luke 22:37 and the detailed quotation from Isa 53:7–8 in Acts 8:32–33. The fact that Jesus is exalted at the right hand of God and thus "glorified" was already

---

17. See Gerhard Schneider, *Die Apostelgeschichte*, 1. Teil: *Einleitung und Kommentar zu Kap 1,1–8,40*, HThK 5.1 (Freiburg im Breisgau: Herder, 1980), 299 n. 27.

18. Strauss, *Davidic Messiah in Luke-Acts*, 138.

"proven" in the Pentecost sermon.[19] This reference to Isa 53 is reinforced with the help of the attribute "just" (Isa 53:11; cf. Luke 23:19). After Acts 1:22 and 2:32, Peter stresses the resurrection for the third time in 3:15.

In Acts 3:18 Peter explicitly notes that God fulfilled "what he preached before through the mouth of all his prophets," that his Christ should suffer (cf. Luke 24:26, 46; cf. Acts 3:21). Interestingly, however, so far no written proof has been given of the necessity of Jesus's suffering. This is reserved for the entire early community in Acts 4.

Peter refers first to all the prophets (Acts 3:18, 21, 24) before he gives an example of the prophetic interpretation of Scripture. Acts 3:22–23 is a mixed quotation from Deut 18:15, 18; and Lev 23:29. There is no doubt that only the earthly Jesus can be meant by the "prophet like Moses" (cf. Luke 4:24; 7:16, 39; 24:19). The threat that those who do not listen to him will be exterminated is not without its problems, but it has a stabilizing function for the Christian community and justifies for Luke the necessity of conversion.[20] Peter thus verifies another aspect mentioned in Luke 24:46–47. In summary, Peter states that "all prophets from Samuel on" had also proclaimed "these days." He alludes to the introduction of the sermon on Pentecost (Acts 2:17). This is the time between the birth of Jesus and his second coming. This time of the call to repentance issued to Israel and the nations is the time of the fulfillment of the Scripture prophecies. The sermon in 3:25 is concluded with a citation of Gen 22:18 and Gen 26:4 with a promise known from the history of Abraham. Here the listeners are addressed as "sons of the prophets and of the covenant," a conceptual allusion to the covenant and the special relationship between Israel and the Lord (Exod 34:10; Ezek 37:26; Isa 55:3; etc.).

Genesis 22:18 comes closest to the wording offered by Luke in the quotation in 3:25 (cf. also Gen 26:4, as well as Gen 12:3). In the quotation, the term ἔθνη τῆς γῆς from the book of Genesis, which is used to refer exclusively to gentiles, is changed to πατριαὶ τῆς γῆς by Luke. This happens because the Jews are included.[21] Gentiles as well as Jews are now in the same way the subject of God's salvation. The only prerogative of the Jews is now that God has awakened his servant Jesus "first" for the Jews (3:26).

---

19. See Dietrich Rusam, *Das Alte Testament bei Lukas*, BZNW 112 (Berlin: de Gruyter, 2003), 341–42.

20. See Günter Wasserberg, *Aus Israels Mitte – Heil für die Welt: Eine narrative-exegetische Studie zur Theologie des Lukas*, BZNW 92 (Berlin: de Gruyter, 1998), 227.

21. Rese, *Alttestamentliche Motive*, 73; Gert J. Steyn, *Septuagint Quotations in the Context of the Petrine and Pauline Speeches of the Acta Apostolorum*, CBET 12 (Kampen: Kok Pharos, 1995), 155; Rusam, *Das Alte Testament*, 358–59.

Before the High Council (Acts 4)

Peter and John had been taken prisoner because of the healing of the paralyzed man and the subsequent riot. On the following day they were brought before the rulers and elders and scribes. The question posed to them, "By what power or in what name did you do this?" gives Peter the opportunity to preach about Jesus again. First, he offers a short summary of Acts 3:6 in verse 10, then he calls Jesus κεφαλὴ γωνίας (cornerstone), using a verbal allusion to Ps 118:22. The marker may be missing because in Luke 20:17-18 Jesus himself had already quoted Ps 118:22-23. It has been assumed that behind the version of Ps 118:22 that Acts 4:11 offers here is the Hebrew text because it is said that the builders "mocked" the stone—and not "rejected" it (as in the Septuagint and in Luke 20:17). But by changing the verb, Luke adapts the psalm to the "mockery" of Jesus by Herod and his soldiers (Luke 23:11; cf. Luke 18:14).[22] This is how Peter addresses his audience directly: they are these people who had "mocked" Jesus. For the first time it is indicated in Luke-Acts that the passion of Jesus is also foretold in the Jewish Scriptures. With the resurrection, Jesus became the cornerstone. Peter's short speech aims to show that the resurrection of Jesus enables him to heal.

The Believers' Prayer (Acts 4)

The healing of the paralyzed man (Acts 3:1-11), with the subsequent speech of Peter (Acts 3:12-26) and the trial (Acts 4:1-22), has shown the reader for the first time that the Jerusalem temple aristocracy is turning against the message of the risen and exalted Christ Jesus. The reaction to this first experience of oppression is an internal stabilization of the first Christian congregation: they come together in order to resist the pressure. That is why Luke says a common prayer at this point. Its introduction (4:24) contains a conceptual allusion since the phrase "lift up the voice" appears in Judg 2:4; 9:7; Ruth 1:9, 14; 1 Sam 11:4; 24:17; 2 Sam 3:32; 13:36. This awakens the expectation that further scriptural evidence will follow. Similarly, the address of God as δεσπότης and the one who "made heaven and earth and the sea and all that is in them" is a conceptual allusion to God's work of creation (Gen 1-2; cf. also Exod 20:11; Ps 146:6).[23] The mention of God's creative activity in the Jewish Bible usually has a soteriological function. Faith

---

22. See J. Ross Wagner, "Psalm 118 in Luke-Acts: Tracing a Narrative Thread," in *Early Christian Interpretation of the Scriptures of Israel: Investigations and Proposals*, ed. Craig A. Evans and James A. Sanders, JSNTSup 148 (Sheffield: Sheffield Academic, 1997), 173 n. 65.

23. See Michael Dömer, *Das Heil Gottes: Studien zur Theologie des lukanischen Doppelwerkes*, BBB 51 (Cologne: Hanstein, 1978), 66.

in creation justifies the confidence that God can and will save his people (cf. Pss 121:2; 124:8; 134:3). The following quotation is introduced as a word of God, which is pronounced by "our father" David (4:25a). The fact that David is referred to here as "our father" alludes to Acts 2:29, where Peter calls David "patriarch." Both times a quotation from the Psalms follows. The idea that the Holy Spirit spoke through David's mouth is already attested in Acts 1:16. The wording of the quotation (4:25-26) corresponds exactly to the version of Ps 2:1-2. The two subjects (ἔθνη καὶ λαοί) represent the gentiles and the tribes of Israel in the Acts of the Apostles (cf. Luke 2:31; Acts 4:27). The designation of Jesus as ἅγιον παῖς ("holy servant"; 4:27) has a similar double function as the note "whom you anointed."[24] The "holy servant" is a verbal allusion to the servant of God from Isa 53 just like at the beginning of Peter's third speech in Acts 3:13 (cf. Acts 3:26). And the "anointing" of Jesus refers to the inaugural sermon of Jesus in Nazareth (Luke 4:18), where Jesus quotes Isa 61:1 and 58:6 as scriptural proof of his baptism (Luke 3:21-22). At the same time, the reader is reminded of the etymology of the word χριστός (Christos): Jesus is "Christos" (the Messiah, or the anointed one) because he is "anointed" by God: Similar to Acts 2:25-32, the actual quotation from the Scriptures is followed by a concrete transfer to the story of Jesus. The mention of the names "Herod" and "Pilate" recalls their role in the history of the passion of Jesus in Luke (Luke 23:1-25). In contrast to Mark's Gospel, Luke offers an interrogation scene before Herod Antipas, the ruler of Galilee (Luke 23:6-12) in addition to the interrogation before the Jewish council (Luke 22:63-71) and the trial before Pilate (Luke 23:1-5, 13-25). This interrogation is fruitless; Jesus refuses to testify. It culminates, after the accused was again handed over to Pilate, in the note, "And Herod and Pilate became friends with each other that very day" (Luke 23:12). Reading Acts 4:24-28, it becomes clear why Luke has included this third interrogation scene. It enables him to see Ps 2:1-2 as proof of the necessity of the suffering of Jesus. Herod is the representative of the "kings of the earth" and Pilate represents the "rulers."[25] This now explains what Peter had prepared in his previous speech with the allusion to Ps 118:22 (the rejected "cornerstone") in Acts 4:11: Jesus Christ had to suffer. This conviction was only generally stated in the words of the Risen One in Luke 24:26, 46. Now, finally, it is exemplified. Acts 4:28 summarizes once again the conformity of the passion of Jesus with Scripture. The

---

24. Cf. Donald Lee Jones, "The Title 'Servant' in Luke-Acts," in *Luke-Acts: New Perspectives from the Society of Biblical Literature Seminar*, ed. Charles H. Talbert (New York: Crossroad, 1984), 157; contra Darrell L. Bock, *Proclamation from Prophecy and Pattern: Lucan Old Testament Christology*, JSNTSup 12 (Sheffield: Sheffield Academic, 1987), 188-90.

25. Wim J. C. Weren, "Psalm 2 in Luke-Acts: An Intertextual Study," in *Intertextuality in Biblical Writings: Essays in Honour of Bas van Iersel*, ed. Sipke Draisma (Kampen: Kok, 1989), 200.

conclusion of the prayer (4:29-30) by using the terms "threaten" (cf. Acts 4:17, 21) and "boldness" (cf. Acts 4:13) again refers to the context, the speech of Peter before the council. Since the healing of the paralyzed man is to be understood as a single example of the "signs and miracles" (cf. Acts 2:19) predicted in Joel 3:1-5, the community expects further "signs and miracles" or "healings" (v. 30).[26] The mention of the "name" of Jesus also refers to Peter's description of the healing of the paralyzed man (Acts 3:6, 16; 4:7, 10, 12). By using the title "holy servant" for Jesus (already known from 4:27; cf. Acts 3:13), Luke reminds us of the quotation. Finally, the last verse (4:31) of the prayer states the fulfillment: the earthquake at the place where the community gathered is another example of "signs and miracles" and thus leads back to Acts 2:17-21 (Joel 3:1-5).

Again before the Jewish Council (Acts 5)

The reason for the last speech of Peter in Acts (Acts 5:29-32) is the liberation of the apostles from the prison into which they had been thrown because of the "signs and miracles" (Acts 5:12) that had happened through their hands. The term "signs and miracles" is, as we have already seen, a conceptual allusion to the (slightly altered) quotation of Joel 3:3 in Peter's sermon at Pentecost (Acts 2:19; cf. also 2:22). The miracles of the apostles "prove" that the Holy Spirit was poured out over the disciples by the Lord Jesus, who was exalted at the right hand of God. The beginning of the christological part of the sermon is structured like the beginning of the third speech of Peter in Acts 3:13-26: The opening formulation "the God of our fathers" is a contextual allusion both to Acts 3:13, and thus also to Exod 3:6, 15 (cf. also Luke 20:37 and Acts 7:32). Each time Peter emphasizes the common starting point between the apostles and the Jewish council. The brevity of the formulations in Acts 5:30 shows that it is important here to remind the reader of the argumentation in Acts 3:13. Peter alludes to Deut 21:22 without marking the allusion. There it is commanded to hang on the wood only those who have committed a sin worthy of death. This allusion is intended to make it clear that the execution of Jesus was not just. The shame of the cross stands in sharp contrast to God's saving action. Peter had pointed to this contrast in Acts 3:13-15. With the note of the exaltation of Jesus to the right hand of God, the following, 5:31, alludes to Acts 2:33 (cf. also Luke 20:42; 22:69; Acts 7:55-56) and thus verbally also to Ps 110:1. With the help of the title "leader," the third speech of Peter is referred to again, in which the salvific-historical necessity of

---

26. See Wolfgang Weiss, *"Zeichen und Wunder": Eine Studie zu der Sprachtradition und ihrer Verwendung im Neuen Testament*, WMANT 67 (Neukirchen-Vluyn: Neukirchener Verlag, 1995), 88.

the penitential sermon was proven. In Acts 5:31 only Israel is the addressee of this sermon because the gentiles in Acts 5 do not belong to Peter's audience. The note about the gift of the Spirit refers not only to the Pentecost event (Acts 1:8; 2:3-4, 17-18, 33) but explicitly to the gift of the Spirit to all church members; they receive the Spirit at their baptism (Acts 2:38; cf. Acts 4:31).

The function of this last sermon of Peter's is to prove the correctness of the *clausula Petri*: we must obey God rather than men (5:29). This thesis had already been hinted at in the end of the first trial of Peter and John before the council (Acts 4:19). Therefore, the topic of "obeying" is taken up again at the end (5:32). In order to avoid redundancy, Luke refrains here from once again summarizing the biblical argument developed in the previous sermons.[27] So, the unmarked scriptural references (with the exception of Deut 21:22 in Acts 5:30) allude to scriptural passages already quoted in Acts. Peter fulfills the task Jesus had given him in Luke 22:32 to strengthen the brethren, as outlined precisely in Luke 24:44-49.

Stephen as "Reliable Character" (Acts 7)

Stephen's speech differs from Peter's sermons in three important points: (1) it does not refer anywhere to its instigation, the attack on Stephen; (2) it has no christological message; and (3) it also contains no call to conversion. For this reason, it has even been assumed that Stephen's speech did not originally belong to Acts of the Apostles.[28] But the differences to Peter's speeches can be explained: Luke refrained from putting his christological message in Stephen's mouth again because this would have been redundant—both for the council and for the readers. Moreover, Stephen is not an apostle (cf. Acts 1:21-22) and therefore does not have to fulfill the task of the Risen One (Luke 24:44-49). The starting point of the speech is the assertion of the false witnesses that Stephen constantly speaks against the temple and Torah (Acts 6:13). In his speech, Stephen offers a historical retrospective that makes clear that the Israelites had shown themselves to be unruly toward God, but also how God had reacted to this stubbornness. So, Stephen's speech is to be interpreted as an integral part of the book of Acts.[29]

Therefore, Stephen can refrain from marking the quotations. Luke deliberately chooses the first six citations in order to name key points of Israel's history

---

27. Roloff, *Die Apostelgeschichte*, 103.
28. See Traugott Holtz, *Untersuchungen über die alttestamentlichen Zitate bei Lukas*, TUGAL 104 (Berlin: Akademie, 1968), 87; Roloff, *Die Apostelgeschichte*, 117; and Bock, *Proclamation from Prophecy and Pattern*, 216.
29. John J. Kilgallen, *The Stephen Speech: A Literary and Redactional Study of Acts 7:2-53*, AnBib 67 (Rome: Biblical Institute Press, 1976), 84; Helmer Ringgren, "Luke's Use of the Old Testament," *HTR* 79, no. 1/3 (1986): 235.

with God: Acts 7:3 (Gen 12:1) deals with the beginning of the history of salvation. In Acts 7:6–7 (Gen 15:13–14; Exod 3:12) the Abrahamic promise is aimed at the temple. Then Stephen reports the (first) opposition of an Israelite to Moses (Acts 7:27–28; cf. Exod 2:14). With the quotation from Exod 3:5–10 in Acts 7:32–34, Moses's vocation is described. The abbreviated but still detailed quotation in this context shows the special relationship between God and Moses. The rejection of Moses by the people becomes clearer. The following allusion to Deut 18:15 in Acts 7:37 is modeled after the third speech of Peter (Acts 3:22). Stephen quotes the same words as Peter. Thus, Luke ensures continuity from Peter to Stephen. The fates of Moses and Jesus are similar: both have been rejected by the people of Israel.[30] The last unmarked quotation in Stephen's speech (Acts 7:39–40; Exod 32:1) is intended to show the audience of Stephen (including the readership of Acts) the general stubbornness of the Israelites toward God. According to Stephen, Israel has repeatedly turned against the messengers of God: Acts 7:9–11 deal with the opposition to Joseph and 7:24–29 and 35–41 with the opposition to Moses.[31]

The following quotation from Amos 5:25–27 in Acts 7:42–43 has the function of justifying God's turning away from Israel as a consequence of their stubbornness. It "functions as an illustration of οὐκ ἐφυλάξατε" (cf. Acts 7:53).[32] The marking shows the key function for the speech: with the reference to the exile, it proves the credibility of Stephen. But at the same time, it connects the main reproach (namely that Israel has repeatedly turned away from God) with the aim of Stephen's speech: to make it clear that the temple has basically no meaning (anymore) for God. This rejection of the temple by God is made clear by a final marked quotation from Isa 66:1–2 in Acts 7:49–50. Often this quotation has been interpreted in such a way that God has generally rejected the temple cult. But this contradicts the positive attitude of Luke toward the temple that we find at other places in his work (cf. Luke 2; 19:45–21:38; 24:53; Acts 2:46; 3:11; 5:20; 7:6–7; 21:26; 22:17; 24:18). But we must note that for the readers of Luke–Acts, the temple has already been destroyed. Thus, the citation has the following double function in the present context: (1) Stephen makes clear that it is not he who is speaking against the temple, it is God himself who has turned against it. (2) Because the last quotation has no time reference, it retains its validity in the present and in the future. On the level of the reader of the Acts of the Apostles, the quotation has the function of playing down the catastrophe of the destruction of the tem-

---

30. Consult Wolfgang Kraus, "Die Bedeutung von Dtn 18,15–18 für das Verständnis Jesu als Prophet," *ZNW* 90, no. 3–4 (1999): 160.

31. According to Kilgallen, *Stephen Speech*, 84, this quotation has a key role in the understanding of Stephen's speech.

32. Jan de Waard, *A Comparative Study of the OT Text in the Dead Sea Scrolls and in the New Testament*, STDJ 4 (Leiden: Brill, 1965), 46.

ple in 70 CE, which is actually not unimportant for the Christian community either. Thus, this is a word of consolation: the temple has been destroyed, but this has no meaning because "the Most High does not dwell in houses made by hands" (7:48).

Philip as "Reliable Character" (Acts 8)

The stoning of Stephen (Acts 7) as an exemplary act of persecution (cf. Acts 8:1-3) showed the situation of the Christian community in Jerusalem. Therefore, Luke describes step by step the turning of the Christian mission to the gentiles, which had to take place (Acts 1:8; 3:25; cf. Gen 22:18). A first act is the mission to the Samaritans by Philip (Acts 6:5; 8:5, 12, 25). However, because Philip is not an apostle but "only" a deacon, this extension of the mission has to be subsequently approved by the apostles (Acts 8:14-17). This is followed by the presentation of the baptism of the Ethiopian eunuch (Acts 8:26-40). It remains open whether Luke imagined this man to be a gentile or a Jew. In any case it seems that he is a man who until this point had been excluded from salvation.[33] The introduction to the quotation of Isa 53:7-8 (Acts 8:32-33) is similarly elegant to the quotation in Luke 4:17: it is not said that the Scripture is read. Thus, Luke blurs the narrated story with the reader's present. Unlike Acts 2:29-33 or Acts 4:27-28, no interpretation is given. The note, according to which Philip began with this Scripture "and told him the good news about Jesus" (8:35), requires the reader to make this interpretation by himself. The quotation refers back to the whole of salvation history (passion, raising from the dead, and exaltation), and so it refers to the earlier quotations (e.g., to the passion in Luke 18:31; 24:27). Because Peter's sermons are in mind, the interpretation of the quotation by Philip in Acts 8 remains colorless.[34] At the same time, the rhetorical question ("Who can describe his generation?") shows that the meaning reaches the present of the readers. According to Luke 8:19-21, the "generation" of Jesus is all "those who hear the word of God and do it." This reflects Peter's call at the end of the Pentecost sermon: "Save yourselves ἀπὸ τῆς γενεᾶς τῆς σκολιᾶς ['from this crooked generation']" (Acts 2:40). This salvation takes place through the incorporation into the family of Jesus through baptism (Acts 2:38, 41; cf. Acts 8:36). The Ethiopian's rhetorical question, "What prevents me from being baptized?" (Acts 8:36) indicates that

---

33. Most scholars guess that he must have been a gentile (cf. already Eusebius, *Hist. eccl.* 2.1.13); cf. Schneider, *Die Apostelgeschichte*, 489; Roloff, *Die Apostelgeschichte*, 139; and F. Scott Spencer, *The Portrait of Philip in Acts: A Study of Roles and Relations*, JSNTSup 67 (Sheffield: JSOT Press, 1992), 173, who argues that the eunuch "fits the same basic category of 'God-fearer' (the absence of the term notwithstanding) as the Roman centurion Cornelius."

34. See Roloff, *Die Apostelgeschichte*, 142.

Israel's Scriptures in Acts

the border of Judaism has fallen. All in all, through his preaching and baptismal practice in the context of Acts, Philip proves himself to be a faithful "disciple" of Peter (Acts 2–3) or Jesus (Luke 24:44–49).

Paul as a "Reliable Character" (Acts 13:13–49)

From Acts 13 forward, the task of the reliable narrative character is continuously performed by Paul. Similar to Jesus in Luke 4:16–29, a synagogue service forms the background for Paul's first sermon, which takes place in the synagogue of Antioch in Pisidia (Acts 13:13–49).

Before Paul speaks of the message of Christ, he describes the most important historical salvation experiences for Israel. He can do without an explicit marking of the quotations. He begins in 13:17–19, similarly to Stephen, with the election of the fathers (cf. Gen 12:1–3), the migration in the desert (cf. Deut 1:31), and the liberation of Israel from Egypt and describes the history of Israel as the history of God's care for his people up to the institution of David as king. The scriptural passage cited here (Acts 13:22) is a mixed quotation of 1 Sam 13:14; Ps 89:21; and Isa 44:28. Whereas long periods of time were previously described with a few sentences, the marked quotation now slows down the narrated time to the speed of the narrative. With the help of this "slow motion," it becomes clear what is important to the narrator: David's special reference to God. According to Luke this is the "forefather" of Jesus (Luke 1:32; 3:31; 18:38–39; 20:41–44; Acts 13:23). The aim of the salvific overview is proving that Jesus is Israel's savior (cf. Luke 2:10). What this salvation consists of will only be shown later (13:38). In verses 26–31 the Pauline message is presented in a similar way to Peter's message. Thus Paul (cf. Peter in Acts 3:17) blames the inhabitants of Jerusalem for the execution of Jesus (Acts 13:27). But this is at the same time the "fulfillment" of the words of the prophets (Acts 3:18; cf. also the quotation from Ps 2:1–2 in Acts 4:25–26). The fact that the action of the Jerusalemites is contrasted with the briefly described resurrection of Jesus (13:30) is reminiscent of Acts 3:15 and 4:10. Finally, Paul refers in 13:31 to the meaning of the "witnesses" (cf. Luke 24:48; Acts 1:22; 2:32; 10:40–41). His sermon is in continuity with the preaching of the witnesses (μάρτυρες) even if Paul cannot claim this title for himself.

In 13:32 Paul's exegetical argumentation begins. And it is not by chance that he immediately speaks of Jesus's appearance on earth. The Greek word used here (ἀνιστάναι) could be interpreted as "resurrect" or simply as "occur."[35] But it appears in Acts 3:22, 26; 7:37 in the second sense, so it becomes clear what is meant

---

35. For "resurrect," see Rese, *Alttestamentliche Motive*, 83; Roloff, *Die Apostelgeschichte*, 207. For "occur," see Strauss, *Davidic Messiah in Luke-Acts*, 162.

here. The corresponding scriptural proof is offered by Paul with the help of the precisely marked Ps 2:7 ("in the second psalm"). According to Wim Weren, this precise indication speaks for the fact "that the verse quoted functions as a *pars pro toto*."[36] Here the text literally follows the Septuagint, too. Immediately after this (13:34), Paul addresses the raising from the dead of Jesus with the help of Isa 55:3.[37] This shows again the fact that in the following, Ps 2:7 cannot speak of David, while the faithfulness of God to the promises made to David is emphasized. The quotation of Ps 16:10 is reminiscent of Peter's sermon on Pentecost (Acts 2:27). Therefore, the argumentation according to which David cannot speak of himself here, but rather Jesus must be meant, can be abbreviated in comparison to Peter's sermon.[38] The difference between the argumentation in Acts 2 and Acts 13 consists only in the aim of the two speeches. Peter wants to prove that the resurrection and exaltation of Jesus had already been predicted in the Jewish Scriptures and that therefore it can be established that the crucified one is the Christ and Lord (Acts 2:36). Paul's sermon in Antioch has as its aim the proof of God's faithfulness to his people. That is why the biblical argument is preceded by a brief outline of salvation history. The christological part of the sermon is under the topic "God fulfills his promises." Both Peter and Paul promise their listeners forgiveness of sins (Acts 2:38; 13:38). Paul's speech ends in 13:41 with the marked citation of Hab 1:5, warning the listeners not to reject the message of Christ. This also has its counterpart in Peter's Pentecost sermon (Acts 2:40). The "work" of God is the inclusion of the gentiles in salvation history. Acts 13:44–45 and 17:4–5 show that the Jewish opposition to the Christian proclamation is ignited by the phenomenon of proclamation to gentiles (cf. also Luke 4:28–29).[39] Paul in Acts 13:46–47 is able to understand the gentile mission with the help of Isa 49:6 as the fulfillment of Jewish Scripture. For the readers of the book of Acts, this legitimizes the actual progress of the Christian mission with its already well-established gentile mission. With the turn to the gentiles, Paul now explicitly poses the question about the reception of salvation by the gentiles and the associated question about possession and observance of the Torah (Acts 13:38–39, 46).

James as "Reliable Character" (Acts 15)

After the first gentile, the centurion Cornelius, had been converted by Peter because of a divine intervention (Acts 10) and after Paul's first mission journey

---

36. Weren, "Psalm 2 in Luke-Acts," 198.
37. Steyn, *Septuagint Quotations*, 179; Bock, *Proclamation from Prophecy and Pattern*, 251.
38. Cf. the parallels of Acts 2:29–31 and 13:36; Rusam, *Das Alte Testament*, 407.
39. Cf. Steyn, *Septuagint Quotations*, 200: "The function of this quotation here is thus to make it clear: this has to happen, they have to turn now from the Jews to the gentiles with the message of salvation."

(Acts 13–14), Luke describes a meeting of the apostles in Jerusalem in which it is to be clarified whether the gentile Christians must be circumcised or not, as already practiced. At this meeting Peter tries to prove the fundamental similarity of gentiles and Jews with regard to salvation (15:7–11). With the help of a verbal allusion—the prohibition of putting the Lord to the test (cf. Deut 6:16; Pss 78:18, 41, 56; 106:14; Mal 3:15)—he rejects the demand for circumcision in general: whoever binds purity to circumcision puts God to the test because he denies the purification of hearts given by the Spirit. Paul and Barnabas use the following silence to tell of the "signs and miracles," an allusion to Joel 3:3 (Acts 2:19), which God had also done among the gentiles through them (cf. also Acts 14:3). Finally, James, the brother of Jesus, speaks. The reader knows his special role among the "brothers" in Jerusalem since Acts 12:17 (cf. also Gal 2:9). This sequence of speakers is carefully considered: Peter gives the direction, Paul may only illustrate, while the affirmative proof of Scripture is led by James. James is thus (after Peter, Stephen, Philip, and Paul) only the fifth person mentioned by name in the book of Acts to quote a passage from the Scriptures. The explicitly marked quotation of Amos 9:11–12 (Acts 15:16–18) also goes back to the version of the Septuagint. The reason for the changes that Luke has made is adaptation to the new context. The aim of the quotation is to show that the people of God (λαός, this noun always refers to the people of Israel in the Scripture) is now also constituted among the gentiles (ἔθνη). So, the previous meaning of λαός is reinterpreted (cf. Luke 1:32–33 and 1:68–79). This new people of God is made up of the remaining Jewish people (cf. Acts 3:23) and of all the gentiles (cf. Acts 3:25). According to Acts 15:17, it is about the people who ask "for the Lord" (these words are inserted and imitate Scripture language [cf. Ps 22:27; Prov 28:5, and many others]). Thus, the insertion "Christianizes" the quotation (cf. Acts 2:21). If God rebuilds "the tent of David that has fallen" in this way, then the conclusion can be drawn that no burden should be placed on the converted gentiles either; that is, they should not be hindered in their search for the Lord. James thus supports the previous speaker Peter in the principled rejection of the Jewish law as a way of salvation. The final sentence, according to which the Lord "makes these things known from old," refers to the scriptural proofs given so far by Peter, Stephen, Philip, and Paul.

In the following twelve chapters of Acts, there is not a single quotation from Scripture. This is because Luke prefers to put scriptural evidence into the mouths of his protagonists at their first appearance (Peter in Acts 1:20; Stephen in Acts 7; Philip in Acts 8:32–33; Paul in Acts 13:33–35; and James in Acts 15:16–18) to show their reliability for the implied author and reader. Moreover, Luke wants to verify the claim of the risen Lord that it is written in Scripture that Christ will suffer and rise from the dead and that preaching in his name should be done among all nations (Luke 24:44–49). In this way, he wants to give biblical reasons for the decisive passages in the history of the mission: the outpouring of the Holy Spirit at Pentecost (Acts 2), the resurrection of Jesus (Acts 2), the necessity of Jesus's suffering (Acts 4 and 5), and the offer of salvation to the gentiles (indicated in Acts 15).

In the following chapters, Luke merely describes Paul's progress on two missionary journeys until his arrival in Rome (Acts 28). There, finally, the last scriptural proof is given, in which the turning to the gentiles is explicitly justified.

Paul in Rome (Acts 28)

At the end of the book of Acts Paul quotes the inaugural vision of Isaiah (Isa 6:9–10 in Acts 28:25–27) in view of the differing opinions of the Roman Jews toward his proclamation. The aorist form in 28:27 (ἐπαχύνθη γὰρ ἡ καρδία) denotes a situational and not a durative state of heart. So, the obduracy is in Luke's view revocable by God at any time. But with the help of this Scripture, Luke is able to explain why the majority of his Jewish brothers and sisters refuse to accept the message of Jesus. It should be noted here that the final sentence of the quotation, "I will heal them" (Acts 28:27), is to be interpreted as God's promise.[40] Luke expresses the hope that the Jewish people will at some point be converted to Jesus by God. Paul proclaims the turning of salvation to the gentiles as provocative competition for the Jews who are "not listening" (28:28); thus the prophetic promise of Luke 3:6 is fulfilled at the end of Acts. The possibility of salvation for the gentiles encompasses Luke-Acts in a large arc (cf. 1:8; 8:26–40; 10:1–48; 15:1–28). A reaction of the Jews is no longer recounted. The Acts of the Apostles concludes open-endedly; the offer of salvation to Jews and gentiles remains (cf. also the quotation of Amos 9:11–12 in Acts 15:16–18). In this way, the present of the Lukan community is reached.

Conclusion

When the Lukan figures refer to Jewish Scripture, it is consistently based on the Septuagint. This is especially evident in the quotation of Ps 16:8–11 in Acts 2:25–28. If we first compare the Hebrew version with the Greek version, we find a total

---

40. Cf. Salvatore Mele, *A Causa della Speranza di Israele: Il finale del libro degli Atti (At 28,17–31) alla luce della predicazione ad Antiochia di Pisidia (At 13,13–52) e a Corinto (At 18,1–18)* (Assisi: Cittadella Editrice 2014), 68; Stefan Schreiber, "Das Schlusswort einer großen Apologie: Paulus, Jesaja und die Juden in Rom (Apg 28,16–31)," in *Antijudaismen in der Exegese? Eine Diskussion 50 Jahre nach Nostra Aetate*, ed. Stefan Schreiber and Thomas Schumacher (Freiburg im Breisgau: Herder, 2015), 221.

of six differences.[41] It is no coincidence that all these differences are incorporated by Luke in Acts 2:25–28. This observation shows that Luke offers the Septuagint version in Acts 2. Often Luke sees no need at all to change the Septuagint text (cf. Ps 110:1 with Acts 2:34–35; Ps 2:1–2 with Acts 4:25–26; Isa 53:7–8 with Acts 8:32–33; Ps 2:7 with Acts 13:33; Ps 16:10b with Acts 2:27 and 13:35; Isa 6:9–10 with Acts 28:26). In Acts, Jewish Scripture is used when individual men who make a decisive contribution to the mission's history (Peter, Stephen, Philip, Paul, and James) are introduced. Luke lets his reliable characters quote either with or without markings. Two quotations are found twice, once marked and once unmarked (Ps 118; Deut 18). The individual quotations are all taken from the Septuagint. If Luke deviates from the text, he does so in order to adapt the scriptural quotation to his concern and his context.

Formally, Luke uses every possibility to refer to the Jewish Scriptures. Interestingly, however, he only refrains from marking quotations if it is clear that the Jewish Scriptures are meant (as in the historical reviews of Acts 7 and 13) or if the alluded scriptural word has already been quoted before with a marking (Ps 16:10 in Acts 2:31 was quoted in Acts 2:25–28; and Joel 3:5b in Acts 2:39 is prepared in Acts 2:16–21). The same observation can be made with nearly every verbal allusion: they also appear in Luke-Acts in the context of a marked quotation. Thus, Luke ensures that the verbal allusions to the Jewish Scriptures are also recognized as such by the reader.

Table 12.1. Uses of Scripture in Acts

Scripture	Verbal allusion	Marked citation
Ps 132:22	Acts 2:30	Luke 1:32–33
Isa 53:7–8	Acts 3:14	Acts 8:32–33
Ps 118:22	Acts 4:11	Luke 20:17
Jes 61:1–2	Acts 4:27	Luke 4:18
Ps 110:1	Acts 5:31	Luke 20:41–44; Acts 2:33–35
Deut 6:16	Acts 15:11	Luke 4:12

In summary, three different ways of using Scripture can be seen in Acts:

1. Luke likes to use Jewish Scripture as a historical illustration and interpretation; especially in the historical overviews given by Stephen in Acts 7 and Paul in Acts 13, quotations appear in order to present the history of God with his people as the history of apostasy from God (Acts 7) or as the history of salvation (Acts 13:16–

---

41. See Bock, *Proclamation from Prophecy and Pattern*, 172–77.

22). The quotation of Joel at the beginning of the Pentecost sermon (Joel 3:1–5 in Acts 2:17–21) belongs in this context as an interpretation of the Pentecost event and the healings recounted in Acts (3:1–10; 4:12–16); so also with the last quotation in the Acts of the Apostles, Isa 6:9–10 in Acts 28:25–28 by Paul. The Jewish opposition to the message of Jesus, already visible in the history of Jesus and becoming more and more apparent in Acts, leads Paul to the realization of the (momentary) hardening, which will, however, be canceled in the future.

2. Central to Luke is the prophetic-Christian interpretation of Jewish Scripture. It is already practiced by Jesus (Luke 18:31–33) and claimed by the risen Lord (Luke 24:26–27, 44–47). Step by step, Peter (or the early church), Philip, and, of course, Paul verify these assertions of the risen Lord: the Christ "had to" suffer (Ps 118:22 in Acts 4:11; Ps 2:1–2 in Acts 4:25–28; Isa 53:7–8 in Acts 8:32–33), must be resurrected (Ps 16:8–11 in 2:24–32; Isa 55:3 and Ps 16:10 in Acts 13:34–35) and exalted (Ps 110:1 in Acts 2:34–35; Isa 52:13 in Acts 3:13; Ps 110:1 in Acts 5:31).

3. Above all, the Scriptures are interpreted as instructions for the Christian missionaries. Formally, this use is shown in the election of a replacement for Judas: in Acts 1:21 Peter quotes Ps 109:8 and concludes that an apostle must be elected. But in the sermon on Pentecost Peter theologically makes clear that the raising from the dead and exaltation of Jesus, founded by quotations from the Scriptures, requires the apostles to call their listeners to repentance (Acts 2:36, 38; cf. Deut 18:15, 18 in Acts 3:22–23). Peter sees the pagan mission justified by Gen 22:18 in Acts 3:25. Then it is in Acts 13:41 where Paul, with the help of Hab 1:5, warns his audience to listen to his words (cf. Acts 13:38). For him Isa 49:6 justifies the necessity of the mission of the gentiles (Acts 13:47). And James establishes this proclamation to the gentiles without observance of Jewish law with the help of Amos 9:11–12 (Acts 15:16–18).

Luke creates in Luke-Acts a new understanding of Jewish Scripture. When the Ethiopian eunuch asks Philip in Acts 8:34: "About whom, I ask you, does the prophet say this, about himself or about someone else?" the answer is obvious for the reader: the Jewish Scripture speaks of the suffering, risen, and exalted Christ. According to Luke, this is the main content of the Christian kerygma to the end of the earth (Acts 1:8).

Bibliography

Adams, Sean A. *The Genre of Acts and Collected Biography*. SNTSMS 156. Cambridge: Cambridge University Press, 2013.

Bock, Darrell L. *Proclamation from Prophecy and Pattern: Lucan Old Testament Christology*. JSNTSup 12. Sheffield: Sheffield Academic, 1987.

Booth, Wayne C. *The Rhetoric of Fiction*. 2nd ed. Chicago: University of Chicago Press, 1983.
Brawley, Robert L. *Text to Text Pours Forth Speech: Voices of Scripture in Luke-Acts*. ISBL. Bloomington: Indiana University Press, 1995.
Cosgrove, Charles H. "The Divine Δεῖ in Luke-Acts: Investigations into the Lukan Understanding of God's Providence." *NovT* 26, no. 2 (1984): 168–90.
Dömer, Michael. *Das Heil Gottes: Studien zur Theologie des lukanischen Doppelwerkes*. BBB 51. Cologne: Hanstein, 1978.
Füglister, Notker. "Die Verwendung und das Verständnis der Psalmen und des Psalters um die Zeitenwende." Pages 319–84 in *Beiträge zur Psalmenforschung: Psalm 2 und 22*. Edited by Josef Schreiner. FB 60. Würzburg: Echter, 1988.
Gibson, Jack J. *Peter between Jerusalem and Antioch: Peter, James and the Gentiles*. WUNT 2/345. Tübingen: Mohr Siebeck, 2013.
Holtz, Traugott. *Untersuchungen über die alttestamentlichen Zitate bei Lukas*. TUGAL 104. Berlin: Akademie, 1968.
Jacob Jervell, *The Theology of the Acts of the Apostles*. New Testament Theology. Cambridge: Cambridge University Press, 1996.
Jones, Donald Lee. "The Title 'Servant' in Luke-Acts." Pages 148–65 in *Luke-Acts: New Perspectives from the Society of Biblical Literature Seminar*. Edited by Charles H. Talbert. New York: Crossroad, 1984.
Kilgallen, John J. *The Stephen Speech: A Literary and Redactional Study of Acts 7:2–53*. AnBib 67. Rome: Biblical Institute Press, 1976.
Kraus, Wolfgang. "Die Bedeutung von Dtn 18,15–18 für das Verständnis Jesu als Prophet." *ZNW* 90, no. 3–4 (1999): 153–76.
Lane, Thomas J. *Luke and the Gentile Mission: Gospel Anticipates Acts*. EHS.T 571. Frankfurt am Main: Lang, 1996.
Mele, Salvatore. *A Causa della Speranza di Israele: Il finale del libro degli Atti (At 28,17-31) alla luce della predicazione ad Antiochia di Pisidia (At 13,13–52) e a Corinto (At 18,1–18)*. Assisi: Cittadella Editrice, 2014.
Neubrand, Maria. *Israel, die Völker und die Kirche: Eine exegetische Studie zu Apg 15*. SBB 55. Stuttgart: Katholisches Bibelwerk, 2006.
Rese, Martin. *Alttestamentliche Motive in der Christologie des Lukas*. Gütersloh: Mohn, 1969.
———. "Die Funktion der alttestamentlichen Zitate und Anspielungen in den Reden der Apostelgeschichte." Pages 61–79 in *Les Actes des Apôtres: Traditions, rédaction, théologie*. Edited by Jacob Kremer. BETL 48. Gembloux: Duculot, 1979.
Ringgren, Helmer. "Luke's Use of the Old Testament." *HTR* 79, no. 1/3 (1986): 227–35.
Roloff, Jürgen. *Die Apostelgeschichte*. NTD 5. Göttingen: Vandenhoeck & Ruprecht, 1981.
Rusam, Dietrich. *Das Alte Testament bei Lukas*. BZNW 112. Berlin: de Gruyter, 2003.
———. "Deuteronomy in Luke-Acts." Pages 63–81 in *Deuteronomy in the New Testa-*

ment. Edited by Maarten J. J. Menken and Steve Moyise. LNTS 358. London: T&T Clark, 2007.

Schneider, Gerhard. *Die Apostelgeschichte*, 1 Teil: *Einleitung und Kommentar zu Kap 1,1–8,40*. HThK 5.1. Freiburg im Breisgau: Herder, 1980.

———. "Gott und Christus als KYRIOS nach der Apostelgeschichte." Pages 213–26 in *Lukas: Theologie der Heilsgeschichte; Aufsätze zum lukanischen Doppelwerk*. BBB 59. Königstein: Hanstein, 1985.

Schreiber, Stefan. "Das Schlusswort einer großen Apologie: Paulus, Jesaja und die Juden in Rom (Apg 28,16–31)." Pages 203–31 in *Antijudaismen in der Exegese? Eine Diskussion 50 Jahre nach Nostra Aetate*. Edited by Stefan Schreiber and Thomas Schumacher. Freiburg im Breisgau: Herder, 2015.

Seul, Peter. *Rettung für alle: Die Romreise des Paulus nach Apg 27,1–28,16*. BBB 146. Berlin: Philo, 2003.

Spencer, F. Scott. *The Portrait of Philip in Acts: A Study of Roles and Relations*. JSNTSup 67. Sheffield: JSOT Press, 1992.

Steyn, Gert J. *Septuagint Quotations in the Context of the Petrine and Pauline Speeches of the Acta Apostolorum*. CBET 12. Kampen: Kok Pharos, 1995.

Strauss, Mark L. *The Davidic Messiah in Luke-Acts: The Promise and Its Fulfillment in Lukan Christology*. JSNTSup 110. Sheffield: Sheffield Academic, 1995.

Tannehill, Robert C. *The Narrative Unity of Luke-Acts. A Literary Interpretation*. 2 vols. Philadelphia: Fortress, 1986–1990.

Waard, Jan de. *A Comparative Study of the OT Text in the Dead Sea Scrolls and in the New Testament*. STDJ 4. Leiden: Brill, 1966.

Wagner, J. Ross. "Psalm 118 in Luke-Acts: Tracing a Narrative Thread." Pages 154–78 in *Early Christian Interpretation of the Scriptures of Israel: Investigations and Proposals*. Edited by Craig A. Evans and James A. Sanders. JSNTSup 148. Sheffield: Sheffield Academic, 1997.

Wasserberg, Günter. *Aus Israels Mitte – Heil für die Welt: Eine narrative-exegetische Studie zur Theologie des Lukas*. BZNW 92. Berlin: de Gruyter, 1998.

Weiss, Wolfgang. *"Zeichen und Wunder": Eine Studie zu der Sprachtradition und ihrer Verwendung im Neuen Testament*. WMANT 67. Neukirchen-Vluyn: Neukirchener Verlag, 1995.

Weren, Wim J. C. "Psalm 2 in Luke-Acts: An Intertextual Study." Pages 189–203 in *Intertextuality in Biblical Writings: Essays in Honour of Bas van Iersel*. Edited by Sipke Draisma. Kampen: Kok, 1989.

B. THE APOSTLE PAUL

13

Israel's Scriptures in Romans

JENS SCHRÖTER

Paul's letter to the Romans holds a special place among his writings. Written around 56 from Corinth as his last letter, Paul addresses the Christ believers in Rome who were for the most part unknown to him.[1] Toward the end of the letter he describes his own situation (Rom 15:22–29): he intends to visit the Roman Christians on his way to Spain and expects to get support from them for his ongoing journey. Before that, he will go to Jerusalem to deliver the collection from Macedonia and Achaia to the community there. From these remarks we can conclude that Paul considers his mission in the east of the Mediterranean world as accomplished and is about to go to the western regions. That the reference to his personal situation and his future plans appears only toward the end of the letter indicates that his upcoming visit in Rome was the occasion for the

---

1. Paul does not use the term ἐκκλησία for the Roman Christ believers as he does for the addressees of his other letters. The reason is probably that he was not well informed about the organizational structure of the Christ groups in Rome and that he himself did not establish a community there. From a historical viewpoint it is likely that the Christian faith in Rome was proclaimed among the Jews and then extended also to non-Jews. In his letter, Paul presupposes non-Jewish readers whom he several times addresses as "gentiles" (ἔθνη). In Rom 1:9–13 and 15:22–25 Paul expresses his longstanding desire to visit the Christ believers in Rome from which he had previously been prevented. In 16:3–15 he greets many people by name, much more than in his other letters. The long list gives the impression of a close relationship between Paul and his addressees in Rome and serves the purpose of justifying why Paul addresses the Roman Christ believers at all.

letter but does not determine its content. Instead, Romans can be characterized as a reflection about the gospel of Jesus Christ against the background of Paul's experiences during his mission in the eastern provinces. Based on the agreement with the apostles in Jerusalem (see Gal 2:7-9), he has preached the gospel to the gentiles in various cities and regions, primarily around the Aegean Sea. During his journeys he experienced resistance and hostility from both Jews and gentiles. Moreover, in the communities of Philippi, Corinth, and Galatia, he had to face opposition from other Jewish missionaries who called Paul's view of the gospel into question and urged the gentile believers to accept Jewish customs, such as circumcision and food laws, an attitude strongly resisted by Paul.

The letter to the Romans has to be interpreted against this background.[2] Paul's expositions can be characterized as an "account of faith" or a "summation of the gospel," since he gives an extensive outline of the gospel as "God's power for salvation to everyone who believes, to the Jew first and also to the Greek" (1:16).[3] He develops this view by way of a general description of the situation of humankind in light of the gospel and the salvation that is brought about by God through faith in Jesus Christ. The reason to expound this view to the Christ believers in Rome is his planned visit to the city and the opportunity to send them a letter in advance via Phoebe who, according to 16:1, was traveling to Rome for some business matters.

In contrast to Paul's other writings, the letter to the Romans is thus primarily prompted by his own situation, whereas the circumstances of his addressees are only of secondary importance. It can even be asked whether Paul had detailed information about specific circumstances among the believers in Rome and the political situation in the city at all. In any case, his main concerns in Romans are to demonstrate that God saves Jews and gentiles through the gospel, the implication of the gospel for God's chosen people Israel, and the consequences of faith in Jesus Christ for the individual believer and the community of Jews and gentiles.

---

2. There is a long-standing debate about the occasion and the reasons for Romans, which can only be briefly touched upon here. For a helpful review of different views, see Karl P. Donfried, ed., *The Romans Debate: Revised and Expanded Edition* (Peabody, MA: Hendrickson, 1991).

3. "Account of faith" and "summation of the gospel" are from Michael Theobald, *Studien zum Römerbrief*, WUNT 136 (Tübingen: Mohr Siebeck, 2001), 23: "Rechenschaft über den Glauben"; similarly Eduard Lohse, *Der Brief an die Römer*, KEK 4 (Göttingen: Vandenhoeck & Ruprecht, 2003), 45-48: "Rechenschaft vom Evangelium" or "Summe des Evangeliums." Günther Bornkamm's characterization of Romans as "Paul's testament" ("Der Römerbrief als Testament des Paulus," in *Geschichte und Glaube: Gesammelte Aufsätze 4*, BEvT 53 [Munich: Kaiser, 1971], 120-39) may be true from the perspective of the modern interpreter but was of course not Paul's own view. Unless otherwise noted, all translations are by the author.

In chapters 1 to 8 Paul discusses with a fictive interlocutor (in all probability an imagined Jew) about the meaning of the gospel for Jews and gentiles. The references to the Scriptures in this part of the letter demonstrate that God saves all humankind, Jews and gentiles, from the dominion of sin by faith without works. In chapters 9 to 11 Paul switches to another topic, which he elaborates in a different mood. He now struggles with the problem that a part of Israel does not believe in the gospel and the consequences of this situation for the salvation of God's elected people. Paul expresses his deep distress about the divide of Israel into a believing and an unbelieving part. The citations from Scripture in these chapters serve the purpose of demonstrating that this divide is in accordance with Israel's history from its beginnings. Moreover, references to Scripture also explain the current disobedience of a part of Israel and the future salvation of all of Israel. In the third part of the letter in chapters 12–15, Paul addresses his readers again in a different way. Now he admonishes them to live according to their new status in Christ. The references to Scripture in these chapters are used to strengthen Paul's exhortations to live in conformity with their faith.

The use of Scripture in Romans thus plays a crucial role in the overall line of thought of the letter. For Paul, it is of vital importance to demonstrate that the gospel of Jesus Christ is in accordance with the Scriptures. Therefore, he refers to them throughout the letter, from chapters 1–15, to demonstrate that the gospel is deeply embedded in God's history with Israel and can only be adequately perceived within the framework of Israel's authoritative writings.[4] Thereby, various usages of the Scriptures can be explored: summary references to "the Scriptures" or to "the law and the prophets" (Rom 1:2 and 3:21); citations of individual sentences and passages (throughout the letter, from 1:17 to 15:21); references to biblical figures and episodes (Abraham's faith and his circumcision in ch. 4; Adam's sin in 5:12–21; Rebecca and her twin sons in 9:10–13), and detailed interpretations of certain motives and stories (the unrighteousness of all human beings in 3:10–18; God's free choice of grace in 9:14–23). Paul's use of Scripture in Romans is characterized by diverse techniques of interpretation that were known and practiced in Second Temple Judaism.[5] These include the interpretation of biblical passages in midrashic form, allegorical and typological interpretations that apply biblical terms and passages to a new situation, and

---

4. According to Mark A. Seifrid, "Romans," in *Commentary on the New Testament Use of the Old Testament*, ed. G. K. Beale and D. A. Carson (Grand Rapids: Baker Academic, 2007), 607, Paul quotes Scripture in Romans roughly sixty times. However, the use of Scripture is not restricted to explicit citations. Instead, there are different ways in which Paul uses Scripture, as will be demonstrated in what follows.

5. See Michael Tilly, "Paulus und die antike jüdische Schriftauslegung," *KD* 63 (2017): 157–81.

eschatological readings that interpret biblical texts in light of God's salvific action at the end of time. Paul is acquainted with these practices and employs them to interpret God's revelation through Jesus Christ. This will be outlined in more detail in the following paragraphs.

Israel's Scriptures in Romans

In the first three chapters of Romans, the references to the Scriptures serve to substantiate the argument that God's righteousness has been revealed through faith in Jesus Christ, without the law, for all humankind.

Right at the beginning of the letter, Paul invokes Scripture for the first time. In 1:2 he characterizes the "gospel of God" (τὸ εὐαγγέλιον θεοῦ) as "promised beforehand through his prophets in the holy scriptures" (ὃ προεπηγγείλατο διὰ τῶν προφητῶν αὐτοῦ ἐν γραφαῖς ἁγίαις). Three aspects of this formulation are particularly important. First, with the rare verb "promised beforehand" Paul declares that through the prophets the gospel was prepared because God announces in the Scriptures what will be realized through the gospel.[6] Thus, Paul does not claim that the Scriptures contain the message of the gospel itself. Instead, he emphasizes the continuity between God's promises in the Scriptures and their fulfillment through the gospel. Second, in the remark that God speaks "through his prophets," Paul characterizes the Scriptures as prophetic testimony of the gospel. This is not restricted to specific writings (e.g., to the books of the prophets), but characterizes Israel's authoritative Scriptures in general. Thus, Paul presupposes collections of such writings, not as a fixed canon but as compilations of the Torah, the prophets, and other writings (such as the Psalms or the book of Proverbs) that gained foundational meaning in Judaism. This is proven by the fact that in Romans Paul quotes from different collections of the Scriptures: from the Torah (e.g., the story of Abraham and Sarah, Jacob and Esau, and the Ten Commandments); the prophets (e.g., Isaiah and the Minor Prophets); the Psalms and Proverbs (see, e.g., 9:36; 12:20). This is in accordance with the Jewish idea that Moses and David are also "prophets" through whom God speaks in the Torah and the Psalms. The reference to "the prophets" thus serves as a principal proposition about the character of the Scriptures. Third, the expression γραφαὶ ἅγιαι is a summary designation for the fundamental writings of Judaism.[7] They

---

6. The only other occurrence of the verb is in the New Testament is 2 Cor 9:5. The verb does not appear in the Septuagint or in any other Jewish writing of the Second Temple period. It denotes things that have been previously announced (see, e.g., Inscr. Priene 113:70–71).

7. The singular γραφὴ ἁγία ("holy Scripture") occurs in T. Naph. 4:1; 5:8. Compatible ex-

are characterized as "holy Scriptures" because they are regarded as the authoritative testimony of God's voice that can be heard through them. Paul thus opens the letter with a general statement about the meaning of Israel's Scriptures as the trustworthy witness of the gospel.

The next reference occurs in 1:16–17, at the transition from the introductory section to the body of the letter. Paul characterizes the gospel as "God's power for salvation to everyone who believes, to the Jew first and also to the Greek" because God's righteousness is revealed in the gospel "through faith for faith." This statement is justified with a quotation from Scripture, introduced by "as it is written" (καθὼς γέγραπται). It is the first explicit quotation from Scripture in the letter and one that is crucial for the overall argument. Unlike in other cases, Paul does not indicate the origin of the quotation.[8] This is due to the fact that he wants to introduce this reference as general proof from Scripture, not from a particular book.

In the phrase ὁ δὲ δίκαιος ἐκ πίστεως ζήσεται, which is derived from Hab 2:4, ἐκ πίστεως can be taken with ὁ δὲ δίκαιος or with ζήσεται.[9] The citation can thus be translated as "the one who is *righteous by faith* will live" or "the righteous one will *live by faith.*" Since Paul has just outlined that God's righteousness will be revealed "from faith to faith," the first option is more likely.[10] That fits with the line

---

pressions are ἱερὰ γράμματα ("holy books") in 2 Tim 3:15 and τὰ βιβλία τὰ ἅγια ("the holy books") in 1 Macc 12:9. Philo and Josephus use the expression ἱεραὶ βίβλοι for the biblical writings or the Torah (see Philo, *Decal.* 154; *Abr.* 157; *Cher.* 124; *Det.* 161; *Post.* 158; *Ebr.* 208, etc.; Josephus, *Ant.* 1.26, 82, 139; 2.347, etc.) or ἱεραὶ γραφαί ("holy writings"; see Philo, *Opif.* 77; *Her.* 106, 159, 286; *Congr.* 34, 90; *Abr.* 61, 121; *Decal.* 8, 37 etc.; see Josephus, *Ag. Ap.* 2.45). Paul also uses ἡ γραφή and αἱ γραφαί for Israel's authoritative writings (Rom 4:3; 9:17; 10:11; 11:2; 15:4; 1 Cor 15:3; Gal 3:8, 22; 4:30).

8. In ch. 9 Paul explicitly identifies citations from Hosea (v. 25) and Isaiah (twice, vv. 27 and 29) to accumulate evidence from Scripture that proves God's election of a people (λαός) from both Jews and gentiles (9:24–25), whereas only a remnant of Israel is left. To substantiate this case, he refers to quotations from different prophetic writings.

9. Paul cites this verse in Gal 3:11 as well to substantiate the difference between "works of the law" and "faith in Jesus Christ."

10. This interpretation is favored, e.g., by Ernst Käsemann, *An die Römer*, HNT 8A (Tübingen: Mohr Siebeck, 1980), 29; C. E. B. Cranfield, *A Critical and Exegetical Commentary on the Epistle to the Romans*, 2 vols., ICC (Edinburgh: T&T Clark, 1975), 1:101–2; Ulrich Wilckens, *Der Brief an die Römer*, 3 vols., EKK 6.1–3 (Zurich: Einsiedeln; Neukirchen-Vluyn: Neukirchener Verlag, 1978–1982), 1:89–90; Douglas J. Moo, *The Epistle to the Romans*, NICNT (Grand Rapids: Eerdmans, 1996), 76–78; and Michael Wolter, *Der Brief an die Römer*, 2 vols., EKKNT 6.1–2 (Neukirchen-Vluyn: Neukirchener Verlag; Ostfildern: Patmos, 2014–2019), 1:126–27 (see also RSV). The other option is preferred, e.g., by Lohse, *Römer*; Joseph A. Fitzmyer, *Romans: A New Translation with Introduction and Commentary*, AB 33 (New York: Doubleday, 1993), 264–65; Klaus Haacker, *Der Brief des Paulus an die Römer*, THKNT 6 (Leipzig: Evangelische

of argument in chapters 1–8 where Paul shows that righteousness comes through faith and leads to salvation and eternal life. With the quotation Paul emphasizes the faith (or confidence) of the believer, whereas in the Septuagint God's πίστις is the basis for the life of the human being.[11] The Hebrew text, by contrast, which is also attested by the Greek translations of Aquila, Symmachus, and Theodotion, as well as in the Minor Prophets scroll from Naḥal Ḥever, reads: "The righteous one will live by his faithfulness."[12] Thus, the μου is dropped entirely only in Paul's version due to his use of the citation as a proof of righteousness by faith as the content of the gospel.

The third statement occurs in 3:21, at the beginning of a new subsection. After having depicted the ungodliness and unrighteousness of all human beings, Paul now states that God's righteousness was made manifest apart from the law as "witnessed by the law and the prophets." The expression "the law and the prophets," which occurs only here in Paul's letters, is a Jewish summary designation for the authoritative writings and is also used in early Christian texts.[13] In Romans it forms an *inclusio* with the quotation in 1:17: The righteous by faith will live, because God's righteousness comes through faith, apart from the law, as it is testified by the law and the prophets. As the summary designation "the law and the prophets" indicates, Israel's Scriptures as a whole bear witness to the gospel.

Other references to the Scriptures in the first part of Romans contribute to this overall argument. In 2:6 Paul uses a phrase that is rooted in Jewish literature: "(God) will render to each person according to that person's deed." The

---

Verlagsanstalt, 2012); and Robert Jewett, *Romans: A Commentary*, Hermeneia (Minneapolis: Fortress, 2007), 145–46 (see also NRSV and KJV).

11. The original reading of the Septuagint probably was: ὁ δὲ δίκαιος ἐκ πίστεώς μου ζήσεται ("the righteous one will live by my [i.e., God's] faithfulness"). For the different versions of the Septuagint text, see Dietrich-Alex Koch, "Der Text von Hab 2,4b in der Septuaginta und im Neuen Testament," in *Hellenistisches Christentum: Schriftverständnis – Ekklesiologie – Geschichte*, ed. Friedrich Wilhelm Horn, NTOA 65 (Göttingen: Vandenhoeck & Ruprecht, 2008), 35–41; Fitzmyer, *Romans*; Moo, *Romans*, 76–77 n. 65.

12. יִחְיֶה בֶּאֱמוּנָתוֹ וְצַדִּיק This reading can also be presupposed for the Habakkuk pesher from Qumran (1QpHab VII and VIII). The version in Heb 10:38 ὁ δὲ δίκαιός μου ἐκ πίστεως ζήσεται ("my righteous one will live by faith") is also attested in the Septuagint manuscripts A and C.

13. In Jewish literature the expression occurs in 2 Macc 15:9; 4 Macc 18:10; T. Lev. 16:2 ("the law and the words of the prophets"). A comparable expression is "Moses and (or: his) prophets" in 1QS I, 3; VIII, 15–16; 4Q397 (4QMMT^d) IV, 15 ("the book of Moses and the books of the prophets"); 4Q504 2 III, 12–14; CD V, 21–VI, 1 (4Q266 3 V, 21–VI, 1: "Moses and the holy anointed ones"). In the New Testament the phrase and similar expressions occur in Matt 5:17; 7:12; 11:13; 22:40; Luke 16:16, 29, 31; 24:27, 44 ("the law of Moses and the prophets and psalms"); Acts 13:15; 24:14; Acts 26:22 ("the prophets and Moses"); 28:23; John 1:45 ("Moses wrote in the law and the prophets").

numerous analogies in Jewish texts with closer parallels in Ps 61:13 LXX and Prov 24:12 indicate that Paul does not directly quote from Scripture, but refers to the common Jewish conviction that God as righteous judge will enforce his righteousness at the final judgment.[14] A similar view is expressed in 3:4. Here Paul quotes explicitly from Ps 50:6 LXX: "As it is written: So that you may be justified in your words and triumph in your judging." God's righteous judgment is a consequence of the opposition outlined immediately before: God is true, whereas every human being is a liar. God's truthfulness and faithfulness (see 3:3) in contrast to human beings is attested in the Scriptures. Again, Paul uses biblical language to express the strong contrast between God and humankind that is crucial for the argument in this part of the letter.[15]

A specific usage of Scripture occurs at the end of this section in 3:10-18. Introduced again by "as it is written," Paul quotes a long passage that proves his overall argument that no human being will be justified before God by works of the law because of the sinfulness of all human beings. With regard to the origin of the quotation—the longest one in the whole Pauline corpus—different possibilities are discussed. Since the entire quotation occurs in Septuagint manuscripts of Ps 13:3 but not in the Hebrew Bible, many scholars argue that the New Testament passage has influenced the textual tradition of the Septuagint.[16] This leaves two possibilities for the origin of the quotation: either Paul compiled the quotation himself from various Scriptural passages, or he used an already existing compilation of Scriptural passages.[17]

The other possibility is that Paul quotes from a Septuagint manuscript that contained the passage in Rom 3:13-18 so that Romans was influenced by the Greek Bible, not the other way around.[18] This solution is more likely for the following reasons: (1) The beginning of Paul's quotation (Rom 3:10-11) did

---

14. See, e.g., Lam 3:64; Isa 3:11; Sir 16:12, 14; Pss. Sol. 2:16, 34; 17:8.

15. For the former (God as ἀληθής or ἀληθινός), see, e.g., Exod 34:6; Isa 65:16; Wis 15:1; for the latter (God's πίστις, God as πιστός), see, e.g., Deut 7:9; 32:4; Ps 32:4 LXX; 144:13 LXX; Jer 39:41 LXX; Hos 2:22. The phrase "every human being is a liar" (πᾶς ἄνθρωπος ψεύστης) occurs in Ps 115:2 LXX (cf. Ps 116:11 MT), although the context in both cases is different.

16. See, e.g., Alfred Rahlfs, ed., *Psalmi cum Odis*, 3rd ed., SVTG 26 (Göttingen: Vandenhoeck & Ruprecht: 1979), 10:30-31, 96; Dietrich-Alex Koch, *Die Schrift als Zeuge des Evangeliums: Untersuchungen zur Verwendung und zum Verständnis der Schrift bei Paulus*, BHT 69 (Tübingen: Mohr Siebeck, 1986), 179-84; and many others.

17. The second option could be confirmed by Justin, *Dial.* 27.3, who quotes a similar compilation of scriptural passages. However, it is also possible that Justin was influenced by the Septuagint version of the psalm or by the passage in Romans.

18. For this solution see especially Martin C. Albl, *"And Scripture Cannot Be Broken": The Form and Function of the Early Christian* Testimonia *Collections*, NovTSup 96 (Leiden: Brill, 1999), 171-77.

not influence Ps 13:1–3 in the Septuagint. (2) The passage from Romans does not occur in the parallel Ps 52:2–4. (3) An influence from the passage in Romans on other Septuagint texts with parallels in Rom 3:13–18, such as Pss 5:10; 139:4; Isa 59:7–8; or Ps 35:2, is not recognizable. (4) The quotation of such a long passage from the New Testament in the Septuagint would be unparalleled. (5) There is no apparent reason for the insertion of such a lengthy quotation about the injustice and ungodliness of the human beings from the New Testament in a Septuagint psalm. (6) The longer version of Ps 13:3 is widely attested in different textual traditions of the Septuagint. (7) Justin may be another witness for the longer version of Ps 13 in the Septuagint.

Hence, if a Christian influence on the Septuagint is unlikely, Paul cites the entire passage from a Greek manuscript to emphasize that no human being is justified before God. He concludes the section of the letter with an allusion to Ps 142:2: "For no human being will be justified before him by works of the law; for through the law comes knowledge of sin" (Rom 3:20). The Septuagint text of this passage reads: "No one living is justified before you." Here, as in Gal 2:16, Paul has adapted the citation to his argument: by adding the phrase "by works of the law," which does not occur in the psalm, he has related justification directly to the law as opposed to justification by faith.[19]

The next section, which begins in 3:21, is focused on God's saving action through Jesus Christ. In 3:24–25 Paul explains that God saves the believers by setting forth Jesus Christ as a propitiatory offering through faith in his blood (ἱλαστήριον διὰ πίστεως ἐν τῷ αὐτοῦ αἵματι). The prepositional phrase ἐν τῷ αὐτοῦ αἵματι serves as an explanation of ἱλαστήριον, indicating that the latter term is used as interpretation of Jesus's death against the background of Israel's Scriptures. Moreover, the prepositional construction διὰ πίστεως makes clear that Jesus's death is a ἱλαστήριον only for the believers, that is, for those who believe in the gospel as God's power for salvation (1:16). The meaning of ἱλαστήριον has to be explained against this background.

ἱλαστήριον, a neuter substantive of the adjective ἱλαστήριος, usually denotes an expiatory offering or a gift to make the gods gracious.[20] In the Septuagint and

---

19. Paul uses ἔργα νόμου also in Rom 3:28; and Gal 2:16; 3:2, 5, 10. The phrase does not appear in the Septuagint or in any other Greek Jewish text. A parallel occurs in 4QMMT, where the author describes the Torah regulations as מעשי התורה whose observation will lead to joy at the end of time and will be reckoned as righteousness (C 27–32). A similar phrase occurs in 1QS V, 21; VI, 18: מעשי התורה.

20. For the usage of the term in non-Jewish Greek texts (including inscriptions) and Josephus, *Ant.* 16.182, see Stefan Schreiber, "Das Weihegeschenk Gottes: Eine Deutung des Todes Jesu in Röm 3,25," *ZNW* 97 (2006): 100–102; Alexander Weiß, "Christus Jesus als Weihegeschenk oder Sühnemal? Anmerkungen zu einer neueren Deutung von hilasterion (Röm

Philo, as well as in Heb 9:5, the term refers to the lid of the ark on which the high priest pours the blood of the sacrificed animals.[21] In the description of the ritual of the Day of Atonement in Lev 16:2, 13–16, God informs Moses that he will appear in a cloud above the ἱλαστήριον, which is on the ark of the testimony in the sanctuary behind the curtain. At the appointed time Aaron should sprinkle the blood of the sacrificial animals on this lid to cleanse the sanctuary from the uncleanness of the Israelites. The usage in Rom 3:25 has to be explained against this background.[22] Paul does not refer directly to the Day of Atonement or the lid of the ark. However, he uses the term in an analogous metaphorical way to describe God's salvific action through the death of Jesus Christ: as God is present in the lid of the ark to cleanse the Israelites from their sins, he is present at Jesus's crucifixion to forgive sins and reconcile the believers with himself. An appropriate translation for ἱλαστήριον would therefore be "place of grace."[23] Thus, in Rom 3:25 Paul takes up a biblical term that evokes God's salvation of Israel to interpret God's saving action through the death of Jesus Christ. The analogy to the lid of the ark is that in both cases God cleanses from sin by way of death (of sacrificed animals or of Jesus Christ).

Another analogy to Rom 3:25 is the interpretation of the death of the Maccabean martyrs as an "atoning death" in 4 Maccabees.[24] In both texts, the death of human beings is interpreted with the term ἱλαστήριον, denoting that God (or the divine providence) made these deaths saving events. Both texts thus share the perspective that God can provide salvation by forgiveness of sins through the death of human beings.[25]

3,25) samt einer Liste der epigraphischen Belege," *ZNW* 105 (2014): 294–302 (although with a different conclusion regarding Rom 3:25). The usual term would be ἀνάθημα ("dedication"), which can be specified as ἱλαστήριον ("expiatory offering").

21. See Exod 25:17–22; 31:7; 35:12; 38:5, 7–8; Num 7:89; Philo, *Cher.* 25; *Her.* 166; *Fug.* 100–101; *Mos.* 2.95, 97.

22. ἱλαστήριον does not denote here a "propitiatory offering" for God, since in the Septuagint as in Philo and the New Testament God is the donator, not the recipient of atonement and propitiation. On this usage, see Adolf Deissmann, "ΙΛΑΣΤΗΡΙΟΣ und ΙΛΑΣΤΗΡΙΟΝ: Eine lexikalische Studie," *ZNW* 4 (1903): 193–212.

23. Luther's translation, "Gnadenstuhl" ("mercy seat"), goes in a similar direction.

24. See 4 Macc 17:21–22. However, the textual transmission of the passage is uncertain. Whereas the Sinaiticus and some other manuscripts read "the propitiation of their death" (τὸ ἱλαστήριον τοῦ θανάτου αὐτῶν), the Alexandrinus and other manuscripts have "their propitiatory death" (τὸ ἱλαστήριος θάνατος αὐτῶν). In the latter case ἱλαστήριον is used as an adjective.

25. It should be noted that in 4 Maccabees the death of the martyr can also be interpreted as a devotion to make God merciful (4 Macc 6:28–29; see 2 Macc 7:37–38). Another difference is that for Paul, Jesus Christ is not just a human being but God's Son who was sent into the world to overcome the power of sin.

In the first section of Romans, Paul emphasizes that the essential content of the gospel is anchored in Scripture. In particular, he demonstrates that God's righteous judgment and the injustice and ungodliness of human beings, as well as God's saving action through the death of Jesus Christ, are attested in the Scriptures. He has not yet shown, however, the proof from Scripture for the justification by faith, without works of the law. This is the content of the story of Abraham to which Paul turns in the next section.

Chapter 4 is an extensive interpretation of Gen 15:6: "Abraham believed in God, and it was reckoned to him as righteousness" (ἐπίστευσεν δὲ Ἀβραὰμ τῷ θεῷ καὶ ἐλογίσθη αὐτῷ εἰς δικαιοσύνην).[26] Paul quotes this verse right at the beginning of the chapter (4:3) and returns to it several times: he explains that to the one who works, wages are reckoned (λογίζεται) as something due, whereas to the one who believes in God who justifies the ungodly, by contrast, faith is reckoned as righteousness (vv. 4 and 5).[27] In 4:9 he repeats the citation and continues (v. 10) by asking *how* Abraham's faith was reckoned to him as righteousness: "For we are saying: Faith was reckoned to Abraham as righteousness. How, then, was it reckoned?" At the end of the chapter, Paul argues that the statement from Scripture is not only for Abraham but also "for us who believe in the one who raised Jesus our Lord from the dead" (4:23-24).

The phrase about Abraham's faith that was reckoned as righteousness is of particular importance to Paul. It proves that the close connection between faith and justification can already be found at the beginning of Israel's history. Paul interprets the story of Abraham from this particular perspective. In 4:7-8 he relates it to another scriptural passage (Ps 31:1-2): The verb "to reckon" (λογίζεσθαι) appears in Gen 15:6 as well as in Ps 31:2 ("Blessed is the man whose sin the Lord does not reckon").[28] Paul connects the passages because in both cases God is the subject and "reckon as righteousness without works" (4:6) is interpreted in the quotation from the psalm as "not reckon sin," "forgive iniquities," and "cover sins."

---

26. Whether the chapter should be called a "midrash" in a narrower sense as many scholars do depends on the definition of "midrash." This question can be left open here.

27. The phrase "who justifies the ungodly" is used from the perspective of Paul's conviction that all human beings are sinners and God saves the believers without the law. It does, by contrast, not imply that Paul would count Abraham among the "ungodly." Instead, 4:4-8 is an exposition of Abraham's faith against the background of what Paul has outlined before, namely, the justification of sinners by faith, without works.

28. Whether Paul is using here the technique of a *gezerah shevah*—an interpretation technique introduced by Hillel that connects two passages of the Torah in which the same term occurs—is disputed. In the present case λογίζεσθαι is used in both passages with a different meaning, in Gen 15:6 as a passive, and in Ps 13:2 in the middle. Moreover, the second quotation is not from the Torah, as is usually the case in a *gezerah shevah* argument. In any case, it is obvious that Paul connects the psalm to the Abraham story via the verb "reckon."

Israel's Scriptures in Romans

In 4:10-11 Paul links Gen 15:6 to another part of the Abraham story by pointing out that Abraham was still uncircumcised when he was justified by faith, whereas his circumcision was a "sign" that he received as "seal of righteousness" only afterward. Thus, Paul establishes a connection between Abraham's faith on the one hand and his circumcision, which is narrated in the Torah only later, on the other. The combination of the two stories allows him to draw the conclusion that there was a period in which Abraham was still uncircumcised (which is of course not mentioned in the Genesis account). Because he already believed in God at that time, Abraham could become the father of both the uncircumcised and the circumcised believers. The designation of Abraham as "our ancestor" (i.e., of "us Jews") at the beginning of the chapter (προπάτωρ ἡμῶν, 4:1) thus receives a new meaning since Abraham is now described as the "father" of all believers (πατήρ, vv. 11-12).

The syntactical construction of 4:11-12 poses an exegetical problem. In particular, it is disputed whether the ambiguous expression in verse 12 "father of the circumcision of those who are not only from circumcision, but also of those who walk in the footsteps of the faith of uncircumcision of our father Abraham" (4:12) refers to one group or two groups.[29] Since in 4:11b Paul characterizes Abraham as "father of all those who believe through uncircumcision," one would expect that in 4:12 he adds those who believe while being circumcised. However, the expression τοῖς οὐκ ἐκ περιτομῆς μόνον ἀλλὰ καὶ τοῖς ("those who are not only from circumcision but also those") is awkward since it should be τοῖς οὐκ ἐκ περιτομῆς μόνον ἀλλὰ τοῖς καὶ ("those who are not only from circumcision but who also"). Therefore, it has been suggested that in 4:11 Paul would refer to Abraham as the father of all believers by characterizing his faith as "faith through uncircumcision," whereas in 4:12 he would divide them into believing Jews and gentiles.[30]

According to another interpretation, in 4:12 Paul refers to the groups of unbelieving and believing Jews. For example, Käsemann argues that in 4:11 Paul refers to gentile believers, whereas in 4:12 he mentions believing and unbelieving Jews and restricts Abraham's fatherhood to the latter group.[31] As in the interpretation mentioned before, Paul uses "circumcision" in a metaphorical sense as circumcision of the heart (see Rom 2:29). Maria Neubrand interprets 4:12 in a similar way but arrives at a different conclusion. According to her view, Paul

---

29. πατέρα περιτομῆς τοῖς οὐκ ἐκ περιτομῆς μόνον ἀλλὰ καὶ τοῖς στοιχοῦσιν τοῖς ἴχνεσιν τῆς ἐν ἀκροβυστίᾳ πίστεως τοῦ πατρὸς ἡμῶν Ἀβραάμ.

30. Benjamin Schliesser, *Abraham's Faith in Romans 4: Paul's Concept of Faith in Light of the History of Reception of Genesis 15:6*, WUNT 2/224 (Tübingen: Mohr Siebeck, 2007), 361-64. A comparable position is taken by Fitzmyer, *Romans*, 381-82, who also thinks that in 4:12 Paul speaks of two groups of believers from Jews and gentiles.

31. Käsemann, *An die Römer*, 109-10.

refers to believing and unbelieving Jews to emphasize that Abraham remains the father of *all* Jews.[32]

The syntactical construction of 4:11–12, however, suggests a different interpretation. Abraham is described as father of those who believe "through uncircumcision" and as father of those who are "from circumcision," which makes it more likely that Paul refers to one group in 4:11 and to another one in 4:12.[33] Moreover, it is improbable that in verse 12a Paul would use "circumcision" in a metaphorical sense, referring to a spiritual circumcision of the heart, and use the same term for physical circumcision in verse 12b. The awkward construction "of those . . . who not only, but also of those" (τοῖς οὐκ . . . μόνον ἀλλὰ καὶ τοῖς) therefore probably refers to the Jews in general, who are then specified as believing in the same way as Abraham, that is, sharing his "faith in uncircumcision." The most likely interpretation of 4:11–12 therefore is that Paul presents Abraham as father of the believers from gentiles and Jews.[34] The problem of those Jews who do not believe in the gospel, by contrast, is dealt with only later (chs. 9–11).

A third interpretation of Abraham's faith arises from the connection with the "promise," introduced in 4:13. The content of the promise is explained with a quotation from Gen 17:5: "As father of many nations I have appointed you" (4:17a). As 4:13–16 point out, this promise is in contrast with the law. Thus, the law (νόμος) now serves as the contrasting term in the same way as "working" and circumcision in the preceding sections. In other words, Paul argues that Scripture is appropriately perceived only if Abraham's faith without works in uncircumcision is related to God's promise that Abraham will become the father of many nations.

In sum, Paul interprets Abraham's faith with reference to three aspects: it is a faith without works; it is a faith in uncircumcision; and it is a faith in accordance with God's promise that does not come through the law. In this way Paul has provided an innovative interpretation of Gen 15:6 that serves his argumentative goal of demonstrating that the gospel is promised beforehand through the Holy Scriptures and that justification without the law is witnessed by the law and the prophets. By referring to Abraham, Paul can demonstrate what he has argued before: that justification through faith in Jesus Christ is open for Jews and gentiles alike (1:16–17) because God is a God not only of the Jews but also of the

---

32. Maria Neubrand, *Abraham, Vater von Juden und Nichtjuden: Eine exegetische Studie zu Röm 4*, FzB 85 (Würzburg: Echter, 1997), 225–45; similarly Haacker, *Römer*, 122–23.

33. εἰς τὸ εἶναι αὐτὸν πατέρα . . . καὶ πατέρα.

34. For this interpretation, see, e.g., Wilckens, *Römer 1*, 265–66; Moo, *Romans*, 269–71; Wolter, *Römer 1*, 291–94; and many others.

gentiles (3:29–30). Abraham's faith is therefore a model of the faith of those who believe in God, who has resurrected Jesus, our Lord, from the dead (4:23–24).

The next reference to the Scriptures occurs at the end of the first section (1:16–5:21) of the first part of the letter (1:16–8:39). In 5:12 Paul introduces "one man" through whom sin and death came to all human beings. In 5:14 the "one man" is identified as Adam, who in 5:18 is contrasted with the "one" Jesus Christ.[35] In 5:12–21 Adam therefore serves as the counterpart or antitype to Christ through whom God's grace (χάρις) came to human beings.[36]

The reference to Adam alludes to the story of the fall of humanity in Gen 3. As in Jewish apocalyptic writings, Adam is characterized as the first sinner who brought about sin to all human beings after him.[37] Remarkably, Paul in a particular way relates Adam's sin (ἁμαρτία, 5:12–13, 20) or his trespass (παράπτωμα, 5:15–18, 20) to the transgression of the law. In 5:13 he notes that the law came only later with Moses, but sin was in the world already before. Adam is therefore a "typos of the coming" (τύπος τοῦ μέλλοντος, 5:14), that is, of sin as transgression of the law.[38] Thus, Paul describes salvation through faith in Jesus Christ against the background of the Genesis account about the trespass of the first human being. As a special accent, he argues that Adam's trespass was a transgression of the law that was given only later at Mount Sinai. This shows that the law is of particular interest to Paul. He describes its role as the benchmark for the reckoning of sin that leads to the situation of humankind under the dominion of sin.

The view developed in 5:12–21 is continued in 7:7–25. Now Paul interprets the dominion of sin and law as an inner conflict of the human being. Because the description is in the first-person singular, it has been argued that the passage is an autobiographical retrospect on Paul's own experience.[39] It is certainly true that

---

35. Ἄρα οὖν ὡς δι᾽ ἑνὸς παραπτώματος εἰς πάντας ἀνθρώπους εἰς κατάκριμα, οὕτως καὶ δι᾽ ἑνὸς δικαιώματος εἰς πάντας ἀνθρώπους εἰς δικαίωσιν ζωῆς.

36. Paul has contrasted Adam and Christ already in 1 Cor 15:21–22: death came through a human being (Adam) as resurrection of the dead came through a human being (Christ). As in Rom 5, Adam and Christ are representatives of humankind under sin and death on the one hand and bestowed with God's grace and the future resurrection on the other. In 1 Cor 15:45, 47, Adam as the "first man," made from earth, is contrasted with Christ as the "last Adam" from heaven.

37. See, e.g., 4 Ezra 3:7, 21; 7:118; 2 Bar. 17:2–3; 48:42; 54:15; 56:5.

38. Most commentators relate τύπος τοῦ μέλλοντος to the coming Christ as the antitype of Adam. However, the context of 5:13–14 makes it more likely that the phrase refers to the future trespasses under the law.

39. Thus, e.g., Jewett, *Romans*, 443, following Jan Lambrecht, *The Wretched I and Its Liberation: Paul in Romans 7 and 8*, LThPM 14 (Leuven: Peeters; Grand Rapids: Eerdmans, 1992); and Troels Engberg-Pedersen, "The Reception of Graeco-Roman Culture in the New Testament: The Case of Romans 7.7–25," in *The New Testament as Reception*, ed. Mogens Müller and Henrik

Paul includes himself among those who have encountered the law and experienced the conflict between willing and doing. However, he certainly does not restrict this situation to himself but describes the conflict between God's commandment that should lead to life and the sin that hinders the human being from a life according to the law in a general way. In other words, Paul regards the human being as God's creation and image, who is confronted with the fact that because of the power of sin s/he cannot live according to what s/he knows to be good.[40]

Paul does not quote the Scriptures in this passage, nor does he allude to a biblical figure. However, it is obvious that his view on the human being developed in this passage is based on the biblical account about humankind under the dominion of sin. The "I" in Rom 7 is therefore the Adamic person living under the sin that came into the world with the first human being, as outlined in 5:12–21.

In 8:36 Paul quotes again from the Scriptures, introduced with "as it is written." In this passage, he describes the situation of the believers under the conditions of the present age: they are already saved, justified, and glorified and await the future glory that will be revealed to them.[41] Thus, they are "saved in hope" (τῇ γὰρ ἐλπίδι ἐσώθημεν, 8:24). The citation from Ps 43:22 LXX illustrates that those who belong to Jesus Christ, despite the confidence of their future salvation, still face death in in their present lives: "For your sake we are being put to death all day long. We are considered as sheep to be slaughtered." In its new context, the quotation substantiates the view that the present sufferings are an integral part of the existence of the believers. This does not call into question their justification and salvation because nothing can separate them from God's love in Jesus Christ (8:38–39). Instead, those who are still suffering from their bodily existence in the present age await the glory of the age to come.

Tronier, JSNTSup 230 (Sheffield: Sheffield Academic, 2002), 32–57. The autobiographical interpretation has a long tradition in scholarship. It was, e.g., favored by Augustine, Jean Calvin, and Adolf Deissmann. See Moo, *Romans*, 425. An overview of the history of interpretation of Rom 7 from antiquity to the twentieth century is provided by Hermann Lichtenberger, *Das Ich Adams und das Ich der Menschheit: Studien zum Menschenbild in Römer 7*, WUNT 164 (Tübingen: Mohr Siebeck, 2004), 17–105.

40. In 7:22 Paul uses the phrase "inner person" (ἔσω ἄνθρωπος) to describe the spiritual dimension of the human being who is in conflict with the "members" and the "flesh" as the outer dimension of the same person. The topic of the inner conflict between willing and doing has parallels in Greek and Roman texts dealing in the figure of Medea. See Reinhard v. Bendemann, "Die kritische Diastase von Wissen, Wollen und Handeln: Traditionsgeschichtliche Spurensuche eines hellenistischen Topos in Römer 7," *ZNW* 95 (2004): 35–63; Jens Schröter, "Der Mensch zwischen Wollen und Tun: Erwägungen zu Römer 7 im Licht der 'New Perspective on Paul,'" in *Paulus – Werk und Wirkung: Festschrift für Andreas Lindemann zum 70. Geburtstag*, ed. Paul-Gerhard Klumbies et al. (Tübingen: Mohr Siebeck, 2013), 195–224.

41. See 8:24: ἐσώθημεν ("saved"); 8:30: ἐδικαίωσεν ("justified"), ἐδόξασεν ("glorified").

In chapters 9–11 Paul deals with the most burning issues of the letter, namely the question of what the revelation of God's righteousness revealed in the gospel means for Israel, God's elect people.[42] This problem arises from Paul's argument that God saves all believers, Jews and gentiles, through Jesus's death as a ἱλαστήριον (3:25) and reconciles them as former enemies to himself (5:6–10). Since for Paul it is at the same time irrevocable that Israel is and remains God's chosen people, that the word of God has not failed (9:6), and that God has not rejected his people (11:1), he must explain how these convictions can be reconciled with each other.

The chapters are framed by an introductory lament (9:1–5) and a closing doxology (11:33–36).[43] This is due to the fact that Paul, in the course of his thoughts, develops an answer to the serious problem raised at the beginning. In his expositions he frequently refers to the Scriptures with extensive quotations as well as by mentioning general topics. In this way, he wants to demonstrate that the split within Israel into a believing and an unbelieving part is by no means against the Scriptures. By contrast, this fissure is in line with Israel's history from the very beginning as is attested by Scripture itself. As a conclusion, Paul formulates that eventually God will heal the divide by also saving the part of Israel that is currently hardened (11:25–26).

Already at the beginning of chapter 9, Paul mentions Israel's privileges attested in the Scriptures: sonship, glory, covenants, giving of the law, worship, promises, the fathers, and the Messiah according to the flesh (9:5). All of these characteristics describe Israel's exclusive relationship to God that distinguishes them from all the other peoples.

The first section (9:6–29) is devoted to a scriptural reasoning about the split within Israel. Right at the beginning Paul uses the term "Israel" twice, each time with a different meaning: "Not all those who are of Israel, these are Israel."[44] Whereas the first "Israel" refers to all who physically descended from Israel, the second use applies only to a specific group within Israel, namely those who believe in the gospel.

The division of Israel into two parts is illustrated with examples from Scripture: not all children (τέκνα) of Abraham are his seed (σπέρμα), but only the descendants of Isaac. As proof, Paul quotes Gen 21:12: "In Isaac your seed [σπέρμα] shall be called." In the background is the story of Abraham's two sons, of which

---

42. In Romans, Paul uses "Israel" and "Israelites" only in these chapters. It can denote all who belong to Israel by their origin (the first usage in 9:6; 9:27; 11:26; the "people" [λαός] in 9:25–26; 11:1), the Jews who believe in Jesus Christ (the second usage in 9:6; Paul as Israelite in 11:1), or those Jews who do not believe in the gospel (9:31; 10:19; 11:7).

43. See Moo, *Romans*, 553.

44. οὐ γὰρ πάντες οἱ ἐξ Ἰσραὴλ οὗτοι Ἰσραήλ (Rom 9:6).

only Isaac is the bearer of God's promise to make Abraham the father of many nations.[45] Thus, Paul makes a distinction within Israel between "the children of the flesh" and the "children of the promise" (9:8). This distinction is further developed by a reference to the story of Jacob and Esau (9:10–13). In both cases, Paul quotes a sentence from Scripture that summarizes the meaning of these episodes for his argument: Sarah's son was born according to the promise (Gen 18:10, 14); God has loved Jacob and hated Esau (Mal 1:2–3).

In the further course of the argument of 9:6–29, Paul emphasizes that it is God's free choice to elect and to harden. This is illustrated by a quotation from Exod 33:19: "I will have mercy on whom I have mercy, and I will have compassion on whom I have compassion" (9:15). Thus, the hardening of a part of Israel is by no means against God's election. By contrast, God has always shown mercy and demonstrated his power according to his will. Another example of this acting of God is the raising of pharaoh to demonstrate God's power through him (9:17, quoting Exod 9:16).

In 9:24–29 Paul compiles three citations from the prophets. Each of them is introduced separately with the name of the prophet: "In Hosea it says"; "Isaiah cries out concerning Israel"; and "It is as Isaiah foretold."[46] Thus, Paul accumulates the prophetic testimony to demonstrate that God may call also others than Israel his people (Hos 2:25 and 2:1); that only a remnant of Israel will be saved (Isa 10:22–23); and that God has left a seed (σπέρμα) for us (Isa 1:9).[47] The clue of the last two quotations is that the "remnant" of Israel will be saved. This does, however, not answer the question whether *all* of Israel will be saved. Instead, Paul's first answer is that Scripture proves the division in Israel and the saving of only a remnant. As will become clear in what follows, this "remnant" consists of those Jews who, like Paul himself, believe in the gospel of Jesus Christ (see 11:1).

The second section (9:30–10:21) is related to Israel's failure in view of the gospel. Again, Paul refers to the Scriptures to explain that Israel "stumbled over the stone of stumbling" as it is written in Isa 28:16, quoted in 9:33 in connection with Isa 8:14. Both citations are combined in a similar way in 1 Pet 2:6, 8

---

45. A similar argument is developed in Gal 4:21–31: of the two sons of Abraham, one was born "according to the flesh" (κατὰ σάρκα), the other one "through promise" (δι' ἐπαγγελίας).

46. Probably, the Hosea introduction refers to it as part of the Book of the Twelve/Minor Prophets.

47. Paul cites the passage from Isaiah in combination with echoes of Hos 2:1 and Isa 28:22. From Isa 10:22 he takes over the idea of a remnant (κατάλειμμα, thus also in the most manuscripts of Romans; Sinaiticus, Alexandrinus, and Vaticanus, and some others have ὑπόλειμμα). The metaphor that the number of the sons of Israel should be as the sand of the sea also appears in Hos 2:1, which has influenced Paul's quotation.

with the same differences from the Septuagint.[48] Since 1 Peter is probably not dependent on Romans, it is likely that both citations were already combined before Paul and 1 Peter in Jewish or early Christian tradition and taken over by both authors independently. The main characteristic of the Pauline text is that he has conflated the "costly, chosen, precious stone" from Isa 28:16 in the LXX (and 1 Pet 2:6) with the "stumbling stone and rock of offense" from Isa 8:14 (and 1 Pet 2:8). Remarkably, Paul's version of Isa 8:14 is closer to the Hebrew text and Symmachus than to the Septuagint.[49]

In Rom 10:5-13 Paul cites several passages from Scripture to prove that the contradiction between righteousness that comes from the law and righteousness that comes from faith is in accordance with what the Scriptures say. In particular, he quotes Lev 18:5 to show that Moses obliges "to do these things," which means: to do what the law requires in order to gain life.[50] The righteousness from faith, by contrast, is oriented toward the confession that Jesus is the resurrected and exalted Lord and that God has resurrected him from the dead (10:9). This is demonstrated by referring to Deut 30:12-14: it is not necessary to ascend to heaven or to descend into the abyss, since the "the word is near to you, in your mouth and in your heart." These references are not cited as words from Scripture. Instead Paul uses them as an expression of the "righteousness of faith." This again shows how he integrates Scripture into his view that God saves through faith in the gospel. In a resumption of Isa 28:16 (see 9:33), Paul concludes that those who believe in him will not be ashamed (10:11). The passage ends with a citation from Joel 3:5: "everyone who calls on the name of the Lord will be saved."

The last part of chapter 10 (vv. 14–21) deals with the failure of the preachers and of God himself to convince Israel of the gospel. Paul composed this passage based on several quotations from Scripture that are interwoven into a speech about Israel's rejection of all efforts for them: Isaiah 52:7 ("how timely are those who bring good news"); 53:1 ("Lord, who has believed our message?"); Ps 18:5 LXX ("Into all the earth their voice has gone forth, and their words unto the ends of the inhabited world"); Deut 32:21 ("I will make you jealous of those who are not a people, of a foolish people I will make you angry"); Isa 65:1 ("I was found by those who were not seeking me; I showed myself to those who were not asking for me"); and 65:2 ("All day long I have held out my hands to a people who are disobedient and obstinate").

---

48. See Dietrich-Alex Koch, "The Quotations of Isaiah 8,14 and 28,16 in Romans 9,33 and 1 Peter 2,6.8 as Test Case for Old Testament Quotations in the New Testament," *ZNW* 101 (2010): 228–34.

49. The Septuagint has transformed the Hebrew text that speaks of a "stumbling stone" and a "rock of falling" into a positive statement about God's behavior toward Israel.

50. See also Gal 3:12 where Lev 18:5 is quoted in a similar sense.

The quotations are used in different ways. The first one is introduced with "as it is written"; the second one is presented as a word of Isaiah to God. The quotation from Ps 18 is introduced by "but I say," that is, as a word of Paul himself. The last three citations are presented as words of Moses and of God who speaks through Isaiah. The two sentences from Isa 65:1–2 are thereby introduced separately with "Isaiah boldly says" and "to Israel he says." Thus, Paul explains Israel's rejection of the gospel by referring to different parts of Scripture that describe their disobedience to God's striving for them and point to another people by whom God will be found. The passage is therefore another example of Paul's view that the gospel is promised beforehand in the Scriptures.

In Rom 11 Paul develops a third answer to the problem of Israel's disobedience to the gospel. Now Israel's destiny as a divided people comes into focus. Quotations from Scripture appear in the first and the last part of the chapter (11:1–10 and 25–36), whereas in the middle part (11:11–24), Paul describes the history of Israel and the believing gentiles in the metaphor of two olive trees: a wild one (ἀγριέλαιος) and a cultivated one (καλλιέλαιος). In this part Paul addresses his gentile readers for the first time since 1:13.[51] Now he describes their relationship to the nonbelieving Jews as that of "wild branches" that have been grafted onto the cultivated olive tree, whereas other branches have been cut off but can be grafted in again.

Paul begins in 11:1–10 by explaining why despite Israel's disobedience God has not rejected his people. A first proof is Paul himself: he is an Israelite, of the seed of Abraham, and he believes in the gospel. A second proof comes from Scripture: the episode of Elijah who alone survived Ahab's slaughter of the prophets (1 Kgs 19:10, quoted in 11:3) serves as an example that not all of Israel will be destroyed, but God will save a remnant. In 11:4 Paul continues with another citation from the same story: "I have kept for myself seven thousand who have not bowed the knee to Baal" (1 Kgs 19:18). The story from 1 Kgs 19 thus serves as proof that God will save a "chosen remnant" (11:5: λεῖμμα κατ' ἐκλογήν). Thus, Paul takes up the idea of a "remnant" of Israel which he had referred to already in 9:27. In what follows this is explained further as a "hardening of the rest," followed by a proof from Scripture: in 11:8 Paul cites Deut 29:3 LXX in combination with Isa 29:10. The text from Deuteronomy is part of Moses's speech to the Israelites before their crossing of the Jordan. Moses reminds them that they cannot completely grasp the great things that the Lord has done for them since God "has not given you a mind to understand, or eyes to see or ears to hear." Paul has transformed this sentence into a positive statement about what God *gave* the Israelites. Moreover, he has replaced the "heart" with the "spirit of

---

51. See 11:13: "I say to you gentiles."

stupor" (πνεῦμα κατανύξεως) from Isa 29:10. Thus, Paul has conflated two passages from Scripture that describe how God has hindered Israel from seeing his mighty deeds into a statement that fits his own line of thought: that Israel did not achieve what they were seeking for is the result of God's hardening of them.

In 11:9 Paul adds another citation from Ps 68:23–24 LXX (with slight variations), introduced by "And David says." As is common in Jewish tradition, the psalms are ascribed to David as an inspired composer. The quotation supports the previous one. The psalm is a prayer that God may bring calamity upon the persecutors. In Paul's usage it is another statement about God's hardening of the nonbelieving part of Israel: "Let their table become a snare and a trap and a stumbling block and a retribution. Let their eyes be darkened so that they cannot see and keep their backs forever bent." Thus, in this paragraph Paul explains the divide within Israel by referring to God's hardening of a part of them. This intensifies the question of how this hardened part can be saved. Again, the quotations demonstrate that Israel's destiny is in accordance with the testimony of Scripture. And again, Paul has compiled citations from different parts of Scripture that are linked by the line of thought of his argument.

In the last part of chapter 11, Paul comes to the most burning issue of these chapters, namely how the divide in Israel can be healed. He takes up the idea of a partial hardening of Israel that is now interpreted as a "mystery" that will last "until the fullness of the gentiles comes in" (11:25). This is continued with a Scriptural quotation, introduced by "as it is written" (καθὼς γέγραπται). The much-discussed phrase "and in this way all Israel will be saved" (καὶ οὕτως πᾶς Ἰσραὴλ σωθήσεται), which precedes the quotation, probably refers to the process through which "all of Israel" will be saved, namely that the hardening of the nonbelieving part of Israel will be removed. The following citation adds another aspect of God's saving activity with Israel: He will come as "the deliverer from Zion, turn away ungodliness from Jacob," and remove their sin as the content of his covenant with them. Paul quotes Isa 59:20–21 in connection with Isa 27:9 with a minor change: instead of "for the sake of Zion" (ἕνεκεν Σιών), Paul writes "from Zion" (ἐκ Σιών).[52] That Paul thinks of God (not Jesus Christ) as the "deliverer from Zion" is not only indicated by several texts from the Scriptures but also by the fact that Paul deals with God's behavior toward Israel.[53] Consequently, it is God who will save Israel by dissolving the hardening and bringing the divide in Israel to an end.

---

52. Whether this goes back to a Pauline modification, a Jewish tradition, or an unknown Greek version of the text can remain open here.

53. See Wolter, *Römer*, 2:212–13. He refers to Pss 13:7 LXX; 19:3 LXX; 49:2 LXX; 109:2 LXX; and others.

In the final section (11:33-36), Paul praises God's wisdom and knowledge that will lead to Israel's salvation, even if it cannot be grasped in detail by human beings. Included in this praise are three rhetorical questions, based on two passages from Scripture. The first two questions ("Who has known the mind of our Lord? Who has been his counselor?" in 11:34) are largely in agreement with Isa 40:13 LXX, whereas the third one ("Who has given him a gift to receive a gift in return?" in 11:35) follows Job 41:3. In this case, however, the Pauline wording deviates from the Septuagint and also from the Hebrew text. It is likely that Paul follows a Greek version of the biblical text that is closer to the Hebrew original than the Septuagint.[54]

In 12:1-15:13 Paul develops instructions for a life according to faith—"a reasonable worship" (λογικὴ λατρεία), as he calls it at the beginning (12:1). These instructions are of a general character and not specifically related to the addressees in Rome (although they are applied to them as well, of course). These admonitions show that for Paul a community of believers usually consists of members with and without a Jewish background. In this part of the letter, too, Paul makes frequent reference to Scripture in order to emphasize that the life of the believers has to be in accordance with God's commandments. The specific contribution to the use of Scriptures in Romans, therefore, is that Paul now interprets Scripture as ethical instruction for the believers.

In 12:9-21 Paul articulates a series of general admonitions for the behavior toward insiders and outsiders on the basis of Jewish and early Christian ethical traditions. Explicit references to Scripture occur in verses 19-21, where he deals with behavior toward enemies. The solicitation not to avenge oneself in 12:19 is substantiated by a citation from Deut 32:35, which is identical with Heb 10:30 but differs from the Hebrew Bible and the Septuagint: γέγραπται γάρ· ἐμοὶ ἐκδίκησις, ἐγὼ ἀνταποδώσω, λέγει κύριος ("For it is written: 'To me is vengeance, I will repay,' says the Lord"). The theme occurs frequently in other Jewish texts also, as, for example, Jer 5:9; Joel 3:4; Nah 1:2. Thus, it is likely that the quotation from Deut 32:35 as it is cited independently by Paul and the author of Hebrews already existed in early Jewish and/or early Christian tradition.

Paul connects this citation with another one from Prov 25:21-22. Unlike in the previous case, however, he does not mark this sentence as a quotation. Thus, it reads as an application of the previous quotation to the addressees; it is an instruction in the second-person singular on how to deal with the enemy: "if your enemy is hungry, feed him; if he is thirsty, give him to drink; for by doing so you will be heaping coals of fire on his head." The citation is not a version of the com-

---

54. See Berndt Schaller, "Zum Textcharakter der Hiobzitate im paulinischen Schrifttum," *ZNW* 71 (1980): 21-26.

mand to love one's enemies from the Jesus tradition. Instead, Paul refers to God's eternal judgment about those who are currently adversaries of the Christian communities to encourage them to a peaceful life together with their enemies (the focus of the love command in the Jesus tradition is somewhat different).

In 13:8–10 Paul establishes the love command as the main principle of the law. In 13:8a he explains that to love one another means to fulfill the law, and in 13:9b he cites the command to love your neighbor as yourself from Lev 19:18. In between these two remarks he cites the last four of the ten commandments from Deut 5:17–21.[55] As the following remark, "and if there is any other commandment," indicates, Paul has cited the four commandments as examples that could be expanded by others. Eventually, in 13:10 he summarizes that love is the fulfillment of the law. Thus, Paul interprets the law—that is, the Torah from Sinai, as the citation from Deut 5 makes clear—from the perspective of love as its most important command. Since love (ἀγάπη) is a leading category in Paul's ethics (besides edification, οἰκοδομή), the passage demonstrates that he interprets the Torah according to his ethics for the life of a community of Christ believers.[56]

In chapters 14 and 15 Paul cites Scripture a few more times. The quotation from Isa 45:23 in 14:11 ("For it is written, 'To me every knee shall bow, and every tongue will praise God'") serves to substantiate the view that observance of food laws is insignificant because all must appear before God's judgment seat. Paul uses this citation in Phil 2:10–11 as well, although with a christological meaning: in Philippians "Lord" (κύριος) refers to Jesus Christ, whereas in Romans it is applied to God, as the preceding reference to God's mercy seat shows. Moreover, Paul introduces the citation with the formula "As I live, says the Lord" (ζῶ ἐγώ, λέγει κύριος).[57] This introduction may be regarded as an accentuation of the theo-logical understanding of the quotation in distinction from the preceding verses which have a christo-logical emphasis.

In 15:3 Paul cites Ps 68:10b from the Septuagint, "The insults of those who insult you have fallen on me," to describe how Christ gave an example of how not to please oneself, but to please one's neighbor for edification. Again, Paul uses Scripture to reinforce his ethical instructions: The citation illustrates Christ's passive behavior toward his adversaries during the passion events. Paul does not refer to these events explicitly, although they serve as the background of his

---

55. Paul leaves out the command not to bear false witness against the neighbor (Deut 5:20) and gives the last command, not to covet one's neighbor's wife, in an abbreviated form ("you shall not covet").

56. See also Gal 5:14, where Paul also cites Lev 19:18 as proof that the law is fulfilled in the love command. See also 1 Cor 13. For edification see Rom 14:19; 15:2; 1 Cor 8:1; 10:23; 14:3–5, 12, 17, 26; 2 Cor 10:8; 12:19; 13:10; 1 Thess 5:11.

57. See, e.g., Num 14:28; Isa 49:18; Jer 22:24; Ezek 5:11.

remark.[58] The clue of his argument, however, is that Christ gave an example of how to behave toward one's neighbor for edification (15:2). This is supported by the beginning of the next paragraph: "Receive one another, just as Christ has received us to the glory of God" (15:7).

A compilation of four citations from Scripture occurs in 15:9–12. Similar to 9:25–29 and in contrast to 3:10–18, Paul introduces each citation separately: "As it is written" (v. 9b); "and again it says" (10a); "and again" (11a); "and again Isaiah says" (12a). The accumulation of references from different parts of Scripture—Psalms, Torah, Prophets—serves to illustrate that the preceding exhortation is in accordance with Israel's Scriptures. All four citations contain the word "gentiles" (ἔθνη). This points to the case that Paul wants to support with this compilation: as he has argued before, Christ has become a servant of the circumcision to confirm the promises of the fathers (15:8), and the gentiles are glorifying God for his mercy (15:9a).[59] The following citations corroborate this statement about the gentiles: God will be praised among the gentiles, the gentiles shall rejoice with God's people, all the gentiles and all peoples shall praise the Lord, the root of Jesse shall rule the gentiles and the gentiles will hope on him. Thus, the compilation serves to illustrate what Paul has demonstrated throughout the letter: God's power for salvation in the gospel is aimed first at the Jews but also at the gentiles.

Conclusion

The references to Scripture play an important role for Paul's argument in Romans. He refers to Scripture throughout the letter in different ways to explore his view of the gospel. In general statements about the "holy Scriptures" or "the law and the prophets" as well as in remarks about God's oracles (τὰ λόγια τοῦ θεοῦ, 3:2) or the word of God (ὁ λόγος τοῦ θεοῦ, 9:6), he emphasizes that the gospel is based on the Scriptures of Israel. This is outlined in more detail in the first part of the letter, where Paul explains that God's righteousness by faith, without works of the law, belongs to the basic content of Israel's Scriptures. Paul quotes from the Torah and the prophets, with particular attention to Hab 2:4 and Gen 15:6, and demonstrates by the example of Abraham that God's saving activity through faith in Jesus Christ is in accordance with Israel's history and

---

58. See a similar description in 1 Pet 2:21–23 with a reference to Isa 53.

59. The relationship of these two sentences is a conundrum since (1) the two sentences do not correspond with each other syntactically, and (2) "Christ" in 15:8 and "the gentiles" in 15:9 are not on the same semantic level. The most probable solution is that both sentences are to be regarded as complementary but independent statements that are both dependent on the introductory "I say" in 15:8a.

the Scriptures. This applies to the situation of humankind under sin before the coming of Christ as well as to the new life in the Spirit under the circumstances of the present age. A particular theme developed on the basis of Scripture is the divide within Israel between those who believe in Jesus Christ and those who are "hardened." Paul demonstrates that this split in Israel is also in accordance with the Scriptures and that in the end all of Israel will be saved, as it is written in the Scriptures. In the last part of the letter, quotations from Scripture serve to illustrate the way of life according to God's commandment in view of the gospel.

The quotations sometimes literally agree with the Septuagint as it is known from the Christian Bible manuscripts of the fourth and fifth centuries, for example, Sinaiticus and Vaticanus, though sometimes they differ from them. These variations are sometimes due to Paul's own interest in the citation, while in other cases Paul apparently cites from revisions of the Greek text that are closer to the Hebrew original (e.g., in 11:35). Particularly striking in this regard is the long citation in Rom 3:10–18 that may go back to a Septuagint version of the psalm. Sometimes Paul seems to take over conflations of biblical passages from early Christian tradition (e.g., in 9:33). The compilation of biblical passages serves Paul's own interest of citing from different writings to prove that Scripture in all its parts testifies to the gospel (e.g., 10:15–21).

Throughout the letter it is evident that Paul uses the Scriptures as proof of his conviction that God saves all humankind through faith in Jesus Christ. In Romans he relates this conviction to the Scriptures of Israel more than in any other of his letters. He wants to demonstrate that the gospel can aptly be understood only if it is interpreted on the basis of Israel's Scriptures because the God of Israel is the same God who saves Jews and gentiles by faith in Jesus Christ. This conviction serves as the hermeneutical paradigm for the interpretation of Scripture. In other words, in Paul's view Scripture is properly understood and interpreted only on the basis of faith in Jesus Christ. Thus, all of the uses of Scripture in Romans—explicit quotations, the midrashic interpretation of Gen 15:6, the allusion to biblical narratives or figures—serve the purpose of developing the insight that Scripture witnesses to the gospel.

Bibliography

Albl, Martin C. *"And Scripture Cannot Be Broken": The Form and Function of the Early Christian Testimonia Collections.* NovTSup 96. Leiden: Brill, 1999.

Bendemann, Reinhard v. "Die kritische Diastase von Wissen, Wollen und Handeln: Traditionsgeschichtliche Spurensuche eines hellenistischen Topos in Römer 7." *ZNW* 95, no. 1 (2004): 35–63.

Bornkamm, Günther. "Der Römerbrief als Testament des Paulus." Pages 120–39 in *Geschichte und Glaube: Gesammelte Aufsätze 4*. BEvT 53. Munich: Kaiser, 1971.

Cranfield, C. E. B. *A Critical and Exegetical Commentary on the Epistle to the Romans*. 2 vols. ICC. Edinburgh: T&T Clark, 1975.

Deissmann, Adolf. "ΙΛΑΣΤΗΡΙΟΣ und ΙΛΑΣΤΗΡΙΟΝ: Eine lexikalische Studie." *ZNW* 4 (1903): 193–212.

Donfried, Karl P., ed. *The Romans Debate: Revised and Expanded Edition*. Peabody, MA: Hendrickson, 1991.

Dunn, James D. G. *Romans*. 2 vols. WBC 38A–B. Waco, TX: Word, 1988.

———. *The Theology of Paul the Apostle*. Grand Rapids: Eerdmans, 1998.

Engberg-Pedersen, Troels. "The Reception of Graeco-Roman Culture in the New Testament: The Case of Romans 7.7–25." Pages 32–57 in *The New Testament as Reception*. Edited by Mogens Müller and Henrik Tronier. JSNTSup 230. Sheffield: Sheffield Academic, 2002.

Fitzmyer, Joseph A. *Romans: A New Translation with Introduction and Commentary*. AB 33. New York: Doubleday, 1993.

Haacker, Klaus. *Der Brief des Paulus an die Römer*. 4th ed. THKNT 6. Leipzig: Evangelische Verlagsanstalt, 2012.

Jewett, Robert. *Romans: A Commentary*. Hermeneia. Minneapolis: Fortress, 2007.

Karrer, Martin, Marcus Sigismund, and Ulrich Schmid. "Textgeschichtliche Beobachtungen zu den Zusätzen in den Septuaginta-Psalmen." Pages 140–61 in *Die Septuaginta: Texte, Theologien, Einflüsse; 2. Internationale Fachtagung veranstaltet von Septuaginta Deutsch (LXX. D), Wuppertal 23.–27.7.2008*. Edited by Wolfgang Kraus, Martin Karrer, and Martin Meiser. WUNT 252. Tübingen: Mohr Siebeck, 2010.

Käsemann, Ernst. *An die Römer*. HNT 8A. Tübingen: Mohr Siebeck, 1980.

Koch, Dietrich-Alex. "Der Text von Hab 2,4b in der Septuaginta und im Neuen Testament." Pages 25–41 in *Hellenistisches Christentum: Schriftverständnis – Ekklesiologie – Geschichte*. Edited by Friedrich Wilhelm Horn. NTOA 65. Göttingen: Vandenhoeck & Ruprecht, 2008.

———. *Die Schrift als Zeuge des Evangeliums: Untersuchungen zur Verwendung und zum Verständnis der Schrift bei Paulus*. BHT 69. Tübingen: Mohr Siebeck, 1986.

———. "The Quotations of Isaiah 8,14 and 28,16 in Romans 9,33 and 1Peter 2,6.8 as Test Case for Old Testament Quotations in the New Testament." *ZNW* 101, no. 2 (2010): 223–40.

Kujanpää, Katja. *The Rhetorical Functions of Scriptural Quotations in Romans: Paul's Argumentation by Quotations*. NovTSup 172. Leiden: Brill, 2019.

Lambrecht, Jan. *The Wretched I and Its Liberation: Paul in Romans 7 and 8*. LThPM 14. Leuven: Peeters; Grand Rapids: Eerdmans, 1992.

Lichtenberger, Hermann. *Das Ich Adams und das ich der Menschheit: Studien zum Menschenbild in Römer 7*. WUNT 164. Tübingen: Mohr Siebeck, 2004.

Lohse, Eduard. *Der Brief an die Römer.* KEK 4. Göttingen: Vandenhoeck & Ruprecht, 2003.

Moo, Douglas J. *The Epistle to the Romans.* NICNT. Grand Rapids: Eerdmans, 1996.

Neubrand, Maria. *Abraham, Vater von Juden und Nichtjuden: Eine exegetische Studie zu Röm 4.* FB 85. Würzburg: Echter, 1997.

Nicklas, Tobias. "Paulus und die Errettung Israels: Röm 11,25–36 in der exegetischen Diskussion und im jüdisch-christlichen Dialog." *EC* 2, no. 2 (2011): 173–97.

Osten-Sacken, Peter von der. "Römer 9–11 als Schibbolet christlicher Theologie." Pages 515–38 in *Der Gott der Hoffnung: Gesammelte Aufsätze zur Theologie des Paulus.* SKI 3. Leipzig: Evangelische Verlagsanstalt, 2014.

Porter, Stanley E., and Christopher D. Land, eds. *Paul and Scripture.* Pauline Studies 10. Leiden: Brill, 2019.

———, eds. *As It Is Written: Studying Paul's Use of Scripture.* SymS 50. Atlanta: Society of Biblical Literature, 2008.

Rahlfs, Alfred, ed. *Psalmi cum Odis.* 3rd ed. SVTG 26. Göttingen: Vandenhoeck & Ruprecht: 1979.

Reasoner, Mark. "'Promised Beforehand through His Prophets in The Holy Scriptures': Composite Citations in Romans." Pages 128–58 in *Composite Citations in Antiquity.* Vol. 2, *New Testament Uses.* Edited by Sean A. Adams and Seth M. Ehorn. LNTS 593. London: Bloomsbury, 2018.

Sandnes, Karl-Olav. "Justification and Abraham: Exegesis of Romans 4." Pages 147–81 in *God's Power for Salvation: Romans 1,1–5,11.* Edited by Cilliers Breytenbach. Colloquium Oecumenicum Paulinum 23. Leuven: Peeters, 2017.

Schaller, Berndt. "Zum Textcharakter der Hiobzitate im paulinischen Schrifttum." *ZNW* 71, no. 1–2 (1980): 21–26.

Schliesser, Benjamin. *Abraham's Faith in Romans 4: Paul's Concept of Faith in Light of the History of Reception of Genesis 15:6.* WUNT 2/224. Tübingen: Mohr Siebeck, 2007.

Schreiber, Stefan. "Das Weihegeschenk Gottes: Eine Deutung des Todes Jesu in Röm 3,25." *ZNW* 97, no. 1–2 (2006): 88–110.

———. "Weitergedacht: Das versöhnende Weihegeschenk Gottes in Röm 3,25." *ZNW* 106, no. 2 (2015): 201–15.

Schreiner, Thomas R. *Romans.* BECNT 6. Grand Rapids: Baker, 1998.

Schröter, Jens. "Der Mensch zwischen Wollen und Tun: Erwägungen zu Römer 7 im Licht der 'New Perspective on Paul.'" Pages 195–223 in *Paulus – Werk und Wirkung: Festschrift für Andreas Lindemann zum 70. Geburtstag.* Edited by Paul-Gerhard Klumbies, David S. Du Toit, Torsten Jantsch, and Nils Neumann. Tübingen: Mohr Siebeck, 2013.

Seifrid, Mark A. "Answered Lament: Paul's Gospel, Israel, and the Scriptures in Romans." Pages 175–215 in *Paulinische Schriftrezeption: Grundlagen – Ausprä-*

gungen – Wirkungen – Wertungen. Edited by Florian Wilk and Marku Öhler. FRLANT 268. Göttingen: Vandenhoeck & Ruprecht, 2017.

———. "Romans." Pages 607–94 in *Commentary on the New Testament Use of the Old Testament*. Edited by G. K. Beale and D. A. Carson. Grand Rapids: Baker Academic, 2007.

Stanley, Christopher D. *Paul and the Language of Scripture: Citation Technique in the Pauline Epistles and Contemporary Literature*. SNTSMS 74. Cambridge: Cambridge University Press, 1992.

———. "'The Redeemer Will Come ἐκ Σιων': Romans 11.26–27 Revisited." Pages 118–142 in *Paul and the Scriptures of Israel*. Edited by Craig A. Evans and James A. Sanders. JSNTSup 83. Sheffield: Sheffield Academic, 1993.

Theobald, Michael. *Römerbrief*. 2 vols. SKKNT 6.1-2. Stuttgart: Katholisches Bibelwerk, 1992–1993.

———. *Studien zum Römerbrief*. WUNT 136. Tübingen: Mohr Siebeck, 2001.

Tilly, Michael. "Paulus und die antike jüdische Schriftauslegung." *KD* 63, no. 3 (2017): 157–81.

Weiß, Alexander. "Christus Jesus als Weihegeschenk oder Sühnemal? Anmerkungen zu einer neueren Deutung von hilasterion (Röm 3,25) samt einer Liste der epigraphischen Belege." *ZNW* 105, no. 2 (2014): 294–302.

Wilckens, Ulrich. *Der Brief an die Römer*. 3 vols. EKKNT 6.1-3. Zürich: Einsiedeln; Neukirchen Vluyn: Neukirchener Verlag, 1978–1982.

Wilk Florian and J. Ross Wagner, ed. *Between Gospel and Election: Explorations in the Interpretation of Romans 9–11*. WUNT 257. Tübingen: Mohr Siebeck, 2010.

Wolter, Michael. "Das Israelproblem nach Gal 4,21–31 und Röm 9–11." *ZTK* 107, no. 1 (2010): 1–30.

———. *Der Brief an die Römer*. 2 vols. EKKNT 6.1-2. Neukirchen-Vluyn: Neukirchener Verlag; Ostfildern: Patmos, 2014–2019.

14

Israel's Scriptures in 1 and 2 Corinthians

KATJA KUJANPÄÄ

In 1 and 2 Corinthians, Israel's Scriptures feature prominently in Paul's argumentation, with about twenty-eight citations, depending on the definition. The most cited books are Isaiah (seven times), Psalms (five times), Deuteronomy (three), Genesis (twice), Exodus (twice), Jeremiah (twice), and 1 Kingdoms (twice). Leviticus, 2 Kingdoms, Job, and Hosea are each cited once. In addition to citations from Israel's Scriptures, Paul also cites Menander once without referring to the source text (1 Cor 15:33). In addition, Paul uses both verbal and conceptual allusions, as well as scriptural motifs and imagery, such as God's vineyard (cf. 1 Cor 3:5–9 and Isa 5:1–7), and occasionally retells entire narratives in his own words (cf. 1 Cor 10). Paul also draws on scriptural language and concepts for which it is not always possible to identify a single source text. Moreover, some of his statements have a scriptural basis, but rather than referring to a specific verse, they reflect traditional interpretations of Israel's Scriptures. The idea of God's people judging the world (1 Cor 6:2), for example, may have its basis in Dan 7:22 but occurs more explicitly in numerous other early Jewish texts.[1]

Citations and allusions accumulate in certain argumentative passages, such as 1 Cor 10 and 15. Yet there are also some sections where Israel's Scriptures do not play a prominent role: in 1 Cor 7 (on marriage); 1 Cor 12 (on spiritual gifts); 2 Cor 1–2 (on Paul's relationship with the Corinthians); and 2 Cor 11:4–12:21

---

1. See Roy E. Ciampa and Brian S. Rosner, "1 Corinthians," in *Commentary on the New Testament Use of the Old Testament*, ed. G. K. Beale and D. A. Carson (Grand Rapids: Baker Academic, 2007), 711.

(Paul's defense of his ministry). While most such sections relate to the context of the letter and are thus situational by nature, the minor role of scriptural material in Paul's discussion of spiritual gifts demonstrates that there is no clear correlation between the theological weight of a topic and the number of scriptural references used when discussing it.

Table 14.1. Citations in 1 and 2 Corinthians

1 Corinthians		2 Corinthians	
1:19	Isa 29:14	4:13	Ps 116:10 (115:1 LXX)
1:31	Jer 9:22–23; 1 Kgdms [=1 Sam] 2:10	6:2	Isa 49:8
		6:16	Lev 26:11–12
2:9	unknown	6:17	Isa 52:11; Ezek 20:34
2:16	Isa 40:13	6:18	2 Kgdms [=2 Sam] 7:8, 14
3:19	Job 5:12	8:15	Exod 16:18
3:20	Ps 94:11 (93:11 LXX)	9:9	Ps 112:9 (111:9 LXX)
5:13	Deut 17:7 etc.	10:17	Jer 9:22–23; 1 Kgdms [=1 Sam] 2:10
6:16	Gen 2:24		
9:9	Deut 25:4	13:1	Deut 19:15
9:10	unknown		
10:7	Exod 32:6		
10:26	Ps 24:1 (23:1 LXX)		
14:21	Isa 28:11–12		
15:27	Ps 8:7 (8:7 LXX)		
15:32	Isa 22:13		
15:33	Menander		
15:45	Gen 2:7		
15:54	Isa 25:8		
15:55	Hos 13:14		

Paul's Use of Introductory Formulas

Paul introduces scriptural references in various ways in his argumentation, and several cases in 1 and 2 Corinthians highlight the problems of identifying citations and distinguishing them from allusions. An introductory formula is not on its own a sufficient criterion for identifying the presence of a citation, given that Paul sometimes cites several words from the Septuagint without an introductory formula (e.g., 1 Cor 2:16). Some such cases can be identified as citations with the help of other signs, such as interpretive comments or clear syntactical discrepancies (e.g., Ps 8:7 in 1 Cor 15:27; see below, under "Paul's Use of Israel's

Scriptures").[2] On the other hand, in 2 Cor 4:6, Paul's formulation looks like an introductory formula, but what follows is no straightforward citation: "For God, who said, 'Let light shine out of darkness.'"[3] Often, the distinction between an unmarked citation and a verbal allusion may be blurry because it is typical of Paul to freely rewrite scriptural passages to fit his argument, as exemplified in 1 Cor 15:25 (see below, under "Paul's Use of Israel's Scriptures").

In two instances, Paul uses an introductory formula, but it is not clear what he is citing. In 1 Cor 2:9, "as it is written" introduces a fascinating citation: "What no eye has seen nor ear heard and what has not risen to the heart of man, what God has prepared for those who love him." While the citation resembles, to some extent, Isa 64:3, it appears unlikely that Paul thoroughly rewrites this verse (or conflates it himself with Isa 65:16; Jer 5:16; Sir 1:10; Pss. Sol. 6:6).[4] This is because a similar citation can be found in a number of other sources, including Pseudo-Philo (LAB 26:13), Gos. Thom. 17 (as Jesus's saying), 1 Clem. 34:8; 2 Clem. 11:7; 14:5, and a series of other Christian texts.[5] To complicate the matter further, Origen claims that the citation can be found "in secretis Eliae prophetae," but the Apocalypse of Elijah contains no such passage.[6] It is possible that the citation is a pre-Pauline Jewish logion that circulated among different groups.[7] The citation is formulated on the basis of Isa 64:3 but not a direct citation of its Hebrew, Greek, or Aramaic form. While it is unclear what Paul himself thought of the origin of his citation, his introductory formula seems to suggest that one way or another he did see it as deriving from Scripture.

In 1 Cor 9:10, Paul appears to signify the presence of a citation: "For it is written for our sake that 'The one who plows should plow in hope and the one who

---

2. Citations can be defined in various ways, and the aptness of the definition depends on its purpose. On this point, see Katja Kujanpää, *The Rhetorical Functions of Scriptural Quotations in Romans: Paul's Argumentation by Quotations*, NovTSup 172 (Leiden: Brill, 2019), 19–20.

3. ὅτι ὁ θεὸς ὁ εἰπών· ἐκ σκότους φῶς λάμψει. Cf. Gen 1:3 Γενηθήτω φῶς ("Let there be light"); Isa 9:1: ὁ λαὸς ὁ πορευόμενος ἐν σκότει, ἴδετε φῶς μέγα· ... φῶς λάμψει ἐφ᾽ ὑμᾶς ("O you people walking in darkness, see a great light! ... light will shine on you"). Unless otherwise noted, all translations are by the author.

4. "From ages past we have not heard, nor have our eyes seen a God besides you, and your works that you will do to those who wait for mercy" (Isa 64:3 LXX).

5. For a comprehensive list, as well as excerpts from the primary texts, see Michael E. Stone and John Strugnell, *The Books of Elijah, Parts 1–2*, SBLTT 18 (Missoula, MT: Scholars Press, 1979), 42–73.

6. Origen, *Matthäuserklärung*, ed. Erich Klostermann, 2nd ed., GCS 38 (Berlin: Akademie, 1976), under Matt 27:9–10 (p. 250, lines 4–6). See Joseph Verheyden, "Origen on the Origin of 1 Cor 2,9," in *The Corinthian Correspondence*, ed. Reimund Bieringer, BETL 125 (Leuven: Leuven University Press, 1996), 491–511.

7. Dietrich-Alex Koch, *Die Schrift als Zeuge des Evangeliums: Untersuchungen zur Verwendung und zum Verständnis der Schrift bei Paulus*, BHT 69 (Tübingen: Mohr Siebeck, 1986), 38–39.

threshes should thresh in hope of sharing in the crop.'" However, no such text is known, which is why many English translations assume that no citation has been introduced and that "it is written" (ἐγράφη) refers to the preceding citation from Deuteronomy (cf. NRSV; ESV). However, the combination of ἐγράφη with ὅτι does look like an introductory formula, and the parallel structure of the citation stands out from Paul's style in the surrounding context.[8] Moreover, γάρ suggests that this citation is supposed to offer additional support for Paul's interpretation that God has decreed that preachers have the right to material comforts (1 Cor 9:4–11). Just before the passage, Paul cites Deut 25:4 ("You shall not muzzle an ox while it is treading out the grain"), arguing that the law is not concerned with oxen but with "us."[9] The second citation, also written "for our sake," confirms that the point of the law is indeed metaphorical rather than a piece of agricultural advice. It appears therefore probable that 1 Cor 9:10 is another example of a scripturally based saying that Paul attributes to Scripture.[10]

Paul's Use of Israel's Scriptures

In 1 and 2 Corinthians, Paul refers to Israel's Scriptures in connection with a vast variety of themes and for manifold reasons. In this chapter, it is possible to discuss only a couple of themes and cases. Here, I draw attention especially to sections in which citations and allusions abound and help to highlight central features in Paul's scriptural argumentation.

Wisdom of the World and Boasting (1 Corinthians 1–3)

Several marked citations at the beginning of 1 Corinthians are related to the interconnected themes of the "wisdom of the world" and "boasting." Paul argues for a fundamental reversal of the social value system and appears to attack popular sophistic rhetoric. The basis for this reversal is the eschatological reality anchored in the Christ event (1 Cor 1:18).[11]

---

8. Koch, *Die Schrift als Zeuge*, 41; Christopher D. Stanley, *Paul and the Language of Scripture: Citation Technique in the Pauline Epistles and Contemporary Literature*, SNTSMS 74 (Cambridge: Cambridge University Press, 1992), 196–97.

9. For this citation, see David Lincicum, *Paul and the Early Jewish Encounter with Deuteronomy*, WUNT 2/284 (Tübingen: Mohr Siebeck, 2010), 131–33.

10. For false attributions of citations in antiquity, see Koch, *Die Schrift als Zeuge*, 42.

11. Richard B. Hays, "The Conversion of the Imagination: Scripture and Eschatology in 1 Corinthians," *NTS* 45, no. 3 (1999): 402–9.

Paul presents several citations to highlight God's disregard for human wisdom. The first occurs in 1 Cor 1:19: "As it is written, 'I will destroy the wisdom of the wise and the discernment of the discerning I will thwart'" (Isa 29:14). Paul further sharpens the message of his source text. In Isa 29:14, God will merely "hide" the discernment of the discerning, whereas in Paul's citation he will "thwart" it, suggesting a sharper contrast between divine plans and human understanding. The citations in 1 Cor 3:19-20 similarly underline the futility of human wisdom in God's eyes: "For it is written, 'He catches the wise in their craftiness'" (1 Cor 3:19/Job 5:13). And again, "The Lord knows the thoughts of the wise, that they are futile" (1 Cor 3:20/Ps 93:11 LXX).[12] In the latter citation, Paul has modified the wording to connect the citation to the theme of wisdom. While in the psalm, the Lord is said to know the thoughts of "human beings," Paul replaces this with knowing the thoughts of "the wise," thus forming a verbal connection with the preceding citation.[13]

The stark contrast between the wisdom of God and the value systems of "this age" is emphasized by the citation in 1 Cor 2:9: "What no eye has seen nor ear heard and what has not risen to the heart of man, what God has prepared for those who love him." The theme resumes in 1 Cor 2:16, where Paul uses an unmarked citation from Isa 40:13 to highlight God's sovereign decisions: "For who has known the mind of the Lord so as to instruct him?"

This belittlement of human wisdom and the fundamental upheaval of systems of worth are closely related to the theme of boasting (καυχάομαι; cf. 1 Cor 1:27-31), a word that can have various connotations in Paul. He uses the word in a negative sense to refer to the bragging of his opponents, but, in many instances, his use of the word reflects connotations of the word in the Septuagint: "The object of boast is what has value in life, what is seen as worth to be striven for, what one is proud of. . . . It is a question of where the centre of one's life lies: whether one puts one's faith in God or relies on worldly supports."[14] According to Paul, the Corinthians should recognize that Christ is their wisdom, "so that, as it is written, 'Let the one who boasts, boast in the Lord'" (1 Cor 1:31). Despite the introductory formula, this concise citation does not match exactly any verse of the Septuagint. It is, however, clearly dependent on 1 Kgdms 2:10 or its parallel passage in Jer 9:22-23, as the following table illustrates.

---

12. The futility of human wisdom in face of divine plans is a theme that occurs in several other early Jewish writings as well; see particularly Wis 17:7; Bar 3:29-37.

13. Koch, *Die Schrift als Zeuge*, 153; Stanley, *Paul and the Language of Scripture*, 195.

14. Anneli Aejmelaeus, "Wisdom Meets Prophecy: The Theme of Boasting and Paul's Quotation of Hannah's Psalm," in *Weisheit und Schöpfung: Festschrift für James Loader zum 65. Geburtstag*, ed. Stefan Fischer and Marianne Grohmann, Wiener Alttestamentliche Studien 7 (Frankfurt am Main: Lang, 2010), 14; see also 25-27.

Table 14.2. The Citation in 1 Corinthians 1:31 and 2 Corinthians 10:17

1 Cor 1:31/2 Cor 10:17[15]	1 Kgdms 2:10[16]	Jer 9:22–23 LXX[17]
ὁ καυχώμενος ἐν κυρίῳ καυχάσθω	ἀλλ' ἢ ἐν τούτῳ καυχάσθω ὁ καυχώμενος, συνίειν καὶ γινώσκειν τὸν Κύριον, καὶ ποιεῖν κρίμα καὶ δικαιοσύνην ἐν μέσῳ τῆς γῆς.	ἀλλ' ἢ ἐν τούτῳ καυχάσθω ὁ καυχώμενος, συνίειν καὶ γινώσκειν ὅτι ἐγώ εἰμι κύριος ποιῶν ἔλεος καὶ κρίμα καὶ δικαιοσύνην ἐπὶ τῆς γῆς
"Let him who boasts, boast in the Lord."	"But let him who boasts boast in this: understanding and knowing the Lord, and executing justice and righteousness in the midst of the earth."	"But let him who boasts boast in this: understanding and knowing that I am the Lord when I execute mercy and justice and righteousness in the earth."

In 1 Kgdms 2, the citation belongs to Hannah's song, a poem that praises God's power to reverse the status of human fortunes: "the Lord makes poor and makes rich; he brings low, and he exalts" (1 Kgdms 2:7). The Lord takes the needy and poor and raises them to power and glory (2:8). Jeremiah 9, for its part, is a warning of the approaching divine judgment. What immediately precedes the citation in both 1 Kingdoms and Jeremiah is a prohibition of boasting with three objects: "Let not the wise boast in his wisdom, and let not the mighty boast in his might, and let not the rich boast in his richness." This triad of wisdom, power, and wealth corresponds with Paul's depiction of the Corinthians at the time of their calling in 1 Cor 1:26 (though Paul speaks of birth rather than wealth): "not many of you were wise according to human standards, not many were powerful, not many were of noble birth."[18] While Paul probably knew both passages, the intertextual links with 1 Kgdms 2 appear stronger than those with Jer 9.[19] It

---

15. Paul repeats the citation in 2 Cor 10:17, although without an introductory formula.

16. The provisional critical text for *Regnorum liber I (Samuelis I)*, ed. Anneli Aejmelaeus, SVTG 5,1 (Göttingen: Vandenhoeck & Ruprecht, forthcoming), used with Aejmelaeus's permission.

17. Unless indicated otherwise, the Septuagint is cited according to the editions published in the series Septuaginta: Vetus Testamentum Graecum (SVTG) by the Göttingen Academy of Sciences.

18. J. Ross Wagner, "'Not Beyond the Things Which Are Written': A Call to Boast Only in the Lord (1 Cor 4.6)," *NTS* 44, no. 2 (1998): 284; Aejmelaeus, "Wisdom Meets Prophecy," 23.

19. Aejmelaeus, "Wisdom Meets Prophecy," 23–24; Wagner, "Not Beyond the Things," 284.

appears probable that Paul himself compressed the source text here, though the possibility cannot be excluded that the summarization had been made already before him.[20]

In 1 Corinthians, Paul discusses boasting because it reflects the factiousness of the congregation. His tone is pastoral, whereas in 2 Cor 10:17 he repeats the same citation in a polemical context, in a fierce defense of himself and his coworkers against the "super-apostles" (2 Cor 11:5). This time, the focus is not so much on the inversion of systems of worth but on "commending oneself." In its new context, the citation that is already familiar to the Corinthians suggests that Paul's opponents are guilty of bragging when they commend themselves (whereas Paul and his coworkers are commended by the Lord).

The Exodus Generation and the Corinthians (1 Corinthians 10)

In 1 Cor 10, Paul combines several wilderness narratives from Exodus and Numbers, retelling them selectively. These narratives are also recounted and interpreted in certain psalms that may have influenced Paul's formulations.[21] By referring to the wilderness generation as "our fathers" (10:1), Paul encourages the Corinthians to view the narratives as their own ancestral tradition that should shape their identity and behavior. Moreover, he explicitly refers to the scriptural incidents that he calls into his audience's mind as τύποι, "prefigurations," that were "written down for our instruction" (1 Cor 10:6, 11). This is one of the rare passages in which Paul explicitly comments on his hermeneutical moves.

Paul begins by listing the impressive experiences of the wilderness generation but soon emphasizes that they did not guarantee God's favor (1 Cor 10:1–5). Similarly, the Corinthians should not be overconfident but learn from the sins of the wilderness generation. Paul then examines these sins individually. The first sin is desiring evil (10:7), an allusion to Num 11:4–34, where the Israelites tire of eating manna and crave meat. When referring to this story, Ps 106:14 (105:14 LXX) omits the object of the craving and underlines the evilness of the wanton, illicit desire itself, and Paul continues this line of interpretation.

When Paul moves on to idolatry, he presents the only direct citation in the section. His introduction already provides the audience an interpretive framework: "Do not become idolaters as some of them did; as it is written, 'The people sat down to eat and drink, and they rose up to play'" (1 Cor 10:7/Exod 32:6). The cita-

---

20. For Paul compressing the text, see Stanley, *Paul and the Language of Scripture*, 188. The passage is cited in 1 Clem. 13:1, but it is probably dependent on Paul.

21. Marika Pulkkinen, "Paul's Use of Psalms: Quotations, Allusions, and Psalm Clusters in Romans and First Corinthians" (PhD diss., University of Helsinki, 2020), 150, 156, 163.

tion derives from the golden calf incident, Israel's sin of sins.[22] This is an example of a case in which the audience needs to connect a citation to its literary context to understand its full implications.[23] Paul's constant references to the wilderness narratives in the immediate context and explicit link of the citation to idolatry help the audience make this connection. The people's untroubled and lively communal celebration of their idols in the citation connects with the reality of the Corinthians and the problem of meat offered to idols, the main topic of 1 Cor 10:14–33.[24] As Paul sees it, when the Corinthians join in cultic feasts, they may be in danger of taking part in idolatrous practices and of associating themselves with demons.

Paul then warns his audience of sexual immorality and its severe consequences: "and twenty-three thousand fell in a single day." This probably refers to the story of the Israelite men having sexual relations with Moabite women, who consequently led the men to idolatry (Num 25:1–9). The next warning poses both hermeneutical and textual problems: "We must not put Christ to the test, as some of them did and were destroyed by serpents" (1 Cor 10:9). It appears that Paul identifies "the Lord" in the narrative as Christ.[25] The serpents occur in Num 21:6 as a deadly punishment after the people have spoken against Moses and complained of the food. The final warning concerns complaining. This motif occurs several times in the wilderness narratives, but Paul appears to have in mind the complaints following Korah's rebellion that result in a plague (Num 17:6–15).[26] According to Paul, the complainers were "destroyed by the destroyer [ὀλοθρευτής]," the angel of divine judgment featured in several biblical narratives.[27] Although Numbers does not attribute the plague following the Korah incident to "the destroyer," Wisdom of Solomon (Wis 18:25) does, and it appears that Paul is familiar with this tradition (see also 4 Macc 7:11).[28]

By selectively retelling certain aspects of the narratives, Paul is able to forge links between Israel's constitutional narratives and the social reality and everyday ethical dilemmas of the Corinthians. The sins that Paul highlights in the narratives are general enough so that the audience can identify with them and "undertake the metaphorical leap of finding their own circumstances figured in the narrative."[29]

---

22. Philo refers to the incident several times, emphasizing the drunkenness of the people and their distasteful dancing (*Mos.* 2.161-6; *Ebr.* 95–96 [the dancing; revelry]; *Spec.* 1.79). Pseudo-Philo recounts the incident in LAB 12:2–3, in which imitation of the nations strongly motivates idolatry.
23. Hays, "Conversion of the Imagination," 398.
24. Francis Watson, *Paul and the Hermeneutics of Faith* (London: T&T Clark, 2004), 365.
25. Ciampa and Rosner, "1 Corinthians," 772.
26. The versification varies: 16:41–50 in some versions.
27. Cf. Exod 12:23; 2 Sam 24:16; 1 Chron 21:12–15; 2 Chron 32:21; Sir 48:21.
28. Watson, *Paul and the Hermeneutics*, 367.
29. Hays, "Conversion of the Imagination," 401.

Bodily Resurrection and Scripture (1 Corinthians 15)

In 1 Corinthians 15, a chapter dense with citations and allusions, Paul defends the notion of the bodily resurrection, which appears to have been questioned by some Corinthians. Bodily resurrection and the eschatological vision of Christ's victory over death appear to be themes for which Paul wishes to present a firm scriptural foundation. For him, the two are intimately connected: resurrection follows directly from Christ's victory.[30]

When Paul presents his eschatological vision, he draws repeatedly on Gen 1–3, striking a contrast between Adam and Christ: "as all die in Adam, so all will be made alive in Christ" (1 Cor 15:22). Later in the argument, Paul cites Gen 2:7, again presenting Christ as Adam's counterpart: "Thus it is written, 'The first man, Adam, became a living being'; the last Adam became a life-giving spirit" (1 Cor 15:45). Here, Paul uses the contrast to highlight that terrestrial bodies must have celestial counterparts.[31]

The discussion of resurrection contains exemplary cases of how Paul intertwines scriptural passages and makes them interact. An excellent example is his use of Pss 110 and 8 in 1 Cor 15:25–27. He rewrites Ps 110:1 (109:1 LXX) to match his description of Christ's victory, changing the person and simplifying the imagery by omitting the "footstool":

Table 14.3. 1 Corinthians 15:25 and Psalm 110:1

1 Cor 15:25	Ps 110:1 (109:1 LXX)
δεῖ γὰρ αὐτὸν βασιλεύειν ἄχρι οὗ θῇ πάντας τοὺς ἐχθροὺς ὑπὸ τοὺς πόδας αὐτοῦ.	ἕως ἂν θῶ τοὺς ἐχθρούς σου ὑποπόδιον τῶν ποδῶν σου.
"For he must reign until he has put all the enemies under his feet."	"until I make your enemies a footstool of your feet."

---

30. Ciampa and Rosner, "1 Corinthians," 748.

31. The questions that Paul anticipates in 1 Cor 15:35 ("But someone will ask, 'How are the dead raised? With what kind of body do they come?'") intrigued other Jewish interpreters as well. Second Baruch (also called the Apocalypse of Baruch, a probably post-70 CE apocalypse) contains similar questions: "In what shape will those live who live in Your day/Or how will the splendor of those who (are) after that time continue?" (2 Bar. 49:2, cited according R. H. Charles, *The Apocrypha and Pseudepigrapha of the Old Testament in English*, 2 vols. [Oxford: Oxford University Press, 1913], 2:481–524). Further interesting early Jewish texts discussing resurrection include 1 En. 51:1; 62:14–16; T. Jud. 25:4–4; T. Benj. 10:6–8.

Paul uses the vivid imagery of the psalm without signaling to the audience that he is citing an external source text. The second psalm (Ps 8:7), on the other hand, he cites explicitly. Although he uses no introductory formula, his way of taking up and interpreting certain words suggests to the audience the presence of a citation: "For 'God has put all things in subjection [ὑπέταξεν] under his feet.' But when it says, 'All things are put in subjection,' it is plain that . . ." It appears that Paul interprets the two psalms in light of one another. Psalm 8 celebrates the special status of humanity over the rest of creation, yet Paul reads it in light of Ps 110, giving it a messianic interpretation. Psalm 8, for its part, influences the wording of Paul's allusion to Ps 110: in Paul's rewritten version, God has placed "all" enemies under Christ's feet, likely influenced by the phrasing of "all things" in Ps 8. Indeed, this all-inclusiveness is significant for Paul, for he seems to include death among the enemies that are brought in subjection. By reading the psalms together, Paul uses them as scriptural witnesses for Christ's ultimate rule.[32]

In 15:32–33, Paul first cites Isaiah and then Menander without signaling the presence of either citation. The verbatim citation from Isa 22:13 depicts how the people of Jerusalem fail to turn to their Lord even in the face of a siege: "Let us eat and drink, for tomorrow we die!" The feasting and drinking in Isaiah reflect the utter despair of the people and their decisive refusal to repent or rely on hope. In 1 Corinthians, the aspect of imminent disaster is absent, and the exhortation to feast appears merely to crystallize the earthly perspective of those living without hope of resurrection. What unites it with the wider context of Isa 22 is the failure of the people to put their trust in God's power. Paul appears to view such a sinful attitude as a collective phenomenon, warning his audience in the words of Menander: "Bad company ruins good morals."[33] Paul implies here that those who deny bodily resurrection are bad company and will lead others into a path of immorality. He does not mention the source of these words, presenting them rather as a common maxim. Since Menander was very popular and much cited in Paul's time, Paul's citation of his words does not imply that he expected a high level of literary education in his audience.[34] What is interesting here is that Paul cites Israel's Scriptures and Menander together and in such a similar

---

32. Similarly, Richard B. Hays, *Echoes of Scripture in the Letters of Paul* (New Haven: Yale University Press, 1989), 84. For closer analysis, see Pulkkinen, "Paul's Use of Psalms," 124–30.

33. The quotation is attributed to Menander by Jerome, Euthalius, and Photios I of Constantinople. Identifying Menander's comedy *Thais* as the more exact source is, however, uncertain; see Koch, *Die Schrift als Zeuge*, 42–45. See also John Granger Cook, "1 Cor 15:33: The *status quaestionis*," *NovT* 62 no. 4 (2020): 375–91, who suggests that Euripides might be an equally probable source or that the proverb might simply be drawn from "the common wisdom of antiquity."

34. Koch, *Die Schrift als Zeuge*, 43–45.

manner. Both citations are rhetorically effective as they are, requiring no further comments from Paul.

In 1 Cor 15:54–55, Paul combines Isa 25:8 with Hos 13:14, presenting them as a single entity: "Death is swallowed up in victory [Isa 25:8]. Where, O death, is your victory? Where, O death, is your sting? [Hos 13:14]" Both citations contain complex textual problems, and those of Isa 25:8 will be discussed below, under "The Textual Character of Paul's Citations." What is important here is that Paul interprets the passage from Hosea in light of the version of Isaiah known to him, and it is probable that he also modifies its wording accordingly.[35] Isaiah 25:8 is part of a joyful eschatological vision. In contrast, in their original literary context, the questions from Hosea are not meant as taunts to death. Instead, they are part of a prophecy of doom to Ephraim, probably representing the Lord's summons to Death and Sheol/Hades, for the continuation of the prophecy makes it clear that it is not a salvific statement (see Hos 13:14–15).[36] However, when Paul combines the questions with Isa 25:8, they appear to be mocking death, which has been vanquished by Christ. This is therefore a good example of how Paul recontextualizes his citations.

Veiled Moses (2 Corinthians 3)

In 2 Cor 3:4–18, Paul alludes to the story of Moses's veil (Exod 34:30–35). His interpretive retelling of some aspects of the story is connected to the question of his own worthiness and integrity (2 Cor 2:14–7:4). Paul compares Moses's ministry (διακονία) with his own ministry in the service of the new covenant.[37] This difficult passage is intriguing for several reasons. First, Paul refers to Moses not only as a minister and a representative of the old covenant but also as a leader comparable to Paul (3:13) and as a text that is being read (2 Cor 3:14).[38] According to Paul, the Jews read Moses with "a veil over their hearts," one that covers the true meaning of the text and that can only be lifted when they turn to Christ (2 Cor 3:15–16). Paul expresses this idea by rewriting a verse from Exodus: "But when one turns to the Lord, the veil is removed" (2 Cor 3:16). "But whenever Moses went in before the Lord to speak with him, he would remove the veil until coming out" (Exod 34:34).

---

35. See Koch, 169–70; Stanley, *Paul and the Language of Scripture*, 214–15.
36. Koch, *Die Schrift als Zeuge*, 175; Ciampa and Rosner, "1 Corinthians," 748.
37. As Jens Schröter, "Schriftauslegung und Hermeneutik in 2 Korinther 3: Ein Beitrag zur Frage der Schriftbenutzung des Paulus," *NovT* 40, no. 3 (1998): 255, summarizes it, Paul seeks to demonstrate that it is his ministry that led the Corinthians to a new relationship with God and relayed to them the life-giving Spirit.
38. Similarly, Michael Benjamin Cover, *Lifting the Veil: 2 Corinthians 3:7–18 in Light of Jewish Homiletic and Commentary Traditions*, BZNW 210 (Berlin: de Gruyter, 2015), 270–71.

Second, Paul's portrayal of Moses's ministry is surprisingly negative. In Paul's dichotomies, it is associated with the ministry of death and condemnation, letters that kill, and glory that passes away, while Paul and his coworkers are "ministers of the new covenant," which is characterized by righteousness, the Spirit, freedom, and greater, permanent glory (2 Cor 3:6–13). Paul relativizes Moses's great moment of glory in Israel's Scriptures and presents it as inferior to the glory of the Christ event.

The third intriguing feature in the passage is Paul's interpretation of Moses's reason for veiling himself. In Exodus, when Moses descends from Sinai, his face "was made glorious," and the Israelites were at first afraid to approach him. Paul's remark that "the Israelites could not gaze at Moses's face because of its glory" (2 Cor 3:7) probably refers to this initial apprehension, although Paul has changed fear to inability.[39] After Moses has relayed the commandments to the Israelites, he places a veil over his face. Every time Moses converses with the Lord, he removes the veil (Exod 34:30–33). Paul seems to imply that Moses veiled himself to hide the fact that the glory on his face was passing away: "Since, then, we have such a hope, we act with great openness, not like Moses, who used to place a veil over his face so that the Israelites might not gaze at the end of what was passing away" (2 Cor 3:13). That the glory on Moses's face was impermanent is also implied by Philo and Pseudo-Philo, whereas in the targumim, the glory of Moses's face does not fade but continues until his death.[40] The surprising idea in Paul's ambiguous statement is therefore not the impermanence of the glory but that Moses would have sought to conceal the fact for some purpose.

While commentators have asked whether Paul introduces an external element into the story, Paul's interpretation may be rooted in the narrative in Exodus, which gives no reason for the habitual use of the veil.[41] Although the Israelites are at first afraid of Moses's appearance, they overcome this fear. Paul offers an exegetical solution to this unmotivated use of the veil. Francis Watson explains: "One would expect the glory to fade with the passing of the immediate occasion of encounter with divinity—as in the later case of the transfigured Jesus. It is just this supposition that the veil makes it impossible to confirm."[42] Thus, in light

---

39. The motif of inability has a parallel in Philo, *Mos.* 2.70, which mentions first the awe of the Israelites and continues that their eyes could not stand Moses's dazzling brightness. Pseudo-Philo, in contrast, changes the awe to failure to recognize Moses because of the glory (LAB 12.1).

40. For Philo and Pseudo-Philo, see Linda L. Belleville, *Reflections of Glory: Paul's Polemical Use of the Moses-Doxa Tradition in 2 Corinthians 3.1–18*, JSNTS 52 (Sheffield: Sheffield Academic, 1991), 32–35, 40–43. As for the targumim, see their renderings of Num 27:20 and Deut 34:7, analyzed by Belleville, 28–30.

41. For an external element, see, e.g., Victor Paul Furnish, *2 Corinthians: Translated with Introduction, Notes and Commentary*, AB 32A (New York: Doubleday, 1984), 226–27.

42. Watson, *Paul and the Hermeneutics*, 269.

of the Christ event, Paul concludes that the splendor of Moses's face was only temporary and that the veil concealed this. Paul does not, therefore, introduce an alien element to the narrative but rather solves an implicit problem in it.[43]

Paul's solution for the exegetical problem (the unmotivated use of the veil) does not present Moses in a flattering light.[44] At the very least, Paul presents Moses's practice of veiling himself as a failure to act in a frank and open manner, whereas his own ministry is characterized by openness and sincerity (2 Cor 4:2–3; 2 Cor 7:4).[45] This passage illuminates that, in light of the Christ event, Paul occasionally reevaluates scriptural tradition. Here, he downplays a significant moment in Israel's narratives.

The Quotation Chain in 2 Corinthians 6

Second Corinthians 6:14–7:1 contains a rhetorically impressive catena of citations that continues to pose a challenge for commentators. This section clearly forms a coherent entity on its own and undeniably disturbs the flow of thought that would otherwise continue seamlessly from 2 Cor 6:13 to 7:2. Scholars hold differing views concerning the origin of the section. Was it composed by Paul? If it was, did Paul dictate the section between 6:13 and 7:2 or was it inserted into its current location by a later editor? These questions are related to larger problems concerning the unity and composition of 2 Corinthians.[46] While they are too complicated to be dealt with here, it is instructive to examine the citation technique and to compare it with Paul's undisputed chains of citations. In the following, I will not try to solve the question of the authorship of the catena but will draw some conclusions that are highly relevant for the problem.

The argument in 2 Cor 6:14–7:1 appears to call for a strict separation of believers from unbelievers. The catena, consisting of five source texts (Lev 26:11–12; Isa 52:11; Ezek 20:34; 2 Kgdms 7:14; and 7:8), first substantiates the statement that "we are the temple of the living God" (2 Cor 6:16), then cites God's commandment

---

43. Watson, *Paul and the Hermeneutics*, 270.

44. Similarly, Margaret E. Thrall, *Introduction and Commentary on II Corinthians I–VII*, vol. 1 of *A Critical and Exegetical Commentary on the Second Epistle to the Corinthians*, ICC (London: T&T Clark, 1994), 258.

45. See Katja Kujanpää, "Paul and the Author of 1 Clement as Entrepreneurs of Identity in Corinthian Crises of Leadership," *JSNT* 44, no. 3 (2022): 368–89.

46. See, e.g., Reimund Bieringer, "Plädoyer für die Einheitlichkeit des 2. Korintherbriefes: Literarkritische und inhaltliche Argumente," in *Studies on 2 Corinthians*, ed. Reimund Bieringer and Jan Lambrecht, BETL 112 (Leuven: Leuven University Press, 1994), 131–79; Lars Aejmelaeus, *Schwachheit als Waffe: Die Argumentation des Paulus im Tränenbrief (2. Kor. 10–13)*, PFES 78 (Helsinki: Finnish Exegetical Society; Göttingen: Vandenhoeck & Ruprecht, 2000), 19–26; Fredrick J. Long, *Ancient Rhetoric and Paul's Apology: The Compositional Unity of 2 Corinthians*, SNTSMS 131 (Cambridge: Cambridge University Press, 2004), 3–10.

for the people to separate themselves from the outsiders, and finally contains a promise of the consequences of such a separation. The first remarkable feature of the citation chain is the introductory formula "as God said" (καθὼς εἶπεν ὁ θεὸς ὅτι). Elsewhere in his undisputed letters, Paul never explicitly names "God" as the subject of the verb λέγω in an introductory formula, and he tends to use the present tense of the verb.[47] The first citation, from Lev 26:11–12, has been modified by the compiler of the catena. The citation also shares similarities with Ezek 37:27.

Table 14.4. The Citation in 2 Corinthians 6:16

2 Cor 6:16	Lev 26:11–12 LXX	Ezek 37:27 LXX
ἐνοικήσω	καὶ θήσω	καὶ ἔσται
	τὴν σκηνήν[48] μου	ἡ κατασκήνωσίς μου
ἐν αὐτοῖς	ἐν ὑμῖν,	ἐν αὐτοῖς,
καὶ ἐμπεριπατήσω	καὶ οὐ βδελύξεται ἡ	
	ψυχή μου ὑμᾶς. καὶ	
	ἐμπεριπατήσω ἐν ὑμῖν	
καὶ ἔσομαι αὐτῶν θεὸς	καὶ ἔσομαι ὑμῶν θεός,	καὶ ἔσομαι αὐτοῖς θεός,
καὶ αὐτοὶ ἔσονταί μου λαός.	καὶ ὑμεῖς ἔσεσθε μου λαός.	καὶ αὐτοὶ ἔσονταί μοι[49] λαός.
"I will live and walk among them, and I will be their God and they shall be my people."	"And I will place my tent among you, and my soul shall not abhor you. And I will walk among you and will be your God, and you shall be my people."	"And my dwelling place shall be among them, and I will be God to them and they shall be my people."

The compiler of the catena systematically changes the second-person pronouns to the third person. The reason for this is unclear since the following parts of the catena use the second person. It is possible that Ezek 37:27 has influenced the citation. The compiler also changes the concrete image of "placing a tent" to "dwelling" to describe God's presence among his people. Finally, he omits the words "and my soul shall not abhor you," the only negative phrase in the passage depicting the intimate connection between God and his people.[50]

---

47. Although see Rom 9:29: καθὼς προείρηκεν Ἡσαΐας ("as Isaiah predicted").
48. Many important manuscripts read διαθήκην (the reading of LXX^Ra) instead of σκηνήν (LXX^Gö).
49. Numerous witnesses read ἔσονταί μου λαός ("they will be my people").
50. Stanley, *Paul and the Language of Scripture*, 200.

Israel's Scriptures in 1 and 2 Corinthians

The second part of the catena is a citation from Isa 52:11, but its exhortations have been reordered.

Table 14.5. The Citation in 2 Corinthians 6:17

2 Cor 6:17	Isa 52:11 LXX
διὸ <u>ἐξέλθατε ἐκ μέσου</u> αὐτῶν καὶ <u>ἀφορίσθητε</u>, λέγει κύριος, καὶ <u>ἀκαθάρτου μὴ ἅπτεσθε</u> "Therefore go out from their midst and be separated, says the Lord, and touch nothing unclean."	ἀπόστητε ἀπόστητε, ἐξέλθατε ἐκεῖθεν καὶ <u>ἀκαθάρτου μὴ ἅπτεσθε</u>, <u>ἐξέλθατε ἐκ μέσου</u> αὐτῆς,[51] <u>ἀφορίσθητε</u> "Depart, depart, go out from there and touch nothing unclean, go out from the midst of it, be separated."

In addition, the compiler of the catena has added the phrase "says the Lord" to clarify the speaker of the imperative (cf. Rom 12:19; 1 Cor 14:21). The addition of the conjunction διό ("therefore") connects this section with the previous citation: since God dwells among his people, the people must separate themselves from the unbelievers. The catena then continues seamlessly with the consequence of this separation: "And I will welcome you." This is probably a citation from Ezek 20:34.[52]

Table 14.6. The Citation in 2 Corinthians 6:17

2 Cor 6:17	Ezek 20:34 LXX
	καὶ ἐξάξω ὑμᾶς ἐκ τῶν λαῶν
κἀγὼ <u>εἰσδέξομαι ὑμᾶς</u> "and I will take you in"	καὶ <u>εἰσδέξομαι ὑμᾶς</u> ἐκ τῶν χωρῶν "and I will bring you out from the peoples and take you in from the countries"

Paul cites the immediate context of Isa 52:11 several times (Rom 2:24; 10:15, 16; 15:21). This passage is full of hope: the Lord has delivered his people, who should now leave the nations among whom they live. The context of delivery and a new exodus is very similar to that of Ezek 20:34. However, Ezek 20:33–38 emphasizes God's sovereign action, and no active decision-making is required from the people. In contrast, the catena makes God's welcome conditional: the way the

---

51. Several Lucianic manuscripts agree with 2 Corinthians in reading αὐτῶν instead of αὐτῆς, but this is probably a case of polygeny—that is, Lucianic editors and the compiler of the catena would have changed the pronoun independently of one another for similar reasons. For the Lucianic editors, the proper antecedent is "all the nations"; in 2 Corinthians "unbelievers" (Stanley, *Paul and the Language of Scripture*, 223–24).

52. For other possibilities, see Peter Balla, "2 Corinthians," in Beale and Carson, *Commentary on the New Testament Use of the Old Testament*, 771.

citations follow each other gives the impression that only if the believers separate themselves will God welcome them. This corresponds with the call for separation from unbelievers in 2 Cor 6:14-16. It thus seems clear that the catena and verses 6:14-16 and 7:1 within the disputed section form a tightly interwoven entity.

The final section of the catena is a combination of 2 Kgdms 7, verses 14 and 8.

Table 14.7. The Citation in 2 Corinthians 6:18

2 Cor 6:18	2 Kgdms 7:14 LXX[53]	2 Kgdms 7:8 LXX
καὶ ἔσομαι ὑμῖν εἰς πατέρα καὶ ὑμεῖς ἔσεσθέ μοι εἰς υἱοὺς καὶ θυγατέρας, λέγει κύριος παντοκράτωρ	ἐγὼ ἔσομαι αὐτῷ εἰς πατέρα, καὶ αὐτὸς ἔσται μοι εἰς υἱόν·	Τάδε λέγει Κύριος παντοκράτωρ
"And I will be a father to you and you shall be sons and daughters to me, says the Lord Almighty."	"I will be a father to him, and he shall be a son to me."	"Thus says the Lord Almighty"

In 2 Kgdms 7, Nathan relays to David the promise that the Lord will be like a father to David's son. The compiler of the catena widens the scope of the promise considerably so that it encompasses all believers, both male and female.[54] The addition of "daughters" may reflect texts such as Isa 43:6.[55] Again, the compiler allows no ambiguity concerning the speaker and moves the introduction of God's speech ("says the Lord Almighty," from 2 Kgdms 7:8) to the end of the promise. The citation is a powerful conclusion to the catena that both begins and ends with a promise of God's presence and of an intimate relationship. Yet this relationship necessitates a separation of God's people from the idolatrous outsiders, as the middle part of the catena exhorts.

The techniques that the compiler of the catena uses when adapting the wording of the citations are very similar to Paul's techniques. Paul also changes personal pronouns and other grammatical forms, omits and adds words, adds explications of the speaker, and changes the word order.[56] Paul undeniably has some skill in combining different source texts into new rhetorically impressive

---

53. The provisional critical text for *Regnorum liber II (Samuelis II)*, ed. Tuukka Kauhanen, SVTG 5.2 (Göttingen: Vandenhoeck & Ruprecht, forthcoming). Used by permission.

54. For an overview of the use of this passage in the Dead Sea Scrolls and Philo, see Balla, "2 Corinthians," 772.

55. Hans Hübner, *Corpus Paulinum*, vol. 2 of *Vetus Testamentum in Novo* (Göttingen: Vandenhoeck & Ruprecht, 1997), 368.

56. See Koch, *Die Schrift als Zeuge*, 103-90; Kujanpää, *Rhetorical Functions*, 339-40.

entities that support his argument.⁵⁷ However, other writers in antiquity had similar skills and employed the same techniques, and Paul's style could otherwise also have been studied and imitated. Analyzing the citation technique cannot therefore on its own solve the question of the authorship of 2 Cor 6:14–7:1, and the separate question of whether the verses are in their correct place is another problem. Nevertheless, two conclusions can be drawn. First, apart from the introductory formula, the catena matches Paul's citation practice. Second, within the disputed section, the catena effectively supports the verses both preceding and following it (6:14–16; 7:1), which suggests that the compiler has carefully composed the entirety of 6:14–7:1 (rather than merely the catena).

The Textual Character of Paul's Citations

How did Paul interact with the scriptural texts? It is important to consider the full range of possibilities. He may have studied scrolls at different stages of his life and at different locations, encountering manuscripts that represent various textual traditions. He memorized passages and possibly compiled written notes, heard texts read aloud and discussed them, engaging in scriptural debates with various discussion partners.⁵⁸ While the possibilities that Paul used Jewish florilegia (or even florilegia complied by Christ followers) and that he interacted directly with Hebrew texts need to be considered, there is little textual evidence for either.⁵⁹

It has long been recognized that Paul primarily cites Scripture and alludes to it according to the Septuagint. There are cases where Paul's use of Scripture only works with the wording of the Septuagint (e.g., 2 Cor 4:13/Ps 115:1 LXX [116:10 MT]). While, in the vast majority of cases, Paul's use of the Septuagint is undeniable, in 1 and 2 Corinthians there are two citations from Isaiah that seem to be based on a Hebraizing revision of the Septuagint. Jewish Hebraizing revision of the Greek translation is a well-documented phenomenon in the textual transmission of the late Second Temple period. The Hebraizing revisers sought to bring the Greek translation into conformity with the Hebrew text they used. The revisions could influence lexical choices, word order, grammatical forms, and details, such as articles and prepositions. The consistency of the revision varies from case to case.⁶⁰ Hebraizing revision is best viewed as a phenomenon, tendency,

---

57. Kujanpää, *Rhetorical Functions*, 53, 129, 200–201, 264, 297.
58. Jonathan D. H. Norton, *Contours in the Text: Textual Variation in the Writings of Paul, Josephus and the Yaḥad*, LNTS 430 (London: Bloomsbury, 2011), 34.
59. See Kujanpää, *Rhetorical Functions*, 335.
60. Anneli Aejmelaeus, "Textual History of the Septuagint and the Principles of Critical Editing," in *The Text of the Hebrew Bible and Its Editions: Studies in Celebration of the Fifth Centennial of the Complutensian Polyglot*, ed. Andrés Piquer Otero and Pablo A. Torijano

and ideal present over some centuries among Greek-speaking Jews. The Greek translations connected to Aquila, Symmachus, and Theodotion can be viewed as slightly later representatives of the same tendency. When one suspects that Paul quotes a verse that has been revised according to the Hebrew, the readings of Aquila, Symmachus, and Theodotion are highly interesting, for agreements with them increase the probability of a Hebraizing source text.[61] The knowledge of Aquila's, Symmachus's, and Theodotion's readings often come through Origen's text-critical work, as is the case in the second example to be discussed below.

The first, unambiguous case of Hebraizing revision of Isaiah is in 1 Cor 15:54. The first part of the combined citation represents a clear case of a Hebraizing revision of the original Greek translation. Paul's wording agrees verbatim with Theodotion and has agreements with Aquila and Symmachus as well. All four deviate clearly from the Septuagint's reading.

Table 14.8. The Citation in 1 Corinthians 15:54

1 Cor 15:54	Isa 25:8 LXX	Isa 25:8 Masoretic Text
κατεπόθη ὁ θάνατος εἰς νῖκος	κατέπιεν ὁ θάνατος ἰσχύσας	בִּלַּע הַמָּוֶת לָנֶצַח
"Death is swallowed up in victory."	"Death, having prevailed, swallowed [them] up."	"He will swallow up death forever."
Theodotion	**Symmachus**	**Aquila**
κατεπόθη ὁ θάνατος εἰς νῖκος = 1 Cor 15:54	καταποθῆναι ποιήσει τὸν θάνατον εἰς τέλος	καταποντίσει τὸν θάνατον εἰς νῖκος
"Death is swallowed up in victory."	"... causes death to be swallowed up in victory."	"He sinks death in victory."

In the Septuagint, death is the subject, whereas in the other Greek texts listed in the table above, death is swallowed up by God.[62] The original translation was corrected by a reviser, who sought to bring the verse to closer correspondence with his understanding of the Hebrew text he used. Κατεπόθη is probably based

---

Morales, THBSup 1 (Leiden: Brill, 2017), 171. For an overview, see Folker Siegert, *Zwischen Hebräischer Bibel und Altem Testament: Eine Einführung in die Septuaginta*, MJSt 9 (Münster: LIT, 2001), 84–87; Jennifer M. Dines, T*he Septuagint*, Understanding the Bible and Its World (London: T&T Clark, 2004), 4, 81–84. On the importance of Hebraizing revision for Pauline studies, see Kujanpää, *Rhetorical Functions*, 5–8.

61. On this point, see Paavo Huotari and Katja Kujanpää, "Hebraizing Revision in Isaiah Quotations in Paul and Matthew," in *Scriptures in the Making: Texts and Their Transmission in Late Second Temple Judaism*, ed. Raimo Hakola, Jessi Orpana, and Paavo Huotari, CBET 109 (Leuven: Peeters, 2022), 313–42.

62. In Symmachus, death is swallowed through the anointing of nations.

on vocalizing בעל as a *pual* perfect, and εἰς νῖκος reflects a reading of לָנֶצַח in light of the Aramaic root נצח, "to overcome."[63] The resulting Hebraizing wording is preserved by Paul and Theodotion and may have been used as a model by Aquila and Symmachus as well.[64] Similar cases of Hebraizing revision in quotations from Isaiah can be found in Rom 9:33 and 10:15.[65]

The other probable case of Hebraizing revision poses a complex problem. Paul's wording differs notably from the reading of the Septuagint, but it is not a faithful translation of the Hebrew preserved in the Masoretic Text either, as table 14.9 indicates.

Table 14.9. The Citation in 1 Corinthians 14:21

1 Cor 14:21	Isa 28:11–12 LXX	Isa 28:11–12 MT
ἐν ἑτερογλώσσοις καὶ ἐν χείλεσιν ἑτέρων λαλήσω τῷ λαῷ τούτῳ	διὰ φαυλισμὸν χειλέων διὰ γλώσσης ἑτέρας, ὅτι λαλήσουσι τῷ λαῷ τούτῳ λέγοντες αὐτῷ Τοῦτο τὸ ἀνάπαυμα τῷ πεινῶντι	כִּי בְּלַעֲגֵי שָׂפָה וּבְלָשׁוֹן אַחֶרֶת יְדַבֵּר אֶל־הָעָם הַזֶּה: אֲשֶׁר אָמַר אֲלֵיהֶם זֹאת הַמְּנוּחָה הָנִיחוּ לֶעָיֵף
καὶ οὐδ' οὕτως εἰσακούσονταί μου, λέγει κύριος	καὶ τοῦτο τὸ σύντριμμα, καὶ οὐκ ἠθέλησαν ἀκούειν	וְזֹאת הַמַּרְגֵּעָה וְלֹא אָבוּא שְׁמוֹעַ
"By people of strange tongues and by the lips of foreigners will I speak to this people,	"because of contempt of lips, through a different tongue, for they will speak to this people, saying to it,	"Therefore, with stammering lip and with different tongue he will speak to this people, to whom he said,
and even then they will not listen to me, says the Lord."	'This is the rest for the hungry, and this is the destruction,' but they did not want to listen."	'This is rest; give rest to the weary; and this is the repose.' But they did not want to listen."

---

63. For details, see Florian Wilk, *Die Bedeutung des Jesajabuches für Paulus*, FRLANT 179 (Göttingen: Vandenhoeck & Ruprecht, 1998), 21 n. 7. Alternatively, κατεπόθη may represent the divine passive, which would make it an adequate translation of the *piel* vocalization.

64. Similarly, Koch, *Die Schrift als Zeuge*, 63; Wilk, *Die Bedeutung*, 21.

65. See Kujanpää, *Rhetorical Functions*, 135–41, 173–77; Huotari and Kujanpää, "Hebraizing Revision in Isaiah."

In the Septuagint, the passage characterizes the incongruous proclamation of the drunken priest and prophet (Isa 28:7), whereas in the Masoretic Text, the words "This is rest; give rest to the weary; and this is the repose" are uttered by God. The readings of Aquila, Symmachus, and Theodotion are not preserved (apart from a few unhelpful fragments), but Origen makes a highly interesting remark concerning 1 Cor 14:21: "for I have found an equivalent to this phrase in Aquila's translation."[66]

Origen's remark may suggest that there was a Hebraizing Greek reading that served as a basis for Paul's citation (and perhaps Aquila's translation). It has been suggested that despite the plural and the different order of the tongue and the lips, ἐν ἑτερογλώσσοις καὶ ἐν χείλεσιν ἑτέρων could be a retranslation of the Hebrew. It is imaginable that a Hebraizing reviser read the Hebrew root as לעז ("to speak unintelligibly") rather than לעג ("to mock") and used the adjective ἑτερόγλωσσος while preserving the Septuagint's use of two different words, γλῶσσα and χεῖλος.[67]

After the first two lines (see table 14.9), the probability that Paul modified the text seems higher, for the deviations from the Septuagint and the Masoretic Text appear to be relevant to the point he makes with the citation. Paul omits most of Isa 28:12 that has no relevance to his argument concerning glossolalia.[68] It appears probable that the use of the first-person singular λαλήσω and the addition of the pronoun μου and the words λέγει κύριος (cf. Rom 12:19) all belong together and represent Paul's adaptation.[69] In Paul's reading it is God (not the priest and the prophet) who uses alien languages, and his adjustments make the speaker explicit. Finally, "even then they will not listen to me" (vs. "they did not want to listen" in the Septuagint) may reflect Paul's emphasis: the problem is not that the hearers of glossolalia are *unwilling* to understand but that glossolalia is an ineffective method for reaching them.[70] The phrase "they will not listen to me" occurs several times in the Septuagint, and Paul may have reformulated the end of Isa 28:12 with the phrase in mind.

In summary, Origen's comment may suggest that Paul's wording is based on a Greek reading that had been revised in light of the Hebrew. Yet Paul has

---

66. εὗρον γὰρ τὰ ἰσοδυναμοῦντα τῇ λέξει ταύτῃ ἐν τῇ τοῦ Ἀκύλου ἑρμηνείᾳ κείμενα. *Philocalia* 9.2, cited according to J. Armitage Robinson, *The Philocalia of Origen: The Text Revised, with a Critical Introduction and Indices* (Cambridge: Cambridge University Press, 1893).

67. See Koch, *Die Schrift als Zeuge*, 64–65; Stanley, *Paul and the Language of Scripture*, 199–201; Wilk, *Die Bedeutung*, 28–29. The word ἑτερόγλωσσος (also used by non-Jewish authors; see LSJ) is used by Aquila in Ps 114:1 (113:1 LXX) to translate the root לעז, which visually resembles the root לעג in Isa 28:11, as well as by Theodotion in Isa 33:19 (MT נִלְעַג לָשׁוֹן).

68. Koch, *Die Schrift als Zeuge*, 65, 123; Stanley, *Paul and the Language of Scripture*, 202.

69. Similarly, see Koch, *Die Schrift als Zeuge*, 65; Wilk, *Die Bedeutung*, 28. For Rom 12:19, see Kujanpää, *Rhetorical Functions*, 325.

70. Koch, *Die Schrift*, 123.

actively modified this version: he omits the superfluous middle part, changes the citation to being God's direct speech, and rewrites the final part to make it better match his point.

In contrast to the two citations from Isaiah, in which a Hebraizing revision seems probable, the textual character of the citation from Job 5:13 in 1 Cor 3:19 is ambiguous.

Table 14.10. The Citation in 1 Corinthians 3:19

1 Cor 3:19	Job 5:13 LXX	Job 5:13 MT
ὁ δρασσόμενος	ὁ καταλαμβάνων	לֹכֵד
τοὺς σοφοὺς	σοφοὺς	חֲכָמִים
ἐν τῇ πανουργίᾳ αὐτῶν	ἐν τῇ φρονήσει	בְּעָרְמָם
"He catches the wise in their craftiness."	"He takes the wise in cleverness."	"He takes the wise in their craftiness."

The pronoun αὐτῶν at the end of the citation matches the Hebrew and could thus be a Hebraizing correction. The use of πανουργία to render the root ערם corresponds with the translation practice of the Septuagint and could thus well represent Hebraizing revision that would have preferred standard equivalents. However, the problem is the use of δράσσομαι to translate לכד. Such a translation has no precedent in the Septuagint, where δράσσομαι translates קמץ three times in the Pentateuch and is thus "reserved" for a different root. The Septuagint's translation of the root לכד with καταλαμβάνω, in contrast, is perfectly unproblematic from the viewpoint of standard equivalents. It is difficult to imagine why a Hebraizing reviser would have changed the verb. It is therefore questionable if 1 Cor 3:19 can be plausibly viewed as a case of a Hebraizing revision of Job.[71] While it is possible that Paul quotes the verse according to a version known to him, the wording could also have resulted from his own modification: "catching" the wise sounds better than merely "taking" them.

Conclusion

In 1 and 2 Corinthians, the ethical orientation of Paul's scriptural argumentation is pronounced. Several scriptural references serve a paraenetic function: Paul's citations call into question human value systems and highlight the importance of putting one's trust in God, and the wilderness generation's sins are immedi-

---

71. Pace Berndt Schaller, "Zum Textcharakter der Hiobzitate im paulinischen Schrifttum," *ZNW* 71, nos. 1–2 (1980): 23–25.

ately relevant to the everyday life of the Corinthians. The scriptural references function in different ways in Paul's instruction. The exodus narratives are an object of step-by-step exegesis, whereas some citations serve to confirm Paul's own statements by offering them scriptural support. In 1 Cor 6:16, for example, a citation from Gen 2:24 confirms Paul's warning that "whoever is united to a prostitute becomes one body with her." Similarly, Paul cites Deut 25:4 to confirm with scriptural authority his view that apostles have the right to enjoy the material support of their congregations (1 Cor 9:9).

The communal and identity-building function of Paul's scriptural argumentation is prominent in passages such as 1 Cor 10 and 2 Cor 3, although these two passages represent different ways of relating to scriptural tradition. In 1 Cor 10, Paul presents the wilderness narratives as "prefigurations" "for us." The Corinthian community needs to be wary of the same dangers that threatened the existence of ancient Israelites. In 2 Cor 3, in contrast, Paul underlines the transient nature of Moses's glory in comparison to the glory of the Christ event that the Corinthians are able to experience. By referring to the story of Moses's veil, Paul reminds the Corinthians of everything they have received through Paul's ministry. Emphasizing their superior situation as members of the new covenant underlines his own merit as their apostle.

Several citations and allusions are connected to eschatological themes. Paul's theological emphasis on bodily resurrection possibly inspired him at some point to reread Israel's Scriptures in light of Christ's resurrection and to search for a scriptural foundation. That scriptural prophecies are being fulfilled in the eschatological time that Paul and his audience are living in is explicitly articulated in 1 Cor 15:54–55: "then the saying that is written shall come to pass" (before a citation from Isa 25:8 and Hos 13:14). Similarly, in 2 Cor 6:2, Paul interprets his own time as the "favorable time" and "the day of salvation" that the citation from Isa 49:8 promises.

From a rhetorical perspective, some citations mainly serve to bring vividness and eloquence to Paul's discourse. A good example is the unmarked citation from Isa 22:13: "Let us eat and drink, for tomorrow we die!" Some citations allow the audience to hear the divine voice speaking in first-person singular (e.g., 1 Cor 1:31; 14:21; 2 Cor 6:2, 16, 18), which is rhetorically impressive and brings additional weight to the letter.

When Paul refers to Israel's Scriptures, he often seeks to guide the Corinthians to read the citations and allusions in a certain way. He chooses the words he quotes and the elements he leaves unquoted. He frames the citation with interpretive elements, such as the introductory formula and his own explanatory remarks. As becomes clear from the examples analyzed, Paul also modifies the wording of citations in order to conform them to their new contexts. It is noteworthy that what is authoritative for Paul is not the exact wording of scriptural passages. What matters for Paul is that he can illuminate the relevance of Israel's Scriptures for his audience, and adjusting the wording of citations serves exactly this function.[72]

Paul's active use of Israel's Scriptures strengthens his ethos and highlights his competence and skill in the eyes of the Corinthian audience, and it is probable that Paul himself was well aware of this. He demonstrates his ability to interact with ancient writings, to find scriptural material relevant to his argumentation, to forge links between different scriptural texts, and to interweave the references and his own discourse. Simultaneously, it appears that referring to Israel's Scriptures is a natural way for Paul to approach questions and solve problems. One should not exaggerate this tendency. As I observed at the beginning of this chapter, 1 and 2 Corinthians also contain theologically weighty sections in which Israel's Scriptures have no visible role to play. Yet one receives the impression that it is personally important for Paul to interweave Scripture into the discourse even when scriptural support is not necessary for the argument. This may reflect his background, but it also reflects his personal interest in and commitment to Israel's Scriptures.

Bibliography

Aejmelaeus, Anneli. *Regnorum liber I (Samuelis I)*. SVTG 5.1. Göttingen: Vandenhoeck & Ruprecht, forthcoming.

———. "Textual History of the Septuagint and the Principles of Critical Editing." Pages 160–79 in *The Text of the Hebrew Bible and Its Editions: Studies in Celebration of the Fifth Centennial of the Complutensian Polyglot*. Edited by Andrés Piquer Otero and Pablo A. Torijano Morales. THBSup 1. Leiden: Brill, 2017.

———. "Wisdom Meets Prophecy: The Theme of Boasting and Paul's Quotation of Hannah's Psalm." Pages 11–28 in *Weisheit und Schöpfung: Festschrift für James Loader zum 65. Geburtstag*. Edited by Stefan Fischer and Marianne Grohmann. Wiener Alttestamentliche Studien 7. Frankfurt am Main: Lang, 2010.

Aejmelaeus, Lars. *Schwachheit als Waffe: Die Argumentation des Paulus im Tränenbrief (2. Kor. 10–13)*. PFES 78. Helsinki: Finnish Exegetical Society; Göttingen: Vandenhoeck & Ruprecht, 2000.

Balla, Peter. "2 Corinthians." Pages 753–83 in *Commentary on the New Testament Use of the Old Testament*. Edited by G. K. Beale and D. A. Carson. Grand Rapids: Baker Academic, 2007.

---

72. For a comparison with Romans, see Kujanpää, *Rhetorical Functions*, 334–36, 339–41.

Belleville, Linda L. *Reflections of Glory: Paul's Polemical Use of the Moses-Doxa Tradition in 2 Corinthians 3.1–18*. JSNTS 52. Sheffield: Sheffield Academic, 1991.

Bieringer, Reimund. "Plädoyer für die Einheitlichkeit des 2. Korintherbriefes: Literarkritische und inhaltliche Argumente." Pages 131–79 in *Studies on 2 Corinthians*. Edited by Reimund Bieringer and Jan Lambrecht. BETL 112. Leuven: Leuven University Press, 1994.

Charles, R. H. *The Apocrypha and Pseudepigrapha of the Old Testament*. 2 vols. Oxford: Clarendon, 1913.

Ciampa, Roy E., and Brian S. Rosner. "1 Corinthians." Pages 695–752 in *Commentary on the New Testament Use of the Old Testament*. Edited by G. K. Beale and D. A. Carson. Grand Rapids: Baker Academic, 2007.

Cook, John Granger. "1 Cor 15:33: The *status quaestionis*." *NovT* 62, no. 4 (2020): 375–91.

Cover, Michael Benjamin. *Lifting the Veil: 2 Corinthians 3:7–18 in Light of Jewish Homiletic and Commentary Traditions*. BZNW 210. Berlin: de Gruyter, 2015.

Dines, Jennifer M. *The Septuagint*. Understanding the Bible and Its World. London: T&T Clark, 2004.

Furnish, Victor Paul. *2 Corinthians: Translated with Introduction, Notes and Commentary*. AB 32A. New York: Doubleday, 1984.

Hays, Richard B. "The Conversion of the Imagination: Scripture and Eschatology in 1 Corinthians." *NTS* 45, no. 3 (1999): 391–412.

———. *Echoes of Scripture in the Letters of Paul*. New Haven: Yale University Press, 1989.

Hübner, Hans. *Corpus Paulinum*. Vol. 2 of *Vetus Testamentum in Novo*. Göttingen: Vandenhoeck & Ruprecht, 1997.

Huotari, Paavo, and Katja Kujanpää. "Hebraizing Revision in Isaiah Quotations in Paul and Matthew." Pages 313–42 in *Scriptures in the Making: Texts and Their Transmission in Late Second Temple Judaism*. Edited by Raimo Hakola, Jessi Orpana, and Paavo Huotari. CBET 109. Leuven: Peeters, 2022.

Kauhanen, Tuukka. *Regnorum liber II (Samuelis II)*. SVTG 5.2. Göttingen: Vandenhoeck & Ruprecht, forthcoming.

Koch, Dietrich-Alex. *Die Schrift als Zeuge des Evangeliums: Untersuchungen zur Verwendung und zum Verständnis der Schrift bei Paulus*. BHT 69. Tübingen: Mohr Siebeck, 1986.

Kujanpää, Katja. *The Rhetorical Functions of Scriptural Quotations in Romans: Paul's Argumentation by Quotations*. NovTSup 172. Leiden: Brill, 2019.

———. "Paul and the Author of 1 Clement as Entrepreneurs of Identity in Corinthian Crises of Leadership." *JSNT* 44, no. 3 (2022): 368–89.

Lincicum, David. *Paul and the Early Jewish Encounter with Deuteronomy*. WUNT 2/284. Tübingen: Mohr Siebeck, 2010.

Long, Fredrick J. *Ancient Rhetoric and Paul's Apology: The Compositional Unity of 2 Corinthians*. SNTSMS 131. Cambridge: Cambridge University Press, 2004.

Norton, Jonathan D. H. *Contours in the Text: Textual Variation in the Writings of Paul, Josephus and the Yaḥad*. LNTS 430. London: Bloomsbury, 2011.

Origen. *Matthäuserklärung*. Edited by Erich Klostermann. 2nd ed. GCS 38. Berlin: Akademie, 1976.

Pulkkinen, Marika. "Paul's Use of Psalms: Quotations, Allusions, and Psalm Clusters in Romans and First Corinthians." PhD diss., University of Helsinki, 2020.

Robinson, J. Armitage. *The Philocalia of Origen: The Text Revised, with a Critical Introduction and Indices*. Cambridge: Cambridge University Press, 1893.

Schaller, Berndt. "Zum Textcharakter der Hiobzitate im paulinischen Schrifttum." *ZNW* 71, no. 1–2 (1980): 21–26.

Schröter, Jens. "Schriftauslegung und Hermeneutik in 2 Korinther 3: Ein Beitrag zur Frage der Schriftbenutzung des Paulus." *NovT* 40, no. 3 (1998): 231–75.

Siegert, Folker. *Zwischen Hebräischer Bibel und Altem Testament: Eine Einführung in die Septuaginta*. MJSt 9. Münster: LIT, 2001.

Stanley, Christopher D. *Paul and the Language of Scripture: Citation Technique in the Pauline Epistles and Contemporary Literature*. SNTSMS 74. Cambridge: Cambridge University Press, 1992.

Stone, Michael E., and John Strugnell. *The Books of Elijah, Parts 1–2*. SBLTT 18. Missoula, MT: Scholars Press, 1979.

Thrall, Margaret E. *Introduction and Commentary on II Corinthians I–VII*. Vol. 1 of *A Critical and Exegetical Commentary on the Second Epistle to the Corinthians*. ICC. London: T&T Clark, 1994.

Verheyden, Joseph. "Origen on the Origin of 1 Cor 2,9." Pages 491–511 in *The Corinthian Correspondence*. Edited by Reimund Bieringer. BETL 125. Leuven: Leuven University Press, 1996.

Wagner, J. Ross. "'Not Beyond the Things Which Are Written': A Call to Boast Only in the Lord (1 Cor 4.6)." *NTS* 44, no. 2 (1998): 279–87.

Watson, Francis. *Paul and the Hermeneutics of Faith*. London: T&T Clark, 2004.

Wilk, Florian. *Die Bedeutung des Jesajabuches für Paulus*. FRLANT 179. Göttingen: Vandenhoeck & Ruprecht, 1998.

15

Israel's Scriptures in Galatians

A. ANDREW DAS

In 1928 Adolf von Harnack, reflecting longstanding presuppositions, explained that the apostle Paul drew on Israel's Scriptures only when responding to Judaizing opponents.[1] An element of truth stands behind the strong claim, at least for the Letter to the Galatians. The apostle received word that another Christ-believing missionary movement had made its way to his newfound congregations in Galatia. In response, he quickly dashes off a letter contrasting his own birthing movement (4:19) with the other (4:21–31). His own leads to children in freedom, whereas the other to offspring in slavery under the law of Mt. Sinai (4:24–25). With a profound sense of urgency, Paul defends a ministry that does not require gentile observance of the Jewish law or circumcision, in the face of rivals who taught otherwise. For the rivals, the one "gospel" (singular) message of the Jewish messiah requires his followers likewise to become Jewish (4:21). This dispute is at the heart of what "we Jews by birth" supposedly "know" (2:15–16a)—an ambiguous claim that the Mosaic law and faith in/of Christ are mutually exclusive (as Paul would interpret it) or that faith and the law are complementary and both necessary (so his rivals at Galatia).[2] The letter teems with emotion against "those" people (third person), who are "casting the evil eye" or

---

1. Adolf von Harnack, "The Old Testament in the Pauline Letters and in the Pauline Churches," in *Understanding Paul's Ethics: Twentieth Century Approaches*, ed. Brian S. Rosner, trans. George S. Rosner and Brian S. Rosner (Grand Rapids: Eerdmans, 1995), 31.

2. A. Andrew Das, "The Ambiguous Common Ground of Galatians 2:16 Revisited," *BR* 58 (2013): 49–61; Das, "Another Look at ἐὰν μή in Galatians 2:16," *JBL* 119, no. 3 (2000): 529–39.

"bewitching" the Galatians (3:1; 1:2-3) as former idolaters who had left those ways behind (4:8). Ultimately, "they" want "you" Galatians to be circumcised (6:12-13).[3] In this heated conflict situation, Paul draws on Israel's Scriptures.

One approach to Paul's use of Scripture is to trace the letter's logic and reasoning to its potential origins—to explain *why* he may have written as he did. Roy Ciampa exhausted the possible scriptural parallels to Paul's thinking in Galatians 1-2.[4] For Richard B. Hays, on the other hand, scriptural echoes inform the text of Galatians regardless of whether Paul was conscious of them or not.[5] Yet another approach, with Christopher Stanley, is to ask how Scripture would have functioned for the ancient *readers* of the letter.[6]

Often researchers have *assumed* that the Galatians were knowledgeable of the Jewish Scriptures, but these are gentiles new to Judaism and its customs. Paul does not identify them as Godfearers from the synagogues but as former idolaters (4:8). Educated pagan authors of the day, by way of contrast, demonstrate no knowledge of the Jewish Scriptures beyond Gen 1 (Pseudo-Longinus, *On the Sublime* 9.9; Ocellus Lucanus [an allusion to Gen 1:28]). One must also consider the very low literacy rate in the ancient Roman world, the high cost and unavailability of scrolls, and the level of exposure (or not) to the Jewish synagogues. Analyses of the role of Scripture in an early Christian document need to weigh the capacities of the audience, and even more in a letter emerging from a conflict situation over the recently introduced law of Moses.

Finally, Galatians has been the subject of intense scrutiny over the years for conceptual allusions, what have also been labeled grand thematic narratives—references to a narratival theme or topic in the Scriptures (with Porter).[7] Conceptual allusions, however, reside at the weakest level of intertextual "signal." Methodologically, it is best to begin with what is known—marked citations—and then progress in order to realms of lesser certainty.

---

3. A. Andrew Das, *Galatians*, ConC (St. Louis: Concordia, 2014), 1-19.

4. Roy E. Ciampa, *The Presence and Function of Scripture in Galatians 1 and 2*, WUNT 2/102 (Tübingen: Mohr Siebeck, 1998).

5. Richard B. Hays, *Echoes of Scripture in the Letters of Paul* (New Haven: Yale University Press, 1989), 29.

6. Christopher D. Stanley, *Arguing with Scripture: The Rhetoric of Quotations in the Letters of Paul* (London: T&T Clark, 2004).

7. Stanley E. Porter, "Further Comments on the Use of the Old Testament in the New Testament," in *The Intertextuality of the Epistles: Explorations of Theory and Practice*, ed. Thomas L. Brodie, Dennis R. MacDonald, and Stanley E. Porter, New Testament Monographs 16 (Sheffield: Sheffield Phoenix, 2007), 98-110; Porter, "The Use of the Old Testament in the New Testament," in *Early Christian Interpretation of the Scriptures of Israel: Investigations and Proposals*, ed. Craig A. Evans and James A. Sanders, JSNTSup 148 (Sheffield: Sheffield Academic, 1997), 87-88, 92-94.

Israel's Scriptures in Galatians

Marked Citations and the Nature of the Scriptural Text

Paul draws consistently from and adapts the Septuagint, not the Masoretic Text. He signals nine of his eleven citations. He was not expecting at least most of the Galatians to recognize citations from Scripture without a cue.

Table 15.1. Marked Citations in Galatians

Gal 3:6	Gen 15:6
Gal 3:8	Gen 12:3
Gal 3:10	Deut 27:26 (28:58/30:10)
Gal 3:12	Lev 18:5
Gal 3:13	Deut 21:23
Gal 3:16	Gen 13:15
Gal 4:27	Isa 54:1
Gal 4:30	Gen 21:10
Gal 5:14	Lev 19:18

Galatians 3:6/Genesis 15:6

Gal 3:6: [καθὼς] ... Ἀβραὰμ ἐπίστευσεν τῷ θεῷ, καὶ ἐλογίσθη αὐτῷ εἰς δικαιοσύνη.[8]
Just like Abraham: he "believed God, and so it was reckoned to him as righteousness."[9]

Gen 15:6 LXX: καὶ ἐπίστευσεν Ἀβραμ τῷ θεῷ, καὶ ἐλογίσθη αὐτῷ εἰς δικαιοσύνη.
And Abram believed God, and it was reckoned to him as righteousness.[10]

Paul's first citation is marked by καθώς ("just as"). He omits the Septuagint's initial καί ("and") in order to connect the citation to the prior argument. He shifts Ἀβραάμ ("Abraham") forward (cf. the nonshift in Rom 4:3, following the LXX word order exactly). Paul may be including the name as part of the citation or using the name to introduce the verse since nowhere else in the New Testament does καθώς ("just as") by itself introduce a quotation: "so it was with Abraham."

---

8. Brackets signal alterations or deletions from the LXX.
9. New Testament translations are by the author.
10. All LXX translations are from NETS.

Second Temple Jews pointed to Abraham as a model for gentile conversion to Judaism in having left behind the idolatrous household of his father (Jub. 11:16–17; 12:2–8, 16–24; Apoc. Ab. 1–8; 27:7; 31:4–8; Philo, *Virt.* 212–16; *Spec.* 1.9; *Abr.* 60–88; Josephus, *Ant.* 1.154–157; LAB 6:4; 23:5; cf. Josh 24:2–3). Second Temple authors stressed Abraham's faithfulness, even to the point of obeying the Mosaic law in its as-yet-unwritten form (e.g., Jub. 23:10; 24:11; T. Levi 9:1–14; T. Benj. 10:4; 2 Bar. 57:1–3; Philo, *Abr.* 275–76; Justin, *Dial.* 10.3–4 [Trypho citing Gen 17 against Justin]; 1 Macc 2:52; Jdt 8:25–27; 4 Macc 16:19–20; CD III, 2–3; Pr Man 8; T. Ab. 10:13 [an ironic witness]; 4QMMT 117 [4Q398 frag. 2 II; 4Q399 frag. 1 II]; m. Qidd. 4:14; Sir 44:20). Philo celebrated Abraham as an example of faithfulness to God's commands in bringing his passions under control through circumcision (see also Jub. 15:9–35; Sir 44:19–20; m. 'Abot 3:11 [ET 3:12]; cf. 1 Macc 1:15, 60–62). Jews saw themselves as Abraham's "seed" (cf. Ps 105:6 [104:6 LXX]; Isa 41:8), an identity conferred on the gentile male through circumcision. Conspicuously, Paul ignores the circumcision of Abraham's household in Gen 17 to stress instead the gentiles' inclusion in Abraham's *faith* (cf. Rom 4:1–12; Josephus, *Ant.* 20.44–45).

That Paul is responding to the Galatian rivals and their use of Abrahamic texts is confirmed by the following verse. Second Temple Jews considered descent from Abraham a matter of pride (Pss. Sol. 9:9; 3 Macc 6:3; Philo, *Her.*; cf. Isa 41:8). Paul emphatically claims in Gal 3:7 that those characterized by faith are the true "sons of Abraham." The apostle does not use this phrase elsewhere in his letters. The phrase appears unprompted. He draws a conclusion about who the sons of Abraham are from premises that do not mention Abrahamic sonship. Galatians 3:6, with its quotation of Gen 15:6, mentions only the patriarch himself. Eventually Paul concludes in 3:29 that those *in Christ* are Abraham's true "seed" with 3:7's unexpected conclusion presaging that later logic. The non sequitur about Abrahamic sonship in 3:7 suggests that the apostle is responding to an assertion made by the rivals about the identity of Abraham's true (law-observant) sons.

Galatians 3:8/Genesis 12:3

Gal 3:8: [προϊδοῦσα δὲ ἡ γραφὴ ὅτι ἐκ πίστεως δικαιοῖ τὰ ἔθνη ὁ θεός, προευηγγελίσατο τῷ Ἀβραὰμ ὅτι] . . . ἐνευλογηθήσονται ἐν σοὶ πᾶσαι πάντα τὰ ἔθνη.

And because the Scripture had foreseen that God would justify the gentiles by faith, [it] proclaimed the gospel in advance to Abraham that "all the gentiles will be blessed in you."

Gen 12:3 LXX: καὶ εὐλογήσω τοὺς εὐλογοῦντάς σε, καὶ τοὺς καταρωμένους σε καταράσομαι· καὶ ἐνευλογηθήσονται ἐν σοὶ πᾶσαι αἱ φυλαὶ τῆς γῆς.

And I will bless those who bless you, and those who curse you I will curse, and in you all the tribes of the earth shall be blessed.

"The Scriptures had foreseen that" (προϊδοῦσα δὲ ἡ γραφὴ ὅτι) signals the citation. The initial καί ("and") in Gen 12:3 is dropped for the sake of transition to the citation. Paul uses ἐνευλογηθήσονται ("will be blessed"), attested in the majority of Septuagintal manuscripts. (The shorter εὐλογηθήσονται ["will be blessed"] in some LXX manuscripts [F G 76 115] is likely a scribal shift to a more customary equivalent.) Paul's use of πάντα τὰ ἔθνη ("all the gentiles") is without precedent in the Septuagintal tradition and likely reflects a conflation with Gen 18:18. The use of πάντα τὰ ἔθνη ("all the gentiles") and the omission of τῆς γῆς ("the earth") reflect Paul's preference for "gentiles" as a label for the non-Jewish world (1:16; 2:2, 8, 9, 12, 14, 15; 3:14) and advance his contention that what God was promising to Abraham was also for the non-Jews.

Conspicuously, Paul does not use Gen 22:18's ἐν τῷ σπέρματί σου ("in your offspring") and thereby avoids any potential allusion to the Second Temple Akedah traditions of Abraham's and/or Isaac's obedience in the near sacrifice. Paul's rivals may have given priority to Gen 22:18 and 26:4–5, but the apostle regards Gen 12:3 (and 18:18) as foundational. God's promises had included the gentiles on the sole basis of faith—from the beginning.

Galatians 3:10/Deuteronomy 27:26 (28:58/30:10)

Gal 3:10: ἐπικατάρατος πᾶς ... ὃς οὐκ ἐμενεῖ ... πᾶσιν + τοῖς γεγραμμένοις ἐν τῷ βιβλίῳ + τοῦ νόμου ... τοῦ ποιῆσαι αὐτά.
Cursed is everyone ... who does not abide ... by all the things written in the book of the Law ... to do them.

Deut 27:26 LXX: ἐπικατάρατος πᾶς ἄνθρωπος, ὅστις οὐκ ἐμμενεῖ ἐν πᾶσιν τοῖς λόγοις τοῦ νόμου τούτου ποιῆσαι αὐτούς.
Cursed be any person who does not remain in all the words of this law to do them.

Deut 28:58 LXX: ἐὰν μὴ εἰσακούσητε ποιεῖν πάντα τὰ ῥήματα τοῦ νόμου τούτου τὰ γεγραμμένα ἐν τῷ βιβλίῳ τούτῳ φοβεῖσθαι τὸ ὄνομα τὸ ἔντιμον καὶ τὸ θαυμαστὸν τοῦτο.
If you do not listen to perform all the words of this law that are written in this book to fear this honorable and marvelous name.

Deut 30:10 LXX: ἐὰν εἰσακούσῃς τῆς φωνῆς κυρίου τοῦ θεοῦ σου φυλάσσεσθαι καὶ ποιεῖν πάσας τὰς ἐντολὰς αὐτοῦ καὶ τὰ δικαιώματα αὐτοῦ καὶ τὰς κρίσεις

αὐτοῦ τὰς γεγραμμένας ἐν τῷ βιβλίῳ τοῦ νόμου τούτου, ἐὰν ἐπιστραφῇς ἐπὶ κύριον τὸν θεόν σου ἐξ ὅλης τῆς καρδίας σου καὶ ὅλης τῆς ψυχῆς σου.
If you listen to the voice of the Lord your God, to keep his commandments and his statutes and his judgments that are written in the book of this law, if you turn to the Lord your God with the whole of your heart and with the whole of your soul.

Paul signals the citation with γέγραπται ("it is written"). The omission of the LXX's ἄνθρωπος ("person") matches the omission of the same word in Gal 3:12b/Lev 18:5. This creates a parallelism between πᾶς ὅς ("everyone who") in 3:10 and πᾶς ὁ ("everyone who") in 3:13, thereby enclosing verses 11–12's ὁ ποιήσας ("the one who does") and ὁ κρεμάμενος ("the one who is hung"). Paul's ὅς ("who") agrees with several LXX manuscripts (cf. ὅστις in others). The omission of ἐν after ἐμενεῖ does not affect meaning and may also reflect the Septuagintal tradition. Paul replaces Deut 27:26's τοῖς λόγοις ("the words") with Deut 28:58's τὰ γεγραμμένα ἐν τῷ βιβλίῳ (at the beginning of the list of curses) and Deut 30:10's τὰς γεγραμμένας ἐν τῷ βιβλίῳ τοῦ νόμου τούτου ("[the things] that are written in the book of this law"). He adapts the language to this context with the dative case (τοῖς γεγραμμένοις ["the things written"]). The omission of τούτου ("this") renders τοῦ νόμου ("the law") with an absolute sense (cf. the repetition of the term in 3:2, 5, 11, 12, and 13). The insertion of τοῦ ("the one") before ποιῆσαι ("doing") matches some Septuagintal tradition.[11] Paul closes the quotation with the neuter αὐτά ("them") rather than the masculine αὐτούς ("them"). This may be an unconscious assimilation to the Deuteronomic ποιῆσαι αὐτά (["to do them"]; 3:13; 5:1; 7:12; 26:16) or a deliberate adaption to the neuter referent implied in "all those things that are written."

The Deuteronomy passage threatens a curse for anyone who fails to do the law. This expresses succinctly the rivals' position. Paul's own point, expressed at the beginning of the verse, is that those who *rely on* the law are under a curse. Galatians 3:10 therefore cites a passage that, on the surface, is at odds with and undermines his own point. This would not be by choice. He appears to be explaining a key proof-text employed by the rival teachers at Galatia to encourage law observance.

Galatians 3:12/Leviticus 18:5

Gal 3:12: [ὁ δὲ νόμος οὐκ ἔστιν ἐκ πίστεως, ἀλλ'] ὁ ποιήσας αὐτὰ . . . ζήσεται ἐν αὐτοῖς.

---

11. Uncials A F M; majority of Hexaplaric manuscripts; majority of texts of minuscule families b d f n s y.

[But the Law is not of faith; rather,] "the one who does these things . . . will live by them."

Lev 18:5 LXX: καὶ φυλάξεσθε πάντα τά προστάγματά μου καὶ πάντα τά κρίματά μου καὶ ποιήσετε αὐτά, ἃ ποιήσας ἄνθρωπος ζήσεται ἐν αὐτοῖς.
And you shall keep all my ordinances and all my judgments, and you shall do them; as for the things a person does, he shall live by them.

The quotation is marked by demonstrable syntactical tension with its context because of the changed subject and the dangling pronouns (αὐτά; αὐτοῖς ["them," "them"]) that lack antecedents.[12] The use of the masculine singular article (ὁ ["the one"]) instead of the relative neuter plural pronoun (ἃ ["the things"]) and the inclusion of αὐτά ("these things") both match how Paul adapted Lev 18:5 in Rom 10:5. The omission of ἄνθρωπος ("person") is a departure from Paul's faithful use of the LXX in Rom 10:5. The omission creates a closer verbal parallel between this verse and the unmarked Hab 2:4 citation in Gal 3:11—thus sharpening the contrast between the two verses, as Paul understands them.

The Leviticus passage promises life to those who do the law's works. The later rabbis seized on the word "man/person" (האדם; ἄνθρωπος) in the Hebrew and Septuagintal texts of Lev 18:5 and concluded that any "man," even a gentile, could be righteous if he or she observed the law (b. Sanh. 59a; b. B. Qam. 38a). In m. ʾAbot 6:7: "Great is the Law, for it gives life to them that practice it both in this world and the world to come" (trans. Danby). Leviticus 18:5's presumed teaching that *any* person may enjoy eternal life by obedience to the law would have been prime fodder for the rivals' teaching at Galatia. The scriptural quotation, like Deut 27:26, is apparently at odds with the apostle's own conclusion: "no one is justified before God by the law" (Gal 3:11). Paul is not using such poor texts for his own position by choice. He is reinterpreting another of the rivals' key passages.

Galatians 3:13/Deuteronomy 21:23

Gal 3:13: ἐπικατάρατος . . . πᾶς ὁ κρεμάμενος ἐπὶ ξύλου.
"Cursed . . . is everyone who is being hung on a tree."

Deut 21:23 LXX: οὐκ ἐπικοιμηθήσεται τὸ σῶμα αὐτοῦ ἐπὶ τοῦ ξύλου, ἀλλὰ

---

12. Christopher D. Stanley, *Paul and the Language of Scripture: Citation Technique in the Pauline Epistles and Contemporary Literature*, SNTSMS 74 (Cambridge: Cambridge University Press, 1992), 35.

ταφῇ θάψετε αὐτὸν ἐν τῇ ἡμέρᾳ ἐκείνῃ, ὅτι κεκατηραμένος ὑπὸ θεοῦ πᾶς κρέμαμενος ἐπὶ ξύλου.
His body shall not sleep upon the tree, but with burial you shall bury him that same day, for anyone hanging on a tree is cursed by a god.

Paul omits Deut 21:23's ὅτι ("for") since it would be unnecessary in his context; he had just used ὅτι γέγραπται ("since it is written") to signal the citation. He changes the LXX's κεκατηραμένος ("cursed") to ἐπικατάρατος ("cursed"), removing any impression that the "curse" fell upon the victim *prior* to being hung on the tree. Christ's death *on* the cross redeemed people from the curse. Paul employs the neuter adjective (ἐπικατάρατος, not κεκατηραμένος) to remove any temporal implication. This also creates a clear link to 3:10 with the same adjective. He removes the LXX's ὑπὸ θεοῦ ("by a god") since in Deuteronomy God's curse rests on those who sin, but Christ is one who had *not* sinned (2 Cor 5:21) and who had become a curse "for us" (Gal 3:13a). Paul may have added ὁ ("who") to κρέμαμενος ("is being hung") to create a verbal parallel with Deut 27:26 in Gal 3:10, but some LXX witnesses include the article.

Galatians 3:13's citation of Deut 21:23, with its reference to a curse, answers the curse for disobedience of the law invoked by Paul's opponents in their use of Deut 27:26 (in Gal 3:10). Paul does not draw on the "curse" word group apart from Gal 3:10 and 13 (κατάρα; ἐπικατάρατος ["cursed," "cursed"]). The Deuteronomic categories of legal blessing and curse do not reflect the apostle's own concerns. Paul's use of Scripture in this verse is in *response* to the rivals.

Galatians 3:16/Genesis 13:15

Gal 3:16: οὐ λέγει· καὶ τοῖς σπέρμασιν, ὡς ἐπὶ πολλῶν ἀλλ᾽ ὡς ἐφ᾽ ἑνός · καὶ τῷ σπέρματί σου, ὅς ἐστιν Χριστός.
It does not say "and to the seeds," as to many, but as to one: "and to your seed," who is Christ.

Gen 13:15 LXX: ὅτι πᾶσαν τὴν γῆν, ἣν σὺ ὁρᾷς, σοὶ δώσω αὐτὴν καὶ τῷ σπέρματί σου ἕως τοῦ αἰῶνος.
For all the land that you see, I will give it to you and to your offspring forever.

Galatians 3:16 quotes exactly what Scripture "says" (λέγει) in Gen 13:15 LXX as Paul returns to the topic of the plural "sons" of Abraham raised in Gal 3:6–7. He clarifies, however, that the words "and to your seed" refer to a single individual. The notion that the "seed/offspring" promised to Abraham is grammatically singular would have surprised Paul's contemporaries. Genesis 13:16 employs the word "seed/offspring" for Abraham's collective descendants. Paul denies the collective sense of the word. As justification for his interpretation, Paul could well have pointed to Isaac as Abraham's single son of promise (Gen 22:2, 12, 16–17; 24:7; cf. Jub. 16:17–18: Jacob as the single seed of Isaac but then his descendants as a collective seed—an interplay). Genesis 22 stresses in three separate instances that Isaac was Abraham's one and only son (Gen 22:2, 12, 16). Yet the apostle completely ignores Isaac in favor of a direct connection between Abraham and Christ. The Galatians are related to Abraham through Christ and not through membership in the Jewish people mediated by Isaac.

Galatians 4:27/Isaiah 54:1

> Gal 4:27: γέγραπται γάρ· εὐφράνθητι, στεῖρα ἡ οὐ τίκτουσα, ῥῆξον καὶ βόησον, ἡ οὐκ δίνουσα· ὅτι πολλὰ τὰ τέκνα τῆς ἐρήμου μᾶλλον ἢ τῆς ἐχούσης τὸν ἄνδρα.
> For it is written: "Rejoice, O barren woman who does not bear [children]; break forth and cry aloud, you who have no labor pains, because the children of the desolate woman [will be] more numerous than [the children] of her who has a husband."
>
> Isa 54:1: Εὐφράνθητι, στεῖρα ἡ οὐ τίκτουσα, ῥῆξον καὶ βόησον, ἡ οὐκ ὠδίνουσα, ὅτι πολλὰ τὰ τέκνα τῆς ἐρήμου μᾶλλον ἢ τῆς ἐχούσης τὸν ἄνδρα, εἶπεν γὰρ κύριος.
> Rejoice, O barren one who does not bear; break forth and shout, you who are not in labor! Because more are the children of the desolate woman that of her that has a husband, for the Lord has spoken.

In Gal 4:21–31 Paul returns to the Abrahamic narrative and associates Mount Sinai not with Isaac, the child of promise, but rather with *Ishmael*, the child of slavery. The association is rhetorically shocking, and so Paul openly signals that he is interpreting the Genesis texts in a nonliteral fashion (Gal 4:24). Many of Paul's unique twists in 4:21–31 confirm that the rivals were teaching the Galatians on the basis of the Abrahamic texts. In Genesis Isaac was the beneficiary of the Abrahamic covenant. Paul, for his part, recognizes the covenant with Isaac (note the single covenant of circumcision in Gen 15:18; 17:7, 10–17, 18–21, 23–27) but speaks also of *another* covenant with Ishmael. Whereas in Genesis Abraham promptly carried out God's command to circumcise his household, the apostle ignores any mention of the eternal covenant of circumcision (Gen 17:7, 13, 19; 21:4). "It is written" in Gal 4:22 introduces an interpretive summary of Gen 16–18, 21, whereas elsewhere Paul draws on γέγραπται ("it is written") to introduce direct quotations of the biblical text (cf. 3:10, 13; 4:27). These departures are telltale signs that circumstances have dictated the discussion. He is not raising the Abrahamic narratives of his own accord. Paul never mentions Sarah or Ishmael by name but assumes the Galatians' awareness of these individuals. Descriptive epithets will apparently suffice. Paul is responding to his rivals' teaching of the Abrahamic stories to promote law observance.

In Gal 4:27 Paul explicitly signals an exact citation of Isa 54:1 LXX. In later centuries the Jews associated the barren woman of Isa 54:1 with Jerusalem (Tg. Isa. 54:1 [Jerusalem]; Song Rab. 1.5; 4.4 [Israel])—an association that may have been current already in Paul's day. 4Q164 cites Isa 54:11–12 in anticipating the Qumran community as the foundation of an eschatologically restored Jerusalem. Jerusalem had been left desolate because her inhabitants *had abandoned Moses's law* (Bar 4:12)! Adherence to the Torah would reverse Jerusalem's fortunes and result in a multitude of children for the barren woman. Isaiah 54:1 would conform neatly to the rivals' teaching. Paul understands this passage in very different terms: a zealous adherence to the law is precisely what led to the present Jerusalem's predicament.

Galatians 4:30/Genesis 21:10

> Gal 4:30: ἔκβαλε τὴν παιδίσκην . . . καὶ τὸν υἱὸν αὐτῆς· οὐ γὰρ μὴ κληρονοήσει ὁ υἱὸς τῆς παιδίσκης . . . μετὰ τοῦ υἱοῦ τῆς ἐλευθέρας.
> "Drive out the slave woman and her son, for the son of the slave woman will by no means inherit with the son of the free woman."

> Gen 21:10 LXX: [καὶ εἶπεν τῷ Ἀβραάμ·]"Ἔκβαλε τὴν παιδίσκην ταύτην καὶ τὸν υἱὸν αὐτῆς· οὐ γὰρ κληρονομήσει ὁ υἱὸς τῆς παιδίσκης ταύτης μετὰ τοῦ υἱοῦ μου Ἰσαακ.
> [Then she said to Abraam,] "Cast out this slave-girl and her son; for the son of this slave-girl shall not inherit together with my son Isaak."

In Gal 4:30 Paul cites Gen 21:10 (καὶ εἶπεν τῷ Ἀβραάμ ["Then she said to Abraam"]). Paul's μή ("not") and his use of the indicative κληρονοήσει ("will inherit") match LXX manuscripts. The omission of *both* demonstrative pronouns is unusual (only the five manuscripts of the b family of minuscules delete both). The deletion of the pronouns advances Paul's application of the "free woman" and the "servant girl" to his hearers (no longer referring to the original women of Genesis). Paul furthers his application to the audience by using τῆς ἐλευθέρας ("the free woman"), matching the freedom language throughout 4:21–5:1 and 5:13.

Paul had just faulted the rival teachers for excluding the Galatians in 4:17, and Gen 21:10 is an excellent text supporting the rivals' case for why the Galatians should abandon the (gentile) heritage of Ishmael in favor of Isaac's. Although Gen 21:10 highlights Isaac as the child of promise, Paul downplays any connection to the Jewish patriarch. He ignored Isaac earlier in Gal 3:15–17 in favor of the single seed of Abraham as Jesus Christ. He ignores Isaac again here as he changes Genesis's "my son Isaac" to "son of the free woman." He also ascribes the words of Sarah in Genesis simply to Scripture. The changes are conspicuous and deliberate.

Galatians 5:14/Leviticus 19:18

Gal 5:14: ὁ γὰρ πᾶς νόμος ἐν ἑνὶ λόγῳ πεπλήρωται, ἐν τῷ· ἀγαπήσεις τὸν πλησίον σου ὡς σεαυτόν.
For the whole law has been fulfilled in one word, namely: "You will love your neighbor as yourself."

Lev 19:18: καὶ οὐκ ἐκδικᾶταί σου ἡ χείρ, καὶ οὐ μηνιεῖς τοῖς υἱοῖς τοῦ λαοῦ σου καὶ ἀγαπήσεις τὸν πλησίον σου ὡς σεαυτόν· ἐγώ εἰμι κύριος.
And your own hand shall not take vengeance, and you shall not be angry against the sons of your people, and you shall love your neighbor as yourself; it is I who am the Lord.

In Gal 5:14 Paul cites (ἐν τῷ) the wording of Lev 19:18 LXX exactly. The later rabbis viewed the Leviticus verse as a summary of all the commands of the law. Hillel, the great Jewish teacher of Jesus's day, reportedly told an aspiring convert: "What is hateful to you, do not do to your neighbor: that is the whole Torah, while the rest is commentary thereof; go and learn it" (b. Šabb. 31a [Soncino ed.]; cf. Tob 4:15; CD IX, 2, 7–8; Rabbi Akiba [50–135 CE] in Sipra on Lev 19:18 [Parashat Qedoshim Pereq 4]). Early Christian texts refer to Lev 19:18 quite frequently (e.g., Rom 13:9; Jas 2:8; Did. 1.2), which suggests an emphasis that may stem from the teaching of Jesus when he summarized the law in these words (Mark 12:31; Matt 5:43; 19:19). Like the later rabbis, the rivals could easily have employed Lev 19:18 to refer to obedience to the entire law, a concrete love in action. Paul takes matters in the opposite direction as he pointedly refuses to place the command to love in a context of taking on the yoke of the Torah (cf. Gal 5:18: not "under" the law).

Unmarked Citations

In addition to the nine marked citations, Paul also cites Israel's Scriptures without a signal in two instances.

Table 15.2. Unmarked Citations in Galatians

Gal 2:16   Ps 143:2
Gal 3:11   Hab 2:4

Galatians 2:16/Psalm 143:2

Ps 143:2 (142:2 LXX): ὅτι οὐ δικαιωθήσεται ἐνώπιόν σου πᾶς ζῶν
because no one living will be justified before you.

Gal 2:16d: ὅτι ἐξ ἔργων νόμου δικαιωθήσεται πᾶσα σάρξ
because no flesh is justified by the works of the law.

Paul concludes 2:16 with Ps 143:2 (142:2 LXX), supporting the antithetical relationship between faith in/of Christ and the works of the law. He does not mark the citation: The ὅτι is likely causal ("because") and deliberate rather than a *recitativum* (cf. Rom 3:20). The causal logic is rendered even more explicitly in some of the textual witnesses.[13] Paul's wording differs from the Septuagint in three regards. First, he substitutes "all flesh" (πᾶσα σάρξ) for "every living being" (πᾶς ζῶν). The Scriptures use πᾶσα σάρξ as a synonym for πᾶς ζῶν (e.g., Ps 65:2 [64:2 LXX]; 136:25 [135:25 LXX]; 145:21 [144:21 LXX]). "Flesh," however, is likely Paul's own alteration, as he draws attention to human "flesh" where circumcision takes place and anticipates what he says about the flesh later in the letter. Flesh serves as the opposite of the Spirit already in the next paragraph (3:3). Second, Paul omits the unnecessary phrase "before you" (ἐνώπιόν σου). Third, he adds the phrase ἐξ ἔργων νόμου in his contrast as activity that stands apart from God's Spirit.

Jewish authors recognized that no one could claim to be righteous before God (Job 9:22; Ps 14:1–3; Isa 59:2–21; 1 En. 81:5 [no flesh is righteous before the Lord]; 1QH VI [=XIV], 14–15). Psalm 143 therefore invokes *God's* righteousness as saving (143:1, 11 [142:1, 11 LXX]). Nevertheless, God's salvation was never divorced from living according to Moses's law. Paul ignores both Ps 143:8's "way" in which one should walk and 143:10's doing the "will" of God. Elsewhere in the Psalms, the "way" in which one should walk and the "will" of God are identified with the Mosaic law (Pss 18:22–24; 40:9; 119:1). The stress, for Paul, is on God's grace. By not signaling the quotation, Paul avoids the potential rejoinder that the psalm, in its entirety, indicates that no one is justified before God *apart from* the law.[14]

13. Including C D² H K L Y.
14. Martinus C. de Boer, *Galatians*, NTL (Louisville: Westminster John Knox, 2011), 152.

Galatians 3:11/Habakkuk 2:4

Gal 3:11: ὅτι ὁ δίκαιος ἐκ πίστεώς μου ζήσεται
Because the righteous one will live by faith

Hab 2:4: MT: וצדיק באמונתו יחיה
But the righteous shall live by their faithfulness
LXX^B (Codex Vaticanus): ὁ δίκαιος ἐκ πίστεώς μου ζήσεται
The righteous one will live by my faithfulness
LXX^A (Codex Alexandrinus): ὁ δίκαιος μου ἐκ πίστεώς ζήσεται
My righteous one shall live by faithfulness

Many Jews of Paul's day understood Hab 2:4's "faith" as *faithfulness* (cf. Rom 1:17; Heb 10:38). The referent to "his" in the Hebrew text is unclear: the pronoun could refer to *God's* faithfulness, to the righteous individual's *own* faith(fulness), or to the messiah's faithfulness. One Greek Septuagintal text (LXX^A) is ambiguous, "My righteous one shall live on the basis of faith/fulness," while another text (LXX^B) translates the verse as referring to *God's* faithfulness (to promises). The Dead Sea Scroll community interpreted the verse as applying to faith in or loyalty to the community's teacher (1QpHab VII, 5–VIII, 3; note: not the teacher's own faithfulness). The Dead Sea passage also mentions "toil," perhaps in obedience to the law. The later rabbis understood Hab 2:4 to promise reward to the faithful (e.g., b. Mak. 24a). This scriptural verse too would serve well the teaching of the rivals.

The notion of faithful law observance, present in most of the textual precursors, is absent in Paul. Interpreting the verse differently than his Second Temple peers, he does not follow either the Masoretic or the Septuagintal text and deletes the pronoun (whether "his" in the MT and "my" in LXX^B) that modifies faith/fulness. He ignores the first clause of the verse about the individual's own integrity and focuses on faith/trust, in agreement with Abraham's believing "faith" in Gal 3:6. Paul remains riveted on the blessings associated with faith apart from the deeds prescribed by the law.

To review: The consistency with which Paul quotes passages that support law observance or juxtaposes scriptural passages directly in response indicates that the Galatians are learning the Scriptures from the rivals. Paul either has learned of their teaching or is assuming the texts that figure in it (cf. the indefinite "whoever the person may be" in 5:9; the interrogative "who" in 3:1 and 5:7). Paul explicitly signals most of his citations, which suggests that they are not familiar enough to be recognized apart from introductory formula. He does not cite passages that the Galatians might have known apart from the dynamic of the rivals' instruction and his response (e.g., any prior teaching of his own).

Again, the Galatians appear to have been learning the Scriptures primarily or exclusively from the rivals.

He avoids the commands to circumcise in Gen 17 (esp. vv. 10–14) and Lev 12:3. Were Paul to cite such clear texts commanding circumcision as an "everlasting covenant," he would surely be playing into the hands of the rivals. He would be conceding that the Scriptures did indeed advocate circumcision as necessary for God's continued acceptance. It is enough that many of the passages he *does* tackle are, on the surface, at odds with his own position (e.g., Deut 27:26 in Gal 3:10; Lev 18:5 in Gal 3:12).

Verbal Allusions

Multiple studies have explored Paul's allusions in the letter to the Scriptures.[15] Scholars debate whether such studies only illumine Paul's own thinking or whether they may point to the audience's competence in the Scriptures. Despite Paul's signaling of quotations, many have contended that the Galatian audience consisted of sophisticated readers of Scripture, thanks to potential synagogue instruction or the cues provided by Paul's associates reading the letter or by the more biblically literate.

Ciampa, for instance, claimed that the term "Christ" would be difficult for the Galatians to understand apart from Paul's prior extensive instruction in the messianic expectations of Israel.[16] The understanding of "Christ," however, is a complicated matter—whether a proper name, a title, or better, an honorific. A long-standing honorific may function like a proper name and not require *any* scriptural literacy on the part of the Galatians. Paul does not make a play on the word "Christ" in Gal 1:1 as he does in 2 Cor 1:21–22; he does not refer to the specific blessings given to the Jewish people as in Rom 9:3–5—two passages where the supernominal associations of Christ as the Messiah come to the fore.[17]

Ciampa interpreted Paul's use of the phrase "churches/assemblies of God" (ἐκκλησία τοῦ θεοῦ) in Gal 1:13 as a "clear" reference to the Israelite assemblies in the Scriptures. Even the word "churches" or "assemblies" (ἐκκλησία) earlier in Gal 1:2 subtly evokes the Galatians' scriptural self-understanding on the basis of Paul's prior instruction.[18] However, *any* gathering of people in the Greco-Roman

---

15. E.g., Ciampa, *Presence*; Matthew S. Harmon, *She Must and Shall Go Free: Paul's Isaianic Gospel in Galatians*, BZNW 168 (Berlin: de Gruyter, 2010).

16. Ciampa, *Presence*, 38–39.

17. A. Andrew Das, "Christ as Messiah in Romans," in *Scripture, Texts, and Tracings in Romans*, ed. Linda L. Belleville and A. Andrew Das (Lanham, MD: Lexington Books/Fortress Academic, 2020), 185–203.

18. Ciampa, *Presence*, 47.

world could be called an "assembly" (ἐκκλησία). Ciampa may be illumining Paul's own thought structures and not what he assumed of his audience.

The term "covenant" (διαθήκη) is another proffered evidence that the Galatians were familiar with scriptural terminology. Greeks and Romans used the word for a last will and testament, but the Jews employed διαθήκη uniquely for an agreement between two parties. Paul himself uses the word in a distinctively Jewish sense for the Abrahamic covenant in Gal 3:17 (430 years prior to Moses's law). How would the Galatians have comprehended Paul's logic without prior instruction in the Scriptures' covenants? On the other hand, when Paul first refers to a διαθήκη in 3:15, the legal terminology finds parallels in Greco-Roman last wills and testaments (e.g., κυρόω διαθήκην ["ratify a will"], ἀθετέω ["annul a will"], ἐπιδιατάσσομαι ["add a codicil"]). Paul "detheologizes" the term before he "retheologizes" it in 3:17—as J. Louis Martyn recognized years ago.[19] Second Temple Jews considered the Abrahamic covenant and Mosaic law two sides of the same coin (e.g., Sir 17:12–13; 24:23; 28:7; 39:8; 4 Ezra 3:32; 4:23; 5:29; 7:46; 8:27), and so Paul *divorces* Moses's law from Abraham's covenant in Gal 3:17. He returns to this shocking separation in Gal 4:21–31, esp. 4:24: the one Abrahamic covenant surprisingly becomes *two* Abrahamic covenants, and the law now is associated with an Abrahamic covenant—the covenant of the slave woman and her child! The inconsistency indicates that διαθήκη is not a term of choice for Paul. He is responding to the rivals' teaching about the Mosaic covenant—again, in connection with their promotion of the law.[20]

Paul does not assume that the Galatians will recognize his quotations of the Scripture apart from explicit introductory cues. He appears to be responding to what would figure in the rivals' own teaching of the Scriptures. If this reconstruction is correct, then one cannot expect of the Galatians sophistication in the detection of allusions or echoes, and yet Paul *does* allude extensively to the Scriptures throughout this letter. This may simply reflect his own background in the heritage of Israel and need not imply anything of the Galatian audiences' competence. Sometimes, however, his scriptural allusions (in contrast to his marked citations) appear to be pointed at his rivals, should they be listening to the Galatian discourse and *should they be competent*—especially in Gal 1–2. The allusions, if detected, would function as Ciampa claimed: to reinforce Paul's ethos and authority.[21]

---

19. J. Louis Martyn, *Galatians: A New Translation with Introduction and Commentary*, AB 33A (New York: Doubleday, 1997), 338.

20. A. Andrew Das, *Paul and the Stories of Israel: Grand Thematic Narratives in Galatians* (Minneapolis: Fortress, 2016), 65–92.

21. Ciampa, *Presence*, 226.

In Gal 1:6, for instance, Paul worries that the Galatians are so "quickly" (ταχύ) "turning away" (μετατίθημι), language reminiscent of Israel's apostasy in the wilderness in Exod 32:8 LXX (ταχύ); Deut 9:12, 16 (cf. Judg 2:17 LXX). The rivals reading over the shoulders of the Galatians may have recognized the allusion—and been incensed. Many Jews were hypersensitive to desertion after their faith had been nearly eradicated by the persecutions of Antiochus IV Epiphanes. The law had prescribed death for apostates (Lev 24:16; Deut 17:1–7; see 11Q19 [11QTª], e.g., LV). Many in Paul's day would have been willing to suffer death rather than forsake their ancestral traditions. Although the rivals thought they were leading the Galatians to a more faithful observance of God's will, ironically, Paul describes the Galatians' path as leading to apostasy. In the next verse, Gal 1:7, Paul refers to "some" people who are "confusing" or "troubling" (οἱ ταράσσοντες) the Galatians. Paul may be alluding to Achar, the "troubler of Israel" in 1 Chr 2:7, who led Israel to apostasy. Again, the allusion, if detected, would be at the expense of the rivals.

In the next paragraph, Paul is clear that he had been called by God from his mother's womb (Gal 1:15–16), an allusion to the Hebrew prophets (Jer 1:5; Isa 49:1), confirmed by the subsequent verses. In Gal 1:24 Paul borrows from the language of Isa 49:3, and in Gal 2:2 (cf. 4:11) he appears to be drawing on Isa 49:4. Paul also quotes Isa 49:8 in 2 Cor 6:2. Thus Paul's call was like that of the prophets of old. The Jewish rivals would have been more likely to have grasped the allusion than the Galatians. Galatians 1:15–16a develops Paul's repeated opening claims to be the recipient of divine and not human revelation (1:1; 1:11b–12). The rivals were teachers of *Moses* (3:19–20), but Paul was the recipient of *direct* revelation! Whereas the rivals might appeal to the human pillars in Jerusalem (2:1–10), Paul derives his authority from God the Father. Again, the reasoning here bears a polemical edge that the rivals may well have grasped—or not. Paul may have delighted in these ironies without assuming anyone would necessarily notice.

Conceptual Allusions

Many specialists have gone a step further to identify conceptual allusions, or what one might call "grand thematic narratives." These are references to a narratival theme or topic in the Scriptures—whether the exodus in Gal 4:1–7; the influx of the gentiles into Zion in Gal 3:10–14; 3:23–26; and 4:3–5; or the Akedah of Gen 22 in Gal 3. Recent work has called most of these into question.[22] Conceptual allusions reside at the weakest level of intertextual "signal," and alternative

---

22. Das, *Paul and the Stories*, which includes examples and discussion of this category, including each of the examples in this section.

explanations are frequently more likely. For instance, in Gal 4:1–7 Paul draws on Greco-Roman inheritance and guardianship language attested in the papyri (esp. P.Ryl. 2.153), not the exodus. The "gentile influx" theme posited for Gal 3:10–14; 3:23–26; and 4:3–5 depends on a distinction in pronouns that is inconsistent and exegetically problematic. Paul *subverts* Akedah traditions in avoiding reference to Isaac in favor of Christ at critical moments in Gal 3. The most likely conceptual allusions are those that are "anchored" in clearer citations or allusions. Paul quotes and alludes to the Isaianic servant passages (e.g., Isa 43:1 in Gal 4:27; Isa 49:1 in Gal 1:15), strengthening confidence in a conceptual allusion at work elsewhere in the letter. Paul quotes and alludes to "Israel-in-exile" with, for instance, Deut 27:26 (/28:58/30:10) in Gal 3:10, again strengthening confidence in this conceptual allusion elsewhere in the letter. A sound methodology would therefore dictate that one work from the known (citations) to the unknown (conceptual allusions).

Conclusion

Many of the sophisticated allusions and echoes scholars have identified may be recognizable only to the modern academic. One need only consider how few of the proposed Galatians allusions a renowned sixteenth-century professor of the Old Testament detected.[23] The more urgent question is at what level *the ancient hearer* would perceive the uses of Scripture, and the situation that motivated the letter must remain firmly in view. The use of introductory formulas assumes that most or all the gentile readers would not otherwise recognize his scriptural citations. Paul does not assume that the readers would know anything about the context of those quotations and, in some instances, interprets the scriptural passage in ways that may seem at odds with the original context without any apparent concern that the audience would notice or object. Paul does frequently allude to the Scriptures. This may only illumine the influences on Paul's own thought structures. At times, the scriptural allusions bear implications that could be pointed against the rival Jewish teachers and their promotion of law observance—were they capable of recognizing them in the ancient context. This raises the possibility that Paul is ostensibly addressing one audience (the Galatian gentiles) while aware that his letter may be overheard by others at a different level of biblical literacy (the Jewish Christian rivals).

---

23. A. Andrew Das, "Luther on the Scriptures in Galatians—and Its Readers," in *Always Reforming: Reflections on Martin Luther and Biblical Studies*, ed. Channing L. Crisler and Robert Plummer (Bellingham, WA: Lexham Press, 2021), 115–25.

Bibliography

Barclay, John M. G. "Mirror-Reading a Polemical Letter: Galatians as a Test Case." *JSNT* 10, no. 31 (1987): 73–93.

Ciampa, Roy E. *The Presence and Function of Scripture in Galatians 1 and 2.* WUNT 2/102. Tübingen: Mohr Siebeck, 1998.

Danby, Herbert. *The Mishnah: Translated from the Hebrew, with Introduction and Brief Explanatory Notes.* London: Oxford University Press, 1933.

Das, A. Andrew. "The Ambiguous Common Ground of Galatians 2:16 Revisited." *BR* 58 (2013): 49–61.

———. "Another Look at ἐὰν μή in Galatians 2:16." *JBL* 119, no. 3 (2000): 529–39.

———. "Christ as Messiah in Romans." Pages 185–203 in *Scripture, Texts, and Tracings in Romans.* Edited by Linda L. Belleville and A. Andrew Das. Lanham, MD: Lexington Books/Fortress Academic, 2020.

———. *Galatians.* ConC. St. Louis: Concordia, 2014.

———. "Galatians 3:10: A 'Newer Perspective' on an Omitted Premise." Pages 203–23 in *Unity and Diversity in the Gospels and Paul: Essays in Honor of Frank J. Matera.* Edited by Christopher W. Skinner and Kelly R. Iverson. ECL 7. Atlanta: Society of Biblical Literature, 2012.

———. "Luther on the Scriptures in Galatians—and Its Readers." Pages 111–25 in *Always Reforming: Reflections on Martin Luther and Biblical Studies.* Edited by Channing L. Crisler and Robert Plummer. Bellingham, WA: Lexham Press, 2021.

———. *Paul and the Stories of Israel: Grand Thematic Narratives in Galatians.* Minneapolis: Fortress, 2016.

De Boer, Martinus C. *Galatians.* NTL. Louisville: Westminster John Knox, 2011.

Goodrich, John K. "'As Long as the Heir Is a Child': The Rhetoric of Inheritance in Galatians 4:1–2 and P.Ryl. 2.153." *NovT* 55, no. 1 (2013): 61–76.

Harmon, Matthew S. *She Must and Shall Go Free: Paul's Isaianic Gospel in Galatians.* BZNW 168. Berlin: de Gruyter, 2010.

Harnack, Adolf von. "The Old Testament in the Pauline Letters and in the Pauline Churches." Pages 27–49 in *Understanding Paul's Ethics: Twentieth Century Approaches.* Edited by Brian S. Rosner. Translated by George S. Rosner and Brian S. Rosner. Grand Rapids: Eerdmans, 1995.

Hays, Richard B. *Echoes of Scripture in the Letters of Paul.* New Haven: Yale University Press, 1989.

Koch, Dietrich-Alex. *Die Schrift als Zeuge des Evangeliums: Untersuchungen zur Verwendung und zum Verständnis der Schrift bei Paulus.* BHT 69. Tübingen: Mohr Siebeck, 1986.

Martyn, J. Louis. "Covenant, Christ, and Church in Galatians." Pages 137–51 in *The*

Future of Christology: Essays in Honor of Leander E. Keck. Edited by Abraham J. Malherbe and Wayne A. Meeks. Minneapolis: Fortress, 1993.

———. *Galatians: A New Translation with Introduction and Commentary*. AB 33A. New York: Doubleday, 1997.

Novenson, Matthew V. *Christ among the Messiahs: Christ Language in Paul and Messiah Language in Ancient Judaism*. Oxford: Oxford University Press, 2012.

Porter, Stanley E. "Allusions and Echoes." Pages 29–40 in *As It Is Written: Studying Paul's Use of Scripture*. Edited by Stanley E. Porter and Christopher D. Stanley. SymS 50. Atlanta: Society of Biblical Literature, 2008.

———. "Further Comments on the Use of the Old Testament in the New Testament." Pages 98–110 in *The Intertextuality of the Epistles: Explorations of Theory and Practice*. Edited by Thomas L. Brodie, Dennis R. MacDonald, and Stanley E. Porter. New Testament Monographs 16. Sheffield: Sheffield Phoenix, 2007.

———. "The Use of the Old Testament in the New Testament: A Brief Comment on Method and Terminology." Pages 79–96 in *Early Christian Interpretation of the Scriptures of Israel: Investigations and Proposals*. Edited by Craig A. Evans and James A. Sanders. JSNTSup 148. Sheffield: Sheffield Academic, 1997.

Stanley, Christopher D. *Arguing with Scripture: The Rhetoric of Quotations in the Letters of Paul*. London: T&T Clark, 2004.

———. *Paul and the Language of Scripture: Citation Technique in the Pauline Epistles and Contemporary Literature*. SNTSMS 74. Cambridge: Cambridge University Press, 1992.

16

Israel's Scriptures in Ephesians and Colossians

PAUL FOSTER

The letters of Ephesians and Colossians are arguably the two most closely related pair of writings in the Pauline corpus. For example, these two letters present the strongest examples of household codes contained in the Pauline writings (Col 3:18–4:1; Eph 5:22–6:9). Admittedly there may be partial or vestigial ideas that relate to contents of typical household codes in 1 Tim 3:4 or Tit 2:2–10, but the form of that material diverges from the classic examples in Greco-Roman literature (Aristotle, *Pol.* 1.3.1; Plutarch, *Lib. ed.* 10; Seneca, *Ep.* 94.1) and more significantly from the examples contained in Col 3:18–4:1 and Eph 5:22–6:9. Apart from household codes, there are several theological ideas expressed in these two letters that appear to have a greater degree of affinity with one another than they do with other letters in the Pauline corpus. Their ecclesiology tends to be more universal in nature (Col 1:18, 24, 25; Eph 1:22; 3:10, 21; 5:23–32). By contrast, a more localized view of the church is found in most of Paul's other writings (see Rom 16:1 "the church which is at Cenchrea"; Rom 16:4 "the churches of the gentiles"; and many other examples; but cf. 1 Tim 3:15 "the church of the living God"). Also, the eschatological perspectives contained in Colossians and Ephesians tend to be more realized in nature (Col 2:12–14; 3:1–3; and Eph 1:7–8; 2:6) than the more typically future-oriented eschatology found in the majority of Paul's letters (Rom 6:5, 8).

However, the most striking affinities between Colossians and Ephesians are not merely thematic or theological, but are to be found in the extensive and extended verbal parallels. Since the predominant (but not universal) view is that Ephesians is in some way dependent on the text of Colossians, in this study the putative scriptural references in Colossians will be considered before turning to the use of Scripture in Ephesians. Without doubt the most noteworthy is the parallel that exists between Col 4:7–8 and Eph 6:21–22. In this case, of the thirty-four Greek words that constitute Col 4:7–8, thirty-two of these are found in Eph 6:21–22 in the same form and sequence.[1]

Table 16.1. Comparing Col 4:7–8 and Eph 6:21–22

Col 4:7–8	Eph 6:21–22
Τὰ κατ᾽ ἐμὲ πάντα γνωρίσει ὑμῖν Τύχικος ὁ ἀγαπητὸς ἀδελφὸς καὶ πιστὸς διάκονος καὶ σύνδουλος ἐν κυρίῳ, ὃν ἔπεμψα πρὸς ὑμᾶς εἰς αὐτὸ τοῦτο, ἵνα γνῶτε τὰ περὶ ἡμῶν καὶ παρακαλέσῃ τὰς καρδίας ὑμῶν	Ἵνα δὲ εἰδῆτε καὶ ὑμεῖς τὰ κατ᾽ ἐμέ, τί πράσσω, πάντα γνωρίσει ὑμῖν Τύχικος ὁ ἀγαπητὸς ἀδελφὸς καὶ πιστὸς διάκονος ἐν κυρίῳ, ὃν ἔπεμψα πρὸς ὑμᾶς εἰς αὐτὸ τοῦτο, ἵνα γνῶτε τὰ περὶ ἡμῶν καὶ παρακαλέσῃ τὰς καρδίας ὑμῶν
"the things concerning me Tychicus, the beloved brother and faithful servant and fellow slave in the Lord, will make known all to you, whom I sent to you for this very reason, in order that you might know the things concerning us, and your hearts might be encouraged."	"But in order also that you might know the things concerning me, how I am doing, Tychicus, the beloved brother and faithful servant in the Lord, will make known all to you, whom I sent to you for this very reason, in order that you might know the things concerning us, and your hearts might be encouraged."

The only difference is that the two-word phrase "and fellow-slave" καὶ σύνδουλος, contained in Col. 4:8 is omitted from Eph. 6:21. This example alone, regardless of questions of authorship, is strongly suggestive of some form of literary dependence. There are other significant parallels involving Col 1:14 // Eph 1:7; and Col 2:13 // Eph 2:5. Together this evidence of similarity in content, theological themes, and precise and extended verbal parallels suggests a close connection between these two letters.

Given these wide-ranging and varied points of similarity, it is striking when one comes to consider the respective use of the Jewish Scriptures in these two letters. Here the evidence drawn from each epistle seems to reflect very divergent

---

1. For a fuller discussion of this example and other cases, see Paul Foster, *Colossians*, BNTC (London: Bloomsbury T&T Clark, 2016), 85–90. Unless otherwise noted, all translations are by the author.

practices. In Colossians the strongest potential allusion to the Jewish Scriptures is the possible use of Gen 1:28 in Col 3:10. This example will be discussed in more detail below. By contrast, in Ephesians there are around half-a-dozen citations of the Jewish Scriptures and probably a similar number of verbal allusions, although the exact enumeration of these is more debatable. Moreover, the following table based on the work of Thorsten Moritz reveals a clear pattern in the compositional practice of the author of Ephesians, whereby scriptural material is introduced into contexts where textual data has been drawn from parallel passages contained in Colossians.[2]

Table 16.2. Textual Parallels

	Colossians		Ephesians	
Parallel from Colossians	Verses with OT material		Parallel from Ephesians	Verses with OT material
Col 1:13	–		1:15–23	*1:20*, 22
Col 1:3–27; 2:9–14	–		2:11–18	2:13, 17
Col 2:15	–		4:8–10	*4:8*
Col 3:5–12	3:10 (?)		4:25–5:2	4:25–26, 30; 5:2
Col 3:16	–		5:13–20	5:14, 18
Col 3:18–19	–		6:1–4	6:2

Therefore, as noted elsewhere, "there is a clear pattern whereby the author of Ephesians supplies a citation from the Jewish Scriptures into a section of text with a parallel in Colossians, even though the parallel section of Colossians does not (in all but one case) allude to the Old Testament."[3]

Hence in these two closely related letters one striking and distinguishing feature is the divergent practice around the use of the Jewish Scriptures. This may have implications for discussions of the authorship of these epistles, or perhaps it might reflect something of the ability of the intended recipients to detect and resonate with the Jewish scriptural heritage. However, before any even tentative conclusions can be drawn, it is necessary to look first at the use or relative nonuse of Scripture in these two letters.

---

2. Moritz, "The Psalms in Ephesians and Colossians," in *The Psalms in the New Testament*, ed. Steve Moyise and Maarten J. J. Menken, NTSI (London: T&T Clark International, 2004), 183. Here he states that "the italicized portions in the fourth column indicate the verses that make use of the Psalms."

3. Foster, *Colossians*, 58.

The Use of Scripture in Colossians

There have been three recent major studies of the use of Scripture in Colossians.[4] These studies adopt similar approaches and methods.[5] However, they have produced widely divergent results. One point of commonality between Gordon Fee, G. K. Beale, and Christopher Beetham (the authors of the three studies on the use of Scripture in Colossians) is that none of the examples they identify is classified as a citation (marked or unmarked) of the Jewish Scriptures in the letter to Colossians. However, here the agreement largely ends. The fainter uses of Scripture that they each detect are variously labeled as allusions or echoes. Fee exclusively employs the term "echo"; Beale exclusively uses the term "allusion"; and Beetham classifies some of the putative uses of Scripture as "echoes," while others that are stronger are deemed to be "allusions." This difference in choice of terminology, however, is by no means the major point of divergence between the three studies. The more fundamental point of disagreement arises in relation to those passages in Colossians that are identified as having material that echoes or alludes to material in Jewish Scriptures.

As can be seen in table 16.3 below, Fee identifies ten echoes, Beale seventeen allusions, and Beetham eleven uses of Scripture, of which two are allusions and nine are echoes.[6] As a useful comparison, the following table also lists those passages identified in NA[28], which are listed in appendix III: Loci Citati vel Allegati, in the category Ex Vetere Testamento. The following table has been presented previously.[7] Here A = allusion, and E = echo, as defined by the scholar in question. References under each scholar's name occur only when the suggested allusion or echoes differs to some degree from the listed intertext.

---

4. Gordon D. Fee, "Old Testament Intertextuality in Colossians: Reflections on Pauline Christology and Gentile Inclusion in God's Story," in *History and Exegesis: New Testament Essays in Honor of Dr. E. Earle Ellis for His 80th Birthday*, ed. Sang-Won Son (London: T&T Clark, 2006), 201–21; G. K. Beale, "Colossians," in *Commentary on the New Testament Use of the Old Testament*, ed. G. K. Beale and D. A. Carson (Grand Rapids: Baker Academic, 2007), 841–70; Christopher A. Beetham, *Echoes of Scripture in the Letter of Paul to the Colossians*, BibInt 96 (Leiden: Brill, 2008).

5. To some degree all three of these studies have been significantly influenced by the works of Richard B. Hays, *Echoes of Scripture in the Letters of Paul* (New Haven: Yale University Press, 1989); and Hays, *The Conversion of the Imagination: Paul as Interpreter of Israel's Scriptures* (Grand Rapids: Eerdmans, 2005).

6. Beale prefers the term "allusion," which he sees as reflecting intentionality on the part of Paul (whereas an echo is seen as more loosely defined, sometimes "as unconscious and unintentional sometimes as conscious and intentional"; Beale, "Colossians," 841).

7. See Paul Foster, "Echoes without Resonance: Critiquing Certain Aspects of Recent Scholarly Trends in the Study of the Jewish Scriptures in the New Testament," *JSNT* 38, no. 1 (2015): 96–111; Foster, *Colossians*, 54–55.

Table 16.3. Intertexts in Colossians

	Passages in Colossians	Intertext from OT	NA[28]	Fee	Beale	Beetham
1	Col 1:6, 10	Gen 1:28			A	E
2	Col 1:9–10	Exod 31:3; 35:31–32; Isa 11:2		E (Isa 11:2)	A	E (Isa 11:2, 9)
3	Col 1:12–14	Exodus motif		E	A	E
4	Col 1:13	2 Sam 7:12–16		E (2 Sam 7:14, 18)	A	E (2 Sam 7:12–18)
5	Col 1:15	Gen 1:26, 28		E		
6	Col 1:15	Gen 1:27			A	
7	Col 1:15	Ps 89:27 [LXX 88:28]		E	A	
8	Col 1:15–17	Wisdom theme			A (poss.)	
9	Col 1:15–20	Prov 8:22–31				A
10	Col 1:17	Prov 8:23–27	A			
11	Col 1:18	Gen 1:1		E		
12	Col 1:19	Ps 68:17 [LXX 67:17]			A	E
13	Col 1:26–27	Dan 2			A	
14	Col 2:2–3	Dan 2; Prov 2:3–6			A	
15	Col 2:3	Sir 1:24–25; 1 En. 46:3; Isa 45:3; Prov 2:3–4	A			
16	Col 2:11	Deut 30:6			A	E
17	Col 2:13	Gen 17:10–27			A	E
18	Col 2:22	Isa 29:13	A	E	A	E
19	Col 3:1	Ps 110:1	A	E	A	E
20	Col 3:9–10	Gen 3:7–21			A	
21	Col 3:9–10	Gen 1:26, 28		E		
22	Col 3:10	Gen 1:26–27	A		A	A
23	Col 3:12	Deut 7:6–8		E		
24	Col 4:1	Lev 25:43–53; Eccl 5:7	A			
25	Col 4:5	Dan 2:8			A	
	Total:		6	10	17	11

Some entries in the table occur as variations of each other, such as the fifth and sixth rows, the fourteenth and fifteenth, and the twenty-first and twenty-second. However, in these cases it was important to reflect the differing formulations of the intertextual link as presented by each scholar.

As is immediately apparent from this table, not only are the numbers of allusions or echoes significantly different between all scholars, yet more striking is the lack of uniformity in the list of passages that each of the three scholars has identified. Given the fact that each is using an approach that is informed by Richard Hays's paradigm, and in the case of Beethem his published study was doctoral research carried out under the supervision of Beale, the divergence is worrying.[8] This suggests that the methods being employed are at this stage incapable of producing a stable or consistent set of results. Including the listing from NA[28], "only three examples have the support in all four lists (taking rows twenty-one and twenty-two together). These are the slight verbal allusions of Isa 29:13 in Col 2:22; Ps 110:1 [LXX 109:1] in Col 3:1; and Gen 1:26–27 in Col 3:[9]–10."[9]

The strongest of these examples involves the statement in Colossians that believers are being renewed in the likeness of the image of the creator. This is seen as alluding to a passage in the first creation account in Genesis. The parallel may be set out as follows:

Table 16.4. Textual Parallels

LXX Gen 1:27	Col 3:10
καὶ ἐποίησεν ὁ θεὸς τὸν ἄνθρωπον <u>κατ' εἰκόνα θεοῦ ἐποίησεν αὐτόν</u> ἄρσεν καὶ θῆλυ ἐποίησεν αὐτούς "And God made man, according to the image of God he made him, male and female he made them."	καὶ ἐνδυσάμενοι τὸν νέον τὸν ἀνακαινούμενον εἰς ἐπίγνωσιν <u>κατ' εἰκόνα τοῦ κτίσαντος αὐτόν</u> "and have put on the new self who is being renewed to a true knowledge according to the image of the one who created him."

For ease of comparison the key five-word phrase in both passages has been highlighted with underlining. Three of the five words are identical. In both pas-

---

8. Hays's paradigm revolves around the seven tests he lists for determining the presence of an echo. These tests are (1) availability (source available to author and readers); (2) volume (agreement in words and syntactic patterns); (3) recurrence (same passage used by author elsewhere); (4) thematic coherence (theme of echoed text fits author's argument); (5) historical plausibility (is the proposed echo historically possible); (6) history of interpretation (have later readers detected the echo); and (7) satisfaction (is the echo appealing and make sense). See Hays, *Echoes of Scripture in the Letters of Paul*, 29–32.

9. Foster, *Colossians*, 55.

sages the expression κατ' εἰκόνα denotes the divine image. The accusative masculine singular pronoun has a different object of reference in the two passages. In Genesis it is a singular but collective pronoun that refers to all humanity, both female and male, being formed in the likeness of God. By contrast, in Col 3:10 individual believers are addressed as needing to "put on" a new self, which is transformed and refashioned after the image of the creator. Here particular members of the community of faith are addressed and instructed to actualize their transformed lives. In Genesis, the statement is one of fact, namely that humanity as a whole is formed in the image of the divine. The elements that differ in these phrases are the anarthrous use of the genitive noun θεοῦ "God" contained in Gen 1:27 LXX, whereas in Col 3:10 a substantivized participle τοῦ κτίσαντος is employed to denote God. This description of God as "the one who created" in Col 3:10 makes any verb describing God's action unnecessary. This stands in contrast to Gen 1:27 LXX since the noun "God" requires an accompanying verb to describe the divine action.

The points of similarity and difference having been described, the question remains as to whether or not this evidence supports the case for Col 3:10 being dependent on Gen 1:27 in some way. Alongside those observations, one must bear in mind the foundational nature of the creation story of Genesis, its retelling in various contexts, and its circulation in forms independent of the text of Genesis. Therefore, the snatches of shared common terminology may be sufficient to suggest only that in some manner Col 3:10 might be directly or indirectly dependent on Gen 1:27. However, there is insufficient evidence to load this fleeting allusion with intertextual meaning by importing themes and ideas either from the wider context of Genesis or from Paul's other references to creation. These are the type of moves that Beetham makes when he states, "the last Adam Messiah Jesus, *is* the image of God and serves as the head and prototype of the new humanity of the new creation."[10] The validity of such a reading might be challenged since the context of Col 3:6–11 does not obviously suggest or necessitate these more developed theological themes.

In the case of the possible use of Isa 29:13 LXX in Col 2:22, the connection is based on a single short parallel phrase: ἐντάλματα ἀνθρώπων καὶ διδασκαλίας (Isa 29:13b) and τὰ ἐντάλματα καὶ διδασκαλίας τῶν ἀνθρώπων (Col 2:22b). There may be some direct connection, but it is equally possible the expression "the precepts and doctrines of men" had become "a stock phrase used to denote human instruction, and circulated independently of its original context."[11]

---

10. Beetham, *Echoes of Scripture in the Letter of Paul to the Colossians*, 244 (emphasis original).

11. Foster, *Colossians*, 55.

The last of the three common examples involves the potential use of Ps 109:1 LXX [= Ps 110:1 MT] in Col 3:1.¹² The link is based on the common idea of sitting at the right of God. However, the verbal correspondence is low.

Table 16.5. Textual Parallels

Ps 109:1 LXX	Col 3:1
εἶπεν ὁ κύριος τῷ κυρίῳ μου κάθου ἐκ δεξιῶν μου ἕως ἂν θῶ τοὺς ἐχθρούς σου ὑποπόδιον τῶν ποδῶν σου "The Lord said to my Lord, Sit on my right, until I make your enemies a footstool for your feet."	Εἰ οὖν συνηγέρθητε τῷ Χριστῷ, τὰ ἄνω ζητεῖτε, οὗ ὁ Χριστός ἐστιν ἐν δεξιᾷ τοῦ θεοῦ καθήμενος "If then you have been raised up with Christ, keep seeking the things above, where Christ is, seated at the right hand of God."

The similarities are obvious and revolve around the notion of sitting at the right hand of the Lord or God. Again, it is not improbable that at some level Col 3:1 has some type of dependence on Ps 109:1, notwithstanding the fact that sitting at the right hand of a powerful figure was a commonplace idea. The prominence of Ps 109:1 LXX in early Christian writing is well known (cf. Matt 22:44 // Mark 12:36 // Luke 20:42; Acts 2:34; 1 Cor 15:25). However, in each of those examples drawn from the New Testament, including the Pauline case in 1 Cor 14:25, the correspondence is far greater.

The use of Jewish Scriptures in Colossians is minimal. At best there are a couple of fleeting verbal allusions. However, the subject matter in those cases involves such commonplace religious ideas that it may be unnecessary to posit either direct or indirect dependence. As Andrew Lincoln notes, "In Colossians, with its direct confrontation of syncretistic teaching, no OT citations are used nor is there any explicit mention of the law."¹³ It may be possible to go even further and simply to say that not just in terms of citations but in regard to the use of Jewish Scriptures as a whole that there is little discernible appeal to this body of tradition.

---

12. The number of the psalms follows a slightly different sequence in the Septuagint from that found in the Masoretic Text. Here Ps 109 LXX is one number lower than the corresponding Masoretic psalm due to Pss 9 and 10 in the MT being combined to form a single psalm in Ps 9 LXX.

13. Lincoln, "The Use of the OT in Ephesians," *JSNT* 4, no. 14 (1982): 48.

Israel's Scriptures in Ephesians and Colossians

The Use of Scripture in Ephesians

In contrast to the negligible use of Scripture in Colossians, there is a significantly greater employment of such traditions in Ephesians. As Moritz has noted, "Ephesians builds on Colossians not least by the addition of Old Testament material."[14] Moreover, whereas the strongest putative example of the use of Scripture in Colossians was the case of the slight verbal allusion in Col 3:10 to Gen 1:27 LXX, in Ephesians one sees the Jewish Scriptures deployed in a range of different ways. This varied usage includes two examples of marked but authorially unattributed citations, as well as unmarked citations and verbal allusions of varying strength. Arguably, there are also some conceptual allusions. However, since the ideas are so broad in nature, it must be concluded that they lack the degree of specificity that would establish a connection with a scriptural base-text. Instead, such broad similarities could be seen as due to general religious ideas that emerged from the wider pluriform thought world of first-century Mediterranean religious culture.

The texts in Ephesians that present a reasonably strong case as providing examples of the use of Jewish Scriptures in a discernible manner are listed in table 16.6 below. Here the passages in Ephesians are listed in the order in which they occur in the letter, this is followed by reference to the scriptural text that is being utilized, and finally the third column lists the type or class of use that is being employed.[15]

Table 16.6. Intertexts in Ephesians

Text from Ephesians	Underlying Scriptural Text	Type of Use of Scripture
Eph 1:20	Ps 109:1 LXX (Ps 110:1)	Verbal allusion
Eph 1:22	Ps 8:7	Unmarked citation / verbal allusion
Eph 2:17	Isa 57:19	Unmarked citation
Eph 4:8	Ps 68:18	Marked unattributed citation
Eph 4:25	Zech 8:16	Unmarked citation
Eph 4:26	Ps 4:4	Unmarked citation
Eph 5:31	Gen 2:24	Unmarked citation
Eph 6:2–3	Exod 20:12 (or Deut 5:16)	Marked unattributed citation

14. Moritz, "Psalms in Ephesians and Colossians," 183.
15. This list draws on multiple earlier lists and discussions and reflects my own perspective on the most convincing examples of the use of scriptural texts in Ephesians.

Eph 6:14	Isa 59:17	Verbal allusion
Eph 6:15	Isa 52:7	Verbal allusion
Eph 6:17	Isa 59:17	Verbal allusion

It needs to be noted that there is not a clear demarcation between the category of unmarked citation and that of the stronger verbal allusions. Such a distinction remains a matter of classification and genuinely open debate. However, what is immediately apparent from the table is that there is not an even distribution of the use of Scripture throughout the letter. Rather, the clustering of scriptural citations reflects the type of argument being made by the author of Ephesians where it is considered that an appeal to the Jewish Scriptures would strengthen the train of thought.

The discussion will examine these examples in sequence. The first case, which is found in Eph 1:20, involves the use of Ps 109:1 LXX, a text that in relation to the discussion pertaining to Col 3:1 has already been noted as occurring with notable prominence in early Christian writings.[16]

Table 16.7. Ps 109:1 and Eph 1:20

Ps 109:1 LXX	Eph 1:20
εἶπεν ὁ κύριος τῷ κυρίῳ μου <u>κάθου ἐκ δεξιῶν</u> μου ἕως ἂν θῶ τοὺς ἐχθρούς σου ὑποπόδιον τῶν ποδῶν σου "The Lord said to my Lord, 'Sit on my right, until I make your enemies a footstool for your feet.'"	Ἣν ἐνήργησεν ἐν τῷ Χριστῷ ἐγείρας αὐτὸν ἐκ νεκρῶν καὶ <u>καθίσας ἐν δεξιᾷ</u> αὐτοῦ ἐν τοῖς ἐπουρανίοις "which he brought about in Christ, when he raised him from the dead, and seated him at his right in the heavenlies."

The key parallel three-word phrase involves the shared verb καθίζω, although in different forms, and, again in different forms, the adjective δεξιός. While sitting at a potentate's right was a key way of denoting the status of a powerful but nonetheless subservient viceroy or vizier in the ancient world, it is the widespread use of Ps 109:1 LXX in early Christian literature that makes some kind of dependence likely in this case, rather than seeing the image as arising from the common stock of divine-kingly ideas. However, the lack of precise verbal agree-

---

16. Moritz has stated that "Ps 110:1 plays a major role in early Christianity, as is evidenced by its frequent use in the New Testament"; Moritz, "Psalms in Ephesians and Colossians," 185. In the same collection of essays Watts suggests that the reason for this prominence might be due to "Psalm 110:1's unique understanding of exaltation"; Rikk E. Watts, "The Psalms in Mark's Gospel," in Moyise and Menken, *Psalms in the New Testament*, 37.

ment means little can be said about the precise form of the text of Ps 109:1 LXX from which the allusion in Eph 1:20 is drawn. In fact, given both the wide circulation of Ps 109:1 LXX in early Christian writings and the use of an equally vague allusion to the same text in Col 3:1—an epistle on which Ephesians appears to be dependent in some way—it is possible that Eph 1:20 is indirectly dependent on this text, rather than directly consulting the Greek text of Ps 109:1 LXX.

The second example, that of the use of Ps 8:7 in Eph 1:22, needs to be considered in connection with the previous example. There is a similar conceptual idea in Ps 109:1b LXX, "until I make your enemies a footstool for your feet," and the statement in Ps 8:7b LXX, "you have subjected all things under his feet." Here dominion is revealed by placing something under the feet of the one who receives divine power. In Ps 110:1 (Ps 109:1 LXX) the idea is that of the royal figure having enemies made as a footstool for the king's feet. In Eph 1:22 the idea is that the representative human, addressed in the singular, has all of creation put in subjection to human dominion.

Table 16.8. Ps 8:7b and Eph 1:22

Ps 8:7b LXX	Eph 1:22
πάντα ὑπέταξας ὑποκάτω τῶν ποδῶν αὐτοῦ	καὶ πάντα ὑπέταξεν ὑπὸ τοὺς πόδας αὐτοῦ
"You have subjected all things under his feet."	"And he subjected all things under his feet."

The verbal parallel is striking, albeit not exact. The differences are the aorist second-person form of ὑποτάσσω in LXX Ps 8:7b as opposed to the third-person form in Eph 1:22. The context of Ephesians requires this change because the divine subject is not being addressed directly as in Ps 8:7, but rather a descriptive statement is being made about divine action. Additionally, the preposition ὑποκάτω contained in Ps 8:7b LXX is replaced with the more common form ὑπό, and consequently in Eph 1:22 the case of the following definite article and noun is changed to that required by the governing preposition ὑπό. Both these changes are most likely stylistic alterations, but this observation may support the case that the text of Ps 8:7b LXX is not being consulted directly. Instead, it may be the case that the author is relying on memory or that the form deployed had already become adapted for early Christian use. While Heb 2:8 preserves the exact wording of Ps 8:7b LXX as given in the table above (πάντα ὑπέταξας ὑποκάτω τῶν ποδῶν αὐτοῦ), when Ps 8:7 is cited in the Pauline writings in 1 Cor 15:27 (πάντα γὰρ ὑπέταξεν ὑπὸ τοὺς πόδας αὐτοῦ) the form is almost identical to that of Eph 1:22, the difference being the postpositive conjunction γάρ replacing the conjunction καί contained in Eph 1:22. Therefore, the author of Ephesians may be citing a form of Ps 8:7b LXX that was already in wider circulation in Pauline circles. Discussing the case of the modification of Ps 8:7b LXX in 1 Cor 15:27, Christopher Stanley notes that "though a pre-Pauline origin cannot be ruled out, all the evidence seems to favor the view that Paul has (perhaps unconsciously) adapted the wording of this common quotation to conform to his own linguistic usage."[17] Furthermore, in the context of Heb 2:5–8 and 1 Cor 15:24–27, "Paul conjoins the same two psalms" (Ps 109:1 LXX and Ps 8:6b LXX) as he does here in Eph 1:20–22. Consequently, it appears that the author of Ephesians is not directly citing either of these psalms, but rather is drawing upon a form of Pauline or early Christian scriptural exegetical interpretation that had already brought together the elements of Ps 109:1 LXX and Ps 8:6b LXX that are utilized in Eph 1:20–22.[18]

The third example moves from the Psalms to Isaiah as the source of the base text being utilized. As can be seen from table 16.6, and in common with early Christianity more generally, the most commonly cited texts drawn from the Jewish Scriptures were Psalms and Isaiah.

Table 16.9. Isa 57:19a and Eph 2:17

Isa 57:19a LXX	Eph 2:17
εἰρήνην ἐπ' εἰρήνην τοῖς μακρὰν καὶ τοῖς ἐγγὺς οὖσιν	καὶ ἐλθὼν εὐηγγελίσατο εἰρήνην ὑμῖν τοῖς μακρὰν καὶ εἰρήνην τοῖς ἐγγύς
"Peace upon peace to those who are far away and those who are near."	"And he came and preached peace to you who were far away and peace to those who were near."

Both texts exhibit the double use of the key term "peace," εἰρήνη, but in different constructions. The string of five words τοῖς μακρὰν καὶ τοῖς ἐγγύς is nearly identical with the sequence from Eph 2:17 of six words, τοῖς μακρὰν καὶ εἰρήνην τοῖς ἐγγύς, apart from the intrusion of the second reference to peace (εἰρήνην). The beginning of Eph 2:17 is perhaps more indebted to Isa 52:7 LXX than Isa 57:19a LXX. Hence, this might account for the restructuring at the beginning of Eph 2:17 with its consequent deviation from the text of Isa 57:19a

---

17. Stanley, *Paul and the Language of Scripture: Citation Technique in the Pauline Epistles and Contemporary Literature*, SNTSMS 74 (Cambridge: Cambridge University Press, 1992), 207.

18. This is the conclusion at which Lincoln arrives: "The use of the OT in the last part of Eph. 1 then appears not to be direct but mediated via traditional formulations and 1 Cor 15:24–28." Lincoln, "Use of the OT in Ephesians," 42.

Israel's Scriptures in Ephesians and Colossians

LXX. The opening of Isa 52:7 LXX heralds one who appears on the mountains "who proclaims news of peace," εὐαγγελιζομένου ἀκοὴν εἰρήνης. Here the LXX form of Isa 52:7 stands closer to Eph 2:17 than does the Masoretic form, which presents two elements—the proclaiming of good news and the announcement of peace. In distinction, in the LXX these two elements have been conflated into one element of "proclaiming news of peace." The wording of Eph 2:17 is not particularly close to that of Isa 52:7 LXX, but this is a text cited elsewhere in the Pauline letters (Rom 10:15).

Therefore, it is possible that the author of Ephesians had received this material as a preformed unit or that the two texts were already closely associated in the wider Pauline tradition. Hence it is unlikely that the author was "thinking of the broad literary contexts in which both of these texts occur in Isaiah."[19] The author of Ephesians presumably recognized the material in Eph 2:17 as a scriptural tradition. Thus the declaration of Christ as the one who breaks down the dividing wall (Eph 2:14) that excluded those who were previously "far away" (Eph 2:13) and the description of Christ as "our peace" (Eph 2:14) were the keyword associations that made the deployment of the scriptural tradition in Eph 2:17 particularly apposite. However, the author appears to have drawn on earlier Pauline precedents for using LXX Isa 52:7 and combined this with a modified version of some of the language in Isa 57:19a LXX to suit the overall argument of Eph 2:11–22.

The most extensive citation of the Jewish Scriptures is the use of LXX Ps 67:19b in Eph 4:8, although the author appears to modify the text to fit the argument being made.

Table 16.10. Ps 67:19a and Eph 4:8

Ps 67:19a LXX	Eph 4:8
ἀνέβης εἰς ὕψος ᾐχμαλώτευσας αἰχμαλωσίαν ἔλαβες δόματα ἐν ἀνθρώπῳ	διὸ λέγει· ἀναβὰς εἰς ὕψος ᾐχμαλώτευσεν αἰχμαλωσίαν, ἔδωκεν δόματα τοῖς ἀνθρώποις.
"You have ascended on high; You have led captive captives; You have received gifts among man."	"Therefore it says, When he ascended on high, he led captive captives, he gave gifts to men."

The first thing to note is that the citation in Ephesians is marked with the formula διὸ λέγει, but this indefinite marker means the citation is not clearly attributed. The attribution formula is also ambiguous. This can be seen in English

---

19. Contra Frank S. Thielman, "Ephesians," in Beale and Carson, *Commentary on the New Testament Use of the Old Testament*, 817.

translations where the διὸ λέγει is rendered either as "wherefore he saith" (KJV) or "therefore it says" (NASB). Presumably the choice of the masculine pronoun sees the referent as the male psalmist, whereas the neuter pronoun takes the referent as being the psalm itself.

In terms of the differences between the textual form of Ps 67:19b LXX and Eph 4:8, the change from the second-person direct address of the psalm to the third-person description is due to the way in which the scriptural tradition is deployed in the epistle. The replacement of the representative singular expression ἐν ἀνθρώπῳ with τοῖς ἀνθρώποις appears to be a stylistic change that not only makes the plurality of the representative singular form explicit, but is better suited to the most significant change: the switch of the verb ἔλαβες to ἔδωκεν. Without doubt the final change is the most striking, and it represents an interpretative challenge with regard to explaining this switch of verbs since this could be seen as a reversal of meaning.[20] A number of interpreters have appealed to the targumic tradition, which contains a similar switch of verbs, in order to claim that the author of Ephesians was not responsible for changing the text but in fact drew upon a tradition that already contained the statement concerning the "giving" rather the "receiving" of gifts.[21] The difficulty with this interpretation is that the targum on the Psalms is a relatively late work, so an earlier stage of that tradition with the verbal change must be inferred. In this vein Lincoln states,

> Since the Targum on the Psalms is a late work, it is probable that the writer has made use of an ancient rabbinic tradition which the Targum has also preserved and that this tradition has interpreted the Hebrew לקח rather than reflected a variant textual tradition which had תלק. The tradition has been taken over by the writer to the Ephesians and incorporated into a midrash pesher rendering of the text in which he integrates his exposition of its meaning in the light of fulfilment in Christ into the actual quotation, a procedure which is of course not unusual in the contemporary Jewish exegetical techniques or elsewhere in the use of the OT in the NT.[22]

---

20. Richard N. Longenecker, *Biblical Exegesis in the Apostolic Period*, 2nd ed. (Grand Rapids: Eerdmans, 1999), 107.

21. The English translation of the Aramaic text of the targum of the Psalms is typically given in the following form: "You ascended to the firmament, O prophet Moses, you took captives, you taught them the words of the Torah, you gave them as gifts to the sons of man; even among the rebellious who are converted and repent does the Shekinah of the Lord God dwell." See, e.g., Henry St. John Thackeray, *The Relation of St. Paul to Contemporary Jewish Thought* (London: Macmillan, 1900), 181–82; Max Wilcox, "The Translation of the Targum of Psalms: A Report," *ByzF* 24 (1997): 153–57; Luis Díez Merino, "Exégesis Targúmica Del Salmo 68," *MEAH* 53 (2004): 108, who lists Eph 4:8 as evidence for a pre-Christian reading related to the targum.

22. Lincoln, "Use of the OT in Ephesians," 19.

However, rather than follow this somewhat convoluted multistage evolution of the tradition, which requires positing several unevidenced stages of development, it seems simpler to attribute the change to the author of Ephesians.[23] As Lincoln and others note, such changes were widely known as part of Jewish exegetical techniques.[24]

It is helpful to treat Eph 4:25–26 together when considering the use of diverse material from the Jewish Scriptures in these verses.

Table 16.11. Zech 8:16 Ps 4:4; and Eph 4:25–26

Zech 8:16 and Ps 4:4 LXX	Eph 4:25–26
οὗτοι οἱ λόγοι οὓς ποιήσετε <u>λαλεῖτε ἀλήθειαν ἕκαστος πρὸς τὸν πλησίον αὐτοῦ</u> καὶ κρίμα εἰρηνικὸν κρίνατε ἐν ταῖς πύλαις ὑμῶν <u>ὀργίζεσθε καὶ μὴ ἁμαρτάνετε</u> λέγετε ἐν ταῖς καρδίαις ὑμῶν καὶ ἐπὶ ταῖς κοίταις ὑμῶν κατανύγητε διάψαλμα	Διὸ ἀποθέμενοι τὸ ψεῦδος <u>λαλεῖτε ἀλήθειαν ἕκαστος μετὰ τοῦ πλησίον αὐτοῦ</u>, ὅτι ἐσμὲν ἀλλήλων μέλη. <u>ὀργίζεσθε καὶ μὴ ἁμαρτάνετε</u>· ὁ ἥλιος μὴ ἐπιδυέτω ἐπὶ [τῷ] παροργισμῷ ὑμῶν
"These are the words which you shall do, speak truth each one with his neighbor and a peaceful judgment offer at your gates. Be angry and do not sin, speak in your hearts and on your beds be pierced."	"Therefore, laying aside falsehood, speak truth each one with his neighbor, for we are members of one another. Be angry, and do not sin; do not let the sun go down on your anger,"

Here the author of Ephesians employs two short phrases from Zech 8:16 LXX and Ps 4:4 respectively. It is not possible to tell whether this combination of scriptural phraseology was the handiwork of the author of the letter or if these traditions had already been combined in early Christian tradition. Here there is agreement with the sentiment expressed in the Jewish Scriptures on the ethical standards of truthful dealing with neighbors and permissible anger unaccompanied by sin. However, there is no direct appeal to Scripture as a source of authority. Rather, the phraseology of the Jewish Scriptures is a convenient medium or form of words through which the author of Ephesians can express the similar ethical thinking communicated in the letter. So here there is a clear

---

23. Cohick also sees the change as being made by the author of Ephesians, whom she identifies as Paul. "Most likely, Paul himself altered the text." See Lynn H. Cohick, *The Letter to the Ephesians*, NICNT (Grand Rapids: Eerdmans, 2020), 259.

24. Lincoln characterizes this as "a pesher quotation of Ps. 68:18" and states further that this is "a rabbinic type of midrash" that "fulfils a typical function of *haggadah*, filling out possible gaps of meaning in the text." Lincoln, "Use of the OT in Ephesians," 24–25.

use of two short scriptural phrases drawn from Septuagintal texts. However, it is not possible to detect whether this is more likely to be the work of the author of Ephesians or whether these texts were combined at an earlier stage.

The material in Eph 5:22–33 parallels and expands the first element of the household code present in Col 3:18–19—the relationship between wives and husbands. In those verses in Colossians there is no use of scriptural material. The author of Ephesians largely preserves the wording of the injunction given to wives (Col 3:18 // Eph 5:22 and 33b) but greatly expands the address to husbands (Col 3:19; cf. Eph 5:23–33a). Part of that expansion includes the unmarked scriptural citation "for this cause a man shall leave his father and mother, and shall cleave to his wife; and the two shall become one flesh" (Eph 5:31). With minor differences, including a different choice of opening preposition, this is virtually identical with the text of Gen 2:24 LXX.[25] It is not entirely clear whether this tradition is deployed as a simple proof text for the train of thought or whether the author wishes to present the understanding of the relationship between husbands and wives as being grounded in the original creation of that relationship. In some ways, citing Gen 2:24 allows the author to bring the digression about Christ's relationship with the church back to the main point of the household code—the nature of the relationship between husbands and wives. As such the citation helps the rhetorical flow of the author's progression of thought.

The case of the use of the material drawn from either Exod 20:12 LXX or Deut 5:16 in Eph 6:2–3 is significant because it is the second of the author's two marked citations in the letter. In some respects the Hebrew text of Deut 5:16 is closer to Eph 6:2–3 than the Hebrew text of Exod 20:12. This has led some commentators to propose that Deut 5:16 is the text being cited.[26] It is "now generally agreed, however, that this is wrong."[27] The reasons for seeing the base text as Exod 20:12 LXX have been clearly laid out by Frank Thielman and depend on the observation that in common with the form in Eph 6:2–3, the text of Exod 20:12 LXX includes the phrase "that it may go well with you" (unlike the MT of Exod 20:12), as well as omitting both the "your" (σου) after "mother" and the phrase "as the Lord your God commanded you."[28] By contrast, both those elements are present in the Masoretic Text of Exod 20:12 and in both the MT and LXX of Deut 5:16. Therefore, the form of the citation in Eph 6:2–3 is demonstrably closer to the form of Exod 20:12 LXX than it is to any of the other forms of this material contained in the Masoretic or Septuagintal texts.

---

25. On this see further Lincoln, "Use of the OT in Ephesians," 32.
26. E. Earle Ellis, *Paul's Use of the Old Testament*, Twin Brooks Series (Grand Rapids: Baker, 1981), 152, 185.
27. Thielman, "Ephesians," 829.
28. Thielman, 829, §D. Paul's Text.

Table 16.12. Exod 20:12a–b and Eph 6:2–3

Exod 20:12a–b LXX	Eph 6:2–3
τίμα τὸν πατέρα σου καὶ τὴν μητέρα . . . ἵνα εὖ σοι γένηται καὶ ἵνα μακροχρόνιος γένῃ ἐπὶ τῆς γῆς "Honor your father and mother . . . that it may be well with you and that you may live long on the earth."	τίμα τὸν πατέρα σου καὶ τὴν μητέρα, ἥτις ἐστὶν ἐντολὴ πρώτη ἐν ἐπαγγελίᾳ, ἵνα εὖ σοι γένηται καὶ ἔσῃ μακροχρόνιος ἐπὶ τῆς γῆς. "Honor your father and mother (which is the first commandment with a promise) that it may be well with you and that you may live long on the earth."

The cited material is virtually identical apart from the replacement of the ἵνα . . . γένῃ construction with the single word ἔσῃ. The description of this material as "the first commandment with a promise" shows the author's awareness that this tradition is drawn from the decalogue, although in this context there is no attribution of Mosaic authorship. Here is a key example where the author of Ephesians has clearly used material drawn from Colossians (Col 3:20–21; cf. Eph 6:1, 4). However, the scriptural citation of Exod 20:12 LXX has been inserted after the command addressed to children, which is drawn from Col 3:1. The scriptural material functions to reinforce and to justify this injunction directed to children. The citation of Exod 20:12 LXX also demonstrates that the command is not innovative and that its observance carries a divine promise. This is more than mere proof texting. While there is a light reference to the wider context from which this material is drawn, the contents of the wider context are not significant for the point the author makes. The form of the household code was drawn from Greco-Roman literature. By introducing a scriptural justification for the commandment that children should obey parents, the author may be implicitly showing that such behavior was not simply an assimilation to wider cultural norms. Rather, it represented the divine will for the character of the relationship between children and their parents.[29]

The last three examples of the use of material are treated together since they are closely connected by the author of Ephesians, and moreover this set of images is drawn from the same scriptural text, the writings of Isaiah.

---

29. For a wider discussion of this passage, see Harold W. Hoehner, *Ephesians: An Exegetical Commentary* (Grand Rapids: Baker, 2002), 785–94.

Table 16.13. Isa 59:17a; 52:7b; 59:17b and Eph 6:14b, 15, 17a

Isa 59:17a; 52:7b; 59:17b LXX	Eph 6:14b, 15, 17a
καὶ ἐνεδύσατο δικαιοσύνην ὡς θώρακα (Isa 59:17a) ὡς πόδες εὐαγγελιζομένου ἀκοὴν εἰρήνης (Isa 52:7b) καὶ περιέθετο περικεφαλαίαν σωτηρίου ἐπὶ τῆς κεφαλῆς (Isa 59:17b).	καὶ ἐνδυσάμενοι τὸν θώρακα τῆς δικαιοσύνης (Eph 6:14b). καὶ ὑποδησάμενοι τοὺς πόδας ἐν ἑτοιμασίᾳ τοῦ εὐαγγελίου τῆς εἰρήνης (Eph 6:15). καὶ τὴν περικεφαλαίαν τοῦ σωτηρίου δέξασθε (Eph 6:17a).
"And He put on righteousness like a breastplate" (Isa 59:17a) "As feet of one bringing glad tidings of a message of peace" (Isa 52:7b) "and he put on a helmet of salvation upon his head" (Isa 59:17b).	"And having put on the breastplate of righteousness" (Eph 6:14b). "And having shod your feet with the preparation of the gospel of peace" (Eph 6:15). "And take the helmet of salvation" (Eph 6:17a).

There is obviously a concatenation of images drawn from Isa 52:7 LXX and 59:17 LXX that are being deployed in Eph 6:14-17. This is, however, no verbatim or facile reproduction of text. In essence, the author of Ephesians exhorts addressees to put on a metaphorical spiritual armor using the images of a breastplate, foot-protection, a shield, a helmet, and a sword. Three of those five elements form some level of verbatim allusion to material in Isaiah, whereas the other two images appear to be part of the author's composition or drawn from another source of tradition. This case is made more complex since there is an earlier, but less developed use of the image of armor in the Pauline tradition: "let us be sober, having put on the breastplate of faith and love, and as a helmet, the hope of salvation" (1 Thess 5:8). It is noticeable that the text in Ephesians has not only expanded the list of elements of armor, but it has rewritten the references to both the "breastplate" and the "helmet" that are shared with 1 Thessalonians in ways that make the descriptions closer in verbal form to the same images in Isaiah. Notwithstanding this, there are significant differences both in verbal form and in terms of the purpose of the armory images. Isaiah 52 describes a single herald who comes by foot to announce glad tidings of peace. Also, Isa 59 describes "the Lord" as the one who "put on righteousness like a breastplate and a helmet of salvation on his head." By contrast, in Eph 6 the martial imagery is applied to believers depicted as warriors struggling against supernatural powers.[30] So there appears

---

30. Ernest Best, *A Critical and Exegetical Commentary on Ephesians*, ICC (Edinburgh: T&T Clark, 1998), 587.

Israel's Scriptures in Ephesians and Colossians

to be an inversion in the use of the image of armor. In Isaiah the supernatural deity puts on armor to fight against earthly opponents on behalf of his people. In Ephesians it is human believers who are to put on armor to fight against supernatural opponents and thereby to demonstrate their loyalty and fidelity to God.

A further complicating factor in the occurrence is the parallel with material in Wis 5:17–20. There are several points where the tradition in Ephesians appears closer to that found in Wisdom of Solomon. Thus, Thielman observes, Paul "is closer to Wisdom than to Isaiah when he uses the term 'whole armor' (*panoplia* [Eph 6:11; Wis 5:17]) and includes the 'shield' (*aspida* [Wis 5:19]; *thōraka* [Eph 6:14]) and 'sword' (*rhomphaia* [Wis 5:20]; *machaira* [Eph 6:17]) in his list of weapons."[31] This overlapping evidence opens up a number of possibilities for explaining the formation of the tradition contained in Eph 6:14b, 15, 17a. Given the strong and close links with material found in Isa 52 and 57 LXX, there does appear to be some direct connection between Isaiah and the redeployment of those ideas in Eph 6. However, the author may have been influenced both by the existing Pauline use of the metaphor of weapons and armor in 1 Thess 5:8 and the points where closer parallels exist with Wis 5:17–20. Giving the complexity of the prior textual traditions and the freedom with which they are reused in Eph 6, it is necessary to conclude that certainty cannot be attained in discerning precisely how this mix of traditions and ideas coalesced into the formation of Eph 6:10–17.

This suggests that the original intention and context of the armor metaphors were not the controlling factor in the way in which the author of Ephesians reused these images. Rather, these obvious verbal allusions supply a set of useful metaphors that are utilized in the new and thematically different context addressed to the recipients of the letter.

Conclusions

Two separate conclusions must be stated since the letters of Colossians and Ephesians display a different use of and relationship to the Jewish Scriptures. In Colossians the use of Scripture is at best minimal. There are two or three passages where there is some level of verbal allusion. In Colossians the wider context of those slight verbal allusions is not important to the author in terms of the arguments being made. Furthermore, because the verbal affinities are slight, it is impossible to determine the form of the Jewish Scriptures from which the author of Colossians is drawing, or even whether the author is drawing directly on scriptural material. Therefore, in Colossians Scripture plays no explicit or significant role in the author's thinking as presented in the letter.

---

31. Thielman, "Ephesians," 832.

The case of Ephesians is significantly different both in terms of the volume of scriptural material used and the types of usages employed by the author. Eleven possible cases of the use of the Jewish Scriptures were considered, and each of these was determined to be a plausible instance where the author of Ephesians has utilized material from the Jewish Scriptures within the letter. There are two marked but unattributed citations of Scripture in the letter: the use of Ps 67:19b LXX in Eph 4:8 and the use of Exod 20:12 LXX in Eph 6:2-3. The first case is striking because the author alters the meaning from "receiving" to the "giving of gifts." This should be seen as a key example of christological exegesis where the meaning of the source text has been reshaped to conform it to an understanding of what Christ has achieved for believers and to show that this is a fulfillment of Scripture. This reading of the source text is what Francis Watson describes as a "construal of the whole from a particular perspective."[32] The other nine cases where Scripture is used are examples that fall on a continuum of the types of use between unmarked citations and verbal allusions. It is a judgment decision as to where the dividing line between those categories might fall. The author of Ephesians employs the Jewish Scriptures to support the argument of the letter at a number of points. However, the original context or primary argumentative purpose of the scriptural tradition is not a noticeable concern of the author.

In terms of the range of scriptural material employed in Ephesians, among the eleven examples discussed, there are four cases where material from the Psalms is used, four cases of the use of Isaiah—although three of those cases are in close combination—and one case each of Genesis, Exodus, and Zechariah being used. However, in the case of decalogue material from Exodus being used in Eph 6:2-3, this is an example of a marked but authorially unattributed citation.

Given the literary relationship between Ephesians and Colossians and the shared themes that exist between the two letters, the use of Scripture in the two letters represents one of the key differences between these two epistles. In essence, at points, Ephesians "scripturalizes" some of the material drawn from Colossians and also uses Scripture in passages in Ephesians that have no parallel with material in Colossians. Whether this says something about the scriptural dexterity of the two authors of these related letters or whether it reflects the authors' assessment of the scriptural receptivity of the recipients of these letters may be debated. What is beyond question is that the use of Scripture in what are perhaps the two most closely related Pauline letters is by contrast an area where these two letters are most fundamentally different.

---

32. Francis Watson, *Paul and the Hermeneutics of Faith* (London: T&T Clark, 2004), 515.

Bibliography

Beale, G. K. "Colossians." Pages 841–70 in *Commentary on the New Testament Use of the Old Testament*. Edited by G. K. Beale and D. A. Carson. Grand Rapids: Baker Academic, 2007.

Beetham, Christopher A. *Echoes of Scripture in the Letter of Paul to the Colossians*. BibInt 96. Leiden: Brill, 2008.

Best, Ernest. *A Critical and Exegetical Commentary on Ephesians*. ICC. Edinburgh: T&T Clark, 1998.

Cohick, Lynn H. *The Letter to the Ephesians*. NICNT. Grand Rapids: Eerdmans, 2020.

Díez Merino, Luis. "Exégesis Targúmica Del Salmo 68." *MEAH* 53 (2004): 97–122.

Ehorn, Seth, "The Use of Psalm 68(67).19 in Ephesians 4.8: A History of Research." *CBR* 12, no. 1 (2012): 96–120.

Ellis, E. Earle. *Paul's Use of the Old Testament*. Twin Brooks Series. Grand Rapids: Baker, 1981.

Fee, Gordon D. "Old Testament Intertextuality in Colossians: Reflections on Pauline Christology and Gentile Inclusion in God's Story." Pages 201–21 in *History and Exegesis: New Testament Essays in Honor of Dr. E. Earle Ellis for His 80th Birthday*. Edited by Sang-Won Son. London: T&T Clark, 2006.

Foster, Paul. *Colossians*. BNTC. London: Bloomsbury T&T Clark, 2016.

———. "Echoes without Resonance: Critiquing Certain Aspects of Recent Scholarly Trends in the Study of the Jewish Scriptures in the New Testament." *JSNT* 38, no. 1 (2015): 96–111.

Hays, Richard B. *The Conversion of the Imagination: Paul as Interpreter of Israel's Scriptures*. Grand Rapids: Eerdmans, 2005.

———. *Echoes of Scripture in the Letters of Paul*. New Haven: Yale University Press, 1989.

Hoehner, Harold W. *Ephesians: An Exegetical Commentary*. Grand Rapids: Baker Academic, 2002.

Lindars, Barnabas. *New Testament Apologetic: The Doctrinal Significance of the Old Testament Quotations*. London: SCM, 1961.

Lincoln, Andrew T. "The Use of the OT in Ephesians." *JSNT* 4, no. 14 (1982): 16–57.

Longenecker, Richard N. *Biblical Exegesis in the Apostolic Period*. 2nd ed. Grand Rapids: Eerdmans, 1999.

Moritz, Thorsten. *A Profound Mystery: The Use of the Old Testament in Ephesians*. NovTSup 85. Leiden: Brill, 1985.

———. "The Psalms in Ephesians and Colossians." Pages 181–95 in *The Psalms in the New Testament*. Edited by Steve Moyise and Maarten J. J. Menken. NTSI. London: T&T Clark, 2004.

Stanley, Christopher D. *Paul and the Language of Scripture: Citation Technique in the Pauline Epistles and Contemporary Literature*. SNTSMS 74. Cambridge: Cambridge University Press, 1992.

Thackeray, Henry St. John. *The Relation of St. Paul to Contemporary Jewish Thought*. London: Macmillan, 1900.

Thielman, Frank S. "Ephesians." Pages 813–33 in *Commentary on the New Testament Use of the Old Testament*. Edited by G. K. Beale and D. A. Carson. Grand Rapids: Baker Academic, 2007.

Watson, Francis. *Paul and the Hermeneutics of Faith*. London: T&T Clark, 2004.

Watts, Rikk E. "The Psalms in Mark's Gospel." Pages 25–45 in *The Psalms in the New Testament*. Edited by Steve Moyise and Maarten J. J. Menken. NTSI. London: T&T Clark, 2004.

Wilcox, Max. "The Translation of the Targum of Psalms: A Report." *ByzF* 24 (1997): 153–57.

17

Israel's Scriptures in Philippians and Philemon

ANGELA STANDHARTINGER

Philippians and Philemon play almost no role in the discussion of Israel's Scriptures in Paul.

Philippians has no marked citations nor direct references to Israel's Scripture. The only unmarked citation from Isa 45:23 in Phil 2:10-11 is part of the pre-Pauline christological hymn in Phil 2:6-11.[1] In his letter to Philemon and Aphia, Paul neither includes a citation nor even any clear allusion to Scripture at all. Yet, both letters are not anomalous with regard to the Pauline corpus.[2] First Thessalonians likewise lacks any citations from Scripture.

Some verbal and conceptual allusions, however, have to be discussed.[3] Indeed, a possible allusion to Job 13:16 and 19:25-6 in Phil 1:19 became the key text for Richard Hays to demonstrate his concept of "intertextual echoes."[4] Some interpreters find a cluster of verbal allusions to Isa 45:18-26 LXX in Phil 1:27-

---

1. Lukas Bormann, "Triple Intertextuality in Philippians," in *The Intertextuality of the Epistles: Explorations of Theory and Practice*, ed. Thomas L. Brodie, Dennis R. MacDonald, and Stanley E. Porter, New Testament Monographs 16 (Sheffield: Sheffield Phoenix, 2006), 93.

2. Pace Stephen Fowl, "The Use of Scripture in Philippians," in *Paul and Scripture: Extending the Conversation*, ed. Christopher D. Stanley, ECL 9 (Atlanta: Society of Biblical Literature, 2012), 165.

3. Moisés Silva, "Philippians," in *Commentary on the New Testament Use of the Old Testament*, ed. G. K. Beale and D. A. Carson (Grand Rapids: Baker Academic, 2011), 835.

4. Richard B. Hays, *Echoes of Scripture in the Letters of Paul* (New Haven: Yale University Press, 1989), 21-29.

2:18. Others discover allusions to the Hebrew text of the fourth Servant Song (Isa 52:13–53:12) in Phil 2:7. Many see another verbal allusion to Deut 32:5 LXX in Phil 2:15. Moreover, Paul may allude to the grumbling of the wilderness generation and to God's servant who has not run in vain (Isa 49:4; 65:23) in the same context (Phil 2:14, 16). Finally, there is an allusion to Ps 8:7 in Phil 3:21, a psalm verse to which Paul also refers in 1 Cor 15:27. Paul cites Isa 45:23 not only in Phil 3:10–11, but also in Rom 14:11, yet in the latter context in a more literal form than in Phil 2:10–11. Quotations and allusions from Isaiah, Deuteronomy, and Psalms appear quite often in Paul's writing. That Paul refers here to the Job tradition likely reflects his suffering in prison while he writes to the Philippians. Yet, most important for the interpretation of Philippians are two conceptional allusions in Phil 3. In this chapter Paul remodels his autobiography into the biography of the ideal wise king and teacher, while he slips into the role of an apocalyptic prophet.

Israel's Scriptures in Philippians

Table 17.1. Israel's Scriptures in Philippians and Philemon

	Philippians		Philemon	
Marked Citation	none		none	
Unmarked Citation	Phil 2:10–11	Isa 45:23	none	
Verbal Allusion	Phil 1:19	Job 13:16	Phlm 5	Exod 19:6
	Phil 1:27–2:18	Isa 45:18–26		
	Phil 2:7	Isa 52:12; 53:12		
	Phil 2:12	Ps 2:11–12; Deut 11:25		
	Phil 2:14	Exod 15:24 etc.		
	Phil 2:15	Deut 32:5 LXX; 1 En. 104:2; Dan 12:3; Isa 42:6; 49:6		
	Phil 2:16	Deut 32:47;		
	Phil 3:21	Ps 8:7		
Conceptual Allusion	Phil 3:4–17	Sir 51:13–30; Wis 6–9	Phlm	Lev 25:39–40; Deut 23:16–17; Philo, Virt. 124
	Phil 3:18–21	Jer 8:23; 9:1; 1 En. 94–96; 62:13–16; 104:2, 4, 6; Dan 12:3		

The Unmarked Citation of Phil 2:10-11

The pre-Pauline hymn in Phil 2:6-11 cites the text from Isa 45:23 LXX. With most, yet not all manuscripts of the LXX, Phil 2:11 translate תִּשָּׁבַע "[every tongue] shall swear" with ἐξομολογήσεται "[every tongue] will confess."[5] Furthermore, Phil 2:10-11 reads with most manuscripts of the LXX and with 1QIsᵃ an "and" between the two verbal actions in Isa 45:23b.[6] At the end of the sentence, the Septuagint moves the object "to God" from the beginning of verse 24 in order to clarify the address of the praise or oath. Some interpreters see a reflection of the Septuagint version in "to the glory of God" (Isa 45:24 LXX).[7]

Philippians 2:10-11 adjusts Isa 45:23b to its context by transforming the verbal action in the future into a ἵνα clause, "in order that." It also identifies those who praise as "those in heaven and on earth and in the underworld" and spells out their acclamation, "Jesus Christ is Lord." This group can neither consist only of humans or of hostile powers but includes all beings everywhere in and beyond this world. Yet, when does their confession happen? The Hebrew text and its Greek translations read both of the verbs "to bow" and "to swear/confess" in the future tense and therefore date the universal reference to Israel's God to the eschaton. The Jewish Sybil follows by prophesying, "then [at the beginning of the Golden Age] they will bend a white knee to the great God, the immortal king" (Sib. Or. 3:616-17). In Rom 14:10-12 Paul cites Isa 45:23b LXX^OG exactly (with the majority of LXX manuscripts) in order to prove the universal judgment of deeds at the end of time. Otfried Hofius pointed to a similar interpretation in the *nishmat* and *aleinu* prayers from the later *Siddur*.[8] Everywhere, Isa 43:23b expresses eschatological hopes in Jewish theology.

In Phil 2:10-11, however, the bowing of knees and the confession explain why God has exalted Jesus and has endowed him with his own holy name. Also, all human, angelic, and demonic beings in heaven, on earth, and in the underworld join the early Christian confession "Jesus Christ is the Lord." For the Christ hymn, the eschatological future of Isa 45:23 has already begun. Whoever reads

---

5. Other manuscripts (Sc and in variants many others) read ὀμεῖται ("swear"), yet Joseph Ziegler, *Isaias*, SVTG 14 (Göttingen: Vandenhoeck & Ruprecht, 1939), 295, follows Sc^mg, Syl, Eusebius, and Rom 14:11. Unless otherwise noted, all translations are by the author.

6. 1QIsaᵃ reads תכרע כול בורך ותשבע כול לשון, cf. 1QIsaᵃ (Isa 45:23); MS 106 (M in Ziegler, *Isaias*, 295) omits καί ("and") with the Hebrew standard text.

7. Florian Wilk, *Die Bedeutung des Jesajabuches für Paulus*, FRLANT 179 (Göttingen: Vandenhoeck & Ruprecht, 1998), 325.

8. Otfried Hofius, *Der Christushymnus Philipper 2,6-11: Untersuchungen zu Gestalt und Aussage eines urchristlichen Psalms*, 2nd ed., WUNT 17 (Tübingen: Mohr Siebeck, 1991), 48-50.

or sings this text connects her- and himself to this universal acclamation of the God of Israel's reign and glory. The poets of the hymn quoted Isa 45:23b because its imagery signals the beginning of the eschatological reign of God. Yet, God's eschatological reign has already begun.

Possible Verbal Allusions in Philippians

In Philippians, as elsewhere in his writings, Paul uses biblical phrases like "God is my witness" (Phil 1:8; Gen 31:44; Wis 1:6), "fruit of righteousness" (Phil 1:11; Amos 6:12; Prov 13:2), "fear and trembling" (Phil 2:12; 1 En. 14:13; 60:3; Mark 16:8), "book of life" (Phil 4:3; Ps 68:29 LXX), "the Lord is near" (Phil 4:5; Pss 33:19 LXX; 144:18 LXX), and more.[9] Offerings reach God's nose as "sweet fragrance" (Phil 4:18; cf. Gen 8:21; Exod 29:18; Lev 1:9, 13; Ezek 20:41). While those expressions come more naturally from a Jewish writer with scriptural training like Paul, few identify them as programmatic and evoking a specific biblical context.

One verbal allusion, though some call it a quotation, consisting of five words, appears in Phil 1:19 (τοῦτό μοι ἀποβήσεται εἰς σωτηρίαν).[10] Job states: "Though the Mighty One overpowers me—inasmuch as he has begun—certainly I will speak and argue my case before him. And this for me will prove to be salvation [τοῦτό μοι ἀποβήσεται εἰς σωτηρίαν], for deceit cannot enter before him" (Job 13:15–16 LXX). Job claims before his friends and God—both are his adversaries in this context—that his apology cannot fail in the heavenly courtroom. A reader who is competent to locate the source of the original voice discovers "intriguing resonances" between Job's plight and Paul's.[11] Writing his letter from prison, Paul assumes the role of Job, who likewise presents himself as a prisoner in a judgment scene (cf. Job 13:18, 27). Furthermore, Hays detects a second allusion to Job 19:25 LXX: "For I know that [οἶδα γὰρ ὅτι] my Redeemer lives," at the beginning of Phil 1:19. Working together, the verbal allusions express a "triumphant assertion of trust in the power and faithfulness of God."[12] Others even think that Paul "desires the Philippians to display a version of Job's confidence without the bitterness of Job."[13]

---

9. For an extensive list, see Hans Hübner, *Corpus Paulinum*, vol. 2 of *Vetus Testamentum in Novo* (Göttingen: Vandenhoeck & Ruprecht, 1997), 481–502.

10. Hays, *Echoes of Scripture in the Letters of Paul*, 21–24; Stanley E. Porter, "Paul and His Use of Scripture: Further Considerations," in *Paul and Scripture*, ed. Stanley E. Porter and Christopher D. Land, Pauline Studies 10 (Leiden: Brill, 2019), 28, identifies the text as a quotation. Yet, see Lau Chi Hing, "The Use of Job 13:16 in Philippians 1:19: Direct Quotation or Allusion?," in Porter and Land, *Paul and Scripture*, 335–49, for the opposite position.

11. Hays, *Echoes of Scripture in the Letters of Paul*, 22.

12. Hays, *Echoes of Scripture in the Letters of Paul*, 22.

13. Fowl, "Use of Scripture," 173.

Yet, the phrase οἶδα γὰρ ὅτι ("For I know that") appears four times in the LXX, three times in the New Testament, and twenty-nine times in the *Thesaurus Linguae Graecae* up to the end of the first century CE. Many critics find Hays's triumphalist christological reading at least in this respect less convincing. In the first century, Job is mostly a prominent suffering righteous person who was famous for his patience and endurance.[14] Indeed, the next verse, Phil 1:20, alludes to the suffering righteous one with the language of the Psalms: "God, you are my hope, never let me be put to shame" (Ps 70:1 LXX). No less famous than Job is Socrates, who likewise is aware "that nothing can be bad for a good man, either alive or dead, and his affairs are not ignored by the gods" (Plato, *Apol.* 41d [Fowler]). The possible verbal allusion to Job 13:16 introduces the widespread motif of the suffering righteous. Yet, apart from the fact that every hearer and reader of the letter is free to bring whatever textual knowledge she or he might have, it may not be so obvious to all readers of the letter that this suffering will automatically be transformed in the final vindication.

Hays finds a verbal allusion in a cluster of texts (Job 13:13, 18, 27; 19:25–26). Likewise, Florian Wilk discovers a contextual-based cluster of verbal allusions to Deutero-Isaiah in Phil 1:28; 2:10, 12–13, 16. Like Isa 45:23, Phil 2:10 points to the universal acclamation of all nations at the return of Christ in the parousia. In Wilk's interpretation, the paraenesis in Phil 1:27–2:18, of which the Christ hymn is a part, starts already in Phil 1:28 with an allusion to Isa 45:16–17: "All who oppose him shall be ashamed and disgraced. . . . Israel is being saved by the Lord with everlasting salvation." When Paul points out in Phil 2:12–13 that God's saving acts include the willing and acting of the Christians, he alludes to Isa 45:21–22: "There is no righteous one except me. . . . Turn to me, and you shall be saved." Finally, Paul contextualizes his own work with the expression "that I neither ran in vain" in Phil 2:16 by alluding to the servant, whose lament "I have labored in vain" (Isa 49:4) is countered by God.[15] Deutero-Isaiah's general proclamation of a turn of an era, in which God had already freed and vindicated his people Israel and established his eschatological reign, is quite close to the *evangelion* proclaimed by New Testament writers. However, at some point one cannot avoid the impression that the presumed allusion to a particular word cluster of Isaiah runs contrary to the meaning in its original context.

Joachim Jeremias argued that the unique expression ἑαυτὸν ἐκένωσεν ("he emptied himself"), which is documented nowhere else, is a spontaneous Greek translation of הֶעֱרָה לַמָּוֶת נַפְשׁוֹ ("he poured himself out to death") from

---

14. See T. Job 4:10; 26:1, and passim; and Jas 5:11.
15. Wilk, *Die Bedeutung*, 301–2, 323–25, 397.

Isa 53:12.[16] James Patrick Ware adds that Aquila translates Isa 53:2, "he had no form or majesty . . . nothing in his appearance," with μορφή ("form"; Phil 2:6), and "my servant" in Isa 52:13 as δοῦλος μοῦ (cf. 53:11; Phil 2:7).[17] Allusions to Isa 52:13–53:12 would connect the hymn to the passion story in the Gospels. However, as many have pointed out, most Greek translations call the servant παῖς θεοῦ ("child/slave of God") and more importantly, God's servant suffers before, because of, and on behalf of others. Christ does not empty himself for soteriological reasons, that is, on behalf of others in the Christ hymn.[18] Strikingly, the Christ hymn of Phil 2:6–11 is not interested in the biography of Jesus beyond the brutal fact of his crucifixion.

Finally, almost all commentators discover a verbal allusion in Phil 2:15: "unblemished children of God in the midst of a crooked and perverse generation" (τέκνα θεοῦ ἄμωμα μέσον γενεᾶς σκολιᾶς καὶ διεστραμμένης) to Deut 32:5 "blemished children, a generation crooked and perverse" (τέκνα μωμητά γενεά σκολιὰ καὶ διεστραμμένη). The allusion is marked by four to six rare words.[19] Already early manuscripts prove the identification of this verbal allusion when they read with Deut 32:5 ἀμώμητα ("unblamed") instead of ἄμωμα ("blameless").[20] At the end of his life, Moses warns Israel not to repeat the grumbling in the wilderness. This is a request. As Ps 77:8 LXX in line with 1 Cor 10:1–13 puts it: "They should not be like their fathers, a generation crooked and embittering" (ἵνα μὴ γένωνται ὡς οἱ πατέρες αὐτῶν γενεὰ σκολιὰ καὶ παραπικραίνουσα γενεά). And indeed, Paul prompts the Philippians in Phil 2:14: "Do all things without grumbling," thereby alluding with the verb γογγύζω ("grumbling") as the catchword of the biblical wilderness stories.[21]

However, the meaning of this allusion is less obvious. Understanding the allusion to Ps 2:11–12, "fear . . . and trembling" (Phil 2:12), as a calling to allegiance to

---

16. Joachim Jeremias, "Zu Philipper 2,7: ἑαυτὸν ἐκένωσεν," in *Abba: Studien zur neutestamentlichen Theologie und Zeitgeschichte* (Göttingen: Vandenhoeck & Ruprecht, 1966), 309.

17. James Patrick Ware, *The Mission of the Church in Paul's Letter to the Philippians in the Context of Ancient Judaism*, NovTSup 120 (Leiden: Brill, 2005), 225–27.

18. Samuel Vollenweider, "Die Metamorphose des Gottessohns: Zum epiphanialen Motivfeld in Phil 2,6–8," in *Horizonte neutestamentlicher Christologie: Studien zu Paulus und zur frühchristlichen Theologie*, WUNT 144 (Tübingen: Mohr Siebeck, 2002), 303–4.

19. See, among others, Guy Prentiss Waters, *The End of Deuteronomy in the Epistles of Paul*, WUNT 2/221 (Tübingen: Mohr Siebeck, 2006), 148–58.

20. The majuscules F, G, K, L, P, Ψ, 075, 0278, and the minuscules 81, 104, 365, 630, 1175, 1505, 1739, 1881, 2646, among others.

21. Exod 15:24; 16:2, 7–8, 12; Num 14:2, 27; Deut 1:27; et al. The two allusions are often discussed; see Fowl, "Use of Scripture"; Silva, "Philippians," 838; Markus Öhler, "Reception of the Old Testament in 1 Thessalonians and in Philippians?," in Land and Porter, *Paul and Scripture*, 367–69.

Christ in the face of opposition and a warning against disloyalty, David McAuley reads our passage as an eschatological prognosis that promises salvation to those who remain steadfast and refuse to capitulate under pressure, in which they will "shine like stars" (Dan 12:3; Phil 2:15).[22] And indeed, "like shining stars" is a typical metaphor for the righteous in the resurrection (1 En. 104:2; Dan 12:3). Yet, McAuley forms the allusions into a story that is not shaped by intertexts but by his own idea of the meaning of Christ's story. The allusions only embellish an already existing story, that is, McAuley's interpretation of Philippians. They serve only as proof texts to enforce Paul's warnings. While "shining stars" are a political image in first century CE, an allusion to Israel as "light to the gentiles" (Isa 42:6; 49:6) fits better in this context.[23]

That Paul is referring to a catena of otherwise unrelated texts is in my view not convincing. Yet, building on an earlier proposal by Francis W. Beare, David Allen recently read Phil 2:12–18 as an updated version of the Song of Moses in Deut 32.[24] For Allen "fear and trembling" refers to Deut 11:25; "grumbling" to Deut 1:27; Phil 2:16 ("hold fast the word of life . . . so that I neither ran in vain") alludes to Deut 32:47: "this is not an empty word for you, since it is your very life"; and, finally, while God declares that Moses has to die because he has not sanctified God, Paul is going to sanctify the Philippians by his own death (Deut 32:51; Phil 2:17–18). By establishing Paul on the one hand as a new Moses and on the other as an anti-Moses who blames Israel—the Exodus generations, the contemporaries of Paul, or even those today (?)—to be the "crooked and perverse generation" of Phil 2:15, this reading leans toward supersessionism, a criticism many have already voiced.[25] In Philippians, the "crooked and perverse generation" are outsiders, not Jews of any generation. The Philippians have learned their lesson from the grumblings of the wilderness generation, as have the readers of Ps 77:8 LXX and 1 Cor 10:11–13. There is no antithetic Moses-Paul, Philippians-Israel typology in Philippians, nor in any other of Paul's letters. In the end, one has to admit that the significance of the allusion to Deut 32:5 in Phil 2:15 remains enigmatic.[26]

---

22. McAuley, *Paul's Covert Use of Scripture: Intertextuality and Rhetorical Situation in Philippians 2:10–16* (Eugene, OR: Pickwick, 2015), 161–242.

23. Fowl, "Use of Scripture," 176–77.

24. Francis W. Beare, *A Commentary on the Epistle to the Philippians*, BNTC (London: Black, 1959), 88–89; David M. Allen, "'Paul Donning Mosaic Garb?' Use of Deuteronomy 32 in Philippians 2:12–18," *EuroJTh* 26 (2017): 135–43.

25. Markus Bockmuehl, *The Epistle to the Philippians*, BNTC (Peabody, MA: Hendrickson, 1998), 156–58; John Reumann, *Philippians: A New Translation with Introduction and Commentary*, AB 33B (New Haven: Yale University Press, 2008), 402–4; Paul A. Holloway, *Philippians: A Commentary*, Hermeneia (Minneapolis: Fortress, 2017), 133–34.

26. Cf. David Lincicum, *Paul and the Early Jewish Encounter with Deuteronomy*, WUNT 2/284 (Tübingen: Mohr Siebeck, 2010), 120.

Conceptual Allusions

While there is only one unmarked citation and a few possible verbal allusions in Philippians, two conceptual allusions are crucial for the letter's interpretation. Both appear in Phil 3:2–21. Philippians 3:5–17 remodels the biography of the ideal sage in Jewish wisdom literature as it is presented in Sir 51:13–30 and Wis 6–9.[27] Instead of relying on the advantages of his noble birth and education (cf. Wis 8:19), Paul and the wise alike aspire to Christ/Wisdom and hope to gain through him/her something more valuable than all other riches (Sir 51:21; Wis 7:7–9; Phil 3:7–8). The sage exerts himself for Lady Wisdom like Paul for Christ but can only receive the goal when she or he approaches him (Sir 6:27–28; 15:2; Wis 6:16; 8:17–21; 9:10, 17; Phil 3:8–14). The process is purposeful but remains open and unfinished. Finally, like the ideal sage, Paul invites his readers in Philippi to imitate this way of life (Sir 6:18–27; 51:23–30; Wis 6:1–21; Phil 3:17). Paul's Christ biography imitates the ideal biography of the Jewish sage.

In Phil 3:18, Paul changes his role. Speaking in tears about the future of the "enemies of the cross," he takes on the part of an apocalyptic prophet, announcing humiliation to the unrighteous as compensation for their injustice and wrong behavior (Jer 8:23; 9:1 LXX; 1 En. 95:1; 96:4–5, 8) and retributive justification to his own group (1 En. 62:13–16; 104:2, 4, 6; Dan 12:3).[28] In Philippians, the eschatological transformation of the suffering righteous into the heavenly figure of glory is carried out not by God but by Christ. This allusion to Ps 8:7 LXX: πάντα ὑπέταξας ("you subjected everything [to him]") in Phil 3:21: ὑποτάξαι αὐτῷ τὰ πάντα ("to subject all things to him") remains exceptional for Paul (cf. 1 Cor 15:27). It likewise evokes the biblical creation stories and the idea of the restoration of paradise prominent in Jewish apocalypticism.[29] The two unmarked allusions or patterns from the wisdom and apocalyptic tradition help to reconstruct the beginning of early christological and eschatological thinking, and not only in Paul.

---

27. Cf. Angela Standhartinger, "Weisheitliche Idealbiografie und Ethik in Phil 3," *NovT* 61, no. 2 (2019): 156–75.

28. Cf. Standhartinger, "Apocalyptic Thought in Philippians," *The Jewish Apocalyptic Tradition and the Shaping of New Testament Thought*, ed. Benjamin E. Reynolds and Loren T. Stuckenbruck (Minneapolis: Fortress, 2017), 233–45.

29. Cf. 2 Bar. 51:11; Lutz Doering, "Urzeit-Endzeit Correlation in the Dead Sea Scrolls and Pseudepigrapha," in *Eschatologie – Eschatology: The Sixth Durham-Tübingen Research Symposium; Eschatology in Old Testament, Ancient Judaism and Early Christianity*, ed. Hans-Joachim Eckstein, Christof Landmesser, and Hermann Lichtenberger, WUNT 272 (Tübingen: Mohr Siebeck, 2011), 19–58.

Conclusion

Several explanations have been given for the striking lack of scriptural reference in Philippians. As shown above, the letter contains no marked and only one unmarked citation in Phil 2:10–11 and two mostly undisputed marked allusions in Phil 1:19 and 2:15. Some interpreters assume that the non-Jewish Philippians had no interest in Scripture. Either they lacked competence, or Scripture had no authority for them, or Paul, writing to the Philippians and Philemon during his imprisonment, had no access to texts or his own notes and excerpts.[30] Or he developed his "Christian" scriptural reasoning only late in his career in his conflicts with opponents in Galatia and Corinth.[31] Or "all letters without the apostolic claim also lack any appeal to biblical warrants for the legitimacy of Paul's theology."[32]

However, as Phil 3:2–21 proves, Paul does not renounce his Jewish learning. Yet, for one who is confined in prison while fearing a death sentence, there is no time left for close readings of Scripture. Whether or not the Philippians were able to understand the allusion to the suffering righteous in Phil 1:19 as a reference to Job, place the quotation from Isa 45:23 in its original context, and identify the manifold allusions in Phil 2:12–18, one can be sure that with the help of their intimate knowledge and that of their apostle Epaphroditus, they understood what Paul wanted to share with them. Even today, the overloaded abundance of possible scriptural allusions in Phil 2:12–18 conveys the impression of an endangered writer who tries to hide certain messages from unentitled readers and prison guards and who says as much as possible in a very short amount of time.

SCRIPTURE IN PHILEMON

The Letter to Philemon lacks any marked and unmarked citations and verbal allusions. Or, as Wilhelm Dittmar states in his collections of Old Testament citations: "Philemon vacat."[33] A few conceptual allusions might be discussed.

---

30. Öhler, "Reception."

31. Dietrich-Alex Koch, "'. . . bezeugt durch das Gesetz und die Propheten': Zur Funktion der Schrift bei Paulus," in *Hellenistisches Christentum: Schriftverständnis - Ekklesiologie - Geschichte*, ed. Dietrich-Alex Koch and Friedrich Wilhelm Horn, NTOA 65 (Göttingen: Vandenhoeck & Ruprecht, 2008), 13–24.

32. M. Eugene Boring, "Philippians and Philemon: Date and Provenance," *CBQ* 81, no. 3 (2019): 491.

33. Wilhelm Dittmar, *Vetus Testamentum in Novo: Die Alttestamentlichen Parallelen des Neuen Testaments in Wortlaut der Urtexte und der Septuaginta* (Göttingen: Vandenhoeck &

Paul praises Philemon's faithful love "to all the holy ones," which might refer to the well-known biblical epithet of Israel as a holy nation (גּוֹי קָדוֹשׁ/ἔθνος ἅγιον, Exod 19:6; cf. Lev 19:2; 2 Sam 7:23). Paul's efforts to mediate between the escaped slave Onesimus and his owner Philemon might, depending on one's general interpretation of the letter, be influenced by or contradict Lev 25:39–40 and Deut 23:16–17: "You shall not hand over to an owner a servant . . . he shall reside with you."[34] The latter biblical command was discussed by Paul's contemporary Philo, who called surrender of a slave to his cruel master a sacrilege, while at the same time he tried to harmonize the biblical commandment with the Greco-Roman legal circumstances of his time (*Virt.* 124). Yet, one has to admit that Paul's petition on behalf of Onesimus does not go deep into Israel's Scriptures.

Bibliography

Allen, David M. "'Paul Donning Mosaic Garb?' The Use of Deuteronomy 32 in Philippians 2:12–18." *EuroJTh* 26, no. 2 (2017): 135–43

Beare, Francis W. *A Commentary on the Epistle to the Philippians*. BNTC. London: Black, 1959.

Bockmuehl, Markus. *The Epistle to the Philippians*. BNTC. Peabody, MA: Hendrickson, 1998.

Boring, M. Eugene. "Philippians and Philemon: Date and Provenance." *CBQ* 81, no. 3 (2019): 470–94.

Bormann, Lukas. "Triple Intertextuality in Philippians." Pages 90–97 in *The Intertextuality of the Epistles: Explorations of Theory and Practice*. Edited by Thomas L. Brodie, Dennis R. MacDonald, and Stanley E. Porter. New Testament Monographs 16. Sheffield: Sheffield Phoenix Press, 2006.

Dittmar, Wilhelm. *Vetus Testamentum in Novo: Die alttestamentlichen Parallelen des Neuen Testaments im Wortlaut der Urtexte und der Septuaginta zusammengestellt*. 2 vols. Göttingen: Vandenhoeck & Ruprecht, 1899–1903.

Doering, Lutz. "Urzeit-Endzeit Correlation in the Dead Sea Scrolls and Pseudepigrapha." Pages 19–58 in *Eschatologie – Eschatology: The Sixth Durham-Tübingen Research Symposium; Eschatology in Old Testament, Ancient Judaism and Early Christianity*. Edited by Hans-Joachim Eckstein, Christof Landmesser, and Hermann Lichtenberger. WUNT 272. Tübingen: Mohr Siebeck, 2011.

Ruprecht, 1903), 239; Hübner, *Corpus Paulinum*, 660–63, names two verbal allusions in Phlm 5 to 4 Macc 15:25; 16:22; and Phlm 7 to Isa 66:10–11.

34. Klaus Wengst, *Der Brief an Philemon*, THKNT 16 (Stuttgart: Kohlhammer, 2005), 41–42; cf. also Lev 25:39–40.

Fowl, Stephen. "The Use of Scripture in Philippians." Pages 163–84 in *Paul and Scripture: Extending the Conversation*. Edited by Christopher D. Stanley. ECL 9. Atlanta: Society of Biblical Literature, 2012.

Hays, Richard B. *Echoes of Scripture in the Letters of Paul*. New Heaven: Yale University Press, 1989.

Hing, Lau Chi. "The Use of Job 13:16 in Philippians 1:19: Direct Quotation or Allusion?" Pages 335–49 in *Paul and Scripture*. Edited by Stanley E. Porter and Christopher D. Land. Pauline Studies 10. Leiden: Brill, 2019.

Hofius, Otfried. *Der Christushymnus Philipper 2,6–11: Untersuchungen zu Gestalt und Aussage eines urchristlichen Psalms*. 2nd ed. WUNT 17. Tübingen: Mohr Siebeck, 1991.

Holloway, Paul A. *Philippians: A Commentary*. Hermeneia. Minneapolis: Fortress, 2017.

Hübner, Hans. *Corpus Paulinum*. Vol. 2 of *Vetus Testamentum in Novo*. Göttingen: Vandenhoeck & Ruprecht, 1997.

Jeremias, Joachim. "Zu Philipper 2,7: ἑαυτὸν ἐκένωσεν." Pages 308–13 in *Abba: Studien zur neutestamentlichen Theologie und Zeitgeschichte*. Göttingen: Vandenhoeck & Ruprecht, 1966.

Koch, Dietrich-Alex. "'. . . bezeugt durch das Gesetz und die Propheten': Zur Funktion der Schrift bei Paulus." Pages 13–24 in *Hellenistisches Christentum: Schriftverständnis – Ekklesiologie – Geschichte*. Edited by Friedrich Wilhelm Horn. NTOA 65. Göttingen: Vandenhoeck & Ruprecht, 2008.

Lincicum, David. *Paul and the Early Jewish Encounter with Deuteronomy*. WUNT 2/284. Tübingen: Mohr Siebeck, 2010.

McAuley, David. *Paul's Covert Use of Scripture: Intertextuality and Rhetorical Situation in Philippians 2:10–16*. Eugene, OR: Pickwick, 2015.

Öhler, Markus. "Reception of the Old Testament in 1 Thessalonians and in Philippians?" Pages 350–71 in *Paul and Scripture*. Edited by Christopher Land and Stanley E. Porter. Pauline Studies 10. Leiden: Brill, 2019.

Plato. *Euthyphro; Apology; Crito; Phaedo; Phaedrus*. Translated by Harold North Fowler. LCL. Cambridge: Harvard University Press, 1960.

Porter, Stanley E. "Paul and His Use of Scripture: Further Considerations." Pages 7–30 in *Paul and Scripture*. Edited by Stanley E. Porter and Christopher D. Land. Pauline Studies 10. Leiden: Brill, 2019.

Reumann, John. *Philippians: A New Translation with Introduction and Commentary*. AB 33B. New Haven: Yale University Press, 2008.

Silva, Moisés. "Philippians." Pages 835–39 in *Commentary on the New Testament Use of the Old Testament*. Edited by G. K. Beale and D. A. Carson. Grand Rapids: Baker Academic, 2011.

Standhartinger, Angela. "Apocalyptic Thought in Philippians." Pages 233–45 in *The*

Jewish Apocalyptic Tradition and the Shaping of New Testament Thought. Edited by Benjamin E. Reynolds and Loren T. Stuckenbruck. Minneapolis: Fortress, 2017.

———. "Weisheitliche Idealbiografie und Ethik in Phil 3." *NovT* 61, no. 2 (2019): 156–75.

Vollenweider, Samuel. "Die Metamorphose des Gottessohns: Zum epiphanialen Motivfeld in Phil 2,6–8." Pages 285–306 in *Horizonte neutestamentlicher Christologie: Studien zu Paulus und zur frühchristlichen Theologie*. WUNT 144. Tübingen: Mohr Siebeck, 2002.

Ware, James Patrick. *The Mission of the Church in Paul's Letter to the Philippians in the Context of Ancient Judaism*. NovTSup 120. Leiden: Brill, 2005.

Waters, Guy Prentiss. *The End of Deuteronomy in the Epistles of Paul*. WUNT 2/221. Tübingen: Mohr Siebeck, 2006.

Wengst, Klaus. *Der Brief an Philemon*. THKNT 16. Stuttgart: Kohlhammer, 2005.

Wilk, Florian. *Die Bedeutung des Jesajabuches für Paulus*. FRLANT 179. Göttingen: Vandenhoeck & Ruprecht, 1998.

Ziegler, Joseph. *Isaias*. SVTG 14. Göttingen: Vandenhoeck & Ruprecht, 1939.

18

Israel's Scriptures in 1 and 2 Thessalonians

TODD D. STILL

Although there are no marked or unmarked citations of Israel's Scriptures in 1 and 2 Thessalonians, there are any number of verbal and conceptual allusions to Scripture in these early Pauline letters.[1] An exhaustive treatment of arguably relevant texts is not possible within the space constraints of this chapter. Herein we will nevertheless be able both to identify and to comment upon many of the more commonly recognized scriptural allusions and themes in 1 and 2 Thessalonians.[2] For the purposes of this chapter, I will presuppose the traditional attribution of 2 Thessalonians to Paul, although nothing posited here necessarily requires as much.[3]

Were one to consider the most widely recognized allusions to Israel's Scriptures within 1 and 2 Thessalonians, one would discover a greater concentration of such among the (Latter) Prophets (esp. Isaiah) and the Writings (esp. Daniel). Additionally, one would find a larger number of allusions to Scripture in 1 Thess 4 and 2 Thess 1 than elsewhere; a number of scriptural themes or conceptual al-

---

1. Among the Pauline Letters, the same can also be said of Philippians, Colossians, Titus, and Philemon. For valuable tables of scriptural citations and allusions in the Pauline corpus, see the classic work of E. Earle Ellis, *Paul's Use of the Old Testament* (Edinburgh: Oliver & Boyd, 1957; repr., Grand Rapids: Baker, 1981), 150-54.

2. For a more expansive treatment, see Jeffrey A. D. Weima, "1-2 Thessalonians," in *Commentary on the New Testament in the Old Testament*, ed. G. K. Beale and D. A. Carson (Grand Rapids: Baker Academic, 2007), 871-89.

3. See further, Todd D. Still, *Conflict at Thessalonica: A Pauline Church and Its Neighbours*, JSNTSup 183 (Sheffield: Sheffield Academic, 1999), 46-60.

lusions in the Thessalonians letters would come to the fore, including election, holiness, the day of the Lord, labor pains, and light/day versus darkness/night.

Thus, while it would be an exaggeration to contend that Scripture is ever on the surface of these letters, it would be accurate to maintain that they are nonetheless indebted to the Jewish Scriptures. As Jeffrey A. D. Weima perceptively observes, "Paul's vocabulary, metaphors, and theological framework in the Thessalonian correspondence betray the influence of the OT in both small and significant ways."[4]

Israel's Scripture in 1 and 2 Thessalonians

Verbal Allusions in 1 Thessalonians

Table 18.1. Verbal Allusions in 1 Thessalonians

1 Thessalonians		Jewish Scripture	
2:4	τῷ δοκιμάζοντι τὰς καρδίας ἡμῶν ("who tests our hearts")[5]	Jer 11:20 Cf. Jer 12:3; 17:19; Ps 138:3; Prov 17:3	δοκιμάζων νεφροὺς καὶ καρδίας ("who tests minds and hearts")
2:16	εἰς τὸ ἀναπληρῶσαι αὐτῶν τὰς ἁμαρτίας πάντοτε ("always filling up the measure of their sins")	Gen 15:16 Cf. Ps 78:6 LXX; 2 Macc 6:14; Dan 8:23	ἀναπεπλήρωνται ("is complete")
3:5	εἰς κενὸν γένηται ὁ κόπος ἡμῶν ("that our labor had been in vain")	Isa 49:4 Cf. Isa 65:23	Κενῶς ἐκοπίασα ("I have labored in vain")
3:13	ἅγιοι ("angels" and/or "believers")	Zech 14:5	πάντες οἱ ἅγιοι μετ' αὐτοῦ ("all the holy ones with him")
4:5	τὰ ἔθνη τὰ μὴ εἰδότα τὸν θεόν ("the gentiles who do not know God")	Jer 10:25 Cf. Job 18:21; Ps 78:6 LXX	ἐπὶ ἔθνη τὰ μὴ εἰδότα σε ("on the nations that do not know you")

---

4. Weima, "1–2 Thessalonians," 871.
5. Unless otherwise noted, all translations are by the author.

4:6	ἔκδικος ("avenger")	Ps 93:1 LXX Cf. Deut 32:35	ὁ θεὸς ἐκδικήσεων ("God of vengeance")
4:8	διδόντα τὸ πνεῦμα αὐτοῦ τὸ ἅγιον εἰς ὑμᾶς ("the one who gives his Holy Spirit to you")	Ezek 37:14 Cf. Ezek 36:27	καὶ δώσω τὸ πνεῦμά μου εἰς ὑμᾶς ("I will put my spirit in you")
4:9	θεοδίδακτος ("God-taught")	Isa 54:13 LXX Cf. Isa 30:20–21; Jer 31:34	διδακτοὺς θεοῦ ("taught by God")
4:17	ἁρπαγησόμεθα ἐν νεφέλαις εἰς ἀπάντησιν τοῦ κυρίου εἰς ἀέρα ("we will be caught up in the clouds to meet the Lord in the air")	Dan 7:13	τῶν νεφελῶν τοῦ οὐρανοῦ ("with the clouds of heaven")
5:8	ἐνδυσάμενοι θώρακα πίστεως καὶ ἀγάπης καὶ περικεφαλαίαν ἐλπίδα σωτηρίας ("let us put on the breastplate of faith and love, and for a helmet the hope of salvation")	Isa 59:17	καὶ ἐνεδύσατο δικαιοσύνην ὡς θώρακα καὶ περιέθετο περικεφαλαίαν σωτηρίου ἐπὶ τῆς κεφαλῆς ("He put on righteousness like a breastplate, and a helmet of salvation on his head")
5:23	ὑμῶν τὸ πνεῦμα καὶ ἡ ψυχὴ καὶ τὸ σῶμα ἀμέμπτως ("may your spirit and soul and body be kept blameless")	Job 1:1 Cf. Job 1:8; 2:3	ἦν ὁ ἄνθρωπος ἐκεῖνος ἀληθινός, ἄμεμπτος ("that man was blameless and upright")

Given that there are no marked or unmarked citations of Scripture in 1 and 2 Thessalonians, interpreters must attune their ears to hear and train their eyes to see the scriptural allusions that are seamlessly, if not unconsciously, woven into the Thessalonian correspondence.[6] This, of course, both presupposes and requires requisite knowledge and reliable tools.

Were one to begin an investigation of the verbal allusions to Israel's Scriptures present in 1 and 2 Thessalonians at the beginning of 1 Thessalonians and carry

---

6. I have been aided in my study of the allusive use of Scripture in the New Testament in general and in Paul in particular by the invaluable volume of Richard B. Hays, *Echoes of Scripture in the Letters of Paul* (New Haven: Yale University Press, 1989), esp. 29–33.

through to the conclusion of 2 Thessalonians, then 1 Thess 2:4 would be the first text to which one would turn where there is broad academic consensus of the presence of a scriptural allusion.⁷ There, in defending both his ministerial message and motives, Paul speaks of God as the one "who tests our hearts" (τῷ δοκιμάζοντι τὰς καρδίας ἡμῶν).⁸ An allusion to Jer 11:20, where the prophet speaks of the Lord as the one who "tests minds and hearts" (δοκιμάζων νεφροὺς καὶ καρδίας), is frequently, if inconclusively, posited.⁹

A second text in 1 Thess 2 where an allusion to Scripture is often detected is in 2:16.¹⁰ There, in a polemically charged passage, Paul refers to certain Jews who in their opposition of the Pauline mission to the gentiles so that they might be saved are always "filling up the measure of their sins" (εἰς τὸ ἀναπληρῶσαι αὐτῶν τὰς ἁμαρτίας πάντοτε). A positive correlation, thought to constitute an allusion, is often made between ἀναπληρῶσαι in 1 Thess 2:16 and ἀναπεπλήρωνται in Gen 15:16, where it is said that the sins of the Amorites have yet to be filled up (cf. Dan 8:23; Wis 19:4; 2 Macc 6:14).¹¹

Turning to 1 Thess 3, one arguably discovers two additional allusions to Scripture. In the first instance, Paul's confession to the Thessalonians in 3:5, that he was fearful that he and his fellow missioners' labor among them might have been in vain (εἰς κενὸν γένηται ὁ κόπος ἡμῶν), may well echo Isa 49:4, where the servant declares, "I have labored in vain" (Κενῶς ἐκοπίασα; cf. Isa 65:23).¹² Furthermore, and more frequently detected, is an allusion to Zech 14:5 in 1 Thess 3:13. Although there is disagreement among commentators as to whom Paul is referring when he speaks of the ἅγιοι in 3:13 (angels and/or believers?), there is broad scholarly

---

7. Meanwhile, see Weima's valuable comments on 1 Thess 1:9b, where he posits the influence of Scripture upon the terminology Paul employs to describe the Thessalonians' conversion and the God to whom they turned ("1–2 Thessalonians," 872). Note also my "'Turning to God from Idols': Conversion in *Joseph and Aseneth* and 1 Thessalonians," in *Anthropologie und Ethik im Frühjudentum und im Neuen Testament: Wechselseitige Wahrnehmungen*, ed. Matthias Konradt and Esther Schläpfer, WUNT 1/322 (Tübingen: Mohr Siebeck, 2014), 493–514.

8. On 1 Thess 2:1–12 as an apology, see, e.g., Still, *Conflict at Thessalonica*, 137–48.

9. Abraham J. Malherbe (*The Letters to the Thessalonians: A New Translation with Introduction and Commentary*, AB 32B [New York: Doubleday, 2000], 141) maintains, "The description of God as the one 'who tests our hearts' is an allusion to Jer 11:30 (cf. 12:3) and once more reveals Paul's prophetic self-understanding." Cf. Weima, "1–2 Thessalonians," 873.

10. On the authenticity of 1 Thess 2:13–16, see Still, *Conflict at Thessalonica*, 24–45.

11. So, Ernest Best, *A Commentary on the First and Second Epistles to the Thessalonians*, BNTC (Peabody, MA: Hendrickson, 1986), 118, remarks, "Paul is using words drawn from Gen. 15.16."

12. See, e.g., F. F. Bruce, *1 & 2 Thessalonians*, WBC 45 (Waco, TX: Word, 1982), 63–64, who also helpfully notes Ps 126:1 LXX in this context.

consensus that he is employing language from Zech 14:5 (πάντες οἱ ἅγιοι μετ᾽ αὐτοῦ) at this juncture in the letter.[13]

As noted in the introduction, 1 Thess 4 is filled with scriptural allusions. Beginning in 4:5, one may detect a scriptural allusion (note esp., e.g., Job 18:21; Ps 78:6 LXX; Jer 10:25) in Paul's admonishing his converts not to live in passionate lust like gentiles who do not know God (τὰ ἔθνη τὰ μὴ εἰδότα τὸν θεόν).[14] One verse later, in speaking of the Lord as an "avenger" regarding πορνεία, Paul may well be alluding to Ps 93:1 LXX, where the Lord is described as a God of vengeance (ὁ θεὸς ἐκδικήσεων). Then, at the conclusion of a section that commences at 4:1 (or perhaps 4:3), which is focused upon holiness or sanctification with special respect to sexual purity, Paul speaks of God as "the one who gives his Holy Spirit to you" (διδόντα τὸ πνεῦμα αὐτοῦ τὸ ἅγιον εἰς ὑμᾶς, 4:8). Here, it appears that the apostle is not only employing language decidedly akin to Ezek 37:14 (καὶ δώσω τὸ πνεῦμά μου εἰς ὑμᾶς) but that he is also maintaining that the eschatological age envisioned by the prophet is coming to pass through the conversion and sanctification of gentile Thessalonian Christ-followers.[15]

Relatedly, and significantly, as Paul begins the next section of the letter, he contends that they had been "God-taught" (θεοδίδακτος) to love one another (4:9). It would appear that this Pauline neologism is an allusion to Isa 54:13 LXX, where the prophet envisions a new Jerusalem, established in beauty and security, where all their children would be "taught by God" (διδακτοὺς θεοῦ; cf. Isa 30:20–21; Jer 31:34). Paul seemingly saw the Thessalonian's φιλαδελφία for one another and other Macedonian believers as a sign of this promised inbreaking.[16]

A final, commonly agreed-upon Old Testament allusion in 1 Thess 4 merits mention here. Paul's assurance that believers who are living at the time of Christ's parousia will be caught up with the dead in Christ "in the clouds to meet the Lord in the air" (4:17) is often thought to be indebted to Dan 7:13, where one likened unto a son of man is seen coming "with the clouds of heaven" (τῶν νεφελῶν τοῦ οὐρανοῦ).[17]

---

13. For the options, note, e.g., Justin D. King, "Paul, Zechariah, and the Identity of the 'Holy Ones' in 1 Thessalonians 3:13: Correcting an Un'Fee'sible Approach," *PRSt* 39, no. 1 (2012): 25–38.

14. See similarly in Paul, Gal 4:8–9; 2 Thess 1:8; 1 Cor 1:21. Note also the essay by George P. Carras, "Jewish Ethics and Gentile Converts: Remarks on 1 Thes 4,3–8," in *The Thessalonian Correspondence*, ed. Raymond F. Collins and Norbert Baumert, BETL 87 (Leuven: Leuven University Press, 1989), 306–15.

15. Note more fully Weima, "1–2 Thessalonians," 878–79.

16. See further Stephen E. Witmer, "θεοδίδακτοι in 1 Thessalonians 4.9: A Pauline Neologism," *NTS* 52, no. 2 (2006): 239–50.

17. An allusion in 1 Thess 4:13 to Wis 3:16 regarding those who are said to have no hope is sometimes suggested. Additionally, for the argument that the Lord's descent from heaven with a shout spoken of in 1 Thess 4:16 echoes Ps 46:6 LXX, see Craig A. Evans, "Ascending and

When turning to the final chapter of the first letter, one arguably finds an allusion to Isa 59:17 at 1 Thess 5:8, where Paul calls Thessalonian Christ-followers to don faith and love as a breastplate and hope as a helmet. The lack of symmetry between the two pieces of armor mentioned and the three theological virtues commended strengthens the likelihood of the apostle's indebtedness to Isaiah.[18] It might also be noted that Paul employs the same terms that Isaiah does (in the LXX) for breastplate (θώρακα) and helmet (περικεφαλαίαν).[19]

Verbal Allusions in 2 Thessalonians

Table 18.2. Verbal Allusions in 2 Thessalonians

2 Thessalonians		Jewish Scripture	
1:6	ἀνταποδοῦναι ("to repay")	Isa 66:6 Cf. Isa 66:15	ἀνταποδιδόντος ("repaying")
1:8	ἐν πυρί ("in fire")	Isa 66:15	ὡς πῦρ ἥξει ("will come in fire")
1:8	μὴ ὑπακούουσιν ("those who do not obey")	Isa 66:4 Cf. Job 18:21; Ps 78:6 LXX; Jer 10:25	οὐχ ὑπήκουσάν μου ("they did not answer me")
1:9	οἵτινες δίκην τίσουσιν ὄλεθρον αἰώνιον ἀπὸ προσώπου τοῦ κυρίου καὶ ἀπὸ τῆς δόξης τῆς ἰσχύος αὐτοῦ ("These will suffer the punishment of eternal destruction, separated from the presence of the Lord and from the glory of his might")	Isa 2:10 Cf. Isa 2:19, 21	κρύπτεσθε εἰς τὴν γῆν ἀπὸ προσώπου τοῦ φόβου κυρίου καὶ ἀπὸ τῆς δόξης τῆς ἰσχύος αὐτοῦ, ὅταν ἀναστῇ θραῦσαι τὴν γῆν ("hide in the dust from the terror of the Lord, and from the glory of his majesty")

Descending with a Shout: Psalm 47.6 and 1 Thessalonians 4.16," in *Paul and the Scriptures of Israel*, ed. Craig A. Evans and James A. Sanders, JSNTSup 83 (Sheffield: Sheffield Academic, 1993), 238–53.

18. So Weima, "1–2 Thessalonians," 882.

19. It is sometimes suggested that Paul draws upon the language of Job 1:1, 8 (ἀπεχόμενος ἀπὸ παντὸς πονηροῦ πράγματος; cf. Job 2:3) when in 1 Thess 5:22 he calls the Thessalonians to "reject every kind of evil" (ἀπὸ παντὸς εἴδους πονηροῦ ἀπέχεσθε). If the argument is not compelling, the shared terminology is striking.

Israel's Scriptures in 1 and 2 Thessalonians

1:10	ὅταν ἔλθῃ ἐνδοξασθῆναι ἐν τοῖς ἁγίοις αὐτοῦ ("when he comes to be glorified by his saints")	Zech 14:5 Cf. Ps 67:36 LXX; Exod 34:10; Sir 38:3, 6	καὶ ἥξει κύριος ὁ θεός μου καὶ πάντες οἱ ἅγιοι μετ' αὐτοῦ ("Then the Lord my God will come, and all the holy ones with him")
1:12	ἐνδοξασθῇ τὸ ὄνομα τοῦ κυρίου ἡμῶν Ἰησοῦ ἐν ὑμῖν ("so that the name of our Lord Jesus may be glorified in you")	Isa 66:5 Cf. Isa 66:13	τὸ ὄνομα κυρίου δοξασθῇ ("Let the Lord be glorified")
2:4	ὁ ἀντικείμενος καὶ ὑπεραιρόμενος ἐπὶ πάντα λεγόμενον θεὸν ἢ σέβασμα, ὥστε αὐτὸν εἰς τὸν ναὸν τοῦ θεοῦ καθίσαι ἀποδεικνύντα ἑαυτὸν ὅτι ἔστιν θεός ("He opposes and exalts himself above every so-called god or object of worship, so that he takes his seat in the temple of God, declaring himself to be God")	Dan 11:36–39 Cf. Ezek 28:2	καὶ ποιήσει κατὰ τὸ θέλημα αὐτοῦ ὁ βασιλεὺς καὶ παροργισθήσεται καὶ ὑψωθήσεται ἐπὶ πάντα θεὸν καὶ ἐπὶ τὸν θεὸν τῶν θεῶν ἔξαλλα λαλήσει ("The king shall act as he pleases. He shall exalt himself and consider himself greater than any god, and shall speak horrendous things against the God of gods")
2:8	καὶ τότε ἀποκαλυφθήσεται ὁ ἄνομος, ὃν ὁ κύριος [Ἰησοῦς] ἀνελεῖ τῷ πνεύματι τοῦ στόματος αὐτοῦ ("And then the lawless one will be revealed, whom the Lord Jesus will destroy with the breath of his mouth")	Isa 11:4 Cf. Ps 88:23; Isa 57:3–4 LXX	καὶ πατάξει γῆν τῷ λόγῳ τοῦ στόματος αὐτοῦ καὶ ἐν πνεύματι διὰ χειλέων ἀνελεῖ ἀσεβῆ ("He will strike the earth with the rod of his mouth, and with the breath of his lips he shall kill the wicked")
2:13	Ἡμεῖς δὲ ὀφείλομεν εὐχαριστεῖν τῷ Θεῷ πάντοτε περὶ ὑμῶν ἀδελφοὶ ἠγαπημένοι ὑπὸ κυρίου	Deut 33:12	Ἠγαπημένος ὑπὸ κυρίου κατασκηνώσει πεποιθώς, καὶ ὁ θεὸς σκιάζει ἐπ' αὐτῷ πάσας τὰς ἡμέρας, καὶ ἀνὰ μέσον τῶν ὤμων αὐτοῦ κατέπαυσεν

	("But we must always give thanks to God for you brothers beloved by the Lord")		("The beloved of the Lord rests in safety—the High God surrounds him all day long—the beloved rests between his shoulders")
3:16	Αὐτὸς δὲ ὁ Κύριος τῆς εἰρήνης δῴη ὑμῖν τὴν εἰρήνην διὰ παντὸς ἐν παντὶ τρόπῳ. ὁ Κύριος μετὰ πάντων ὑμῶν ("Now may the Lord of peace himself give you peace at all times in all ways. The Lord be with all of you")	Num 6:26 LXX and Judg 6:12 Cf. Ruth 2:4	ἐπάραι κύριος τὸ πρόσωπον αὐτοῦ ἐπὶ σὲ καὶ δῴη σοι εἰρήνην ("The Lord lift up his countenance upon you, and give you peace") Κύριος μετὰ σοῦ, δυνατὸς τῇ ἰσχύι ("The Lord is with you, you mighty warrior")

In 2 Thess 1, interpreters often note the influence of and allusions to Isa 66.[20] In particular, exegetes posit that the term ἀνταποδοῦναι employed in 2 Thess 1:6 may allude to Isa 66:6, where the same verb appears (cf. Isa 66:15). Another allusion to Isa 66 is frequently seen in 2 Thess 1:8, where it states that Lord Jesus will be revealed ἐν πυρί (cf. Isa 66:15: ὡς πῦρ ἥξει). Yet a third allusion to Isa 66 is sometimes detected in 2 Thess 1:8, where it is said that at the time of his revelation from heaven, the Lord Jesus will inflict vengeance on those who do not obey (μὴ ὑπακούουσιν) the gospel. In Isa 66:4, the Lord laments Israel's unwillingness to hear and heed his word (οὐχ ὑπήκουσάν μου). A fourth and final allusion to Isa 66 is often found in 2 Thess 1:12, where Paul speaks of the name of the Lord Jesus being glorified among the Thessalonians (ἐνδοξασθῇ τὸ ὄνομα τοῦ κυρίου ἡμῶν Ἰησοῦ ἐν ὑμῖν). Commentators commonly agree that the apostle is alluding to Isa 66:5 (τὸ ὄνομα κυρίου δοξασθῇ) here.

Remaining in 2 Thess 1 and turning to Isa 2, one arguably discovers a verbal allusion to Isa 2:10, 19, 21 respectively when Paul employs in 2 Thess 1:9 the precise phrase found in those verses, namely, ἀπὸ τῆς δόξης τῆς ἰσχύος αὐτοῦ. Two additional scriptural allusions, both from the Psalms, seemingly occur in 2 Thess 1:10. In the first instance, when speaking of the Lord being "glorified in his holy people" (ἐνδοξασθῆναι ἐν τοῖς ἁγίοις αὐτοῦ) at his coming, Paul appears to be alluding to Ps 88:8 LXX (ὁ θεὸς ἐνδοξαζόμενος ἐν βουλῇ ἁγίων). Additionally, Paul's declaration in 2 Thess 1:10b that the Lord will "be marveled

---

20. See esp. Roger D. Aus, "The Relevance of Isaiah 66:7 to Revelation 12 and 2 Thessalonians 1," *ZNW* 67, no. 3–4 (1971): 252–68.

at by all who have believed" (θαυμασθῆναι ἐν πᾶσιν τοῖς πιστεύσασιν) arguably echoes θαυμαστὸς ὁ θεὸς ἐν τοῖς ἁγίοις αὐτοῦ in Ps 67:36 LXX.

Turning to 2 Thess 2, Paul employs scriptural terms and texts to describe and depict "the man of lawlessness, the son of destruction" (note, e.g., Ps 88:23; Isa 57:3–4 LXX). In addition, this sinister figure's actions spoken of in 2 Thess 2:4 are in keeping with the actions taken by the king (typically thought to be Antiochus IV Epiphanes) of whom Dan 11:36–39 speaks. Moving further into the chapter, interpreters often correlate the destruction wrought by the Lord Jesus "with the breath of his mouth" with Isa 11:4 LXX and Ps 32:6 LXX.

Paul's wish-prayer in 2 Thess 3:16, that the Lord would give the Thessalonians peace and would be with them, arguably constitutes the final scriptural allusion in 2 Thessalonians. Numbers 6:26 LXX and Judg 6:12 (cf. Ruth 2:4) are often regarded to be probative parallels.[21]

Conceptual Allusions in the Thessalonian Correspondence

Election. God's election of and covenant with Israel is a scriptural commonplace. Among other pertinent passages, one might point to such texts as 1 Chr 16:13; Pss 89:3–4; 105:6; and Isa 42:1; 43:20; 45:4; 65:9 as illustrative. The theme of election also recurs in 1 and 2 Thessalonians. Of particular importance and relevance are 1 Thess 1:1, 4; 2:12; 4:7; 5:24; and 2 Thess 2:13. Karl P. Donfried adjudges the motif of election to be a key theological component within the Thessalonian letters and observes that "Paul reminds the Thessalonian Christians that God has chosen them and that as a result of that selection they must now live out the consequences of that choice and accept the privileges and responsibilities of the call into the kingdom of God."[22]

Holiness. Decided theological and contextual differences notwithstanding, another clear connection between and influence of Scripture upon the Thessalonian letters regards a call and commitment to be holy. Even as Israel is instructed to be holy as God is holy (see esp. Lev 11:44–45; 19:2; 20:7, 26; 22:32; cf. Exod 19:5–6; Deut 26:18–19; Isa 35:8; Ezek 36:23), Paul calls the Thessalonians to lead holy lives, not least with respect to their sexual conduct (note 1 Thess 4:3–4, 7;

---

21. For a reading of 1 and 2 Thessalonians focused upon peace, see Jouette M. Bassler, "Peace in All Ways: Theology in the Thessalonian Letters; A Response to R. Jewett, E. Krentz, and E. Richard," in *Pauline Theology*, vol. 1, *Thessalonians, Philippians, Galatians, Philemon*, ed. Jouette M. Bassler (Minneapolis: Fortress, 1991), 71–85.

22. Karl P. Donfried, "The Theology of 1 Thessalonians," in *The Theology of the Shorter Pauline Letters*, by Karl P. Donfried and I. Howard Marshall (Cambridge: Cambridge University Press, 1993), 29.

cf. 5:26). For Paul, the empowering presence of the Holy Spirit given by God to Christ followers established, expected, and enabled the same (so 1 Thess 4:8; 2 Thess 3:13; cf. 1 Thess 1:5–6; 3:13; 5:23).[23]

The Day of the Lord. The phrase [ἡ] ἡμέρα [τοῦ] κυρίου appears in 1 Thess 5:2 and 2 Thess 2:2 (and but two other times in Paul [1 Cor 5:5; 2 Cor 1:14; cf. 2 Pet 3:10]). In the former verse, Paul indicates that the Thessalonians were well aware that the "day of the Lord" would come like a thief in the night (cf. 1 Thess 5:4). Meanwhile, the latter verse reveals that some among the assembly were declaring that the day was already dawning, a claim that Paul was eager to counter in chapter 2 of that letter. While not desiring to downplay or to discount the interpretative challenges inherent to each of the aforementioned passages, our present remit is to observe the scriptural roots of the "day of the Lord" concept.

Time and again, Israel's prophets warned the people that the "day of the Lord" and the judgment associated therewith would come soon and with sudden surety.[24] Paul appears to have adopted and adapted this concept to convey to his converts (at least those in Thessalonica and Corinth) that the Lord Jesus's coming (parousia), which might well be sooner than later (1 Thess 4:17; 5:10), would result in "destruction" and "wrath" for outsiders and salvation for believers (so 1 Thess 1:10; 5:2, 9; 2 Thess 1:9–10).

Labor pains. In describing the "day of the Lord" to the Thessalonians, Paul likens the destruction that will come upon those who are declaring "peace and security" to the labor pains (ὠδίν) that come suddenly, if expectedly, upon a pregnant woman. Although ὠδίν is a Pauline hapax legomenon and occurs only three other times in the entire New Testament (see Matt 24:8; Mark 13:8; Acts 2:24), the term appears thirty-five times in the LXX. As in 1 Thess 5:3, not infrequently ὠδίν is employed in the LXX, particularly in Isaiah and Jeremiah, to depict the labor pains that come upon a pregnant woman (note esp. 1 Sam 4:19; Ps 47:7; Isa 13:6; 21:3; 26:17; 66:7; Jer 6:24; 13:21; Mic 4:9). It is plausible, and perhaps even probable, that Paul was indebted to Scripture for this imagery, which he then applies eschatologically with respect to the final judgment.[25]

Light/Day versus Darkness/Night. An additional and final conceptual allusion that is on full display in 1 Thess 5:4–8 (cf., e.g., Rom 2:19; 1 Cor 4:5; 2 Cor 4:6) is the contrast between light and day on the one hand with darkness and

---

23. See more fully, e.g., Jeffrey A. D. Weima, "'How You Must Walk to Please God': Holiness and Discipleship in 1 Thessalonians," in *Discipleship in the New Testament*, ed. Richard N. Longenecker (Grand Rapids: Eerdmans, 1996), 98–119.

24. Among other relevant scriptural texts, see Isa 13:6, 9; Jer 46:10; Ezek 13:5; 30:3; Joel 1:15; 2:1, 11, 31; 3:14; Amos 5:18, 20; Obad 15; Zeph 1:7, 14; Mal 4:5.

25. On the image of labor pains both within and beyond the New Testament, see Conrad Gempf, "The Imagery of Birth Pangs in the New Testament," *TynBul* 45, no. 1 (1994): 119–35.

night on the other. This contrast occurs regularly in Israel's Scriptures. In such prophetic texts as Isa 5:20; 9:2; 42:16; 52:10; 58:10; Jer 13:16; Amos 5:8, 20; and Mic 3:6; 7:8, this dichotomous pairing carries a moral valance not unlike that found in 1 Thess 5. The likelihood is high that such scriptural passages shaped Paul's thinking and impacted his writing.[26]

Conclusion

What may be said by way of conclusion regarding Paul's use of Israel's Scriptures in 1 and 2 Thessalonians? Given that there are no scriptural citations in these early Pauline letters, one might be inclined to think that the influence of Israel's Scriptures is negligible if not lacking altogether with respect to these early Pauline missives. Such an assessment, however, would not only neglect the verbal and conceptual allusions that are found throughout the letters but would also fail to appreciate fully the extent to which Israel's Scriptures penetrated Paul's thought and shaped his written communication.

Even if Paul's dependence upon Scripture is not readily apparent to the majority of people who read 1 and 2 Thessalonians, this study has shown nonetheless his indebtedness to Israel's Scriptures in these letters. Furthermore, even though Scripture does not appear to feature in these letters as it does, for example, in Paul's longer, later letter to the Romans, one gathers that it was part and parcel of the apostle's proclamation of the gospel to gentile Thessalonians "who turned to God from idols to serve a living and true God" (1 Thess 1:9; cf. Acts 17:2–3) and was foundational to both his initial and subsequent instruction of those converts, not least along eschatological and moral lines (see, e.g., 1 Thess 4:1–8).

Bibliography

Aus, Roger D. "The Relevance of Isaiah 66:7 to Revelation 12 and 2 Thessalonians 1." *ZNW* 67, no. 3–4 (1971): 252–68.

Bassler, Jouette M. "Peace in All Ways: Theology in the Thessalonian Letters; A Response to R. Jewett, E. Krentz, and E. Richard." Pages 71–85 in *Pauline Theology*. Vol. 1, *Thessalonians, Philippians, Galatians, Philemon*. Edited by Jouette M. Bassler. Minneapolis: Fortress, 1991.

Best, Ernest. *A Commentary on the First and Second Epistles to the Thessalonians*. BNTC. Peabody, MA: Hendrickson, 1986.

---

26. So also, e.g., Weima, "1–2 Thessalonians," 882.

Bruce, F. F. *1 & 2 Thessalonians*. WBC 45. Waco, TX: Word, 1982.
Carras, George P. "Jewish Ethics and Gentile Converts: Remarks on 1 Thes 4,3–8." Pages 306–15 in *The Thessalonian Correspondence*. Edited by Raymond F. Collins and Norbert Baumert. BETL 87. Leuven: Leuven University Press, 1989.
Donfried, Karl P. "The Theology of 1 Thessalonians." Pages 28–63 in *The Theology of the Shorter Pauline Letters*. By Karl P. Donfried and I. Howard Marshall. Cambridge: Cambridge University Press, 1993.
Ellis, E. Earle. *Paul's Use of the Old Testament*. Edinburgh: Oliver & Boyd, 1957. Repr., Grand Rapids: Baker, 1981.
Evans, Craig A. "Ascending and Descending with a Shout: Psalm 47.6 and 1 Thessalonians 4.16." Pages 238–53 in *Paul and the Scriptures of Israel*. Edited by Craig A. Evans and James A. Sanders. JSNTSup 83. Sheffield: Sheffield Academic, 1993.
Gempf, Conrad. "The Imagery of Birth Pangs in the New Testament." *TynBul* 45, no. 1 (1994): 119–35.
Hays, Richard B. *Echoes of Scripture in the Letters of Paul*. New Haven: Yale University Press, 1989.
King, Justin D. "Paul, Zechariah, and the Identity of the 'Holy Ones' in 1 Thessalonians 3:13: Correcting an Un'Fee'sible Approach." *PRSt* 39, no. 1 (2012): 25–38.
Malherbe, Abraham J. *The Letters to the Thessalonians: A New Translation with Introduction and Commentary*. AB 32B. New York: Doubleday, 2000.
Still, Todd D. *Conflict at Thessalonica: A Pauline Church and Its Neighbours*. JSNTSup 183. Sheffield: Sheffield Academic, 1999.
———. "'Turning to God from Idols': Conversion in *Joseph and Aseneth* and 1 Thessalonians." Pages 493–514 in *Anthropologie und Ethik im Frühjudentum und im Neuen Testament: Wechselseitige Wahrnehmungen*. Edited by Matthias Konradt and Esther Schläpfer. WUNT 1/322. Tübingen: Mohr Siebeck, 2014.
Weima, Jeffrey A. D. "1–2 Thessalonians." Pages 871–89 in *Commentary on the New Testament in the Old Testament*. Edited by G. K. Beale and D. A. Carson. Grand Rapids: Baker Academic, 2007.
———. "'How You Must Walk to Please God': Holiness and Discipleship in 1 Thessalonians." Pages 98–119 in *Discipleship in the New Testament*. Edited by Richard N. Longenecker. Grand Rapids: Eerdmans, 1996.
Witmer, Stephen E. "θεοδίδακτοι in 1 Thessalonians 4.9: A Pauline Neologism." *NTS* 52, no. 2 (2006): 239–50.

19

Israel's Scriptures in the Pastoral Epistles

GERD HÄFNER

In the Pastoral Epistles, a tension can be found with regard to the use of Israel's Scriptures: only rarely are the writings used explicitly or with recognizable intention, and yet in 2 Tim 3:16 a fundamental statement about their importance is made that is rarely found in the New Testament: "Every scripture inspired by God is also useful for teaching, rebuking, correcting, and training in righteousness."[1] This discrepancy cannot be resolved by claiming a multitude of scriptural references or by seeing the concept of γραφή ("Scripture") as extending to early Christian literature. The author of the Pastoral Epistles does not reflect on the canon or the status of early Christian writings. And his use of Scripture does not go beyond the five cases discussed hereafter.

It is not the quotation that is characteristic of the use of Scripture in the Pastoral Epistles, but the paraphrase, that is, the free reproduction of a passage from Scripture. It allows a reference text to be sharpened in a way that corresponds to the author's intention. Strictly speaking, this form of reference to Scripture stands between verbal allusion and conceptual allusion: it alludes to a particular scriptural passage, but this cannot be determined by recourse to a word or a string of words. The reference to Scripture is rather derived from the content of the passage. However, since the reference to the content is usually associated with

---

1. The following considerations are based on the assumption that 1 Timothy, 2 Timothy, and Titus were written as a pseudepigraphic corpus, at the earliest in the period around the turn of the first to the second century CE, more likely in the first third of the second century CE. Unless otherwise noted, all translations are by the author.

at least subtle terminological echoes, the paraphrase is best attributed to verbal allusion in the system of this book. Such a scriptural reference can be recognized especially, despite limited literal conformity, when it refers to prominent topics. This is the case throughout the Pastoral Epistles: they deal with creation and the fall of humanity (1 Tim 4:3–4; 2:13–14) as well as with an event from the story of Moses, the conflict with the Egyptian magicians in the context of the plague narrative (2 Tim 3:8–9). All references are taken exclusively from the Pentateuch (Genesis, Exodus, Numbers, and Deuteronomy).

What can be ascribed to conceptual allusion in the Pastoral Epistles is not a form of scriptural reference by the author but an expression of his attachment to tradition. Undoubtedly, one can find many formulations, motives, or themes that are found in Israel's Scriptures. However, they are usually nonspecific to the concerns of the letters, so that one does not get the impression that it is the author who brings in such thematic or linguistic allusions because of his familiarity with the Scriptures. Rather, he seems to stand in an early Christian tradition that is essentially influenced by Hellenistic Judaism. What can be interpreted in the Pastoral Epistles as conceptual allusion is in essence a mediated reference to Scripture.[2] This view is confirmed by the fact that even the unambiguous scriptural references are largely integrated into given traditions (see "Using Scripture," below).

The tension mentioned at the beginning cannot be avoided. Whoever deals with Israel's Scriptures in the Pastoral Epistles must find an answer to the question: How do the great reserve in the concrete use of Scripture and the fundamental statement about its importance fit together?

Israel's Scripture in the Pastoral Epistles

Table 19.1. Marked Citations and Verbal Allusions in the Pastoral Epistles

Marked citation	1 Tim 5:18	Deut 25:4
	2 Tim 2:19	Num 16:5

---

2. This is to be recorded against the assertion that in the Pastoral Epistles frequent recourse to the Scriptures is found. Cf. Anthony T. Hanson, "The Use of the Old Testament in the Pastoral Epistles," *IBS* 3, no. 3 (1981): 201–19; Beate Kowalski, "Zur Funktion und Bedeutung der alttestamentlichen Zitate und Anspielungen in den Pastoralbriefen," *SNTSU* 19 (1994): 45–68. For more detail see my *"Nützlich zur Belehrung" (2 Tim 3,16): Die Rolle der Schrift in den Pastoralbriefen im Rahmen der Paulusrezeption*, HBS 25 (Freiburg im Breisgau: Herder, 2000), 91–123.

Verbal allusion	1 Tim 2:13–14	Gen 2 and Gen 3
	1 Tim 4:3	Gen 1:29 and Gen 1:31
	2 Tim 3:8–9	Exod 7–9

Introducing Scripture

Only in two cases is Scripture cited, each announced by an introductory formula, but in different ways. In 1 Tim 5:18 the quotation from Deut 25:4 is introduced with the remark "for Scripture says" (λέγει γὰρ ἡ γραφή); so, the testimony of Scripture is clearly used to justify a statement. By contrast, in 2 Tim 2:19 a metaphor appears to introduce the scriptural quotation: the saying from Num 16:5 is called "the seal" (σφραγίς). This fits into the train of thought in that figurative language has already been introduced to speak of the church as "God's firm foundation" (στερεὸς θεμέλιος τοῦ θεοῦ), which has this seal—in contrast to the false teachers criticized earlier. Admittedly, the two metaphors do not go well together, as foundations do not bear a seal. But this discrepancy can probably be explained by the assumption that the author, when speaking of "foundation," was no longer aware that he was using a metaphor at all. This is not unlikely due to the frequency of the imagery of house building in the early Christian tradition. Therefore, one does not have to harmonize the two metaphors, but can concentrate on the metaphor used for Scripture. With this introduction, the author implicitly claims Scripture for his own position. That is why he does not use the neutral term γραφή. By using the seal metaphor, he claims that the scriptural testimony quoted confirms that the actions of the false teachers cannot harm the church. This procedure alone indicates that Scripture plays an important role in the debates that are in the background of the Pastoral Epistles.

That Scripture is quoted in 2 Tim 2:19 is beyond question. And, as we have seen, it can also be justified that the quotation is not introduced with the usual term. Nevertheless, the text gives cause for discussion as to whether the author really *wanted* to quote Scripture. Following the quotation from Num 16:5, in fact, we find a text that is not attested in Scripture, but is obviously intended as a quotation ("Let everyone who names the name of the Lord depart from iniquity"). So, are sentences quoted here that have authority but not necessarily the authority of *Scripture*? The question must be answered in the negative for two reasons. (1) From the findings in the Pastoral Epistles as a whole, not least from 2 Tim 3:16, their interest in the authority of Scripture is evident. It is unlikely that the author could have attributed a comparable role to early Christian sayings. Although the two quotations in 2 Tim 2:19 may have been conveyed to him by the early Christian tradition, he does not bring them in *as* early Christian tradition, but as a testimony of Scripture. (2) First Timothy 5:18 shows that the term

"Scripture" can also introduce statements that are not documented in Scripture. The quotation from Deut 25:4 is followed by the sentence that the laborer deserves his wages. Although this sentence is found in the synoptic tradition (Luke 10:7), it cannot be concluded from this that the status of Holy Scripture should be attributed to early Christian literature.[3] In the Pastoral Epistles, there is otherwise no indication for such an interest. Moreover, the content of the sentence in question is not particularly distinctive and could well be objectively connected with statements from Scripture or Jewish tradition (Lev 19:13; Deut 24:14–15; Sir 34:22 LXX; T. Job 12:3).

The unmarked reference to Scripture in the verbal allusions acquires its peculiarity through the fact that the scriptural statements are completely integrated into the argumentation of the letters. It is true that the author is no master of the text of Scripture, as he must provide sufficient indicators in terms of content for the reference to be recognized by the recipients. But he is able, through his own emphasis, to draw conclusions that are not found in the text itself and that could not have been gained at all by means of quotation. This form of scriptural reference, the free handling of the text, can be regarded as the profile of the Pastoral Epistles.

Using Scripture

According to what has been said so far, it is appropriate to begin the investigation of the use of Scripture in the Pastoral Epistles with the special form of verbal allusions. We find the first recourse to the statements of Scripture in connection with remarks about the role of women in the congregation. That role is determined above all by two limitations: Women are not to teach or to rule over men (1 Tim 2:12), but rather to learn and submit (1 Tim 2:11). This role model is justified by a reference to the story of creation and the fall: "For Adam was formed first, then Eve. And Adam was not deceived, but the woman was deceived and became a transgressor" (1 Tim 2:13–14). The literal echoes of Gen 2 and 3 in the LXX are quantitatively low: Adam, woman (γυνή), form (πλάσσειν), deceive (ἀπατᾶν). But they are so specific in content that there is no doubt about the scriptural text they allude to. But this applies only to the two verses quoted. The subsequent statement that woman will be saved by childbearing (1 Tim 2:15) is no longer part of the paraphrasing of the biblical text.

The way in which the testimony of Scripture is presented makes the advantages of verbal allusion clear. (1) The fact that Adam was created before Eve is

---

3. See, e.g., Benjamin P. Wolfe, "Scripture in the Pastoral Epistles: Premarcion Marcionism?," *PrSt* 16, no. 1 (1989): 5–16, for whom Paul's letters are to be included in the term "Scripture."

completely consistent with Gen 2, but no conclusion is drawn from it regarding the relationship of the sexes to one another in the scriptural text.[4] The author of the Pastoral Epistles, however, places the narrative of the second creation report in the context of a principle that was widespread and accepted in antiquity: the former is the more valuable. This principle had not been explicitly applied in the interpretation of Gen 2 prior to this point, although there is a certain parallel in 1 Cor 11:8–9 (the woman was created out of man and for man's sake). In the reception by the Pastoral Epistles, the fact that Adam was created before Eve justifies the subordination of the woman to the man in the church. (2) The reference to the narrative of the fall of humanity in 1 Tim 2:14 also shows a striking emphasis on the scriptural text: "Adam was not deceived." This is correct insofar as the verb "to deceive" (ἀπατᾶν) is applied solely to Eve in Gen 3. However, the narrative leaves no doubt that Adam also transgressed the divine commandment. In the Pastoral Epistles, this remains hidden, in that the transgression is tied to the seduction, and so the woman alone is burdened with the transgression. In the context this is primarily intended to underpin the prohibition of teaching: whoever has proven to be easily deceived in the origin, unsolidified in keeping the divine commandment, cannot teach others, but must be taught (1 Tim 2:11–12). The plausibility of such an emphasis might have been strengthened in the situation of the Pastoral Epistles by the history of interpretation. This history is marked by the fact that Eve's guilt is emphasized and Adam's role in Gen 3 is left out. In Sir 25:24 it says: "With a woman sin had a beginning, and because of her we all die." Since this is not explained in detail, Sirach seems to be building on an already established tradition. Later texts confirm the picture (LAE 3:3; Gk. Apoc. Ezra 2:16; Sib. Or. 1:42–45). Philo of Alexandria also believes that women are more easily deceived (QG 33).

The reference to Gen 2 and 3 is primarily intended to strengthen the order of the church that the author of the Pastoral Epistles has in mind as an ideal. He does not describe already existing conditions but wants to enforce the exclusion of women from responsible positions. This concern may overlap with a second one: the fight against false teachers. This results above all from the observation that the opponents rejected the role of women propagated by the Pastoral Epistles. If salvation is opened up to women by fulfilling their role in the family (1 Tim 2:15), the opponents virtually rule out such a role: "They forbid marriage" (1 Tim 4:3). The antiheretical thrust is confirmed by a further observation. A second conviction is attributed to the opponents in 1 Tim 4:3: the observance of food taboos. In the

---

4. Benjamin L. Merkle, "Paul's Arguments from Creation in 1 Corinthians 11:8–9 and in 1 Timothy 2:13–14: An Apparent Inconsistency Answered," *JETS* 49, no. 3 (2006): 543 n. 54, inserts this into Gen 2.

following, however, only this second point is argued against. This is best explained by the fact that the author assumes that he has already taken a stand against the prohibition of marriage—by his scriptural argumentation in 1 Tim 2:13–15.

The author also uses Scripture against the opponents' dietary requirements, again by freely reproducing the text. Two theological judgments about what has been created are thereby introduced. "God has created for acceptance" (1 Tim 4:3) the food that the opponents reject; "everything created by God is good and nothing is to be rejected" (4:4). Behind the second statement is Gen 1:31: "God saw *all* that he had *made*, and it was very *good*." The scriptural reference of the first statement is less clear. Probably Gen 1:29 should be considered, where "food" (βρῶμα) is a terminological reference point. Furthermore, this verse is formed by a saying of God that gives created things to humanity as food—a clue for the phrase "for acceptance" in 1 Tim 4:3. The content of 1 Tim 4:3, however, seems to refer rather to Gen 9:3 because only there are the animals also given as food. On the other hand, the author seems to be concerned with the reference to creation rather than with later concessions, therefore Gen 1:29 is to be favored as the scriptural reference.[5]

This is probably why the characterization of the opponents' position remains deliberately unclear. If the opponents abstained from eating meat, recourse to Gen 1 with the purely vegetarian diet would be argumentatively contestable. This is somewhat obscured by the fact that the text refers to *food* in general without introducing any differentiation. If the opponents' dietary asceticism was not aimed exclusively at the renunciation of meat (but also included wine, for instance; see 1 Tim 5:23), it could be concealed that the Scriptural text does not cover everything for which the author uses it as an argument.

The opposition to food taboos leads to the statement that food was created for acceptance (1 Tim 4:3: εἰς μετάλημψιν) and that nothing is unclean (οὐδὲν ἀπόβλητον). The reference text itself does not provide this emphasis. In the biblical tradition, the conviction that everything is well-made has undoubtedly been associated with dietary restrictions (so, e.g., Lev 11). The free rendering of the scriptural text, in which the boundaries between rendering and interpretation become blurred, attempts to conceal the weakness of the argument as far as possible. Nevertheless, the question arises: Why does the author argue with a scriptural text that seems to be of only limited use as an argument? Probably he wanted to stress the good creation because he saw here the decisive point of

---

5. Cf. also Markus Lang, "Nützlich in den richtigen Händen: Schriftrezeption in den Pastoralbriefen," in *Paulinische Schriftrezeption: Grundlagen – Ausprägungen – Wirkungen – Wertungen*, ed. Florian Wilk and Markus Öhler, FRLANT 268 (Göttingen: Vandenhoeck & Ruprecht, 2017), 244 n. 30.

Israel's Scriptures in the Pastoral Epistles

conflict. Therefore, he wants to strike at the theological basis of the opponents with his argumentation. Incidentally, this is the only place where arguments are made directly against the position of the false teachers. Typical for the Pastoral Epistles is the delimitation, not the content-related argument. But when "sound doctrine" is not only asserted for one's own side but also justified, Scripture comes into play (see also 1 Tim 2:13–14, which is indirectly criticizing the rejected false doctrine).

The third case of verbal allusion in 2 Tim 3:8–9, on the other hand, relies solely on demarcation and dispenses with any argumentation from Scripture. From the plague narratives in Exod 7–9 the confrontation of Moses and Aaron with the Egyptian magicians is taken up but read in light of a tradition that has made the nameless magicians the pair of brothers Jannes and Jambres. Apart from this identification, however, there is no element in the Pastoral Epistles that could not be derived from the stories in the book Exodus. The point of reference is therefore the book of Exodus, not the Targum Ps.-Jonathan with its reference to Jannes and Jambres or the book Jannes and Jambres, which is indirectly attested and survived in manuscripts in a very fragmentary state.[6]

The paraphrase of the scriptural text aims at a comparison between the Egyptian sorcerers and the false teachers against whom the Pastoral Epistles are directed. The reference to the false teachers cannot be rejected because in 2 Tim 3:1–5 the moral decline of all humankind before the end is described.[7] It is certainly not intended to claim for all humankind that it has the "form of piety" (3:5). Moreover, 3:6 makes it clear that a particular group is picked out of a larger number.

---

6. Cf. Albert Pietersma, *The Apocryphon of Jannes and Jambres the Magicians: P. Chester Beatty XVI (with New Editions of Papyrus Vindobonensis Greek inv. 29456 + 29828 verso and British Library Cotton Tiberius B. v f. 87)*, RGRW 119 (Leiden: Brill, 1994). For discussion of further fragments identified as witnesses of the apocryphon, see Georg Schmelz, "Zwei neue Fragmente des Apokryphons über die Zauberer Jannes und Jambres," *Atti del XXII Congresso Internazionale di Papirologia*, 3 vols. (Florence: Istituto papirologico G. Vitelli, 2001), 2:1199–1212; Albert Pietersma, "Two More Fragments of the Vienna 'Jannes and Jambres,'" *BASP* 49 (2012): 21–29. For the possible contribution of the Ethiopian version for the reconstruction of the Greek text, see Ted M. Erho and W. Benjamin Henry, "The Ethiopic Jannes and Jambres and the Greek Original," *APF* 65, no. 1 (2019): 176–223. A translation into German based on the Greek and Latin text including a detailed introduction is to be found in Albert Pietersma, *Jannes und Jambres*, trans. Gerbern S. Oegema, JSHRZ 2.4 (Gütersloh: Gütersloher Verlagshaus, 2013).

7. Thus Johannes Tromp, "Jannes and Jambres (2 Timothy 3,8–9)," in *Moses in Biblical and Extra-Biblical Traditions*, ed. Axel Graupner and Michael Wolter, BZAW 372 (Berlin: de Gruyter, 2007), 221, does not connect the brothers Jannes and Jambres to the Egyptian sorcerers but to an inner-Israelite opposition against Moses and Aaron documented in CD V, 17–19 ("Jannes and his brother").

Two points are emphasized in the comparison: (1) The sorcerers resisted Moses (ἀντέστησαν); (2) their "folly" (ἄνοια) has become apparent. For the opponents, correspondingly it is stated: (1) they resist the truth (ἀνθίστανται); (2) their folly (ἄνοια) will be evident. The fact that it has not yet become evident in the present but will only become apparent in the future confirms the picture of the successful activity of the opponents that results from the context. They creep into homes, as is stated in polemical distortion, and capture weak women (γυναικάρια). To put it unpolemically: it is precisely women who accept the doctrine, and it is this to an extent that worries the author. This very success might have led to the example from the story of Moses. The sorcerers are initially able to keep up with Moses and Aaron by repeating their miracles (Exod 7:11–12; 7:22; 8:3). Eventually, however, they fail because of the plague of flies and disappear from the scene because of the plague of boils (Exod 9:11). This sequence of successful activity and eventual failure is probably the reason for the choice of the scriptural reference. The opponents are to be perceived like the Egyptian sorcerers. The false teachers' success is the first step toward destruction. Here, then, Scripture is placed entirely in the service of the polemics against the opponents; there is no objective argument for the assertion that the opponents are to be understood according to the example of those magicians.

Scripture is expressly quoted in 1 Tim 5:18, with two peculiarities. First, a phrase that is not documented in Scripture is quoted (see "Introducing Scripture," above), and second, Paul has already quoted the rule concerning animal protection from Deut 25:4 ("You shall not muzzle an ox when it is treading out the grain") in a figurative sense: to justify the right of the apostles to material support by the churches (1 Cor 9:9). Nor are the Pastoral Epistles concerned with the welfare of the animal but rather want "the elders who rule well" to be "considered worthy of double honor" (1 Tim 5:17). While Paul explicitly explains why the meaning of the quoted text is not to be found in the concern for the animal ("Is it for oxen that God is concerned?"), the scriptural text is referred to in a completely different context without comment in the Pastoral Epistles. Probably the scriptural text was thus conveyed to the author by the Pauline tradition.

This hypothesis is also supported by the fact that a second sentence is added as Scripture, which actually comes from the Jesus tradition and was already used by Paul in the same context as Deut 25:4—though not as Scripture, but as a saying of the Lord (see 1 Cor 9:14). Probably the author of the Pastoral Epistles used a stock justification for the support of the apostles, following Paul's example, arguing with reference to Deut 25:4 and a saying from the Jesus tradition ("the laborer deserves his wages"). Whether the misunderstanding that the second sentence is also a scriptural saying goes back to that tradition or to the author of the letters can no longer be clarified. A further observation strengthens the assessment that the use of the Scriptures in the Pastoral Epistles is less determined by independent recourse than by given tradition. The rule of the two or three witnesses (1 Tim 5:19) is clearly set apart from the scriptural testimony, even though it originates objectively from Deut 19:15. Moreover, there is no sign of any effort to adapt the wording to the reference text. The fact that the wording of the quotation deviates from 1 Cor 9:9 in two respects does not speak against the mediation by the Pauline tradition (see "The Nature of the Scriptural Text," below).

The new context in which the scriptural quotation is placed can be attributed to the author. It is no longer a matter of supplying the needs of locally unattached preachers of the gospel, but rather a matter of the elders who rule well over the church. Scripture says that they shall "be considered worthy of double honor" (1 Tim 5:17). The exact understanding of this phrase is controversial. It is probably not primarily a matter of salary or remuneration, but rather of the recognition that should be given to church leaders—"double" as compared to the widows mentioned before (1 Tim 5:3–16). The saying about the threshing ox is interpreted in light of the specific situation. Paul had referred it to the question of the apostles' maintenance and had given reasons for this understanding. The Pastoral Epistles build on this foundation; they no longer need to justify the figurative meaning but even increase the extent to which the rule of Deut 25:4 is transferred to other circumstances: now it is no longer a question of provision for survival but rather of the *recognition* that is necessary for the fruitful work of the church leaders. Scripture becomes an argument in the enforcement of the church order that the author of the letters has in mind as an ideal.

The second quotation explicitly introduced in 2 Tim 2:19 was probably also given to the author by the early Christian tradition. There are two observations supporting this judgment. (1) The biblical reference text is treated quite differently in the two parts of the scriptural testimony. While Num 16:5 is quoted literally ("the Lord knows those who are his"), the second part, joined with "and," cannot be assigned to any particular text: "let everyone who names the name of the Lord depart from iniquity." (2) The context of Num 16:5, the uprising of Korah and his company, is not evaluated, although it would have fit perfectly into the context of the author's polemics against the opppenents. Therefore, one can hardly say that 2 Tim 2:19 is "drawing on the Numbers 16 *narrative*."[8] Probably a single verse was the only reference point for the quotation.

---

8. Gregory A. Couser, "'How Firm a Foundation': The Ecclesiology of 2 Timothy 2:19–21," BSac 173 (2016): 474 (emphasis added).

The quotation of Num 16:5 is on the one hand used similarly to the example of Jannes and Jambres in 2 Tim 3:8–9. The scriptural saying is not part of a substantive argumentation against the position of the opponents but is simply claimed for one's own side. The success of the opponents (2 Tim 2:17–18) does not lead to the downfall of the firmly established church because "the Lord knows those who are his," that is, he distinguishes between the orthodox and the false teachers and their followers. On the other hand, there is a difference from the passage already discussed, in so far as the connection with the history of Israel is now completely ignored. The opposition of Jannes and Jambres to Moses came up as an example from the past; in 2 Tim 2:19 the scriptural text directly applies to the church.

In the conflict with the opponents, Scripture is used as an authority even if it cannot contribute anything factually to the dispute being dealt with, and the opponents could have just as rightly referred to the text quoted. This scriptural saying has absolutely nothing to do with the aforementioned content of false doctrine (2 Tim 2:18: "the resurrection has already taken place"). It serves only as a demarcation.

This also applies to the second part: "let everyone who names the name of the Lord depart from iniquity." In context, this has to be read as a call to stay away or separate from false doctrine. The following picture of the different vessels in the house (2 Tim 2:20–21) especially points to this meaning. What characterizes a person as a "vessel for dishonor" or "vessel for honor" is not clarified by the scriptural quotation.

The statement about the Scriptures in 2 Tim 3:15–16 is surprising in view of the generally sparse use of Scripture in the Pastoral Epistles; but it fits into the lines recognized so far. This applies, first, to the context of the *polemics against the opponents*, in which the statement is embedded. What is said about the Scriptures appears to be in contrast to the actions of "evildoers" who act as "deceived deceivers" (2 Tim 3:13). Second, the writings are placed within the *church tradition* from which the author of the letters himself has in some cases taken his recourse to the Scriptures. The addressee Timothy is reminded that he knew the Scriptures from childhood—and this after he was asked to continue in what he has learned (3:14–15). Thus, even before anything is said about them in terms of content, the Scriptures appear as a moment in the church's teaching tradition. What is said about the importance of the Scriptures can be attributed, third, to the issue of *church order*, or more precisely, to the ministry of the church leader. For it is possible to interpret 2 Tim 3:15–17 as *one* coherent thought. As the fictitious addressee of the letter, Timothy is not only a disciple of the apostle but also a type of church leader, so what is said to him also concerns church order. Timothy is enabled by the Holy Scriptures to work for salvation through faith in Christ (3:15b). This thought is then developed by explaining the usefulness of "every scripture breathed out by God" (parallel to the "Holy Scriptures") for the ministry of the church leader: He works for salvation by faith when he teaches, rebukes, corrects, and trains in righteousness (3:16). Thus, the minister is equipped by the Scriptures to carry out his task well (3:17).

The Nature of the Scriptural Text

From the above discussion, it follows that it is difficult to make well-founded judgments about the scriptural text used. The preferred form is verbal allusion with free reproduction of the reference text (1 Tim 2:13–14; 4:3–4; 2 Tim 3:8–9). Some quotations cannot be found in the Scriptures despite the introductory formula (the respective second sayings in 1 Tim 5:18 and 2 Tim 2:19 added with καί ["and"]). In the two cases that remain, it seems likely that the author of the Pastoral Epistles is dependent on an early Christian tradition and does not independently refer to the scriptural text. This, however, must still be substantiated by argument here.

In 1 Tim 5:18 the sentence begins with the object (βοῦν ἀλοῶντα, "treading ox"); in addition, a verb is chosen for the muzzling of the ox that corresponds to the tradition of the LXX (φιμοῦν), whereas for 1 Cor 9:9 usually κημοῦν ("muzzle") is preferred. The version of 1 Tim 5:18 cannot be traced back to a will to adapt the wording to the scriptural text, for the prefixing of the object is not documented in any other available text tradition of Deut 25:4. One can hardly see any motive for a conscious change, for in view of the brevity of the sentence, no significant clarification or emphasis is associated with the change. The Hebrew text offers the same word order as the LXX. The differences between 1 Tim 5:18 on the one hand and Deut 25:4 and 1 Cor 9:9 on the other are best attributed to processes of transmission that cannot be reconstructed in detail.

The quotation of Num 16:5 in 2 Tim 2:19 shows only one difference with the LXX text: θεός ("God") is replaced by κύριος ("Lord"). At first glance, this appears to be an adaptation to the Hebrew text, which at this point offers the tetragram. What speaks against such a conclusion, however, is that the quotation follows the LXX in the formulation of the predicate: "The Lord *knows* (ἔγνω) those who are his." The Hebrew text, on the other hand, has a *hiphil* form: "The Lord *will show* who belongs to Him." So here, too, hardly any conclusions can be drawn for the text form used in the Pastoral Epistles.

Conclusion

With regard to content, the Pastoral Epistles refer to the Scriptures in two contexts: the fight against the opponents and questions of church order. From a formal point of view, it is noticeable that the use of the Scriptures is bound by tradition. The two explicit quotations show dependence on specifications from early Christian tradition. The programmatic sentence 2 Tim 3:15–16 confirms this integration on a fundamental level: The "Holy Scriptures" are perceived as part of the church tradition, the original connection with Israel no longer plays a role. There is no reflection on this shift of addressees; the Scriptures are directly addressed to believers and speak into the present situation.

The three factors mentioned are inwardly connected. The church leader is supposed to represent "sound doctrine," that is, that tradition that, according to the concept of the Pastoral Epistles, can be traced back to Paul: What was heard from Paul should be entrusted to reliable people who are capable of teaching (2 Tim 2:2). Such a church leader has the task of opposing false teachers (e.g., 2 Tim 2:24–25; Tit 1:9). The Holy Scriptures are useful for this purpose.[9]

However, this basic statement does not correspond to the very reserved use of the Scriptures we observe in practice. The author of the letters himself does not seem to know how "every scripture breathed out by God" can be used for the task mentioned. The fact that he nevertheless makes such a fundamental statement about the Scriptures is probably connected with the historical situation in which he wrote his letters under the name of Paul. His main concern was to fight against opponents for whom the Scriptures had been of great importance (see 1 Tim 1:7; Tit 3:9). Therefore, he claims the Scriptures for his own side. The riddle of the programmatic sentence in 2 Tim 3:15–16 can thus be explained: precisely *because* the Scriptures are rarely used but are not to be left to the opponents, the principle about the importance of the "Holy Scriptures" appears. The principle takes the place of the implementation. For the theology of the Pastoral Epistles, recourse to the Scriptures is practically irrelevant, but for the purpose of the letters, they are of great importance.[10] This, at least, can be observed: there is no contradiction between principle and actual recourse to the Scriptures. All elements of the program are realized in the actual use of the

---

9. In general, Predrag Dragutinovic interprets the findings likewise: the interpretation of Scripture is institutionalized "in order to take Scripture away from the opponents and to keep it within the framework of tradition by an institutionally controllable interpretation practice" ("Die Schrift im Dienst der gesunden Lehre: Text-pragmatische Erwägungen zu 2 Tim 3,14–17," *ASEs* 32 [2015]: 323).

10. Cf. also Lang, "Schriftrezeption," 246–47.

Scriptures. The "Scriptures of Israel" are not elaborated as a theological theme and are only rarely quoted or alluded to and are yet of great importance for the purpose of the Pastoral Epistles.

Bibliography

Couser, Gregory A. "'How Firm a Foundation': The Ecclesiology of 2 Timothy 2:19–21." *BSac* 173 (2016): 460–75.
Dragutinovic, Predrag. "Die Schrift im Dienst der gesunden Lehre: Text-pragmatische Erwägungen zu 2 Tim 3,14–17." *ASEs* 32, no. 2 (2015): 309–24.
Erho, Ted M., and W. Benjamin Henry. "The Ethiopic Jannes and Jambres and the Greek Original." *APF* 65, no. 1 (2019): 176–223.
Häfner, Gerd. *"Nützlich zur Belehrung" (2 Tim 3,16): Die Rolle der Schrift in den Pastoralbriefen im Rahmen der Paulusrezeption*. HBS 25. Freiburg im Breisgau: Herder, 2000.
Hanson, Anthony T. "The Use of the Old Testament in the Pastoral Epistles." *IBS* 3, no. 3 (1981): 201–19.
Kowalski, Beate. "Zur Funktion und Bedeutung der alttestamentlichen Zitate und Anspielungen in den Pastoralbriefen." *SNTSU* 19 (1994): 45–68.
Lang, Markus. "Nützlich in den richtigen Händen: Schriftrezeption in den Pastoralbriefen." Pages 235–47 in *Paulinische Schriftrezeption: Grundlagen – Ausprägungen – Wirkungen – Wertungen*. Edited by Florian Wilk and Markus Öhler. FRLANT 268. Göttingen: Vandenhoeck & Ruprecht, 2017.
Merkle, Benjamin L. "Paul's Arguments from Creation in 1 Corinthians 11:8–9 and in 1 Timothy 2:13–14: An Apparent Inconsistency Answered." *JETS* 49, no. 3 (2006): 527–48.
Pietersma, Albert. *The Apocryphon of Jannes and Jambres the Magicians: P. Chester Beatty XVI (with New Editions of Papyrus Vindobonensis Greek inv. 29456 + 29828 verso and British Library Cotton Tiberius B. v f. 87)*. RGRW 119. Leiden: Brill, 1994.
———. *Jannes und Jambres*. Translated by Gerbern S. Oegema. JSHRZ 2.4. Gütersloh: Gütersloher Verlagshaus, 2013.
———. "Two More Fragments of the Vienna 'Jannes and Jambres.'" *BASP* 49 (2012): 21–29.
Schmelz, Georg. "Zwei neue Fragmente des Apokryphons über die Zauberer Jannes und Jambres." Pages 1199–1212 in vol. 2 of *Atti del XXII Congresso Internazionale di Papirologia*. 3 vols. Florence: Istituto papirologico G. Vitelli, 2001.
Tromp, Johannes. "Jannes and Jambres (2 Timothy 3,8–9)." Pages 211–26 in *Moses in*

Biblical and Extra-Biblical Traditions. Edited by Axel Graupner and Michael Wolter. BZAW 372. Berlin: de Gruyter, 2007.

Wolfe, Benjamin P. "Scripture in the Pastoral Epistles: Premarcion Marcionism?" *PrSt* 16, no. 1 (1989): 5–16.

C. HEBREWS AND THE CATHOLIC LETTERS

20

Israel's Scriptures in Hebrews

GABRIELLA GELARDINI

The role of Scripture in Hebrews is not merely a pronounced but an outstanding one. In the words of Hans-Friedrich Weiss in the last Hebrews volume of the famous *Kritisch-exegetischer Kommentar über das Neue Testament*, published in 1991,

> This is already evident in formal-quantitative terms from the multitude of explicit quotations from Scripture, furthermore from the abundance of virtual quotations and references to biblical texts and subjects, which are difficult to define in detail, but not least also from the fact that Hebrews—as a letter of consolation and exhortation in the tradition of the Scripture-led sermon of the Diaspora synagogue—presents itself to a large degree as an exposition of Scripture or as a sermon based on certain passages of Scripture.[1]

Important and central issues are addressed here, taken from a commentary that has matured over a period of more than 130 years and stands for comprehensive scholarship, in which—apart from Weiss—greats such as Gottlieb Lünemann, Bernhard Weiss, and Otto Michel have contributed their knowledge and insight.

I am grateful to Dr. David E. Orton for proofreading this chapter.

1. Hans-Friedrich Weiss, *Der Brief an die Hebräer*, KEK 13 (Göttingen: Vandenhoeck & Ruprecht, 1991), 171–72. Unless otherwise noted, translations are by the author; biblical quotations follow the NRSV unless otherwise indicated.

Weiss first speaks of a "multitude of explicit quotations," and indeed there is no chapter in Hebrews that is not adorned with at least one quotation, the long tenth chapter having as many as eight. If we follow NA²⁸, there are forty-five quotations, which puts Hebrews third in the New Testament in this regard, after the Gospel of Matthew (with 82) and the Epistle to the Romans (with 74). All explicit quotations are taken from the Old Testament canon, most of them from the Ketuvim (19), secondly from the Torah (17), and least frequently from the Nevi'im (9). As far as their placement is concerned, the majority of the quotations are found in the first third of the text, that is, the introduction. Their form is also varied: we find long quotations, including the longest in the entire New Testament, very short ones, pairs, compound ones, as well as several repetitions. With regard to the allusions, Weiss even speaks of an "abundance of virtual quotations and references to biblical texts and subjects." Rightly so, because appendix III in NA²⁸, entitled "Loci citati vel allegati" (Passages cited or alluded to), counts no less than 282 of them. Here the sources from which they are drawn are clearly different, as most references are to the Torah (126), followed by those to the Nevi'im (75), then to the Ketuvim (43), and beyond the canonical margins, extending in some cases to the deuterocanonical works or the Old Testament Pseudepigrapha (38).[2]

That Hebrews "presents itself to a large degree as exposition of Scripture" is further noted by Weiss. In fact, there is hardly a sentence in the letter that cannot be assigned to one of the three artfully interwoven genres of quotation, scriptural exposition, or adaptation of the same aimed at the addressees.

It is understandable, then, that the topic of the use of Scripture in Hebrews scholarship has not only produced countless essays in the last twenty years but has recently also increasingly filled books.[3] This fact is also, of course, an expression of a paradigm shift within New Testament research, which today reads the New Testament less in contrast to Second Temple Judaism and its writings than more in continuity with the same.

Moreover, Weiss uses the term "letter of consolation and exhortation" for the rhetoricity of the letter, also recognized by many after him, referring, of course, to

---

2. That the whole Torah is important for the author of Hebrews has been shown by Gudrun Holtz, regardless of the fact that it is not quoted excessively, in "Pentateuchrezeption im Hebräerbrief," in *Die Septuaginta und das frühe*, ed. Thomas Scott Caulley and Hermann Lichtenberger, WUNT 277 (Tübingen: Mohr Siebeck, 2011), 358–80.

3. Bryan R. Dyer, e.g., has presented a useful essay, albeit one that is limited in scope and no longer entirely up to date: "The Epistle to the Hebrews in Recent Research: Studies on the Author's Identity, His Use of the Old Testament, and Theology," *JGRChJ* 9 (2013): 104–31. In this chapter, and in view of what is to be presented here, the most helpful from the last twenty years or so will be mentioned.

the ambiguous self-designation of the text as a "word of exhortation [τοῦ λόγου τῆς παρακλήσεως]" (Heb 13:22). It may explain, for instance, the fact that quotations in Hebrews are introduced less—as is usual in the rest of the New Testament—with words of writing, and instead consistently with those of speaking. Weiss is even more specific and speaks of a "sermon of the diaspora synagogue," which reminds us that such sermons had to follow certain rules of the aesthetics of production. With regard to Hebrews, the symmetries recognized by many deserve a special mention here, which is why, for the same reasons of production and reception aesthetics, it also matters *where* the author places a particular quotation.

Finally, Weiss discerningly emphasizes that Hebrews represents an "exposition of Scripture and preaching on the basis of certain passages of Scripture." Here he is referring to the readings from Scripture that underlie the sermon and are taken from a reading cycle. They are to be interpreted—and this is the central function of the sermon—regardless of whether they are explicitly mentioned in the homily or not. If the latter is the case, for example, a Torah reading is not quoted in the sermon because the reading was given before the delivery of the sermon, then it is of central importance to try to identify this reading because in it lies the hermeneutical key that unlocks not only the meaning of the entire text but also that of its individual parts, including the function of the quotations and allusions. Indications of the existence of a Torah reading that may underlie the sermon and that is not cited in the text can be provided, among other things, by the quotations because quite often they are not themselves pre-texts, but rather corresponding receptions of an older pre-text, that is, a certain narrative from Scripture, which may well be the Torah reading sought. If this is true, and I assume it is in Hebrews, then the "backbone" of Hebrews would not be the quotations but the underlying texts mentioned by Weiss.[4]

Israel's Scripture in Hebrews

Introducing Scripture

Quotations

Following NA[28], we start with a tabular overview of the marked as well as unmarked quotations, which makes various things optically visible as an aid to

---

4. That the quotations are the "backbone" of Hebrews has been asserted by Gert J. Steyn, e.g., in "An Overview of the Extent and Diversity of Methods Utilised by the Author of Hebrews When Using the Old Testament," *Neot* 42, no. 2 (2008): 327–52, esp. 327, 329.

understanding.[5] First of all, the placement of the quotations within the text. There are of course different views on the structure of Hebrews, but for present purposes I choose to follow Erich Grässer's compromise formula, according to which, in Hebrews "irrespective of all possible differentiated dispositions, a three-level basic scheme in the structure becomes apparent": Heb 1:1–6:20; 7:1–10:18; and 10:19–13:25.[6] This fits well with the genre criticism of synagogal homilies, which usually assumes a division into three parts, an introduction, a central part, and a conclusion, while introductions as well as conclusions can be in two parts, as in my proposal.[7] In a concentric structure like that of Hebrews, however, the main statement lies in the middle of the text, in my view in the eighth chapter, where the exposition must begin, and the text to the right of it mirrors—and contrasts with—that to the left. A quotation placed in the center is thus of special importance from the point of view of genre as well as structural criticism.

Table 20.1. Marked and Unmarked Citations in Hebrews

Hebrews	Marked Citations	Unmarked Citations	Persons in Hebrews	Original Context
1:5a	Ps 2:7 LXX		Jesus	Royal Psalm
1:5b	2 Sam 7:14 (1 Chr 17:13)		Jesus	David
1:6	Deut 32:43 LXX (Ps 96:7 LXX)		Jesus (angels)	Song of Moses
1:7	Ps 103:4 LXX		Angels	Psalm of David
1:8–9	Ps 44:7–8 LXX		Jesus	

---

5. I have decided to follow NA[28] because the research often offers slightly different counts while failing to provide the criteria on which they are based. I am interested in transparency, and I am aware of the fact that in certain places the counting can be different, e.g., that the compound quotations in Heb 2:13; 10:30; or 10:37–38 may not be counted as two, but only as single quotations.

6. Erich Grässer, *An die Hebräer*, 3 vols., EKK 17 (Zurich: Benziger; Neukirchen-Vluyn: Neukirchener Verlag, 1990–1997), 1:28–29. I have dealt in depth with the structure of Hebrews and its research in, among other places, Gelardini, *"Verhärtet eure Herzen nicht": Der Hebräer, eine Synagogenhomilie zu Tischa be-Aw*, BibInt 83 (Leiden: Brill, 2007), 11–84, 353–57.

7. For more details on the topic of synagogue homilies, cf. Gelardini, *"Verhärtet eure Herzen nicht,"* 123–68, esp. 138; but also Gelardini, "Hebrews, Homiletics, and Liturgical Scripture Interpretation," in *Reading the Epistle to the Hebrews: A Resource for Students*, ed. Eric F. Mason and Kevin B. McCruden, RBS 66 (Atlanta: Society of Biblical Literature, 2011), 121–43.

Israel's Scriptures in Hebrews

1:10–12	Ps 101:26–28 LXX		Jesus	
1:13	Ps 109:1 LXX		Jesus	Psalm of David
2:6–8	Ps 8:5–7 LXX		Jesus	Psalm of David
2:12	Ps 21:23 LXX		Jesus	Psalm of David
2:13a	Isa 8:17 (12:2 LXX; 2 Sam 22:3)		Jesus	
2:13b	Isa 8:18 LXX		Jesus	
3:5		Num 12:7 LXX	Exodus generation	
3:7–11	Ps 95:7–11		Exodus generation	Kadesh-Barnea (Num 13–14)
3:15	Ps 95:7–8		Exodus generation	Kadesh-Barnea (Num 13–14)
4:3	Ps 95:11		Exodus generation	Kadesh-Barnea (Num 13–14)
4:4	Gen 2:2 LXX		God	Sinai (Exod 31:12–17; 35:1–3)
4:5	Ps 95:11		Exodus generation	Kadesh-Barnea (Num 13–14)
4:7	Ps 95:7–8		Exodus generation	Kadesh-Barnea (Num 13–14)
5:5	Ps 2:7 LXX		Jesus	Royal Psalm
5:6	Ps 110:4		Jesus	Psalm of David
6:14	Gen 22:17		Abraham	Moriah
Subtotal Introduction 20		1		
7:1–3		Gen 14:17–20	Abraham (Melchizedek)	Delivery of Lot
7:4		Gen 14:20	Abraham (Melchizedek)	Delivery of Lot
7:17	Ps 110:4		Jesus	Psalm of David
7:21	Ps 110:4		Jesus	Psalm of David
8:5	Exod 25:40		Exodus generation	Sinai (Exod 32–34)
8:8–12	Jer 31:31–34 (longest)		Exodus generation	Sinai (Exod 32–34) Kadesh-Barnea (Num 13–14)
9:20	Exod 24:8		Exodus generation	Sinai (Exod 32–34)

10:5–7	Ps 40:7–9		Jesus	
10:16–17	Jer 31:33–34		Exodus generation	Sinai (Exod 32–34) Kadesh-Barnea (Num 13–14)
Subtotal center 7		*2*		
10:28		Deut 17:6	Exodus generation	Idolatry
10:30a	Deut 32:35		Exodus generation	Idolatry
10:30b	Deut 32:36 LXX (Ps 134:14 LXX)		Exodus generation	Song of Moses, idolatry
10:37a		Isa 26:20 LXX	Exodus generation	God's wrath
10:37b		Hab 2:3 LXX	Exodus generation	God's wrath
10:38		Hab 2:4 LXX	Exodus generation	God's wrath
11:18	Gen 21:12 LXX		Isaac (Abraham)	
11:21		Gen 47:31 LXX	Jacob (Abraham)	
12:5–6	Prov 3:11–12		Exodus generation	
12:15		Deut 29:17 LXX	Exodus generation	Idolatry
12:21	Deut 9:19 (shortest)		Exodus generation	Sinai (Exod 33)
12:26	Hag 2:6 LXX		Exodus generation	Second Temple
12:29		Deut 4:24 (9:3)	Exodus generation	Idolatry
13:5	Deut 31:6, 8 (1 Chr 28:20)		Exodus generation	Moab
13:6	Ps 117:6 LXX		Exodus generation	
Subtotal conclusion 8		*7*		
Total	**35**	**10**		

Israel's Scriptures in Hebrews

From the bottom column of totals in table 20.1, we see that there are a total of forty-five citations in the text, thirty-five marked and ten unmarked, with a minimum of one and a maximum of eight of them in each chapter.[8]

Most of the marked quotations are in the introduction, Heb 1–6 (twenty); they are the second most numerous in the concluding section, 10:19–13 (eight), and the least numerous in the short middle section, 7–10:18 (seven). What is immediately noticeable are the numerous Psalms citations in the introduction (fourteen), which reminds us of the (later frequently attested) rules of production aesthetics related to synagogue homilies, which expects a stringing together of psalms, not seldom in the form of catenae, as in Heb 1, and often as a lead-in to the opening verse of the Torah reading, usually included toward the end of the introduction.[9] In contrast, most of the unmarked quotations are found in the final section (seven); they are the second most numerous in the middle section (two) and least numerous in the opening section (one).

Also noticeable are the relatively frequent (underlined) repetitions of some marked quotations, without which they would number only twenty-seven in total. There are repetitions only in the introduction and in the center, not in the conclusion. They are the following: twice Ps 2:7 LXX as well as thrice each Ps 95:7–8 and 95:11; and in the center thrice Ps 110:4 (once in the introduction) as well as twice Jer 31:33–34.[10] Repetitions represent emphases, and priority is given to Jer 31:(31)33–34 not only because of its double repetition but also because of its length—with 135 words, it is the longest scriptural quotation in the whole of the New Testament (the shortest comprises three words)—and also because of its central position. Here we are reminded of (later) reconstructions of the triennial reading cycle, which has a prophetic reading from Jer 31:33–40 at the beginning of the month of Av, a text portion that according to production aesthetics had to be placed in the middle section of the homily.[11] Second most important among the repeated quotations is Ps 95:7–11 in the second part of the introduction (Heb 3–6) also because of its striking length and its pairing with

---

8. In the case of various marked quotations, NA[28] offers several possibilities without deciding on one or the other, such as 2 Sam 7:14 in Heb 1:5, where it also gives 1 Chr 17:13. Although I list the variants in the table, they are not included in the count here.

9. Even if such catenae lead to a Torah opening verse, they do not have to carry the theme of the Torah reading; on the contrary, the further away from it they were, the more artistic a peticha was considered to be; the conclusion that the citations could refer to a "possible liturgical background or context" is also reached by Gert J. Steyn in *A Quest for the Assumed LXX Vorlage of the Explicit Quotations in Hebrews*, FRLANT 235 (Göttingen: Vandenhoeck & Ruprecht, 2011), 407–12 et passim.

10. The Song of Moses is also quoted three times (Deut 32:1–43), but different verses.

11. For more details on readings from the prophets and its placement in the text, cf. Gelardini, "*Verhärtet eure Herzen nicht*," 123–68, esp. 135, 139.

Gen 2:2. The third most important quotation is Ps 110:4, not because of its length, but because of its pairing with Gen 14:17–20.

Sources of Quotations

Next, we examine which books of the Tanak Hebrews quotes or does not quote from. Again I follow appendix III of NA[28].

Table 20.2. Works Quoted in Hebrews

Tanak	Hebrews Marked Citations	Unmarked Citations	Total
Tanak	35	10	45[12]
Torah[13]	10	7	17
Genesis	3	3	6
Exodus	2		2
Numbers		1	1
Deuteronomy	5	3	8
Nevi'im[14]	6	3	9
1–2 Samuel	1		1
Isaiah	2	1	3
Jeremiah	2		2
Habakkuk		2	2
Haggai	1		1
Ketuvim[15]	19		19
Psalms	18		18
Proverbs	1		1

The thirty-five marked quotations consist of 807 words, the ten unmarked ones of 88, together totaling 895 words. This results in a very considerable share of 18 percent of the total text, consisting of 4,955 words.

From the Torah, Hebrews quotes Deuteronomy the most, as the other New Testament texts do (forty-seven). With regard to the Nevi'im, there are no conspi-

---

12. The citations in the other New Testament writings sum to 416, which includes the variants, but since NA[28] does not specifically identify them in appendix III, this produces some inaccuracy in comparison with Hebrews.

13. There are no quotations from Leviticus.

14. There are no quotations from Joshua, Judges, 1–2 Kings, Ezekiel, Hosea, Joel, Amos, Obadiah, Jonah, Micah, Nahum, Zephaniah, Zechariah, or Malachi.

15. There are no quotations from Job, Song of Songs, Ruth, Lamentations, Ecclesiastes, Esther, Daniel, Ezra-Nehemiah, or 1–2 Chronicles.

cuities, except in comparison with the rest of the New Testament, which quotes with striking frequency from Isaiah (eighty-six), while Hebrews hardly quotes from it at all. With regard to the Ketuvim, Hebrews is in line with the rest of the New Testament, with both giving the most space to the Psalms (eighty-two). With regard to psalm citations in Hebrews, it is worth noting that a relatively large number of Davidic psalms are used (Pss 8; 21; 40; 103; 109; 110), as well as two royal psalms (Pss 2; 40) that are particularly relevant to the temple cult and its liturgy.[16] Hebrews—unlike some other texts of the New Testament—quotes only from the canonical writings and not from the deuterocanonical works or the Old Testament Pseudepigrapha (six), nor from the other writings of Second Temple Judaism, nor—unlike Philo, for example—from the Greek writings.

Only nine of the quotations used in Hebrews are found in the rest of the New Testament, with the greatest overlaps in relation to Romans (four) and Acts (three): Ps 2:7 LXX (Acts), 2 Sam 7:14 (2 Corinthians, Revelation), Deut 32:43 LXX (Romans), Ps 109:1 LXX (Matthew twice; Mark; Luke; Acts; 1 Corinthians), Ps 8:5–7 LXX (1 Corinthians, Ephesians [8:7]), Deut 32:35 (Luke, Romans), Hab 2:4 LXX (Galatians, Romans), Gen 21:12 LXX (Romans), Deut 29:17 (Acts).

Introductory Formulas of Quotations

Let us now turn to the introductory formulas of the marked quotations. The example from Heb 1:8, for instance, reads, "But of the Son he says, 'Your throne, O God, is forever and ever, and the righteous scepter is the scepter of your kingdom.'" Compared to introductory formulas in the rest of the New Testament, it is noticeable that the usual elements of formula quotations, such as the noun "Scripture" (γραφή), or corresponding verbal usage, such as "it is written" (γέγραπται), are absent. A special feature of Hebrews is that it prefers to use *verba dicendi* throughout instead, and mostly in the present tense actualizing the pre-text, that is, "say" (twenty-three times λέγω: fifteen times pres., thrice aor., five times pf.; twice λαλέω in aor.; once φημί, pres.), "address" (once διαλέγομαι, pres.) and "attest" (once μαρτυρέω, pres.). In two cases these verbs are in combination with other verbs, namely "testify" (διαμαρτύρομαι, aor.) and "promise" (ἐπαγγέλλομαι, pf.). In some cases (four times) an introductory formula is applied to two (thrice) or three quotations (once). Often—as in the example above—either the addressee or the speaker is mentioned, rarely both and also often neither of them; what is missing (in parentheses in table 20.3) has to be reconstructed from the near context, which is not always possible with certainty.

---

16. Erich Zenger, Heinz-Josef Fabry, and Georg Braulik, *Einleitung in das Alte Testament*, 3rd ed., Kohlhammer Studienbücher Theologie 1.1 (Stuttgart: Kohlhammer, 1998), 309–26, esp. 318.

The extraction and recontextualization of pre-texts presents an opportunity for modification with regard to speakers as well as addressees, which the author is not slow to make use of.[17] We shall examine a concrete example and its implications for hermeneutics in more detail below, in "Using Scripture." In total, seven speakers present themselves of whom God speaks most often (sixteen times), then—and evidently on behalf of the former—the Holy Spirit (six times), then Jesus and Moses (twice each), the addressees, a someone as well as an it (once each). God addresses different ones, but most often his Son (six times), then the church (five times), then the angels and Abraham (twice each), and Moses (once). The Holy Spirit always speaks to the addressees, Jesus to God, Moses to the fathers, the addressees to themselves, the someone to God, and the it to the Son. In overview, the introductory formulas of the thirty-five marked quotations in Hebrews appear as follows:

Table 20.3. Introductory Formulas of Marked Quotations in Hebrews

Hebrews	Passage	Speaker	Verb (tense)	Addressees
1:5a	Ps 2:7 LXX	(God)	said (λέγω, aor.)	Son
1:5b	2 Sam 7:14			
1:6	Deut 32:43 LXX	(God)	says (λέγω, pres.)	angels
1:7	Ps 103:4 LXX	(God)	λέγω (pres.)	angels
1:8–9	Ps 44:7–8 LXX	(God)	(λέγω)	Son
1:10–12	Ps 101:26–28 LXX			
1:13	Ps 109:1 LXX	(God)	has said (λέγω, pf.)	(Son)
2:6–8	Ps 8:5–7 LXX	someone	testified (διαμαρτύρομαι, aor.), λέγω (pres.)	(God)
2:12	Ps 21:23 LXX	(Son)	λέγω (pres.)	(God)
2:13a	Isa 8:17			
2:13b	Isa 8:18 LXX			
3:7–11	Ps 95:7–11	(God through Holy Spirit)	λέγω (pres.)	(addressees)

---

17. An overview of speakers and addressees of all quotations in the original context is provided by Markus-Liborius Hermann, *Die "hermeneutische Stunde" des Hebräerbriefs: Schriftauslegung in Spannungsfeldern*, HBS 72 (Freiburg im Breisgau: Herder, 2013), 60–61.

3:15	Ps 95:7–8	(God through Holy Spirit)	λέγω (pres.)	(addressees)
4:3	Ps 95:11	(God through Holy Spirit)	λέγω (pf.)	(addressees)
4:4	Gen 2:2 LXX	(God through Holy Spirit)	λέγω (pf.)	(addressees)
4:5	Ps 95:11			
4:7	Ps 95:7–8	(Holy Spirit through David)	λέγω (pres.)	(addressees)
5:5	Ps 2:7 LXX	(God)	said (λαλέω, aor.)	Son
5:6	Ps 110:4	(God)	λέγω (pres.)	(Son)
6:14	Gen 22:17	God	λέγω (pres.)	Abraham
7:17	Ps 110:4	it is	attested (μαρτυρέω, pres.)	priest (Jesus)
7:21	Ps 110:4	Lord (God)	λέγω (pres.)	Priest (Jesus)
8:5	Exod 25:40	(God)	says (φημί, pres.)	Moses
8:8–12	Jer 31:31–34	Lord (God)	λέγω (pres.)	his house (addressees)
9:20	Exod 24:8	Moses	λέγω (pres.)	people (fathers)
10:5–7	Ps 40:7–9	(Jesus)	λέγω (pres.)	God
10:16–17	Jer 31:33–34	Holy Spirit	λέγω (pf.)	(addressees)
10:30a	Deut 32:35	Lord (God)	λέγω (aor.)	people (addressees)
10:30b	Deut 32:36 LXX			
11:18	Gen 21:12 LXX	(God)	λαλέω (aor.)	Abraham
12:5–6	Prov 3:11–12	Lord (God)	addresses (διαλέγομαι, pres.)	sons [and daughters] (addressees)
12:21	Deut 9:19	Moses	λέγω (aor.)	(fathers)
12:26	Hag 2:6 LXX	(God)	has promised (ἐπαγγέλλομαι, pf.), λέγω (pres.)	(addressees)
13:5	Deut 31:6, 8	(God)	λέγω (pf.)	(addressees)
13:6	Ps 117:6 LXX	(addressees)	λέγω (pres.)	(themselves)

The author's handling of unmarked quotations is much freer. Often he rearranges sentences of the pre-text, and sometimes he adapts or supplements quotations or omits something or takes only a part of it. As an example of a rearrangement, we may compare the quotation from Hab 2:4 LXX in Heb 10:38:

> Heb 10:38
> But my righteous one will live by faith,
> and if he shrinks back, I take no pleasure in him. (NET)

> Hab 2:4 LXX
> If it draws back, my soul is not pleased in it.
> But the just shall live by my faith. (NETS)

Allusions

With regard to verbal as well as conceptual allusions, NA[28] has done good preliminary work and compiled the findings in the apparatus of the outer margin and in the aforementioned appendix III, respectively. The latter, as mentioned in our introduction, counts 282 allusions, but does not distinguish between verbal and conceptual ones.[18] Most of the allusions listed in NA[28] are verbal, however, and often several sources are listed for one allusion. To illustrate them in detail would go beyond the scope of this chapter, but it seems important to mention that at first sight they represent a counterweight to the quotations taken mainly from the Ketuvim. Here, with 126 entries, the Torah clearly has the upper hand, most notably Genesis (38), followed by Exodus (36), then Leviticus and Numbers (20 each), and finally Deuteronomy (12). In second place are the Nevi'im with 75 entries, with most from Isaiah (19)—barely represented in the citations as we recall—followed by Jeremiah (10), and Joshua and Judges (9 each). The Ketuvim come to 43 entries, and as with the quotations, the Psalms again take top place (26), followed by Daniel as well as the Chronicles (6 each). Finally, unequal to the quotations, here come entries from the deuterocanonical works as well as the Old Testament Pseudepigrapha (38), most from the books of Maccabees (12), followed by Sirach (9), and again no entries for the Greek writings. There are quite a few of the allusions listed in NA[28] that I cannot follow. On the other hand, I repeatedly see gaps. In view of the "abundance of virtual quotations and references to biblical texts and subjects" mentioned by Weiss, I want to show at selected places in "Using Scripture," below, where in my view NA[28] is to be confirmed, questioned, or supplemented.

In conclusion to this formal overview, it should be mentioned that Hebrews makes references to Scripture not merely by quotations and allusions but also by

---

18. The number of allusions differs from the apparatus on the outer margin, which counts four allusions more, namely 286.

explicit mention of it or parts of it. Thus, for example, the author refers to Scripture as a whole as "word" (λόγος, 2:2; ῥῆμα, 6:5), "book, scroll" (βιβλίον, 9:19; κεφαλίδι βιβλίου, 10:7), or "law" (νόμος, νομοθετέω, 7:5, 11, 12, 16, 19, 28 [twice]; 8:4, 10; 9:19, 22; 10:1, 8, 16, 28). And to parts of it as "commandment(s)" (ἐντολή, 7:5, 16, 18; 9:19) or "regulations" (δικαίωμα, 9:1, 10). We are now equipped to turn next to the contents of the quotations, including those contents to which the quotations are referring beyond themselves.

Using Scripture

Major Themes in and beyond Hebrews' Citations

Let us begin with the content of the longest, repeated, and most weighty quotation because of its central position, Jer 31:(31)33–34. It belongs to the so-called book of consolation comprising Jer 30–31, which has as its basic theme the return of the exiles of Israel to their homeland as well as the rebuilding of Jerusalem.[19] The quotation begins with a promise of a new covenant addressed to Jeremiah's addressees, one that is made to apply to the addressees of Hebrews: "The days are surely coming, says the Lord, when I will establish a new covenant with the house of Israel and with the house of Judah" (8:8). It is to be a different covenant, and here comes the reference to the older narrative, "not like the covenant that I made with their ancestors [πατράσιν αὐτῶν], on the day when I took them by the hand to lead them out of the land of Egypt; for they did not continue in my covenant, and so I had no concern for them, says the Lord" (8:9). In this covenant, God will put the laws into the minds of each of his household and write them on their hearts, so that everyone—"from the least of them to the greatest"—will know God and he will be their God and they will be his people (8:10-11). The result will be God's forgiveness of all their sins because of his mercy (8:12). The time referred to by "out of Egypt" is clear: it is the time of the wilderness, as is clear from the beginning of this Jeremiah chapter, "The people who survived the sword found grace in the wilderness; when Israel sought for rest" (Jer 31:2).[20] The exodus community, however, passed through many deserts during the forty years, from that one to the Reed Sea (Exod 13:18) and on to the steppes of Moab (Num 33:50). Which desert is meant in the quotation does not take long to guess, for that too is clear, namely, the one where "I made the covenant with their ancestors," and that is the

---

19. Roland Gradwohl, *Bibelauslegungen aus jüdischen Quellen*, 4 vols., CTB 37–38 (Stuttgart: Calwer, 2017), 2:293.

20. Susan E. Docherty, *The Use of the Old Testament in Hebrews: A Case Study in Early Jewish Bible Interpretation*, WUNT 2/260 (Tübingen: Mohr Siebeck, 2009), 194.

wilderness of Sinai (Exod 19:1; Num 33:15). And it is to this place, and *only* this place, that the statement "for they did not continue in my covenant" applies, for here the exodus community had broken the covenant through idolatry (Exod 32). In the wilderness of Kadesh, on the other hand, it was God who abandoned the covenant with the adults of the exodus community and no longer wished to fulfill the promise of giving the land to them (Num 13:26; 33:37). Taken out of its context, Jer 31:31-34 gives the impression that "grace" befell only Jeremiah's addressees, but this is by no means so, as is clear from the Jeremiah context of the quotation and especially from the aforementioned Jer 31:2, for God's people did not remain without covenant from the time at Sinai until the time of Jeremiah. Grace was also experienced by the sinful exodus community at Sinai (Exod 34:6-7), where the covenant had been renewed by God despite the serious transgression against him (Exod 34:10), through the mediation of Moses. This grace of God is thus the central message for all three contexts and addressees, for those at Sinai, for those in Babylonian exile after the destruction of the First Temple (Jer 31:34 in Heb 8:12), as well as for those in Roman exile after the destruction of the Second Temple (4:16). Weiss was thus once again correct in his prioritization of consolation over exhortation. For Jeremiah's addressees grace is connected with the promise of the return home and the rebuilding of Jerusalem, as it may be for the addressees of Hebrews as well.[21] Three contexts, three times and places, are distinguished from one another, and it is important to take note of this differentiation. At the same time, however, these three contexts are brought into relationship with one another by their superimposition. In this way, hermeneutically speaking, the adaptation of the quoted text for the addressees in Hebrews functions by integrating the present into two points in past time while interpreting the former through the latter two. Jeremiah 31:(31)33-34 in Heb 8:8-12 and 10:16-17 thus refers to the events at Sinai, the covenant making there, the covenant breaking through idolatry as well as God's consequent wrath, Moses's mediation, as well as God's gracious covenant renewal.

The Jeremiah quotation, however, is not the only one that refers to Sinai; explicit mention of covenant worship is also made in Exod 24:8 in Heb 9:20, of the instructions for establishing worship in Exod 25:40 in Heb 8:5, and of Moses's fear after idolatry in Deut 9:19 in Heb 12:21. As David Allen correctly notes, the statement in Deut 9:19 is one that does not occur in Exod 32-34 in this fashion and therefore probably carries elements of Oral Torah.[22] I will return to this be-

---

21. I have commented extensively on the possible historical situation in Gelardini, "Verhärtet eure Herzen nicht," parts 2 and 3.
22. David M. Allen, *Deuteronomy and Exhortation in Hebrews: A Study in Narrative Re-Presentation*, WUNT 2/238 (Tübingen: Mohr Siebeck, 2008), 62-66.

low. A whole series of other quotations speak of God's wrath, judgment as well as punishment, and, as the additional information in table 20.1 shows, stand in the context of and as a consequence of idolatry so that they too refer directly or indirectly to Sinai. These are Deut 17:6 in Heb 10:28; Deut 32:35 in Heb 10:30a; Deut 32:36 LXX in Heb 10:30b; Isa 26:20 LXX in Heb 10:37a; Hab 2:3 LXX in Heb 10:37b; Hab 2:4 LXX in Heb 10:38; Prov 3:11–12 in Heb 12:5–6; Deut 29:17 LXX in Heb 12:15; Hag 2:6 LXX in Heb 12:26; and Deut 4:24 in Heb 12:29. Finally, the texts in Heb 12:18–21 as well as Heb 13 also refer to Sinai, as I have recently shown with regard to the latter.[23] Not counting allusions and less obvious passages, we come to a total of at least fifteen quotations and two passages that refer to Sinai. It is thus the place most frequently referred to in Hebrews, both directly and indirectly, especially the events surrounding the making of the covenant there, the breaking of the covenant—including its consequences—as well as the gracious renewal of the covenant. Thus, there are good reasons to assume a Torah reading from Exod 32–34 underlies Hebrews.[24]

Like Jer 31:(31)33–34, the second longest and most repeated quotation in Hebrews, Ps 95:7–11, refers to an older narrative:[25] It begins with a warning to the psalm's addressees not to do the same as their ancestors, meaning the same exodus generation to which the Jeremiah quotation had already referred: "Today, if you hear his voice, do not harden your hearts as in the rebellion, as on the day of testing in the wilderness, where your ancestors [πατέρες ὑμῶν] put me to the test, though they had seen my works" (3:7–9). The psalmist goes on to say in 3:10 that God was angry with that generation, for going astray they had not been able to discern his ways, whereupon God had made the decision, "in my anger I swore, 'They will not enter my rest'" (3:11). In the word "wilderness" the place is named, and with the statement "They will not enter my rest," it is also clear of which wilderness we are speaking here, namely, the above-mentioned one

---

23. Gabriella Gelardini, "Charting 'Outside the Camp' with Edward W. Soja: Critical Spatiality and Hebrews 13," in *Hebrews in Contexts*, ed. Gabriella Gelardini and Harold W. Attridge, AJEC 91 (Leiden: Brill, 2016), 210–37.

24. More recent reconstructions of the triennial reading cycle show the presence of readings from these chapters, even paired with passages from Jer 31, which logically unites the themes of covenant breaking and renewal. For more on the Torah reading and its pairings, see Gelardini, *"Verhärtet eure Herzen nicht,"* 128–47.

25. A very good article on the text and reception of this psalm has been presented by Martin Karrer, "Die Väter in der Wüste: Text und Rezeption von LXX Ps 94 in Hebr 3," in *Text - Textgeschichte - Textwirkung: Festschrift zum 65. Geburtstag von Siegfried Kreuzer*, ed. Thomas Wagner, Jonathan M. Robker, and Frank Ueberschaer, AOAT 419 (Münster: Ugarit-Verlag, 2014), 427–58. Robert G. Rayburn II too has drawn attention to the underlying narrative of Ps 95 (*"Yesterday, Today and Forever": The Narrative World of Ψ 94 [Ps 95] as a Hermeneutical Key to Hebrews* [Berlin: Lang, 2019]).

called Kadesh, where God had made this decision with the exodus generation in mind, with the exception of Caleb and Joshua. Since this decision comes in the form of an oath, which cancels the central promise of the giving of the land for the adults of the exodus generation, this statement is also to be understood as a termination of the renewed Sinai covenant with them. While this generation of fathers still experienced grace at Sinai, that is, were given a second chance, they no longer do so in Kadesh.

The quoted verses form the conclusion of Ps 95, and in the context of its beginning, verses 1–6, it becomes clear that the violation is ultimately the consequence of not having recognized and acknowledged God as the one he is, namely "a great king above all gods" (Ps 95:3). The example of the exodus generation in Kadesh, then, is used to suggest knowledge of God to the addressees of the psalm as well as to those of Hebrews because it is the very expression of a covenant relationship. So here again we see how three contexts are superimposed and related. If we take the twenty quotations that refer to Sinai (fifteen) and Kadesh (five) and add those that take place in Hazeroth, Num 12:7 LXX in Heb 3:5—where Moses's siblings, Miriam and Aaron, question his authority—as well as in Moab (Deut 31:6, 8 in Heb 13:5) and with a similar theme Ps 117:6 LXX in Heb 13:6, we arrive at a total of twenty-three quotations, which is more than half of those that refer to the "wilderness generation" (see table 20.1).

The largest group of quotations, which refers to the desert generation, is followed by the second largest, namely those sixteen quotations that have "Jesus" (see table 20.1)—in contrast to the angels, among other things—as their content. They establish Jesus's divinity (twice Ps 2:7 LXX in Heb 1:5a; 5:5; 2 Sam 7:14 in Heb 1:5b), as well as his righteous and eternal rule (Ps 44:7–8 LXX in Heb 1:8–9; Ps 101:26–28 LXX in Heb 1:10–12), his mediatorial role as royal priest on behalf of the children entrusted to him (Ps 21:23 LXX in Heb 2:12; Isa 8: 17 in Heb 2:13a; Isa 8:18 LXX in Heb 2:13b; thrice Ps 110:4 in Heb 5:6; 7:17, 21), which includes his humiliation below the angels and sacrifices (Deut 32:43 LXX in Heb 1:6; Ps 103:4 LXX in Heb 1:7; Ps 8:5–7 LXX in Heb 2:6–8; Ps 40:7–9 in Heb 10:5–7), as well as his consequent exaltation to God's side (Ps 109:1 LXX in Heb 1:13). Significantly, Jesus is compared positively to Moses in 3:1–6. Just as Moses was faithful to his house—once again the exodus community—Jesus is faithful to his house, the addressees of Hebrews. In other words, for the addressees of Hebrews, Jesus seems to do something comparable to what Moses did for the exodus generation at Sinai: covenant renewal after apostasy (3:12). I will return to this below.

A third group of five quotations has "Abraham" (see table 20.1) and his descendants as its theme, that is, God's covenant with Abraham (Gen 22:17 in Heb 6:14), including the promise of his numerous posterity via Isaac (Gen 21:12 LXX in Heb 11:18), his blessing by Melchizedek (twice Gen 14:[17–]20 in

Heb 7:1–3, 4), and the blessing of Joseph's sons by Abraham's grandson Jacob (Gen 47:31 LXX in Heb 11:21). While a connection between the first and second groups of quotations is more obvious, the role of this group is less readily apparent. There is one connection, however, and that is in God's covenant with Abraham, on the basis of which the exodus from Egypt had taken place. I will also come back to this below.

A final quotation has "God" as its content (see table 20.1), speaking of his rest (Gen 2:2 LXX in Heb 4:4), admittedly in an ambiguous sense. "Rest" can also, in fact, as we recall from Jer 31:2, for example, stand for the promised land. But the observance of Sabbath rest is also a "covenant sign" (Exod 31:17); it frames the narrative of Exod 32–34 (Exod 31:12–17; 35:1–3) and is by its very essence precisely the opposite of denial of God and apostasy, namely, acknowledgment of God and faith in him as the Creator who brought forth the world out of nothing. Again, therefore, we see a connection with the desert generation, to whom the assurance of this rest had been given a second time at Sinai, though it was denied the third time at Kadesh. However, the author does not yet seem to see his addressees at Kadesh, which is why he promises them the remaining rest for a second time in analogy to the narrative at Sinai.

The content of the quotations and to what it refers has thus shown that virtually all of them can be placed in the context of the exodus, especially with the covenant breaking and covenant renewal at Sinai. So let us next examine the narrative events of the desert section from the Sea of Reeds to Kadesh, but especially those of Exod 32–34, to see what thematic overlap there is between the events at Sinai and Hebrews with its quotations, interpretations, and adaptations.

The Underlying Narrative's Themes Compared to Hebrews

God's relationship with Israel is a covenant relationship from the beginning. God makes a covenant with Abraham, promising him two things, "descendants as numerous as the stars of heaven" (Gen 15:5) and the "land from the river of Egypt to the great river, the river Euphrates" for those descendants (Gen 15:18). Four generations later (Gen 15:16), Israel being in Egypt at this time, the first of the two promises—their multiplication—has been fulfilled (Exod 1:7). However, their enslavement there by the Egyptians is hard on them, and "God heard their groaning, and God remembered his covenant with Abraham, Isaac, and Jacob" (Exod 2:24; cf. also 6:5). God sees the time has come to fulfill the second part of his promise, and for this very purpose (Exod 3:8, 17) he calls his "servant" Moses (Exod 14:31; cf. Heb 2; 3:1–6; 13:7–8, 17), announcing to him his will for Israel: "I will bring you into the land that I swore to give to Abraham, Isaac, and Jacob; I will give it to you for a possession. I am the Lord" (Exod 6:8; cf. also 13:11). The exodus from Egypt is then based on the Abrahamic covenant (cf. Heb 6:13–18), with the goal of fulfilling God's second promise to Abraham—the giving of the land (cf. Heb 6:19–20)![26]

The exodus occurs miraculously and is the occasion for great praise of God (Exod 7–15), but the passage through the first stretches of the desert—Shur (Mara), Sin, and Rephidim (Massah and Meribah)—to Sinai is less so (Exod 15:22–17:7), for Israel finds it difficult to trust God and repeatedly puts him to the test because of fearing a lack of provisions (cf. Heb 3–4). However, God proves patient; he wants the descendants of Abraham to become his people at Sinai, and in return he wants to become their God (Exod 6:7). So, after arriving there, he prepares them for a covenant with him (cf. Heb 12:18–21) by laws he imparts to them through Moses but also warnings (Exod 19–23), especially against idolatry (Exod 23:24), and affirms this with the words: "I am going to send an angel in front of you, to guard you on the way and to bring you to the place that I have prepared. Be attentive to him and listen to his voice; do not rebel against him, for he will not pardon your transgression; for my name is in him" (Exod 23:20–21).

After the covenant is established (Exod 24; cf. Heb 9:18–22), Moses goes to the mountain to receive instructions, especially for the establishment of God's abode (cf. Heb 8:5), so that he might dwell in the midst of his covenanted people, but also to receive the material sign of the covenant, the two covenant tablets (Exod 25–31). But when Moses is "delayed" from the people's point of view, they asked Aaron to make them a god in the form of a golden calf, which they worship as soon as it is finished (Exod 32:1–6). God is not unaware of this imminent apostasy (cf. Heb 3:12; 6:6), reveals it to Moses, and in his anger declares to him his intention to destroy Israel (Exod 32:7–10; cf. Heb 10:19–39). Moses recalls this moment in Deut 9:19 (cited in Heb 12:21), "And I was terrified on account of the wrath and the anger, because the Lord had been provoked against you to destroy you utterly" (NETS), and remembers God's warning, "for he will not pardon [Israel's] transgressions, for my name is in [the angel]" (Exod 23:21; cf. Heb 1:7; 2:2). Consequently, oral tradition has personified God's "wrath and anger" as God's angels, according to a variant from Pesiq. Rab. 10:9 that closely parallels Deut 9:19:

> When they made the golden calf, the angels came bringing accusations against them. Then it was that Moses said: For I was in dread of the (angels of) anger and hot displeasure (Deut 9:19). It was then also that Moses rose up forthwith, girded his loins with prayer and speaking in defense of Israel, sought mercy of

---

26. Gradwohl, *Bibelauslegungen aus jüdischen Quellen*, 2:294.

the Holy One, blessed be He. . . . Moses meant: Master of the universe, I know that they deserve death, in keeping with what thou didst say to me: He that sacrificeth unto the gods . . . shall be utterly destroyed (Exod 22:19). Nevertheless, I beseech Thee, deliver them from the destroying angels. Remember the merit of the Fathers: Remember Abraham, Isaac, and Israel, Thy servants to whom Thou didst swear by Thine own self (Exod 32:13).[27]

The quotation anticipates what Moses does in view of God's plan to destroy Israel by angels: He implores God for its sparing and its salvation (Exod 32:1–13; cf. Heb 1–2; 5:7–10; 9:28). Moses makes two arguments in this regard: first, that the Egyptians should not be able to say that God brought Israel out of Egypt to kill them, and second, he reminds God of his covenant with Abraham, Isaac, and Israel, including the two promises of numerous descendants and the giving of the land. The second argument makes clear that although the Sinai covenant is breached, the older Abrahamic covenant still exists and is still legally valid. Turning again to the above quotation, another midrashic elaboration emerges, for in his invocation, Moses emphasizes to God the "(faith) merits" of the patriarchs and uses them forensically as a means to atonement (cf. Heb 11–12:3).[28]

The seemingly impossible is achieved: God disregards his plan, and the one who prevented Israel's "deserved" destruction and made their salvation possible is the servant of God, Moses (Exod 32:14; cf. Heb 2:3, 10). But by no means does this let the Israelites off the hook, for the "covenant with the first" (בְּרִית רִאשֹׁנִים), as Lev 26:45 calls it, is broken (cf. Heb 8:7, 13; 9:1, 15, 18), and punishments for this grave offense cannot escape it.[29] Returning to the camp, Moses consequently breaks the tablets of the covenant, confronts Aaron, and calls those who are for the Lord—the Levites gather around him—to slay the guilty by the sword, about three thousand losing their lives that day (Exod 32:15–29; cf. Heb 4:12–13). Yet even those who "escaped the sword" (we recall Jer 31:2) are not safe in their covenant-breaking condition, so—after Moses has scolded them for their "great sin" (cf. Heb 3:13; 13:22)—he returns to God on the mountain in hopes of obtaining atonement (cf. Heb 2:17). To this end, he offers his own life to God (e.g., Exod 33:11; Deut 34:10–12; cf. Heb 9:15–10:18), but God refuses. The guilty

---

27. *Pesikta Rabbati: Discourses for Feasts, Fasts, and Special Sabbaths*, 2 vols., ed. William G. Braude, Yale Judaica series 18 (New Haven, CT: Yale University Press, 1968). For a rendering of Deut 9:19 that departs somewhat more from the original, see, e.g., Tg. Ps.-J.; and for listings of other examples Gelardini, "Verhärtet eure Herzen nicht," 214–18.

28. For further midrashic elaboration of this motif, see Gelardini, "Verhärtet eure Herzen nicht," 343–45.

29. Gradwohl, *Bibelauslegungen aus jüdischen Quellen*, 2:295.

would be called to account, God argues, and accordingly he strikes the Israelites with an additional calamity, a plague (cf. Heb 12:4–11).

Neither will he lead the people into the land any longer; his angel is to do so in his stead, a judgment that sends Israel into a state of immense grief (Exod 32:30–33:6; cf. Heb 12:11). Moses then takes his tent, pitching it outside the defiled camp and calling it the Tent of Meeting (cf. Heb. 9:23; 10:19–23; 13:9–16).[30] Here God speaks to Moses, showing him favor (Exod 33:12–17; cf. Heb 13:9), which the latter uses to plead for God's assistance—in place of the angel—in going up to the promised land. As a guarantee of God's favor, he asks to be allowed to see God's glory, which the latter grants him (Exod 33:7–23). Exodus 34 tells of this extraordinary encounter (cf. Heb 6:19–20), and furthermore of God's gracious forgiveness (cf. Heb 4:16), of the renewal of the Sinai covenant (Exod 34:10, 27; cf. Heb 8:6–12; 9:15; 10:16), including the new covenant tablets (Exod 34:1), and of the renewal of the pending covenant promise—the giving of the land or rest—in consequence (Exod 33:1–3, 14; cf. Heb 9:15).[31]

Moses's tireless dedication on behalf of Israel, at the risk of his life, earns him respect in the Torah, and even more so in the Oral Torah; and Philo dignifies him not only with the title of prophet (cf. Heb 1:1–2) but also with that of king (cf. Heb 1) and high priest (e.g., *Praem.* 53–54; *Mos.* 1.148; cf. Heb 2:17; 7), comparing, for example, his intercession in the tent outside with that of the high priest in the holy of holies on Yom Kippur (*Leg.* 2.54–56; cf. Heb 6:20; 8:1–2; 9:7, 25; 13:7–17). Indeed, Philo even wants him to be understood as divine, and Josephus also paraphrases him as suprahuman (*Ant.* 3.318, 320) and partaker and heir of all creation (cf. Heb 1; 2:5)![32] As Philo writes:

> And so, as he abjured the accumulation of lucre, and the wealth whose influence is mighty among men, God rewarded him by giving him instead the greatest and most perfect wealth. That is the wealth of the whole earth . . . as a portion well fitted for His heir. Therefore, each element obeyed him as its master, changed its natural properties and submitted to his command, and

---

30. A correlation of Heb 13 and Exod 33:7–11 has also been noted by David M. Allen, in "Why Bother Going Outside? The Use of the Old Testament in Heb 13:10–16," in *The Scriptures of Israel in Jewish and Christian Tradition: Essays in Honour of Maarten J. J. Menken*, ed. Bart J. Koet, Steve Moyise, and Joseph Verheyden, NovTSup 148 (Leiden: Brill, 2013), 239–52.

31. Jewish exegetes consistently hold that the "new" covenant is not really a new covenant but merely a renewed one. They base this on Jer 11:1–8, where "cursed" may be the one "who does not heed the words of this covenant, which I commanded your ancestors when I brought them out of the land of Egypt (Jer 11:3–4)." The goal of this covenant, too, remains the same, unchanged: "I will be their God, and they shall be my people" (Jer 31:33; Gradwohl, *Bibelauslegungen aus jüdischen Quellen*, 2:297–98). For the identity of these exegetes, see Gradwohl, 2:18–20.

32. Cf. in this regard also John Lierman, "Moses as Priest and Apostle in Hebrews 3:1–6," in Gelardini and Attridge, *Hebrews in Contexts*, 47–62.

this perhaps is no wonder. For if, as the proverb says, what belongs to friends is common, and the prophet is called the friend of God [Exod 33:11], . . . [a]gain, was not the joy of his partnership with the Father and Maker of all magnified also by the honour of being deemed worthy to bear the same title? For he was named god and king of the whole nation, and entered, we are told, into the darkness where God was. . . . Thus he beheld what is hidden from the sight of mortal nature, and, in himself and his life displayed for all to see, he has set before us, like some well-wrought picture, a piece of work beautiful and godlike, a model for those who are willing to copy it. (*Mos.* 1:155–158 [Colson])

The rest of the story is quickly told. After the covenant renewal (cf. Heb 12:22–29)—with the Sabbath rest as the sign of the covenant (Exod 31:12–17; 35:1–3; cf. Heb 4:4)—what had already been decreed before the breaking of the covenant is carried out, namely, the erection and inauguration of the tabernacle of God, also called the Tent of Meeting, like that of Moses outside the camp (Exod 33:7; 40:29), and the assumption of the cultic service by Aaron and his sons (Exod 35–40; cf. Heb 9:1–10:17). This is followed by the gift of all laws and ordinances (Lev 1–Num 10:10), and finally, in Num 10:11, the departure from Sinai. But Israel seems not to have learned from the grace and continues with complaining (Num 11). At Kadesh, within sight of the promised land, Moses sends out scouts, and their report again sets the people in revolt against God. Once again God wants to eliminate them, and once again Moses pleads for them to be spared. God hears him anew, but in view of his tenth testing by the people (Num 14:22), God's patience is irrevocably at its end, whereupon he terminates the Sinai covenant definitively—not with Israel and neither with the children of the exodus generation—but only with the adult ones among them (Num 12–14; cf. Heb 3–4; 6:4–8; 10:26–31).

Retellings of the Underlying Narrative

The above comparative remarks have, I hope, made it clear that Hebrews has great overlaps with the narrative of the desert generation and that this homily joins the chorus of those voices that retell the tragic events at Sinai in midrashic fashion and adapt them for their own addressees. Early examples of such retellings are already found in the Torah, especially in Deuteronomy (esp. 9:7–10:7), but then also in the prophetic book of Ezekiel (20:5–26), among the Scriptures also in Nehemiah (9:9–23), and most frequently in the Psalms (e.g., 78; 95 cited in Hebrews; 105–106; 135–136).[33] Josephus too picks up the desert tradition (cf. *Ant.* 3, while omitting Exod 32–34), and extensively so does Philo, as well as later

---

33. Examples of such retellings have been nicely collected, not least with regard to Heb 11,

targumim and midrashim, and the list could easily be extended.[34] The many retellings—which underline the importance of this narrative—vary, some closer to the original, others adding the later story, others again changing the order, and still others adding their own touches, for example, by linking the narrative to David. The latter is also important to Hebrews, more precisely, David's messianic descendant, whom the author sees—as other New Testament writings do—in Jesus. Like Moses at Sinai, Jesus acts as a royal high priest for the salvation of the people entrusted to him. But since Jesus, unlike Moses, does not belong to the tribe that was intended for the priesthood according to the law, we want finally to examine, as an example, the author's exegetical modus operandi, especially in chapter 7, by means of which he artfully overcomes this "flaw."

Genesis 12–15, Especially 14:17–20

The pairing of the unmarked quotation from Gen 14:17–20 with the marked quotation from Ps 110:4 is a distinctive feature of Hebrews. Not only because, according to NA[28], neither Gen 14 nor Ps 110:4 is cited in any other New Testament text but also because, with the inclusion of this pair, the only two passages in the Tanak that mention Melchizedek are here united with the third, intrabiblical mention. The author attaches special weight to Ps 110 in this regard not only because he quotes the fourth verse three times but also because he cites the first verse, which is much quoted in the New Testament, as well (see table 20.1), apart from several allusions to both verses in various other places in the text. So let us see what the author does with this pair of quotations, working our way chronologically through the three levels: first that in Genesis, followed by that in the psalm, and finally that of Heb 7 itself.

After his call, Abra(ha)m set out from Haran in the direction of Canaan, taking with him his nephew Lot, from his extended family. When he arrived at his destination, however, a famine that soon occurred forced him and his family to flee south to Egypt (Gen 12). When this had passed, Abraham—and Lot with him—returned wealthy, and "the land could not support both of them living together" (13:6). Hereupon, at Abraham's suggestion, they separated amicably, Lot choosing the fertile Jordan plain to the east near Sodom, while Abraham was content with Hebron to the west (Gen 13). At that time, however, the peasant king of Sodom—named Bera—formed an alliance with four other peasant kings of

---

by Pamela M. Eisenbaum, e.g., in *The Jewish Heroes of Christian History: Hebrews 11 in Literary Context*, SBLDS 156 (Atlanta: Scholars Press, 1997).

34. For examples see Gelardini, *"Verhärtet eure Herzen nicht,"* 211–29, 258–72, 303–15, 341–45, 364–73.

the surrounding area—those of Gomorrah, Admah, Zeboiim, and Bela—against their patron and Great King Chedorlaomer of Elam in the east, whereupon the latter, together with three allies, went to war against them.

As was to be expected, the renegades were defeated and plundered, with Abraham's nephew Lot among the captives taken away (14:1–12). The events were reported to Abraham by an escapee, whereupon he set out with 318 able-bodied men of his household, defeated Chedorlaomer and his allies, and brought back all the captives—Lot included—along with their possessions (14:13–16). On his return, the defeated vassal king of Sodom met him in the King's Valley near Jerusalem (cf. Josephus, *Ant.* 7.243), and so did Melchizedek—king of Salem (later Jerusalem, cf. Ps 76:3) and priest of God Most High—and not empty-handed like the loser Bera, but with bread and wine. This Melchizedek then blessed the victor Abraham in the name of the Most High God and also blessed the latter for delivering the oppressors into Abraham's hands. In response, Abraham gave him one tenth of his spoils (14:17–20).

Following this blessing, the defeated Bera demanded that Abraham return the prisoners of war but keep the booty. However, the king of Sodom did not seem to be entitled to make this demand because what Abraham had recaptured belonged to him as the victor. Abraham could then have seen himself as having reached his goal because before these events the possession of the country had already twice been promised to him by God (12:7, 14–17). But he reacted unexpectedly, and in this his true greatness was revealed, for it was not from the hand of Bera that he wanted to receive the gift of the land, but from the one in whose name he had been blessed by Melchizedek, God Most High (14:21–24). What also distinguished Abraham in this situation was the fact that he did not go to war because of apostasy, as Bera did, but, worthy of a progenitor, took the rescue of Lot as the occasion for his campaign. The victory made him proleptically "royal" and his renunciation "priestly," following the example of Melchizedek.[35] It is understandable that God immediately rewarded this attitude with a covenant (cf. Josephus *Ant.* 1.183), which included not only the promise of descendants but also the one of the land (Gen 15).

Psalm 110

It may be assumed that the author of the royal Ps 110, which comprises only seven verses, was aware of Gen 14 as well as a Melchizedek tradition extending beyond it; the important points of reference here seem to be Jerusalem and the kingship of David, to whom this psalm was attributed.

---

35. Benno Jacob, *Das Buch Genesis*, ed. in collaboration with the Leo Baeck Institute (Berlin: Schocken, 1934; repr., Stuttgart: Calwer, 2000), 367–89, esp. 386.

According to Hans-Joachim Kraus, there are four features that have given rise to the paramount importance of this psalm:[36] First, God, by means of a speaker, possibly an officiating prophet, invites the enthroned king to his side in verse 1. The "sitting at the right hand of God" then, together with the statement "the Lord sends out from Zion your mighty scepter" in verse 2, has a very specific meaning, namely, that the king is appointed to coregency in Jerusalem and receives a share in God's military might and victory through his exaltation and position of honor in God's sphere of power. Second, the king is accorded, among other things, a heavenly birth in verse 3, which is tantamount to a declaration of adoption. Third, the enthroned one is furthermore—and this is vouchsafed in the oath of God—in verse 4 irrevocably and eternally declared a priest "according to the order of Melchizedek." In pre-Israelite Jerusalem, the city king must have exercised priestly activity, which is why this official dignity is now conferred on the Israelite city king of Jerusalem. The "priesthood forever" ascribed, however, should not be misunderstood as messianic, Kraus argues, because it refers to the reigning and enthroned king of Israel and Judah. And fourth, finally, in verse 7 it is said that through the enthroned king and in front of him God, the world judge and war hero, will overcome all enemies.

Extrabiblical Melchizedek Traditions

Israel's Scriptures tell us only of a "priest-king" Abraham proleptically elevated by Melchizedek near Jerusalem and of the priest-king David enthroned there in the order of Melchizedek. It is therefore understandable that the information gaps left by these two texts with regard to such an important person have given rise to considerable narrative and theological creativity, some of it extrabiblical.[37]

There are remarks on Melchizedek in numerous Second Temple Judaism texts, in addition to Hebrews in the New Testament, and also in various Qumran texts, most extensively in 11Q13 (11QMelch). Here, for example, Melchizedek is a just and merciful ruler who promises redemption to captives and bears their sins. He is given divine or messianic attributes, will come at the end of days, on the day of atonement, and will deliver people from the hand of Belial. Mention of Melchizedek is also found in Philo as well as Josephus, and furthermore in 2 En. 71–72, the apocryphal history of Melchizedek, which sees him as a Canaanite, but as one who turned away from idolatry and toward the knowledge of

---

36. No psalm has triggered as many hypotheses and discussions in research as Ps 110; a good introduction to this psalm has been offered by Kraus, *Psalmen 60–150*, 7th ed., BKAT 15.2 (Neukirchen-Vluyn: Neukirchener Verlag, 2003), 925–38.

37. For a detailed presentation of these creative approaches, see Christfried Böttrich and Miriam von Nordheim-Diehl, "Melchisedek" (WiBiLex, 2012), http://www.bibelwissenschaft.de/stichwort/26809/.

the one Creator God. Melchizedek also found reception and elaboration in the targumim and in the rabbinic writings, as well as in patristic and gnostic texts, in iconography, and even in Islam. In summary, it can be said that in relation to Melchizedek there are rereadings in a historical-political as well as a messianic-eschatological context. Josephus takes the former line and Philo even goes in both directions. A look at their reception is worthwhile, especially since they are close to Hebrews in time and content.

Josephus refers to Melichizedek in *J.W.* 6.438 as a "righteous king" and also identifies him as the founder and name giver of Jerusalem, furthermore as the first builder of the temple and first priest in the service of God, although he was a "Canaanite chief," and repeats both the first and the fourth aspects in his retelling of the Genesis narrative in *Ant.* 1.180.

In contrast, Philo mentions Melchizedek in three places, *Abr.* 235, *Congr.* 99, and *Leg.* 3.79–82. While the first two reflect an understanding of Melchizedek as a historical-political figure, the third follows a messianic-eschatological line of tradition. In *Abr.* 235 Philo remains quite close to the Genesis text but emphasizes the joy of victory, has him moreover prepare victory offerings, and concludes, "for 'the belongings of friends are held in common,' as the proverb says, and this is far more true of the belongings of the good whose one end is to be well-pleasing to God" (Colson). In other words, Melchizedek and Abraham share ownership and dignity. In *Congr.* 99, Philo emphasizes the tithe and says of Melchizedek in passing, "the holder of that priesthood, whose tradition he had learned from none other but himself" (Colson), thereby ascribing to him—like Abraham—an independent knowledge of God. In *Leg.* 3.79–82 Philo identifies Melchizedek by means of etymological analysis of the place name Salem as "king of peace," in view of whom God had "not fashioned beforehand any deed of his, but produced him to begin with as such a king, peaceable and worthy of His own priesthood" (Colson), which is why his name would mean "righteous king." Philo takes this epithet as the starting point of an extended allegory that leads to the conclusion that Melchizedek is the priestly, and hence divine, Logos that helps people—symbolized in wine—to become intoxicated with God, that is, the knowledge of God. Thus, Philo has transformed Melchizedek to a peaceable and just priest-king, created by God especially for his service.

Hebrews 7

The characterization of Melchizedek as a messianic-eschatological figure, appearing especially on Yom Kippur, is shared by Hebrews with Philo as well as 11Q13 or 2 En. 71–72. Let us now turn to Ps 110:4 in Hebrews, which is found three times as a marked quotation in the text (see "The Nature of the Scriptural Text").

Psalm 110:4 is paired with Gen 14:17–20 in Heb 7:1–2, with a repetition of Gen 14:20 in Heb 7:4. Scholars dispute whether Gen 14:17–20 is an unmarked quotation or more of a paraphrase, for the content is recounted but with some omissions.[38] Genesis 14:17–20 also seems closer to the LXX than to the MT. First, the rearrangement is notable, as Hebrews begins with Gen 14:18, then inserts 14:17, and ends with 14:19–20. Also obvious is the omission of the king of Sodom, who is of no interest to the author; likewise bread and wine are missing, and it seems that for the author the priestly aspect is sufficiently covered by the blessing. Now the author not only omits but also adds extrabiblical traditions, those that we encountered in both Josephus and Philo, namely the characterization of Melchizedek as a righteous person as well as a peaceable king. But the author goes beyond this and describes him in 7:3 as having no parents and no family tree, without beginning or end, resembling the Son of God and priest forever, although alluding—as NA[28] correctly recognizes—to Ps 110:4, which—unlike the psalmist—he had not attributed to David, but to his messianic descendant Jesus back in 5:5–6.[39] So here Ps 110:4 interprets Gen 14:17–20 and not vice versa!

The placement of the first quotation from Ps 110:4 is in the context of the interpretation of Ps 95:7–11, namely where it is adapted to the addressees (4:14–6:12).[40] It is said here that they need a high priestly commitment, as did the exodus community at Sinai, after the sin of idolatry there. It is further said that there is such a high priest for them, Jesus, who was not only begotten of God—which the author expresses by means of Ps 2:7 instead of Ps 110:3—but was also appointed by him, which is why it is—unlike in the psalm—that God attributes Ps 110:4 to Jesus in Heb 5:6. While 4:14–5:10 deals with the necessity and existence of such a high priest, the author—in continuing adaptation of Ps 95:7–11 LXX—warns in 5:11–6:12 that after the covenant renewal in prospect, there is—as in Kadesh—no more room for renewed apostasy, repentance, and grace. In the cultic central section, 7–10:18, the author deals with the renewal of the covenant.[41] It requires a high priest according to the order of Melchizedek, which is compared with that according to the order of Aaron (Heb 7), who can subsequently mediate the new covenant (Heb 8:7–9:10), and for this he needs a (his) sacrifice (9:15–10:18).

---

38. Steyn, *Quest for the Assumed LXX Vorlage*, 219–34, esp. 219.

39. Father- and motherlessness is widely known for the description of divine beings in ancient literature (Steyn, *Quest for the Assumed LXX Vorlage*, 230). The author also alludes to Ps 110:4 in Heb 5:10; 6:20; 7:11, 20, 24, and 28, although unaccountably NA[28] does not list the first and last three passages.

40. Gelardini, "Verhärtet eure Herzen nicht," 354; on the context of Heb 3–6 see also the good article by Randall C. Gleason, "The Old Testament Background of the Warning in Hebrews 6:4–8," *BSac* 155 (1998): 62–91.

41. Gelardini, "Verhärtet eure Herzen nicht," 355.

In Heb 7:1–3, Melchizedek is presented as a superhuman being who resembles the Son, Jesus. What follows in 7:4–10 is a midrashic reworking of the tithing theme in Gen 14:20, whereby Melchizedek as the recipient of tithes and dispenser of blessings is presented as superior to Abraham and his Levitical descendants.[42] The next section, 7:11–17, explains the need for another priest, according to the order of Melchizedek, not the order of Aaron, since perfection was not achieved through the latter. And since Jesus was also of the tribe of Judah, this also required a change of law, namely a calling "not through a legal requirement concerning physical descent," "but through the power of an indestructible life" (7:16), whereupon Ps 110:4 is quoted for the second time in 7:17. Hebrews 7:18–21 explains that Ps 110:4 is equivalent to an oath of God, and thus Jesus—unlike the priests after the order of Aaron—became a priest on the basis of a divine oath, whereupon Ps 110:4 is quoted for a third time. Hebrews 7:22–24 transfers the word "eternity" in Ps 110:4 to Jesus—unlike in the psalm—as one who lives forever, thus constructing a messianization of the one addressed. And since he does not die like the earthly ones, but lives and thus remains eternally, Jesus has become the guarantor of a better covenant. Finally, 7:25–28 elaborates, in conjunction with his sinlessness, that Jesus is thereby better able to save those who approach. In conclusion, I will interpret the statements of Heb 7 in the light of what has been said but shall first turn to a short section on the nature of the scriptural text in Hebrews, exemplified by Ps 110:4 (109:4 LXX).

The Nature of the Scriptural Text

Table 20.4. Psalm 110:4 in LXX, Hebrews 5:6; 7:17, 21

Psalm 109:4 LXX	Hebrews 5:6 Introduction	Hebrews 7:17 Center	Hebrews 7:21b Center
ὤμοσεν κύριος καὶ οὐ μεταμεληθήσεται	καθὼς καὶ ἐν ἑτέρῳ λέγει·	μαρτυρεῖται γὰρ ὅτι	ὤμοσεν κύριος καὶ οὐ μεταμεληθήσεται·

---

42. Although at various points a proximity to Philo can be observed in terms of his exegetical and hermeneutical methods, the author of Hebrews does not follow his allegorical approach, but, as Daniel Boyarin says, "Hebrews is midrash, midrash in style, midrash even in structure, not pesher, not allegory, certainly not paraphrase or rewritten Bible—to name some of the ancient Jewish, Greek, and Christian modes of interpretation. Hence, the practices of midrash are considerably older than their earliest rabbinic attestation" ("Midrash in Hebrews/Hebrews as Midrash," in Gelardini and Attridge, *Hebrews in Contexts*, 15–30, esp. 15, 17); and a little more generally, Docherty: "Hebrews must be taken seriously as an important exemplar of early post-biblical Jewish exegesis" (*Use of the Old Testament in Hebrews*, e.g., 2, 81).

Σὺ εἶ ἱερεὺς εἰς τὸν αἰῶνα κατὰ τὴν τάξιν Μελχισεδεκ.	σὺ ἱερεὺς εἰς τὸν αἰῶνα κατὰ τὴν τάξιν Μελχισέδεκ.	σὺ ἱερεὺς εἰς τὸν αἰῶνα κατὰ τὴν τάξιν Μελχισέδεκ.	σὺ ἱερεὺς εἰς τὸν αἰῶνα.⁴³
The Lord swore and will not change his mind, "You are a priest forever according to the order of Melchisedek." (NETS)	[A]s he says also in another place, "You are a priest forever, according to the order of Melchizedek."	For it is attested of him, "You are a priest forever, according to the order of Melchizedek."	"The Lord has sworn and will not change his mind, 'You are a priest forever.'"

As table 20.4 shows, the text of the quotations in Hebrews—as well as in the MT—is virtually identical with the witnesses in LXX. The main difference in all three versions of this quotation in Hebrews is the possible inclusion of εἶ by some witnesses between σύ and ἱερεύς. There are good reasons to assume that this word was in fact included in the *Vorlage* of Hebrews. It is present in most of the important LXX witnesses and is also consistently attested by 𝔓⁴⁶, the oldest textual witness of Hebrews.⁴⁴

In addition, the following can be said in principle about the subject of *Vorlage* in Hebrews, which Gert J. Steyn has investigated in detail: "It can be assumed that the versions... of the quotations in Hebrews... represent a written *Vorlage*. This can be observed in light of the fact that those readings are closer to the Greek version(s) of the Old Testament. This *Vorlage* differs at some points from the reconstructed eclectic LXX editions today, but traces of these 'differences' were found in textual witnesses."⁴⁵ The investigation of the differences leads Steyn to conclude that Hebrews displays similarities to texts of Philo and those of Qumran. But the author himself too seems to be creatively involved in some stylistic and theological changes to his quotations.⁴⁶

---

43. According to NA²⁸ some manuscripts insert τὴν τάξιν Μελχισέδεκ here, too, to harmonize it with the other two mentions.

44. Steyn, *Quest for the Assumed LXX Vorlage*, 205-34, esp. 209-10.

45. See also in this regard Gert J. Steyn, "Which 'LXX' Are We Talking about in NT Scholarship? Two Examples from Hebrews," in *Die Septuaginta - Texte, Kontexte, Lebenswelten*, ed. Martin Karrer and Wolfgang Kraus, WUNT 219 (Tübingen: Mohr Siebeck, 2008), 697-707; Martin Karrer, "The Epistle to the Hebrews and the Septuagint," in *Septuagint Research: Issues and Challenges in the Study of the Greek Jewish Scriptures*, ed. Wolfgang Kraus and R. Glenn Wooden, SCS 53 (Atlanta: Society of Biblical Literature, 2006), 335-53.

46. Steyn, *Quest for the Assumed LXX Vorlage*, 378-412, esp. 407, 412.

Conclusion

Hebrews scholarship has frequently—and prominently so in the voice of Weiss—assigned Hebrews to the genre of synagogue homily.[47] This genre definition takes into account the central aspect of production aesthetics, that the main task of a homily is the interpretation of an underlying text or texts, that is, the reading of the Torah and/or the prophets, which are interpreted with the help of, among other things, quotations. Since a Torah reading does not have to appear explicitly in the homily, quotations can refer to it, which seems to be precisely the case in Hebrews, for in many cases they refer to the wilderness generation, more specifically to the narrative at Sinai concerning the breaking of the covenant caused by idolatry as well as the subsequent renewal of the covenant mediated by Moses (Exod 32–34).[48] If we now interpret the statements made in Heb 7 against this background, we notice the correspondence in the fact that the original situation at Sinai, after the sin of the golden calf, also required a "different priest" because, as Moses recalls in Deut 9:20: "The LORD was so angry with Aaron that he was ready to destroy him, but I interceded also on behalf of Aaron at that same time."

Moses acted on the basis of the Abrahamic covenant after Aaron's breaking of the Sinai covenant, as I have set out above, so it could be argued—although the author of Hebrews does not explicitly say so—that Moses, too, acted according to the order of Melchizedek, not merely "royally" like Abraham, for Moses was concerned with the salvation of the people, just as Abraham was concerned with the salvation of Lot, but also "priestly," in that he regarded salvation as more important than the promise of the gift of the land, for he, like Aaron, was ultimately denied a share of it (Num 20:12).[49] Therefore, as shown above, Jewish tradition has seen Moses as a "high priest avant la lettre," one who ascended to heaven for the entrusted

---

47. Recently also, e.g., by Boyarin, "Midrash in Hebrews/Hebrews as Midrash," 29: "I wouldn't dream of thinking of a rabbinic 'background' or even of so-called Jewish influence. I would rather see the epistle *as* a Jewish text, a homily presumably closely related to other Jewish homilies of the time in style and to great extent, in content as well" (emphasis original).

48. According to this view, Ps 110 cannot be understood as the underlying text of Hebrews, as, e.g., Gert J. C. Jordaan and Pieter Nel do in the tradition of George W. Buchanan ("From Priest-King to King-Priest: Psalm 110 and the Basic Structure of Hebrews," in *Psalms and Hebrews: Studies in Reception*, ed. Dirk J. Human and Gert J. Steyn, LHBOTS 527 [New York: T&T Clark, 2010], 229–40; but also Jared Compton (*Psalm 110 and the Logic of Hebrews*, LNTS 537 [London: T&T Clark, 2015]). It would also be illogical because a savior needs entrusted people as well as an occasion, and this is preeminently the case in the covenant breaking and covenant renewal.

49. Wolfgang Kraus has arrived at another proposal regarding the function of the figure of Melchizedek, in "Zur Aufnahme und Funktion von Gen 14,18–20 und Ps 109 LXX im Hebräerbrief," in Wagner, Robker, and Ueberschaer, *Text – Textgeschichte – Textwirkung*, 459–74.

ones threatened by the wrath of God and obtained atonement as well as salvation on Yom Kippur. For this he was praised in Jewish tradition, beginning with Philo, not only as priest-king, but as divine. So there are good reasons to believe that the author of Hebrews was inspired by this oral tradition in his characterization of Jesus. Numerous allusions to Exod 32–34 in NA[28] are to be discovered here.

There are, however, also differences between Moses with the desert generation and Jesus and his addressees. A new crisis, at a different time and place, requires a new savior. Similar to Moses, Jesus is presented as divine, but unlike Moses, eternally alive, which pronounces the messianic. Jesus also offers his life to God, which God—unlike in the case of Moses—accepts as a sacrifice, and he therefore also ascended to God in heaven (Sinai), where he remains, however, not returning to earth as Moses did; creation is his inheritance, as in the case of Moses, to be available for ever for his entrusted ones before God (Heb 7:25). Jesus is thus presented as one who is to supplement the earthly, Levitical cult and, it seems, even replace it sooner or later. This can be interpreted as a relativization of the Levitical cult, but it seems more plausible to interpret it against the background of the narrative context in Exod 32–34 as a justified criticism of Aaron and in historical perspective, after the destruction of the Second Temple, as a pastoral attempt to relativize not the Levitical cult, but its loss.

The author imagines the place of covenant renewal on Zion in the heavenly Jerusalem, a locality that he virtually superimposes on Sinai. He sees the addressees as guilty of the sin of apostasy, like the exodus community; it seems to be the author's central theological concern, and because they are not yet in Kadesh, he considers the possibility of covenant renewal as still available.[50] But this gracious gift, offered by God and dearly purchased by Jesus through his life, must not be disregarded, as this would result in God's wrath. The appropriate attitude is therefore to look up to Jesus and, encouraged by the example of the witnesses of faith, to endure God's chastening—like the exodus generation at Sinai—and in due repentance to return to God, in the outside, as an expression of the one and only covenant relationship.

Bibliography

Allen, David M. *Deuteronomy and Exhortation in Hebrews: A Study in Narrative Re-Presentation.* WUNT 2/238. Tübingen: Mohr Siebeck, 2008.

---

50. Apostasy and breach of the covenant are shown in God's turning away, and this can also express itself in a destroyed temple, the house of God that has become uninhabitable for him in the midst of his people—at least this is how Josephus argues countless times and in varying ways in his war report.

———. "Why Bother Going Outside? The Use of the Old Testament in Heb 13:10–16." Pages 239–52 in *The Scriptures of Israel in Jewish and Christian Tradition: Essays in Honour of Maarten J. J. Menken*. Edited by Bart J. Koet, Steve Moyise, and Jozef Verheyden. NovTSup 148. Leiden: Brill, 2013.

Böttrich, Christfried, and Miriam von Nordheim-Diehl. "Melchisedek." *WiBiLex*, 2012. http://www.bibelwissenschaft.de/stichwort/26809/.

Boyarin, Daniel. "Midrash in Hebrews/Hebrews as Midrash." Pages 15–30 in *Hebrews in Contexts*. Edited by Gabriella Gelardini and Harold W. Attridge. AJEC 91. Leiden: Brill, 2016.

Compton, Jared. *Psalm 110 and the Logic of Hebrews*. LNTS 537. London: T&T Clark, 2015.

Docherty, Susan E. *The Use of the Old Testament in Hebrews: A Case Study in Early Jewish Bible Interpretation*. WUNT 2/260. Tübingen: Mohr Siebeck, 2009.

Dyer, Bryan R. "The Epistle to the Hebrews in Recent Research: Studies on the Author's Identity, His Use of the Old Testament, and Theology." *JGRChJ* 9 (2013): 104–31.

Eisenbaum, Pamela M. *The Jewish Heroes of Christian History: Hebrews 11 in Literary Context*. SBLDS 156. Atlanta: Scholars Press, 1997.

Gelardini, Gabriella. "Charting 'Outside the Camp' with Edward W. Soja: Critical Spatiality and Hebrews 13." Pages 210–37 in *Hebrews in Contexts*. Edited by Gabriella Gelardini and Harold W. Attridge. AJEC 91. Leiden: Brill, 2016.

———. "Hebrews, Homiletics, and Liturgical Scripture Interpretation." Pages 121–43 in *Reading the Epistle to the Hebrews: A Resource for Students*. Edited by Eric F. Mason and Kevin B. McCruden. RBS 66. Atlanta: Society of Biblical Literature, 2011.

———. *"Verhärtet eure Herzen nicht": Der Hebräer, eine Synagogenhomilie zu Tischa be-Aw*. BibInt 83. Leiden: Brill, 2007.

Gleason, Randall C. "The Old Testament Background of the Warning in Hebrews 6:4–8." *BSac* 155 (1998): 62–91.

Gradwohl, Roland. *Bibelauslegungen aus jüdischen Quellen*. 4 vols. CTB 37–38. Stuttgart: Calwer, 2017.

Grässer, Erich. *An die Hebräer*. 3 vols. EKKNT 17. Zurich: Benziger; Neukirchen-Vluyn: Neukirchener Verlag, 1990–1997.

Hermann, Markus-Liborius. *Die "hermeneutische Stunde" des Hebräerbriefs: Schriftauslegung in Spannungsfeldern*. HBS 72. Freiburg im Breisgau: Herder, 2013.

Holtz, Gudrun. "Pentateuchrezeption im Hebräerbrief." Pages 358–80 in *Die Septuaginta und das frühe Christentum*. Edited by Thomas Scott Caulley and Hermann Lichtenberger. WUNT 277. Tübingen: Mohr Siebeck, 2011.

Jacob, Benno. *Das Buch Genesis*. Edited in collaboration with the Leo Baeck Institute. Berlin: Schocken, 1934. Repr., Stuttgart: Calwer, 2000.

Jordaan, Gert J. C., and Pieter Nel. "From Priest-King to King-Priest: Psalm 110 and the Basic Structure of Hebrews." Pages 229–40 in *Psalms and Hebrews: Studies in Reception*. Edited by Dirk J. Human and Gert J. Steyn. LHBOTS 527. New York: T&T Clark, 2010.

Karrer, Martin. "Die Väter in der Wüste: Text und Rezeption von LXX Ps 94 in Hebr 3." Pages 427–58 in *Text – Textgeschichte – Textwirkung: Festschrift zum 65. Geburtstag von Siegfried Kreuzer*. Edited by Thomas Wagner, Jonathan M. Robker, and Frank Ueberschaer. AOAT 419. Münster: Ugarit-Verlag, 2014.

———. "The Epistle to the Hebrews and the Septuagint." Pages 335–53 in *Septuagint Research: Issues and Challenges in the Study of the Greek Jewish Scriptures*. Edited by Wolfgang Kraus and R. Glenn Wooden. SCS 53. Atlanta: Society of Biblical Literature, 2006.

Kraus, Hans-Joachim. *Psalmen 60–150*. 7th ed. BKAT 15.2. Neukirchen-Vluyn: Neukirchener Verlag, 2003.

Kraus, Wolfgang. "Zur Aufnahme und Funktion von Gen 14,18–20 und Ps 109 LXX im Hebräerbrief." Pages 459–74 in *Text – Textgeschichte – Textwirkung: Festschrift zum 65. Geburtstag von Siegfried Kreuzer*. Edited by Thomas Wagner, Jonathan M. Robker, and Frank Ueberschaer. AOAT 419. Münster: Ugarit-Verlag, 2014.

Lierman, John. "Moses as Priest and Apostle in Hebrews 3:1–6." Pages 47–62 in *Hebrews in Contexts*. Edited by Gabriella Gelardini and Harold W. Attridge. AJEC 91. Leiden: Brill, 2016.

Philo. *On Abraham; On Joseph; On Moses*. Translated by F. H. Colson. LCL. Cambridge: Harvard University Press, 1935.

———. *On the Confusion of Tongues; On the Migration of Abraham; Who Is the Heir of Divine Things? On Mating with the Preliminary Studies*. Translated by F. H. Colson and G. H. Whitaker. LCL. Cambridge: Harvard University Press, 1932.

———. *On the Creation; Allegorical Interpretations*. Translated by F. H. Colson and G. H. Whitaker. LCL. Cambridge: Harvard University Press, 1929.

Rayburn, Robert G., II. *"Yesterday, Today and Forever": The Narrative World of Ψ 94 [Ps 95] as a Hermeneutical Key to Hebrews*. Berlin: Lang, 2019.

Steyn, Gert J. "An Overview of the Extent and Diversity of Methods Utilised by the Author of Hebrews When Using the Old Testament." *Neot* 42, no. 2 (2008): 327–52.

———. *A Quest for the Assumed LXX Vorlage of the Explicit Quotations in Hebrews*. FRLANT 235. Göttingen: Vandenhoeck & Ruprecht, 2011.

———. "Which 'LXX' Are We Talking about in NT Scholarship? Two Examples from Hebrews." Pages 697–707 in *Die Septuaginta: Texte, Kontexte, Lebenswelten*. Edited by Martin Karrer and Wolfgang Kraus. WUNT 219. Tübingen: Mohr Siebeck, 2008.

Weiss, Hans-Friedrich. *Der Brief an die Hebräer.* KEK 13. Göttingen: Vandenhoeck & Ruprecht, 1991.

Zenger, Erich, Heinz-Josef Fabry, and Georg Braulik. *Einleitung in das Alte Testament.* 3rd ed. Kohlhammer Studienbücher Theologie 1.1. Stuttgart: Kohlhammer, 1998.

21

Israel's Scriptures in James

KARL-WILHELM NIEBUHR

Like many other books of the New Testament, the Epistle of James cannot be understood adequately without a deeper knowledge of the Scriptures of Israel. From the beginning to the end, the author uses concepts, terminology, or even word-for-word quotations from these writings to express his own ideas and intentions, with and without marking it. Most of the important books of Scripture are used or referred to in his letter; omissions are not significant in view of the rather short text. Out of four exact citations, three are from the Torah (Jas 2:8, 11, 23) and one is from the book of Proverbs (4:6). A fifth is introduced as such, but is not found in any of the Scriptures of Israel (4:5). With regard to the three main sections of Hebrew Scripture (Torah, Prophets, Writings), there are neither particular hot spots nor glaring lacunae noticeable in the letter. Taken together the ratio of all references to the three traditional sections mentioned is about twenty-two (Torah), twenty-five (Prophets), seventeen (Writings), plus seventeen from the Apocrypha.[1]

To avoid an anachronistic misunderstanding, I have to make clear in advance, however, that the author of the Epistle of James did not have at his

---

I am grateful to Vincent Hirschi, MDiv and ThM of Regent College, Vancouver, a PhD student in Biblical Studies at the University of Fribourg (Switzerland), for his extremely helpful comments on an earlier draft of this chapter and for correcting my English.

1. Jewish texts originating in Greek and belonging to the Septuagint are considered part of the Scriptures of Israel in this chapter because this corresponds to the circumstances relevant to the Epistle of James.

disposal a well-defined "canon" of Scripture in distinction to a broader pool of religious writings that had grown out of the Scriptures of Israel in ancient Judaism. Such a thing as a canon was created only later in ancient Christian circles. Therefore, every text, figure, or motif stemming from the Scriptures appeared to James embedded in a lively tradition of reading Scripture as testified abundantly in contemporary ancient Jewish sources. However, to maintain the limits of this contribution and to meet the focus of the volume at hand, I restrict my survey to references to the Scriptures as identified in the Epistle of James and include extrabiblical sources only by pointing to selected references in the footnotes.

Nevertheless, the use of Scripture belongs to the preferred rhetorical and strategic means the author uses with emphasis to express his intentions. This not only results from the frequency with which he points to Scripture explicitly, but from other markers as well (see "Introducing Scripture," below). He uses the term "Scripture" (ἡ γραφή) several times, quotes it in its exact wording, alludes to biblical concepts by using a kind of "loaded language," or points to biblical stories by dropping a biblical name to evoke a model represented by that figure. Even though Scripture is not the only ideological background and stock of ideas the author uses, he does not refer to any other sources for his arguments explicitly. This even applies to the so-called Jesus tradition, which the author possibly knew and used but never identifies as such.[2] Moreover, the author presupposes that his audience will be able to recognize his use of Scripture and to fill in the blanks when he omits ideas, phrases, or concepts that belong to the passages from Scripture to which he alludes.

In the letter prescript the author introduces himself by name as James from Jerusalem—who was well known as the brother of Jesus (cf. Gal 1:19; 1 Cor 15:7; Acts 15:13–21)—and thereby pretends to stem from a Galilean family background (cf. Mark 6:3). However, the language of his letter turns out to be a cultivated and colorful *koine* Greek that does not show any signs of a non-Greek original anywhere. Therefore, it is not surprising that all citations from or allusions to Scripture point to the Greek of the Septuagint as well.[3]

---

2. Cf. Karl-Wilhelm Niebuhr, "James," in *The Reception of Jesus in the First Three Centuries*, vol. 1 of *From Paul to Josephus: Literary Receptions of Jesus in the First Century CE*, ed. Helen K. Bond (London: T&T Clark, 2020), 259–75, esp. 267–74.

3. The historical quest for the authorship of the letter need not occupy us here. For my own view, see Niebuhr, "James," 259–65.

Israel's Scriptures in the Epistle of James

Introducing Scripture

The term ἡ γραφή ("Scripture," only singular) for Israel's Scriptures occurs three times in the letter of James (2:8, 23; 4:5). There are no other formulaic markers for references to Scripture (like, e.g., γέγραπται ["it is written"], Μωϋσῆς ... γράφει ["Moses writes"], ὅπως πληρωθῇ τὸ ῥηθὲν διὰ τῶν προφητῶν ["to fulfill what is spoken through the prophets"], or the like; but see below, "Epistolary Arguments and Reflections [Marked Citations]" for 2:23). However, the author refers to Scripture by formulations common for "oral" statements (2:11, ὁ γὰρ εἰπών ["who said"]; 2:23, ἡ γραφὴ ἡ λέγουσα ["the Scripture saying"]; 4:5, ἡ γραφὴ λέγει ["Scripture says"]; 4:6, διὸ λέγει ["therefore it says"]; 5:11, τὴν ὑπομονὴν Ἰὼβ ἠκούσατε ["you have heard of the steadfastness of Job"]).[4] For the author and his audience, therefore, Scripture has a voice one must listen to, a sounding tone that enters the hearer. It is a spoken word to be heard and followed, not a written book to be read (the verbs γράφειν ["to write"] and ἀναγινώσκειν ["to read"] are missing in the letter). This observation may imply a practice of reading and understanding Scripture in the circles of early Christian communities that cannot be treated further here.

The phrases that introduce the references to Scripture are not formulaic, but individually induce citations of, phrases from, or allusions to Scripture. Therefore, to unlock the meaning of the introductory formulas requires interpreting first the context of the argument they are a part of (see "Using Scripture [Examples]," below). From semantic and grammatical perspectives, the use of κατά plus the accusative in Jas 2:8 may imply that Scripture is used as standard or yardstick. In 2:23, the word πληροῦσθαι ("to be fulfilled"), particularly in company with πιστεύειν ("to believe or trust"), δικαιοσύνη ("righteousness"), and Ἀβραάμ ("Abraham"), may evoke the eschatological completion of Scripture by turning to faith in Christ, as Paul develops it in Galatians and Romans. However, the aim of this chapter is restricted to understanding James on his own terms, without comparing his methods with those of Paul.[5] The rhetorical question in 4:5, by implicitly denying the possibility that Scripture may speak in vain (κενῶς ἡ γραφὴ λέγει), implies the authority of Scripture over its addressees.

This also refers to the relationship between Scripture and law as described in Jas 2:8. Here, γραφή ("Scripture") and νόμος ("law") stand closely together

---

4. Unless otherwise noted, all translations are by the author.
5. For my view on the relationship to Paul, cf. Karl-Wilhelm Niebuhr, "Jakobus und Paulus über das Innere des Menschen und den Ursprung seiner ethischen Entscheidungen," *NTS* 62, no. 1 (2016): 22–30.

and are almost identified (νόμον τελεῖν βασιλικὸν κατὰ τὴν γραφήν, "to fulfill the royal law according to the Scripture"). The qualification of the Torah as "royal," according to this formulation, follows the standards of Scripture (κατά) and is explained by a citation of the love command from Lev 19:18 (ἀγαπήσεις τὸν πλησίον σου ὡς σεαυτόν, "you shall love your neighbor as yourself"), one of the core commandments of the Torah. However, even there, the compound sentence in Jas 2:8 is a conditioned injunction with an imperative function directed to the audience (εἰ μέντοι . . . καλῶς ποιεῖτε, "if . . . you do well") that contributes to the overall intention of the paragraph not to show partiality in favor of the rich against the poor (see "Epistolary Arguments and Reflections [Marked Citations]," below).

When the author drops names of biblical figures (Abraham, Rahab, Job, Elijah), certain narrative elements of the passages from Scripture alluded to remain in the background but are presupposed as known to the addressees in order to strengthen the argument of the author. Obviously, he can trust that the letter recipients know the stories behind the names. They are able to draw conclusions from them with regard to the intentions of his arguments even if the stories are not told. Sometimes one gets the impression that the author and the readers know even more than what is written in Scripture by having access to common narrative motives or instructive patterns from early Jewish literature and tradition. For example, when the author calls Abraham a "friend of God" (2:23), he probably follows a tradition that has its roots in 2 Chr 20:7 (καὶ ἔδωκας αὐτὴν [i.e., τὴν γῆν] σπέρματι Αβρααμ τῷ ἠγαπημένῳ σου εἰς τὸν αἰῶνα, "and gave it [the land] forever to the seed of Abraham, your beloved"; cf. Isa 41:8). In fact, similar motives occur frequently in early Jewish, rabbinic, and ancient Christian texts (see "The Common Ground of Thinking and Believing [Evoked Stories]," below), but the qualification of Abraham as "friend of God" is not found anywhere in these terms in Scripture.[6]

The most important function of the Scriptures of Israel for the Epistle of James is to create a space of convictions and ideas into which the author wants to invite his audience. This refers primarily, but not only, to the field of religious and theological thinking and ethical instruction. Adopting this proposition presupposes that one interprets the letter as a whole because it is grounded in Scripture not only by citations, allusions, and concepts but also by its origin in the way of life and the religious convictions of ancient Judaism that unite the author and the recipients. This is already visible in the formulation of the letter prescript

---

6. For nonscriptural evidence, see n. 26 below. For "friend of God," see Dale C. Allison Jr., *A Critical and Exegetical Commentary on the Epistle of James*, ICC (New York: Bloomsbury, 2013), 493–96.

where the author qualifies himself as "a slave of God and the Lord Jesus Christ" and calls his audience "the twelve tribes in dispersion."[7] The confession of the Lord Jesus Christ occurs twice in the letter (1:1; 2:1). It determines the intentions of the author right from the beginning and belongs to the system of convictions shared by his addressees.

Using Scripture (Examples)

I have structured the following section by using, on the one hand, the four categories introduced by the editors of this volume (marked citation, unmarked citation, verbal allusion, conceptual allusion). On the other hand, I have tried to do justice to the particular way that James is dealing with Scripture, as I attempted to identify by studying this letter. Therefore, I decided to begin my presentation of the material by pointing to the letter prescript as an example of "conceptual allusions." Then follows a discussion of "marked citations" in Jas 2 because here the outstanding importance of the testimony of Scripture for the theological and ethical argument of the author can be clarified. The third section ("The Common Ground of Thinking and Believing [Evoked Stories]") is devoted to references to biblical figures in Jas 2 and 5. This is a preeminent way of using Scripture in the letter that cannot be classified readily in one of the four categories mentioned. It relates to "conceptual allusions" in that it refers to particular passages from Scripture without quoting them. On the other hand, a figure includes more than a concept by pointing to the whole story as told in Scripture about the biblical person in view. That is why I use the term "evoked stories" for that paragraph. At the end ("Prophetic Paraenesis and Eschatological Exhortation [Verbal Allusions or Unmarked Citations]") I deal with "verbal allusions" and "unmarked citations" together because these two categories are least clearly to be distinguished with regard to the letter of James.

The Biblical Frame of Communication (Conceptual Allusions)

Table 21.1. The Biblical Frame of Communication (Conceptual Allusions)

1:1	Ἰάκωβος "Jacob/James"	Gen 25–50

---

7. See, for interpretation, Karl-Wilhelm Niebuhr, "One God, One Lord in James," in *Monotheism and Christology in Greco-Roman Antiquity*, ed. Matthew V. Novenson, NovTSup 180 (Leiden: Brill, 2020), 173–75.

θεοῦ ... δοῦλος "servant of God"	Isa 49:1–6	
αἱ δώδεκα φυλαί "the twelve tribes"	Exod 24:4	ὀρθρίσας δὲ Μωυσῆς τὸ πρωὶ ᾠκοδόμησεν θυσιαστήριον ὑπὸ τὸ ὄρος καὶ δώδεκα λίθους εἰς τὰς δώδεκα φυλὰς τοῦ Ισραηλ "Now, early in the morning, Moyses constructed an altar at the foot of the mountain and twelve stones for the twelve tribes of Israel"[8]
	1 Kgs 18:31 (cf. Exod 28:21; 36:21 [MT 39:14]; Josh 4:5; 2 Esd 6:17; Ezek 47:13; Sir 44:23; 45:11)	καὶ ἔλαβεν Ηλιου δώδεκα λίθους κατ' ἀριθμὸν φυλῶν τοῦ Ισραηλ (v.l. *recensio* Orig. Ιακωβ, MT בְּנֵי־יַעֲקֹב), ὡς ἐλάλησεν κύριος πρὸς αὐτὸν λέγων Ισραηλ ἔσται τὸ ὄνομά σου. "And Elijah took twelve stones according to the number of the tribes of Israel, as the Lord had spoken to him, saying, 'Israel shall be your name'"
διασπορά "dispersion"	Jer 15:7	καὶ διασπερῶ αὐτοὺς ἐν διασπορᾷ· ἐν πύλαις λαοῦ μου ἠτεκνώθησαν, ἀπώλεσαν τὸν λαόν μου διὰ τὰς κακίας αὐτῶν "And I will disperse them in a dispersion in the gates of my people. I was made childless; I destroyed my people because of their evils"
	2 Macc 1:27	ἐπισυνάγαγε τὴν διασπορὰν ἡμῶν, ἐλευθέρωσον τοὺς δουλεύοντας ἐν τοῖς ἔθνεσιν, τοὺς ἐξουθενημένους καὶ βδελυκτοὺς ἔπιδε, καὶ γνώτωσαν τὰ ἔθνη ὅτι σὺ εἶ ὁ θεὸς ἡμῶν "Gather together our scattered people; set free those who are slaves among the nations; look on those who are rejected and despised, and let the nations know that you are our God"

---

8. All quotations from the Septuagint are from NETS.

To distinguish strictly between conceptual allusions, verbal allusions, and unmarked citations (see "Prophetic Paraenesis and Eschatological Exhortation [Verbal Allusions or Unmarked Citations]," below) would call for an elaborate methodological substantiation and may be questioned as operable in several cases in the letter of James. As conceptual allusions, one could include, for instance, the conviction that God chose the poor (Jas 2:5; cf. Ps 112:7-8 LXX) or that the rich will be judged by God at the end of time (Jas 5:1-6, cf. Amos 5:7-20). As verbal allusions, one may count the announcement of the eschatological "day of slaughter" (5:5; cf. Jer 12:3) or the "passing away of the flower of the grass" (Jas 1:10-11; cf. Isa 40:6). However, in every single case such classifications are not strict and often both categories could apply. Therefore, I treat here in more detail only the letter prescript because here the author starts a "play of meanings" intelligible only by disclosing its references to Scripture.

By introducing himself as "James" and by addressing the recipients as "the twelve tribes in the dispersion," the author evokes, already in the letter prescript, a set of associations that is deeply rooted in and substantially filled with traditions from Scripture. Although in New Testament Greek the spelling Ἰάκωβος for the brother of Jesus or for other contemporary bearers of that name is strictly distinct from Ἰακώβ for the biblical patriarch, readers would not avoid catching an allusion to the very prominent biblical figure well known by that name (cf. Gen 25-36). The Septuagint and Philo only know the name Ἰακώβ, used almost exclusively for the patriarch, but Josephus has only Ἰάκωβος, for the patriarch as for other bearers of the name.[9] However, the primary association evoked by the name Ἰάκωβος in the prescript of the letter would be to think of the brother of Jesus known as one of the leaders of the Jerusalem original church after Easter (cf. Mark 6:3; 1 Cor 15:7; Gal 1:19; 2:1-13; Acts 12:17; 15:13-21; 21:18-26; Jude 1).[10] Similarly, the term δοῦλος ("servant") used to characterize the author in relation to God and Jesus Christ may include allusions to the servant of God (παῖς θεοῦ) in prophetic tradition (cf. Isa 41:8-9; 42:1; 49:3, 5; 52:13; Wis 2:13). Probably, more striking for the letter recipients in their social context is the opposition in the prescript between slave (δοῦλος) and lord (κύριος). Thus, by carefully choosing his words in the letter prescript, the author provides an image of himself deeply colored by biblical language.

---

9. The only exception to Ἰακώβ is Ἰάκουβος in 1 Esd 9:48 (LXX). For the Septuagint, cf. Gen 25-50; Exod 1:1 etc.; Lev 26:42; Num 23:7; etc.; Deut 1:8 etc.; Josh 24:4, 32; 1 Kgs 12:8; etc.; for Philo, cf. *Mut.* 12-13, 81-83; *Somn.* 1.168-172; *Leg.* 2, 59; for Josephus, cf. *Ant.* 1.258 etc. (the son of Isaak); 20.102 (the son of Jude the Galilee); 20.200 (the brother of Jesus); *J.W.* 4.235 etc. (a military leader of the Idumaeans); *Life* 96.240 (a friend of Josephus).

10. Cf. Karl-Wilhelm Niebuhr, "James and the Historical Jesus," in *Oxford Handbook of Hebrews and the Catholic Epistles*, ed. Patrick Gray (New York: Oxford University Press, forthcoming).

The qualification of the letter recipients as "the twelve tribes in the dispersion," however, certainly evokes associations exclusively directed to Scripture. The full number of the twelve tribes forming the people of Israel does not correspond to the historical-political state of the time of the author, but relies only on its roots in Scripture and on eschatological expectations targeted at it. To amplify this impression, we briefly follow the use of the phrase αἱ δώδεκα φυλαί ("the twelve tribes") in the Scriptures of Israel.

According to Exod 24:3-8, Moses "built an altar at the foot of the mountain and arranged twelve standing stones—according to the twelve tribes of Israel" (δώδεκα λίθους εἰς τὰς δώδεκα φυλὰς τοῦ Ισραηλ, 24:4). By reading to the people the "Book of the Covenant," he places the Israelites under covenantal obligations, and they reply: "We are willing to do and obey all that the LORD has spoken" (24:7; cf. v. 3).

The motif of twelve pillars or stones representing the twelve tribes of Israel recurs in Scripture at several places. Most prominently for the letter of James, it also occurs in the story of Elijah who confronted the prophets of Baal (1 Kgs 18).[11] Before he turned to God in prayer to invoke God for help, he "took twelve stones, corresponding to the number of tribes that descended from Jacob [δώδεκα λίθους κατ᾽ ἀριθμὸν φυλῶν τοῦ Ισραηλ (v.l. Origen: Ιακωβ, MT בְּנֵי־יַעֲקֹב)], to whom the LORD had said, 'Israel will be your new name'" (18:31).

The symbol of twelve stones is prominent in Scripture elsewhere. According to Exod 28:21 and 36:21 (MT 39:14), the priestly garments are decorated with "twelve stones with their names according to the names of the sons of Israel" (cf. Sir 45:11). When Joshua led the people into the promised land, he erected a memorial in the river Jordan from twelve stones "according to the number of the Israelite tribes" (Josh 4:5). To explain that action he declared: "When your children ask someday, 'Why are these stones important to you?' tell them how the water of the Jordan stopped flowing before the ark of the covenant of the Lord.... These stones will be a lasting memorial for the Israelites" (4:6-7).

According to 2 Esd 6, after having returned from the Babylonian exile, "the people of Israel, the priests and the Levites, and the rest of the sons of the exile, celebrated the rededication of the house of God with joy." They "offered ... twelve male goats for sin on behalf of all Israel, for the number of the tribes of Israel" (ὑπὲρ παντὸς Ισραηλ δώδεκα εἰς ἀριθμὸν φυλῶν Ισραηλ, 6:16-18).

In Ezek 47:13-23, by pointing to the depression at the Babylonian exile, the prophet announces the future distribution of the land, when "the twelve tribes of the sons of Israel will have an addition of allotment" (ταῖς δώδεκα φυλαῖς τῶν υἱῶν Ισραηλ πρόσθεσις σχοινίσματος, 47:13). Ben Sira proves that such hopes

---

11. The story is recalled in Jas 5:17-18; see below.

remained alive in the Hellenistic period when he mentions that God blessed Jacob by giving to him the land as an inheritance and "divided his portions; and he allotted among twelve tribes" (ἐν φυλαῖς ἐμέρισεν δέκα δύο, Sir 44:23).

In the prescript of the letter of James, the twelve tribes of Israel closely relate to the qualification of the addressees as presently living in the "diaspora." This term too is full of associations, for the events of Israel's exile and return are prominent in all sections of the Scriptures of Israel. To mention only two references where the term διασπορά is used, I point to Jer 15:7 and 2 Macc 1:27. For Jeremiah, the dispersion is the result of Israel's wickedness and God's punishment (διασπερῶ αὐτοὺς ἐν διασπορᾷ· . . . διὰ τὰς κακίας αὐτῶν ["and I will disperse them in a dispersion . . . because of their evils"]). The author of 2 Maccabees, at the beginning of his historical report about the successful uprising of the Jews, quotes a letter from Jerusalem to the Jews in Egypt according to which the priests before reinstalling the worship in the temple prayed to God: "Accept this sacrifice on behalf of all your people Israel [ὑπὲρ παντὸς τοῦ λαοῦ σου Ισραηλ]. . . . Gather together our scattered people [ἐπισυνάγαγε τὴν διασπορὰν ἡμῶν], set free those who are slaves among the nations."[12]

Taken together, the evidence from the early Jewish period for the concept of the twelve tribes of Israel in dispersion is strong. It is rooted in pivotal narrative elements of the Torah and actualized in prophetic and sapiential traditions.[13] By carefully selecting meaningful traditions from Scripture and applying conventions of Jewish letter writing, James forms a frame of communication that predetermines the content and the intentions of his letter.[14] The address to "the twelve tribes in the dispersion" in the letter prescript together with the final reference to Elijah in 5:18–19 (who had built an altar from twelve stones to remember the full number of Israel) form an *inclusio* of allusions to the restored people of Israel according to Scripture.[15] Without explicitly citing from or pointing to Scripture, the author already with his first and again with his last words reminds his epistolary audience of the fundamentals of their faith and hopes. Both the

---

12. See Willem C. van Unnik, *Das Selbstverständnis der jüdischen Diaspora in der hellenistisch-römischen Zeit*, ed. Pieter W. van der Horst, AGJU 17 (Leiden: Brill, 1993), 89–107.

13. For prophetic traditions on a "new covenant," consult Mariam J. Kamell, "Incarnating Jeremiah's Promised New Covenant in the 'Law' of James," *EvQ* 83, no. 1 (2011): 19–28. However, James does not actualize the concept of the covenant explicitly.

14. Cf. Lutz Doering, *Ancient Jewish Letters and the Beginnings of Christian Epistolography*, WUNT 298 (Tübingen: Mohr Siebeck, 2012), 452–63; Karl-Wilhelm Niebuhr, "The Epistle of James in Light of Early Jewish Diaspora Letters," in *The Catholic Epistles: Critical Readings*, ed. Darian Lockett (Bloomsbury: T&T Clark, 2021), 70–75.

15. Cf. Mariam Kamell Kovalishyn, "The Prayer of Elijah in James 5: An Example of Intertextuality," *JBL* 137, no. 4 (2018): 1040–42.

writer and the recipients rest upon convictions of the people of Israel. However, they qualify their confession by faith in "God and the Lord Jesus Christ" (1:1).

Epistolary Arguments and Reflections (Marked Citations)

Table 21.2. *Epistolary Arguments and Reflections (Marked Citations)*

2:8	ἀγαπήσεις τὸν πλησίον σου ὡς σεαυτόν "You shall love your neighbor as yourself"	Lev 19:18	καὶ ἀγαπήσεις τὸν πλησίον σου ὡς σεαυτόν· "And you shall love your neighbor as yourself"
2:23	Ἐπίστευσεν δὲ Ἀβραὰμ τῷ θεῷ, καὶ ἐλογίσθη αὐτῷ εἰς δικαιοσύνην "Abraham believed God, and it was reckoned to him as righteousness"	Gen 15:6	καὶ ἐπίστευσεν Αβραμ τῷ θεῷ, καὶ ἐλογίσθη αὐτῷ εἰς δικαιοσύνην. "And Abram believed God, and it was reckoned to him as righteousness"
4:6	Ὁ θεὸς ὑπερηφάνοις ἀντιτάσσεται, ταπεινοῖς δὲ δίδωσιν χάριν "God opposes the proud, but gives grace to the humble"	Prov 3:34	κύριος ὑπερηφάνοις ἀντιτάσσεται, ταπεινοῖς δὲ δίδωσιν χάριν. "The Lord opposes the proud, but gives grace to the humble"

I consider Jas 1:2–27 to be the introduction (epitome) to the following main argumentative section (exposition), consisting of two parts, the probation of faith by hearing and doing the word of God (2:1–3:12) and by right social behavior (3:13–5:6). James 5:7–20 is the concluding section (epilogue). James quotes verses or parts of verses from Scripture four times in three sections of his letter. The first marked citation (2:8, cf. Lev 19:18, see below) is part of the initial section of the main argument (2:1–13). In his argument about Abraham as a model for the unity of faith and works (Jas 2:21–24), the author quotes Gen 15:6: "Abraham believed God, and it was counted to him as righteousness" (Ἐπίστευσεν δὲ Ἀβραὰμ τῷ θεῷ, καὶ ἐλογίσθη αὐτῷ εἰς δικαιοσύνην, 2:23; we will deal with this passage later, see "The Common Ground of Thinking and Believing [Evoked Stories]"). A third quotation is from the book of Proverbs (Jas 4:6; cf. Prov 3:34). It belongs to an argument difficult to reconstruct exactly because of several textual, syntactical, and semantic problems (Jas 4:1–12).[16] By quoting "God opposes the proud, but

---

16. See Allison, *James*, 588–639; Christoph Burchard, *Der Jakobusbrief*, HNT 15.1 (Tübingen: Mohr Siebeck, 2000), 164–80.

gives grace to the humble" ([κύριος]¹⁷ ὑπερηφάνοις ἀντιτάσσεται, ταπεινοῖς δὲ δίδωσιν χάριν), the author underlines his main exhortation to withdraw from quarrels in the congregation (4:4). Another marked citation follows (ἢ δοκεῖτε ὅτι κενῶς ἡ γραφὴ λέγει ["or do you think that the Scripture speaks in vain"], 4:5) that, however, does not occur in Scripture. In the rest of this section, I focus on citations in the first argumentative section (2:8–11).

In Jas 2:1–3:12 the author displays his basic intent of fostering the unity of hearing, believing, and doing. By an example that refers to the behavior in the congregation toward rich and poor people inside or outside the church, he criticizes partiality in their conduct (2:1–13). Based on religious traditions from Scripture about God who "has chosen those who are poor in the world to be rich in faith" (2:5), James turns against that partiality. When they make distinctions by favoritism toward the rich and disdain toward the poor, their conduct is in contrast to the will of God, who promised that the poor would be heirs of the kingdom. Moreover, it contradicts "the royal law according to the Scripture, 'You shall love your neighbor as yourself'" (2:8; cf. Lev 19:18). To substantiate his argument, James adds a series of reasons introduced by conjunctions like εἰ (2:8, 9, 11) or γάρ (2:10, 11, 13). Among these reasons, once more two brief citations of commandments of the Torah occur, this time from the Decalogue (μὴ μοιχεύσῃς, μὴ φονεύσῃς ["you shall not commit adultery," "you shall not murder"], 2:11; cf. Exod 20:13–14; Deut 5:17–18). The argumentative section ends with a fundamental admonition "to speak and to act as those who are to be judged under the law of liberty" (2:12), and with an announcement of the severe, yet merciful, judgment of God (2:13).

The structure and order of the argument in this section makes clear that its focus is to exhort the congregation. They must avoid partiality (2:1) and direct their faith and conduct in speaking and doing the will of God as expressed in the Torah. Moreover, they must keep in mind God's eschatological judgment (2:12–13). Therefore, they are to orient their practice and belief according to the Mosaic law distinguished as "the royal law according to the Scripture" (2:8) and "the law of liberty" (2:12; cf. 1:25: "the perfect law, the law of liberty"). The author selects for citation the love command (Lev 19:18) and parts of the Decalogue (Exod 20:13–14/Deut 5:17–18), that is, commandments that are particularly distinguished in early Jewish and Christian traditions. By doing that he underlines the normative role of the Torah for those who "hold their faith in our Lord Jesus Christ, the Lord of glory."[18] In other words, his main argument is not to make

---

17. The Septuagint reads ὁ θεός. That variant also occurs in the quotation from Prov 3:34 in 1 Pet 5:5.

18. See Karl-Wilhelm Niebuhr, *Gesetz und Paränese: Katechismusartige Weisungsreihen in*

a selection of particularly important commandments of the Torah or to quote a specific text from Scripture, but to emphasize the unity of the law taken as a whole (cf. 2:10). The author does not argue halakhically, by discussing individual situations where particular commandments of the Torah are valid or not, but rather theologically or paraenetically. His intention is to prompt his audience to consider and to reflect on the will of God altogether, not just to take orders or to follow particular commandments in special cases. Thus, in James we meet a Christian author (cf. 1:1; 2:1!) who bases his arguments on the Scriptures of Israel because the will of God for the practice and the belief of his people is found there comprehensively and is binding for the Christian community as well.

The Common Ground of Thinking and Believing (Evoked Stories)

Table 21.3. The Common Ground of Thinking and Believing (Evoked Stories)

2:21	Ἀβραάμ ... ἀνενέγκας Ἰσαὰκ ... ἐπὶ τὸ θυσιαστήριον "Abraham ... offered his son Isaac ... upon the altar"	Gen 22:2, 9	2 Λαβὲ τὸν υἱόν σου τὸν ἀγαπητόν, ὃν ἠγάπησας, τὸν Ισαακ, καὶ πορεύθητι εἰς τὴν γῆν τὴν ὑψηλὴν καὶ ἀνένεγκον αὐτὸν ἐκεῖ εἰς ὁλοκάρπωσιν ἐφ᾽ ἓν τῶν ὀρέων, ὧν ἄν σοι εἴπω. ... 9 καὶ ᾠκοδόμησεν ἐκεῖ Αβρααμ θυσιαστήριον καὶ ἐπέθηκεν τὰ ξύλα καὶ συμποδίσας Ισαακ τὸν υἱὸν αὐτοῦ ἐπέθηκεν αὐτὸν ἐπὶ τὸ θυσιαστήριον ἐπάνω τῶν ξύλων "Take your beloved son Isaak, whom you love, and go into the high land, and offer him as a whole burnt offering on one of the mountains, whichever I mention to you. ... And Abraam built the altar there and laid on the wood, and when he had bound his son Isaak hand and foot, he laid him on the altar atop the wood."

---

der frühjüdischen Literatur, WUNT 2/28 (Tübingen: Mohr Siebeck, 1987), 7–31; J. Cornelis de Vos, *Rezeption und Wirkung des Dekalogs in jüdischen und christlichen Schriften bis 200 n.Chr.*, AGJU 95 (Leiden: Brill, 2016), 87–269. For New Testament references to the love commandment and to the Decalogue, cf. Mark 10:19 par.; 12:31 par.; Rom 13:9; Gal 5:14.

2:25	Ῥαὰβ ἡ πόρνη ... ὑποδεξαμένη τοὺς ἀγγέλους καὶ ἑτέρᾳ ὁδῷ ἐκβαλοῦσα "Rahab the prostitute ... welcomed the messengers and sent them out by another road"	Josh 2:1–16 (cf. 6:22–25)	2:1 εἰσήλθοσαν εἰς οἰκίαν γυναικὸς πόρνης, ᾗ ὄνομα Ρααβ ... 16 εἰς τὴν ὀρεινὴν ἀπέλθετε, μὴ συναντήσωσιν ὑμῖν οἱ καταδιώκοντες ... καὶ μετὰ ταῦτα ἀπελεύσεσθε εἰς τὴν ὁδὸν ὑμῶν "they entered the house of a prostitute whose name was Rahab.... Depart into the hill country so that the pursuers may not come upon you ... and afterward you shall depart on your way"
5:10	προφῆται οἳ ἐλάλησαν ἐν τῷ ὀνόματι κυρίου "prophets who spoke in the name of the Lord"	Dan 9:6	καὶ οὐκ ἠκούσαμεν τῶν παίδων σου τῶν προφητῶν, ἃ ἐλάλησαν ἐπὶ τῷ ὀνόματί σου "And we have not obeyed your servants the prophets, what they spoke in your name"
	Ἰὼβ "Job"	Job passim	
5:17	Ἠλίας ... προσευχῇ προσηύξατο "Elijah prayed a prayer"	1 Kgs 18:1–45	1 καὶ ῥῆμα κυρίου ἐγένετο πρὸς Ηλιου ... καὶ δώσω ὑετὸν ἐπὶ πρόσωπον τῆς γῆς.... 24 καὶ ἐγὼ ἐπικαλέσομαι ἐν ὀνόματι κυρίου τοῦ θεοῦ μου, καὶ ἔσται ὁ θεός, ὃς ἐὰν ἐπακούσῃ ἐν πυρί, οὗτος θεός ... 36 καὶ ἀνεβόησεν Ηλιου εἰς τὸν οὐρανὸν καὶ εἶπεν Κύριε ὁ θεὸς Αβρααμ καὶ Ισαακ καὶ Ισραηλ, ἐπάκουσόν μου, κύριε ... 45 καὶ ἐγένετο ὑετὸς μέγας 1 "And it happened ... that a word of the Lord came to Eliou ... and I will give rain on the surface of the earth.... 24 and I will call on the name of the Lord, my God, and it will be, the god who answers by fire, he is God.... 36 And Eliou cried aloud to heaven and said, O Lord, God of Abraam and Isaak and Israel, heed me, O Lord ... 45 and there was a heavy rain"

At several places, the author mentions the names of figures prominent in Scripture. Throughout the letter, they form important parts of his argument.

In Jas 2:14-26, an excursus subordinated to his thesis that hearing, believing, and doing are not to be separated, James compiles two examples from Scripture (Abraham and Rahab). Later in the letter, the prophets are lumped together as examples of suffering and patience (5:10) and Job comes into play as a model of endurance or "steadfastness" (ὑπομονή, 5:11).[19] Elijah, who was particularly popular not only as a prophet but also as a fiery warrior for God (cf. 1 Kgs 17-19; 21; 2 Kgs 1-2; 2 Chr 21; Mal 3; Sir 48:1-11), as a model for trustful and enduring prayer concludes the letter exhortations (Jas 5:17-18). In each case, the references are very short, often consisting of nothing more than the names of the figures and a few words recollecting the story behind them. Taken together, however, these figures form something like a squad of people from Scripture who embody the qualities put forward in the exhortations of the letter.[20]

Again, I chose only one example to discuss in more detail. In his argument relating to the (false) opposition between faith and works, the author first points to Abraham, who "was justified by works" (2:21). By means of the Scripture he attempts to substantiate his thesis that faith without works is "dead" or "useless" (2:17, 20, 26).[21] Obviously, by the phrase "when he offered up his son Isaac on the altar" James alludes to Gen 22. He trusts that the letter recipients are aware of the whole story without repeating it. From the Greek text of the Septuagint, he picks up just one word (θυσιαστήριον), in addition to the names of Abraham and Isaac. This suffices to evoke the course of events retold not only in Scripture but in early Jewish writings as well.[22] However, the conclusion the author

---

19. Cf. Christopher R. Seitz, "The Patience of Job in the Epistle of James," in *Konsequente Traditionsgeschichte: Festschrift für Klaus Baltzer zum 65. Geburtstag*, ed. Rüdiger Bartelmus, OBO 126 (Fribourg: Universitätsverlag; Göttingen: Vandenhoeck & Ruprecht, 1993), 373-82; Nicholas J. Ellis, *The Hermeneutics of Divine Testing: Cosmic Trials and Biblical Interpretation in the Epistle of James and Other Jewish Literature*, WUNT 2/396 (Tübingen: Mohr Siebeck, 2015), 211-16.

20. It is impossible to enter here the extremely large field of receptions of biblical figures in early Jewish literature, although that field provides the supply for James's arguments and forms the horizon under which he had encountered them. Corresponding parts of the works of Philo and Josephus, who both, however, develop their own interpretations, provide rich material. Elaborate retellings of biblical stories belong to literary compositions as the Book of Jubilees, the Liber Antiquitatum Biblicarum, or the Testaments of the Twelve Patriarchs and to texts preserved only in the Qumran scrolls as well (e.g., the Genesis Apocryhon, 1Q20). See for textual evidence on Abraham: Jub. 11-23; Philo, *Virt.* 212-17; *Migr.*; *Abr.*; Josephus, *Ant.* 1.154-256; LAB 6-8; on Rahab: Josephus, *Ant.* 5.1-15; on Elijah: Sir 48:1-11; Josephus, *Ant.* 13.316-362; 9.20-28; Liv. Pro. 21; on Job: Aristeas the Exegete; Testament of Job.

21. Cf. Ellis, *Hermeneutics of Divine Testing*, 199-211.

22. For Abraham in early Jewish literature, see Robert J. Foster, *The Significance of Exemplars for the Interpretation of the Letter of James*, WUNT 2/376 (Tübingen: Mohr Siebeck, 2014), 62-75; Peter H. Davids, "The Pseudepigrapha in the Catholic Epistles," in *The Pseudepigrapha*

draws—that Abraham's "faith was active along with his works, and faith was completed by his works" (2:22)—is what matters for his argument. Moreover, he underlines that conclusion by quoting Gen 15:6, "Abraham believed God, and it was counted to him as righteousness," introduced by the phrase "the Scripture was fulfilled that says."[23] Finally, he adds, "he [i.e., Abraham] was called a friend of God" (2:23). Whether the letter recipients are aware that this phrase does not belong to the text of Scripture is difficult to say.[24] Syntactically, it continues the sentence without division (ἐπίστευσεν δὲ Ἀβραάμ ... καὶ ἐλογίσθη ... καὶ φίλος θεοῦ ἐκλήθη). Only in 2:24 does the author address the audience again by repeating his thesis. Possibly, by calling Abraham "friend of God," he wanted to allude to narrative traditions alive in Jewish literature, but this remains unproven.[25]

The second example from Scripture occurring as an argument for the thesis that "faith apart from works is dead" (2:26) is Rahab the prostitute (cf. Josh 2:1–16; 6:22–25). Although Rahab is a quite prominent figure in early Christian literature (cf. Matt 1:5) and her faith was regarded as paradigmatic (cf. Heb 11:31; 1 Clem. 12:1–8), only James puts her on par with Abraham and emphasizes her "being justified" (ἐδικαιώθη). Again, the name and a short phrase alluding to a single scene from the biblical story suffice to recollect the full course of events: Rahab "received the messengers and sent them out by another way" (ὑποδεξαμένη τοὺς ἀγγέλους καὶ ἑτέρᾳ ὁδῷ ἐκβαλοῦσα, 2:25). Only readers who knew the story could make any sense out of this brief excerpt.

Thus, the whole section of the argument in Jas 2:21–26 exemplarily demonstrates how James knows and uses the Scriptures of Israel. To substantiate his arguments and intentions, in this single paragraph he combines different ways of referring to Scripture. He mentions names known from Scripture, alludes to stories or texts by using short phrases, quotes a phrase verbatim, points explicitly to what Scripture says, or does all that at once. Scripture offers a stock of examples and ideas useful to refer to and to justify what the author wants to express or explain by his letter. In other cases mentioned above, the function of figures

---

and Early Biblical Interpretation, ed. James H. Charlesworth and Craig A. Evans, JSPSup 14 (Sheffield: JSOT Press, 1993), 228–45, esp. 228–31.

23. The quotation of Gen 15:6, combined with an argument about "faith" and "works," reminds any reader of Paul's argument in his letters to the Galatians and to the Romans on justification by faith in Christ without "works of the law" (cf. Gal 3:6; Rom 4:3). However, James does not speak of "works of the law" or have in mind any problems of gentiles belonging to the Christ believers, which is the background of Paul's argument on justification. Therefore, I assume that both independently of each other refer to the same passage from Scripture to corroborate their particular arguments.

24. But cf. 2 Chr 20:7; Isa 41:8.

25. Cf. Jub. 19:9; CD III, 2; Philo, *Abr.* 273; *Migr.* 44–45 (referring to Gen 15:6!).

Israel's Scriptures in James

summoned from Scripture is less argumentative. Job, Elijah, or the prophets are role models for the readers to identify with and to apply in their personal decisions of everyday life.[26]

Prophetic Paraenesis and Eschatological Exhortation (Verbal Allusions or Unmarked Citations)

Table 21.4. Prophetic Paraenesis and Eschatological Exhortation (Verbal Allusions or Unmarked Citations)

1:10–11	ὡς ἄνθος χόρτου ... ὁ ἥλιος ... ἐξήρανεν τὸν χόρτον, καὶ τὸ ἄνθος αὐτοῦ ἐξέπεσεν "like a flower in the field ... the sun ... withers the grass, and its flower falls"	Isa 40:6–7 Job 14:2	6 Πᾶσα σὰρξ χόρτος, καὶ πᾶσα δόξα ἀνθρώπου ὡς ἄνθος χόρτου· 7 ἐξηράνθη ὁ χόρτος, καὶ τὸ ἄνθος ἐξέπεσεν 6 "All flesh is grass; and all the glory of man is like the flower of grass. 7 The grass has withered, and the flower has fallen" ὥσπερ ἄνθος ἀνθῆσαν ἐξέπεσεν "like a flower that has bloomed, drops off"
1:27	ἐπισκέπτεσθαι ὀρφανοὺς καὶ χήρας "to care for orphans and widows"	Isa 1:17, 23 Jer 22:3; cf. Ezek 22:7	μάθετε καλὸν ποιεῖν ... κρίνατε ὀρφανῷ καὶ δικαιώσατε χήραν· "learn to do good ... defend the orphan and do justice to the widow" Ποιεῖτε κρίσιν καὶ δικαιοσύνην ... καὶ ὀρφανὸν καὶ χήραν μὴ καταδυναστεύετε "Do justice and righteousness ... and do not act impiously against ... orphan and widow"
4:4	Μοιχαλίδες "adulterers"	Hos 3:1	πορεύθητι καὶ ἀγάπησον γυναῖκα ἀγαπῶσαν πονηρὰ καὶ μοιχαλίν, καθὼς ἀγαπᾷ ὁ θεὸς τοὺς υἱοὺς Ισραηλ καὶ αὐτοὶ ἀποβλέπουσιν ἐπὶ θεοὺς ἀλλοτρίους

---

26. Comment of Vincent Hirschi, private communication. Cf. also Foster, *Exemplars*, 59–204.

			"Go again and love a woman who loves evil things and is an adulteress, just as God loves the sons of Israel, but they turn their attention to foreign gods"
5:3	φάγεται τὰς σάρκας ὑμῶν ὡς πῦρ ἐθησαυρίσατε ἐν ἐσχάταις ἡμέραις "it will eat your flesh like fire. You have laid up treasure for the last days"	Ps 20:10	Κύριος ἐν ὀργῇ αὐτοῦ συνταράξει αὐτούς, καὶ καταφάγεται αὐτοὺς πῦρ. "The Lord will confound them in his wrath, and fire will devour them"
		Jdt 16:17	κύριος παντοκράτωρ ἐκδικήσει αὐτοὺς ἐν ἡμέρᾳ κρίσεως δοῦναι πῦρ καὶ σκώληκας εἰς σάρκας αὐτῶν "the omnipotent Lord will punish them in the day of judgment, to send fire and worms for their flesh"
5:7	ἕως λάβῃ πρόϊμον καὶ ὄψιμον "until it receives the early and the late rains"	Deut 11:14	καὶ δώσει τὸν ὑετὸν τῇ γῇ σου καθ' ὥραν πρόϊμον καὶ ὄψιμον "he too will give the rain for your land in season, early rain and later rain"
		Jer 5:24	Φοβηθῶμεν δὴ κύριον τὸν θεὸν ἡμῶν τὸν διδόντα ἡμῖν ὑετὸν πρόϊμον καὶ ὄψιμον "Do let us fear the Lord our God, who gives us rain, early rain and late rain"
		Hos 6:3	τοῦ γνῶναι τὸν κύριον, ὡς ὄρθρον ἕτοιμον εὑρήσομεν αὐτόν, καὶ ἥξει ὡς ὑετὸς ἡμῖν πρόϊμος καὶ ὄψιμος τῇ γῇ "to know the Lord; we will find him ready as dawn, and he will come to us like the early and the latter rain to the earth"
5:10	προφῆται οἳ ἐλάλησαν ἐν τῷ ὀνόματι κυρίου "the prophets who spoke in the name of the Lord"	Dan 9:6	καὶ οὐκ ἠκούσαμεν τῶν παίδων σου τῶν προφητῶν, ἃ ἐλάλησαν ἐπὶ τῷ ὀνόματί σου "we have not obeyed your servants the prophets, what they spoke in your name"

Most of the references to Scripture in the Letter of James belong to the category of verbal allusion. I use this term as proposed by the editors of this volume to mark a reference to a specific word or string of words without an explicit marker. However, this category is most difficult to define exactly. There are several phrases used in the letter that are typical to express particular motifs of scriptural and early Jewish traditions, like "orphans and widows" (1:27), "in the last days" (5:3), or "in the name of the Lord" (5:10). However, to decide whether such a word or phrase represents an allusion to Scripture often depends on the feeling of the exegete (or on the technology applied by searching the texts). I here limit my inspection to phrases that point to prophetic traditions and that highlight the paraenetical and eschatological perspective of the letter.

The clearest case for a verbal concordance with a prophetic saying is Jas 1:10–11: "like a flower of the grass he [i.e., the rich man] will pass away. For the sun rises with its scorching heat and withers the grass; its flower falls, and its beauty perishes."[27] In the exposition of his argument, the author takes up a popular metaphor and turns it toward the lowly brother and the rich in the congregation. Thereby he admonishes them not to trust to fading values like wealth or high rank. The metaphor of withering grass and fading flowers occurs prominently in Isa 40:6–7 (ὡς ἄνθος χόρτου· ἐξηράνθη ὁ χόρτος, καὶ τὸ ἄνθος ἐξέπεσεν). However, Isaiah uses the metaphor to point to the transiency of all human beings (πᾶσα σὰρξ χόρτος καὶ πᾶσα δόξα ἀνθρώπου, 40:6), in contrast to the word of God that will stand forever (40:8). Therefore, he proclaims: "the glory of the Lord shall be revealed" (40:5). James, on the other hand, focuses on God's judgment over the rich, in particular, who will "fade away in the midst of his pursuits" (ὁ πλούσιος ἐν ταῖς πορείαις αὐτοῦ μαρανθήσεται, 1:11). By taking up the metaphor, he creates a little story about the events in which the sun rises and the flower fades.[28] If we take into account that the metaphor occurs several times in Scripture and beyond, it remains doubtful whether James intended to allude to Scripture at all.[29]

Other references to prophetic texts are even less clear. Often it is a single word or a short phrase that reminds the reader of passages from Scripture, but sometimes the motifs evoked are so common that one doubts whether any reference to the Scriptures is intended. In this paragraph, I refer to some phrases that sound particularly biblical, without arguing that the author intended to remind his audience of Scripture in every case.

The pair consisting of "orphans and widows" several times in Scripture represents people in social need or people who risk being oppressed.[30] By using that

---

27. Cf. Michael Glöckner, *Bildhafte Sprache im Jakobusbrief: Form, Inhalt und Erschließungspotential der metaphorischen Rede einer frühchristlichen Schrift*, ABIG 69 (Leipzig: Evangelische Verlagsanstalt, 2021), 159–74.

28. Cf. aorist forms like ἀνέτειλεν, ἐξήρανεν, ἐξέπεσεν, ἀπώλετο.

29. Cf. Job 14:2; 1 Pet 1:24; Matt 6:30 // Luke 12:28.

30. Most notably in the Prophets (cf. Isa 1:17, 23; Jer 7:6; 22:3; Ezek 22:7), but in the Torah (cf. Exod 22:21; Deut 10:18; 14:29) and the Writings as well (cf. Pss 67:6; 145:9).

phrase, James intends to characterize the right way of piety (θρησκεία, 1:27). In Jas 4:4, he picks up the term μοιχαλίς ("adulterer") used by prophets to describe the wrong relationship between Israel and God. Thus, the prophet Hosea shall marry an adulterous woman (γυναῖκα ἀγαπῶσαν πονηρὰ καὶ μοιχαλίν) to symbolize how "the Lord loves the children of Israel, though they turn to other gods and love cakes of raisins" (Hos 3:1). The same metaphor (and term) occurs in Ezekiel and Malachi (cf. Ezek 16:38; 23:45; Mal 3:5). James, by using the unusual feminine form of the word, probably intended to remind his audience of that prophetic tradition, but not a specific text in the prophets. A similar reference to prophetic literature seems to be manifest in Jas 5:7. Here, the author admonishes his audience to be patient like a farmer "who waits for the precious fruit of the earth, being patient about it, until it receives the early and the late rains" (ἕως λάβῃ πρόϊμον καὶ ὄψιμον). The last phrase may remind them of terms used in Jer 5:24 and Hos 6:3. Yet, the motif occurs in the Torah as well to motivate Israel to keep the commandments of the law in the promised land (Deut 11:14).[31] However, the metaphor looks too common and natural to prove a conscious reference to Scripture.

A full cluster of terms and phrases alluding to prophetic traditions governs the last argumentative section of the letter (Jas 5:1–6).[32] The paragraph consists of a series of sharp polemics against the rich who oppress the day laborer and live in luxury and self-indulgence (5:5). Several of the motifs are conventional in prophetic proclamations of God's judgment over those who oppress the poor or over the enemies of God's people. Thus, Isaiah threatens those who deride the righteous that "the moth will eat them up like a garment, and the worm will eat them like wool" (ἱμάτιον ... βρωθήσεται ὑπὸ σητός, Isa 51:8; cf. τὰ ἱμάτια ὑμῶν σητόβρωτα γέγονεν, Jas 5:2). That the Lord will punish Israel's enemies is a promise to Israel's king according to Ps 20:10: "the Lord will swallow them up in his wrath, and fire will consume them" (κύριος ἐν ὀργῇ αὐτοῦ συνταράξει αὐτούς, καὶ καταφάγεται αὐτοὺς πῦρ; cf. φάγεται τὰς σάρκας ὑμῶν ὡς πῦρ, Jas 5:3). In Jdt 16:17, a similar threat against the gentiles occurs: "The omnipotent Lord will punish them in the day of judgment, to send fire and worms to their flesh" (δοῦναι πῦρ καὶ σκώληκας εἰς σάρκας αὐτῶν). The judgment day is called "a day of slaughter" (ἡμέρα σφαγῆς) in Jer 12:3, like in Jas 5:5. Particularly eye-catching is the term κύριος Σαβαώθ (Lord of hosts) in Jas 5:4, for Σαβαώθ is the only non-Greek word occurring in the letter. The phrase εἰς τὰ ὦτα (κυρίου) ("to the ears [of the Lord]") appears several times in Scripture (cf. Isa 5:9; Ps 17:7) to express the assurance that God will listen to the prayers of the oppressed.

---

31. Cf. Vincent Hirschi, *Friendship or Enmity? The Christian and the World in the Letter of James* (Eugene, OR: Resource Publications, 2019), 91–94.

32. See Glöckner, *Bildhafte Sprache im Jakobusbrief*, 205–48.

To conclude this section, verbal allusions to Scripture presumably occur in all parts of the letter but rarely appear in a way that would make allusions to any particular texts definite. Often, the language of James appears influenced by common motifs without the need to assume any references to particular verses or chapters. Words or phrases that may originally go back to texts or concepts from Scripture have become a part of current arguments and intentions of the letter writer. The sound of that language may remind the recipients of what they are accustomed to read in or to receive from Scripture. This refers especially to expressions related to ethical admonitions or to proclamations about God's eschatological judgment. The particular religious character of the letter emerges from that language.

The Nature of the Scriptural Text

Taking into account the brevity of the letter and the low number of exact citations, one has to be cautious with regard to any conclusions about the textual character of the writings used in James. The few citations in Jas 2:8, 11, 23 and 4:6 do not show any peculiarities. The change of κύριος from Prov 3:34 into ὁ θεός in Jas 4:6 cannot prove a different version of the textual tradition, but follows the variable use of terms for God and Jesus Christ in the letter.[33] All remaining citations resemble Septuagint readings. Therefore, there is no hint that the author had access to Greek versions of Scripture other than the Septuagint.

Conclusion

The use of the Scriptures of Israel in the Epistle of James is multifaceted, more than the few marked references to Scripture would suggest. By calling the addressees the twelve tribes in dispersion, in the prescript of the letter the author creates a scriptural frame for his communication that is needed to understand the following corpus. In all of its parts, he points or alludes to Scripture in different ways to strengthen his arguments and intentions. Toward the end of the letter, such references become still denser so as to conclude that there is communication on that common basis of understanding. Obviously, the author presumes that the letter recipients are educated well enough in the Scriptures to follow his arguments. Even when he leaves open gaps in stories or uses only short phrases from Scripture, he can trust that the readers will fill them in from their previous knowledge or add the thoughts implied.

---

33. The same change occurs in 1 Pet 5:5; 1 Clem. 30:2; Ign. *Eph.* 5:3. This may speak for an early Christian collection of quotations from Scripture that James used.

Although some of the marked citations are part of his argument, James does not refer to Scripture from a halakic or more technically exegetical point of view. He does not intend to make clear the exact meaning of particular wordings of the texts or to explain different expressions in Scripture. Scripture for him is a pool of ideas or examples useful for developing and underlining his own ideas and intentions. He is not interested primarily in particularly notable passages of Scripture, but he selects quotations or allusions according to their usefulness for his argument. In any case, he attributes to the Scriptures of Israel an extraordinary authority. There is no doubt for him that Scripture speaks the truth, and there is no other external authority he wants his readers to accept (not even the Jesus tradition!). Therefore, his way of dealing with Scripture is, essentially, interpretation.

Beyond particular references to Scripture, the language of the letter and the thoughts of the author are framed by the convictional world of the people of Israel that in itself is based on Scripture. This also applies to his confession of the Lord Jesus Christ, which he shares with his audience. For both the author and his audience, the Scriptures of Israel do not consist of written texts from prior ages, but are the living word of God to be heard and followed today.

Bibliography

Albertz, Rainer. *Elia: Ein feuriger Kämpfer für Gott*. 3rd ed. Biblische Gestalten 13. Leipzig: Evangelische Verlagsanstalt, 2012.

Allison, Dale C., Jr. *A Critical and Exegetical Commentary on the Epistle of James*. ICC. New York: Bloomsbury, 2013.

Burchard, Christoph. *Der Jakobusbrief*. HNT 15.1. Tübingen: Mohr Siebeck, 2000.

Davids, Peter H. "The Pseudepigrapha in the Catholic Epistles." Pages 228–45 in *The Pseudepigrapha and Early Biblical Interpretation*. Edited by James H. Charlesworth and Craig A. Evans. JSPSup 14. Sheffield: JSOT Press, 1993.

DeSilva, David A. *The Jewish Teacher of Jesus, James, and Jude: What Earliest Christianity Learned from the Apocrypha and Pseudepigrapha*. New York: Oxford University Press, 2012.

Doering, Lutz. *Ancient Jewish Letters and the Beginnings of Christian Epistolography*. WUNT 298. Tübingen: Mohr Siebeck, 2012.

Ellis, Nicholas J. *The Hermeneutics of Divine Testing: Cosmic Trials and Biblical Interpretation in the Epistle of James and Other Jewish Literature*. WUNT 2/396. Tübingen: Mohr Siebeck, 2015.

Foster, Robert J. *The Significance of Exemplars for the Interpretation of the Letter of James*. WUNT 2/376. Tübingen: Mohr Siebeck, 2014.

Glöckner, Michael. *Bildhafte Sprache im Jakobusbrief: Form, Inhalt und Erschließungspotential der metaphorischen Rede einer frühchristlichen Schrift*. ABIG 69. Leipzig: Evangelische Verlagsanstalt, 2021.

Hirschi, Vincent. *Friendship or Enmity? The Christian and the World in the Letter of James*. Eugene, OR: Resource Publications, 2019.

Jobes, Karen H. "The Minor Prophets in James, 1 and 2 Peter and Jude." Pages 135–53 in *The Minor Prophets in the New Testament*. Edited by Maarten J. J. Menken and Steve Moyise. LNTS 377. London: T&T Clark, 2009.

Johnson, Luke Timothy. "The Use of Leviticus 19 in the Letter of James." *JBL* 101, no. 3 (1982): 391–401.

Kamell, Mariam J. "Incarnating Jeremiah's Promised New Covenant in the 'Law' of James." *EvQ* 83, no. 1 (2011): 19–28.

Kamell Kovalishyn, Mariam. "The Prayer of Elijah in James 5: An Example of Intertextuality." *JBL* 137, no. 4 (2018): 1027–45.

Konradt, Matthias. "The Love Command in Matthew, James, and the Didache." Pages 271–88 in *Matthew, James, and the Didache: Three Related Documents in Their Jewish and Christian Settings*. Edited by Huub van de Sandt and Jürgen Zangenberg. SymS 45. Atlanta: Society of Biblical Literature, 2009.

Luther, Susanne. "Strategies of Authorizing Tradition in the Letter of James." Pages 209–23 in *Authoritative Writings in Early Judaism and Early Christianity: Their Origin, Collection, and Meaning*. Edited by Tobias Nicklas and Jens Schröter. WUNT 441. Tübingen: Mohr Siebeck, 2020.

Mason, Eric F. "Use of Biblical and Other Jewish Traditions in James." Pages 27–43 in *Reading the Epistle of James: A Resource for Students*. Edited by Eric F. Mason and Darian R. Lockett. Atlanta: SBL Press, 2019.

Niebuhr, Karl-Wilhelm. "The Epistle of James in Light of Early Jewish Diaspora Letters." Pages 67–83 in *The Catholic Epistles: Critical Readings*. Edited by Darian R. Lockett. Edinburgh: T&T Clark, 2021.

———. *Gesetz und Paränese: Katechismusartige Weisungsreihen in der frühjüdischen Literatur*. WUNT 2/28. Tübingen: Mohr Siebeck, 1987.

———. "Jakobus und Paulus über das Innere des Menschen und den Ursprung seiner ethischen Entscheidungen." *NTS* 62, no. 1 (2016): 1–30.

———. "James." Pages 259–75 in *The Reception of Jesus in the First Three Centuries*. Vol. 1 of *From Paul to Josephus: Literary Receptions of Jesus in the First Century CE*. Edited by Helen K. Bond. London: T&T Clark, 2020.

———. "James and the Historical Jesus." In *Oxford Handbook of Hebrews and the Catholic Epistles*. Edited by Patrick Gray. New York: Oxford University Press, forthcoming.

———. "One God, One Lord in James." Pages 172–88 in *Monotheism and Christology in Greco-Roman Antiquity*. Edited by Matthew V. Novenson. NovTSup 180. Leiden: Brill, 2020.

Popkes, Wiard. "James and Scripture: An Exercise in Intertextuality." *NTS* 45, no. 2 (1999): 213–29.

Seitz, Christopher R. "The Patience of Job in the Epistle of James." Pages 373–82 in *Konsequente Traditionsgeschichte: Festschrift für Klaus Baltzer zum 65. Geburtstag*. Edited by Rüdiger Bartelmus. OBO 126. Fribourg: Universitätsverlag; Göttingen: Vandenhoeck & Ruprecht, 1993.

Unnik, Willem C. van. *Das Selbstverständnis der jüdischen Diaspora in der hellenistisch-römischen Zeit*. Edited by Pieter W. van der Horst. AGJU 17. Leiden: Brill, 1993.

Vos, J. Cornelis de. *Rezeption und Wirkung des Dekalogs in jüdischen und christlichen Schriften bis 200 n.Chr*. AGJU 95. Leiden: Brill, 2016.

Wick, Peter. "'You Shall Not Murder. . . . You Shall Not Commit Adultery': Theological and Anthropological Radicalization in the Letter of James and in the Sermon on the Mount." Pages 88–96 in *The Decalogue in Jewish and Christian Tradition*. Edited by Henning Graf Reventlow and Yair Hoffman. LHBOTS 509. New York: T&T Clark, 2011.

22

Israel's Scriptures in 1 Peter, Jude, and 2 Peter

JÖRG FREY

Discussing 1–2 Peter and Jude in a single chapter means putting together quite different items. The three writings, assembled in the collection of the Catholic Epistles, are written by different authors who were not part of a common "school."[1] They represent different theological interests and address different audiences. First and Second Peter are both ascribed to Simon Peter, but the marked differences in language, themes, and theology demonstrate that they cannot originate from the same author. In the view of critical scholarship, 2 Peter is probably the last writing that made it into the New Testament canon. It is certainly pseudonymous, designed as a literary testament of Peter. First Peter is probably also pseudonymous and written after Peter's martyrdom in Rome (cf. 1 Pet 5:13). The author of 2 Peter refers to 1 Peter, which was apparently known to his audience and accepted as a Petrine testimony. But, strikingly, he feels no need to imitate the form or style of 1 Peter.[2] This may suggest that 2 Peter not only relates itself to the Peter of 1 Peter but more widely to Petrine images from the Gospels and Acts and possibly even later texts, such as the Apocalypse of

---

1. This was suggested by Richard Bauckham, *Jude, 2 Peter*, WBC 50 (Waco, TX: Word, 1983); Marion L. Soards, "1 Peter, 2 Peter, and Jude as Evidence for a Petrine School," *ANRW* 25.5:3827–49; but cf. Jörg Frey, "Von der 'petrinischen Schule' zum 'petrinischen Diskurs,'" in *Petrusliteratur und Petrusarchäologie: Römische Begegnungen*, ed. Jörg Frey and Martin Wallraff, Rom und der Protestantismus 4 (Tübingen: Mohr Siebeck, 2020), 87–124.

2. The marked differences were already perceived in antiquity, e.g., by Jerome, *Vir. ill.* 1.

Peter or even the Kerygma of Peter.[3] Thus, 2 Peter is part of a "Petrine discourse" in the mid-second century.[4]

With regard to 2 Peter and Jude, the literary relationship has been thoroughly discussed with the result that 2 Peter extensively draws on Jude, adopting its central part (Jude 3–18), albeit with significant changes (2 Pet 2:1–3:4).[5] But 2 Peter was probably composed at a different place and in a different community context and with different problems and opponents in view, and the addressees probably did not know Jude. No direct relationship can be shown between Jude and 1 Peter. Jude and 2 Peter are usually treated together in commentaries due to their dependence.[6] Combining even 1 and 2 Peter and Jude in one investigation mirrors the more traditional view of a common authorship between 1 and 2 Peter or a common school context, which has been thoroughly revised in more recent scholarship.[7]

1 Peter

Introduction

First Peter is a paraenetic and consolatory "diaspora letter," addressed to predominantly gentile (1 Pet 1:14) Jesus followers in Asia Minor who are characterized as living in the dispersion (1 Pet 1:1), that is, who through their new religious orientation have become outsiders in their non-Christian environment and thus share the Jewish diaspora experience.[8] The letter, composed in the name of Pe-

---

3. See Wolfgang Grünstäudl, *Petrus Alexandrinus: Studien zum historischen und theologischen Ort des zweiten Petrusbriefes*, WUNT 2/353 (Tübingen: Mohr Siebeck, 2013); Jörg Frey, Matthijs den Dulk, and Jan G. van der Watt, eds., *2 Peter and the Apocalypse of Peter: Towards a New Perspective*, BibInt 174 (Leiden: Brill, 2019).

4. See Frey, "Von der 'petrinischen Schule.'"

5. See Jörg Frey, *The Letter of Jude and the Second Letter of Peter: A Theological Commentary*, trans. Kathleen Ess (Waco, TX: Baylor University Press, 2018), 182–92.

6. Cf. Bauckham, *Jude, 2 Peter*; Anton Vögtle, *Der Judasbrief, Der zweite Petrusbrief*, EKKNT 22 (Solothurn: Benziger; Neukirchen-Vluyn: Neukirchener Verlag, 1994); Henning Paulsen, *Der zweite Petrusbrief und der Judasbrief*, KEK 12.2 (Göttingen: Vandenhoeck & Ruprecht, 1992); Peter H. Davids, *The Letters of 2 Peter and Jude*, PNTC (Grand Rapids: Eerdmans, 2006); Frey, *Letter of Jude and the Second Letter of Peter*.

7. For the older view, see Charles Bigg, *A Critical and Exegetical Commentary on the Epistles of St. Peter and St. Jude*, ICC (Edinburgh: T&T Clark, 1901); Karl-Hermann Schelkle, *Die Petrusbriefe. Der Judasbrief*, HThKNT 13.2 (Freiburg im Breisgau: Herder, 1961); J. N. D. Kelly, *The Epistles of Peter and of Jude*, BNTC (London: Black, 1969).

8. Cf. 1 Pet 1:1; 2:11; 4:4, etc. See Reinhard Feldmeier, *Die Christen als Fremde: Die Metapher*

ter, the "witness of Jesus's sufferings and participant in the glory to be revealed" (1 Pet 5:1), probably presupposes Peter's martyrdom in Rome (1 Pet 5:13) and aims at consoling and consolidating the addressees in various experiences of hostility and suffering (cf. 1 Pet 1:6; 2:20; 4:12–14). Whereas earlier scholars often considered 1 Peter as mainly influenced by Paul, more recent interpreters perceive a wider range of early Christian traditions in the background.[9]

First Peter includes a dense web of scriptural citations and allusions, which cannot always be clearly identified.[10] Scripture is the only source of the author's thought world that is explicitly named.[11] Yet, only two citations are clearly marked as Scripture, namely 1 Pet 1:16, where διότι γέγραπται, "wherefore it is written," introduces the command of holiness from Lev 19:2 and 1 Pet 2:6–8 with διότι περιέχει ἐν γραφῇ, "wherefore it is contained in Scripture," introducing a sequence of quotations from Isa 28:16; Ps 118:22; and Isa 8:14 related to the motif of the λίθος ("stone"). Two more citations are only briefly marked, with διότι, "wherefore," introducing Isa 40:6–8 in 1 Pet 1:24–25a, or γάρ, "for, because," which connects the long citation of Ps 34:13–17 in 1 Pet 3:10–12 with its context.[12] First Peter utilizes all parts of the Scriptures of Israel, the Pentateuch, the Prophets, and the Writings, with a preference for Isaiah and—somewhat less—Psalms and Proverbs.[13] There are long citations, such as Ps 34:13–17; combinations, such as 2:4; 2:6–8; and 2:9–10; and midrashic expositions, such as 1 Pet 2:4–8, where

---

der Fremde in der antiken Welt, im Urchristentum und im 1. Petrusbrief, WUNT 64 (Tübingen: Mohr Siebeck, 1992); Reinhard Feldmeier, *Der erste Brief des Petrus*, THKNT 15.1 (Leipzig: Evangelische Verlagsanstalt, 2005) (ET: *The First Letter of Peter: A Commentary on the Greek Text*, trans. Peter H. Davids [Waco, TX: Baylor University Press, 2008]). For diaspora letters, see Lutz Doering, *Ancient Jewish Letters and the Beginning of Christian Epistolography*, WUNT 298 (Tübingen: Mohr Siebeck, 2012), 430–52.

9. Norbert Brox, *Der erste Petrusbrief*, EKKNT 21 (Zurich: Einsiedeln; Cologne: Benziger, 1979), 47–51; Jens Herzer, *Petrus oder Paulus? Studien über das Verhältnis des Ersten Petrusbriefes zur paulinischen Tradition*, WUNT 103 (Tübingen: Mohr Siebeck, 1998).

10. Cf. Reinhard Feldmeier, *Der erste Brief des Petrus*, 18 (ET: *The First Letter of Peter* [Waco: Baylor University Press, 2008], 26). The density of references is perhaps only matched by Revelation where there are, however, no marked citations at all, and by the Epistle to the Hebrews.

11. Paul J. Achtemeier, *1 Peter: A Commentary on First Peter*, Hermeneia (Minneapolis: Fortress, 1996), 12.

12. Achtemeier, *1 Peter*, 12.

13. From Isaiah: Isa 40:6 in 1:24; Isa 40:8–9 in 1:25; Isa 28:16 in 2:6; Isa 8:14 in 2:18; Isa 43:21 in 2:9; Isa 10:3 in 2:12; Isa 53:9 in 2:22; Isa 53:4, 12 in 2:24; Isa 53:5 in 2:24; Isa 53:6 in 2:25; Isa 8:12–13 in 3:14–15; Isa 11:2 in 4:14; cf. further the allusions to Isa 52:3 in 1:18; and to Isa 28:16 in 2:4. See Feldmeier, *Brief*, 18 (*The First Letter of Peter*, 26). From Psalms: Ps 33:9 in 2:3; Ps 118:22 in 2:7; Ps 34:13–17 in 3:10–12; Ps 22:14 in 5:8; cf. the allusions to Ps 118:22 in 2:4; Ps 39:13 in 2:11; Ps 89:51 in 4:14; Ps 55:23 in 5:7. See Feldmeier, *Brief*, 18 (*The First Letter of Peter*, 26). From Proverbs: Prov 10:12 in 4:8; Prov 11:31 in 4:18; Prov 3:34 LXX in 5:5; cf. the allusions to

various elements from Isa 53 are adopted and expounded. The entire thought world and all of the imagery of the author appears to be informed and shaped by the Scriptures, although they only "furnish illustrations for, but do not prove, the validity of the Christian faith."[14] This marks a decisive difference from, for example, the Pauline usage of the Scriptures in specific arguments about topics such as the legacy of Christ or the law.

Israel's Scriptures in 1 Peter

Table 22.1. Israel's Scriptures in 1 Peter

	Marked Quotations	Unmarked Quotations	Allusions	Paradigms and References
1:2			Exod 24:7–8	
1:7			Prov 17:3	
1:10				Prophets
1:13			Prov 31:17	
1:16			Lev 11:44–45; 19:2	
1:18			Isa 52:3	
1:34–25a	Isa 40:6–8			
2:3		Ps 33:9 LXX		
2:4			Isa 28:16; Ps 118:22	
2:6–8	Isa 28:16; Ps 118(117):22 LXX; Isa 8:14			
2:9		Exod 23, 22 LXX; Isa 43:21	Exod 19:6; 23:22	
2:10			Hos 1:6, 9	
2:11			Gen 23:4; Ps 39:13	
2:12		Isa 10:3		
2:17			Prov 24:21	
2:22		Isa 53:9		

Prov 17:3 in 1:7; Prov 31:17 in 1:13; Prov 24:21 in 2:17; Prov 3:25 in 3:6. See Feldmeier, *Brief*, 18 (*The First Letter of Peter*, 26).

14. Achtemeier, *1 Peter*, 12–13 n. 117.

2:24		Isa 53:4, 12; 53:5	
2:25		Isa 53:6	
3:5–6			Sarah
3:6		Gen 18:12; Prov 3:25	
3:10–12	Ps 34:13–17	Ps 34:13–17	
3:14–15		Isa 8:12–13	
3:20		Gen 7:13–23	
3:20–21			Noah/flood
4:8		Prov 10:12	
4:14		Isa 11:2	Ps 89:51
4:18		Prov 11:31 LXX	
5:5		Prov 3:34 LXX	
5:7			Ps 55:23
5:8		Ps 22:14	Exod 22:25; Job 1:7

In 1 Pet 1:10, there is an important conceptual reference to the prophets (1 Pet 1:10). Although their number and names are unspecified, the hint may refer to the authors of the prophetic books, understood as historical figures, in whom the Spirit—notably "the Spirit of Christ" (1:11)—was active in authoring their words. The content of their prophecy is specified: It is "the grace" (1:10) and, more specifically, the sufferings of Christ and the glory that should follow. While the prophets themselves sought to know what time and which person their words referred to, the addressees now know that reference, as they live in the time of fulfillment. Thus 1 Peter shares the conviction widely held in the early Jesus movement that prophecy refers to Christ and to the present state of the community of Jesus followers. Thus, the prophets were actually to serve not their contemporaries but the present community, and the Scriptures were written for the instruction of the present generation. It was already the Spirit of Christ who inspired the prophetic words related to the Christ event, and while the prophets themselves did not know the true reference of their words, this is now revealed. This prophetic and eschatological understanding of the Scriptures (not only the Prophets but also the Pentateuch and the Writings) has close parallels not only at Qumran (1QpHab VII, 1–5) but also in Paul (1 Cor 10:11).

Further explicit references to biblical stories are the mention of Sarah as an example of a decent "holy woman" (1 Pet 3:5–6) and the reference to Noah and the flood as an example of God's patience (1 Pet 3:20–21). Here, another pattern of the relationship between scriptural phenomena and the present of the addressees is established: The salvation of eight persons ("souls") through the water is called an ἀντίτυπος ("antitype") of the present salvation through baptism, so that a typological correspondence is established between the scriptural reality and the present reality in faith. But here, in notable difference from the only other passage where this term is used in the New Testament (Heb 9:24), the present reality is not an inferior copy of the original but rather an equal or even superior continuation in God's salvific activity.[15] There is similarity or even continuity between then and now, but the old is not considered or quoted for its own sake, but merely due to its importance for the present.

This can be shown from the citation of Isa 40:6–9 in 1 Pet 1:24. The quoted verses stress the aspect of the abiding validity of God's word. However, in the context, the "living and abiding word of God" (1:23) is the generative power that caused the rebegetting of the addressees. Thus, when quoting the passage about the eternity of God's word, the author is not interested in the abiding quality of the scriptural word of God but rather in the abiding and eternal quality of the new word, through which the readers received their new life in Christ. Thus, the old is completely utilized for qualifying the new. Unlike, for example, in Paul or in the Gospels, there is no argument about the scriptural legacy of Christ or aspects of Christian life. Nor is there any reflection about the relationship between biblical Israel and the present situation of the gentile believers in Jesus.

The vast variety of scriptural motifs and images can be presented only in a small selection: the motif of "inheritance" (κληρονομία) in 1:4 recalls the division of the land in Joshua but is now related to the heavenly inheritance of the Jesus followers, who are dispersed foreigners on earth. The motif of trials and temptations in which faith will prove genuine "like gold in fire" (1:6–7) has numerous analogies in the wisdom literature (cf. Wis 3:5–6) but was already adopted in other early Christian traditions (1 Cor 3:13; Rev 3:18). The image of the believers as newborn infants (2:2) is linked with a shortened psalm verse about tasting the kindness of the Lord (Ps 34:9 [33:9 LXX]). The quotation is not marked, but it is a clear adoption and adaption of scriptural language.

Most important is the dense appropriation of Isa 53 in 2:21–25, which is read without any hesitation as a description of the passion of Jesus. Various parts of Isa 53:4, 5, 9, 12 are inserted into the paraenetic text of the author as unmarked citations; thus the author appropriates the scriptural narrative of Christ's suffering for his own exhortation: Christ suffered for the sake and healing of the addressees, but in his suffering he also left an example of behavior they should follow (2:21). Soteriological and ethical aspects are closely interwoven and related to the present situation of the addressees and their sufferings.

---

15. Cf. Achtemeier, *1 Peter*, 267.

The complex web of scriptural images can be demonstrated in the dense passage 2:4-10: The image of the believers as living stones of a spiritual house (1 Pet 2:5) adopts scriptural temple imagery in a way that has striking parallels in the Dead Sea Scrolls where the pure community, living in separation from the Jerusalem temple cult, was also considered a "temple of humans" (4Q174 1-2 I, 6; cf. also Paul in 1 Cor 3:9-17). The image is combined with the qualification of the addressees as a "holy priesthood" bringing spiritual sacrifices (1 Pet 2:5), "royal priesthood" (Exod 19:6), "holy nation," "people for God's own possession" (Isa 43:21), and "people of God" (Hos 1:6, 9). By the author's adopting a whole cluster of scriptural motifs, the particular quality of Israel as the elected and holy nation is completely transferred to the gentile believers in Jesus. The connection between Jesus and the believers is established by the christological application of the scriptural prophecy of the chosen and precious stone or the cornerstone in Zion (Isa 28:16) and of the saying about the stone that was rejected by many and thus became a stumbling stone (Ps 118:22 [117:22 LXX]). So the identity of the believers as living stones in a spiritual temple is related to and based on the identity of Christ as the chosen cornerstone.

First Peter, thus, shows the quick adaption of various techniques of scriptural interpretation in the early Christian tradition (possibly independent from Paul) and the liberty of combining different texts and adapting them for creating a new thought world made from a mosaic or patchwork of biblical motifs and ideas that were now altogether related to life in Christ. There is no argument with Jews or alternative readings of the Scriptures; instead, the Jewish side is almost excluded and the Scriptures are completely appropriated for Christian reading.

JUDE

Introduction

Jude is a brief polemical letter ascribed to Judas the brother of Jesus (and of James, see Jude 1) but written in a postapostolic period that looks back to the time of the apostles (Jude 18). The author addresses a particular community situation in which he saw the need to distance his audience from other teachers who still participated in community meals (Jude 12).[16] The clearest point of dispute is about the status of angels: While the author holds angelic beings in high esteem and repeatedly refers to angel traditions (Jude 6, 9), he accuses his

---

16. This means that Jude is not a "catholic" epistle in the sense that it is not addressed to a wider audience (as, e.g., James, 1 and 2 Peter).

opponents of "slandering" or rejecting angelic beings (Jude 8, 10; 16).[17] Such a disregard of angels might even be a view or practice in the line of Pauline (Rom 8:38-9; cf. 1 Cor 6:3; 15:24) or post-Pauline (Col 2:15-18) thought. It is uncertain to what extent the other charges against the opponents are merely polemical stereotypes because "heretics" are quite often considered arrogant, deceptive, and full of immoral behavior. The suggestion that the opponents turn grace into licentiousness (Jude 4) has caused interpreters to see the opponents as libertinists or antinomians, but it could also be a hint that those community members actually followed Pauline views, which appeared disrespectful in the eyes of the author, not only with regard to angelic beings but also to other aspects of the order of the world, law, and ethics. According to his views, such disrespectful people cannot be legitimate members of the community but are destined to death and destruction.

The assertion that for such people judgment is predetermined, that they are "long beforehand written down" (πάλαι προγεγραμμένοι) for judgment, is taken from the Scriptures, yet the entirety of scriptural argument in Jude is formed to prove the threat of judgment on the ungodly. Jude 5-7 and Jude 11 each provide three examples of judgment that are subsequently (Jude 8, 12) applied to the opponents (οὗτοι, "these," vv. 8, 12, 16). The only marked citation, in Jude 14-15, comes from the book of Enoch (1 En. 1:9), which for the author was indeed Scripture of highest authority. Enochic traditions are further referred to in Jude 6 and likely in Jude 12b-13; another apocalyptic tradition, probably from the lost end of the Assumption of Moses, is prominently referred to in Jude 9. Actually, Enoch is the only scriptural tradition that could be adduced as a proof for the idea that sinners are not punished immediately or at the time of their death but are kept imprisoned until the day of judgment. This is stated with regard to the angelic Watchers (1 En. 10:12), and this is presupposed when verse 6 says that the angels who had not kept their proper domain are kept in chains and darkness beneath the earth until the final judgment. Whereas the mention of the sin of the angels in Gen 6:1-4 is very brief and enigmatic, the extensive tale of the Watchers (1 En. 6-12) is the source of Jude 6. Enoch, as the scribe who proclaims the judgment over the Watchers (1 En. 12:4; 15:3) and the others who follow their sins, is the most important prophet.

The other scriptural episodes alluded to are the death of the wilderness generation (Jude 5: Num 14), then, linked with the Watchers episode (Jude 6: Gen

---

17. For introductory matters, consult Jörg Frey, "The Epistle of Jude between Judaism and Hellenism," in *The Catholic Epistles and the Apostolic Tradition*, ed. Karl-Wilhelm Niebuhr and Rob Wall (Waco, TX: Baylor University Press, 2009), 309-30; Frey, *Letter of Jude and the Second Letter of Peter*, 3-56.

6:1–4; 1 En. 6–12), the judgment over the Sodomites (Gen 19), and in Jude 11 the paradigmatically negative figures of Cain (Gen 4), Balaam (Num 22–24), and Korah (Num 16). These examples of sin and judgment are all taken from the narrative of the Pentateuch but read in the light of the later Jewish history of interpretation. There are no further citations or clear allusions to other Scriptures of the Prophets (other than Enoch) or the Writings. With its programmatic and well-structured use of examples (vv. 5–7, 11) culminating in the quotation from Enoch (v. 14–15) and, finally, an apostolic prophecy about the "scoffers" (vv. 17–18), Jude is a unique example of the paraenetic use of Scripture. It is, indeed, remarkable that there is no reference to scriptural promises, salvation history, or covenant, nor is there any reflection of the relation between the Scriptures and "our Lord Jesus Christ" (v. 21) in the brief polemical letter.

Israel's Scriptures in Jude

Table 22.2. Israel's Scriptures in Jude

	Marked Quotations	Unmarked Quotations	Allusions	Paradigms and References
5				Wilderness (Num 14)
6				Angels (Gen 6:1–4 + 1 En. 6–12!)
7				Sodomites (Gen 19)
9			Zech 3:2	Michael/Satan (Assumption of Moses?)
11				Cain (Gen 4); Balaam (Num 22–24); Korah (Num 16)
12–13			1 En. 80 (cf. 2:1–5:4)	
14	1 En. 1:9			

The author's technique of introducing scriptural examples proceeds by way of very brief reference. He combines examples with an eye to his argument, subtly hints at similarities (e.g., between the sin of the Watchers and that of the Sodomites) that bind the stories together and characterizes the figures mentioned, drawing on a wide range of scriptural and later interpretations.

The only explicit introduction is given for Enoch as a prophet, before his words are quoted: "But the seventh after Adam, Enoch, also prophesied about these [people; τούτοις], saying." Enoch is not only qualified as a prophet but solemnly introduced as the seventh after Adam (= 1 En. 60:8), which seems to substantiate his particular authority. His prophecy announcing the judgment of the ungodly is directly related to the opponents. But whereas the Enochic context refers to a theophany in which God will appear with myriads of his holy ones (i.e., angels), the subject in Jude 14 is κύριος (without article) which might now, in its Christian context, refer to Christ and his parousia with a host of angels.[18] For Jude, Enoch is a prophet of Christ's coming to judge the ungodly—and this is what the author wants to proclaim with regard to his opponents. If they disrespect the angels (and thus the created order of the world), Christ will come with myriads of angels to convict them because of their ungodly words and deeds.

The textual form of the quotation differs from our only extant Greek version of (parts of) 1 Enoch from the late sixth century (Codex Panopolitanus) and also from the Aramaic text as preserved at Qumran.[19] The citation is clearly translation Greek, but the differences from the extant Greek version cannot prove that our author directly translated from the Aramaic.[20] We must assume, instead, that in the first century 1 Enoch was widely available in Greek, but as there was no standardized text, there is no certainty about the exact textual form that was available to the author of Jude. Some elements of his quotation (such as the insertion of κύριος) might also be due to himself when he adjusted a version and shortened it for the present context.

In his brief references to various stories and figures from the pentateuchal narrative, the author presupposes a detailed knowledge of the Scriptures. He also utilizes postbiblical traditions of interpretation from Second Temple Judaism (and/or parts of the Jesus movement). In particular the presentation of

---

18. Cf. 1 Thess 3:13; 2 Thess 1:7; Mark 8:38; 14:62.

19. Panopolitanus is the codex in which we also find the only extant Greek manuscript of the Gospel of Peter and the large Greek manuscript of the Apocalypse of Peter; see George W. E. Nickelsburg, "Two Enochic Manuscripts: Unstudied Evidence for Egyptian Christianity," in *Of Scribes and Scrolls: Studies on the Hebrew Bible, Intertestamental Judaism, and Christian Origins, Presented to John Strugnell on the Occasion of His Sixtieth Birthday*, ed. Harold W. Attridge, John J. Collins, and Thomas H. Tobin, Resources in Religion 5 (Lanham, MD: University Press of America, 1991), 251–60. The Qumran evidence is 4Q204 (4QEn^c) 1 I, 15–17. For a synopsis of the versions, see Bauckham, *Jude, 2 Peter*, 95; and Vögtle, *Der Judasbrief, Der zweite Petrusbrief*, 74–75.

20. This was suggested by Carroll D. Osburn, "The Christological Use of 1 Enoch 1.9 in Jude 14, 15," *NTS* 23, no. 3 (1977): 340; Bauckham, *Jude, 2 Peter*, 96.

Cain and Balaam as paradigms of ungodliness goes far beyond their scriptural presentation and is only paralleled in later Jewish and early Christian traditions. It has been suggested that the author adopted preexisting patterns of warning examples, but the nonchronological sequence points to a deliberate composition: the apostasy of the desert generation comes first and is then associated with the references to the fallen angels (v. 6) and with Sodom and Gomorrah "and the surrounding cities" (v. 7).[21]

The utilization of Scripture is selective and subtle. Based on the view that the addressees have been granted salvific knowledge once and for all, the author reminds his addressees (v. 5) of the exodus generation that was saved from Egypt but focuses on the fact that those who murmured in unbelief (that is, all except Joshua and Caleb) were not saved "a second time" but had to die in the desert (Num 14:22-24).[22] Thus, an apostasy of the once enlightened ones would inevitably lead to death and perdition.[23] The two further examples are also focused on the judgment aspect: the tale of the Watchers (1 En. 6-12) is correctly interpreted in Enochic categories as the main sin of the angels is seen in their transgression from their heavenly realm into a realm that was not assigned to them, that is, in a neglect of a cosmic order.[24] The focus is on the preservation of those sinners in a prison of the "underworld" until the "great day" of judgment. The phrase draws on various elements of 1 Enoch: chains are mentioned in 1 En. 54:5; the binding of the angelic leaders in darkness is described in 1 En. 10:4-5, 12, 14. But the brief allusion to details of the episode aims at the present, as a warning against a certain kind of sin. Most significant is the connection between the Watchers (v.6) and the Sodom episode (v.7) by the comparative ὡς ("as, likewise") and an additional τὸν ὅμοιον τρόπον ("in a similar manner") indicating that the sins of the Watchers and the Sodomites were comparable. If the Sodomites went "after different flesh" in their desire to abuse Lot's angelic guests (cf. Gen 19:5), this was not merely fornication, but again a transgression of the border between humans

---

21. For preexisting patterns, see Bauckham, 46. Cf. Sir 16:7-10; 3 Macc 2:4-7; T. Naph. 3:4-5; CD II, 17-III, 13.

22. The textual problems of v. 5 cannot be discussed here; see Frey, *Letter of Jude and the Second Letter of Peter*, 79-82. In my view, the reading Ἰησοῦς (= Joshua), preferred by NA[28] and the ECM is an early typological wordplay but not the initial text. The preferable reading is κύριος, which functions as grammatical subject for vv. 5 and 6 and thus primarily refers to God, although the use of κύριος in Jude may imply a reference to the Lord on a second level. We cannot preclude the view that it was already the preexistent Christ who was active in those episodes.

23. 1 En. 12:4 and 15:3: "who have abandoned the high heaven."

24. See Monika E. Götte, *Von den Wächtern zu Adam: Frühjüdische Mythen über die Ursprünge des Bösen und ihre frühchristliche Rezeption*, WUNT 2/426 (Tübingen: Mohr Siebeck, 2016), 70-77.

and angels.²⁵ Thus, the author invokes both scriptural examples in a manner that fits his charge against the opponents, who are accused of disrespectful behavior against angelic beings. He shapes the examples as present signs of warning for his addressees. As the prison under the earth is considered a present reality, the smoky relics of Sodom and Gomorrah serve as a present warning sign (δεῖγμα) of the eternal punishment.²⁶

The other three scriptural examples in Jude 11 simply mention scriptural figures: Cain, Balaam, and Korah. All three are also adopted as negative examples in other early Christian texts.²⁷ In Jude 11, all three are considered examples of ungodliness, and the author simply needs to mention their name with a brief characterization. His aim is to state that his opponents are actually in their footsteps and thus also under the threat of the judgment and destruction they suffered. But the author obviously presupposes more than merely the scriptural narrative. He draws on later traditions in which these figures were further denigrated and made paradigms of apostasy and false teaching and examples of judgment.

In Gen 4, Cain is not simply punished but also protected by God against being slain (Gen 4:14–15). Later traditions consider him a prototypical sinner and one who tempts to sin (Wis 10:3; Philo, *Post.* 38–39; Josephus, *Ant.* 1.61). The targumim even depict him as a typical atheist who denies God, judgment, and the coming world and, consequently, has no share in that coming world.²⁸ Jude 11 clearly presupposes that walking "in the path of Cain" leads to judgment and destruction.

Similarly, Balaam is not a completely negative figure in the narrative of Num 22–24: He does not curse but blesses the Israelites (Num 24:2–4, 15–16), whereas other scriptural passages consider that he actually cursed them (Deut 23:5; Josh 24:9–10; Neh 13:2). Later interpretation characterizes him as an "impious" man (Philo, *Migr.* 113), a false prophet who was ultimately destroyed (Philo, *Mut.* 203), and a tempter to idol worship (LAB 18:13) who received a reward for the death of twenty-four thousand Israelites caused by his tempting.²⁹

---

25. According to Gen 19:8, Lot wants to avoid this violation of hospitality by presenting his daughters to them for sexual abuse. In T. Naph. 3:4–5, it is also said with reference to both episodes that they altered or exchanged "the order of their nature."

26. According to Wis 10:7, the smell of the smoke can be perceived at present.

27. Cain in 1 John 3:12; 1 Clem. 4:1–7; Balaam in Rev 2:14 and 2 Pet 2:15–16 (dependent on Jude 11); Korah in 1 Clem. 51:3–4 (cf. 2 Tim 2:19).

28. According to Tg. Yer. I, Tg. Neof., and the Tosefta on the targum (each on Gen 4:8), Cain says: "There is no judgment, there is no judge, there is no other world, there is no good reward for the righteous and no punishment for the wicked," whereas Abel acknowledges all these things. See Geza Vermes, "The Targumic Versions of Gen 4:3–16," in *Post-Biblical Jewish Studies*, SJLA 8 (Leiden: Brill, 1975), 98.

29. b. Sanh. 106a; Num. Rab. 22:5; Sipre Num. 157.

Balaam has no share in the future world (m. Sanh. 10:2), and his followers are characterized by "an envious eye, a greedy mind, and an arrogant spirit; they are going to hell" (m. 'Abot 5:19). This denigrated image is also presupposed when Rev 2:14 uses Balaam as a name for temptation into licentiousness and idol worship. When Jude 11 says that the opponents have turned themselves "to the deceit of Balaam for the sake of payment," he draws on some of those interpretations, not merely the scriptural story.

From the three figures mentioned in Jude 11, only Korah and his group experience a clear and immediate punishment (Num 16:32-35), being swallowed by the earth and destroyed by fire. From the biblical account, Korah was already an instigator of contradiction and rebellion; later traditions developed this even further. Due to the narrative of immediate judgment, the Korah episode was often used as a cautionary example, and the author of Jude could effectively place it at the end of his series.[30]

Apart from these clear adoptions of scriptural examples used as proof of the threat of judgment against sinners like the opponents were considered to be and as a warning example for the addressees not to follow their path, Jude does not openly refer to other motifs or phenomena from the Scriptures of the later Hebrew or Greek canon. But considering that for Jude, at least Enoch (and perhaps also other apocalyptic traditions) had scriptural authority, we can further mention the adoption of the imagery from 1 En. 80 (possibly viewed through the lens of 1 En. 2:1-5:4) in Jude 12b-13.[31] The metaphorical description of the opponents draws on images of the change of the natural phenomena in the days of the sinners. The climax is the description of the false teachers as wandering stars, that is, as planets. In antiquity, the orbits of the planets were considered irregular, and in apocalyptic thought they are a sign that the order of the cosmos is crumbling (1 En. 80:6; 82:6). When the author finally mentions "for whom the gloom of darkness has been preserved for eternity" (v. 13), the fate of wandering stars, fallen angels, and the opponents is merged into a rhetorically effective image of doom and destruction.

One last tradition should not be left unmentioned. In Jude 9, the author inserts an example from another apocalyptic writing, probably the lost end of the Assumption of Moses, where the archangel Michael and the Satan are in a dispute and—importantly—Michael does not curse the Satan (who is simply another an-

---

30. Sir 15:19; Josephus, *J.W.* 5.566; LAB 57:2; 1 Clem. 4:12; 51:4; Prot. Jas. 9:2.
31. Thus Bauckham, *Jude, 2 Peter*, 90-91; Bauckham, *Jude and the Relatives of Jesus* (Edinburgh: T&T Clark, 1990), 191-94.

gelic being) but just says: "The Lord rebuke you!"[32] The example is important for the conflict in the background, as it shows that not even the archangel Michael dares to slander or accurse another angelic being, while the opponents do not show that kind of respect with regard to angelic beings. The phrase "The Lord rebuke you!" is a verbal quotation from a similar scene in Zech 3:2, where in a heavenly court scene the High Priest Joshua is accused by Satan, and not Joshua but the Lord himself silences the accuser with these words. In Jewish and Christian apocalyptic tradition, there are a number of similar scenes, and the author obviously does not draw on Zech 3:1–5 but on a later episode, possibly dependent on Zech 3.[33] Again, a text that did not make it into the Hebrew canon nor into the LXX is the source for an important, possibly also scriptural, example in Jude.

The scriptural and "apocryphal" examples in Jude are some of the most interesting phenomena in the usage of the Scriptures of Israel in the New Testament. They ultimately question many of our traditional ideas of the growth and limitations of the "canon" or of "Israel's Scripture(s)," thus calling for new questions and perspectives far beyond the concepts in the present book.

2 Peter

Introduction

Second Peter is linguistically and theologically unique in the New Testament.[34] Shaped as a testament of Peter, it is addressed to all faithful Christians in a time after Peter's death (2 Pet 1:12–15), and in its closing it even tries to negotiate the adequate understanding of the Pauline epistles for which "Peter" now claims to give the correct interpretation (2 Pet 3:15–16).[35] Following Jude, the letter considers the rise of false teachers as a sign of the end time (2 Pet 3:3), and this might be a reason why the author could adopt Jude's polemical passage. The main issue, however, differs from Jude. The false teachers rejected in 2 Peter are not accused of slandering angelic beings; their main characteristic seems to be the skeptical denial of the parousia of Christ (2 Pet 3:4), phrased in a philosophical context of the unchangeability of the world, or, more generally, the validity of the escha-

---

32. On the textual versions, see Bauckham, *Jude, 2 Peter*, 65–75; Bauckham, *Jude and the Relatives*, 235–80.

33. For similar scenes, see Jub. 17:15–18:16 with Abraham and the Prince Mastema; 4QVisions of Amram (4Q543–549) with a bright angel whose name is lost and a dark angel named Malki-resha; later Yalqut Rubeni 43:3 with Michael and Satan.

34. On the linguistic features of the writing, see Thomas J. Kraus, *Sprache, Stil und historischer Ort des zweiten Petrusbriefes*, WUNT 2/136 (Tübingen: Mohr Siebeck, 2001).

35. See Frey, *Letter of Jude and the Second Letter of Peter*, 419–31.

tological hope in view of the "delay" of the parousia. Against such skepticism, 2 Peter reaffirms the reliability of the prophetic word and the hope for a "new heaven and earth" (2 Pet 3:13) but rejects any kind of calculation (2 Pet 3:8) as might have been circulated in Peter's name in other traditions, for example, the Apocalypse of Peter. In his adoption of the argument from Jude, the author blurs the issues about angels and omits the quotation from 1 Enoch.

Among the numerous texts in the background of 2 Peter, the Scriptures—in their Greek version—take a prominent place. The author presupposes a general knowledge of biblical salvation history and refers to some of its episodes and figures: the creation (2 Pet 3:5), the fall of the angels (2:4), the flood (2:5; 3:6), Noah (2:5), the Sodomites episode (2:6) and Lot (2:7), and Balaam (2:15).

Marked scriptural quotations, however, are completely missing in 2 Peter. The only quotation, which is unmarked, is a few words from Ps 89:4 LXX (= Ps 90:4 MT) in 2 Pet 3:8. Aside from this, there are only scant allusions of varying clarity, ranging from the Torah (Num 24:17 in 2 Pet 1:19) and the Prophets (Isa 65:17 in 2 Pet 3:17; Hab 2:3 in 2 Pet 3:9, 13-14) to Psalms and Proverbs (Prov 26:11 in 2 Pet 2:22).[36] The author makes creative new associations with scriptural motifs and provides readings that go far beyond the biblical narrative, for example, when stating that the whole cosmos was destroyed in the flood (2 Pet 3:6). The authority of Scripture does not preclude an independent reception and an adaption to the present argument.

In 2 Peter, scriptural examples and a biblical diction are meant to demonstrate the validity of the author's point of view. The best parallels of some motifs (e.g., the series of examples in 2:4-10) are found in late texts such as Sirach LXX, Wisdom, or 3 Maccabees. Occasionally, the biblical diction is also formed by use of a language that finds its patterns even beyond the LXX, in Hellenistic Jewish and early Christian texts.

Israel's Scriptures in 2 Peter

Table 22.3. *Israel's Scriptures in 2 Peter*

	Marked Quotations	Unmarked Quotations	Allusions	Paradigms and References
1:19			Num 24:17	Prophets
2:4				Angels (Gen 6:1-4 + 1 En. 6-12)

---

36. See Martin G. Ruf, *Die heiligen Propheten, eure Apostel und ich: Metatextuelle Studien zum zweiten Petrusbrief*, WUNT 2/300 (Tübingen: Mohr Siebeck, 2011), 561-65; and Bauckham, *Jude, 2 Peter*, 138.

2:5		Noah (Gen 7–9)
2:6		Sodomites (Gen 19)
2:7		Lot (Gen 19)
2:15–16		Balaam (Num 22–24 etc.)
2:22	Prov 26:11	
3:6		Flood (Gen 7)
3:8	Ps 90 (89):4 LXX	
3:9	Hab 2:3	
3:13–14	Hab 2:3	
3:17	Isa 65:17	

A first important statement concerning the validity of the Scriptures is made in 2 Pet 1:19–21. Following the "eyewitness" testimony about the vision of the glory of Jesus (2 Pet 1:16–18), the author in the apostolic mantle now points to the even more reliable "prophetic word." In view of early Christian usage, this term refers not merely to the books of the prophets but to the entirety of the Scriptures read as prophetic testimony. The Scriptures are considered even more reliable than the eyewitness, characterized as a lamp in the night before daybreak, so that attentiveness to the prophetic word is a matter of survival. Christological fulfilment has even confirmed and strengthened the expectation of the fulfilment of the yet unfulfilled promises, such as Jesus's second coming (3:4) or the new world shaped by justice (3:13). It is quite generally stated that biblical prophecy has not been fabricated by the prophets' or authors' own interpretation, but was spoken by people who were borne by the Holy Spirit, and this is the reason for its enduring validity. However, the christological testimony and the prophetic word are only important to confirm that in the end "the Lord" (God or Christ) has the power to save the just and judge the wicked.[37] The attention to the prophetic word, thus, already prepares for the decisive argument against the denial of the parousia by the opponents in chapter 3.

In the series of examples, basically adopted from Jude, the changes made by the author are significant. Instead of three examples of judgment, 2 Peter provides four examples, two of judgment and two of salvation (2 Pet 2:4–7). While the example of the wilderness generation is left aside, the author inserts Noah as the paradigm of salvation after the sin of the watchers and the flood, and Lot as the example of salvation after the Sodom episode. Unlike in Jude, the para-

---

37. In 2 Peter, there is no clear distinction between God and Christ, so "the Lord" can refer to both divine figures.

digms are listed in the correct chronological order. The whole series is presented and linked in one extended phrase (2:4–10a) with the aim of the demonstration stated in 2:9: "that the Lord knows how to save the pious... and to preserve the unrighteous for the day of judgment." So, the scriptural examples do not merely function as a proof of the reality of judgment, although this is still stressed at the end (2:10a). They are to demonstrate the double reality of judgment *and* salvation and the eschatological readiness of the Lord to bring about both.

With regard to the sinning angels (2:4) the details Jude had provided in dependence on the Enoch tradition are largely erased in 2 Peter. With the verb ταρταρόω ("hurl into Tartarus"), the author even changes the mythological framework from the Enochic context to the (closely related) myth of the Titans. The sin of the angels, characterized precisely in Jude as a transgression of the boundary between angels and humans and thus a breach of the divine cosmic order, is now mentioned without any specification. The angels just sinned. Likewise, in the example of the Sodomites (2:6), their sin is left unspecified. Thus, the author deletes all specific elements that were phrased with regard to the opponents of Jude and the charge of slandering angels. On the other hand, the examples of Noah and Lot are elaborated with new aspects: Noah (2:5) is characterized not merely as righteous (Gen 6:9) but—like in later interpretation—as the "herald of righteousness," and the author stresses that he was rescued as the eighth person (cf. Gen 8:18; 1 Pet 3:20), which is possibly inspired by Sib. Or. 1:280–81, according to which Noah steps as "the eighth" from the ark into the new world.[38] Lot (2:7) is characterized as "righteous," which goes beyond the biblical narrative (where Lot's behavior bears clearly negative aspects) and adopts the later, more positive shaping of his image as presented in Wis 10:6 and 19:17, as well as in Philo, *Mos.* 2.58, and 1 Clem. 11:19. In a striking parenthetical digression that aims at his faithful readers, the author further expands the description of Lot with regard to the sufferings of the pious among the ungodly (2:8). The examples of Noah and Lot demonstrate that the author of 2 Peter also creatively draws on the postbiblical history of interpretation and independently shapes his examples to serve his argument.

In the following polemical passage, 2 Peter shortens and generalizes the passage about Michael and the Satan from Jude 9 (2 Pet 2:11). Now, the mighty angels are simply an example of decency, demonstrating the indecency and boldness of the false teachers. From the three examples of Jude 11, Cain and Korah are omitted and just Balaam is kept and expanded (2:15–16): The phrase "he loved the wages of unrighteousness" adopts the idea that Balaam received some reward for his damaging activities. But while the biblical account says that he

---

38. For Noah as the "herald of righteousness," see Jub. 7:20–39; Josephus, *Ant.* 1.74; Sib. Or. 1:148–98, cf. 1:129: "he preached repentance."

refused to curse Israel for the wages offered by Balak (Num 22:18; 24:13), later interpretations in Philo and the rabbis depict him as greedy or speculate about his reward.[39] The further haggadic expansion that Balaam was convicted by the speech of a mute beast speaking in human voice inserts additional elements from the narrative of the talking donkey (Num 22:28–38) and helps to shape the image of Balaam as an antitype of the false prophets.

In his refutation of the skeptical argument of the scoffers who point to the permanence of the world, the author presents a creative interpretation of the creation and the deluge (3:5–7). First, he verbally alludes to the creation from Gen 1 ("heavens and earth," "water," "God's word") and states that the heavens and the earth were once made of water and through water and were sustained through God's word.[40] The use of the verb συνίστημι shows, however, that the author reads the creation story within the context of contemporary Hellenistic cosmologies. Then, he states that "through these (two)," that is, through water and the word of God, the "world" was destroyed in the flood. This is a first argument against the idea of the immutability of the world that aims at creating plausibility for the reality of a further destruction through fire or, more generally, a last judgment. However, when the author states that "the world of that time" (ὁ τότε κόσμος) was destroyed, this goes far beyond the biblical account (Gen 6), according to which only the life on the surface of the earth was annihilated, but not "the world" or "the heavens and the earth." Here, the flood is reinterpreted in terms of a cosmic catastrophe according to the pattern of the cosmic catastrophe still to be expected, the conflagration of the word. Deluge and conflagration are, thus, linked as two analogous cosmic catastrophes in which the entirety of the world (heavens and earth) is destroyed and a new world (heavens and earth) emerges. While the biblical account of the flood is reinterpreted in cosmological terms, conversely a philosophical (Stoic) cosmology of an infinite sequence of worlds and conflagrations is "corrected" according to the biblical accounts of merely three worlds: the antediluvial world, the present world, and the world to come. The author of 2 Peter thus enters a creative interaction between the biblical data of creation, flood, and eschatological expectation, and contemporary cosmology, providing a reasonable argument for the plausibility of the eschatological expectation of a "new heaven and earth" (3:13). With this final expectation, the author alludes to Isa 65:17 and 66:22 LXX.[41]

---

39. Cf. Frey, *Letter of Jude and the Second Letter of Peter*, 351.

40. The grammatical structure in 3:5 is not completely clear. See Frey, *Letter of Jude and the Second Letter of Peter*, 387–88.

41. Cf. also the early Jewish and Christian reception in 1 En. 91:16; LAB 3:10; Jub. 1:29; 4:26; and Rev 21:1.

The only verbal quotation from the Scriptures in 2 Peter is embedded in this argument in order to refute the idea that God could delay his promise "as some believe it is a delay" (3:9). Thus, the author states the incommensurability of human and divine measures of time, quoting Ps 90:4 (89:4 LXX), which was probably familiar to the addressees, but in an independent interpretation. While the psalm addresses God ("For a thousand years in your sight are like yesterday when it is past"), the author transforms this into a statement about how "before the Lord" things are different. He further expands the quotation into a twofold "conversion ratio"; as for his argument against the alleged "delay," he must show that one day "before God" could be a thousand years. Such a usage of Ps 90:4 could draw an a longer exegetical tradition that had also included speculations about the duration of the world based on the creation week and was adopted probably somewhat before 2 Peter in Barn. 15.3–4 and then in later Christian traditions.[42] But the quotation only confirms that the author of 2 Peter, who is probably the philosophically most educated author of the New Testament, draws on the Scriptures quite independently and with creative new interpretations.

Conclusion

As has been demonstrated, the reception of Israel's Scriptures in these three letters is very different. All three letters show an intense adoption of scriptural motifs and texts, but whereas the Scriptures shape the entire thought world of 1 Peter, the usage of the Scriptures in Jude as a proof for the judgment of the ungodly is very specific, and the high regard for the Enochic traditions is unique in the New Testament. In 2 Peter, finally, the Scriptures are considered "inspired" by the Holy Spirit and therefore highly authoritative, but their interpretation is again quite free and unique, in debate with current philosophical views. In all those writings, Scripture does not serve to prove the legacy of the Christian faith, nor is there any debate with contemporary non-Christian Jews. Instead, the Scriptures of Israel are fully appropriated and freely used as examples for paraenetic purposes or to provide arguments for the authors' theological views. As Jude in particular demonstrates, the range of authoritative Scriptures is still variable and negotiated at the end of the first and the beginning of the second century CE.

---

42. For the exegetical tradition, cf. Jub. 4:30; Justin, *Dial.* 81.8; Irenaeus, *Haer.* 5.23.2. For duration of the world, see 2 En. 33:1–2; LAB 28:2; GLAE 42; and further rabbinic traditions.

Bibliography

Achtemeier, Paul J. *1 Peter: A Commentary on First Peter*. Hermeneia. Minneapolis: Fortress, 1996.

Bauckham, Richard. *Jude, 2 Peter*. WBC 50. Waco, TX: Word, 1983.

———. *Jude and the Relatives of Jesus*. Edinburgh: T&T Clark, 1990.

Bigg, Charles. *A Critical and Exegetical Commentary on the Epistles of St. Peter and St. Jude*. ICC. Edinburgh: T&T Clark, 1901.

Brox, Norbert. *Der erste Petrusbrief*. EKKNT 21. Zurich: Einsiedeln; Cologne: Benziger, 1979.

Davids, Peter H. *The Letters of 2 Peter and Jude*. PNTC. Grand Rapids: Eerdmans, 2006.

Doering, Lutz. *Ancient Jewish Letters and the Beginnings of Christian Epistolography*. WUNT 298. Tübingen: Mohr Siebeck, 2012.

Feldmeier, Reinhard. *Der erste Brief des Petrus*. THKNT 15.1. Leipzig: Evangelische Verlagsanstalt, 2005.

———. *Die Christen als Fremde: Die Metapher der Fremde in der antiken Welt, im Urchristentum und im 1. Petrusbrief*. WUNT 64. Tübingen: Mohr Siebeck, 1992.

———. *The First Letter of Peter: A Commentary on the Greek Text*. Translated by Peter H. Davids. Waco, TX: Baylor University Press, 2008.

Frey, Jörg. "The Epistle of Jude between Judaism and Hellenism." Pages 309–30 in *The Catholic Epistles and the Apostolic Tradition*. Edited by Karl-Wilhelm Niebuhr and Rob Wall. Waco, TX: Baylor University Press, 2009.

———. *The Letter of Jude and the Second Letter of Peter: A Theological Commentary*. Translated by Kathleen Ess. Waco, TX: Baylor University Press, 2018.

———. "Von der 'petrinischen Schule' zum 'petrinischen Diskurs.'" Pages 87–124 in *Petrusliteratur und Petrusarchäologie: Römische Begegnungen*. Edited by Jörg Frey and Martin Wallraff. Rom und der Protestantismus 4. Tübingen: Mohr Siebeck, 2020.

Frey, Jörg, Matthijs den Dulk, and Jan G. van der Watt, eds. *2 Peter and the Apocalypse of Peter: Towards a New Perspective*. BibInt 174. Leiden: Brill, 2019.

Götte, Monika E. *Von den Wächtern zu Adam: Frühjüdische Mythen über die Ursprünge des Bösen und ihre frühchristliche Rezeption*. WUNT 2/426. Tübingen: Mohr Siebeck, 2016.

Grünstäudl, Wolfgang. *Petrus Alexandrinus: Studien zum historischen und theologischen Ort des zweiten Petrusbriefes*. WUNT 2/353. Tübingen: Mohr Siebeck, 2013.

Herzer, Jens. *Petrus oder Paulus? Studien über das Verhältnis des Ersten Petrusbriefes zur paulinischen Tradition*. WUNT 103. Tübingen: Mohr Siebeck, 1998.

Kelly, J. N. D. *The Epistles of Peter and of Jude*. BNTC. London: Black, 1969.

Kraus, Thomas J. *Sprache, Stil und historischer Ort des zweiten Petrusbriefes.* WUNT 2/136. Tübingen: Mohr Siebeck, 2001.

Nickelsburg, George W. E. "Two Enochic Manuscripts: Unstudied Evidence for Egyptian Christianity." Pages 251–60 in *Of Scribes and Scroll: Studies on the Hebrew Bible, Intertestamental Judaism, and Christian Origins, Presented to John Strugnell on the Occasion of His Sixtieth Birthday.* Edited by Harold W. Attridge, John J. Collins, and Thomas H. Tobin. Resources in Religion 5. Lanham, MD: University Press of America, 1991.

Osburn, Carroll D. "The Christological Use of 1 Enoch 1.9 in Jude 14, 15." *NTS* 23, no. 3 (1977): 334–41.

Paulsen, Henning. *Der zweite Petrusbrief und der Judasbrief.* KEK 12.2. Göttingen: Vandenhoeck & Ruprecht, 1992.

Ruf, Martin G. *Die heiligen Propheten, eure Apostel und ich: Metatextuelle Studien zum zweiten Petrusbrief.* WUNT 2/300. Tübingen: Mohr Siebeck, 2011.

Schelkle, Karl-Hermann. *Die Petrusbriefe, Der Judasbrief.* HThKNT 13.2. Freiburg im Breisgau: Herder, 1961.

Soards, Marion L. "1 Peter, 2 Peter, and Jude as Evidence for a Petrine School." *ANRW* 25.5:3827–49.

Vermes, Geza. "The Targumic Versions of Gen 4:3–16." Pages 92–126 in *Post-Biblical Jewish Studies.* SJLA 8. Leiden: Brill, 1975.

Vögtle, Anton. *Der Judasbrief, Der zweite Petrusbrief.* EKKNT 22. Solothurn: Benziger; Neukirchen-Vluyn: Neukirchener Verlag, 1994.

23

Israel's Scriptures in the Johannine Letters

GEORGE PARSENIOS

The Gospel of John binds itself closely and obviously to the Scriptures of Israel, with numerous scriptural citations and even more allusions to scriptural themes and people. The Letters of John are different. These letters contain no citations of Scripture, and the clearest allusion to Scripture is a verbal allusion to Cain the murderer in 1 John 3:12. If one were to judge merely on the basis of scriptural citations, one could easily conclude that 1–3 John were written with little regard for the Scriptures of Israel.[1] But this appearance is misleading.[2] These letters contain several verbal and conceptual allusions to Scripture. Here is a table of the allusions to Scripture in 1–2 John (there are no allusions to Scripture in 3 John).

Table 23.1. Allusions to Scripture in 1 John

1 John		Scriptural Text	
1:1	"What was from the beginning"[3]	Gen 1:1	"In the beginning"

---

1. C. H. Dodd, *The Johannine Epistles* (London: Hodder & Stoughton, 1946), lii–liii.
2. Judith Lieu, *Theology of the Johannine Epistles* (Cambridge: Cambridge University Press, 1991), 20.
3. Unless otherwise noted, all translations are by the author.

Israel's Scriptures in the Johannine Letters

1:7	"But if we walk in the light as he himself is in the light"	Isa 2:5	"Come, let us walk in the light of the Lord"
1:8	"If we say that we have no sin, we deceive ourselves, and the truth is not in us"	2 Chr 6:36 Cf. Prov 20:9	"If they sin against you— for there is no one who does not sin"
1:9	"If we confess our sins, he who is faithful and just will forgive us our sins and cleanse us from all unrighteousness"	Deut 32:4 Cf. Exod 34:6; Prov 28:13; Mic 7:18–20	"God, his work is perfect, and all his ways are just. A faithful God, without deceit, just and upright is he"
2:2	"He is the atoning sacrifice for our sins"	Lev 16:16 Cf. Lev 25:9; Ps 130:4	"Thus he shall make atonement for the sanctuary . . . because of their transgressions"
2:9–10	"Whoever says, 'I am in the light,' while hating a brother or sister, is still in the darkness"	Eccl 2:14	"The wise have eyes in their head, but fools walk in darkness"
2:17	"And the world and its desire are passing away, but those who do the will of God live forever"	Isa 40:8	"The grass withers, the flower fades; but the word of our God will stand forever"
2:18	"Children, it is the last hour!"	Dan 8:19 Cf. Dan 10:14; 11:40	"He said, 'Listen, and I will tell you what will take place later in the period of wrath; for it refers to the appointed time of the end'"
3:5	"and in him there is no sin"	Isa 53:9	"and there was no deceit in his mouth"
3:12	"We must not be like Cain who was from the evil one and murdered his brother"	Gen 4:8	"Cain rose up against his brother Abel, and killed him"
3:14	"We know that we have passed from death to life because we love one another. Whoever does not love abides in death"	Lev 19:17	"You shall not hate in your heart anyone of your kin; you shall reprove your neighbor, or you will incur guilt yourself"

3:17	"How does God's love abide in anyone who has the world's goods and sees a brother or sister in need and yet refuses help?"	Deut 15:7 Cf. Deut 15:11	"If there is among you anyone in need... do not be hard-hearted or tight-fisted toward your needy neighbor"
4:10	"In this is love, not that we loved God but that he loved us and sent his Son to be the atoning sacrifice for our sins"	Lev 16:16 Cf. Lev 25:9; Ps 130:4	"Thus he shall make atonement for the sanctuary... because of their transgressions"
5:3	"For the love of God is this, that we obey his commandments. And his commandments are not burdensome"	Deut 30:11	"Surely, this commandment that I am commanding you today is not too hard for you, nor is it too far away"
5:7	"There are three that testify"	Deut 19:15	"only on the evidence of two or three witnesses shall a charge be sustained"
5:21	"Little children, keep yourselves from idols"	Exod 20:2–6	"You shall not make for yourself an idol"

Table 23.2. Allusions to Scripture in 2 John

2 John		Scriptural Text	
12	"Although I have much to write to you, I would rather not use paper and ink; instead I hope to come to you and talk with you face to face, so that our joy may be complete"	Num 12:8; Jer 32:4	"With him I speak face to face—clearly, not in riddles"

In most cases, these allusions are not immediately obvious from reading 1–3 John. When we read the letters of John in tandem with other documents from early Christianity, however, and with other texts from Second Temple Jewish literature, the connections rise closer to the surface. In various ways, Scripture and the history of its interpretation in the Second Temple period are critical elements in the rhetoric and theology of the Letters of John.

Before this fact can be demonstrated, a further comment is needed in order to clarify the relationship between the Letters of John and the Gospel of John. Scholars have long debated how the letters relate to the gospel, but the following three options are most often offered as explanations: (1) the letters precede the production of the gospel; (2) the letters are contemporary with the writing of the gospel; (3) the letters follow the completion of the gospel. The present chapter will presuppose that the letters are written after the gospel was completed and that the letters are the byproduct of a struggle between two groups that disagree over the proper interpretation of the Johannine tradition. Evidence for this struggle appears in verses like 1 John 2:19, which says, "They went out from us, but they did not really belong to us. For if they had belonged to us, they would have remained with us; but their going showed that none of them belonged to us." A group has left the community, apparently because of a dispute over Christology. The precipitating problem seems to be the question of whether Jesus truly took on flesh or not (1 John 4:2; 2 John 7), although the exact nature of the dispute is unclear. We can speculate by comparing the opponents in 1 John to near contemporaries who similarly rejected the incarnation, like the figure of Cerinthus mentioned by Irenaeus (*Haer.* 1.26.1) or the Docetists mentioned by Ignatius of Antioch (*Trall.* 9–10). Cerinthus was especially elaborate in his theology, arguing that the divine Christ alighted onto the man Jesus in his baptism and then departed before the crucifixion. In this way, he protected the divine nature from suffering in the body of the human Jesus. Specific connections are impossible to establish between 1–3 John and any specific figure in early Christianity since the Johannine letters describe only briefly the beliefs of their opponents. And yet, Cerinthus, the Docetists, and other figures indicate that various people and groups struggled in the second century to reconcile the human and divine in the person of Jesus. The same struggle to see Christ as both human and divine animates the Letters of John. The letters, therefore, respond to the opposite problem of the gospel. In the gospel, the opponents argue that Jesus is only a man and not divine (John 5:18; 10:33; 19:7). In the letters, the opponents argue that Jesus is God but not really a man. According to the anonymous author of 1–3 John, much is at stake in how one defines the identity of Jesus because those who do not believe properly in the Son lose their union with the Father (1 John 2:23). This is the first issue that drives the argument of the letters, the issue of Christology. The second issue is related. If false believers lose their union with the Father, they lose as well their union with other believers, an issue that introduces the second concern of the letters: the love command. In order to have union with God, one must be united to the group associated with the author of these letters (1 John 1:3), and such a union with fellow believers fulfills the "love command." With this basic background in hand, we can now turn to the use of Scripture in 1–3 John with greater understanding.

Israel's Scripture in the Letters of John

First John 3:12 contains the only verbal allusion to a biblical text in 1–3 John, when it says, "We must not be like Cain who was from the evil one and murdered his brother. And why did he murder him? Because his own deeds were evil and his brother's righteous." Because 1–3 John contain no marked or unmarked citations of Scripture, this allusion in 1 John 3 to Cain is the most explicit reference to the Scriptures of Israel in the Johannine letters. We will see below that there are several other verbal allusions and conceptual allusions to Scripture, but the allusion to Cain in 1 John 3 is the most explicit reference to a biblical text or theme in these letters and so will receive attention first. Once we have read the allusion to Cain in 1 John in the light of ancient traditions about Cain, we will see that this allusion has great significance for the schism that has torn the community.

Although 1 John 3:12 clearly refers to the figure of Cain from Gen 4:1–16, the passage in 1 John is unusual inasmuch as it says both more and less than is said about Cain in Gen 4.[4] It says less than the text of Genesis because, although Cain is mentioned by name, his brother Abel is not. Abel receives only a vague conceptual allusion in the next verse. The details of the story in Genesis are also completely ignored, with no reference to the two sacrifices that the brothers offered to God and no mention of God's response. Little interest is shown, therefore, in the frame or details of the story from Genesis itself. Cain seems to be important here simply and exclusively because he is a murderer and for reasons particular to the concerns of 1 John.

On the other hand, if details from the actual text of Genesis are rare in 1 John 3:12, other elements that are alien to Genesis are added. Two items especially stand out: that Cain "belonged to the evil one" and that "his deeds were evil" (3:12). What accounts for this added material? It does not seem possible to understand 1 John as merely reflecting on the text of Genesis.[5]

Indeed, several factors suggest that the image of Cain in 1 John resembles portraits of Cain from elsewhere in Second Temple Jewish texts. Jude 10–11, for

---

4. Several unsuccessful attempts from a previous generation to argue that 1 John 3 was simply interpreting Gen 4 are discussed in Raymond Brown, *The Epistles of John: A New Translation with Introduction and Commentary*, AB 30 (New York: Doubleday, 1982), 442–43.

5. For discussion of various proposals, as well as the inherent flaws in each, see Brown, *Epistles of John*, 442–43.

example, resembles 1 John because in Jude Cain exemplifies a path to be avoided. Similarly, Heb 11:4 offers Abel as a positive example to imitate. Philo writes several treatises that deal with Cain and Abel (*On the Cherubim*, *On the Sacrifices of Abel and Cain*, *The Worse Attacks the Better*, and *On the Posterity of Cain*), but Josephus is most helpful for reading 1 John because Josephus's treatment of Cain in *Ant.* 1.52–62 bears an interesting relation to the present text. He describes Abel as being concerned with righteousness (δικαιοσύνη) and Cain as being most evil (πονηρότατος), language that mirrors 1 John 3:12, where Abel's works are said to be righteous (δίκαια) and those of Cain are evil (πονηρά). Matthew 23:35 also refers to the "blood of Abel the righteous" (Ἄβελ τοῦ δικαίου). Cain and Abel serve in 1 John as general paradigms of righteous and wicked behavior, just as they do in several other contemporary texts, using even the same language to define them.

Our real concern, however, focuses on the comments in 1 John that say that Cain "belonged to the evil one" and that his "deeds were evil." These comments can be understood more clearly against the backdrop of other ancient Jewish and Christian texts. The sin of Cain was viewed in some early Christian and Jewish writings as qualitatively different from the sin of Adam and Eve. Where Adam and Eve fell from their original condition into something sinful when they disobeyed God, Cain was understood not to have deviated from his original state by committing murder. He actualized his true self. He was already evil before he killed his brother.[6] How can this be? Certain features in the text of Genesis suggested to ancient interpreters that the birth of Cain was unusual.[7] Eve announces his birth in Gen 4:1, for instance, by saying that she gave birth to a "man" (אִישׁ) "with the help of the Lord" (אֶת־יְהוָה). Why, exegetes wondered, did Eve refer to her baby with the word usually reserved for an adult (אִישׁ) and not as a mere son (בֵּן)? And what did it mean to say that he was born "with the help of the Lord"? The various recensions of the Life of Adam and Eve show how speculation developed to resolve these exegetical puzzles. Cain is described, for example, as being able at the moment of birth to gather food for his mother

---

6. For this insight and for further references and discussion, see John Byron, *Cain and Abel in Text and Tradition: Jewish and Christian Interpretations of the First Sibling Rivalry*, TBN 14 (Leiden: Brill, 2011), 17.

7. The issues are discussed at length in James L. Kugel, *Traditions of the Bible: A Guide to the Bible as It Was at the Start of the Common Era* (Cambridge: Harvard University Press, 1998), 147; Johannes Tromp, "Cain and Abel in the Greek and Armenian/Georgian Recensions of the Life of Adam and Eve," in *Literature on Adam and Eve: Collected Essays*, ed. Gary A. Anderson, Michael E. Stone, and Johannes Tromp, SVTP 15 (Leiden: Brill, 2000), 277–96; Robert Hayward, "Pirqe de Rabbi Eliezer and Targum Pseudo-Jonathan," *JJS* 42, no. 2 (1991): 215–46; Byron, *Cain and Abel*, 11–17.

(LAE 21.3): "And she bore a son and he was shining; and at once the babe rose up and ran and bore a blade of grass in his hands, and gave it to his mother, and his name was called Cain" (trans. Wells). If Cain is so advanced even at birth, then he should already be called a "man," and such a capable child could be born only through "the help of the Lord." This is at least one tradition of how to deal with the unusual statements in Gen 4.

A very common manner of reflecting on Cain's unusual birth took a far less optimistic direction, however, projecting his later career as a murderer onto his origin. Cain was evil even from the womb. In the Armenian version of the Life of Adam and Eve, infertility overtakes the land after the birth of Cain (21:3a) and he is called a murderer as soon as he is born (21:3b). In the Georgian version, he is not only called a murderer of good people but is described as one who gathers food for himself and deprives others of it (21:3b).[8] He is, thus, a paradigm of evil behavior of all kinds as soon as he enters the world and engages in murderous greed from his first breath.

A broadly attested tradition takes this speculation one step further, arguing that the supernatural intervention in Cain's birth was not "with the help of God" but through the agency of the devil. The Gospel of Philip says that Cain was a murderer because he was the son of the serpent (61:5–10; see also Tertullian, *Pat.*, 5.15). When Gen 4:1 says that "Adam knew Eve his wife," this is not taken in certain Jewish traditions in the typical biblical sense of referring to marital relations, but in the sense that Adam knew something about his wife, that is, that Cain was the son of Sammael (Tg. Ps.-J. on Gen 41; Pirque Rabbi Eliezer 21).

We now have a very different perspective on the cryptic comments in 1 John 3:12 that Cain "belonged to the evil one" and that his "deeds were evil." These comments are just the visible tip of a very large iceberg of speculative interpretation of the text of Genesis and reflection on the character of Cain. There is no question as to why Cain is the one figure mentioned explicitly in these letters. The murder of a brother is a critical image for these letters, arising as they do from within a community rent by schism. First John 3:15 calls everyone who hates his brother a murderer. This is a reference to those who have left the community. They do not merely reject their fellow believers, but bring the ruin on them that Cain did in the case of his brother. And, like Cain, who was evil from the very beginning, those who leave the community show that they were never really *of* the community (1 John 2:19).

An equally significant allusion, which is also not given context or elaboration, is related to the christological issues that animate the letter. In 1 John 2:2 and 4:10, Jesus is called a ἱλασμός ("atoning sacrifice," NRSV). Possible translations

---

8. See Tromp, "Cain and Abel," 289.

of ἱλασμός extend along a very broad spectrum, from a cultic sense referring to sacrifices in the temple to a neutral, completely nonsacramental sense. The noun ἱλασμός occurs in the LXX, where it can mean simply "forgiveness." Psalm 130:4 (129:4 LXX) reads, for instance, "For with you is forgiveness." This is the sense that Judith Lieu applies to the usage by the epistolary author.[9] There are better reasons to think, however, that ἱλασμός refers to the sacrificial death of Jesus on the cross and carries a more cultic meaning. First John 1:7 says, "The blood of Jesus cleanses us from every sin," a phrase that we must bear in mind when, only a few verses later in 2:2, we read that Jesus is a ἱλασμός concerning our sins. The term conveys this meaning of sacrifice when it is used in Lev 25:9, where the Day of Atonement is called ἡμέρα τοῦ ἱλασμοῦ.[10]

The reference to the blood of Jesus in 1:7 colors the mention of the term in 1 John, making a sacrificial sense of the term the most probable and obvious meaning. The sacrificial sense here also seems to evoke the statement of John the Baptist in the Fourth Gospel, when John says, "Here is the Lamb of God, who takes away the sin of the world" (John 1:29), which seems to refer to the fact that Jesus is slaughtered on the cross at the same time as the lambs prepared for Passover (John 19:31). Raymond Brown argues that 1 John alludes to the sacrifice on the Day of Atonement, ἡμέρα τοῦ ἱλασμοῦ (LXX Lev 25:9).[11] The high priest sacrificed a bull and a goat "concerning all their sins" (περὶ πασῶν τῶν ἁμαρτιῶν αὐτῶν; LXX Lev 16:16), just as the death of Jesus took place "concerning our sins" (περὶ τῶν ἁμαρτιῶν ἡμῶν; 1 John 2:2). The emphasis on Jesus's sacrificial death has a very specific sense in 1 John because the death of Jesus on the cross is the furthest expression of his appearance in the flesh. If the opponents do not accept that Jesus truly took on flesh, then the author of 1 John emphasizes the value of his sacrificial death in order to underscore the reality of his life in the flesh. Again, the profundity of the allusion and its significance for the theology of 1 John are not immediately obvious and not explained. But the allusion is very meaningful for the letter.

Other allusive language is harder to correlate for certain with the Old Testament, despite efforts to make such a connection. First John 2:18, for example, re-

---

9. Judith Lieu, *I, II and III John: A Commentary*, NTL (Louisville: Westminster John Knox, 2008), 64.

10. Attending to cognates does not really help to resolve the issue. The specific term ἱλασμός occurs in the New Testament only in 1 John 2:2 and 4:10, but several cognate forms of ἱλασμός are common in the New Testament: ἱλάσκεσθαι in Luke 18:13 and Heb 2:17; ἱλαστήριον is found twice in the New Testament, in Rom 3:25 and Heb. 9:5; ἵλεως is used twice in Matt 16:22 and Heb 8:12. Accounting for these words does not necessarily solve the dilemma, though, because their meanings are arrayed along the same spectrum as ἱλασμός. They sometimes carry sacrificial imagery but need not necessarily do so (Brown, *Epistles of John*, 217–21).

11. Brown, *Epistles of John*, 221–22.

fers twice to the "last hour" (ἐσχάτη ὥρα), when the antichrists will appear, which may be connected to prophecies in Dan 8:17-19; 10:14; and 11:40, which refer to both the "hour" and the "end time," but the relevant words are only used in proximity to one another, and not in the precise formulation seen in 1 John. A specific allusion to Scripture seems unlikely. It is more likely that the direct source of this imagery is the Gospel of John, which connects the hour (5:25) of Jesus to the last days (6:40).[12] Reflection on the end of days, of course, is common in apocalyptic literature in ancient Judaism (e.g., 4QMMT C 13-15; 1QpHab VII, 6-13).

All of the above are verbal allusions, and they rely on specific words from Scripture for their significance. There are also conceptual allusions to Scripture in the Letters of John. We can see most clearly how this is so when we read the Johannine letters in conjunction with other Second Temple Jewish texts.[13] The dualism of 1-3 John is a case in point. First John refers to "the spirit of truth" and "the spirit of error" (1 John 4:6) and then adds that "those who have fellowship with God walk in the light," while "those who walk in darkness do not do what is true" (1:6-7). Similar is 1 John 2:11, which says, "But whoever hates his brother is in the darkness, walks in the darkness, and does not know the way to go, because the darkness has brought on blindness." The emphasis on darkness in these two texts is an allusion to Isa 6:10, which says, "He has blinded their eyes and hardened their heart." The text is regularly used in the New Testament for those who reject Jesus (John 12:40; Mark 4:11-12). But the resulting dualism in the formulas of 1 John develops this imagery further than what appears in Scripture and in a way that resembles similar language in the Dead Sea Scrolls. For instance, 1QS III, 17-19, says that God put within human beings "two spirits . . . to walk according to them until the time of his visitation; these are the spirits of truth and of deceit." To confine the discussion to the Dead Sea Scrolls is to miss the larger point. The expressions shared in common between 1-3 John and Qumran literature is found as well in other bodies of contemporary Jewish literature. For instance, T. Jud. 20:1 says, "Two spirits are active in humanity, that of truth and that of error." The Testaments of the Twelve Patriarchs also resembled the Johannine command to love one another and the warning against idols (1 John 5:21).[14] The purpose of this dualism in the Johannine letters is not to define firm boundaries between people of the light and people of the darkness, so that "never the twain shall meet." The goal is rather to urge the readers of the letters to see what separates darkness from light in order to choose the light.

---

12. For further discussion, see G. K. Beale, "The Old Testament Background of the 'Last Hour' in 1 John 2,18," *Bib* 92, no. 2 (2011): 231-54.

13. Lieu, *Theology*, 87.

14. Lieu, *1, 2, 3 John*, 174.

A final category of allusions is a group of scriptural terms or images that are clearly drawing on Scripture but only loosely and sometimes in indirect ways. They are verbal allusions, but vaguely so. For example, 1 John 1:1 opens in its first words by referring to "That which was from the beginning." This clearly refers to the opening line of the gospel, "In the beginning," which clearly refers to the opening line of Genesis: "In the beginning." First John speaks of what was "from the beginning," and not "in the beginning," but to open a text by referring to the "beginning" seems like a clear, if indirect, reference to John 1 and therefore Gen 1. Similarly, the opponents are cast as "false prophets" (1 John 4:1–2) who engage in deceit (4:6) or as "antichrists" (2:18). Various figures from the Scriptures might provide the model for these deceptive figures, such as the Satan or angelic adversary in Job 1:6 and Zech 3:1, a human ruler embodying evil, such as Antiochus Epiphanes (175–164 BCE), or the false prophet, such as the one described in Deut 13:2–6 and 18:20. Warnings against false prophets exist throughout the Scriptures of Israel, as in 1 Kgs 22.

Conclusion

First John ends with an enigmatic warning (5:21): "Children, guard yourselves from idols." This exhortation concludes the argument of the letter with one final conceptual allusion. The most basic feature of Jewish religion was single devotion to the one God of Israel (Exod 20:2–6). No text of Scripture is actually quoted here, but the obvious theological background of the exhortation to avoid idols is repeated throughout the Scriptures.[15] The same applies to all of the scriptural allusions in the Johannine letters. Behind all of the major theological and ethical concerns of the letter lie scriptural allusions. Scripture provides the basic conceptual framework within which the epistolary author constructs his argument. The argument itself has two points of foci: the appearance of Christ in the flesh and the need to love one another. The exhortation to believe that Jesus appeared in the flesh and the command to love one another are articulated within an entirely scriptural vision of reality. The relevant allusions are not always immediately obvious, but they become clearer when read against the backdrop of the Gospel of John and of other Second Temple Jewish literature. When the letters are read in this context, it becomes quite clear that Scripture provides the underlying structure for the theology of 1–3 John.

---

15. See, of course, the commandment from the Decalogue (Exod 20:2–17; Deut 5:6–21), as well as warnings in the prophets, such as Jer 10:11, which gave rise to the production of the Epistle of Jeremiah, which is in general a warning against falling into idolatry. More generally for early Jewish references, see T. Reub. 4:5–6 and T. Jos. 6:5.

Bibliography

Bauckham, Richard. "The Qumran Community and the Gospel of John." Pages 105–15 in *The Dead Sea Scrolls Fifty Years After Their Discovery: Proceedings of the Jerusalem Congress, July 20–25, 1997*. Edited by Lawrence H. Schiffman, Emanuel Tov, and James C. VanderKam. Jerusalem: Israel Exploration Society, 2000.

Beale, G. K. "The Old Testament Background of the 'Last Hour' in 1 John 2,18." *Bib* 92, no. 2 (2011): 231–54.

Brown, Raymond. *The Epistles of John: A New Translation with Introduction and Commentary*. AB 30. New York: Doubleday, 1982.

Byron, John. *Cain and Abel in Text and Tradition: Jewish and Christian Interpretations of the First Sibling Rivalry*. TBN 14. Leiden: Brill, 2011.

Dodd, C. H. *The Johannine Epistles*. MNTC. London: Houlder & Stoughton, 1946.

Fitzmyer, Joseph A. "Qumran Literature and the Johannine Writings." Pages 117–33 in *Life in Abundance: Studies of John's Gospel in Tribute to Raymond Brown*. Edited by John R. Donahue. Collegeville, MN: Liturgical Press, 2005.

Hayward, Robert. "Pirqe de Rabbi Eliezer and Targum Pseudo-Jonathan." *JJS* 42, no. 2 (1991): 215–46.

Kugel, James L. *Traditions of the Bible: A Guide to the Bible as It Was at the Start of the Common Era*. Cambridge: Harvard University Press, 1998.

Lieu, Judith. *1, 2, 3 John*. NTL. Louisville: Westminster John Knox, 2008.

———. *The Theology of the Johannine Epistles*. Cambridge: Cambridge University Press, 1991.

Schnelle, Udo. *Die Johannesbriefe*. THKNT 17. Leipzig: Evangelische Verlagsanstalt, 2010.

Tromp, Johannes. "Cain and Abel in the Greek and Armenian/Georgian Recensions of the Life of Adam and Eve." Pages 277–96 in *Literature on Adam and Eve: Collected Essays*. Edited by Gary A. Anderson, Michael E. Stone, and Johannes Tromp. SVTP 15. Leiden: Brill, 2000.

Wells, L. S. "Books of Adam and Eve." Pages 123–54 in vol. 2 of *The Apocrypha and Pseudepigrapha of the Old Testament*. Edited by R. H. Charles. 2 vols. Oxford: Clarendon, 1913.

D. THE BOOK OF REVELATION

24

Israel's Scriptures in the Revelation of John

IAN K. BOXALL

Any discussion of the use of Israel's Scriptures in the Revelation of John is beset with challenges particular to this biblical book. On the one hand, Revelation is one of the most scripturally rich texts in the New Testament canon. Many of its 405 verses are saturated with phrases drawn from Israel's Scriptures, echoes of specific texts, and allusions to whole scriptural narratives. Indeed, in the assessment of one of John of Patmos's classic interpreters, "no writer of the Apostolic age makes larger use of his predecessors."[1] On the other hand, this lengthy book (only slightly shorter than the Gospel of Mark) contains not a single marked citation from Israel's Scriptures, while many of its scriptural allusions and echoes arguably evoke multiple biblical intertexts simultaneously.

This complexity, and disagreement as to what counts as a scriptural allusion, explains the huge variation in scholarly estimates of the use of Israel's Scriptures in this book (ranging from 250 to over 1000).[2] To cite just a couple of examples: the fourth edition of UBS's *Greek New Testament* identifies 658 scriptural allusions in Revelation (plus a few more from extracanonical works such as 1 Enoch and the Psalms of Solomon). The twenty-eighth edition of Nestle-Aland's *Novum Testamentum Graece* identifies almost 800 possible allusions to books found in

---

1. Henry Barclay Swete, *The Apocalypse of St John: The Greek Text with Introduction, Notes and Indices*, 3rd ed. (London: Macmillan, 1922), cxl.
2. Steve Moyise, *The Later New Testament Writers and Scripture: The Old Testament in Acts, Hebrews, the Catholic Epistles, and Revelation* (London: SPCK, 2012), 111.

the Greek canon, located in 284 verses in Revelation. This is in addition to potential allusions to the Jesus tradition (e.g., Rev 3:3; 16:15; cf. Matt 24:43; Luke 12:39; 1 Thess 5:2, 4; Rev 6:1–17: cf. Mark 13 and par.), Jewish pseudepigrapha (e.g., Rev 2:4; 3:10; 8:3: cf. 1 Enoch 5:4; 9:3; Rev 12:10; cf. Jub 1:20), and Greco-Roman sources (e.g., the Leto-Apollo-Python myth in Rev 12:1–6).

The challenges are compounded by the Apocalypse's generic complexity. This includes its visionary and auditory character. The author claims to have "seen" and "heard" much of what he describes (e.g., Rev 1:2, 10, 12; 4:1; 5:1–2, 6, 13), and several scholars take seriously such claims in interpreting the complex literary work John has constructed. Moreover, this visionary dimension is closely related to another generic feature: Revelation's appeal to Israel's prophetic tradition, which includes visions as well as auditory revelation (e.g., Num 12:6; 1 Kgs 22:17; Isa 1:1; 2:1; 6:1; Amos 9:1; Obad 1; Nah 1:1; Hab 1:1).[3] John of Patmos places his own work on an equal footing with those of Israel's prophets. His book contains "words of prophecy" (Rev 1:3; 22:7, 10), some of them dictated directly by the heavenly Son of Man (Rev 2–3). John himself is a divinely commissioned prophet (Rev 10:8–11), and member of the brotherhood of prophets (Rev 22:9). Echoing the authoritative Mosaic Pentateuch, he imposes stern warnings against tampering with his words (Rev 22:18–19; cf. Deut 4:2). These prophetic and visionary claims raise the possibility that, in some cases, the interweaving of scriptural allusions may be the result of well-learned scriptural texts "erupting into consciousness" in a trance-like state, whether that is understood as reception of visions or prophetic utterance.

Nor is authorial recall the only dynamic at work in studying Israel's Scriptures in the Apocalypse. Recent scholarly debates have often focused on the weight to be given to John on the one hand, and his readers or audiences (both ancient and modern) on the other. In such a richly textured book, which scriptural intertexts are heard in specific acts of reading? The answer depends in no small part on the education and scriptural "memory bank" of specific readers/hearers. Moreover, are any of these intertexts dominant voices, and, if so, how can the more marginal voices be heard? How many are intentional, and how many unconscious, and how might one decide?[4] Clear distinctions are not always possible: as Richard Hays, a key practitioner of intertextuality in New Testament studies, notes, his

---

3. On the close relationship between apocalyptic and prophecy, see e.g., Elisabeth Schüssler Fiorenza, *The Book of Revelation: Justice and Judgment* (Philadelphia: Fortress, 1986), 133–56.

4. For different voices in this debate, see, e.g., G. K. Beale, *The Use of Daniel in Jewish Apocalyptic Literature and in the Revelation of St. John* (Lanham, MD: University Press of America, 1984); Steve Moyise, *The Old Testament in the Book of Revelation*, JSNTSup 115 (Sheffield: Sheffield Academic, 1995); Jon Paulien, *Decoding Revelation's Trumpets: Literary Allusions and the Interpretation of Revelation 8:7–12*, Andrews University Seminary Doctoral Dissertation 11

own preferred categories of quotation, allusion, and echo are only "approximate markers on the spectrum of intertextual linkage."[5]

These considerations complicate the task of this chapter. None of them, however, undermine the prominence of Israel's Scriptures for the author of Revelation. John of Patmos draws on a wide range of texts subsequently to be defined as canonical. Unsurprisingly for a self-conscious work of prophecy, Israel's prophetic literature is an important source, with Isaiah, Ezekiel, and Daniel (the latter understood as a prophetic book) as particular favorites. The prominence of Isaiah, early Christianity's de facto "fifth gospel," is unsurprising.[6] The importance of Ezekiel and Daniel, books attributed to exiled prophets, may reflect John's self-understanding as a prophet in exile (whether enforced or self-imposed: Rev 1:9). R. H. Charles includes Jeremiah among Revelation's dominant prophets, while others also give an important role to Zechariah.[7] Other minor prophets (Joel, Amos, Hosea, Zephaniah, Habakkuk) are less prominent. The strong influence of the Psalter is also widely acknowledged: on G. K. Beale's figures, more than half the allusions come from Isaiah, the Psalms, Ezekiel, and Daniel combined.[8] Interestingly, this consensus on the prominence of the prophets and Psalms in Revelation is broadly shared by modern exegetes and both Latin and Greek patristic commentators (e.g., Tyconius of Carthage, Oecumenius, and Andrew of Caesarea). The centrality of heavenly worship in Revelation, and frequent inclusion of liturgical-type canticles (e.g., Rev 4:11; 5:9–10; 11:17–18), offers a partial explanation for John's liking for the Psalter. Yet allusions to the Psalms are not restricted to Revelation's canticles or visions of the heavenly temple, suggesting that other concerns are also at play.[9]

(Berrien Springs, MI: Andrews University Press, 1988); Michelle Fletcher, *Reading Revelation as Pastiche: Imitating the Past*, LNTS 571 (London: Bloomsbury T&T Clark, 2017).

5. Richard B. Hays, *Echoes of Scripture in the Gospels* (Waco, TX: Baylor University Press, 2016), 10.

6. On the use of Isaiah, see esp. Jan Fekkes III, *Isaiah and Prophetic Traditions in the Book of Revelation: Visionary Antecedents and Their Development*, JSNTSup 93 (Sheffield: JSOT Press, 1994).

7. R. H. Charles, *A Critical and Exegetical Commentary on the Revelation of St. John*, 2 vols., ICC (Edinburgh: T&T Clark, 1920), 1:lxv; Marko Jauhiainen, *The Use of Zechariah in Revelation*, WUNT 2/199 (Tübingen: Mohr Siebeck, 2005); Garrick V. Allen, *The Book of Revelation and Early Jewish Textual Culture*, SNTSMS 168 (Cambridge: Cambridge University Press, 2017).

8. Beale, *The Book of Revelation: A Commentary on the Greek Text*, NIGTC (Grand Rapids: Eerdmans, 1999), 77; see also Swete, *Apocalypse*, cliii.

9. On the Psalms in Revelation, see, e.g., Steve Moyise, "The Psalms in the Book of Revelation," in *The Psalms in the New Testament*, ed. Steve Moyise and Maarten J. J. Menken, NTSI (London: T&T Clark, 2004), 231–46.

Of the books of the Pentateuch, allusions to Exodus are primary, a reflection of the importance of the exodus narrative for the story that John describes. The widely acknowledged allusions to Genesis focus especially on Eden (the tree and river of life, e.g., Gen 2:9–10; 3:3, 22, 24; Rev 2:7; 22:1–2; the serpent and the woman, Gen 3:1, 14–19; Rev 12:9, 17), the promises to Abraham (e.g., Gen 12:3; 15:18; 28:14; Rev 1:7; 9:14), and Jacob's blessing of Judah (Gen 49:9, 11; Rev 5:5; 7:14). There is less agreement on allusions to other scriptural texts, though several scholars detect use of books preserved in the OG/LXX but not the MT (e.g., Tobit; Wisdom of Solomon).[10]

The modes of scriptural allusion throughout Revelation are also diverse. In many cases, multiple allusions are combined in the same passage, or even in the same verse (e.g., Dan 7:13 and Zech 12:10 at Rev 1:7), raising questions as to which should be given priority in interpretation. In others, a scriptural book (e.g., Ezekiel) may help shape the macrostructure of John's composition. Alternatively, the influence is more thematic, sometimes evoking whole scriptural narratives, thus making allusions to specific texts less certain. Examples include the pervasive exodus motif and allusions to the Egyptian plagues (e.g., Rev 12:6, 14; 15:2–4; 16:1–21), the prophetic announcement of the demise of Babylon (Rev 18, drawing on prophetic taunt songs against both Tyre and Babylon, Isa 23–24; 47; Jer 50–51; Ezek 26–27), and the new creation of Rev 21–22 (with influence from both Genesis and Isaiah). Finally, scriptural characters can function as "types" to illuminate the contemporary situation of John's first century congregations (e.g., the characters of Balaam and Jezebel in Rev 2:14, 20). Attention will be paid to each of these dimensions in what follows.

Israel's Scriptures in the Revelation of John

Introducing Scripture

How does John of Patmos introduce Israel's Scriptures in his book? We have already noted the striking absence of clearly marked citations, introduced by explicit quotation formulas. John Sweet writes of Revelation's author: "He never quotes a passage verbatim, but paraphrases, alludes and weaves together motifs in such a way that to follow up each allusion usually brings out further dimen-

---

10. Though Hebrew and Aramaic fragments of Tobit were discovered at Qumran. For lists of biblical books used in Revelation, see, e.g., Swete, *Apocalypse*, cxl–clviii; Craig R. Koester, *Revelation: A New Translation with Introduction and Commentary*, AB 38A (New Haven: Yale University Press, 2014), 123.

sions of meaning."[11] On the contrary, verbs that function elsewhere as citation markers, such as γράφω or λέγω, serve in the Apocalypse to introduce John's own prophetic mediation of divine revelation rather than previous Scriptures (e.g., Rev 1:8, 11, 17, 19; 2:1; 7:13; 9:14; 10:4; 19:9).[12] The nearest thing to an "introductory formula" is the reference to "the song of Moses, the servant of God" at Rev 15:3, although this introduces not a direct quotation from either Exod 15:1–18 or Deut 32:1–43 but a catena of textual allusions drawn from the Psalms, Isaiah, Jeremiah, and Amos as well as the Pentateuch.

The question of unmarked citations is more contested. Many Revelation scholars follow Sweet in denying the presence even of these, viewing all usage of Israel's Scriptures as allusion or echo. Some distinguish between *dependency* on scriptural texts (from memory) and *copying* from manuscripts, arguing that the former is a better model for understanding Revelation.[13] But this either/or distinction obscures the complexity of the evidence, which makes a combination of manuscript usage (representing a variety of textual traditions) and recall from memory more probable.[14]

A minority of scholars identify actual quotations, noting that the presence of these is not dependent on an introductory formula, so long as (following Hays) one finds "the verbatim reproduction of an extended chain of words" from the source text.[15] Of the nearly eight hundred scriptural references in the margins of NA[28], twenty-eight are italicized, that is, identified as direct quotations.[16] The spread of these reflects the general spread of the scriptural allusions: Psalms (six), prophets (sixteen, with the largest number drawn from Isaiah [five], Ezekiel [three] and Amos [three]), plus two each from Genesis and 2 Kings, and one each from Deuteronomy and 2 Samuel. More focused studies identify additional direction quotations in specific books. In his study of John's use of Ezekiel, Albert Vanhoye identifies three "citations exactes" from that prophet (Rev 1:15 =

---

11. John Sweet, *Revelation*, SCM Pelican Commentaries (London: SCM, 1979), 39.

12. Darius Müller, "Zitatmarkierungen und die Gegenwart der Schrift im Neuen Testament," in *Textual History and the Reception of Scripture in Early Christianity/Textgeschichte und Schriftrezeption im frühen Christentum*, ed. Johannes de Vries and Martin Karrer, SCS 60 (Atlanta: Society of Biblical Literature, 2013), 189–99.

13. E.g., Louis Arthur Vos, *The Synoptic Traditions in the Apocalypse* (Kampen: Kok, 1965), 16–53.

14. See esp. Allen, *Early Jewish Textual Culture*, 254–67.

15. Hays, *Echoes of Scripture in the Gospels*, 10.

16. Robert Bratcher also has a list of fifteen Old Testament passages (drawn from the Psalms [five], Daniel [three], Isaiah [two], Exodus [two], Hosea [one], Zechariah [one], and Proverbs [one]) in his study of Old Testament quotations in the New Testament, although he redefines these as allusions rather than actual quotations. Bratcher, ed., *Old Testament Quotations in the New Testament*, rev. ed., Helps for Translators 3 (London: United Bible Societies, 1967), 74–76.

Ezek 43:2; Rev 10:10 = Ezek 3:3; Rev 18:1 = Ezek 43:2), together with another four exhibiting only "légères retouches" (Rev 7:14 = Ezek 37:3; Rev 11:11 = Ezek 37:10; Rev 18:19 = Ezek 27:30; Rev 18:21 = Ezek 26:21).[17] In addition, he finds "un total d'une trentaine d'utilisations difficilement contestable."[18]

Similarly, Steve Moyise finds four unmarked quotations from the Psalms in the Apocalypse (Ps 2:1–2 = Rev 11:15, 18; Ps 2:8–9 = Rev 2:26–27; 12:5; 19:15; Ps 86:8–10 = Rev 15:3–4; Ps 89:28, 38 = Rev 1:5), the second and third of which are also designated by NA[28] as citations.[19] All four of them, moreover, share a thematic link in "the fate of the nations." The case of John's use of Ezekiel raises its own particular issues and will be discussed separately below.

One example will suffice to demonstrate the complexity. The oracle of the "one like a son of man" to Thyatira (Rev 2:26b–27) shows clear dependence on Ps 2:8–9, as does the description of the Divine Warrior at Rev 19:15, while verbal echoes of this psalm are also strong at Rev 12:5. In these different contexts it is read ecclesiologically (a promise to the victor, Rev 2:26b–27) and christologically (the authority given to Christ, Rev 12:5 and 19:15). The latter reflects a messianic interpretation of this psalm (e.g., Pss. Sol. 17:23–24; Acts 13:33; Heb 1:5; 5:5), while the former mirrors Revelation's conviction that God's people, especially the martyrs, share in Christ's royal rule (e.g., Rev 1:6, 9; 20:4–6). Moreover, the christological interpretation is not completely absent from this first passage, for its words are spoken by "the Son of God" (Rev 2:18; cf. Ps 2:7).

The wording at Rev 2:27 (repeated in part at Rev 19:15) is more than a verbal allusion according to common criteria for detecting citations, for it is identical to the OG/LXX of Ps 2:9 in six of its eleven words (except that the 2nd pers. sg., addressed by God to the king, has become the 3rd pers. ποιμανεῖ to fit its new context) and relatively close to the Hebrew (particularly given the ambiguity of תרעם in the unpointed consonantal text).[20] The remaining five words retain significant verbal similarity (though the "vessels" are now plural, and the verb is in the passive voice).

---

17. Albert Vanhoye, "L'utilisation du livre d'Ézéchiel dans l'Apocalypse," *Bib* 43, no. 3 (1962): 437–38.

18. Vanhoye, "L'utilisation," 440 [ET: "a total of around thirty uses that are difficult to dispute."].

19. Moyise, "Psalms in the Book of Revelation," 231–46. NA[28] treats Ps 2:2 (Rev 11:15) and Ps 89:28, 38 (Rev 1:5) as allusions rather than citations.

20. David E. Aune, *Revelation 1–5*, WBC 52 (Dallas: Word, 1997), 210. Trudinger argues for dependence on a Semitic source here. L. Paul Trudinger, "Some Observations concerning the Text of the Old Testament in the Book of Revelation," *JTS* 17, no. 1 (1966): 84.

δώσω αὐτῷ ἐξουσίαν ἐπὶ τῶν ἐθνῶν καὶ <u>ποιμανεῖ αὐτοὺς ἐν ῥάβδῳ σιδηρᾷ ὡς τὰ σκεύη τὰ κεραμικὰ συντρίβεται</u> (Rev. 2:26b–27).

שְׁאַל מִמֶּנִּי וְאֶתְּנָה גוֹיִם נַחֲלָתֶךָ וַאֲחֻזָּתְךָ אַפְסֵי־אָרֶץ:

תְּרֹעֵם בְּשֵׁבֶט בַּרְזֶל כִּכְלִי יוֹצֵר תְּנַפְּצֵם:

αἴτησαι παρ' ἐμοῦ καὶ δώσω σοι ἔθνη τὴν κληρονομίαν σου καὶ τὴν κατάσχεσίν σου τὰ πέρατα τῆς γῆς. <u>ποιμανεῖς αὐτοὺς ἐν ῥάβδῳ σιδηρᾷ ὡς σκεῦος κεραμέως συντρίψεις αὐτούς</u> (Ps 2:8–9).

Yet, as is typical for John, precise verbal agreement is combined with a more paraphrastic treatment of Ps 2:8 in Rev 2:26b (Charles calls it a "free rendering").[21] John interprets the Psalm's statement that the king will be given "the nations" as an "inheritance" or "possession" (נַחֲלָה; LXX κληρονομία), in terms of being granted "authority," one of his favorite words (also Rev 6:8; 9:3, 19; 11:6; 12:10; 13:2; 14:18; 16:9; 17:12; 18:1; 20:6; 22:14).[22]

Besides this example, the following are also strong candidates for containing unmarked citations. Revelation 1:15 (describing "his voice like the sound of many waters") is particularly close to the Hebrew of Ezek 43:2 (וְקוֹלוֹ כְּקוֹל מַיִם רַבִּים). The song of the four living creatures at Rev 4:8 picks up word for word the Trisagion of the seraphim at Isa 6:3, including the divine title (translating יְהוָה צְבָאוֹת as κύριος ὁ θεὸς ὁ παντοκράτωρ, the addition of ὁ θεός perhaps under the influence of Amos 3:13). The cry of "the kings of the earth" and their companions at Rev 6:16 is arguably an extended citation from Hos 10:8. John's description of the scroll's effects at Rev 10:10 (καὶ ἦν ἐν τῷ στόματί μου ὡς μέλι γλυκὺ) draws fairly precisely on Ezek 3:3, a potential citation that is supported by other allusions to Ezek 3 in Rev 10. Another probable citation from Ezek 43:2, again closer to the Hebrew than the OG/LXX, is found in Rev 18:1 (καὶ ἡ γῆ ἐφωτίσθη ἐκ τῆς δόξης αὐτοῦ; MT has וְהָאָרֶץ הֵאִירָה מִכְּבֹדוֹ).

More contested are the prophetic oracle at Rev 1:7 and the cluster of potential citations in the "Song of Moses" at Rev 15:3–4. Revelation 1:7 combines phrases from Dan 7:13 and Zech 12:10 and 14 (possibly modified in a more universalistic way by Gen 12:3 and 28:14: πᾶσαι αἱ φυλαὶ τῆς γῆς). Here the relationship with the earlier texts is more paraphrastic. That John may be drawing upon an existing tradition at this point is supported by the same combination of Daniel and Zechariah, albeit in reverse order, in Matt 24:30. As regards Rev 15:3–4, NA[28] finds

---

21. Charles, *Revelation*, 1:74.
22. Unless otherwise noted, all translations are by the author.

no less than eight potential citations (Pss 111:2; 139:14; Amos 3:13; 4:13; Deut 32:4; Ps 145:17; Jer 10:7; Ps 86:9), together with eleven allusions. That this is the only place in Revelation where John provides something like a citation marker certainly strengthens the case for a citation at this point. Yet the degree of correspondence with the source text is in most of the proposed examples minimal. A strong case, however, can be made for a quotation from Ps 86:9 at Rev 15:4: πάντα τὰ ἔθνη ἥξουσιν καὶ προσκυνήσουσιν ἐνώπιόν σου closely follows the source text, with a total of eight words in the same sequence.

The presence of unmarked citations in the Apocalypse, then, is minimal (and contested). The bulk of Revelation's use of Israel's Scriptures occurs in either verbal or conceptual allusions. As will be demonstrated below, these multiple allusions function in several different ways.

Using Scripture

Given that John's appeal to Israel's Scriptures is often highly allusive and rarely explicitly marked, how is he using them? Moyise has identified three different models used by scholars to answer this question.[23] Some (e.g., George Caird and Elisabeth Schüssler Fiorenza) employ a rhetorical model, viewing the author as using Scripture to articulate his own vision of the future, particularly shaped by his convictions about Jesus Christ. According to this model, John can use Israel's Scriptures with little attention to original context. Scholars such as Richard Bauckham and Beale work with a scribal or exegetical model, envisaging John's vision as rooted in his careful exegesis of the scriptural text. A third, mystical model (which Moyise finds, e.g., in the work of Christopher Rowland) emphasizes the foundational role of meditation on biblical texts as preparatory to the visions John describes.[24] These models are helpful in identifying emphases. However, as will become clear, they are not watertight.

We shall begin our discussion with a more detailed consideration of Revelation's visionary and prophetic character before examining different kinds of usage: John's preference for mixed allusions; the structural role of certain biblical books, notably Ezekiel; more thematic or conceptual allusions; specific typological usage. Our discussion will include consideration of how John's convictions

---

23. Moyise, *Later New Testament Writers*, 140-42.
24. Caird, *A Commentary on the Revelation of St. John the Divine*, BNTC (London: Black, 1966); Schüssler Fiorenza, *Justice and Judgment*; Bauckham, *The Climax of Prophecy: Studies on the Book of Revelation* (Edinburgh: T&T Clark, 1993); Beale, *Use of Daniel*; Rowland, *The Open Heaven: A Study of the Apocalyptic in Judaism and Early Christianity* (London: SPCK, 1982), 214-47.

concerning Jesus Christ impact his use of Israel's Scriptures and its potential rhetorical effect on his readers/audiences.

Visionary-Prophetic Exegesis

Revelation makes robust claims of standing in continuity with Israelite prophecy. John describes his book as "words of prophecy" (Rev 1:3; 22:7), in which the words of the exalted Christ are introduced by the prophetic Τάδε λέγει formula (Rev 2:1, 8, 12, 18; 3:1, 7, 14; cf. e.g., Isa 1:24; Amos 1:6; Mic 2:3; Obad 1). He receives a prophetic commissioning from the mighty angel with the little scroll (Rev 10:11) and is exhorted to regard other prophets as his "brothers" (Rev 22:9). Moreover, he has a prophetic rival in the congregation at Thyatira, whom he names disparagingly as "Jezebel" (Rev 2:20).

Such claims to prophetic insight and visionary experience lead to a blurring of categories often treated as mutually exclusive by biblical scholars, such as prophet, visionary, and scribe or exegete. (This blurring should already be obvious in the attribution of Jewish apocalypses to scribes such as Enoch, Baruch, and Ezra.) It also complicates the quest for conscious authorial intention, and thus the common scholarly distinction between allusion and echo where that distinction is made on the basis of authorial intent. While the text in its final form contains evidence of conscious organization and *post eventum* reflection (e.g., the sequences of sevens, the explicit interpretations of the stars and lampstands, or the heads and horns of the beast, Rev 1:20; 17:9–10, 12), this is combined with a fluidity and chaotic character to be expected of a text rooted in actual visionary experience. Furthermore, visionaries not only shape their understanding of what they have seen and heard in light of their own traditions; those traditions have already coalesced as preexisting patterns to which those original visionary experiences conform. Moreover, far from being antithetical to visionary and prophetic activity, careful exegetical study of specific texts (e.g., Ezek 1) seems to have played a preparatory role for at least some Jewish visionaries.[25]

The influence of Israel's Scriptures could therefore be felt at each stage of the process: shaping what the experience would be, both in terms of received patterns and juxtapositions of scriptural texts and in highlighting precise exegetical ambiguities; allowing the seer to interpret what was seen *in eventu*; and provid-

---

25. E.g., Rowland, *Open Heaven*, 214–47; Christopher Rowland and Christopher R. A. Morray-Jones, *The Mystery of God: Early Jewish Mysticism and the New Testament*, CRINT 12 (Leiden: Brill, 2009), 63–90. On the postexilic perception that prophets fasted and meditated on Scripture prior to reception of visions, see e.g., John Barton, *Oracles of God: Perceptions of Ancient Prophecy in Israel After the Exile* (Oxford: Oxford University Press, 1986), 124–28.

ing the *post eventum* language to describe and interpret that event. Moreover, the visionary material in Revelation need not have been the result of a single visionary experience, but a complex body of several vision reports subsequently reworked into the current text, sent as a prophetic-apocalyptic letter to the seven churches of Asia.

The dynamic of such a "visionary exegesis" may be illustrated by a comparison of John's vision of the heavenly throne room (Rev 4–5) with both antecedents in Israel's Scriptures and parallels in Jewish apocalypses. By common consent, the main scriptural intertext is Ezekiel's vision of the merkavah or throne-chariot (Ezek 1:1–28). Strong similarities, both thematic (e.g., the throne, the four living creatures, the sound of mighty waters, the rainbow) and verbal, point to this prophetic text as inspiration for what John describes. Yet, like parallel throne visions (e.g., 1 En. 14; Apoc. Ab. 18), this is no straightforward literary borrowing from Ezek 1. Rather, it contains a different sequence of details, looser verbal echoes, and striking changes from the source text (notably the attribution of a different face to each living creature, Rev 4:7; cf. Ezek 1:10), together with the influence of other scriptural intertexts (e.g., Isa 6; 1 Kgs 22:19; and Dan 7). A more satisfying explanation is that Ezekiel's opening chapter has functioned as one key text for meditation and exegetical speculation in the seer's preparation for visionary experience, as well as shaping the subsequent verbal articulation of that experience.

A visionary model therefore presupposes a more dynamic interplay of conscious and unconscious use of scriptural texts, as well as the author's christological convictions, in a memory "which is so charged with Old Testament words and thoughts that they arrange themselves in his visions like the changing patterns of a kaleidoscope, without conscious effort on his own part."[26] The metaphor of "kaleidoscope," indeed, is regularly used of the fluidity of Revelation's inaugural vision (Rev 1:12–20), where the complex description of the "one like a son of man" combines a rich crop of scriptural images and verbal allusions with theological claims for Jesus of Nazareth as "the Living One" who now holds the keys of death and Hades (Rev 1:18).[27]

Combined Verbal Allusions

Many allusions to Israel's Scriptures in Revelation come from multiple scriptural texts simultaneously. As Beale famously noted, "Sometimes, four, five, or more

---

26. Swete, *Apocalypse*, cliv.
27. Commentators frequently find the following passages evoked in this Patmos vision: Isa 49:2; Ezek 1:24; 9:11; Dan 3:6; 7:9, 13; 10:5–6; Zech 4:2. For a discussion, see, e.g., Moyise, *Old Testament in the Book of Revelation*, 37–44.

OT references are merged into one picture."[28] The most obvious example is the "Song of Moses the servant of God and the Song of the Lamb" (Rev 15:3-4), in which NA[28] detects nineteen citations and allusions. This represents a rich interweaving of phrases drawn from the Psalter, prophetic books, and the Pentateuch, rather than drawing substantially from either of the biblical songs attributed to Moses, Exod 15:1-18 and Deut 32:1-43 (though the former provides the basic thematic outline, and Revelation's canticle echoes words from Deut 32:4).[29]

As Bauckham has argued, Rev 15:3-4 provides evidence for John's use of Jewish exegetical techniques, such as *gezērâ šāwâ*, interpreting scriptural passages in light of others containing the same or similar words. His use of Jer 10:6-7 and Ps 86:8-10 depends on their containing a phrase similar to Exod 15:11 ("Who is like you, O Lord, among the gods?"). Similar techniques may help explain other combined allusions, as in the vision report of Rev 1:9-20. For example, the merging of Daniel's figures of "the Ancient of Days" and "one like a son of man" (Dan 7:9, 13) at Rev 1:14 ("his head and his hair were white as wool which is white as snow") may have a partially exegetical explanation. The OG/LXX of Dan 7:13 understands the son of man figure coming not "to" but "as" the Ancient of Days (ὡς παλαιὸς ἡμερῶν). Similarly, the reference to the "sharp double-edged sword" emerging from the son of man's mouth (Rev 1:16; an image for God's word, cf. Heb 4:12) apparently combines Isa 11:4 and 49:2, perhaps through *gezērâ šāwâ*. The image will recur later in the book to describe the means by which Christ conquers his enemies (Rev 2:12, 16; 19:15, 21). Such exegetical possibilities, however, do not preclude a visionary origin to much of this "kaleidoscopic" passage.

Further combined allusions also function to describe Revelation's Christ or occur in divine titles. Hence the description of God as "Lord God Almighty" in the song of the four living creatures (Rev 4:8) apparently combines Isa 6:3 with Amos 3:13. The appearance of the Lamb in heaven is preceded by the voice of an elder interweaving two messianic titles: "the Lion of the tribe of Judah, the Root of David" (Rev 5:5 = Gen 49:9; Isa 11:1, 10). Yet both titles are immediately reworked in light of John's convictions about Jesus, for in the next verse he describes seeing "a lamb standing as if slaughtered" (Rev 5:6). This sets up a christological dynamic in which the two animal metaphors—one signifying power, the other weakness—stand in tension. Rhetorically, it poses the question as to what true power looks like for those who follow the crucified Christ.

A more extensive example occurs in the vision of the returning Jesus as the rider on the white horse (Rev 19:11-16). This looks like a combination not only of specific allusions from Israel's Scriptures (e.g., Pss 9:9; 72:2; Isa 11:1; Dan 10:6)

---

28. Beale, *Book of Revelation*, 79.
29. Bauckham, *Climax of Prophecy*, 296-307.

but of substantial passages: Isaiah's vision of YHWH as Divine Warrior returning from defeating the Edomites and the descent of God's word upon Egypt in the Wisdom of Solomon (Isa 63:1-6; Wis 18:14-16). Again, the combined texts are radically reshaped by the story of Jesus, for, in contrast to the Isaiah passage, the rider's robe is dipped in blood prior to the battle being engaged (Rev 19:13a). This suggests victory through sacrifice, the blood being either Christ's own or that of his martyr-soldiers. Christology has reframed the interpretation of scriptural antecedents.

Structural Role of Israel's Scriptures

But the use of Israel's Scriptures is not confined to specific quotations and allusions, whether single or combined. It is widely acknowledged that certain biblical books play a more prominent role in Revelation, impacting the book's order and structure. Both Daniel and Ezekiel have been seen to function in this way, though scholarship is divided as to their respective prominence. The number of verbal allusions to Daniel is especially noteworthy, proportionate to its size (NA[28] identifies 80, compared with 138 and 100 for the much-longer Isaiah and Ezekiel respectively). For Beale, parts of Revelation can even be viewed as "midrash" on Danielic passages.[30]

Allusions to Daniel appear as early as the opening verse, where John's "revelation of Jesus Christ [Ἀποκάλυψις Ἰησοῦ Χριστοῦ]," whose content reveals "what must happen soon" (ἃ δεῖ γενέσθαι ἐν τάχει, Rev 1:1) recalls Daniel's words to king Nebuchadnezzar about a God in heaven revealing mysteries (Theodotion: ἀποκαλύπτων μυστήρια) concerning what must happen in the last days (ἃ δεῖ γενέσθαι ἐπ' ἐσχάτων τῶν ἡμερῶν, Dan 2:28). Similar allusions to Dan 2:28-29 appear at strategic points through the book (also Rev 1:19; 4:1; 22:6).

This passage is important for at least three reasons. First, it is concerned, like the Apocalypse, with a God who reveals heavenly mysteries. Second, its usage here points to John's conviction that Daniel's "last days" have now come to pass and that what had been sealed (Dan 12:4) is now to be unveiled. Third, its appearance in the opening verse of Revelation gives Daniel particular prominence. There may be a further, thematic reason for the importance of Dan 2:28-29: it comes from the section of Daniel describing the fidelity of Judean exiles in Babylon, appropriate given that Revelation also reflects an exile's "point of view," including a command that God's people come out of Babylon (Rev 18:4).

---

30. Beale, *Use of Daniel*, 313-20; Beale, *John's Use of the Old Testament in Revelation*, JSNTSup 166 (Sheffield: Sheffield Academic, 1998). For a critique, see the review by Adela Yarbro Collins in *JBL* 105, no. 4 (1986): 734-35.

Israel's Scriptures in the Revelation of John

The influence of Daniel on the Apocalypse, however, is limited. Revelation draws on a select group of Danielic passages, several of which have shaped key vision reports: the ten-day testing of Daniel and his companions (Dan 1:12-14; Rev 2:10), the Nebuchadnezzar story (Dan 2-4; Rev 1:1, 19; 4:1; 13:15; 16:7; 19:2; 22:6), and the angelic figure of Dan 8; 10; and 12 (Rev 1:13, 17; 10:6). Most prominent is Dan 7, providing the son of man figure (Dan 7:13-14; Rev 1:7, 13; 14:14), the myriads of angels around the throne (Dan 7:10; Rev 5:11), and the beast from the sea (Dan 7:1-8, 15-27; Rev 11:7; 13:1-10; 14:11; 17:12; cf. 12:3). This is unsurprising, given the centrality of the Son of Man, and the motif of the vindication of the holy ones, in the portrayal of Jesus in the Gospels. In addition, the time period at Rev 12:14 (καιρόν καὶ καιρούς καὶ ἥμισυ καιροῦ) is clearly derived from Daniel (ἕως καιροῦ καὶ καιρῶν καὶ ἥμισυ καιροῦ, Dan 7:25; 12:7 Theodotion). Moreover, in both Daniel and Revelation, this period refers to the persecution of God's people prior to the end, rephrased by John variously as forty-two months and 1,260 days (Rev 11:2, 3; 12:6; 13:5).

An even stronger case may be made for Ezekiel as *Vorlage* for Revelation. The influence of this prophetic book has already been noted (e.g., in the throne room vision of Rev 4-5), albeit often combined with allusions to other texts. NA[28] identifies approximately one hundred allusions to Ezekiel, including two unmarked citations (Ezek 37:5, 10 at Rev 11:11; Ezek 11:20 at Rev 21:7).[31] Beate Kowalski identifies around 130, drawn from thirty-five of the book's forty-eight chapters.[32] But numerous scholars have noted a more extensive correlation between the order of Ezekiel and the Apocalypse, even if few have followed Michael Goulder in positing a lectionary explanation.[33] David Mathewson's table plots out substantial agreement among scholars:[34]

---

31. Though stronger cases can be made for those identified by Vanhoye: Rev 1:15 = Ezek 43:2; Rev 10:10 = Ezek 3:3; Rev 18:1 = Ezek 43:2.

32. Kowalski, *Die Rezeption des Propheten Ezechiel in der Offenbarung des Johannes*, SBB 52 (Stuttgart: Katholisches Bibelwerk, 2004), 252-62.

33. See e.g., Vanhoye, "L'utilisation"; Goulder, "The Apocalypse as an Annual Cycle of Prophecies," NTS 27, no. 3 (1981): 342-67; Jeffrey M. Vogelgesang, "The Interpretation of Ezekiel in the Book of Revelation" (PhD diss., Harvard University, 1985); Jean-Pierre Ruiz, *Ezekiel in the Apocalypse: The Transformation of Prophetic Language in Revelation 16,17-19,10*, EHS.T 376 (Frankfurt am Main: Lang, 1989); Kowalski, *Rezeption*; Ian K. Boxall, "Exile, Prophet, Visionary: Ezekiel's Influence on the Book of Revelation," in *The Book of Ezekiel and Its Influence*, ed. Henk Jan de Jonge and Johannes Tromp (Aldershot: Ashgate, 2007), 147-64; Steve Moyise, "Ezekiel and the Book of Revelation," in *After Ezekiel: Essays on the Reception of a Difficult Prophet*, ed. Andrew Mein and Paul M. Joyce, LHBOTS 535 (London: T&T Clark, 2011), 45-57.

34. Mathewson, *A New Heaven and a New Earth: The Meaning and Function of the Old Testament in Revelation 21.1-22.5*, JSNTSup 238 (London: Sheffield Academic, 2003), 29.

Table 24.1. The Structural Influence of Ezekiel

Ezek 1	Rev 1
Ezek 2	Rev 5 (and Rev 10)
Ezek 9–10	Rev 7–8
Ezek 16, 23	Rev 17
Ezek 26–28	Rev 18
Ezek 38–39	Rev 19–20
Ezek 40–48	Rev 21–22 (and Rev 11)

Particularly striking is the close correlation between the final visions of Ezekiel (Ezek 38–48) and John's climactic visions of the millennium, Gog and Magog, and the New Jerusalem. Other Ezekielian passages might also be added to bolster the structural parallels: for example, Ezek 5–7 influencing Rev 6 (especially Ezek 6:11; 7:2–3, 15), verbal echoes of Ezek 12:25 at Rev 10:6 and of Ezek 14:3–11 at Rev 13:11–18, and elements of Ezek 29 and 32 (the slaying of the great dragon/pharaoh to provide food for the "animals of the earth" and "the birds of the air") influencing Rev 19:17–21.[35] The latter observation allows an interpreter of Revelation to find an even stronger structural parallel with Ezekiel in this section. As commentators regularly note, the strongest verbal intertext for the "great supper of God" (Rev 19:17–21) is Ezek 39:17–20, which in Ezekiel's order comes *after* the appearance of Gog from the land of Magog (Ezek 38), not before as in Revelation (Gog and Magog only appear after the millennium at Rev 20:8). Bringing in Ezek 29 and 32 restores the Ezekielian sequence.

Though the structural parallels with Ezekiel are more pervasive than those with Daniel, the Apocalypse is no "new Ezekiel" either. Some of the Ezekiel passages are used more than once, demonstrating thematic as well as structural influence. Moreover, the dynamic relationship between John's text and his Ezekielian hypotext means that the latter is frequently reworked in light of John's other intertexts, as well as his theological convictions. As noted above, the vision of God's throne (Rev 4) varies significantly from Ezek 1, with strong verbal allusions to, for example, Isa 6; 1 Kgs 22:19; and Dan 7. Perhaps the most striking variation comes in the extended allusion to Ezekiel's final visions of the new temple and city. John's reworking is notable for the absence of a temple ("I saw no temple in it, for the Lord God Almighty is its temple, and the Lamb"; Rev 21:22), or rather for its merging of temple and city (the latter is cuboid, recalling the holy of holies in Solomon's temple, Rev 21:16; cf. 1 Kgs 6:20). Ezekiel's city and temple are also dwarfed by the massive size of John's visionary city (twelve thousand stadia in

---

35. Boxall, "Exile, Prophet, Visionary," 149–55.

length, height, and breadth, or approximately fifteen hundred miles: Rev 21:16; cf. Ezek 40:1–42:20). In addition, Ezekiel's focus on the restoration of Israel is transformed in Revelation by a more universal outlook shaped by intertexts from Trito-Isaiah, with promises made for "the kings of the earth" (Rev 21:24–26; cf. Isa 60:3–11).[36] Such may be overlooked in undue concentration on Ezekiel's structural role. As Michelle Fletcher reminds us, concentrating on the role of a particular book risks "splitting Revelation up into constituent parts rather than reading its multivocal text holistically."[37]

Conceptual Allusions

Arguably more important than the role of specific scriptural books are conceptual allusions, which cannot be attributed to a single scriptural text.[38] These include the christological titles of the book (e.g., the Son of God, "one like a son of man," and, preeminently, "the Lamb"), the myth of the Divine Warrior and related day of the Lord, and motifs such as the new creation (e.g., Rev 21:1–5; 22:1–2; cf. Gen 1–2; Isa 43:19; 65:17; 66:22) or destructive locusts (e.g., Rev 9:1–11; cf. Exod 10:1–20; Joel 1–2; Wis 16:9).

In certain cases, these conceptual allusions are so extensive as to evoke complete narratives. Holistic readings of Revelation typical of narrative criticism, and arguably the book's earliest reception as an aural experience (Rev 1:3), draw attention to extended biblical stories embedded in the text, functioning as overlapping and mutually reinforcing subplots.[39] The story of the exodus is particularly pervasive, providing a narrative coherence to otherwise disparate elements scattered throughout the book. Revelation tells the story of God's people being "loosed" or "freed" from their sins by the blood of a slaughtered lamb (e.g., Rev 1:5; 5:6; 6:1; cf. Exod 12). Later, those victorious over the beast stand by a sea of glass, singing "the song of Moses, the servant of God, and the song of the Lamb" (Rev 15:2–4; cf. Exod 15:1–18). Elsewhere, the dragon-Satan functions as another pharaoh (cf. Ezek 29:3), pursuing the woman, a potent symbol of God's people, into the wilderness (Rev 12:6, 13; cf. Exod 14). Like Israel at the exodus, the

---

36. On Revelation's universalizing tendency, see, e.g., Vanhoye, "L'utilisation," 446–67; Beale, *Book of Revelation*, 91–92; Fekkes, *Isaiah and Prophetic Traditions*.

37. Fletcher, *Reading Revelation as Pastiche*, 23.

38. Jon Paulien, "Criteria and the Assessment of Allusions to the Old Testament in the Book of Revelation," in *Studies in the Book of Revelation*, ed. Steve Moyise (Edinburgh: T&T Clark, 2001), 119.

39. See, e.g., David L. Barr, *Tales of the End: A Narrative Commentary on the Book of Revelation*, Storytellers Bible 1 (Santa Rosa, CA: Polebridge, 1998); James L. Resseguie, *The Revelation of John: A Narrative Commentary* (Grand Rapids: Baker Academic, 2009).

woman is given eagle's wings to aid her flight to safety in that wilderness, where she is fed by God (Rev 12:14; Exod 16:4-36; 19:4). Other Exodus details include the repeated reference to Sinai-like lightning and thunder emanating from God's throne (Rev 4:5; 8:5; 11:19; 16:18; cf. Exod 19:16) and the influence of the Egyptian plagues tradition on Revelation's septets of trumpets and bowls (Rev 8-9; 16; cf. Exod 7:14-11:10; Wis 11-19). Revelation thus tells the story of a new exodus, inaugurated by the slaughter of Christ the Lamb.

Another subplot, suggested by the exodus story, serves as a connecting thread for Rev 17:1-22:5. This "Tale of Two Cities" motif seems to be shaped by Deutero-Isaiah's prophecy of a glorious return from exile in Babylon to Jerusalem/Zion, which the prophet presents as a new exodus (e.g., Isa 40:3; 43:14-21), with Babylon as the new Egypt. Similarly, the last chapters of the Apocalypse set up both a parallel and a contrast between two women-cities, Babylon the great city (currently incarnated in the city of Rome) and the New Jerusalem. With this wider Isaianic narrative in view, the heavenly cry "Come out of her, my people" (Rev 18:4) functions as a call to God's exiled people to leave Babylon for the New Jerusalem. This is a good example of how conceptual and thematic allusions may be missed by exclusive attention to identifying scriptural citations and allusions. Though the editors of NA[28] find several allusions to Deutero-Isaiah (especially the taunt-song to Babylon in Isa 47) in Revelation's own declaration of Babylon's fall (Rev 18), there are hardly any in the corresponding New Jerusalem vision, where it is Isa 56-66 that dominates. Yet many commentators would agree that the broader pattern of Deutero-Isaiah sheds important light on the function of Revelation's closing section.

Scriptural Figures and Places as Types

A final set of examples pertains to use of scriptural characters and geographical locations as "types" or "patterns" for contemporary figures, events, and political realities. Particularly striking is the use of the characters Balaam and Jezebel to target John's rivals in two of the seven congregations, Pergamum and Thyatira (Rev 2:14, 20). Both figures are sufficiently well-known to be identified by name without precise verbal allusions to specific passages. Balaam, a pagan prophet at the time of Moses (Num 31:8), is an ambiguous figure. He uttered a messianic prophecy about a star from Jacob (Num 24:15-19) yet was also blamed for Israel's apostasy at Shittim (Num 25:1-9; 31:16), giving him particular potency as a type for false teachers (e.g., 2 Pet 2:14-16; Jude 11; Philo, *Mos.* 1.264-314). The biblical Jezebel, Phoenician princess and consort to King Ahab of Israel (1 Kgs 16:31), is negatively portrayed in Israel's Scriptures as nemesis to the prophet Elijah (1 Kgs 19:1-8; 21:23-24).

In Revelation, both "Balaam" and "Jezebel" function as types for believers regarded as compromised by their association with the pagan culture of their cities. In the case of "Jezebel" in Thyatira, she is a prophet, like John himself. The typology may be even broader, therefore, given Revelation's association of true prophetic witness with both Elijah and Moses (preventing rain and turning water to blood, Rev 11:5–6; cf. 1 Kgs 17:1–7; 18:1, 41–46; Exod 7:14–24). John then functions as "Elijah" to Thyatira's "Jezebel," and "Moses" to Pergamum's "Balaam."

Places can also function typologically, especially in Revelation's geography, which is as mythic as it is terrestrial. The "great city" at Rev 11:8 (variously interpreted as a cipher for Rome, or Jerusalem, or the archetypal corrupt city) is "spiritually called 'Sodom' and 'Egypt,' where also their Lord was crucified." Thus, it embodies all the negative associations of those previous locations, including the memory of Egypt as land of bondage. "Babylon," currently incarnated in imperial Rome, is molded to the pattern of the first Babylon, whether as arrogant city, place of exile, or destroyer of God's temple. Revelation's Har Mageddon ("the mountain of Megiddo") may be difficult to locate on a literal map, given its expansive role. Rather, it now functions as a mythic location for the last great battle, encapsulating the memories of all those crucial battles fought across the centuries in the Jezreel Valley within sight of the city of Megiddo (e.g., Judg 5:19; 2 Kgs 9:27; 23:29).

Nature of the Scriptural Text

Our final question is also complicated by John's aversion to marked scriptural citations and preference for allusion and paraphrase: what textual form(s) did John utilize? Discussion of this topic often contrasts the divergent views of the two great Revelation commentators of the early twentieth century: Henry Barclay Swete and Robert Henry Charles. For Swete, John's scriptural *Vorlage* was the LXX; for Charles, John worked with the Hebrew text (or Hebrew and Aramaic in the case of Daniel). Yet, in fact, both had slightly more nuanced views. Though Charles thought that John made his own translation from Hebrew, he also acknowledged that this translation is often influenced by the wording of the LXX and the revision later incorporated into Theodotion.[40] Swete allowed that in places where his wording departs from the LXX, John "rendered independently," or used another Greek version, and that the names Abaddon and Har Mageddon (Rev 9:11; 16:16) imply at least knowledge of Hebrew or Aramaic.[41]

Some general observations are pertinent here before exploring concrete evidence for the use of specific textual *Vorlagen*. First, John writes in Greek, and

---

40. Charles, *Revelation*, 1:lxvi, and detailed tables in lxviii–lxxxii.
41. Swete, *Apocalypse*, clv–clvi.

addresses his prophetic letter to congregations of Christ followers in western Asia Minor, territory where Jews spoke Greek and read their Scriptures in that language. Thus the probability is strong that John knew Greek translations of at least some biblical books and expected such familiarity on the part of at least some of his original audiences. Second, however, his Greek is idiosyncratic, leading to the conclusion that the author is a Semitic speaker who thinks in Hebrew or Aramaic, has consciously "biblicized" his Greek style to reflect his claims to prophetic inspiration, or has deliberating bowdlerized the language to demonstrate his outsider status.[42] Charles's observation that John frequently diverges from readings found in the LXX (e.g., Rev 1:15 = Ezek 43:2; Rev 18:1 = Ezek 43:2; Rev 19:11 = Isa 11:4) supports his knowledge of Hebrew textual traditions. In addition, John may also know Aramaic interpretative traditions reflected in the later targumim. Such targumic expansion may underlie the divine title at Rev 1:8 (ὁ ὢν καὶ ὁ ἦν καὶ ὁ ἐρχόμενος; cf. Rev 4:8; 11:17; 16:5) and the reading "kingdom, priests" in the allusion to Exod 19:6 at Rev 1:6 (βασιλείαν ἱερεῖς; MT has "kingdom of priests"; LXX "royal priesthood").[43] Thus a bilingual (or even trilingual) background for our author is quite possible, especially given evidence for textual pluriformity in the first century and for scribal practice of combining careful exegesis of manuscripts, including consonantal Hebrew texts, inherited exegetical traditions, and recall from memory.[44]

For many recent scholars, the complex evidence supports John's use of both Hebrew and Greek textual traditions.[45] We have already noted evidence for John's knowledge of a Hebrew text of Ezekiel (e.g., Rev 1:15; 18:1 = Ezek 43:2), and there are multiple other examples that are either clearly derived from the Hebrew (e.g., Rev 22:2, where the leaves of the trees are for healing, dependent on the Hebrew of Ezek 47:12) or could come either from the Hebrew or the Greek. But influence from the Greek seems stronger in a small number of cases (e.g., Rev 11:11 = Ezek 37:5, 10 LXX). The allusion to Isa 22:22 at Rev 3:7 appears to be dependent on either the Hebrew or a Theodotion-type text since "key of the house of David" is absent from Isa 22:22 LXX (which reads τὴν δόξαν Δαυιδ and lacks the reference to opening and shutting). John's description of the colors of the four horses at Rev 6:1-8 (especially χλωρός in v. 8) also seems dependent on a Hebrew textual tradition for Zechariah.[46] Yet NA[28] finds multiple correspondences between Revelation and Theodotion's

---

42. E.g., R. H. Charles, *Studies in the Apocalypse: Being Lectures Delivered before the University of London* (Edinburgh: T&T Clark, 1913), 79–102; Sweet, *Revelation*, 16; Harry O. Maier, *Apocalypse Recalled: The Book of Revelation after Christendom* (Minneapolis: Fortress, 2002).

43. Martin McNamara, *The New Testament and the Palestinian Targum to the Pentateuch*, AnBib 27A (Rome: Pontifical Biblical Institute, 1966), 97–125, 227–30.

44. Allen, *Early Jewish Textual Culture*, 39–104.

45. See, e.g., Steve Moyise, "The Language of the Old Testament in the Apocalypse," *JSNT* 22, no. 76 (1999): 97–113.

46. Allen, *Early Jewish Textual Culture*, 138.

Greek text of Daniel (at Rev 1:1, 7, 17, 19; 4:1, 9; 10:4; 20:4, 11). Evidence that John knew the Wisdom of Solomon, a text composed in Greek, further underscores his capacity to work with texts in different languages (Rev 2:12 = Wis 18:16; Rev 4:11 = Wis 1:14; Rev 8:1 = Wis 18:14; Rev 9:3 = Wis 16:9; Rev 19:11–16 = Wis 18:14–16). John of Patmos emerges as a skillful reader and hearer of Scripture, sometimes quoting, more often alluding to multiple texts simultaneously, perhaps at times from memory, at times through sophisticated exegesis of written texts.

Conclusion

The Apocalypse of John of Patmos is a scripturally rich and multilayered text drawing widely and creatively on Israel's Scriptures. This richness is in part the result of complex interweaving of allusions, recall of biblical narratives, and repetition of scriptural concepts and motifs. It is also the result of a mind saturated with scriptural language and imagery, exegetically sophisticated, shaped by visionary experience and conviction of prophetic inspiration. This significantly blurs distinctions frequently made in Revelation scholarship, whether between visionary, constructive theologian, and scribal exegete, or between conscious allusion and unconscious echo. In a text that claims prophetic inspiration and origins in ecstatic visions, the influence of Israel's Scriptures could occur at every stage of the process: prevision exegesis and meditation on key texts, complex interweaving of texts and images in visionary state or prophetic utterance, and *post eventum* reflection on the visions, shaped by further exegetical study.

The finished form, however, certainly conveys the author's preference for specific books, especially prophetic books, such as Isaiah, Ezekiel, Daniel, and Zechariah, and the liturgical language of the Psalms, albeit reshaped by his convictions about Jesus Christ. Prophetic motifs, such as judgment and salvation, are pervasive, and certain prophets, notably Ezekiel, have contributed to the overall structure of his epistolary apocalypse. But Revelation is no new Ezekiel, for at almost every point Ezekiel's visions are brought into dynamic dialogue with other scriptural intertexts and in places (such as the vision of the templeless New Jerusalem in Rev 21–22) dramatically reshaped as a consequence. One should not underestimate here the influence of John's Christology and soteriology, resulting in what Austin Farrer once called a "rebirth of images."[47]

Finally, Revelation's use of Israel's Scriptures, especially the more subtle but sustained allusions to earlier scriptural narratives, serves a powerful rhetorical purpose. The book seems to have been written for small congregations of Christ

---

47. Austin Farrer, *A Rebirth of Images: The Making of St. John's Apocalypse* (Westminster: Dacre Press, 1949).

believers in cities of western Asia Minor, some (including the local "Balaam" and "Jezebel") dazzled by what Rome had to offer, few able to see what, to the seer's eyes, were its beastly, demonic features. John's interweaving of these older stories into his prophetic-visionary book gives them fresh meaning for these young communities. They are invited to eschew the bondage of a new Egypt under the sway of a pharaoh-like dragon and embark on a new exodus, inaugurated by the slaughter of a new paschal lamb. As an exiled prophet on Patmos, John proposes to the seven churches their own exilic status. Revelation thus represents an urgent summons to "come out of Babylon," a radical cultural disengagement, which paradoxically means a return from exile, a summons to begin the journey home to the New Jerusalem, already "coming down out of heaven from God" (Rev 21:2).

Bibliography

Allen, Garrick V. *The Book of Revelation and Early Jewish Textual Culture*. SNTSMS 168. Cambridge: Cambridge University Press, 2017.

Aune, David E. *Revelation 1–5*. WBC 52. Dallas: Word, 1997.

Barr, David L. *Tales of the End: A Narrative Commentary on the Book of Revelation*. Storytellers Bible 1. Santa Rosa, CA: Polebridge, 1998.

Barton, John. *Oracles of God: Perceptions of Ancient Prophecy in Israel after the Exile*. Oxford: Oxford University Press, 1986.

Bauckham, Richard. *The Climax of Prophecy: Studies on the Book of Revelation*. Edinburgh: T&T Clark, 1993.

Beale, G. K. *The Book of Revelation: A Commentary on the Greek Text*. NIGTC. Grand Rapids: Eerdmans, 1999.

———. *John's Use of the Old Testament in Revelation*. JSNTSup 166. Sheffield: Sheffield Academic, 1998.

———. *The Use of Daniel in Jewish Apocalyptic Literature and in the Revelation of St. John*. Lanham, MD: University Press of America, 1984.

Boxall, Ian K. "Exile, Prophet, Visionary: Ezekiel's Influence on the Book of Revelation." Pages 147–64 in *The Book of Ezekiel and Its Influence*. Edited by Henk Jan de Jonge and Johannes Tromp. Aldershot: Ashgate, 2007.

Bratcher, Robert G., ed. *Old Testament Quotations in the New Testament*. Rev. ed. Helps for Translators 3. London: United Bible Societies, 1967.

Caird, George B. *A Commentary on the Revelation of St. John the Divine*. BNTC. London: Black, 1966.

Charles, R. H. *A Critical and Exegetical Commentary on the Revelation of St. John*. 2 vols. ICC. Edinburgh: T&T Clark, 1920.

———. *Studies in the Apocalypse: Being Lectures Delivered before the University of London*. Edinburgh: T&T Clark, 1913.

Collins, Adela Yarbro. Review of *The Use of Daniel in Jewish Apocalyptic Literature and in the Revelation of St. John*, by G. K. Beale. *JBL* 105, no. 4 (1986): 734–35.
———. "The Use of Scripture in the Book of Revelation." Pages 11–32 in *New Perspectives on the Book of Revelation*. Edited by Adela Yarbro Collins. BETL 291. Leuven: Peeters, 2017.
Farrer, Austin. *A Rebirth of Images: The Making of St. John's Apocalypse*. Westminster: Dacre Press, 1949.
Fekkes, Jan, III. *Isaiah and Prophetic Traditions in the Book of Revelation: Visionary Antecedents and Their Development*. JSNTSup 93. Sheffield: JSOT Press, 1994.
Fletcher, Michelle. *Reading Revelation as Pastiche: Imitating the Past*. LNTS 571. London: Bloomsbury T&T Clark, 2017.
Goulder, Michael D. "The Apocalypse as an Annual Cycle of Prophecies." *NTS* 27, no. 3 (1981): 342–67.
Hays, Richard B. *Echoes of Scripture in the Gospels*. Waco, TX: Baylor University Press, 2016.
Jauhiainen, Marko. *The Use of Zechariah in Revelation*. WUNT 2/199. Tübingen: Mohr Siebeck, 2005.
Koester, Craig R. *Revelation: A New Translation with Introduction and Commentary*. AB 38A. New Haven: Yale University Press, 2014.
Kowalski, Beate. *Die Rezeption des Propheten Ezechiel in der Offenbarung des Johannes*. SBB 52. Stuttgart: Katholisches Bibelwerk, 2004.
Maier, Harry O. *Apocalypse Recalled: The Book of Revelation after Christendom*. Minneapolis: Fortress, 2002.
Mathewson, David. *A New Heaven and a New Earth: The Meaning and Function of the Old Testament in Revelation 21.1–22.5*. JSNTSup 238. London: Sheffield Academic, 2003.
McNamara, Martin. *The New Testament and the Palestinian Targum to the Pentateuch*. AnBib 27A. Rome: Pontifical Biblical Institute, 1966.
Moyise, Steve. "Ezekiel and the Book of Revelation." Pages 45–57 in *After Ezekiel: Essays on the Reception of a Difficult Prophet*. Edited by Andrew Mein and Paul M. Joyce. LHBOTS 535. London: T&T Clark, 2011.
———. "The Language of the Old Testament in the Apocalypse." *JSNT* 22, no. 76 (1999): 97–113.
———. *The Later New Testament Writers and Scripture: The Old Testament in Acts, Hebrews, the Catholic Epistles, and Revelation*. London: SPCK, 2012.
———. *The Old Testament in the Book of Revelation*. JSNTSup 115. Sheffield: Sheffield Academic, 1995.
———. "The Psalms in the Book of Revelation." Pages 231–46 in *The Psalms in the New Testament*. Edited by Steve Moyise and Maarten J. J. Menken. NTSI. London: T&T Clark, 2004.
Müller, Darius. "Zitatmarkierungen und die Gegenwart der Schrift im Neuen Tes-

tament." Pages 189-99 in *Textual History and the Reception of Scripture in Early Christianity/Textgeschichte und Schriftrezeption im frühen Christentum*. Edited by Johannes de Vries and Martin Karrer. SCS 60. Atlanta: Society of Biblical Literature, 2013.

Paulien, Jon. "Criteria and the Assessment of Allusions to the Old Testament in the Book of Revelation." Pages 113-29 in *Studies in the Book of Revelation*. Edited by Steve Moyise. Edinburgh: T&T Clark, 2001.

———. *Decoding Revelation's Trumpets: Literary Allusions and the Interpretation of Revelation 8:7-12*. Andrews University Seminary Doctoral Dissertation Series 11. Berrien Springs, MI: Andrews University Press, 1988.

Resseguie, James L. *The Revelation of John: A Narrative Commentary*. Grand Rapids: Baker Academic, 2009.

Rowland, Christopher. *The Open Heaven: A Study of the Apocalyptic in Judaism and Early Christianity*. London: SPCK, 1982.

Rowland, Christopher, and Christopher R. A. Morray-Jones. *The Mystery of God: Early Jewish Mysticism and the New Testament*. CRINT 12. Leiden: Brill, 2009.

Ruiz, Jean-Pierre. *Ezekiel in the Apocalypse: The Transformation of Prophetic Language in Revelation 16,17-19,10*. EHS.T 376. Frankfurt am Main: Lang, 1989.

Schüssler Fiorenza, Elisabeth. *The Book of Revelation: Justice and Judgment*. Philadelphia: Fortress, 1986.

Sweet, John. *Revelation*. SCM Pelican Commentaries. London: SCM, 1979.

Swete, Henry Barclay. *The Apocalypse of St John: The Greek Text with Introduction, Notes and Indices*. 3rd ed. London: Macmillan, 1922.

Trudinger, L. Paul. "Some Observations concerning the Text of the Old Testament in the Book of Revelation." *JTS* 17, no. 1 (1966): 82-88.

Vanhoye, Albert. "L'utilisation du livre d'Ézéchiel dans l'Apocalypse." *Bib* 43, no. 3 (1962): 436-76.

Vogelgesang, Jeffrey M. "The Interpretation of Ezekiel in the Book of Revelation." PhD diss., Harvard University, 1985.

Vos, Louis Arthur. *The Synoptic Traditions in the Apocalypse*. Kampen: Kok, 1965.

PART 3

Themes and Topics from Israel's Scriptures in the New Testament

In this third section, "Themes and Topics from Israel's Scriptures in the New Testament," we move from a close reading of the New Testament books to an investigation of various themes. The eight chapters consider major topics that cut across the New Testament: God, Messiah, Holy Spirit, covenant, law, wisdom, liturgy and prayer, and eschatology. These are not exhaustive surveys of the topics but focused analyses of the way in which the Scriptures of Israel function for the authors of the New Testament as determinative resources in conceptualizing a given theme.

To underscore again the early Jewish context of the Jesus movement, the chapters consider not simply their respective subjects in the scriptural texts themselves but also the ways in which these subjects are received and debated in early Jewish literature. This allows the authors to cast into sharp relief the extent to which the New Testament authors follow the interpretive scriptural conventions of their day and where they part company and develop their own novel readings. There is, of course, also a great variety in the understanding of these subjects among the New Testament writers. By considering one theme across the New Testament, these chapters illuminate both the commonalities and distinctives among the ways in which these various authors understand and actualize their scriptural heritage.

∽

25

God

ARCHIE T. WRIGHT

God has been the topic of many a monograph, essay, or article, but rarely has the subject been evaluated within Israel's Scriptures, other Second Temple–period Jewish literature, and the New Testament. In what follows, I will attempt to touch on just a small piece of the person of God from these three collections of literature. Even within that scope, my examination will be limited due to the constraints on the length of the chapter. In order to make the task manageable, I have chosen to examine just two natures of God: Creator and Father. Characteristics of God that can be found in Israel's Scriptures, the New Testament, along with some transitional material in other Second Temple–period literature may help us understand, at least partially, the development of these ideas about God in the early Christian period.

GOD AS CREATOR IN ISRAEL'S SCRIPTURES

We are told from the beginning that the God of Israel's Scriptures is the creator God: Gen 1:1, "In the beginning, God [אלהים] created [ברא] the heavens and the earth."[1] The term used here for "creating" is in the *qal* form and is used only to designate the activity of God (see, e.g., Num 16:30; Jer 31:22; Isa 4:5; 65:18; Ps 51:12). The term is most often used when describing the creation of the cosmos

---

1. Unless otherwise noted, all translations of Scripture and of the Dead Sea Scrolls texts are by the author.

by God, that is, the heavens and the earth and all living beings (see, e.g., Gen 1:1, 21; 2:3). Máire Byrne contends that YHWH's creation is a continuing process that involves maintaining the cosmos, not just something that takes place in Gen 1–3. In Job 38:12–41:34 God reminds Job and his friends who is responsible for the creation and maintenance of the cosmos.[2] The wisdom literature of the Bible often speaks of God in terms of creator and less about his relationship with Israel.[3] We find the authors of Job, Proverbs, and Ecclesiastes referring to God's creation and stating that part of this creation includes human cultures. Leo G. Perdue has argued that wisdom literature "finds its theological center in creation."[4] The psalmists in Pss 8, 19, 24, 74, 89, and 104, who continually sing of the creation by YHWH, often speak of the God of Israel as the creator of the world. Israel is called upon to worship him as creator (Pss 148 and 149). We see from this small sampling of texts that the authors of the Jewish Scriptures were very much focused on the creative activity of God.

As mentioned, the God of Israel is acknowledged throughout the Jewish biblical tradition as the creator of the cosmos and all that it contains. However, it appears that the biblical authors were perhaps aware of other ancient traditions in developing their story of God's role in creation. For example, we see the ancient Near Eastern concept of *Chaoskampf* in the Enuma Elish, in which God takes on and overcomes chaos on the earth in the creation process (see Gen 1).[5] This is particularly prominent in Job (Job 3:8; 7:12; 9:8, 13; 26:12–13). In Job 38:8–11, we read of the creation of the great sea monster Leviathan in the midst of the chaos of the sea. Psalm 104 describes the great pleasure with which God created such creatures, but at the same time Leviathan is very much a part of the ancient myth of *Chaoskampf*.

One of the more interesting "God as Creator" texts is found in Prov 8:22–31, in which God creates Wisdom as a female character (see Prov 8:22; perhaps Wisdom has some connection to the Spirit), who describes how God brings forth all of creation, while Wisdom is standing at God's side as an apparent part of the

---

2. Máire Byrne, *The Names of God in Judaism, Christianity, and Islam: A Basis for Interfaith Dialogue* (London: Bloomsbury, 2011), 34.

3. Kathryn Schifferdecker, "Creation Theology," in *Dictionary of the Old Testament: Wisdom, Poetry and Writings*, ed. Tremper Longman III and Peter Enns (Downers Grove, IL: InterVarsity Press, 2008), 63–71.

4. Leo G. Perdue, *Wisdom and Creation: The Theology of Wisdom Literature* (Nashville: Abingdon, 1994), 340.

5. For the ancient Near East, see John H. Walton, "Creation in Genesis 1:1–2:3 and the Ancient Near East," *CTJ* 43, no. 1 (2008): 48–63. For God overcoming chaos, see, e.g., Gregory Mobley, *The Return of the Chaos Monster and Other Backstories of the Bible* (Grand Rapids: Eerdmans, 2012); Debra Scoggins Ballentine, *The Conflict Myth and Biblical Tradition* (Oxford: Oxford University Press, 2015).

process (Prov 8:30). There is some debate as to Wisdom's specific role in creation. Terrence E. Fretheim contends that Wisdom is a "created co-creator" (described as an אמון, "craftsman" in Prov 8:30), who helps God in the creation process. According to John's Gospel, this would perhaps draw a parallel between Wisdom and Christ.[6] In Wis 7:22, Wisdom is described as the "fashioner of everything" (πάντων τεχνῖτις). Again, this may have connections to John 1:3, in which the author tells us that all things came into being through the Logos, that is, the Christ. However, Perdue argues that the Hebrew in Prov 8:30 should be read as "little child," in which case Wisdom is acting as a child who plays before God and delights in all his creation.[7] Perdue supports this reading by pointing at language such as "beget" in 8:22 and 24. What is clear from Proverbs' understanding of Wisdom is that she is with God throughout the process of creation, including the earth and all living creatures, but her position in the hierarchy of divine beings is unclear. One might argue that Wisdom here is synonymous with the Spirit.

A significant question in the story of God as creator is exactly what the role of humanity is in all of it. Both the psalmist in Ps 8:4 and the author of Job in 7:17 ask the question, "What is humanity's role in maintaining God's creation?" From the beginning we are told it is one of stewardship—Adam is told to serve (לעבד, this could also mean "to work") the earth from which he was taken (Gen 1:1–2:3; 3:23; and Ps 8:8). One might ask, as the psalmist seemingly does: Was the universe created for humanity? And was humanity chosen to represent God on the earth as the "image of God" and, as a result, rules over the earth in a position that is a little less than God?[8] Job 38–41 paints a little different picture of humanity, one that is a bit more humbling. In this section, God speaks in first person and offers a detailed account of what God has created. Humanity does not hold the central focus of the narrative, and, in fact, God seems to think little of them in relation to the rest of his creation.

One issue that is often raised about God as creator is the phrase *creatio ex nihilo*, "created out of nothing." God created the entire universe from no existing matter because at the time of creation, only God existed. The argument emerges from Gen 1:1–2:4, which states that when God created the heavens and the earth, the earth was formless and void. Nevertheless, apparently תהום, "the deep," and מים, "water," existed upon the surface of the earth. We are not told where these two items came from, nor are we told what is meant by "the deep." The beginning of 1:2 could be read to mean that the earth did not yet exist (תה

---

6. Terrence E. Fretheim, *God and World in the Old Testament: A Relational Theology of Creation* (Nashville: Abingdon, 2005), 214–15.
7. Perdue, *Wisdom and Creation*, 91.
8. The Hebrew בני האלהים can also be translated "gods."

וָבֹהוּ, "formless and void"), or at least it did not yet have any shape. "The deep" could be understood as the darkness of what would become the universe. This could suggest that there was nothing in existence except YHWH. Some scholars argue that Gen 1:1–2 states this otherwise.[9] The argument suggests that "the deep" and the water were preexistent materials with which God worked to create the cosmos. We will see that this issue also appears in other literature of the Second Temple period and in the New Testament.

God as Creator in the Second Temple Jewish Literature

As we move to other literature of the Second Temple period, there are several texts that speak of the God of Israel as creator or a term closely related to it. We do not see any distinct themes in this literature that diverge from Israel's Scriptures, that is, there is no "new creation" or no new figure who was assisting God in creation, although one might argue that Wisdom is a concept developed in the Second Temple period (see, e.g., Wisdom of Solomon, Sirach, and Song of Songs).[10] In fact there is a sense that God created the cosmos *ex nihilo* at the end of Jub. 2:2, which reads, "And [He created] the abysses and darkness—both evening and night—and light—both dawn and daylight—which He prepared in the knowledge of His heart."[11] The author seems to suggest that things came into being through the thoughts of God rather than some material substance. This point is also supported by 2 Macc 7:28, which states, "Look at the heaven and the earth and everything that is in them and recognize that God did not make them out of things that existed."

In another stream of the God as creator tradition, in Jub. 2:2 (cf. 1 En. 60:12–22), we are told that there are heavenly beings who are possibly assisting God in creation, or at least are present on the first day of creation, although their role is not made clear. The author states in 2:2,

---

9. Gary A. Anderson and Markus Bockmuehl, eds., *Creation ex nihilo: Origins, Development, Contemporary Challenges* (Notre Dame: University of Notre Dame Press, 2018); Markus Bockmuehl, "*Creatio ex nihilo* in Palestinian Judaism and Early Christianity," *SJT* 65 (2012): 253–70; Nathan J. Chambers, *Reconsidering Creation Ex Nihilo in Genesis 1*, JTISup 19 (University Park, PA: Eisenbrauns, 2020).

10. Louis H. Feldman, James L. Kugel, and Lawrence H. Schiffman, eds., *Outside the Bible: Ancient Jewish Writings Related to Scripture*, 3 vols. (Philadelphia: Jewish Publication Society, 2013).

11. See James L. Kugel, "Jubilees," in Feldman, Kugel, and Schiffman, *Outside the Bible*, 1:289–90.

For on the first day He created the heavens, which are above, and the earth, and the waters, and all of the spirits which minister before Him: the angels of the Presence, and the angels of sanctification, and the angels of the spirit of fire, and the angels of the spirit of the winds, and the angels of the spirit of the clouds and darkness and snow and hail and frost, the angels of resoundings and thunder and lightning, and the angels of the spirits of cold and heat and winter and springtime and harvest and summer and all the spirits of his creatures which are in heaven and on earth.[12]

There are seven spirits mentioned in Jub. 2:2 that may be similar to if not the same seven spirits as those mentioned in Rev 1:4, "From the seven spirits that are before his throne." Although it could be argued that there are fifteen spirits listed in Jub. 2, depending on how one reads the portions with multiple items following the word "spirit." For example, the "spirit of the clouds and darkness and snow and hail and frost" could be five distinct spirits. One might ask if the author of John 1 was aware of this tradition when speaking of the Logos being at the creation with God. As will be seen below, other authors may have been thinking along similar lines.

Overall, the theme of God as creator is sparsely attested in the texts from the period. Pseudo-Orpheus (second c. BCE) 1:8–10 (recension C) makes note of the Immortal One who has formed the cosmos: "He is one, of himself, self-generated, and by whom all things are completed."[13] In T. Ab. 10:14 the author contends that God is the creator of the cosmos. He notes that while Abraham is being shown all the earth, Abraham asked God to destroy the wickedness he sees on his journey. As a result, God tells Abraham's angelic guide, Michael, to stop the journey before Abraham asks for the destruction of the entire world because he is the only righteous one who has not sinned (this is an interesting shift from Noah being the sinless/righteous one in Genesis). The author of Testament of Abraham continues in 10:14, "I have made the world, I desire not to destroy any of them," further supporting the central theological position of God as creator.[14] The author of T. Job 39:12 tells us that following the death of Job's children other people are looking for them, but Job tells them to stop looking: "Do not trouble yourselves in vain, for you will not find my children since they were taken up to heaven by the Creator their king." Testament of Job shows that even in the

---

12. Kugel, "Jubilees," 289.
13. See David E. Aune, "Pseudo-Orpheus," in Feldman, Kugel, and Schiffman, *Outside the Bible*, 1:743–49. Cf. John 1:3, which reads, "All things came into being through him, and without him not one thing came into being."
14. See Annette Yoshiko Reed, "Testament of Abraham," in Feldman, Kugel, and Schiffman, *Outside the Bible*, 2:1671–96.

diaspora, we see the centrality of God as creator. The term used in Testament of Job for "creator" is δημιουργός; although used in a positive sense here, the term later takes on negative implications in the creation accounts of the second century CE gnostic groups. However, in Heb 11:10 δημιουργός speaks of God as the architect and builder in a very positive sense: "For he [Abraham] was waiting for the city that has foundations whose architect and builder [δημιουργός] is God."[15] Second Maccabees 7:23 states: "Therefore, the creator of the world, who shaped the beginning of humanity and devised the origin of all things, will in his mercy give life and breath back to you again." It is clear from these few selected passages that the authors of the Second Temple period understood God as creator as a central theological component in their worldview(s).

The Dead Sea Scrolls also offer a similar understanding of the creative nature of God. In the Community Rule, 1QS III, 17–18, from Qumran, the author, the Maskil, speaks of God as the creator of humanity, which was to govern the world, והואה ברא אנוש לממשלת תבל, "he created humankind to have dominion over the world" (cf. 4 Ezra 6:54; Wis 9:2–3; Jub. 2:14; 2 Bar. 14:18; 1Q34 3 II, 3). This statement draws on Gen 1:28, "Be fruitful and multiply and fill the earth and subdue it." Once again, the God of Israel is the creator who cares about all the small details in how the cosmos functions.

A significant component of God's creative activity that arises from the scrolls is the anthropological dualism. One can argue that this anthropological understanding is one of the key focus points of some of the authors of the Qumran scrolls. However, in 1QS III, 13–IV, 26, the Treatise on the Two Spirits, we are told that God created humanity with two spirits that are influenced by two powerful spirits, the Prince of Light and the Angel of Darkness. These spirits guide humanity to rule over the world. The dualism of the human being in 1QS is likely something developed from either Zoroastrianism or possibly an internal Israelite biblical tradition from texts such as 1 Sam 16:14–16 (two spirits of Saul); 1 Kgs 22:13–28 (the lying spirit in the story of Micaiah); Isa 45:7 (God formed light and created darkness); Sir 33:14–15 ("Good is the opposite of evil . . . look at all the works of the Most High, they come in pairs, one the opposite of the other"); T. Jud. 20:1–4 (the two spirits of 1QS III–IV); T. Ash. 1:3–9 (two inclinations given to humanity); and T. Benj. 4:1–7:2 (the two inclinations). However, we may also see this dualistic anthropology in the New Testament writings of Paul and his concept of "spirit and flesh" against which humans are battling. In the Treatise on the Two Spirits, the author makes clear that God is behind the

---

15. See Harold W. Attridge, "The Testament of Job," in Feldman, Kugel, and Schiffman, *Outside the Bible*, 2:1872–99.

creation of humanity as in the Genesis creation story, but with a very different twist to explain the origins of the sinful human nature.

The concept of God creating the cosmos *ex nihilo* is also mentioned in texts from the Second Temple period. In Jos. Asen. 12:1–2 (100 BCE–115 CE), we can identify a possible influence of 2 Macc 7:28. The author states, "O Lord, God of the Ages, who created and brought to life everything, who gave the breath of life to all your creation [Gen 2:7], who brought forth the unseen to light [Gen 1:2], who made that which exists and that which is visible out of the invisible and nonexistent." As will become apparent, this same *creatio ex nihilo* tradition is part of the New Testament authors' understanding of God as creator (e.g., Rom 4:17, "he [God] calls the things that do not exist into existence"). The remainder of the prayer in Jos. Asen. 12:1–2 speaks of the creation account and paraphrases the Genesis account with beautiful poetic language: "O Lord, God of the ages, who created and brought to life everything, who gave breath of life to all your creation."[16]

Further evidence can be found in the diaspora writings of Philo of Alexandria, who speaks of God the Creator in two of his writings, *Contempl.* 90 and *Migr.* 91. One might argue that the theme of God as creator is discussed in *Questions and Answers on Genesis*, but there Philo does not appear to call God "creator" but rather uses the term ποιητής, "maker." In *Somn.* 1.135 Philo speaks of God as the "maker" who fills all parts of the cosmos with living beings (cf. *Abr.* 9, where God is called father and creator). In *Contempl.* 90, while speaking about the Therapeutae, Philo mentions God as ποιητῇ, "creator," the Greek translation for the Hebrew term ברא: "Such are the Therapeutae, who have embraced the contemplative nature and the things in it. They live in the soul alone as citizens of both heaven and earth. Their virtue commends them to the Father and Maker [ποιητῇ] of the universe, making them friends of God and adding the most suitable reward." The term ποιητῇ is derived from the verb ποιέω, which when used in reference to God and his creative characteristics in the New Testament is translated "to create." In *Migr.* 91, Philo shifts his focus to the origins of this creator God and identifies him as the "Unoriginate" (ἀγένητον, lit. "Uncreated One"; see also 157; 192). God is the one who brought the world into being and he maintains his creation. Philo notes, "the Seventh Day is meant to teach the power inherent in the Unoriginate and the nonactivity of created beings."[17] In

---

16. According to Patricia Ahearne-Kroll, psalms of lament, such as we see here, "often use the mythical language of creation and chaos . . . in describing the psalmist's condition, the adversary, or the power of God" to find deliverance. See Ahearne-Kroll, "Joseph and Aseneth," in Feldman, Kugel, and Schiffman, *Outside the Bible*, 3:2551.

17. Translations for Philo from Loeb Classical Library.

other words, for Philo, humanity is totally reliant on God for its very existence. We can see from Philo's writing that he viewed the God of Israel as the creator of the cosmos, and at the same time argues that he has no beginning as the "Uncreated One."

One final text to mention is 4 Ezra 6:1–6. Here, the angel Uriel describes all the things that God had created prior to the establishment of Israel and Zion and tells Ezra that the same God who brought about the created world will be the one to bring it to an end. These few examples of writings of the Second Temple period share a similar theological understanding of God as creator. At the same time, they have a nuanced view of the origins of humanity with two spirits, a concept that appears to be central to the sinful nature of humanity.

God as Creator in the New Testament

As we move to the New Testament and God's role as creator, the issue of *creatio ex nihilo* arises. Some scholars argue that it is unlikely that "created out of nothing" was the intention of the author of Genesis.[18] We read nothing of the creation of water in Genesis, but it becomes a major part of the narrative. In fact, the author of 2 Pet 3:5 states that the "earth was formed from water and through water by the word of God." The concept of *creatio ex nihilo* is implied in Rom 4:17, "he [God] calls the things that do not exist into existence." This does not necessarily suggest that God used "nothing" to create things, but rather that God called/spoke them into existence. In addition, in Heb 11:3, the author states, "so that what is visible came into existence from things that are not seen." Again, because something is not visible does not mean it does not exist, for example, things that exist in the divine realm are certainly invisible, but most would argue that they do exist. From these few texts it seems likely the authors of the New Testament were aware of the tradition of *creatio ex nihilo* that was being passed down through the writings of the Second Temple period.

In the New Testament there are many references to "creator" and "creation." In what follows, we will attempt to see how the New Testament authors were following the tradition of the God of Israel as creator of the cosmos. In Mark 10:6 (// Matt 19:4), the author draws on Gen 1:27, stating that ἀπὸ δὲ ἀρχῆς κτίσεως ἄρσεν καὶ θῆλυ ἐποίησεν αὐτούς "and from the beginning of creation male and female he [God] created them." The Greek word ἐποίησεν is one of the terms used by the LXX translators for the Hebrew word ברא, "create." As mentioned previously, this is a term that

---

18. See Anderson and Bockmuehl, *Creation ex nihilo*; Bockmuehl, "Creatio ex nihilo"; Chambers, *Reconsidering Creation Ex Nihilo*.

is only applied to the action of God himself. In other words, God is the sole creator of the cosmos. Mark 13:19 (// Matt 24:21) speaks again of God the creator, but in this reference the author uses a different Greek term for "created," ἔκτισεν (from κτίζω), which is used in the LXX to translate both ברא ("create") and קנה ("possess"). It is clear, though, that the author of Mark understands God is the creator of all creation: ἀπ' ἀρχῆς κτίσεως ἣν ἔκτισεν ὁ θεὸς ἕως τοῦ νῦν, "from the beginning of creation which God created until now." Although the following passage does not speak directly to the issue of God as creator, the author of Rom 1:20 states that ever since the creation of the world, God's divine power, although invisible, is here in creation. From this passage one might argue that God's divine power is what is maintaining the cosmos. This is similar to Philo's *Migr.* 91.[19]

In the New Testament, unlike the Jewish Scriptures and other writings of the Second Temple period, there is an interesting shift in the theological understanding of creation, in that the focus of the authors moves to God's actions in and through Christ. The authors of several New Testament texts speak of a "new creation" in Christ (2 Cor 5:17), although some might argue that this is still God at work in creation. John 1:1–9 states that Jesus was at the beginning of creation (much like the concept of Wisdom existing at creation in the Jewish Scriptures), and he is the foundation of all things created. Similarly in Col 1:15–17 the writer tells us that Christ is the image of the invisible God, and "in him all things in heaven and on earth were created, things visible and invisible. . . . He himself is before all things and in him all things hold together" (cf. Heb 1:1–2 and John 1:1–9). Here we may have a declaration of Christ's divinity or some kind of substitutionary creation theology in which Christ (or Wisdom) played a major role in the creation of the cosmos, a significant shift from the creation account in Israel's Scriptures and other writings of the Second Temple period.

God the Father in Israel's Scriptures

Much of the scholarship written on God the Father has been written through a "christological" lens rather than the "Father God motif" as seen in the Jewish Scriptures.[20] References to God the Father in the Jewish Scriptures appear no fewer than

---

19. Other notions of God creating the cosmos can be found in Rom 8:18–30; 1 Tim 4:4 says that everything God created is good; 1 Pet 4:19 calls God a faithful creator; Rev 4:11 states that God created all things; Rev 10:6 also states that God created the heavens and earth and all that is in them. All these passages point to an ongoing tradition that the God of Israel created and maintains the cosmos.

20. See David R. Tasker, *Ancient Near Eastern Literature and the Hebrew Scriptures about the Fatherhood of God*, StBibLit 69 (New York: Lang, 2004), 4.

sixteen times, including Deut 32:5; 2 Sam 7:14; 1 Chr 17:13; 22:10; 28:6; 29:10; Pss 68:5; 89:26; 103:13; Prov 3:12; Jer 3:4–5, 7–8; 31:9; Isa 63:16 (twice); 64:8; and Mal 1:6; 2:10.[21] However, in addition to the references that include the term "father," there are numerous instances in which the idea of God as father appears without direct use of the Hebrew term אב. For example, God is referred to as the "father of Israel" in Exod 4:22 without using the term "father": "Thus says the LORD: Israel is my firstborn," which implies that God is the father of Israel the nation. The author of Deut 14:1 declares to Israel, "You are children of the LORD your God." In Isa 45:11, we discover a connection between God as father and our previous characteristic of creator. The author states: "Thus says the LORD, the Holy One of Israel and its maker [ויצרו]: will you question me about my children?" (also Isa 45:12). In Jer 31:9, following the exile, we are told "for I have become a father to Israel, and Ephraim is my firstborn." In Hos 11:1, we hear of God calling out his son (Israel) from Egypt: "When Israel was a child, I loved him, and out of Egypt I called my son." This is perhaps also to be understood as a prophetic text concerning Jesus coming out of Egypt with Mary and Joseph in Matt 2:14–15. It is said that Israel continually turned from God to worship idols and the Baals. As can be seen from these few examples, the authors of the Jewish Scriptures understood YHWH to be the father of a nation, but as we will see below, this fatherhood does become more individualized toward the king of Israel and later in the New Testament for the Messiah.

Perhaps in an effort to emphasize the fatherhood of God, members of the community were giving their children names that spoke of God the Father. As such, we see the name of the father appearing as part of the name of individuals throughout ancient Israel. In 1 Sam 8:2, we read of the second son of Samuel was named Abiyah (אביה), "God, my father." Beginning in 2 Sam 8:16 we have several names that contain the Hebrew word "father": Joab (יואב), meaning "he will be/is my father"; in 2 Sam 8:17 Abithar (אביתר), which means "my father who is very generous," who is the father of Abimelech, meaning "my father is king," a priest of YHWH. From these few examples we can see the importance of recognizing and reminding people that God is the father to Israel and to individuals.

Svetlana Knobnya has argued that there is a close connection between the exodus motif and God as father and redeemer of the nation.[22] She contends that the concept of "father and redeemer of Israel" is supported in Isa 63:16, "You, O LORD, are our father [אבינו], our redeemer from old is your name." Further support is suggested in Exod 4:22–23, in which God is the father of all Israel. Again, this is in relation to the redemption of the nation and the coming out of slavery in Egypt as children of God.[23] A similar redemptive theme is found

---

21. Svetlana Knobnya, "God the Father in the Old Testament," *EJT* 20, no. 2 (2011): 139.
22. Knobnya, "God the Father," 140.
23. On the "firstborn sons," בני בכרי, see further Exod 19–24.

in Deut 1:31, where God the Father takes his son into the wilderness to redeem him following his time of enslavement in Egypt. In Deut 32:5–6, we discover that Moses has similar ideas concerning God's relationship with the nation of Israel despite their unfaithfulness. In Deut 32:5 we read, "His degenerate children were corrupt toward him, a perverted and crooked generation. Do you repay the Lord this way? O foolish and unwise people; is he not your father who created you?" Also see Mal 2:10, "Do we not all have one father? Did not one God create us?" Here we see both of the characteristics we are discussing of God, God the Father, and God the Creator. Francis Martin agrees with Knobnya. He argues that God is the father who emerges from the exodus tradition and rescues Israel, his firstborn son, from slavery in Egypt.[24] Thomas F. Torrance proposes that the "colorful figurative language reflecting qualities characteristic of the parental authority and care of a human fatherhood" are present in the figure of God but without the human nature being part of the nature of God.[25] Marianne Meye Thompson suggests that there is a danger in attempting to turn the theology of God the Father in Scripture into an anthropology of the father.[26] We cannot apply our understanding of human fatherhood upon God the Father, as the authors of the Jewish Scriptures make clear despite their use of anthropological language.

Thompson identifies three assumptions about God the Father in the Jewish Scriptures: (1) God is the source or origin of the family of God (Jer 31:9; Deut 32:4–6, 8) in that he provides an inheritance for his children Israel (Isa 63:16; 64:8; Jer 3:19; 31:9); (2) God protects and provides for his children at times miraculously (Ps 41:2; Nah 1:7; Jer 31:10; Jdt 9:14); and (3) God expects that obedience and honor are due him as the creator of the cosmos, while disobedience requires the correction by the Father (Jer 3:4–5, 19; Deut 32:6).[27] One should understand that Israel was not the first nation to identify God with a father figure. Two of their archnemeses, Egypt and Babylon, each depict their gods as fathers due to their roles as creators of the world. In addition, the gods of Egypt and Babylon are fathers to the king and to the other gods of these nations.[28]

A well-known title for the kings of Israel is God's son, beginning with David and following, while at the same time God remains the father of the nation. Da-

---

24. See Martin, *The Feminist Question: Feminist Theology in the Light of Christian Tradition* (Grand Rapids: Eerdmans, 1994), 271.

25. Torrance, "The Christian Apprehension of God the Father," in *Speaking the Christian God: The Holy Trinity and the Challenge of Feminism*, ed. Alvin F. Kimel Jr. (Grand Rapids: Eerdmans, 1992), 130.

26. Thompson, *The Promise of the Father: Jesus and God in the New Testament* (Louisville: Westminster John Knox, 2000), 38.

27. Thompson, *Promise of the Father*, 39.

28. Here one might find a connection to the בני האלהים in Israel's Scriptures and later Second Temple Judaism.

vid is designated as God's son in 2 Sam 7:14: "I will be his father and he will be my son" (cf. 1 Chr 17:13; 22:10; 28:6; Pss 2; 89:26–27; and Prov 3:11–12). However, from this kingly relationship that perhaps evolved from God's relationship with Israel as his firstborn son, the king now becomes the representative of Israel and thus he is now identified as the son. But when we move to the New Testament, we see another major shift in that Jesus becomes the "only Begotten Son" of God, although God is still father to the people of God, Israel. Deuteronomy 14:1–2 identifies the nation of Israel as the children of the Lord and his inheritance. This of course speaks to the language of election and adoption that we discover in the writings of the New Testament.

God the Father in the Second Temple Jewish Literature

According to Thompson, there are similar themes that run not only from the Jewish Scriptures to the New Testament, but these same themes are taken up by authors during the Second Temple period.[29] The idea of the God of Israel as father to the nation is found in numerous texts from the period. Like God the Father in the Jewish Scriptures, God is the father of the nation in 1 Chr 29:10, "You are blessed, LORD, the God of Israel, our father from age to age." In Tob 13:4 he is acknowledged as the father of Israel and God forever. Wisdom of Solomon 11:10 states that God, like a father, tested Israel as a warning against following the path of the other nations. In Wis 11, in particular, we see the father protecting his child from acts of disobedience, a similar protection we saw in the Jewish Scriptures.

The theme of God as father to Israel is taken up in the second century BCE text of Jub. 1:24–25. Here, God says, "And I shall be a father to them, and they will be sons to me. And they will be called 'sons of the living God.' And every angel and spirit will know and acknowledge that they are my sons, and I am their father in uprightness and righteousness."[30] In Jub. 19:29, the author notes Abraham's comments to Jacob: "May the Lord be to you and the people a father always and may you be a/the firstborn son." The first century CE author Josephus, in his *Antiquities of the Jews*, retells the stories of Israel's history, in which he carries on the tradition of the God of Israel as father of the nation and individuals (*Ant.* 1.20; 1.230; 2.152; 4.62; 5.93; 7.380).[31]

---

29. Thompson, *Promise of the Father*, 40.
30. Kugel, "Jubilees," 287. See also 3 Macc 2:21; 5:7; 7:6.
31. See also Philo, who uses similarly language as he speaks of God the Father in *Spec.* 2.197; *Opif.* 74, 76; *Mut.* 29. In *Cher.* 49, God is "Father of all things for he begat them"; he is "Father and Maker" in *Opif.* 77 and *Decal.* 51.

God

We see in Sir 23:1, 4 a similar tradition to Jesus's instructions to his disciples in Matt 6:9 to pray to God, "Our Father," for mercy and help. In Sir 23, the prayer begins: "Lord, Father, and ruler of my life." We also discover in Sirach that God the Father is equated to God the Creator (Sir 10:12; 32:13; 33:13; 47:8). Thompson contends that there is a "corresponding universalizing of God as Father" in which he is father of all individuals, but he is understood as "Father of all righteous Israelites."[32] Wisdom 2:16–18 supports this idea in that the righteous person is God's child, while the unrighteous person lies in wait for the righteous person to see if God will help the righteous one who is supposedly his child (2:18).

The Dead Sea Scrolls show a similar idea of God as father of the nation and the individual. In the Hodayot (1QH^a XVII, 35), the author states: "You are the father to all your children of your truth," thus identifying himself most likely as the father of those in the Qumran community. In the quite fragmentary text of 4Q511 (4QSongs of the Sage^b) 127 1, God is identified through a reconstruction as "] our father [," but it seems clear the author is speaking of the God of Israel. Similarly in the fragmentary 4Q502 (4QRitual of Marriage) 39 3, the author describes God thus: "h]e is [our?] father." In a scroll identified as "The Calendar" (4Q327) 1 16; the author is describing the struggles of Joseph and his brothers, during which Joseph calls out to God: "O Father, my God, leave me not forsaken, in the power of the nations" (cf. 4Q460 [4QNarrative Work and Prayer] 9 I, 5). There are approximately six references in the Dead Sea Scrolls in which God is compared to "a father": In 4Q378 (4QApocryphon of Joshua) 6 I, 8, the author states, "he will speak like a father to his son"; in 4Q379 18 4, "to] be for me, O o[ur] Lord, like a father"; 4Q448 (4QApocryphal Psalm and Prayer) I, 2 contains the reconstructed phrase in the form of "you loved as a fat[her . . .]." It is likely that each of these is referring to God's love for the children of Israel. A further scroll that contains similar language is 4Q392 (4QWorks of God) 6 IX, 6, again fragmentary, which may read "[as a fat]her for/to his son (?)." One might read this as reflecting the sustaining love of God the Father for his son Israel, similar language that we see in the New Testament in God's love to his only begotten Son.

The next reference to God as a father is found in the fragmentary 4Q418 (4QInstruction) 86 1, which reads "[. . .] for his service and as a father over [his] [dau]ght[er]s." The final reference to a father in the Dead Sea Scrolls is found in 4Q423 (4QInstruction) 7 3, which appears to parallel a saying found in Ps 103:13, "As a father has compassion upon his children, the Lord has compassion upon those who fear him." Here we see two things: (1) the father is being equated to

---

32. Thompson, *Promise of the Father*, 51.

YHWH, the Lord; and (2) this compassion is a gift to the righteous who fear him. Both ideas are similar to those espoused in the Jewish Scriptures.[33]

The theme of adoption of individuals into the family of God, found in such New Testament passages as Rom 8:15; 9:26; and Gal 3:26, is also represented in the book of Jubilees and some texts from Qumran. Jubilees 1:24 appears to be drawing on 2 Sam 7:14, "I will be a father to him, and he shall be a son to me." However, the Jubilees text appears to be speaking of the nation of Israel as the son rather than of an individual. It reads: "And I shall be a father to them, and they will be sons to me. And they will be called 'sons of the living God.'" Both texts seem to suggest that God is adopting the individual or the nation as his son(s). This concept of adoption may have its roots in Israel's election in Gen 25:28, retold in Jub. 19:18. There Abraham tells Rebecca that God will choose Jacob (Israel) as his people (cf. Jub. 19:29).[34] 4Q504 (4QWords of the Luminaries) frag. 1–2 III, 6–7 also speaks of this sense of adoption by God of Israel as his child, based on Exod 4:22: "[to I]srael 'My son, my firstborn,' and you have chastened us as a man chastens his child." One should keep in mind that 4Q504 does not use the word "father" but reflects that characterization with the use of the firstborn son. A similar adoption theme is possible in 4Q382 (4QpapParaphrase of Kings) frag. 104.3, which reads: "Surely you are the bestower of an inheritance; you have become their master, their father." The term "inheritance" here seems to indicate the concept of adoption along with the phrase "you have become ... their father."

Messianic adoption language also appears in the scrolls, and it may be reflected later in the New Testament in the sonship of Jesus. In 4Q174 (4QEschatological Commentary A) frag. i, 21, 11, citing 2 Sam 7:11–14, the author speaks of the shoot of David who will arise in the last days: "I will be a father to him, and he will be my son." In 4Q246 (4QAramaic Apocalypse) II, 1, the author takes this messianic language further; he writes, "He will be called the Son of God, they will call him Son of the Most High." This may be compared with Luke 1:32–35, which refers to Jesus as "Son of the Most High/Son of God."

The phrase "my Father" is also used in the scrolls to invoke prayer, similar to the disciples' prayer spoken by Jesus in Matt 6:9 ("Our Father").[35] In 4Q372 (4QNarrative and Poetic Composition) frag 1.15–19, the author recalls the sending of Joseph to Egypt by his brothers. He cries out to YHWH to save him: "My

---

33. For further references to mercy and the father, see Tob. 13:4; Jub. 1:24; 19:29; LAE 32:2; 35:2; and 37:4. See Lutz Doering, "God as Father in the Texts from Qumran," in *The Divine Father: Religious and Philosophical Concepts of Divine Parenthood in Antiquity*, ed. Felix Albrecht and Reinhard Feldmeier, TBN 18 (Leiden: Brill, 2014), 112.

34. Kugel, "Jubilees," 287, 362–63.

35. See Doering, "God as Father," 125–26.

Father, my God, leave me not forsaken in the power of the nations." In the scrolls we see father language being used in prayer by individuals to call upon God in a personal way for redemption, deliverance, and for empowerment.

God the Father in the New Testament

According to Larry Hurtado, "God as Father is the most characteristic designation of God in the New Testament."[36] He suggests that the increased presence of the Father is due to the appearance of the Son, Jesus Christ. As we will see below, it is Jesus himself who raises the prominence of the Father in the Gospels, first to make it clear who Jesus is, and second, to assure the disciples that God the Father of Israel is the one who has sent him. Matthew only uses the term father in what are known as the Jesus sayings. It appears seventeen times in the Sermon on the Mount, in which Jesus is giving instructions to the disciples on living a proper life of faith. In Matt 6:9, the Disciples' Prayer, Jesus teaches them to invoke the name of the Father in prayer similar to what we have seen in the Dead Sea Scrolls. This suggests that God is not only the father of Jesus but also of the disciples. Matthew also chooses to insert πατήρ where Mark has used θεός (e.g., Matt 12:50 // Mark 3:35; Matt 26:29 // Mark 14:25). A somewhat similar pattern is seen in the readings of Matthew over against Luke in the teaching of loving one's neighbor. This would suggest that Matthew and his community think that God is the father of the nation. Matthew states in 5:43: "You have heard that it was said 'you will love your neighbor and you will hate your enemy.' But I say to you, Love [imperative] your enemies and pray for those who persecute you, so that you may be sons of our Father in heaven." This seems to imply that forgiving others is a prerequisite for becoming members of God's family, which is reiterated in the Disciples' Prayer in Matt 6. Luke 6:35 offers quite a different reading, which may indicate another tradition: "But love your enemies, do good, and lend, expecting nothing in return. Your reward will be great, and you will be children of the Most High [υἱοὶ ὑψίστου]" (see also Matt 6:26 // Luke 12:24; Matt 10:29–32 // Luke 12:6–8).

John's Gospel offers the most occurrences of God the Father, some 109 times, most of those, as in the Synoptics, in the sayings of Jesus. A significant number is found in his conversation with the Samaritan woman at the well (esp. in John 4:21–23), in which he tells her that they will worship the Father neither on this mountain nor in Jerusalem. This language seems to suggest that the Samari-

---

36. Larry W. Hurtado, *God in New Testament Theology*, Library of Biblical Theology (Nashville: Abingdon, 2010), 38.

tans also identified God as father. Jesus also uses the phrase "my Father" in John 5:17, when he finds himself in conflict with the Jews (οἱ Ἰουδαῖοι) concerning Sabbath practices, and they accuse him of equating himself with God simply by calling God his father. This seems unusual, considering what we have seen in Israel's Scriptures about God's fatherly relationship with the nation and individuals. Perhaps the issue is that Jesus was covertly calling himself "Son of God," that is, the king. In John 5:19–23, Jesus also draws a correlation between his sonship with God the Father in all the works and miracles that he performs during his ministry on the earth. In John 6:25–65, Jesus again identifies God as his father, but this time the fact that he equates himself with God does not appear to be the issue. Rather, the issue is the Eucharist and how Jesus can offer his body and blood to bring spirit and life to the people. As a result, many of his followers depart and no longer follow him. It is possible that these individuals, in certain contexts, are identified as οἱ Ἰουδαῖοι who are persecuting Jesus for various reasons.

John also identifies God as the father of the disciples in 20:17: "Jesus said to her, 'Do not hold on to me, because I have not yet ascended to the Father. But go to my brothers and say to them, I am ascending to my Father and your Father, to my God and your God.'" Here, one might ask if the disciples are being identified as the nation (based on the use of "father" in the Jewish Scriptures) and the true sons of Israel who are following the Messiah. So also in Rom 8:29, "For those whom he foreknew he also chose beforehand to have the same image of his Son, in order that he is the firstborn among many brothers and sisters." Paul also advocates this view in Gal 4:6–7 and Rom 8:15–16, where he exhorts believers to call upon God using the term "Abba Father."[37] It appears that in the New Testament writings, the authors have identified God's fatherhood with the followers of Jesus and with Jesus himself.

With the arrival of Jesus as the Messiah and the Son of God, we see a shift from the view(s) of God the Father in the Jewish Scriptures and the writings of the Second Temple period. God is the father of the ruling king over Israel who is also identified as the son of God. This may explain the disturbance among some of the leadership of the Jews and the opponents of Jesus with his declaration of being the son of the Father, that is, "I am the king." Otherwise, we see some very familiar features of the Father, in that he is the father of the disciples, father of the nation, and he is adopting the followers of the Son of God into the family of God.

Conclusion

From this brief overview of the figure of God, we have discovered various connections between the God of the Jewish Scriptures, the writings of the Second

---

37. See discussion in Hurtado, *God in New Testament Theology*, 40.

Temple period, and the New Testament. Due to the enormity of this subject of God in Scripture and other early Jewish texts, we have elaborated on only two characteristics of God: God as creator and God as father. There are many more that could be identified and discussed in the Scriptures and writings in the Second Temple period: God as spirit, God as healer, God as wisdom, God as judge, God as redeemer, and the list could go on.

We have identified God's main role as that of the creator of the cosmos and of all that is in it. This, in various ways, was the common theme in all three collections of writings. In the wisdom texts in particular, such as Job, Proverbs, Wisdom, and Ecclesiastes, the authors' focus is on God's role as creator rather than on his relationship with Israel or with an individual (although the idea of a relationship is not completely absent). In addition, we have seen that the concept of *creatio ex nihilo* was known to the authors in the three collections of texts, which establish God as the origin of all things. At the same time, there appeared to be spiritual beings cooperating with God during creation, such as the spirits in Jubilees and the Logos in John 1. Finally, we have also seen that the Creator God is closely connected to the concept of God the Father of an individual and of the nation. In the Jewish Scriptures and in the New Testament, God establishes a special father/child relationship with the kings of Israel. In the New Testament, the relationship is with Christ and the followers of Christ. These two characterizations of God, along with the other possible natures of God listed above, establish a close relationship between the God of Israel as creator and father, with the cosmos, and with humanity from the beginning in Genesis to the end in John's Apocalypse.

BIBLIOGRAPHY

Ahearne-Kroll, Patricia. "Joseph and Aseneth." Pages 2525–89 in vol. 3 of *Outside the Bible: Ancient Jewish Writings Related to Scripture*. Edited by Louis H. Feldman, James L. Kugel, and Lawrence H. Schiffman. 3 vols. Philadelphia: Jewish Publication Society, 2013.

Anderson, Gary A., and Markus Bockmuehl, eds. *Creation* ex nihilo: *Origins, Development, Contemporary Challenges*. Notre Dame: University of Notre Dame, 2018.

Attridge, Harold W. "The Testament of Job." Pages 1872–99 in vol. 2 of *Outside the Bible: Ancient Jewish Writings Related to Scripture*. Edited by Louis H. Feldman, James L. Kugel, and Lawrence H. Schiffman. 3 vols. Philadelphia: Jewish Publication Society, 2013.

Aune, David E. "Pseudo-Orpheus." Pages 743–49 in vol. 1 of *Outside the Bible: Ancient Jewish Writings Related to Scripture*. Edited by Louis H. Feldman, James L.

Kugel, and Lawrence H. Schiffman. 3 vols. Philadelphia: Jewish Publication Society, 2013.

Ballentine, Debra Scoggins. *The Conflict Myth and Biblical Tradition*. Oxford: Oxford University, 2015.

Bockmuehl, Markus. "*Creatio ex nihilo* in Palestinian Judaism and Early Christianity." *SJT* 65, no. 3 (2012): 253–70.

Byrne, Máire. *The Names of God in Judaism, Christianity, and Islam: A Basis for Interfaith Dialogue*. London: Bloomsbury, 2011.

Chambers, Nathan J. *Reconsidering Creation* Ex Nihilo *in Genesis 1*. JTISup 19. University Park, PA: Eisenbrauns, 2020.

Doering, Lutz. "God as Father in the Texts from Qumran." Pages 107–36 in *The Divine Father: Religious and Philosophical Concepts of Divine Parenthood in Antiquity*. Edited by Felix Albrecht and Reinhard Feldmeier. TBN 18. Leiden: Brill, 2014.

Feldman, Louis H., James L. Kugel, and Lawrence H. Schiffman, eds. *Outside the Bible: Ancient Jewish Writings Related to Scripture*. 3 vols. Philadelphia: Jewish Publication Society, 2013.

Fretheim, Terrence E. *God and World in the Old Testament: A Relational Theology of Creation*. Nashville: Abingdon, 2005.

Hurtado, Larry W. *God in New Testament Theology*. Library of Biblical Theology. Nashville: Abingdon, 2010.

Knobnya, Svetlana. "God the Father in the Old Testament." *EJT* 20, no. 2 (2011): 139–48.

Kugel, James L. "Jubilees." Pages 272–465 in vol. 1 of *Outside the Bible: Ancient Jewish Writings Related to Scripture*. Edited by Louis H. Feldman, James L. Kugel, and Lawrence H. Schiffman. 3 vols. Philadelphia: Jewish Publication Society, 2013.

Martin, Francis. *The Feminist Question: Feminist Theology in the Light of Christian Tradition*. Grand Rapids: Eerdmans, 1994.

Mobley, Gregory. *The Return of the Chaos Monster and Other Backstories of the Bible*. Grand Rapids: Eerdmans, 2012.

Perdue, Leo G. *Wisdom and Creation: The Theology of Wisdom Literature*. Nashville: Abingdon, 1994.

Philo. *Every Good Man Is Free; On the Contemplative Life; On the Eternity of the World; Flaccus; Hypothetica; On Providence*. Translated by F. H. Colson and G. H. Whitaker. LCL. Cambridge: Harvard University Press, 1935.

Philo. *On the Confusion of Tongues; On the Migration of Abraham; Who Is the Heir of Divine Things? On Mating with the Preliminary Studies*. Translated by F. H. Colson and G. H. Whitaker. LCL. Cambridge: Harvard University Press, 1932.

Reed, Annette Yoshiko. "Testament of Abraham." Pages 1671–96 in vol. 2 of *Outside the Bible: Ancient Jewish Writings Related to Scripture*. Edited by Louis H. Feldman, James L. Kugel, and Lawrence H. Schiffman. 3 vols. Philadelphia: Jewish Publication Society, 2013.

Schifferdecker, Kathryn. "Creation Theology." Pages 63–71 in *Dictionary of the Old Testament: Wisdom, Poetry and Writings*. Edited by Tremper Longman III and Peter Enns. Downers Grove, IL: InterVarsity Press, 2008.

Tasker, David R. *Ancient Near Eastern Literature and the Hebrew Scriptures about the Fatherhood of God*. StBibLit 69. New York: Lang, 2004.

Thompson, Marianne Meye. *The Promise of the Father: Jesus and God in the New Testament*. Louisville: Westminster John Knox, 2000.

Torrance, Thomas F. "The Christian Apprehension of God the Father." Pages 120–43 in *Speaking the Christian God: The Holy Trinity and the Challenge of Feminism*. Edited by Alvin F. Kimel Jr. Grand Rapids: Eerdmans, 1992.

Walton, John H. "Creation in Genesis 1:1–2:3 and the Ancient Near East." *CTJ* 43, no. 1 (2008): 48–63.

26

Messiah

J. THOMAS HEWITT

All ancient Jewish messiah discourse is interpretative discourse. The Scriptures of Israel provided the words, diction, and imagery for describing the person and import of each figure of antiquity styled an "anointed one," whether Simon ben Kosiba, Qumran's Coming One(s) of Aaron and Israel, the Righteous One of the Similitudes of Enoch, or, indeed, Jesus of Nazareth. Thus investigation of the use of Israel's Scriptures by the authors of the New Testament to portray Jesus is an investigation of a significant way in which the early Jesus movement is similar to, indebted to, and indeed *part of*, the Jewish milieu in which it began.

But this is not to say that all messiahs were the same, that their portraits were each, in one way or another, manifestations of an ostensible "messianic idea" shaping the perspectives and expectations of every ancient author who penned a text about a messiah.[1] Indeed, no two christs were ever quite alike, and this so much so that some have deemed ancient messianism an incoherent phenomenon and the epithet "messiah" an indeterminate locution.[2] Jacob Neusner, for instance, decries any effort to delineate a set of messianic beliefs held across ancient Judaism as a misguided attempt to harmonize texts "that do not speak

---

1. See J. Thomas Hewitt, *Messiah and Scripture: Paul's "in Christ" Idiom in Its Ancient Jewish Context*, WUNT 2/522 (Tübingen: Mohr Siebeck, 2020), 45–54, and the literature cited therein.

2. See William Scott Green, "Introduction: Messiah in Judaism: Rethinking the Question," in *Judaisms and Their Messiahs at the Turn of the Christian Era*, ed. Jacob Neusner, William Scott Green, and Ernest S. Frerichs (Cambridge: Cambridge University Press, 1987), 1–14; and Jacob Neusner, preface to *Judaisms and Their Messiahs*, ed. Neusner, Green, and Frerichs, ix–xiv.

the same language of thought."³ This claim is part and parcel of Neusner's well-known insistence that in antiquity there were actually a number of Judaisms, not just one Judaism. Significantly, however, Neusner admits that in their literature these Judaisms "universally appeal to the same Hebrew Scriptures."⁴ Ancient messiah texts do not evince a singular messianic idea, but they are nevertheless a parade example of this universal appeal to Israel's Scriptures in early Jewish literary production.⁵ And this is no small thing.

Why then are there as many messianic portraits as there are messiah texts? It is because every appropriation of Scripture is an interpretative act, and in every interpretative act Scripture and historical circumstance meet. The interpretative results of that encounter therefore vary as circumstances vary, even while the Scriptures themselves may be regarded as more or less fixed entities relative to the exigencies of authors' diverse situations and aims. Hence, if the christ of John's Apocalypse is different from the christ of 4 Ezra, that does not make the Christian messiah a species different from a Jewish messiah. For also the messiah of 2 Baruch is distinct from the messiah of 4 Ezra, who is distinct from the messiah of 1 Enoch, who is distinct from the messiah(s) of the Damascus Document, and so on. In short, one trait common to all ancient messiahs is that they are each distinctive.⁶

We may therefore speak of at least two marks of all ancient messiah speculation. One, all ancient Jewish messiah discourse, including that of the early Jesus movement, is interpretative discourse. But two, the results of those interpretative acts are unpredictable and varied. To use Loren Stuckenbruck's felicitous turn of phrase, all ancient messiah speculation is "creatively biblical."⁷ The aim of this chapter is to illustrate how this is so among the texts of the New Testament and thereby to demonstrate a significant affinity between early Christian messianic interpretation and that of early Judaism. There already exist good treatments of the main scriptural texts that were formative for early Christian messiah spec-

---

3. Neusner, preface, xiii.

4. Neusner, preface, xii.

5. The term "messiah texts" denotes the specific category of early Jewish literature employing the term "messiah," not the general category of literature portraying eschatological redeemers who may or may not carry the epithet. See the admonitions of Marinus de Jonge, "The Use of the Word 'Anointed' in the Time of Jesus," *NovT* 8, no. 2/4 (1966): 132–48.

6. This also holds true, as we will see, for the various portraits of Jesus of Nazareth found within the New Testament, though to what degree the New Testament authors' distinct messianologies are complementary or contradictory is a separate question.

7. Loren T. Stuckenbruck, "Messianic Ideas in the Apocalyptic and Related Literature of Early Judaism," in *The Messiah in the Old and New Testaments*, ed. Stanley E. Porter, McMaster New Testament Studies (Grand Rapids: Eerdmans, 2007), 113. The whole essay is a fine illustration of how this is so within early Jewish literature.

ulation and how they were read by early Christian authors.⁸ So in this chapter I need not be comprehensive, nor do I necessarily focus on the readings of Scripture that many may regard as most influential. Further, my contention that the messiah texts of both early Judaism and early Christianity evince comparable interpretative ingenuity is not wholly original.⁹ I do, however, consider this factor to have been underemphasized and insufficiently explored. Therefore, to illuminate the "creatively biblical" character of messiah speculation not only in ancient Judaism but also early Christianity, I want to illustrate three characteristics of messianic interpretation that are prevalent among both early Jewish messiah texts and the texts of the New Testament: (1) the proliferation of scriptural idioms, (2) the variegated reception of the same scriptural sources, and (3) the integrative appropriation of different scriptural sources. It is important to note that these are *formal* characteristics, which concern the modes in which scriptural sources are retrieved in messiah speculation rather than the specific content of messianic interpretations. Even so, there are also many points of contact, which I will often note, between the content of early Christian messianic readings and interpretative traditions attested elsewhere in early Jewish literature. It is the formal characteristics of messianic interpretation, though, that constitute the focus of this chapter. Before defining and illustrating those characteristics, we turn first to the scriptural sources themselves.

Messiah in Israel's Scriptures

Discussion about a messiah in Israel's Scriptures has traditionally churned around the question of whether or not there is one.¹⁰ How can this be, given the thirty-eight occurrences of משיח in the Hebrew Bible? It is because scholarly

---

8. See the bibliography. Especially good is Donald Juel, *Messianic Exegesis: Christological Interpretation of the Old Testament in Early Christianity* (Philadelphia: Fortress, 1988). Many such treatments also acknowledge variation in how Israel's Scriptures are appropriated within early Christianity. See, e.g., the conclusion of the classic study of Ps 110, David M. Hay, *Glory at the Right Hand: Psalm 110 in Early Christianity*, SBLMS 18 (Nashville: Abingdon, 1973).

9. See, e.g., Stuckenbruck, "Messianic Ideas," 113 n. 44. Contrast Gershom Scholem, "Toward an Understanding of the Messianic Idea in Judaism," in *The Messianic Idea in Judaism and Other Essays on Jewish Spirituality* (New York: Shocken, 1971), 1–2, who emphasizes interpretative innovation as a trait unique to early Christian reading practices over and against those of roughly contemporary Jewish authors. On the fallaciousness of such a "Jewish messiah-Christian messiah distinction," see Matthew V. Novenson, *The Grammar of Messianism: An Ancient Jewish Political Idiom and Its Users* (Oxford: Oxford University Press, 2017), 187–216.

10. Cf., e.g., the classic treatment of Joseph Klausner, *The Messianic Idea in Israel from Its Beginning to the Completion of the Mishnah*, trans. W. F. Stinespring (New York: Macmillan,

Messiah

tradition has, until recently, been satisfied to use the word "messiah" as a technical term denoting eschatological redeemers, who in early Jewish literature are in some places "messiahs" and in some places not, but who in Israel's Scriptures are never the referent of the term "messiah." The impetus and evolution of this terminological finessing is aptly surveyed and critiqued by Matthew Novenson, who contends that actually "it is entirely possible and methodologically far preferable to describe the various ancient uses of the word 'messiah' and the pertinent differences without privileging one [the later 'technical term'] as the ostensibly real, ... fully evolved definition."[11] In this spirit, I present some basic observations about the use of the word "messiah" in Israel's Scriptures rather than attempting to trace the development of some conception allegedly invoked by the word "messiah" in later Jewish literature.

The word משיח itself and its translation equivalencies and transliterations (Aramaic משיחא; Greek χριστός, μεσσίας; Latin *unctus, christus*; etc.) are designations of distinctly Jewish scriptural provenance.[12] Further, despite protestations that there is no discernable messianology in Israel's Scriptures or that, if there is, it is not to be found in contexts mentioning a messiah as such, the usage of "messiah" in Israel's Scriptures is in some fundamental ways reflected in the usage of "messiah" in New Testament literature.[13] For example, the thirty-eight occurrences of the term משיח in the Hebrew Bible denote either priests, kings, prophets, or (only twice) an ambiguous, expected figure who is either a priest or a ruler.[14] Comparably, the χριστός of the New Testament is also variously charac-

---

1955); with that of Sigmund Mowinckel, *He That Cometh: The Messiah Concept in the Old Testament and Later Judaism*, trans. G. W. Anderson (Grand Rapids: Eerdmans, 2005).

11. Novenson, *Grammar of Messianism*, 34–64, quotation from 63.

12. Most pertinent for New Testament literature is the noun χριστός, a *TLG* search of which confirms only two instances antedating the LXX, both of the neuter χριστόν, meaning "ointment" (Aeschylus, *Prom.* 480; Euripides, *Hipp.* 516).

13. The usage of χριστός in the LXX follows quite closely the usage of משיח in the Hebrew Bible, and therefore on this particular point the generalization "Israel's Scriptures" will suffice, regardless of which text form it appears a given New Testament author may have used. For the details of how the LXX and the Hebrew Bible correspond on this matter, including a few exceptions (the more interesting of which concern OG Dan 9:25 and 26), see Novenson, *Christ among the Messiahs: Christ Language in Paul and Messiah Language in Ancient Judaism* (Oxford: Oxford University Press, 2012), 49 n. 68.

14. Priests: Lev 4:3, 5, 16; 6:15. Kings: 1 Sam 2:10, 35; 12:3, 5; 16:6; 24:7 (twice), 11; 26:9, 11, 16, 23; 2 Sam 1:14, 16; 19:22; 22:51; 23:1; Isa 45:1 (a gentile ruler, Cyrus); Hab 3:13; Pss 2:2; 18:51; 20:7; 28:8; 84:10; 89:39, 52; 132:10, 17; Lam 4:20; 2 Chr 6:42. Prophets: Ps 105:15; 1 Chr 16:22 (the "prophets" in both cases are Israel's patriarchs). Ambiguous: Dan 9:25, 26. The ambiguous instances in Daniel are usually understood as referring to historical figures of the past. Even so, the diction of phrases in which the term is embedded is future oriented—a linguistic feature, if not a historiographical feature, presenting interpretative possibilities to later readers. For a

terized as a priest, king, prophet, and expected one.¹⁵ My point is not that these New Testament uses of "messiah" necessarily constitute interpretations of Jewish scriptural texts containing the word "messiah," but rather that early Christian characterizations of the anointed one follow in a general way the various profiles of anointed ones in Israel's Scriptures. Moreover, the proportionality of the types of anointed ones in Israel's Scriptures corresponds to that of the profiles of the messiah in the New Testament. The term מָשִׁיחַ in the Hebrew Bible most often denotes royal figures, less frequently priests, and very seldom prophets. And in New Testament literature Jesus is most regularly portrayed as a royal figure, less commonly a priest, and only occasionally a prophet.¹⁶

In pointing out these correspondences, I do not mean to imply that the authors of the New Testament deliberately and collectively sought to emulate a pattern in Israel's Scriptures. Instead, I merely observe that early Christian reflection on the roles of the christ appears to have run along the same lines as the portraits of christs in Israel's Scriptures in both type and proportion. This is a "use" of Israel's Scriptures in the sense that it is a linguistic phenomenon within early Christian literary production that conforms in a fundamental way to a linguistic feature of Israel's Scriptures.¹⁷ Thus the formative influence of Israel's Scriptures on early Christian messiah speculation, even at the lexical level, is significant.

Looking beyond the term "messiah," there are obviously other portions of Israel's Scriptures that were influential in later messiah speculation. This influence, however, is not the function of an ideological phenomenon in which messianic streams run through Israel's Scriptures and inevitably empty out into a river of later messianism. Rather, the influence of Israel's Scriptures is a linguistic phenomenon in which those Scriptures' words, phrases, and images became springs of textual-interpretative possibilities variously drawn upon by authors

---

more detailed overview of מָשִׁיחַ in the Hebrew Bible, see J. J. M. Roberts, "The Old Testament's Contribution to Messianic Expectations," in *The Messiah: Developments in Earliest Judaism and Christianity*, ed. James H. Charlesworth (Minneapolis: Fortress, 1992), 39-41.

15. E.g., as priest: Heb 9:11; Rom 8:34; as king: Mark 15:2, 32; Eph 5:5; 2 Pet 1:11; Rev 11:5; as prophet: Luke 4:24, 41; Acts 3:18, 22; and as expected one: Phil 3:20; 1 Pet 1:7.

16. Regarding the perhaps unexpected uses of "messiah" to denote a gentile ruler (Isa 45:1) and the prophet-patriarchs (Ps 105:15; 1 Chr 16:22), it may be significant that Matthew includes gentile women in Jesus's genealogy—Ruth and Rahab (perhaps also Bathsheba and Tamar)—and that Paul insists that Jesus is Abraham's single "seed," a position traditionally occupied by the patriarch Isaac. On the former point see John Nolland, "The Four (Five) Women and Other Annotations in Matthew's Genealogy," *NTS* 43, no. 4 (1997): 527-39; and on the latter see Jon D. Levenson, *The Death and Resurrection of the Beloved Son: The Transformation of Child Sacrifice in Judaism and Christianity* (New Haven: Yale University Press, 1993), esp. chs. 14-16.

17. I thus part ways here with, e.g., the classic study Mowinckel, *He That Cometh*, 3-9; and the more recent survey Roberts, "Old Testament's Contribution," 39.

Messiah

developing the assorted profiles of the messiahs we find in early Jewish literature, profiles as indebted to Israel's Scriptures as they were diverse in form.[18]

Messiah in Early Jewish Literature

The coherence of messianism in early Judaism consists not in a single messianic conception to which various texts witness, but rather in a common mode of discourse that is interpretative. Looking to early Jewish literature, I want to illustrate the three formal characteristics delineated above concerning how Israel's Scriptures are drawn upon in messiah texts.[19] As I have already contended and will show in the next section, these modes of interpretation also characterize the messianic readings of Scripture evinced in the New Testament. To observe this is to ameliorate accounts of early messianism unduly emphasizing the purported uniqueness of early Christian messianic interpretation. And of course, by virtue of their authors' cultural situatedness, most, if not all, of the texts of the New Testament are themselves specimens of early Jewish literature and should therefore be factored into any comprehensive description of early Jewish messiah speculation. However, in this section I foreground non-Christian Jewish texts to establish a point of reference for describing early Christian messianic interpretation vis-à-vis that of other contemporary non-Christian messiah speculators. But ultimately that description reveals affinity rather than disparity, and so along the way I will note points of contact in both form and content between the reading practices evinced in early Jewish literature and in the texts of the New Testament.

Proliferation of Scriptural Idioms

In early Jewish messiah texts the word "messiah," or another designation of the figure called "messiah" in the same text, often appears in an idiom borrowed from Israel's Scriptures. The scriptural sources of these idioms are themselves sometimes messiah texts *sensu stricto*, but they are also sometimes non-messiah texts interpreted messianically. For example, m. Soṭah 9:15 borrows from Ps 89:52 MT the idiom עקבות משיחא. Mishnah Soṭah 9:15 reads, "With the footprints

---

18. On watersheds, springs, and messianic language, see Nils A. Dahl, "Sources of Christological Language," in *Jesus the Christ: The Historical Origins of Christological Debate*, ed. Donald H. Juel (Minneapolis: Fortress, 1991), esp. 115–17, 132–33.

19. For a more detailed exploration of some of the following illustrations, see Hewitt, *Messiah and Scripture*, 58–76.

of the messiah [בעקבות משיחא] presumption shall increase," and Ps 89:52 MT reads, "Your enemies mock, O YHWH, they mock the heels of your anointed one [עקבות משיחך]."[20] Curiously, this idiom does not mean the same thing in its respective contexts. In m. Soṭah it is part of an adverbial phrase denoting the future arrival of a messiah, while in Ps 89:52 it is a synecdoche for the messiah. This simple connotative difference illustrates a broader feature of the interpretative ingenuity of early Jewish messiah discourse: scriptural material is occasionally appropriated in ways that yield novel connotations extending beyond that in the scriptural source. Another instance of the proliferation of a scriptural idiom is the recurrence of temporal clauses with "messiah" as the subject (either grammatically or conceptually) of a verb of "coming."[21] This can be seen in CD XII, 23–XIII, 1; and XIV, 19: "until there comes [עד עמוד] the messiah of Aaron and Israel"; 4Q252 V, 3: "until comes [עד בוא] the messiah of righteousness"; and 2 Bar. 72:2: "when . . . the time of my messiah comes [Syriac *ʾty*]."[22] These turns of phrase are likely appropriated from a scriptural source that is not itself a messiah text but that is frequently interpreted messianically in early Judaism—Gen 49:10: "The scepter shall not depart from Judah, nor the ruler's staff from between his feet, until Shiloh comes [עד כי־יבא שילה, ἕως ἂν ἔλθῃ]."[23] A final illustration of the reuse of a scriptural idiom is the repeated phraseology of a messiah "rising" or being "raised up." This appears in 4 Ezra 12:32: "This is the messiah . . . , who will arise [Syriac *dnḥ*, lit. "shine"] from the posterity of David";[24] Ps. Sol. 17:21, 32: "Behold, O Lord, and raise [ἀνάστησον] for them their king, the son of David . . . and their king will be the messiah lord [χριστὸς κύριος]" (cf. 18:5);[25] Tg. Ps.-J. Gen 49:11:

20. See Novenson, *Christ among the Messiahs*, 55. Mishnah translation modified from Herbert Danby, *The Mishnah: Translated from the Hebrew, with Introduction and Brief Explanatory Notes* (Oxford: Oxford University Press, 1933). Unless otherwise indicated, all other translations are my own.

21. This also is discussed by Novenson, *Christ among the Messiahs*, 54, who follows Joseph A. Fitzmyer, *The One Who Is to Come* (Grand Rapids: Eerdmans, 2007), 62, in wrongly accounting for this idiom in terms of the influence of Dan 9:25, which, while containing the temporal phrase עד־משיח/ἕως χριστοῦ, lacks a verb of "coming" (but cf. Matt 1:17, which also lacks such a verb).

22. Translations of 2 Baruch modified from that of A. F. J. Klijn, *OTP* 1:615-52.

23. This idiom also appears in several New Testament writings to be discussed below (e.g., Gal 3:19; Matt 10:23; Rev 2:25). On the messianic interpretation of Gen 49:10 in early Judaism and early Christianity, see Dennis C. Duling, "The Promises to David and Their Entrance into Christianity—Nailing Down a Likely Hypothesis," *NTS* 20, no. 1 (1973): 59, 64.

24. The Latin omits the clause "who . . . David." Translations of 4 Ezra modified from that of Bruce M. Metzger, *OTP* 1:217-60.

25. Alfred Rahlfs, ed., *Psalmi cum Odis*, SVTG 10 (Göttingen: Vandenhoeck & Ruprecht, 1931) emends χριστὸς κύριος to read χριστὸς κυρίου, correcting a purported Christian interpolation. Against this, R. B. Wright, *OTP* 2:669, observes that there is no manuscript evidence

"How beautiful is the king messiah who is destined to arise [לְמָקוֹם] from the house of Judah!"; and Tg. Neb. Mic 5:1, 3: "From you shall come forth before me the messiah ... and he shall arise [וִיקוּם] and rule."[26] This idiom is likely drawn from Num 24:17: "A star will come out of Jacob and a scepter will arise [וְקָם, ἀναστήσεται] out of Israel."[27] Thus the diction of, though not always the sense of, early Jewish messiah texts is shaped by the diction of Israel's Scriptures.

Variegated Reception of the Same Scriptural Sources

Early Jewish messiah speculation is also marked by the variegated reception of the same scriptural sources among multiple messiah texts. In other words, it is common for the same scriptural source to be used by more than one messiah speculator but in different ways. I have already mentioned that Gen 49:10 and Num 24:17 repeatedly feature in early Jewish messiah texts, and to these we may add 2 Sam 7:12-14; Isa 11:2-4; and Dan 7:12-14 (and often portions of these verses' immediate contexts).[28] But while these texts are common sources of literary fodder for depicting messiahs, they are not often read in the same way. Note, for instance, the distinct uses of Isa 11:2-4 in the Psalms of Solomon and in the Similitudes of Enoch:

> Behold, O Lord, and raise for them their king, the son of David ... *in wisdom of righteousness* to drive out sinners from the inheritance ... *with a rod of iron to shatter all their substance, to destroy the lawless nations by the word of his mouth* [Isa 11:2, 4] ... and their king will be the messiah lord. (Pss. Sol. 17:21, 23-24, 32)[29]

---

in Greek or Syriac supporting the reading χριστὸς κυρίου and that Luke 2:11 suggests that χριστὸς κύριος was an "available ... messianic title" in the era.

26. Micah 5:3 MT reads, "and he shall stand [וְעָמַד]." Translations of targumim modified from Samson H. Levey, *The Messiah: An Aramaic Interpretation; The Messianic Exegesis of the Targum*, HUCM 2 (Cincinnati: Hebrew Union College Press, 1974).

27. Other possibilities include 2 Sam 7:12; Isa 11:10 LXX; Jer 23:5; and Amos 9:11. A less likely candidate, given its obscurity relative to early Jewish messiah texts, is 2 Sam 23:1. Talk of an anointed one "rising" or "being raised" also features prominently among several texts of the New Testament to be discussed below (e.g., Luke 24:46; Acts 2:32; Heb 7:15-16).

28. Similar lists are compiled by John J. Collins, "Messiahs in Context: Method in the Study of Messianism in the Dead Sea Scrolls," in *Methods of Investigation of the Dead Sea Scrolls and the Khirbet Qumran Site: Present Realities and Future Prospects*, ed. Michael O. Wise et al. (New York: New York Academy of Sciences, 1994), 213-30; and Gerbern S. Oegema, *The Anointed and His People: Messianic Expectations from the Maccabees to Bar Kochba*, JSPSup 27 (Sheffield: Sheffield Academic, 1998), 302-3.

29. Italics in primary text quotations indicate appropriated scriptural material.

> For they have denied the Lord of spirits and his anointed one.... For the chosen one has taken his stand in the presence of the Lord of spirits; ... *And in him dwell the spirit of wisdom and the spirit of insight, and the spirit of instruction and might*, and the spirit of those who have fallen asleep in righteousness. *And he will judge the things that are secret* [Isa 11:2, 3]. (1 En. 48:10; 49:2–4)[30]

The author of the Psalms of Solomon borrows Isaiah's "rod" and "word" to depict the messiah's punishing of the nations, while the author of the Similitudes appropriates Isaiah's spirits of virtue to portray the messiah's wisdom.[31] Or consider the ways in which the oracle of Gen 49 is drawn upon differently in 4 Ezra and in the Talmud Bavli:

> And as for *the lion* [Gen 49:9] that you saw rousing up out of the forest and roaring ... this is the messiah whom the Most High has kept until the end of days, who will arise from the posterity of David. (4 Ezra 12:31–32)[32]

> What is [the messiah's] name? The school of R. Shila said: His name is *Shiloh*, for it is written, *Until Shiloh comes* [Gen 49:10]. (b. Sanh. 98b)[33]

The author of 4 Ezra finds in the oracle of Gen 49 a beast worthy of standing in for the messiah, while the rabbis play with the ambiguity of Gen 49's enigmatic term שילה and the resemblance it bears to the name of the rabbi in question.[34]

---

30. Translation modified from George W. E. Nickelsburg and James C. VanderKam, *1 Enoch: The Hermeneia Translation* (Minneapolis: Fortress, 2012).

31. Alongside these examples we might add Rom 15:8–9, 12, where Paul appropriates Isa 11 in yet another way, to portray his messiah as the hope of the gentiles: "Christ has become a servant of circumcision for the truth of God, to confirm the promises to the patriarchs and so that the gentiles might glorify God for mercy. Just as it has been written, ... *The root of Jesse will be, even he who rises up to rule the nations; upon him the nations will hope* [Isa 11:10]." All three of these texts are noted in Novenson, *Christ among the Messiahs*, 59–60, but his point is a different and more basic one—namely, that Isa 11 commonly received a messianic interpretation.

32. On this lion as the lion of Judah, see Michael E. Stone, *Fourth Ezra: A Commentary on the Book of Fourth Ezra*, Hermeneia (Minneapolis: Fortress, 1990), 209.

33. On this "language game," see Novenson, *Grammar of Messianism*, 15–16. On the term "Shiloh" and messianic interpretation, see Emmanouela Grypeou and Helen Spurling, *The Book of Genesis in Late Antiquity: Encounters between Jewish and Christian Exegesis*, JCPS 24 (Leiden: Brill, 2013), 376–79. Translations of the Talmud Bavli modified from Isidore Epstein, ed., *Hebrew-English Edition of the Babylonian Talmud*, 30 vols. (London: Soncino, 1960–1990).

34. Paul in Gal 3:16, 19 offers yet another reading of Gen 49:10, finding in it a reference to the coming "seed of Abraham," the messiah. See J. Thomas Hewitt, "Ancient Messiah Discourse and Paul's Expression ἄχρις οὗ ἔλθῃ τὸ σπέρμα in Galatians 3.19," *NTS* 65, no. 3 (2019): 398–411.

Messiah

Notice finally how the scene of Dan 7 is used to develop diverse messianic portraits in the visions of 4 Ezra and 2 Baruch:

> And I looked, and behold, this wind made *something like the figure of a man* [Dan 7:13] *come up out* of the heart *of the sea* [Dan 7:3]. And I looked, *and behold, that man flew with the clouds of heaven* [Dan 7:13]. (4 Ezra 13:3)[35]

> *The last [fourth] ruler* [Dan 7:7, 19-23] who is left alive at that time will be bound, whereas the entire host will be destroyed. And they will carry him on Mount Zion, *and* my messiah *will convict him* [Dan 7:26] of all his wicked deeds and will assemble and set before him all the works of his hosts.... *And [my messiah's] dominion will last forever* [Dan 7:14, 27]. (2 Bar. 40:1-3)

While in both of these texts messiahs overcome God's opponents, 4 Ezra exploits imagery from Dan 7 to convey the otherworldliness of the messiah, while 2 Baruch draws on different imagery to construct a messianic tribunal.[36] Thus, while several scriptural sources may feature repeatedly among early Jewish messiah texts, the reception of those sources is often variegated, evincing both the interpretative ingenuity of messiah speculators and the interpretative possibilities presented by Israel's Scriptures.

Integrative Appropriation of Different Scriptural Sources

The third and final trait of early Jewish messianic interpretation to illustrate is the integrative appropriation of different scriptural sources in individual messiah texts. By this I do not mean merely that the author of a given messiah text might draw upon more than one scriptural source in developing his messianology; that is virtually a given. Rather, I refer to the amalgamation of two or more scriptural texts in the portrayal of a messiah. A well-known rabbinic example of this is R. Akiba's explanation in b. Sanh. 38b of the thrones of Dan 7:9—"one for the Ancient of Days and one for David"—an explanation incorporating the heavenly seating arrangement of Ps 110:1.[37] Or in 4 Ezra 11-13 there is a fusing of imagery from the oracle of Gen 49 and the vision of Dan 7 when

---

35. On the correlation of this figure with the messiah of 4 Ezra 12:32, see Michael E. Stone, "The Concept of the Messiah in IV Ezra," in *Religions in Antiquity: Essays in Memory of Erwin Ramsdell Goodenough*, ed. Jacob Neusner, SHR 14 (Leiden: Brill, 1968), 309.

36. Daniel 7 also features prominently, though differently, in the Synoptics. E.g., Matt 25:31-32 draws on Dan 7:9-10, 13-14 to depict an assembly of the nations, not to be eradicated as in 4 Ezra 13:37-40, but rather to be sorted.

37. See Juel, *Messianic Exegesis*, 137-38; and Hay, *Glory at the Right Hand*, 26, who is in-

the "lion" (4 Ezra 11:37; 12:1; cf. Gen 49:9), who confronts an eagle, the "fourth beast" (4 Ezra 11:39; cf. Dan 7:7), is explained to be the messiah (4 Ezra 12:32) and is then beheld as "something like the figure of a man" who "flew with the clouds of heaven" (4 Ezra 13:3; cf. Dan 7:13), later revealed by the Most High as "my son" (4 Ezra 7:32, 37; cf. Ps 2:2, 7).³⁸ Thus, the lion of Judah is the messiah, is the seed of David (according to the Syriac), is the heavenly man, is the son of God—a scripturally composite messianic vignette if ever there were one.³⁹ Comparably, we find in Pss. Sol. 17:23–24 the activity of the messiah (cf. 17:32) depicted by an integration of imagery from Ps 2 and Isa 11: "With a *rod of iron* [Ps 2:9] he will break in pieces all their substance. He will destroy the godless nations *with the word of his mouth* [Isa 11:4 LXX]."⁴⁰ This collocation of Ps 2:9 and Isa 11:4 is perhaps prompted by the common term שבט, "rod," in the MT, though the author of the Psalms of Solomon follows Isa 11:4 LXX, λόγῳ στόματος αὐτοῦ, allowing the "word" of Isa 11:4 to define the "rod" of Ps 2:9.⁴¹ A slightly different example is found in 4Q252 V, 2–4. The author is self-consciously interpreting the meaning of the words המחקק, "the staff," and הדגלים, "the standards," from the second clause of Gen 49:10 (cf. רגליו, "his feet" in the MT). But then arriving at the enigmatic MT phrase עד כי־יבא שילה, he simply glosses it with עד בוא משיח הצדק צמח דוד, "until comes the messiah of righteousness, the branch of David." This is a transparent incorporation of the verbiage לדוד צמח צדיק, "for David a righteous branch," from Jer 23:5 and 33:15 into a messianic interpretation of the ambiguous word שילה from Gen 49:10.⁴² Thus early Jewish messiah texts (even when their form is "commentary") commonly integrate multiple and diverse sources appropriated from Israel's Scriptures into single messianic portraits. This trait, in addition to the proliferation of scriptural idioms and the variegated reception of the same scriptural sources, also characterizes the messianic interpretation of Israel's Scriptures in the literature of the New Testament.

---

debted to Nils Dahl for this observation. The coalescing of Dan 7 and Ps 110 also appears in several New Testament texts to be discussed below (e.g., Mark 14:62; Acts 7:55–56; 1 Cor 15:24–25).

38. On this "blending" of scriptural sources, see Peter Schäfer, "Diversity and Interaction: Messiahs in Early Judaism," in *Toward the Millennium: Messianic Expectations from the Bible to Waco*, ed. Peter Schäfer and Mark Cohen, SHR 77 (Leiden: Brill, 1998), 33.

39. One is reminded here of the many guises of the messiah in Revelation: lion of Judah, progeny of David (both 5:5), heavenly man (1:12–16), and son of God (2:18).

40. See Stuckenbruck, "Messianic Ideas," 95–96.

41. There is a comparable collocation of imagery from Ps 2:9 and Isa 11:4 in Rev 19:15: "And from *his mouth* comes a sharp sword, so that by it he might *strike* [Isa 11:4] the nations, and he *will rule them with a rod of iron* [Ps 2:9]."

42. See John J. Collins, *The Scepter and the Star: Messianism in Light of the Dead Sea Scrolls*, 2nd ed. (Grand Rapids: Eerdmans, 2010), 70.

Messiah

Messiah in the New Testament

Turning to the New Testament, we see how its authors participated in the broader ancient Jewish interpretative enterprise of messiah discourse, and in particular how the texts they produced exhibit the same three formal characteristics that I have shown mark the messianic use of Israel's Scriptures in early non-Christian Jewish literature.[43] As in the previous section, I will note along the way points of contact between reading practices evinced in the texts of the New Testament and those found in early non-Christian Jewish literature.

Proliferation of Scriptural Idioms

One of the most prominent idioms used to describe the Christian messiah is the frequently recurring designation "son." But why should the messiah be called the son of God? Explanations abound: He is called God's son because David's seed was to be God's son, and the messiah is a Davidide. He is called God's son because Israel is God's son, and the messiah is Israel incorporate. He is called God's son because the emperor is styled God's son, and the messiah is a foil to earthly sovereigns. And so on. One or more of these and other explanations may well be historically valid, but more fundamental is the fact that there is an obvious linguistic precedent set by Israel's Scriptures for referring to a messiah as God's son. This precedent is set by Ps 2 in which "the Lord's anointed" (v. 2) is declared "my son" (v. 7) by Israel's deity. Explorations of why in Israel's ancient Near Eastern context her king (2:6) should be called God's son, or discussions of the impetus for, and import of, the early Christian habit of calling the messiah God's son are welcome complements to this simple observation about Ps 2. But the linguistic precedent itself is foundational to this prominent feature of the messianic diction we find in early Christian literature.[44]

Nils Dahl expands on this understanding of the influence of Ps 2 by contending that the psalm also supplied the idiom for a "dyadic formula" proliferated among the texts of the New Testament: "the God and Father of our Lord Jesus

---

43. Any use of Scripture in the New Testament to describe Jesus is a use of Scripture to describe the messiah, since every New Testament author who refers to Jesus calls him χριστός (3 John neither contains the word χριστός nor refers to Jesus [though cf. v. 7]). This is not to say, however, that epithets applied to Jesus (lord, christ, king, etc.) are applied indiscriminately.

44. The designation of a messiah as the "son of God" may not be unique to early Christian literature. 1QSa II, 11–12 and 4 Ezra 13:32, 37 both appear to describe a messiah as God's son, but see Adela Yarbro Collins and John J. Collins, *King and Messiah as Son of God: Divine, Human, and Angelic Messianic Figures in Biblical and Related Literature* (Grand Rapids: Eerdmans, 2008), 65, 96 on relevant textual ambiguities.

Christ" (and variants).⁴⁵ This expression is an adaption of the binary phraseology of the final clause of Ps 2:2, κατὰ τοῦ κυρίου καὶ κατὰ τοῦ χριστοῦ αὐτοῦ, "against the Lord and against his anointed." We can expand further on Dahl's observation by noting that the same idiom is also likely influential for Luke's report in Acts 2:36 of Peter's assertion, "God made him both Lord and messiah." If these observations are correct, the use of these dyadic formulas are a case in which the proliferation of a scriptural idiom entails a significant divergence from the idiom's original context in Israel's Scriptures, a divergence of some import for the question of early divine christology. This divergence is the transfer of the title κύριος from the deity of Israel, to whom it refers in Ps 2:2, to the messiah while maintaining Israel's God as a distinct person referred to as "the Father" (a characterization that is the obvious implication of Ps 2:7). The plausibility of this use of Ps 2 is confirmed by a similar interpretative move evinced in the creedal material of 1 Cor 8:6, where the Shema of Deut 6:4 appears to have been reworked to incorporate the messiah, again by applying to him the title κύριος, which in the scriptural source refers to Israel's deity.⁴⁶

Returning to the designation "son," Jon Levenson contends that its well-known modifier ἀγαπητός, "beloved," is also an idiom transparently borrowed from Israel's Scriptures.⁴⁷ In particular, he argues that the word ἀγαπητός would have evoked for early audiences the Akedah, in which the adjective is prominently applied to Isaac three times (Gen 22:2, 12, 16 LXX; MT: יחיד, "only"). The effect, Levenson argues, of applying the idiom "my beloved son" to the messiah would be to liken Jesus to Isaac, thus framing Jesus's sacrifice as evidence of his beloved status rather than a negation of it, just as Isaac's endangerment is inextricably bound to his beloved status.⁴⁸

Also drawing upon the Abraham saga is the proliferation of the idiom ἐν χριστῷ, "in Christ," in the Pauline epistles. I have argued at length elsewhere that this is a scripturally formed idiom in several important respects.⁴⁹ Regarding

---

45. Dahl, "Sources of Christological Language," 130. Related idioms occur twenty-four times in various New Testament epistles.

46. See David Lincicum, *Paul and the Early Jewish Encounter with Deuteronomy*, WUNT 2/284 (Tübingen: Mohr Siebeck, 2010), 138–40.

47. "Beloved son" occurs eight times in the Synoptics and 2 Peter, but there are really only two literary contexts for the phrase—the heavenly pronouncement at Jesus's baptism and the parable of the vineyard.

48. Levenson, *Death and Resurrection*, 30–31, 200–202. Levenson postulates that an association between "the beloved son" of the Akedah and the Passover lamb underlies a number of early Christian portrayals of Jesus (200–219). Levenson also demonstrates that this association is not unique to Christian messianic interpretation but is also evinced in Jub. 17:15–18:19 as well as later rabbinic literature (176–99).

49. Hewitt, *Messiah and Scripture*, esp. chs. 3–4.

the structure of the expression itself, Paul has appropriated the recurring qualification of the promise to Abraham, that the nations would be blessed ἐν τῷ σπέρματί σου, "in your seed" (Gen 22:18; 26:4; 28:14 LXX), substituting χριστός for σπέρμα σου. This use of Scripture is clear from Paul's explicit identification of Abraham's seed as the messiah in Gal 3:16, following a paraphrase in Gal 3:14 of the promise to Abraham into which Paul inserts the messiah: "so that the blessing of Abraham might come into the gentiles in Christ Jesus."[50] "In Christ" is a hallmark of Pauline idiolect, picked up already in other New Testament texts, such as 1 Peter, but even more so by the time of Apostolic Fathers.[51]

Returning to one of the scriptural idioms already encountered in our survey of early Jewish literature, we find expressions analogous to "until the messiah comes" among the texts of the New Testament. As discussed above, this idiom appears to derive from Gen 49:10 and typically consists of a temporal clause with the messiah as the subject of a verb of coming. This phraseology appears across a range of New Testament texts, including Gal 3:19: "until comes [ἄχρις οὗ ἔλθῃ] the seed [i.e., the messiah per 3:16] to whom it was promised"; 1 Cor 11:26: "you proclaim the Lord's death until he comes [ἄχρι οὗ ἔλθῃ]"; Matt 10:23: "until comes [ἕως ἂν ἔλθῃ] the son of man"; John 21:22, 23: "until I come [ἕως ἔρχομαι]"; and Rev 2:25: "until I have come [ἄχρι(ς) οὗ ἂν ἥξω]." It is interesting to note that several, though not all (cf. Gal 3:19), of these instances draw upon the phraseology of Gen 49:10 not to articulate something regarding the messiah's initial appearance, but to describe the expectation of the messiah's second appearance. This particular connotation of the idiom is perhaps a distinctive mark of early Christian messiah speculation, but the proliferation of the idiom is not distinctive, and the impulse of interpretative innovation is itself typical of all early Jewish messiah speculation.

Another example of such innovation is the early Christian proliferation of a second idiom discussed in the previous section, that of a messiah "rising" or "being raised" up. This is apparent in New Testament texts that use ἀνίστημι, "to raise up, to rise," or its cognate ἀνάστασις, "a rising up" to describe not merely the messiah's ascendancy, but the messiah's resurrection. Note, for instance, Luke 24:46: "Thus it is written that the messiah is to suffer and to be raised up [ἀναστῆναι]"; Acts 2:32: "This Jesus God raised up [ἀνέστησεν]"; and Heb 7:15–16: "when ac-

---

50. While the expression "in Christ" was unprecedented in the first century, the interpretative logic by which Paul identifies Abraham's seed as the messiah—namely, the conflation of Abraham's seed with David's seed—and thus authorizes his paraphrase of the idiom "in your seed" with "in messiah" is already traditional in Jewish interpretation. Note, e.g., the innerbiblical allusions to the Abraham saga in descriptions of the Davidic dynasty in Jer 33:22 and Ps 72:17. See further Hewitt, *Messiah and Scripture*, 100–105.

51. The idiom appears repeatedly, e.g., in 1 Clement and the writings of Ignatius.

cording to the likeness of Melchizedek another priest arises [ἀνίσταται] who has become a priest . . . according to the power of an indestructible life."[52] Max Wilcox and Dennis Duling note that Rom 1:3-4 appears to appropriate a pre-Pauline tradition in which the phrase "I will raise up [ἀναστήσω] your seed after you" in 2 Sam 7:12 was read by early Christian interpreters as a reference to the messiah's resurrection.[53] Thus the idiom of a messiah "rising" may not necessarily be drawn from Num 24:17, as it seems to be in some of the other early Jewish messiah texts discussed above. Moreover, other New Testament texts suggest there are actually a number of Israel's Scriptures that seem to have catalyzed a creative use of ἀνίστημι as a sort of double entendre. Ross Wagner points to Paul's use in Rom 15:12 of Isa 11:10—"and in that day there will be a root of Jesse, even the one who will arise [ὁ ἀνιστάμενος] to rule the gentiles"—contending that "it would be ludicrous to suggest . . . that Paul would not have recognized the paronomastic potential of ἀνίστημι."[54] And in Acts 3:22 (cf. 7:37) the quotation of Deut 18:15—"the Lord your God will raise up [ἀναστήσει] for you a prophet like me from your brethren"—referring to the messiah indicates that at least for Luke the language of the Pentateuch was comparably influential.[55] Taken together, these examples demonstrate that the proliferation of scriptural idioms we observed among early Jewish messiah texts is also a mark of early Christian literature. Furthermore, although in early Christian literature the "rising" of the messiah often denotes the messiah's resurrection, not merely his ascendancy— certainly a distinctive interpretative innovation—such a connotative deviation from the obvious meaning of ἀνίστημι in Num 24:17; or 2 Sam 7:12; or Isa 11:10 is not formally different from the rabbis' reconfiguration of the sense of עקבות in m. Soṭah 9:15 described in our survey of early Jewish literature. In both cases, the

---

52. On Heb 7:15 as a reference to resurrection, see David M. Moffitt, *Atonement and the Logic of Resurrection in the Epistle to the Hebrews*, NovTSup 141 (Leiden: Brill, 2011), 202-3.

53. See Wilcox, "The Promise of the 'Seed' in the New Testament and the Targumim," in *New Testament Text and Language: A Sheffield Reader*, ed. Stanley E. Porter and Craig A. Evans, BibSem 44 (Sheffield: Sheffield Academic, 1997), 284, 292-93; and Duling, "Promises to David," 71, 74-77.

54. J. Ross Wagner, *Heralds of the Good News: Isaiah and Paul "In Concert" in the Letter to the Romans*, NovTSup 101 (Leiden: Brill, 2003), 319 n. 44.

55. The scene in Acts also plays with a double entendre. Peter's assertion that "God raised up [ἀναστήσας] a servant" (3:26) appears to carry the mundane sense of simply establishing the messiah. But directly after, Luke reports that this assertion annoyed the Sadducees, who took Peter as "proclaiming the resurrection [ἀνάστασιν] of the dead in Jesus" (4:2). Thus according to Luke the Sadducees, at least, heard more in the term ἀνίστημι than meets the eye. In this connection, note Tg. Ps.-J. Hos 6:2, where the simple "raising up" (יקם/ἀναστησόμεθα) of Israel found in the MT/LXX is explicitly framed as resurrection. See Matthew Black, "The Christological Use of the Old Testament in the New Testament," *NTS* 18, no. 1 (1971): 6.

innate ambiguity of figural speech, whether of a description of empowerment as vertical motion or the designation of a whole person by a body part, is exploited to depict a new situation. The early Christian proliferation of this idiom of the messiah "arising" is thus a case in which the mode of messianic interpretation is conventional even as the particular interpretative result is distinctive.

Variegated Reception of the Same Scriptural Sources

We have seen above that the variegated reception of the same scriptural sources characterizes the use of Israel's Scriptures across early Jewish messiah texts, themselves representing distinct expressions of Judaism. To show that certain scriptural sources were read by authors of the early Jesus movement somewhat differently than they were elsewhere in early Judaism would reinforce this point but would also be rather obvious. Instead, my aim here is to demonstrate that even *within* the early Jesus movement there was variation in how certain texts were received.

The interpretation of Daniel in the New Testament is a clear example of such variegated reception. For instance, in the Synoptics Dan 7 supplies imagery for the exaltation of the messiah, while in Paul Dan 7 inspires the depiction of the messiah's foes, and in Revelation Dan 7 furnishes a description of the messiah's countenance:

> And then they will see the *son of man coming in the clouds* [Dan 7:13] with much power and glory. (Mark 13:62; cf. par.)

> Then comes the end, when he [Christ] hands over the kingdom to God the Father, having *destroyed every rule and every authority and power* [Dan 7:27 OG]. (1 Cor 15:24)[56]

> And in the midst of the lampstands *one like a son of man.... And his head and hair were white, as white wool, as snow, and his eyes like flame of fire* [Dan 7:9] (Rev 1:13–14).[57]

---

56. For details on this appropriation of imagery from Dan 7, including consideration of an analogous retrieval of Danielic material in 4Q246, see Hewitt, *Messiah and Scripture*, ch. 4.

57. This use of Dan 7:9 is also significant for questions of early Christian divine christology since these features of appearance belong to the Ancient of Days in Dan 7 but to the messiah in Rev 1. On the possible interpretation of the Dan 7's "one like a son of man" as divine also in early Judaism, see Loren T. Stuckenbruck, "'One Like a Son of Man as the Ancient of Days' in the Old Greek Recension of Daniel 7,13: Scribal Error or Theological Translation?," *ZNW* 86, no. 3–4 (1995): 268–76.

Voluminous discussion of an alleged title "son of man" obscures the fact, but the reception of Dan 7 in early Christianity was quite varied and concerned with much more than the epithet.[58] This variegated reception of Dan 7 to describe the Christian messiah is perhaps unsurprising given its distinct appropriations also in the early Jewish messiah texts already described, 4 Ezra and 2 Baruch.

The retrievals of Ps 110 (Ps 109 OG) among the texts of the New Testament are another clear example of variegated reception. At the most general level, the psalm stimulated two notably diverse messianologies—one royal, one priestly. Thus, the figure at God's right hand in Ps 110:1 is used to depict the vindicated messiah's ruling authority in the Synoptics, Acts, and 1 Peter, and the psalm's imagery of enemies underfoot is used by Paul to the same end.[59] Yet in Hebrews, Ps 110:4's mention of the enigmatic figure Melchizedek is capitalized upon to defend and define the priesthood of a (Judahite) messiah.[60]

There are also finer distinctions at play in the early Christian reception of Ps 110. As just mentioned, Paul reaches for Ps 110:1's indication of an implied period of waiting for the subjection of the messiah's enemies—"Sit at my hand until [ἕως ἄν] I make your enemies your footstool"[61]—and he does so to explain the delay between the messiah's resurrection and that of the messiah's people (1 Cor 15:23–28). This is a "royal" reading of Ps 110:1 but a reading of a different part of the psalm for a different purpose than what we see in the Gospels. Or consider Stephen's anomalous vision reported in Acts 7:55–56 of Jesus not sitting but *standing* at God's right hand. Though the import of this deviation from the posture depicted in Ps 110:1 is not explained in Acts, it appears that the distinctive situation of Stephen's being martyred prompts the unconventional reception of the psalm's image of presence at God's right hand.[62] Yet another use of the psalm appears in Mark 12:35–37 par., where it is neither the posture nor the temporal clause of Ps 110:1 that is exploited, but rather the characters of the dialogue. The Synoptics report that Jesus subverts the Pharisees' conception of the messiah as

---

58. For a foray into debates about the "son of man," see the essays in Larry W. Hurtado and Paul L. Owen, eds., *'Who Is This Son of Man?' The Latest Scholarship on a Puzzling Expression of the Historical Jesus*, LNTS 390 (London: T&T Clark, 2011).

59. Cf. Matt 26:64; Mark 14:62; 16:19; Luke 22:69; Acts 2:33–35; 5:31; 7:55–56; 1 Cor 15:25–27; 1 Pet 3:22. See also T. Job 33:3, where the benighted Job points to his throne of glory "at the right hand of God."

60. See Heb 7; Moffitt, *Atonement and the Logic of Resurrection*, 200–208. Cf. Rom 8:34, where Paul evinces awareness of a priestly-messianic reading of Ps 110.

61. Paul has ἄχρι οὗ (1 Cor 15:25).

62. See Nicole Chibici-Revneanu, "Ein himmlischer Stehplatz: Die Haltung Jesu in der Stephanusvision (Apg 7.55–56) und ihre Bedeutung," *NTS* 53, no. 4 (2007): 459–88.

David's son by asking how then can David, the presumed author of the psalm, refer to the addressee of God's speech as "my Lord."[63]

The uses of Isa 28:16 in Rom 9:33 and 1 Pet 2:6 constitute a somewhat different instance of variegated reception. One immediately notices that while the quotation of Isa 28:16 in 1 Pet 2:6 is unaltered (though more similar to the MT than the LXX), the wording of Isa 8:14 has been substituted into the quotation in Rom 9:33. Thus the stone of 1 Pet 2:6 is, as Isa 28:16 has it, "a cornerstone chosen and precious," but the stone of Rom 9:33 is a stone "of stumbling, and a rock of offence [Isa 8:14]."[64] These different depictions of the "stone," whose referent is the messiah, correlate with the different purposes of the letters.[65] Paul is emphasizing the tragedy of Israel's disbelief in Jesus, disbelief thrown into sharp relief by the gentiles' attainment by faith of righteousness (Rom 9:30). And so, while Paul would surely agree that the stone of Isa 28:16 is "chosen and precious" to God, and while he wants to retain Isa 28:16's depiction of God's agency in the placement of the stone (cf. Rom 11:11–12), the "stumbling stone" of Isa 8:14 better fits his purpose of explaining his kinsmen's response to the messiah. First Peter also addresses disbelief (1 Pet 2:8), but probably gentile disbelief (cf. 1 Pet 2:12; 4:3), and that only very briefly. Instead, the emphasis there is on the participation of believers in the "chosen and precious" status of the messiah, the cornerstone of a temple into which they are integrated as "living stones" (1 Pet 2:5). These uses of Isa 28:16 are conceptually similar in some respects, but the forms and emphases are divergent, evincing a variegated reception of the text in early Christianity.[66]

Integrative Appropriation of Different Scriptural Sources

We have seen the integrative appropriation of different scriptural sources already in two Pauline texts: in Gal 3:19 the embedding of Abraham's seed (i.e., the messiah as Paul understood it) in the phraseology of the oracle of Gen 49:10; and in Rom 9:33, as just discussed, the merging of Isa 28:16 and 8:14. For comparably terse

63. See Juel, *Messianic Exegesis*, 142–44.

64. This same phrase from Isa 8:14 appears in 1 Pet 2:8, but it is left separate from the quotation of Isa 28:16.

65. On Paul's composite citation, the possibility of a *testimonium*, and some disagreement about the referent of the "stone" in Rom 9:33, see Joseph A. Fitzmyer, *Romans: A New Translation with Introduction and Commentary*, AB 33 (New York: Doubleday, 1993), 612–14. For my part, the repetition of the phrase "everyone who believes in him will not be put to shame" in Rom 10:11, where clearly the messiah is in view, is sufficient evidence for understanding the stone of Rom 9:33 as the messiah.

66. See Richard Bauckham, "James, 1 and 2 Peter, Jude," in *It Is Written: Scripture Citing Scripture*, ed. D. A. Carson and H. G. M. Williamson (Cambridge: Cambridge University Press, 1988), 310–12.

instances of this trait, one could also point to the drama of Rev 5 in which the visionary hears that the *"lion of the tribe of Judah* [Gen 49:9] *has conquered"* (5:5) but then turns and sees not a lion but *"a lamb* placed as having been *slaughtered* [Isa 53:7; cf. Gen 22:7-8; Exod 12:21]" (5:6). This depiction of the messiah of Revelation is a merging of two seemingly disparate figurations, the effect of which is an implicitly subversive commentary on notions of messianic power and authority.

Another, relatively widespread example of such integrative appropriation concerns the aforementioned depictions of the exalted messiah in the Synoptics and Acts.[67] In each case the messiah, "son of man," is at God's "right hand," and in Matthew and Mark he is "coming on the clouds of heaven." These portraits comprise clear integrations of imagery from Ps 110:1 with imagery from Dan 7:13.[68] Further, material from Ps 8 is also collocated with imagery from Ps 110 and Dan 7 in three New Testament epistles:

> Then comes the end, when [the messiah] hands over the kingdom to God the Father, having *destroyed every rule and every authority and power* [Dan 7:27 OG]. For it is necessary that he reign until *"he has put all his enemies under his feet"* [Ps 110:1]. The last enemy to be destroyed is death. For *"[God] has subjected all things under his feet"* [Ps 8:6]. (1 Cor 15:24-27)

> [God] seated [the messiah] *at his right hand* [Ps 110:1] in the heavenlies, far above *every rule and authority and power* [Dan 7:27 OG] ... and *"he subjected all things under his feet"* [Ps 8:6]. (Eph 1:20-22)

> [messiah Jesus] is *at the right hand* [Ps 110:1] of God, having gone into heaven, angels and *authorities and powers having been subjected to him* [Dan 7:27 OG; Ps 8:6]. (1 Pet 3:22)

Each of these messianic tableaux integrates material from three different scriptural sources. The inclusion of Ps 8:6 in this amalgamation may be authorized by the terminology "son of man" shared between Dan 7:13 and Ps 8:4, but about this we can do no more than speculate since that expression itself appears in none of these New Testament epistles.

A more extensive instance of the integrative appropriation of diverse scriptural sources is found in the parable of the wicked husbandmen (Mark 12:1-12; cf. Matt 21:33-46; Luke 20:9-19).[69] The parable is an innovative adaptation of Isaiah's

---

67. See Mark 14:62; Matt 26:64; Luke 22:69; Acts 7:55-56.
68. Hay, *Glory at the Right Hand*, 26, suggests that Dan 7 itself may have been influenced by Ps 110.
69. On this parable see the intriguing discussion in Levenson, *Death and Resurrection*, 226-32.

Song of the Vineyard (Isa 5:1–7), closing with a citation of Ps 118:22–23. Levenson notes that perhaps the most significant difference between the Isaianic song and Synoptic parable is that while in Isaiah the problem is the unproductive vineyard (Isa 5:2), in the parable the problem has become the wicked tenants. This alteration allows the issue of repeated violence against the owner's messengers to be introduced, violence culminating in the murder of the owner's "beloved [ἀγαπητός] son" (i.e., the messiah).[70] According to Levenson, this description of the son as "beloved" introduces a third scriptural source, the Akedah, the interpretative result being what he calls a "Joseph christology . . . a pattern in which the emphasis lies on the malignancy of the slayers rather than on the pious intentions of the father who gave up his beloved son [as with Isaac]."[71] In other words, the son in the parable is like Isaac in that he is an iteration of the pattern of endangered beloved sons, the scriptural archetype of which is Isaac. But the son is even more similar to Joseph, another beloved son in peril, because those who endanger him are wicked *unlike* Abraham. If Levenson's reading is correct, this "Joseph christology" further illuminates the integration of Ps 118:22–23—"The stone that the builders rejected has become the cornerstone; this was the Lord's doing, and it is marvelous in our eyes"—and resolves the "tension" that Joel Marcus detects between the apparent positivity of the psalm and pessimism of the parable.[72] Just as those who endangered Joseph unwittingly furthered God's purposes, so also those who would kill "the beloved son," who would reject "the stone," the messiah, ultimately further "the Lord's doing." Levenson's admittedly "allegorical" reading of the parable may be subject to criticism. At the very least, though, it highlights the parable's complex and integrative appropriation of scriptural sources, a mode of messianic interpretation evident across the literature of the New Testament and elsewhere in early Judaism.

Conclusion

When ancient authors penned portraits, paeans, and predictions about their messiahs, their oeuvre spoke in the diction of ancient oracles as they proliferated scriptural turns of phrase, as their situations impinged on their readings of the same Scriptures in diverse ways, and as their minds forged new connections between di-

---

70. Levenson, *Death and Resurrection*, 227–28.
71. Levenson, *Death and Resurrection*, 226. This reception of the Akedah would be an early Christian innovation. However, Levenson's broader point is that any such interpretative development would be premised on a correlation of Isaac with the paschal lamb, an association already drawn in early Judaism (see n. 54).
72. Joel Marcus, *The Way of the Lord: Christological Exegesis of the Old Testament in the Gospel of Mark* (Louisville: Westminster John Knox, 1992), 111.

vergent Scriptures coalescing in the production of new literature. Thus all ancient Jewish messiah speculation, including that witnessed to by the texts of the New Testament, may be characterized as an interpretative enterprise marked by ingenuity—a series of encounters between traditional texts and novel circumstances. The increasing recognition of this in some quarters marks a tectonic shift in the study of early Judaism and Christian origins. On the one hand, we can no longer postulate a monolithic Jewish messianic ideology only to spar over whether that ideology is reflected in early Christian writings. For there is no "messianic idea," only multiple messianologies. And on the other hand, we can no longer dismiss ancient Jewish messianism as nothing but a scholarly construct ill-suited to the evidence only to frame early Christology as sui generis vis-à-vis the Jewish milieu in which the Jesus movement began. The coherence of ancient messianism consists in its mode of discourse, which is consistently interpretative.

To study, then, the messianic interpretation of Scripture in the New Testament is first to examine a profound way in which early Jesus followers remained in dialogue with other Jews and second to discover the remarkable phenomenon of the inclusion of gentiles in that otherwise intra-Jewish dialogue. It is this latter historical phenomenon alongside belief in the resurrection of Jesus of Nazareth that constitute perhaps the two most consequential *nova* of circumstance that refracted the Scriptures of Israel in the early Christian imagination. If so, then exploration of the uses of those Scriptures in the New Testament should eschew any notion that early Christian interpretation ran in straight lines toward exegetical inevitabilities, and instead it should foster curiosity for discovering how scriptural tradition was cherished even in the face of such change. The early Jesus movement, like the other Judaism(s) of its day, contended ingeniously with the space between text and history, always finding in Israel's Scriptures vitality enough for a new moment.

Bibliography

Bauckham, Richard. "James, 1 and 2 Peter, Jude." Pages 303–17 in *It Is Written: Scripture Citing Scripture*. Edited by D. A. Carson and H. G. M. Williamson. Cambridge: Cambridge University Press, 1988.

Black, Matthew. "The Christological Use of the Old Testament in the New Testament." *NTS* 18, no. 1 (1971): 1–14.

Chibici-Revneanu, Nicole. "Ein himmlischer Stehplatz: Die Haltung Jesu in der Stephanusvision (Apg 7.55–56) und ihre Bedeutung." *NTS* 53, no. 4 (2007): 459–88.

Collins, Adela Yarbro, and John J. Collins. *King and Messiah as Son of God: Divine,*

Human, and Angelic Messianic Figures in Biblical and Related Literature. Grand Rapids: Eerdmans, 2008.

Collins, John J. "Messiahs in Context: Method in the Study of Messianism in the Dead Sea Scrolls." Pages 213–30 in *Methods of Investigation of the Dead Sea Scrolls and the Khirbet Qumran Site: Present Realities and Future Prospects*. Edited by Michael O. Wise, Norman Golb, John J. Collins, and Dennis Pardee. New York: New York Academy of Sciences, 1994.

———. *The Scepter and the Star: Messianism in Light of the Dead Sea Scrolls*. 2nd ed. Grand Rapids: Eerdmans, 2010.

Dahl, Nils A. "Sources of Christological Language." Pages 113–36 in *Jesus the Christ: The Historical Origins of Christological Debate*. Edited by Donald H. Juel. Minneapolis: Fortress, 1991.

Danby, Herbert. *The Mishnah: Translated from the Hebrew, with Introduction and Brief Explanatory Notes*. Oxford: Oxford University Press, 1933.

Duling, Dennis C. "The Promises to David and Their Entrance into Christianity—Nailing Down a Likely Hypothesis." *NTS* 20, no. 1 (1973): 55–77.

Epstein, Isibore, ed. *Hebrew-English Edition of the Babylonian Talmud*. 30 vols. London: Soncino, 1960–1990.

Fitzmyer, Joseph A. *The One Who Is to Come*. Grand Rapids: Eerdmans, 2007.

———. *Romans: A New Translation with Introduction and Commentary*. AB 33. New York: Doubleday, 1993.

Green, William Scott. "Introduction: Messiah in Judaism: Rethinking the Question." Pages 1–14 in *Judaisms and Their Messiahs at the Turn of the Christian Era*. Edited by Jacob Neusner, William Scott Green, and Ernest S. Frerichs. Cambridge: Cambridge University Press, 1987.

Grypeou, Emmanouela, and Helen Spurling. *The Book of Genesis in Late Antiquity: Encounters between Jewish and Christian Exegesis*. JCPS 24. Leiden: Brill, 2013.

Hay, David M. *Glory at the Right Hand: Psalm 110 in Early Christianity*. SBLMS 18. Nashville: Abingdon, 1973.

Hengel, Martin. *Studies in Early Christology*. Edinburgh: T&T Clark, 1995.

Hewitt, J. Thomas, "Ancient Messiah Discourse and Paul's Expression ἄχρις οὗ ἔλθῃ τὸ σπέρμα in Galatians 3.19." *NTS* 65, no. 3 (2019): 398–411

———. *Messiah and Scripture: Paul's "in Christ" Idiom in Its Ancient Jewish Context*. WUNT 2/522. Tübingen: Mohr Siebeck, 2020.

Horbury, William. *Jewish Messianism and the Cult of Christ*. London: SCM, 1998.

Hurtado, Larry, and Paul L. Owen, eds. *'Who Is This Son of Man?' The Latest Scholarship on a Puzzling Expression of the Historical Jesus*. LNTS 390. London: T&T Clark, 2011.

Jonge, Marinus de. "The Use of the Word 'Anointed' in the Time of Jesus." *NovT* 8, no. 2/4 (1966): 132–48.

Juel, Donald. *Messianic Exegesis: Christological Interpretation of the Old Testament in Early Christianity*. Philadelphia: Fortress, 1988.

Klausner, Joseph. *The Messianic Idea in Israel from Its Beginning to the Completion of the Mishnah*. Translated by W. F. Stinespring. New York: Macmillan, 1955.

Klijn, A. F. J. "2 (Syriac Apocalypse of) Baruch (Early Second Century A.D.)." *OTP* 1:615–52.

Levenson, Jon D. *The Death and Resurrection of the Beloved Son: The Transformation of Child Sacrifice in Judaism and Christianity*. New Haven: Yale University Press, 1993.

Levey, Samson H. *The Messiah: An Aramaic Interpretation; The Messianic Exegesis of the Targum*. HUCM 2. Cincinnati: Hebrew Union College Press, 1974.

Lincicum, David. *Paul and the Early Jewish Encounter with Deuteronomy*. WUNT 2/284. Tübingen: Mohr Siebeck, 2010.

Marcus, Joel. *The Way of the Lord: Christological Exegesis of the Old Testament in the Gospel of Mark*. Louisville: Westminster John Knox, 1992.

Metzger, Bruce M. "The Fourth Book of Ezra (Late First Century A.D.)." *OTP* 1:517–60.

Moffitt, David M. *Atonement and the Logic of Resurrection in the Epistle to the Hebrews*. NovTSup 141. Leiden: Brill, 2011.

Mowinckel, Sigmund. *He That Cometh: The Messiah Concept in the Old Testament and Later Judaism*. Translated by G. W. Anderson. Grand Rapids: Eerdmans, 2005.

Neusner, Jacob. Preface to *Judaisms and Their Messiahs at the Turn of the Christian Era*. Edited by Jacob Neusner, William Scott Green, and Ernest S. Frerichs. Cambridge: Cambridge University Press, 1987.

Neusner, Jacob, William S. Green, and Ernest Frerichs, eds. *Judaisms and Their Messiahs at the Turn of the Christian Era*. Cambridge: Cambridge University Press, 1987.

Nickelsburg, George W. E., and James C. VanderKam. *1 Enoch: The Hermeneia Translation*. Minneapolis: Fortress, 2012.

Nolland, John. "The Four (Five) Women and Other Annotations in Matthew's Genealogy." *NTS* 43, no. 4 (1997): 527–39.

Novenson, Matthew V. *Christ among the Messiahs: Christ Language in Paul and Messiah Language in Ancient Judaism*. Oxford: Oxford University Press, 2012.

———. *The Grammar of Messianism: An Ancient Jewish Political Idiom and Its Users*. Oxford: Oxford University Press, 2017.

Oegema, Gerbern S. *The Anointed and His People: Messianic Expectations from the Maccabees to Bar Kochba*. JSPSup 27. Sheffield: Sheffield Academic, 1998.

Rahlfs, Alfred, ed. *Psalmi cum Odis*. 3rd ed. SVTG 26. Göttingen: Vandenhoeck & Ruprecht, 1979.

Roberts, J. J. M. "The Old Testament's Contribution to Messianic Expectations." Pages 39–51 in *The Messiah: Developments in Earliest Judaism and Christianity*. Edited by James H. Charlesworth. Minneapolis: Fortress, 1992.

Schäfer, Peter. "Diversity and Interaction: Messiahs in Early Judaism." Pages 15–35 in *Toward the Millennium: Messianic Expectations from the Bible to Waco*. Edited by Peter Schäfer and Mark Cohen. SHR 77. Leiden: Brill, 1998.

Scholem, Gershom. "Toward an Understanding of the Messianic Idea in Judaism." Pages 1–36 in *The Messianic Idea in Judaism and Other Essays on Jewish Spirituality*. New York: Shocken, 1971.

Stone, Michael E. "The Concept of the Messiah in IV Ezra." Pages 295–312 in *Religions in Antiquity: Essays in Memory of Erwin Ramsdell Goodenough*. Edited by Jacob Neusner. SHR 14. Leiden: Brill, 1968.

———. *Fourth Ezra: A Commentary on the Book of Fourth Ezra*. Hermeneia. Minneapolis: Fortress, 1990.

Strauss, Mark L. *The Davidic Messiah in Luke-Acts: The Promise and Its Fulfillment in Lukan Christology*. JSNTSup 110. Sheffield: Sheffield Academic, 1995.

Stuckenbruck, Loren T. "Messianic Ideas in the Apocalyptic and Related Literature of Early Judaism." Pages 90–113 in *The Messiah in the Old and New Testaments*. Edited by Stanley E. Porter. McMaster New Testament Studies. Grand Rapids: Eerdmans, 2007.

———. "'One Like a Son of Man as the Ancient of Days' in the Old Greek Recension of Daniel 7,13: Scribal Error or Theological Translation?" *ZNW* 86, no. 3–4 (1995): 268–76.

Wagner, J. Ross. *Heralds of the Good News: Isaiah and Paul "In Concert" in the Letter to the Romans*. NovTSup 101. Leiden: Brill, 2002.

Wilcox, Max. "The Promise of the 'Seed' in the New Testament and the Targumim." Pages 275–93 in *New Testament Text and Language: A Sheffield Reader*. Edited by Stanley E. Porter and Craig A. Evans. BibSem 44. Sheffield: Sheffield Academic, 1997.

Wright, R. B. "Psalms of Solomon (First Century B.C.)." *OTP* 2:639–70.

27

Holy Spirit

JOHN R. LEVISON

The Jewish Scriptures contain 389 references (378 in Hebrew, 11 in Aramaic) to the word רוּחַ, which is variously translated in English as "spirit," "Spirit," "breath," or "wind." Nonbiblical manuscripts from the Judean desert—the Dead Sea Scrolls—contain nearly 600 references to the word רוּחַ. The first-century Jewish philosopher Philo of Alexandria refers over 150 times to πνεῦμα. And the New Testament contains 379 references to the word πνεῦμα.[1] Add to these the writings in the Apocrypha, pseudepigrapha, and Josephus, and the numbers swell further. Simply by the numbers, therefore, any effort to address the topic of the holy spirit is a formidable undertaking.[2] Still, if approached selectively and cautiously, it is possible to say something of significance. In this chapter, we will look at five themes as they are interpreted in portions of Israel's Scriptures, Second Temple Jewish literature, and the New Testament: ecstasy, wisdom, purification, outpouring, and exodus. Each theme illuminates different dimensions of the relationship between Jewish Scripture, select literature of Second Temple Judaism, and the New Testament.

---

1. Tabulations are from Accordance software.

2. While I retain capitalization in quotations, I do not otherwise capitalize "spirit" throughout this chapter because it is too difficult to distinguish in English between spirit, Spirit, wind, and breath and because often the word רוּחַ communicates a combination of these, such as Spirit-breath or wind-Spirit. It is best, therefore, to be consistent in English. Further, capitalization is often done on the basis of theological rationales, such as whether this is the divine Spirit versus the human spirit. This is, in my opinion, a false dichotomy. For further discussion, see Levison, *Filled with the Spirit* (Grand Rapids: Eerdmans, 2009), 3–13; Levison, *A Boundless God: The Spirit according to the Old Testament* (Grand Rapids: Baker Academic, 2020), 15–32.

Holy Spirit

Spirit and Ecstasy

A cursory reading of the apostle Paul's letters to the Corinthians offers a clear impression: many participants of this church were in the throes of ecstasy.[3] He repeatedly addresses the problem—it is indeed a *problem* within the Corinthian spiritual hierarchy—of glossolalia (1 Cor 12–14). He warns that outsiders who observe worship in a community taken with glossolalia will think the worshipers out of their minds (οὐκ ἐροῦσιν ὅτι μαίνεσθε in 1 Cor 14:23). And he cautions that worship should be done in order, with tongues speakers offering their garbled words one by one with an interpreter present (1 Cor 14:27). The elevation of allegedly inspired ecstasy at Corinth, we will see, underscores the indispensability of Second Temple literature for understanding early Christian claims to an experience of the holy spirit.

The prominence of an ecstatic experience of the spirit has only a slim foothold in the Jewish Scriptures, in which inspiration, particularly prophetic inspiration, tends to be associated not with an ecstatic impulse but with a compelling message intended to sway Israel toward Torah. During the postexilic era, writers looked back to a swath of inspired prophets, which Israel had ignored. Ezra prayed, "Many years you were patient with them, and warned them by your spirit through your prophets; yet they would not listen" (Neh 9:30).[4] Zechariah said, "They made their hearts adamant in order not to hear the law and the words that the Lord of hosts had sent by his spirit through the former prophets" (Zech 7:12). This sweeping retrospect is apparent as well in the Dead Sea Scrolls, such as in 1QS VIII, 16, which traces the study of Torah to "what the prophets have revealed by His holy spirit."[5] In the book of Acts, Stephen followed suit in a speech prior to martyrdom. "You stiff-necked people, uncircumcised in heart and ears," he cried, "you are forever opposing the Holy Spirit, just as your ancestors used to do. Which of the prophets did your ancestors not persecute?" (Acts 7:51–52; see also 2 Pet 1:20–21). Inspiration, in these overviews, is about a comprehensible message, to which, in their estimation, Israel failed to respond.

---

3. For a definition of ecstasy in the New Testament, see Levison, *Inspired: The Holy Spirit and the Mind of Faith* (Grand Rapids: Eerdmans, 2013), 9–11; also Levison, "Ecstasy, New Testament," in *The Encyclopedia of the Bible and Its Reception*, ed. H.-J. Klauck et al. (Berlin: de Gruyter, 2013), 7:338–40.

4. Unless otherwise specified, translations of Scripture, including the Apocrypha, are from the NRSV, occasionally with alterations. Citations of Philo of Alexandria and Josephus are from Loeb Classical Library.

5. Except for Hodayot, translations of the Dead Sea Scrolls are from Michael O. Wise, Martin Abegg, and Edward Cook, *The Dead Sea Scrolls: A New Translation*, rev. ed. (New York: HarperCollins, 2005).

There is relatively little of the ecstatic even in Israel's prophetic corpus.[6] In the mid-eighth century BCE, Hosea quoted his opponents, who said, "the prophet is a fool, the man of the Spirit is mad" (Hos 9:7). Why they thought prophets were mad is not clear; this may have had less to do with prophetic frenzy than with Hosea and Amos's tendency, during the affluent Omride dynasty, to confront their contemporaries with social critique and impending destruction. Ezekiel may be an exception when it comes to an ecstatic experience of the spirit. Ezekiel laid claim to multiple experiences of the spirit; at one point, he recalled, "the spirit lifted me up" (Ezek 3:12, 14); at another, "the spirit of the LORD fell upon me" (Ezek 11:5).

This sort of ecstasy seems to be associated with bands of prophets, such as the prophets of Baal, who inflicted wounds on themselves in their confrontation with Elijah (1 Kgs 18:28). Approached by a roving band of prophets, Saul, who would be king, fell into some sort of a prophetic trance (1 Sam 10:6-11). And, in the rural regions of the south during the late eighth century BCE, the prophet Micah rejected the visions and revelations of prophetic clans mustered in support of the king and claimed instead to be filled "with power, with the spirit of the LORD, and with justice and might" (Mic 3:1-8).[7] Those prophets who left a literary legacy, apart from Ezekiel, seem to have been less enamored of ecstasy than the bands, Israelite or otherwise, that circulated in Palestine.

This scenario changed dramatically during the Second Temple period, with the advent of Hellenistic culture—the Delphic priestess, sibyls, the disembodied flight of the soul—and its appreciation for ecstasy. Philo of Alexandria drank deep of ecstasy. In his interpretation of ἔκστασις in Gen 15:12 LXX, he wrote, "This is what regularly befalls the fellowship of the prophets. The mind is evicted at the arrival of the divine Spirit, but when that departs the mind returns to its tenancy" (*Her.* 265).[8] The phenomenon of prophecy, in the writings of Philo, is drenched in the language of ecstasy. This marks a departure from Israel's Scriptures.

Philo discovered the quintessence of ecstasy in the story of Balaam, in which the angel predicts: "I shall prompt the needful words without your mind's consent, and direct your organs of speech as justice and convenience require. I shall guide the reins of speech, and, though you understand it not, employ your tongue for each prophetic utterance" (*Mos.* 1.274; see Num 22:35). This

---

6. See Johannes Lindblom, *Prophecy in Ancient Israel* (Oxford: Blackwell, 1962).
7. For detailed discussion, see Levison, *Filled with the Spirit*, 41-47.
8. Also *Spec.* 1.65; 4.49; QG 3.9. See Levison, "Philo's Personal Experience and the Persistence of Prophecy," in *Prophets, Prophecy, and Prophetic Texts in Second Temple Judaism*, ed. Michael H. Floyd and Robert D. Haak, LHBOTS 427 (London: T&T Clark, 2006), 194-209; Levison, "Inspiration and the Divine Spirit in the Writings of Philo Judaeus," *JSJ* 26, no. 3 (1995): 271-323.

prediction is fulfilled when Balaam "advanced outside, and straightway became possessed, and there fell upon him the truly prophetic spirit which banished utterly from his soul his art of wizardry" (*Mos.* 1.277). Josephus, too, imported a similar model of inspiration in his iteration of the Balaam story when an angel explains to Balak, who had summoned Balaam, "that spirit gives utterance to such language and words as it will, whereof we are all unconscious" (*Ant.* 4.119). This form of inspiration was a product of the Greco-Roman era; it resembles a view held by Ammonius in Plutarch's *On the Defection of Oracles*, in which "the god himself after the manner of ventriloquists . . . enters into the bodies of his prophets and prompts their utterances, employing their mouths and voices as instruments" (414E).[9]

Even the author of the Palestinian composition Liber Antiquitatum Biblicarum succumbed to the allure of ecstasy. The spirit, not surprisingly, inspires prophecy: Miriam has a dream in which the birth of Moses is predicted (LAB 9:10); Deborah predicts Sisera's demise by the inspiration of the spirit (31:9); an abbreviated account of Saul's pursuit of David contains this detail: "And (a) spirit abided in Saul, and he prophesied" (LAB 62:2). Most startling of all, to the military feats of the first judge, Othniel (Judg 3:9–10), identified in Liber Antiquitatum Biblicarum as Kenaz, are added a prophetic experience (LAB 28:6): "when they had sat down, a holy spirit came upon Kenaz . . . and he began to prophesy." Afterward, Kenaz could not recall what he had said—a clear sign of ecstasy in the Greco-Roman world.[10]

This swell of ecstasy during the Second Temple Jewish era may serve to explain why early Christians, despite their indebtedness to the Jewish Scriptures, could place such an emphasis upon the ecstatic impulse. Absent the literature of Second Temple Judaism, it would not be possible fully to understand this shift from comprehensibility to ecstasy.

While early Christians appear to have succumbed to the allure of ecstasy, New Testament authors do not. The apostle Paul responds to the Corinthian overvaluation of glossolalia with several correctives. First, in a list of spiritual gifts, Paul refers first to wisdom and knowledge and last to glossolalia and their interpretation (1 Cor 12:4–11). Second, Paul challenges the Corinthians' priorities by

---

9. For detailed discussion, see Levison, "The Debut of the Divine Spirit in Josephus' *Antiquities*," *HTR* 87 (1994): 123–38; Levison, "The Prophetic Spirit as an Angel according to Philo," *HTR* 88, no. 2 (1995): 189–207.

10. E.g., Plato, *Apol.* 22C; *Meno* 99C; Aelius Aristides, *In Defense of Oratory* 43; Pseudo-Justin, *Cohortatio ad Graecos* 37.2–3; John Cassian, *Collationes* 12. Further details can be found in Levison, "Prophetic Inspiration in Pseudo-Philo's *Liber Antiquitatum Biblicarum*," *JQR* 85, no. 3/4 (1995): 297–329. Translations of Liber Antiquitatum Biblicarum are from D. J. Harrington, "Pseudo-Philo," *OTP* 2:297–377.

advising them to pursue a comprehensible form of prophetic inspiration rather than tongues precisely because prophecy edifies the church (1 Cor 14:2–6). Third, he demands that the gift of glossolalia be accompanied by the gift of interpretation (14:13–19). Fourth, in order to draw the Corinthians to the clear priority that everything should be done "for building up" the community (14:26), Paul offers practical advice: every gift in worship should be exercised one at a time, while others remain silent (14:26–33). Finally, based upon his own experience, Paul suggests that the clearest arena for the exercise of glossolalia is private, personal prayer (14:18–20). All of these exhortations reflect a tendency to dampen the enthusiastic spirit, to align the Corinthian experience of the spirit less with the proclivities of latter-day Balaams and more with the impulse of Israel's literary prophets, as they came to be understood in retrospect during the Persian, Greek, and Roman eras.

Luke, in the book of Acts, also evinces a reluctance to endorse an experience of the spirit that is principally ecstatic. At three junctures in the book of Acts—the beginning of the church (Acts 2:4), the inclusion of gentiles (10:44–46), and the completion of John the Baptist's promise of baptism with the Holy Spirit (19:6)—Luke tamps down the possibility that speaking in tongues is an ecstatic experience—or at least a *wholly* ecstatic experience.

Acts 2 conveys an experience in which the early believers, on the day of Pentecost, "were filled with the Holy Spirit and began to speak in other tongues" (Acts 2:4). With the word "other" the miracle of Pentecost becomes one of comprehension; Jews who had gathered from around the world could understand the disciples' recitation of God's powerful acts in their own dialects (2:5–7). Luke affirms this through narrative—"each one heard them speaking in the native language of each" (2:6)—and dialogue, "And how is it that we hear, each of us, in our own native language? . . . in our own languages we hear them speaking about God's deeds of power" (2:8, 11). This, according to the sermon of Peter, is not a late-in-time event, a novelty, an innovation. It is the fulfillment of the grand prophecy of Joel, which would transform everyone, including slaves, both male and female, into prophets capable of speaking the praiseworthy acts of God (Acts 2:17–21; see 2:11).

When, in the second instance, the holy spirit came upon Cornelius and his gentile friends, Peter and his coterie heard them "speaking in tongues and praising God." The association of speaking in tongues with praise draws readers back to speaking in *other* tongues in Acts 2. The verb "praise" (μεγαλύνειν) in Acts 10:46 is related to the noun "praiseworthy acts" (τὰ μεγαλεῖα) in Acts 2:11. This literary parallel suggests that this second instance of speaking in (other) tongues, as at Pentecost, consists of a litany of praise in foreign languages that was comprehensible to bystanders. Peter and his Jewish coterie of believers certainly saw this, in the book of Acts, as an experience similar to their own speaking in other tongues (11:17).

A similar scenario characterizes the third instance of speaking in (other) tongues, which features a band of "disciples" who had not heard of the holy spirit; when Paul laid his hands upon them, "the Holy Spirit came upon them, and they spoke in tongues and prophesied." This, too, avoids the onslaught of ecstasy because prophesying in Acts, like praise, is invariably comprehensible. Prophets punctuated the history of the early church with occasional but certain clarity about the future. For example, the prophet Agabus correctly predicted a famine (Acts 11:27–28). Judas and Silas, themselves prophets, were sent to Antioch with a letter to interpret the Jerusalem Council's decision "by word of mouth." When they arrived in Antioch, they encouraged and strengthened the believers with intelligible words (15:22, 27, 32).

The effort both Paul and Luke make to curtail the ecstatic impulse suggests that ecstasy was alive and well in the early church. This impulse did not rise readily from the Jewish Scriptures, but it easily could have arisen from the world of Second Temple Judaism if the writings of Philo, Josephus, and the Liber Antiquitatum Biblicarum offer a reliable window into that world. The appreciation for ecstasy expressed by early Christians, to which Paul and Luke respond, in fact, would be more difficult to explain without an awareness of the literature of Second Temple Judaism. These authors imported into their revisions of Scripture a fresh impulse toward ecstasy. Paul and Luke appear, in contrast, to have tamped down this impulse, though their efforts reveal that there existed in the early church a penchant for ecstasy that would persist, not only within second-century Montanism, but in enthusiastic movements throughout the duration of the Christian church.

Spirit and Wisdom

Early in his first extant letter to the Corinthians—long before he broaches the topic of ecstasy in worship later in the letter—Paul draws an essential connection between spirit and wisdom. He begins with a reminiscence: "When I came to you, brothers and sisters . . . I came to you in weakness and in fear and in much trembling. My speech and my proclamation were not with plausible words of wisdom, but with a demonstration of the Spirit and of power, so that your faith might rest not on human wisdom but on the power of God" (1 Cor 2:1–5). The pairing of spirit and power (πνεύματος καὶ δυνάμεως) in this text can evoke, of course, signs and wonders, as in Rom 15:19, where Paul describes the obedience of the nations that have been won "by the power of signs and wonders, by the power of the Spirit of God." Yet something more is at play in 1 Corinthians, where the spirit inspires the *content* of Paul's preaching: "For I decided to know nothing among you except Jesus Christ, and him crucified" (1 Cor 2:2). The content of Paul's message, the cross, is the wisdom that the rulers of this age cannot grasp. The cross is what the spirit, which "comprehends what is truly God's," transforms into a powerful message (2:8–11).

The presence of inspired wisdom constituted a longstanding tradition in Israelite and Second Temple Jewish literature. As early as the story of Joseph, who interprets a cryptic dream, an Egyptian pharaoh asks the question, "Can we find anyone else like this—one in whom is the spirit of God?" (Gen 41:38). Pharaoh, as rulers are wont to do, answers his own question: "Since God is making known all of this to you, there is no one discerning and wise like you" (41:39). When pharaoh affirms both the presence of the spirit in Joseph and his remarkable wisdom, he draws the first indisputable connection between the spirit and wisdom in Israel's Scriptures.

This association peppers Israelite literature. Joshua is full of a spirit of wisdom because Moses laid his hands upon him (Deut 34:9). In Isaiah's imagination, the spirit that rests on an inspired ruler is, first and foremost, a spirit of wisdom and understanding (Isa 11:2). In wisdom literature, of course, the association of the spirit with wisdom flourishes. An embittered Job claims, "as long as my breath is in me and the spirit of God is in my nostrils, my lips will not speak falsehood, and my tongue will not utter deceit . . . until I die I will not put away my integrity from me" (Job 27:2–5). The subtle implication of Job's claim, that the spirit of God inspires wisdom, blooms in young Elihu's claim to possess wisdom: "I am young in years, and you are aged. . . . But truly it is the spirit in a mortal, the breath of the Almighty that makes for understanding. It is not the old that are wise, nor the aged that understand what is right" (Job 32:6–9). The connection between the spirit and wisdom persisted well into the Persian era, in the narrative of the construction of the tabernacle (Exod 25:1–31:11 and 35:4–33), in which God tells Moses, "And you shall speak to all the wise of heart whom I have filled with a spirit of wisdom [רוּחַ חָכְמָה], and they will make Aaron's vestments" (Exod 28:3; my translation). The skilled, the wise-of-heart, are now to be filled to the brim with the spirit of wisdom—and their inspired leaders, Bezalel and Oholiab, even more so (Exod 31:1–6; 35:30–36:3).

The latest exemplar of this association in Israel's Scriptures is a product of the Maccabean era—and consequently a representative of Second Temple Judaism. Set in the context of exile, the story of Daniel spans three generations. During the second, Nebuchadnezzar's daughter-in-law recalls, "There is a man in your kingdom who is endowed with a spirit of the holy gods. In the days of your father he was found to have enlightenment, understanding, and wisdom like the wisdom of the gods." She recalls that "an excellent spirit, knowledge, and understanding to interpret dreams, explain riddles, and solve problems were found in this Daniel" (Dan 5:11–12). Her husband, Nebuchadnezzar's son, Belshazzar, is also aware of Daniel's *spirit of God* (5:14) and *excellent wisdom*. In this story, a conspicuous verbal correspondence between spirit and wisdom surges to the surface:

רוּחַ יַתִּירָה ("excellent spirit"; 5:12)
וְחָכְמָה יַתִּירָה ("excellent wisdom"; 5:14)

The association of the spirit with wisdom in the book of Daniel is both a galvanization of Israelite thought and an expression of Second Temple Jewish thought because it both takes the reader back to the story of Joseph and underscores through repetition the pivotal theme of the relationship between wisdom and spirit that was latent in the ancient story of Joseph. It functions as a key shift, therefore, from an ancient Israelite story to its iteration in Second Temple Judaism.

The accentuation of this connection is hardly surprising in the context of Second Temple Judaism since, a few decades earlier, the Jerusalem scribe and headmaster of sorts Ben Sira, in a thinly veiled autobiographical description, laid claim to a spirit of wisdom: "he will be filled with the spirit of understanding/ he will pour forth words of wisdom of his own. . . . He will show the wisdom of what he has learned" (Sir 39:6, 8). *How* exactly one is filled with this spirit Ben Sira does not say. He does repudiate visions and claims to revelation, and he believes rather that serious study and life experiences alone are legitimate sources of wisdom (39:1–5). This portrait of the scribe, therefore, shares affinities with the story of Daniel and the artisans who constructed the tabernacle, as well as Job and Elihu; all champion the conviction that the spirit is a reservoir of wisdom.

The devotees at Qumran also believed that they possessed inspired wisdom. One hymn reads, "And I, the Instructor, I know you, my God, by the spirit that you have placed in me. Faithfully have I heeded your wondrous secret counsel. By your holy spirit you have [o]pened up knowledge within me through the mystery of your wisdom and the fountainhead of [your] power" (1QH^a XX, 14–16).[11] This hymn evokes powerful images of inspired wisdom. The words, "your holy spirit," are sandwiched between references to "your wondrous secret counsel" and "the mystery of your wisdom."

Philo of Alexandria's commentaries on Torah drip with learning, which he attributes to an experience of being wafted on the winds of knowledge during

---

11. Translations of the hymns are from Eileen Schuller and Carol Newsom, *The Hodayot (Thanksgiving Psalms): A Study Edition of 1QH^a*, EJL 36 (Atlanta: Society of Biblical Literature, 2012).

much-needed breaks from civic duties (*Spec.* 3.1–6). Philo's writings fuse no less than two disparate modes of inspiration in a single experience of sober intoxication: prophetic ecstasy, in which the mind is replaced by the spirit (e.g., *Mos.* 1.274), and experiences in which the spirit instructs an alert mind, such as in *Gig.* 23, where Philo defines "spirit of God," at least in part, as "the pure knowledge in which every wise man naturally shares" (*Gig.* 23). Both modes of inspiration, claims Philo, happen to him in his effort to interpret Torah: ecstasy in *Cher.* 27–29 and alert learning from the spirit in *Somn.* 2.252. Along the same vein, Moses differs from the prophetic race, with its purely ecstatic experience, in his ability to be inspired without losing mental control. Like Philo, Moses experiences sober intoxication: a mind which, alert, experiences "that divine possession in virtue of which he is chiefly and in the strict sense considered a prophet" (*Mos.* 2.191).

The author of the Wisdom of Solomon shares with Philo a penchant for wisdom understood through the lens of Greco-Roman philosophies, particularly Stoicism. The author retains the traditional perspective on the spirit as a gift: "I prayed ... and the spirit of wisdom came to me" (Wis 7:7); and "who has learned your counsel, unless you ... sent your holy spirit from on high" (Wis 9:17). Yet this gift is Stoic in character: "the spirit of the Lord has filled the world, and that which holds all things together knows what is said" (Wis 1:7–8). In Stoicism, πνεῦμα is the cohesive force of the universe. Alexander of Aphrodisias, for example, summarizing the view of renowned Stoic thinker, Chrysippus, explains that πνεῦμα pervades the cosmos and makes it coherent (*On Mixture* 216.14–17).

This association between spirit and wisdom, which reached many geographically far-flung corners of Second Temple Judaism, persisted in early Christianity, though more obliquely than in many writings of the Second Temple period. A story tucked into the earliest chapters of Luke's gospel attests to its perseverance (Luke 2:25–35). Joseph and Mary, while bringing Jesus to the temple for his dedication, are met by an old man, who, Luke tells his readers, is inspired by the spirit: the spirit rests on him; the spirit reveals to him; the spirit guides him into the temple. Simeon is genuinely inspired. As he gathers the baby Jesus in his arms, Simeon gathers up words he has long since memorized. His simple prayer is drenched in the language of Isaiah 40–55: "a light for revelation to the nations" (Isa 42:6 and 49:6) and "glory to your people Israel" (46:13). Simeon, inconspicuous to the powers that be, is nonetheless deeply inspired and learned—both.

In the book of Acts, deacons selected to take care of widows are people of good standing "full of the Spirit and of wisdom." One of them, Stephen, debated with his contemporaries, who, Luke tells Theophilus, "could not withstand the wisdom and the Spirit with which he spoke" (6:10). In those heady, if precarious, early days, Peter stood up in the Jewish council and, "filled with the Holy Spirit," delivered a compelling speech, grounded in Ps 118:22, that caused his hearers to be amazed at these uneducated companions of Jesus (Acts 4:8–12). Wisdom and spirit, learning and inspiration, are here joined at the hip.

We have seen already that Paul too seems to embrace this association, if indirectly, when he claims that his speech and proclamation "were not with plausible words of wisdom, but with a demonstration of the Spirit and of power" (1 Cor 2:4). Paul's wisdom is not the wisdom of the world but the wisdom of the cross (1:17). To this end, he cites an amalgamation of Isa 64:3; 52:15; and 65:16 to make the point that what God has prepared for those who love him is unknown to human eyes and hearts. He caps this off with a clear reference to the spirit: "these things God has revealed to us through the Spirit; for the Spirit searches everything, even the depths of God" (1 Cor 2:9–10; see also Eph 1:17).

The Fourth Gospel, too, evinces this association. On his last evening with them, Jesus offers his students, his disciples, one final, protracted stint of teaching. In the course of this stretch, Jesus delivers four distinctive blocks of teaching on the spirit (John 14:16; 14:26; 16:7–11; 16:13–15). He promises the presence of the spirit of truth, another paraclete, whose vocation will mirror what Jesus's own vocation has been throughout the Fourth Gospel—to *teach*: "But the paraclete, the Holy Spirit, whom the Father will send in my name, will teach you everything" (John 14:26). In a final saying about the spirit, Jesus promises that "when the Spirit of truth comes, it will guide you into [in] all the truth" (16:13).[12] Such promises are reminiscent of the psalmists' prayers, "Teach me to do your will, for you are my God. Let your good spirit lead me on a level path" (Ps 143:10), and "Lead me in your truth, and teach me, for you are the God of my salvation" (Ps 25:5).

We see in the association of spirit and wisdom another model that is slightly different from the model represented by the association of spirit and ecstasy. With respect to ecstasy, Second Temple Jewish authors were instrumental in *introducing* the ecstatic dimension, which Christians adopted as well, into their latter-day interpretations of Scripture. The element of inspired wisdom, in contrast, was already present in Jewish Scripture. When Christians adopted this association, they did so both in accordance with the Jewish Scriptures and in harmony with Second Temple Judaism.

Further, we know that Paul and Luke attempted to tamp down the ecstatic impulse; with respect to wisdom, New Testament authors attempted instead to fan the flames of inspired wisdom. They hoped, in short, to curtail ecstasy but

---

12. Textual uncertainty makes it difficult to determine whether the spirit, in the original text, is said to lead "in" or "into" truth. Of the major codices, Alexandrinus and Vaticanus read "into," while Sinaiticus and Bezae read "in."

to cultivate wisdom. To put this yet another way: the predilections of New Testament writers vis-à-vis inspired ecstasy lay in *contradistinction* to other authors of the Second Temple period, while their partiality toward inspired wisdom lay in *continuity* with other Second Temple authors. Second Temple literature, then, allows us to discern how New Testament writers both resisted their Second Temple environment with respect to allegedly inspired ecstasy and embraced it with respect to inspired wisdom and knowledge.

Spirit and Purification

In his letter to the Thessalonians, the apostle Paul concludes an exhortation to sexual sanctification with these words: "Therefore whoever rejects this rejects not human authority but God, who also gives his Holy Spirit to you" (1 Thess 4:1–8, esp. 8). This, like the association between spirit and wisdom, reflects Paul's long-standing Israelite and early Jewish heritage.

The association of the spirit with purification arises in two different corners of Israel's Scriptures. In Ps 51, the poet prays:

> Create in me a clean heart, O God,
> and put a new and right spirit within me.
> Do not cast me away from your presence,
> and do not take your holy spirit from me.
> Restore to me the joy of your salvation,
> and sustain in me a willing spirit.
> (Ps 51:10–12 [51:12–14 MT])

Despite the poet's conviction that he was conceived in sin, successive pleas in this psalm point to the possibility of rehabilitation: the belief that God can teach the poet wisdom deep within (51:6 [51:8 MT]); the conviction that cleansing is still available (51:7 [51:9 MT]); and the assumption that physical healing is still possible, that crushed bones can again rejoice (51:8 [51:10 MT]). The poet holds on for dear life. Consequently, the urgent plea, "Create in me a clean heart" is a prayer for cleansing, for transformation, for instruction in wisdom rather than for a miraculous transformation that does away with the old heart altogether. The basis for this belief is that God will accept a broken spirit, a broken and contrite heart (Ps 51:16–17 [51:18–19 MT]). Therefore, God does not have to turn away God's presence or take away God's holy spirit from the beleaguered poet.

Ezekiel, too, imagines the possibility of a new heart and spirit, though not in exactly the same way as the psalmist. In three related passages representing different phases in his prophetic life, Ezekiel speaks of a new heart and spirit. In the earliest and most hopeful phase, he tells Israel to make for themselves a new heart and spirit (18:31–32); it is *their* ability, *their* responsibility. In the next phase, perhaps closer to the fall of Jerusalem in 587 BCE, he promises that God will put a new heart and spirit within Israel (11:17–20); it is no longer *their* responsibility but *God's*. In the final phase, in the wake of the destruction of Jerusalem, he adds cleansing to the mix:

> I will take you from the nations, and gather you from all the countries, and bring you into your own land. I will sprinkle clean water upon you, and you shall be clean from all your uncleannesses, and from all your idols I will cleanse you. A new heart I will give you, and a new spirit I will put within you; and I will remove from your body the heart of stone and give you a heart of flesh. I will put my spirit within you, and make you follow my statutes and be careful to observe my ordinances. Then you shall live in the land that I gave to your ancestors; and you shall be my people, and I will be your God. (Ezek 36:24–28)

The new element in this iteration of the promise of a new heart and a new spirit is the imperative of cleansing, which precedes the gift of the spirit and heart. The translation, "sprinkle," is altogether too benign to express the character of purification. This Hebrew verb, זָרַק, tends to be used of the splattering of the blood of sacrificial animals against the altar. If Israel is to have a new heart and spirit, it needs to have water not so much sprinkled upon them as splattered all over them.[13]

During the Second Temple period, purity became paramount in the Dead Sea Scrolls, where the spirit is not the result, as in Ezekiel's promise, but the *source* of purification. The hymns are particularly rich with such language: "I know that no one can be righteous apart from you, and so I entreat you with the spirit that you have placed in me that you make your kindness to your servant complete [for]ever, cleansing me by your holy spirit and drawing me nearer by your good favor" (1QH^a VIII, 29–30). In the Community Rule, as well, the spirit is associated with purity, this time during initiation into the community: "For only through the spirit pervading God's true society can there be atonement for a man's ways, all of his iniquities; thus only can he gaze upon the light of life and so be joined to His truth by His holy spirit, purified from all iniquity. Through an upright and humble attitude his sin may be covered, and by humbling himself before all God's laws his flesh can be made clean. Only thus can he really receive

---

13. For details, see Levison, *Boundless God*, 138.

the purifying waters and be purged by the cleansing flow" (1QS III, 6–9; see 1QS IX, 3–4). The spirit in this context of initiation (1QS I, 21–III, 12) is laser focused upon the purification demanded of initiates.

In Jub. 1:20–21, portions of which were also found in the Judean Desert, the figure of Moses, recalling Ps 51, intercedes for Israel, "O Lord, let your mercy be lifted up upon your people, and create for them an upright spirit.... Create a pure heart and a holy spirit for them. And do not let them be ensnared by their sin henceforth and forever." God responds in turn by recalling Ps 51 and Ezek 11:19–20: "And I shall create for them a holy spirit, and I shall purify them so that they will not turn away from following me from that day and forever. And their souls will cleave to me and to all my commandments" (Jub. 1:22–25).[14]

In light of the integral association of the spirit with purification in the Dead Sea Scrolls, it may be somewhat surprising that, in the New Testament, the spirit is only obliquely associated with purification. John the Baptist's prediction that Jesus will baptize with holy spirit and fire suggests judgment, of course, but judgment as purification, too, as in the words of Isaiah, which may have inspired the Baptist's warning: "once the Lord has washed away the filth of the daughters of Zion and cleansed the bloodstains of Jerusalem from its midst by a spirit of judgment and by a spirit of burning" (Isa 4:4; modified).[15]

The apostle Paul, despite referring frequently to πνεῦμα, generates only muted associations between the spirit and purification. Even when he writes that "the law of the Spirit of life in Christ Jesus has set you free from the law of sin and of death" (Rom 8:2), he taps principally into the exodus tradition, with its emphasis upon liberation rather than purification. Perhaps the closest Paul's letters come to this association occurs in his discussion of sex with prostitutes: "Shun fornication! Every sin that a person commits is outside the body; but the fornicator sins against the body itself. Or do you not know that your body is a temple of the Holy Spirit within you, which you have from God, and that you are not your own?" (1 Cor 6:18–19). Paul's rare but forceful exhortations to sexual purity in 1 Thess 4:8 and 1 Cor 6:18–19 may hint at the unfortunate reality that early churches did not make the association between spirit and sanctity, which was pivotal in both the Jewish Scriptures and Second Temple Jewish literature, quite so forcefully.

In a more general sense, though purification is relatively rarely attributed to the holy spirit in the New Testament, sanctification on several occasions is the province of the holy spirit. Paul functions as a priest, a servant of the gospel, so that the offering of the gentiles will be "sanctified by the Holy Spirit" (Rom 15:16).

---

14. Translations of Jubilees are from O. S. Wintermute, "Jubilees (Second Century B.C.)," *OTP* 2:35–142. See also m. Soṭah 9:15.

15. For further discussion, see Levison, *An Unconventional God: The Spirit according to Jesus* (Grand Rapids: Baker Academic, 2020), 35–39.

This is the language of ritual consecration—though perhaps also, if obliquely, the language of purification. The author of the letter to the Hebrews also underscores the ritual dimension of purification: "For if the blood of goats and bulls, with the sprinkling of the ashes of a heifer, sanctifies those who have been defiled so that their flesh is purified, how much more will the blood of Christ, who through the eternal Spirit offered himself without blemish to God, purify our conscience from dead works to worship the living God!" (Heb 9:13–14).[16] The letter of 1 Peter also contains the language of ritual consecration; its recipients "have been chosen and destined by God the Father and sanctified by the Spirit to be obedient to Jesus Christ and to be sprinkled with his blood" (1 Pet 1:2). In all of these cases, the association of the spirit with purification is set within a ritual context. The outlier with respect to ritual purification is 2 Thess 2:13, in which the author tells readers to be thankful "because God chose you as the first fruits for salvation through sanctification by the Spirit and through belief in the truth" (2 Thess 2:13).

We encounter in the association of spirit with purification a relationship between the New Testament, the Jewish Scriptures, and Second Temple literature that is slightly different from what we have seen so far in this study. In the first section, we saw how Second Temple Jewish literature helps to explain a penchant for ecstasy in the early church: early Christian experience may have been funded by a form of Judaism that embraced ecstasy during the Greek and Roman eras. In the second section, we noted how New Testament authors championed an association between wisdom and spirit that had characterized both the Jewish Scriptures and Second Temple Judaism. Once again, Christianity followed suit, though none of the New Testament authors attempted to tamp this association down, as they did with respect to the spirit and ecstasy. In this section, we have observed how the association of the spirit with purification in the New Testament, in comparison with Israelite and Second Temple Jewish literature, tends to play a limited role. In this respect, the New Testament is consistent with both corpora, but with less apparent emphasis. Nonetheless, the forcefulness with which these few New Testament references are made suggests, too, that Christian communities may not have regarded as quite so axiomatic the association between the spirit and purification that characterized (other) Second Temple Jewish communities.

Spirit and Outpouring

When Peter, on the day of Pentecost, attempts to explain the remarkable impact of the holy spirit upon Jesus's followers, he cites Joel 3:1–4 (2:28–32 LXX

---

16. For a fuller analysis, see Levison, "A Theology of the Spirit in the Letter to the Hebrews," *CBQ* 78, no. 1 (2016): 105–7.

and ET), in which the spirit is outpoured on all, both old and young, male and female, slave and free. The promise of Joel belongs to a line of predictions in the Jewish Scriptures of the spirit outpoured. A desert will become a forest (Isa 32:9–20). Offspring will become a green tamarisk and willows by flowing streams (Isa 44:1–5). Exiles will return to their homeland (Ezek 39:17–29). Heartfelt penitence will bring reconciliation in its train (Zech 12:1–13:6).[17]

The notion of the outpouring of the spirit persisted in Second Temple Judaism, though not always with a communal emphasis. One section of the Enoch cycle begins when Enoch commands Methuselah to "gather together to me all the sons of your mother; for a voice calls me, and the spirit is poured over me so that I may show you everything that shall happen to you forever" (1 En. 91:1).[18] In contrast, in the Dead Sea Scrolls, the outpouring is communal: "[In]deed, You have poured out Your holy spirit upon us, [br]inging Your blessings to us" (4Q504 XVIII, 15–16). The verb expressing outpouring in this text, יָצַק, is reminiscent of Isa 44 but not Ezek 39:29; Joel 3:1; and Zech 12:10, which imagine outpouring with the verb שָׁפַךְ.

There is no question in Acts 2 about which of these Israelite texts proved pivotal, though, as with so many New Testament citations of Israelite Scripture, this is not verbatim. Noticeable modifications in Acts 2:16–21 emerge from a close comparison of Acts 2 and Joel 3. First, while the portents in the book of Joel are on heaven and earth, Peter divides these into portents above and signs on earth. Second, Peter emphasizes prophecy; to the words, "I will pour out my spirit," Peter adds, "and they shall prophesy." While this never actually transpires in Acts, the connection between Israel's Scriptures and the New Testament could not be more visible than in Peter's citation from the book of Joel. Third, Peter sets these events "in the last days" rather than at an indefinite point of time; he sees this outpouring as fulfilled in their midst.

This temporal shift from future to recent past could be seen as a Lukan innovation—except for the presence of a similar conception in Second Temple Jewish literature. Peter differs from Joel by claiming that the outpouring has *already* taken place among the community of believers who followed Jesus. In this respect, Peter's conception of outpouring aligns with that of the people responsible for 4Q504, who believed that the spirit had already been poured out upon them. While the author of 4Q504 adopts the language of Isa 44:3 and Peter the language of Joel, both shift the chronological point of reference from the future to the past. Once again, then, Second Temple literature explains a shift that takes place from the Scriptures of Israel to the New Testament, allowing us

---

17. See Levison, *Boundless God*, 89–103.
18. Translations of 1 Enoch are from E. Isaac, "1 (Ethiopic Apocalypse of) Enoch (Second Century B.C.–First Century A.D.)," *OTP* 1:5–90.

to see with utter clarity how a New Testament rendering of a scriptural passage is not a novelty but part and parcel of Second Temple Jewish faith. New Testament authors, in other words, were not the first to modify a scriptural conception in order to make a certain point. This interpretative context, which may be invisible to many readers of the New Testament, is supplied by the varied and vast corpora of Second Temple Jewish literature.

Spirit and Exodus

A fifth and final construal of the relationship between Israel's Scriptures, Second Temple Jewish literature, and the New Testament emerges when we explore the impact of the later chapters of the book of Isaiah on the New Testament. Of this, there are salient instances. At Jesus's baptism, for example, the words that follow the descent of the spirit like a dove are a fusion of Ps 2:7 and Isa 42:1, which describe the servant upon whom the spirit is said to rest: "You are my Son, the Beloved; with you I am well pleased" (Mark 1:11). The inspired servant of Isa 42—"I have put my spirit upon him"—is in view, as Jesus's vocation merges kingship and service.

The impact of Isa 61:1–4 is also in plain sight when Jesus, in Luke's Gospel, reads this text at the beginning of his opening sermon in the synagogue of Nazareth (Luke 4:18–19). Like Peter's citation of Joel in the book of Acts, this is not verbatim. Jesus, according to Luke's gospel, adds words from Isa 58:6, "let the oppressed go free," and omits a reference to the brokenhearted. Notwithstanding these modifications, Isa 61:1–4 provides Jesus, in Luke's Gospel, with a straightforward manifesto to bring good news to the poor, sight to the blind, and release to prisoners. This is not surprising, as Isa 61:1–4 had provided other Second Temple Jews—those who preserved the Dead Sea Scrolls, at least—with a similar vision of what the messiah would be like:

> [for the heav]ens and the earth will listen to his anointed one. . . . For the Lord will consider the pious, and call the righteous by name, and his spirit will hover upon the poor, and he will renew the faithful with his strength. For he will honor the pious upon the throne of an eternal kingdom, freeing prisoners, giving sight to the blind, straightening out the twisted. . . . And the Lord will perform marvelous acts such as have not existed, just as he sa[id,] [for] he will heal the badly wounded and will make the dead live, he will proclaim good news to the poor . . . and enrich the hungry. (4Q521 2 II, 5–8, 11–13)

Once again, the literature of Second Temple Judaism anticipates the impulses of the New Testament.

Yet another text, a less conspicuous one, had an appreciable impact upon New Testament conceptions of the spirit. Tucked into Isa 63 is a prophetic lament, in which the story of the exodus is transformed in a startling way. The actions of the angel of God's presence—a fusion of two distinct agents of the exodus, God's angel (Exod 23:20–24) and God's presence (Exod 33:14–15)—devolve, in quick sequence, upon the holy spirit. This lament is riddled by interpretive questions prompted by differences between the Hebrew and its Greek translation, but this much is clear: the holy spirit supplants the agents of the exodus and becomes the sole divine deliverer of Israel at the exodus. The Hebrew lament, in part, reads:

> *The angel of his presence saved them;*
> in his love and in his pity he redeemed them;
> he lifted them up and carried them all the days of old.
> *But they rebelled and grieved his holy spirit;*
> therefore he became their enemy; he himself fought against them.
> Then they remembered the days of old, of Moses his servant.
> Where is the one who brought them up out of the sea with the shepherds of his flock?
> *Where is the one who put within them his holy spirit,*
> who caused his glorious arm to march at the right hand of Moses,
> who divided the waters before them to make for himself an everlasting name,
> who led them through the depths?
> Like a horse in the desert, they did not stumble.
> Like cattle that go down into the valley, *the spirit of the Lord gave them rest.*
> Thus you led your people, to make for yourself a glorious name.
> (Isa 63:9–14; modified, based exclusively on the Hebrew, italics added)

The Hebrew text and its Greek translation differ from one another. The Hebrew of Isa 63:9 reads: "In all their distress, the angel of his presence saved them" (my translation). The Greek, in contrast, says that it was *not* an angel but God's presence that saved them.[19] The Hebrew of 63:14 has the spirit giving Israel rest, like

---

19. The Greek translators opted instead for, "It was no ambassador or angel but the Lord himself that saved them" (Isa 63:9 NETS). The Greek translators took the opposite interpretation of the Hebrew—it was *not* an angel that saved Israel—perhaps because they were reluctant to attribute salvation to an angel rather than to God. A detailed discussion can be found in

the presence of Exod 33:14–15, but the Greek has the spirit guide the fledgling nation, rather more like the pillars and cloud: "A spirit came down from the Lord and guided them. Thus you led your people, to make for yourself a glorious name" (Isa 63:14 NETS).[20] Despite differences between Hebrew and Greek, the perspective of this lament is clear: *the activities of the agents of the exodus are now the work of the holy spirit*. Rebellion against the angel of the exodus (Exod 23:20–23) becomes rebellion against the holy spirit (Isa 63:10). It is not an angel or pillar (e.g., Exod 13:21–22; 14:19) that was placed within Israel; it was God's holy spirit (Isa 63:11). Finally, the spirit rather than God's presence (Exod 33:14) gave Israel rest (Isa 63:14) or, in Greek, the spirit rather than a pillar or cloud guided them in the wilderness (Isa 63:14 LXX).[21] In short, in Isa 63, the elements associated with the agents of the exodus coalesce around a new agent: the holy spirit.

This lament had negligible impact upon conceptions of the holy spirit in extant Second Temple Jewish literature. The angel of God's presence—not the holy spirit—reemerged in the book of Jubilees (e.g., Jub. 1:27, 29; see 2:1–2). This is the angel who led Israel; there is not the merest mention of the pillars, the cloud, the presence (פָּנִים) as guides—or, for that matter, the spirit.

It is difficult, then, to discern appreciable traces of the lament of Isa 63:7–14 in Second Temple Judaism—except for the segment of Second Temple Judaism represented by the New Testament. In a letter to believers in Galatia, the apostle Paul launches a volley of images to argue that something fundamental has changed in the lives of believers: "heirs, as long as they are minors, are no better than slaves. . . . But when the fullness of time had come, God sent his Son, born of a woman, born under the law, in order to redeem those who were under the law, so that we might receive adoption as children. And because you are children, God has sent the Spirit of his Son into our hearts, crying, 'Abba! Father!' So you are no longer a slave but a child, and if a child then also an heir, through God" (Gal 4:1–7). There is an exodus subplot in this text. Like the Israelites, the Galatians were once slaves. Like the Israelites, the Galatians have been liberated—male and female, slave and free, Jew and gentile. Like the Israelites, the Galatians were redeemed. And, like the Israelites, the Galatians are no longer slaves but children and, if children, then heirs.[22]

Levison, *The Holy Spirit before Christianity* (Waco, TX: Baylor University Press, 2019); for a briefer exposé, see also Levison, *Boundless God*, 139–55.

20. On the originality of the Hebrew text, see Levison, *Holy Spirit before Christianity*, 134–37.
21. On this cloud, see Levison, *Holy Spirit before Christianity*, 130–34.
22. For discussions of this dimension of Paul's thought, see N. T. Wright, *Paul and the Faithfulness of God*, Christian Origins and the Question of God 4 (Minneapolis: Fortress, 2013), 657; James Scott, *Adoption as Sons of God: An Exegetical Investigation in the Background of ΥΙΟΘΕΣΙΑ in the Pauline Corpus*, WUNT 2/48 (Tübingen: Mohr Siebeck, 1992); Rodrigo

It is not the exodus story itself that is the foreground of Galatians; it is the exodus story *pressed through the sieve of the prophetic lament in Isa 63*, which places the spirit at the center of the exodus. On this basis, Paul is able to write that it is not a pillar or angel that leads in this new exodus; it is the spirit of God's son. The sending of the spirit into the hearts of believers mirrors the conviction, expressed in the prophetic lament, that God put the holy spirit within a people who passed through the sea. If God put the holy spirit into the heart of slaves in Egypt, this same God can send the spirit into the hearts of people enslaved to the elements of the cosmos. Even the emphasis upon God as father may have an antecedent in Isa 63:16: "For you are our father . . . you, O Lord, are our father; our Redeemer from of old is your name."[23]

Through these allusions to Isa 63:7–14 in the letters of Paul, we discern still a fifth model of how Israel's Scriptures, Second Temple Jewish literature, and the New Testament relate to one another with respect to the holy spirit. In this case, Second Temple Judaism plays only a small role, if it plays a role at all. Rather, a prophetic lament from the Neo-Babylonian (exilic) or Persian (postexilic) eras creates a bridge of sorts between the Scriptures of Israel and the New Testament. Yet the scenario is not so simple: leapfrogging from the Old, over Second Temple Judaism, to the New. What has taken place in the Jewish Scriptures is more complex than this scenario would suggest. In New Testament conceptions of a new exodus, the holy spirit, rather than various agents, such as pillars, an angel, or a cloud, is central. The centrality of the spirit in the New Testament did not arise from a Second Temple Jewish context. Nor did it arise from the exodus tradition in Torah. The bridge rather between the exodus traditions and the New Testament is supplied by a lament in Isa 63:7–14, in which already, centuries before the rise of Christianity, the spirit had supplanted other agents of liberation. The bridge from Old to New Testament, then, is not in this case found in Second Temple Judaism but in an exilic or postexilic prophetic lament. This is an altogether different construal of the relationship between Jewish Scripture, Second Temple Jewish literature, and the New Testament from all prior four sections in this chapter. In each of those sections, Second Temple Judaism proved formative for the formation of conceptions—and perhaps experiences—of the holy spirit in the early church. In this, the final section, inner-biblical exegesis is the font of pneumatology; Second Temple Judaism is not.

Morales, *The Spirit and the Restoration of Israel: New Exodus and New Creation Motifs in Galatians*, WUNT 2/282 (Tübingen: Mohr Siebeck, 2010), 78–131; Sylvia C. Keesmaat, *Paul and His Story: (Re)Interpreting the Exodus Tradition*, JSNTSup 181 (Sheffield: Sheffield Academic, 1999), 155–215. See also Rom 8:14–17.

23. For a discussion of the influence of Isa 63:7–14 on the synoptic gospels, see Levison, *Holy Spirit before Christianity*, 118–21.

Holy Spirit

Conclusion

This study has given us the opportunity to identify five models of the relationship between the Jewish Scriptures, Second Temple Jewish literature, and the New Testament. These models have much in common, but each is also distinctive. All five offer insight, not only into the emergence of belief in the holy spirit in the early church but also into the relationship that existed, to varying degrees, between the early church, its Second Temple Jewish context, and the Jewish Scriptures that lay at the root of both.

1. *Ecstasy*. Second Temple Jewish literature allows us to grasp why ecstasy became so important to many believers in the early church. Second Temple Jewish authors lent a prominence to the association of the spirit with ecstasy that was not present in the Jewish Scriptures. Early followers of Jesus inherited this penchant for ecstasy, but New Testament authors, such as Luke and Paul, were compelled to tamp down the impulse, perhaps in an effort to align early Christian impulses with the Jewish Scriptures.

2. *Wisdom*. Second Temple Jewish literature allows us to see clear continuity between the three corpora explored in this chapter. Second Temple Jewish authors inherited an association of the spirit with wisdom that had characterized as well the Jewish Scriptures. While it is not possible to ascertain whether early followers of Jesus embraced a similar appreciation for inspired wisdom, several New Testament authors, including Paul, Luke, and the author of the Fourth Gospel, affirmed this scriptural and Second Temple Jewish instinct to associate the spirit with wisdom.

3. *Outpouring*. This would seem to be a straightforward instance of an Old Testament quotation (Joel 3:1–4) in the New. But this is not the case. In Peter's citation of the prophecy from Joel, outpouring is fulfilled rather than future, recent rather than impending, as it is in the book of Joel. This shift from future to recent past is illuminated, not by Joel itself, but by a passage in the Dead Sea Scrolls, in which the outpouring of the spirit is deemed already to have taken place. In this case, Second Temple Jewish literature is essential for acknowledging that the modification of Joel's prophecy in Acts is not novel; it belongs to a world in which others saw the promise of the spirit's outpouring fulfilled within the confines of a faithful community.

4. *Purification*. Second Temple Jewish literature allows us to discern levels of intensity in the embrace of certain scriptural themes throughout diverse corpora. Early Jewish authors incorporated an association of the spirit with purification that was present earlier in Jewish Scripture. Jesus's early followers may not have been inclined to make this association, if the vigorous exhortations

of the apostle Paul are any indication. Paul, in the most forceful of terms, is compelled to urge believers to sanctification by the spirit, yet even Paul, while vigorous in exhortation, issues these appeals relatively rarely.

5. *The exodus.* Second Temple Judaism plays a diminished role in the formation of a New Testament association between spirit and exodus. That role belongs instead to an exilic or postexilic lament in Isa 63:7–14, in which the spirit accomplishes what various agents—pillars, angel, presence, and cloud—had done in the exodus tradition. The bridge between the Scriptures of Israel and the New Testament is provided in this last instance, not by Second Temple Jewish literature, but by a later iteration of the exodus within the Hebrew and Greek Scriptures themselves.

Bibliography

Carroll, John T. *The Holy Spirit in the New Testament.* Core Biblical Studies. Nashville: Abingdon, 2018.

Dunn, James D. G. *Baptism in the Holy Spirit: A Re-examination of the New Testament Teaching on the Gift of the Spirit in Relation to Pentecostalism Today.* 2nd ed. London: SCM, 2011.

Harrington, D. J. "Pseudo-Philo." *OTP* 2:297–377.

Hildebrandt, Wilf. *An Old Testament Theology of the Spirit of God.* Peabody, MA: Hendrickson, 1995.

Horn, Friedrich Wilhelm. *Das Angeld des Geistes: Studien zur paulinischen Pneumatologie.* FRLANT 154. Göttingen: Vandenhoeck & Ruprecht, 1992.

Isaac, E. "1 (Ethiopic Apocalypse of) Enoch (Second Century B.C.–First Century A.D.)." *OTP* 1:5–90.

Keesmaat, Sylvia C. *Paul and His Story: (Re)Interpreting the Exodus Tradition.* JSNTSup 181. Sheffield: Sheffield Academic 1999.

Levison, John R. *A Boundless God: The Spirit according to the Old Testament.* Grand Rapids: Baker Academic, 2020.

———. "The Debut of the Divine Spirit in Josephus' *Antiquities.*" *HTR* 87 (1994): 123–38.

———. "Ecstasy, New Testament." Pages 338–40 in vol. 7 of *The Encyclopedia of the Bible and Its Reception.* Edited by H.-J. Klauck, B. McGinn, C.-L. Seow, H. Spieckermann, B. Dov Walfish, and E. Ziolkowski. Berlin: de Gruyter, 2009–.

———. *Filled with the Spirit.* Grand Rapids: Eerdmans, 2009.

———. *The Holy Spirit before Christianity.* Waco, TX: Baylor University Press, 2019.

———. "Inspiration and the Divine Spirit in the Writings of Philo Judaeus." *JSJ* 26, no. 3 (1995): 271–323.

———. *Inspired: The Holy Spirit and the Mind of Faith*. Grand Rapids: Eerdmans, 2013.

———. "Philo's Personal Experience and the Persistence of Prophecy." Pages 194–209 in *Prophets, Prophecy, and Prophetic Texts in Second Temple Judaism*. Edited by Michael H. Floyd and Robert D. Haak. LHBOTS 427. London: T&T Clark, 2006.

———. "Prophetic Inspiration in Pseudo-Philo's *Liber Antiquitatum Biblicarum*." *JQR* 85, no. 3/4 (1995): 297–329.

———. "The Prophetic Spirit as an Angel according to Philo." *HTR* 88, no. 2 (1995): 189–207.

———. "A Theology of the Spirit in the Letter to the Hebrews." *CBQ* 78, no. 1 (2016): 90–110.

———. *An Unconventional God: The Spirit according to Jesus*. Grand Rapids: Baker Academic, 2020.

Lindblom, Johannes. *Prophecy in Ancient Israel*. Oxford: Blackwell, 1962.

Montague, George T. *Holy Spirit: Growth of a Biblical Tradition*. Eugene, OR: Wipf & Stock, 2006.

Morales, Rodrigo. *The Spirit and the Restoration of Israel: New Exodus and New Creation Motifs in Galatians*. WUNT 2/282. Tübingen: Mohr Siebeck, 2010.

Nasrallah, Laura Salah. *An Ecstasy of Folly: Prophecy and Authority in Early Christianity*. HTS 52. Cambridge: Harvard University Press, 2003.

Rabens, Volker. *The Holy Spirit and Ethics in Paul: Transformation and Empowering for Religious-Ethical Life*. Minneapolis: Fortress, 2014.

Schäfer, Peter. *Die Vorstellung vom Heiligen Geist in der rabbinischen Literatur*. SANT 28. Munich: Kösel, 1972.

Schuller, Eileen, and Carol Newsom. *The Hodayot (Thanksgiving Psalms): A Study Edition of 1QH^a*. EJL 36. Atlanta: Society of Biblical Literature, 2012.

Scott, James. *Adoption as Sons of God: An Exegetical Investigation in the Background of UIOΘESIA in the Pauline Corpus*. WUNT 2/48. Tübingen: Mohr Siebeck, 1992.

Shoemaker, W. R. "The Use of רוּחַ in the Old Testament, and of πνεῦμα in the New Testament: A Lexicographical Study." *JBL* 23, no. 1 (1904): 13–67.

Tigchelaar, Eibert J. C. "Historical Origins of the Early Christian Concept of the Holy Spirit." Pages 167–240 in *The Holy Spirit, Inspiration, and the Cultures of Antiquity: Multidisciplinary Perspectives*. Edited by Jörg Frey and John R. Levison. Ekstasis 5. Berlin: de Gruyter, 2017.

Turner, Max. *Power from on High: The Spirit in Israel's Restoration and Witness in Luke-Acts*. JPTSup 9. Sheffield: Sheffield Academic, 1996.

Volz, Paul. *Der Geist Gottes und die verwandten Erscheinungen im Alten Testament und im anschließenden Judentum.* Tübingen: Mohr, 1910.

Wintermute, O. S. "Jubilees (Second Century B.C.)." *OTP* 2:35–142.

Wise, Michael O., Martin Abegg, and Edward Cook. *The Dead Sea Scrolls: A New Translation.* Rev. ed. New York: HarperCollins, 2005.

Wright, N. T. *Paul and the Faithfulness of God.* Christian Origins and the Question of God 4. Minneapolis: Fortress, 2013.

28

Covenant

RICHARD J. BAUTCH

In the Second Temple period, covenant became synonymous with creativity. New Testament writers embraced older covenantal forms but set them within contemporary patterns of theological thought that were especially meaningful to early Christian communities. Exegetes par excellence, those responsible for the Gospels, Epistles, and the book of Revelation, took up the covenantal traditions of ancient Israel as pliable concepts that could bend one way or another and join together with uniquely Christian insights in service of the kerygma. As a result, the covenants of Abraham, Moses, and David, to name but a few, played an important role in the nascent thinking around Jesus Christ and the ecclesial ministries that arose as his early followers proclaimed his death and resurrection.

As the New Testament witness developed in terms of covenantal forms and themes, it extended a phenomenon that began centuries earlier in the wake of the Babylonian exile (587–539 BCE). The return from exile occasioned a quest to recover legacies from monarchic Israel in order to fashion a new identity for the people of God. They had been a covenantal people and would remain so if that were possible.[1] The key to envisioning the future would be an innovative approach to covenant and to other touchstones of faith brought forward from pre-

---

1. During reconstruction after the Babylonian exile, various groups of Judeans sought to articulate a coherent foundational narrative so that their visions for Second Temple Judaism would have a firm basis in covenant. See Richard J. Bautch, *Glory and Power, Ritual and Relationship: The Sinai Covenant in the Postexilic Period*, LHBOTS 471 (London: T&T Clark, 2009), 4.

monarchic and monarchic times. Covenant would assume a fresh purpose while maintaining vital links with the past, and other social constructs by which Israel had defined its relationship with the God YHWH would be articulated anew as well. Indeed, as Archibald van Wieringen has demonstrated, "The theologoumenon 'new,' which arises in the Old Testament prophetic post-exilic literature and in which continuity and discontinuity play an important role, proves itself to be fertile and fruitful in Biblical writings and significant for the interpretation of similar literary expressions in New Testament texts."[2] That is, "new" was new well before the New Testament, and the endeavor to address current issues through an appeal to the past constituted a "theologoumenon" because it endured over several centuries. Noteworthy is the observation that when later writers take up concepts such as covenant, there is both continuity and discontinuity with the earlier context. Van Wieringen notes, "'New' as a theologoumenon . . . is not meant as a *novum* in opposition to something that is old, but rather expressing a continuity, which is closer to our word 'anew,' however in a different form, also implying a kind of discontinuity."[3] He adds, "Continuity and discontinuity both play their own specific role."[4]

The covenants in the New Testament, then, were part of a larger theological effort over centuries to establish continuities—with discontinuity evident as well—between a religious community's focus at present and ancient beliefs that have their origins in premonarchic and monarchic Israel. This study will demonstrate that there are five continuities, or facets, of Israel's covenant that stand out because they prove to be highly influential for the New Testament writers. The five facets of covenant are discussed at length below, under "Summary," and they include: (1) enhanced divine agency, exemplified by God writing instruction on the human heart; (2) confession of sin prompting divine mercy and forgiveness; (3) the bestowal of the Holy Spirit; (4) the fusing together of covenantal traditions; (5) a group making a single belief the core of its covenant while at the same time projecting externally a more broadly based notion of

---

2. Van Wieringen, "The Theologoumenon 'New': Bridging the Old and New Testament," in *The Scriptures of Israel in Jewish and Christian Tradition: Essays in Honour of Martin J. J. Menken*, ed. Bart J. Koet, Steve Moyise, and Joseph Verheyden, NovTSup 148 (Leiden: Brill, 2013), 286.

3. Van Wieringen, "Theologoumenon 'New,'" 289.

4. Van Wieringen, "Theologoumenon 'New,'" 289. The stress upon continuity mitigates supersessionist readings of New Testament texts while making clear that the two testaments are inseparable: "By 'Old Testament' the Christian Church has no wish to suggest that the Jewish Scriptures are outdated or surpassed. On the contrary, it has always affirmed that the Old Testament and the New Testament are inseparable. Their first relationship is precisely that"; Pontificia Commissione Biblica, *Le peuple juif et ses Saintes Écritures dans le Bible chrétienne* (Città del Vaticano: Libreria Editrice Vaticana, 2001), §1.

Covenant

the covenant. Covenant in the Hebrew Bible is a diamond with many facets, yet these five facets in particular allow one to appreciate how the Hebrew Bible has refracted light forward onto the New Testament writings.

In this sense, the concept of covenant in the New Testament epitomizes the notion of a whole greater than the sum of its parts. To appreciate the whole fully, however, one must consider carefully the parts, or the texts where covenant is articulated anew and Christian Scripture takes shape. This chapter presents four studies of covenant as it is attested in Luke/Acts (Luke 1:72; 22:20; Acts 3:25; 7:8), the Pauline letters (Rom 11:27; 1 Cor 11:25; 2 Cor 3:6–14), the letter to the Hebrews (8:7–13; 9:15–22; 10:11–18), and Revelation (11:19).[5] To place these New Testament texts in perspective, this chapter begins with a review of covenant in Israel's Scriptures and related Jewish texts, with emphasis on the exegetical developments that point forward to the Christian formulations of covenant in the New Testament.[6]

Covenant in Israel's Scripture

Beginning in premonarchic Israel and continuing through the seventh century BCE, there were prominent covenants that extended over generations. Their significance lay in the fact that they were preeminent vehicles for the ancient writers to construe the ongoing relationship between God and Israel. The first example is the covenant (ברית) with Noah (Gen 9:9), who receives God's promise not to destroy the earth again.[7] God further promises to provide Noah multitudinous progeny (Gen 9:1, 9) and a habitat where they may dwell (Gen 9:11). A divine promise to

---

5. The New Testament material is ordered canonically, and that choice was made in the absence of a genetic connection among the Gospels, Epistles, and Revelation with respect to covenant. Each New Testament book/epistle is a case study unto itself. To begin with Luke 1:72 highlights the "bridge" function of John the Baptist in the Synoptic Gospels, especially in Luke where Zechariah's prayer both highlights the John-to-Jesus connection and brings Israel's concept of covenant into focus.

6. In contrast to the canonically ordered New Testament texts, here the order of the material is topical (Sinai, followed by Abraham, followed by special interest groups) in order to build on van Wieringen's premise that the Babylonian exile provided the impetus for important developments in covenant. As the above introduction has illustrated the need to construe covenants in new ways during the postexilic period and following, the Sinai covenant rightly opens the discussion as the parade example of that phenomenon (with Jeremiah's new covenant leading the way). On the relative importance of the Abrahamic covenant in the postexilic period, see Richard J. Bautch, "An Appraisal of Abraham in Postexilic Covenants," *CBQ* 71, no. 1 (2009): 42–63.

7. Biblical citations follow the NRSV translation.

sustain humankind also characterizes the subsequent covenant between God and Abraham. The Noachian and Abrahamic covenants are parallel in many respects. Like Noah, Abraham is promised progeny (Gen 15:5) and a special place where his family may live (Gen 15:7, 16–21). As the covenant with Abraham is realized, it indeed spans generations and is associated with his son and grandson, Isaac and Jacob respectively. Later the book of Jeremiah comprehensively refers to God's covenant partners as "the seed" (זרע) of Abraham, Isaac, and Jacob (Jer 33:26).

Another covenant with special significance is that concluded with Moses on Mt. Sinai (Exod 19:5; 24:7–8). In this covenant, the unique relationship between God and Israel is more clearly aligned with Israel heeding God's voice (Exod 19:5–6). To those who keep the divine commandments, God extends steadfast love (חסד) to the thousandth generation. Those who serve other gods, however, God requites to the fourth generation (Exod 20:5–6).[8] The Sinai covenant's longevity becomes apparent when it is rearticulated for the subsequent generation (Deut 4:13) and still later by Moses's successor, Joshua (Josh 24:25). In the eighth century BCE, the prophets judge social behavior according to what the Sinai covenant permits and proscribes in terms of both the ten "words" (דברים) or commandments (Hos 4:2) and the broader legislation associated with Sinai. Amos 2:12, for example, condemns the Northern Kingdom of Israel for leading Nazirites to violate vows that are stipulated in Torah (Num 6:3–4).

A final covenant of importance is that made with King David and his successors (2 Sam 7; 23:5). That David's heir will long reign on the throne of Judah is the thrust of this agreement, which requires relatively little in return from the Davidic line. God's promise stipulates obedience and loyalty by the king, but in a manner different from that of the Sinai covenant. Whereas the Sinai covenant obliges Israel to obey the commandments, the Davidic covenant does not strictly require this of the king: "If he does wrong, I will reprove him with blows from a human rod, but my steadfast love [חסד] will not leave him" (2 Sam 7:14–15). Indeed, it would appear that for more than three hundred years the Davidic covenant was in effect, until the fall of Judah in 587 BCE, which led directly to the Babylonian exile. The remarkably long tenure of the Davidic kings is explained in part by the terms of this covenant.

---

8. Regarding the so-called conditionality of the Sinai covenant (and other pacts as well), interpreters in the twenty-first century have reframed the issue as follows: conditionality differs from text to text, but it resides in virtually every covenantal text. See Richard J. Bautch and Gary N. Knoppers, eds., *Covenant in the Persian Period: From Genesis to Chronicles* (Winona Lake, IN: Eisenbrauns, 2015), 5. See also the work of Joachim Krause, who rightly argues that the longstanding, binary-coded question of "conditioned" versus "unconditioned" forms proves to be insufficient; covenants in the Hebrew Bible are each conditionally structured in their own way; Krause, *Die Bedingungen des Bundes: Studien zur konditionalen Struktur alttestamentlicher Bundeskonzeption*, FAT 140 (Tübingen: Mohr Siebeck, 2020), 207–24.

In the sixth century and following, with the return from exile of various groups of Judeans, the concept of covenant was in resurgence. In these circumstances, covenant became a catalyst for Jewish thought throughout the Second Temple period. While the covenants associated with the patriarchs and David retained a degree of currency, there were fresh perspectives on covenant that emerged at this time, and each must be understood within its religious and historical context. Collectively, the tradents who were rearticulating various covenantal forms in the wake of the exile gave birth to the notion of covenant *as new*, and it is at this time that Jeremiah or one of his scribes describes the Sinai covenant in such radically different terms that it is now "a new covenant" (Jer 31:31–34, which is discussed in detail below). New covenant, as understood by van Wieringen and others, is a community's assertion of its continuity with the past: they will continue to be a people to whom God has promised progeny and a homeland while giving them the laws and commandments as a way of life. At the same time, new implies discontinuity: monarchic Israel is gone, and their way of life is to be transformed, updated, and made theologically relevant in any number of ways. After exile, the literature exhibited a striking diversity of ideas related to covenant; there were covenantal developments associated with certain prophetic circles, with the Priestly school of biblical authors, with scribes responsible for wisdom writings, and with other groups of distinction. Eventually, various trajectories of covenantal thinking developed and helped give shape to the Second Temple period as an epoch.

Covenant in Second Temple Literature

To some, the term "Second Temple literature" indicates texts written no earlier than the second century BCE. For the purposes of this chapter, however, such literature is understood more broadly to begin in the late sixth century at the end of the exile, and it includes biblical as well as nonbiblical texts. A caveat to the reader: in the following discussion, references to Isaiah and Jeremiah do not indicate a historical prophet who lived in ancient Israel, except possibly in the case of Jer 31:31–34. Rather, Isaiah and Jeremiah denote large prophetic corpora that developed over centuries as redactors shaped these collections and supplemented them with oracles that reflect the issues and theological concerns of the Second Temple period.

The Sinai Covenant

The Sinai covenant associated with Moses evolved as a response to the unthinkable destruction and human loss experienced at the hands of the Babylonians.

The exile shook the covenant to its foundations. Consequently, beginning in the postexilic period, a restored and renewed Sinai covenant emerged with ritual, kinship, and creation among its dominant features.[9] The conclusion of the Sinai theophany (Exod 24:3–8) is a prime example of a late and highly ritualized depiction of covenant making; Moses takes animal blood from a sacrificial victim and dashes it upon the people, saying: "See the blood of the covenant that the LORD has made with you in accordance with all these words" (Exod 24:8). The ritual action highlights how a creature who has suffered bloodshed comes to play a central role in reifying the covenant. Kinship is recalled in terms of Israel's twelve tribes (Exod 24:4), which express an ethos of family that is highly constructed. In turn, the people's refrain, "We will do everything the Lord has told us" (Exod 24:3, 7), parallels the covenantal pledge voiced by Joshua's family (Josh 24:15, 24).

Another portion of the Sinai account in Exodus, 19:16–25, underscores God's awesome power and its marvelous effects. The text, a theophany richly set in the topography of Sinai itself, may predate the exile. It is important to focus, therefore, on reflexes of Exod 19:16–25 in the exilic and postexilic writings associated with the prophet Isaiah. In chapters 63–64, the tradents of Isaiah announce the omnipotence of Israel's God in the context of covenant. Key expressions in Isa 63:19b describe God coming down from the skies and the mountains trembling; significantly, the same two actions occur when God descends upon a quaking Mt. Sinai (Exod 19:18). The Isaian writer reports these actions again in Isa 64:2, likely to emphasize the oracle's link to the Sinai theophany. Moreover, the prophetic verses in question, Isa 63:19 and 64:2, form part of a prayer (Isa 63:7–64:11) that is informed by the concept of covenant. Another prophetic corpus, that of Jeremiah, similarly explores at this time the notion that the Lord of the Sinai covenant is omnipotent and creator par excellence. Both Isaiah and Jeremiah bring enhanced divine agency into sharp focus.

Divine agency is on display in the new covenant associated with Jeremiah (Jer 31:31–34), which has traditionally been dated to the sixth century.[10] Literarily, this rendering of the Sinai covenant comprises the following motifs: making a new covenant (31:31), the failure of the exodus generation/YHWH as Lord (31:32), writing Torah on the heart (31:33), the lack of need for teachers (31:34a), forgiveness (31:34b). The third and fourth motifs in particular reveal a fundamental

---

9. Bautch, *Glory and Power*, 57–86.
10. On dating Jer 31:31–34 to the sixth century, see William L. Holladay, *Jeremiah: A Commentary on the Book of the Prophet Jeremiah*, vol. 2, *Chapters 26–52*, Hermeneia (Philadelphia: Fortress, 1989), 165; Jack R. Lundbom, *Jeremiah 21–36: A New Translation with Introduction and Commentary*, AB 21B (New York: Doubleday, 2004), 465, 471.

change in the understanding of the divine-human relationship. No longer is there a process of teaching and learning Torah from generation to generation (Jer 31:34a). A heightened divine initiative provides humans with a more direct means to grasp and meet their moral obligations. Into the most explicitly conditional covenant, the Sinai covenant, Jeremiah is infusing the idea that covenant compliance is now completely in God's hands. An overwhelming sense of divine agency supplants the tutelage in Torah that had long been in place. Jeremiah's ideas about pedagogy—or the lack thereof—appear in subsequent writings of the Second Temple period. These further articulations of covenant recall the bilateral pact associated with Sinai but pivot on unilateral action by God that inclines the people to do the will of their creator (e.g., Jer 32:36–41).

Jeremiah's new covenant also emphasizes the forgiveness of sin as a correlative to the people having bonded with the Lord at the level of their hearts. The final words of the passage read: "For I will forgive their iniquity, and remember their sins no more" (Jer 31:34b). The words for iniquity (עָוֺן) and sin (חטא) appear in the same order in Jer 5:25. Inasmuch as the base text, Jer 5, initiates the call to turn back to the Lord with all of one's heart, the new covenant consummates such renewal. Forgiveness of sin is a salient feature of the restored Sinai covenant associated with Jeremiah after the return from exile.

The Abrahamic Covenant

In the late fifth and fourth centuries BCE, a scribal culture emerged around the Jerusalem temple, and shortly thereafter one observes in works such as Isaiah and Chronicles "a Levitical-Priestly stream of scribalism broadly conceived."[11] The Priestly writers gravitated to the figure of Abraham and drew attention to this patriarch as a conduit for covenantal thinking in the Second Temple period. With the exile ever in the background, they sought an enduring Abrahamic framework within which to explore God's relationship with humanity and with Israel. Specifically, these Priestly writers favored the concept of an "eternal covenant" (ברית עולם) that could withstand exile and similar misfortune, and they associated this eternal covenant with Abraham (Gen 17:7) in particular. There are contemporary texts, such as Lev 26, whose exilic setting is simply an effect (retrojection) by Priestly scribes writing in the Second Temple period.[12] Leviti-

---

11. David M. Carr, "Criteria and Periodization for Dating Biblical Texts to Parts of the Persian Period," in *On Dating Biblical Texts to the Persian Period: Discerning Criteria and Establishing Epochs*, ed. Richard J. Bautch and Mark Lackowski, FAT 2/101 (Tübingen: Mohr Siebeck, 2019), 15.

12. The copious references to covenant (Lev 26:9, 15, 25, 42, 44, 45) in Lev 26 are conspicuous in that the book of Leviticus rarely mentions covenant otherwise (Lev 2:13; 24:8). The

cus 26 reports that God "remembered" the covenant with Abraham (Lev 26:42), a divine act tantamount to reaffirming the people and assuring them that they will fare better in the future than they have in the past. The Abrahamic covenant alone, however, does not ensure future blessing.

More is involved as the Abrahamic covenant in Lev 26:42 is preceded by a penitential expression (26:40) in which the people confess their iniquity (עון), their treachery (מעל), and their hostility (קרי) toward God. The tripartite confession of sin, patterned along the lines of Second Temple prayers found in Dan 9 (9:4–19) and 1QS (I, 21–26), indicates that God's willingness to restore and fulfill the covenant is tied to Israel's penitence. As was evidenced above in Jeremiah's new covenant, penitence and divine mercy, like ritual, kinship, and creation, become prominent in the covenantal matrix of the Second Temple period.

Moreover, another feature of the Abrahamic covenant stands out in Lev 26. The Priestly writers responsible for this text are also interested in other patriarchal covenants, with Jacob and Isaac (26:42), and especially in the covenant with the Israelites at Sinai (26:15, 25, 44, 45). At the chapter's climax, God vows not to abandon the land of Israel or the people who have been sent from it into exile because God remembers (זכר) the *Sinai* covenant (26:45). In this case, the figure of Abraham serves as a springboard to fresh thinking about the Mosaic covenant, and the final verses of Lev 26 advance a symbiotic relationship between the Abrahamic and Mosaic traditions of covenant. Going forward, God will not break God's covenant with this people (26:44), understood as the Abrahamic and Mosaic pacts now fashioned into one.[13]

The Covenants of Special-Interest Groups

Increasingly, scholars are considering how special-interest groups employed the concept of covenant in the Second Temple period. At this time, there were segments within society that defined themselves around issues such as intermarriage, circumcision, Sabbath observance, and celebrating festivals. Typically, the

---

lexical shift suggests that the book's penultimate chapter is redactional and the exilic setting is a retrojection.

13. In a parallel development, elsewhere the biblical writers blend language reminiscent of the Davidic promises with the Abrahamic covenant, described allusively in terms of heavenly stars and grains of sand (Jer 33:22). That is, writers responsible for Jer 33:14–26 harmonize two major covenantal traditions that were largely kept separate through the monarchic period. Such a fusing of the Davidic and Abrahamic systems manifests a larger point: in the time of the Second Temple, covenantal thought reflected diversity, multiplicity, and creativity. See Bernard Gosse, "Abraham comme figure de substitution à la royauté davidique, et sa dimension internationale à l'époque postexilique," *Thf* 33, no. 2 (2002): 163–86.

groups maintained a sharply drawn, single-issue profile but tempered any exclusivism and tried to keep within the mainstream of greater Israel.[14] The members of the groups in question at times made an agreement among themselves not to waver on their single issue, such as opposition to intermarriage in the case of those responsible for Ezra 9–10. This group, and others like it, often spoke of its internal agreement as a covenant that they linked to the broader covenant that God gave to Israel through Moses on Mt. Sinai (Ezra 10:3). There was, in fact, specialized language to elevate the group's key issue to the level of Torah and bestow upon it Mosaic authority: "Let it be done *according to Torah*" (Ezra 10:3 [emphasis added]; see also Ezra 6:18). The covenant thus ran in two correlative directions; it ensured right conduct on the issue of utmost concern, as it offered the prospects of broad unity to all the peoples entering the pact started by this group. Similarly, Neh 10 suggests that a Judean group had been energized around a few select issues (intermarriage and the Sabbath, Neh 10:30, 33) that factored into their covenantal agreement. The same group, however, simultaneously understood itself more globally and projected its covenant broadly; in Neh 10:30, the group members bind themselves together in a pact to follow *all the laws of Moses* (emphasis added).

The Dead Sea Scrolls reflect the phenomenon highlighted in Ezra and Nehemiah, that of a group's covenant running in two quite different directions. In the Damascus Document (CD), covenant ensures right conduct on a group's key issue while at the same time offering the prospects of broad unity to all who would enter the group's pact. Maxine Grossman notes how the claim in CD III, 13 that "God's new covenant with this community is a covenant with Israel forever" is repeated several times in the text.[15] Her analysis of this language identifies "an overlay of two covenants upon one another. The first is the covenant at Sinai, which the people of Israel swore to uphold. The second is the covenant of the community, which causes the people to engage in proper Torah practices."[16] The ancient reader of CD, however, apprehends a single covenant, "the special possession of the community described in the text and also fundamentally tied to the Sinai experience of the people of Israel."[17] An isolated group's covenant claims to embrace all of Israel. The Dead Sea Scrolls provide other examples of

---

14. See Bautch and Knoppers, *Covenant in the Persian Period*, 6, 263–65.
15. See Maxine Grossman, *Reading for History in the Damascus Document: A Methodological Study*, STDJ 45 (Leiden: Brill, 2002), 163. While Grossman refers to the covenant as "God's new covenant," the word "new" is not attested in CD III, 13. Nonetheless, it is a new covenant in the broader sense of the theologoumenon "new" that emerged during the Second Temple period.
16. Grossman, *Reading for History*, 163–64.
17. Grossman, *Reading for History*, 164.

this effect, such as the covenant in 1QSa (I, 1–5), which points toward both the priestly group with which it originated and Israel at the eschaton.

Among the Dead Sea Scrolls, CD provides a second, additional window on covenant as the highly pneumatized relationship between God and God's people: CD II, 12 describes a member of the covenant as someone "anointed in God's holy spirit" and thereby given divine perspective. In Grossman's words, "A covenanter is someone who can step outside of human time and has perspective on all that has been and will be."[18] This broader reality is tantamount to the divine plan, and one glimpses it by receiving God's holy spirit. Carol Newsom, in her discussion of the Hodayot, emphasizes that no activity stands outside the divine plan, which is only made visible to God's chosen people, the covenanters of the Dead Sea Scrolls.[19] The Hodayot, like CD, indicate that such special knowledge, the divine perspective or plan, is gained via God's holy spirit. Indeed, one portion of this hymnic collection (1QH[a] VIII, 26–37) contains five references to God's holy spirit, a clustering of pneumatological mentions in the context of a covenant renewal. Of this passage, Judith Newman notes: "God is addressed using the language of covenant faithfulness (*chesed*), and the one who prays acknowledges that his entreaty comes only by means of the spirit/breath that God had already given him. His request is to make the covenant relationship an eternal one: 'make your kindness (*chesed*) to your servant complete forever, cleansing me by your holy spirit and drawing me nearer by your good favor.'"[20]

Making the covenantal relationship eternal would allow the human partner to step outside earthly time forever and enjoy God's perspective limitlessly. The means to this end is God's spirit. Significantly, the spirit of God both enlightens and cleanses. The cleansing is decidedly moral, of the sort referred to in Exod 34:6, to which 1QH[a] VIII, 34 alludes: "And I kno[w that you are a God] gracious and compassionate, patient and abounding, in kindness and faithfulness, one who forgives transgressions and unfaithful[ness]." The forgiveness of transgressions and unfaithfulness is not a passing reference.

Newman points out that repentance played an outsized role in the self-conception of the Qumran communities, with reinforcement from Exod 34:6, as well as a verse from Isaiah, 59:20.[21] The Isaian oracle describes those who belong to Jacob and who have turned back from sin as the group of שבי פשע

---

18. Grossman, *Reading for History*, 106.
19. Carol Newsom, "The Case of the Blinking I: Discourse of the Self at Qumran," *Semeia* 57 (1992): 17.
20. Newman, "Covenant Renewal and Transformational Scripts in the Performance of the Hodayot and 2 Corinthians," in *Jesus, Paulus und die Texte von Qumran*, ed. Jörg Frey and Enno Edzard Popkes, WUNT 2/390 (Tübingen: Mohr Siebeck, 2015), 302.
21. Newman, "Covenant Renewal," 302–3, 303 n. 42.

("those who turn from transgression"). The members of the שׁבי פשׁע form a pneumatic covenant (Isa 59:21) based upon "my Spirit that I put upon you, my words that I have put in your mouth." The idiom שׁבי פשׁע recurs in the Hodayot (6:35; 10:11; 14:9; cf. 8:35 "those who return to you") to suggest a connection with this community's self-understanding. In turning back from sin, the individual turns to God, and 1QHª VIII, 36 appropriately adds: "Do not turn away the face of your servant [and do no]t reject the son of your handmaid." The reference to the hymnist's face indicates how the body can reflect light and glory when its inward parts are cleansed and oriented to God's own face.

Summary

The review of the Hebrew Bible and Second Temple literature has yielded a wealth of information about the concept of covenant. Within this data set, can one identify the antecedents to covenant as it appears in the New Testament? There are five facets of covenant that emerge as highly influential for the writers of the Gospels, the Epistles, and Revelation. These points of continuity are as follows:

1. Enhanced divine agency, exemplified by God writing instruction on the human heart. In response to the defeat Israel suffered when the Babylonians sacked Jerusalem, divine omnipotence became fundamental to postexilic covenants (Isa 63:19; 64:2). Often expressed theophanically or through the imagery of creation, God's power and initiative were as well the impetus for something unprecedented: writing instruction on the human heart (Jer 31:33).
2. Confession of sin prompting divine mercy and forgiveness. Also foundational to many of the covenants articulated in the Second Temple period was the confession of sin followed by divine mercy and forgiveness. In the wake of the exile, penitence allowed for an understanding of covenant as broken, but not irrevocably so (Isa 59:21; 64:3–6; Jer 31:34b; 1QHª VIII, 34). Such formulations of covenant often used patterned penitential language to recount the people's misdeeds (Lev 26:40).
3. The bestowal of the Holy Spirit. In the context of covenant, the desire to confess sin was an interior gift associated at times with the bestowal of God's holy spirit (Isa 59:20–21; CD II, 12; 1QHª VIII, 34). At other times, the divine spirit was given in a more general way to orient and support the people as they endeavored to live the pattern of life revealed to them at Mt. Sinai (Isa 63:10, 11, 14; Neh 9:20).
4. The fusing together of covenantal traditions. The fusion of hamartiology/soteriology with pneumatology indicates how covenant in the Second Temple

period became a crossroads where different perspectives could meet and be combined. Most salient in this regard were the blending of patriarchal traditions into a composite expression of covenant: the Abrahamic and Mosaic covenants (Lev 26:45), the Abrahamic and Davidic covenants (Jer 33:22), and analogously the Davidic and priestly covenants (Jer 33:21–22).

5. A group making a single belief the core of its covenant while at the same time projecting externally a more broadly based notion of the covenant. Covenant was expressive of community and its identity. In a number of cases, the group in question was relatively small, and it gravitated to a single belief as the core of its covenant. At the same time, it projected a much larger image of itself, again in terms of covenant. To outsiders, the group sought to appear as *the* Jewish ethnos that embodied ancient Israel and preserved its way of life, especially its legal tradition, in the subsequent age (i.e., the Second Temple period; Ezra 10:3; Neh 10:30–33; CD III, 13; 1QS I, 1–5).

Covenant in the New Testament

Luke-Acts

It is auspicious to begin with Luke-Acts, where the first mention of covenant (διαθήκη) occurs in the context of John the Baptist. The canticle (1:68–79) associated with John's father, Zechariah, refers to John as the "prophet of the Most High" (1:76), and Israel's "prophets of old" are indicated as well (1:70). Between the two references to prophets, covenant appears as an expression of the salvation (σωτηρία) that was promised to the ancients (1:72).[22] John, as a high point in the prophetic line, sheds light on the continuity of covenant across the ages. At the same time, John's profile is in contrast to that of Jesus by design.[23] The discontinuity of the two, and of the old and new covenants, is also suggested.

In Zechariah's canticle, the key word σωτηρία ("salvation") is associated with God keeping the covenant and its promises (Luke 1:72). In the words of one commentator, John Carroll, "The salvation that Zechariah celebrates is the culmination of a story that began long ago."[24] What is at the heart of that story?

---

22. See John T. Carroll, *Luke: A Commentary*, NTL (Louisville: Westminster John Knox, 2012), 59.
23. To indicate the contrast, Augustine writes: "John is born of a woman too old for childbirth; Christ was born of a youthful virgin. The news of John's birth was met with incredulity, and his father was struck dumb. Christ's birth was believed, and he was conceived through faith." Augustine, Sermon 289, §1–3, PL 38:1327–28.
24. Carroll, *Luke*, 59.

Throughout the course of Luke's Gospel, covenantal salvation becomes synonymous with the forgiveness of sin and other facets of human redemption. Indeed, mercy, reconciliation, and restoration are conjoined themes in Luke, and they punctuate many of the sayings and parables in the Third Gospel (Luke 5:32; 13:5; 15:9, 17–24; 16:30; 23:43; 24:47). In Luke 5:32, which is a programmatic statement of Jesus's mission, Luke actually adds a reference to repentance: "I have come to call not the righteous but sinners to repentance" (cf. Mark 2:17; Matt 8:13). The Lukan turn to mercy and forgiveness is a development that parallels the postexilic Jewish writings referred to above. In the Pentateuch (Lev 26:40), as well as the Prophets (Isa 59:21; 64:3–6; Jer 31:34b) and the Dead Sea Scrolls (1QH^a VIII, 34), divine clemency is key to renewal and a new beginning. These pre-Christian texts have in common the theme of repentance and as well a focus on covenant. Similarly, in Luke the evangelist establishes two primary themes, salvation and divine mercy, while covenant plays its part by reinforcing the antiquity of the central ideas.

The Lukan configuration of salvation and divine forgiveness recurs in the Acts of the Apostles. In chapter three, Peter heals a man who had been lame from birth (Acts 3:1–10). Immediately, the apostle delivers a christological oration to the amazed crowd at the temple (3:11–4:4). His final words are decisive: "You are the descendants of the prophets and of the covenant that God gave to your ancestors, saying to Abraham, 'And in your descendants all the families of the earth shall be *blessed*.' When God raised up his servant, he sent him first to you, to *bless* you by turning each of you from your wicked ways" (Acts 3:25–26, emphasis added). The servant raised up is Jesus, who was referred to as such in the first part of the oration (3:13), where Abraham is also mentioned. The two references to Jesus as servant unify Peter's speech and frame the salvific mission of Jesus. In Acts 3:26, the servant's blessing ushers in salvation in a specific way, as every recipient of the blessing is able to turn from their wicked ways.[25] The core Lukan elements of salvation (via blessing) and forgiveness recur, again with covenant playing a conspicuous role theologically. The blessing extended by the servant, Jesus, is one and the same as the Abrahamic benediction bestowed covenantally on the patriarch's family, yet intended for all peoples. There is continuity between the blessing received by Abraham's family in the Scriptures of Israel and that given by Jesus in the New Testament. The latter transforms the former inasmuch as those now wishing to share in the promise to Abraham are called to repentance.[26]

---

25. The process of turning from one's wicked ways (Acts 3:26) is introduced in a preceding verse, Acts 3:19, where Peter issues the imperative: "Repent and turn to God, so that your sins may be wiped out, so that times of refreshing may come from the Lord."

26. Richard I. Pervo, *Acts: A Commentary*, Hermeneia (Minneapolis: Fortress, 2009),

In the oration, Peter tells the hearers of his words that they are descendants of the prophets and as well heirs of the Abrahamic covenant (Acts 3:25). While the introduction of covenant at this point strikes some as abrupt, the connection to what precedes it, Mosaic prophecy, is more integral than it might first appear to be.[27] Acts 3:21b–24, as part of the inner workings of Peter's speech, develops the notion that Jesus is the prophet "like Moses" as indicated in Deut 18:15. In Acts, however, the treatment of the scriptural text from Deuteronomy is not especially christological and emphasizes rather the importance of acting in accordance with the words of this prophet lest a person be rooted out from his community. That is, a Deuteronomic sequence of commandment, transgression, and consequence is presented in a manner that harks back to the Mosaic covenant.[28] While the term ברית does not appear in Deut 18:15–22, the text contains echoes of the Sinai covenant. These echoes, when placed in the context of Acts, harmonize with the presentation of the Abrahamic pact in Acts 3:25. Peter's oration comes to a crescendo in the synthesis of the two covenants, the Mosaic and the Abrahamic. The New Testament writer's creativity is impressive but not wholly original, as the text recalls Lev 26:45 and similar scriptural verses that blend patriarchal traditions into a composite expression of covenant, the Abrahamic *and* Mosaic covenants, in tandem with one another.

The composite covenant appears again in Acts 7 as part of Stephen's oration before he is put to death. Addressing the council in Jerusalem, Stephen recites a history of Israel, beginning with Abraham, who received from God "the covenant of circumcision" and who, when Isaac was born, circumcised his son on the eighth day (Acts 7:8). Circumcision is established as the sign of the Abrahamic covenant in Gen 17:10–14, which also makes undergoing this rite the criterion for membership in the community. Proceeding from Abraham,

---

109. The phenomenon of repentance here requires context and a careful differentiation between the collective experiences of Jewish and Christian communities. It is especially important to interrogate the work of earlier scholars, who imposed Christian concepts of conversion on ancient Judaism and to see "each religion's idea of change or reorientation or initiation in its own context. In doing so, we gain a more nuanced and differentiated view on the religious life in antiquity." Birgitte Secher Bøgh, introduction to *Conversion and Initiation in Antiquity: Shifting Identities, Creating Change*, ed. Birgitte Secher Bøgh, Early Christianity in the Context of Antiquity 16 (Frankfurt am Main: Lang, 2014), 9.

27. On the abruptness, see Bøgh, introduction, 9.

28. In the words of Jeffrey Tigay, "The prophet's primary role [as indicated in Deut 18:18, 'all that I commanded him'] is as God's messenger and spokesman... [the prophet] conveyed God's *demarche* when Israel violated the terms of His covenant. The prophets served, in sum, as the monitors of Israel's fulfillment of its covenant obligations to God"; Tigay, *Deuteronomy: The Traditional Hebrew Text with the New JPS Translation*, JPS Torah Commentary (Philadelphia: Jewish Publication Society, 1996), 176.

Stephen touches on stories of Joseph and especially Moses, as well as David and Solomon. The martyr concludes his speech with a pointed accusation: "You stiff-necked people, uncircumcised in heart and ears, you are forever opposing the Holy Spirit, just as your ancestors used to do" (Acts 7:51). The statement is designed to evoke the Abrahamic covenant of circumcision and more. Next, the death of Jesus at the hands of those who are now about to stone Stephen is characterized as betrayal and murder: "You are the ones that received the law as ordained by angels, and yet you have not kept it" (Acts 7:53). Rejecting the law is tantamount to undoing the covenant, as indicated by the charge of "uncircumcised in heart and ears." The Abrahamic pact is clearly referenced, but "uncircumcised" in this case also echoes the Mosaic covenant of right teaching in Deuteronomy. Resonant in the words attributed to Stephen is Deut 10:16: "Circumcise, then, the foreskin of your heart, and do not be stubborn [literally, stiff-necked] any longer." The injunction forms part of Deut 10:12–21, a sermon with Deuteronomic flavoring (Deut 10:12–13) and references to Egypt that recall Moses (Deut 10:18–19). In this pentateuchal source text for Acts 7, the Mosaic covenant is visible to the degree that one commentator of Acts translates "uncircumcised" as "cut off from the covenant" and deems it a reference to the "Deuteronomic tradition" as well as Abraham.[29] The translation is apt as Stephen's speech climaxes at the concept of covenant, here understood as both the bestowal of blessed community through Abraham and the right teaching imparted by Moses and the prophets. The former requires circumcision, the latter engenders a circumcised heart.

Stephen's speech intones another important note, in terms of covenant. The key verse, Acts 7:51, accuses the council and those in attendance: "You are forever opposing the Holy Spirit, just as your ancestors used to do." The Hebrew Bible, as well as the Dead Sea Scrolls, characterizes the divine Spirit in similar terms, with repentant sinners in Isa 59:21 and the Hodayot serving as a leitmotif, the שׁבי פשׁע, "those who turn from transgression." Recall that in these earlier texts the Spirit starts to become a hypostasis of the Divine, similar in this regard to God's angel who, interestingly, also plays an outsized role in Acts 7 when it alludes to the Sinai covenant (Acts 7:53 as noted above; see also 7:30, 35, 38). Following revealed teaching or, conversely, sinning against God are matters of the covenant now involving angels and the Holy Spirit. By the same token, covenant is God's own gift to a repentant people, as the oracle in Isa 59:15b–21 establishes. In this text of the Second Temple period, Isaiah's God declares "my covenant" with Zion and Jacob, who have turned away from sin and now receive the Spirit of the Lord. The Holy Spirit is as an eternal gift, ever on their mouths in the form of God's

---

29. Pervo, *Acts*, 192.

words. Informed by Scripture and notably Isaiah, Christian pneumatology has a modest place in Acts 7 but to a much greater degree informs other covenant texts in the New Testament, as shown below in the study of Paul's letters.

In sum, John the Baptist appears early in the Third Gospel as a bridge linking the old to the new. Subsequently, Luke-Acts follows a trajectory of repentance/forgiveness toward a telos of salvation. To enhance this focus, the writer employs covenant, understood as a complex of different traditions in the Hebrew Scriptures related to both Abraham and Moses at Sinai. Covenant also draws from the literary past an understanding of God's Spirit as vital to the communion now offered afresh to the followers of Jesus. Luke-Acts brings its multifaceted view of covenant into sharp relief in the account of the last supper (Luke 22:17–20), which concludes: "And he did the same with the cup after supper, saying, 'This cup that is poured out for you is the new covenant in my blood'" (Luke 22:20). The cup poured out reflects the Passover meal at hand, a ritual recalling the Passover Seder as well as the deliverance from Egypt. "New covenant" describes, on the one hand, Luke's retrieval and transformation of Israel's covenant. "New covenant" also alludes to Jer 31:31–34, where the prophet announces a *new* covenant that is interior, or inspirited, and whose result is the forgiveness of sins. Explicitly and implicitly, different aspects of the Luke-Acts covenant come to light in the words spoken at table by Jesus. One could not find a clearer example of Israel's Scriptures in the New Testament vis-à-vis covenant: "The Passover meal's call to remembrance of God's liberation of the people from slavery in Egypt (e.g., Exod 12:14) is merged with memory of Jesus, whose body and blood constitute a renewed covenant people for whom the experience of God's Spirit will work the obedience to God and God's Torah that participation in the covenant entails."[30]

Covenant in Paul

As a reader of the New Testament turns the page from Acts to the letters of Paul, covenant appears with some now-familiar features evoking the Hebrew Scriptures that the apostle knew intimately. In his passages about covenant, Paul incorporates several important themes: the forgiveness of sins, becoming a child of Abraham, and the new covenant that stands at the center of ministry. In addition, Paul aligns covenant with the descent of the Holy Spirit, through whom gentiles as well as Jews participate in divine life with Jesus Christ. Such union with Christ is both pneumatic and eschatological; for Paul, it is the pinnacle of Christian experience, and it is decidedly covenantal.

30. Carroll, *Luke*, 435.

Covenant

The letter to the Romans is a theologically rich treatise, and Paul in Rom 11 likens Israel to an olive tree with diverse branches.[31] The "natural branches" represent Jews, some of whom were "broken off" so that a wild olive shoot (the gentiles) could be grafted on (Rom 11:17–19). Paul observes that certain natural branches remain on the olive tree, and even those that were removed may be restored "if they do not persist in unbelief" (11:23).[32] The mature tree, representing the complete community of faith at the parousia, is "all Israel" poised to receive salvation (11:26). In addition to the branches, Paul describes the root of the olive tree. The root is uniquely Jewish as the wild shoots that were grafted on subsequently do not share in the root (11:17). It is the root that supports the entire tree and undergirds the covenant (11:27).

In the context of Rom 11, Paul draws on passages from the Hebrew Scriptures to make a point about covenant. Isaiah 59:20–21 contains the prophetic oracle that informed the Hodayot found at Qumran (see above). The Isaiah text functions here in a similar role: to capture the eschatological moment. In Rom 11:26–27, Paul's point of reference is the final community comprising Israel and the nations at the parousia when Christ returns. The end-time scenario in Romans is influenced by Isaiah, which Paul paraphrases: "Out of Zion will come the deliverer; he will banish ungodliness [ἀσεβείας] from Jacob." The citation continues: "And this is my covenant with them," although rather than continuing with Isa 59:21 and introducing the Spirit, as the prophet does, Paul interjects a phrase from Isa 27:9, "when I take away their sins" (ὅταν ἀφέλωμαι τὰς ἁμαρτίας αὐτῶν). Here Paul's understanding of the relationship between covenant and the remission of sin must be taken carefully. Paula Fredriksen observes, "By the time Paul reaches his paean of praise in Romans 11, the human sinners, whether pagans or Jews, seem excused; all humanity at the Parousia are saved."[33] The Greek confirms Fredriksen's insight, as the verb "take away" (ἀφέλωμαι) their sins is an aorist subjunctive that indicates action *preceding* the main clause. "When" I take away their sins refers to some earlier period of

---

31. Paul's inspiration for the plant metaphor to explain God's disciplining and restoration of the Jewish people can be traced back to works such as Philo's *Praem.* 162–171. See Thomas H. Tobin, *Paul's Rhetoric in Its Contexts: The Argument of Romans* (Peabody, MA: Hendrickson, 2004), 366.

32. It is not that Jews were expected to believe in Jesus; their unbelief is rather their denial that the gifts and calling of God are irrevocable (Rom 11:29). See Beverly Roberts Gaventa, *When in Romans: An Invitation to Linger with the Gospel according to Paul*, Theological Explorations for the Church Catholic (Grand Rapids: Baker Academic, 2016), 47–76.

33. Paula Fredriksen, "The Question of Worship: Gods, Pagans and the Redemption of Israel," in *Paul within Judaism: Restoring the First-Century Context to the Apostle*, ed. Mark D. Nanos and Magnus Zetterholm (Minneapolis: Fortress, 2015), 199.

remediation, prior to the covenant's enactment but presumably important if not essential to its overall efficacy.

Paul's construal of covenant in Rom 11 can be contrasted with one of the eschatological passages in 1QH^a that alludes to Isa 59:21.[34] 1QH^a VIII, 20 describes God lavishing loving-kindness upon God's covenant partner eternally while simultaneously the Spirit purifies the covenanter in question. In this scenario, purification is pivotal to covenant, and it is ongoing, through the action of the Spirit. Paul, in contrast, detaches forgiveness from covenant, if ever so slightly. Furthermore, Paul opts against introducing the Holy Spirit into Rom 11:27, even though the Spirit is attested in his source text (Isa 59:21) and has elsewhere been cited as a means of taking away sins (1QH^a VIII, 20).[35] Romans 11 shows that the influence of the Hebrew Bible's covenant texts upon later writers was not univocal, and there are unique details in Paul's exegesis that in turn shape his theology.

Paul's letter to the Galatians is similarly important to an understanding of covenant in the New Testament. A cursory reading of Galatians could suggest Paul is disparaging Israel's legacy, particularly with regard to the Mosaic law associated with the covenant at Sinai (Gal 3:1–5, 10–12, 24). In this vein, statements elsewhere in the chapter (Gal 3:17–18) portray the Mosaic law as diminishing the Abrahamic covenant, which is referred to as a "promise" (ἐπαγγελία). Whereas other exegetes contemporary with Paul were harmonizing the Sinai and Abrahamic covenants, Paul appears to juxtapose the two as part of a larger critique of the Mosaic law. Such is a misreading of Paul, however, as there was emerging a novel view of interior transformation that informs the Pauline corpus and is especially pronounced in Galatians.[36] Rather than conjoin the Abrahamic and Sinaitic legacies as his contemporaries were doing, Paul in fact repositions them as the basis for a new promise: "In Christ Jesus the blessing of Abraham might come to the gentiles, so that we might receive the promise of the Spirit through faith" (Gal 3:14). For gentiles in particular, faith and belief now serve the function previously assigned to the law. No less momentous is that Paul makes the Spirit preeminent, and going

---

34. See Newman's argument that this text, at 1QH^a VIII, 35, makes reference to Isa 59:21; Newman, "Covenant Renewal," 303.

35. Moreover, the Holy Spirit is hardly understated in Romans (Rom 1:4; 6:5, 11–14; 7:25; 8:2, 9, 11, 14–15). The Spirit indwells those who belong to Christ and provides them with many benefits, including resurrection (Rom 8:11) and divine inheritance (Rom 8:15).

36. "The new element in v 14b is that the promise God made to Abraham is now called 'the promise of the Spirit.' . . . When the Galatians received the Spirit, this could not have been an illegitimate, premature or deficient event; they must have experienced nothing less than the fulfillment of the solemn promise God had made to Abraham"; Hans Dieter Betz, *Galatians: A Commentary on Paul's Letter to the Church in Galatia*, Hermeneia (Philadelphia: Fortress, 1979), 152–53.

forward covenant will be synonymous with a sharing in the Spirit of Jesus Christ. The "apostle to the gentiles" has repositioned and redefined Israel's covenant as wholly pneumatic and christological, and in this he stands alongside other New Testament writers proclaiming an inspired covenant in Christ.

Second Corinthians expounds upon Paul's inspired covenant in Christ, which the apostle further describes as a "new covenant" in language that is theologically rich: "Such is the confidence that we have through Christ toward God. Not that we are competent of ourselves to claim anything as coming from us; our competence is from God, who has made us competent to be ministers of a new covenant, not of letter but of spirit; for the letter kills, but the Spirit gives life" (2 Cor 3:4–6). Again, a first-level reading can be deceptive. It might appear that Paul opposes the ministries of letter and spirit and the covenants of death and life as a prelude to later (2 Cor 3:10) countering passing glory with permanent glory. Paul's point, however, is not these antitheses but the new covenant as a radical development of the covenantal frameworks found variously in Israel's Scriptures. The opposing pairs, in the words of Gregory Tatum, "indicate the radicality of the development," but they hardly remove Paul from the realm of Judaism.[37] Tatum adds, "The actual covenant texts [in Paul] reveal a re-location of the Abrahamic and Mosaic covenants before, within, over against, and alongside the New Covenant."[38] That is to say, one should conceive the relationship of covenant and new covenant not along typological lines but as a "quantum leap" from the former to the latter. Although reading the Scriptures of Israel pneumatologically transforms and christologically transfigures the believer, it does not displace the originating Jewish context. With Paul, the development of the new covenant is a "fully Jewish development," and "the 'covenantal life of Israel' cannot be separated from circumcision and Torah."[39] Tatum's reading of 2 Cor 3:4–6 captures the text's paradox, and it is consistent with the instruction of the Pontifical Biblical Commission, which suggests a twofold manner of reading the Old Testament, in its original meaning at the time of writing and through a subsequent interpretation in the light of Christ (see n. 4).

In 2 Cor 3, another source text from Scripture is Exod 34:29–35. In this passage Moses descends Mt. Sinai with the two tablets and is met by the Israelites.

---

37. Gregory Tatum, "Law and Covenant in *Paul and the Faithfulness of God*," in *God and the Faithfulness of Paul: A Critical Examination of the Faithfulness of N. T. Wright*, ed. Christoph Heilig, J. Thomas Hewitt, and Michael F. Bird, WUNT 2/413 (Tübingen: Mohr Siebeck, 2016), 315.

38. Tatum, "Law and Covenant," 315.

39. Tatum, "Law and Covenant," 313. For further perspective on Paul's continuity with Judaism, see Emmanuel Nathan, *Re-membering the New Covenant at Corinth*, WUNT 2/514 (Tübingen: Mohr Siebeck, 2020), 2, 137–55.

He relates to them, in the form of commandments, all that God had spoken to him on the mountain. In 2 Cor 3:7–18, Paul evokes the Exodus passage in the context of his new covenant because the goal remains to live the pattern of life originally revealed at Mt. Sinai and newly available through communion with Jesus Christ. In the new covenant, the divine Spirit is given to orient and support the people as they endeavor to follow all the commandments (2 Cor 3:8). Participatory pneumatology of this sort is anticipated in Israel's Scriptures (Isa 63:10, 11, 14; Neh 9:20).[40] Paul evokes this ancient pattern not only in 2 Corinthians but also through a second treatment of the new covenant in 1 Cor 11:24–25, the apostle's account of the Last Supper.[41] The Pauline scholar Jerome Murphy-O'Connor focuses on the expression "new covenant in my blood" (1 Cor 11:25) and emphasizes "the Jewish comprehension of covenant" in his analysis.[42] The new covenant would have been understood "realistically" as the new form of relationship between God and humanity that was inaugurated through the death of Christ and is given anew to each person who proclaims Christ's death and resurrection. In the Jewish comprehension of covenant, exemplified by Exod 24:8, "there could be no covenant without a real relationship to the victim sacrificed to seal the covenant."[43] Just as Moses takes blood and throws it upon the people to effect their covenant with the Lord, the substance of Christ's blood in each instance of the Eucharist situates those who receive it in a new pattern of life.

Covenant in Hebrews

At the compositional center of the Letter to the Hebrews is an extended discussion of Christ's high-priestly ministry (Heb 8:1–10:18). While replete with the language of sacrifice and cult, Hebrews here explores the new covenant that Christ is mediating as the prime expression of his redemptive work. An earthly high priest in the Jerusalem temple would by definition offer sacrifice, but the high priest in heaven expunges sin through actions that are categorically different: he mediates a new covenant that is better (κρείττονός) than its predecessors (Heb 8:6).[44] Hebrews 8:1–10:18 contains three passages on the new covenant at

---

40. See John R. Levison, *The Holy Spirit before Christianity* (Waco, TX: Baylor University Press, 2019), 32–39. Levison provides a discussion of Isa 63:7–14 and concludes that the oracle provides evidence of the historical emergence of pneumatology in Scripture.

41. For a comparison, see above the analysis of Luke 22:17–20, the gospel account to which Paul's version of the Eucharist is most closely related.

42. Jerome Murphy-O'Connor, *Keys to First Corinthians: Revisiting the Major Issues* (Oxford: Oxford University Press, 2009), 208.

43. Murphy-O'Connor, *Keys to First Corinthians*, 208.

44. See the commentary on Heb 8:6 in Peter Gräbe, "The New Covenant and Christian

its beginning (Heb 8:7–13), middle (Heb 9:15–22), and end (Heb 10:11–18). Moreover, parallelism between Heb 8:7–13 and 10:11–18, the first and final passages, provides a covenantal framework around the portrait of Christ the high priest while highlighting key elements in the new covenant that he mediates.[45]

Hebrews 8:1–6 serves as an introduction to these three chapters and provides the initial reference to the new covenant (Heb 8:6). There follows (Heb 8:7–13) an exegetical treatment of the new covenant in Jeremiah (Jer 31:31–34). Hebrews 8:7–13 parses the prophet's words and phrases while quoting at length the Septuagintal version preserved in Codex Alexandrinus and other major witnesses. Two exegetical points bear scrutiny because they figure prominently in the larger argument of this New Testament writer. First, the new covenant is interior, engraved not on tablets but on the human heart (Heb 8:10–11). Interiority here means more than a memorization or inculcation of Torah; it involves, according to Harold Attridge, the cleansing of the conscience and true spiritual worship.[46] Second, the new covenant effectively removes iniquities and sins by means of God's mercy (ἵλεως), a divine attribute not referenced in Jer 31:31–34, although it is implied there by Jeremiah's conciliatory tone. It was earlier noted, in the analysis of Luke-Acts, that the turn to forgiveness and mercy is a development that parallels the postexilic Jewish writings (Lev 26:40; Isa 59:21; 64:3–6; Jer 31:34b; 1QH^a VIII, 34). In covenantal contexts, divine clemency has become synonymous with a new beginning and, in Hebrews, a new covenant. The two facets brought forward from Jeremiah, interiorization and forgiveness, will prove to be key in the covenant of Hebrews.

At the conclusion of this passage, Heb 8:13 states that the first covenant is "obsolete and growing old will soon disappear." Attridge notes that in Hebrews the covenant of Jeremiah has "a negative function," which is to say there is discontinuity with the Old Testament.[47] Hebrews uses various antitheses (Heb 8:2, 6) to express the discontinuity, which is further manifest through the dichotomy of the old and new covenants. Continuity, however, is also asserted in terms of interiorization and forgiveness forming part of the new sacrificial system reflected in Christ's highpriestly ministry. The system, as well as the argument of Hebrews, comes to light more fully in the next of the three covenantal passages, Heb 9:15–22.

Identity in Hebrews," in *A Cloud of Witnesses: The Theology of Hebrews in Its Ancient Contexts*, ed. Richard Bauckham, Trevor Hart, and Nathan MacDonald, LNTS 387 (London: T&T Clark, 2008), 121–23.

45. There are common themes indicated in the first and third passages, such as the interiority of the new covenant (Heb 8:10; 10:16) and God's mercy, along with the forgiveness of sins (Heb 8:12; 10:17).

46. Harold W. Attridge, *The Epistle to the Hebrews: A Commentary on the Epistle to the Hebrews*, Hermeneia (Philadelphia: Fortress, 1989), 227.

47. Attridge, *Hebrews*, 226.

The pericope in Heb 9 provides information not available through Jeremiah, namely *how* Christ's sacrificial death serves as the atoning sacrifice and the basis for the new covenant. First, there are two complementary explanations given to Christ's death. Hebrews 9:15 states that Christ's atoning death places him in the role of covenant mediator. The mediatorial role recalls the scriptural tradition that Moses at Sinai did not simply interpret the Torah; he mediated it as well. For the Pentateuchal scholar Eckart Otto, after Moses's death "the role of mediator of divine revelation was assumed by the written Torah itself. . . . Moses had to die so that the transcribed Torah could assume Moses' function of mediating the divine will to the generations of addressees of the Torah in the Promised Land."[48] The Jesus of Hebrews is like Moses in that his death also inaugurates a new and greater means of mediating God's will to humankind. With such continuity there is also discontinuity: Jesus Christ *is* the new mediation. Christ's death does not open the way for another mediator, as did Moses, but rather it establishes Christ as mediator par excellence.

In the second explanation, Heb 9 illuminates the cause-and-effect relationship of Christ to the new covenant from an exegetical angle. Recalling Exod 24:5–8, the covenant rite at Sinai, the writer highlights "the blood of the covenant that God has ordained for you" (Heb 9:20). Just as the Sinai covenant required a blood sacrifice when it was issued, the new covenant comes forth from the Christ who suffered and died: "Without the shedding of blood, there is no forgiveness of sins" (Heb 9:22). Commentators note the several details added to this scene by the New Testament writer: sacrificial goats as well as calves, implements for sprinkling such as scarlet wool and hyssop, blood being splashed on the book as well as the altar. Hebrews is harmonizing the received text with other scriptural traditions such as Lev 14:3–7 and Num 19:6–18. In this vein, the expression "according to the law" (κατὰ τὸν νόμον) is especially significant. Hebrews states that Moses read *every* command according to the law (Heb 9:19, emphasis added) and that *everything* is cleansed by blood according to the law (Heb 9:22, emphasis added). "According to the law" is not attested in Exod 24:5–8, but it recalls how social groups in the Hebrew Bible would make an agreement among themselves to remain staunch on a single issue, such as opposition to intermarriage (Ezra 9–10). The group in question would speak of its internal agreement as a covenant that they linked to the broader covenant that God gave to Israel through Moses on Mt. Sinai (Ezra 10:3). As was noted earlier in this chapter, specialized language would elevate the group's key issue to the level of Torah and bestow upon it Mo-

---

48. Eckart Otto, "Deuteronomy as the Legal Completion and Prophetic Finale of the Pentateuch," in *Paradigm Change in Pentateuchal Research*, ed. Matthias Armgardt, Benjamin Kilchör, and Markus Zehnder, BZABR 22 (Wiesbaden: Harrassowitz, 2019), 182–83.

saic authority: "Let it be done *according to Torah*" (Ezra 10:3 [emphasis added]; see also Ezra 6:18; Neh 10:30). In the examples provided by Ezra and Nehemiah from earlier in the Second Temple period, covenant as a concept ensured right conduct on the issue of utmost concern, as it offered the prospects of broad unity to all the peoples entering the pact of this group.[49] To achieve this double effect, the phrase "according to Torah" was crucial. While it is unlikely that Hebrews is appealing to Mosaic legal authority in the narrower sense, the phrase "according to the law" (κατὰ τὸν νόμον) invokes the textual authority of revelation to further elucidate the cause-and-effect relationship of Christ to the new covenant. It was an innovation for Hebrews to construe the covenant as based upon Christ's work as high priest, but this idea is normalized when it is squared with the concept of Torah as the scriptural expression of God's will for humankind.

Hebrews 10:11–18 concludes the exposition of the heavenly high priest, Jesus Christ, and the new covenant that he mediates. The pericope is a recapitulation and synthesis of points previously made. The new sacrificial system is heavenly based because Christ as high priest offered himself for the forgiveness of sins, once and for all. Those on earth access this system spiritually, with God's own Spirit (τὸ πνεῦμα τὸ ἅγιον) enacting the words of Jeremiah: "I will put my laws in their hearts, and I will write them on their minds" (Heb 10:16). The interiority that the ancient prophet introduced into covenantal thinking has become the access point, and his accent on the forgiveness of sins has become the defining feature of the new covenant (Heb 10:17–18). Forgiveness to such an unprecedented degree makes a person worthy to enter into an intimate covenant relationship with God, through both the Spirit and through Christ the mediator. Interiority and forgiveness are mutually reinforcing as Hebrews brings forth from Scripture and specifically from Jeremiah the keys to its new covenant.

If we recall the five facets of covenant in the Hebrew Bible that highly influenced the New Testament writers (listed above in "Summary"), Heb 8:1–10:18 incorporates them all: writing instruction on the human heart (Heb 8:10; 10:16), confession of sin prompting divine mercy and forgiveness (Heb 8:12; 10:17), the bestowal of the Holy Spirit (Heb 10:15), the fusion of covenantal traditions (the cultic Priestly tradition and the legal typology associated with Sinai), and making a single belief the core of covenant while at the same time projecting a larger concept of the covenant (the expression κατὰ τὸν νόμον in Heb 9:19, 22). Based on its robust appropriation of scriptural thought, the *new* covenant in Heb 8:1–10:18 is a bit of a misnomer as it reflects the *antiquity* of covenant in Scripture five times over.

---

49. As noted above, this stance is also characteristic of the community responsible for the Damascus Document.

Covenant in Revelation

In the book of Revelation, the scriptural concept of covenant is both everywhere and nowhere. It is nowhere in that it is simply not attested lexically, nor are there allusions to compacts with Abraham, Moses, or David in any of the twenty-two chapters. The word διαθήκη appears only once, in Rev 11:19, which follows the account of the two witnesses (Rev 11:1–14) and anticipates the conflict between the woman and the dragon (Rev 12:1–17). Rev 11:19 reads: "Then God's temple in heaven was opened, and the ark of his covenant was seen within his temple; and there were flashes of lightning, rumblings, peals of thunder, an earthquake, and heavy hail." Although the reader is jolted by the image of the ark of the covenant set within the heavenly temple—much like the souls of the slaughtered discovered beneath an altar in Rev 6:9—the scene is otherwise static and theologically shallow. What does "the ark of the covenant" mean in this context? Revelation is silent.

On the other hand, the concept of covenant is everywhere in Revelation inasmuch as the book is saturated with the realia of Scripture, from prophetic oracles to cultic rituals to primordial conflicts. In terms of continuity and discontinuity with scriptural tradition, the book of Revelation is so continuous that the writer could transpose an ancient covenant into his Christian context without reconfiguring it. Thus, many read "the ark of the covenant" in Rev 11:19 as a loaded term that connotes a unilateral sense of "covenant" issued by the divine partner. For example, Mitchell Reddish comments that "the ark serves as a reminder of the promises of God and specifically the faithfulness of God in fulfilling God's covenant promises. The ark is therefore not a sign of eschatological consummation, but a sign of assurance to the faithful that God will always be with them and protect them."[50] Similarly, Charles Talbert writes, "When the prophet John sees the ark in the heavenly temple, it is the ultimate promise that God's love is steadfast and that the kingdom is coming."[51] Such interpretations are consistent with the theology of Revelation, although their basis in the text is minimal. Modern commentaries aside, how does Revelation connect the ark in Rev 11:19 to the scriptural idea of covenant? The answer may be hiding in plain sight.

It is important to read Rev 11:19 together with the verse that precedes it:

The nations raged, but your wrath has come, and the time for judging the dead, for rewarding your servants, the prophets and saints and all who fear

---

50. Mitchell G. Reddish, *Revelation*, SHBC (Macon, GA: Smyth & Helwys, 2001), 219.
51. Charles H. Talbert, *The Apocalypse: A Reading of the Revelation of John* (Louisville: Westminster John Knox, 1994), 47.

your name, both small and great, and for destroying those who destroy the earth. Then God's temple in heaven was opened, and the ark of his covenant was seen within his temple; and there were flashes of lightning, rumblings, peals of thunder, an earthquake, and heavy hail. (Rev 11:18–19)

In keeping with the apocalyptic genre, there is a moral dichotomy between the nations and "all those who fear your name" (τοῖς φοβουμένοις τὸ ὄνομά σου). It is the latter, the ones who fear God's name, who see the ark of the covenant revealed in the heavenly temple. The question becomes, Who are these individuals who "fear God's name"? Clearly they include servants, prophets and saints, but what is the identity taken on by someone in Revelation who fears (φοβέω) God's name (τὸ ὄνομά)? In Rev 14:6–7, an angel in heaven proclaims "good news" (εὐαγγέλιον) to all those on earth: "Fear God and give him glory." Here another term, "glory" (δόξα), is added to create a theological dyad. Old Testament scholars have written much about the fear of God expressed in combinations of terms, typically two in number, that complement one another.[52] These studies contribute much to our understanding of theology in ancient Israel, although none have examined the lexical pair of *glorifying* God and *fearing* God's name in any depth. The writer of Revelation, however, is oriented to this line of thought, as evidenced by Rev 15:4: "Lord, who will not fear and glorify your name? For you alone are holy. All nations will come and worship before you, for your judgments have been revealed." This verse encapsulates the key ideas surrounding covenant: those who fear and glorify God's name, such that it becomes their identity, are one and the same with all who are in right relationship with God and grasp the holiness of the deity. It is this group to whom the ark of the covenant is revealed in situ, with heaven now serving as its context and as the final destination of all who fear and glorify God's name.

These encouraging words about covenant in Revelation, the final book of the New Testament, are illumined by a comparison to Malachi, the final book of the Christian Old Testament. The oracles of the prophet Malachi criticize, but they also instruct. "Cursed be the knave who vows to his lord one of his flock but sacrifices a spoiled animal" (Mal 1:14), begins one oracle, which continues, "I am a great king, and my name is feared among the nations [ושמי נורא בגוים]," with emphasis, for our purposes, on fearing the name. One then reads, "And

---

52. A seminal study is Joachim Becker, *Gottesfurcht im Alten Testament*, AnBib 25 (Rome: Pontifical Biblical Institute, 1965). Becker studies the concept of fear of the divine through analysis of the Hebrew root ירא and its derivative forms. He posits a semantic and conceptual relationship between ירא and קדוש, the Hebrew term for holiness and specifically for holiness as a divine attribute. On this basis, many scholars have defined "fear of God" as the experience of encountering God as holy.

now, I [give] to you the priests this commandment," whereupon the priests are told "to give glory to my name [לשמי כבוד לתת]," lest God curse them and turn their blessings to curses (Mal 2:1). In this oracle, the repetition of glorifying and fearing God's name establishes in Malachi the model of right response to God. A motif is emerging, and it will become the leitmotif (see Mal 2:4–9; 3:5, 16). Taken together, these verses indicate that those who fear God's name are at the center of the book of Malachi. They fear and glorify God's name in order to occasion blessing and deflect curses. This constellation of ideas forms the text's leitmotif, which at times is referred to as a commandment (Mal 2:1, 4).

The preeminent commandment in Malachi, to fear and glorify God's name, is also expressed as a covenant. That is, the group responsible for this text and its theology is the champion of the covenant of Levi (Mal 2:4, 8), a pact that should not be overlooked even though it is not attested elsewhere in the Hebrew Bible. The covenant of Levi exists to reinforce Malachi's leitmotif of fearing and glorifying God's name, and to do so in a way that imparts identity to the priestly group here associating itself with Levi. Through their association with Levi, they gain the role of God's messengers (Mal 2:7b).[53] Among the scriptural prophets, Ezekiel and Daniel have influenced Revelation to a great degree, but Malachi resonates there as well. It would be fruitful to compare and contrast the Levitical covenanters in Malachi with those in Revelation who fear and glorify God's name. At this late point in the chapter, however, there is neither time nor space to explore Malachi's implications for Revelation. It suffices to say, however, that the covenant of Levi near the conclusion of the Hebrew Bible sheds light on how God is construed in Revelation and how covenant in the New Testament is a creative continuation of Israel's Scriptures.

Conclusion

In this journey through the biblical concept of covenant in its earlier and later iterations, two key features emerged: creativity and continuity. Paradoxically, the creativity was inspired by the exile, itself a destruction that brought an end to ancient Israel. In the wake of loss, however, there was a resurgence of covenant that came to reflect diversity, multiplicity, and fresh thinking. As the Second Temple period extended over decades and centuries, the continuity of certain

---

53. On the relationship between the covenant of Levi and Malachi's leitmotif of fearing and glorifying God's name, see Richard J. Bautch, "Priestly Polemics in the Covenant of Levi," in *Covenant—Concepts of Berith, Diatheke, and Testamentum: Proceedings of the Conference at the Lanier Theological Library in Houston, Texas, November 2019*, ed. Christian Eberhart and Wolfgang Kraus in collaboration with Richard J. Bautch, Matthias Henze, and Martin Rösel, WUNT (Tübingen: Mohr Siebeck, 2022), 93–112.

covenantal traditions influenced how communities Jewish and Christian articulated their relationship with their deity—their covenant. A focal point has been the bridge between the Old and New Testaments, marked as it were by the five facets of covenant that were perennial on both sides of the boundary: enhanced divine agency/writing instruction on the human heart; confession of sin prompting divine mercy and forgiveness; the bestowal of the Holy Spirit; the fusion of covenantal traditions; and a group making a single belief the core of its covenant while at the same time projecting externally a more broadly based notion of the covenant. The five facets were more than precursors of Christianity; they were vital to the formation of covenant in the New Testament. Furthermore, readers of the New Testament will appreciate how the writers adapted these facets to their own context and modified them in light of theological insights they were gaining; the dynamics of discontinuity were also important. Two facets in particular, the forgiveness of sins and the bestowal of the Spirit, are essential to all the covenants in question, with a few exceptions (Rom 9; Rev 11) that serve, as the saying goes, to prove the rule. Forgiveness and mercy are especially prominent in the covenants of Luke-Acts. Paul assigns the Spirit a major role in his covenants and so lays the foundation for Christian pneumatology. Hebrews celebrates the interiority of the new covenant that was first proclaimed by Jeremiah. There is much yet to be written about covenant, but the New Testament witnesses show that covenant joins together not merely God and God's people but as well the traditions of Israel and the identities of the earliest Christian communities.

Bibliography

Attridge, Harold W. *The Epistle to the Hebrews: A Commentary on the Epistle to the Hebrews*. Hermeneia. Philadelphia: Fortress, 1989.

Bautch, Richard J. "An Appraisal of Abraham in Postexilic Covenants." *CBQ* 71, no. 1 (2009): 42–63.

———. *Glory and Power, Ritual and Relationship: The Sinai Covenant in the Postexilic Period*. LHBOTS 471. London: T&T Clark, 2009.

———. "Priestly Polemics in the Covenant of Levi." Pages 93–112 in *Covenant—Concepts of Berith, Diatheke, and Testamentum: Proceedings of the Conference at the Lanier Theological Library in Houston, Texas, November 2019*. Edited by Christian Eberhart and Wolfgang Kraus in collaboration with Richard J. Bautch, Matthias Henze, and Martin Rösel. WUNT. Tübingen: Mohr Siebeck, 2022.

Bautch, Richard J., and Gary N. Knoppers, eds. *Covenant in the Persian Period: From Genesis to Chronicles*. Winona Lake, IN: Eisenbrauns, 2015.

Becker, Joachim. *Gottesfurcht im Alten Testament*. AnBib 25. Rome: Pontifical Biblical Institute, 1965.

Betz, Hans Dieter. *Galatians: A Commentary on Paul's Letter to the Church in Galatia*. Hermeneia. Philadelphia: Fortress, 1979.

Bøgh, Birgitte Secher. Introduction to *Conversion and Initiation in Antiquity: Shifting Identities, Creating Change*. Edited by Brigitte Secher Bøgh. Early Christianity in the Context of Antiquity 16. Frankfurt am Main: Lang, 2014.

Carr, David M. "Criteria and Periodization for Dating Biblical Texts to Parts of the Persian Period." Pages 11–18 in *On Dating Biblical Texts to the Persian Period: Discerning Criteria and Establishing Epochs*. Edited by Richard J. Bautch and Mark Lackowski. FAT 2/101. Tübingen: Mohr Siebeck, 2019.

Carroll, John T. *Luke: A Commentary*. NTL. Louisville: Westminster John Knox, 2012.

Fredriksen, Paula. "The Question of Worship: Gods, Pagans and the Redemption of Israel." Pages 175–201 in *Paul within Judaism: Restoring the First-Century Context to the Apostle*. Edited by Mark D. Nanos and Magnus Zetterholm. Minneapolis: Fortress, 2015.

Gaventa, Beverly Roberts. *When in Romans: An Invitation to Linger with the Gospel according to Paul*. Theological Explorations for the Church Catholic. Grand Rapids: Baker Academic, 2016.

Gosse, Bernard. "Abraham comme figure de substitution à la royauté davidique, et sa dimension internationale à l'époque postexilique." *Thf* 33, no. 2 (2002): 163–86.

Gräbe, Peter. "The New Covenant and Christian Identity in Hebrews." Pages 118–27 in *A Cloud of Witnesses: The Theology of Hebrews in Its Ancient Contexts*. Edited by Richard Bauckham, Trevor Hart, and Nathan MacDonald. LNTS 387. London: T&T Clark, 2008.

Grossman, Maxine L. *Reading for History in the Damascus Document: A Methodological Study*. STDJ 45. Leiden: Brill, 2002.

Holladay, *Jeremiah: A Commentary on the Book of the Prophet Jeremiah; 2, Chapters 26–52*. Hermeneia. Philadelphia: Fortress, 1989.

Krause, Joachim J. *Die Bedingungen des Bundes: Studien zur konditionalen Struktur alttestamentlicher Bundeskonzeptionen*. FAT 140. Tübingen: Mohr Siebeck, 2020.

Levison, John R. *The Holy Spirit before Christianity*. Waco, TX: Baylor University Press, 2019.

Lundbom, Jack R. *Jeremiah 21–36: A New Translation with Introduction and Commentary*. AB 21B. New York: Doubleday, 2004.

Murphy-O'Connor, Jerome. *Keys to First Corinthians: Revisiting the Major Issues*. Oxford: Oxford University Press, 2009.

Nathan, Emmanuel. *Re-membering the New Covenant at Corinth*. WUNT 2/514. Tübingen: Mohr Siebeck, 2020.

Newman, Judith H. "Covenant Renewal and Transformational Scripts in the Performance of the Hodayot and 2 Corinthians." Pages 291–330 in *Jesus, Paulus und die Texte von Qumran*. Edited by Jörg Frey and Enno Edzard Popkes. WUNT 2/390. Tübingen: Mohr Siebeck, 2015.

Newsom, Carol A. "The Case of the Blinking I: Discourse of the Self at Qumran." *Semeia* 57 (1992): 13–23.

Otto, Eckart. "Deuteronomy as the Legal Completion and Prophetic Finale of the Pentateuch." Pages 179–88 in *Paradigm Change in Pentateuchal Research*. Edited by Matthias Armgardt, Benjamin Kilchör, and Markus Zehnder. BZABR 22. Wiesbaden: Harrassowitz, 2019.

Pervo, Richard I. *Acts: A Commentary*. Hermeneia. Minneapolis: Fortress, 2009.

Pontificia Commissione Biblica. *Le peuple juif et ses Saintes Écritures dans le Bible chrétienne*. Vatican City: Libreria Editrice Vaticana, 2001.

Reddish, Mitchell G. *Revelation*. SHBC. Macon, GA: Smyth & Helwys, 2001.

Talbert, Charles H. *The Apocalypse: A Reading of the Revelation of John*. Louisville: Westminster John Knox, 1994.

Tatum, Gregory. "Law and Covenant in Paul and the Faithfulness of God." Pages 311–27 in *God and the Faithfulness of Paul: A Critical Examination of the Faithfulness of N. T. Wright*. Edited by Christoph Heilig, J. Thomas Hewitt, and Michael F. Bird. WUNT 2/413. Tübingen: Mohr Siebeck, 2016.

Tigay, Jeffrey. *Deuteronomy: The Traditional Hebrew Text with the New JPS Translation*. JPS Torah Commentary. Philadelphia: Jewish Publication Society, 1996.

Tobin, Thomas H. *Paul's Rhetoric in Its Contexts: The Argument of Romans*. Peabody, MA: Hendrickson, 2004.

Wieringen, Archibald L. H. M. van. "The Theologoumenon 'New' Bridging the Old and New Testament." Pages 285–301 in *The Scriptures of Israel in Jewish and Christian Tradition: Essays in Honour of Martin J. J. Menken*. Edited by Bart J. Koet, Steve Moyise, and Joseph Verhyden. NovTSup 148. Leiden: Brill, 2013.

29

Law

CLAUDIA SETZER

"Torah" both in its narrow sense as the Pentateuch and its capacious sense as ongoing revelation and interpretation means much more than "law." It includes narratives, poetry, and blessings. The New Testament rendering of Torah as *nomos*, following the Septuagint and other Greek references, thus narrows its meaning to "law" or "custom," inviting a more legalistic understanding.

What did New Testament writers mean by *nomos*? Multiple references to "the law and the prophets" in the New Testament imply consensus as to its content. But despite the *idea* of a stable canon in the first century, no one lists the included books. Josephus reports there are twenty-two books in the Bible (vs. the traditional grouping of twenty-four, possibly reflecting disputes over some books or their grouping) and describes the five books of Moses (*Ag. Ap.* 1.37–40), and 4 Ezra refers to twenty-four books that "were written first" to be revealed to the public (4 Ezra 14:45–46). Furthermore, the idea of a fixed canon and "reverence for our Scriptures" serves an apologetic aim for Josephus, who is answering pagan criticism of Judaism (*Ag. Ap.* 1.42–43).

Recent scholars have questioned both the reality of a fixed Torah in the imagination of first-century Jewish writers and the existence of a clear line between text and interpretation. Brennan Breed discusses the diversity in textual transmission and argues against the truth or utility of an "original" or fixed version of biblical text.[1] Eva Mroczek demonstrates that Second Temple Jewish writers

---

1. Brennan Breed, *Nomadic Text: A Theory of Biblical Reception History*, ISBL (Bloomington: University of Indiana Press, 2014).

drew on and revered texts like Enoch and Jubilees in ways similar to their treatment of later biblical books, bespeaking a much broader and multiform plane of revelation.[2]

We do not need to posit an absolutely fixed canon, however, to recognize a wellspring of interpretive activity around recurring laws, activity that recognizes their authority because of their origin in the Lawgiver while showing considerable dynamism and leeway in interpretation. Later rabbinic midrashim and the Mishnah attest to two distinct and creative ways that interpreters worked with the inherited texts. Mark's mention of the παράδοσις τῶν πρεσβυτέρων "tradition of the elders" (7:3) developing in "Pharisaic" circles suggests he is aware of similar practices in his own time.

Laws from Israel's Scriptures make their way into the New Testament via biography and teachings. They are embedded in references to Jesus and his family's own observance of its commands, his teaching of his own interpretation of some of its laws (e.g., Mark 12:28–31; Matt 5:21–48), and disputes between Jesus and other Jews who also revere the Torah (e.g., Mark 3:1–6; 7:1–13). Paul touts his own Jewish pedigree as law observer (Phil 3:6, Acts 22:3) even as he frets about gentile believers taking on observance of the law in Galatia. Paul contemplates the law in the abstract, as an agent outmatched by the forces of sin, as well as God's irrevocable gift to Israel (Rom 7:16–17; 9:4; 11:29). James refers to "the royal law in Scripture" (2:8, referring to Lev 19:18). Hebrews borrows imagery from the priestly and temple regulations but views the law as a shadowy precursor of Christ, the true high priest in the heavenly sanctuary (Heb 10:1). Scripture as a whole is invoked as a form of legitimation, using terms like the "Scripture(s)," "Moses," or "Moses and the prophets," a topic beyond the scope of this chapter.

Because Israel's laws in the New Testament link primarily to biography, ministry, and preaching, certain ones figure prominently. Most relate to Sabbath, purity, circumcision, and temple practice, or are about laws related to love of God and neighbor. A majority of the Torah's laws never make an appearance in the New Testament, including ones related to agriculture, buying and selling, loaning money, payment of damages, and more. Distinction in value between kinds of laws, say "ritual" versus "ethical" does not appear in Scripture itself, nor in first century Judaism. Jesus does not abrogate laws by category but rather puts his own distinctive interpretation on many of them.

---

2. Eva Mroczek, *The Literary Imagination in Jewish Antiquity* (New York: Oxford University Press, 2016). Mroczek goes beyond simply saying that the borders of canon were fuzzy. She draws a picture of a broad, dynamic, and open set of practices that situate revelation in many more writings.

Themes and Topics from Israel's Scriptures in the New Testament

Laws Prominent in the New Testament

Love of God and Neighbor

Frequently overlooked is the fact that the commands of love of God and love of neighbor are also laws in Israel's Scriptures (Deut 6:4–5; Lev 19:18). The half verse "you shall love your neighbor as yourself" is cited explicitly as one of the two great commandments identified by Jesus as summing up the whole of them in Mark 12:28–31 (// Matt 22:34–40; Luke 10:25–28).[3] It is also cited in the last of Matthew's antitheses (5:21–48) and in James (2:8) as "the royal law." Many other references seem to point to it, often juxtaposing the word "commandment" and "love" (John 13:34–35; 1 John 2:7–11; 3:23; 5:2–3; 2 John 6; Rom 13:8; 1 Cor 13). John presents the command to love as "new" and from Jesus, which informs the many Johannine references, and may connote insider language.

John Meier argues the double love commandment in its Markan and Q forms goes back to the historical Jesus, whose reflection on the whole of Torah gives pride of place to these two commands.[4] Meier is careful to warn against a devaluing of the rest of the Torah's commandments, but his view is an unnecessarily narrow bridge to walk. Reflection on the broader meaning of the Torah's commands, while not minimizing their observance, will appear throughout Jewish history, from the famous aphorism attributed to Hillel the Elder to the teaching of Harvard's Isadore Twersky.[5]

Purity Laws

Laws in Israel's Scripture divide the world into categories of טהור (καθαρός) "pure" or "clean," and טמא (ἀκάθαρος), "impure" or "unclean," as well as קדוש (ἅγιος), "holy," and חול (κοινός), "common" or "profane," modeling a system relatively foreign to us, but perhaps somewhat less so after experiencing a pandemic where managing contagion through washing and distancing are connected to care for society. Within the categories of impurity, scholars have delineated two

---

3. Unless otherwise noted, all translations are by the author.
4. John Meier, *Law and Love*, vol. 4 of *A Marginal Jew: Rethinking the Historical Jesus*, ABRL (New Haven: Yale University Press, 2009), 572–76.
5. Regarding the story of a gentile who asks Hillel to teach him the whole of Torah while standing on one foot, b. Šabb. 31a, "What is hateful to you do not do to another. That is the whole of Torah. The rest is commentary. Go and learn." Isadore Twersky discusses what he calls "supercategories," principles like *kedushah*, "holiness," or *tmimut*, "perfection," for which there is no specific commandment because the whole of the Torah embodies them; Twersky, "Make a Fence Around the Torah," *The Torah U-Madda Journal* 8 (1998–1999): 33–35.

kinds, one ritual and the other moral, coming from the Priestly Code (Lev 1–16) and the Holiness Code (Lev 17–26). The first relates to some bodily processes, like discharge of semen, menstrual blood, or blood after giving birth; some illnesses, including skin disease (often incorrectly translated as leprosy); something like fungus or mold that grows on houses and cloth; and death, where a corpse transmits the highest level of impurity. Most processes are unavoidable for most people, do not carry a moral charge, and are rectified by washing or immersion, offering sacrifice, passage of time, and/or examination by a priest. Some animals are impure and cannot be eaten. The second category of pure/impure distinctions, from the Holiness Code (Lev 17–26), attaches morality to these categories. Sins such as idolatry, murder, manslaughter, and leaving a corpse overnight on a tree defile not only the person but the land.

The distinctions between holy and common relate to the temple cult and access to the altar. Holiness implies separation and fitness to approach the divine: "You [Aaron and sons] are to distinguish between the holy and the common, and between the unclean and the clean" (Lev 10:10; Ezek 22:26). Priests serving at the altar must be both pure *and* holy.

Ritual purity laws appear in narratives around Jesus's birth and ministry. In Luke's Gospel Mary and Joseph bring the newborn Jesus to the temple both to offer a sacrifice of two doves according to the ritual of purification after childbirth (Lev 12) and to perform the ritual of פדיון הבן, the redemption of the first-born son from service to the priesthood (Num 18:15–16). Luke notes that the parents performed this ceremony "to do for him what was customary under the law" (Luke 2:27) and that they did "everything required by the law of the Lord" (2:39).

Jesus begins his ministry with immersion by the Baptist, a purification ritual (Mark 1:9–11; Matt 3:13–17; Luke 3:21). After healing a leper (Mark 1:40–45), Jesus "sternly warns" him to go straight to the priest to complete the rituals for restorative cleansing after healing "what Moses commanded, as a testimony to them" (Lev 14:2–32; Mark 1:44).[6] Corpse impurity is an issue in the raising of a young woman (Mark 5:35–43; Matt 9:18–26; Luke 8:40–56) and also the son of the widow of Nain (Luke 7:11–17), but nothing suggests that Jesus rejects the overall system. Rather he, like the mourners and those who will prepare the body, willingly contracts ritual impurity. Nor does Jesus's reaction to the woman with abnormal bleeding suggest he or the woman reject purity laws (Mark 5:25–34; Matt 9:20–22; Luke 8:42–48). Matthew Thiessen submits the passages around

---

6. Myrick C. Shinall Jr. argues that Jesus's treatment of the leper is in line with Second Temple Judaism and rejects the image of lepers being utterly shunned by Jewish society; Shinall, "The Social Condition of Lepers in the Gospels," *JBL* 137 (2018): 915–34.

healings to rigorous analysis, showing that Jesus is not recalled as someone who abrogates the laws around maintaining ritual purity nor openly flouts them. Rather, Jesus destroys the *sources* of impurity by his own bodily presence, emitting a "contagion of holiness." All of Jesus's actions and his very being are a rebuke to the forces of death, the ultimate source of impurity.[7]

Jesus's Battle with Unclean Spirits

Although references to demons and evil spirits in Israel's Scriptures are limited, Jewish texts of the Second Temple period like Tobit, Jubilees, and 1 Enoch see a cosmos roiling with demons who attack weak humans, sending pain, illness, and death.[8] Later rabbinic material placed demons everywhere, in abandoned buildings, in palm trees, and in crowds where rabbis taught, threatening humanity's well-being.[9] Readers of Mark and early Christ followers would be attuned to Jesus's visceral power over these forces of pollution, even as these powers are passed on to his followers (Mark 3:15; 6:7; Matt 10:1).

Jesus battles against "unclean spirits," another identification for the demons Jesus casts out in his many healings/exorcisms. The Gospel of Mark casts Jesus as locked in combat with Satan and his demons from the beginning of his ministry, starting with the power struggle in the wilderness (Mark 1:12–13). In the first chapter alone, Jesus seemingly heals hundreds of their illnesses by exorcising demons. Unlike his own disciples and many others in the gospel, the demons know Jesus's identity and understand his power (Mark 1:23–24, 34; 3:11; 5:7). Even Jesus's detractors recognize the efficacy of his exorcisms but say he dabbles in the demonic himself, possessed by an "unclean spirit" (Mark 3:22, 30). He replies that his power to "bind the strong man" can only come from his power outside of Satan's realm. Thiessen notes that in the incident of Jesus confronting the unclean spirit in the Gerasene demoniac (Mark 5:1–13) "impurity saturates the entire scene," from the man roaming in a graveyard full of corpses to the evil spirits sent into the pigs.[10]

---

7. Matthew Thiessen, *Jesus and the Forces of Death: The Gospels' Portrayal of Ritual Impurity within First-Century Judaism* (Grand Rapids: Baker Academic, 2020), 88–93, 108–22.

8. E.g., in Israel's Scriptures: שדים (Deut 32:17; Ps 106:37) and שעירים (Lev 17:7; 2 Chr 11:15), both associated with prohibited cult practices, the child-stealing Lilith (Isa 34:14), and Azazel, the scapegoat possibly associated with a desert demon (Lev 16). Thiessen, *Jesus and the Forces of Death*, 132–39.

9. Sara Ronis describes demonology as much more evident in the Babylonian material than the Palestinian, part of rabbinic conceptualizing of space; Ronis, "Space, Place, and the Race for Power: Rabbis, Demons, and the Construction of Babylonia," *HTR* 110, no. 4 (2017): 588–603.

10. Thiessen, *Jesus and the Forces of Death*, 145.

The logion of Mark 7:15, "there is nothing outside a person that by going in can defile, but the things that come out are what defile," suggests that one's actions and behavior must not be neglected in observance of laws around ritual purity and impurity. In the surrounding narrative, both Pharisees, concerned about ritual purity, and Jesus's own disciples, presumably less concerned about purity matters, fail to understand his teaching (7:1–23). The person who challenges Jesus and wins approval is the Syro-Phoenician woman, who, as a foreigner and a non-Jew, is outside the whole system of purity since gentiles do not carry ritual impurity. Mark 7:19b, "thus he declared all foods clean," is understood by most as a Markan gloss. Luke presents three examples of Jesus's joining a Pharisee at table in the Pharisee's home (Luke 7:36; 11:37; 14:1), which suggests that Jesus did not reject their purity practices, even if he argued they did not substitute for ethical behavior or could have been observed more stringently.[11]

Paul uses the pure/impure and holy/common distinctions to explain his mission to the gentiles, sometimes conflating categories. Non-Jews, though not impure in the ritual sense (contrary to popular belief, only Jews can be ritually impure) and welcome in certain parts of the temple precincts, are by definition *not* a holy (קדוש) people. This status is reserved for Israel. Since Paul did not think gentiles should convert to Judaism to join the people of God (as evidenced by Galatians and Luke's version of the Apostolic Council), he must argue for transformation of gentiles *qua* gentiles into a holy people.

Paula Fredriksen shows that English translations have obscured Paul's heavy use of categories of the language of purity, holiness, and temple service in relation to the gentiles. Christ's death is a sacrifice that atones (2 Cor 5:21; Rom 3:25). In Rom 15:15b–16, Paul speaks of "the grace given me by God to be a minister [λειτουργόν, or 'temple functionary'] of Christ Jesus to the gentiles in the priestly service [ἱερουργοῦντα] of the gospel of God, so that the offering [προσφορά] of the gentiles may be acceptable, sanctified by the Holy Spirit," using three words of temple service. The result is to render gentiles now holy and fit for service to God.[12] Paul

---

11. Yair Furstenberg argues that Jesus's criticism of the Pharisees matches complaints from multiple Second Temple groups that Pharisees are too lenient in purity and other legal matters or overturn natural hierarchies of sacredness, leading to the creation of an early "anti-Pharisaic literature" in Second Temple Judaism, evident in 4QMMT, the Mishnah, and the Gospel of Matthew; Furstenberg, "Jesus against the Laws of Pharisees: The Legal Woe Sayings and Second Temple Intersectarian Discourse," *JBL* 139, no. 4 (2020): 769–88. In an earlier article, Furstenberg shows that the Pharisees differed from their contemporaries by ascribing purity and impurity to human activity and God's control. Other groups saw categories of purity and impurity in more ontological or cosmic terms; Furstenberg, "Controlling Impurity: The Natures of Impurity in Second Temple Debates," *Dine Israel* 30 (2015): 163–96.

12. Paula Fredriksen, "Paul, Purity, and the *Ekklēsia* of the Gentiles," in *The Beginnings of Christianity*, ed. Jack Pastor and Menachem Mor (Jerusalem: Yad Ben-Zvi, 2005), 213–14.

frequently speaks of the gentile believers using sanctification language (1 Thess 1:9; 4:3–7) and of the community as God's temple (1 Cor 3:16–17; 2 Cor 6:16).

Pamela Eisenbaum further illustrates Paul's embrace of these categories to bring gentiles as gentiles into the holy people of God via moral behavior. She notes that he stresses the kinds of sins that impart impurity, namely idolatry and sexual sins, the same sins emphasized in the Holiness Code that caused Canaanites to be expelled and that polluted the earth (Lev 18:24–25). Paul emphasizes discipline in sexual practices and in avoidance of idolatry, two categories prominent in Israel's Scriptures.[13] Eisenbaum's argument goes a long way toward explaining Paul's strictness in sexual matters, a strictness that is not apparent in Jesus's preaching. Paul counsels the Corinthians to expel the man sleeping with his stepmother (1 Cor 5:1–8) and is horrified that his congregants are going to prostitutes (1 Cor 6:12–20). Presumably Jesus did not approve of these things either, but as a preacher to Jews who had the Torah, he did not need to emphasize these sins over others. For Paul, moral purity is the ticket for gentiles' elevation to an עַם קָדוֹשׁ, a "holy people."

Behind the many references throughout the New Testament to Jesus's death as a purifying or atoning sacrifice stands the sacrificial system. Its categories and rituals provide the symbolic language to explain Jesus's death and a cosmic transformation to Christ followers—to translate legal prescriptions into theological ones. In Hebrews, Jesus is both the atoning sacrifice and the high priest (Heb 1:3; 2:17; 3:1; 4:14–16; 5:1–10; 7:26–28; 8:6; 9:11–14, 25–28; 10:1–13; 10:19–22; 13:11–12). Its theology is pure replacement theology, arguing that the Levitical priesthood and its sacrifices have been superseded by Jesus and his followers while retaining the categories of purity and atonement (Heb 2:11; 9:22). Hebrews 2:14 shows Jesus's atoning sacrifice brings the defeat of the devil, who wields the power of death.[14]

The role of ritual purity in first-century Judaism and in the early Christ followers' understanding of Jesus's ministry is crucial for dismantling negative stereotypes of early Judaism. Amy-Jill Levine shows how the purity laws are relentlessly invoked in parables scholarship to depict Pharisees and the Judaism

---

13. Pamela Eisenbaum, *Paul Was Not a Christian: The Original Message of a Misunderstood Apostle* (San Francisco: HarperOne, 2009), 155–67.

14. David Moffitt argues for the postresurrection incarnate Jesus's presence in the heavenly sanctuary to effect atonement, in line with the Yom Kippur sacrifice; Moffitt, *Atonement and the Logic of Resurrection in the Epistle to the Hebrews*, NovTSup 141 (Leiden: Brill, 2013). But any nonsupersessionist argument founders on Heb 10:11–12. A. J. M. Wedderburn suggests that the author undermines his own purposes by rejecting the efficacy of the cultic system while retaining cultic categories; Wedderburn, "Sawing Off the Branches: Theologizing Dangerously Ad Hebraeos," *JTS* 56, no. 2 (2005): 393–414.

of Jesus's time as unfeeling and legalistic compared to a compassionate Jesus, noting such views come from conservative and liberationist interpreters alike.[15] Care to follow laws of ritual purity does not signal lack of compassion, nor does it seem that Jesus rejected these laws.

Sabbath Laws

While the command to observe and remember the Sabbath and to do no work appears in three places in the Torah (Exod 20:8–11; 35:2–3; Deut 5:12–15), it gives virtually no guidance as to what that means (except Exod 35:3, Num 15:32–36). Naturally, questions arose over what constituted prohibited work on the Sabbath, leading the later rabbis to develop the thirty-nine kinds of prohibited labor, as well as the inevitable instances in which they may override the prohibitions to save a life. In the Mekilta, a tannaitic midrash, a discussion between rabbis begins: "From where is it derived that saving a life overrides the Sabbath?" Numerous verses are brought forward and arguments put forth. Rabbi Simeon ben Menissia says: "The Sabbath is given over to you [לכם שבת מסורה], you are not surrendered to the Sabbath" (Mek. 31.13). The idea of overriding observance of a Sabbath law to preserve life and serve human needs is derived from Lev 18:5, "you shall keep my statutes and my ordinances; by doing so one may live. I am the Lord." In one typical use in b. Yoma 85b, interpreters add: "You shall live by them, not die by them."[16]

Despite a popular sense that Jesus and the Pharisees battled one another over Sabbath observance, probative examples are few. Mark's Gospel records two incidents where Jesus's Sabbath practice engenders conflict, one where the disciples pluck grain (Mark 2:23–28) and another where Jesus heals a man with a withered hand (Mark 3:2–4). In 1:21–31 Jesus heals in and out of the synagogue on the Sabbath, including Peter's mother-in-law, without provoking complaint. Nor is Sabbath breaking one of the charges against Jesus by the priests or Sanhedrin. Matthew adds no new examples, but removes one healing story from the Sabbath (Matt 8:14–15). In Matt 23, overly punctilious Sabbath observance is *not* one of the charges associated with Pharisaic excess or hypocrisy. Luke adds two controversies around Sabbath healing: Jesus's healing the woman with the spirit of weakness (Luke 13:10–16) and the healing of a man with edema (Luke 14:1–5). In

---

15. Amy-Jill Levine, *Short Stories by Jesus: The Enigmatic Parables of a Controversial Rabbi* (San Francisco: HarperOne, 2015).

16. See Lutz Doering, who also argues for the judicious use of rabbinic materials in understanding New Testament traditions; Doering, "Sabbath Laws in the New Testament," in *The New Testament and Rabbinic Literature*, ed. Reimund Bieringer et al., JSJSup 136 (Leiden: Brill, 2009), 207–53.

the latter story, Jesus seems to dare the "lawyers and Pharisees" he is eating with to object. They do not. When he makes his argument for healing on the Sabbath from the rule of pulling an ox out of a pit on the Sabbath, they remain silent. Although the narrative is crafted to imply dissent, Luke does not produce any.

John does not transmit these narratives but presents two new ones—the paralytic healed by Jesus who is censured for carrying his mat (John 5:1–18) and the man born blind (John 9:1–40). In both Johannine stories, the mention of the Sabbath appears as a secondary addition to a simple healing story, coming after the healing is complete. John expands the objection to Sabbath healing into a dispute about Jesus's identity and status: "this is why the Jews sought all the more to kill him, because he not only broke the Sabbath but also called God his own Father, making himself equal with God" (5:18). John may reflect a tradition of disputes over Sabbath observance, but his concerns are christological, not halakic.

Jesus was not a Sabbath breaker, neither did he minimize its importance or encourage its violation. On the contrary, a quick read of the Synoptics shows Jesus matter-of-factly observing the Sabbath; eating with Pharisees and leaders of the Pharisees and with his disciples; a "regular" in synagogue who teaches and chants from the prophets (Mark 1:21–29; 3:1–6; Matt 4:23; 13:54; Luke 4:16–20; 4:31–37; 13:10–17). We assume that as religious Jews, Jesus and his disciples observed Sabbath laws, otherwise controversies over their Sabbath observance would not make sense. Something else is at work in John: Sabbath observance is a gateway to larger objections to high christological claims, a reason that John's hearers are no longer at home in some synagogues.[17] Adele Reinhartz argues that John intentionally appropriates Jewish institutions as a rhetorical strategy to repudiate Jews and Judaism and promote a gentile mission.[18]

Acts presents Paul touring diaspora synagogues to win converts (Acts 13:5; 14:1–2; 16:13; 17:1, 10, 17; 18:4, 19, 26; 19:8), at times spending multiple Sabbaths in one place. In one case, he stays for three months! The well-known Theodotus inscription from first-century Jerusalem indicates a synagogue could function as a gathering place for study and a hostel for travelers (*CIJ* 2.1404). Luke shows how Paul incites plenty of controversy even as he enjoys missionary success. But while Paul is accused of "turning the world upside down" (Acts 17:6), Luke presents no charges of Sabbath violation or lack of reverence for it.

---

17. John's identification of Jesus as the Logos, multiple references to Jesus as the Son of Man, references to his oneness with the Father, and use of the "I am" sayings indicate a uniquely high Christology, which may help explain a rift with some local Jewish groups.

18. Adele Reinhartz, *Cast Out of the Covenant: Jews and Anti-Judaism in the Gospel of John* (Lanham, MD: Lexington Books; Fortress Academic, 2018).

Circumcision

Circumcision is simply a given for Jesus as the son of a Jewish family. Luke is careful to note that Jesus was circumcised on the eighth day as commanded in the Torah (Lev 12:3; Luke 2:21). Paul includes his own circumcision on the eighth day within a list of his Jewish bona fides (Phil 3:5).

When Paul writes to gentile Christ believers in Galatia, circumcision becomes a metonymy for the commandments of the Torah as a whole. But he says nothing about Jews circumcising their sons or ceasing to do so. Elsewhere he allows the practice to stand, presumably for Jews who believe in Jesus (1 Cor 7:18–20). Acts 21:20–25 implies that the charge that Paul teaches against circumcision is false.

According to Acts 16:3, Paul circumcised his fellow worker Timothy, the son of a Jewish mother and a non-Jewish father, in deference to the Jews in the area. Gentile Christians, according to Paul's rendering, were never required to be circumcised (Gal 2:1–9; Acts 15:1–21; 21:25), and it only became an issue when Jerusalem church leaders were pressured by false brethren (Gal 2:4). Rebuffed there for the time being, they, or those like them, later made headway with Galatian Christ believers.

Paul's heated rhetoric against circumcision only appears when he speaks of gentiles taking on circumcision. According to J. Louis Martyn's careful reconstruction of the situation in Galatia, Paul's apostolic status and teaching are under assault by a group Martyn terms "the Teachers," Jewish believers in Jesus who believe gentiles who join the Jesus believers should be circumcised in accordance with the Torah law.[19] Paul's fury seems fueled by a sense of apocalyptic emergency as Jesus's return is imminent. Nor have the gentile believers been briefed on the full rigors of a Torah-observant lifestyle; he implies that they have been pressured to take on circumcision, a requirement for males to join the Jewish people, but not informed that the law would then also demand observance of food laws, Sabbath, temple offerings, and more.

Gentiles who were baptized Christ followers had their own "Torah." Frederiksen calls them "ex-pagan pagans," because Paul *did* make certain demands of them, that they refrain from idolatry and take on strictures in sexual matters.[20] The Apostolic Council, whether real or idealized, also points to certain demands levied on gentile converts to the church. Such people probably had precedents in the non-Jewish

---

19. J. Louis Martyn, *Galatians: A New Translation with Introduction and Commentary*, AB 33A (New York: Doubleday, 1997), 117–26.

20. Paula Fredriksen, *Paul: The Pagans' Apostle* (New Haven: Yale University Press, 2017), 117–22.

donors and regular visitors to diaspora synagogues testified to by inscriptions and incidents in Acts (Acts 15:21, 25). It is difficult to imagine that gentiles attracted to synagogues did not observe some minimum standards of conduct regarding worship, food, and sexual behavior, at least when in community with Jews.

Outside of the conflict in Galatia and the report of the Apostolic Council in Acts, circumcision does not seem to emerge as a concern in New Testament texts. The situation in Galatia is idiosyncratic, the result of some kind of alternative Christian mission, not a continuation of earlier practice. Fredriksen speculates that a mid-century alarm, perhaps over Jesus's delayed return and the failure of the mission to the Jews, may have fueled one group's efforts to bring gentiles into Israel via circumcision.[21] They did not succeed. Later works like the Pseudo-Clementine Homilies and Recognitions impose further demands of purity regulations on Christians from Lev 17–18 but do not impose circumcision.

Temple Practice

Jesus and his family appear as pious Jews observing laws relating to the Jerusalem temple in line with other Jews. His family brings sacrifices as purification after birth and also performs the redemption of the first-born son in Luke's Gospel. Jesus is one of a crowd of pilgrims coming to Jerusalem to celebrate Passover at the time of his arrest. At his arrest he alludes to teaching frequently in the temple without harassment (Mark 14:49; Luke 19:47; John 18:20).

The puzzling incident of the overturning of the money changers' tables is not a legal matter (Mark 11:15–19; Matt 21:12–13; Luke 19:45–48; John 2:13–16). A system of exchanging foreign money for the silver Tyrian shekel was part of a functioning system. People exchanged money to make offerings or buy animals to offer sacrifice at the temple. Several explanations are offered as to the cause of Jesus's outburst. Money changers may have been gouging people, much like exchanges in foreign currency today, or offering different rates to different people. Trade may have spilled over from the outer court of the gentiles into the sacred inner court. Jesus may have protested Roman control of the temple and priesthood. In line with his apocalyptic and prophetic stance, he may have been predicting the destruction of the temple and Jerusalem, particularly since he alludes to Isa 56:7 and Jer 7:11. Frederiksen notes, however, that Paul, the only writer before 70, knows nothing of such a prediction.[22] Nor do we see evidence that the Jerusalem church, coalescing after Jesus's death, rejected temple practice or the temple itself.

---

21. Paula Fredriksen, *When Christians Were Jews: The First Generation* (New Haven: Yale University Press, 2018), 102–3.

22. Fredriksen, *When Christians Were Jews*, 50–51.

In any case, the force of Jesus's actions and statements are not against the temple and its practices but against actions of some money changers. If anything, his stance seems to be one of restoration and purification of temple practices.

Food Laws

We cannot imagine Jesus abandoning the laws of *kashrut*, or kosher food. The Gospels show him eating with Pharisees without comment. Nor can we imagine a charismatic preacher to other Jews traversing this significant boundary marker and retaining any authority. Furthermore, such a radical departure from a fundamental religious practice would leave deep memories, and neither he nor the disciples are accused of eating nonkosher food. Mark 7:1–5 is about eating in a state of ritual purity, a practice associated with Pharisees and not, as Mark inaccurately states, extending to all Jews. The decisions at the Apostolic Council relate to gentiles, but stating their abstention from certain foods would not need mentioning if all food laws were abrogated.

Mark 7:15, if it is authentic, needs explanation. We can imagine such a saying from Jesus along prophetic lines that rejects ritual unless accompanied by acts of social justice. "I desire mercy and not sacrifice" (Hos 6:6) does not mean that sacrifice is canceled but that mercy is more important. Although Meier ultimately rejects this "dialectical negation" argument as only a possibility, he concludes that Mark 7:15, and by extension Mark's editorial comment in 17b, are products of the early church.[23] Yet Mark may have an early saying expressing something like "I desire not (just) eating kosher food, but ethical behavior," which he revises for his own universalizing purposes.[24] For the same reason he editorializes, "thus he declared all foods clean."

The vision of Peter in Acts, repeated three times, presents a more difficult puzzle (Acts 10:11–16, 28; 11:5–10). On the face of it, it seems to erase the boundaries between different kinds of animals and allows the Jew Peter to eat any animal, kosher or nonkosher. Confusing the issue is the contrast between "clean" and "common" (Acts 10:15), when the natural opposite of "clean" would be "unclean," and the elision of the two different categories, "common" and "unclean" in 11:8.

Thiessen outlines the problems that arise if we assume this ambiguous vision abrogates the food laws: (1) Peter does not follow it up by consuming such nonkosher, impure, or common food. In spite of the narrative beginning with his hunger and others preparing food, he never does eat anything. (2) Peter cannot understand the saying in its literal sense, refusing its literal meaning three or four

---

23. Meier, *Law and Love*, 384–99.
24. Meier, *Law and Love*, 386–87.

times (Acts 10:14–16) and continuing to wonder about its meaning (Acts 10:17, 19) until its metaphorical sense unfolds in the narrative. (3) Peter's bafflement ends when he affirms the vision is about human beings, "God has shown me [in the vision] that I should not call any person common or unclean" (Acts 10:28). He confirms the fitness of the gentiles before God (Acts 10:34–35; 45, 47). (4) Peter is not remembered by Luke or accused by anyone of eating nonkosher food. Objections are to with whom he eats, or in Paul's case, with whom he suddenly refuses to eat (Acts 11:1–2; Gal 2:11–13). The Apostolic Council's minimal strictures on gentile believers' food would not make sense if Jews were no longer bound by *any* food laws. (5) The vision(s) are embedded in narratives not about food or eating at all but inclusion of gentiles as gentiles.[25] Thiessen argues that the division is allegorical, explaining Luke's rather conservative vision that gentiles must be brought in as gentiles, and this is only possible if they become holy.[26]

While we keep coming up short in our search for examples of law observance as a firm boundary marker or point of serious contention with other Jews for either the historical Jesus or in early Christ-believing groups, two possible exceptions stand out—Jesus's teaching on oaths and divorce.

Special Cases: Oaths and Divorce

Divorce is assumed in the Torah and little detail is given except to mention a writ of divorce, a prohibition for a twice-divorced woman to return to her first husband (Deut 24:1–4), and a prohibition for a priest to marry a divorced woman (Lev 21:7, 13). Later, the rabbinic schools of Hillel and Shammai will wrangle over the circumstances in which a man may exercise this right (m. Giṭ. 9:10). Limited evidence in first-century materials like Philo, Josephus, and the Dead Sea Scrolls affirm the legal right of divorce.

Jesus seems to depart from the Torah teaching, forbidding divorce and labeling remarriage as adultery. Five sayings on divorce by Jesus provide multiple attestations, strengthening the idea that some stricture or prohibition goes back to Jesus (Mark 10:11–12; Matt 19: 3–9; the Q logion extracted from Matt 5:32 and Luke 16:18; 1 Cor 7:10–11). The examples do not say exactly the same thing, but the aphorism of Mark 10:9, "therefore what God has joined together let no one separate," is likely authentic, and Jesus forbade divorce and declared remarriage to be a form of adultery.[27]

---

25. Matthew Thiessen, *Contesting Conversion: Genealogy, Circumcision, and Identity in Ancient Judaism and Christianity* (New York: Oxford University Press, 2011), 124–26.
26. Thiessen, *Jesus and the Forces of Death*, 195.
27. Meier, *Law and Love*, 95–128, provides the exegetical brush clearing to get to this prohibition.

Note that this apparent change in the Torah law reveals a Jesus considerably stricter and more demanding than other Second Temple and rabbinic interpreters. As an apocalyptic thinker, he expects the imminent coming of the kingdom, so celibacy and punctiliousness in sexual matters is called for. Paul, Jesus, and some at Qumran reacted with celibacy; others, already married, were to retain marriage.

An even more surprising example of Jesus's departing from the Torah's laws is his prohibiting the taking of oaths. Unlike divorce, which is voluntary, oaths are required in the Bible and rabbinic materials to resolve certain disputes (Exod 22:9–11; Num 5:11–28).[28] Oaths and swearing appear throughout the Torah, Prophets, and Writings as a necessary feature of a functioning legal system, just as today's law courts rely on witnesses swearing or affirming to tell the truth in their testimonies. Similarly, they appear in Qumran literature (e.g., CD XV, 1–8; XVI, 1–12) and throughout the New Testament (e.g., Luke 1:73; Acts 2:29–35; Heb 7:21–28). Paul himself swears an oath or two (Gal 1:20; Rom 1:9). Yet two places in the New Testament forbid taking oaths, one put in a direct statement from Jesus (Matt 5:34–37), and another as early Christian paraenesis (Jas 5:12). Their dissimilarity from the usual acceptance of oaths in the New Testament, coupled with dual attestation in very different works, argues for authenticity as teaching from the historical Jesus.[29]

Assuming their authenticity, we must ask: Is Jesus revoking the law in these cases? His commands are far from the apparent meaning of the text. But a discomfort with oaths appears in Eccl 5:1–6 and 8:2, in Philo, *Decal.* 17.84, and in Sir 23:9, works earlier than or contemporary with Jesus. Could a tiptoeing around oaths not also be a stricter interpretation of the law, treating all speech as if it has God as witness, being extremely scrupulous about even everyday talk? The coming of the kingdom requires living in a state of readiness, just as the people of Israel at the foot of the mountain observed extra strictures to ready themselves to see God. Given the apocalyptic framework, Jesus is less likely to be recommending a free-for-all from the law than an ascetic abstention. Perhaps everything that comes out of one's mouth should carry the weight and clarity of an oath (Matt 5:37).

The later rabbinic concept of סיג התורה, of making a fence around the Torah (m. 'Abot 1.1), can mean adding strictures to avoid sin. For example, the sages say that the evening Shema prayer should be recited before midnight, despite the fact that technically one has until dawn. The explanation given is "to distance a person from transgression" (m. Ber. 1.1). Furthermore, we must appreciate

---

28. Moshe Greenberg, Haim Hermann Cohn, and Menachem Elon, "Oath," *EncJud* 15:358–64.
29. Meier, *Law and Love*, 198–206.

the elasticity of interpretation that allowed interpreters to stray far from the literal sense of the text while retaining allegiance to it. In the famous story of the oven of Akhnai, for example, the sages assert their authority to interpret the text independent of God's heavenly voice (b. B. Meṣ. 59a–b) with the half-verse from Exod 23:2: "You shall follow a majority," unfazed by the presence of a negative in the biblical verse that makes it "you shall *not* follow after a majority in wrongdoing." In the cases of divorce and oaths, Jesus and his followers may have understood themselves as continuing to uphold the Torah's commands.

Three Approaches to Nomos: Jesus, Paul, and Matthew

Jesus was certainly a Jew who observed the laws of the Torah as he understood them. We cannot imagine otherwise. A charismatic apocalyptic preacher to Israel would lack all credibility if he rejected the Torah's commands, and none of Jesus's sayings suggest an antinomian approach. But this statement alone does not get us as far as we would like. It is equivalent to saying a citizen of the United States believes in the Constitution. What kind of halakic Jew might he have been? We hear more of the laws that suggest disagreement, and some of these are introduced at the level of the gospel's composition. Mark provides one such example, regarding fasting, where the disciples' failure to fast is at odds with some other Jewish groups and practices of Mark's own time (Mark 2:18–20). We have outlined a Jesus whose practice and interpretation fall within the parameters of Second Temple Judaism, fueled by an apocalyptic and prophetic outlook.

Most recent discussions of Jesus and the law note three things: the diversity of interpretation in first-century Judaism, the inability to live by the law without interpreting it to apply to new situations, and the hostile rhetoric that typifies different groups when talking about others with whom they disagree. Multiple voluntary associations in Second Temple Judaism produced different practices stemming from their interpretations of Israel's Scriptures. Invariably they disapproved of other understandings. The Dead Sea Scrolls tout multiple pejorative references to the "seekers after smooth things," probably Pharisees, for their text interpretations and practical laxity in the Damascus Document, the Hodayot, and Pesher Habakkuk (CD I, 18; 1QH^a II, 14; 4Q169 3–4).[30] Philo railed against the extreme allegorizers (*Migr.* 86–93), Josephus attacked the Zealots (*J.W.* 4.193–208; 4.355–357), and Sadducees made fun of Jesus who, along with the Pharisees,

---

30. See Albert Baumgarten, "Seekers After Smooth Things," in *Encyclopedia of the Dead Sea Scrolls*, ed. Lawrence H. Schiffman and James C. VanderKam (Oxford: Oxford University Press, 2000), 2:857–59.

preached resurrection of the dead (Mark 12:18–23). His response was that they did not understand their own Scriptures or the nature of God (Mark 12:24–27). Matthew's Jesus called Pharisees "blind guides" and "hypocrites." Later rabbis disparage the ignorant "people of the land," the *Am ha'aretz* (e.g., m. 'Abot 2.5; 5.10; b. Ber. 47b; b. Soṭah 22a). Many without titles probably simply disagreed with one another.[31] We should not see the examples of Jesus in dispute about law observance with Pharisees, Sadducees, or others as out of the ordinary.

Interpreting and applying the Torah's law is inevitable and part of every group's forging of its identity. For the rabbis, coming after Jesus, the appearance of a second "Oral Law," given a status alongside the Written Torah as also revealed at Sinai (m. 'Abot 1.1), significantly revised the plain meaning of many of the laws. A protoversion of such interpretation is probably behind the "tradition of the elders" in Mark 7:5, with which Jesus disagrees. To give an example of the latitude of interpretation, the many transgressions in Israel's Scriptures that earn the death penalty are modified by rabbinic laws of examination of witnesses and exceptions to the degree that the death penalty was significantly undermined. The Mishnah says a court that executed one person in seven years was considered bloodthirsty. Rabbi Eleazar ben Azariah quickly revised it again to mean one execution in seventy years (m. Mak. 1.10). Similar latitude in Jesus's interpretation should not surprise us, especially in light of an expectation of an imminent apocalyptic change.

Paul speaks more about the law in the abstract and the particular than any other New Testament writer, but because he addresses different groups and crises, no unified picture emerges. He leaves us three kinds of material about Jewish law: his references to his own observance and sense of election, his intense response to his gentile Christ followers in Galatia, and his more measured reflections on the Torah's place in the new cosmos created by Jesus's death. He never comments on whether Jews must observe the Torah commandments. We are familiar with his own self-confidence in his Torah observance (Phil 3:5–6) where he makes an astounding claim that he was "under the law, blameless." He maintains Israel's advantage in God's plan and invidious distinctions between Jews and gentiles (Rom 1:16; 2:9–10; 3:1–2; 9:4; Gal 2:15).

Paul's letters, however, are not addressed to Jews, and he sees himself as the prophet to the gentiles who, like Jeremiah, was set apart by God before birth (Gal 1:15–16). Non-Jews have a place in God's plan for redemption, but the Torah does not command them in the same way it commands Jews. His remarks on the law revolve around this reality. His challenge is to bring gentiles into the people

---

31. Multiple authors on Judaism's first-century diversity. See, e.g., https://www.pbs.org/wgbh/pages/frontline/shows/religion/portrait/judaism.html.

of God as gentiles, a possibility now because Jesus's death brought a change in the cosmic power balance.

As Fredriksen shows us, Paul's pagan converts to Christ were not "law-free" but were bound by certain commandments, namely the first and second of the Ten Commandments, the prohibition against worshiping other gods and the making of graven images, as well as those against murder, adultery, theft, and coveting (Rom 13:9), and a host of others, like "love your neighbor as yourself," and the prohibition against a son having sexual relations with his stepmother (Lev 18:8; 1 Cor 5:1). He introduces numerous other strictures on sexual and social behavior (1 Cor 6) and issues guides to proper behavior (1 Cor 7).[32] These "expagan pagans" assumed a different level of adherence to and support from the Torah. His remarks that circumcised or not, one should keep the commandments of God (1 Cor 7:19) show that all are commanded in some way. Jews and gentiles had different relations to Torah and its laws, but neither group could be entirely without it. It is foundational to understanding Christ's mission, and its laws impose obligations on all who follow him.

In his heated rhetoric in Galatians, Paul argues that the teachers promoting circumcision to gentile believers have made a mistake and blurred ethnic boundaries. In light of the apocalyptic emergency, full conversion to Judaism is not possible or desirable. The conflict shows that circumcision had never been required to enter Christian assemblies, just as gentiles were not required to be circumcised to hold some status in diaspora synagogues.[33] Paul, a diaspora Jew, would have been familiar with such assemblies. These competitors are likely more conservative Jewish Christians, perhaps the same or similar to "men from James" or "those of the circumcision" in Gal 2:12.

Finally, Paul reflects on the law in the abstract. Paul never abandons the idea of the law's value and Israel's privilege as its recipient, but Rom 7 shows him wrestling with the question of whether it remains binding, wondering if it is an unwitting tool of sin, that malevolent force and vehicle of death. Yet he maintains the law is "holy, just, and good" (Rom 7:12).

Who is the "I" of Rom 7? As Fredriksen points out, if it is Paul speaking for himself, it contradicts the other places where he touts his "blamelessness under the law" (Phil 3:4–5) and zealousness for ancestral traditions (Gal 1:14), or what Krister Stendahl calls his "robust" conscience vis-à-vis the law. Fredriksen sug-

---

32. Fredriksen, *Paul: Pagans' Apostle*, 117–22.

33. Donor lists in synagogue inscriptions mention non-Jewish contributions, and references in Acts suggest gentiles in synagogues were commonplace (Acts 14:1; 18:4). See the relevant sources in Irina Levinskaya, *The Book of Acts in Its Diaspora Setting*, vol. 5 of *The Book of Acts in Its First Century Setting*, ed. Bruce W. Winter (Grand Rapids: Eerdmans, 1996).

gests he is adopting the rhetorical device of "speech in character," speaking as a gentile who tries to grapple with the law outside of following Christ. Such a person, he advises, will find a rough road. If we adopt this approach, his remarks are not about universal experiences nor his own inner struggles but about gentiles who try to go it alone, looking for salvation by following the law without Christ. It is not appropriate or adequate for gentiles, despite reassurances that the law itself is not a sin (Rom 7:7), is good (7:12, 13, 16), a source of delight (7:22), and a vehicle to serve God (7:25). This approach requires accepting Paul's speaking in another's voice, but this device appears throughout his letters, especially when dealing with questions of law and Israel (Rom 9–11).[34]

Stendahl, in his article "The Apostle Paul and the Introspective Conscience of the West," began a new era in scholarship on Paul, rejecting an outworn image of Paul as a guilt-wracked wrestler with sin as the legacy of Lutheran and Reformation thinking. Paul shows a "robust" sense of self, not a person battling a works righteousness or earning points for salvation, a system foreign to first-century Judaism.[35] The New Perspective on Paul scholars like E. P. Sanders replaced the stereotypic legalism with a more accurate picture of a rich and confident first-century "Palestinian" Judaism but did not grant to Paul that following commandments in the law brought one to salvation; only faith in Christ did.[36] John Gager's work moves the question by attention to audience, arguing a two-track system, that Paul sees the Torah and its continued observance as efficacious for Jews, while faith in Christ is the way for gentiles.[37]

Relieved of the earlier, constricting works/grace dichotomy, contemporary scholars, especially a group sometimes called the "Paul within Judaism" school, ask the (to some) radical question, "What if Paul never repudiated his Jewishness, nor abandoned his love of and observance of Torah?"[38] Have we taken his preaching to gentiles too far, assuming he meant the same things for Jews and

34. Fredriksen, *Paul: Pagan's Apostle*, 125–26; Stanley Stowers, *A Rereading of Romans: Justice, Jews, and Gentiles* (New Haven: Yale University Press, 1994), 9–10.

35. Krister Stendahl, "The Apostle Paul and the Introspective Conscience of the West," *HTR* 56, no. 3 (1963): 199–215.

36. E. P. Sanders, *Paul and Palestinian Judaism: A Comparison of Patterns of Religion* (Minneapolis: Fortress, 1977). For reflection on the impact of Sanders's and Gager's work and a consideration of the contemporary "Paul within Judaism" school, see *JJMJS* 5 (2018), http://www.jjmjs.org/issues.html.

37. John Gager, *The Origins of Anti-Semitism: Attitudes towards Judaism in Pagan and Christian Antiquity* (New York: Oxford University Press, 1983); Gager, *Reinventing Paul* (New York: Oxford University Press, 2000).

38. A brief and nonexhaustive list of these scholars includes Paula Fredriksen, Mark Nanos, Pamela Eisenbaum, Matthew Novenson, and Kathy Ehrensperger. See the recent edited volume, *Israel and the Nations: Paul's Gospel in the Context of Jewish Expectation*, ed. František

himself? Have we turned Paul the law-abiding Jew into Paul the Christian, a term he never used?

Matthew is intensely interested in the Torah, in narratives, laws, and the broader text that includes the prophets, taking every opportunity to underline its continuity with Jesus and Jesus's continuity with it. The fulfillment citations (Matt 1:22–23; 2:15, 17, 23; 4:14–16; 8:17; 12:17–21; 13:35; 21:4–5; 26:54, 56; 27:9), the parallels between Jesus and Moses, the programmatic statement from Jesus that he has not come to abolish but to fulfill the law and the prophets (5:17–20), and the grounding of Jesus's radical interpretation in Torah evident in the six antitheses in chapter 5 show the Torah as a constant guidebook.

Matthew 5:17–48 provides us a look at Matthew's view of Jesus, the teacher and interpreter of Torah. As Meier has shown, this early Christian catechism turns on the language of fulfillment of Scripture that is Matthew's theme throughout the gospel.[39] The Sermon on the Mount exhibits Jesus as one like Moses, who teaches the law from the mountain (Matt 5:1).

The six so-called "antitheses" in chapter 5 are better understood not as oppositions between the Torah laws and Jesus's teaching, but as his halakic midrash, or his radical extrapolation of those laws. Several of them, such as the ones about murder (5:21–26) and adultery (5:27–30), qualify as extending the commandments to include lesser offenses, similar to stringencies produced by the later rabbis in their attempts to "create a fence around the Torah." To prohibit anger and name-calling, as Jesus commands, is to distance a person more fully from a chance to commit murder (Matt 5:21–22). Avoiding adultery is more likely if one avoids looking at a woman lustfully (5:27–28). Even the last example, "love your enemies," seems to broaden the categories of neighbor and obligation to love them (5:43–44). "Hate your enemy" is not a verse in the Torah but could hint at a local interpretation circulating in Matthew's time. While the teaching of Matthew's Jesus seems to some modern interpreters sufficiently radical as to reverse the plain sense of the text and overturn the Torah's commandments, such arguments fail to appreciate the elasticity of ancient interpretation, the professed link to the biblical text, and the programmatic claim of Matt 5:17–20 to fulfill, not abolish the law.

Thiessen argues that Matthew is responding to accusations that his community members are law abolishers whose anarchy helped bring down the temple.

Ábel (Lanham, MD: Lexington Books/Fortress Academic, 2021); and *JJMJS* 5 (2018), http://www.jjmjs.org/issues.html.

39. Meier, *Law and Love*, 41–43. Meier insists that this material should not be put in the mouth of the historical Jesus, especially as the key to solving the enigma of Jesus and the law.

He shows that the frequency of forms of λύω, "to loosen," and καταλύω, "to abolish," in Matthew echo others at the time (1, 2 Maccabees; 4 Maccabees; Josephus's description of the Zealots) who accuse one another of being law abolishers who brought ruin to Israel (*J.W.* 4.184, 348, 381–382, 388). Matthew responds with a "halakic" Jesus, who is even more demanding on law observance on his followers, "exceeding the scribes and Pharisees" (Matt 5:20).[40] Indeed, he argues they be "perfect" or "whole" in their practice (Matt 5:48).

Celia Deutsch argues that the programmatic statement of Matt 5:17–20, as well as the parallels in language of interpretation, are meant to counter both antinomian urges in the group as well as accusations by others of departure from the Torah. She shows the prevalence and variety of the metaphor of Lady Wisdom among the learned groups in early Judaism, a version of Greco-Roman ideas of virtues personified by females. Matthew, clearly from the learned class, adapts the image and weaves together Q material to present Jesus as personified Wisdom.[41] Jesus-Wisdom teaches and interprets Torah in the gospel, his authority augmented by the strength of this freighted metaphor.

Jesus's conflicts with "the Pharisees" are often explained as stand-ins for conflicts between Matthew and some local rabbis towards the end of the first century. Following Anders Runesson, and in line with the suggestions of Thiessen and Deutsch, I suggest that some who identify with the Pharisees may still be around, and Matthew himself may have been one.[42] This does not entitle us to see them as "Jewish authorities" but rather one of multiple groups with different takes on the Torah. Furthermore, the evangelist takes pains to add a certain "people" language at crisis points in the gospel, for example, "the chief priests and elders *of the* people" (Matt 26:3), blurring the distinction between the leaders and the people.[43]

Matthew 23

Oddly enough, despite its bitter invective against the Pharisees for the nature of their law observance, this chapter provides no evidence that Matthew disagrees with their observance of the Torah laws per se. On the contrary, the opening

---

40. Matthew Thiessen, "Abolishers of the Law in Early Judaism and Matthew 5:17–20," *Bib* 93, no. 4 (2012): 543–56.

41. Celia M. Deutsch, *Lady Wisdom, Jesus, and the Sages: Metaphor and Social Context in Matthew's Gospel* (Valley Forge, PA: Trinity Press International, 1996), 81–96.

42. Anders Runesson, "Rethinking Early Jewish-Christian Relations: Matthean Community History as Pharisaic Intragroup Conflict," *JBL* 127, no. 1 (2008): 95–132.

43. Claudia Setzer, "Sinai, Covenant and Innocent Blood Traditions in Matthew's Blood Cry (Matt 27:25)," in *The Ways That Often Parted: Essays in Honor of Joel Marcus*, ed. Lori Baron, Jill Hicks-Keeton, and Matthew Thiessen, ECL 24 (Atlanta: SBL Press, 2018), 169–85.

salvo affirms their accuracy in understanding and teaching Torah, "the scribes and Pharisees sit on Moses's seat, so observe whatever they tell you" (23:2–3). The problem is their hypocrisy, their blindness in being distracted from larger principles, "the weightier matters of the law," by punctiliousness in observing the law's details, and finally, their culpability in the shedding of innocent blood. This final charge links them to those who killed the prophets and to the execution of Jesus. A standard intra-Jewish critique in this period was that the prophets sent to Israel were persecuted and killed (Isaiah in Ascen. Isa. 1–5; Isaiah, Jeremiah, Ezekiel, Amos, Zechariah ben Jehoiada in Lives of the Prophets). Deutsch shows that Wisdom's disciples also court humility and suffer martyrdom, in contrast to her opponents who seek public regard.[44] For Matthew, the blood of the innocent cascades continuously from Abel to Jesus, bringing down God's wrath (Matt 23:29–36).[45] The wrath that the evangelist predicts for them, most interpreters agree, is the disaster of 70 CE.

The "woes" that castigate the scribes and Pharisees as "hypocrites" (Matt 23:13, 15, 23, 25, 27, 29) and "blind" (23:16, 17, 19, 24) are followed by examples of their meticulous observance of the Torah's details while missing its moral force. But nowhere does it suggest that they should stop observing these details. On the contrary, the woes beg for greater congruence between small matters and more abstract virtues but affirm continued care for details: "Woe to you, scribes and Pharisees, hypocrites! You tithe dill and mint and cumin [presumably small amounts] and have neglected the weightier matters of the law, justice and mercy and faith; *these you ought to have done*, without neglecting the others" (Matt 23:23, emphasis added). Similarly, a critique of outward shows of purity accompanied by inner "extortion and rapacity" affirms greater care for both: "You blind Pharisee! First cleanse the inside of the cup and of the plate, *that the outside may also be clean*" (23:26, emphasis added). Similar arguments against ritual unaccompanied by social justice and concern for the poor infuse the Hebrew prophets, who are not recommending jettisoning Torah observance. Later traditions in the Jerusalem Talmud offer critique of *perushim*, "separatists" or "Pharisees," as causing harm, hairsplitting, and performing acts of charity for the wrong reasons, but seem to be from insiders calling others to account.[46]

---

44. Deutsch, *Lady Wisdom*, 89–95.

45. See Catherine Sider Hamilton, *The Death of Jesus in Matthew: Innocent Blood and the End of Exile*, SNTSMS 166 (Cambridge: Cambridge University Press, 2017).

46. See discussion of these references in y. Soṭa 3:4 (19a) and y. Ber. 9:5 (14b) in Richard Kalmin, *Migrating Tales: The Talmud's Narratives and Their Historical Context* (Oakland: University of California Press, 2014), 170–72.

Conclusion

In some ways, the laws of Israel's Scriptures are so ubiquitous in the New Testament as to be invisible. They are submerged in many narratives where their presence is assumed, behind language about covenant, temple, God's promises, and commandments. Neither Jesus nor his interlocutors dispute the laws' importance nor whether they should be observed.

The idea of Jesus in continual conflict with Pharisees over matters of biblical law is an exaggeration unsupported by the texts. The conflicts are surprisingly few, and the differences are no more severe than those between other Jewish groups of the time. Paul sustains argument over circumcision and eating around gentiles, but both are offshoots of the question of inclusion of gentiles in the church. Matthew presents more friction between Jesus and other Jewish teachers but shows Jesus to be superior in interpretation and fulfillment of the law's obligations.

Biblical law itself is not the focus for New Testament writers. The laws are carriers of other larger ideas. Purity laws help show Jesus facing down the forces of death. Sabbath laws reflect eschatological hopes. Circumcision acts as a symbol of Israel's covenant status. Uses of law, whether to refute, support, or amplify, allow interpreters proclaiming Jesus's story to take their places in a line of tradition rooted in Israel's Scriptures.

New Testament writers supply more evidence of an early and ongoing quest for meaning through interpretation. They participate in the processes of interpretation of Israel's Scriptures that also result in rabbinic midrash halakah and midrash haggadah, Mishnah, pesher commentary at Qumran, and targum, where interpreters shape and are shaped by the biblical material.[47] This chapter considers the laws found in Israel's written Scriptures, but we note that the beginnings of what will later be called "the Oral Law" by the rabbis also surface in the New Testament. The dispute over the "tradition of the elders" (Mark 7:3), references to the authoritative teaching of the scribes and Pharisees (Matt 23:2–3), and the uses of Jesus's sayings on Sabbath, divorce, oaths, and other matters as determinative betray an emerging body of interpretation that begins to take on the force of the Written Torah.

---

47. Ishay Rosen-Zvi suggests that the Mishnah is the fashioning of a new Torah; "Mishnah, Midrash, and How to Read Tannaitic Literature," *Ancient Jew Review*, September 2, 2020, https://www.ancientjewreview.com/read/2020/9/2/mishnah-midrash-and-how-to-read-tannaitic-literature. Book in Hebrew: *Between Midrash and Mishna: Reading Tannatic Literature* (Ra'ananah: Open University, 2019).

Bibliography

Ábel, František. *Israel and the Nations: Paul's Gospel in the Context of Jewish Expectation*. Lanham, MD: Lexington Books/Fortress Academic, 2021.

Baumgarten, Albert. "Seekers After Smooth Things." Pages 857–59 in vol. 2 of *Encyclopedia of the Dead Sea Scrolls*. Edited by Lawrence H. Schiffman and James C. VanderKam. 2 vols. Oxford: Oxford University Press, 2000.

Breed, Brennan. *Nomadic Text: A Theory of Biblical Reception History*. ISBL. Bloomington: University of Indiana Press, 2014.

Deutsch, Celia M. *Lady Wisdom, Jesus, and the Sages: Metaphor and Social Context in Matthew's Gospel*. Valley Forge, PA: Trinity Press International, 1996.

Doering, Lutz. "Sabbath Laws in the New Testament Gospels." Pages 207–53 in *The New Testament and Rabbinic Literature*. Edited by Reimund Bieringer, Florentino García Martínez, Didier Pollefeyt, and Peter Tomson. JSJSup 136. Leiden: Brill, 2009.

Eisenbaum, Pamela M. *Paul Was Not a Christian: The Original Message of a Misunderstood Apostle*. San Francisco: HarperOne, 2009.

Fredriksen, Paula. "Paul, Purity, and the Ekklēsia of the Gentiles." Pages 205–17 in *The Beginnings of Christianity: A Collection of Articles*. Edited by Jack Pastor and Menachem Mor. Jerusalem: Yad Ben-Zvi, 2005.

———. *Paul: The Pagans' Apostle*. New Haven: Yale University Press, 2017.

———. *When Christians Were Jews: The First Generation*. New Haven: Yale University Press, 2018.

Furstenberg, Yair. "Controlling Impurity: The Natures of Impurity in Second Temple Debates." *Dine Israel* 30 (2015): 163–96.

———. "Jesus against the Laws of the Pharisees: The Legal Woe Sayings and Second Temple Intersectarian Discourse." *JBL* 139, no. 4 (2020): 769–88.

Gager, John. *The Origins of Anti-Semitism: Attitudes towards Judaism in Pagan and Christian Antiquity*. New York: Oxford University Press, 1983.

———. *Reinventing Paul*. New York: Oxford University Press, 2000.

Greenberg, Moshe, Haim Hermann Cohn, and Menachem Elon. "Oath." *EncJud* 15:358–64.

Hamilton, Catherine Sider. *The Death of Jesus in Matthew: Innocent Blood and the End of Exile*. SNTSMS 166. Cambridge: Cambridge University Press, 2017.

Kalmin, Richard. *Migrating Tales: The Talmud's Narratives and Their Historical Context*. Oakland: University of California Press, 2014.

Klawans, Jonathan. "The Law." Pages 655–58 in *The Jewish Annotated New Testament*. Edited by Amy-Jill Levine and Marc Z. Brettler. 2nd ed. Oxford: Oxford University Press, 2017.

Levine, Amy-Jill. *Short Stories by Jesus: The Enigmatic Parables of a Controversial Rabbi*. San Francisco: HarperOne, 2015.

Levinskaya, Irina. *The Book of Acts in Its Diasporma Setting*. Vol. 5 of *The Book of Acts in Its First Century Setting*. Edited by Bruce W. Winter. Grand Rapids: Eerdmans, 1996.

Martyn, J. Louis. *Galatians: A New Translation with Introduction and Commentary*. AB 33A. New York: Doubleday, 1997.

Meier, John P. *Law and Love*. Vol. 4 of *A Marginal Jew: Rethinking the Historical Jesus*. ABRL. New Haven: Yale University Press, 2009.

Mroczek, Eva. *The Literary Imagination in Jewish Antiquity*. Oxford: Oxford University Press, 2016.

Novenson, Matthew. "Whither the Paul within Judaism Schule?" *JJMJS* 5 (2018): 79–88. http://www.jjmjs.org/uploads/1/1/9/0/11908749/novenson_-_whither_the_paul.pdf.

Reinhartz, Adele. *Cast Out of the Covenant: Jews and Anti-Judaism in the Gospel of John*. Lanham, MD: Lexington Books/Fortress Academic, 2018.

Ronis, Sara. "Space, Place, and the Race for Power: Rabbis, Demons, and the Construction of Babylonia." *HTR* 110, no. 4 (2017): 588–603.

Rosen-Zvi, Ishay. *Between Midrash and Mishna: Reading Tannaic Literature*. Raʿananah: Open University, 2019. [Hebrew]

———. "Mishnah, Midrash, and How to Read Tannaitic Literature." *Ancient Jew Review*, September 2, 2020. https://www.ancientjewreview.com/read/2020/9/2/mishnah-midrash-and-how-to-read-tannaitic-literature.

Runesson, Anders. "Re-thinking Early Jewish–Christian Relations: Matthean Community History as Pharisaic Intragroup Conflict." *JBL* 127, no. 1 (2008): 95–132.

Sanders, E. P. *Paul and Palestinian Judaism: A Comparison of Patterns of Religion*. Minneapolis: Fortress, 1977.

Setzer, Claudia. "Sinai, Covenant and Innocent Blood Traditions in Matthew's Blood Cry (Matt 27:25)." Pages 169–85 in *The Ways That Often Parted: Essays in Honor of Joel Marcus*. Edited by Lori Baron, Jill Hicks-Keeton, and Matthew Thiessen. ECL 24. Atlanta: SBL Press, 2018.

Shinall, Myrick C., Jr. "The Social Condition of Lepers in the Gospels." *JBL* 137, no. 4 (2018): 915–34.

Stendahl, Krister. "The Apostle Paul and the Introspective Conscience of the West." *HTR* 56, no. 3 (1963): 199–215.

Stowers, Stanley. *A Rereading of Romans: Justice, Jews, and Gentiles*. New Haven: Yale University Press, 1994.

Thiessen, Matthew. "Abolishers of the Law in Early Judaism and Matthew 5:17–20." *Bib* 93, no. 4 (2012): 543–56.

———. *Contesting Conversion: Genealogy, Circumcision, and Identity in Ancient Judaism and Christianity*. New York: Oxford University Press, 2011.

———. *Jesus and the Forces of Death: The Gospels' Portrayal of Ritual Impurity within First-Century Judaism*. Grand Rapids: Baker Academic, 2020.

Twersky, Isadore. "Make a Fence Around the Torah." *The Torah U-Madda Journal* 8 (1998–1999): 25–42.

Wedderburn, A. J. M. "Sawing Off the Branches: Theologizing Dangerously *Ad Hebraeos*." *JTS* 56, no. 2 (2005): 393–414.

30

Wisdom

BENJAMIN WOLD

New Testament authors use, both explicitly and nonexplicitly, the traditional wisdom books of Israel's Scripture, including apocryphal wisdom compositions found in the Septuagint. They are also influenced, probably indirectly, by wisdom literature known only from discoveries at Qumran. In addition to the intertextual presence of wisdom literature in the New Testament, Israel's wisdom traditions exert influence in a number of different ways. This is mainly observable when studying particular topics and themes as well as distinct intellectual currents in the Second Temple era. Early Christians participated in the ongoing activity of teaching about wisdom and instructing how to live wisely as part of the warp and weave of early Jewish sapiential discourse.

Wisdom in Israel's Scripture

In order to discuss wisdom in Israel's Scripture, we are required first to address thorny issues related to how the term "wisdom" is used and what it means.[1] As a term of convenience, we may speak of "wisdom literature" while highlighting that

---

1. Some would go so far as to question whether we can speak of "wisdom literature" at all; e.g., Will Kynes, *An Obituary for "Wisdom Literature": The Birth, Death, and Intertextual Reintegration of a Biblical Corpus* (Oxford: Oxford University Press, 2019), who critically discusses wisdom as a genre invented by nineteenth-century scholarship. A helpful collection of essays on this topic is found in Mark R. Sneed, ed., *Was There a Wisdom Tradition? New Prospects in Israelite Wisdom Studies*, AIL 23 (Atlanta: SBL Press, 2015).

we are not marking out a form-critical category.² The three traditional wisdom books in the Hebrew Bible are Job, Proverbs, and Qohelet (Ecclesiastes), which are grouped as such because of their common concern with חכמה ("wisdom"), instructional themes, and use of genre types (e.g., sayings and admonitions). In addition to these three books, Song of Songs and Psalms are often discussed under the umbrella of "wisdom literature"; however, our focus here is primarily on the three traditional books.

The sapiential worldview is typically concerned with teachings about how to conduct oneself based upon lessons derived from observations on how the world works. It is rooted in the created order and this-worldly cause and effect. Associated ideas include creation, individualism, universalism, and empiricism. Moreover, one characteristic of this literature is that it does not look to the past or to the future. As such, one finds a sage's instruction in the form of, for example, proverbs. However, proverbs may be found across Israel's Scripture and not only in our so-called wisdom books. It merits noting that our three wisdom books are dissimilar from most of the rest of Israel's Scripture because they are not interested in Israel's relationship with God. Rather, their focus is typically on the individual and how to live a life of happiness and prosperity in general terms, with Job a clear exception. Therefore, "wisdom" is in many respects amorphous and may be found in any number of exhortations, sayings, or in paraenesis. Any treatment of wisdom is bogged down when approached as an issue of genre, and to speak of a common worldview is challenged by heterogenous views of wisdom (i.e., ideas found in Job, Proverbs, and Qohelet often do not agree with one another). Consequently, one way to approach the study of wisdom, as Stuart Weeks addresses it, is to focus on common issues rather than on shared attitudes or literary forms.³

Modern definitions of wisdom literature and approaches to it are overwhelmingly shaped by studies on the canonical compositions, when in fact so many of our sapiential texts are found elsewhere. Indeed, larger issues related to definitions and categories, especially with regard to the study of the New Testament, require that we include early Jewish traditions in the conversation.

---

2. The last two decades have seen a robust conversation about "conflicted boundaries between wisdom and apocalyptic" as part of a larger recognition within biblical studies that genres are not exclusive but overlap; see Benjamin G. Wright III and Lawrence M. Wills, eds., *Conflicted Boundaries in Wisdom and Apocalypticism*, SymS 35 (Atlanta: Society of Biblical Literature, 2005). Processes of categorization require decisions about like kind, asking in what respect things are dis/similar and what unites and divides them. The natural sciences, too, debate their categories; see the popular treatment in Lulu Miller, *Why Fish Don't Exist: A Story of Loss, Love, and the Hidden Order of Life* (New York: Simon & Schuster, 2020).

3. Weeks, *An Introduction to the Study of Wisdom Literature* (London: T&T Clark, 2010), 1.

Wisdom in Early Jewish Literature

Wisdom in the Apocrypha: Ben Sira and Wisdom of Solomon

Looking beyond Israel's wisdom tradition in the Hebrew Bible to the early Jewish nonbiblical literature, several compositions are noteworthy. Here we find two important compositions: Ben Sira and the Wisdom of Solomon.

Ben Sira was composed in the mid-second century BCE in Hebrew and was translated first into Greek ("Sirach") and then into Latin ("Ecclesiasticus"). Ben Sira is remarkable not only for its considerable length (fifty-one chapters in modern editions) but also for its influence.[4] The date and provenance of the Wisdom of Solomon are more complicated, as it may be a composite of two or more compositions; these were written in Greek somewhat later than Ben Sira, most likely in the late first century BCE or early first century CE.[5]

Sirach, the grandson of Ben Sira, writes in the preface of his Greek translation that his grandfather devoted himself to reading the law, the prophets, and the other ancestral books. Ben Sira is not interested in explicitly interpreting Israel's Scripture; he never directly cites it but rather prefers to write in the form of proverbs. In this sense, Ben Sira draws upon the traditional wisdom books in order to shape his own poetics.[6] Ben Sira is well known for equating Mosaic Torah with wisdom (Sir 15:1; 24:8; 24:23); however, it is debated whether Ben Sira is "sapientializing Torah" or "Torah-izing wisdom." Summarizing Ben Sira's relationship to the Torah, Jack Sanders writes that "he simply assumes that it supports his traditional sapiential morality" and that he "could not conceive that its morality could be other than his traditional sapiential morality."[7] Ben Sira integrates legal, prophetic, and historical strands of Israel's tradition into his own wisdom. While Ben Sira presents creation as the basis of wisdom, he also writes that one may acquire it in the company of the wise (Sir 6:36) or by meditating on the commandments (Sir 6:37).[8] Ben Sira's attention to Israel's Scripture sets

---

4. David A. deSilva, *The Jewish Teachers of Jesus, James, and Jude: What Earliest Christianity Learned from the Apocrypha and Pseudepigrapha* (New York: Oxford University Press, 2012), 58–85.

5. See William Horbury, "The Wisdom of Solomon," in *The Oxford Bible Commentary*, ed. John Barton and John Muddiman (Oxford: Oxford University Press, 2001), 661; a number of recent studies argue for the unity of Wisdom of Solomon; see Luca Mazzinghi, *Wisdom*, IECOT (Stuttgart: Kohlhammer, 2019), 19–20.

6. E.g., Eric D. Reymond, *Innovations in Hebrew Poetry: Parallelism and the Poems of Sirach*, SBLStBL 9 (Atlanta: Society of Biblical Literature, 2004).

7. Sanders, "When Sacred Canopies Collide: The Reception of the Torah of Moses in the Wisdom Literature of the Second-Temple Period," *JSJ* 32, no. 2 (2001): 124.

8. John J. Collins, *Jewish Wisdom in the Hellenistic Age*, OTL (Louisville: Westminster John Knox, 1997), 55.

him in sharp contrast to the biblical wisdom books, which are distinctive for not referring to Israel's traditions. The best-known, and most explicit, example is the Praise of the Fathers (Sir 44–50). Here, Israel's most eminent leaders, beginning with Noah and concluding with Simon the high priest, are eulogized. An epic recounting of Israel's history located in Ben Sira is remarkable in itself; also noteworthy is the emphasis on temple sacrifice offered by a high priest because wisdom tradition is often viewed as uninterested in cult.[9]

In the Wisdom of Solomon, wisdom is not simply derived from biblical laws but is a cosmic principle. Much of the Wisdom of Solomon's instruction is rooted in Stoicism, particularly the idea of the world soul, where wisdom stretches across the earth and orders all things.[10] Wisdom 7:24–26 expresses wisdom as "pervading all things"; it is the "breadth of the power of God." When in chapters 10–19 the biblical history is recounted from creation to the exodus, Joseph Blenkinsopp describes wisdom as a "principle of interpretation or reinterpretation"; the author is "sapientializing" sacred history.[11] Wisdom of Solomon mentions the law only in passing (Wis 2:12; 6:4; 16:6; 18:4). When Moses is referred to, he is a leader in the wilderness and a prophet (Wis 10:15–11:4) but not the lawgiver.[12] In Wisdom of Solomon wisdom is never equated with the Mosaic Torah. Indeed, Torah is brought in only to the degree that its laws are made wisdom's laws, thereby maintaining the preeminence of wisdom.[13]

Wisdom at Qumran

A neat division between the Apocrypha and the Qumran discoveries is not possible because the categories refer to, respectively, a traditional grouping of compositions and an archaeological discovery that has multiple groupings within it. That is, some of the Apocrypha were discovered at Qumran, notably fragments of Ben Sira (i.e., 2Q18; cf. Mas1h; 11Q5). Here, "Qumran wisdom" refers to those compositions that were not known prior to their discovery alongside the Dead Sea.[14]

---

9. Burton L. Mack, *Wisdom and the Hebrew Epic: Ben Sira's Hymn in Praise of the Fathers*, CSHJ (Chicago: University of Chicago Press, 1985), 1.

10. Joseph Blenkinsopp, *Wisdom and Law in the Old Testament: The Ordering of Life in Israel and Early Judaism*, 2nd ed., OBS (Oxford: Oxford University Press, 2003), 170.

11. Blenkinsopp, *Wisdom and Law*, 172.

12. Blenkinsopp, *Wisdom and Law*, 169; Wis 18:4 refers to the Torah as the "imperishable light" that was "given to the world."

13. Sanders, "Sacred Canopies," 129.

14. See John Kampen, *Wisdom Literature*, ECDSS 14 (Grand Rapids: Eerdmans, 2011); Matthew J. Goff, *Discerning Wisdom: The Sapiential Literature of the Dead Sea Scrolls*, VTSup 116 (Leiden: Brill, 2007).

Wisdom

Wisdom literature preserved in the Qumran discoveries comes primarily from Cave 4, with several copies also found in Cave 1. These Cave 4 compositions were first published in critical editions in the mid- to late 1990s. These previously unknown texts have subsequently produced a profound shift in our understanding of the transformation of Israel's wisdom tradition in the Hellenistic and Roman periods. The category of Qumran wisdom faces similar challenges to those observed previously, namely that the parameters are unclear.

The scrolls that are typically categorized as "wisdom" were composed in Hebrew and likely date to the mid-second century BCE and first century BCE. These include the following works:

- 1Q/4QInstruction (1Q26; 4Q415–418, 423) is the longest of these documents; originally it was about thirty columns long and is preserved in at least eight manuscripts that are found in hundreds of fragments.
- 1Q/4QMysteries (1Q27; 4Q299–301) may also be categorized as sapiential texts.
- 4QBeatitudes (4Q525; note similarities with 4Q185), as the title suggests, uses the formulation "blessed" in its didactic discourse.
- 4Q184 ("Wiles of the Wicked Woman") reworks parts of Prov 1–9.

There are several texts that are simply titled as Sapiential Works (4Q474–476) or Instruction-like compositions (4Q424–426). Other compositions include 4QWays of Righteousness (4Q420–421) and Sapiential Hymns (4Q411; 4Q498). The more substantive of these manuscripts are reviewed briefly here.

4QInstruction, published in 1999, has had the largest impact on our reassessment of Jewish wisdom. One reason for this is that before the discovery of this composition, eschatology and cosmology, which one might term "otherworldly" or apocalyptic points of view, were seen to be at odds with "this-worldly" thought that characterizes the wisdom books found in Israel's Scripture. Before the discovery of 4QInstruction, this-worldly and other-worldly views were seen, by and large, to be incompatible. In the last two decades it has become commonplace to speak of conflicted boundaries between wisdom and apocalyptic. This shift in scholarly categories and the attempt to redraw the paradigms significantly impact any assessment of wisdom in the New Testament. 4QInstruction includes the view that consequences for individual actions are found in the hereafter—reward for the righteous and destruction for the wicked. Moreover, otherworldly beings, namely angels, are an important part of the discourse. Human and angelic beings share a relationship in 4QInstruction: (1) angels are seen as role models to be followed in the pursuit of understanding, and (2) the community's sage serves as a mediator between angels and humans. 4QInstruction offers an explicit cosmology (4Q416 1) that provides a framework for how to live in this world.

The source of wisdom is presented as revelation, called "mystery of existence" (רז נהיה).¹⁵ In its most basic form, this mystery is knowledge of good and evil, which is found in the created order itself; however, understanding its depths is an ongoing pursuit. Part of humanity fails to acknowledge good and evil. There is also the concern that the one who is addressed could grow weary in seeking it. In summary, teaching about how to live in this world in light of the hereafter, other-worldly beings, and wisdom, all common topoi within apocalyptic thought, all derive from more than simple human experience. They are based on revelation. 4QInstruction evidences a compatibility in early Jewish wisdom that has broken well-established scholarly molds.¹⁶

Israel's Scripture is never cited verbatim in 4QInstruction, although it is alluded to frequently and at times paraphrased or rewritten. Mosaic Torah is never mentioned, and it is not thematized. I have argued elsewhere that the reason for this is that revelation at Sinai is subordinate to the revelation of the created order.¹⁷ Therefore, Israel's Scripture is used nonexplicitly when establishing a universal wisdom for all humanity. Most often the author alludes to and rewrites Gen 2–3. For instance, the creation narrative is foundational for teaching about marriage and family relations (4Q416 2 III–IV). It also sets up the metaphor that the pursuit of wisdom is like tending an Edenic garden (4Q423 1). In summary, in 4QInstruction wisdom instruction adapts biblical ruling and uses it as a consideration in sapiential advice, without, however, appealing to the authority of the Torah or explicitly citing it.¹⁸

1Q/4QMysteries shares several key terms in common with 1Q/4QInstruction, such as "mysteries" (רזים), "inheritance" (נחלה), and "birth times" (בית מולדים). "Mysteries" relate to the mysteries of creation and of the natural order. We find, too, that God has an active role in the process of history. Together, natural phenomena and historical events are part of divine wisdom. Similar to 4QInstruction is the concern to distinguish between truth and falsehood, good and evil. There is also an eschatological horizon: the end is imminent, wickedness will be destroyed, and knowledge of God will fill the earth.

---

15. The repeated expression is used that this mystery has been "revealed" (גלה) to the addressee.

16. Florentino García Martínez, "Wisdom at Qumran: Worldly or Heavenly?," in *Wisdom and Apocalypticism in the Dead Sea Scrolls and in the Biblical Tradition*, ed. Florentino García Martínez, BETL 168 (Leuven: Peeters, 2003), 1–16; cf. Matthew J. Goff, *The Worldly and Heavenly Wisdom of 4QInstruction*, STDJ 50 (Leiden: Brill, 2003).

17. Benjamin Wold, *4QInstruction: Divisions and Hierarchies*, STDJ 123 (Leiden: Brill, 2018), 146–95.

18. Daniel J. Harrington, *Wisdom Texts from Qumran*, Literature of the Dead Sea Scrolls (London: Routledge, 1996), 59.

4QBeatitudes (4Q525) is broadly concerned with how to live a wise life, offering instruction about the need for wisdom, describing the ways of folly, and urging for a return to wisdom. Moreover, 4Q525 2 II, 3–4 equates Torah with wisdom: "Blessed is the man who obtains wisdom [חכמה], who walks in the torah of the Most High, and establishes her ways in his heart."[19] Elisa Uusimäki concludes that 4QBeatitudes reconfigures wisdom to cohere and resonate within its own context by introducing "torah devotion and dualistic elements" to its discourse.[20] A key characteristic of the composition, as indicated by the title, is a series of "blessed" statements. In scholarly parlance, these statements are referred to as "macarisms," from the Greek μακάριος, while the Latin term "beatitudes" is used more popularly. Such a collection of macarisms has no counterpart in Israel's Scripture, and there is otherwise no extant instance of continuous macarisms in the literary tradition until the Sermon on the Mount (Matt 5). Of the wisdom teachings in Israel's Scripture that begin with the pronouncement "blessed," about twenty occur in the Psalms (e.g., Ps 1:1, "Blessed is the man who walks not in the counsel of the wicked"). This formulation is found less frequently in Job and Proverbs. In 4Q525, Psalms are particularly important (e.g., 2 II + 3 I is strongly reminiscent of Ps 15:3 in regard to not slandering with the tongue).

4QWiles of the Wicked Woman (4Q184) reconfigures the promiscuous woman of Prov 7, who entices men to commit adultery. The presentation and identity of a female who walks the city streets and encourages sin has been widely debated. One possibility is that the female figure in 4Q184 is a demon, although there are convincing counter arguments.[21] There is little contention that this composition poetically reworks parts of Prov 1–9 in order to emphasize the activities of wickedness.[22] Here, 4Q184 is an important example of a running allusion to an important wisdom motif: the "Wicked Woman" of Proverbs who stands in contrast to Lady Wisdom. This is significant because a crucial aspect of wisdom Christology (cf. "Conceptual Allusions: Wisdom Christology," below) is a conceptual allusion to personified wisdom.

---

19. Collins, *Jewish Wisdom*, 49. 11Q5 (11QPsa), 154, explicitly identifies Torah with wisdom.

20. Uusimäki, *Turning Proverbs towards Torah: An Analysis of 4Q525*, STDJ 117 (Leiden: Brill, 2016), 268: "The Hebrew language of 4Q525 even serves as a way to extend the existing Torah, i.e., a body of teachings of some sort."

21. Joseph M. Baumgarten, "On the Nature of the Seductress in 4Q184," *RevQ* 15, no. 1/2 (1991): 133–43.

22. Matthew J. Goff, "A Seductive Demoness at Qumran? Lilith, Female Demons and 4Q184," in *Das Böse, der Teufel, und Dämonen – Evil, the Devil, and Demons: Dualistic Characteristics in the Religion of Israel, Ancient Judaism, and Christianity*, ed. Benjamin Wold, Jan Dochhorn, and Susanne Rudnig-Zelt, WUNT 2/412 (Tübingen: Mohr Siebeck, 2016), 76.

The Apocrypha and Qumran: Shared Features

In the Second Temple era we observe wisdom in transition.[23] Ben Sira, Wisdom of Solomon, and previously unknown sapiential literature discovered at Qumran incorporate aspects of Israel's Scripture into their compositions while simultaneously maintaining wisdom's preeminence.[24] Generally speaking, the sapiential traditions in the Hellenistic and Roman era develop the biblical tradition further without adopting it by way of direct citation. However, Ben Sira, Wisdom of Solomon (Wis 2:12; 6:4; 16:6), and much of the Qumran sapiential literature (e.g., 4Q525 2 II, 3–4; 4Q185 II, 8–11) refer explicitly to the theme of Mosaic Torah or, in the case of Sirach and the Wisdom of Solomon, to its Greek equivalent, νόμος. However, this is not a constant: in 4QInstruction and 1Q/4QMysteries, Mosaic Torah is never thematized or even explicitly referred to even if they nonexplicitly incorporate Scripture. Another feature of early Jewish literature is a concern for the relationship of, and fine lines between, sapiential universalism and Jewish particularism. Different compositions reflect this concern for creation and universal laws while finding different ways of accommodating particularistic tones.[25] Moreover, cosmology and eschatology play an ever-increasing role in wisdom instruction. This observation is true not only of 4QInstruction but also the apocryphal literature.[26] These three issues—the place of Mosaic Torah in wisdom instruction, universalism and particularism, and wisdom and apocalyptic—also feature prominently in theologies found in New Testament literature.

Wisdom in the New Testament

As noted, it is problematic to speak of wisdom literature along the lines of genre. Therefore, any attempt to identify compositions or treat subsections of New Testament literature along these lines runs into major obstacles. Nonetheless, it is safe to observe that among New Testament writings there is not a single com-

---

23. Samuel L. Adams, *Wisdom in Transition: Act and Consequence in Second Temple Instruction*, JSJSup 125 (Leiden: Brill, 2008), 273–77.

24. Sanders, "Sacred Canopies," 129.

25. See Daniele Pevarello, "Looking for Wisdom in Wis. 11:2–19:2: Between Universalism and Particularism," *JSP* 30, no. 1 (2020): 21–34; Wold, *4QInstruction*, 142–45.

26. Benjamin G. Wright III, "Conflicted Boundaries: Ben Sira, Sage and Seer," in *Congress Volume Helsinki 2010*, ed. Martti Nissinen, VTSup 148 (Leiden: Brill, 2012), 229–53; Wright, "1 Enoch and Ben Sira: Wisdom and Apocalyptic in Relationship," in *The Early Enoch Literature*, ed. Gabriele Boccaccini and John J. Collins, JSJSup 121 (Leiden: Brill, 2007), 159–76; Michael Kolarcik, "Sapiential Values and Apocalyptic Imagery in the Wisdom of Solomon," in *Studies in the Book of Wisdom*, ed. Géza G. Xeravits and József Zsengellér, JSJSup 142 (Leiden: Brill, 2010), 23–36.

position dedicated to imparting wisdom within a genre that mirrors Proverbs, Qohelet, or Job, nor do any present themselves poetically as do the Psalms and Song of Songs. However, there are forms of wisdom teaching known from the wisdom tradition of Israel's Scripture, and their development in early Judaism, that are taken up in the New Testament (e.g., paraenesis and macarisms). If any composition in the New Testament were to be categorized as "wisdom," then it would be the letter of James. Within the New Testament, we find some interest in the three traditional wisdom books of the Hebrew Scripture, but citations are relatively few, as we shall see below. If one includes the Psalms among the wisdom writings of the Hebrew Scripture, then the influence upon New Testament authors is profound because the Psalms, and certainly not just the wisdom Psalms, are cited and alluded to more than any other part of Israel's Scripture. The Jewish wisdom tradition is also taken up nonexplicitly. Conceptual allusions are found primarily in the various ways that Jesus is identified with personified wisdom ("wisdom Christology"). These three topics come into focus below: (1) James as wisdom, (2) explicit citation, and (3) conceptual allusion.[27]

Another possible way to address how the New Testament develops, modifies, and relates to the wisdom tradition of Israel's Scripture is to consider the teaching about "wisdom" (חכמה); however, since the Greek New Testament is only concerned with σοφία ("wisdom"), distinguishing between influence from Hellenistic wisdom traditions, Greek philosophy, Israel's Scripture, and early Judaism is nearly impossible. Indeed, when the sages teach about חכמה in early Jewish literature, they are actively integrating Greek ideas about σοφία with it. In the New Testament, the most dominant way in which σοφία is adapted is vis-à-vis wisdom Christology.[28]

The Letter of James as a Wisdom Composition

Martin Dibelius argued that James should be understood within a genre of hortatory literature characterized by paraenesis.[29] Following on from Dibelius,

---

27. Verbal allusions to the Israelite wisdom tradition are found especially in James and within different wisdom Christologies and are, therefore, referred to in these two sections.

28. Yet another important topic is Jesus as sage. Because any treatment of this topic requires an assessment of the sayings source Q and complex arguments about the historical Jesus as "sage" or "apocalyptic prophet" (or a combination of both), it is beyond the scope of this study. However, two important developments in this regard may be noted. First, the sayings source Q has been reassessed in light of 4QInstruction (see Matthew J. Goff, "Discerning Trajectories: 4QInstruction and the Sapiential Background of the Sayings Source Q," *JBL* 124, no. 4 [2005]: 657–73); *in nuce*, conflicted boundaries in 4QInstruction challenge assumptions in Q scholarship about wisdom. Second, our understanding of the sages (i.e., the Maskil) at Qumran has expanded our paradigm for understanding this role (e.g., the exalted sage of 4Q491c).

29. Dibelius, *James: A Commentary on the Epistle of James*, trans. Michael A. Williams, Hermeneia (Philadelphia: Fortress, 1976), 3–4.

Frederick Francis posited that James is a didactic letter, common in antiquity. Since then this view has been widely accepted.[30] Dale Allison addressed what it means to read James in this light, noting how as a didactic letter it "moves one to anticipate words for a broad audience as opposed to a small, well-defined community" and that "as a listener one expects to hear exhortations that disallow discussion and instead call for obedience."[31]

James appears to be impersonal, which is typical of wisdom writings. Following Weeks's thematic treatment of wisdom, we find instruction throughout that teaches conventional sapiential topics, such as humility (4:6b, 10; cf. Prov 11:2; Sir 3:17–24), the folly of wealth (Jas 1:10–11; cf. Prov 14:24), care for widows and orphans (Jas 1:27; cf. Sir 4:10), and God's authority (Jas 4:14; cf. Prov 8:15). Exhortations take on typical wisdom forms, including several proverbial teachings, such as Jas 1:19: "Let every man be quick to hear, slow to speak, slow to anger" (cf. Prov 17:27: "One who spares words is knowledgeable; one who is cool in spirit has understanding"); Jas 3:8: "But no human being can tame the tongue—a restless evil, full of deadly poison" (cf. Prov 10:19: "When words are many, transgression is not lacking, but the prudent are restrained in speech"); and Jas 4:14: "You boast in your arrogance, all such boasting is evil" (cf. Prov 27:1: "Do not boast about tomorrow, for you do not know what a day may bring"). James frequently uses admonitions and exhortations, such as "be doers of the word" (Jas 1:22), "let not many of you become teachers" (Jas 3:1), "do not boast and be false to the truth" (Jas 3:14), and "do not speak evil against one another" (Jas 4:11).[32]

There is an eschatological dimension to James's teachings that is not found in the wisdom books of Israel's Scripture. James 1:12 begins with "blessed is the man who endures trial," which is followed by a promise of future reward: "for when he has stood the test he will receive the crown of life that God has promised to those who love him." Eschatological reward for the righteous is also found in Jas 5:3 ("you have treasures laid up for the last days") and in 2:5, where the righteous are "heirs of the kingdom." End-time judgment for the wicked is also found in Jas 5:8–9, where the impending coming of the Lord is described as "the judge standing at the doors" (cf. Jas 1:21; 5:20). James's teaching about wisdom places consequences for wise and ethical behavior not only found in the here and now but also as a reward and punishment in the future; this is also a characteristic of the development of the wisdom tradition in early Judaism (esp. 4QInstruction).

---

30. Francis, "The Form and Function of the Opening and Closing Paragraphs of James and 1 John," *ZNW* 61 (1970): 110–25.

31. Allison, *A Critical and Exegetical Commentary on the Epistle of James*, ICC (London: Bloomsbury, 2013), 76.

32. Unless otherwise noted, all translations are by the author.

One of the most striking features of James's paraenesis is the nature of wisdom as something that can be revealed (Jas 1:5) and given by God from above (Jas 3:15), a feature that indicates an apocalyptic transcendence by deriving understanding from the heavenly realm as opposed to the earthly. The shift in the wisdom paradigm extends beyond eschatologizing wisdom. 4QInstruction shares a number of notable commonalities with James, including revealed wisdom (i.e., "mystery of existence"), eschatology, and especially a cosmological framework. The first column of 4QInstruction (4Q416 1) describes the heavenly hosts, God's rule over the cosmos, future reward for the righteous, punishment for the wicked, and humanity's responsibility to live rightly in light of how the cosmos has been ordered. James differs from 4QInstruction in that its cosmology is more implicit than explicit. In both compositions otherworldly beings have a prominent role. Whereas 4QInstruction is concerned with angels, James is concerned with demons. These two writings also evidence a reification of evil.[33] Both wrestle, each in their own way, with sapiential universalism and the particularism of the Torah/law.[34] Reading James in light of 4QInstruction provides the opportunity to appreciate the relationship of cosmology with sapiential teaching as it develops in early Judaism and early Christianity.

Explicit Citations in the New Testament

The most straightforward evidence for the New Testament authors' engagement with wisdom literature comes in the form the explicit citations of the wisdom books in the Hebrew Scriptures. Proverbs is by far the most frequently cited wisdom book by the New Testament authors.[35] The letter of James, in addition to participating in the sapiential tradition, which we have just seen, also cites the book of Proverbs once and does not explicitly refer to any other wisdom book. James 4:6, teaching about humility, evokes the proverb "God opposes the proud, but gives grace to the humble" (Prov 33:34; cf. Job 22:29). On another occasion, James may have Prov 10:12 ("Hatred stirs up strife, but love covers all offenses") in mind when teaching about bringing a sinner back from wandering, an action he says saves a soul from death and "covers a multitude of sins" (Jas 5:20). First Peter 4:18 draws on Prov 11:31 to underscore judgment upon those who do not live according to the gospel. First Peter reworks an a fortiori statement while

---

33. Benjamin Wold, "Sin and Evil in the Letter of James in Light of Qumran Discoveries," *NTS* 65, no. 1 (2019): 78–93.

34. Benjamin Wold, "Universal and Particular Law in James and Early Judaism," *JSNT* 41, no. 1 (2018): 95–106.

35. NA[28] lists eight citations and over a hundred allusions in its "Loci Citati vel Allegati."

emphasizing that if salvation (or reward) is difficult for the righteous, then how much more so for the wicked. Hebrews 12:5 addresses struggle against sin and encourages enduring in trials; here, Prov 3:11 is brought to bear where God's discipline of his children is presented as chastisement of those whom God loves.

Paul, too, is indebted to the wisdom tradition, as can be seen in a number of occasions. He draws upon Prov 24:12 when teaching about the wicked and righteous receiving punishment and reward in Rom 2:6. While Prov 24:12 presents the basic principle that God repays each according to their deeds, Paul sets this teaching within an apocalyptic worldview, where consequences are in the hereafter. The "day of wrath" will bring judgment to some and immortality and eternal life to others. Paul also cites Prov 25:21 ("If your enemies are hungry, give them bread to eat; and if they are thirsty, give them water to drink") in Rom 12:20, when exhorting his readers to live peaceably with all and not to seek vengeance. Job and Ecclesiastes are only explicitly recollected once in the New Testament, both by Paul. In 1 Cor 3:19 Paul argues that "the wisdom of this world is foolishness with God, for it is written, 'He catches the wise in their craftiness'" (cf. Job 5:12–13). In Rom 3:10 Paul establishes the guilt of all humanity before offering his solution to it (i.e., Christ Jesus); he cites Eccl 7:20, that there is no one righteous who does not sin.

Conceptual Allusions: Wisdom Christology

Christ is identified with the personification of wisdom in a number of places in the New Testament. In early Judaism, wisdom was one of a few key philosophical or theological concepts that were used to bridge the divine and human beings. Divine wisdom is often equated with Mosaic Torah, most notably in Ben Sira 24, where Lady Wisdom issues forth from the mouth of God, in heaven, down to Israel. Other bridging concepts that at times overlap or merge with wisdom are the divine Logos ("Word"), spirit, and mysteries; together, these were ways of portraying God's revelatory activity in an intelligible way within the context of the ancient Mediterranean world. Wisdom personified expressed God's activity in the world, his nearness to his people and involvement in creation. Wisdom was also a way to communicate God's involvement with humanity within a monotheistic framework. Personified wisdom was often portrayed as preexistent (e.g., Prov 8:2–31; Job 28; Bar 3:9–4:4; Wis 6:12–11:1; 1 En. 42:1–3) and as participating with God in creation. James Dunn concludes that personified wisdom is "a function of Yahweh, a way of speaking about God himself, of expressing God's active involvement with his world and his people without compromising his transcendence."[36]

---

36. James D. G. Dunn, *Christology in the Making: A New Testament Inquiry into the Origins of the Doctrine of the Incarnation* (Grand Rapids: Eerdmans, 1980), 176.

Wisdom

We see throughout much of New Testament literature that authors allude to concepts related to wisdom personified. This is by far the most prevalent way in which early Christians participated in the wisdom tradition. Indeed, the nonexplicit framework drawn upon is not limited to the "wisdom" tradition per se but is widespread in the intellectual currents of the time. They include Philo of Alexandria, the apocryphal literature, and the Enochic traditions. Here the focus is on how Paul and the Gospels variously characterize Christ within this tradition.

Paul uses divine wisdom in 1 Cor 1–2 to proclaim Christ crucified. The cross is the very definition of God's wisdom; as such, it is part of God's plan for salvation. Paul identifies Christ with personified wisdom in two passages, in Col 1:15–20 and 1 Cor 1–2 (cf. 8:6).[37] First Corinthians is the most prominent and earliest example of Paul speaking about Christ with wisdom terminology. He refers to Christ as "the power of God and the wisdom of God" (1 Cor 1:24) and Christ "whom God made our wisdom" (1:30). Paul writes that "we impart a secret and hidden wisdom of God, which God decreed before the ages for our glorification" (1 Cor 2:7). Wisdom terminology is used of Christ and his role in creation: "there is one God, the Father . . . and one Lord, Jesus Christ, through whom are all things and through whom we exist" (1 Cor 8:6). Another important feature of wisdom in these first two chapters is that wisdom is hidden and revealed not in the Torah (the "law") but rather in the Christ event. First Corinthians 8:6 is striking because it is a statement about Christ's cosmic significance framed within a declaration that God is one (Deut 6:4; cf. Jas 2:19). By appealing to the Jewish wisdom tradition, Paul is able to present Jesus as Lord through whom all things came into being. The creative activity of God is shared with wisdom (e.g., Ps 104:24, "in wisdom you have made them all"; Philo, *Her.* 199, "the whole world which was created by divine wisdom"; cf. *Det.* 54; Prov 3:19, "the Lord by wisdom founded the earth"; Wis 8:4–6).

Colossians 1:15–20 describes Christ in a hymn that is widely regarded as having been composed prior to the rest of the letter and originally applied to wisdom. Colossians itself is likely not one of Paul's letters but rather reflects "Paulinism." The final form may be attributed to one of his followers, perhaps within Paul's lifetime or shortly afterward. Even if the hymn is pre-Pauline and interpolated at a later stage to refer to Christ, it has been integrated into the whole

---

37. Some would list Rom 10:6–10 as a third passage, in which Paul refers to Deut 30:12–14 when he asks: "'Who will ascend into heaven?' (that is, to bring Christ down)." Baruch 3:29 also uses Deut 30:12–14 and interprets it in regard to wisdom: "Who has gone up in heaven and taken her, and brought her down from the clouds?" However, despite this commonality, the identification with wisdom found in Baruch is likely not made in Romans. Instead, both interpret Deuteronomy but to different ends. For Paul it serves to form a contrast between what is far and near, not to identify Christ with wisdom.

of the letter. The hymn celebrates Jesus as the fullest extent of God's wisdom, and directly after the hymn the author speaks of a "mystery hidden for ages and generations but now made known to his saints" (Col 1:26), "which is Christ in you" (1:27), and that in Christ "all the treasures of wisdom and knowledge" are hidden (2:3). Near the end of the letter the speaker urges his audience to "walk in wisdom" (4:5).

The hymn of Col 1:15–20 consists of two stanzas, verses 15–18a and verses 18b–20, both heavily influenced by wisdom motifs. The first stanza of the hymn portrays Christ as personified wisdom who plays a role in creation. He is "the image of the invisible God, the firstborn of all creation" (1:15). In the first line of the second stanza, Christ is also a firstborn son: "the beginning, the firstborn of the dead" (1:18b). Wisdom as firstborn is a development from other wisdom traditions, most likely Prov 8:22–27 and Sir 24:1–9, where wisdom is the first created work of God. Philo similarly describes personified wisdom as "firstborn mother of all things" (QG 4.97). Wisdom as the "image" of God's goodness is known from Wis 7:26 (cf. Philo, Leg. 1.43). Colossians 1:16 ("in him all things are created") alludes to wisdom as the agent through which God creates. Christ is "before all things and in him all things hold together" (1:17), which also evokes the divine Logos (Sir 43:26, "by his word all things hold together"). In the second stanza, the statement that in Christ "all the fullness of God was pleased to dwell" (Col 1:19) expresses a notion that is suited to wisdom, Logos, or spirit, namely, the manifestation of the presence of God. However, these personifications do not typically reside in a single being (as with Christ) but pervade the whole world (e.g., Wis 7:24, "because of her [Wisdom's] pureness she pervades and penetrates all things"; cf. Ps 139:7). There are exceptions: Philo's description of Moses, "the spirit which is upon him is the wise, the divine, the indivisible . . . the spirit which is everywhere diffused, so as to fill the universe" (Gig. 27); and 4QInstruction's presentation of an exalted sage as firstborn and apotheosis of attaining wisdom (4Q418 81+81a).[38] The Colossians hymn identifies Christ with divine wisdom in order to assert his significance in terms his audience would have understood.

Wisdom as a bridging concept (i.e., mediating the divine/human relationship), which is significantly developed in early Jewish tradition, exerted considerable influence on Paul's presentation of Christ in some key Pauline passages (1 Cor 1:25, 30; 8:6; Col 1:15–20). Divine wisdom, already part of the philosophical texture and common language of the time, developed as a category in which Paul could consider the cosmic and universal significance of Christ. For Paul, Jesus is the embodiment of divine wisdom sent to all humanity.

---

38. Translation from C. D. Yonge, *The Works of Philo: Completed and Unabridged* (Peabody: Hendrickson, 1993).

Wisdom

Paul sets the stage so that by the time the Letter to the Hebrews was composed, it had likely already become traditional to describe Christ's cosmic significance in terms drawn from the portrayals of personified wisdom in the sapiential tradition. The incipit of Hebrews (Heb 1:1–3) is a prominent expression of wisdom Christology. Here Christ is the "son" through whom God makes the world. He is the "radiance" (ἀπαύγασμα) of God's glory, "stamp" or "exact imprint" (χαρακτήρ) of God's being, and through him God sustains the world. Similar to Col 1:15–18, the influence of depictions of wisdom as God's companion and cocreator is discernible. Creation is sustained by the son (cf. 1:17, "in him all things hold together"), which evokes an association of wisdom with the Logos (cf. Philo, *Migr.* 6).

By the time the evangelists began to edit and adapt their sources, Paul had already identified Christ with wisdom in his letter to the Corinthians. Matthew in particular can be seen to develop an emerging wisdom Christology. One of the most notable passages is Matt 8:20, which portrays the Son of Man as having nowhere to lay his head. This seemingly alludes to embodied and personified wisdom dwelling with humanity (cf. 1 En. 42:1–2). Indeed, as part of Jesus's teachings in Matthew, we find a number of sayings that explicitly recall the wisdom tradition, such as Matt 5:42 (cf. Sir 4:4–6); Matt 24:28 (cf. Job 39:30); and Matt 12:42 ("someone greater than Solomon is here"). Among the Synoptic Gospels, Matthew has been frequently noted for its particular interest in wisdom. Jack Suggs demonstrates that wisdom is a basic part of Matthew's theology and that Christ and wisdom are clearly identified.[39] Ben Witherington suggests that Matthew is thoroughly sapiential with its focus on "teacher" and "disciple," as well as his interest to teach about wisdom. Jesus as a teacher of wisdom reflects an Israelite sage who "dealt with and drew deductions from the repeatable patterns and moral patterns of ordinary life, both of human life and the life of the larger natural world."[40] Celia Deutsch argues against a thoroughgoing sapiential reading of Matthew. She is interested in the evangelist's "sage-Jesus" in light of the Lady Wisdom motif.[41] She argues that Matthew adapts Lady Wisdom into Jesus,

---

39. Suggs, *Wisdom, Christology and Law in Mathew's Gospel* (Cambridge: Harvard University Press, 1970).

40. See Witherington, *Matthew*, SHBC (Macon, GA: Smyth & Helwys, 2006), 10; Witherington, *Jesus the Sage: The Pilgrimage of Wisdom* (Minneapolis: Fortress, 2000), 341–68, argues that Matthew is presented as a scribe so that the wisdom teachings are Jesus's own and not the result of editorial activity by Matthew. See the reviews of Witherington by Grant Macaskill, *Revealed Wisdom and Inaugurated Eschatology in Ancient Christianity*, JSJSup 115 (Leiden: Brill, 2007), 253–58, who rightly focuses on his thoroughgoing wisdom Christology as unconvincing.

41. Deutsch, *Lady Wisdom, Jesus, and the Sages: Metaphor and Social Context in Matthew's Gospel* (Valley Forge, PA: Trinity Press International, 1996).

and explores implications of the gender exchange and the social context that may have inspired it. While there are objections to the idea that wisdom Christology is even present in Matthew, the case for it remains reasonably strong.

Understanding Matthew's use of the wisdom tradition requires an analysis of the evangelist within the double tradition. That is, Matthew's redactional activity maintains a wisdom Christology that reflects significant differences with Luke as reflected in four passages: Matt 11:19 (= Luke 7:35); Matt 11:25–30 (= Luke 10:21–22); Matt 23:34–36 (= Luke 11:49–51); and Matt 23:37–39 (= Luke 13:34). When Jesus prays in Matt 11:25–30, he thanks the Father because he has "hidden these things from the wise and understanding and revealed them to babes" (11:25). Jesus claims a unique relationship to the Father, as Son, and thereby limits the possibility that wisdom can reach humanity by any other means. Indeed, this is explicit in Jesus's declaration that "no one knows the Son except the Father, and no one knows the Father except the Son and any one to whom the Son chooses to reveal him" (Matt 11:27). Furthermore, the saying of Jesus in Matt 11:28–30 ("Come to me, all who labor and are heavy laden, and I will give you rest. Take my yoke upon you, and learn from me; for I am gentle and lowly in heart, and you will find rest for your souls. For my yoke is easy, and my burden is light") is remarkably similar to the words of the speaker in Sir 51:23–26, who teaches about wisdom: "Draw near to me, you who are uneducated, and lodge in the house of instruction. Why do you say you are lacking in these things, and why do you endure such great thirst? I opened my mouth and said, 'Acquire wisdom for yourselves without money. Put your neck under her yoke, and let your souls receive instruction; it is to be found close by'" (cf. 11Q5 XVIII, 3a–4, where wisdom is a gift to the simple without understanding). In Ben Sira, the sage invites students to put their neck under wisdom's yoke, whereas in Matthew it is Jesus's own yoke that he calls people to take upon themselves, which is quite convincingly interpreted by Dunn as equating Jesus with wisdom.[42]

For Matthew, Jesus the divine wisdom helps to establish the authority of his disciples, who become wisdom's emissaries. This likely functions within a wider polemic between his community and the Jewish communities that rejected its Christian message. In Luke 11:49 the wisdom of God says, "I will send them prophets and apostles," whereas in Matt 23:34 Jesus himself speaks saying, "I send you prophets and wise men and scribes." Matthew transforms the saying of personified wisdom into a saying about Jesus himself, and the messengers he sends suffer persecution, are killed, and some are scourged in "your synagogues" (Matt 23:34). Finally, the lament over Jerusalem in Matt 23:37–39 (Luke 13:34) is a direct speech in which a simile is made about a hen that gathers her brood under her

---

42. Dunn, *Christology*, 200–201.

wings. In this speech, the first-person singular form is used when posing the question: "How often would I have gathered (you prophets)?" The "I" in this statement holds an allusion to personified wisdom because she is the one who sends prophets (Prov 9:3; Sir 24:7–12; 1 En. 42:1–3) and is also motherly (Sir 1:15). 11Q11 (11QApocryphal Psalms) VI, 5–6 uses similar imagery in reference to God as protector ("with his feathers he will cover you and under his wings you shall lodge"), which makes it more difficult to discern how the Gospel of Matthew uses this allusion. If Matthew attributes the "I" of this statement to Jesus, the context may suggest that God is speaking, which would reinforce the conclusion that Matthew has a developed wisdom Christology.

The opening hymn of John's Gospel (1:1–18) is considered by many to have been written by early Christians and later adapted by the evangelist as the prologue.[43] The hymn's message is particularly suited to present the message of Christ in terms that Greek readers would have understood. The poetic style and several themes in the prologue—for example, the incarnational theology (John 1:1, 14, "the logos became flesh")—are not shared by the rest of the gospel. However, the preexistence of Christ in 1:1–2 ("He was in the beginning with God") is also found in John 17:5 when Jesus prays: "glorify me . . . with the glory that I had before the world was made." As we have seen, Lady Wisdom existed with God from the beginning even before there was an earth (Prov 8:22–23; Sir 24:9; Wis 6:22); Christ as the Logos, a parallel bridging concept in the Hellenistic world with wisdom, is "with God" and "was God" (John 1:1) and as such participated with God in the creation of the world (1:3, "all things were made through him"; cf. 1 Cor 8:6; Col 1:15–18a). The presentation of personified wisdom in Wis 7:25–26 shares important commonalities with the portrayal of Christ as the Logos in John's prologue. In the hymn and elsewhere in the gospel, Christ has the Father's glory (John 1:14; cf. 8:50; 11:4; 17:5, 22, 24). Wisdom is the pure emanation of God's glory in Wis 7:25. In John 1:4–5 and throughout the Johannine literature (8:12; 11:5; 1 John 1:5), God is light and Jesus comes forth from God as the light of the world and men. Wisdom is said to be a reflection of the everlasting light of God in Wis 7:26. Wisdom is also preferred to any natural light (Wis 7:10, 29; cf. Bar 3:33). The Logos as the "only son from the father" comes down from heaven to earth (John 1:14), which is a theme related to wisdom making her habitation with God's people (Sir 24:8) and humanity (Bar 3:37; Wis 9:10).

---

43. See Daniel Boyarin, "The Gospel of the Memra: Jewish Binitarianism and the Prologue to John," *HTR* 94, no. 3 (2001): 243–84; cf. Matthew J. Gordley, "The Johannine Prologue and Jewish Didactic Hymn Traditions: A New Case for Reading the Prologue as a Hymn," *JBL* 128, no. 4 (2009): 781–802. For an overview on these issues, see Ernst Haenchen, *John 1: A Commentary on the Gospel of John Chapters 1–6*, Hermeneia (Philadelphia: Fortress, 1984), 131–40.

There are indications that even after the prologue, the Fourth Gospel identifies Christ with wisdom. In John 3:13 it is written of the Son of Man that only he has ascended and descended from heaven, an activity explicitly associated elsewhere with personified wisdom (Bar 3:29; Wis 9:16–17). On several occasions in John's Gospel, Jesus foretells his return to the Father (John 13:3; 16:28; 20:17), which is similar to the return of wisdom to heaven in the Similitudes of Enoch (1 En. 42:2). At the end of the prologue (John 1:18), Jesus is the one who exclusively reveals God to humanity, which is a function of wisdom among humankind, instructing in ways pleasing to God (Wis 8:4; 9:9–10; Sir 4:12; Bar 4:1) and teaching what is from above (Job 11:6–7; Wis 9:16–18). Finally, the "I am" statements that are found more than forty times in the gospel, often express Jesus's divine and celestial origins, further strengthening the view that Jesus is purposefully identified with divine wisdom.[44]

Conclusion

What wisdom is and how it should be treated is far from straightforward. To speak of wisdom in Israel's Scripture is to draw upon a category of convenience that consists of the books of Proverbs, Job, and Qohelet. Among these three compositions, New Testament authors most frequently cite and allude to Proverbs, but compared with other parts of Israel's Scripture these traditions exert less influence (e.g., Genesis or Isaiah). However, intertextuality is only one way to consider wisdom in the New Testament. Another approach is to take into account common themes and instructional formulations (e.g., proverbs or paraenesis). While exhortations to act wisely occur in a number of places in the New Testament, they are concentrated especially in James and in parts of Matthew. Moreover, the wisdom books of Israel's Scripture teach about wisdom, at times personified as Lady Wisdom, which is a multifaceted concept that authors in the New Testament (esp. Paul, Matthew, and John) allude to. By equating personified wisdom with Christ, God seeks to communicate knowledge of himself with humanity. The portrayal of Christ as wisdom is part of a broader philosophical trajectory, well known in Jewish thought, that was concerned with divine wisdom and creation, the architecture of the world, and the relationship of humanity to the divine. Appreciation of wisdom Christology is significantly enhanced when reading it as part of early Jewish wisdom traditions.

New Testament and early Jewish wisdom literature are anachronistic categories that blur historical undertakings. These are entities of the same sapiential

---

44. Raymond E. Brown, *The Gospel according to John (I–XII): A New Translation with Introduction and Commentary*, AB 29 (Garden City, NY: Doubleday, 1966), cxxii–cxxvi.

ecosystem. They are distinguishable by the gravitational weight of Christology in the New Testament, but when scrutinized, these christological conceptual frameworks are well known in early Jewish literature—even though they are not limited to the wisdom tradition. When studied together, especially in light of previously unknown wisdom literature from Qumran, greater appreciation is gained for an important development during the Second Temple era: the boundaries between wisdom and apocalyptic continue to blur. These conflicted boundaries may be seen in instructions and teachings operating with a cosmology, sometimes explicitly, other times implicitly, that includes both a temporal and spatial axis. Act and consequence are not limited to one's own life; rather, reward and punishment for one's behavior will come in the hereafter. Moreover, understanding may be derived from observing the created order, but knowledge is also revealed and transcendent. Otherworldly beings, such as angels and demons, play roles in the lives of human beings. Therefore, the pursuit of wisdom acknowledges their presence and activities. The erosion of categories is also an erasure of paradigms that requires assumptions about such weighty topics as the hypothetical saying, source Q, conceptualizations of evil, or anthropology to be checked.

While the specific textual traditions found at Qumran may not have been known or read by Jesus, his followers, and the early Christians, they nonetheless shared a number of intellectual and literary patterns. Previously unknown materials from Qumran Cave 4 that are relatively new to the academic community have changed, and continue to transform, our understanding of the reception and development of wisdom in the Greco-Roman period. As such, our appreciation for sapiential discourse in the New Testament is currently being reassessed.

Bibliography

Adams, Samuel L. *Wisdom in Transition: Act and Consequence in Second Temple Instructions.* JSJSup 125. Leiden: Brill, 2008.

Allison, Dale C., Jr. *A Critical and Exegetical Commentary on the Epistle of James.* ICC. New York: Bloomsbury, 2013.

Bauckham, Richard. *James: Wisdom of James, Disciple of Jesus the Sage.* New Testament Readings. London: Routledge, 1999.

Baumgarten, Joseph M. "On the Nature of the Seductress in 4Q184." *RevQ* 15, no. 1/2 (1991): 133–43.

Blenkinsopp, Joseph. *Wisdom and Law in the Old Testament: The Ordering of Life in Israel and Early Judaism.* 2nd ed. OBS. Oxford: Oxford University Press, 2003.

Boyarin, Daniel. "The Gospel of the Memra: Jewish Binitarianism and the Prologue to John." *HTR* 94, no. 3 (2001): 243–84.

Brown, Raymond E. *The Gospel according to John (I–XII): A New Translation with Introduction and Commentary*. AB 29. Garden City, NY: Doubleday, 1966.

Charlesworth, James H., and Michael A. Daise, eds. *Light in a Spotless Mirror: Reflections on Wisdom Traditions in Judaism and Early Christianity*. Faith and Scholarship Colloquies. Harrisburg, PA: Trinity Press International, 2003.

Collins, John J. *Jewish Wisdom in the Hellenistic Age*. OTL. Louisville: Westminster John Knox, 1997.

DeSilva, David A. *The Jewish Teachers of Jesus, James, and Jude: What Earliest Christianity Learned from the Apocrypha and Pseudepigrapha*. New York: Oxford University Press, 2012.

Deutsch, Celia M. *Lady Wisdom, Jesus, and the Sages: Metaphor and Social Context in Matthew's Gospel*. Valley Forge, PA: Trinity Press International, 1996.

Dibelius, Martin. *James: A Commentary on the Epistle of James*. Translated by Michael A. Williams. Hermeneia. Philadelphia: Fortress, 1976.

Dunn, James D. G. *Christology in the Making: A New Testament Inquiry into the Origins of the Doctrine of the Incarnation*. Philadelphia: Westminster, 1980.

Francis, Frederick O. "The Form and Function of the Opening and Closing Paragraphs of James and 1 John." *ZNW* 61, no. 1/2 (1970): 110–25.

García Martínez, Florentino. "Wisdom at Qumran: Worldly or Heavenly?" Pages 1–16 in *Wisdom and Apocalypticism in the Dead Sea Scrolls and in the Biblical Tradition*. Edited by Florentino García Martínez. BETL 168. Leuven: Peeters, 2003.

Goff, Matthew J. "Discerning Trajectories: 4QInstruction and the Sapiential Background of the Sayings Source Q." *JBL* 124, no. 4 (2005): 657–73.

———. *Discerning Wisdom: The Sapiential Literature of the Dead Sea Scrolls*. VTSup 116. Leiden: Brill, 2007.

———. "A Seductive Demoness at Qumran? Lilith, Female Demons and 4Q184." Pages 59–76 in *Das Böse, der Teufel, und Dämonen – Evil, the Devil, and Demons: Dualistic Characteristics in the Religion of Israel, Ancient Judaism, and Christianity*. Edited by Benjamin Wold, Jan Dochhorn, and Susanne Rudnig-Zelt. WUNT 2/412. Tübingen: Mohr Siebeck, 2016.

———. *The Worldly and Heavenly Wisdom of 4QInstruction*. STDJ 50. Leiden: Brill, 2003.

Gordley, Matthew J. "The Johannine Prologue and Jewish Didactic Hymn Traditions: A New Case for Reading the Prologue as a Hymn." *JBL* 128, no. 4 (2009): 781–802.

Haenchen, Ernst. *John 1: A Commentary on the Gospel of John Chapters 1–6*. Hermeneia. Philadelphia: Fortress, 1984.

Harrington, Daniel J. "Wisdom in the NT." *NIDB* 5:865–69.

———. *Wisdom Texts from Qumran*. Literature of the Dead Sea Scrolls. London: Routledge, 1996.

Hedrick, Charles W. *The Wisdom of Jesus: Between the Sages of Israel and the Apostles of the Church.* Eugene, OR: Wipf & Stock, 2014.

Horbury, William. "The Wisdom of Solomon." Pages 650–67 in *The Oxford Bible Commentary.* Edited by John Barton and John Muddiman. Oxford: Oxford University Press, 2001.

Horsley, Richard A., and Patrick A. Tiller. *After Apocalyptic and Wisdom: Rethinking Texts in Contexts.* Eugene, OR: Cascade, 2012.

Kampen, John. *Wisdom Literature.* ECDSS 14. Grand Rapids: Eerdmans, 2011.

Kloppenborg, John S. *The Formation of Q: Trajectories in Ancient Wisdom Collections.* Minneapolis: Fortress, 1987.

Kolarcik, Michael. "Sapiential Values and Apocalyptic Imagery in the Wisdom of Solomon." Pages 23–36 in *Studies in the Book of Wisdom.* Edited by Géza G. Xeravits and József Zsengellér. JSJSup 142. Leiden: Brill, 2010.

Kynes, Will. *An Obituary for "Wisdom Literature": The Birth, Death, and Intertextual Reintegration of a Biblical Corpus.* Oxford: Oxford University Press, 2019.

Lips, Hermann von. *Weisheitliche Traditionen im Neuen Testament.* WMANT 64. Neukirchen-Vluyn: Neukirchener Verlag, 1990.

Macaskill, Grant. *Revealed Wisdom and Inaugurated Eschatology in Ancient Judaism and Early Christianity.* JSJSup 115. Leiden: Brill, 2007.

Mack, Burton L. *Wisdom and the Hebrew Epic: Ben Sira's Hymn in Praise of the Fathers.* CSHJ. Chicago: University of Chicago Press, 1985.

Mazzinghi, Luca. *Wisdom.* IECOT. Stuttgart: Kohlhammer, 2019.

Miller, Lulu. *Why Fish Don't Exist: A Story of Loss, Love, and the Hidden Order of Life.* New York: Simon & Schuster, 2020.

Pevarello, Daniele. "Looking for Wisdom in Wis. 11:2–19:2: Between Universalism and Particularism." *JSP* 30, no. 1 (2020): 21–34.

Reymond, Eric D. *Innovations in Hebrew Poetry: Parallelism and the Poems of Sirach.* SBLStBL 9. Atlanta: Society of Biblical Literature, 2004.

Sanders, Jack T. "When Sacred Canopies Collide: The Reception of the Torah of Moses in the Wisdom Literature of the Second-Temple Period." *JSJ* 32, no. 2 (2001): 121–36.

Sneed, Mark R., ed. *Was There a Wisdom Tradition? New Prospects in Israelite Wisdom Studies.* AIL 23. Atlanta: SBL Press, 2015.

Suggs, Jack M. *Wisdom, Christology and Law in Matthew's Gospel.* Cambridge: Harvard University Press, 1970.

Uusimäki, Elisa. *Turning Proverbs towards Torah: An Analysis of 4Q525.* STDJ 117. Leiden: Brill, 2016.

Weeks, Stuart. *An Introduction to the Study of Wisdom Literature.* London: T&T Clark, 2010.

Witherington, Ben, III. *Jesus the Sage: The Pilgrimage of Wisdom*. Minneapolis: Fortress, 2000.

———. *Matthew*. SHBC. Macon, GA: Smyth & Helwys, 2006.

Wold, Benjamin. *4QInstruction: Divisions and Hierarchies*. STDJ 123. Leiden: Brill, 2018.

———. "Sin and Evil in the Letter of James in Light of Qumran Discoveries." *NTS* 65, no. 1 (2019): 78–93.

———. "Universal and Particular Law in James and Early Judaism." *JSNT* 41, no. 1 (2018): 95–106.

———. "Wisdom in the New Testament." Pages 349–67 in *The Wiley-Blackwell Companion to Wisdom Literature*. Edited by Matthew J. Goff and Samuel L. Adams. Hoboken, NJ: Wiley-Blackwell, 2019.

Wright, Benjamin G., III. "1 Enoch and Ben Sira: Wisdom and Apocalyptic in Relationship." Pages 159–76 in *The Early Enoch Literature*. Edited by Gabriele Boccaccini and John J. Collins. JSJSup 121. Leiden: Brill, 2007.

———. "Conflicted Boundaries: Ben Sira, Sage and Seer." Pages 229–53 in *Congress Volume Helsinki 2010*. Edited by Martti Nissinen. VTSup 148. Leiden: Brill.

Wright, Benjamin G., III, and Lawrence M. Wills, eds. *Conflicted Boundaries in Wisdom and Apocalypticism*. SymS 35. Atlanta: Society of Biblical Literature, 2005.

31

Liturgy and Prayer

RODNEY A. WERLINE

The Jesus movement emerged in the era of Second Temple Judaism. The earliest members of the movement were Jews and continued to identify as such. Into this new movement they brought with them many aspects of their Jewish life and faith, and these included Jewish authoritative traditions, including Scripture and worship practices. These facets of their faith had long been closely related to one another—even intertwined. The Hebrew Bible itself bears evidence of the interplay between authoritative tradition and worship, and the literature produced by Jews in the Second Temple period shows that they preserved and developed this relationship. The New Testament documents testify that the early church followed the same course. Both the shape and the content of the liturgical material in the New Testament resemble the products of the church's predecessors and Jewish contemporaries. While the unique agenda of the earliest followers of Jesus becomes apparent in their incorporation of Scripture into their liturgical pieces, they obviously adapted and deployed the methods and tactics they found within their own cultural traditions.

Prayers and Liturgies in the Hebrew Bible

The Hebrew Bible contains an extensive amount of liturgical material. While the Psalter forms the largest, most obvious collection, the literature is dotted with prayers, liturgies, blessings, and hymns, many embedded within narratives or collections of prophetic oracles and traditions. Unfortunately, reconstructing original settings for these liturgical pieces or the settings in which they were repeatedly used remains fraught with methodological and evidential roadblocks. The problem has been notorious and well-known in psalms studies. The language of many psalms suggests contexts such as royal enthronements, individual and communal complaints or laments, ascents, general worship and praise within the temple, and various festivals. However, scholars possess very little in regard to scenes depicting these ceremonies or the fuller liturgies for these ceremonies. Conclusions that various psalms found their homes in such settings sometimes rely on parallels with other ancient Near Eastern texts and contexts, especially those from the Canaanites and the Babylonians. The psalms themselves, of course, refer to the temple and aspects related to the temple. Still, interpreters could benefit from more information than what these texts yield; the picture is limited and little is certain. Similar problems emerge in the examination of the prophetic corpus and the liturgical units located within the collections.

However, even within this literature interpreters have begun to see that prayers and liturgical material take up older traditions or build new practices to address gaps in the logic of Hebrew Bible traditions and directives. For example, the confession in Exod 34:6–7, "The LORD, the LORD, a God merciful and gracious, slow to anger, and abounding in steadfast love and faithfulness, keeping steadfast love for the thousandth generation, forgiving iniquity and transgression and sin, yet by no means clearing the guilty, but visiting the iniquity of the parents upon the children and the children's children, to the third and the fourth generation," seems to have made its mark on several other liturgical pieces and narratives within the Hebrew Bible (cf., e.g., Pss 100:5; 107:1, 8, 15, 21, 31, 43; 136; Dan 9:4; Jonah 4:2).[1] While evidence is scant, the passages obviously reveal that some learned and liturgically minded circles within ancient Israel and Judah had already begun to reappropriate authoritative traditions. This kind of work, as I have argued elsewhere, becomes especially evident in the penitential prayer traditions that stretch from probably the exilic period into the Second Temple era and beyond.[2] These prayers grow out of an interpretation of the meaning of and proper way to fulfill the expectations in Deut 4:27–31 and 30:1–4 that the people of Israel would one day "turn" (שׁוב) and "seek" (דרשׁ) God "with their whole heart." First Kings 8 represents an early attempt to explain this tradition and understands "to seek" as prayer directed toward the temple. The scene is Solomon's dedication of the temple, but the king gives his primary attention to directions for alleviating the covenantal curses found in Deut 28 when they are visited upon the people. As

---

1. Unless otherwise noted, all translations are from the NRSV.
2. Rodney A. Werline, *Penitential Prayer in Second Temple Judaism: The Development of a Religious Institution*, EJL 13 (Atlanta: Scholars Press, 1998).

Judith Newman explains, the prayer also recalls the promises made to David (2 Sam 7:14–16; 1 Kgs 8:25).[3] Interpreters now see the influence of Levitical and perhaps Ezekielian circles on the penitential prayer in Neh 9, as this penitential tradition develops and grows.[4] Other traditions begin to make their way into the expressions of penitential prayer, such as the warnings about rejecting the words of the prophets (cf. Jer 7:25; 35:15; 44:4; Dan 9:6, 10; cf. Bar 2:20, 24; 1 Esd 8:82). One can add to this the frequent inclusion of what Gerhard von Rad labeled a *Gerichtsdoxologie*, "You are righteous, O Lord" (e.g., Dan 9:14; cf. Tob 3:2).[5] Finally, authors and editors combine these traditions with the particular agendas and perspectives of their respective groups, while also incorporating other traditions into the liturgical material. Throughout the Second Temple era, this tradition expands and includes an even wider array of authoritative texts (cf., e.g., Dan 9; Bar 1:15–3:8; 4Q504).[6] The point here, however, is that this particular prayer practice in the Hebrew Bible already displays the incorporation of older and authoritative traditions into the prayers. Thus, when we encounter the phenomenon in the New Testament, the practice is in no way new.

Prayers and Liturgies in the Second Temple Era

As stated above, this phenomenon of incorporating authoritative traditions into prayers and liturgies continues throughout the Second Temple era. This literature contains numerous prayer texts and liturgical pieces. The number, of course, significantly expanded with the discovery of the Dead Sea Scrolls. While there was no fixed or standardized prayer in this period, just as there were no standardized times for prayer, liturgical specialists and practitioners turned to authoritative traditions for the language of their prayers and liturgies. Some communities may have observed fixed times for prayers within their own circles (e.g., Dan 6:10; 9:21; 1QS X), but no standardization existed across the boundaries of social groups and throughout the Judaism of the era.[7] Groups may have created their times for prayer based on certain passages from the Psalms.

---

3. Judith H. Newman, *Praying by the Book: The Scripturalization of Prayer in Second Temple Judaism*, EJL 14 (Atlanta: Scholars Press, 1999), 38–54.

4. See Mark J. Boda, *Praying the Tradition: The Origin and Use of Tradition in Nehemiah 9*, BZAW 277 (Berlin: de Gruyter, 1999).

5. Cf. Gerhard von Rad, *Old Testament Theology*, trans. D. M. G. Stalker, 2 vols. (New York: Harper & Row, 1962), 1:354–55. See also Boda, *Praying the Tradition*, 55.

6. See Werline, *Penitential Prayer*, 75, 91–92, 151–52.

7. Jeremy Penner, *Patterns of Daily Prayer in Second Temple Period Judaism*, STDJ 104 (Leiden: Brill, 2012).

Even without the language of prayers being fixed, one can see the tremendous influence that texts now in the Hebrew Bible had on the language and rhetoric of Second Temple prayers.

Studies like those from Newman have explained that these texts suggest a close relationship between prayer and the study of authoritative traditions, which she has labeled "Scripture."[8] Two texts from the era especially showcase this connection and the process. First, as Ben Sira explains the life of the scribe, he places study, interpretation, prayer, and instruction at the heart of the scribal office (Sir 39:1–11). Assuming that Ben Sira is the author, or editor, of the prayer in Sir 36:1–22, which focuses on the deliverance of Israel from its enemies, one can see the product of the scribe who interprets authoritative traditions and incorporates them into a prayer. The prayer in Sir 36 is filled with traditional language that refers to God's past deliverances, especially the exodus: "Give new signs, and work other wonders; / make your hand and right arm glorious. / Rouse your anger and pour out your wrath" (Sir 36:6–8; cf., e.g., Deut 4:34; 26:8; Neh 9:10; Dan 4:2–3; Pss 44:3; 89:13; 135:9; Isa 62:8; 63:12; Jer 10:25; Ezek 7:8; 9:8). The people are "called by your name" (36:17; cf. Deut 28:10; Isa 43:1; Jer 14:9), and they are the "firstborn" (36:17; cf. Exod 4:22). The concern in the text for Israel's return appears in numerous texts in the Hebrew Bible.

Daniel 9 provides another example of this close relationship between prayer and interpretation (see vv. 2, 24). In this passage, the seer contemplates Jeremiah's prophecy that the exile would last seventy years (Jer 25:12; 29:10). Obviously, at the time of the actual writing of Dan 9 during the crisis with Antiochus IV (167–164 BCE), it seemed as though the prophecy had failed. While the visionary contemplates this problem and prays, God sends Gabriel to explain that Jeremiah's seventy years should actually be interpreted as seventy weeks of years. Between Daniel's reflection on the meaning of Jeremiah and Gabriel's interpretation stands a prayer. The prayer is packed with penitential language and traditions from established authoritative, traditional speech. The author certainly thought that the covenantal curses from Deut 28 had been activated. However, in the midst of the traditional language one can also spot the special interests of the *maskilim*, presumably the circle behind the production, preservation, and transmission of the tradition, as Daniel confesses to God that the people did not "ponder [שׂכל] your truth" (Dan 9:13).

While examples of the use of traditional language in the era abound, one final example from a Dead Sea Scroll titled Barki Nafshi (4Q434–439) will suffice. In this

---

8. Newman, *Praying by the Book*; and Judith H. Newman, *Before the Bible: The Liturgical Body and the Formation of Scriptures in Early Judaism* (New York: Oxford University Press, 2018).

Liturgy and Prayer

text, the author expresses concern about evil powers that have taken up residence in his body. His hope is that God will remove these forces and offer protection from them. The prayer draws on the image from Ezek 11:19 and 36:26 about replacing a heart of stone within the petitioner, as well as the "clean heart" from Ps 51:10–12.[9]

Prayers and Liturgies in the New Testament

The New Testament's use of these authoritative traditions that become part of the Hebrew Bible presents nothing particularly new. Of course, as mentioned about the reference to the *maskilim* in Dan 9, New Testament prayers will reveal their own particular agendas that arise from the authors' understandings about Jesus. However, some prayers, or portions of prayers, exhibit little or no particularly "Christian" features outside of the overall context in which they appear.[10]

Luke's Praise for Deliverance

Luke opens his Gospel with several blessings, prayers, and songs. These liturgical pieces primarily respond to God's actions manifested in the birth of Jesus. In line with material from the Second Temple period, those offering their praises draw on traditional language and themes. The author's goal in this section of the Gospel does not simply seem to apply a prophecy-fulfillment pattern. Instead, the traditional language provides the narrative with the aura of the sacred past. As a result, the author led the audience to understand the birth of Jesus and John the Baptist in continuity with, and as the fulfillment of, expectations in Scripture. Further, the audience must now hear or view the past in light of the author's interpretation of it through the Jesus story.[11]

Mary's Song in Luke 1:46–55

Mary's prayer stands as the first of four canticles in Luke's opening two chapters. Notably, Luke does not use the word "prayed" or "sang" but instead simply states "Mary said." Interpreters might question if Mary directs her speech toward God.

---

9. Miryam T. Brand, *Evil Within and Without: The Source of Sin and Its Nature as Portrayed in Second Temple Judaism*, JAJSup 9 (Göttingen: Vandenhoeck & Ruprecht, 2013), 44–46; Rodney A. Werline, *Whenever They Prayed: Dimensions of New Testament Prayer* (Lanham, MD: Lexington Books/Fortress Academic, 2021), 101.

10. In writing this chapter, I greatly benefited from the references supplied in the margins in NA^{28}.

11. Werline, *Whenever They Prayed*, 40–55.

After all, the immediate audience is Elizabeth. However, the line between second-person speech directed to God and third-person speech is not always as significant as one might expect, as prayers and psalms can alternate between second and third person. In its basic force, Mary's prayer mostly recalls Hannah's prayer in 1 Sam 2:1–10. Hannah engages with the high priest when she uncontrollably weeps at the shrine and Eli mistakes her actions as signs that she is drunk. Both prayers emphasize the theme of reversal—God brings down the mighty while the humble are exalted. However, the reversals in each context differ. Samuel's birth reverses Hannah's barrenness and social shame, especially in regard to her rival wife, and Samuel will see the fall of Eli and his sons. Mary's song in Luke introduces the theme of reversal in this gospel, which will take various shapes and meanings, for example, the fate of the wealthy as compared to the poor, and the movement of the marginalized into the community while the socially respected insiders will eventually be cast out. However, as the narrative moves along, the reader must also wonder if one of the most profound reversals is connected with the success that the church will have among gentile audiences as compared to Jewish. In fact, Jesus will introduce this possibility in his inaugural sermon in the synagogue in Nazareth by drawing on passages from Third Isaiah (Isa 61:1–2; 58:6), as well as stories from the lives of Elijah and Elisha (1 Kgs 17:8–16; 2 Kgs 5:1–14).

The opening lines of Mary's praise echoes Hannah's opening words: "My heart exults in the LORD; my strength is exalted in my God" (1 Sam 2:1). However, one can also hear praises that arise from the Psalms, such as "O magnify the LORD with me, and let us exalt his name together" (Ps 34:3) and "Then my soul shall rejoice in the LORD, exulting in his deliverance" (Ps 35:9). In fact, for nearly every phrase one can locate parallel language in the Psalms. Raymond Brown has provided an extensive list of these similarities.[12]

Mary's praise climaxes by recalling the promises God made to Abraham, a theme that appears in several of Luke's opening canticles: "According to the promise he made to our ancestors, to Abraham and to his descendants forever" (Luke 1:55). In 1:48b, Mary might be co-opting the words of the promise made to Abraham in Gen 12:3: "In you all the families of the earth shall be blessed"; "Surely, from now on all generations will call me blessed" (Luke 1:48).

Zechariah's Benedictus (Luke 1:67–79)

In response to John's birth, his father, Zechariah, spoke a "prophecy," which takes the form of a blessing or hymn to God, the Benedictus (Luke 1:67–79). Except for the lines that refer to John's birth (1:76–77), nothing in the hymn's content would

---

12. Raymond E. Brown, *The Birth of the Messiah: A Commentary on the Infancy Narratives in Matthew and Luke*, updated ed., ABRL (Garden City, NY: Doubleday, 1993), 58–60.

preclude its existence prior to the Gospel of Luke. Like the Magnificat, nearly every line in the piece parallels language or themes from the Hebrew Bible. The opening blessing mirrors formulations found throughout the Psalms and in many other texts. The focus in 1:68–71 is on Jesus's birth, not John's, as the fulfillment of the promise that God would raise up a descendent of David who would bring salvation. Unfortunately, the NRSV has decided to translate κέρας σωτηρίας (1:69) as "mighty savior," instead of "horn of salvation," though they have provided a footnote with this translation. Their translation obscures the obvious allusion to 2 Sam 22:3: "My God, my rock, in whom I take refuge, my shield and the horn of my salvation." The hymn then connects the promise to David to the covenantal promise made to Abraham (1:72–73). However, the language of being rescued from the "hands of our enemies" (v. 74b) seems to be influenced by Mic 4:10. The lines that refer to John, 1:76–77, depict him and his work as the fulfillment of Isa 40:3 and Mal 3:1—the one who "will go before the Lord to prepare his ways" (1:76; cf. Mal 3:4–6). Zechariah concludes his blessing (1:78–79) with phrases that echo the expectation of Isaiah that God's light will shine on the people (Isa 9:1; 60:1) and that they will finally walk in the "way of peace" (cf. Isa 59:8).

Simeon's Nunc Dimittis (Luke 2:29–32)

Simeon delivers the final liturgical response to seeing God's "salvation" when he encounters Jesus and his parents when they bring him to be presented at the temple (Luke 2:21–38). Simeon is described as one who was "looking forward to the consolation of Israel" (2:25). This phrase evokes the "Book of Consolation" in Isa 40–55, which anticipates Israel's salvation and restoration. As will be seen below in the discussion of 2 Corinthians, the memory of the exile left a profound collective traumatic mark on Israel's memory. Luke's words appear to evoke that memory and to connect the healing from it to the arrival of Jesus. Simeon picks up the child and offers what we now call the Nunc Dimittis (Luke 2:29–32). His words are brimming with allusions to texts from Isaiah:[13] for Luke 2:30, "for my eyes have seen your salvation," compare "and all people shall see it together" (Isa 40:5) and 2:31, "which you have prepared in the presence of all peoples" (cf. Isa 52:10); for 2:32, "a light for revelation to the Gentiles," compare "I will give you as a light to the nations, that my salvation may reach to the end of the earth" (Isa 49:6); and 2:32, "and for glory to your people Israel," probably alludes to Isa 49:13 LXX. Luke will refer to some of these Hebrew Bible texts again later in his work.[14] Simeon blesses the child (Luke 2:34). In his final words, directed to

---

13. For these parallels, see Joseph Fitzmyer, *The Gospel according to Luke I–IX: A New Translation with Introduction and Commentary*, AB 28 (Garden City, NY: Doubleday, 1981), 428.

14. Fitzmyer, *Luke I–IX*, 428.

Mary, one cannot avoid recalling Mary's song from earlier in the birth narrative about God bringing down the mighty and lifting up the lowly (1:52).

Acts 4

In Acts 4:24–30, the church prays together with Peter and John after the two are released from having been arrested by "the priests, the captain of the temple, and the Sadducees" for preaching in the temple (Acts 4:1). This arrest led to an appearance and defense before a council that might be identified as the Sanhedrin (cf. 4:15).

> When they heard it, they raised their voices together to God and said, "Sovereign Lord, who made the heaven and the earth, the sea, and everything in them, it is you who said by the Holy Spirit through our ancestor David, your servant: 'Why did the Gentiles rage, and the peoples imagine vain things? The kings of the earth took their stand, and the rulers have gathered together against the Lord and against his Messiah.' For in this city, in fact, both Herod and Pontius Pilate, with the Gentiles and the peoples of Israel, gathered together against your holy servant Jesus, whom you anointed, to do whatever your hand and your plan had predestined to take place. And now, Lord, look at their threats, and grant to your servants to speak your word with all boldness, while you stretch out your hand to heal, and signs and wonders are performed through the name of your holy servant Jesus." (Act 4:24–30)

The group addresses God as "Sovereign Lord" (δέσποτα; 4:24). Simeon uses this same title in Luke 2:29. This appellation for God occurs in several prayers in the LXX (e.g., Dan 9:8, 15, 17, 19; Jdt 5:20, 24; 7:11; 9:12; 11:10; Tob 3:14; Sir 36:1; 2 Macc 15:2; 3 Macc 2:2) and Josephus (e.g., *Ant.* 1.272; 4.40, 46; 5.41). The title may have sometimes translated or stood for the tetragrammaton (see, e.g., Dan 9:8; Jonah 4:3; Jer 15:11), but it also might have simply translated *'adonai*. The praise to God as creator occurs in many of the Psalms, but it also opens the prayers for deliverance of Simon in 3 Maccabees and fills the Song of the Three Young Men. The invocation of the prayer by the high priest Simon in 3 Macc 2:1–20 most closely resembles Acts 4, as both designate God as δέσποτα and refer to God's status as creator (cf. 3 Macc 2:2–3; but cf. also Ps 146:6). All three prayers (Acts 4; 3 Maccabees; Prayer of Azariah) appear within the context of dealing with violence. Placed here in Acts, Luke's prayer functions as thanksgiving or praise for the release of the two, but it also sounds a strongly defiant tone that challenges the power and authority of the so-called earthly powers and the will of the people.

The nature of the prayer in Acts 4 actually better matches the characteristics of the speeches in the early portions of Acts. In those speeches, the speakers interpret Hebrew Bible texts as predictions of Jesus's suffering and resurrection in reference to the features of the immediate setting. However, the odd thing about this choice is that prayers do not typically include a formulaic method within the prayer. This whole prayer hinges on an interpretation of Ps 2:1–2: "It is you who said by the Holy Spirit through our ancestor David, your servant: 'Why did the Gentiles rage, and the peoples imagine vain things?'" (Acts 4:25). Luke inserts the text into the prayer with the use of a prophecy-fulfillment formula. The closest parallel of this formula, though, occurs in Mark 12:36. This type of explicit citation of Scripture followed by its interpretation does not frequently occur within a prayer. Typically, prayers either borrow language from a Hebrew Bible text or they work in the quotation in a smoother fashion. Psalm 2, as we have come to recognize, was apparently a favorite in the early church. The church applied the pronouncement originally said over Israel's king to Jesus (cf. Matt 3:17; 4:3; 17:5; Mark 1:11; 9:7; Luke 3:22; 9:35; John 1:49; Acts 13:33; Heb 1:5; 5:5). Luke's mode of interpretation of the text somewhat resembles the formulations found in the Qumran pesharim. Many of these texts arrive at the meaning of the passage for the community by explaining that X is Y. The pesharim often interpret a name of a person or place within the text with a sobriquet, which often leaves the intended meaning of the interpretation quite obscure for an interpreter outside the community, including a modern interpreter. Luke does not follow that particular practice of obscuring the identity of the persons here in Acts. Instead, he attempts to match the opponents to the community and various groups of people to references in Ps 2. However, his interpretation does not work out as neatly as he seems to think, and it becomes difficult to match each reference in the story to the psalm. The prayer identifies each of these parties in the events leading to Jesus's death. The "gentiles" are seemingly the Romans; the "peoples" are the Jewish people; "kings of the earth" and "rulers" are Herod and Pontius Pilate (4:25–26). Obviously, the original psalm had none of this in mind and clearly focused on the king in Jerusalem as under assault from neighboring kingdoms. The final declaration of praise—"stretch out your hand to heal, and signs and wonders are performed"—recalls descriptions of God's salvation in the exodus, as the discussion above of Sir 36 demonstrated.

Scripture in the Prayers in the Passion Narrative

The abundance of prayer and liturgical material in the era, its frequent use in practice and formation of members of the culture, and the close relationship between worship and the use and production of Scripture also shaped the language and thought patterns of authors in the crafting of the literature now within the New Testament. For a long time, interpreters have recognized that the Psalms and Isaiah influence the construction of the passion narratives. As Stephen

Ahearne-Kroll has shown, Mark borrows especially from Pss 22; 41; 42-43; and 69 as he constructs his narrative of Jesus's death.[15] Some of the allusions to the Psalms occur in the actions or narratival statements, but the text also gives a few lines from the Psalms to Jesus. Ahearne-Kroll has explained the significance of the Psalms for the passion narrative in Mark as a way to portray Jesus as a suffering royal figure. In the Gethsemane scene, he has shown the influence of Ps 42 (Ps 41 LXX) on Jesus's words, actions, and emotions. According to Ahearne-Kroll, Pss 42:6, 12; 43:5, "Why are you cast down, O my soul, and why are you disquieted within me? Hope in God; for I shall again praise him, my help and my God. My soul is cast down within me," has shaped Mark 14:33b-34a: "[He] began to be distressed and agitated. And he said to them, 'I am deeply grieved, even to death'" (Matt 26:38 follows Mark exactly; missing in Luke).[16] Also apparent is the parallel between the threefold repetition of the phrase in Pss 42-43 and Jesus's instructing his disciples to pray three times.[17] Adela Yarbro Collins also argues that Jesus here employs the language of lament like that found in Pss 6:2-3 (6:3-4 LXX); 42:5 (41:6 LXX).[18] Luke's omission of the statement might demonstrate his attempt to avoid attributing doubt and emotion to Jesus. Further, his prayer in the garden in which he asks God to "let this cup pass from me" might harken back to a passage in Isaiah: "See, I have taken from your hand the cup of staggering; you shall drink no more from the bowl of my wrath" (Isa 51:22). The language casts Jesus as a righteous figure suffering at the hands of wicked enemies. It might also be possible to think that the prominent metaphor "watch" for praying could arise from a text like Ps 130:5-6: "I wait for the LORD, my soul waits, and in his word I hope; my soul waits for the Lord more than those who watch for the morning, more than those who watch for the morning." As mentioned above, the idea of praying at night or in the middle of the night is attested in the Dead Sea Scrolls (e.g., 1QS IX, 26-X, 7a) and in Pss. Sol. 6. Also worth noting is the way in which "watch" becomes attached to alertness to the arrival of the eschaton; preparation for that event includes prayer.

The most famous line from the Psalms that Jesus speaks as a prayer to God comes while he is on the cross and cries out very near the point of his death. The words do not originate from Pss 42-43 but from Ps 22:1: "At three o'clock Jesus

---

15. Stephen Ahearne-Kroll, *The Psalms of Lament in Mark's Passion: Jesus' Davidic Suffering*, SNTSMS 142 (Cambridge: Cambridge University Press, 2007).

16. Ahearne-Kroll, *Psalms of Lament*, 181-83.

17. Ahearne-Kroll, *Psalms of Lament*, 183.

18. Yarbro Collins, *Mark: A Commentary*, Hermeneia (Minneapolis: Fortress, 2007), 676-77; cf. also Werner H. Kelber, "The Hour of the Son of Man and the Temptation of the Disciples (Mark 14:32-42)," in *The Passion in Mark: Studies in Mark 14-16*, ed. Werner H. Kelber (Philadelphia: Fortress, 1976), 43.

cried out with a loud voice, 'Eloi, Eloi, lema sabachthani?' which means, 'My God, my God, why have you forsaken me?'" (Mark 15:34 // Matt 27:46; missing in Luke). Here, again, Luke's omission of the citation probably constitutes an attempt to remove any hint of doubt within Jesus. In Luke, Jesus dies as a faithful and resolute martyr, a model that Stephen will follow in Acts 7. Some of the features of these scenes resonate with depictions of a righteous person who suffers in some Second Temple texts.[19] In the Dead Sea Scrolls, 1QH^a IX–XI recounts the suffering that befell the speaker when his enemies came upon them. The columns are replete with allusions to the Psalms and other Hebrew Bible texts as he explains his struggles and praises God for his ultimate deliverance.

Perhaps Mark wished to identify Jesus with David. Many would have simply assumed that David authored the Psalms and that, therefore, an "I" in a passage must have referred to the king. However, the passages also raise issues of theodicy and the place of God in the scene and invites an audience to reflect on God's silence throughout the scenes and how the resurrection might in the end supply vindication, not only for Jesus's mission, but for God who did not intervene during the passion.[20]

Paul

Paul possessed a well-developed knowledge of traditions from the Hebrew Bible. The apostle could work these traditions seamlessly into his prayers and liturgical pieces. This ability required a substantial amount of cultural knowledge and technical skill. As Newman has demonstrated, Paul presented himself in a liturgical body, where all these skills met and he became the expert who constructed the bodies of members of his congregations.[21]

As is well known, Paul's letters follow the letter-writing conventions of the Greco-Roman world. As a result, in his opening lines Paul assures his recipients that he constantly remembered them in his prayers, of course except for the Galatians. On three occasions, his report includes the phrase "I thank my God" (εὐχαριστῶ τῷ θεῷ μου; Rom 1:18; Phil 1:3; Phlm 4). Similar language appears in many prayers and hymns in the period, and one especially thinks of the title of the Qumran Hodayot, so named because of the recurrence of the phrase: "I thank you, O Lord" (אודכה אדוני). However, as Gordon Wiles reminded in-

---

19. Georg W. E. Nickelsburg, *Resurrection, Immortality, and Eternal Life in Intertestamental Judaism and Early Christianity*, exp. ed., HTS 56 (Cambridge: Harvard University Press, 2006), 119–62.

20. Ahearne-Kroll, *Psalms of Lament*, 82–136.

21. Newman, *Before the Bible*, 75–105.

terpreters, we wrongly overlook the influence of the Psalms on Paul's speech and the practice of praise and thanksgiving preceding petitions.[22] Wiles turns to Ps 9 for an example of this practice in the Psalms. Of course, the phrase "I will give thanks to you, O Lord" (ἐξομολογήσομαί σοι κύριε) appears many times in the LXX tradition (e.g., see LXX Pss 7:18; 17:50; 27:7; 29:13; 34:18; 41:6, 12; 42:4–5; 51:11; 53:8; 56:10; Sir 51:1, 12; Pss. Sol. 16:5).

Newman has proposed a fascinating and convincing reading of the opening blessing in 2 Cor 1:3–8 and Paul's use of the trauma of the cultural memory of the exile upon Jews. Paul then seems to align this with the trauma in Corinth's own history—the destruction by the Romans in 44 BCE and the eventual repopulation of the city with a large number of freed slaves who carried their own trauma.[23] As she argues, the basic form in 2 Corinthians matches a traditional Jewish blessing of the era. However, the content of the remainder of the blessing is not exactly a "prayer report" as one might expect but rather a thanksgiving to God for the consolation that God gives Paul and his colleagues as they suffer on behalf of the Corinthians. Newman follows the interpreters who see the language of Isaiah's "Book of Consolation" behind Paul's words.[24] One can immediately recall the opening words in Second Isaiah: "'Comfort, O comfort my people,' says your God. 'Speak tenderly to Jerusalem, and cry to her that she has served her term, that her penalty is paid, that she has received from the LORD's hand double for all her sins'" (Isa 40:1–2). She encourages her readers also to compare Isa 49:13; 51:3, 12, 19; 52:9; 54:11; 57:18; 61:2; 66:13. The language responds to the kind of trauma of cultural memory captured in the lament in Jer 31:15: "Thus says the LORD: 'A voice is heard in Ramah, lamentation and bitter weeping. Rachel is weeping for her children; she refuses to be comforted for her children, because they are no more.'" The impact of this memory and these themes stretch to many other Second Temple texts. For example, recently, in addition to the many passages that Newman explores, I have noticed a series of exhortations in Baruch that direct the audience to "take courage" (Bar 4:5, 21, 27, 30). Exile and the hope for return provide the setting for this book in the Apocrypha that is basically a collection of liturgical prayers and poems.[25]

Paul inserts liturgical pieces into his lengthy disquisition in Rom 9–11. The influence of the Hebrew Bible and the general liturgical formulas of the era once again leave their mark. A blessing of God stands in the opening statements of the

---

22. Gordon Wiles, *Paul's Intercessory Prayers: The Significance of the Intercessory Prayer Passages in the Letters of St. Paul*, SNTSMS 24 (Cambridge: Cambridge University Press, 1974), 160–65.
23. Newman, *Before the Bible*, 86–100; cf. Werline, *Whenever They Prayed*, 38–40.
24. Newman, *Before the Bible*, 92.
25. Werline, *Whenever They Prayed*, 51–52.

section: "and from them, according to the flesh, comes the Messiah, who is over all, God blessed forever. Amen" (Rom 9:5). Unfortunately, how to translate the blessing in the text is not quite clear. Paul concludes the section with a doxology in 11:33–36 that includes quotations from LXX Isa 40:13 and Job 41:3: "For who has known the mind of the Lord? Or who has been his counselor? Or who has given a gift to him, to receive a gift in return?" (Rom 11:34–35). The language in the other verses of the doxology also ring with language from the Hebrew Bible and parallels to other literature from the era (e.g., Job 5:9; 15:8; Wis 17:1). The brief praise to God's wisdom fits the much lengthier poetic pieces in Prov 8; Sir 24; and Bar 3:9–4:4 (cf. also 1 En. 42). In fact, Baruch also plays with the theme of wisdom's inscrutability and inaccessibility in the poetic reflection about her (Bar 3:29–37). For Baruch, however, God graciously provides access to this wisdom through "the book of the commandments of God," that is, the Torah (Bar 4:1).

Paul closes the overarching argument of his letter to the congregation with quotations that direct the gentiles to fulfill their liturgical role of praising God, as Scripture promised: "as it is written, 'Therefore I will confess you among the Gentiles, and sing praises to your name'; and again he says, 'Rejoice, O Gentiles, with his people'; and again, 'Praise the Lord, all you Gentiles, and let all the peoples praise him'; and again Isaiah says, 'The root of Jesse shall come, the one who rises to rule the Gentiles; in him the Gentiles shall hope'" (Rom 15:9b–12). The citations originate in the following passages: 15:9 from Ps 18:50 LXX, verse 10 from Deut 32:43 LXX, verse 11 from Ps 117:1, verse 12 from Isa 11:10 LXX. Paul follows these directives with a wish-prayer (Rom 15:13). The insertion of the liturgical features confirms Newman's thesis that interpretation and prayer or liturgy seem never far apart from one another, or that interpretation does not occur in a space apart from worship. Further, the reading of the letter aloud to a congregation also constructed Paul as the absent worship leader and interpreter for the community.[26]

The two most recognizable liturgical pieces in Paul's letters that may have not originated with the apostle are the hymn in Phil 2:5–11 and the confession in Rom 1:3–4.[27] Whether the Christ hymn in Philippians employs themes from the Hebrew Bible largely depends on the interpreter.[28] The first matter resides in the use of the term ἁρπαγμόν (2:6) and whether one should read the term as "something to hold onto" or "something to be grasped" or "stolen." If the inter-

---

26. Newman, *Before the Bible*, 100–105.

27. In the deutero-Pauline letters, Col 1:15–20 is also often considered a liturgical piece.

28. Substantial opposition against the idea that Phil 2:5–11 should be classified as a hymn or that it is anything more than "heightened prose" has been recently argued by Benjamin Edsall and Jennifer R. Strawbridge, "The Songs We Used to Sing? Hymn 'Traditions' and Reception in Pauline Letters," *JSNT* 37, no. 3 (2015): 290–311.

preter accepts the latter understanding of the term, then the hymn might refer to the idea of Adam attempting to "steal" what God forbade, eating of the tree of life. Second, among the many possibilities for the image of the Christ emptying himself, taking the form of a servant, and becoming obedient even to death, is the servant tradition in Isaiah. Complicating this possibility, however, is the fact that the LXX uses παῖς (Isa 41:8, 9; 42:1, 19; 43:10; 44:1, 2, 21, 26; 45:4; 49:6; 50:10; 52:13) and not δοῦλος (Phil 2:7). Nevertheless, the thematic similarities between Isaiah, especially 52:13–53:12, and Phil 2 remain striking. Further, the theme of the vindication of the righteous sufferer appears in many Jewish texts in the era.[29]

According to Robert Jewett, the especially balanced participial constructions and the parallelism shared between phrases in Rom 1:3–4 mark the verses as an early creed.[30] The identification of Jesus as from the one "who was descended from David according to the flesh" (Rom 1:3; literally "from the seed of David" [τοῦ γενομένου ἐκ σπέρματος Δαυὶδ κατὰ σάρκα]) provides a rare example of Paul's interest in Jesus as descended from the Davidic line and perhaps stands in tension with some of Paul's other statements.[31] One should note, though, that an expectation of a Davidic Messiah does not permeate the literature of the era. The Davidic theme might continue in the passage's use of the phrase "and was declared to be Son of God" (τοῦ ὁρισθέντος υἱοῦ θεοῦ Rom 1:4), which might be drawn from Ps 2.[32] According to Nathan C. Johnson, Paul does not consider Jesus's Davidic descent as inferior and antithetical to being proclaimed "Son of God" through the resurrection.[33] Instead, he produces several examples from Second Temple texts that he understands as evidence of authors who thought that the designation of "Son of David" indicated the divinity of the messiah (he suggests, e.g., 4Q174 I, 10–13; 4Q246; 4Q369; 4 Ezra 11–13).

Revelation

Revelation contains a large collection of liturgical material. While not every apocalyptic text shares this feature with Revelation, several do. For example, 1 En. 1–36 contains an assortment of prayers and other ritual or liturgical practices, and the Songs of the Sabbath Sacrifice (4Q400–407) record the angelic liturgies that take place in the heavenly worship, in which, apparently, the members of the Qumran community believed they participated. This increase in instances

---

29. Nickelsburg, *Resurrection, Immortality, and Eternal Life*.
30. Robert Jewett, *Romans: A Commentary*, Hermeneia (Minneapolis: Fortress, 2007), 97–98.
31. Jewett, *Romans*, 98.
32. Jewett, *Romans*, 104, citing Leslie C. Allen, "The Old Testament Background of (προ)-ορίζειν in the New Testament," *NTS* 17, no. 1 (1970): 104–8.
33. Johnson, "Romans 1:3–4: Beyond Antithetical Parallelism," *JBL* 136, no. 2 (2017): 467–90.

of prayer and liturgical elements in this type of literature is not surprising for several reasons. First, some apocalypses open up a view of heaven and the activities there. This is God's realm, and a visionary could imagine it as a heavenly, kingly court, as a heavenly temple where angelic worship takes place, or as a combination of both. These are the primary metaphors that carry on into the mystical traditions of *merkabah* and *hekhalot* Judaism. These imagined settings would both require a number of rituals in order to describe scenes and to move the scenes along. Second, Revelation presents a lot of activity taking place on earth, most of which can be categorized as catastrophic. Thus, the reader can expect either ritual anticipation of looming disasters or responses to such disasters. The language of the prayers and liturgies in Revelation draws extensively on the Hebrew Bible. Again, this is the tendency of Jewish and early Christian prayers in the era. A complete account of every citation of a Hebrew Bible text is not possible here. Instead, I will provide a brief overview and a few examples.

The author begins the letters to the seven churches with a traditional epistolary formula, which also resembles the Pauline correspondences. This includes an A-to-B greeting and, like Paul, the greeting of "grace" and "peace" (Rev 1:4). Revelation does not contain a traditional prayer report. However, the text includes an extended doxology to Christ (1:5b–6). Prominent in the verses stands the allusion to Exod 19:6: "But you shall be for me a priestly kingdom" / Rev 1:6: "And made us to be a kingdom, priests serving his God and Father." This Exodus passage also appears in 1 Pet 2:9. If both Revelation and 1 Peter share an Asia Minor provenance, then interpreters have to wonder if the text was popular in the region around the turn of the first and second centuries. Elisabeth Schüssler Fiorenza has argued that 1:5–6, and probably 5:9–10, sprang from a baptismal liturgy.[34] The doxology closes with a praise to God's glory and dominion: "To him be glory and dominion forever and ever. Amen" (1:6). Various versions of this kind of praise recur throughout Revelation. In this instance, Dan 7:14 may have influenced the author since the author quotes Dan 7:13 in the following verse. Similar collections of terms for praise to God occur in 4:11, "You are worthy, our Lord and God, to receive glory and honor and power"; 5:12, "Worthy is the Lamb that was slaughtered to receive power and wealth and wisdom and might and honor and glory and blessing!"; 5:13, "To the one seated on the throne and to the Lamb be blessing and honor and glory and might forever and ever!" Jewish literature begins to pile up these kinds of lists of praise to God during the Persian period. The doxologies by pagan kings in Daniel probably reflect this practice (e.g., Dan 4:2–3, 34–35; 6:26–27). Practices arising from a text like 1 Chr 29:11 also

---

34. Elisabeth Schüssler Fiorenza, *The Book of Revelation: Justice and Judgment*, 2nd ed. (Minneapolis: Fortress, 1998), 68–81.

stand behind such acclamations as these in Revelation: "Yours, O Lord, are the greatness, the power, the glory, the victory, and the majesty; for all that is in the heavens and on the earth is yours; yours is the kingdom, O Lord, and you are exalted as head above all." Members of the early church may have encountered the practice through these traditions. Of course, the passage from the 1 Chr 29 may have given shape to the doxology added later to the Matthean version of the Lord's Prayer (Matt 6:13).

As Revelation transitions from the letters to the churches to the cosmic eschatological drama, the opening scene depicted in chapter 4 features the worship occurring in heaven. The visionary sees God sitting on a throne, which means that the dominating metaphor for the image is that of a royal court. For the description of the throne (Rev 4:1–8), the text draws from Ezekiel's vision of the chariot throne (Ezek 1:26–28). The influence of this description had spread through Judaism by this time, for Daniel's vision of the Ancient of Days contains elements from the Ezekiel tradition as well (Dan 7:9–10). The author also draws on Zech 4:2–3 for the detail of the "seven burning torches" in "front of the throne," which represent the "seven spirits of God." While many other allusions could be identified, our focus should shift to the four living creatures, which the author merges with the description of the seraphim in Isa 6. Their liturgical language in Rev 4 derives directly from Isa 6:3: "And one called to another and said: 'Holy, holy, holy is the Lord of hosts.'" In Rev 4:9, the text describes the four living creatures as giving "glory and honor and thanks to the one who is seated on the throne, who lives forever and ever," language that closely resembles Nebuchadnezzar's doxology in Dan 4:34: "I blessed the Most High, and praised and honored the one who lives forever." As discussed above, the liturgy offered by the twenty-four elders resembles doxologies like that in 1 Chr 29:11.

The appearance of the lamb who is slain in Rev 5 incorporates metaphors from a temple setting and the exodus story. Upon the appearance of the lamb, the twenty-four elders each have a harp and golden bowls of incense, which we learn "are the prayers of the saints" (5:8). Together, they sing a "new song" (5:9). This term occurs many times in Hebrew Bible texts (Pss 33:3; 40:3; 96:1; 98:1; 144:9; 149:1; Isa 42:10; cf. also Jdt 16:1, 13). Revelation 14:3 also uses the term in the context of the deliverance of the 144,000. In all these texts, the speaker sings as a result of God's deliverance, which the performer believes inaugurates a new era. The text depicts Christ as a lamb that was slaughtered (Rev 5:9, 12). The lamb's death effected the "ransom" of the "saints": "For you were slaughtered and by your blood you ransomed for God [καὶ ἠγόρασας τῷ θεῷ ἐν τῷ αἵματί σου] saints from every tribe and language and people and nation" (5:9). While the typical term used in connection with the exodus is "redeem" (λύτρον, λυτρόω), the combination of "buy" with the reference to Exod 19:6 evokes the images of

Israel's redemption from Egypt.³⁵ As described above, similar language appears in the opening doxology to Christ in 1:5–6. That passage praised Christ as the one who "freed us from our sins by his blood" (λύσαντι ἡμᾶς ἐκ τῶν ἁμαρτιῶν ἡμῶν ἐν τῷ αἵματι αὐτοῦ; Rev 1:5). As Schüssler Fiorenza explains, the participle λύσαντι comes from the same root as λύτρον.³⁶ Thus, despite the change and slight differences in terminology, Revelation still has the exodus in mind. The author of Revelation also likes the phrase "tribe and language and people and nation" (Rev 5:9; cf. 7:9; 13:7; 14:6; 17:15), which might have also been influenced by a similar formula in Dan 3:4, 7, 29; 5:19; 6:25; 7:14.³⁷ A final liturgical moment happens in 5:11–14, as a large throng worships the lamb. Similar to other passages in Revelation, the content and structure of the praise bear close resemblance to 1 Chr 16:27–28; 19:11.

Additional liturgies of deliverance are included in chapters 7, 11, and 12. The celebration in chapter 7 responds to the sealing of the 144,000 and the appearance of the great multitude in heaven, which the reader discovers consists of those who have survived the "great ordeal." They wave palm branches (cf. 1 Macc 13:51; 2 Macc 10:7; 14:4), and the blessing resembles those that gather God's attributes into praise. The thanksgiving in 11:17–18 is a response to the opening of the seventh seal. Their song reflects features of Ps 2. Frederick Murphy identifies several similarities with Ps 79:1–6, 10–11, 13.³⁸ Further, in the description of God as "who are and who were" (11:17), he sees an allusion to the revelation of God in Exod 3. The liturgical declaration about Satan's expulsion from heaven in 12:10–12 features language similar to Isa 44:23: "Sing, O heavens, for the LORD has done it; shout, O depths of the earth; break forth into singing, O mountains, O forest, and every tree in it!"; also, Isa 49:13: "Sing for joy, O heavens, and exult, O earth; break forth, O mountains, into singing!" (cf. Ps 96:11).

A scene by a "sea of glass" returns in Rev 15, along with the exodus motif. Those who stand there, the conquerors of the beast, "sing the song of Moses"— like Moses did upon the destruction of Pharoah's army (Exod 15:1–18). Almost every word in their song derives from the Hebrew Bible. The language affirms more than God's power; it lauds God's justice and right to judge the enemy, an example of what, again, von Rad designated as *Gerichtsdoxologie*. Another declaration of God's righteousness follows in chapter 16 after the third angel pours out the bowl of God's wrath that turns all the rivers and springs into blood

---

35. Schüssler Fiorenza, *Book of Revelation*, 73–75.
36. Schüssler Fiorenza, *Book of Revelation*, 71–72.
37. Frederick J. Murphy, *Fallen Is Babylon: The Revelation to John*, New Testament in Context (Valley Forge, PA: Trinity Press International, 1998), 197.
38. Murphy, *Fallen Is Babylon*, 272–73.

THEMES AND TOPICS FROM ISRAEL'S SCRIPTURES IN THE NEW TESTAMENT

(16:4–7). The punishment recalls the plague against Egypt of turning water into blood, and the language of the doxology draws on the Deuteronomic traditions (cf. Deut 32:4), including the theme of persecuting and killing the prophets.

Revelation 18:1–8 contains a taunt over the fall of "Babylon," that is, Rome, that imitates the prophetic speech form (cf. taunt over Babylon in Isa 13 and over Tyre in Ezek 37). In 18:9–24, various groups lament over the destruction of the city and the end of their livelihoods. In contrast, in heaven the voice of a loud multitude praises God's righteousness (18:1–3, 6–8) and the twenty-four elders along with the four living creatures offer their own "Hallelujah" to God (18:7–8).

Liturgical Language and Literary Structuring

Besides the Hebrew Bible influencing the language choices of New Testament authors or these writers directly borrowing language from these traditions, careful examinations of larger units of texts reveal that liturgical texts and practices could give shape to passages. Here I point to only two examples. First, Daniel Harrington in his work on Matt 8:23–27 (// Mark 4:35–41; Luke 8:22–25) notes extensive similarities between Jesus calming the storm in the Synoptic Gospels and Ps 107:[39]

> Some went down to the sea in ships,
> doing business on the mighty waters;
> they saw the deeds of the LORD,
> his wondrous works in the deep.
> For he commanded and raised the stormy wind,
> which lifted up the waves of the sea.
> They mounted up to heaven, they went down to the depths;
> their courage melted away in their calamity;
> they reeled and staggered like drunkards,
> and were at their wits' end.
> Then they cried to the LORD in their trouble,
> and he brought them out from their distress;
> he made the storm be still,
> and the waves of the sea were hushed. (Ps 107:23–29)

---

39. Daniel Harrington, *The Gospel of Matthew*, Sacra Pagina 1 (Collegeville, MN: Liturgical Press, 1991), 123.

The parallels between the synoptic tradition and the psalm appear quite obvious. The disciples are in the boat with Jesus when a storm begins to rage on the Sea of Galilee. Fearing for their lives, they cry out to Jesus, who, because he is asleep in the boat, seems completely uncaring to them. Jesus rebukes the waves and "a great calm" comes upon the water. Psalm 107 evokes images of the primordial chaos waters that threaten humanity and the orderly creation. These images might also linger in the synoptic tradition, and perhaps Jesus walking on the water suggests the same possibility.

Second, an odd feature of the texts in the New Testament is the absence of penitential prayers like those in Ezra 9; Neh 1; 9; and Dan 9. The form occupied a dominant place in the liturgies of the Second Temple period. The form influenced the daily prayers in The Words of the Heavenly Lights (4Q504), as well as elements of the annual covenant ceremony at Qumran in the Community Rule (1QS). But the New Testament contains no such prayer and they do not figure into the liturgy of the early church in the following centuries. Instead, the church eventually identifies Pss 6, 32, 38, 51, 102, 130, and 143 as penitential psalms. Still, the penitential traditions certainly influence several texts in the New Testament.[40]

One of the most obvious examples comes from 1 John 1:8–10: "If we say that we have no sin, we deceive ourselves, and the truth is not in us. If we confess our sins, he who is faithful and just will forgive us our sins and cleanse us from all unrighteousness. If we say that we have not sinned, we make him a liar, and his word is not in us." The language describing God as "faithful and just" derives from the declarations of God's righteousness that frequently appears in the penitential prayer traditions, von Rad's *Gerichtsdoxologie*. Thus, while the New Testament does not offer a full penitential prayer like those of the Second Temple period, the trail of its influence is undeniable. The early church at some point began to extract some features from the Hebrew Bible penitential tradition and combined these with their own emerging practices. The transformation might be detectable as early as Paul's arguments in Galatians and Romans. In Galatians, Paul argues that the curse of the law has been lifted through Jesus taking on that curse. Behind Paul's idea might stand the frequent reference in penitential prayers that the Deuteronomic curses cling to the people (e.g., Bar 1:20; 3:4; 4Q504 1–2 III, 10b–11a), an idea based on Deut 28:21 and 60: "The Lord will make the pestilence cling to you" (28:21); "He will bring back upon you all

---

40. For more on this influence of penitential prayer, see Rodney A. Werline, "The Impact of the Penitential Prayer Tradition on New Testament Theology," in *Seeking the Favor of God*, vol. 3, *The Impact of Penitential Prayer beyond Second Temple Judaism*, ed. Mark J. Boda, Daniel K. Falk, and Rodney A. Werline, EJL 23 (Atlanta: Society of Biblical Literature, 2008), 149–83.

the diseases of Egypt, of which you were in dread, and they shall cling to you" (28:60). Paul's argument that both Jews and gentiles are sinners and only God is righteous in Rom 1–3 might also bear the influence of the penitential prayer tradition. He supports his argument with a catena of verses from the Hebrew Bible that all emphasize human sinfulness, beginning with the declaration "There is no one who is righteous, not even one" (Rom 3:10–17, in order: Pss 14:4 [cf. also 53:1–2]; 5:9; 140:3; 10:7; Isa 59:7–8; Prov 1:16; Ps 36:1). It is also possible that Paul's quote from Ps 51:4 might also belong to the catena: "So that you may be justified in your words, and prevail in your judging" (Rom 3:4). Whether Paul adopted an existing catena or creates this himself is not clear. Since precious little is known about religious practices in the synagogue in that era, suggestions that Paul took the catena from synagogue worship can only be regarded as speculation. Following the catena, Paul brings the portion of his argument that "God's righteousness has been revealed" (Rom 1:16–17) to a close and is able to declare God's righteousness in the work in Christ: "But now, apart from law, the righteousness of God has been disclosed, and is attested by the law and the prophets, the righteousness of God through faith in Jesus Christ for all who believe. For there is no distinction, since all have sinned and fall short of the glory of God; they are now justified by his grace as a gift, through the redemption that is in Christ Jesus" (3:21–24).

Conclusion

When placed within its correct social and literary context, the literature now in the New Testament does not differ from the Jewish literature of the era in regard to its use of traditional language found in the Hebrew Bible. Certainly, the New Testament authors employ that language in prayers and liturgies to support their own agendas related to understanding Jesus of Nazareth as the Christ. However, the authors of every Jewish text had their own agendas as well, and they put prayer, liturgies, and traditional language from the Hebrew Bible in service of that agenda. Perhaps one of the clearest examples of this is the confession that Israel "did not ponder [שׂכל] your (YHWH's) truth" in Dan 9:13 (my translation). With the selection of this particular verb, the interests of the *maskilim* become unmasked, and the insertion levels a critique against the group's contemporaries. Not only has Israel not obeyed Torah, but they have not listened to the teachings of the *maskilim*. Beyond the simple adoption of Hebrew Bible language, if one were to explore the functions of the uses of prayers and liturgies and their traditional speech, one would again uncover that no surprising differences exist between the New Testament texts and the literature of the Second Temple era.[41] While no standardized or fixed prayers occur within the literature of this era—neither in Jewish texts nor those in the New Testament—the practice of drawing on traditional, authoritative language had become standard and had been so for a long time, perhaps even before the Babylonian exile. Thus, following this practice, the authors of the New Testament look, act, and sound like their predecessors and their contemporaries.

Bibliography

Ahearne-Kroll, Stephen P. *The Psalms of Lament in Mark's Passion: Jesus' Davidic Suffering*. SNTSMS 142. Cambridge: Cambridge University Press, 2007.

Allen, Leslie C. "The Old Testament Background of (προ)ορίζειν in the New Testament." *NTS* 17, no. 1 (1970): 104–8.

Boda, Mark J. *Praying the Tradition: The Origin and Use of Tradition in Nehemiah 9*. BZAW 277. Berlin: de Gruyter, 1999.

Brand, Miryam T. *Evil Within and Without: The Source of Sin and Its Nature as Portrayed in Second Temple Judaism*. JAJSup 9. Göttingen: Vandenhoeck & Ruprecht, 2013.

Brown, Raymond E. *The Birth of the Messiah: A Commentary on the Infancy Narratives in Matthew and Luke*. Updated ed. ABRL. Garden City, NY: Doubleday, 1993.

Collins, Adela Yarbro. *Mark: A Commentary*. Hermeneia. Minneapolis: Fortress, 2007.

Edsall, Benjamin, and Jennifer R. Strawbridge. "The Songs We Used to Sing? Hymn 'Traditions' and Reception in Pauline Letters." *JSNT* 37, no. 3 (2015): 290–311.

Falk, Daniel K. *Daily, Sabbath, and Festival Prayers in the Dead Sea Scrolls*. STDJ 27. Leiden: Brill, 1998.

Falk, Daniel K., and Angela Kim Harkins. "Early Jewish Prayer." Pages 461–87 in *Early Judaism and Its Modern Interpreters*. Edited by Matthias Henze and Rodney A. Werline. 2nd ed. Atlanta: SBL Press, 2020.

Fitzmyer, Joseph. *The Gospel according to Luke I–IX: A New Translation with Introduction and Commentary*. AB 28. Garden City, NY: Doubleday, 1981.

Harrington, Daniel J. *The Gospel of Matthew*. Sacra Pagina 1. Collegeville, MN: Liturgical Press, 1991.

Jewett, Robert. *Romans: A Commentary*. Hermeneia. Minneapolis: Fortress, 2007.

---

41. Newman, *Before the Bible*; Werline, *Whenever They Prayed*.

Johnson, Nathan C. "Romans 1:3–4: Beyond Antithetical Parallelism." *JBL* 136, no. 2 (2017): 467–90.

Kelber, Werner H. "The Hour of the Son of Man and the Temptation of the Disciples (Mark 14:32–42)." Pages 41–60 in *The Passion in Mark: Studies in Mark 14–16*. Edited by Werner H. Kelber. Philadelphia: Fortress, 1976.

Murphy, Frederick J. *Fallen Is Babylon: The Revelation to John*. New Testament in Context. Valley Forge, PA: Trinity Press International, 1998.

Newman, Judith H. *Before the Bible: The Liturgical Body and the Formation of Scriptures in Early Judaism*. New York: Oxford University Press, 2018.

———. *Praying by the Book: The Scripturalization of Prayer in Second Temple Judaism*. EJL 14. Atlanta: Scholars Press, 1999.

Nickelsburg, Georg W. E. *Resurrection, Immortality, and Eternal Life in Intertestamental Judaism and Early Christianity*. Exp. ed. HTS 56. Cambridge: Harvard University Press, 2006.

Penner, Jeremy. *Patterns of Daily Prayer in Second Temple Period Judaism*. STDJ 104. Leiden: Brill, 2012.

Rad, Gerhard von. *Old Testament Theology*. Translated by D. M. G. Stalker. 2 vols. New York: Harper & Row, 1962.

Schüssler Fiorenza, Elisabeth. *The Book of Revelation: Justice and Judgment*. 2nd ed. Minneapolis: Fortress, 1998.

Werline, Rodney A. "The Impact of the Penitential Prayer Tradition on New Testament Theology." Pages 149–83 in *Seeking the Favor of God*. Vol. 3, *The Impact of Penitential Prayer beyond Second Temple Judaism*. Edited by Mark J. Boda, Daniel K. Falk, and Rodney A. Werline. EJL 23. Atlanta: Society of Biblical Literature, 2008.

———. *Penitential Prayer in Second Temple Judaism: The Development of a Religious Institution*. EJL 13. Atlanta: Scholars Press, 1998.

———. *Whenever They Prayed: Dimensions of New Testament Prayer*. Lanham, MD: Lexington Books/Fortress Academic, 2021.

Wiles, Gordon P. *Paul's Intercessory Prayers: The Significance of the Intercessory Prayer Passages in the Letters of St. Paul*. SNTSMS 24. Cambridge: Cambridge University Press, 1974.

32

Eschatology

GARRICK V. ALLEN

The New Testament is relentlessly eschatological in its outlook, and the potential avenues for examining the influence of Jewish Scriptures on the eschatologies of the New Testament are legion. Early Christian writers mediated their memories of Jesus and the experiences of their communities through the matrix of Jewish Scripture and contemporary interpretive traditions and practices, usually concluding that the current age was drawing to its end (or had already begun to do so) with certainty and speed. Indeed, the oldest surviving Christian writing, a letter written by Paul, Silvanus, and Timothy, now known as 1 Thessalonians, deals explicitly with eschatological questions: the fate of the dead (4:13–15), resurrection (4:16–18), and the timing of the day of the Lord (5:1–11). The fact that Paul feels compelled to respond to these questions suggests that the Thessalonians were grappling with the death of members of their community who had passed before the expected return of Jesus. Already the quotidian realities of daily life and expectation of the end were colliding in unexpected ways for the nascent community in Thessalonica and presumably elsewhere.

Importantly, the eschatological orientation of early Christianity reflected in the New Testament did not materialize out of thin air. The ways that early Christians conceived of the end of the age are deeply rooted in Jewish Scripture and traditions of their interpretation. Paul's description of the time of the end in 1 Thess 5:2 as the "day of the Lord" (ἡμέρα κυρίου) is a collocation borrowed from prophetic literature, a body of texts that speak often of "this day" or the "day of YHWH," a day usually associated with cosmic cataclysm, destruction, judgment, God's direct engagement with the world, and the end of exile. In the context of a longer call for repentance in light of God's imminent coming, Joel 1:15 describes this day thus (with special emphasis in the Greek version): "O this day [אהה ליום // Οἴμμοι οἴμμοι οἴμμοι εἰς ἡμέραν], for the day of the Lord [יום יהוה // ἡμέρα κυρίου] is near."[1] The appropriation and reinterpretation of motifs from Jewish tradition extends also to important concepts that have eschatological dimensions in the New Testament, like the kingdom of God, the end of exile, divine sonship, and messiah.[2] The influence of the Jewish scriptural tradition on the eschatologies of the New Testament is substantial and indelible; its texts and concepts are reused ubiquitously and woven throughout the works of the New Testament in the form of explicit quotations, allusions, and more elusive and indirect types of literary reuse. New Testament eschatology is unintelligible apart from knowledge of the details of Jewish Scripture and traditions of its interpretation operative in the late Second Temple period.

Doing justice to the complex dynamics of the relationship between Jewish Scripture and the eschatologies of the New Testament would require a number of book-length treatments. So what I want to do in this context is to trace the way that interpretive traditions around particular Jewish scriptural texts develop from their initial literary and historical contexts through to their deployment by the New Testament authors. The possible test cases for this type of study are copious, but it is useful here, after a brief overview of the different forms of engagement with Jewish Scripture in the New Testament, to focus specifically on two concrete examples, which I take from Isa 40, Dan 7, and the postexilic prophet Zechariah.[3] This selection of texts is far from exhaustive, but it allows us to begin to see the variegated ways that New Testament authors incorporated Jewish scriptural texts and ideas into their works and the ways in which these texts are foundational to their modes of literary composition and patterns of thought.

The Indebtedness of New Testament Eschatologies to Jewish Scripture

In addition to Paul's use of eschatological concepts like the "day of the Lord" in 1 Thessalonians, various New Testament authors appealed to or referenced a

---

1. See Elie Assis, *The Book of Joel: A Prophet between Calamity and Hope*, LHBOTS 581 (London: T&T Clark, 2013), 57–70, 105–10. See also Isa 2:10–22; Zeph 1:14–16; Amos 5:18–20. Unless otherwise noted, all translations are by the author.

2. On these themes, see the recent studies Adela Yarbro Collins and John J. Collins, *King and Messiah as Son of God: Divine, Human, and Angelic Figures in Biblical and Related Literature* (Grand Rapids: Eerdmans, 2008); Garrick V. Allen et al., eds., *Son of God: Divine Sonship in Jewish and Christian Antiquity* (University Park, PA: Eisenbrauns, 2019).

3. On Zechariah see Garrick V. Allen, *The Book of Revelation and Early Jewish Textual Culture*, SNTSMS 168 (Cambridge: Cambridge University Press, 2017).

variety of Jewish scriptural traditions with different levels of explicitness. First, allusions are common throughout the narratives and letters of the New Testament, an implicit form of reference that directly engages a particular text through reformulation. Allusions are not signaled in the text. But they do reference particular texts (or particular constellations of text) that were central to early Christian eschatology. A good example is the book of Revelation, which is notoriously and relentlessly allusive in its texture. Many of the details of John's description of the New Jerusalem in Rev 22:1–2—an eschatological text if there ever was one—correspond to features of the city described in both Hebrew and Greek forms of Ezek 47:1–12.[4] Like Ezekiel, John sees "a river of living water [ποταμὸν ὕδατος ζωῆς] clear as crystal coming from the throne of God and of the lamb in the middle of her street, and on either side of the river were trees of life [ξύλον ζωῆς], producing twelve fruits, each giving its fruit according to the month, and the leaves of the trees are for the healing of the nations [τὰ φύλλα τοῦ ξύλου εἰς θεραπείαν τῶν ἐθνῶν]" (Rev 22:1–2). John does not signal it explicitly, but his description is not unlike Ezekiel's, where water flows from the threshold of the temple (47:1), on its banks are numerous trees (47:7; δένδρα πολλὰ σφόδρα) that will bear all kinds of fruit for eating (πᾶν ξύλον βρώσιμον) in great fecundity due to their proximity to the water (47:12), and their leaves (וְעָלֵהוּ) will be for healing (47:12). The description of these items in Ezekiel, whether in Greek or Hebrew, does not correspond precisely to John's wording, but the extended reference to this cluster of ideas signals an allusion to a scriptural tradition that is key to John's vision of the age to come. And, of course, John's engagement with Ezekiel is mediated through other early Jewish traditions that partake in this same discourse (e.g., 11Q18 frag. 14; 2 Bar. 4:1–7; 1 En. 47:12; 90:33–36; Pss. Sol. 14:3).

Another, more direct form of reference that occurs in the New Testament in relation to eschatology (and many other topics) is what I call implicit quotation (what the editors of this volume call unmarked citation)—a more direct type of reference that is not explicitly signaled with a formal quotation marker, but which carries such a correspondence of wording between quoted text and target text that little doubt remains as to the source of the reference. A good example of implicit quotation appears in 1 Pet 4:18. In chapter 4, Peter continues his string of paraenetic instructions but now in relation to suffering and judgment because, as he says in 4:7, "the end of all things is near" (πάντων δὲ τὸ τέλος ἤγγικεν). He goes on to urge his readers to persevere through suffering as an intrinsic part of their faithful life (4:12) and to rejoice in suffering as participatory in Christ's suffering (4:13) because "the time has come for judgment to begin with the household of God" (4:17). The situation of Peter's readers and their reac-

---

4. See the extended in discussion in David E. Aune, *Revelation 17–22*, WBC 52C (Nashville: Nelson, 1998), 1175–79.

tions to suffering are necessitated by their close proximity to the end and their impending deliverance. To normalize further their suffering, Peter references a Greek form of Prov 11:31 nearly word for word, the only difference being the presence of μέν in the Proverbs text. Suffering is an unavoidable aspect of salvation, which is no easy thing.

Table 32.1. First Peter 4:18 Compared to Proverbs 11:31

1 Peter 4:18	Proverbs 11:31
εἰ ὁ δίκαιος μόλις σῴζεται, ὁ ἀσεβὴς καὶ ἁμαρτωλὸς ποῦ φανεῖται "If it is hard for the righteous to be saved, what will become of the ungodly and the sinner?"	εἰ ὁ μὲν δίκαιος μόλις σῴζεται, ὁ ἀσεβὴς καὶ ἁμαρτωλὸς ποῦ φανεῖται "If it is hard for the righteous to be saved, what will become of the ungodly and the sinner?"

While Peter's reference is set off from the text of the letter in editions and modern translations by italics or indentation, there is nothing in the text itself that signals this reference, which makes it an implicit or unmarked quotation.

A final form of reference that occurs in some New Testament works is the explicit or marked quotation. Although rare in early Jewish literature in comparison with more allusive forms of reference, multiple quotations in the New Testament pertain in some way to eschatology. One such example occurs in 2 Pet 3:8. In chapter 3, the author warns readers that they are "in the last days" (ἐσχάτων τῶν ἡμερῶν), evidenced by the multitude of scoffers and their licentiousness (3:3). They question the imminence of Jesus's return because life continues as usual by all appearances (3:4). The author appeals to God's creation as evidence of the world's impending unmaking (3:5–7), going on to critique his opponents' conception of time. God is not slow in fulfilling all things because "with the Lord one day is a like a thousand years, and a thousand years like a day" (ὅτι μία ἡμέρα παρὰ κυρίῳ ὡς χίλια ἔτη καὶ χίλια ἔτη ὡς ἡμέρα μία). Although the wording does not correspond exactly to the Hebrew or Greek text, this phrase represents an explicit quotation to Ps 90:4 (89:4 LXX), where the psalmist says, "a thousand years in your sight are like the day of yesterday that passed and a watch in the night" (NETS). The quotation is signaled in 2 Peter with the marker ὅτι ("because"), which creates a modest level of discretion between the quote and the rest of the letter's text, even if the wording of the quotation does not exactly match any known source text.

Like any other topic, the New Testament writers constructed their eschatological perspectives by drawing upon, referencing, and reworking Jewish scriptural traditions. The evidences of their activity were shaped by the explicitness of their

Eschatology

reuse, the level of correspondence to the wording of their sources, and the rhetorical function of these references in their own compositions. Scriptural reuse and literary engagement of many kinds are central to what constitutes the textual culture in which the New Testament was written. It is no surprise then, that these processes were complex, varied, and ubiquitous when it comes to eschatology. In order to explore these dynamics more closely, we now turn to two examples in greater detail, beginning with Deutero-Isaiah.

Isaiah 40:3–5 and the End of Exile

The book of Isaiah is a major locus of exegetical attention for constructing eschatological ideas in early Christianity, especially chapters 40–55 and 56–66 (Deutero- and Trito-Isaiah respectively).[5] Although important nuances exist (e.g., Isa 11:1–16), the tone and message of Isa 1–39 is largely pessimistic, promising exile as just punishment for Israel's sins, while Isa 40–66 foresees an impending restoration of the exilic condition and God's manifestation among his people. Within the consolatory framework of Deutero-Isaiah, the four Servant Songs (42:1–4; 49:1–6; 50:4–9; 52:13–53:12) have garnered special attention in the context of New Testament studies primarily because of their import for understanding the development of messianic traditions and the language that early Christian writers deployed to present their portraits of Jesus (e.g., Rom 4:25; 1 Cor 15:2–5; 1 Pet 2:22–25; Heb 9:28) or to portray Jesus's self-understanding in the Gospels.[6]

But in this section, I want to examine Deutero-Isaiah's influence on another topic that is central to New Testament eschatology: the end of exile. The anonymous prophetic voice of Deutero-Isaiah presupposes a Babylonian exilic context, promising the impending end of exile couched in the language of judgment, restoration, topographic upheaval, and divine action.[7] While God is presented as a just threat to the community in Isa 1–39, promising exile for the sins of the people and their leaders, in chapters 40–55 it is clear that he is also the agent of

---

5. On the relationship of Deutero-Isaiah to the rest of the book, see John Goldingay and David Payne, *Isaiah 40–55: A Critical and Exegetical Commentary*, ICC (London: T&T Clark, 2014), 1–8.

6. E.g., see the classic study of Morna D. Hooker, *Jesus and the Servant: The Influence of the Servant Concept of Deutero-Isaiah in the New Testament* (London: SPCK, 1959); and, more recently, Peter Stuhlmacher, "Isaiah 53 in the Gospels and Acts," in *The Suffering Servant: Isaiah 53 in Jewish and Christian Sources*, ed. Bernd Janowski and Peter Stuhlmacher (Grand Rapids: Eerdmans, 2004), 147–62.

7. See H. G. M. Williamson, *The Book Called Isaiah: Deutero-Isaiah's Role in Composition and Redaction* (Oxford: Clarendon, 1994), 1–18.

Israel's imminent reconstitution. Because the end of exile is depicted as a fast approaching but nonetheless future event, Deutero-Isaiah became a useful medium for the transmission of eschatological perspectives in early Christian writings.

While there is much to say about the reception of Deutero-Isaiah in later literature, I want to focus here specifically on the role of Isa 40:3–5 and its appropriation in the eschatology of early Jewish works and the New Testament.[8] This text appears at the very outset of Deutero-Isaiah, a literary division that is preceded in chapter 39 by Isaiah's prediction to Hezekiah that all the treasures of his kingdom (39:1–4) would in the next generation be carried away to Babylon (39:6). Some of Hezekiah's sons would also be carried off and serve as eunuchs in the Babylonian court (39:7). In response to Isaiah's prophecy of doom, Hezekiah shortsightedly muses, "The word of the Lord that you have spoken is good . . . for there will be peace and security in my days" (39:8). Isaiah 40 then shifts, its anonymous governing voice assuming that Isaiah's promise to Hezekiah has already come to pass and that God is now preparing to reverse Jerusalem's fortunes (40:1; 41:27). God himself will appear, lead his people, and restore Jerusalem, culminating in a significant and momentous event: "see, the Lord God comes with might, and his arm rules for him; his reward is with him, and his recompense before him. He will feed his flock like a shepherd; he will gather the lambs in his arms, and carry them in his bosom, and gently lead the mother sheep" (40:10–11). Babylon will be judged (47:1–15; 48:14) and Jerusalem restored (44:26; 51:11; 51:21–52:2); a kind of new exodus is on the horizon (43:16–17; 44:21; 48:21; 52:4–6).[9]

Although not necessarily explicitly eschatological in its initial literary and historical context, God's manifestation as a leader of his exiled people returning to Zion (e.g., 52:7–10) eventually became the stuff of eschatological expectation in early Judaism. The prophet expects the imminent fulfillment of the end of exile and regathering of the people (e.g., 44:26, 28), accompanied by natural phenomena like the leveling of mountains and raising of valleys. God, we are told, is preparing to do something new (42:9; 43:19), bringing about a salvation that is everlasting (46:13) and restoring Zion to Edenic conditions (51:3). Part and parcel of this looming event is the destruction of Babylon (43:14; 49:26) and the return of exiles from the four corners of the earth to Jerusalem (43:4–7; 51:11).

---

8. For Deutero-Isaiah's reception in later literature, see, e.g., see Darrell D. Hannah, "Isaiah within Judaism of the Second Temple Period," in *Isaiah in the New Testament*, ed. Steve Moyise and Maarten J. J. Menken (London: T&T Clark, 2005), 7–33; Florian Wilk, *Die Bedeutung des Jesajabuches für Paulus*, FRLANT 179 (Göttingen: Vandenhoeck & Ruprecht, 1998).

9. On the development of restoration traditions in the prophets and Isaiah's place within that development, see Konrad Schmid and Odil Hannes Steck, "Restoration Expectations in the Prophetic Tradition of the Old Testament," in *Restoration: Old Testament, Jewish, and Christian Perspectives*, ed. James M. Scott, JSJSup 72 (Leiden: Brill, 2001), 41–81.

Eschatology

But under what circumstances will the captives return to Jerusalem? After a call from God for comfort for his people and an assurance that Jerusalem has been properly punished (40:1–2), Isa 40:3–5 describes a sort of migration that functions in some ways as a summary for the whole of Isa 40–55: A voice cries out: "In the wilderness prepare the way of YHWH, make straight in the desert a highway for our God. Every valley shall be lifted up, and every mountain and hill be made low; the uneven ground shall become level, and the rough places a plain. Then the glory of YHWH shall be revealed, and all people shall see it together, for the mouth of YHWH has spoken." Connected to other traditions of divine manifestation (e.g., Isa 11:11–16; Mal 3:1; Ps 68), Isa 40:3–5 envisions YHWH's triumphant return to Jerusalem in view of all humanity.

Along with a number of other texts that speak of preparing a path for God and his people to return (Isa 42:15–16; 43:19; 49:9–12), 40:3–5 is paradigmatic of the outlook of Deutero-Isaiah: Jerusalem's sins that led to exile have been paid, and God will reveal his glory to all people through the restoration of Israel, a restoration that includes the leveling of desert terrain and the making of a road in the wilderness. This, for the anonymous author of Deutero-Isaiah, is what the end of exile looks like—an event modeled in part on the exodus in which God reveals himself to all people.

The depiction of God's return described in Isa 40:3–5 becomes a key passage for further reflection on the significance of the end of exile, an expectation that becomes more explicitly eschatological as time progresses from the mid-sixth century BCE.[10] For example, the Jerusalem psalm in the book of Baruch (4:5–5:9), likely composed in the second century BCE, makes use of a Greek form of Isa 40:3–5 to describe God's enthronement in Jerusalem following the judgment of Israel's oppressors (Bar 4:31–35). Deutero-Isaiah plays a key role in the composition of the Baruchan psalm, and Isa 40:4–5a in particular is important for its climactic moment, summed up in Bar 5:9:[11] "For God will lead Israel with joy, in the light of his glory, with the mercy and righteousness that come from him."[12] The use of Isa 40:4–5a in Bar 5:7 is further influenced by Pss. Sol. 11:4 (cf. Pss. Sol. 8:17),

---

10. See the note in Sir 48:24 that Isaiah "saw the last things" (εἶδεν τὰ ἔσχατα), signifying that all of Isaiah might be understood as eschatological by at least some in the late Second Temple period.

11. For Deutero-Isaiah's role in the Baruchan psalm, see Marko Marttila, "The Deuteronomistic Ideology and Phraseology in the Book of Baruch," in *Changes in Scripture: Rewriting and Interpreting Authoritative Traditions in the Second Temple Period*, ed. Hanne von Weissenberg, Juha Pakkala, and Marko Marttila, BZAW 419 (Berlin: de Gruyter, 2011), 321–46.

12. On the relationship of dependence between Pss. Sol. 11 and Bar 5, see Carey A. Moore, *Daniel, Esther and Jeremiah: The Additions; A New Translation with Introduction and Commentary*, AB 44 (Garden City, NY: Doubleday, 1984), 314–16.

which also speaks of high mountains being leveled. But the imagery of Isa 40:3–5 is extended further by both texts; both Bar 5:8 and Pss. Sol. 11:5 note that God will make fragrant trees (πᾶν ξύλον εὐωδίας) to shade the exiles on their march home, perhaps tapping into a tradition in 1 En. 25:4–5 that equates the fragrant tree with the Edenic tree of life. Connecting the end of exile to Eden highlights the eschatological nature of this interpretation: *Endzeit* echoes *Urzeit*.

Table 32.2. Comparison of Isaiah 40:4–5 (OG), Baruch 5:7, and Psalms of Solomon 11:4

Isaiah 40:4–5^{OG}	Baruch 5:7	Psalms of Solomon 11:4[13]
πᾶσα <u>φάραγξ</u> <u>πληρωθήσεται</u> καὶ <u>πᾶν ὄρος</u> καὶ βουνὸς <u>ταπεινωθήσεται</u>, καὶ ἔσται πάντα τὰ σκολιὰ εἰς εὐθεῖαν καὶ ἡ τραχεῖα εἰς ὁδοὺς λείας, καὶ ὀφθήσεται <u>ἡ δόξα κυρίου</u>, καὶ ὄψεται πᾶσα σὰρξ τὸ σωτήριον τοῦ θεοῦ, ὅτι κύριος ἐλάλησε	συνέταξε γὰρ ὁ θεὸς <u>ταπεινοῦσθαι πᾶν ὄρος</u> ὑψηλὸν καὶ θῖνας ἀενάους καὶ <u>φάραγγας πληροῦσθαι</u> εἰς ὁμαλισμὸν τῆς γῆς, ἵνα βαδίσῃ Ισραηλ ἀσφαλῶς <u>τῇ τοῦ θεοῦ δόξῃ</u>	<u>ὄρη</u> ὑψηλὰ <u>ἐταπείνωσεν εἰς</u> ὁμαλισμὸν αὐτοῖς οἱ βουνοὶ ἐφύγοσαν ἀπὸ εἰσόδου αὐτῶν
"Every <u>ravine shall be filled up</u>, and <u>every mountain</u> and hill <u>be made low</u>, and all crooked ways shall become smooth roads. Then <u>the glory of the Lord</u> shall appear, and all flesh will see the salvation of God, because the Lord has spoken" (NETS, with minor alterations)	"For God has instructed that <u>every high mountain</u> and the everlasting mounds <u>be made low</u> and <u>the valleys be filled</u> to make level the ground so that Israel might walk safely by <u>the glory of God</u>" (NETS)	"<u>He made low</u> high mountains into level ground for them, the hills fled at their coming"

Apart from the introduction to Bar 5:7 (συνέταξε γὰρ ὁ θεός, "for God has instructed"), the remainder of the verse is closely engaged with Isa 40:4–5 infused

---

13. Text and translation (with alteration) from Robert B. Wright, *The Psalms of Solomon: A Critical Edition of the Greek Text*, Jewish and Christian Texts in Context 1 (London: T&T Clark, 2007). Underlines denote agreement with Isa 40:4–5.

Eschatology

with material from other scriptural sources. The author of the psalm inverted the two main clauses in Isaiah, reversing the order of the main verbs ταπεινόω ("to humble, make low") and πληρόω ("to fill, fulfill"). In addition to other changes, Bar 5:7 includes the collocation "everlasting mounds" (θῖνας ἀενάους) as a parallel to "every high mountain" (πᾶν ὄρος ὑψηλόν), a collocation that can be traced to the blessing of Jacob in Gen 49:26^OG, implicitly connecting the promised bounty of God's blessing upon Joseph with the end of exile. The end of Bar 5:7 notes that "Israel will walk safely by the glory of God" (τῇ τοῦ θεοῦ δόξῃ, see also Bar 4:37), an image derived from the manifestation of God's glory to all people in Isa 40:5 ("the glory of the Lord shall appear," ὀφθήσεται ἡ δόξα κυρίου). Psalms of Solomon 11, too, clearly alludes to Isa 40:4–5a, and, in addition to the shared mention of fragrant tress along the road (Bar 5:8; Pss. Sol. 11:5), both texts assume the perspective that the road in the wilderness is for the exiles of Israel to return to Jerusalem. In Isa 40:3, however, the road appears to be for God's use: "prepare the way of the Lord" and "make straight in the desert a highway for our God." In both Baruch and the Psalms of Solomon, YHWH's road becomes a means of passage for the exiles returning to Jerusalem.

The text of Isa 40:3–5 is further referenced in works discovered among the Dead Sea Scrolls and utilized as one of many avenues to describe the eschatology of the *Yaḥad* and early Judaism more broadly.[14] Isaiah 40:3 is quoted twice in the Serek Hayaḥad (1QS VIII, 14; IX, 19–21), and its deployment in these cases differs from its reuse in Pss. Sol. 11 and Baruch.[15] In 1QS VIII, 14, the quotation explains the motivation behind the *Yaḥad*'s removal to the wilderness to separate themselves from the "session of perverse men" (הנשי העול, VIII, 13). This separation "prepares the way of the Lord" by the "expounding of the Torah" (מדרש התורה), which leads to the revealing knowledge once hidden from Israel to the *Yaḥad* through the work of the Interpreter (הדורש, VIII, 12).[16] The *Yaḥad* views the activity of their community as accomplishing the imperatives of Isa 40:3: the

---

14. See John J. Collins, "The Expectation of the End in the Dead Sea Scrolls," in *Eschatology, Messianism, and the Dead Sea Scrolls*, ed. Craig A. Evans and Peter W. Flint (Grand Rapids: Eerdmans, 1997), 74–90.

15. On the use of Scripture in 1QS and the history of scholarship on this question see George J. Brooke, "Isaiah 40:3 and the Wilderness Community," in *New Qumran Texts and Studies*, ed. George J. Brooke and Florentino García Martínez, STDJ 15 (Leiden: Brill, 1994), 117–32; Sarianna Metso, "The Use of Old Testament Quotations in the Qumran Community Rule," in *Qumran between the Old and New Testaments*, ed. Frederick H. Cryer and Thomas L. Thompson, JSOTSup 290 (Sheffield: Sheffield Academic, 1998), 217–31.

16. See Hanne von Weissenberg and Elisa Uusimäki, "Are There Sacred Texts in Qumran? The Concept of Sacred Text in Light of the Qumran Collection," in *Is There a Text in This Cave? Studies in the Textuality of the Dead Sea Scrolls in Honour of George J. Brooke*, ed. Ariel Feldman, Maria Cioata, and Charlotte Hempel, STDJ 119 (Leiden: Brill, 2017), 33–35.

regulations of their communal life are attempts to "prepare the way of the Lord" and "make straight [literally] in the desert a highway for our God."

The use of Isa 40:3 in 1QS IX, 19–20 functions similarly, describing a time of preparation when "the men of the Yaḥad . . . will walk blamelessly with his fellow, guided by what has been revealed to them" (1QS IX, 19).[17] Instead of describing the anticipated end of exile and the return of the people to Jerusalem, the Serek Hayaḥad deploys Isa 40:3 as a way to legitimate the community's move from Jerusalem to the wilderness. Exile allows them to undertake interpretive activity apart from any "perverse men." And these actions are obedient to the call of Isa 40:3 because they are preparing the way of the Lord—the life of the community is inextricable from the expectation of YHWH's return. Obedience to Torah is a necessary condition for restoration, and the sectarian authors of 1QS seem to have taken literally the call of Isa 40:3 to "in the wilderness prepare the way of the Lord."

Isaiah 40:3–5 is also quoted in full in 4Q176 (4QTanḥumim), a work that, although opaque due to its fragmentary state, seeks to comfort the righteous during the "trials and tribulations of the righteous in the end of days."[18] The genre of 4Q176 is not easy to define, but it has long been viewed as an exegetical work due to its substantial chain of explicit quotations.[19] Isaiah 40:1–5, the first quoted text in the sequence, appears in I, 15–20, followed by an uninterrupted string of quotations from Deutero-Isaiah: Isa 41:8–10 (I, 20–II, 2); 43:1–7 (II, 3–11); 44:3 (II, 11–13); 49:7, 13–17 (II, 13–20); 51:22–23 (II, 20–III, 1); 52:1–3 (III, 2–4); 54:4–10 (III, 5–12). Isaiah 51:23 and 52:1–2, along with Zech 13:9, are also partially preserved in column IV (frags. 12, 13, 15, 42). Although the beginning and end of the work are no longer extant, a literary framework is preserved around this string of juxtaposed quotations. The start of 4Q176 appears to be a prayer, which then introduces "consolations from the book of Isaiah" (תנחומים ומין ספר ישעיה, I, 15), which immediately introduced the quotation of Isa 40:1–5.

---

17. See Tucker S. Ferda, "John the Baptist, Isaiah 40, and the Ingathering of the Exiles," *JSHJ* 10, no. 2 (2012): 161–62.

18. Jonathan G. Campbell, *The Exegetical Texts*, Companion to the Qumran Scrolls 4 (London: T&T Clark, 2004), 85.

19. See Campbell, *Exegetical Texts*, 78–85; Jesper Høgenhaven, "4QTanḥumim (4Q176): Between Exegesis and Treatise?," in *The Mermaid and the Partridge: Essays from the Copenhagen Conference on Revising Texts from Cave Four*, ed. George J. Brooke and Jesper Høgenhaven, STDJ 96 (Leiden: Brill, 2011), 151–67; Christopher D. Stanley, "The Importance of 4QTanḥumim (4Q176)," *RevQ* 15, no. 4 (60) (1992): 569–82; Høgenhaven, "The Literary Character of 4QTanhumim," *DSD* 14, no. 1 (2007): 99–123. Citations of 4Q176 follow the reconstruction in Høgenhaven, "Literary Character."

Eschatology

The quotations are again referred to as "words of consolation" (דברי תנחומים) in III, 13, and each quoted text reports divine speech directed to Jerusalem, Israel, or the people of God.[20] The framework of 4Q176, insofar as it can be reconstructed, reflects a "transition from a state of humiliation for the righteous who constitute the people of God . . . to a state where the glory of God is revealed and judgement passed upon all mankind according to the divine plan that goes back to before the time of creation."[21] The quotations from Deutero-Isaiah, beginning with Isa 40:1-5, are presented as divine utterances of consolation in the context of humiliation on the verge of impending eschatological fulfillment. For the author or compiler of 4Q176, YHWH's plan from creation is coming to fruition; deliverance for the righteous is coming, but it remains an eschatological event. In the meantime, Isaiah comforts those who suffer under the oppression of the wicked by ensuring their eschatological vindication.

The variegated deployment of Isa 40:3-5 in early Judaism demonstrates the flexibility of scriptural traditions in the construction of eschatological ideologies.[22] The prophetic declaration of this text can be deployed to envision Jerusalem's joy at the return of her children, who traverse a straight road in the wilderness shaded by fragrant trees. Although God leads his people along the road (Bar 5:9), the path is also for those who partake in an eschatological regathering. The community responsible for the sectarian rule preserved in 1QS also took Isa 40:3-5 as an eschatological event, one that was being fulfilled in the community's retreat to the desert and continued interpretation of Torah. The life of the community as the genuine arbiter of Israel's tradition was actively preparing the way for YHWH's return.[23] Regardless of the mechanics of reuse, Isa 40:3-5 (and Deutero-Isaiah more generally) was interpreted as part of an eschatological expectation of salvation for God's people, resulting in the end of exile and the restoration of Israel to Jerusalem. This trajectory represents the larger traditional resource from which early Christian eschatologies developed.

Perhaps this is why parts of Isa 40:3-5 are variously quoted in each of the New Testament gospels as statements by the anonymous narrators of the Synoptics describing the activity of John the Baptist and as first-person speech of the Baptist

---

20. Høgenhaven, "Literary Character," 107-8.

21. Høgenhaven, "Literary Character," 122.

22. See also the overview in Albert L. A. Hogeterp, *Expectations of the End: A Comparative Traditio-Historical Study of Eschatological, Apocalyptic and Messianic Ideas in the Dead Sea Scrolls and the New Testament*, STDJ 83 (Leiden: Brill, 2008), 117-19.

23. See generally, Lawrence H. Schiffman, "The Concept of Restoration in the Dead Sea Scrolls," in Scott, *Restoration*, 203-21.

in John.[24] Because Luke expands the quotation from Mark and Matthew to include the entirety of Isa 40:3–5, I focus on the Lukan version in this section.[25]

As the Lukan infancy narratives come to a close (1:1–2:52), we meet John the Baptist at the river Jordan. There he begins to proclaim baptism of the forgiveness of sins, an activity that is supported by the quotation of Isa 40:3–5, set apart from the narrative as it is in each Gospel with a clear introductory statement (Luke 3:4, "as it is written in the book of the words of Isaiah the prophet," ὡς γέγραπται ἐν βίβλῳ λόγων Ἡσαΐου τοῦ προφήτου). The quotation implicitly identifies the "voice of one crying out in the wilderness" (φωνὴ βοῶντος ἐν τῇ ἐρήμῳ) as John's, a point made explicit in the Fourth Gospel's reworking of the quotation as first-person speech ("I am the voice of one calling out in the wilderness," Ἐγὼ φωνὴ βοῶντος ἐν τῇ ἐρήμῳ, John 1:23). Luke's inclusion of a larger portion of Isa 40 than Matthew or Mark clarifies the ultimate, eschatological goal of John's ministry. Not only is the Baptist's activity preparatory for the ministry of Jesus and a symbolic enactment of Isaiah's description of preparing a smooth path for God in the desert, but the inclusion of text from Isa 40:5 clarifies that the quoted text functions as an explanation for John's activity: a path is made in the desert for the Lord, referring here to Jesus, who becomes the protagonist of the narrative in 3:23, for the purpose that "all flesh will see the salvation of God" (ὄψεται πᾶσα σὰρξ τὸ σωτήριον τοῦ θεοῦ).[26]

Other aspects of John's ministry are eschatologically oriented, focusing on impending judgment. He asks the crowds who warned them "to flee from the wrath that is to come" (3:7) and warns that the axe is laid at the root of the tree and that trees that do not bear fruit will be tossed into the fire (3:9). His focus on judgment, coupled with his teaching on just living (3:10–14), leads the crowd to wonder whether John is a messiah (3:15). He assures them that he is not, but that one is coming after him who will clear the threshing floor and burn the chaff (3:17).

The use of Isa 40 in each of the gospels, and specifically in Luke, speaks not only to John's preparatory role, but to the significance of Jesus's activity. The quo-

---

24. On the use of Isaiah in the New Testament, with a focus on the Gospels, see Craig A. Evans, "From Gospel to Gospel: The Function of Isaiah in the New Testament," in *Writing and Reading the Scroll of Isaiah: Studies of an Interpretive Tradition*, ed. Craig C. Broyles and Craig A. Evans, 2 vols., VTSup 70 (Leiden: Brill, 1997), 2:651–91.

25. Mark 1:2–3 quotes only Isa 40:3 in a composite citation with Exod 23:20 and Mal 3:1; Matt 3:3 quotes only Isa 40:3; the Baptist cites only Isa 40:3 in John 1:23. The text of W032 expands the quotation in Mark even further, including Isa 40:4–8. See Krister Stendahl, *The School of St. Matthew and Its Use of the Old Testament*, 2nd ed., ASNU 20 (Lund: Gleerup, 1968), 47–54. These instances are the only time that Isa 40:3–5 is referenced in the New Testament, with the possible exception of Acts 1:5; 18:6; 28:8; Ferda, "John the Baptist," 175–76. Klyne R. Snodgrass, "Streams of Tradition Emerging from Isaiah 40:1–5 and Their Adaptation in the New Testament," *JSNT* 2, no. 8 (1980): 24–45, also makes the case that this quotation and the use of Isaiah more broadly is especially important for Luke vis-à-vis the other gospels.

26. John's preparatory role is a fact also foretold to John's father Zechariah in Luke 1:16–17.

tation places Jesus's ministry in the context of the end of exile and the consolation of God's people in a period before the fulfillment of this promise. The reference to Isa 40 places the evangelists' narratives within the larger context of early Jewish eschatological thought as it related to the end of exile. John's baptizing in the desert prepares the way for Jesus, who reconstitutes Israel, a point reinforced by many of Jesus's symbolic actions and teachings.[27]

Beyond the intimation inherent in the quotation itself, exile and restoration are not explicit topics in John's engagement with the crowd in Luke 3:3–20. But the larger interpretive history of the Isaiah passage in early Judaism necessitates that John's activity be understood within this larger framework. In Baruch and the Psalms of Solomon, Isa 40:3–5 is clearly interpreted as a reference to the end of exile, and in 4Q176 it is deployed to comfort a beleaguered people as a promise of future deliverance. And like the evangelists' portrayal of the Baptist, the sectarian community in 1QS viewed themselves as actively partaking in the fulfilling of this Isaianic promise by locating themselves in the wilderness. For Luke, it is not the community that acts as the precursor to God's return, but John who functions as a prophetic and transitional figure for Jesus's activity.[28]

The interpretive path of Isa 40:3–5 from the sixth century BCE to the first CE is winding. Initially composed by an anonymous prophet, it was redeployed in the second century BCE in Baruch as an expression of hope in a regathering of all Israel to Jerusalem, used to describe the activities of a sectarian group who separated themselves from the priestly hierarchy in Jerusalem, and by the evangelists as a way to frame Jesus's activities as the, by this point, long-awaited end of exile. Despite the geopolitical changes in Judea during this period, many viewed the exile as an ongoing reality and used Deutero-Isaiah as a matrix for understanding their place on the cusp of the impending age. Isaiah 40:3–5 became the eschatological text *par excellence* for anticipating the reversal of the exilic condition.

DANIEL 7:13 AND ZECHARIAH 12:10: ESCHATOLOGICAL JUXTAPOSITIONS

The final, and brief, example of Jewish scriptural texts deployed to construct eschatologies in early Judaism and Christianity that I explore here is the combi-

---

27. E.g., the selection of twelve disciples. See the texts assembled in Ferda, "John the Baptist," 156.

28. See Joseph A. Fitzmyer, *The Gospel according to Luke I–IX: A New Translation with Introduction and Commentary*, AB 28 (Garden City, NY: Doubleday, 1981), 450–51.

nation of Dan 7:13 and Zech 12:10 that appears as part of the Synoptic apocalyptic discourse in Matt 24:30 and Rev 1:7.[29]

In its literary context, Dan 7 inaugurates an apocalyptic turn in the work whose purported setting remains in the Babylonian court like the preceding tales (7:1). The apocalyptic turn takes the form of night visions. Daniel's vision concerns four beasts rising out of the sea, representing successive kingdoms (see Dan 2:24–45). Attention is focused on the fourth and final beast, who is exceedingly frightening and powerful, devouring with iron teeth and smashing whatever remains with his feet (7:7). More troubling still is the manifestation of the beast's blasphemous horn. It removes the three preceding horns and has eyes like a human and a blaspheming mouth (7:8). The arrival of the horn leads immediately to judgment and the setting up of thrones. An Ancient One attended by a legion of angels appears, books are opened, and court sits in session (7:9–10). The beast with the arrogant horn is killed and thrown in the fire.[30]

A second figure arrives on the scene in 7:13: he is "one like a Son of Man" (ὡς υἱὸς ἀνθρώπου) who comes "with [or on] the clouds of heaven" (μετὰ [ἐπὶ] τῶν νεφελῶν τοῦ οὐρανοῦ).[31] He comes before the Ancient of Days and is given dominion, glory, honor, and kingship over many tribes, tongues, and nations: "His dominion is an everlasting dominion that shall not pass away, and his kingship is one that shall never be destroyed" (7:14).

The vision is then interpreted by an angelic guide, who tells us that although the beasts arising from the earth represent earthly kingdoms, "the holy ones of the Most High shall receive the kingdom and possess the kingdom forever—forever and ever" (7:18), corresponding to the reign of the one like a Son of Man. But again, focus is centered on the fourth beast, who makes war with the holy ones (7:19–27). He is given power for a time but makes changes to the sacred calendar and persecutes the holy ones, leading to the judgment laid out in the heavenly court. The kingdom will then pass to the holy ones of the Most High (7:28).

Within this narrative, Dan 7:13 is significant because it introduces a divine agent—the one like a Son of Man or one like a human being—into the heavenly court judgment scene who "comes with the clouds of heaven" and who receives dominion following the demise of the beast. There has been significant critical

---

29. See also John 19:36–37. On the place of Zech 12:10 in the Johannine tradition, see Wm. Randolph Bynum, *The Fourth Gospel and the Scriptures: Illuminating the Form and Meaning of Scriptural Citation in John 19:37*, NovTSup 144 (Leiden: Brill, 2012).

30. See Michael Segal, *Dreams, Riddles, and Visions: Textual, Contextual, and Intertextual Approaches to the Book of Daniel*, BZAW 455 (Berlin: de Gruyter, 2016), 132–54.

31. I reference the Greek version of Daniel here because these are the forms referenced in the New Testament.

debate as to the identity of this figure, but it is clear at least that this vision depicts eschatological divine judgments from the heavenly court on an earthly kingdom represented by the Seleucid king Antiochus IV Epiphanes.[32]

While Dan 7 is visionary, Zech 12 is oracular, designating itself as an "utterance" (משׂא), "the word of YHWH concerning Israel" (12:1). YHWH is about to make Jerusalem a stumbling block to all who lay siege against her, a heavy stone that will harm all who attempt to lift her. "On that day" (ביום ההוא), all the nations will come to stand against Jerusalem (12:3), but YHWH will strike their armies with madness and their horses with panic, leading the Jerusalemites to say that they are safe because YHWH is their God (12:4–5). Judah will become a fire that devours her neighbors (12:6), victory will be given to them, and "on that day YHWH will shield the inhabitants of Jerusalem so that the feeblest among them on that day shall be like David, and the house of David shall be like God, like the angel of YHWH, at their head" (12:8).

The oracle's focus on David, his house, and divine military conflict describes an eschatological scenario in which Jerusalem and Judah are maintained by God's intervention. But the oracle ends on a note of woe, describing the mourning for a pierced one in Jerusalem "on that day" that extends to the families of David, Nathan, Levi, and Shimei (12:11–14). There are a number of interesting intertextual links in this final section of the oracle, but most interesting is the figure described in 12:10.[33] This passage is complicated by a number of textual and transmissional issues, but the text can be read:

> And I will pour out a spirit of compassion and supplication on the house of David and the inhabitants of Jerusalem, and they will look upon me, to the one they have pierced, and they will wail over him, as one mourns for an only child, and weep bitterly over him, as one weeps over a firstborn.[34]

Although different in genre and structure, both texts describe enigmatic figures who make appearances in eschatological scenarios, be it judgment in the heavenly court or following a military conflict in which YHWH protects Jerusalem and destroys her enemies. In Zech 12:10, the passage could be understand as describing the return of a previously slain figure.

---

32. On the interpretations of the Son of Man figure and its afterlife in early Jewish literature, see John J. Collins, *The Scepter and the Star: Messianism in Light of the Dead Sea Scrolls*, 2nd ed. (Grand Rapids: Eerdmans, 2010), 191–96; Segal, *Dreams, Riddles, and Visions*, 134–39.

33. For the intertextual links, see Rex Mason, "Zechariah 12.1–13.6," in *Bringing out the Treasure: Inner Biblical Allusion in Zechariah 9–14*, ed. Mark J. Boda and Michael H. Floyd, JSOTSup 370 (Sheffield: Sheffield Academic, 2003), 131–71.

34. See Allen, *Book of Revelation*, 112–22.

Both Dan 7:13 and Zech 12:10 are only sparingly referenced in early Jewish literature, even though other parts of Dan 7 and Zech 12 are alluded to in other locations.[35] The most obvious allusion in Dan 7:13 occurs in 1 En. 46, part of the second parable in the Similitudes.[36] First Enoch 45 describes the remaking of heaven and earth, where God's chosen one will dwell (45:4). The chosen one will make judgments, give rest to the righteous, and remove the unrighteous from the face of the earth (45:6). The seer then describes the judgment scene in more detail, modeled in part on Dan 7. The scene includes an ancient one with white hair and another figure who appears like a human standing among the angels (46:1). This figure is identified by an interpreting angel as the Son of Man; he is righteous, does the will of the ancient one, removes kings from their thrones, and breaks the teeth of sinners (46:3–4). He is the source of the authority of earthly kings.

Within the context of a larger passage on eschatological judgment that draws on multiple Danielic traditions in the Similitudes, the one like a Son of Man from Dan 7:13 becomes a prototypical agent of judgment. The role of this figure is extended further in 1 En. 46: he is angelomorphic and preexistent, exercises control over the heavenly storerooms, acts as God's agent of authority over all the earth, and executes final judgment. It is not hard to see why this figure in Dan 7, especially when interpreted through the matrix of Enochic traditions, becomes important for early Christian understandings of Jesus.

In contrast to the Danielic Son of Man, the pierced figure in Zech 12:10 receives surprisingly little play in extant early Jewish literature. The only clear source for tracing his reception is in Targum Jonathan, where a major interpretive alteration exists. Instead of the house of Jerusalem and the house of David looking "to me whom they pierced" (in the proto-MT and Greek revising versions), the text in Targum Jonathan depicts this group as asking a question: "and they will ask me about their going into exile" (ויבעון מן קדמי על דאטלטלו), connecting this oracle to an ongoing area of concern in early Judaism. This translation is also possibly aware of existing associations of the pierced one (אשר דקרו) with Jesus and the use of this text in Christian literature, sidestepping a potentially problematic rendering.

An interesting Aramaic marginal note in Codex Reuchlinianus at Zech 12:10 (twelfth century CE), however, reintroduces piercing into the equation:[37]

---

35. Daniel 7 is alluded to in 1 En. 90:20; Apoc. Zeph. 4:2; and Zech 12 in 1QHª IX, 10–17; 1QM XI, 10; 1 En. 56:6.

36. See George W. E. Nickelsburg and James C. VanderKam, *1 Enoch 2: A Commentary on the Book of 1 Enoch Chapters 37–82*, Hermeneia (Minneapolis: Fortress, 2012), 153–61; Collins, *Scepter*, 196–205.

37. See Allen, *Book of Revelation*, 248–50 for further detail; and the apparatus of Alexander

> And I shall cause to rest upon the house of David and upon the inhabitants of Jerusalem the spirit of prophecy and true prayer. And afterward the messiah son of Ephraim [משיח בר אפרים] will go out and do battle with Gog, and Gog will slay him in front of the gate of Jerusalem. And they shall look to me and shall inquire of me [ויבעון] why the nations pierced [דקרו] the messiah son of Ephraim.

This comment describes an eschatological battle between Gog and a messiah son of Ephraim, who becomes the pierced figure mentioned in the Hebrew text, fleshing out the relationship between the two parts of the oracle in Zech 12. The final sentence of the note includes the verbs of both of the parallel clauses in Targum Jonathan and the Masoretic Text, reconciling the initial difference between these traditions by juxtaposition. The marginal note clearly identifies the pierced one as a messianic figure who will be martyred at the gates of Jerusalem.

Although the reception of Dan 7:13 and Zech 12:10 is spotty in early Judaism, both texts are understood in eschatological terms. The one like a Son of Man functions as an agent of divine judgment and the pierced one becomes an object of mourning "on that day." Both become connected to messiahs. There are no concrete lexical linkages between the description of these two figures, but it is not surprising that they were combined and eventually transmitted as an independent interpretive tradition in early Christianity, appearing in many early Christian writings (Rev 1:7; Justin, *Dial.* 14.8; *1 Apol.* 52.12; Did. 16.8; Barn. 7.9; Apoc. Pet. 6).[38]

Matthew 24:30 represents another early example of the combination of these two traditions. In 24:3, part of the larger apocalyptic discourse of the Synoptic Gospels (cf. Mark 13 // Luke 21), Jesus sits on the Mount of Olives and is approached by some disciples who ask him to "tell us, when will this be, and what will be the sign of your coming and of the end of the age [τὸ σημεῖον τῆς σῆς παρουσίας καὶ συντελείας τοῦ αἰῶνος]." This two-pronged question initiates a lengthy speech from Jesus that continues until Matt 25:46, where he describes the "sign of his coming" and the "end of the age" as defined by conflict, famine,

---

Sperber, ed., *The Bible in Aramaic: Based on Old Manuscripts and Printed Texts*, vol. 3 (Leiden: Brill, 1962). On the marginalia in Codex Reuchlinianus (Badische Hof- und Landesbibliothek, Karlsruhe), see Hector M. Patmore, "The Marginal Notes to the Targum Text of Codex Reuchlinianus No. 3," *AS* 10, no. 1 (2012): 53–85.

38. See Daniele Tripaldi, "'Discrepat evangelista et Septuaginta nostraque translatio' (*Hieronymus*, Briefe, 57,7,5): Bemerkungen zur Textvorlage des Sacharja-Zitats in Offb 1,7," in *Die Johannesoffenbarung: Ihr Text und ihre Auslegung*, ed. Michael Labahn and Martin Karrer, ABIG 38 (Leipzig: Evangelische Verlagsanstalt, 2012), 131–43, for further information on the reception of this tradition.

natural disasters, persecution, false prophecy, false messiahs, and a desolating sacrilege, among other things. The Son of Man, Matthew's Jesus reports, will come unexpectedly, like a flash of lightning (24:27), but he will be preceded by a darkened sun and moon, stars falling from heaven, and the shaking of the heavens (24:29), borrowing language from Isa 13:10 and 34:4.[39] Following these signs, the "sign of the Son of Man will appear in heaven and then all the tribes of the earth will mourn [Zech 12:10], and they will see the Son of Man coming on the clouds of heaven [Dan 7:13] with power and great glory" (Matt 24:30).

Central to Matthew's description of the coming of the Son of Man is this combination of Zech 12:10 and Dan 7:13, apparently because the author views the figures described here as related in some way to the Son of Man's identity. The "sign of the Son of Man" (τὸ σημεῖον τοῦ υἱοῦ τοῦ ἀνθρώπου) is a combination of Zechariah's mysterious pierced figure, although the explicit reference to piercing is omitted in Matthew, and one like the Son of Man from Dan 7. Although unclear from Zech 12 when taken in isolation, Matthew's Jesus implies that the mourning in the oracle is the result of the fear of judgment, exercised by the Son of Man at the end of the age. For Jesus, or whoever it was that first juxtaposed these traditions, the eschatological figures in Zech 12 and Dan 7 were mutually interpretive, describing the same figure and his future involvement in God's judgment.

Jesus's eschatological speech in Matt 24:3–25:46 is deeply indebted to Jewish Scripture, particularly as it relates to the Son of Man. The combination of Isa 13:10; 34:4; Zech 12:10; and Dan 7:13 in Matt 24:29–31 is paradigmatic of this proclivity: Jesus's description of the coming of the Son of Man is unintelligible without recourse to Jewish scriptural traditions, reflecting the thoughtful interpretation and juxtaposition of texts that ancient Christian writers viewed as closely related. The combination of these traditions in this passage is one of any number of examples that demonstrates that the early Christian eschatological imagination is integrally tied to interpretative imagination, the careful scrutiny of Jewish Scripture as a corpus of related texts, and the operative eschatologies of early Judaism.

Conclusion

Eschatological expectations were ubiquitous in early Judaism and Christianity, an orientation influenced by the political machinations of the period and,

---

39. On the problem of Son of Man language in Matthew, see Ulrich Luz, "The Son of Man in Matthew: Heavenly Judge or Human Christ?," *JSNT* 15, no. 48 (1992): 3–21.

perhaps more forcefully, by the interpretation of Jewish scriptural traditions. The routes that these texts and their interpretive traditions traveled are circuitous and branching, due in large part to the ubiquity of Jewish Scripture as the building blocks of literary composition. In some instances, early Christian authors demonstrate a clear awareness of existing Jewish interpretive practices when it comes to specific texts. The evangelists' ascription of Isa 40:3–5 to the activity of John the Baptist runs parallel to the interpretation of the same passage quoted in 1QS, and the eschatological reality of the end of exile in the Gospels is coterminous with the perspective of a number of early Jewish works.[40] The interpretation of the first few verses of Deutero-Isaiah in early Christianity is directly conditioned by contemporary Jewish perspectives. The same goes for the identification of the one like a Son of Man in Dan 7:13 as an eschatological agent of judgment as witnessed in 1 Enoch. However, early Christian authors maintained the interpretive agency to extend existing interpretive traditions; for example, the juxtaposition of the pierced one from Zech 12:10 with the one like a Son of Man based on the perception of their shared activity as agents of judgment who appear at the end of the age. The rich eschatological tapestry of early Judaism and Christianity is deeply connected to the rich interpretive imagination at play in the literary works composed in this period.

Bibliography

Allen, Garrick V. *The Book of Revelation and Early Jewish Textual Culture*. SNTSMS 168. Cambridge: Cambridge University Press, 2017.

Allen, Garrick V., Kai Akagi, Paul Sloan, and Madhavi Nevader, eds. *Son of God: Divine Sonship in Jewish and Christian Antiquity*. University Park, PA: Eisenbrauns, 2019.

Assis, Elie. *The Book of Joel: A Prophet between Calamity and Hope*. LHBOTS 581. London: T&T Clark, 2013.

Aune, David E. *Revelation 17–22*. WBC 52C. Nashville: Nelson, 1998.

Brooke, George J. "Isaiah 40:3 and the Wilderness Community." Pages 117–32 in *New Qumran Texts and Studies: Proceedings of the First Meeting of the International Organization for Qumran Studies, Paris 1992*. Edited by George J. Brooke and Florentino García Martínez. STDJ 15. Leiden: Brill, 1994.

Bynum, Wm. Randolph. *The Fourth Gospel and the Scriptures: Illuminating the Form and Meaning of Scriptural Citation in John 19:37*. NovTSup 144. Leiden: Brill, 2012.

---

40. See Brooke, "Isaiah 40:3," 131–32.

Campbell, Jonathan G. *The Exegetical Texts*. Companion to the Qumran Scrolls 4. London: T&T Clark, 2004.

Collins, Adela Yarbro, and John J. Collins. *King and Messiah as Son of God: Divine, Human, and Angelic Figures in Biblical and Related Literature*. Grand Rapids: Eerdmans, 2008.

Collins, John J. "The Expectation of the End in the Dead Sea Scrolls." Pages 74–90 in *Eschatology, Messianism, and the Dead Sea Scrolls*. Edited by Craig A. Evans and Peter W. Flint. Grand Rapids: Eerdmans, 1997.

———. *The Scepter and the Star: Messianism in Light of the Dead Sea Scrolls*. 2nd ed. Grand Rapids: Eerdmans, 2010.

Evans, Craig A. "From Gospel to Gospel: The Function of Isaiah in the New Testament." Pages 651–91 in vol. 2 of *Writing and Reading the Scroll of Isaiah: Studies of an Interpretive Tradition*. Edited by Craig C. Broyles and Craig A. Evans. 2 vols. VTSup 70. Leiden: Brill, 1997.

Ferda, Tucker S. "John the Baptist, Isaiah 40, and the Ingathering of the Exiles." *JSHJ* 10, no. 2 (2012): 154–88.

Fitzmyer, Joseph. *The Gospel according to Luke I–IX: A New Translation with Introduction and Commentary*. AB 28. Garden City, NY: Doubleday, 1981.

Goldingay, John, and David Payne. *Isaiah 40–55: A Critical and Exegetical Commentary*. ICC. London: T&T Clark, 2014.

Hannah, Darrell D. "Isaiah within Judaism of the Second Temple Period." Pages 7–33 in *Isaiah in the New Testament*. Edited by Steve Moyise and Maarten J. J. Menken. London: T&T Clark, 2005.

Høgenhaven, Jesper. "4QTanḥumim (4Q176): Between Exegesis and Treatise?" Pages 151–67 in *The Mermaid and the Partridge: Essays from the Copenhagen Conference on Revising Texts from Cave Four*. Edited by George J. Brooke and Jesper Høgenhaven. STDJ 96. Leiden: Brill, 2011.

———. "The Literary Character of 4QTanhumim." *DSD* 14, no. 1 (2007): 99–123.

Hogeterp, Albert L. A. *Expectations of the End: A Comparative Traditio-Historical Study of Eschatological, Apocalyptic and Messianic Ideas in the Dead Sea Scrolls and the New Testament*. STDJ 83. Leiden: Brill, 2009.

Hooker, Morna. *Jesus and the Servant: The Influence of the Servant Concept of Deutero-Isaiah in the New Testament*. London: SPCK, 1959.

Luz, Ulrich. "The Son of Man in Matthew: Heavenly Judge or Human Christ?" *JSNT* 15, no. 48 (1992): 3–21.

Marttila, Marko. "The Deuteronomistic Ideology and Phraseology in the Book of Baruch." Pages 321–46 in *Changes in Scripture: Rewriting and Interpreting Authoritative Traditions in the Second Temple Period*. Edited by Hanne von Weissenberg, Juha Pakkala, and Marko Marttila. BZAW 419. Berlin: de Gruyter, 2011.

Mason, Rex. "Zechariah 12.1–13.6." Pages 131–71 in *Bringing out the Treasure: Inner Biblical Allusion in Zechariah 9–14*. Edited by Mark J. Boda and Michael H. Floyd. JSOTSup 370. Sheffield: Sheffield Academic, 2003.

Metso, Sarianna. "The Use of Old Testament Quotations in the Qumran Community Rule." Pages 217–31 in *Qumran between the Old and New Testaments*. Edited by Frederick H. Cryer and Thomas L. Thompson. JSOTSup 290. Sheffield: Sheffield Academic, 1998.

Moore, Carey A. *Daniel, Esther and Jeremiah: The Additions; A New Translation with Introduction and Commentary*. AB 44. Garden City, NY: Doubleday, 1984.

Nickelsburg, George, and James C. VanderKam. *1 Enoch 2: A Commentary on the Book of 1 Enoch Chapters 37–82*. Hermeneia. Minneapolis: Fortress, 2012.

Patmore, Hector M. "The Marginal Notes to the Targum Text of Codex Reuchlinianus No. 3." *AS* 10, no. 1 (2012): 53–85.

Schiffman, Lawrence H. "The Concept of Restoration in the Dead Sea Scrolls." Pages 203–21 in *Restoration: Old Testament, Jewish, and Christian Perspective*. Edited by James M. Scott. JSJSup 72. Leiden: Brill, 2001.

Schmid, Konrad, and Odil Hannes Steck. "Restoration Expectations in the Prophetic Tradition of the Old Testament." Pages 41–81 in *Restoration: Old Testament, Jewish, and Christian Perspectives*. Edited by James M. Scott. JSJSup 72. Leiden: Brill, 2001.

Segal, Michael. *Dreams, Riddles, and Visions: Textual, Contextual and Intertextual Approaches to the Book of Daniel*. BZAW 455. Berlin: de Gruyter, 2016.

Snodgrass, Klyne R. "Streams of Tradition Emerging from Isaiah 40:1–5 and Their Adaptation in the New Testament." *JSNT* 2, no. 8 (1980): 24–45.

Sperber, Alexander, ed. *The Bible in Aramaic: Based on Old Manuscripts and Printed Texts*. 3 vols. Leiden: Brill, 1962.

Stanley, Christopher D. "The Importance of 4QTanḥumim (4Q176)." *RevQ* 15, no. 4 (60) (1992): 569–82.

Stendahl, Krister. *The School of St. Matthew, and Its Use of the Old Testament*. 2nd ed. ASNU 20. Lund: Gleerup, 1968.

Stuhlmacher, Peter. "Isaiah 53 in the Gospels and Acts." Pages 147–62 in *The Suffering Servant: Isaiah 53 in Jewish and Christian Sources*. Edited by Bernd Janowski and Peter Stuhlmacher. Grand Rapids: Eerdmans, 2004.

Tripaldi, Daniele. "'Discrepat evangelista et Septuaginta nostraque translatio' (Hieronymus, Briefe, 57,7,5): Bemerkungen zur Textvorlage des Sacharja-Zitats in Offb 1,7." Pages 131–43 in *Die Johannesoffenbarung: Ihr Text und ihre Auslegung*. Edited by Michael Labahn and Martin Karrer. ABIG 38. Leipzig: Evangelische Verlagsanstalt, 2012.

Weissenberg, Hanne von, and Elisa Uusimäki. "Are There Sacred Texts in Qumran? The Concept of Sacred Text in Light of the Qumran Collection." Pages 21–41 in *Is There a Text in This Cave? Studies in the Textuality of the Dead Sea Scrolls in Honour of George J. Brooke*. Edited by Ariel Feldman, Maria Cioata, and Charlotte Hempel. STDJ 119. Leiden: Brill, 2017.

Wilk, Florian. *Die Bedeutung des Jesajabuches für Paulus*. FRLANT 179. Göttingen: Vandenhoeck & Ruprecht, 1998.

Williamson, H. G. M. *The Book Called Isaiah: Deutero-Isaiah's Role in Composition and Redaction*. Oxford: Clarendon, 1994.

Wright, Robert B. *The Psalms of Solomon: A Critical Edition of the Greek Text*. Jewish and Christian Texts in Context 1. London: T&T Clark, 2007.

PART 4

Tracing Israel's Scriptures

In this fourth section, "Tracing Israel's Scriptures," we flip the direction of our reading. Instead of beginning with a particular New Testament book and then reading backward in search of its scriptural predecessor texts, our point of departure now is four books from Israel's Scripture that are among the most commonly cited books in the New Testament: Deuteronomy, Isaiah, Psalms, and Daniel. The chapters take up the influence of scriptural texts in the New Testament from a related but distinctive angle: How were individual books from Israel's Scriptures received across the New Testament? The final chapter in the section, the longest in our volume, also traces the use of Israel's Scriptures in the New Testament—only the focus is not on a particular book, but on individual figures.

Each chapter advances in three steps. It begins with a short consideration of the scriptural book itself, then turns to the book's history of reading in early Judaism, and finally traces its impact across various corpora and authors that make up the New Testament. Given the enormous number of references to, and forms of engagement with scriptural books and characters in early Jewish writings, these chapters necessarily have to remain selective. The point cannot be to provide a comprehensive overview of Second Temple Jewish literature. Instead, the chapters highlight those aspects in the book's or individual's early Jewish interpretive life that provide the necessary context for our reading of the New Testament.

Similar to the third section, the chapters devote particular attention to the question of whether there are significant commonalities with, or differences from the early Jewish interpretations of the same book and character. What appears to be shared, and what is distinctive in the New Testament's use of Scripture? In other words, these chapters shed light on the sorts of hermeneutical trajectories that accompany their respective books or figures in early Judaism, and on what is common and what is distinctive in the ways in which individual authors of the New Testament negotiate that heritage and participate in the process of interpretation and counterinterpretation.

33

Deuteronomy in the New Testament

GERT J. STEYN

The New Testament authors interpreted their Scriptures christologically (through "retrodiction") in the light of Jesus of Nazareth—his origin and birth, his public performances, his humiliating death by means of crucifixion, the empty tomb reports, and his postmortem appearances.[1] Earlier New Testament literature, such as Paul and Mark, display a high frequency of citations and allusions to Israel's Scriptures, but relatively few of those are specifically applicable to the Jesus events. The percentage of citations directly applicable to Jesus is significantly greater in later New Testament literature—a phenomenon that indicates that the further early Christianity developed, the more its proponents tried to make sense of the Jesus events based on their Jewish Scriptures. It is particularly citations from the Psalms, Isaiah, and some Minor Prophets that were used to understand and interpret the Jesus events. However, very few Pentateuch passages were proportionally utilized as *christological* substantiation of the Jesus events.

The early Christian movement, being itself a branch of Judaism during New Testament times, needed to demarcate itself in finding and formulating its own identity. It needed to define its overlaps and differences with mainline Judaism. Particularly the Deuteronomic legal and cultic codes would become increasingly debated and controversial in New Testament times, as this movement expanded in non-Jewish and pagan environments. Which laws would still be valid and how

---

1. For retrodiction, see Gert J. Steyn, "'Retrodiction' of the Old Testament in the New: The Case of Deut 21:23 in Paul's Letter to the Galatians and the Crucifixion of Yehoshua ben Yoseph," *HvTS* 71, no. 3 (2015): a3091; DOI: 10.4102/hts.v71i3.3091.

should they be interpreted? Which aspects of the Jewish cult would still apply and in what manner? Hence, the interpretation of the Scriptures, inherited from Israel's history, remained important for the early Christians, which meant that early Christianity did not, in this aspect, differ at all from other Jewish groups. Deuteronomy had an immense impact on the origins and development of early Christian doctrine and ethics. It is thus no surprise that Deuteronomy is the third most frequently cited scriptural book in the New Testament—after Psalms and Isaiah—and the most cited and alluded to from the Pentateuch by the New Testament writers.

The Textual Status of LXX Deuteronomy

The scope of LXX Deuteronomy is the same as MT Deuteronomy so that the compositional and thematic outline is basically the same in both.[2] There are hardly any major deviations, except for Deut 32:40, 43–45. Numerous small deviations between the Greek and the Hebrew are, however, present.

The large number of LXX Deuteronomy textual witnesses includes some fragmentary papyri, the complete LXX Deuteronomy in five different majuscules, as well as nearly one hundred minuscules. Papyrus Fouad 266b (Deut 17–33)—one of the oldest LXX Deuteronomy witnesses that predates the Christian era—is particularly marked by its use of the tetragrammaton, in contrast to fragment PFouad 266c (Deut 10–33), dating from the same period.[3] It contains fragments with four pieces of Deuteronomy that occur in Hebrews (Deut 29:17–20; 31:5–7; 32:1–7; and 32:39–43). PFouad shows signs of a text tradition that aligns closer to the later Deuteronomy^{MT}.[4]

Further Deuteronomy textual witnesses include a large number Dead Sea Scrolls fragments—most from Qumran and some from Naḥal Ḥever.[5] It also includes a Greek fragment containing Deut 11:4 (4Q122). Some of these, such as

---

2. For the textual status of LXX Deuteronomy, see Sidnie White Crawford, "Deuteronomy," in *Pentateuch, Former and Latter Prophets*, ed. Armin Lange and Emanuel Tov, THB 1B (Leiden: Brill, 2016), 148–52; Melvin K. H. Peters, "Deuteronomion/Deuteronomium/Das fünfte Buch Mose," in *Einleitung in die Septuaginta*, ed. Siegfried Kreuzer, vol. 1 of *Handbuch zur Septuaginta/Handbook of the Septuagint*, ed. Martin Karrer, Wolfgang Kraus, and Siegfried Kreuzer (Gütersloh: Gütersloher Verlagshaus, 2016), 161–63.

3. Zaki Aly and Ludwig Koenen, eds., *Three Rolls of the Early Septuagint: Genesis and Deuteronomy; A Photographic Edition*, PTA 27 (Bonn: Habelt, 1980), 1; for the Tetragrammaton, see p. 5.

4. Martin Karrer and Wolfgang Kraus, eds., *Septuaginta Deutsch: Erläuterungen und Kommentare zum griechischen Alten Testament*, vol. 1, *Genesis bis Makkabäer* (Stuttgart: Deutsche Bibelgesellschaft, 2011), 524.

5. These include 1Q4–5; 1Q13; 1Q33; 2Q10–12; 4Q28–44; 4Q122 (LXX); 5Q1; 6Q3; 6Q20; 8Q3–4; 11Q3; 11Q13.

4Q44, support a text that is closer to the Old Greek version of the Pentateuch (LXX) than to that of the MT. Interesting textual differences have been identified in the *Canticum Mosis*, where Deut 32:43 consists of four stichs in MT Deuteronomy, six in 4Q44, and eight in LXX Deut and Ode 2.

Deuteronomy in Early Jewish Literature

Deuteronomy took a central role in Jewish Torah observance and shaped the Jewish cultic tradition in its liturgical and festival expressions. It became much more than literary history in early Judaism. It was perceived as divine instruction being mediated through prophetic Mosaic discourses and intended "as a pedagogical tool to instruct each generation on what it means to be part of God's chosen people."[6] It was considered to contain catechism on the doctrine of God, as the law book on ethical behavior, and as the liturgical source for Jewish worship, containing formulas, prayers, and instructions on the Jewish festivals, as well as eschatological traits for future generations. Its *Wirkungsgeschichte* in the Jewish tradition and early Jewish literature was substantial.[7] The assumption that Deuteronomy (or an earlier version of it) was the law book that was discovered by the high priest Hilkiah in the temple and that it provided the basis for the reforms under King Josiah (2 Kgs 22–23), though not undisputed, remains a popular hypothesis. Many of the basic ideas in Deuteronomy became decisive for the historical books. Deuteronomy had a powerful impact on later Jewish tradition. In fact, the historical books (Joshua, Judges, Samuel, Kings) are all considered to be "Deuteronomistic History" due to similarities in language, style, and content.[8] Later (mostly postexilic) Deuteronomistic editorial activities have further been suggested. Jeremiah, too, is "suffused with Deuteronomistic language and allusions," while Deuteronomic echoes are to be found in Ezekiel and Second Isaiah.[9]

---

6. Duane L. Christensen, *Deuteronomy 1–21:9*, WBC 6A (Dallas: Word, 2001), 137.

7. For *Wirkungsgeschichte*, see Peters, "Deuteronomium," 171–72. For Deuteronomy's substantial influence, see Sarah J. K. Pearce, *The Words of Moses: Studies in the Reception of Deuteronomy in the Second Temple Period*, TSAJ 152 (Tübingen: Mohr Siebeck, 2013); Timothy Lim, "Deuteronomy in the Judaism of the Second Temple Period," in *Deuteronomy in the New Testament: The New Testament and the Scriptures of Israel*, ed. Maarten J. J. Menken and Steve Moyise, LNTS 358 (London: T&T Clark, 2007), 6–26.

8. See, e.g., Konrad Schmid and Raymond Person, eds., *Deuteronomy in the Pentateuch, Hexateuch, and the Deuteronomistic History*, FAT 2/56 (Tübingen: Mohr Siebeck, 2012); Eckhart Otto and Reinhard Achenbach, eds., *Das Deuteronomium zwischen Pentateuch und deuteronomistischem Geschichtswerk*, FRLANT 206 (Göttingen: Vandenhoeck & Ruprecht, 2004).

9. Jeffrey H. Tigay, *Deuteronomy: The Traditional Hebrew Text with the New JPS Translation*, JPS Torah Commentary (Philadelphia: Jewish Publication Society, 1996), xxvi.

Studies on the reception of Deuteronomy among the Dead Sea Scrolls, such as those by Sidnie White Crawford on 4QReworkedPentateuch and the Temple Scroll, "testify to the importance and popularity of the book of Deuteronomy in the Second Temple period."[10] It is impossible to present here a comprehensive overview of Deuteronomy's influence in early Jewish literature due to its broad and dense intertexture of citations and allusions. The Dead Sea Scrolls, Philo of Alexandria, and Josephus all cited or alluded numerous times to virtually every single chapter of Deuteronomy.[11] In an attempt to provide a manageable and representative survey, we will rather briefly identify four main trajectories of Deuteronomy in terms of its tradition-reception, namely, (1) as Jewish law book, (2) as compendium on the Jewish cult and worship practice, (3) as pedagogical instruction manual, and (4) as an eschatological tractate.

Deuteronomy as a Jewish Law Book

The Decalogue

The Decalogue (Deut 5:6-21) closely connects the elements of early Jewish doctrine and ethics. Fragments of the text are retained among the Dead Sea Scrolls with some witnesses being closer to the MT (4Q37; 4Q134; 4Q142), others closer to the LXX (4Q128; 4Q137), and others in-between (1Q13; 4Q41; 4Q129). The Nash Papyrus (ca. 150 BCE) serves as an example that the Decalogue might have circulated originally in combination with the Shema (Deut 6:4-6) as a unified collection (see also the Mishnah, Tamid 5:1).[12] Philo elaborates and comments extensively on

---

10. Crawford, "Reading Deuteronomy in the Second Temple Period," in *Reading the Present in the Qumran Library: The Perception of the Contemporary by Means of Scriptural Interpretations*, ed. Kristin de Troyer and Armin Lange, SymS 30 (Atlanta: Society of Biblical Literature, 2005), 127-40. For Deuteronomy among the Dead Sea Scrolls, see, e.g., Joshua M. Matson, "Employing Deuteronomy: An Analysis of the Quotations and Allusions to Deuteronomy in the Dead Sea Scrolls" (master's thesis, Trinity Western University, 2015). For the Temple Scroll, see also David Lincicum, "Paul and the Temple Scroll: Reflections on a Shared Engagement with Deuteronomy," in *"What Does the Scripture Say?" Studies in the Function of Scripture in Early Judaism and Christianity*, vol. 2, *The Letters and Liturgical Traditions*, ed. Craig A. Evans and H. Daniel Zacharias, LNTS 470 (London: T&T Clark, 2012), 51-69.

11. For the Dead Sea Scrolls, see David L. Washburn, *A Catalog of Biblical Passages in the Dead Sea Scrolls*, TCS 2 (Atlanta: Society of Biblical Literature, 2002), 56-75. For Philo, see Francis H. Colson and J. W. Earp, *Philo: The Embassy to Gaius; Indices to Vols. I-X*, LCL (Cambridge: Harvard University 1962), 249-59. For Josephus, see *Josephus*, trans. Henry St. John Thackery et al., 13 vols., LCL (Cambridge: Harvard University Press, 1926-1965); William Whiston, *The Works of Josephus: Complete and Unabridged* (Peabody, MA: Hendrickson, 1987).

12. Martin McNamara, *Targum and Testament Revisited: Aramaic Paraphrases of the Hebrew Bible: A Light on the New Testament*, 2nd ed. (Grand Rapids: Eerdmans, 2010), 68.

the Ten Commandments in his *De decalogo*. Particularly the second table of the Decalogue (Exod 20:12–16; Deut 5:16–20) is cited by Philo (*Det.* 52; *Spec.* 2.261). Philo also presents expositions on the commands about parent respect, theft, false witness, and coveting in his four-volume *De specialibus legibus*. Intertextual connections with several of the individual commandments surface again in Second Temple Jewish literature. The fifth commandment (honoring one's parents), for instance, is cited by Philo (*Det.* 52; *Spec.* 2.261), Josephus (*Ag. Ap.* 2.206), and Pseudo-Philo, LAB 11.9–10.[13] Josephus, too, in discussing the Jewish precepts, includes sanctity of marriage (cf. *Against Apion*) as a reflection of the adultery commandment. Several other allusions have further been identified:[14]

Table 33.1. References and Allusions to the Ten Commandments

Commandment		References and allusions
Second	Idolatry	Exod 20:4–6 / Deut 5:8–10 = Jub. 20:8; 23:31; CD B XX, 21–22
Third	Lord's Name	Exod 20:7 / Deut 5:11 = 1 En. 60:6
Fourth	Sabbath	Exod 20:8–11 / Deut 5:12–15 = Neh 9:14; 13:22; Ps 136:11–12; 2 Macc 15:3–4; Jub. 2:26 [4Q218]; CD A VI, 18 [4Q266]
Fifth	Parents	Exod 20:12 / Deut 5:16 = 4Q416; 4Q418; Mal 1:6; Sir 3:1–16; 7:27; Tob 4:3; Jub. 7:20; 35:12–13; Let. Aris. 228; Sib. Or. 3:593–94
Tenth	Covetousness	Exod 20:17 / Deut 5:21 = 4 Macc 2:5; T. Iss. 7:3

Lex talionis: *The Law of Retaliation*

The eighteenth-century BCE retaliation law from the Code of Hammurabi, king of Babylon, found its way into Israel's Torah. It is especially the reception of the two lines on the blinding of an eye and the fracturing of the bone of another *awīlum* that is noticeable in the Torah. The retaliation of "eye for eye, tooth for tooth" is cited in Deut 19:21; Exod 21:24; and Lev 24:20. The text is also retained in 4Q365 and probably in 4Q35. It is interesting that Philo nowhere refers to this law in his extant corpus of literature. An allusion might be present in Josephus (*Ant.* 4.278: "the law judging it equitable that life should go for life").

---

13. Bradley H. McLean, *Citations and Allusions to Jewish Scripture in Early Christian and Jewish Writings through 180 C.E.* (Lewiston, NY: Mellen, 1992), 35.

14. Armin Lange and Matthias Weigold, *Biblical Quotations and Allusions in Second Temple Jewish Literature*, JAJSup 5 (Göttingen: Vandenhoeck & Ruprecht, 2011), 97–98.

Deuteronomy as Compendium on Jewish Cult and Worship Practice

The Shema Yisrael as Daily Prayer

The Shema Yisrael (Deut 6:4) is a brief creedal statement and one of the most significant expressions of Jewish identity. Being recited by Jews in the morning and evening as a daily prayer, it is a clear confessional statement that expresses in its repetition the doctrinal belief in the oneness of Israel's God. The second-century BCE Letter of Aristeas (§160) confirms that priests were reciting the Shema during their temple service.[15] The Shema survives among the Dead Sea Scrolls on witnesses that show closer proximity to the MT (Mur4; 4Q43; 4Q130). Allusions to the Shema have further been identified in Zech 14:9 and Bar 3:9.

The Sabbath, Sabbatical Year, and Pilgrimage Festivals

The Sabbath (Deut 5:12–15; Exod 20:8–11), Sabbatical Year (Deut 15:1–18; Exod 21:2–6; 23:10–12; Lev 25), and pilgrimage festivals (Passover, Festival of the Booths and of the Weeks; Deut 16:1–17; Exod 23:10–19; 34:18–24) found important places on the Jewish cultic calendar based on their substantiation and instructions for implementation in the Torah.[16] Some scholars have understood Deut 31:9–13 to connect the reading of the law primarily with the Sabbatical Year and secondarily with the Feast of Tents (Sukkoth) in that year.[17]

Allusions to the Sabbath abound in Second Temple Jewish literature with representative occurrences in Neh 9:14; 13:22; Ps 136:11–12; 2 Macc 15:3–4; Jub. 2:26 (4Q218); CD A VI, 18 (// 4Q266); and CD A X, 16–17. Allusions to the Sabbatical Year are present in Neh 10:31; 4 Macc 2:8; and the Dead Sea Scrolls (11Q13; 4Q16; 4Q17; 4Q18; 4Q19), while allusions to the pilgrimage festivals occur in 2 Chronicles (30:5; 35:13; 8:12–13) and in Tob 1:6. Prescriptions of particular

---

15. Douglas S. Huffman and Jamie N. Hausherr, "Shema, The," in *The Lexham Bible Dictionary*, ed. John D. Barry et al. (Bellingham, WA: Lexham Press, 2016).

16. See Christensen, *Deuteronomy 1–21:9*; and Christensen, *Deuteronomy 21:10–34:11*, WBC 6B (Nashville: Nelson, 2002). He understands Deuteronomy as a didactic poem within a liturgical setting. See also Donn F. Morgan, "The So-Called Cultic Calendars in the Pentateuch (Ex 23:10–19, 34:18–26, Lev 23, Nu 28–29, Deut 16:1–17): A Morphological and Typological Study" (PhD diss., Claremont, 1974). For the calendar, see Martin G. Abegg, "The Calendar at Qumran," in *The Judaism of Qumran: A Systemic Reading of the Dead Sea Scrolls*, vol. 5 of *Judaism in Late Antiquity*, ed. Alan J. Avery-Peck, Jacob Neusner, and Bruce D. Chilton, HdO 56 (Leiden: Brill, 2001), 145–71; Roger T. Beckwith, *Calendar and Chronology, Jewish and Christian: Biblical, Intertestamental and Patristic Studies* (Leiden: Brill, 2001).

17. Roland de Vaux, *Ancient Israel: Its Life and Institutions*, 2nd ed. (London: Darton, Longman & Todd, 1980), 502.

celebrations or specific festivals are further alluded to in Josh 5:10-12; 1 Sam 20:5, 24-27; 2 Kgs 23:21-23; Isa 1:13-14; Amos 8:5; Zech 14:16-19; Ezra 3:1-6; 6:19-22; Neh 8:14-18. Jubilees, too, gives instructions for and accounts of the festivals (cf. Jub. 6:17-31; 15:1-2; 16:20-31; 22:1-9; 32:4-9, 27-29; 34:18-19; 44:1-4; 49).[18] The Feast of Tents "was the most important and the most crowded of the three annual pilgrimages to the sanctuary," and referred to by Josephus as the "holiest and the greatest of Hebrew feasts" (*Ant.* 8.100).[19]

Song of Moses

The Song of Moses (Deut 32:1-43) became one of the most well-known and important hymns in the Jewish and early Christian traditions.[20] Its history is complicated and represents a complex textual tradition.[21] It is assumed that "the so-called Song of Moses is a long, widely ranging poem which came into existence quite independently of Deuteronomy."[22] Its composition in Deuteronomy is dated on the basis of its linguistic characteristics during the transitional period in poetic Hebrew between the tenth and eighth century BCE.[23] Deuteronomy 32:40-43 presents Israel's God as "warrior" and describes the last revelation of God for judgment to take place.[24]

Three pieces of evidence testify to the importance of the *Canticum Mosis* for early Judaism. These include the references in Philo and the Testament (also known as Apocalypse) of Moses, which is framed around the end of the book (Deut 31-34) with evidence of an existing second-century BCE original of the Testament.[25] This is in itself an indication of the importance that this section in Deuteronomy had for early Judaism. The third is to be found in 4 Macc 18:18-19

---

18. James R. Davila, *Liturgical Works*, ECDSS 6 (Grand Rapids: Eerdmans, 2000), 17.
19. Quotation from de Vaux, *Ancient Israel*, 495; Everett Ferguson, *Backgrounds of Early Christianity*, 2nd ed. (Grand Rapids: Eerdmans, 1993), 525.
20. See Gert J. Steyn, *A Quest for the Assumed Septuagint Vorlage of the Explicit Quotations in Hebrews*, FRLANT 235 (Göttingen: Vandenhoeck & Ruprecht, 2011), 57-72.
21. Martin Karrer, *Der Brief an die Hebräer: Kapitel 1,1-5,10*, ÖTK 20.1 (Gütersloh: Gütersloher Verlagshaus, 2002), 135-36.
22. Gerhard von Rad, *Deuteronomy: A Commentary*, OTL (London: SCM, 1988), 195.
23. Solomon Nigosian, "Linguistic Patterns of Deuteronomy 32," *Bib* 78, no. 2 (1997): 206-24.
24. H. A. J. Kruger, "A Sword over His Head or in His Hand? Luke 22,35-38," in *Scriptures in the Gospels*, ed. Christopher Tuckett, BETL 131 (Leuven: Leuven University Press, 1997), 598-99. The other places where God is described as warrior are Exod 15:3; Ps 24:8; Isa 27:1; 42:13; 51:9; 59:17; 63:3; 66:16; Ezek 21:3, 4, 5.
25. For Philo, see *Det.*, 114 (Deut 32:13); *Leg.* 3, 105 (Deut 32:34, 35); *Plant.* 59 (Deut 32:7-9). For the Apocalypse of Moses, see John Priest, "Testament of Moses (First Century A.D.),"

(probably written during the first century CE), where the mother of the seven sons reminds them about the importance of the Song of Moses. This case has been used as evidence that the *Canticum Mosis* was sung during the Jewish diaspora around the turn of the century.[26]

Connections between the *Canticum Mosis* and the largely hypothetical cultic ritual of the "Covenant Festival" were made in the past. This covenant festival was seen to be an annually repeated sacred act of the renewal of the covenant which might have attestation in the Qumran Manual of Discipline/Rule of the Community (1QS II, 15).[27] Alfons Weiser states that "the description of the liturgy used by the sect of Qumran at the annual celebration of the feast of the renewal of the Covenant, however, enables us to draw from it valuable conclusions as to the existence of corresponding elements in the Old Testament tradition" and refers to Deut 32 among other texts.[28]

Some scholars have identified structural and thematic similarities between Deut 32 and Joel 1–2, while others consider the *Canticum Mosis* as background for Ps 58 with intertextual connections to Ps 82:2–4; Mic 2:1; Ps 3:8; Job 3:16; 11:16; 27:21; Mal 3:18.[29] In fact, the Song of Moses served as the source text of several later scriptural intertexts.[30]

Deuteronomy as Pedagogical Instruction Manual

The citation formula of the Shema was later expanded to include the lines directly following it (6:5–9). The expansion embraced the great commandment (Deut 6:5; see also 10:12–13), which is not only closely linked with the doctrinal statement about monotheism but particularly an ethical statement as behavioral consequence of the believer's relation and attitude to God. The expansion also incorporated the obligation to learn and teach the Torah (Deut 6:6–9; see also 5:1; 11:19–21; 1QS X, 10). It is this instruction of Deut 6:8–9 that led to the practice of presenting the text of Deut 6:4–9 (with Deut 11:13–21; Exod 13:1–10, 11–16)

OTP 1:919–34. For dating, see James L. Kugel and Rowan A. Greer, *Early Biblical Interpretation* (Philadelphia: Westminster, 1986), 76.

26. See Heinrich Schneider, "Die biblischen Oden im christlichen Altertum," *Bib* 30, no. 1 (1949): 28–65.

27. Cf., e.g., Alfons Weiser, *The Psalms: A Commentary*, OTL (London: SCM, 1982).

28. Weiser, *Psalms*, 35.

29. For ties to Joel, see Douglas Stuart, *Hosea–Jonah*, WBC 31 (Dallas: Word, 1987), 228. For Psalms, see Beat Weber, *Werkbuch Psalmen I: Die Psalmen 1 bis 72* (Stuttgart: Kohlhammer, 2001), 260.

30. Wilhelm Dittmar, *Vetus Testamentum in Novo: Die alttestamentlichen Parallelen des Neuen Testaments im Wortlaut der Urtexte und der Septuaginta*, 2 vols. (Göttingen: Vandenhoeck & Ruprecht, 1903), 304.

in tefillin and mezuzahs as a reminder of Israel's covenant relationship. There are also indications in early Judaism—represented by Philo—that Deut 6:5 was linked with Lev 19:18.[31] The Shema functions as a kind of literary hinge in Deuteronomy by connecting the Decalogue (Deut 5) and the great commandment (Deut 6) with each other.[32] Luke L. Cheung reminds us that "there is a strong connection between loving God and keeping his commandments throughout the Jewish tradition (e.g., Deut. 6:5–9; 10:12–13; 11:22; Neh. 1:5; Sir. 2:15; 14:1; Pss. Sol. 14:1–2; with the Decalogues: Exod. 20:6; Deut. 5:10; cf. 1 Jn 4:21; 5:2)."[33]

The Eschatological Notion of Deuteronomy

An eschatological dimension is especially present in Deut 18:15–22. In this passage "a prophet like Moses" is promised, who will be raised and in whose mouth God will put his words (18:18). Deuteronomy ends with the reference to "a prophet like Moses" (34:10). Although Deut 18:18–19 was used very seldom in other Jewish literature, it is to be found in 4Q175 and 1QS IX, 11.[34] Despite Philo's possible reference (*Leg.* 1.65) to Deut 18:15, there is no indication that this refers for him to an expected prophet.

Although Deut 18 stands out as perhaps the most prominent eschatological passage, it is certainly not the only place where the eschatological horizon comes into view. Eschatological traces surface especially in the latter part of Deuteronomy, such as in 30:1–10, in the reference ἔσχατον τῶν ἡμερῶν (31:29), the *Canticum Mosis*, and maybe even in the blessing of Moses (Deut 33).

Summary

This very brief survey about Deuteronomy's role in early Jewish literature makes it vividly clear that its impact on this literature can hardly be overestimated. Its influence dovetailed into endless allusions, numerous citations, and many thematic trajectories. Its theological, ethical (law codes), cultic (liturgic elements), pedagogical, and eschatological facets made a lasting impression on the written tradition and its execution in everyday praxis.

---

31. Craig S. Keener, *The IVP Bible Background Commentary: New Testament* (Downers Grove, IL: InterVarsity Press, 1993), Matt 22:34–40.

32. See also Jack R. Lundbom, *Deuteronomy: A Commentary* (Grand Rapids: Eerdmans, 2013).

33. Cheung, *The Genre, Composition and Hermeneutics of the Epistle of James*, PBTM (Carlisle: Paternoster, 2003), 186.

34. The readings of 4Q175 and that of the MT are identical with the exception of וידבר for the ודבר of the MT.

The early Christian movement, as a new branch of Judaism, would proceed within this Deuteronomic framework, but it would realign the parameters, reinterpret its theology and ethics, while rethinking and readapting its cultic fabric. Christianity's paradigmatic shift would create increasing tension with traditional Judaism, contributing to an ever-widening gap as it defined its own identity from Deuteronomy as one of the most important Scriptures of Israel.

Deuteronomy in the New Testament

At least thirty-six explicit Deuteronomy citations have been identified in fifty-four places in the Greek New Testament.[35] It is explicitly cited in some Pauline literature (Galatians, 1–2 Corinthians, Romans, 1 Timothy), the synoptic writers (Q, Mark, Matthew, Luke-Acts), and some of the General Epistles (James, Hebrews).[36] Deuteronomy citations are, however, very rare in the Johannine writings and totally absent in the rest of the Pauline literature (1–2 Thessalonians, Philippians, Colossians, Philemon, 2 Timothy, Titus) and remainder of the General Epistles (1–2 Peter, Jude).

Table 33.2. Deuteronomy in the New Testament

Deuteronomy	New Testament	Deuteronomy	New Testament
4:24	Heb 12:29	17:6	Heb 10:28
4:35	Mark 12:32	17:7	1 Cor 5:13
5:16	Mark 7:10; Matt 15:4; 19:19; Eph 6:2	18:15	Act 3:22; 7:37
5:16–20	Mark 10:19; Luke 18:20	19:15	2 Cor 13:1; Matt 18:16
5:17	Rom 13:9; Matt 5:21; Jas 2:11	19:21	Matt 5:38
5:17–20	Rom 13:9; Matt 19:18	21:23	Gal 3:13
5:17–21	Rom 13:9	25:4	1 Cor 9:9; 1 Tim 5:18
5:18	Rom 13:9; Matt 5:27	27:26	Gal 3:10, 13
5:21	Rom 7:7	29:3	Rom 11:8
6:4	Mark 12:29	29:17	Heb 12:15
6:5	Mark 12:30, 33; Matt 22:37; Luke 10:27	30:12	Rom 10:6

---

35. NA[28], 843–45.
36. For a comprehensive commentary on the New Testament citations, see G. K. Beale and D. A. Carson, eds., *Commentary on the New Testament Use of the Old Testament* (Grand Rapids: Baker Academic, 2007).

6:13	Matt 4:10; Luke 4:8	30:14	Rom 10:8
6:16	Matt 4:7; Luke 4:12	31:6, 8	Heb 13:5
8:3	Matt 4:4; Luke 4:4	32:4	Rev 15:3
9:3	Heb 12:29	32:21	Rom 10:19
8:17 / 9:4	Rom 10:6	32:35	Rom 12:19; Heb 10:30
9:19	Heb 12:21	32:36	Heb 10:30
10:2	Matt 4:10; Luke 4:8	32:43	Rom 15:10; Heb 1:6

Many of these Deuteronomy citations appeared already in documents that predated the New Testament. Matthew has the most citations from Deuteronomy, and all of them had already been cited in literature that predates him.[37] This might point to common knowledge regarding established scriptural (Deuteronomic) traditions in especially Q, Mark, and Pauline exegetical traditions. The same applies to all the Deuteronomy citations in Luke's Gospel. Those in Acts (Acts 3:22; 7:37), however, occur there for the first time.

Hebrews is usually seen as one of the New Testament books that cites the most from Deuteronomy.[38] However, a closer look at those previously identified "citations," confirms, strictly speaking, actually only four clearly identified marked citations.[39] At least four other instances usually identified to be citations could rather be counted as conceptual allusions (all in Heb 12), with a fifth one (Deut 17:6 in Heb 10:28) as an intended verbal allusion.[40] As with Matthew and Luke, also all the Deuteronomy citations already appeared prior to Hebrews in early Christian literature that predates it except for the very last citation, which was used by the early Jewish writer Philo (*Conf.* 166). Hebrews contains the citations closest to the beginning and to the end of Deuteronomy, and all its Deuteronomy citations are short and fragmentary. Other New Testament books that also frequently cite from Deuteronomy are Romans and Mark's Gospel.

Given the fact that it has been noted in the previous section that Deuteronomy served as a law code, it comes as no surprise that the Jewish Shema and the Decalogue occur in many of the New Testament books that cite from Deuteronomy.

---

37. Predated by the Pauline letters (Romans, 2 Corinthians), Mark, and Q.

38. See Susan E. Docherty, *The Use of the Old Testament in Hebrews: A Case Study in Early Jewish Bible Interpretation*, WUNT 2/260 (Tübingen: Mohr Siebeck, 2009); David M. Allen, *Deuteronomy and Exhortation in Hebrews: A Study in Narrative Re-presentation*, WUNT 2/238 (Tübingen: Mohr Siebeck, 2008).

39. Deut 32:43 (Heb 1:6); Deut 32:35–6 (Heb 10:30–31); Deut 9:19 (Heb 12:21); Deut 31:6 (Heb 13:5). See Gert J. Steyn, "Deuteronomy in Hebrews," in Menken and Moyise, *Deuteronomy*, 153.

40. Deut 20:3 (Heb 12:3); Deut 29:17 (Heb 12:15); Deut 4:11–12 (Heb 12:18–19); Deut 4:24/9:3 (Heb 12:29). See Steyn, "Deuteronomy," 154.

The Shema Yisrael is furthermore combined with the great commandment as an early Christian pedagogical instruction. But the status and function of Deuteronomy as a compendium on the Jewish cult and worship practices were also noted. It is therefore no surprise to see how Deuteronomy unfolds as a template for early Christian ritual practices—especially in relation to the Jewish festivals and the liturgical role of the Song of Moses. Most fascinating to observe, however, is the deployment of the eschatological notion of Deuteronomy, which serves in the New Testament as a lens through which the Christ events unfold in a new interpretative manner. As it is impossible to discuss all Deuteronomy occurrences in the New Testament, we will pursue these four trajectories in the New Testament as we limit our attention to some selected citations closely linked to each of these.

A Law Book as Orientation for Christian Ethics

As an established ethical code, Deuteronomy naturally formed the basis of orientation for early Christian ethics. With clear references to the Decalogue and the *lex talionis*, a new direction is taken within its christological reception.

The Decalogue

Without repeating here previous studies on the order, structure, and formulation of the commandments in the New Testament, it is important to note that several versions of the Decalogue could be identified, such as the parallels in Exod 20 and Deut 5 and their versions in Codices Alexandrinus and Vaticanus.[41] The New Testament citations of the commandments can all be traced back clearly to these different versions.

The second table of the Decalogue (Exod 20:12–16; Deut 5:16–20) is cited by Paul, the Synoptics, and James. Among these, Mark (7:10a; 10:19) and Matthew (15:4a; 19:18–19) cite five commandments (parent respect, murder, adultery, theft, false witness), while Paul (Rom 13:9), Luke 18:20; and James 2:11 only list the latter four.[42] The citation in Mark 7:10a and Matt 15:4a concerns only the parent-respect commandment and belongs to the broader context of Mark 7:1–23 on purity and impurity. The second part of the citation, which deals with the consequences

---

41. Gert J. Steyn, "Pretexts of the Second Table of the Decalogue and Early Christian Intertexts," *Neot* 30, no. 2 (1996): 451–64; William R. G. Loader, *The Septuagint, Sexuality and the New Testament: Case Studies on the Impact of the LXX in Philo and the New Testament* (Grand Rapids: Eerdmans, 2004), 15–17.

42. See Gert J. Steyn, "A Comparison of the Septuagint Textual Form in the Torah Quotations Common to Philo of Alexandria and the Gospels of Mark and Matthew," in *XIV Congress of the IOSCS, Helsinki 2010*, ed. Melvin K. H. Peters, SCS 59 (Atlanta: Society of Biblical Literature, 2013), 605–24.

of the commandment, shows some interesting features. The two LXX versions (Exod 20:12; Deut 5:16)—in contrast to the other commandments—formulate the consequences in a positive statement, whereas Mark 7:10a and Matt 15:4a present it in a negative statement. The Gospels most probably represent here an alternative early Christian tradition with the negative consequences should the commandment not be obeyed.

Reinterpreting the Law of Retaliation

The New Testament reception of the *lex talionis* (Deut 19:21) is only found in Jesus's citation in Matt 5:38, when he reinterprets it (Matt 5:39–42) in the Sermon on the Mount. The *lex talionis* "was given as a directive for the court, not (as in the misunderstanding Jesus counters in Matt. 5:38) as a permission for private revenge."[43] Matthew's citation follows the identical readings of LXX Exod 21:24; Lev 24:20; and Deut 19:21, although he has editorially linked the "eye for eye" part with καί ("and") to the "tooth for tooth" part. Exodus 21:24 lists eight bodily harms (life, eye, tooth, hand, foot, burn, wound, bruise), while Lev 24:18–20 lists only four (life, fracture, eye, tooth), and Deut 19:21 lists five (life, eye, tooth, hand, foot). Matthew, in turn, selected only the two that are explicitly linked to the face (eye, tooth). The Matthean Jesus extends the reaction to include the other cheek, the cloak, a second mile, beggars, and borrowers.

Early Christian Pedagogical Instruction

As an established pedagogical instruction, Deuteronomy naturally formed the basis of orientation for early Christian instruction. Probably rooted in a Jesus logion, the New Testament writers found their "golden rule" in Jesus's citation of the Shema itself—now combined with the great commandment of Lev 19:18.

The Citation of the Shema Yisrael and the Great Commandment

A citation from Deut 6:4–5 (+ Lev 19:18) surfaces in Jesus's discussion of the great commandment in Mark 12:28–34 (// Matt 22:36–40).[44] In comparison to Mark's version, the variation of Matthew (22:37)—keeping "mind" but dropping "strength"—has been explained by some, though unconvincingly, to be the result

---

43. J. Alec Motyer, "Judgment," in *New Dictionary of Biblical Theology*, ed. T. Desmond Alexander and Brian S. Rosner (Downers Grove, IL: InterVarsity Press, 2000), 613.

44. Cf. Erik Waaler, *The "Shema" and the First Commandment in First Corinthians: An Intertextual Approach to Paul's Re-reading of Deuteronomy*, WUNT 2/253 (Tübingen: Mohr Siebeck, 2008).

of Matthew being a gentile.⁴⁵ Aside from this variation, there are two significant additions to the citation of Deut 6:4-5 in the synoptic tradition, namely the phrases "with all your mind" and "to love your neighbor as yourself"—probably taken from Lev 19:18 and thus presenting the combination as a composite citation with regard to the love commandment. The two commandments are linked with the key word "love." The New Testament writers probably traced the origins of the "golden rule" back to a logion in the Jesus tradition that contained Jesus's own summary of the law. The Didache also combines Deut 6:5 and Lev 19:18, where "the 'Two Ways' (Did. 1.2) begins with a citation of the two commandments to love God (Deut 6:5) and to love your neighbor (Lev 19:18) as refracted through Jesus's teaching."⁴⁶

Deuteronomy's Eschatological Notion as a Lens for the Christ

With established eschatological dimensions in Deuteronomy, New Testament writers such as Luke, Paul, and the author of Hebrews used it as an eschatological lens to interpret (retrospectively and in retrodiction) the Jesus events as the unfolding of God's plan of salvation.

The Testing of God's Son

The so-called temptation, or testing, of God's Son is briefly referred to by Mark 1:12-13 without any specific temptations or explicit citations.⁴⁷ Matthew 4:1-11 and Luke 4:1-13, however, present a longer version that includes three temptations with citations from Deut 6 and 8.⁴⁸ Matthew and Luke differ in wording from each other on some points as the result of each writer's own stylistic preferences. However, the main point of difference between their accounts is to be found in the structure of the motif, where the order of the temptations is changed. Matthew's second temptation became the third in Luke's account and vice versa. Focusing on the Lukan account, Luke's order could be explained in the context of Deut 6-8. The Lukan context makes it clear that the original compiler of this nar-

---

45. Paul Foster, "Why Did Matthew Get the Shema Wrong? A Study of Matthew 22:37," *JBL* 122, no. 2 (2003): 309-33.
46. Everett Ferguson, "Old Testament in Apostolic Fathers," in *Dictionary of the Later New Testament and Its Developments*, ed. Ralph P. Martin and Peter H. Davids (Downers Grove, IL: InterVarsity Press, 1997), 827.
47. For the temptation, see Brandon D. Crowe, *The Obedient Son: Deuteronomy and Christology in the Gospel of Matthew*, BZNW 188 (Berlin: de Gruyter, 2012).
48. See, e.g., David S. New, *Old Testament Quotations in the Synoptic Gospels, and the Two-Document Hypothesis*, SCS 37 (Atlanta: Scholars Press, 1993), 54-59.

rative surely knew the motif of Israel's wandering and testing in the desert. Luke reapplies this motif with the ancient rhetorical technique *mimēsis* (or *imitatio*) and applies it to Jesus. The testing of Jesus as God's Son (Luke 4:1–13) is now based on the context of the testing of Israel as God's son (Deut 6–8). The following elements between the two versions became prominent and emphasize the linguistic similarities between the two versions (better observed in the Greek texts):[49]

Table 33.3. Deuteronomy in Luke's Version of the Temptation of Jesus

Narrative element	Deuteronomy	Luke's Gospel
Situational context		
In the desert and guidance of God	8:2	4:1
Forty years/days	8:4	4:2
Testing	8:2	4:2
Son of God	8:5	4:3, 9
Bread		
Bread temptation	8:3	4:2–4
Jesus's citation 1	8:3	4:4
Promised land		
Promised land for God's son	8:7–10	4:5–6
Condition of the promise—obey God!	8:11–14, 17–20	4:7
Satan demands worship by God's Son	6:12	
Jesus's citation 2	6:13	4:8
God's protection		
Citing LXX Ps 90:11–12, Satan debates with Jesus in a typical Jewish midrash on God's protection		
Jesus's citation 3	6:16	4:12

The three Deuteronomy citations (6:13, 16; 8:3) might thus be labeled "representative quotation"—which means that only a phrase is cited in the new text, but the whole original context (Deut 6:10–16; 8:2–20) is supposed.[50] It surely is no coincidence that the New Testament temptation narrative alludes to and cites from the section immediately following (Deut 6:10–25) the Shema with its

---

49. Gert J. Steyn, "Luke's Use of Mimesis? Re-opening the Debate," in Tuckett, *Scriptures in the Gospels*, 551–58; and Steyn, "Intertextual Similarities between Septuagint Pretexts and Luke's Gospel," *Neot* 24, no. 2 (1990): 229–46.

50. Henry M. Shires, *Finding the Old Testament in the New* (Philadelphia: Westminster, 1974), 6.

expansion of the great commandment (Deut 6:5–9). It points to the theological importance of Jesus's obedience as Son to God alone—an eschatological rewriting of the disobedience of God's son Israel during the exodus in the desert.

A Prophet like Moses

There might be allusions to Deut 18:15 present in Mark 9:4, 7 (// Matt 17:5; Luke 9:35), Luke 7:39; 24:25; John 1:21; and 5:46. Leaving those cases here, the paraphrased version of Deut 18:15–20 in Acts 3:22–23 needs our attention.[51] Deuteronomy 18:15, 18 is to be found once more in Acts in a shorter citation in Acts 7:37. Further striking intratextual resemblances occur between Acts 3:18, 21–24; and Luke 24:25–27.

Acts 3:21 refers to the words of God, spoken in the distant past, through his prophets. Moses's words are used to indicate that, as God raised him up, so will God also raise up a prophet like Moses. It is unclear whether this motif of "the Mosaic prophet" was a pre-Lukan concept that was passed on as early church tradition or whether it was Luke himself who applied the concept to Jesus. It is striking that nowhere else is Jesus explicitly referred to as the eschatological "prophet like Moses."

The composite citation in Acts 3:22–23 is introduced by a single introductory formula. The unit in Acts 3:22–23 is the combination of several conflated phrases, mainly from two different text units, traditionally accepted to be Deut 18:15–20 and Lev 23:29. It is assumed that Acts 3:23 is most likely based on Lev 23:29, with phrases taken from Deut 18:19 and probably from Exod 30:33/Lev 18:29 due to the syntactical similarities between the phrases.[52] Acts 3:22 cites almost verbatim from Deut 18:15 LXX, while Acts 3:23 is a reminder to listen to the words of the prophet (Deut 18:19)—which Luke adapts to now read "*that* prophet." There are two interesting differences between the Hebrew of the MT and the LXX translation. First, whereas the MT and 4Q175 read "*my* words" (דְּבָרַי), the LXX has "*his* words" (τῶν λόγων αὐτοῦ).[53] The LXX reading is also supported by the Samaritan Pentateuch. Second, the reference to "the prophet" is absent in the MT but present in 4Q175 and in Deut 18:19 LXX. There is no LXX textual support in favor of the changes in Acts 3:23, and they can relatively safely be ascribed to the hand of Luke.

---

51. See Gert J. Steyn, *Septuagint Quotations in the Context of the Petrine and Pauline Speeches of the Acta Apostolorum*, CBET 12 (Kampen: Kok Pharos, 1995), 129–58.

52. For citations from Deut 18:19 among the Dead Sea Scrolls, see Deut 18:18–19 (4Q175) and Deut 18:18–20 (4Q158); Lange and Weigold, *Biblical Quotations*, 104.

53. So also Karrer and Kraus, *Erläuterungen*, 572.

New Testament textual changes are all most likely due to the hand of Luke as part of stylistic and contextual adaptation to the new audience. The cited phrases were carefully selected from their original contexts, and those in the cited section that did not fit the new context were omitted on contextual grounds. Stylistic changes were also made, such as the personal pronouns, which were changed to fit the audience to whom this composite citation was directed, and the transposition that placed "prophet" at the beginning and thus in an emphatic position. It is interesting that although this cited section is not part of "the Prophets," Luke uses it similarly to the prophetic material. The bridge is already made within the broader context of Deut 18:15–22. Luke finds in those words some kind of foretelling, with Moses typifying himself as "a prophet" (Acts 3:22). For Luke, then, Moses is a prophet, just as Joel, Isaiah, and the other prophets were. The cited phrases from Deut 18 are now presented as an example of such a promise of the times of restoration, as implied in the previous verses. The first part of the composite citation is presented as a fulfilled promise made to Moses (Acts 3:22a), while the last two parts—containing the as yet unfulfilled aspects of the promise—have the nature of an appeal to the listeners (Acts 3:22b–23).

Although space does not allow to point to further traces of an eschatological reading of Deuteronomy in the New Testament, the brief discussion of the *Canticum Mosis* below draws attention to how Paul seems to have read Deut 32 eschatologically in Rom 9–11—especially in the christological text of Rom 10:5–8. Paul's eschatological reading seems, however, mostly to be about negotiating the status of gentiles within his communities.

The Crucifixion

The two citations from Deut 27:26 in Gal 3:10 and Deut 21:23 in Gal 3:13 are probably the earliest engagements with Deuteronomy in New Testament literature.[54] We will focus here only on the latter; Jesus's crucifixion was problematic within the theological framework of early Christianity. It communicated the policy of no tolerance by the Roman Empire against anyone who had not complied with their laws—whether due to criminal offenses or political resistance. The tragic end of a Jewish messiah, who was expected to liberate his people and to triumph over foreign rulership, would have been difficult to explain to outsiders by those devoted followers of this movement.

The most acceptable reason for Paul's selection of Deut 21:23 points to his Jewish exegetical method of *gezerah shewah* in Gal 3:13, where verbal analogy is used

---

54. Similarly, David Lincicum, *Paul and the Early Jewish Encounter with Deuteronomy*, WUNT 2/284 (Tübingen: Mohr Siebeck, 2010), 142.

with the same words being applied to two separate cases.⁵⁵ With or without any connection to a possible debate about the negative perception of the crucifixion, Paul links the law about those who hang "upon a tree" with the event of Jesus's crucifixion.⁵⁶ Just prior to quoting this passage, Paul makes the statement in Gal 3:12: "Christ redeemed us from the curse of the law [ἐκ τῆς κατάρας τοῦ νόμου] by becoming a curse for us [γενόμενος ὑπὲρ ἡμῶν κατάρα]." The citation from Deut 21:23 is then introduced with the well-known and common introductory formula regularly used by Paul: "for it is written." Introductory formulas are powerful indicators of hermeneutical activity by an author. This indicates the authority of the Torah for Paul, on the one hand, and his intention, on the other hand, to explicitly draw attention to this specific passage. By citing from a Greek version of his Scriptures (LXX), he links the "curse" referred to in his statement (κατάρα) with that of the citation itself (ἐπικατάρατος). But the actual word used by all the LXX manuscripts at this place reads κεκατηραμένος and not the word ἐπικατάρατος that Paul uses in his citation. Paul's word occurs frequently elsewhere in Deuteronomy, whereas the LXX word is found only once more (Deut 23:4). It is difficult to determine whether this is due to Paul's use of another *Textvorlage* of the same passage or whether this is merely part of his "consistently inconsistent citation of scripture."⁵⁷ Whereas Paul's citation in Gal 3:13 differs from Deut 21:23, his contemporary Philo of Alexandria is very close to the reading of Deut 21:23 LXX in *Post.* 26. Both the LXX and Philo have the perfect participle (the LXX in the nominative, Philo in the accusative) + ὑπὸ θεοῦ, whereas Gal 3:13 uses the adjective ἐπικατάρατος and lacks ὑπὸ θεοῦ. However, in the latter part of the citation, the LXX and Galatians are closer when both use πᾶς + present participle *nominative* (Gal 3:13 with the masculine article)—whereas Philo lacks πᾶς and follows the present participle *accusative* with the article.

The citation from Deut 21:23 is part of Paul's larger argument in Galatians (3:6–14) "that gentiles are children of Abraham through faith in Christ rather than by Torah observance."⁵⁸ Both before and after the citation from Deut 21:23, Paul refers to "Christ"—a denomination adapted from the confession that "Jesus is the Christ." He applies the citation at the end of his citation list as "Christo-

---

55. Ardel Caneday, "'Redeemed from Curse of the Law': The Use of Deut 21:22–23 in Gal 3:13," *TJ* 10 (1989): 187.

56. See also Timothy W. Reardon, "'Hanging on a Tree': Deuteronomy 21.22–23 and the Rhetoric of Jesus' Crucifixion in Acts 15.12–42," *JSNT* 37, no. 4 (2015): 407–31.

57. Andrew H. Wakefield, *Where to Live: The Hermeneutical Significance of Paul's Citations from Scripture in Galatians 3:1–14*, AcBib 14 (Atlanta: Society of Biblical Literature, 2003), 58.

58. "Paul seeks to ground in Scripture his assertion that the Galatian Gentile believers received the Spirit through the hearing of faith and not by law observance (3:2)." Lincicum, *Deuteronomy*, 143.

logical punchline."[59] He addresses the crucifixion by explicitly linking the Christ event to God's curse on everyone who "hangs on a tree." Paul explains Jesus's crucifixion death to be an intermediary role that he took between God and humanity. By means of the act of his substitutionary death on the cross, this messiah (Christ) redeemed Paul and the Galatians from the curse of the law by becoming the curse of God. David Lincicum argues convincingly that, according to Paul, it is "only by enduring the curse himself [that] Christ [was] then able to nullify its power and release the blessing that is the curse's structural opposite."[60] This redemption turned out not to be of a political nature but of a religious nature. In his interpretation of Deut 21:23, Paul does not negate or deny the fact that everyone who is executed by crucifixion is cursed by God according to Deuteronomy, but, according to Paul's interpretation of the passage, precisely because of God's curse of the crucified Jesus, two consequences resulted from that action:[61] (1) it happened so that (ἵνα) in Christ Jesus (ἐν Χριστῷ Ἰησοῦ) Abraham's blessing could now also reach the non-Jews and (2) so that (ἵνα) Paul and the Galatians might receive the promise of the Spirit through faith (διὰ τῆς πίστεως).

There is no reference whatsoever, neither implicit nor explicit, to the crucifixion of a messiah or to Jesus as crucified Christ in the legal code of Deut 21:22–23.[62] However, "the scriptural text functions as a valid piece of legislation, and not as a prophecy of Christ."[63] The hermeneutical link with the death of Jesus by crucifixion is only made in the New Testament by Paul himself, who reinterprets the passage in the light of the Christ event when "Paul found a unique connection between curse and crucifixion."[64] It is correct that "Paul does not say the verse *refers* to Christ ... but indicates that we can learn from it how Christ's death might provide a means of redemption from a curse."[65] Deuteronomy 21:23 clearly is no prediction of Jesus's death, but rather a Pauline interpretation in the light of Jesus's crucifixion.

---

59. Lincicum, *Deuteronomy*, 145.

60. Lincicum, *Deuteronomy*, 146.

61. Cf. Daniel R. Streett, "Cursed by God? Galatians 3:13, Social Status, and Atonement Theory in the Context of Early Jewish Readings of Deuteronomy 21:23," *JSPL* 5, no. 2 (2015): 189–209.

62. So also Christopher D. Stanley: "the verse Paul quotes actually refers to the ancient practice of hanging the dead body of a convicted criminal on a tree for public display, not the redeeming death of a crucified Messiah." *Arguing with Scripture: The Rhetoric of Quotations in the Letters of Paul* (London: Continuum, 2004), 125–26.

63. Paul reflects "on the scriptural connection between public execution and the divine curse," asking "what light that connection sheds on the redemption Christ has achieved." Francis Watson, *Paul and the Hermeneutics of Faith* (London: T&T Clark, 2004), 420–21.

64. Lincicum, *Deuteronomy*, 146.

65. Roy E. Ciampa, "Deuteronomy in Galatians and Romans," in Menken and Moyise, *Deuteronomy*, 103 (emphasis original).

Deuteronomy as Cultic Template for Early Christianity

As an established cultic code, Deuteronomy naturally formed the template for early Christian cultic and liturgical orientation. With clear references to the cultic tradition of the Jewish festivals, as well as the liturgical role of the *Canticum Mosis*, among others, the New Testament writers pursued established traditions, although now with christological dimensions in their reception of these Deuteronomic cultic and liturgical trajectories.

The Sabbatical Year and Festivals

In Deut 31, Moses announces Joshua's future leadership and reminds Israel about God's promises—God, who will never leave nor forsake them (31:6, 8). The Levite priests are then instructed to read the Law at the end of every seventh year (Deut 31:10–12). The two maxims in Heb 13 became clearer against this backdrop of Deut 31: "Do not forget to entertain strangers" (Heb 13:2) and especially that they "should keep their lives free from the love of money and be content with what they have" (Heb 13:5)—after which follows the citation from Deut 31:6. The context of the Sabbatical Year, during which the "canceling of debt" takes place, referred to in Deut 31:9–13, contrasts the reference to the "love of money" referred to in Heb 13:5. Hebrews then presents the citation from Ps 117:6 LXX as a conclusion to the preceding discussion on the love of money with its reference to Deut 31:6. The focus of the argument shifts to contentment. This is done by the connecting phrase "so we can say with confidence," which combines the two citations as part of the same argument and as part of the same sentence.

There is sufficient evidence from early Judaism and early Christianity that Ps 118 (Ps 117 LXX) played a key role in the liturgies of the Jewish festivals as a Hallel psalm. Hebrews builds on this tradition, creating a close link between the citations from Deut 31:6 and Ps 117:6 LXX in Heb 13:5–6. Structurally both citations are being presented by means of a single sentence and a single introductory formula. The occurrence of ἐγκαταλίπω strengthens this link. Behind this structural connection lies a deeply rooted Jewish festival tradition that combined the two citations. The Sabbatical Year and Feast of Tents, which were testified about in Deut 31, provides a liturgical link for the author with Ps 117 LXX, which was sung at these occasions as well as during the Passover. The dialogical nature of the two citations, "*God said*" (possible *pars dei* through Deut 31:6 in Heb 13:5) and "*we say*" (possible *pars populi* through Ps 117:6 LXX in Heb 13:6), has a liturgical tone. When one adds to this the preceding context of the love for money (Heb 13:5) in the light of a Sabbatical Year motif in Deut 31, as well as the possible motif of the Eucharist (esp. Heb 13:10–12) in the light of the Passover festival, the author and his readers' familiarity with these intertexts from a liturgical tradition becomes clear.

The Song of Moses in Hebrews and Romans

The *Canticum Mosis* was a familiar song to the Jews, as its inclusion through the Christian textual tradition among the Odes (in LXX Codex A) also testifies. Being appended to the Greek Psalter is probably an indication of its liturgical significance, which ran through the history of the temple and continued in the early church. It probably played a particular role during the cultic rituals and liturgical actions of early Judaism during the celebration of some festivals. Possible connections existed with the controversial festival of the covenant renewal, an annually repeated sacred act, attested in the Dead Sea Scrolls (1QS II, 15). The liturgical connections of the *Canticum Mosis* and Ps 135 with the festival cult of the Israelite covenant community might even throw some light on the covenant motif as found in Hebrews. Furthermore, the *Canticum Mosis* was probably also used during the festival of the Day of Atonement, as testified in a Samaritan liturgical poem.[66]

Among all the New Testament books that contain Deuteronomy citations, the *Canticum Mosis* is cited only by Heb 1:6; 10:30 (Deut 32:35, 36); Rom 10:19 (Deut 32:21); 12:19 (Deut 32:35); 15:10 (Deut 32:43); and Rev 15:3 (Deut 32:4).[67] Apart from these citations, allusions to Deut 32 are found in Matt 4:10; 25:31; Rev 6:10; 12:12; 19:2. Paul must have had, consciously or subconsciously, the broader context of Deut 30–32 in mind—especially during the composition of Rom 10–15, as it alludes to the same sequence found in Deut 30–32.

Table 33.4. Deuteronomy 30–32 in Romans 10–15

Deuteronomy	Romans
30:12	10:6
30:14	10:8
32:21	10:19
32:35	12:19
32:43	15:10

---

66. Daniel K. Falk, *Daily, Sabbath, and Festival Prayers in the Dead Sea Scrolls*, STDJ 27 (Leiden: Brill, 1998), 164.

67. See Steve Moyise, "Singing the Song of Moses and the Lamb: John's Dialogical Use of Scripture," *AUSS* 42, no. 2 (2004): 347–60.

In Hebrews, too, the density of similarities in the form of citations and allusions to Deut 31–33, in particular, is certainly interesting—a trend similar to that of the Testament of Moses. It can be accepted that the last part of Deuteronomy was well known because it contained the *Canticum Mosis*.[68] It is interesting that four of the instances in Hebrews overlap with or come from close proximity from passages already referred to in Romans. Hebrews also uses the context immediately *preceding* a passage that already occurred in Romans (Deut 9:3 in Heb 12:29; Deut 9:4 in Rom 10:6) and the context *following* a passage that occurred in Romans (Deut 29:17 in Heb 12:15; Deut 29:3 in Rom 11:8).[69]

Although Deut 32:43 is also cited in Rom 15:10, it is not the same phrase as that found in Heb 1:6. The phrase cited in Hebrews is the immediately preceding phrase to that which occurs in Romans. Among the Hebrew versions, the cited line in Hebrews is absent in Deut 32:43 MT, which consists only of four stichoi, but is present in 4Q44, where it reads similar to Heb 1:6. The line cited in Rom 15:10 is absent, though it is in 4Q44. The occurrence of six of the lines in 4Q44 confirms that the LXX might have had a similar Hebrew *Vorlage* to that of Qumran. Whether 4Q44 was a copy made for personal reading or a "special use" liturgical text, it seems to have contained only the Song of Moses (Deut 32:1–43).[70] Among the Greek versions of the *Canticum Mosis*, one finds the expanded reading, now covering more lines, "of which it is not easy to decide how many belong to the original translator."[71] Also here scholars suspected the possibility of a liturgical fragment.[72]

Conclusion

The impact of Deuteronomy on the New Testament authors is strikingly evident. Its influence as a law code on the development of New Testament ethics is attested by several authors in their many references to the second table of the Decalogue and the christological reinterpretation of the *lex talionis*. The influence of Deuteronomy's Shema as pedagogical instruction left its imprint on the

---

68. George A. F. Knight, *The Song of Moses: A Theological Quarry* (Grand Rapids: Eerdmans, 1994).

69. See also Clare Rothschild on the "Imitation of Paul in Hebrews," in *Hebrews as Pseudepigraphon: The History and Significance of the Pauline Attribution of Hebrews*, WUNT 235 (Tübingen: Mohr Siebeck, 2009), 63–118.

70. Peter W. Flint, *The Dead Sea Psalms Scroll and the Book of Psalms*, STDJ 17 (Leiden: Brill, 1997), 167, 218.

71. Peter Katz, "The Quotations from Deuteronomy in Hebrews," ZNW 49 (1958): 217.

72. Wouter J. Hanegraaff, *Met de Torah is het begonnen. II: De voortgang van het Woord in Tenach en Septuagint* (Nijkerk: Callenbach, 1989), 137.

"golden rule" of a new Jesus logion. Deuteronomy's influence as a compendium of Jewish cult and worship practices has been noted on early Christian ritual practices—especially in relation to the Jewish festivals and the liturgical role of the Song of Moses. But it is especially the eschatological notion of Deuteronomy that had been intensively adopted and intentionally adapted in a christological manner by the New Testament writers. This eschatological notion became an interpretative lens for Christ. The New Testament mirrors the testing of God's Son in the desert, just like God's son Israel in Deuteronomy. The New Testament also identifies Christ with the eschatological prophet like Moses of Deut 18. The most paradigmatic shift, however, is probably to be found in Paul's interpretation of one of the oldest and earliest Deuteronomy citations in the New Testament, namely Deut 21:23 in Gal 3:13. Through God's curse of the crucified Jesus, Abraham's blessing can now also reach non-Jews and enables everyone to receive the promise of the Spirit through faith.

Jewish and early Christian authors used Deuteronomy as their authoritative religious Scripture for specific hermeneutical purposes by interpreting and reinterpreting its normativity for them within the contexts in which they found themselves. In this reception history of Deuteronomy within Second Temple Jewish literature, the New Testament writers continued with this tradition to engage in the Jewish conversation about the interpretation of Deuteronomy. They continue to do so for largely the same purposes as other contemporary Jewish authors, albeit, of course, with a christological hermeneutic.

Bibliography

Abegg, Martin G. "The Calendar at Qumran." Pages 145–71 in *The Judaism of Qumran: A Systemic Reading of the Dead Sea Scrolls*. Vol. 5 of *Judaism in Late Antiquity*. Edited by Alan J. Avery-Peck, Jacob Neusner, and Bruce D. Chilton. HdO 56. Leiden: Brill, 2001.

Allen, David M. *Deuteronomy and Exhortation in Hebrews: A Study in Narrative Re-presentation*. WUNT 2/238. Tübingen: Mohr Siebeck, 2008.

Aly, Zaki, and Ludwig Koenen, eds. *Three Rolls of the Early Septuagint: Genesis and Deuteronomy; A Photographic Edition*. PTA 27. Bonn: Habelt, 1980.

Arnold, Bill T. "Number Switching in Deuteronomy 12–26 and the Quest for *Urdeuteronomium*." *ZABR* 23 (2017): 163–80.

Ausloos, Hans. *The Deuteronomist's History: The Role of the Deuteronomist in Historical-Critical Research into Genesis–Numbers*. OTS 67. Leiden: Brill, 2015.

Beale, G. K., and D. A. Carson, eds. *Commentary on the New Testament Use of the Old Testament*. Grand Rapids: Baker Academic, 2007.

Beckwith, Roger T. *Calendar and Chronology, Jewish and Christian: Biblical, Intertestamental and Patristic Studies*. Leiden: Brill, 2001.

Caneday, Ardel. "'Redeemed from Curse of the Law': The Use of Deut 21:22–23 in Gal 3:13." *TJ* 10 (1989): 185–209.

Cheung, Luke L. *The Genre, Composition and Hermeneutics of the Epistle of James*. PBTM. Carlisle: Paternoster, 2003.

Christensen, Duane L. *Deuteronomy 1–21:9*. WBC 6A. Dallas: Word, 2001.

———. *Deuteronomy 21:10–34:11*. WBC 6B. Nashville: Nelson, 2002.

Ciampa, Roy E. "Deuteronomy in Galatians and Romans." Pages 99–117 in *Deuteronomy in the New Testament*. Edited by Maarten J. J. Menken and Steve Moyise. LNTS 358. London: T&T Clark, 2007.

Colson, Francis H, and J. W. Earp. *Philo: The Embassy to Gaius; Indices to Vols. I–X*. LCL. Cambridge: Harvard University Press, 1962.

Crawford, Sidnie White. "Deuteronomy." Pages 148–52 in *Pentatateuch, Former and Latter Prophets*. Edited by Armin Lange and Emmanuel Tov. THB 1B. Leiden: Brill, 2016.

———. "Reading Deuteronomy in the Second Temple Period." Pages 127–40 in *Reading the Present in the Qumran Library: The Perception of the Contemporary by Means of Scriptural Interpretations*. Edited by Kristin de Troyer and Armin Lange. SymS 30. Atlanta: Society of Biblical Literature, 2005.

Crowe, Brandon D. *The Obedient Son: Deuteronomy and Christology in the Gospel of Matthew*. BZNW 188. Berlin: de Gruyter, 2012.

Davila, James R. *Liturgical Works*. ECDSS 6. Grand Rapids: Eerdmans, 2000.

Dittmar, Wilhelm. *Vetus Testamentum in Novo: Die alttestamentlichen Parallelen des Neuen Testaments im Wortlaut der Urtexte und der Septuaginta zusammengestellt*. 2 vols. Göttingen: Vandenhoeck & Ruprecht, 1899–1903.

Docherty, Susan E. *The Use of the Old Testament in Hebrews: A Case Study in Early Jewish Bible Interpretation*. WUNT 2/260. Tübingen: Mohr Siebeck, 2009.

Falk, Daniel K. *Daily, Sabbath, and Festival Prayers in the Dead Sea Scrolls*. STDJ 27. Leiden: Brill, 1998.

Ferguson, Everett. *Backgrounds of Early Christianity*. 2nd ed. Grand Rapids: Eerdmans, 1993.

———. "Old Testament in Apostolic Fathers." Pages 826–34 in *Dictionary of the Later New Testament and Its Developments*. Edited by Ralph P. Martin and Peter H. Davids. Downers Grove, IL: InterVarsity Press, 1997.

Foster, Paul. "Why Did Matthew Get the Shema Wrong? A Study of Matthew 22:37." *JBL* 122, no. 2 (2003): 309–33.

Hanegraaff, Wouter J. *Met de Torah is het begonnen. II: De voortgang van het Woord in Tenach en Septuagint*. Nijkerk: Callenbach, 1989.

Huffman, Douglas S., and Jamie N. Hausherr. "Shema, The." In *The Lexham Bible Dictionary*. Edited by John D. Barry et al. Bellingham, WA: Lexham Press, 2016.

Josephus. *Josephus*. Translated by Henry St. John Thackery et al. 13 vols. LCL. Cambridge: Harvard University Press, 1926–1965.

Karrer, Martin. *Der Brief an die Hebräer: Kapitel 1,1–5,10*. ÖTK 20.1. Gütersloh: Gütersloher Verlagshaus, 2002.

Karrer, Martin, and Wolfgang Kraus, eds. *Septuaginta Deutsch: Erläuterungen und Kommentare zum griechischen Alten Testament*. Vol. 1, *Genesis bis Makkabäer*. Stuttgart: Deutsche Bibelgesellschaft, 2011.

Katz, Peter. "The Quotations from Deuteronomy in Hebrews." ZNW 49 (1958): 213–23.

Keener, Craig S. *The IVP Bible Background Commentary: New Testament*. Downers Grove, IL: InterVarsity, 1993.

Knight, George A. F. *The Song of Moses: A Theological Quarry*. Grand Rapids: Eerdmans, 1994.

Kruger, H. A. J. "A Sword over His Head or in His Hand? Luke 22,35–38." Pages 597–604 in *Scriptures in the Gospels*. Edited by Christopher Tuckett. BETL 131. Leuven: Leuven University Press, 1997.

Kugel, James L., and Rowan A. Greer. *Early Biblical Interpretation*. LEC. Philadelphia: Westminster, 1986.

Lange, Armin, and Matthias Weingold. *Biblical Quotations and Allusions in Second Temple Jewish Literature*. JAJSup 5. Göttingen: Vandenhoeck & Ruprecht, 2011.

Lim, Timothy H. "Deuteronomy in the Judaism of the Second Temple Period." Pages 6–26 in *Deuteronomy in the New Testament*. Edited by Maarten J. J. Menken and Steve Moyise. LNTS 358. London: T&T Clark, 2007.

Lincicum, David. *Paul and the Early Jewish Encounter with Deuteronomy*. WUNT 2/284. Tübingen: Mohr Siebeck, 2010.

———. "Paul and the Temple Scroll: Reflections on a Shared Engagement with Deuteronomy." Pages 51–69 in *"What Does the Scripture Say?" Studies in the Function of Scripture in Early Judaism and Christianity*. Vol. 2, *The Letters and Liturgical Traditions*. Edited by Craig A. Evans and H. Daniel Zacharias. LNTS 470. London: T&T Clark, 2012.

Loader, William R. G. *The Septuagint, Sexuality and the New Testament: Case Studies on the Impact of the LXX in Philo and the New Testament*. Grand Rapids: Eerdmans, 2004.

Lundbom, Jack R. *Deuteronomy: A Commentary*. Grand Rapids: Eerdmans, 2013.

Matson, Joshua M. "Employing Deuteronomy: An Analysis of the Quotations and Allusions to Deuteronomy in the Dead Sea Scrolls." Master's thesis, Trinity Western University, 2015.

McLean, Bradley H. *Citations and Allusions to Jewish Scripture in Early Christian and Jewish Writings through 180 C.E.* Lewiston, NY: Mellen, 1992.

McNamara, Martin. *Targum and Testament Revisited: Aramaic Paraphrases of the Hebrew Bible: A Light on the New Testament.* 2nd ed. Grand Rapids: Eerdmans, 2010.

Morgan, Donna F. "The So-Called Cultic Calendars in the Pentateuch (Ex 23:10-19, 34:18-26, Lev 23, Nu 28-29, Deut 16:1-17): A Morphological and Typological Study." PhD diss., Claremont, 1974.

Motyer, J. Alec. "Judgment." Pages 612-15 in *New Dictionary of Biblical Theology.* Edited by T. Desmond Alexander and Brian S. Rosner. Downers Grove, IL: InterVarsity Press, 2000.

Moyise, Steve. "Singing the Song of Moses and the Lamb: John's Dialogical Use of Scripture." *AUSS* 42, no. 2 (2004): 347-60.

New, David S. *Old Testament Quotations in the Synoptic Gospels, and the Two-Document Hypothesis.* SCS 37. Atlanta: Scholars Press, 1993.

Nigosian, Solomon. "Linguistic Patterns of Deuteronomy 32." *Bib* 78, no. 2 (1997): 206-24.

Otto, Eckhart. *Deuteronomium.* 4 vols. HThKAT. Freiburg im Breisgau: Herder, 2012-2017.

Otto, Eckhart, and Reinhard Achenbach, eds. *Das Deuteronomium zwischen Pentateuch und deuteronomistischem Geschichtswerk.* FRLANT 206. Göttingen: Vandenhoeck & Ruprecht, 2004.

Pearce, Sarah J. K. *The Words of Moses: Studies in the Reception of Deuteronomy in the Second Temple Period.* TSAJ 152. Tübingen: Mohr Siebeck, 2013.

Peters, Melvin K. H. "Deuteronomion/ Deuteronomium/ Das fünfte Buch Mose." Pages 161-73 in *Einleitung in die Septuaginta.* Edited by Siegfried Kreuzer. Vol. 1 of *Handbuch zur Septuaginta/Handbook of the Septuagint.* Edited by Martin Karrer, Wolfgang Kraus, and Siegfried Kreuzer. Gütersloh: Gütersloher Verlagshaus, 2016.

Priest, John. "Testament of Moses (First Century A.D.)." *OTP* 1:919-34.

Rad, Gerhard von. *Deuteronomy: A Commentary.* OTL. London: SCM, 1988.

Reardon, Timothy W. "'Hanging on a Tree': Deuteronomy 21.22-23 and the Rhetoric of Jesus' Crucifixion in Acts 5.12-42." *JSNT* 37, no. 4 (2015): 407-31.

Rothschild, Clare. "Imitation of Paul in Hebrews." Pages 63-118 in *Hebrews as Pseudepigraphon: The History and Significance of the Pauline Attribution of Hebrews.* WUNT 235. Tübingen: Mohr Siebeck, 2009.

Schmid, Konrad, and Raymond Person, eds. *Deuteronomy in the Pentateuch, Hexateuch, and the Deuteronomistic History.* FAT 2/56. Tübingen: Mohr Siebeck, 2012.

Schneider, Heinrich. "Die biblischen Oden im christlichen Altertum." *Bib* 30, no. 1 (1949): 28-65.

Shires, Henry M. *Finding the Old Testament in the New*. Philadelphia: Westminster, 1974.
Stanley, Christopher D. *Arguing with Scripture: The Rhetoric of Quotations in the Letters of Paul*. London: T&T Clark, 2004.
Steyn, Gert J. "A Comparison of the Septuagint Textual Form in the Torah Quotations Common to Philo of Alexandria and the Gospels of Mark and Matthew." Pages 605–24 in *XIV Congress of the IOSCS, Helsinki 2010*. Edited by Melvin K. H. Peters. SCS 59. Atlanta: Society of Biblical Literature, 2013.
———. "Deuteronomy in Hebrews." Pages 152–68 in *Deuteronomy in the New Testament*. Edited by Maarten J. J. Menken and Steve Moyise. LNTS 358. London: T&T Clark, 2007.
———. "Intertextual Similarities between Septuagint Pretexts and Luke's Gospel." *Neot* 24, no. 2 (1990): 229–46.
———. "Luke's Use of Mimesis? Re-opening the Debate." Pages 551–58 in *Scriptures in the Gospels*. Edited by Christopher Tuckett. BETL 131. Leuven: Leuven University Press, 1997.
———. "Pretexts of the Second Table of the Decalogue and Early Christian Intertexts." *Neot* 30, no. 2 (1996): 451–64.
———. *A Quest for the Assumed Septuagint Vorlage of the Explicit Quotations in Hebrews*. FRLANT 235. Göttingen: Vandenhoeck & Ruprecht, 2011.
———. "'Retrodiction' of the Old Testament in the New: The Case of Deut 21:23 in Paul's Letter to the Galatians and the Crucifixion of Yehoshua ben Yoseph." *HvTS* 71, no. 3 (2015): a3091. DOI: 10.4102/hts.v71i3.3091.
———. *Septuagint Quotations in the Context of the Petrine and Pauline Speeches of the Acta Apostolorum*. CBET 12. Kampen: Kok Pharos, 1995.
Streett, Daniel R. "Cursed by God? Galatians 3:13, Social Status, and Atonement Theory in the Context of Early Jewish Readings of Deuteronomy 21:23." *JSPL* 5, no. 2 (2015): 189–209.
Stuart, Douglas. *Hosea–Jonah*. WBC 31. Dallas: Word, 1987.
Tigay, Jeffrey. *Deuteronomy: The Traditional Hebrew Text with the New JPS Translation*. JPS Torah Commentary. Philadelphia: Jewish Publication Society, 1996.
Vaux, Roland de. *Ancient Israel: Its Life and Institutions*. 2nd ed. London: Darton, Longman & Todd, 1980.
Waaler, Erik. *The "Shema" and the First Commandment in First Corinthians: An Intertextual Approach to Paul's Re-reading of Deuteronomy*. WUNT 2/253. Tübingen: Mohr Siebeck, 2008.
Wakefield, Andrew H. *Where to Live: The Hermeneutical Significance of Paul's Citations from Scripture in Galatians 3:1–14*. AcBib 14. Atlanta: Society of Biblical Literature, 2003.
Washburn, David L. *A Catalog of Biblical Passages in the Dead Sea Scrolls*. TCS 2. Atlanta: Society of Biblical Literature, 2002.

Watson, Francis. *Paul and the Hermeneutics of Faith*. London: T&T Clark, 2004.
Weber, Beat. *Werkbuch Psalmen I: Die Psalmen 1 bis 72*. Stuttgart: Kohlhammer, 2001.
Weiser, Alfons. *The Psalms*. OTL. London: SCM, 1982.
Whiston, William. *The Works of Josephus: Complete and Unabridged*. Peabody, MA: Hendrickson, 1987.

34

Isaiah in the New Testament

BENJAMIN E. REYNOLDS

Along with Deuteronomy and Psalms, Isaiah is one of the most cited texts from the Scriptures of Israel in the New Testament. The citations and allusions to Isaiah are drawn from across the book of Isaiah (e.g., Isa 1:9; 6:9–10; 7:14; 11:1; 22:13; 35:5; 40:3; 45:3; 49:18; 53:1; 54:13; 61:1; 66:1–2), and they are found in all four gospels, Acts, Paul's epistles (especially Romans, 1 and 2 Corinthians), Hebrews, 1 Peter, and Revelation. This breadth of use indicates Isaiah's profound influence on the thought of early Jesus believers. Isaiah's depiction of the Lord's punishment of his people, judgment against the nations, and yet his promised mercy and redemption reverberates throughout early Jewish literature, including the New Testament.

My approach in this chapter will be to examine the influence of Isaiah on the New Testament in terms of Isaiah's order rather than follow the New Testament order.[1] In modern critical scholarship, Isaiah is often divided into two or three sections: First Isaiah (1–39), Second Isaiah (40–55), and Third Isaiah (56–66). While convenient, these divisions were not necessarily how ancient readers heard or read Isaiah. The references to the kings of Judah (1:1; 6:1; 7:1; 36:1; 38:1), to or-

---

1. See Steve Moyise and Maarten J. J. Menken, eds., *Isaiah in the New Testament* (London: T&T Clark, 2005); Rikk E. Watts, "Isaiah in the New Testament," in *Interpreting Isaiah: Issues and Approaches*, ed. David G. Firth and H. G. M. Williamson (Downers Grove, IL: IVP Academic, 2009), 213–33, for excellent studies that examine Isaiah following the New Testament order.

acles (משא, 13:1; 14:28; 15:1; 17:1; 19:1; 21:1, 11, 13; 22:1; 23:1; 30:6), and to woes (הוי, 1:4, 24; 5:8, 11, 20, 21, 22; 10:1, 5; 17:12; 18:1; 28:1; 29:1, 15; 30:1; 31:1; 33:1; 45:9, 10), as well as phrases like "Listen" (חרש, 41:1; 42:18; 49:1; 51:1), "Hear" (שמע, 39:5; 44:1; 48:1; cf. 41:26), and "Thus says the Lord" (כה אמר־יהוה, 8:11; 18:4; 29:22; 31:4; 37:6, 21, 33; 38:1, 5; 43:1, 14, 16; 44:2, 6; 45:1, 11, 14, 18; 48:17; 49:7, 8, 25; 50:1; 52:3; 56:1, 4; 65:8; 66:1, 12), may have had greater influence on shaping ancient audiences' understandings of Isaiah by creating textual markers whether that be the characters of kings or calls to listen and hear what the Lord says.

A guide to one such early Jewish reading of Isaiah is evident in the Great Isaiah Scroll (1QIsaᵃ). William Brownlee noted that Isaiah 1–33 and 34–66 were written on two separate scrolls that were sewn together to form 1QIsaᵃ. A unique three-line space ends the first scroll (Isa 33). Both scrolls have twenty-seven columns each, and Brownlee argued that this division demarcated two volumes of Isaiah.[2] While the division of Isaiah into two scrolls may have been a practical scribal decision concerning writing materials, this physical division may have influenced the reading of Isaiah as do modern Bible divisions of chapter and verse. Such a two-volume reading of Isaiah at Qumran is evidenced by the majority of extant Qumran Isaiah manuscripts that contain material from either Isaiah 1–33 or 34–66.[3] In addition, all but one Isaiah pesher discuss passages only from Isaiah 1–33, adding further support to the 1–33 and 34–66 division.[4] In contrast to modern divisions of Isaiah, the Qumran manuscripts present an intriguing insight on how Isaiah may have been written, preserved, and likely read at Qumran.

Adapting Brownlee's structure, I will use the following for my examination of the use of Isaiah in early Jewish literature and the New Testament: Isaiah 1–12; 13–33; 34–48; 49–66.[5] While this structure combines many of Brownlee's sections, it draws attention to the parallel narrative sections concerning King Ahaz and King Hezekiah, the arc of the Lord's judgments and woes against Israel, Judah,

---

2. Brownlee, "The Literary Significance for the Bisection of Isaiah," in *The Meaning of the Qumrân Scrolls for the Bible: With Special Attention to the Book of Isaiah* (New York: Oxford University Press, 1964), 247–59.

3. George J. Brooke, "On Isaiah at Qumran," in *"As Those Who Are Taught": The Interpretation of Isaiah from the LXX to the SBL*, ed. Claire Mathews McGinnis and Patricia K. Tull, SymS 27 (Atlanta: Society of Biblical Literature, 2006), 79.

4. Peter W. Flint, "The Interpretations of Scriptural Isaiah in the Qumran Scrolls: Quotations, Citations, Allusions, and the Form of the Scriptural Source Text," in *A Teacher for All Generations: Essays in Honor of James C. VanderKam*, ed. Eric F. Mason et al., 2 vols., JSJSup 153 (Leiden: Brill, 2012), 1:402.

5. Brownlee, "Literary Significance," 247–49: vol. 1: Isa 1–5; 6–8; 9–12; 13–23; 24–27; 28–31; 32–33; vol. 2: 34–35; 36–40; 41–45; 46–48; 49–55*; 56–59; 60–66.

and the nations, and the Lord's redemption of his people.⁶ In the first section, I will briefly survey citations and allusions to Isaiah in early Jewish literature, and in the second section, I will examine illustrative examples of the New Testament's use of Isaiah. What will become apparent from this examination of citations and allusions to Isaiah in early Jewish literature, in which the New Testament is included, are the eschatological and messianic interpretations of Isaiah that were understood in the context of the present situations of the authors and their audiences.

Isaiah in Early Jewish Literature

Isaiah's influence in Second Temple Judaism is evident across early Jewish literature and is the most prevalent book from the Scriptures of Israel found among the Dead Sea Scrolls, after Psalms and Deuteronomy. Twenty-one manuscripts of Isaiah were discovered at Qumran, although the Great Isaiah Scroll (1QIsa^a) is the only complete copy of Isaiah. The majority of the manuscripts are fragments, but some contain more extensive portions of Isaiah (1Q8 [1QIsa^b]; 4Q56 [4QIsa^b]; 4Q57 [4QIsa^c]; 4Q59 [4QIsa^e]).⁷ Six extant pesharim on the book of Isaiah further indicate the book's significance at Qumran (3Q4 [3QpIsa]; 4Q161 [4QpIsa^a]; 4Q162 [4QpIsa^b]; 4Q163 [4QpIsa^c]; 4Q164 [4QpIsa^d]; 4Q165 [4QpIsa^e]). The pesharim offer Qumran community interpretations of Isaiah, such as explaining the one carrying lambs as the Teacher of Righteousness (4Q165 1–2, 2–3; Isa 40:11) and explaining Jerusalem's sapphire foundations as the council of the community and the ruby battlements as the chief priests (4Q164 I, 1–5; Isa 54:11–12). While the Isaiah pesharim interpret Isaiah one phrase at a time, other early Jewish texts cite and allude to Isaiah in different ways. In what follows, I will summarize various citations and allusions in early Jewish literature following the order of Isaiah.

Isaiah 1–12

While Isaiah is evident in many places in early Jewish literature, the Dead Sea scrolls commonly evidence interpretation of certain Isaiah texts directed to-

---

6. Christopher R. Seitz, "How Is the Prophet Isaiah Present in the Latter Half of the Book? The Logic of Chapters 40–66 within the Book of Isaiah," *JBL* 115, no. 2 (1996): 219–40, notes parallels between the calling of Isaiah in Isa 6 and the apparent calling in Isa 40.

7. Brooke, "On Isaiah at Qumran," 72–74; Dwight Swanson, "The Text of Isaiah at Qumran," in Firth and Williamson, *Interpreting Isaiah: Issues and Approaches*, 192–96.

ward the Qumran community. One example includes the interpretation of the "Song of the Vineyard" from Isa 5, where the Lord says that the vineyard is Israel (Isa 5:7). In a conceptual allusion to Isa 5, 1QS VIII, 5 interprets the "community council" as "an everlasting plantation [למטעת עולם], a holy house for Israel" (נטע, Isa 5:7).[8] Similarly, 4Q174 (4QFlorilegium) cites Isa 8:11 in a marked citation and emphasizes avoiding the path of the wicked. The other texts cited along with Isa 8:11 in 4Q174 emphasize the righteous as those who belong to the community and the wicked as those who do not.

Isaiah's throne room vision in Isa 6 is conceptually alluded to in many early Jewish texts and became an important text in Jewish apocalyptic throne room visions (cf. Ezek 1; Dan 7:9–14). The Book of the Watchers combines Isa 6's angels, the lofty throne, and the Lord's appearance as the "Great Glory" (1 En. 14:8–23; cf. T. Levi 2–5; 2 En. 22; Apoc. Ab. 17–19). In an unmarked citation, the Parables of Enoch quotes Isaiah's seraphim (Isa 6:3), although with slight variation: "Holy, holy, holy is the Lord of Spirits, he fills the earth with his spirits" (1 En. 39:12).[9]

Isaiah 10:33–11:16 had an overwhelming influence on early Jewish messianic expectations. 4Q161 8–10 III, 1–25 interprets the shoot of Jesse as a figure who will appear in the final days, rule, and judge all peoples (Isa 10:33–11:5). The references to "[. . . thro]ne of glory, h[oly] crown and multi-colour[ed] vestments [. . .] in his hand" (4Q161 8–10 III, 20–21) are suggestive of kingship and priesthood. The interpretation reflects an eschatological understanding of the shoot of David's defeat of the Kittim and ruling over all people (also 4Q285 5; 11Q14 1 I). Although Isa 11 is not cited in 4Q174, the "branch of David" reference suggests a verbal allusion to the branch from Jesse's stump (4Q174 1 I, 11; Isa 11:1; cf. Jer 23:5; 33:15; Zech 3:8). 1Q28b (1QRule of Benedictions) makes numerous verbal allusions to Isa 11 in its blessing of the "prince of the congregation" (1Q28b V, 20–29; cf. Isa 11:2, 4).

Psalms of Solomon 17, the Parables of Enoch (1 En. 49), and 2 Baruch use imagery from Isa 10–11 in their presentations of their anointed figures. Psalms of Solomon uses Isa 11 in its portrayal of the Davidic "Lord Messiah" as one who will destroy the nations with the word of his mouth, judge with righteousness, and will have a spirit of wisdom and counsel (Pss. Sol. 17:24, 29, 37; cf. 18:7). First Enoch 49:3–4 contains verbal allusions to Isa 11:2–3 in the phrases "spirit of wisdom and understanding" and "spirit of counsel and might." In 1 En. 62:2, the spirit of righteousness is poured out on the Chosen One, who slays sinners with

---

8. DSS citations from Florentino García Martínez and Eibert J. C. Tigchelaar, *The Dead Sea Scrolls Study Edition*, 2 vols. (Grand Rapids: Eerdmans, 1997–1998). Translations of Scripture are by the author.

9. George W. E. Nickelsburg and James C. VanderKam, *1 Enoch: The Hermeneia Translation* (Minneapolis: Fortress, 2012), 53–54.

the word of his mouth (Isa 11:4). Second Baruch contains a conceptual allusion to Isa 10:34–11:1 in its imagery of the forest's destruction and the cedar that is defeated by the vine (2 Bar. 36–40). The conceptual influence of Isa 11:6–10 is also evident in the eschatological consummation in 2 Bar. 70–74. Fourth Ezra's man from the sea who breaths fire from his mouth (4 Ezra 13:10–11), which is interpreted as judgment against the multitude (13:37–38), is a conceptual allusion to Isa 11:4. These texts highlight the significant influence that Isa 11 had on early Jewish messianic interpretation.

Isaiah 13–33

Compared to Isa 1–12, early Jewish literature reflects fewer citations and allusions to the judgment oracles and woe oracles in Isa 13–33. The Parables of Enoch conceptually alludes to Isa 14:3–23 in its references to the kings of the earth, including their having a bed of worms (Isa 14:11; 1 En. 46:6).[10] In a marked citation in 4Q177 (4QCatena A) I, 2–5, Isa 22:13 is used negatively with other Scriptures of Israel against those with whom the community disagrees (also Ps 11:1; Mic 2:10–11; Ps 12:1). 4Q177 also cites Isa 32:7 (4Q177 I, 6–7) and Isa 37:30 (4Q177 I, 1–4) to explain the community's enemies and coming trial. Isaiah 31:8 is cited in an unmarked citation in 1QM XI, 11–12, where it is understood as prophecy concerning the timing of God's judgment against the Kittim.

Isaiah 34–48

The second half of Isaiah is referenced more frequently in early Jewish literature. A conceptual allusion to Isa 35:5–6 is evident in 4Q521's (4QMessianic Apocalypse's) description of the acts of the anointed one (also Isa 61:1; cf. 52:7). According to 4Q521, the anointed one will give sight to the blind (Isa 35:5–6) and will free prisoners and proclaim good news to the poor (Isa 61:1; 4Q521 2 II, 7, 12). 4Q176 (4QTanḥûmîm) contains a string of marked and unmarked citations from Isaiah, beginning with Isa 40:1–5, which is followed directly by Isa 48:1–9 (4Q176 1–2 I, 4–9). The marked citation of Isa 40:1–5 offers comfort regarding the "blood of [. . .] Jerusalem" and "the corpses of your priests." In 1QS VIII, 14 (the Community Rule), the Qumran community interprets its wilderness location and study of the Torah as the preparation of the Lord's way in the wilderness as prophesied in Isa 40:3.[11] The citation represents both a literal understanding of

---

10. Darrell D. Hannah, "Isaiah within Judaism of the Second Temple Period," in Moyise and Menken, *Isaiah in the New Testament*, 17.
11. Sarianna Metso, "Biblical Quotations in the Community Rule," in *The Bible as Book:*

במדבר ("in the wilderness") and a metaphorical understanding of what preparing the way of the Lord means, and it is interpreted in terms of the community's experience. Baruch 5:7 verbally alludes to Isa 40:3–5 and interprets the leveling of mountains as the Lord's restoration of his people to Jerusalem (see Bar 5:6–9; 1 En. 1:6).[12]

Isaiah's servant who is referred to as "my servant" and "my chosen" by the Lord (Isa 41:8; 42:1; 43:10; 44:1, 2; 49:3, 6; 52:13; 53:1) significantly influenced the figure of the messianic "Chosen One" in the Parables of Enoch (1 En. 39:6; 45:3, 4; 49:2, 4; 51:3, 5; etc.). The initial description of the Chosen One "of righteousness and faith" (1 En. 39:6) reflects the depiction of the Isaianic servant who will bring justice to the nations (Isa 42:1) and is interpreted messianically.[13]

Isaiah 49–66

The Parables of Enoch's messianic interpretation of Isaiah's servant also alludes to Isa 49–66. The Parables of Enoch's depiction of the Chosen One as a light of the nations and hidden in the presence of the Lord of Spirits are verbal allusions to Isa 49:2, 6 (1 En. 48:4, 6).[14] Similar messianic interpretations of Isa 49 are evident in Pss. Sol. 17:24's verbal allusion to the Davidic ruler destroying the nations with the word of his mouth (Isa 49:2; cf. Isa 11:4). There are also non-messianic interpretations of the servant of Isa 49 in early Jewish texts. The unmarked citations of Isa 49:2 in 4Q436 1 I, 7 and 4Q437 2 I, 8–9 are placed in the mouth of the speaker of these texts, which may have been used generally in praise.[15] Similarly, 4Q176 contains unmarked citations of Isa 40:1–5; 48:1–9; 49:13–17; 52:1–3; and 54:4–10 that view the servant corporately as the people of God and emphasize God's compassion on them (4Q176 1–2 I, 1–11; 1–2 II, 4–9; 8–11, 1–12; cf. 4Q164 I, 1–5).

Yet, 11Q13 (11QMelch) interprets language from Isa 52:7 as messianic. In the first of two marked citations, 11Q13 (II, 15–16, 23–24) quotes: "[How] beautiful upon the mountains are the feet [of] the messen[ger who] announces peace, the mess[enger of good news." 11Q13 interprets the mountains as the prophets and the messenger as the anointed one prophesied in Dan 9:25 (11Q13 II, 17–18).

The Hebrew Bible and the Judean Desert Discoveries, ed. Edward D. Herbert and Emanuel Tov (London: British Library; New Castle: Oak Knoll Press, 2002), 81–92.

12. David W. Pao, *Acts and the Isaianic New Exodus*, WUNT 2/130 (Tübingen: Mohr Siebeck, 2000), 42.

13. See Holly Beers, *The Followers of Jesus as the Servant: Luke's Model from Isaiah for the Disciples in Luke-Acts*, LNTS 535 (London: Bloomsbury T&T Clark, 2016), 63–80, on Isa 40–61 in early Jewish literature.

14. Hannah, "Isaiah within Judaism," 31.

15. See Hannah, "Isaiah within Judaism," 28–29.

The second citation repeats the line, "Saying to Zion: your God reigns." In this quotation, Zion is interpreted as "the congregation of all the sons of justice."

Throughout early Jewish literature there are citations and allusions to the entirety of Isaiah, although there are multiple references to Isaiah's vision of the Lord (Isa 6), the root of Jesse (Isa 11), and the servant of the Lord (Isa 42–61). Non-messianic interpretations apply Isaiah's language to the Lord's people. The messianic interpretations of these passages are often eschatological and look forward to the consummation of the Lord's judgment and redemption. The present realities of the writers and audiences, however, are apparent in the application of Isaiah's judgment passages to their own enemies and the redemption passages to themselves. As we turn to the examples of Isaiah in the New Testament, we will see similar early Jewish application of Isaiah.

ISAIAH IN THE NEW TESTAMENT

In the New Testament, Isaiah is cited 87 times and alluded to 553 times.[16] An examination of these references to Isaiah indicates that there are striking similarities with other early Jewish texts. First, Isaiah was not cited in isolation but was referenced alongside other texts from Israel's Scriptures. And second, Isa 6, 11, 40, and 42–61 are also the commonly cited and alluded to sections of Isaiah in the New Testament. Matthew, Romans, and 1 Peter have the highest concentration of Isaiah citations, with the pole position going to 1 Peter with 13 citations plus numerous allusions in its five chapters. Romans contains the highest numerical count of citations with 20, and notably 13 of Roman's 20 citations of Isaiah are found in Rom 9–11 (Isa 1:9; 8:14; 10:22–23; 27:9; 28:16 [twice]; 29:10; 40:13; 52:7; 53:1; 59:20–21; 65:1, 2). The book of Revelation, however, is arguably the most influenced by Isaiah with nearly 140 allusions.[17] The Gospel of Luke comes the next highest in allusions with 104, followed by Matthew with 85 and Romans with 49. Our focus in what follows will be on the Isaiah citations and allusions in the New Testament, and as in the last section, we will follow Isaiah's order. The New Testament texts, like other early Jewish texts, interpret Isaiah messianically and

---

16. The numbers of citations and allusions must be held lightly since it is evident that there are various perspectives on what constitutes a citation and an allusion and on what may be considered evidence for Isaianic influence. For the sake of simplicity, I have used the "Loci Citati vel Allegati" from NA[28], and I have compared it with the indices provided in the United Bible Societies, 5th ed., and the lists in Moyise and Menken, *Isaiah in the New Testament*, 211–14.

17. Jan Fekkes, *Isaiah and Prophetic Traditions in the Book of Revelation: Visionary Antecedents and Their Development*, JSNTSup 93 (Sheffield: JSOT Press, 1994), 279–82, counts only fifty as authentic allusions.

eschatologically in relation to present circumstances. The major difference from other early Jewish texts is the New Testament's naming of Jesus as Messiah.

Isaiah 1–12

Isaiah 1:9 is the earliest text of Isaiah cited in the New Testament; Paul cites Isa 1:9 LXX exactly in a marked citation in Rom 9:29. In Isa 1:9–11, Judah is said to be like Sodom and Gomorrah if the Lord had not left "seed," that is, a surviving remnant (Isa 1:9 LXX), but the Lord still calls Judah "Sodom" and "Gomorrah" and is unhappy with their sacrifices (Isa 1:10–11). Paul cites Isa 1:9 as evidence that only a remnant of Israel will be saved (also Hos 1:10; 2:23; Isa 10:22, 23; 28:16). For Paul, Isa 1:9 is evidence that the Lord will judge those who do not repent and that the Lord will save his people Israel (Rom 9:29), yet Paul understands that salvation as dependent upon acceptance of Jesus as Lord and as available to gentiles.[18]

The Lord's judgment against a nation that has rejected him is also evident in Isa 5:1–7, the "Song of the Vineyard." In Isaiah, the vineyard is an image of the Lord's relationship and care of his people, and Israel is the Lord's vineyard and Judah his planting (Isa 5:7). Jesus alludes to the metaphor of Israel as vineyard in his parables (Mark 12:1–11; Matt 21:33; Luke 13:6–9; 20:9–18;). Like 1QS's application of the planting to the community council (1QS VIII, 5), Jesus applies the vineyard imagery to a narrower selection of Israel rather than all Israel. John's Gospel reflects a conceptual allusion to the vineyard tradition in Jesus's statement that he is the true vine (John 15:1–4).

As with the various allusions to Isaiah's throne room vision in early Jewish literature, Rev 4:8 verbally alludes to Isaiah's visionary experience in Isa 6:2–3. David Matthewson states that this is the "only clear example of John's reliance on Isaiah for his language of visionary experience."[19] John's description of the four angels around the throne draws on Ezekiel's vision, but the angels' six wings in Revelation are an allusion to the six wings of the seraphim in Isaiah's throne vision. The opening words of Revelation's four living creatures may reflect an unmarked citation of Isa 6:3: "Holy, Holy, Holy, Lord" (ἅγιος ἅγιος ἅγιος κύριος, Rev 4:8), not unlike the unmarked citation in 1 En. 39:12.[20] The second half of the four living creatures' song, however, differs from that of the seraphim and

---

18. J. Ross Wagner, *Heralds of the Good News: Isaiah and Paul "In Concert" in the Letter to the Romans*, NovTSup 101 (Leiden: Brill, 2003), 115–16.

19. Matthewson, "Isaiah in Revelation," in Moyise and Menken, *Isaiah in the New Testament*, 190.

20. Fekkes, *Isaiah and Prophetic Traditions*, 142–49.

highlights the Lord's power (ὁ παντοκράτωρ) not just in terms of spatial categories but also temporal categories, as "the one who was and is and is coming" (cf. Isa 41:4; 44:6; 48:12).

Isaiah's commission in Isa 6:9–10 is cited in all four gospels (Mark 4:12; Matt 13:14; Luke 8:10; John 12:40) and in Acts 28:26–27 as reason for unbelief. Mark, Matthew, and Luke all cite Isa 6:9 in the context of Jesus's parable of the sower, but Matthew follows his unmarked citation of Isa 6:9 with a word-for-word marked citation of Isa 6:9–10 LXX (Matt 13:14–15). The Gospel of John contains a marked citation of Isa 6:10 in John 12:39–40 as an explanation for the lack of belief in Jesus's signs (John 12:37). The Johannine citation of Isa 6:10 in 12:39–40 is followed by conceptual allusion to Isaiah's vision of the Lord's glory in Isa 6:1–6 (John 12:41; see Isa 53:1 in John 12:38). In Acts 28:26–27, Paul quotes Isa 6:9–10 LXX word for word in a marked citation to explain why some lack belief in Jesus.[21] In all five of these citations of Isa 6:9–10, the failure to heed Isaiah's message is cited as the reason Jesus's or Paul's teaching is not believed.

In Isa 7, King Ahaz is told by the Lord to ask for a sign (Isa 7:10). Because he refuses to do so, Isaiah says that the Lord will give Ahaz a sign anyway, namely that הָעַלְמָה ("the young woman"; LXX: ἡ παρθένος, "the virgin") will conceive and bear a son and that the son's name will be "Immanuel," or "God with us" (עִמָּנוּ אֵל; Εμμανουηλ; Isa 7:14). Matthew cites Isa 7:14 LXX in a marked citation (Matt 1:23), which is the first of many marked citations in the opening chapters of Matthew's Gospel (2:5–6, 15, 17–18; 3:3; 4:6, 14–16). Matthew quotes Isa 7:14 LXX word for word apart from the change of subject (καλέσεις, Isa 7:14; καλέσουσιν, Matt 1:23). The "they" of Matthew's citation are "his people," whom Mary's son will save from their sins (Matt 1:21).[22] Matthew verbally alludes to the name "Immanuel" in Matthew's explanation of the name: "God with us" (Matt 1:23b; Isa 7:14; 8:8, 10). Unlike other extant early Jewish texts, Matthew interprets the sign to Ahaz as messianic prophecy fulfilled in God working to save his people through Jesus.

Messianic interpretation is also evident in New Testament use of Isa 8:14, which along with Isa 28:16 mentions a stone. First Peter cites both Isaiah passages: Isa 28:16 in a marked citation (1 Pet 2:6) and Isa 8:14 in an unmarked citation (1 Pet 2:8). Placed between them is an unmarked citation of Ps 118:22 (117:22 LXX), which is another stone passage. Like the contrast of faithful and unfaithful in Isa 8:14 LXX, Peter speaks of the stone as precious (ἁγίασμα; cf. "sanctuary" in Isa 8:14 LXX) for those who believe, but for those who do not, the stone causes people to stumble because of their disobedience (1 Pet 2:7–8).

---

21. Pao, *Acts and the Isaianic New Exodus*, 105–9.
22. Richard Beaton, *Isaiah's Christ in Matthew's Gospel*, SNTSMS 123 (Cambridge: Cambridge University Press, 2002), 95.

Paul cites the same passage in a marked citation (Rom 9:33) but in a composite citation with Isa 28:16. Paul's wording—"I lay a stone in Zion" and "the one who believes in him will not be put to shame"—derives from Isa 28:16. The language about the stone causing people to stumble and the rock of offense comes from Isa 8:14. Paul appears to have conflated the two passages to highlight Isaiah's message concerning those who reject the Lord and stumble against his stone.[23] The stone imagery in 1 Peter concentrates on the building of people as living stones with Jesus as the foundation stone (1 Pet 2:5; cf. the interpretation of the stone as the community in 1QS VIII, 7–8) and less on Paul's interest in lack of belief.

Isaiah 8:23–9:1 LXX is cited as a marked citation and is one of the fulfillment passages in Matthew's Gospel (Matt 4:15–16). The Isaiah text offers hope to the remnant and promises the Lord's removal of the rod and yoke. Isaiah's references to the throne of David (Isa 9:6 LXX) and later the shoot of Jesse (Isa 11:1) imply a Davidic expectation. Matthew cites Isa 8:23–9:1 LXX to indicate that Jesus's dwelling in Capernaum by the Sea of Galilee (Matt 4:13) was fulfillment of Isaiah's words. Jesus, whom Matthew has declared as the Messiah (Matt 1:1, 17, 18), brings hope and light by living in this land, as prophesied by Isaiah.

Continuing Isaiah's hopes for a Davidic ruler, Isa 11 speaks of a "rod from the root of Jesse" (חֹטֶר מִגֵּזַע יִשָׁי; ῥάβδος ἐκ τῆς ῥίζης Ιεσσαι) and "a shoot/blossom from the root" (וְנֵצֶר מִשָּׁרָשָׁיו יִפְרֶה; καὶ ἄνθος ἐκ τῆς ῥίζης; cf. ἡ ῥίζα τοῦ Ιεσσαι, Isa 11:10). One of the clearest verbal allusions to Isa 11:1 in the New Testament is Revelation's naming of Jesus as the "root of David" (ἡ ῥίζα Δαυίδ, Rev 5:5; ἡ ῥίζα καὶ τὸ γένος Δαυίδ, 22:16; cf. Matt 2:23). Isaiah 11 also influences some of Revelation's imagery of the rider on the white horse (Rev 19:11, 15, 21). The description of the rider judging with righteousness is a conceptual allusion to the root of Jesse judging with righteousness (Isa 11:4a MT). Isaiah also describes Jesse's descendant as striking the earth (πατάξει γῆν) with the word of his mouth and destroying the ungodly with the breath of his lips (Isa 11:4b LXX). A verbal allusion to this description is evident in the portrayal of the rider of Rev 19 with a double-edged sword coming from his mouth so that he might strike the nations (πατάξῃ τὰ ἔθνη, Rev 19:15, 21; cf. Isa 49:2). Revelation's interpretation of the Davidic figure in Isa 11 belongs with other early Jewish messianic interpretations of Isa 11 (Pss. Sol. 17; 4 Ezra 13; cf. Rom 15:12).

Isaiah 13–33

The language of Isaiah's judgment oracles and woes against the nations (Isa 13–33) are cited and alluded to in New Testament judgment and salvation texts.

---

23. Wagner, *Heralds of the Good News*, 127–36, argues for the probability that Paul originated the conflation.

Isaiah in the New Testament

Part of the opening of Isaiah's oracle against Babylon (Isa 13:10) appears in Mark 13:24 and Matt 24:29 in an unmarked citation (see the conceptual allusion in Luke 21:25). The wording and order do not match the LXX or the MT perfectly. The sun is darkened, and the moon will not give its light on the day of the Lord (Isa 13:9). In Jesus's eschatological discourse, Isaiah's cosmological events take place "in those days" after that tribulation (ἐν ἐκείναις ταῖς ἡμέραις, Mark 13:24; Matt 24:29), and Jesus says they are the days when the abomination that causes desolation is set up in the temple (cf. Dan 9:27). The Gospels interpret Isaiah's judgment oracle as a still future judgment that will take place after Jesus (cf. Isa 14:13, 15 with Matt 11:23; Luke 10:21).

The book of Revelation also uses the language and imagery of Isaiah's oracles to describe judgment. Isaiah 13:20 states that Babylon will not be inhabited (לֹא־תֵשֵׁב; οὐ κατοικηθήσεται, Isa 13:20 LXX) but wild animals (θηρία) will rest there. Isaiah 13:20 LXX says demons (δαιμόνια) will dance in the dwellings and sirens will rest. The MT speaks of wild animals, howling creatures, ostriches/owls, wild goats, hyenas/foxes, and jackals (Isa 13:21–22; cf. 34:13). Revelation 18:2 conceptually alludes to this deterioration of Babylon when the mighty angel declares that Babylon has become a dwelling place for demons (κατοικητήριον δαιμονίων) and a lair for all unclean spirits, unclean birds, and unclean beasts. The first line that the mighty angel cries out—"Fallen, Fallen is Babylon the great"—is an unmarked citation from Isaiah's vision of the wilderness of the sea (נָפְלָה נָפְלָה בָּבֶל, Isa 21:9 MT; cf. πέπτωκεν Βαβυλών, Isa 21:9 LXX). Revelation also conceptually alludes to the merchants of Isaiah's oracle concerning Tyre (Isa 23:1–18). Tyre is said to prostitute herself with all the kingdoms of the world (Isa 23:17 MT). Revelation makes the same critique against Babylon, who is portrayed as the great prostitute with whom the kings of the earth have committed sexual immorality (Rev 17:1–2).[24] The judgment oracles of Isa 13–23 influenced Revelation's depiction of the destruction of Babylon (Rev 17:2; 18:3), which is another example of how New Testament authors used Isaiah's language of judgment against Israel's enemies to describe the present and future expectations of followers of Jesus.

In the oracles of Isa 24–27, the Lord declares judgments against the earth but also coming redemption. Isaiah 25 concerns the eschatological feast on Mount Zion and the coming of the nations to Jerusalem. Isaiah 25:8a is cited in a marked citation in 1 Cor 15:54 where Paul completes his argument for the resurrection of the dead: "death is swallowed up in victory" (κατεπόθη ὁ θάνατος εἰς νῖκος). Although a marked citation, Paul's wording differs from the MT and the LXX (בִּלַּע הַמָּוֶת לָנֶצַח; κατέπιεν ὁ θάνατος ἰσχύσας). Paul, reflecting Isaiah's eschatological context, cites the text to speak of the eschatological resurrection. The second half of Isa 25:8 is cited in an unmarked citation in Rev 7:17's eschatological

---

24. Fekkes, *Isaiah and Prophetic Traditions*, 210–17, also 86–91.

context. Isaiah 25:8b reads: "the Lord God will wipe away tears from all faces/ every face" (וּמָחָה אֲדֹנָי יְהוִה דִּמְעָה מֵעַל כָּל־פָּנִים; καὶ πάλιν ἀφεῖλεν Κύριος ὁ θεὸς πᾶν δάκρυον ἀπὸ παντὸς προσώπου). At the end of the great multitude scene, Rev 7:17 states: "And God will wipe away every tear from their eyes" (καὶ ἐξαλείψει ὁ θεὸς πᾶν δάκρυον ἐκ τῶν ὀφθαλμῶν αὐτῶν; cf. Rev 21:4). Both Paul and Revelation understand Isa 25:8 as depicting the consummation of time.

In Isa 26:19 we have one of the few references in the Scriptures of Israel to what may be interpreted as bodily resurrection. While Jesus's speech in John 5:28–29 contains a verbal allusion to Dan 12:2, John 5:28 also shares similar wording with Isa 26:19 LXX in the phrase "those in the tombs" (οἱ ἐν τοῖς μνημείοις). In Matt 11:5 // Luke 7:22, Jesus tells John the Baptist's disciples to tell John that the dead are raised (νεκροὶ ἐγείρονται) in an apparent verbal allusion to Isa 26:19 LXX (ἀναστήσονται οἱ νεκροί, καὶ ἐγερθήσονται). Jesus's use here is either a condensed allusion to the Isaiah text or reflects a different Greek text or a free translation of the Hebrew (cf. Dan 12:2). Isaiah 26's eschatological coming of the Lord is interpreted by John and Matthew // Luke as taking place in Jesus's coming. The eschatological timing is connected to the Messiah not unlike 4Q521, which also lists raising the dead as an action of the Messiah.

Isaiah's judgment oracles (Isa 13–27) are followed by a series of woes (Isa 28–33), which clearly influenced Paul's arguments. Paul cites or alludes to them in Rom 9:33 (Isa 28:16 with 8:14, see above), Rom 11:8 (Isa 29:10), and 1 Cor 1:19 (Isa 29:14). Paul refers to Isaiah's woes in contexts where he addresses unbelief yet God's enduring promise to his people; however, Isaiah's imagery of potter and clay in Isa 29:16 offers support for Paul's claims of the Lord's mercy.[25] Paul verbally alludes to the imagery from Isa 29:16 in Rom 9:20–24 to address questions concerning those on whom God has mercy and compassion (Rom 9:15–19). Of Isa 29:16's four phrases, Paul uses the wording from the first and fourth phrases. He cites the first phrase of Isa 29:16 LXX word for word: "what is molded does not say to the molder" (μὴ ἐρεῖ τὸ πλάσμα τῷ πλάσαντι), but Paul changes the fourth phrase—"you did not make me" wise/clever (οὐ συνετῶς με ἐποίησας, Isa 29:16 LXX)—into a question: "Why did you make me thus?" (τί με ἐποίησας οὕτως; Rom 9:20).[26] Isaiah's woe oracle against those claiming to hide their actions from God is used by Paul to describe God's ability to show compassion on those whom he chooses.

The judgment oracles and woes in Isa 13–33 influenced various New Testament references to judgment and eschatological events. The language used against Israel's enemies shapes the language used against the enemies of God's

---

25. Florian Wilk, *Die Bedeutung des Jesajabuches für Paulus*, FRLANT 179 (Göttingen: Vandenhoeck & Ruprecht, 1998), 139.
26. Wagner, *Heralds of the Good News*, 58–60, suggests Paul is influenced by Isa 45:9 LXX.

new covenant people. The New Testament authors, particularly Paul, refer to Isaiah's judgment oracles and woes to explain the way the Lord will judge their enemies and restore Israel even though they did not believe. The New Testament indicates that Isaiah's prophecies are fulfilled in Jesus and his followers.

Isaiah 34–40

Isaiah 34 begins the second half of the Great Isaiah Scroll (1QIsa^a). In reading Isaiah in these two parts, Isa 34–35 introduces the second half of Isaiah much like Isa 1–5 does Isa 6–33. Isaiah 34 relates the Lord's wrath against the nations and declares that the heavens will be rolled up and the stars will fall. This eschatological language influences both Jesus's language and the book of Revelation. Jesus quotes Isa 34:4 in an unmarked citation, when he declares that these events will take place after the tribulation (Mark 13:25; Matt 24:29; cf. Isa 13:10, see above). Revelation makes conceptual and verbal allusions to portrayals of the Lord's day of vengeance (Isa 34:8–15), specifically the "smoke of the unquenchable fire" (Isa 34:10 LXX; Rev 14:11; 19:3) and the animals that will live in the ruins caused by the Lord's judgment (Isa 34:11–15; Rev 18:2–3; cf. Isa 31:21, see above). Jesus verbally and conceptually alludes to the language of redemption in Isa 35, when he responds to John the Baptist's question. Jesus answers that the lame walk, the blind see, and the deaf hear (Isa 35:10; Matt 11:5–6; Luke 7:22; cf. Isa 26:19; 29:18; 4Q521). Again, in all three instances, we see Isaiah's language informing the present and future circumstances of Jesus and his followers.

Following the Lord's declaration of comfort and pardon in Isa 40:1–2, a voice cries in the wilderness declaring the preparation of the Lord's way and the revelation of his glory (Isa 40:3–5). All four gospels cite Isa 40:3 and interpret John the Baptist as the voice in the wilderness. The Synoptic Gospels cite the text in marked citations (Mark 1:3; Matt 3:3; Luke 3:4–6). Mark cites Isa 40:3 along with Mal 3:1, but Luke cites the entirety of Isa 40:3–5 LXX (cf. Luke 1:76).[27] The Gospel of John cites Isa 40:3 in an unmarked citation, but John the Baptist, rather than the narrator, quotes the text in response to the question, "Who are you?" (John 1:22–23). Similar to the Qumran community's interpretation, "wilderness" is understood as the physical wilderness, but whereas at Qumran the study of Torah prepares the Lord's way (1QS VIII), the Gospels present John the Baptist's preaching about the kingdom and his baptizing as doing so. Both the Synoptic Gospels' and Qumran's use of Isa 40:3 understands Isaiah's words as promise of renewal.

The first of the Servant Songs is cited in an extensive marked citation in Matt 12:18–21 (Isa 42:1–4 LXX). Craig Blomberg notes that it is "the longest sus-

---

27. Pao, *Acts and the Isaianic New Exodus*, 38–39.

tained quotation of the OT in Matthew."[28] The context for the citation comes after Jesus has healed a man with a withered hand on the Sabbath, and the Pharisees respond by conspiring to destroy Jesus (Matt 12:9–14). The crowds follow Jesus when he withdraws, but Jesus still heals the sick. After Jesus tells the crowds not to speak about him, Matthew quotes Isa 42:1–4 LXX as fulfillment (Matt 12:15–17). In Isaiah, this text is the first of the Lord's speeches to his servant (cf. Isa 41:9). The servant is chosen, God will put his spirit on him, and the servant will bring judgment to the gentiles/nations (cf. Isa 11:1–4). Isaiah 42:1 LXX explicitly names Jacob and Israel as the servant, but the MT does not. Matthew is closer to the MT than the LXX. The first part of Isa 42:4 is not present in Matthew, but Matt 12:21 includes the final line from Isa 42:4 and is closer to the LXX here, departing from the MT.[29] Matthew interprets Jesus and not the nation of Israel as God's servant, which highlights the way Jesus, the humble servant, does not meet the crowd's expectations.[30]

Wording from Isa 43:20–21 LXX is cited in an unmarked citation in 1 Pet 2:9. Peter, no longer speaking about those who stumble against the rejected stone (2:6–8; cf. Isa 8:14; 28:16), describes his audience as a "chosen people, a royal priesthood, a holy nation, a people belonging to God" (1 Pet 2:9). The first and last of Peter's descriptors (γένος ἐκλεκτόν; λαὸς εἰς περιποίησιν) reflect wording from Isa 43:20–21 (τὸ γένος μου τὸ ἐκλεκτόν; λαόν μου ὃν περιεποιησάμην). Whereas the "chosen people" of Isaiah are Israel (Isa 43:1, 22), Peter uses Isaiah's descriptors to speak of those who have accepted Jesus as the living stone (1 Pet 2:4; Isa 8:14; 28:16), whether Jew or gentile (1 Pet 1:1, 14).

Isaiah 49–66

The Servant Songs continue in Isa 49, but whereas the Lord spoke in Isa 42 and 45, the servant speaks in 49:1: "The Lord called me from the womb, from the belly of my mother he named me" (also 49:2, 4). The New Testament use of the passage indicates differing interpretations and understandings of the servant. Paul uses the servant's language in Isa 49:1–6 to speak about himself when he defends himself to the Galatians (Gal 1–2), specifically that he was set apart from birth (Gal 1:15; Isa 49:1, 5), that God is glorified through the servant (Gal 1:16, 24; Isa 49:3), that he serves the gentiles (Isa 49:6; Gal 1:16), and that he has not

---

28. Craig L. Blomberg, "Matthew," in *Commentary on the New Testament Use of the Old Testament*, ed. G. K. Beale and D. A. Carson (Grand Rapids: Baker Academic, 2007), 42.

29. Beaton, *Isaiah's Christ*, 139–41, argues that Matthew altered a Greek text that was revised toward the LXX.

30. See Beaton, *Isaiah's Christ*, 122–73.

run in vain (Gal 2:2; Isa 49:4).³¹ In a marked citation in Acts 13:47, Paul and Barnabas cite the words of the servant to explain why they will turn to the gentiles (Isa 49:6 LXX). While Paul and Barnabas use the words of Isa 49 to claim that they are servants of the Lord, Revelation interprets the servant as Jesus the Messiah. Revelation 1:16 and 19:15 both conceptually allude to the description of the servant's mouth as a sharp sword (Isa 49:2) in their visionary portrayals of Jesus with a sharp, double-edged sword in his mouth (cf. Isa 11:4). Both the non-messianic and messianic interpretations of Isa 49 are present in other early Jewish texts (cf. 4Q436; 4Q437; 1 En. 48; Pss. Sol. 17).

In one of the numerous Isaiah citations in Rom 9–11, Paul cites Isa 52:7 in a marked citation in Rom 10:15b. Just prior to this, Paul cites Isa 28:11 (Rom 10:11) and Joel 2:32 (Rom 10:13). Paul argues that there is no difference between Jew and gentile and that all who call on the name of the Lord will be saved. The citation of Isa 52:7 answers Paul's questions about how they will know the Lord and believe (Rom 10:14–15a): some, those with beautiful feet, will proclaim good news to them. In the Isaiah context, the Lord says that the feet of those who bring good news of peace and salvation are lovely or beautiful (נָאווּ Isa 52:7; the LXX does not have an equivalent). Paul's citation follows the MT more closely (Rom 10:15b), although he does not cite the wording "on the mountains," "announcing," "peace," and "salvation." Paul's emphasis is on the Lord's sending of those who bring good news and that the good news concerns Jesus.³² For Paul, "messenger" includes himself and others, which differs from the messianic interpretation of the messenger in 11Q13.

As the Lord continues to speak in Isa 52, the Lord says that he will reveal his arm to all the nations and that the earth will see his salvation (Isa 52:10). Later, the question is asked, "Who has heard our report; to whom has the arm of the Lord been revealed?" (Isa 53:1). Given Isa 52:10–15, the question implies that even though the nations saw the Lord's arm, the report was not believed. John 12:38 cites Isa 53:1 in a marked citation, indicating that Jesus as the servant of the Lord is the Lord's arm. Isaiah's question implies that Jesus, in what he has done and said, has not been believed.³³ John follows the marked citation of Isa 53:1 with a marked citation of Isa 6:9–10 and a conceptual allusion to Isaiah's vision in Isa 6:1–3 (John 12:40–41). Paul also cites the question in Isa 53:1 in a marked citation in Rom 10:16, directly following his citation of Isa 52:7 (Rom 10:15b).

---

31. Matthew S. Harmon, *She Must and Shall Go Free: Paul's Isaianic Gospel in Galatians*, BZNW 168 (Berlin: de Gruyter, 2010), 75–91.

32. Wilk, *Die Bedeutung*, 177.

33. Adam W. Day, *Jesus, the Isaianic Servant: Quotations and Allusions in the Gospel of John*, Gorgias Biblical Studies 67 (Piscataway, NJ: Gorgias, 2018), 94–101.

Both Paul and John interpret the Lord's arm and report in relation to Jesus and lack of belief in him.

The rest of the servant song in Isa 53 is referenced in multiple places in the New Testament. First Peter 2:22–25 contains numerous references to Isa 53. Peter's citations and allusions do not follow the order of Isa 53: Isa 53:9 (1 Pet 2:22); Isa 53:4, 12 (1 Pet 2:24a); Isa 53:5 (1 Pet 2:24b); Isa 53:6 (1 Pet 2:25). Using Isa 53's language, Peter presents Jesus as an example of how to suffer. In a marked citation of Isa 53:4, Matt 8:17 interprets Jesus's healing the sick as fulfillment of Isa 53. In Acts 8:27–33, the Ethiopian eunuch reads Isa 53:7–8 LXX (Acts 8:32–33), and Philip explains from Israel's Scriptures that the servant is Jesus (Acts 8:34–35). In Luke 22:37, Jesus cites Isa 53:12 in a marked citation. Jesus quotes "he was counted among the lawless" as fulfillment concerning himself. Holly Beers argues that Luke includes the citation to indicate Jesus's role as servant.[34] The New Testament interpretations of Isa 52:13–53:12 explain Jesus's suffering as fulfillment of messianic prophecy and to point to that suffering as an example for his followers.

After Isa 53, Isa 54:1 declares, "Rejoice, O barren one" in an address to Jerusalem. Jerusalem, who has drunk from the cup of the Lord's wrath (51:17) and should loose her bonds (52:1–2), has the Lord as her husband and redeemer (54:5–7); she is a poor and uncomforted city whose foundations God will rebuild (54:11–12). In Paul's allegory concerning Hagar and Sarah, Paul cites Isa 54:1 LXX in a marked citation (Gal 4:21–31). Paul associates Sarah and the heavenly Jerusalem with Isaiah's barren woman whose children faithfully follow the Lord. Paul interprets the prophesied prosperity of the barren one and her many children as redemption through Jesus (Isa 54:1–3).[35]

In Acts 13:34, Paul interprets Isa 55:3 LXX in relation to Jesus. While speaking in Pisidian Antioch, Paul cites Isa 55:3 and Ps 16:10 to argue that the Messiah's resurrection was prophesied. Isaiah 55:3 LXX refers to the covenant that God made with David (2 Sam 7:12–14) and states that God "will covenant with you (pl.) the eternal covenant of the holy things of David, the faithful/sure things" (διαθήσομαι ὑμῖν διαθήκην αἰώνιον τὰ ὅσια Δαυιδ τὰ πιστά). For Paul, the promises to David include the resurrection of the Messiah "because" (διότι, Acts 13:35) in Ps 16:10 God said he would not let his holy one see decay (cf. Acts 2:25–28). Paul interprets the promised covenant to David as fulfilled in Jesus's resurrection.

Jesus cites the final line of Isa 56:7 LXX during the temple action, along with Jer 7:11 (Matt 21:13; Mark 11:17; Luke 19:46). The wording of Matthew and Mark

---

34. Beers, *Followers of Jesus as the Servant*, 114–18.
35. See Moisés Silva, "Galatians," in Beale and Carson, *Commentary on the New Testament Use of the Old Testament*, 809, on the complexity of this comparison.

follows the LXX exactly for the first part of the statement (ὁ οἶκός μου οἶκος προσευχῆς κληθήσεται; Luke 19:46: ἔσται). Matthew and Luke, however, do not include the final phrase "for all the nations" (πᾶσιν τοῖς ἔθνεσιν, Isa 56:7), which highlights the shift from Isaiah's emphasis on inclusion to Jesus's on the temple as a place of prayer. Peter Mallen suggests that Luke omitted the phrase because he was interested in movement away from Jerusalem rather than the nations coming to Jerusalem.[36] Whether or not that is the reason, Matthew's and Luke's omissions of "for all the nations" heighten the tension between the commerce taking place in the temple and the Lord's desire for the temple as a house of prayer. The Isaianic emphasis on the coming nations to Jerusalem gives way in the Gospels to an emphasis on what the temple should be but is not.

Isaiah 59:20–21 is cited at the end of Rom 9–11 (Rom 11:26–27). Isaiah speaks of the Lord as a redeemer who will redeem those who turn to the Lord. The Lord will put his spirit on them and his words in their mouths. Paul's citation of these verses comes in his argument that all Israel will be saved (Rom 11:26), saying, "The redeemer will come from Zion" (ἥξει ἐκ Σιὼν ὁ ῥυόμενος, Rom 11:26). The MT reads that he will come "to Zion" (וּבָא לְצִיּוֹן גּוֹאֵל, Isa 59:20), and the LXX "for the sake of Zion" (καὶ ἥξει ἕνεκεν Σιων ὁ ῥυόμενος, Isa 59:20 LXX). The rest of Paul's citation matches the LXX exactly apart from an addition from Isa 27:9 LXX. Paul emphasizes that the Lord will bring salvation to Israel, yet mercy is for all (Rom 11:30–32). As Ross Wagner notes, Paul's emphasis is on the Lord's role in this redemption, yet for Paul, that redemption has been revealed in Jesus.[37]

The eschatological hopefulness of the Lord's redeeming work in Isaiah continues in the preaching of good news to the poor, the restoration of ruins, and the Lord's giving of joy and a double portion (Isa 61:1, 4, 7). In Luke 4:18–19, Jesus quotes Isa 61:1–2 (with Isa 58:6) in the Nazareth synagogue. Jesus recites that the spirit of the Lord is on him to proclaim good news to the poor, to release the captives, restore sight to the blind, and to proclaim the year of the Lord's favor. Jesus declares that this event has been fulfilled in his reciting of Isa 61 (Luke 4:21). In the Qumran text 4Q521, Isa 61 is cited to describe the actions of the messiah. Similarly, for Luke, Jesus is the Messiah and the one on whom the spirit rests (cf. Luke 3:22; 4:1). The events of Isaiah's eschatological hope begin in Jesus's life and work.

In Isa 65, the Lord complains about the people of Israel. While God was present to a people that did not call to him, they sinned and broke his law

---

36. Peter Mallen, *The Reading and Transformation of Isaiah in Luke–Acts*, LNTS 367 (London: T&T Clark, 2008), 150–51.

37. Wagner, *Heralds of the Good News*, 298.

(65:1–5), and he will not be silent and leave sins unpunished (65:6–7). Paul, in a marked citation, quotes the Lord's words in Isa 65:1–2 as evidence that Israel heard the Lord's message (also Isa 53:1; Rom 10:16). Paul quotes the LXX almost exactly, apart from reversing the order of "I was revealed" and "I was found" (Isa 65:1 LXX: ἐμφανὴς ἐγενόμην ... εὑρέθην). Paul emphasizes the Lord's speech to his disobedient people, their rejection of God, and that God did not reject them. The Lord's lack of rejection indicates his promises and mercy to his people (Isa 62–64).

The latter part of Isa 65 contains numerous texts that are alluded to in Revelation. In Isa 65:8–12, 13–16, the Lord speaks against those who disobey and says that his servants will be called a new name (δουλεύουσιν αὐτῷ κληθήσεται ὄνομα καινόν, Isa 65:15 LXX). In Revelation, Jesus tells the church in Pergamum that those who overcome will be given a white stone with a new name on it (Rev 2:17). In Rev 3:14, Jesus is called the "Amen," which may be a conceptual allusion to Isa 65:16 MT: "the God of amen" or "of faithfulness" (בֵּאלֹהֵי אָמֵן). The LXX reads "God of truth" (θεὸν τὸν ἀληθινόν). A verbal allusion to Isa 65:17–20 is evident in Rev 21:1, 4, where John the Seer of Revelation sees Isaiah's new heaven and new earth in his vision of the heavenly Jerusalem (cf. Isa 66:22; 2 Pet 3:13; 1 En. 91:16).[38] In the New Jerusalem, there will be joy and no more weeping (Rev 21:4; Isa 65:19; cf. Rev 7:17 and Isa 25:18). Again, the eschatological and restoration language of Isaiah is interpreted of Jesus and his followers.

Conclusion

The book of Isaiah held an important place in early Judaism and informed early Jewish understandings of the Lord's judgment and redemption. Isaiah is cited and alluded to in various genres of early Jewish literature (pesharim, rules, catenae, narratives, letters, and apocalypses), and the language of Isaiah is drawn upon for various reasons (supporting arguments, imagery, descriptions of the messiah, and eschatological hopes).

Consistently throughout early Jewish citations and allusions to Isaiah's judgment passages is the early Jewish expectation that the enemies of the current audience will be the ones to receive the Lord's judgment, whether they are the enemies of the Qumran community, the kings of the earth, or those who do not acknowledge Jesus as Lord and Messiah. At the same time, the faithful who follow the Lord—through faithful study of the Torah, dwelling with the Chosen One, or believing that Jesus is Lord—will be redeemed. Often, these early Jewish

---

38. Fekkes, *Isaiah and Prophetic Traditions*, 227–31.

texts interpret Isaiah's foretold redemption as taking place at the consummation of time when the Lord will defeat his enemies, reestablish Jerusalem, and dwell with his people.

In the New Testament specifically, the judgment and woe oracles in Isa 13–27 shaped many judgment passages, especially in Revelation. Similarly, much of the language regarding the Lord's servant and the Lord's redemption of his people (Isa 41–55; 56–66) shaped New Testament interpretations of Jesus as Messiah and the eschatological hopes of his followers. Intriguingly, Paul cites Isaiah most often to describe how the gentiles are included in the Lord's salvation and that all Israel will be saved (esp. Rom 9–11). Paul also applies servant-of-the-Lord passages to himself as a proclaimer of Jesus (Gal 1–2; Acts 13:47; Rom 10:15–16; 15:21). In contrast to Paul, the Gospels, 1 Peter, and Revelation interpret Isaiah with christological and eschatological emphases. First Peter cites Isaiah to portray Jesus as an example of suffering while also presenting Jesus as the stone who may be accepted or rejected. The Gospels present Jesus as the servant of the Lord whom Isaiah foretold, and Isaiah's language shapes Revelation's description of the root of David, the great multitude, the New Jerusalem, and the new heavens and earth.

The New Testament texts interpret Isaiah's prophecies as fulfilled in the life, death, and resurrection of Jesus. The Lord's promised redemption of his people and the judgment of their enemies was understood to apply to those who were faithful to Jesus and those who were not. Isaiah's message that the nations will come to Zion was interpreted in the New Testament as the inclusion of the gentiles; Israel's stumbling was interpreted as the rejection of Jesus, yet as in Isaiah, there was hope that God would redeem all who were faithful to the Lord.

Bibliography

Beaton, Richard. *Isaiah's Christ in Matthew's Gospel*. SNTSMS 123. Cambridge: Cambridge University Press, 2002.

Beers, Holly. *The Followers of Jesus as the Servant: Luke's Model from Isaiah for the Disciples in Luke-Acts*. LNTS 535. London: Bloomsbury T&T Clark, 2016.

Blomberg, Craig L. "Matthew." Pages 1–109 in *Commentary on the New Testament Use of the Old Testament*. Edited by G. K. Beale and D. A. Carson. Grand Rapids: Baker Academic, 2007.

Brooke, George J. "On Isaiah at Qumran." Pages 69–85 in *"As Those Who Are Taught": The Interpretation of Isaiah from the LXX to the SBL*. Edited by Claire Mathews McGinnis and Patricia K. Tull. SymS 27. Atlanta: Society of Biblical Literature, 2006.

Brownlee, William Hugh. "The Literary Significance for the Bisection of Isaiah." Pages 247–59 in *The Meaning of the Qumrân Scrolls for the Bible: With Special Attention to the Book of Isaiah*. New York: Oxford University Press, 1964.

Day, Adam W. *Jesus, the Isaianic Servant: Quotations and Allusions in the Gospel of John*. Gorgias Biblical Studies 67. Piscataway, NJ: Gorgias, 2018.

Fekkes, Jan. *Isaiah and Prophetic Traditions in the Book of Revelation: Visionary Antecedents and Their Development*. JSNTSup 93. Sheffield: JSOT Press, 1994.

Flint, Peter W. "The Interpretations of Scriptural Isaiah in the Qumran Scrolls: Quotations, Citations, Allusions, and the Form of the Scriptural Source Text." Pages 389–406 in vol. 1 of *A Teacher for All Generations: Essays in Honor of James C. VanderKam*. Edited by Eric F. Mason, Samuel I. Thomas, Alison Schofield, and Eugene Ulrich. 2 vols. JSJSup 153. Leiden: Brill, 2012.

García Martínez, Florentino, and Eibert J. C. Tigchelaar, eds. *The Dead Sea Scrolls Study Edition*. 2 vols. Grand Rapids: Eerdmans, 1997–1998.

Hannah, Darrell D. "Isaiah within Judaism of the Second Temple Period." Pages 7–33 in *Isaiah in the New Testament*. Edited by Steve Moyise and Maarten J. J. Menken. London: T&T Clark, 2005.

Harmon, Matthew S. *She Must and Shall Go Free: Paul's Isaianic Gospel in Galatians*. BZNW 168. Berlin: de Gruyter, 2010.

Mallen, Peter. *The Reading and Transformation of Isaiah in Luke-Acts*. LNTS 367. London: T&T Clark, 2008.

Matthewson, David. "Isaiah in Revelation." Pages 189–210 in *Isaiah in the New Testament*. Edited by Steve Moyise and Maarten J. J. Menken. London: T&T Clark, 2005.

Metso, Sarianna. "Biblical Quotations in the Community Rule." Pages 81–92 in *The Bible as Book: The Hebrew Bible and the Judean Desert Discoveries*. Edited by Edward D. Herbert and Emanuel Tov. London: British Library; New Castle: Oak Knoll Press, 2002.

Moyise, Steve, and Maarten J. J. Menken, eds. *Isaiah in the New Testament*. London: T&T Clark, 2005.

Nickelsburg, George W. E., and James C. VanderKam. *1 Enoch: The Hermeneia Translation*. Minneapolis: Fortress, 2012.

Pao, David W. *Acts and the Isaianic New Exodus*. WUNT 2/130. Tübingen: Mohr Siebeck, 2000.

Seitz, Christopher R. "How Is the Prophet Isaiah Present in the Latter Half of the Book? The Logic of Chapters 40–66 within the Book of Isaiah." *JBL* 115, no. 2 (1996): 219–40.

Silva, Moisés. "Galatians." Pages 785–812 in *Commentary on the New Testament Use of the Old Testament*. Edited by G. K. Beale and D. A. Carson. Grand Rapids: Baker Academic, 2007.

Swanson, Dwight. "The Text of Isaiah at Qumran." Pages 191–212 in *Interpreting Isaiah: Issues and Approaches*. Edited by David G. Firth and H. G. M. Williamson. Downers Grove, IL: IVP Academic, 2009.

Wagner, J. Ross. *Heralds of the Good News: Isaiah and Paul "In Concert" in the Letter to the Romans*. NovTSup 101. Leiden: Brill, 2003.

Watts, Rikk E. "Isaiah in the New Testament." Pages 213–33 in *Interpreting Isaiah: Issues and Approaches*. Edited by David G. Firth and H. G. M. Williamson. Downers Grove, IL: IVP Academic, 2009.

Wilk, Florian. *Die Bedeutung des Jesajabuches für Paulus*. FRLANT 179. Göttingen: Vandenhoeck & Ruprecht, 1998.

35

The Psalms in the New Testament

MATTHIAS HENZE

Jesus's followers constantly engaged with Israel's Scripture—reading it, praying it, interpreting it, and recasting it according to their theological needs and preferences. The single most popular book among Israel's authoritative writings, both in Second Temple Judaism and among the writers of the New Testament, is the book of Psalms. More Hebrew copies of Psalms were recovered from Qumran than of any other book. No other book of the Hebrew Bible is cited more often in the New Testament than Psalms. And the trend continues in later manuscript traditions. There are more manuscripts of the LXX Psalter than of any other Septuagintal book, with no fewer than ten times as many copies extant of Psalms than of the second most popular book, the book of Genesis.[1]

In some respects, the followers of Jesus engaged with Psalms much like other Jewish groups at the time. A "book of Psalms" that is part of a collection of authoritative writings is mentioned in Second Temple texts and in the New Testament. Though the evidence is scant, it appears that psalms were part of the earliest worship life of the Jesus movement. The New Testament writers also shared with their contemporaries some general conceptual assumptions about Psalms. David was widely thought to be the author of the book of Psalms as a whole, and his name became synonymous with the Psalter. Psalms was considered an oracular text, initially unfulfilled, whose prophecies came true during the days of the interpreter. And the first-person singular, the "I" of the psalmist that is so prominent in many psalms, was not an anonymous, unknown individual

---

1. Brent A. Strawn, "Textual History of Psalms," in *Writings*, ed. Armin Lange and Emanuel Tov, THB 1C (Leiden: Brill, 2017), 5.

who participated in a liturgical ceremony in ancient Israel, as modern form-critics would have it, but an authoritative figure of Israel's past, whose identity can be recovered and who uttered these precise words at a particular moment in time, which can also be recovered. On these conceptual assumptions there was wide agreement.

In other respects, however, the followers of Jesus parted company with their fellow interpreters and soon developed their own, distinct ways of reading Psalms. They chose their own psalms and gave the familiar texts their own interpretation. An obvious example is Ps 110 (109 LXX), a brief and cryptic composition more often quoted in the New Testament than any other scriptural text, which does not appear to have attracted much interpretive curiosity among pre-Christian Jews.[2] Significantly, and yet unsurprisingly, it was the same set of conceptual assumptions that the Jesus followers shared with other groups—that the Psalms are oracular texts, that they were composed by David through prophecy, that they include the words of an authoritative figure, and that the prophecies have been fulfilled at the time of the readers—that soon led them to develop their own christological readings.

An examination of the role of Psalms in the New Testament is instructive in at least two ways. It is an investigation into how the followers of Jesus, while sharing some of the basic thinking about Psalms with other Jewish groups of their time, from the very beginning forged new and distinct ways of reading Israel's Scriptures. And it examines the particular role played by Psalms in the first attempts to articulate the meaning of Jesus's teaching, suffering, and resurrection. Jesus's followers interpreted his crucifixion and resurrection with the help of Scripture, particularly through the lens of Psalms. Their earliest confessional articulations, which may well predate our written documents in the New Testament, and which need to be understood against the background of the Psalms' pervasive presence in liturgy and study, became foundational in the formation of early Christology.

The Place of the Psalms in the Hebrew Bible

Our investigation of Psalms has to begin within the Hebrew Bible itself, as the book of Psalms occupies a particular place among Israel's Scriptures. Whereas

---

2. Armin Lange and Matthias Weigold, *Biblical Quotations and Allusions in Second Temple Jewish Literature*, JAJSup 5 (Göttingen: Vandenhoeck & Ruprecht, 2011), do not list any early Jewish references to Ps 110. The case for the allusions listed in Bradley H. McLean, *Citations and Allusions to Jewish Scripture in Early Christian and Jewish Writings Through 180 C.E.* (Lewiston, NY: Mellen, 1992), 77, is weak.

the Torah and the Prophets consist largely of narratives, the Psalms are poems, liturgical prayers of the individual or the community, that often, though not always, originated at the temple in Jerusalem. It would be impossible to appreciate the rich reception history of Psalms in Second Temple times, including their use in the New Testament, without being mindful of their liturgical nature and poetic force. Another aspect that sets Psalms apart from the other books in the Bible is their profoundly personal tone. While reaching out to God, the psalmist speaks of extreme joy and distress, reflecting the complex range of human emotions. "The psalms," writes Nahum Sarna, "constitute a revealing portrayal of the human condition."[3] This aspect becomes especially poignant when in the Gospels the words of the psalmist become the last words of Jesus. What does it mean theologically when some of the deepest expressions in Scripture of what it means to be human become Jesus's final words, when Old Testament anthropology becomes New Testament Christology?

But it is a third aspect that concerns us here: the ways in which Psalms refer to, and interact with, the Jewish Scriptures, particularly with the Torah. As has often been observed, biblical interpretation begins within the Hebrew Bible itself.[4] The Scriptures of Israel are self-referential, with the later books interpreting the earlier ones. The Psalms make use of Israel's past in a number of ways. The so-called historical psalms, for example, most notably Pss 78, 105, 106, 135, and 136, recall the narrative traditions that are preserved in the Torah and, to a lesser extent, in the Deuteronomistic History. In particular, they recount the creation accounts, the stories of the patriarchs, the exodus, and the taking of the land, and recast these traditions according to their own theological liking.[5] Other psalms borrow certain language or a particular phrase or recognizable term from earlier texts. In time, the Psalms themselves became Scripture and were cited by the authors of the New Testament.

Some examples may illustrate the point.[6] In John 6:31, the crowd is in discussion with Jesus. They recall the exodus story and, specifically, how God gave the Israelites manna to eat: "as it is written, 'He gave them bread from heaven to eat'" (John 6:31). This is a marked citation, taken from Ps 78:24 (77:24 LXX), one

---

3. Nahum M. Sarna, *On the Book of Psalms: Exploring the Prayers of Ancient Israel* (New York: Schocken, 1993), 3.

4. See Marc Zvi Brettler, "Israel's Scriptures in the Hebrew Bible," ch. 2 in this volume.

5. Adele Berlin, "Interpreting Torah Traditions in Psalm 105," in *Jewish Biblical Interpretation and Cultural Exchange: Comparative Exegesis in Context*, ed. Natalie B. Dohrman and David Stern (Philadelphia: University of Pennsylvania Press, 2008), 20–36.

6. Throughout this chapter, chapter and verse numbers of Psalms follow the MT unless noted otherwise. Unless indicated otherwise, Bible translations follow NRSV.

of the historical psalms.[7] But the psalm, in turn, recalls the same episode from Exod 16.[8]

Table 35.1. John 6:31 and Its Precursor Text(s)

John 6:31	ἄρτον ἐκ τοῦ οὐρανοῦ ἔδωκεν αὐτοῖς φαγεῖν	"He gave them bread from heaven to eat."
Ps 77:24 LXX	καὶ ἔβρεξεν αὐτοῖς μαννα φαγεῖν καὶ ἄρτον οὐρανοῦ ἔδωκεν αὐτοῖς	"And he rained down mana for them to eat, and bread from heaven he gave them."[9]
Exod 16:4	ἐγὼ ὕω ὑμῖν ἄρτους ἐκ τοῦ οὐρανοῦ	"I am going to rain bread from heaven for you."
Exod 16:15	οὗτος ὁ ἄρτος ὃν ἔδωκεν κύριος ὑμῖν φαγεῖν	"This is the bread that the Lord has given you to eat."[10]

To Jesus's interlocutors, who invoke the manna episode, it matters greatly that they are the direct descendants of the Israelites who received the manna in the wilderness. The wandering Israelites were, as they put it, "our ancestors" (οἱ πατέρες ἡμῶν; John 6:31). Like the psalmist before them whose words they cite, they claim the exodus generation as their ancestors.

The next example comes from the book of Acts. After Peter and John are released from prison, they rejoin their friends and pray. Their prayer begins with an invocation, using a familiar formula: "Sovereign Lord, who made the heaven and the earth, the sea, and everything in them" (Acts 4:24; repeated verbatim in Acts 14:15). The author of Luke/Acts is here drawing on prayer language from the

---

7. Margaret Daly-Denton, *David in the Fourth Gospel: The Johannine Reception of the Psalms*, AGJU 47 (Leiden: Brill, 2000). On Ps 78, see Anja Klein, *Geschichte und Gebet: Die Rezeption der biblischen Geschichte in den Psalmen des Alten Testaments*, FAT 94 (Tübingen: Mohr Siebeck, 2014), 86–110.

8. We find a similar phenomenon in the Dead Sea Scrolls. The exhortatory parts of the Damascus Document make use of the historical psalms as well, in particular of Pss 78; 105; and 106, "to enable a particular formulation of the identity of its readers within a broader set of identity markers than those belonging to the sect alone." George J. Brooke, "Praying History in the Dead Sea Scrolls: Memory, Identity, Fulfilment," in *Functions of Psalms and Prayers in the Late Second Temple Period*, ed. Mika S. Pajunen and Jeremy Penner, BZAW 486 (Berlin: de Gruyter, 2017), 314.

9. All translations of the Septuagint are taken from NETS.

10. Michael Fishbane, *Biblical Interpretation in Ancient Israel* (Oxford: Clarendon, 1988), 326–29.

Hebrew Bible. One possible precursor text is Ps 145:6 LXX. But the same formula is also found in four other places in the Hebrew Bible, some predating the psalm (Exod 20:11; 2 Kgs 19:15; Neh 9:6; Isa 37:16).

Table 35.2. Acts 4:24 and Its Precursor Text(s)

Acts 4:24	ὁ ποιήσας τὸν οὐρανὸν καὶ τὴν γῆν καὶ τὴν θάλασσαν καὶ πάντα τὰ ἐν αὐτοῖς	"who made the heaven and the earth, the sea, and everything in them"
Ps 145:6 LXX	τὸν ποιήσαντα τὸν οὐρανὸν καὶ τὴν γῆν τὴν θάλασσαν καὶ πάντα τὰ ἐν αὐτοῖς	"who made the sky and the earth, the sea and all that is in them"
Exod 20:11	ἐποίησεν κύριος τὸν οὐρανὸν καὶ τὴν γῆν καὶ τὴν θάλασσαν καὶ πάντα τὰ ἐν αὐτοῖς	"the Lord made the heaven and the earth and the sea and all things in them"
Neh 9:6 (2 Esd. 19:6 LXX)	σὺ ἐποίησας τὸν οὐρανὸν καὶ . . . τὴν γῆν καὶ πάντα ὅσα ἐστὶν ἐν αὐτῇ τὰς θαλάσσας καὶ πάντα τὰ ἐν αὐταῖς	"you made heaven and . . . the earth and all that is on it, the seas and all that is in them"

The psalmist, whose language is cited in Acts 4:24, already adopted the divine epithet from Israel's traditional lore. By using familiar prayer language with deep roots in Scripture, Luke places Peter, John, and the followers of Jesus in the prayer tradition of ancient Israel that ultimately reaches back all the way to the revelation on Mount Sinai (Exod 20:11).

One last example. In a paraenetic section in Heb 10:26–31, the writer warns the audience of God's final judgment. The punishment for those who repudiate Christ's sacrifice will be dire, we are told, "For we know the one who said, . . . 'The Lord will judge his people'" (Heb 10:30). This is a marked citation, but of which precursor text? The reference may be to Ps 134:14 LXX, which agrees verbatim with Heb 10:30. But the psalmist, in turn, has adopted the same phrase from another ancient poem, the famed Song of Moses in Deut 32.

Table 35.3. Heb 10:30 and Its Precursor Text(s)

Heb 10:30	κρινεῖ κύριος τὸν λαὸν αὐτοῦ	"The Lord will judge his people."
Ps 134:14 LXX	κρινεῖ κύριος τὸν λαὸν αὐτοῦ	"The Lord will judge his people."
Deut 32:36 LXX	κρινεῖ κύριος τὸν λαὸν αὐτοῦ	"The Lord will judge his people."

Which text, then, does the author of Heb 10:30 have in mind? It could be Ps 134. But in the same verse in Hebrews, the writer uses another citation ("Vengeance is mine, I will repay"), this one from Deut 32:35, which tips the balance in favor of Deut 32.

Other examples could be added.[11] All of these citations have in common that the Psalms reuse language and motifs from earlier Scripture. By citing these passages, the New Testament writers continue a rich tradition of interpretation and counterinterpretation, of reading and claiming Israel's authoritative past. That tradition begins already in the Hebrew Bible. We may speculate that the New Testament authors chose these citations in full awareness of their intertextual significance, so that, by citing them, they themselves became part of and contributed to a rich, continuous history of recasting Israel's Scriptures. For them, turning to Psalms meant applying the scriptural past to their own time and laying claim to it.

THE PSALMS IN EARLY JUDAISM

The Daily Psalms at the Temple

Even though our evidence about the use of Psalms in communal worship during the Second Temple period is sparse at best, it is instructive to take note of a few references. Writing after the exile, possibly in the fifth or fourth century BCE, the Chronicler relates how King Hezekiah restored the temple worship in Jerusalem. According to 2 Chr 29:26–28, the Levites accompanied the presentation of burnt offerings at the temple with music on "the instruments of David." The entire nation was divided into twenty-four divisions, and Levitical delegates served in weekly rotation in Jerusalem as the representatives of the people (cf. Josephus, *Ant.* 7.367; m. Tamid 1:1–4; 3:2–5).[12] It appears that the assembled congregation

---

11. (1) In John 19:31–37, the evangelist tells the story of the soldiers, who did not break Jesus bones. John comments: "These things occurred so that the scripture might be fulfilled, 'None of his bones shall be broken'" (19:36). The Scripture in question may be Ps 34:21 (33:21 LXX), though the psalm itself is adopting the language and motif from Exod 12:10, 46, in which case John would connect the motif to Israel's first Passover in Egypt; see Richard B. Hays, *Echoes of Scripture in the Gospels* (Waco, TX: Baylor University Press, 2016), 316–18. (2) In Rom 11:2, Paul states emphatically, "God has not rejected his people whom he foreknew." The same line is found in Ps 94:14 (93:14 LXX), which in turn likely derives from 1 Sam 12:22, Samuel's famed farewell address. (3) One of the scriptural texts in the catena in Heb 1 says about Christ, "Let all God's angels worship him" (Heb 1:6). This may be a marked citation of Ps 97:7 (96:7 LXX), but this is yet another New Testament citation of the Song of Moses, this time of Deut 32:43 LXX.

12. Emil Schürer, *The History of the Jewish People in the Age of Jesus Christ (175 B.C.–A.D. 135)*, rev. Geza Vermes and Fergus Millar (Edinburgh: T&T Clark, 1979), 2:292–308; Günter

joined in the singing (cf. Num 10:10; Luke 1:10; Acts 3:1). While the words of their singing are not preserved, m. Tamid 7:4 reports that each day during the week the Levites recited a particular psalm in the temple. The same tradition is preserved in the superscriptions of the LXX Psalter.[13] For five of the seven days of the week, the superscriptions in the LXX agree with the psalm assignments in m. Tamid 7:4 (in the MT Psalter, by contrast, only Ps 92 is assigned to a particular day of the week, "A Song for the Sabbath Day").[14]

Table 35.4. Psalm of the Day

Day of the Week	m. Tamid 7:4	Superscription in the LXX Psalter	
Sunday	Psalm 24	Ψαλμὸς τῷ Δαυιδ· τῆς μιᾶς σαββάτων.	"A Psalm. Pertaining to Dauid. Of the first day of the week."
Monday	Psalm 48	Ψαλμὸς ᾠδῆς τοῖς υἱοῖς Κορε· δευτέρᾳ σαββάτου.	"A Psalm. Of an Ode. Pertaining to the sons of Kore. Pertaining to the second day of the week."
Tuesday	Psalm 82	*The psalm is not assigned to a particular day of the week.*	
Wednesday	Psalm 94	Ψαλμὸς τῷ Δαυιδ, τετράδι σαββάτων.	"A Psalm. Pertaining to Dauid. Pertaining to the fourth day of the week."
Thursday	Psalm 81	*The psalm is not assigned to a particular day of the week.*	

Stemberger, "Psalmen in Liturgie und Predigt der rabbinischen Zeit," in *Der Psalter in Judentum und Christentum*, ed. Erich Zenger, HBS 18 (Freiburg im Breisgau: Herder, 1998), 200–201.

13. Henry Barclay Swete, *An Introduction to the Old Testament in Greek*, 2nd ed. (Cambridge: Cambridge University Press, 1914), 250–51; Albert Pietersma, "Septuagintal Exegesis and the Superscriptions of the Greek Psalter," in *The Book of Psalms: Composition and Reception*, ed. Peter W. Flint and Patrick D. Miller, VTSup 99 (Leiden: Brill, 2005), 443–75; Gilles Dorival, "Titres hébreux et titres grecs des Psaumes," in *Textual Research on the Psalms and Gospels/Recherches textuelles sur les Psaumes et les Évangiles: Papers from the Tbilisi Colloquium on the Editing and History of Biblical Manuscripts; Actes du Colloque de Tbilisi, 19–20 septembre 2007*, ed. Christian-B. Amphoux and James Keith Elliott, NovTSup 142 (Leiden: Brill, 2012), 3–18.

14. Joachim Schaper, "Der Septuaginta-Psalter: Interpretation, Aktualisierung und liturgische Verwendung der biblischen Psalmen im hellenistischen Judentum," in *Der Septuaginta-Psalter: Sprachliche und Theologische Aspekte*, ed. Erich Zenger, HBS 32 (Freiburg im Breisgau: Herder, 2001), 178.

Friday	Psalm 93	Εἰς τὴν ἡμέραν τοῦ προσαββάτου, ὅτε κατῴκισται ἡ γῆ· αἶνος ᾠδῆς τῷ Δαυιδ.	"Regarding the day of the presabbath, when the earth had been settled. A laudation. Of an Ode. Pertaining to Dauid."
Saturday	Psalm 92	Ψαλμὸς ᾠδῆς, εἰς τὴν ἡμέραν τοῦ σαββάτου.	"A Psalm. Of an Ode. Regarding the day of the sabbath."

Ben Sira ends his Hymn of the Ancestors with a paean to the high priest Simon son of Onias (Sir 50:1–24). The praise includes a detailed description of a ritual at the temple, though it remains unclear whether this is a description of the Day of Atonement or of the daily offerings (similarities with m. Tamid 6–7 favor the latter). After the offerings were brought, "the singers praised him [God] with their voices [καὶ ᾔνεσαν οἱ ψαλτῳδοὶ ἐν φωναῖς αὐτῶν] in sweet and full-toned melody" (Sir 50:18). Again, the words of their praises are not preserved, but we may assume that the ritual included the recitation of Psalms.[15]

The Psalms at Qumran

The most significant evidence about Psalms during the Second Temple period, their textual history, and their use comes from the Dead Sea Scrolls.[16] The discovery of no fewer than forty-two Psalm manuscripts from in and around Qumran has generated a lively debate about the nature of these scrolls, their intended purposes, uses, and significance.[17]

---

15. Note also the conclusion to the account of Judas's victorious battle at Emmaus in 1 Macc 4:24: "On their return they sang hymns and praises to Heaven—'For he is God, for his mercy endures forever' (Ps 136 [135 LXX])." See also 3 Macc 6:32; 4 Macc 18:15 (citing Ps 34:20 [33:20 LXX]).

16. General overviews of the Psalms in late Second Temple times, including but not limited to the scrolls, are provided by George J. Brooke, "The Psalms in Early Jewish Literature in the Light of the Dead Sea Scrolls," in *The Psalms in the New Testament*, ed. Steven Moyise and Maarten J. J. Menken, NTSI (London: T&T Clark, 2004), 5–24; and Eileen Schuller, "Functions of Psalms and Prayers in the Late Second Temple Period," in Pajunen and Penner, *Functions of Psalms*, 5–24.

17. Peter W. Flint published an early list of all the Psalms manuscripts, "Appendix: Psalms Scrolls from the Judean Desert," in *Pseudepigraphic and Non-Masoretic Psalms and Prayers*, ed. James H. Charlesworth, PTSDSSP 4A (Tübingen: Mohr Siebeck, 1997), 287–90; for a detailed description, see Armin Lange, "Psalms: Ancient Hebrew Texts," in *Writings*, ed. Armin Lange and Emanuel Tov, THB 1C (Leiden: Brill, 2017), 25–42.

Much of this debate has focused on the largest of these scrolls, the Great Psalms Scroll from Cave 11, 11Q5 (11QPs^a). Originally published in 1965 by James A. Sanders, the scroll has been much discussed.[18] One reason for this attention is the scroll's peculiar sequencing of the psalms. In its current form, 11Q5 includes psalms exclusively from books 4 and 5 of the MT Psalter, but it arranges them in an altogether different order. Peter W. Flint, the premier scholar on the Qumran Psalms scrolls, argues that 11Q5 is an alternative edition to the MT Psalter and that it proves the existence of multiple editions of the book of Psalms that existed simultaneously at Qumran. Specifically, Flint distinguishes between three Psalters: Pss 1–89, that is, the first three books of the MT Psalter; Pss 1–89 + books 4 and 5 of the Psalter in the arrangement found in 11Q5 (and also in 11Q6 [11QPs^b] and 4Q87 [4QPs^e]), which Flint labels the "11QPs^a-Psalter"; and the MT Psalter.[19] Several other interpretations of 11Q5 have since been offered, most notably that 11Q5 is not a Psalter at all but a collection of excerpted texts. Regardless of one's view of the nature of 11Q5, Flint is certainly correct to emphasize that the scrolls prove the existence of multiple Psalms editions that coexisted at the time of the Qumran community.[20]

Another distinctive feature of 11Q5 is the inclusion of several compositions that are not part of the MT Psalter and that are mixed in with the psalms. One of them is a brief prose text, dubbed "David's Compositions" (11Q5 XXVII, 2–11). It tells of David, a wise man, whom God gave a discerning and enlightened spirit. The text then goes on to list the "psalms" (תהלים) and other songs that David composed, totaling 4,050 compositions. The brief text closes with the line:

כול אלה דבר כנבואה אשר נתן לו מלפני העליון

"All these he [David] composed through prophecy given him by the Most High" (XXVII, 11).[21]

---

18. James A. Sanders, *The Psalms Scroll of Qumrân Cave 11 (11QPsa)*, DJD 4 (Oxford: Clarendon, 1965).

19. Peter W. Flint, *The Dead Sea Psalms Scrolls and the Book of Psalms*, STDJ 17 (Leiden: Brill, 1997). See also Eva Jain, *Psalmen oder Psalter? Materielle Rekonstruktion und inhaltliche Untersuchung der Psalmenhandschriften aus der Wüste Juda*, STDJ 109 (Leiden: Brill, 2014); and Mika S. Pajunen, "Perspectives on the Existence of a Particular Authoritative Book of Psalms in the Late Second Temple Period," *JSOT* 39, no. 2 (2014): 139–63.

20. Flint's suggestion of three different Psalters turns out to be minimalistic. Lange, "Psalms. Ancient Hebrew Texts," 24, lists seven different psalms collections, each with its distinct psalms sequence.

21. All quotations from the Dead Sea Scrolls are taken from Donald W. Parry and Emanuel Tov, *The Dead Sea Scrolls Reader*, 2nd ed., rev. and expanded, 2 vols. (Leiden: Brill, 2014).

"David's Composition" is placed toward the end of 11Q5 as one of four compositions that all focus on David: "David's Last Words" (XXI, 11–XXII, 1), "David's Compositions," and "Psalms 151 A and B." Such emphasis on David, as well as his remarkable depiction as a most prolific composer, allows us to draw some conclusions. Flint argues that, taken together, these four compositions "assert Davidic authorship of the 11QPs^a-Psalter."[22] In other words, while David is certainly a prominent figure in the MT Psalter, with 73 psalms ascribed to him in their superscriptions, David's role is even further emphasized in 11Q5: he is considered the author of *all* of its psalms. The writer claims, furthermore, that David wrote 4,050 psalms and hymns, significantly more than are preserved in either the 11QPs^a-Psalter or in the MT. David was able to write all of these texts "through prophecy" (כנבואה). The psalms are prophecies, oracular poems whose exact meaning would not have been evident even to David himself when he wrote them but that came true in the respective times of the interpreters.[23]

One other text from Qumran needs to be mentioned, 4QMMT, a text from the late second century BCE, which, in its third and final part, makes reference to some collections of writings that were considered authoritative by the community.

10 [כתב]נו אליכה שתבין בספר מושה] ו[בספר]י הנ[ביאים ובדוי[ד]
11 [מעשי] דור ודור

10 "to you we have [written] that you must understand the book of Moses[and] the book[s of the pr]ophets and of Davi[d]
11 [the annals of] each generation" (4Q397 IV, 10–11).

The passage is typically seen as an early proof of the existence of a Hebrew canon at Qumran. Exactly how many parts made up this collection of author-

---

22. Peter W. Flint, "The Prophet David at Qumran," in *Biblical Interpretation at Qumran*, ed. Matthias Henze (Grand Rapids: Eerdmans, 2005), 163.

23. We need to note Flint's cautionary note, however. After listing several texts, including the continuous pesharim on the Psalms, 1Q16 (1QpPs); 4Q83 (4QPs^a); and 4Q84 (4QPs^b), as well as texts from the New Testament, the Psalms targum, and some rabbinic writings that all call David a prophet, Flint warns that naming David a prophet and associating him with prophecy "is relatively rare in the Qumran corpus." And yet, Flint concludes that "the psalmist David was viewed as a prophet to whom God revealed later and significant events in their lives and community" (Flint, "Prophet David at Qumran," 166–67). See also James L. Kugel, "David the Prophet," in *Poetry and Prophecy: The Beginning of a Literary Tradition*, ed. James L. Kugel (Ithaca, NY: Cornell University Press, 1990), 45–55; and Jesper Høgenhaven, "Psalms as Prophecy: Qumran Evidence for the Reading of Psalms as Prophetic Text and the Formation of the Canon," in Pajunen and Penner, *Functions of Psalms*, 229–51.

itative books remains a matter of some dispute. The references to the Mosaic Torah and to the Prophets seem clear, even if we cannot know which books were included among the Prophets. The question is what to do with the mention of David at the end of line 10. Does "David" here stand for a third part of the canon that subsequently would become the Writings, or does MMT bear witness to two groups of Scripture only, the Law and the Prophets, and David is simply an example of one of the books or collections subsumed under the Prophets?[24] In either case, it seems clear that "David" here has become synonymous with a collection of psalms, either with what Flint calls the 11QPs^a-Psalter or with another psalms collection, and that that collection was considered authoritative by the members of the community during the second century BCE, either as the third part of an emerging canon or as part of the Prophets.

The Psalms in the New Testament

According to the *loci citati vel allegati* in NA[28], Psalms clearly lead the list of Hebrew Bible books cited and alluded to in the New Testament. No fewer than 606 New Testament uses of Psalms are listed, 101 "direct quotations" and 505 "allusions."[25] According to that list, 129 of the 150 psalms in the MT Psalter are either cited or alluded to at least once in the New Testament.[26] Even though those numbers are almost certainly exaggerated, there can be no doubt that Psalms enjoyed immense popularity among the followers of Jesus.[27] Even if we leave the

---

24. See Brooke, "Psalms in Early Jewish Literature," 12–14; and Eugene Ulrich, *The Dead Sea Scrolls and the Developmental Composition of the Bible*, VTSup 169 (Leiden: Brill, 2015), 300–304, who argues that the most commonly used term for a collection of authoritative writings at Qumran was "the Law and the Prophets."

25. NA[28], 851–55.

26. Harold W. Attridge, "Giving Voice to Jesus: Use of the Psalms in the New Testament," in *Psalms in Community: Jewish and Christian Textual, Liturgical, and Artistic Traditions*, ed. Harold W. Attridge and Margot E. Fassler, SymS 25 (Atlanta: Society of Biblical Literature, 2004), 101–12, lists the psalms that, according to NA[28], are not attested in the New Testament: Pss 3; 12; 13; 30; 52; 56; 57; 58; 59; 60; 64; 81; 83; 120; 121; 124; 127; 129; 131; 133; 142.

27. The exaggeration is especially true of the allusions in the list. Take the example of Ps 1, a text that was both cited and alluded to in early Judaism: e.g., 4Q174 (4QMidrEschat^a) 1–2 I, 14 (citation of Ps 1:1); 1QS VI, 6; and 4Q418 (4QInstruction^d) 43–45 I, 9 (allusions to Ps 1:2); 1QH^a XVIII, 27–28; X, 25–26 (allusion to Ps 1:3); Wis 5:14 (a possible allusion to Ps 1:4). Is Ps 1 ever mentioned in the New Testament? Nestle-Aland lists three allusions, in Acts 24:5 (to Ps 1:1); Matt 21:41 (Ps 1:3); and Matt 13:49 (Ps 1:5), but all three are doubtful. There is no evidence that Ps 1 is mentioned in the New Testament; similarly, Susan E. Gillingham, *A Journey of Two Psalms: The Reception of Psalms 1 and 2 in Jewish and Christian Tradition* (Oxford: Oxford University Press, 2013), 39: "Psalm 1 is never explicitly referred to [in the New Testament]."

allusions aside for a moment, the number of citations alone is impressive. Psalms from all five books of the Psalter are cited across the New Testament, in Matthew (12 times), Mark (6 times), Luke (8 times), John (8 times), Acts (10 times), Romans (15 times), 1 Corinthians (4 times), 2 Corinthians (2 times), Ephesians (3 times), Hebrews (20 times), 1 Peter (3 times), and Revelation (3 times). Table 35.7, "The Psalms in the New Testament," at the end of this chapter provides a more cautious overview, with a focus on the citations. Where appropriate, I have added references to those Psalms passages in early Jewish and Christian texts that are cited or alluded to in the New Testament.[28]

How Did the Followers of Jesus Know the Psalms?

The recitation of Psalms appears to have been a fixed part of the worship life of the early Jesus movement. Their liturgies included the singing of "psalms and hymns and spiritual songs" ([ἐν] ψαλμοῖς καὶ ὕμνοις καὶ ᾠδαῖς πνευματικαῖς, Eph 5:19; similarly in Col 3:16; see also 1 Cor 14:26; Jas 5:13; Rev 5:8–10). We may assume that the "psalms" (ψαλμόι) included the recitation of what we know as the biblical psalms, though the mention of additional "hymns and spiritual songs" makes clear that the early liturgy included hymns other than the Psalms.[29] According to the book of Acts, communal prayer was a part of major events (Acts 1:14, 24). It is noteworthy that the brief narrative in Acts 1:15–26 about the reconstitution of the disciples following the death of Judas includes an allusion to, and two citations of, Psalms (Acts 1:16 alludes to Ps 41:10 [40:10 LXX]; Acts 1:20 cites Ps 69:26 [68:26] LXX and Ps 109:8 [108:8 LXX]), the only scriptural book mentioned in the account.

All references to a "book of Psalms" (βίβλος ψαλμῶν) in the New Testament come from Luke/Acts. In the Gospel of Luke, Jesus is involved in a disputatious exchange with the scribes over the correct interpretation of Ps 110. Introducing the first verse of the psalm, Jesus says: "For David himself says in the book of

---

28. In addition to NA[28], I have consulted the following lists: "Index of Quotations and Allusions—Psalm Order (MT)," in Moyise and Menken, *Psalms in the New Testament*, 249–50; Lange and Weigold, *Biblical Quotations*, 163–78; and McLean, *Citations and Allusions*, 67–81. See also Franz Stuhlhofer, *Der Gebrauch der Bibel von Jesu bis Euseb: Eine statistische Untersuchung zur Kanonsgeschichte* (Wuppertal: Brockhaus, 1988); on Philo, David T. Runia, "Philo's Reading of the Psalms," *SPhiloA* 13 (2001): 102–21; and Christiane Böhm, *Die Rezeption der Psalmen in den Qumranschriften, bei Philo von Alexandrien und im* Corpus Paulinum, WUNT 2/437 (Tübingen: Mohr Siebeck, 2017), 85–91.

29. Robert F. Taft, SJ, "Christian Liturgical Psalmody: Origins, Development, Decomposition, Collapse," in Attridge and Fassler, *Psalms in Community*, 8–9; Michael Cameron, "Psalms," in *The Oxford Handbook of Early Christian Biblical Interpretation*, ed. Paul M. Blowers and Peter W. Martens, Oxford Handbooks (Oxford: Oxford University Press, 2019), 575–76.

Psalms" (αὐτὸς γὰρ Δαυὶδ λέγει ἐν βίβλῳ ψαλμῶν, Luke 20:42). Four chapters later, the risen Christ explains to his disciples "that everything written about me in the law of Moses, the prophets, and the psalms [ἐν τῷ νόμῳ Μωϋσέως καὶ τοῖς προφήταις καὶ ψαλμοῖς] must be fulfilled" (Luke 24:44). The implication is that Scripture consists of two or three parts: Moses and the Prophets, and possibly Psalms.[30] Each part contains christological prophecies that, according to Luke, "must be fulfilled." In Acts 1:20, Luke comments on the death of Judas by citing Ps 109:8 (108:8 LXX), which he introduces with the words, "For it is written in the book of Psalms" (γέγραπται γὰρ ἐν βίβλῳ ψαλμῶν). The reference to "the second psalm" (ἐν τῷ ψαλμῷ ... τῷ δευτέρῳ) in Acts 13:33, as well as the phrase, "Therefore he has also said in another psalm" (διότι καὶ ἐν ἑτέρῳ λέγει) just a couple of verses later (Acts 13:35), presuppose the existence of a written Psalms collection.[31]

For other New Testament authors, too, a reference to David becomes synonymous with a reference to the book of Psalms. In order to explain Jesus's use of parables, for example, Matthew puts a quotation from Ps 78:2 into the mouth of Jesus. For the evangelist, Jesus's manner of teaching "what has been hidden from the foundation of the world" (Ps 78:2 [77:2 LXX], cited in Matt 13:35) is in fulfillment of scriptural prophecy: "This was to fulfill what had been spoken through the prophet" (ὅπως πληρωθῇ τὸ ῥηθὲν διὰ τοῦ προφήτου λέγοντος, Matt 13:35). The "prophet," of course, is David, even though in both the MT and LXX, Ps 78 is attributed to Asaph, not David. For Matthew, David was the author even of those psalms that do not bear his name.[32] Similarly we read in Acts 1:16 that "the scripture had to be fulfilled, which the Holy Spirit through David foretold" (ἔδει πληρωθῆναι τὴν γραφὴν ἣν προεῖπεν τὸ πνεῦμα τὸ ἅγιον διὰ στόματος Δαυὶδ περὶ Ἰούδα).[33] In other words, the Psalter is a book of prophecy containing the

---

30. The passage is often discussed as part of the canon debate. Other pertinent texts are the Prologue to Ben Sira; 2 Macc 2:13–15; Philo, *Contempl.* 25; Josephus, *Ag. Ap.* 1.37–43; and Luke 24:44. See Edmon L. Gallagher, "What Were the Scriptures in the Time of Jesus?," ch. 1 in this volume.

31. Cf. the reference to "the Psalms of David" in Ques. Ezra A35; Ascen. Isa. 4:21 mentions several collections of poetic compositions in addition to Psalms: "the rest of the psalms which the angel of the spirit has inspired."

32. Matthew is not alone in attributing psalms to David that do not have a Davidic heading. See 11Q13 (11QMelch) II, 9–10, which introduces a citation of Ps 82, like Ps 78 a psalm attributed to Asaph, with the words: "as is written about him in the songs of David, who said" (כאשר כתוב עליו בשירי דויד אשר אמר); cf. Eva Mroczek, *The Literary Imagination in Jewish Antiquity* (Oxford: Oxford University Press, 2016), 67.

33. Note how David is explicitly called a "prophet" (προφήτης) in Acts 2:29–31, who foresaw the resurrection of the messiah. See also Luke 20:42; Acts 2:25, 34; Rom 11:9; Heb 4:7; cf. T. Adam 4:3 ("the words of David the prophet"); Apoc. Sedr. 14:4; Apoc. Dan. 14:11.

words of David, which he spoke "by the Holy Spirit" (ἐν τῷ πνεύματι τῷ ἁγίῳ, Mark 12:36) or "by the Spirit" (ἐν πνεύματι, Matt 22:43; cf. Acts 2:34; 4:25–26; Rom 4:6).[34] We are reminded of the line in "David's Compositions" that David composed all these psalms "in prophecy" (כול אלה דבר כנבואה).

Finally, we should make note of another verse in the Gospel of Matthew. Following the Lord's Supper, the Evangelist writes about the disciples, "When they had sung the hymn [Καὶ ὑμνήσαντες], they went out to the Mount of Olives" (Matt 26:30). Since in Matthew's view the last supper is a Passover meal, we may assume that "the hymn" is a reference to Pss 113–118 (or possibly only to Pss 113–114), known as the Egyptian Hallel or the Great Hallel, which is recited during Passover.[35] If this is correct, then Matt 26:30 would give us a rare glimpse of the liturgical practice of the Jesus followers.

How did the followers of Jesus know the Psalms? References to a "book of Psalms" and to "David" as their supposed author demonstrate that written Psalms collections were available and readily served as source texts, even if there is no way of knowing exactly which form these collections took. Dale Allison lists a number of texts in which early Jewish and Christian writers boast of their knowledge of Scripture, suggesting that the Scriptures "were presumably the centerpiece of whatever elementary education [Jews and] Jewish Christians may have had" (cf. 4 Macc 18:10; Acts 17:11; 18:24; 2 Tim 3:15; Josephus, *Ag. Ap.* 2.175, 178; 1 Clem. 53:1; Polycarp, *Phil.* 12:1).[36] To Allison's list we may add Paul's own testimony, "a Hebrew born of Hebrews" (Phil 3:5), who insists that he was "zealous for the traditions of [his] ancestors" (Gal 1:14), a zeal that undoubtedly meant that Paul was intimately familiar with Israel's scriptural traditions.[37]

---

34. Among the Dead Sea Scrolls, continuous pesharim were found only of prophetic books, including Isaiah, Hosea, Micah, Nahum, Habakkuk, Zephaniah, and Psalms: 1Q16 (1QpPs) and 4Q171, 4Q173. Ulrich, *Dead Sea Scrolls*, 288, goes so far as to claim that "the Psalter's transformation to the status of Scripture was evidently due to its prophetic character."

35. B. Pesaḥ. 116b includes a dispute between the School of Hillel and the School of Shammai about which portions of the Hallel to recite before and after the meal. On Psalms in Matthew, see Frank-Lothar Hossfeld and Erich Zenger, "Das Matthäusevangelium im Lichte der Psalmen," in *"Dies ist das Buch . . . ,": Das Matthäusevangelium; Interpretation – Rezeption – Rezeptionsgeschichte; für Hubert Frankmölle*, ed. Rainer Kampling (Paderborn: Schöningh, 2004), 129–40; Maarten J. J. Menken, "The Psalms in Matthew's Gospel," in Moyise and Menken, *Psalms in the New Testament*, 61–82.

36. Dale C. Allison, "The Old Testament in the New Testament," in *From the Beginnings to 600*, vol. 1 of *The New Cambridge History of the Bible*, ed. James Carleton Paget and Joachim Schaper (Cambridge: Cambridge University Press, 2013), 496.

37. David Lincicum, "How Did Paul Read Scripture?," in *The New Cambridge Companion to St. Paul*, ed. Bruce W. Longenecker, Cambridge Companions to Religion (Cambridge: Cambridge University Press, 2020), 225–26.

The followers of Jesus must have known Psalms not only from study but also from worship and regular participation in the liturgy. "There can be an oral literacy as well as a visual literacy," writes Allison, "and within the context of formative Christianity, an inability to read scripture cannot be equated with an ignorance of scripture."[38] This is nowhere truer than of Psalms.

Introducing the Psalms: Marked Citations

The authors of the New Testament use a variety of introductory formulas to mark their psalm citations. The majority of the formulas name a particular precursor text. Above we already noticed the mention of a "book of Psalms" (Luke 20:42; Acts 1:20) or simply of "David"/"the prophet" (Matt 13:35; 22:43; Mark 12:36; Luke 20:42; Acts 1:16; 2:34; Rom 4:6) as the scriptural source. Other writers speak more vaguely of "the Scripture(s)" when introducing a psalm, for example, in Mark 12:10, where the main character of the parable says, "Have you not read this scripture" (οὐδὲ τὴν γραφὴν ταύτην ἀνέγνωτε; also Matt 21:42; Luke 20:17 rephrases the rhetorical question slightly, "What then does this text mean?" [τί οὖν ἐστιν τὸ γεγραμμένον τοῦτο]). Similarly in John 13:18, Jesus alludes to his betrayal by drawing on Ps 41:10, which he introduces with the words, "But it is to fulfill the scripture" (ἀλλ᾽ ἵνα ἡ γραφὴ πληρωθῇ).[39] John uses yet another term to refer to Psalms. Twice in his Gospel he subsumes certain psalms under the "law," in John 10:34 ("Is it not written in your law?"; οὐκ ἔστιν γεγραμμένον ἐν τῷ νόμῳ ὑμῶν) and in 15:25 ("It was to fulfill the word that is written in their law"; ἀλλ᾽ ἵνα πληρωθῇ ὁ λόγος ὁ ἐν τῷ νόμῳ αὐτῶν γεγραμμένος), introducing citations from Ps 82:6 (81:6 LXX), and 69:5 (68:5 LXX), respectively.[40]

Other introductory formulas are less specific and do not identify the scriptural precursor text. A good example is Paul. When the apostle cites a passage from Psalms in Romans or 1 and 2 Corinthians, he often introduces it with the words, "As it is written" (καθὼς γέγραπται), never naming the text in question (Rom 3:4, 10; 8:36; 11:8; 15:3, 9; 1 Cor 3:19; 2 Cor 9:9; however, see also Rom 4:7; 10:18; 11:2; 1 Cor 10:26; 2 Cor 4:13). Unspecific references to a written source can take different forms: "for it is written" (γέγραπται γὰρ, Matt 4:6 // Luke 4:10; cf. John 6:31), "Have you never read?" (οὐδέποτε ἀνέγνωτε ὅτι,

---

38. Allison, "Old Testament in the New Testament," 497.

39. The fulfillment formula is repeated in John 12:38; 13:18; 15:25; 17:12; 19:24, 28, 36. Significantly, with the exception of 12:38, the source texts from Scripture in all of these cases are from Psalms, and the context is always the Johannine passion story.

40. Hays, *Echoes of Scripture in the Gospels*, 338, argues that "law" is "a comprehensive descriptor for all of Israel's Scripture." To support his case, Hays refers the reader to John 10:34; 12:34; 15:25; Rom 3:19; cf. 1 Cor 14:21; Gal 4:21.

Matt 21:16; cf. Matt 21:42), "What then does this text mean?" (τί οὖν ἐστιν τὸ γεγραμμένον τοῦτο, Luke 20:17), and "His disciples remembered that it was written" (ἐμνήσθησαν οἱ μαθηταὶ αὐτοῦ ὅτι γεγραμμένον ἐστίν, John 2:17), all introducing a citation from Psalms. Note also how Heb 2:6–8a includes a long citation of Ps 8:5–7 but curiously leaves the identity of the speaker indefinite, even though in the MT the psalm has a Davidic heading: "But someone has testified somewhere" (διεμαρτύρατο δέ πού τις λέγων, Heb 2:6; cf. 4:4). Occasionally we find references to the psalms as *spoken* words, for example in Eph 4:8, "Therefore it is said" (διὸ λέγει), introducing a quotation from Ps 68:19 (67:19 LXX). More often, David is said to have spoken the words of the psalms. See, for example, Mark 12:23, "David himself said" (αὐτὸς Δαυὶδ εἶπεν; cf. Matt 22:43; Luke 20:42; Acts 2:25, 31, 34; 4:25 Rom 4:6; Rom 11:9; Heb 4:7).[41]

The purpose of marked citations is to illustrate or, more typically, to support a certain claim by quoting an authoritative text. The precursor text can either be identified (e.g., "the book of Psalms," "David," "the Scriptures"), or it remains indefinite (e.g., "As it is written," "Have you never read?," "But someone has testified somewhere"). In either case, the point is to appeal to the received (written) tradition and to draw on its authority. The fulfillment quotations (e.g., "This was to fulfill") present a special case. Here the precursor text is authoritative because it is oracular (e.g., "David himself by the Holy Spirit declared"). According to the New Testament writers, the prophecies have been fulfilled in Jesus.

Unmarked Citations

Unmarked psalm citations fall into two groups. The first group comprises texts in which a New Testament author puts a citation into the mouth of an individual or a group without signaling that the direct speech is a verbatim quotation from Psalms. This is probably the best-known use of Psalms in the New Testament since it includes Jesus's last words, "My God, my God, why have you forsaken me" (Mark 15:34 // Matt 27:46, citing Ps 22:2 [21:2 LXX]). There are several other examples in which Jesus is the speaker of the Psalms. While in Gethsemane, Jesus expresses his profound distress in words of Ps 42:6, "I am deeply grieved, even to death" (Mark 14:34 // Matt 26:38). In his lament over Jerusalem, Jesus cites the makarism from Ps 118:26 (117:26 LXX), "Blessed is the one who comes in the

---

41. 4Q177 (4QCatena A) frags. 12–13 introduces a quotation from Ps 6:2–3 with "David said" (אמר דויד); 11Q13 (11QMelch) II, 9–12 is a series of three quotations from Psalms (Pss 82:1; 7:8–9; 82:2), each introduced with "he said"; 4 Macc 18:15. Margaret Daly-Denton, "David the Psalmist, Inspired Prophet: Jewish Antecedents of a New Testament *Datum*," *ABR* 52 (2004): 32–47; see Valérie Nicolet, "Figures of Ancient Israel in the New Testament," ch. 37 in this volume.

name of the Lord" (Luke 13:35), thereby anticipating his triumphant entry into the city a few chapters later (Luke 19:38).[42] When questioned by the high priest about the accusations brought against him, Jesus responds by quoting Ps 110:1 (109:1 LXX), and Dan 7:13, a potent combination of Hebrew Bible images that look to Jesus's ascension and eschatological enthronement on the heavenly seat of judgment (Matt 26:64).

Jesus is not the only person in the New Testament whose words include citations from the Psalms. The crowd famously greets Jesus upon his entry into the city with the words of Ps 118:25–26 (117:25–26 LXX), "Blessed is the one who comes in the name of the Lord" (Mark 11:9–10 // Matt 21:9 // Luke 19:38; John 12:13). In Acts 4, Peter, "filled with the Holy Spirit" (Acts 4:8), gives a speech in which he describes Jesus as the stone that was rejected by the builders (Acts 4:11), citing Ps 118:22 (117:22 LXX), only that Peter adds the words "[rejected] by you" (ὑφ' ὑμῶν) to place the blame on the council members for having rejected Jesus. Just a few verses later, in Acts 4:24, the Jesus followers pray in the words of Ps 146:6 (145:6 LXX) (cf. Acts 14:15), "Sovereign Lord, who made the heaven and the earth."

The Epistle to the Hebrews presents a special case.[43] With the exception of Heb 4:7, Hebrews does not attribute any psalm to David.[44] Instead, it is God, the exalted Son, and the Holy Spirit who speak in the words of Psalms. God is the implied speaker of the catena in Heb 1, including the quotations of Ps 2:7 in Heb 1:5; Ps 97:7 (96:7 LXX) in Heb 1:6; Ps 104:4 (103:4 LXX) in Heb 1:7; Ps 45:7–8 (44:7–8 LXX) in Heb 1:8–9; Ps 102:26–28 (101:26–28 LXX) in Heb 1:10–12; and Ps 110:1 (109:1 LXX) in Heb 1:13. That Heb 4:3 attributes Ps 95:11 (94:11 LXX) to God is not surprising since God also speaks the words of Ps 95:8–11, possibly originally recited by a priest as part of a temple liturgy.

The Son is quoted twice in Hebrews with words from Psalms. The first reference is in Heb 2:12. Jesus addresses God in prayer in the words of Ps 22:23 (21:23 LXX): "I will proclaim your name to my brothers and sisters, in the midst of the congregation I will praise you" (Heb 2:12). Psalm 22 is used by all four evange-

---

42. Matthew and Luke both draw on Ps 118:25–26 twice (as opposed to Mark and John, who each quote it once, in Mark 11:9–10 and John 12:13). Luke uses it first in Jesus's lament over Jerusalem (Luke 13:31–35) and then again at his entry (Luke 19:38). Matthew reverses the two episodes and has Jesus enter into Jerusalem first (Matt 21:9), before he laments the city (Matt 23:39).

43. See Gabriella Gelardini, "Israel's Scriptures in Hebrews," ch. 20 in this volume.

44. The case of Heb 4:7 is puzzling. The writer explicitly cites a line from "David," though the exact source text remains unclear. A likely candidate is Ps 95:7–8 since Heb 3:7–4:7 is an extended homily on Ps 95; cf. Harold W. Attridge, "The Psalms in Hebrews," in Moyise and Menken, *Psalms in the New Testament*, 205–8; Simon J. Kistemaker, *The Psalm Citations in the Epistle to the Hebrews* (Amsterdam: van Soest, 1961).

lists in their passion narratives (Matt 27:43, 46; Mark 15:24, 34, 43; Luke 23:34; John 19:24). Whereas the evangelists were drawn to the psalm because of the petitioner's urgent plea in the first half of the psalm (Ps 22:1–22a), Hebrews cites a line from the recovery and thanksgiving part in the second half of the psalm (Ps 22:22b–32).[45] Psalm 22 thus provides Hebrews with the words in which Jesus confesses his unity with, and fidelity to, God. Jesus expresses his intention to proclaim God's name in the midst of the congregation. The second reference to Jesus comes in Heb 10:5–7. Jesus is quoted saying, in the words of Ps 40:7–9 (39:7–9 LXX), that God has no desire for sacrifices and burnt offerings. In the context of Ps 40, which mimics similar sentiments expressed by the Prophets, proclaiming God's steadfast love in the great congregation is to be preferred over the presentation of sacrifices. In Heb 10:5–7, Jesus has become the ultimate sacrificial offering that replaces all other sacrifices.[46] Harold Attridge makes the astute observation that the quotation ends with the speaker's statement of commitment, "See, God, I have come to do your will, O God" (Heb 10:7, citing Ps 40:9 [39:9 LXX]). These words are a model of fidelity, first expressed by the psalmist, then cited and embodied by Christ, and consequentially to be emulated by the faithful. "Just as the Son's earlier words in ch. 2 modelled the kind of behavior expected of all God's sons and daughters, this final comment of the dutiful, priestly Son models the fidelity that his siblings should exhibit."[47]

Finally, the quotation of Ps 95:7–11 (94:7–11 LXX) in Heb 3:7–11 is explicitly ascribed to the Holy Spirit, "Therefore, as the Holy Spirit says" (Διό καθὼς λέγει τὸ πνεῦμα τὸ ἅγιον; Heb 3:7). As already noted, Heb 3:7–4:7 is part of an extended homily on Ps 95. For the author of Hebrews, the speaker of the psalm can be both God and the Holy Spirit.[48]

The second, significantly smaller group of unmarked citations consists of text passages in which the authors write, using words from the Psalms (as opposed to putting them into the mouths of their protagonists) without marking these words as direct quotations. In Rom 2:1–11, for example, Paul discusses God's

---

45. This is one of several examples in the New Testament in which the same psalm, in this case Ps 22, was used differently by different New Testament authors. Günter Reim, "Vom Hebräerbrief zum Johannesevangelium, anhand der Psalmzitate," *BZ* 44, no. 1 (2000): 92–100, discusses two other cases, the interpretation of Pss 45 and 95 in the Fourth Gospel and in Hebrews.

46. Benjamin J. Ribbens, "The Sacrifice God Desired: Psalm 40.6–8 in Hebrews 10," *NTS* 67, no. 2 (2021): 289–93.

47. Attridge, "Psalms in Hebrews," 210; see also Dirk J. Human and Gert J. Steyn, eds., *Psalms and Hebrews: Studies in Reception*, LHBOTS 527 (New York: T&T Clark, 2010).

48. This may be compared to Acts 1:16, where the Holy Spirit foretold Jesus's betrayal by Judas "through David" (the allusion is to Ps 41:10 [40:10 LXX]).

impartiality in judgment with an (imaginary) interlocutor. Insisting that nothing will remain hidden from God on the day of judgment, Paul writes, "For he will repay according to each one's deeds" (Rom 2:6), a quotation of Ps 62:13 (61:13 LXX), or possibly Prov 24:12. In his extended discussion of the resurrection, Paul provides a step-by-step description of the final days, including the final reign of the risen Christ. Paul insists that Christ must "reign until he [God] has put all enemies under his feet" (1 Cor 15:25), citing Ps 110:1 (109:1 LXX), a royal psalm apparently so well known that Paul didn't deem it necessary to mark it as such. First Peter draws on Psalms with some frequency.[49] First Peter 2:3 cites an abbreviated form of Ps 34:9 (33:9 LXX), "O taste and see that the Lord is good," again without marking it, possibly because the origin of these words would have been self-evident to the readers/hearers.

Unmarked citations can have multiple purposes. In the case of the first group, the New Testament authors find in the Psalms the actual words spoken by God, by Jesus, by the Holy Spirit, or by the people of Jerusalem. The writers cite the words and supply the specific historical contexts in which these words were spoken. For the second group of unmarked citations, authors who write in the words of the Psalms, the purpose is similar to that of the marked citations: to appeal to the authority of Scripture when making their case. In the three examples we have listed, we may wonder whether the source texts were so well known that the authors thought it unnecessary to mark them as citations.

Verbal and Conceptual Allusions

Nestle-Aland lists more than five hundred allusions to Psalms in the New Testament, far more than to any other scriptural book. Regardless of the methodological problems involved in determining what exactly constitutes an allusion and how to distinguish an allusion from a citation, it is evident that allusions to Psalms in the New Testament by far outnumber the citations.[50]

In this volume we distinguish between verbal and conceptual allusions. In a verbal allusion, the evoked and the alluding text share a certain language, such as a particular word or a brief phrase. Verbal allusions can be short. In Mark's version of the feeding of the five thousand, for example, Jesus tells the people "to sit down in groups on the green grass" (ἐπὶ τῷ χλωρῷ χόρτῳ, Mark 6:39). Why does Mark emphasize that the grass was green? Rather than finding here the words of an eyewitness or an indication that the scene is set during Israel's springtime, Dale

---

49. Sue Woan, "The Psalms in 1 Peter," in Moyise and Menken, *Psalms in the New Testament*, 213–29; Jörg Frey, "Israel's Scriptures in 1 and 2 Peter, Jude," ch. 22 in this volume.

50. See the introduction to this volume for a summary of the debate.

Allison prefers an intertextual explanation. Mark alludes to Ps 23 and the idyllic image of God the Good Shepherd, who leads the psalmist "in green pastures" (εἰς τόπον χλόης, Ps 23:2 [22:2 LXX]).[51] In this christological reading, Jesus provides for the faithful much like the Good Shepherd in Ps 23 does for the poet.

Another example comes from Jesus's prayer in John 17. Jesus relates to the Father how the disciples will fare once they are sent into the world: they will be met with rejection and hatred. "The world has hated them because they do not belong to the world, just as I do not belong to the world" (John 17:14). In other words, the hostility the followers of Jesus will encounter is an extension of the same hostility toward Jesus. The use of the word "hatred" goes back to John 15:18, where Jesus had already explained, "If the world hates you, be aware that it hated me before it hated you." This language, in turn, is drawn from Ps 69. "It was to fulfill the word that is written in their law, 'They hated me without a cause'" (Ps 69:5 [68:5 LXX]). In chapter 15, the psalm is cited to explain the unwarranted hatred toward Jesus "without a cause," which, a couple of chapters later, is transferred to the disciples.[52]

In conceptual allusions, precursor text and intertext are linked by a common motif, theme, or recognizable image. A good example comes from Ps 107, a psalm of thanksgiving (Ps 107:1). The psalmist mentions four groups whom God has redeemed from adversity: the hungry and thirsty (107:4–9), the imprisoned (107:10–16), the grievously ill (107:17–22), and seafarers who survived a major storm (107:23–32). The psalm's message is made clear in its last verse: "those who are wise give heed to these things" (Ps 107:43), that is, the wise know that God intervenes and rescues the downtrodden. Mark's story of the stilling of the storm (Mark 4:35–41 // Matt 8:23–27 // Luke 8:22–25) is often compared with Jonah 1–2. But the allusions to the depiction of the fourth group in Ps 107:22–32 (106:22–32 LXX) are more telling: the waves of the sea surge (Mark 4:37; Ps 107:25); the sailors' courage melts (Mark 4:38; Ps 107:26); they cry for help (Mark 4:38; Ps 107:26–27); Jesus rebukes the wind (Mark 4:39; Ps 107:29); and the sailors are filled with great awe (Mark 4:41; Ps 107:30–32). Whereas in the Hebrew Bible it is God who alone has mastery over the wind and who commands the chaotic waters (cf., e.g., Isa 51:9–11; Job 38:8–11; Pss 89:9; 106:8–12), in Mark's story Jesus possesses equal powers and embodies God's presence in Israel.[53]

Another example: the line in Ps 41:10 (40:10 LXX), "Even my bosom friend in whom I trusted, who ate of my bread, has lifted the heel against me," originally

---

51. Dale C. Allison Jr., "Psalm 23 (22) in Early Christianity: A Suggestion," *IBS* 5 (1983): 132–37.
52. Hays, *Echoes of Scripture in the Gospels*, 338–39.
53. Hays, *Echoes of Scripture in the Gospels*, 69.

spoken by the psalmist about a friend who ended up betraying the psalmist, is invoked three times in the New Testament, in Mark, John, and Acts. In each case the context is Judas's betrayal of Jesus, but each of the three New Testament authors finds his own way of connecting the psalm with Jesus's betrayal. We begin with Mark. When Jesus sits down with the Twelve for the Lord's Supper, he announces, "Truly I tell you, one of you will betray me, one who is eating with me" (Mark 14:18). Mark never says as much, but Jesus's enigmatic words are an allusion to Ps 41:10 (40:10 LXX). This may not be clear in Mark, but the connection is made explicit by John, who knew of the same textual tradition. After Jesus has washed his disciples' feet in John 13, Jesus says to them: "I am not speaking of all of you; I know whom I have chosen. But it is to fulfill the scripture (ἵνα ἡ γραφὴ πληρωθῇ), 'The one who ate my bread has lifted his heel against me'" (John 13:18).[54] Jesus's statement is surprising since John has not yet mentioned any food, only the washing of feet. The Johannine Jesus explicitly cites Ps 41:10 (40:10 LXX), which has become a prophecy that has been fulfilled in Jesus's betrayal.[55] The third reference comes from Acts 1. Peter begins his speech in Jerusalem by recalling the infamous scene: "Friends, the scripture had to be fulfilled, which the Holy Spirit through David foretold concerning Judas, who became a guide for those who arrested Jesus" (Acts 1:16). Like Mark, Luke never cites the psalm. But unlike Mark, Luke mentions David and Judas and assumes that the hearer/reader recognizes the precursor text to which he is alluding. But Luke goes one step further: Not only was Jesus's betrayal foretold by "the Holy Spirit through David," but "the scripture had to be fulfilled" (ἔδει πληρωθῆναι τὴν γραφήν).[56] In other words, Judas *had to* betray Jesus because the Holy Spirit had prophesied his betrayal already through David in Ps 41.[57]

Our last example of a conceptual allusion comes from the passion story. In all four Gospels, Jesus is given vinegar to drink while he is hanging on the cross

54. Maarten J. J. Menken, "The Translation of Psalm 41.10 in John 13.18," *JSNT* 13, no. 40 (1990): 61–79.

55. Four chapters later, in his prayer in John 17, Jesus yet again refers to Judas: "While I was with them, I protected them in your name that you have given me. I guarded them, and not one of them was lost except the one destined to be lost, so that the scripture might be fulfilled" (John 17:12; cf. 18:9). That Scripture, though not further identified, would seem to be Ps 41:10.

56. Peter's choice of language is highly reminiscent of the summary of David's activities in 11Q5: "All these he [David] composed through prophecy given him by the Most High" (XXVII, 11).

57. In a hodayah in 1QHª XIII, 22–41, a beleaguered individual, possibly the Teacher of Righteousness, bemoans that the other members of the community, who are closely associated with him, nonetheless speak ill of him. "Al[so those] who eat my bread have lifted the heel against me" (1QHª XIII, 25–26, citing Ps 41:10). Cf. Carol A. Newsom, *The Self as Symbolic Space: Constructing Identity and Community at Qumran*, STDJ 52 (Leiden: Brill, 2004), 332–46.

(Matt 27:48; Mark 15:36; Luke 23:36; John 19:28–29). Only John reveals to his readers that the scene is an allusion to a verse from the Psalms: "he [Jesus] said in order to fulfill the scripture" (ἵνα τελειωθῇ ἡ γραφή, John 19:28). The motif is taken from Ps 69:22 (68:22 LXX), a prayer of a suffering innocent "servant" (ואל־תסתר פניך מעבדך; "do not hide your face from your servant," Ps 69:18; cf. Isa 52:13), who is insulted and persecuted by his enemies. The psalmist laments the humiliation of asking for help and being offered poison instead. "They gave me poison for food, and for my thirst they gave me vinegar to drink" (Ps 69:22). Together with Ps 22, Ps 69 is a central text for the account of Jesus's last moments. The psalm opens with a cry of invocation, "Save me, O God" (Ps 69:1), recounts in detail the psalmist's neglect and suffering, and ends with the psalmist's thanksgiving (Ps 69:30–36). Surely, the attentive reader/listener of the passion story would have recognized the precursor text and would have known that Ps 69 ends with the ultimate vindication of the suffering servant.

The purpose of allusions is more subtle than that of citations. They add a depth to the text, a deeper level of intentionality. A good example are the laments of the individual and their use in the passion story.

Mark's Passion Narrative

Esther Menn begins her incisive study of Ps 22 in Jewish and Christian interpretation with a look at the ways modern form-critics and premodern interpreters have understood the use of the first-person voice, the "I" frequently found in many Psalms.[58] For form critics, the speaker of the psalm is an anonymous individual who participated in a worship setting to express feelings of extreme distress and thanksgiving. As many psalms are liturgical formulas, over time any individual can pray the psalm and effectively adopt the psalmist's persona. For premodern readers, by contrast, the voice of the individual initially was David, as evidenced already in the psalm superscriptions that attribute particular psalms to certain moments in the life of David (e.g., Pss 3; 51; 54; 56–57; 59–60). Subsequently, other biblical figures of Israel's past also came to be identified with the psalmist. Menn calls this move from poetry to history a "historicizing movement." The poetic language of the psalm becomes the "historicized" narrative of a particular moment in time. The purpose is to harmonize different parts of Scripture: "it draws the Psalter into the scope of the overarching narrative recounted elsewhere in scripture."[59]

---

58. Esther M. Menn, "No Ordinary Lament: Relecture and the Identity of the Distressed in Psalm 22," *HTR* 93, no. 4 (2000): 301–41.

59. Menn, "No Ordinary Lament," 302.

The followers of Jesus understood the first-person speaker in the Psalms in much the same way. The classic example is Mark's passion narrative.[60] During his arrest, Jesus declares, somewhat cryptically, "Let the scriptures be fulfilled" (ἵνα πληρωθῶσιν αἱ γραφαί, Mark 14:49; cf. 14:21), with no further hint or explanation. The reader is never told which Scriptures exactly are fulfilled in Jesus's passion. The mystery is solved when Jesus cries the words of Ps 22:2 (21:2 LXX) from the cross, "My God, my God, why have you forsaken me?" (Mark 15:34). But the attentive reader will have long noticed that Mark's passion and crucifixion narratives form a tight web of Psalms allusions and citations, as the following table illustrates.[61]

Table 35.5. Mark's Passion Narrative

Mark	The Psalms	The Motif
14:18	41:10	One who is eating with Jesus betrays him.
14:34	42:6, 12; 43:5	Jesus's soul is deeply grieved.
14:57	27:12; 35:11	False witnesses speak out against Jesus.
14:61; 15:5	38:14–15	Jesus remains silent before his accusers.
14:62	110:1 [cf. Dan 7:13]	Jesus seated at God's right hand.
15:23, 36	69:22	Jesus is given wine mixed with myrrh/vinegar.
15:24	22:19	The soldiers divide Jesus's clothes among them.
15:24	22:19	The soldiers cast lots.
15:29, 32	22:7–8 [cf. Lam 2:15; Ps 109:25]	Jesus is derided.
15:30–31	22:9	"Save yourself."
15:34	22:2	"My God, my God, why have you forsaken me?"
15:37	22:2, 5, 24	Jesus gives a loud cry.
15:39	22:28–29	The centurion represents "the nations."
15:40	38:12	The bystanders stand far off.

Telling his story of Jesus's betrayal, trial, and crucifixion, Mark draws extensively on Scripture. The first thing to notice is what is not here. Whereas some

---

60. Rikk E. Watts, "The Psalms in Mark's Gospel," in Moyise and Menken, *Psalms in the New Testament*, 25–45.

61. The table is adapted and expanded from Allison, "Old Testament in the New Testament," 494. In the list of psalms, chapter and verse numbers follow the MT, even when the citation is from the LXX. Joel Marcus, *The Way of the Lord: Christological Exegesis of the Old Testament in the Gospel of Mark* (London: T&T Clark, 2004), 172–86, finds additional allusions in Mark. See Craig A. Evans, "Praise and Prophecy in the Psalter and in the New Testament," in Miller and Flint, *Book of Psalms: Composition and Reception*, 565–66, for a general list of the laments of the individual in the passion narratives.

modern interpreters have found in Mark's narrative allusions to Isaiah's suffering servant of Isa 52:13–53:12, there are, in fact, no unambiguous allusions to, or citations of, Isaiah here. The case that has been made for such allusions is not convincing (e.g., Mark 10:45 and Isa 53:12; Mark 14:61 and Isa 53:7) and reflects the theological interpretations of Jesus's death by other New Testament authors.[62]

Instead, Mark draws heavily on Psalms, and also on the apocalyptic visions of Daniel (Mark 2:28; 13:24–27; 14:62) and Zechariah (Mark 11:1–11; 14:26–28), to find the language and framework for his account of Jesus's last hours. In particular, he uses a group of psalms Hermann Gunkel labels the Laments of the Individual, which Joel Marcus prefers to call Psalms of the Righteous Sufferer.[63] In them, an individual, who speaks in the first person, calls on God for deliverance, laments persecutions from the enemies, and claims to be innocent. The psalms typically end with the ultimate vindication of the righteous sufferer and a prayer of thanksgiving.

The central psalm in Mark's passion narrative is Ps 22.[64] Like other Psalms of the Righteous Sufferer, Ps 22 consists of two parts: a lament in the first half (Ps 22:1–22a [21:1–22a LXX]) and the vindication of the psalmist in the second (Ps 22:22b–32 [21:22b–32 LXX]). Apart from the possible allusion to Ps 22:28–29 (21:28–29 LXX) in Mark 15:39, with the centurion representing "the ends of the earth" (Ps 22:28) who now turn to the God of Israel, all references to Ps 22 in Mark 14–15 are to the first, the lament section. We are left to wonder: Is it Mark's intention to draw his readers' attention only to those psalm verses to which he alludes, all of which happen to be in the lament part of the psalm, or are we to assume that by alluding to these verses, Mark is, in fact, invoking Ps 22 as a whole? The answer to this question will have

---

62. Hays, *Echoes of Scripture in the Gospels*, 86–87, observes that Paul, Luke, and John explicitly point to Isa 53, but not Mark. For a different view on Mark, see Marcus, *Way of the Lord*, 186–96; and Elizabeth Shively, "Israel's Scriptures in Mark," ch. 9 in this volume.

63. Marcus, *Way of the Lord*, 172–86; Adela Yarbro Collins, "The Appropriation of the Psalms of Individual Lament by Mark," in *The Scriptures in the Gospels*, ed. Christopher Tuckett, BETL 131 (Louvain: Leuven University Press, 1997), 223–41; Stephen Ahearne-Kroll, *The Psalms of Lament in Mark's Passion: Jesus' Davidic Suffering*, SNTSMS 142 (Cambridge: Cambridge University Press, 2007), 59–81.

64. Hans-Josef Fabry, "Die Wirkungsgeschichte des Psalms 22," in *Beiträge zur Psalmenforschung: Psalm 2 und 22*, ed. Josef Schreiner, FB 60 (Würzburg: Echter, 1988), 279–317; Bernd Janowski, "Die jüdischen Psalmen in der christlichen Passionsgeschichte: Eine rezeptionsgeschichtliche Skizze," in *Freiheit und Recht: Festschrift für Frank Crüsemann zum 65. Geburtstag*, ed. Christof Hardmeier, Rainer Kessler, and Andreas Ruwe (Gütersloh: Kaiser; Gütersloher Verlagshaus, 2003), 397–413; Dieter Sänger, ed., *Psalm 22 und die Passionsgeschichte der Evangelien*, BThSt 88 (Neukirchen-Vluyn: Neukirchener Verlag, 2007); Holly J. Carey, *Jesus' Cry from the Cross: Towards a First-Century Understanding of the Intertextual Relationship between Psalm 22 and the Narrative of Mark's Gospel*, LNTS 398 (London: T&T Clark, 2009).

significant consequences, not only for Mark's use of Psalms but also for how we view his interpretation of Jesus's death and resurrection. If Mark is interested in specific verses only, then Ps 22 would provide the details of Jesus's suffering and give us a glimpse into Jesus's inner life. The evangelist would find in Ps 22 the words spoken by Jesus (Mark 15:34), as well as a description of the circumstances surrounding the crucifixion (Mark 15:24, 29, 32, 37, 39, 40). But there would be no message of hope.[65] If, on the other hand, it was Mark's intention to invoke the psalm as a whole, then his choice of Ps 22 would have much larger implications. As already noted, the tone of the speaker changes in the latter half of the psalm: the psalmist now speaks in the past tense and, no longer imploring God for help, thanks God who has answered the psalmist's prayer (Ps 22:24). Next, the speaker calls on an ever-larger circle of worshipers to join in God's praise, first the immediate congregation (Ps 22:26), then all nations (Ps 22:28–29), and finally even the deceased (Ps 22:30), which some interpreters have seen as a reference to the resurrection of the dead.[66] The psalm ends, rather abruptly, with the triumphant acclamation, "he [God] has done it" (Ps 22:32), affirming that God has fully vindicated the righteous sufferer. If Mark considers Ps 22 as a whole to be the scriptural subtext for his passion story, as does indeed seem likely, and not just the specific verses to which he alludes, then the alert reader would have immediately known that Jesus's cry on the cross during his darkest hour is not the final word. God vindicates the righteous sufferer, as prophesied by the psalmist. All the nations, including the gentile world, will come to realize that God "has done it" (Ps 22:32) in the crucifixion. In a Gospel that lacks an Easter story, this is a powerful message.

Mark's account of Jesus's passion and crucifixion is a collage of references to Psalms. Indeed, his use of Psalms is so pervasive that it is impossible to imagine Jesus's passion story without them. Is that Mark's invention? In other words, was it Mark who first interpreted Jesus's suffering and death through the lens of Psalms? Rudolf Bultmann argued that the earliest account of Jesus's passion was a matter-of-fact, historical account. In Bultmann's reading, any typological correspondences between Jesus's suffering and Psalms, including any allusion to Scripture, are secondary additions, motivated by the dogmatic or apologetic motifs of the early church.[67] It is not clear, though, why any reference to Scripture

---

65. Without referencing Ps 22, Rudolf Bultmann, *Das Verhältnis der urchristlichen Christusbotschaft zum historischen Jesus*, SHAW (Heidelberg: Winter, 1961), 12, argued that we cannot exclude the possibility that Jesus died in utter resignation and despair. "Die Möglichkeit, daß er zusammengebrochen ist, darf man sich nicht verschleiern."

66. See, e.g., Hartmut Gese, "Psalm 22 und das Neue Testament: Der älteste Bericht vom Tode Jesu und die Entstehung des Herrenmahls," *ZTK* 65, no. 1 (1968): 1–22.

67. Rudolf Bultmann, *The History of the Synoptic Tradition*, trans. John Marsh, 2nd ed. (New York: Harper & Row, 1968) 273–81; Adela Yarbro Collins, *Mark: A Commentary*, Hermeneia (Minneapolis: Fortress, 2007), 732–35, for a summary of the debate.

would make the account less historical and therefore needs to be considered an addition. Instead of deeming the use of Psalms an addition to Jesus's passion narrative, the opposite case seems more likely: already the earliest followers of Jesus, who needed to make sense of the crucifixion and resurrection, turned to Psalms as their hermeneutical lens. Psalms gave them the tools to make sense of the nonsensical. "The interpretation of Jesus' death and resurrection," writes Richard Hays, "as far back as we can trace it, grows organically out of the matrix of the psalms of the Righteous Sufferer."[68] A christological reading of Psalms emerged from the desire to understand the crucified Messiah. Psalms provided the Jesus followers with both language and framework. We are reminded of the oldest resurrection account in the New Testament, Paul's summary in 1 Cor 15. Paul writes that on the third day Christ was resurrected "in accordance with the scriptures" (κατὰ τὰς γραφὰς, 1 Cor 15:4; cf. Rom 1:3–4). If we are correct that the connection between Jesus's passion narrative and Psalms is traditional and already predates Mark, we might wonder, with Hays, whether "the Scriptures" to which Paul refers, are not, in fact, the Psalms.[69]

A final thought. So far, our reading has been unilinear, tracing the use of Psalms in Mark. The complex web of Psalms allusions shows that, according to Mark, Jesus's crucifixion had been prophesied in several texts in the Hebrew Bible and that, far from demonstrating the power of Rome, it had been part of God's plan all along. Once the connection between the Psalms of the Righteous Sufferer and Jesus's passion has been made, it is impossible for the Christian reader to hear the passion narrative without hearing the Psalms and vice versa. Passion and Psalms are now irrevocably linked and mutually interpret each other.[70] That connection is theologically meaningful not merely in terms of prophecy and fulfillment but because the most dire expressions of human suffering in the Hebrew Bible are now inextricably tied to Jesus's suffering, death, and resurrection. That is Mark's good news.

Paul

The use of Psalms across the *corpus Paulinum* is rather uneven. It includes twenty-two Psalms citations total, sixteen in Romans, four in 1 Corinthians, two in 2 Corinthians, and none in the other Pauline epistles.[71] This uneven distribution

---

68. Richard Hays, "Christ Prays the Psalms: Israel's Psalter as Matrix of Early Christology," in *The Conversion of the Imagination: Paul as Interpreter of Israel's Scripture* (Grand Rapids: Eerdmans, 2005), 118.
69. Hays, "Christ Prays the Psalms," 118.
70. Allison, "Old Testament in the New Testament," 494.
71. To these we might add the evidence from Ephesians. Ephesians 1:20 alludes to Ps 110:1 (109:1 LXX); Eph 1:22 cites Ps 8:7 (cf. 1 Cor 15:27); Eph 4:8 cites Ps 68:19 (67:19 LXX); and

does not appear to be particular to Psalms but rather reflects Paul's use of Scripture in general.[72] The table below lists all citations (and some allusions) in the Pauline epistles, and, where appropriate, adds the relevant citation markers.[73]

Table 35.6. *Psalms in the Corpus Paulinum*

Paul	The Psalms	Citation Markers	
Rom 2:6	Ps 62:13 [also Prov 24:12]	*Unmarked citation*	
Rom 3:4	Ps 116:11 [115:2 LXX]	δέ	"but"
Rom 3:4	Ps 51:6	καθὼς γέγραπται	"as it is written"
Rom 3:10–12	Ps 14:2–3; cf. Ps 53:3–4	καθὼς γέγραπται	"as it is written"
Rom 3:13	Ps 5:10		
Rom 3:13	Ps 140:4		
Rom 3:14	Ps 10:7		
Rom 3:18	Ps 36:2		
Rom 3:20	Ps 143:2	*Verbal allusion*	
Rom 4:7–8	Ps 32:1–2	καθάπερ καὶ Δαυὶδ λέγει	"So also David speaks" (Rom 4:6)
Rom 8:34	Ps 110:1	*Verbal allusion*	
Rom 8:36	Ps 44:23	καθὼς γέγραπται	"as it is written"
Rom 10:18	Ps 19:5	*Unmarked citation*	
Rom 11:2	Ps 94:14 [cf. 1 Sam 12:22 LXX]	*Unmarked citation*	
Rom 11:9–10	Ps 69:23–24	καὶ Δαυὶδ λέγει	"And David says"

Eph 4:26 cites Ps 4:5; Paul Foster, "Israel's Scriptures in Ephesians and Colossians," ch. 16 in this volume.

72. Cf. Steve Moyise, *Paul and Scripture: Studying the New Testament Use of the Old Testament* (Grand Rapids: Baker Academic, 2010), 18–19, who provides this list of "Scriptural references" in the Pauline epistles: Romans (sixty); 1 Corinthians (seventeen); 2 Corinthians (ten); Galatians (ten); Ephesians (five); Philippians (none); 1 Thessalonians (none); 2 Thessalonians (none); 1 Timothy (one); 2 Timothy (one); Titus (none); Philemon (none).

73. The table is adapted, with some changes, from Böhm, *Die Rezeption der Psalmen*, 130. Chapter and verse numbers follow the MT, even when the citation is from the LXX. Böhm finds an additional citation of Ps 143:2 (142:2 LXX) in Gal 2:16. Sylvia C. Keesmaat, "The Psalms in Romans and Galatians," in Moyise and Menken, *Psalms in the New Testament*, 158–60, adds two allusions to our list, in Gal 2:16 to Ps 143:2 (142:2 LXX), and in Gal 3:16 to Ps 89:38–39, 47, 51–52 (88:38–39, 47, 51–52 LXX).

Rom 15:3	Ps 69:10	ἀλλὰ καθὼς γέγραπται	"but, as it is written"
Rom 15:9	Ps 18:50 = 2 Sam 22:50	καθὼς γέγραπται	"as it is written"
Rom 15:11	Ps 117:1	καὶ πάλιν	"and again"
1 Cor 3:20	Ps 94:11 [cf. 1 Sam 12:22 LXX]	γέγραπται γάρ	"For it is written" (1 Cor 3:19)
1 Cor 10:26	Ps 24:1	γάρ	"for"
1 Cor 15:25	Ps 110:1	Unmarked citation	
1 Cor 15:27 [cf. Eph 1:22]	Ps 8:7	γάρ	"for"
2 Cor 4:13	Ps 116:10 [115:1 LXX]	κατὰ τὸ γεγραμμένον	"that is in accordance with scripture"
2 Cor 9:9	Ps 112:9	καθὼς γέγραπται	"as it is written"

Of the twenty-two Psalms citations in the Pauline epistles, four are unmarked (Rom 2:6; 10:18; 11:2; 1 Cor 15:25) and eighteen are marked (Rom 3:4, 10–18; 4:7–8; 8:36; 10:18; 11:2, 9–10; 15:3, 9, 11; 1 Cor 3:20; 10:26; 15:27; 2 Cor 4:13; 9:9). Paul makes use of a variety of citation formulas. As already noted, the most common are variations of the phrase "as it is written" (καθὼς γέγραπται, Rom 3:4, 10; 8:36; 15:3, 9; 1 Cor 3:20; 2 Cor 4:13; 9:9). Others can be as short as a single word (δέ, "but," in Rom 3:4; γάρ, "for," in 1 Cor 10:26; 15:27) or a brief phrase (καὶ πάλιν, "and again," in Rom 15:11). Twice Paul uses "David says" (Δαυὶδ λέγει in Rom 4:6; 11:9). Not surprisingly, Paul cites a version of Psalms closely aligned with the LXX, with only a few stylistic and grammatical alterations to adapt the precursor text to its new context.[74]

The significant majority of Psalms citations in Paul's writings occur in Romans.[75] Roughly half of them are part of catenae, that is, four clusters of scrip-

---

74. The changes are listed in Böhm, *Die Rezeption der Psalmen*, 131–33; see also Dietrich-Alex Koch, *Die Schrift als Zeuge des Evangeliums: Untersuchungen zur Verwendung und zum Verständnis der Schrift bei Paulus*, BHT 69 (Tübingen: Mohr Siebeck, 1986), 11–101 (on Psalms, 55–56).

75. Richard B. Hays, "Intertextual Echo in Romans," in *Echoes of Scripture in the Letters of Paul* (New Haven: Yale University Press, 1989), 34–83; David Lincicum, "Intertextuality, Effective History, and Memory: Conceptualizing Paul's Use of Scripture," in *Paulinische Schriftrezeption: Grundlage – Ausprägungen – Wirkungen – Wertungen*, ed. Florian Wilk and Markus Öhler, FRLANT 268 (Göttingen: Vandenhoeck & Ruprecht, 2017), 9–22; Jens Schröter, "Israel's Scriptures in Romans," ch. 13 in this volume.

tural citations embedded in the epistle. In the first catena in Rom 3:10–18, which is also the longest in Romans, Paul combines no fewer than five Psalms citations (Ps 14:2–3 [13:2–3 LXX] in Rom 3:10–12; Ps 5:10 in Rom 3:13; Ps 140:4 [139:4 LXX] in Rom 3:13; Ps 10:7 [9:28 LXX] in Rom 3:14; and Ps 36:2 [35:2 LXX] in Rom 3:18), a citation from Isaiah (Isa 59:7–8 in Rom 3:15–17), and possibly one from Proverbs (Prov 1:16 in Rom 3:15), without identifying each citation separately. Psalms is the dominant source text in this first catena (noticeably, there is no citation from the Torah), whereas in the other three catenae that follow, Paul combines quotations from what will become the three parts of the Hebrew canon: in Rom 10:18–20 from Psalms (Ps 19:5 [18:5 LXX] in Rom 10:18), Deuteronomy, and Isaiah; in Rom 11:8–10 from Deuteronomy, Isaiah, and Psalms (Ps 69:23–24 [68:23–24 LXX] in Rom 11:9–10); and in Rom 15:9–12 from Psalms (Ps 18:50 [17:50 LXX] in Rom 15:9), Deuteronomy, Psalms again (Ps 117:1 [116:1 LXX] in Rom 15:11), and Isaiah. We find similar clusters of scriptural citations, or *testimonia*, among the fragments from Qumran.[76] Whether Paul created the catenae in Romans himself or whether he already inherited them can be debated. What is clear from the evidence at Qumran, however, is that the catenae are a literary form of scriptural engagement that well predates Paul.[77]

Paul draws on Psalms for several reasons, though mainly to seek scriptural support for his argument. The text passages that include Psalms citations have different topics. In them, Paul discusses the nature of God (Rom 2:6; 1 Cor 3:20; 2 Cor 9:9), Israel's chosenness (Rom 10:18; 11:2, 9–10), his theology of justification apart from works (Rom 3:4, 10–18, 20; 4:7–8; 15:9, 11), and the need for him to speak (2 Cor 4:13), or he offers some advice (Rom 8:36; 15:9–11; 1 Cor 10:26). The citations are not mere proof texts but form an integral part of Paul's argument. In each case, Paul weaves a Psalms citation into his narrative to draw on its scriptural support. It may be no coincidence that Paul leans on Psalms particularly when he gets to the more controversial parts of his letters and needs a boost of authority.

Another reason why Paul turns to Psalms is that they serve as the scriptural foundation for his Christology. His allusion to Ps 110:1 (109:1 LXX) in Rom 8:34,

---

76. This was already noticed, while the first scrolls were only beginning to be published, by Joseph A. Fitzmyer, "'4QTestimonia' and the New Testament," *TS* 18 (1957): 513–37 (repr., *Essays on the Semitic Background of the New Testament*, SBLSBS 5 [Missoula, MT: Scholars Press, 1974], 59–89). Fitzmyer finds three *testimonia* in Romans, in 3:10–18; 9:25–29; and 15:9–12.

77. Enno Edzard Popkes, "Essenisch-qumranische und paulinische Psalmen-Rezeptionen: Ein Beitrag zur frühjüdischen Schrifthermeneutik," in *Jesus, Paulus und die Texte von Qumran*, ed. Jörg Frey and Enno Edzard Popkes, WUNT 2/390 (Tübingen: Mohr Siebeck, 2015), 248.

for example, is the oldest christological use of Ps 110 and the confession that the risen Christ is seated at the right hand of God.[78]

| Ps 109:1 LXX | κάθου ἐκ δεξιῶν μου | "Sit on my right" |
| Rom 8:34 | ὅς καί ἐστιν ἐν δεξιᾷ τοῦ θεοῦ | "who is at the right hand of God" |

In Rom 15:3, Paul cites Ps 69:10 (68:10 LXX), a Psalm of the Righteous Sufferer, to demonstrate that Christ, who "did not please himself," is an example for the faithful, who, likewise, should not act on their own behalf but build up their neighbors. In 1 Cor 15:20–28, Paul gives a detailed account of the events at the end of time. In this eschatological scenario, Pss 110:1 (109:1 LXX) and 8:7 provide the language for Paul's description of the messianic kingdom and Christ's ultimate defeat of all enemies.

There does not appear to be any particular psalm, or group of psalms, to which Paul returns repeatedly. The apostle never cites the same phrase or psalm motif more than once, though there are four psalms that he uses twice: Ps 69 (Ps 69:10 [68:10 LXX] in Rom 15:3, and Ps 69:23–24 [68:23–24 LXX] in Rom 11:9–10); Ps 94 (Ps 94:11 [93:11 LXX] in 1 Cor 3:20, and Ps 94:14 [93:14 LXX] in Rom 11:2); Ps 110 (Ps 110:1 [109:1 LXX] in Rom 8:34 "at the right hand of God," as well as in 1 Cor 15:26 "[God] put all his enemies under his [the Messiah's] feet"); and Ps 116 (Ps 116:10 [115:1 LXX] in 2 Cor 4:13, and Ps 116:11 [115:2 LXX] in Rom 3:4). All other psalms Paul uses only once.

It is also instructive to compare Paul's choice of psalms with that of the other New Testament authors. Noticeably, there are only four psalms referenced in the Pauline letters that are also used by other New Testament writers. They are Pss 8 and 110, which enjoy great popularity among the writers of the New Testament (see table 35.7 at the end of the chapter). Psalm 62 is a meditation on the trustworthiness of God; in Rom 2:6, Paul quotes the psalm's final line, "For he will repay according to each one's deeds," which is also alluded to in Matt 16:27 and Rev 2:23. And Ps 69, finally, which Paul cites twice, in Rom 11:9–10 and 15:3, both times with proper citation markers, is a Psalm of the Righteous Sufferer that is also cited by John (John 2:17; 15:25) and alluded to by all evangelists. This means that the clear majority of psalms to which Paul turns are not used by any other writer in the New Testament.[79] Equally interesting is which psalms that

---

78. See also 1 Pet 3:22, ὅς ἐστιν ἐν δεξιᾷ [τοῦ] θεοῦ, "who is at the right hand of God." Martin Hengel, "Psalm 110 und die Erhöhung des Auferstandenen zur Rechten Gottes," in *Anfänge der Christologie: Festschrift für Ferdinand Hahn zum 65. Geburtstag*, ed. Cilliers Breytenbach and Henning Paulsen (Göttingen: Vandenhoeck & Ruprecht, 1991), 45–51.

79. They are Pss 5; 10; 14; 18; 19; 24; 32; 36; 44; 51; 53; 94; 106; 112; 116; 117; 140; and 143.

are referenced elsewhere in the New Testament Paul does not use. These include some of the most prominent and widely used psalms, such as Pss 2; 22; and 118. It may be presumptuous to speculate about the reasons for this silence. It appears that certain psalms came to be associated with specific aspects of the earliest Christology. Psalms 22 and 118 provide the scriptural basis for the narrative descriptions of Jesus's passion and crucifixion, aspects of lesser concern for Paul.

The Psalms in the Early Church

The use of Psalms in the New Testament is altogether remarkable—for its pervasiveness, diversity, and innovation. The authors of the New Testament frequently turned to Psalms, more so, in fact, than to any other book of the Hebrew Bible.[80] They engaged with Psalms in remarkably diverse ways and for many different reasons: to borrow a certain phrase from Psalms or allude to a particular motif; to remember Israel's past by citing words from Psalms; to pray in the idiom of Psalms; to claim the scriptural authority of Psalms; to invoke Psalms' promises; or to demonstrate that Jesus's passion and crucifixion were no accidents but the fulfillment of prophecies found throughout Psalms. To these early interpreters, "interpretation" did not mean to try to figure out what a particular psalm meant by using a certain exegetical method. Rather, interpretation meant reapplication and reappropriation.

The followers of Jesus shared with their Jewish contemporaries a set of conceptual assumptions about Psalms. Staying true to these assumptions, they made sense of their own situation with the help of Psalms. To them, the Psalter was a prophetic book composed by David under divine inspiration that bears testimony of Christ, includes his words, prophesies his passion and crucifixion, and speaks of his ascension into heaven. Studying the use of Psalms in the New Testament is thus an exercise in tracing the origin of a distinctively Christian reading of Scripture. Depending on how one dates the connection between the Psalms of the Righteous Sufferer and Mark's passion story or the cluster of Psalms in Paul's catenae, it is conceivable that such a christological understanding of Psalms goes back to the earliest Christian witness that predates our oldest written documents in the New Testament. In the second century, early Christian writers,

---

80. Following table 35.7 below, the New Testament books that lack any reference to Psalms are Galatians (as noted, two possible allusions are Gal 2:16 to Ps 143:2 [142:2 LXX], and in Gal 3:16 to Ps 89:51–52 [88:51–52 LXX]), Colossians, 1–2 Thessalonians, 1–2 Timothy, Titus, Philemon, James, 2 Peter, 1–3 John, and Jude.

chief among them Justin Martyr, significantly advanced and changed the christological reading of Psalms, at times following the New Testament precedent, and at times breaking with it and forging new ways of reading.[81] But it was the writers of the New Testament who laid the foundation for what became a long and distinctly Christian reading of Psalms.

Table 35.7. The Psalms in the New Testament

The Psalms[82]	The New Testament	Early Jewish Texts[83]	Early Christian Texts
Ps 2:1–2	Acts 4:25–26	4Q174 (4QMidr-Eschat^a) 1–2 I, 18–19; 1 En. 48:10	Melito, *Pasc.* 62
Ps 2:7	Matt 3:17; Mark 1:11; 9:7; Luke 3:22; John 1:34, 49; *Acts 13:33*; *Heb 1:5; 5:5*		Justin, *Dial.* 88.8; 103.6; 122.6; *1 Apol.* 40 [Ps 2:7–12]; 1 Clem. 36:4 [Ps 2:7–8]; Gos. Heb. frag. 2
Ps 2:8–9	*Rev 2:26–27; 12:5; 19:15*	Pss. Sol. 17:23–24	Irenaeus, *Haer.* 4.21.3
Ps 4:5	*Eph 4:26*		Polycarp, *Phil.* 12:1
Ps 5:10	*Rom 3:13*		
Ps 6:4	John 12:27	4Q177 (4QMidr-Eschat^b) 12–13 I, 3; Jdt 14:19	
Ps 6:9	*Matt 7:23; Luke 13:27*		
Ps 8:3	Matt 21:16		Irenaeus, *Haer.* 1.14.8; 4.9.3
Ps 8:5–7	*Heb 2:6–8*		Tatian, *Oratio ad Graecos* 15

---

81. Judith M. Lieu, "Justin Martyr and the Transformation of Psalm 22," in *Biblical Traditions in Transmission: Essays in Honour of Michael A. Knibb*, ed. Charlotte Hempel and Judith M. Lieu, JSJSup 111 (Leiden: Brill, 2006), 195–211.

82. Chapter and verse numbers in the table follow the MT, even when the citation is from the LXX. Following the convention in NA[28], citations are in *italics* and allusions in roman print.

83. The biblical scrolls from Qumran are not included in this list. See the "Index of Passages in the Biblical Scrolls from the Judean Desert," in James VanderKam and Peter Flint, *The Meaning of the Dead Sea Scrolls: Their Significance for Understanding the Bible, Judaism, Jesus, and Christianity* (San Francisco: Harper San Francisco, 2002), 419–22.

Ps 8:7	*1 Cor 15:27; Eph 1:22*		
Ps 10:7	*Rom 3:14*		Justin, *Dial.* 27.3
Ps 14:2–3; cf. Ps 53:3–4	*Rom 3:10–12*		Justin, *Dial.* 27.3; Irenaeus, *Haer.* 1.19.1
Ps 16:8–11	*Acts 2:25–28*		
Ps 16:10	*Acts 2:31; 13:35*		
Ps 18:50// 2 Sam 22:50	*Rom 15:9*		
Ps 19:5	*Rom 10:18*		Justin, *Dial.* 42.1; 64.8 [Ps 19:1–7]; Justin, *1 Apol.* 40 [Ps 19:3–6]
Ps 22:2	*Matt 27:46; Mark 15:34*		Justin, *Dial.* 98 [Ps 22 in its entirety]; 99.1
Ps 22:7–8 [cf. Ps 109:25]	*Matt 27:39; Mark 15:29, 32; Luke 23:35*		Justin, *Dial.* 101.1–3 [Ps 22:5–7]; 1 Clem. 16:15–16 [Ps 22:7–9]; Irenaeus, *Haer.* 4.33.12
Ps 22:9	*Matt 27:43*	Sir 7:17 (MS A); Wis 2:18	Justin, *1 Apol.* 38
Ps 22:14	*1 Pet 5:8*	1QH^a XIII, 12–13 (V, 10–11)	Justin, *Dial.* 102.1 [Ps 22:10–16]; 103.1 [Ps 22:15–18]
Ps 22:19	*Matt 27:35; Mark 15:24; Luke 23:34; John 19:24*		Justin, *1 Apol.* 35; 38; Justin, *Dial.* 97.3 [Ps 22:17–19]; Barn. 6.6; Irenaeus, *Haer.* 3.33.12
Ps 22:23	*Heb 2:12*		Barn. 6.16
Ps 23:2	*Rev 7:17*		
Ps 24:1	*1 Cor 10:26*		1 Clem. 54:3; Justin, *Dial.* 36.3; Irenaeus, *Haer.* 4.36.6
Ps 27:12	*Mark 14:57*		
Ps 31:6	*Luke 23:46*	1QH^a VII, 38 (XV, 25)	Justin, *Dial.* 105.5

Ps 32:1–2	*Rom 4:7–8*		1 Clem. 50:6; Justin, *Dial.* 141.2; Irenaeus, *Haer.* 5.17.3
Ps 34:9	*1 Pet 2:3*		
Ps 34:13–17	*1 Pet 3:10–12*	1Q33 (1QM) X, 17 [Ps 34:16]	1 Clem. 22:1–8 [Ps 34:12–18, 20]; Barn. 9.2 [Ps 34:13–14; cf. Exod 15:26; Isa 50:10]; Irenaeus, *Haer.* 4.17.3; 4.28.1; 4.36.2
Ps 34:21 [cf. Exod 12:10, 46]	*John 19:36*		
Ps 35:11	*Mark 14:57*		
Ps 35:19; cf. 69:5	*John 15:25*	Pss. Sol. 7:1	
Ps 36:2	*Rom 3:18*		
Ps 37:11	*Matt 5:5*		Did. 3:7
Ps 38:12	*Mark 15:40; Luke 23:49*		
Ps 39:13	*1 Pet 2:11; Heb 11:13*	1 Chr 29:15; Philo, *Spec.* 1:295	
Ps 40:7–9	*Heb 10:5–7*		Irenaeus, *Haer.* 4.17.1
Ps 41:10	*Mark 14:18; John 13:18; Acts 1:16*	1QHª XIII, 25–26 (V, 23–24)	
Pss 42:6, 12; 43:5	*Matt 26:38; Mark 14:34*		
Ps 44:23	*Rom 8:36*		
Ps 45:7–8	*Heb 1:8–9*		Justin, *Dial.* 38.3–5 [Ps 45:1–18]; 56.14; 63.4–5 [Ps 45:7–13] [Ps 45:11–12]; 86.3; Irenaeus, *Haer.* 3.6.1; 4.33.11
Ps 48:3	*Matt 5:35*		

Ps 51:6	Rom 3:4	4Q393 (4QCommunal Confession) 1 II, 2–4; Pr Man 10	1 Clem. 18 [Ps 51:3–19]
Ps 53:3–4; cf. Ps 14:2–3	Rom 3:10–12		Justin, Dial. 27.3
Ps 55:23	1 Pet 5:7		
Ps 62:13 [cf. Prov 24:12]	Matt 16:27; Rom 2:6; Rev 2:23		1 Clem. 34:3
Ps 68:19	Eph 4:8		Justin, Dial. 87.6; Irenaeus, Haer. 2.20.3
Ps 69:5 [cf. 35:19]	John 15:25		
Ps 69:10	John 2:17; Rom 15:3		
Ps 69:22	Matt 27:48; Mark 15:36; Luke 23:36; John 19:28–29	1QH^a XII, 12 (IV, 11); Sib. Or. 6:25; 8:303	Irenaeus, Haer. 4.33.12
Ps 69:23–24	Rom 11:9–10		
Ps 69:26	Acts 1:20		Irenaeus, Haer. 3.12.1
Ps 69:29	Phil 4:3; Rev 3:5	4Q381 (4QNon-Canonical Psalms B) 31 8; 1 En. 108:3; ALD 10:12–13; Odes Sol. 9:11	
Ps 75:9	Rev 14:10	Philo, Deus 77	
Ps 78:2	Matt 13:35		
Ps 78:24	John 6:31	Wis 16:20; LAB 10:7	
Ps 82:6	John 10:34		Justin, Dial. 124.2 [Ps 82:1–8]; Irenaeus, Haer. 3.6.2; 3.19.1; 4.38.
Ps 86:9	Rev 15:4		
Ps 89:21	Acts 13:22		
Ps 90:4	2 Pet 3:8		Barn. 15.4; Justin, Dial. 81.3

Ps 91:11–12	Matt 4:6; Luke 4:10–11	11Q11 (11QapocrPs) VI, 10–11; Philo, Deus 182	Irenaeus, Haer. 5.21.2
Ps 94:11 [cf. 1 Sam 12:22 LXX]	1 Cor 3:20		
Ps 94:14 [cf. 1 Sam 12:22 LXX]	Rom 11:2	4Q393 (4QCommunal Confession) 3 3–4	
Ps 95:7–11	Heb 3:7–11, 15; 4:3 [Ps 95:11], 5 [Ps 95:11], 7 [Ps 95:7–8]	Jos. Asen. 8:9 (11)	
Ps 97:7 [cf. Deut 32:43 LXX]	Heb 1:6		
Ps 102:26–28	Heb 1:10–12	Sir 14:17 (MS A); Lad. Jac. 7:35	Irenaeus, Haer. 4.3.1
Ps 103:17	Luke 1:50		
Ps 104:4	Heb 1:7	1 En. 17:1; Jub. 2:2; 2 Bar. 48:8	1 Clem. 36:3
Ps 107:3	Luke 13:29	Bar 4:37	
Ps 107:9	Luke 1:53		
Ps 107:23–32	Matt 8:23–27; Mark 4:35–41; Luke 8:22–25	1QH^a XI, 15–16 (III, 14–15) // 4Q432 (4QpapH^f) 5 1–2; 1QH^a XIII, 20 (V, 18) // 4Q429 (4QH^c) 1 II, 5; Sir 43:24 (MasSir, MS B); 4Q418b (4QText with Quotation from Psalm 107?) 1 3; 4Q374 (4QExodus/Conquest Tradition) 2 II, 9	

Ps 109:8	Acts 1:20		Irenaeus, *Haer.* 3.12.1
Ps 110:1	Matt 22:44; 26:64; Mark 12:36; 14:62; 16:19; *Luke 20:42–43;* 22:69; *Acts 2:34;* Rom 8:34; 1 Cor 15:25; Eph 1:20; Heb 1:3, *13;* 8:1; 10:12; 1 Pet 3:22		Barn. 12.10; 1 Clem. 36:5; Justin, *1 Apol.* 45; *Dial.* 32.6 [Ps 110:1–7]; 56.14; 83.2; 127.5; Irenaeus, *Haer.* 2.28.8; 3.6.1; 3.10.5; 3.16.3; 4.33.11
Ps 110:4	*Heb 5:6, 10; 6:20; 7:11, 17, 21*		Justin, *Dial.* 32.6; 33.1–2; 42.1; 63.3; 83.2 [Ps 110:1–4]; 113.5; 118.1
Ps 112:9	2 Cor 9:9	ALD 13:3	
Pss 113–118	Matt 26:30	1 En. 51:4 [Ps 114:4]	
Ps 116:10 [115:1 LXX]	2 Cor 4:13		
Ps 116:11 [115:2 LXX]	Rom 3:4		
Ps 117:1	*Rom 15:11*		
Ps 118:6	Heb 13:6		
Ps 118:22	1 Pet 2:4, *7*		Acts Pet. 24; Barn. 6.4
Ps 118:22–23	Matt 21:42; Mark 12:10–11; Luke 20:17; Acts 4:11		T. Sol. 22:6–8; 23:1–4[84]
Ps 118:25–26	Matt 21:9; *23:39;* Mark 11:9–10; *Luke 13:35; 19:38; John 12:13*		Did. 12:1
Ps 132:11	Acts 2:30		Justin, *Dial.* 68.5; Irenaeus, *Haer.* 3.9.2; 3.16.2
Ps 135:14 [cf. LXX Deut 32:36]	Heb 10:30		

84. It is presumed that Testament of Solomon in its present form is a Christian text.

Ps 140:4	*Rom 3:13*		
Ps 143:2	Rom 3:20	11Q5 (11QPsª) XXIV, 7 (Syriac Psalm III = Ps 155:8); 1 En. 81:5	
Ps 146:6 [cf. Exod 20:11 LXX; 2 Kgs 19:15 LXX; Isa 37:16 LXX; Neh 9:6 LXX]	Acts 4:24; *14:15*; Rev 10:6		Diogn. 3:4

Bibliography

Ahearne-Kroll, Stephen P. "Psalms in the New Testament." Pages 269–80 in *The Oxford Handbook of the Psalms*. Edited by William P. Brown. Oxford Handbooks. Oxford: Oxford University Press, 2014.

———. *The Psalms of Lament in Mark's Passion: Jesus' Davidic Suffering*. SNTSMS 142. Cambridge: Cambridge University Press, 2007.

Allison, Dale C., Jr. "The Old Testament in the New Testament." Pages 479–502 in *From the Beginnings to 600*. Vol. 1 of *The New Cambridge History of the Bible*. Edited by James Carlton Paget and Joachim Schaper. Cambridge: Cambridge University Press, 2013.

———. "Psalm 23 (22) in Early Christianity: A Suggestion." IBS 5 (1983): 132–37.

Attridge, Harold W. "Giving Voice to Jesus: Use of the Psalms in the New Testament." Pages 101–12 in *Psalms in Community: Jewish and Christian Textual, Liturgical, and Artistic Traditions*. Edited by Harold W. Attridge and Margot E. Fassler. SymS 25. Altanta: Society of Biblical Literature, 2004.

———. "The Psalms in Hebrews." Pages 197–212 in *The Psalms in the New Testament*. Edited by Steven Moyise and Maarten J. J. Menken. NTSI. London: T&T Clark, 2004.

Attridge, Harold W., and Margot E. Fassler, eds., *Psalms in Community: Jewish and Christian Textual, Liturgical, and Artistic Traditions*. SBLSS 25. Leiden: Brill, 2004.

Berlin, Adele. "Interpreting Torah Traditions in Psalm 105." Pages 20–36 in *Jewish Biblical Interpretation and Cultural Exchange: Comparative Exegesis in Context*. Edited by Natalie B. Dohrman and David Stern. Jewish Culture and Context. Philadelphia: University of Pennsylvania Press, 2008.

Böhm, Christiane. *Die Rezeption der Psalmen in den Qumranschriften, bei Philo von Alexandrien und im Corpus Paulinum*. WUNT 2/437. Tübingen: Mohr Siebeck, 2017.

Brooke, George J. "Praying History in the Dead Sea Scrolls: Memory, Identity, Fulfilment." Pages 305–19 in *Functions of Psalms and Prayers in the Late Second Temple Period*. Edited by Mika S. Pajunen and Jeremy Penner. BZAW 486. Berlin: de Gruyter, 2017.

———. "The Psalms in Early Jewish Literature in the Light of the Dead Sea Scrolls." Pages 5–24 in *The Psalms in the New Testament*. Edited by Steven Moyise and Maarten J. J. Menken. NTSI. London: T&T Clark, 2004.

Brunson, Andrew C. *Psalm 118 in the Gospel of John: An Intertextual Study on the New Exodus Pattern in the Theology of John*. WUNT 2/158. Tübingen: Mohr Siebeck, 2003.

Bultmann, Rudolf. *Das Verhältnis der urchristlichen Christusbotschaft zum historischen Jesus*. SHAW. Heidelberg: Winter, 1961.

———. *The History of the Synoptic Tradition*. Translated by John Marsh. 2nd ed. New York: Harper & Row, 1968.

Cameron, Michael. "Psalms." Pages 572–87 in *The Oxford Handbook of Early Christian Biblical Interpretation*. Edited by Paul M. Blowers and Peter W. Martens. Oxford Handbooks. Oxford: Oxford University Press, 2019.

Carey, Holly J. *Jesus' Cry from the Cross: Towards a First-Century Understanding of the Intertextual Relationship between Psalm 22 and the Narrative of Mark's Gospel*. LNTS 398. London: T&T Clark, 2009.

Collins, Adela Yarbro. "The Appropriation of the Psalms of Individual Lament by Mark." Pages 223–41 in *Scriptures in the Gospels*. Edited by Christopher Tuckett. BETL 131. Leuven: Leuven University Press, 1997.

———. *Mark: A Commentary*. Hermeneia. Minneapolis: Fortress, 2007.

Daly-Denton, Margaret. *David in the Fourth Gospel: The Johannine Reception of the Psalms*. AGJU 47. Leiden: Brill, 2000.

———. "David the Psalmist, Inspired Prophet: Jewish Antecedents of a New Testament Datum." *ABR* 52 (2004): 32–47.

Dorival, Gilles. "Titres hébreux et titres grecs des Psaumes." Pages 3–18 in *Textual Research on the Psalms and Gospels/Recherches textuelles sur les Psaumes et les Évangiles: Papers from the Tbilisi Colloquium on the Editing and History of Biblical Manuscripts; Actes du Colloque de Tbilisi, 19–20 septembre 2007*. Edited by Christian-B. Amphoux and James Keith Elliott. NovTSup 142. Leiden: Brill, 2012.

Evans, Craig A. "Praise and Prophecy in the Psalter and in the New Testament." Pages 551–79 in *The Book of Psalms: Composition and Reception*. Edited by Patrick D. Miller and Peter W. Flint. VTSup 99. Leiden: Brill, 2005.

Fabry, Hans-Josef. "Die Wirkungsgeschichte des Psalms 22." Pages 279–317 in *Beiträge zur Psalmenforschung: Psalm 2 und 22*. Edited by Josef Schreiner. FB 60. Würzburg: Echter, 1988.

Fishbane, Michael. *Biblical Interpretation in Ancient Israel*. Oxford: Clarendon, 1985.

Fitzmyer, Joseph A. "'4QTestimonia' and the New Testament." *TS* 18 (1957): 513–38. Repr., pages 59–89 in *Essays on the Semitic Background of the New Testament*. SBLSBS 5. Missoula, MT: Scholars Press, 1974.

Flint, Peter W. "Appendix: Psalms Scrolls from the Judean Desert." Pages 287–90 in *Pseudepigraphic and Non-Masoretic Psalms and Prayers*. Edit by James H. Charlesworth. PTSDSSP 4A. Tübingen: Mohr Siebeck, 1997.

———. *The Dead Sea Psalms Scrolls and the Book of Psalms*. STDJ 17. Leiden: Brill, 1997.

———. "The Prophet David at Qumran." Pages 158–67 in *Biblical Interpretation at Qumran*. Edited by Matthias Henze. Grand Rapids: Eerdmans, 2005.

Flint, Peter W., and Patrick D. Miller, eds. *The Book of Psalms: Composition and Reception*. VTSup 99. Leiden: Brill, 2005.

Gese, Hartmut. "Psalm 22 und das Neue Testament: Der älteste Bericht vom Tode Jesu und die Entstehung des Herrenmahls." *ZTK* 65, no. 1 (1968): 1–22.

Gillingham, Susan E., ed. *Jewish and Christian Approaches to the Psalms: Conflict and Convergence*. Oxford: Oxford University Press, 2013.

———. *A Journey of Two Psalms: The Reception of Psalms 1 and 2 in Jewish and Christian Tradition*. Oxford: Oxford University Press, 2013.

———. *Psalms through the Centuries*. Vol. 1. Blackwell Bible Commentaries. Malden, MA: Blackwell, 2008.

Hays, Richard B. "Christ Prays the Psalms: Israel's Psalter as Matrix of Early Christology." Pages 101–18 in *The Conversion of the Imagination: Paul as Interpreter of Israel's Scripture*. Grand Rapids: Eerdmans, 2005.

———. *Echoes of Scripture in the Gospels*. Waco, TX: Baylor University Press, 2016.

———. "Intertextual Echo in Romans." Pages 34–83 in *Echoes of Scripture in the Letters of Paul*. New Haven: Yale University Press, 1989.

Hengel, Martin. "Psalm 110 und die Erhöhung des Auferstandenen zur Rechten Gottes." Pages 43–73 in *Anfänge der Christologie: Festschrift für Ferdinand Hahn zum 65. Geburtstag*. Edited by Cilliers Breytenbach and Henning Paulsen. Göttingen: Vandenhoeck & Ruprecht, 1991.

Høgenhaven, Jesper. "Psalms as Prophecy: Qumran Evidence for the Reading of Psalms as Prophetic Text and the Formation of the Canon." Pages 229–51 in *Functions of Psalms and Prayers in the Late Second Temple Period*. Edited by Mika S. Pajunen and Jeremy Penner. BZAW 486. Berlin: de Gruyter, 2017.

Hossfeld, Frank-Lothar, and Erich Zenger. "Das Matthäusevangelium im Lichte der Psalmen." Pages 129–40 in *"Dies ist das Buch . . . ": Das Matthäusevangelium;*

Interpretation – Rezeption – Rezeptionsgeschichte; für Hubert Frankmölle. Edited by Rainer Kampling. Paderborn: Schöningh, 2004.

Human, Dirk J., and Gert J. Steyn, eds. *Psalms and Hebrews: Studies in Reception.* LHBOTS 527. New York: T&T Clark, 2010.

Jain, Eva. *Psalmen oder Psalter? Materielle Rekonstruktion und inhaltliche Untersuchung der Psalmenhandschriften aus der Wüste Juda.* STDJ 109. Leiden: Brill, 2014.

Janowski, Bernd. "Die jüdischen Psalmen in der christlichen Passionsgeschichte: Eine rezeptionsgeschichtliche Skizze." Pages 397–413 in *Freiheit und Recht: Festschrift für Frank Crüsemann zum 65. Geburtstag.* Edited by Christof Hardmeier, Rainer Kessler, and Andreas Ruwe. Gütersloh: Kaiser; Gütersloher Verlagshaus, 2003.

Janse, Sam. *"You Are My Son": The Reception History of Psalm 2 in Early Judaism and the Early Church.* CBET 51. Leuven: Peeters, 2009.

Keesmaat, Sylvia. "The Psalms in Romans and Galatians." Pages 139–61 in *The Psalms in the New Testament.* Edited by Steve Moyise and Maarten J. J. Menken. NTSI. London: T&T Clark, 2004.

Kistemaker, Simon J. *The Psalm Citations in the Epistle to the Hebrews.* Amsterdam: van Soest, 1961.

Klein, Anja. *Geschichte und Gebet: Die Rezeption der biblischen Geschichte in den Psalmen des Alten Testaments.* FAT 94. Tübingen: Mohr Siebeck, 2014.

Koch, Dietrich-Alex. *Die Schrift als Zeuge des Evangeliums: Untersuchungen zur Verwendung und zum Verständnis der Schrift bei Paulus.* BHT 69. Tübingen: Mohr Siebeck, 1986.

Kugel, James. "David the Prophet." Pages 45–55 in *Poetry and Prophecy: The Beginning of a Literary Tradition.* Edited by James L. Kugel. Ithaca, NY: Cornell University Press, 1990.

Lange, Armin. "Psalms. Ancient Hebrew Texts." Pages 25–42 in *Writings.* Edited by Armin Lange and Emanuel Tov. THB 1C. Leiden: Brill, 2017.

Lange, Armin, and Matthias Weingold. *Biblical Quotations and Allusions in Second Temple Jewish Literature.* JAJSup 5. Göttingen: Vandenhoeck & Ruprecht, 2011.

Lee, Aquila H. I. *From Messiah to Preexistent Son: Jesus' Self-Consciousness and Early Christian Exegesis of Messianic Psalms.* WUNT 2/192. Tübingen: Mohr Siebeck, 2005.

Lieu, Judith M. "Justin Martyr and the Transformation of Psalm 22." Pages 195–211 in *Biblical Traditions in Transmission: Essays in Honour of Michael A. Knibb.* Edited by Charlotte Hempel and Judith M. Lieu. JSJSup 111. Leiden: Brill, 2006.

Lincicum, David. "How Did Paul Read Scripture?" Pages 225–38 in *The New Cambridge Companion to St. Paul.* Edited by Bruce W. Longenecker. Cambridge Companions to Religion. Cambridge: Cambridge University Press, 2020.

———. "Intertextuality, Effective History, and Memory: Conceptualizing Paul's Use of Scripture." Pages 9–22 in *Paulinische Schriftrezeption: Grundlagen – Ausprägungen – Wirkungen – Wertungen*. Edited by Florian Wilk and Markus Öhler. FRLANT 268. Göttingen: Vandenhoeck & Ruprecht, 2017.

Marcus, Joel. *The Way of the Lord: Christological Exegesis of the Old Testament in the Gospel of Mark*. Louisville: Westminster John Knox, 1992.

McLean, Bradley H. *Citations and Allusions to Jewish Scripture in Early Christian and Jewish Writings through 180 C.E.* Lewiston, NY: Mellen 1992.

Menken, Maarten J. J. "The Psalms in Matthew's Gospel." Pages 61–82 in *The Psalms in the New Testament*. Edited by Steven Moyise and Maarten J. J. Menken. NTSI. London: T&T Clark, 2004.

———. "The Translation of Psalm 41.10 in John 13.18." *JSNT* 13, no. 40 (1990): 61–79.

Menn, Esther M. "No Ordinary Lament: Relecture and the Identity of the Distressed in Psalm 22." *HTR* 93, no. 4 (2000): 301–41.

———. "Sweet Singer of Israel: David and the Psalms in Early Judaism." Pages 61–74 in *Psalms in Community: Jewish and Christian Textual, Liturgical, and Artistic Traditions*. Edited by Harold W. Attridge and Margot E. Fassler. SymS 25. Atlanta: Society of Biblical Literature, 2004.

Moyise, Steve. "The Language of the Psalms in the Book of Revelation." *Neot* 37, no. 2 (2003): 246–61.

———. *Paul and Scripture: Studying the New Testament Use of the Old Testament*. Grand Rapids: Baker Academic, 2010.

Moyise, Steve, and Maarten J. J. Menken, eds. *The Psalms in the New Testament*. NTSI. London: T&T Clark, 2004.

Mroczek, Eva. *The Literary Imagination in Jewish Antiquity*. Oxford: Oxford University Press, 2016.

Newsom, Carol A. *The Self as Symbolic Space: Constructing Identity and Community at Qumran*. STDJ 52. Leiden: Brill, 2004.

Niehoff, Maren. "Paul and Philo on the Psalms: Towards a Spiritual Notion of Scripture." *NovT* 62, no. 4 (2020): 392–415.

Pajunen, Mika S. "Perspectives on the Existence of a Particular Authoritative Book of Psalms in the Late Second Temple Period." *JSOT* 39, no. 2 (2014): 139–63.

Pajunen, Mika S., and Jeremy Penner, eds., *Functions of Psalms and Prayers in the Late Second Temple Period*. BZAW 486. Berlin: de Gruyter, 2017.

Parry, Donald W., and Emanuel Tov. *The Dead Sea Scrolls Reader*. 2nd ed., rev. and exp. 2 vols. Leiden: Brill, 2014.

Pietersma, Albert. "Septuagintal Exegesis and the Superscriptions of the Greek Psalter." Pages 443–75 in *The Book of Psalms: Composition and Reception*. Edited by Peter W. Flint and Patrick D. Miller. VTSup 99. Leiden: Brill, 2005.

Popkes, Enno Edzard. "Essenisch-qumranische und paulinische Psalmen-

Rezeptionen: Ein Beitrag zur frühjüdischen Schrifthermeneutik." Pages 231–50 in *Jesus, Paulus und die Texte von Qumran*. Edited by Jörg Frey and Enno Edzard Popkes. WUNT 2/390. Tübingen: Mohr Siebeck, 2015.

Pulkkinen, Marika. "Paul's Use of Psalms: Quotations, Allusions, and Psalm Clusters in Romans and First Corinthians." PhD diss., University of Helsinki, 2020.

Reim, Günter. "Vom Hebräerbrief zum Johannesevangelium, anhand der Psalmzitate." *BZ* 44, no. 1 (2000): 92–100.

Ribbens, Benjamin J. "The Sacrifice God Desired: Psalm 40.6–8 in Hebrews 10." *NTS* 67, no. 2 (2021): 284–304.

Runia, David T. "Philo's Reading of the Psalms." *SPhiloA* 13 (2001): 102–21.

Rüsen-Weinhold, Ulrich. *Der Septuagintapsalter im Neuen Testament: Eine textgeschichtliche Untersuchung*. Neukirchen-Vluyn: Neukirchener Verlag, 2004.

Sanders, James A. *The Psalms Scroll of Qumrân Cave 11 (11QPsª)*. DJD 4. Oxford: Clarendon, 1965.

Sänger, Dieter, ed. *Psalm 22 und die Passionsgeschichte der Evangelien*. BThSt 88. Neukirchen-Vluyn: Neukirchener Verlag, 2007.

Sarna, Nahum M. *On the Book of Psalms: Exploring the Prayers of Ancient Israel*. New York: Schocken, 1993.

Schaper, Joachim. "Der Septuaginta-Psalter: Interpretation, Aktualisierung und liturgische Verwendung der biblischen Psalmen im hellenistischen Judentum." Pages 165–83 in *Der Septuaginta-Psalter: Sprachliche und Theologische Aspekte*. Edited by Erich Zenger. HBS 32. Freiburg im Breisgau: Herder, 2001.

Schuller, Eileen. "Functions of Psalms and Prayers in the Late Second Temple Period." Pages 5–24 in *Functions of Psalms and Prayers in the Late Second Temple Period*. Edited by Mika S. Pajunen and Jeremy Penner. BZAW 486. Berlin: de Gruyter, 2017.

Schürer, Emil. *The History of the Jewish People in the Age of Jesus Christ (175 BC–AD 135)*. Revised by Geza Vermes and Fergus Millar. 3 vols. in 4. Edinburgh: T&T Clark, 1973–1987.

Scott, Matthew. *The Hermeneutics of Christological Psalmody in Paul: An Intertextual Enquiry*. STNSMS 158. New York: Cambridge University Press, 2014.

Stemberger, Günter. "Psalmen in Liturgie und Predigt der rabbinischen Zeit." Pages 199–213 in *Der Psalter in Judentum und Christentum*. Edited by Erich Zenger. HBS 18. Freiburg im Breisgau: Herder, 1998.

Strawn, Brent A. "Textual History of Psalms." Pages 5–23 in *Writings*. Edited by Armin Lange and Emanuel Tov. THB 1C. Leiden: Brill, 2017.

Stuhlhofer, Franz. *Der Gebrauch der Bibel von Jesu bis Euseb: Eine statistische Untersuchung zur Kanonsgeschichte*. Wuppertal: Brockhaus, 1988.

Subramanian, J. Samuel. *The Synoptic Gospels and the Psalms as Prophecy*. LNTS 351. London: T&T Clark, 2007.

Swete, Henry Barclay. *An Introduction to the Old Testament in Greek.* 2nd ed. Cambridge: Cambridge University Press, 1914.

Taft, Robert F. "Christian Liturgical Psalmody: Origins, Development, Decomposition, Collapse." Pages 7–32 in *Psalms in Community: Jewish and Christian Textual, Liturgical, and Artistic Traditions.* Edited by Harold W. Attridge and Margot E. Fassler. SymS 25. Atlanta: Society of Biblical Literature, 2004.

Ulrich, Eugene. *The Dead Sea Scrolls and the Developmental Composition of the Bible.* VTSup 169. Leiden: Brill, 2015.

VanderKam, James C., and Peter W. Flint. "Index of Passages in the Biblical Scrolls from the Judean Desert." Pages 407–23 in *The Meaning of the Dead Sea Scrolls: Their Significance for Understanding the Bible, Judaism, Jesus and Christianity.* San Francisco: Harper, 2002.

Watts, Rikk E. "The Psalms in Mark's Gospel." Pages 25–45 in *The Psalms in the New Testament.* Edited by Steve Moyise and Maarten J. J. Menken. NTSI. London: T&T Clark, 2004.

Witherington, Ben, III. *Psalms Old and New: Exegesis, Intertextuality, and Hermeneutics.* Minneapolis: Fortress, 2017.

Woan, Sue. "The Psalms in 1 Peter." Pages 213–29 in *The Psalms in the New Testament.* Edited by Steven Moyise and Maarten J. J. Menken. NTSI. London: T&T Clark, 2004.

Zemanek, Josef. *Psalmentheologie in den synoptischen Evangelienschriften: Eine innerbiblische Exegese und geschichtliche Analyse.* Heiligenkreuz: Be&Be, 2011.

Zenger, Erich, ed. *Der Psalter in Judentum und Christentum.* Herders biblische Studien 18. Freiburg: Herder, 1998.

———, ed. *Der Septuaginta-Psalter: Sprachliche und Theologische Aspekte.* Herders biblische Studien 32. Freiburg: Herder, 2001.

36

Daniel in the New Testament

ALEXANDRIA FRISCH AND JENNIE GRILLO

The book of Daniel, more than any other book of the Hebrew Bible/Old Testament, is already at home within the literary milieu of early Judaism and the New Testament. Among the books that would eventually go to make up the collection of the rabbinic Hebrew Bible, Daniel is surely the latest to reach its final form. Large parts of Daniel are scribal productions contemporaneous with, or even later than, works outside the eventual Jewish canon, such as the Book of the Watchers or the Book of Giants.[1] Daniel therefore belongs to a world that feels familiar to the reader of the New Testament: this book, unlike most of the rest of the Old Testament, shares with later works features like a belief in resurrection, a detailed angelology, an elaborate periodization of history that offers a theological account of the Hellenistic empires, an interest in sealed visions and secret words, a heavenly figure called the son of man, and an idea of the celestial court as no longer mainly a place for deliberation but as a place of angelic worship. The three centuries that separate Daniel from the New Testament were in many ways more like each other than like the preceding centuries, and thus to read Daniel in relationship to the New Testament is in part to study parallel phenomena, and not only influence.

Nevertheless, there is also a specifically interpretive relationship between Daniel and the New Testament. The book of Daniel is self-consciously a work of scriptural interpretation, which in turn presents itself to later interpreters

---

1. For an introduction to Daniel within its early Jewish milieu, including discussion of dates for these works, see John J. Collins, *The Apocalyptic Imagination: An Introduction to Jewish Apocalyptic Literature*, 3rd ed. (Grand Rapids: Eerdmans, 2016), 107–42.

for further unravelling. Daniel's third vision, in chapter 9, offers an exegesis of Jeremiah's prophecy of a seventy-year exile that in turn projects the end of exile forward into the book's own imagined future, to be deciphered later (Dan 9:24–27). In parallel to this set of Jeremianic connections, the book of Daniel also has a closely exegetical relationship to Isaiah, and this, too, is understood as an interpretive task to be handed on to Daniel's own readers. Joseph Blenkinsopp, detailing the web of connections between and around Daniel and Isaiah, points to an interpretive trajectory stretching from Isaiah to Daniel *and beyond*.[2] In particular, the book of Daniel can be seen as an opening of the sealed book of Isa 8:16 and 29:11, as the *maskilim* ("the wise among the people") of Dan 11:33 replicate the work of Isaiah's servant, described with the same terminology (Isa 52:13).[3] In turn, Daniel's end-time prophecies become a sealed message to be opened by future interpreters (Dan 8:26; 9:24; 12:4), and the New Testament's treatment reads the book of Daniel within this wider tradition of sealed or secret prophetic books (Matt 24:15).

The Book of Daniel in Early Judaism

The book of Daniel was certainly felt to be important in Second Temple Judaism, to take at least the evidence of Qumran. Eight scrolls of Daniel were found distributed between Caves 1, 4, and 6: among Israel's Scriptures, only the Pentateuch, the Psalms, and Isaiah are attested at Qumran in more copies.[4] But to a greater extent than books like Deuteronomy or most of the Psalms, the book of Daniel is itself a product of the literary culture of early Judaism. Although the tales collection in chapters 1–6 shows signs of Neo-Babylonian roots, the final redaction of these tales together with the bulk of the apocalypses in the latter half of the book must date to the last quarter of the second century BCE: The final form of Daniel contains oblique but unmistakable references to the suppression of Jewish worship under Antiochus IV Epiphanes in 167–164 BCE (see Dan 8:9–14, 23–25; 11:21–45; 12:11; and perhaps 7:8, 20–22, 24–25; and Dan 3:32–33, 38–40 LXX). The book of Daniel therefore coalesced alongside many of the texts and traditions that we think of as characteristic of early Judaism, so that

---

2. Blenkinsopp, *Opening the Sealed Book: Interpretations of the Book of Isaiah in Late Antiquity* (Grand Rapids: Eerdmans, 2006), 14–27.

3. Blenkinsopp, *Opening the Sealed Book*, 22.

4. See Eugene Ulrich, "The Text of Daniel in the Qumran Scrolls," in *The Book of Daniel: Composition and Reception*, ed. John J. Collins and Peter W. Flint, 2 vols., VTSup 83 (Leiden: Brill, 2002), 2:573–85. The Qumran copies reflect the same text type as MT, lacking the additions of the Greek versions.

the influence sometimes goes both ways.[5] This is made particularly clear by the textual history of the book: alongside the Hebrew and Aramaic book of Daniel among the literary productions of early Judaism, there are two Greek versions of Daniel. These are the Old Greek (OG) and the version known as Theodotion, which by the time of Jerome had replaced the OG in the LXX. The Old Greek is presumed to date from the second half of the second century BCE; Theodotion probably originates no later than the first half of the first century CE, and not from the second-century CE figure of that name.[6] Among their significant differences from the MT, both Greek versions contain more material in various arrangements: the Prayer of Azariah and the Song of the Three Jews in the fiery furnace, the tale of Susanna, and the tale of Bel and the Dragon. Although these parts are only known in Greek, some or all of them may well have had Semitic originals, and parts of them may be at least as old as the Hebrew and Aramaic parts of Daniel.[7] Chapters 4–6 of Daniel are especially different in OG, reflecting an independent and possibly even older collection. All this variety is part of the story of the book of Daniel in early Judaism, and we will note where possible which version particular writers seem to be using; but these developments are themselves part of the picture of early Jewish scribal activity around the book of Daniel. Daniel emerges from, as well as acts upon, an early Jewish milieu.

The use of the book of Daniel elsewhere in early Jewish literature falls into several patterns. Here, we survey the following patterns for which the book acts as a source: images of deliverance; examples of martyrdom; the motif of the Jew at the court of a foreign king; Daniel as a prophet; Daniel as an intercessor; images of empires; the four kingdoms series; and various eschatological themes. Sometimes, the use made of the book of Daniel is specific and even exegetical; at other times, Daniel is one among other exemplars of much wider traditions and motifs.

Deliverance

The earliest Jewish and Christian art depicts Daniel and his friends as paradigms of deliverance, standing in flames or between lions, hands upraised in prayer.[8]

---

5. See Loren T. Stuckenbruck, "The Formation and Re-formation of Daniel in the Dead Sea Scrolls," in *The Bible and the Dead Sea Scrolls*, vol. 1: *Scripture and the Scrolls; The Second Princeton Symposium on the Dead Sea Scrolls*, ed. James H. Charlesworth (Waco, TX: Baylor University Press, 2006), 102–3.

6. See Alexander A. Di Lella, "The Textual History of Septuagint-Daniel and Theodotion-Daniel," in Collins and Flint, *Book of Daniel: Composition and Reception*, 2:586–607.

7. See Reinhard Gregor Kratz, *Translatio Imperii: Untersuchungen zu den aramäischen Danielerzählungen und ihrem theologiegeschichtlichen Umfeld*, WMANT 63 (Neukirchen-Vluyn: Neukirchener Verlag, 1991), 12, 74–76, 111–19, 130–40.

8. Robin Margaret Jensen, *Understanding Early Christian Art* (London: Routledge, 2000),

Even earlier, Second Temple Jewish texts set these characters in lists of those God has delivered from peril. In "a time of ruin and furious anger," 1 Macc 2 recalls Daniel and his three friends among the ancestors who were set free from danger: "Hananiah, Azariah, and Mishael believed and were saved from the flame; Daniel, because of his innocence, was delivered from the mouth of the lions"—here the mention of Daniel's "innocence," or "simplicity" (ἁπλότης), honors the youthful judge who had been the means of Susanna's rescue in the Old Greek version.[9] The dew that cools the furnace of the Greek versions is recalled, alongside Daniel in the lions' den and Jonah in the whale, in a prayer from the Hellenistic synagogue borrowed into early Christian liturgy in the Apostolic Constitutions: "For your eternal power even cools flames, and muzzles lions and tames sea monsters."[10] The seer of the Apocalypse of Zephaniah, terrified before the accusing angel, prays in these words: "You are the one who saved Israel from the hand of Pharaoh, the king of Egypt. You saved Susanna from the hand of the elders of injustice. You saved the three holy men, Shadrach, Meshach, Abednego, from the furnace of burning fire. I beg you to save me from this distress."[11]

Martyrdom

Although Daniel and his friends are saved from death, their stories nevertheless come to serve as inspiration for the developing idea of martyrdom in early Judaism.[12] The author of 3 Maccabees celebrates their deliverance but emphasizes their willingness to sacrifice life: "The three companions in Babylon who had voluntarily surrendered their lives to the flames so as not to serve vain things, you rescued unharmed, even to a hair, moistening the fiery furnace with dew and turning the flame against all their enemies" (3 Macc 6:6–7). Here, the stress on a surrender that is voluntary (αὐθαιρέτως) belongs to the discourse of Jewish martyrdom.[13] By the time of 4 Maccabees, the theme of martyrdom has muted that of deliverance in the story of Daniel and his friends: the seven brothers about

---

79–84; Lee I. Levine, *Visual Judaism in Late Antiquity: Historical Contexts of Jewish Art* (New Haven: Yale University Press, 2012), 350–51, 293 n. 62.

9. 1 Macc 2:60; cf. Sus 62a, OG: "For this reason youths are beloved by Iakob, because of their simplicity" (ἁπλότης). Unless otherwise noted, all LXX translations are from NETS.

10. Apos. Con. 7.35.7, trans. D. R. Darnell in *OTP* 2:681.

11. Apoc. Zeph. 6:10, trans. O. S. Wintermute, in *OTP* 1:513. This text is dated to c. 125 BCE–275 CE by Bernd Jörg Diebner, *Zephanjas Apokalypsen*, JSHRZ 5.9 (Gütersloh: Mohn, 2003).

12. See Ulrich Kellermann, "Das Danielbuch und die Märtyrertheologie der Auferstehung," in *Die Entstehung der jüdischen Martyrertheologie*, ed. Jan Willem van Henten, StPB 38 (Leiden: Brill, 1989), 51–75.

13. See, e.g., the death of Eleazar in 2 Macc 6:19: "But he, welcoming death with honor rather than life with pollution, went up to the rack of his own accord [αὐθαιρέτως]." Cf.

to be executed say to each other: "Brothers, let us die like brothers for the sake of the law; let us imitate the three youths in Assyria who despised the same ordeal of the furnace" (4 Macc 13:9). Their mother urges them to die using the example of Daniel and the three: "'Daniel the righteous was thrown to the lions, and Hananiah, Azariah, and Mishael were hurled into the fiery furnace and endured it for the sake of God. You too must have the same faith in God and not be grieved.' By these words the mother of the seven encouraged and persuaded each of her sons to die rather than violate God's commandment" (4 Macc 16:21-22, 24).[14]

The Jew at the Court of a Foreign King

The beginning of a work found at Qumran and known as Pseudo-Daniel (4Q243-244) mentions Daniel "before Belshazzar," though it is difficult to make out much more.[15] But in this work the name of Daniel recurs; the text also contains eschatological prophecy about a series of kingdoms and blames the exile on the sins of Israel, so it is in some way Danielic, though it is hard to say whether it represents a parallel or a successor to what are now the biblical Daniel traditions. One of the ways that the book of Daniel is remembered in early Jewish texts is this repeated cameo of Daniel before a king. This is of course a much broader motif: the book of Daniel both receives and shapes large stereotypes about oriental monarchs and their wise advisers.[16] When the book of Daniel shows the rage of a Nebuchadnezzar or the jealousy of his experts, it participates in and adds its own contribution to this developing cultural pattern.[17] The motif emerges particularly clearly in Josephus's rendition of Daniel (*Ant.* 10.186-281; with two supplementary notices in 11.337 and 12.322). Josephus's Daniel is part Greco-Roman philosophical sage, his abstinence a training of the mind and body for attaining wisdom.[18] But he also serves Josephus as an exemplar of the

---

W. H. C. Frend, *Martyrdom and Persecution in the Early Church: A Study of a Conflict from the Maccabees to Donatus* (Oxford: Blackwell, 1965), 46-47.

14. See Jan Willem van Henten, *The Maccabean Martyrs as Saviours of the Jewish People: A Study of 2 and 4 Maccabees*, JSJSup 57 (Leiden: Brill, 1997), 129-32.

15. See Peter W. Flint, "The Daniel Tradition at Qumran," in *Eschatology, Messianism, and the Dead Sea Scrolls*, ed. Craig A. Evans and Peter W. Flint (Grand Rapids: Eerdmans, 1997), 41-60.

16. The classic study is Lawrence M. Wills, *The Jew in the Court of the Foreign King: Ancient Jewish Court Legends*, HDR 26 (Minneapolis: Fortress, 1990).

17. See Tessa Rajak, "The Angry Tyrant," in *Jewish Perspectives on Hellenistic Rulers*, ed. Tessa Rajak et al., HCS 50 (Berkeley: University of California Press, 2007), 110-27.

18. David Satran, "Daniel: Seer, Philosopher, Holy Man," in *Ideal Figures in Ancient Judaism: Profiles and Paradigms*, ed. John J. Collins and George W. E. Nickelsburg, SCS 12 (Chico, CA: Scholars Press, 1980), 33-48.

Jew who serves a foreign king: Josephus stresses Daniel's life at court, giving an expanded version of Dan 1 with some embellishments, such as the tradition that some among the exiled Jews at court were made eunuchs. Daniel is a model for success in the role of royal adviser: Josephus amplifies the esteem of the king, the extent to which Daniel is a prophet of weal rather than woe, and the exemplary qualities of the three Jews, their soundness in mind and body.[19] In all of this, Daniel offers Josephus a precedent for his own career as an exiled Jewish adviser to a foreign imperial dynasty; in David Daube's words, "No one could have been more alive to the nature of this situation, the occupant of which remains faithful to his origins, yet also has sympathy with the—fundamentally hostile—ruling power."[20]

Daniel as Prophet

Although none of the versions of the book of Daniel calls Daniel a prophet, for Josephus Daniel is a prophet like one of the greatest of the Hebrew prophets (*Ant.* 10.267), fully worthy of the divine honors paid to him, because he "conversed with God"; Josephus emphasizes the accuracy of Daniel's finely timed long-range historical predictions, like the rise of Alexander and later of Rome.[21] 4Q174 (4QFlorilegium 1–3 II, 3) also speaks of "the book of the prophet Daniel" in one of the two explicit citations of Daniel at Qumran; what is cited is a combination of Dan 12:10 and 11:32, and the manner of citation puts Daniel on a par with other prophetic books cited as authoritative Scriptures in this document, like Isaiah (4Q174 I, 15) and Ezekiel (4Q174 I, 16).[22] The idea that Daniel was a prophet is also an assumption behind his inclusion in the Lives of the Prophets: this collection of material about prophets sets Daniel alongside all the major prophetic figures of Israel's Scriptures, like Isaiah and Jeremiah, Nathan and Elijah.[23]

---

19. The comparisons are fully set out in Geza Vermes, "Josephus' Treatment of the Book of Daniel," *JJS* 42, no. 2 (1991): 149–66, who also points out that Josephus's Greek text seems to be a mixture of OG and Theodotion (152), though it is interesting that Josephus makes no reference to the additions of the Greek text. For a wider context in the concerns of Josephus, see Louis H. Feldman, "Josephus' Portrait of Daniel," *Hen* 14 (1992): 37–96.

20. Daube, "Typology in Josephus," *JJS* 31, no. 1 (1980): 33.

21. See Steve Mason, "Josephus, Daniel, and the Flavian House," in *Josephus and the History of the Greco-Roman Period: Essays in Memory of Morton Smith*, ed. Fausto Parente and Joseph Sievers, StPB 41 (Leiden: Brill, 1994), 161–91.

22. See Stuckenbruck, "Formation and Re-formation of Daniel," 122–23.

23. This work is hard to date: it has traditionally been dated to the first century CE, at least in its original form, but David Satran has argued for a date as late as the fourth–fifth centuries CE; see Satran, *Biblical Prophets in Byzantine Palestine: Reassessing the Lives of the Prophets*, SVTP 11 (Leiden: Brill, 1995).

Daniel's prophetic medium is that of the dream vision, either as interpreter of others' dreams or the bearer of his own. Josephus prefers to focus on Daniel's interpretation of dreams in Dan 1–6, most likely avoiding the visions of Dan 7–12 because they, too, explicitly pointed to Rome's downfall and were dangerous for him as a guest of Roman patrons.[24] In contrast, the apocalyptic 4 Ezra includes an updated version of Daniel's dream, even citing Dan 7 (12:11).

Daniel as Intercessor, Nebuchadnezzar as Penitent

As well as being a prophet, Daniel is also an intercessor in the Lives of the Prophets, where he becomes something of a holy man. He is a eunuch, gaunt, fasting, and praying for Jerusalem and then praying for Nebuchadnezzar (Liv. Pro. 4:3–4).[25] Here the motif of Daniel's intercession has been imported into the Nebuchadnezzar story; in both Hebrew and Greek Daniel it belongs to chapter 9. Similarly, in the Testament of Moses, an intercessor called "one who is over them" is generally thought to be Daniel: this figure prays for the nation (T. Mos. 4:2–4) in a prayer similar to Daniel's prayer in Dan 9.[26] The complement to Daniel's intercession in the Lives of the Prophets is Nebuchadnezzar's own development as a model of penitence: Nebuchadnezzar "used to weep and honor the Lord, praying forty times each day and night" (Liv. Pro. 4:9).[27] The same motif is attested in the OG of Dan 4, where Nebuchadnezzar's penitence is amplified in prayers and grateful testimony, given in obedience to the command of an angel (4:30, 34 OG). A penitent Nebuchadnezzar probably also shares something with the Prayer of Nabonidus, 4Q242: this text seems to preserve other, parallel traditions about Daniel, if he is to be identified as the text's Jewish diviner/exorcist (*gazer*, like those at the Babylonian court in Dan 2:27; 4:4; and 5:7; of whom Daniel is in charge in 5:11). The Babylonian king in this text is afflicted, forgiven, restored, and commanded by the Daniel-like figure to "declare and write down this story, and so ascribe glory and gre[at]ness to the name of G[od Most High" (4Q242 1–3 I, 5). The Nabonidus of these traditions appears differently as Nebuchadnezzar in the book of Daniel, but both are early Jewish reflexes of Babylonian mythological material that has crystallized around the figure of Daniel at all these different points across the Jewish tradition.[28]

---

24. John M. G. Barclay, "The Empire Writes Back: Josephan Rhetoric in Flavian Rome," in *Flavius Josephus and Flavian Rome*, ed. Jonathan Edmondson, Steve Mason, and James Rives (Oxford: Oxford University Press, 2005), 315–32.
25. See the translation in *OTP* 2:389–91 (trans. D. R. A. Hare).
26. *OTP* 1:929 (trans. J. Priest).
27. For both of these see Satran, "Daniel: Seer, Philosopher, Holy Man."
28. See Matthias Henze, *The Madness of King Nebuchadnezzar: The Ancient Near Eastern Origins and Early History of Interpretation of Daniel 4*, JSJSup 61 (Leiden: Brill, 1999).

Images of Empires

The second half of Daniel is notable for the vivid imagery used to depict foreign empires. Daniel's vision in Dan 7 depicts four kingdoms as four beasts rising from the sea. An emphasis is placed on their hybrid natures, which makes them appear particularly menacing. The fourth creature is the most fearsome with its many horns and iron teeth, with which it devours everything, and stomps on anything left over (7:7). Verbal allusions to this beast, in particular, appear in later texts to reflect the danger of empire in a similar way. The earliest is that of Sib. Or. 3:397 (ca. second century BCE), which predicts the punishment of the "daughters of the west," an invading imperial force, who threaten the temple when they "chewed it terribly with iron teeth" (Sib. Or. 3:324, 329).[29] There is another allusion to Dan 7 a few lines later in the depiction of a royal figure who "from ten horns, he will sprout another shoot on the side" (3:397). In the Psalms of Solomon the Roman general Pompey is portrayed as an arrogant dragon (Pss. Sol. 2:25). In addition to the beastly characterization, the arrogance is a verbal allusion to the symbol of Antiochus IV as one of the fourth beast's horns with a mouth "speaking arrogantly" in Dan 7:8. Finally, a reimagined version of the fourth beast appears in 4 Ezra 11–12 as an eagle with twelve wings and three heads. In a marked citation, the angel Uriel tells Ezra: "The eagle which you saw coming up from the sea is the fourth kingdom which appeared in a vision to your brother Daniel. But it was not explained to him as I now explain it to you" (4 Ezra 12:11–12).[30] The use of the eagle is particularly noteworthy since it reflects the merging of Danielic imagery with Rome's own imperial image of itself as an eagle.[31]

The Four Kingdoms Motif

In Daniel, both the narrative and the apocalyptic imagery incorporate a series of empires. The narrative settings shift from the court of the Babylonians (Dan 1–5) to the Medes (Dan 5:31) and then, finally, to Cyrus the Persian's (Dan 6:28). The same three settings repeat in Dan 7–12. A critical part of the vision in Dan 7 is the series of four beasts that symbolize four empires—the Babylonians, Medes, Per-

---

29. See John J. Collins, "Sibylline Oracles," *OTP* 1:354–61.

30. Trans. from Michael E. Stone and Matthias Henze, *4 Ezra and 2 Baruch: Translations, Introductions, and Notes* (Minneapolis: Fortress, 2013).

31. In 106 BCE, Consul Marius made the eagle the sole symbol of the Roman army's legions as part of his military reform (see Henry M. D. Parker, "Signa militaria," *OCD*, 1406). The eagle, likewise, figures prominently in Roman mythology. E.g., the eagle carried the thunderbolts of Jupiter, the patron deity of the Roman state, and was also the bearer of omens (see, e.g., Livy, *Ab urbe condita* 1.34; Pliny, *Nat.* 15.136–37).

sians, and Greeks. A similar sequence appears in the dream in Dan 2 as a statue with a golden head, a silver upper body, a bronze torso and thighs, and iron/clay feet and legs (Dan 2:32–33). The motif of an imperial series is common to the ancient Near Eastern world and was originally distinct from Daniel. For example, Herodotus, in the fifth century BCE, includes a sequence of Assyrians, Medes and Persians (*Hist.* 1.95, 130) to illustrate Cyrus's rise to power.[32] In its original form the series conveyed the inevitability of Persian rule as it followed previous empires. During the Hellenistic period, Daniel, the Fourth Sibylline Oracle, and the Animal Apocalypse added the Greeks, turning it into a four-kingdom motif.[33] Moreover, these Jewish writers highlighted the end of the fourth kingdom, changing a motif that served as imperial propaganda into anti-imperial rhetoric. This pattern continues into the Roman period, with Rome replacing Greece as the fourth kingdom. Among the Dead Sea Scrolls, the fragmentary "Four Kingdoms" text (4Q552 and 4Q553) depicts the kingdoms as trees and hints at influence from Daniel in its reference, among other things, to a seer.[34] The pseudepigraphic 2 Baruch also imagines the four kingdoms as trees with Rome as a cedar (36:7). Fourth Ezra 11–12, as we saw above, predicts the downfall of the Roman eagle, the fourth kingdom. With this motif, we see how Daniel both participated in a widespread non-Jewish discourse and, subsequently, influenced its use in Jewish circles.

The End of Times

As mentioned above, the four-kingdoms motif ends in the destruction of the series. In Daniel, this end comes via a fifth, divine, and eternal kingdom represented by a stone uncut by human hands in Dan 2 and the Ancient of Days ushering in one like a son of man in Dan 7. Not only do these images represent uniquely Jewish additions to the four kingdoms series, but they reflect

---

32. See also the work of Ctesias in Diodorus Siculus, *Bib. hist.* 2.1–34. For a full overview of the history of the four kingdoms motif, see Brennan W. Breed, "Daniel's Four Kingdoms Schema: A History of Re-writing World History," *Int* 71, no. 2 (2017): 178–89, esp. 181–82.

33. See David Flusser, "The Four Empires in the Fourth Sibyl and in the Book of Daniel," *IOS* 2 (1972): 150–51. The Oracle divides a ten-generation span of humanity into imperial periods under the Assyrians, Medes, Persians, and Macedonians (Sib. Or. 4:49–101). Like the Oracle, the Animal Apocalypse reviews human history, dividing it into four imperial periods of Babylonians, Persians, Ptolemies, and Seleucids (1 En. 89:65–72a; 89:72b–90:1; 90:2–5; and 90:6–19).

34. Collins sees the Four Kingdoms text as an example of the "contemporizing" of Daniel at Qumran ("The Book of Daniel and the Dead Sea Scrolls," in *The Hebrew Bible in Light of the Dead Sea Scrolls*, ed. Nóra Dávid et al., FRLANT 239 [Göttingen: Vandenhoeck & Ruprecht, 2012], 217).

the growing eschatological concerns of Second Temple literature. Fourth Ezra combines both Dan 2 and 7 to predict an apocalyptic end to the fourth kingdom—much like the son of man in Dan 7, a man arrives on clouds from heaven to lead (4 Ezra 13:3, 12, 37). He then carves out a mountain for himself (paralleling Dan 2:35, 45), which is Mount Zion (4 Ezra 13:35–36). In contrast, the Similitudes of Enoch only verbally allude to Dan 7 with a white-haired "head of days" (1 En. 46:1) and a "son of man" (1 En. 46:4) who will destroy kings. At Qumran, 4Q246 (the Son of God text) refers to "an eternal kingdom" (II, 5) and a figure called the son of God who will rule (II, 1, 9). While Collins cautions against reading Daniel's son of man as anything other than one like a human being who symbolizes either an angel or a collective Israel, this text "may well represent the earliest interpretation, or reinterpretation, of the enigmatic 'one like a son of man'" as some sort of transcendent, messianic individual.[35]

Another eschatological theme in Daniel is the anticipation of divine warfare. In Dan 10, an angel visits Daniel after taking leave from a battle in heaven: "And now I will return to fight with the prince of Persia, and behold, when I go out the prince of Greece will come. But I will tell you what is written in the book of truth. There is no one who supports me against these except Michael your prince" (Dan 10:20–21). In Dan 11:40–12:3, a simultaneous battle occurs on earth between a king of the north and a king of the south and includes the "ships of the Kittim" (Dan 11:30), Edom, Moab, and the Ammonites (Dan 11:41). Daniel glimpses the true nature of imperial conflict, one in which earthly events are not only paralleled in heaven, but determined there. Because of this, Daniel does not represent a call to arms and is often contrasted to the militarism of the Maccabees, who are only "a little help" (Dan 11:34). A similar focus on heavenly and earthly battles is found in Qumran's War Scroll (1QM), but this eschatological text extends Daniel's concepts in new directions. The embattled forces of light and darkness are full of direct allusions to Daniel; the sectarian sons of light are led by none other than the angel Michael of Dan 10 and 12 (1QM XIII, 6–7) whereas their enemies, the sons of darkness, include the nations Edom, Moab, Ammon, Philistia, and the Kittim of Ashur (1QM I, 1–2, 4), direct allusions to Dan 11.[36] However, the scroll does not envision parallel battles in heaven and on earth, but instead merges the two so that "holy angels are together with their armies" (1QM VII, 6).[37] Columns 2–9 are

---

35. John J. Collins, *Daniel: A Commentary on the Book of Daniel*, Hermeneia (Minneapolis: Fortress, 1993), 78.

36. See David Flusser, "Apocalyptic Elements in the War Scroll," in *Judaism of the Second Temple Period: Qumran and Apocalypticism*, trans. Azzan Yadin (Grand Rapids: Eerdmans, 2007), 140–58.

37. Trans. Lawrence H. Schiffman, *Eschatological Community of the Dead Sea Scrolls: A Study of the Rule of the Congregation*, SBLMS 38 (Atlanta: Scholars Press, 1989), 50.

so full of descriptions of the necessary military equipment, battle formations, and the various types of soldiers that Yigael Yadin proposed that we understand the scroll as an actual military manual that would be used in the future war.[38] While there is no archaeological evidence that indicates the sectarians were preparing implements for battle, their preoccupation with ritual purity does suggest that they anticipated needing to be pure to fight alongside angels. Thus, it seems that the Qumran community used Daniel's apocalyptic visions to construct their self-understanding as a sect, but, in doing so, they also transformed the quietism of Daniel into a more militant eschatology.

The Book of Daniel in the New Testament

In several places, the New Testament seems to allude to the tales of the book of Daniel, most prominently the story of Daniel in the lions' den. Most explicitly, the Letter to the Hebrews recalls the deliverance of Daniel and his friends in the list of heroes of faith in chapter 11.[39] Among the deeds of "the prophets" is the memory of one who shut (φράσσω) the lions' mouths (Heb 11:33), suggesting Dan 6:23 in Theodotion's version, where the angel shuts (ἐμφράσσω) the lions' mouths. In the verse that follows, other anonymous prophets "quenched raging fires," which echoes—though in different words—the experience of the three in the furnace, cooled by the moist wind in the Greek versions of Dan 3:49–50. In Mark's puzzling little narrative of Jesus's wilderness temptations, there is perhaps a memory of Daniel's second sojourn in a lions' den: "He was with the wild beasts, and the angels waited on him" (Mark 1:13).[40] Commentators have sought a background to this in midrashic or magical traditions, but it may reflect the lions' den story of Bel and the Dragon, where an angel and also the prophet Habakkuk stay with Daniel in the den while Daniel eats the food that Habakkuk has brought (Dan 14:38 Theodotion; OG Dan 14:38, 39).[41] Lonely among the lions, Daniel, like Jesus, finds heavenly messengers there with him. In 2 Timothy, a cameo of Paul on trial makes dramatic use of the parallel of Daniel in the lions' den: "At

---

38. Yigael Yadin, *The Scroll of the War of the Sons of Light against the Sons of Darkness*, trans. Batya Rabin and Chaim Rabin (Oxford: Oxford University Press, 1962), 4–6.

39. See Craig R. Koester, *Hebrews: A New Translation with Introduction and Commentary*, AB 36 (New York: Doubleday, 2001), 512–13.

40. Unless otherwise noted, all New Testament translations are from the NRSV.

41. Joel Marcus prefers a concrete sense for διηκόνουν ("they attended" or "served") in Mark 1:13, so that the angels were serving Jesus with food and drink, which is just what Habakkuk and the angel do to Daniel. See Marcus, *Mark 1–8: A New Translation with Introduction and Commentary*, AB 27 (New York: Doubleday, 1999), 168.

my first defense no one came to my support, but all deserted me. May it not be counted against them! But the Lord stood by me and gave me strength, so that through me the message might be fully proclaimed and all the Gentiles might hear it. So I was rescued from the lion's mouth. The Lord will rescue me from every evil attack and save me for his heavenly kingdom" (2 Tim 4:16–18). Here, the language of lions' mouths and of being saved (σῴζω) recalls Dan 6:21, 22 in the Greek versions.[42] We might also wonder whether Paul's divine companion in the place of danger draws in the memory of the angelic visitors in the Greek texts of Dan 3 and Dan 14. Finally, some scholars have noted a series of parallels between the trial of Susanna and the legal process against Jesus in the Synoptic Gospels: elders who plot a death sentence after an ambush in a garden, two trials, false witnesses, a silent innocent victim, and especially the matching phrase "I am innocent of the blood of this one" (Καθαρὸς ἐγὼ ἀπὸ τοῦ αἵματος ταύτης, Sus (Theodotion) 46; ἀθῷός εἰμι ἀπὸ τοῦ αἵματος τούτου, Matt 27:24).[43]

More than the narratives of Dan 1–6, however, the writers of the New Testament found the visions of Dan 7–12 relevant, employing both verbal and conceptual allusions to shape their criticisms of Roman imperial rule and to foreshadow its apocalyptic end. The book of Revelation features these visions prominently, picking up on the same patterns that were established in early Jewish literature. This is not surprising, given that the text is apocalyptic in nature and, like 4 Ezra and 2 Baruch, dates to the late first century CE after the Roman destruction of the temple. Since Revelation "was written to awaken and intensify Christian exclusiveness, particularly vis-à-vis the imperial cult," allusions to the shocking imperial imagery of Dan 7 appear throughout the text.[44] Revelation 12:3 introduces a dragon with seven heads and ten horns, and, in Rev 13:1, this dragon stands by as a beast with seven heads and ten horns comes out of the sea. Not only are these clear verbal allusions to the hybrid creatures of Dan 7, but the dragon gives the beast his authority and throne (Rev 13:2), indicating that, like the four kingdoms of Dan 7, this beast also represents imperial power.[45] Indeed,

---

42. See Luke Timothy Johnson, *The First and Second Letters to Timothy: A New Translation with Introduction and Commentary*, AB 35a (New York: Doubleday, 2001), 442–43.

43. See Raymond E. Brown, *The Death of the Messiah: From Gethsemane to the Grave: A Commentary on the Passion Narratives in the Four Gospels*, 1st ed., 2 vols., ABRL (New York: Doubleday, 1994), 1:640 n. 9, 1:835, and 2:1451; Robert H. Gundry, *The Use of the Old Testament in St. Matthew's Gospel with Special Reference to the Messianic Hope*, NovTSup 18 (Leiden: Brill, 1967), 144, 149–50; the correspondences are fully laid out in Catherine Brown Tkacz, "Ἀνεβόησεν φωνῇ μεγάλῃ: Susanna and the Synoptic Passion Narratives," *Gregorianum* 87, no. 3 (2006): 449–86.

44. Adela Yarbro Collins, *Crisis and Catharsis: The Power of the Apocalypse* (Philadelphia: Westminster, 1984), 73.

45. See G. K. Beale, *The Use of Daniel in Jewish Apocalyptic Literature and in the Revelation*

the connection between the beast and empire is further supported by the detail that one of the heads of the beast has a lethal but healed wound (Rev 13:3), an allusion to Nero, whose throat, according to legend, was slit. Finally, the association between the beast and empire is confirmed in Rev 17, which interprets the beast's seven heads as "seven mountains . . . and they are also seven kings" (Rev 17:9-10), a reference to the seven hills on which Rome was built.[46]

Just as in Daniel, Revelation's creatures engage in divine warfare. The dragon's arrival on earth is precipitated by a heavenly battle with an angelic force led by Michael, the same chief angel fighting in Daniel (Dan 10:21; 12:1). A parallel battle also occurs as the beast wages war on earth against God's holy people (Rev 13:7), which thematically alludes to the fourth beast's horn making war on the holy ones (Dan 7:21). Since there are dual locales for warfare in heaven and earth, both Scriptures indicate that losing the battle in heaven means losing one's place there. In Rev 12 the dragon is hurled down to earth after its defeat, and in Dan 8 the goat's horn "grew until it reached the host of the heavens, and it threw some of the starry host down to the earth and trampled on them" (8:10). The final destruction of the beast is also based on the four kingdoms motif as it appears in Daniel and 4 Ezra. The horns of the beast and the beast itself will "hate the whore; they will devour her flesh and burn her up with fire" (Rev 17:16). The whore, however, is physically conjoined with the beast she rides upon. The conceptual parallel with the eagle of 4 Ezra is striking. Both the eagle and the whore/beast first devour themselves and then are burned up (4 Ezra 11:35; 12:3). While this downfall matches the fourth beast's body being thrown into the fire in Dan 7:11, further descriptions of the beast's death allude to the destruction of the statue in Dan 2: "A mighty angel took up a stone like a great millstone and threw it into the sea, saying, 'With such violence Babylon the great city will be thrown down, and will be found no more'" (Rev 18:21).

Revelation's use of the visions of Daniel demonstrates the flexibility of the symbolism of historical apocalypses. Given that these "visions convey a sense of mystery, which is not dispelled by the angelic interpretations," they are easily updated

---

of St. John (Lanham, MD: University Press of America, 1984), 229-48. The beast has ten horns (Rev 13:1) like the fourth beast (Dan 7:7). It has a total of seven heads (Rev 13:1), the same as the four beasts combined. It has parts from a leopard, bear, and lion (Rev 13:2) like the first three beasts (Dan 7:4-6). Revelation's monster speaks "haughty and blasphemous words" (Rev 13:5) just as the smallest horn speaks "great things" against God (Dan 7:8, 20). Finally, the beast's authority will last forty-two months (Rev 13:5), which is equivalent to three and a half years, the same amount of time that the small horn will rule (Dan 7:25).

46. Robert H. Mounce, *The Book of Revelation*, NICNT (Grand Rapids: Eerdmans, 1977), 315.

to reflect new historical realities.⁴⁷ The Greek fourth beast of Daniel becomes an analogous Roman Empire in Revelation. However, there are two noteworthy changes. The first is the addition of the satanic element. The dragon who falls from heaven is called the devil and Satan, Διάβολος and Σατανᾶς (Rev 12:9). Revelation 13:18 reveals that the beast's number is 666, which most likely stems from the numerical value of the name Nero, thereby equating Rome with the antichrist.⁴⁸ Also amplifying this new supernatural element is the fact that the Christ figure in the text is the mirror of the beast. It is a lamb but also has horns and multiple eyes and, despite its seeming passivity, will triumph over the beast (Rev 5:6; 17:14). While the beasts in Daniel are vicious, they only reflect human enemies of Israel. The second change is that the danger represented by Rome is concentrated in its imperial cult. Both the dragon and the first beast are worshiped (Rev 13:4). Moreover, Rev 13 depicts a second beast, one that represents the imperial cult and whose role is to enforce the worship of the first beast under the threat of death (Rev 13:12, 15). This beast alludes to Dan 3 and the requirement to worship the king's statue or be killed.⁴⁹ Therefore, we can see that the author of Revelation has appropriated Daniel to present the contemporary, imperial context as inherently dangerous to the welfare of the early Christian community.

In contrast to Revelation's more diffuse allusions to Daniel, Matthew includes a marked citation to signal the end of days. In Matt 24:15 (// Mark 13:14), we read, "Therefore when you see the abomination of desolation which was spoken of through Daniel the prophet, standing in the holy place (let the reader understand) then let those who are in Judea flee to the mountains." The phrase "the abomination of desolation" (שקוץ משומם/βδέλυγμα τῶν ἐρημώσεων and cognate expressions) appears in Dan 9:27; 11:31; and 12:11 and refers to Antiochus IV's desecration of the temple's altar. However, in Matthew the reference is clearly to the Romans' destruction of the temple.⁵⁰ The parenthetical aside, "let the reader understand," further alerts us to the necessity of keeping Daniel in mind when reading what follows in the list of eschatological signs.

In a verbal allusion to Dan 7:13, Matt 24:30 goes on to reveal the arrival of the Son of Man approaching on clouds of heaven. The son of man is by far the most frequently cited and alluded to concept from Daniel throughout the New Testa-

---

47. Collins, *Commentary*, 55.

48. Yarbro Collins, *Crisis and Catharsis*, 59.

49. Jan Willem van Henten, "Dragon Myth and Imperial Ideology in Revelation 12–13," in *Reality of Apocalypse: Rhetoric and Politics in the Book of Revelation*, ed. David L. Barr, SymS 39 (Atlanta: Scholars Press, 2006), 198.

50. Michael Theophilos, *The Abomination of Desolation in Matthew 24.15*, LNTS 437 (London: T&T Clark, 2012).

ment.⁵¹ While in Daniel the Aramaic (כבר אנש) means only "one like a human being," in the New Testament the Son of Man has become more of a designation than a description. Although there are instances where the Son of Man appears to have nothing to do with the apocalyptic tradition, most examples clearly allude verbally or conceptually to themes in Dan 7.⁵² Much like Matt 24:30, a few passages speak of his heavenly descent: "At that time people will see the Son of Man coming in clouds with great power and glory. And he will send his angels and gather his elect from the four winds, from the ends of the earth to the ends of the heavens" (Mark 13:26–27).⁵³ Not only does the Son of Man arrive on clouds, but there is the mention of the four winds, which echoes the winds that stirred up the four beasts (Dan 7:2). Similarly, he possesses power, a theme from Dan 7:14.⁵⁴ Other Son of Man references lack verbal allusions to Daniel but insert him into an eschatological setting that, like Dan 7, anticipates some sort of divine judgment: "And I tell you, everyone who acknowledges me before others, the Son of Man also will acknowledge before the angels of God; but whoever denies me before others will be denied before the angels of God" (Luke 12:8–9).⁵⁵ It is worth noting that many of these statements differentiate between the speaker, Jesus, and the object of his statement, the Son of Man, raising the question of whether they share an identity. Although it seems likely that early Christians viewed them as one and the same, some passages are more explicit that Jesus, Christ, and the Son of Man are interchangeable titles. For example, in response to the high priest's direct questioning of Jesus as to whether he is the Messiah, Jesus answers, "I am; and you will see the Son of Man seated at the right hand

---

51. While, as evidenced in what follows, we see the strong influence of Daniel on the son of man tradition, there has been a long debate as to whether such a Jewish concept existed independent of Daniel and prior to the New Testament. For overviews of this debate in New Testament studies, see Geza Vermes, "The 'Son of Man' Debate," *JSNT* 1 (1978): 28–29; Maurice Casey, *Son of Man: The Interpretation and Influence of Daniel 7* (London: SPCK, 1979); Chrys C. Caragounis, *The Son of Man: Vision and Interpretation*, WUNT 38 (Tübingen: Mohr Siebeck, 1986); Delbert Burkett, *The Son of Man Debate: A History and Evaluation*, SNTSMS 107 (Cambridge: Cambridge University Press, 1999); and Benjamin E. Reynolds, *The Son of Man Problem: Critical Readings*, T&T Clark Critical Readings in Biblical Studies (London: T&T Clark, 2018).

52. For non-Danielic references, take, e.g., the wisdom saying: "And Jesus said to him, 'Foxes have holes, and birds of the air have nests; but the Son of Man has nowhere to lay his head'" (Luke 9:58); or this legal interpretation: "The Sabbath was made for humankind, and not humankind for the Sabbath; so the Son of Man is lord even of the Sabbath" (Mark 2:27–28).

53. In addition to this passage, Matt 24 has numerous eschatological signs associated with the Son of Man's coming. See also Mark 14:62 for another reference to clouds of heaven.

54. For references to the Son of Man's kingdom, see Matt 16:28 and the parable in 13:37–38.

55. See also Matt 16:27; 19:28; Mark 2:9–11; Luke 12:40; and 17:30.

of the Power, and coming with the clouds of heaven" (Mark 14:62).[56] Mark also predicts that the Son of Man will be betrayed, suffer, die, and rise again, drawing direct parallels between the experience of the Son of Man and that of Jesus in the passion narrative (see Mark 8:31; 9:31; 10:33–34; 14:21, 41).[57] Similarly, details of Jesus's life are echoed in what the Son of Man does, such as forgiving sins to heal the sick (Luke 5:24) and befriending the tax collectors (Luke 7:34). There are a few instances in which Matthew leaves out the Son of Man from the Q equivalent in Luke (Matt 5:11; 10:32–33), suggesting that "the omission may be due to the fact that, by the time of Matthew, 'Son of Man' had become a name for Jesus just as 'Messiah' and 'Christ' had."[58]

Conclusion

While the New Testament writers were aware of the court tales of Daniel, the turbulent Roman imperial context of the beginning of the Common Era meant that it was the apocalyptic visions of Daniel that most resonated with them. The near-ubiquitous use of Dan 7's son of man title throughout the Gospels underscores Jesus's divine power to bring about a new kingdom in the midst of imperial power. More than any other New Testament book, however, it is Revelation that features the vision of Dan 7 prominently, picking up on the same patterns that were established in early Jewish literature—ferocious beasts and impending destruction at the end of times color the entire book. This is not surprising given that the text is apocalyptic in nature and, like 4 Ezra and 2 Baruch, dates to the late first century CE after the Roman destruction of the temple. Allusions to the shocking imperial imagery of Dan 7 appear throughout the text and work to sharpen the boundaries between the Christian community and the imperial cult. Revelation, therefore, serves as a prime example of the ways in which the concepts and images of Daniel provided the foundation for a discourse to challenge Roman hegemony.[59] Although the Roman Empire might have appeared as powerful as dragons and beasts, Revelation reveals to its readers the same truth that Daniel had disclosed centuries earlier about empire—its great strength belies its great fall.

---

56. Matthew 19:28 seems to imply heavily that Jesus and the Son of Man are the same, given that Jesus's own disciples will sit on thrones along with the Son of Man.

57. See also Luke 9:21–22, 44; 17:24–25.

58. Adela Yarbro Collins, "The Influence of Daniel on the New Testament," in *A Commentary on the Book of Daniel*, by John J. Collins, Hermeneia (Minneapolis: Fortress, 1993), 99.

59. Alexandria Frisch, *The Danielic Discourse on Empire in Second Temple Literature*, JSJSup 176 (Leiden: Brill, 2017).

This New Testament preference for Dan 7–12 as apocalyptic inspiration not only testifies to the enduring relevance of the Scripture itself but also to the significance of the contributions made by other Second Temple period texts in the intervening years. Texts as diverse in provenance as 4 Ezra, 2 Baruch, the War Scroll, the Four Kingdoms text, and 1 Enoch make use of images and motifs from Daniel's visions. The popularity of Daniel's beastly empires, four kingdoms, and eschatological battles throughout early Jewish literature meant that Jews in Judea and throughout the diaspora knew Daniel and continued to update its apocalyptic forecasts for their contemporary, imperial situations. Therefore, the allusions to Daniel in the New Testament should come as no surprise. Although the New Testament writers tailored Daniel to fit their specific theological needs—the Son of Man as Jesus, for example—their familiarity with Dan 7 meant that they were participating in a larger discourse within early Jewish literature: one that helped them to make sense of imperial power and of their own future, divine kingdom.

Bibliography

Barclay, John M. G. "The Empire Writes Back: Josephan Rhetoric in Flavian Rome." Pages 315–32 in *Flavius Josephus and Flavian Rome*. Edited by Jonathan Edmondson, Steve Mason, and James Rives. Oxford: Oxford University Press, 2005.

Beale, G. K. *The Use of Daniel in Jewish Apocalyptic Literature and in the Revelation of St. John*. Lanham, MD: University Press of America, 1984.

Blenkinsopp, Joseph. *Opening the Sealed Book: Interpretations of the Book of Isaiah in Late Antiquity*. Grand Rapids: Eerdmans, 2006.

Breed, Brennan W. "Daniel's Four Kingdoms Schema: A History of Re-writing World History." *Int* 71, no. 2 (2017): 178–89.

Brown, Raymond E. *The Death of the Messiah: From Gethsemane to the Grave; A Commentary on the Passion Narratives in the Four Gospels*. 1st ed. 2 vols. ABRL. New York: Doubleday, 1994.

Burkett, Delbert. *The Son of Man Debate: A History and Evaluation*. SNTSMS 107. Cambridge: Cambridge University Press, 1999.

Caragounis, Chrys C. *The Son of Man: Vision and Interpretation*. WUNT 38. Tübingen: Mohr Siebeck, 1986.

Carey, Greg. "The Book of Revelation as Counter-Imperial Script." Pages 157–76 *In the Shadow of Empire: Reclaiming the Bible as a History of Faithful Resistance*. Edited by Richard Horsley. Louisville: Westminster John Knox Press, 2008.

Casey, Maurice. *Son of Man: The Interpretation and Influence of Daniel 7*. London: SPCK, 1979.

Collins, Adela Yarbro. *Crisis and Catharsis: The Power of the Apocalypse*. Philadelphia: Westminster, 1984.

———. "The Influence of Daniel on the New Testament." Pages 90–112 in *A Commentary on the Book of Daniel*. Edited by John J. Collins. Hermeneia. Minneapolis: Fortress, 1993.

Collins, John J. *The Apocalyptic Imagination: An Introduction to Jewish Apocalyptic Literature*. 3rd ed. Grand Rapids: Eerdmans, 2016.

———. "The Book of Daniel and the Dead Sea Scrolls." Pages 203–17 in *The Hebrew Bible in Light of the Dead Sea Scrolls*. Edited by Nóra Dávid, Armin Lange, Kristin De Troyer, and Shani Tzoref. FRLANT 239. Göttingen: Vandenhoeck & Ruprecht, 2012.

———. *Daniel: A Commentary on the Book of Daniel*. Hermeneia. Minneapolis: Fortress, 1993.

Daube, David. "Typology in Josephus." *JJS* 31, no. 1 (1980): 18–36.

Dehandschutter, Boudewijn. "Example and Discipleship: Some Comments on the Biblical Background of the Early Christian Theology of Martyrdom." Pages 20–26 in *The Impact of Scripture in Early Christianity*. Edited by Jan den Boeft and M. L. van Poll-van de Lisdonk. VCSup 44. Leiden: Brill, 1999.

Diebner, Bernd Jörg. *Zephanjas Apokalypsen*. JSHRZ 5.9. Gütersloh: Mohn, 2003.

Di Lella, Alexander A. "The Textual History of Septuagint-Daniel and Theodotion-Daniel." Pages 586–607 in vol. 2 of *The Book of Daniel: Composition and Reception*. Edited by John J. Collins and Peter W. Flint. 2 vols. VTSup 83. Leiden: Brill, 2001.

Evans, Craig A. "Daniel in the New Testament: Visions of God's Kingdom." Pages 490–527 in vol. 2 of *The Book of Daniel: Composition and Reception*. Edited by John J. Collins and Peter W. Flint. 2 vols. VTSup 83. Leiden: Brill, 2001.

Feldman, Louis H. "Josephus' Portrait of Daniel." *Hen* 14 (1992): 37–96.

Flint, Peter W. "The Daniel Tradition at Qumran." Pages 41–60 in *Eschatology, Messianism, and the Dead Sea Scrolls*. Edited by Craig A. Evans and Peter W. Flint. Grand Rapids: Eerdmans, 1997.

Flusser, David. "Apocalyptic Elements in the War Scroll." Pages 140–58 in *Judaism of the Second Temple Period: Qumran and Apocalypticism*. Translated by Azzan Yadin. Grand Rapids: Eerdmans, 2007.

———. "The Four Empires in the Fourth Sibyl and in the Book of Daniel." *IOS* 2 (1972): 148–75.

Frend, W. H. C. *Martyrdom and Persecution in the Early Church: A Study of a Conflict from the Maccabees to Donatus*. Oxford: Blackwell, 1965.

Frisch, Alexandria. *The Danielic Discourse on Empire in Second Temple Literature*. JSJSup 176. Leiden: Brill, 2017.

Gundry, Robert H. *The Use of the Old Testament in St. Matthew's Gospel with Special Reference to the Messianic Hope.* NovTSup 18. Leiden: Brill, 1967.

Henten, Jan Willem van. "Dragon Myth and Imperial Ideology in Revelation 12–13." Pages 181–203 in *Reality of Apocalypse: Rhetoric and Politics in the Book of Revelation.* Edited by David L. Barr. SymS 39. Atlanta: Scholars Press, 2006.

———. *The Maccabean Martyrs as Saviours of the Jewish People: A Study of 2 and 4 Maccabees.* JSJSup 57. Leiden: Brill, 1997.

———. "The Tradition-Historical Background of Romans 3:25: A Search for Pagan and Jewish Parallels." Pages 101–28 in *From Jesus to John: Essays on Jesus and New Testament Christology in Honour of Marinus de Jonge.* Edited by Martinus C. de Boer. JSNTSup 84. Sheffield: Sheffield Academic, 1993.

Henze, Matthias. *The Madness of King Nebuchadnezzar: The Ancient Near Eastern Origins and Early History of Interpretation of Daniel 4.* JSJSup 61. Leiden: Brill, 1999.

Jensen, Robin Margaret. *Understanding Early Christian Art.* London: Routledge, 2000.

Johnson, Luke Timothy. *The First and Second Letters to Timothy: A New Translation with Introduction and Commentary.* AB 35A. New York: Doubleday, 2001.

Kellermann, Ulrich. "Das Danielbuch und die Märtyrertheologie der Auferstehung." Pages 51–75 in *Die Entstehung der jüdischen Martyrertheologie.* Edited by Jan Willem van Henten. StPB 38. Leiden: Brill, 1989.

Koester, Craig R. *Hebrews: A New Translation with Introduction and Commentary.* AB 36. New York: Doubleday, 2001.

Kratz, Reinhard Gregor. *Translatio Imperii: Untersuchungen zu den aramäischen Danielerzählungen und ihrem theologiegeschichtlichen Umfeld.* WMANT 63. Neukirchen-Vluyn: Neukirchener Verlag, 1991.

Levine, Lee I. *Visual Judaism in Late Antiquity: Historical Contexts of Jewish Art.* New Haven: Yale University Press, 2012.

Marcus, Joel. *Mark 1–8: A New Translation with Introduction and Commentary.* AB 27. New York: Doubleday, 1999.

Mason, Steve. "Josephus, Daniel, and the Flavian House." Pages 161–91 in *Josephus and the History of the Greco-Roman Period: Essays in Memory of Morton Smith.* Edited by Fausto Parente and Joseph Sievers. StPB 41. Leiden: Brill, 1994.

Mounce, Robert H. *The Book of Revelation.* NICNT. Grand Rapids: Eerdmans, 1977.

Newsom, Carol A., and Brennan W. Breed. *Daniel: A Commentary.* OTL. Louisville: Westminster John Knox, 2014.

Parker, Henry M. D. "Signa militaria." *OCD*, 1406.

Rajak, Tessa. "The Angry Tyrant." Pages 110–27 in *Jewish Perspectives on Hellenistic Rulers.* Edited by Tessa Rajak, Sarah Pearce, James Aitken, and Jennifer Dines. HCS 50. Berkeley: University of California Press, 2007.

Reynolds, Benjamin E. *The Son of Man Problem: Critical Readings*. T&T Clark Critical Readings in Biblical Studies. London: T&T Clark, 2018.
Satran, David. *Biblical Prophets in Byzantine Palestine: Reassessing the Lives of the Prophets*. SVTP 11. Leiden: Brill, 1995.
———. "Daniel: Seer, Philosopher, Holy Man." Pages 33–48 in *Ideal Figures in Ancient Judaism: Profiles and Paradigms*. Edited by John J. Collins and George W. E. Nickelsburg. SCS 12. Chico, CA: Scholars Press, 1980.
Schiffman, Lawrence H. *Eschatological Community of the Dead Sea Scrolls: A Study of the Rule of the Congregation*. SBLMS 38. Atlanta: Scholars Press, 1989.
Stone, Michael E., and Matthias Henze. *4 Ezra and 2 Baruch: Translations, Introductions, and Notes*. Minneapolis: Fortress, 2013.
Stuckenbruck, Loren T. "The Formation and Re-formation of Daniel in the Dead Sea Scrolls." Pages 101–30 in *The Bible and the Dead Sea Scrolls*. Vol. 1, *Scripture and the Scrolls; The Second Princeton Symposium on the Dead Sea Scrolls*. Edited by James H. Charlesworth. Waco, TX: Baylor University Press, 2006.
Theophilos, Michael. *The Abomination of Desolation in Matthew 24.15*. LNTS 437. London: T&T Clark, 2012.
Tkacz, Catherine Brown. "Ἀνεβόησεν φωνῇ μεγάλῃ: Susanna and the Synoptic Passion Narratives." *Gregorianum* 87, no. 3 (2006): 449–86.
Ulrich, Eugene. "The Text of Daniel in the Qumran Scrolls." Pages 573–85 in vol. 2 of *The Book of Daniel: Composition and Reception*. Edited by John J. Collins and Peter W. Flint. 2 vols. VTSup 83. Leiden: Brill, 2001.
Vermes, Geza. "Josephus' Treatment of the Book of Daniel." *JJS* 42, no. 2 (1991): 149–66.
———. "The 'Son of Man' Debate." *JSNT* 1 (1978): 19–32.
Wills, Lawrence M. *The Jew in the Court of the Foreign King: Ancient Jewish Court Legends*. HDR 26. Minneapolis: Fortress, 1990.
Yadin, Yigael. *The Scroll of the War of the Sons of Light against the Sons of Darkness*. Translated by Batya Rabin and Chaim Rabin. Oxford: Oxford University Press, 1962.

37

Figures of Ancient Israel in the New Testament

VALÉRIE NICOLET

When constructing the identity of their communities, early Jewish groups relied on figures found in Israel's Scriptures and focused on the great patriarchs, Abraham, Moses, David, and sometimes Isaac and Jacob.[1] In the details of the texts, however, the situation is more complex, for at least three reasons.

First, one must clarify what is meant by a figure. A figure is created when a historical person or a narrative character is used, reused, reinterpreted in different texts, at different times, and for different contexts. From their origins in Scripture, biblical figures accumulate various dimensions and aspects and allow a plurality of readings.[2] Second, not all uses of figures would have functioned similarly for everyone, nor would they have been identified clearly by all addressees. In the case of an explicit citation, the reader would have known that a figure was used. Allusions might have been less immediately perceptible. Would all audiences have perceived the construction of John the Baptist through Elijah in Matt 3:1–4 and Mark 1:6; 6:15? Allusions we see might not always have been there for the audi-

---

Many thanks are due here to the editors of this volume for their patience and support, and to the Biblical Studies Seminar at Uppsala University, particularly Cecilia Wassén, whose response to an earlier version of this chapter helped reshape the material. As always, Mikael Larsson has read first drafts and provided support. All shortcomings remain mine.

1. If one looks at the New Testament as main material, Moses (eighty times), Abraham (seventy-three times), and David (fifty-nine times) are the most frequently named figures, along with Elijah (twenty-nine times).

2. See Thomas Römer, "Qui est Abraham? Les différentes figures du patriarche dans la Bible hébraïque," in *Abraham: Nouvelle jeunesse d'un ancêtre*, ed. Thomas Römer, Essais bibliques 28 (Geneva: Labor et Fides, 1997), 13.

ences or the authors. While this should not keep us from mapping these allusions, we cannot reconstruct with certainty how they would have worked in their initial context. The third and final reason for the complexity is the mass of data. We are confronted with many figures used in a large corpus and with great variety.[3]

I curtail the multiplicity and complexity of usages by taking the New Testament uses as guide and by focusing on explicit quotations of the figures. This creates a problem. Choosing the New Testament as guide is arbitrary. It reflects the artificial predominance of the New Testament as a late Second Temple collection of Jewish texts because of the adoption of these texts as canonical by the later Christian church. A different picture would emerge if one were to take the Pseudepigrapha or the Dead Sea Scrolls as the main basis for inquiry. For example, Jacob, Noah, or Aaron would be more important figures. It also artificially skews the discussion toward presenting the New Testament as unique among early Jewish texts. To the extent that it will become the canonical text of Christianity, that is of course true, but in the first century this was not the case. One way of addressing this problem is to first delineate the uses of figures of Israel in other early Jewish literature. Additionally, the organization of the material means that greater importance is given to the patriarchal figures used in the New Testament. Less common figures, such as Sarah, Hagar, Tamar, Rahab, and Ruth, all but disappear. This effacement of ancient female figures is addressed below in the discussion of "minor," or less frequently attested, figures.

An Initial Overview: Abraham, Moses, and David

This overview shows initial similarities and differences between uses in the New Testament and in early Jewish texts. It also indicates that the principal uses of figures are rather repetitive. Rarer and more interesting uses will be discussed in the sections concerned with each figure. In this overview, I am also providing a few observations about types of uses. All types of uses identified by this book—marked or explicit citation, unmarked or implicit citation, verbal allusion, and conceptual allusion—are found in the ways early Jewish texts enlist figures of Israel. Explicit quotations are easiest to trace.

In the New Testament, Abraham is mentioned in the expression "the God of Abraham, Isaac and Jacob" and is invoked, along with Isaac and Jacob, as

---

3. For the Pseudepigrapha, I use *OTP*. For the Dead Sea Scrolls, I use Michael O. Wise, Martin G. Abegg Jr., and Edward M. Cook, eds., *The Dead Sea Scrolls: A New Translation*, rev. ed. (New York: Harper Collins, 2005); and Geza Vermes, *The Complete Dead Sea Scrolls* (London: Penguin, 2004). I use the Apocrypha as edited in the NRSV.

forefather.[4] In this usage, Abraham, Isaac, and Jacob lose their individuality to become an entity that facilitates the inscription of a community in a common heritage. This use is found occasionally in texts from Qumran, in the Apocrypha, and in the Pseudepigrapha. The uses of Jacob as a reference to Israel are much more common in these texts and appear only rarely in the New Testament.[5] This use is most widespread in the Apocrypha (particularly for Sirach and 2 Esdras, but also in 1 Maccabees) and in the Pseudepigrapha (in particular for 2 Baruch, Jubilees, and Liber Antiquitatum Biblicarum).[6]

Concerning Moses, a widespread use is to describe the law as the law of Moses, or to identify Moses as the author of a quotation of the Torah. It is found often in the New Testament and the Apocrypha.[7] For the Pseudepigrapha, this use is not developed as much. There is one use in T. Zeb. 3:4 (second century BCE). Concerning the Qumran material, the Damascus Document testifies to this use when quoting the Pentateuch. In the discussion concerning who can enter the community, the covenant is presented as being made between Moses and Israel and its content is the return to the law of Moses (CD XV, 9). The law as a specific feature of Moses also appears in the Community Rule (1QS V, 8; VIII, 22) and in the War Scroll (1QM X, 1–4).[8]

Similarly, David is sometimes presented as "saying" when a psalm is quoted.[9] The only parallel to this formula in the Dead Sea Scrolls is found in fragments 12–13

---

4. For "the God of Abraham, Isaac and Jacob," see Mark 12:26 // Matt 22:32; Luke 20:37; Acts 3:13. For "forefather," see Matt 8:11 // Luke 13:28.

5. Out of the twenty-six uses of the name Jacob (the name Jacob is used twenty-seven times in the New Testament, but Matt 1:15–16 is a reference to a different Jacob, also the father of a Joseph, the husband of Mary), only three connect it to Israel (Luke 1:33; Acts 7:46; and Rom 11:26). Seven uses of Jacob are connected to Abraham and Isaac.

6. At Qumran, we find this use in the Damascus Document (CD III, 4; VII, 19; XX, 17); in the War Scroll (1QM XI, 6); in 4Q163; 4Q174–176; and 11Q5 XVIII, 7, 16.

7. Mark 1:44 // Matt 8:4 and Luke 5:14; Mark 10:3, 4 // Matt 19:7, 8; Mark 12:19 // Matt 22:24 and Luke 20:28; Mark 7:10; Luke 2:22; 16:29, 31; 24:27, 44; John 1:17, 45; 5:46; 7:19; 8:5; Acts 3:22; 6:14; 13:38; 15:1, 5, 21; 26:22; 28:23; Rom 10:5, 19; 1 Cor 9:9; 2 Cor 3:15; Heb 10:28. In the Apocrypha, 1 Esdras uses Moses seven times. Except for 1 Esd 1:6, the other uses refer to what is written in the book of Moses or to the law of Moses (1 Esd 1:11; 5:48; 7:6, 9; 8:3; 9:39). The same is true of the five uses of the names in the book of Tobit or of the two uses in the story of Susanna (Tob 1:8 [codex Sinaiticus]; 6:13; 7:11, 12, 13; Sus 3 and 62 [Theodotion]). In Bar 2:28 Moses is presented as the one who is writing the law of God.

8. This legislative role of Moses is also found in a polytheistic text, Hecateus of Abdera (fourth century BCE), known through Diodorus of Sicily (90–30 BCE) and Photios (810–91 CE). It is the oldest polytheistic mention of the Scripture of Israel. See Jean-Daniel Kaestli, "Moïse et les institutions chez Hécatée d'Abdère," in *La construction de la figure de Moïse/The Construction of the Figure of Moses*, ed. Thomas Römer, TranseuSup 13 (Paris: Gabalda, 2007), 131–43.

9. Mark 12:36 // Matt 22:43 and Luke 20:42; Acts 2:25, 31, 34; 4:25; Rom 4:6; 11:9; Heb 4:7. On the construction of David as author of the Psalms and his subsequent identification with

of 4Q177, which quotes Ps 6:2–3.[10] There is a similar use in the Apocrypha (4 Macc 18:15, quoting Ps 34:19). This use of David as "saying" is not found in the Pseudepigrapha.[11] Compared to the New Testament, other Second Temple Jewish texts associate the figure of David more frequently with the temple, such as in the expression "house of David," or with Jerusalem, in the expression "City of David."[12] The most widespread use of the name David in the New Testament (eighteen out of fifty-nine mentions) is to present Jesus as the son of David.[13] In addition, David can be associated with the notion of a "branch of David," "shoot of David," "root of David," also with messianic undertones. In the New Testament, this is found in Rev 5:5. Luke uses the expression "house of David" to refer to the family of Jesus (Luke 1:27, 69; 2:4). Among the occurrences of David in the Dead Sea Scrolls, this use is also frequent.[14]

Explicit quotations also occur in retellings of episodes of the story of Israel (Acts 7:2–53), lists of heroes (Heb 11:4–40), several briefer mentions of some

---

prophecy, see Margaret Daly-Denton, "David the Psalmist, Inspired Prophet: Jewish Antecedents of a New Testament *Datum*," *ABR* 52 (2004): 32–47.

10. In 11Q13 II, 9–10, which introduces a quotation of Ps 82:1, we have the formula "as it is written concerning him in the Songs of David." Possibly a similar use is intended in two fragments of 4Q397 frag. 14 and 4Q398 frag. 14, but the text is too fragmentary to be sure.

11. The uses of expressions that recall the New Testament (such as "the prophet David spoke" or "the words of David the prophet") are only found in pseudepigraphic works that were redacted by Christians or are Christian compositions, such as Ques. Ezra, recension A 35; Apoc. Sedr. 14:4; Apoc. Dan. 14:11; T. Adam 4:3; and Ascen. Isa. 4:21. First Esdras 1:5 speaks of the directions given by David when it comes to worship in the temple.

12. In the Dead Sea Scrolls, one finds the idea of "house of David" most clearly in CD VII, 16. "House of David" refers to the temple in Tob 1:4, but in Sirach and 1 Esdras, it is related to the lineage of David (Sir 48:15; 51:12 [in the Hebrew addition]; 1 Esd 5:5). The expression "City of David" is not found in the Dead Sea Scrolls or in the Pseudepigrapha. It is characteristic of 1 Maccabees, which uses it for Jerusalem four times (1 Macc 1:33; 2:31; 7:32; 14:36). Luke and John also use "city (or village) of David" (Luke 2:4, 11; John 7:42) but to refer to Bethlehem. The expression "house of David" to indicate the temple does not appear in the New Testament, except perhaps in Acts 15:16, which, using Amos 9:11 LXX as in CD VII, 16 to talk about the "dwelling of David," might refer to the temple.

13. It is particularly frequent in Matthew, for whom "Son of David" is an appropriate messianic title: Matt 1:1; 9:27; 12:33; 15:22; 20:30, 31; 21:9, 15; 22:42. Mark 10:47, 48 and Luke 18:38 (twice) are parallels to Matt 20:30–31. John 7:42 affirms that the messiah is descended from David. It is found also in Rom 1:3 and 2 Tim 2:8. In Rev 22:16, Jesus presents himself as the root and descendant of David.

14. Out of the thirty-six occurrences of the name David, nine are linked to the notion of a branch of David. 4Q252 V, 2–3 is a particularly clear example. In the Apocrypha and Pseudepigrapha, only 4 Ezra 12:32 has this usage, also in an explicit association with the messiah. The three other references in the Pseudepigrapha that allude to the lineage of David (twice through the image of the "house of David" and once through the "family of David") are found in texts that might be Jewish in origin but were redacted by Christians, such as Sib. Or. 6:16 and 7:31, as well as Ascen. Isa. 11:2, which echoes Luke 1:27.

characters in various stories, genealogies, and uses of figures in arguments. Among conceptual allusions, we find examples of figures being constructed through another. All these uses have parallels in other Second Temple Jewish texts. The reappropriation of figures of Israel in "rewritten Scriptures" is specific to literature outside of the New Testament.[15] Also absent in the New Testament is what one could call "fan fiction."[16] "Fan fiction," a term borrowed from popular culture, where it designates the continuing of stories about important characters of video games or television series by fans, can qualify ancient works that develop the life of characters, whether in narrative form (like Joseph and Aseneth) or in a more apocalyptic literary genre (various testaments or martyrdoms, apocalypses). Among the Apocrypha and the Pseudepigrapha, the genre is popular. It appears in Christian literature as well, in the forms of various apocryphal acts and stories about martyrs, but is not present in the New Testament (although one could read Acts as an example of fan fiction about Paul).

Figures of Israel in Early Jewish Literature

The most used figures in early Jewish literature outside the New Testament and the Dead Sea Scrolls are Abraham, Jacob, Joseph, and Moses.[17] Even though Jacob and Joseph are practically nonexistent in the New Testament and will thus not be discussed in the New Testament section, they are included here because of the former's importance in Jubilees and the latter's in Joseph and Aseneth.

Concerning figures of Israel in general, early Jewish literature tends to include various uses. For Abraham, two aspects related to his role in the Scriptures of Israel are discussed in early Jewish literature: God's choice of Abraham as the recipient of the covenant and Abraham's faithfulness. Abraham's faithfulness is sometimes connected with his willingness to sacrifice Isaac in early Jewish texts. For Moses, early Jewish texts discuss three elements: Moses's relationship to the

---

15. After Geza Vermes, who speaks of "Rewritten Bible" in *Scripture and Tradition in Judaism: Haggadic Studies*, 2nd ed., StPB 4 (Leiden: Brill, 1973). For a discussion of the label, see George J. Brooke, "Genre Theory, Rewritten Bible and Pesher," *DSD* 17, no. 3 (2010): 361–86; and Pierluigi Piovanelli, "'Rewritten Bible' ou 'Bible in Progress'? La réécriture des traditions mémoriales bibliques dans le judaïsme et le christianisme anciens," *RTP* 139, no. 4 (2007): 295–310.

16. About fan fiction in biblical scholarship, see Frauke Uhlenbruch and Sonja Ammann, eds., "Fan Fiction and Ancient Scribal Cultures," *Transformative Works and Cultures* 31 (2019), DOI: 10.3983/twc.2019.1887.

17. In the Dead Sea Scrolls, the names most used are Moses (around 170 times), Jacob (around 150 times), and Abraham (about seventy times). Characteristic of the Qumran material is the occurrence of Aaron (twenty-eight times in four different texts). Enoch also appears quite often, mostly, of course, in manuscripts of Enochic literature (4Q201; 203; 212; 530; and 531), as well as in the Genesis Apocryphon (1Q20).

apocalyptic revelation of a new law, Moses's relationship with Egypt, and Moses's special relationship to God. Liber Antiquitatum Biblicarum (first century CE) also insists on Moses's importance for maintaining the cult.

Additionally, early Jewish literature takes the liberty to develop the stories of Moses and Abraham outside their canonical appearances, as Testament of Abraham (first to second century CE) or Liber Antiquitatum Biblicarum exemplify. This is absent from New Testament texts.

Abraham in Early Jewish Literature

When one looks at the trajectory of Abraham in the Scriptures of Israel, two elements are particularly striking.[18] First, the great majority of the mentions of Abraham are concentrated in Genesis and cannot be dated before the exile.[19] The promises of land and descendants are designed to quiet the anxieties of the exiled and contribute to building Abraham as the ancestor of the exiled part of Israel.[20] The second element is the variety of Abraham's portrayal:[21] rural aristocrat established in Hebron, nomadic ancestor who takes on "exotic" features, first recipient of a covenant symbolized by circumcision, figure who lives outside the land and represents the diaspora, ancestor of all the faithful people, and representative of the possibility of openness to the nations with the story of Hagar.[22]

Early Jewish literature focuses on two aspects.[23] First, several texts in the Apocrypha and the Pseudepigrapha seek to justify the election of Abraham as the ancestor and explain why and how Abraham renounces idolatry. Second, ancient Jewish texts highlight the faithfulness and obedience of Abraham, which form the basis for the eternal covenant and the promise of descendants. In some Qumran texts, the obedience is shown in the respect of the ritual of circumcision (CD XVI, 6 // 4Q271 4 II, 7).

Before discussing these two common receptions of Abraham, I mention one specific use, found in the Testament of Abraham.[24] The text focuses on Abraham's

---

18. See Römer, "Qui est Abraham?," 19 and 20.

19. Out of the 175 mentions of the name Abraham, 133 appear in Genesis; and of the 61 mentions of Abram, 59 are found in Genesis.

20. Römer, "Qui est Abraham?," 20–22.

21. Römer, "Qui est Abraham?," 20–22.

22. For exotic features, see Römer, "Qui est Abraham?," 26. Römer, 24–31, gives a chronological development of the features of Abraham, but for our texts, it is reasonable to assume that the cycle of Abraham would be understood as a unity.

23. For a detailed treatment of Abraham in Jewish and Christian literature, see Sean A. Adams and Zanne Domoney-Lyttle, eds., *Abraham in Jewish and Early Christian Literature*, LSTS 93 (London: T&T Clark, 2019).

24. See the introduction to the Testament of Abraham by E. P. Sanders in *OTP* 1:871–81.

absence of sin and his death. Amid the colorful description of Abraham in the Testament of Abraham, one can mention the whirlwind tour of the world which God accords to Abraham as a last wish before his death. The tour is cut short because Abraham, who does not know sin, cannot tolerate it in others and thus makes judgment rain on them and destroy them. God intervenes and asks that Michael show to Abraham what happens after death. This allows Abraham to change his mind about sinners and to intervene for souls through prayer and help them reach salvation (T. Ab. 14:6–8, 14). This episode emphasizes the positive aspect of praying for those who are already dead, using blameless Abraham as an example, while preserving the sovereignty of God, who remains in control of souls after death.[25]

Abraham's Reasons for Abandoning Idolatry and His Election

The retelling of the history of Israel in Jdt 5:5–21 alludes to Abraham in verses 6–9.[26] The retelling is placed in the mouth of Achior, who explains to Holofernes who his enemy is. Achior selects a few elements to tell Holofernes, without naming characters, even though for someone familiar with the biblical story told in the Pentateuch, it is not difficult to identify individuals. Judith 5:7–8 indicates that Abraham and his people "did not wish to follow the gods of their ancestors" and turned to the God of heaven. This abandonment of the ancestors' ways led to persecution and to Abraham's move to Mesopotamia. According to Adolfo Roitman, Judith provides an explanation for an unclear fact in Gen 11:31, namely why Abraham and his family leave Ur. Judith suggests "that they left for religious reasons," abandoning their polytheistic practices for worship of the one true God.[27]

This is also found in Jub. 11:16–17, which presents Abraham as knowing from his early years that idols are impure, so much so that he leaves his father to avoid

---

25. Annette Yoshiko Reed, "The Construction and Subversion of Patriarchal Perfection: Abraham and Exemplarity in Philo, Josephus, and the *Testament of Abraham*," *JSJ* 40, no. 2 (2009): 185–212, sees in the Abraham of the Testament of Abraham a negative exemplum and emphasizes its humoristic dimension. While I agree that the text is funny, it still presents Abraham in a rather positive light.

26. Judith was probably composed at the end of the second century BCE or beginning of the first century BCE. See Adolfo Roitman, "The Traditions about Abraham's Early Life in the Book of Judith," in *Things Revealed: Studies in Early Jewish and Christian Literature in Honor of Michael E. Stone*, ed. Esther G. Chazon, David Satran, and Ruth Clements, JSJSup 89 (Leiden: Brill, 2004), 73–87. Contra Roger Gil and Eberhard Bons, "Judith 5:5–21 ou le récit d'Akhior: Les mémoires dans la construction de l'identité narrative du peuple d'Israël," *VT* 64, no. 4 (2014): 573–87, who date Judith to the Persian period.

27. Roitman, "Traditions about Abraham's Early Life," 80. This could, as Roitman indicates, depend upon the tradition found in Josh 24:2–3.

worshiping idols with him. Jubilees 12:1–15 elaborates on Abraham's critique of idols and presents Abraham as delivering a plea to convince Terah to abandon idol worship. A bit further, Jubilees gives another explanation for Abraham's enlightenment about the one God. Jubilees 12:16–24 introduces the covenant between God and Abraham and the departure to Canaan. In Jub. 12:16–24, Abraham, while stargazing, realizes that the portents contained in the sky are in the hands of the Lord (Jub. 12:17). He then prays and asks to be established forever, with his seed (Jub. 12:20). God's answer (Jub. 12:22–24) is Jubilees's version of Gen 12:1–3 and relates the promise of the land and of becoming a great and numerous people (Jub. 12:22). Consequently, Abraham leaves Haran for Canaan. Before Abraham's call by God, Abraham already recognized the one God and abandoned idolatry.

The motif of Abraham's knowledge of astronomy is found elsewhere in Jewish literature of the time.[28] Apocalypse of Abraham 7:1–7 uses it in Abraham's discourse designed to dismantle Terah's faith in false idols. The Apocalypse of Abraham showcases Abraham's interrogation about idols in several examples. Abraham is perplexed by the fate of Marumath, who loses its head and is refashioned by Abraham's father (Apoc. Ab. 1:4–9) and is distraught when three statues (Apoc. Ab. 2:4, or five according to 3:7) fabricated by his father sink in the river. A further experience with a wooden statue of a god, Barisat, which burns in a fire, convinces Abraham that the gods of his father are nothing but idols (Apoc. Ab. 5). He then appeals to God who created all things (Apoc. Ab. 7:10) and asks for a revelation (Apoc. Ab. 7:12), granted to him in the next chapter, which results in his election (Apoc. Ab. 8:1–5).

These passages emphasize how Abraham, even before he is called by God, realizes the falsity of idol worship and turns to the one true creator God. This makes God's choice of Abraham as recipient of the two promises associated with the covenant (land and descendants) more understandable. One text offers a different reason. For Liber Antiquitatum Biblicarum, Abraham is never associated with idolatry since it explicitly indicates that the descendants of Serug (which include Terah and Abraham) do not join in the practice of astrology (LAB 4:16, contrary to Jub. 11). Liber Antiquitatum Biblicarum thus does not need to explain why Abraham would need to turn away from idol worship. Liber Antiquitatum Biblicarum derives its explanation for Abraham's choice from the proximity be-

---

28. Josephus mentions it in *Ant.* 1.156. One sees it in one of two quotations of Pseudo-Eupolemus (first century BCE) found in Alexander Polyhistor's *On the Jews* and transmitted through Eusebius's *Praeparatio evangelica*. Knowledge of astrology is acceptable since it is combined with reverence for the one true God. On Pseudo-Eupolemus, see the introduction by R. Doran, *OTP* 2:873–79.

tween the first mention of Abram in Gen 11:26 and the episode of the tower of Babel (Gen 11:1–9). As the dispersed inhabitants of the earth come together to build a tower (LAB 6:1), Abram and a few others refuse to participate.[29] Subsequently, the leaders condemn them to be burned. One of the chiefs plots to help Abram and his fellow rebels escape. Abram declines to flee and gives a reason based on his complete trust in God and his willingness to recognize God as the only judge (LAB 6:11). Abram is then led away to be burned, but God intervenes, saving Abram and burning those around the furnace. A bit later, God affirms what the story had already shown, God's preference for Abram (LAB 7:4) and God's gift of the covenant to Abram (LAB 7:4). Liber Antiquitatum Biblicarum does not indicate that God's choice derives from this episode, but the narrative unfolding of the episodes supports the interpretation according to which Abraham's faithfulness to the one true God precedes his election.

Faithfulness and Obedience of Abraham; Covenant and Promise

Abraham's faithfulness is practically a convention of the description of Abraham in early Jewish texts. Sirach's long list of heroes emphasizes it. Abraham appears in Sir 44:19–21. Several elements are highlighted about him, which will be found in most texts: Abraham as father of a great nation (Sir 44:19); the covenant between God and Abraham marked by circumcision (Sir 44:20); Abraham's faithfulness to the covenant, despite a test (Sir 44:20); the blessing of the nations through him, which means numerous offspring (Sir 44:21).[30]

Abraham's faithfulness and perfection are exemplified through his resistance to trials. This is explicit in Jub. 17:15–18, where the request to sacrifice Isaac stems from a challenge by Mastema. It represents the ultimate trial (Jub. 18) after those recounted in 17:17–18. The angel of the presence mentioned in Jub. 1:27 stops Abraham, and his obedience puts Mastema to shame. God then reiterates the promise made in Jub. 12:22–23 and recognizes Abraham's faithfulness (Jub. 18:16).[31] The Damascus Document also underscores Abraham's faithfulness

---

29. Except for the brief genealogical mention in LAB 4:15, this is the first mention of Abram in Liber Antiquitatum Biblicarum.

30. Fourth Ezra 3:13–15 also insists on God's choice of Abraham, whom God loves. Fourth Ezra indicates that Abraham is the recipient not only of an everlasting covenant but also of revelations about the end of times. This is also found in 2 Bar. 57:1–2.

31. Fourth Maccabees 16:20 also contains a reference to the sacrifice of Isaac. In 4 Maccabees, Abraham becomes an example of zeal while Isaac embodies courage. The sacrifice of Isaac is also recounted in a fragment by Demetrius the Chronographer (third century BCE). This fragment only recounts the story of the sacrifice, without commenting on Abraham or Isaac's character (frag. 1; *Praep. ev.* 9.19.4). Finally, in the list of unnamed heroes helped by Wisdom

and righteousness with two explanations. Damascus Document III, 2 presents him as a "friend of God because he kept the commandments of God and did not choose his own will."[32] Similarly, CD XVI, 6 insists on Abraham's respect for the law of circumcision as soon as he is made aware of it. This should be an example for the people who return to the law of Moses to remain faithful. Abraham's pre-Sinaitic respect for the commandments serves as a reminder that the members of the Qumran community should also fulfill the law of Moses.[33]

Jacob in Early Jewish Literature

The use of Jacob to refer to Israel notwithstanding, Jacob is particularly significant in the book of Jubilees, which contains 261 uses of the name. Jubilees's concern for the necessity of Israel's separation from the other nations colors the entire perspective of the book and is explicit in the treatment of the stories of Jacob and his sons, as well as in the farewell speeches of various characters.[34] Jacob's importance in Jubilees might be related to his symbolic representation of all of Israel, made concrete by his name change, from Jacob to Israel (Jub. 32:17, which parallels Gen 35:9–12 rather than Gen 32:28 since Jubilees does not relate the struggle at Jabbok), but might also be connected to the fact that he is presented as the one who, in contrast to Esau, is opposed to intermarriage.

In Jub. 25:1–10 (which develops Gen 27:46–28:5), for example, the initiative of Jacob's planned marriage lies entirely with Rebecca (Jub. 25:1), who calls Jacob and forbids him to marry a daughter of Canaan, an unnecessary precaution since Jacob himself has already rejected this option.[35] Mother and son share the same

---

(Wis 10:1–11:1), Abraham is presented as a "righteous man," "blameless before God," and one whom Wisdom helped to keep "strong in the face of his compassion for his child" (Wis 10:5). Without this last allusion to the sacrifice of Isaac, it would be less evident to identify Abraham, although Wis 10:5 also suggests the context of Babel and Wis 10:6 alludes to the story of Sodom.

32. Vermes, *Complete Dead Sea Scrolls*, 131.

33. This is also seen in Jubilees, which has Abraham celebrating various feasts that are only ordained after Moses (first fruits in Jub. 15:1; Tabernacles in Jub. 16:20–31). Jubilees's discussion of circumcision in the context of the story of Abraham also testifies to this point (Jub. 15:11–34).

34. See also Jacques T. A. G. M. van Ruiten, *Abraham in the Book of Jubilees: The Rewriting of Genesis 11:26–25:10 in the Book of "Jubilees" 11:14–23:8*, JSJSup 161 (Leiden: Brill, 2012), 343–44.

35. Outside of Genesis, Rebecca is mentioned only once in the biblical corpus (Rom 9:10). In the Dead Sea Scrolls, her name appears eight times: three times in fragments related to Jubilees (4Q222; 4Q223–224), four times in the Reworked Pentateuch (4Q364), and once in T. Naph. (4Q215). In the Pseudepigrapha, she is named forty-three times: thirty-nine times in Jubilees and once each in Testament of Levi, Testament of Naphtali, Testament of Jacob, and Joseph and Aseneth. In Jubilees, Rebecca might even be a more significant character than Isaac. Jubilees adds to Genesis the story of Rebecca's death (Jub. 35:1–27) and agrees with Gen 49:31

opposition to foreign women. Jacob never thought about taking a wife among the Canaanites because he remembers the words of Abraham, who blessed him before his death (Jub. 25:5). Even when his brother, against the commandments of Abraham, entreats him to take a foreign wife (Jub. 25:8), Jacob has no desire to do so. Jacob represents the righteous, uncorrupted son, while Esau is tainted, justifying Rebecca and Abraham's preference for Jacob. In Jubilees, Abraham blesses Jacob twice (Jub. 19:15–31 and 22:10–23). This is an innovation in comparison to Genesis, which does not tell of a blessing of Jacob by Abraham.[36] In Abraham's first blessing (Jub. 19:15–31), the condemnation of intermarriage does not appear. Abraham recognizes the superiority of Jacob, even indicating that he loves him more than his own sons (Jub. 19:21), and asks for God's blessing on Jacob. In the second blessing (Jub. 22:10–23), Abraham severely condemns the gentiles and issues a commandment to separate from the gentiles. This is followed by a lengthy critique of the gentiles (Jub. 22:16–18) that should convince Jacob to separate from them and to avoid marriage with a Canaanite (Jub. 22:20). Abraham then dies, with Jacob resting on his chest (Jub. 23:1–3). Jacob is thus presented as pure and respectful of his ancestors and of his God.

Joseph in Early Jewish Literature

The high number of references to Joseph is related to Joseph and Aseneth, a fanfiction development of Gen 41:45, where Joseph marries a foreign woman, who is also the daughter of the priest of another god.[37] The characteristics of Joseph are stable across early Jewish literature. He is a good, pious man.[38] This good character is described differently by different works, but it concentrates on the absence of evil, his piety, as well as his meekness and mercy (Jos. Asen. 8:9 [short recension]; T. Zeb. 8:4). In Joseph and Aseneth, this piety is enhanced by his temperance and his virginity (Jos. Asen. 4:8 [short recension]). Fourth Macca-

---

that she was buried in Machpelah. Jubilees mentions that Rebecca was buried by Esau and Jacob, just like Isaac (Gen 35:29), but even more like Abraham, who is also buried in Machpelah by his two rival sons, Ishmael and Isaac (Gen 25:9). Rebecca's burial emphasizes that she shares Abraham's characteristics, especially when it comes to recognizing Jacob's qualities over against Esau and to separating from the nations.

36. Römer, "Qui est Abraham?," 20, indicates that there might well have been a tradition anterior to the formation of the stories of the patriarchs that considered Jacob as the son of Abraham.

37. There are also several mentions of Joseph in the Testament of the Twelve Patriarchs (second century BCE to first century CE). When the patriarchs reflect on their lives, they must give an account of the treatment they inflicted on Joseph.

38. Testament of Simon 4:4 and 5:1; T. Levi 13:9; T. Dan 1:4; T. Benj. 3:1 and 5:4; and Joseph the one beloved of Israel in T. Jos. 1:2. In Ascen. Isa. 4:22, Joseph is presented as righteous.

bees 2:2, with T. Reub. 4:8, also mentions his temperance as an example to follow. Along with Joseph's goodness goes his beauty (cf. Gen 39:6).[39] Finally, Joseph is presented as a leader, able to teach kings (Sir 49:15 LXX; 1 Macc 2:53; 4Q213). 4Q213 associates these leadership skills with Joseph's abilities to write and with his discipline, while 1 Macc 2:53, in a short list of heroes, connects Joseph's leadership anachronistically with the respect for the commandments.

Joseph's exemplary character is seldom picked up in the New Testament. Joseph is mentioned twice anecdotally in John 4:5 and Rev 7:8. He might stand behind the figure of Joseph in Matt 1–2 since both have premonitory dreams and a father named Jacob and spent time in Egypt. He is used as a figure only in Acts 7 and Heb 11. Acts 7:9–19 recalls the Joseph story and emphasizes two aspects. First, a leitmotiv of Acts 7, Joseph is used to show that God rescues those whom God has chosen from their afflictions (Acts 7:9–10). Afflictions are not a sign of having fallen away from God's grace. If one remains faithful to God throughout sufferings, God will be faithful also. Second, Joseph prepares the next episode, namely the rise of Moses. Acts 7:18 concludes the retelling of Joseph's story with an explicit quotation of Exod 1:8 LXX, which then leads to Moses's story. The mention in Heb 11:22 is more surprising since it introduces an aspect of Joseph not discussed by other texts, his last words in Gen 50:24–25, where he announces the exodus and asks to be buried in the promised land. For Hebrews, what matters is Joseph's trust in God's promises that allows him to see what is to come.

Moses in Early Jewish Literature

In the Scriptures of Israel, Moses appears mostly in the Pentateuch and the book of Joshua. Four features stand out. In Exodus and Deuteronomy, Moses is primarily the mediator between God and the people.[40] Deuteronomy furthermore presents him as a prophet (Deut 34:10). Moses is also the "lawgiver, teacher of all

---

39. The Testament of Gad mentions that Joseph was delicate (T. Gad 1:4), which can be construed as a critique since Joseph immediately becomes faint and abandons Gad while they are tending the flocks. Of course, Gad is not the most objective of brothers when it comes to Joseph. In T. Sim. 5:1, Joseph's beauty is presented as an external manifestation of his inner uprightness. With his characteristic boastfulness, Joseph brags about his beauty in T. Jos. 18:4, where his beauty is constructed as reflecting the character of Jacob and associated with strength. Understandably, Joseph's beauty and his unapologetic attitude toward it elicits jealousy, something evidenced in a couple of occurrences in Testament of the Twelve Patriarchs (T. Gad 1:5, 9; T. Dan 1:5; T. Sim. 2:6).

40. See Tina Dykesteen Nilsen, "Memories of Moses: A Survey through Genres," *JSOT* 41, no. 3 (2017): 290.

the commandments, statutes and ordinances."⁴¹ Finally, Moses is God's servant, a formula found particularly in the book of Joshua (fourteen times), matching the description of Deut 34:5. Yet, in the Pentateuch, a couple of passages also point to Moses's failure.⁴² This is particularly apparent in Num 20:2–13 (it resurfaces in Deut 32:51), where Moses's disobedience at Meribah explains why Moses cannot enter the promised land.

Even though the number of references to Moses is not as high as it is for Jacob or Joseph, Moses is a particularly important figure for late Second Temple Jewish literature. As was the case for Abraham, the uses of Moses touch upon several elements of his character. The most common use is to associate Moses with the law. In addition, the following features of Moses appear in early Jewish texts: Moses as giver of a new law, Moses and Egypt, and Moses as God's beloved. I will discuss these features first and then give two brief accounts of the use of Moses at Qumran and in Liber Antiquitatum Biblicarum.

Moses and the Apocalyptic Revelation of a New Law

In early Jewish texts, such as Jubilees, Moses is used as a figure to support the claim that the Torah revealed at Sinai and transmitted through Moses can be enhanced by new apocalyptic revelations, sometimes conceived as a new Torah. Jubilees builds on Exod 24:18, which mentions that Moses spent forty days and nights on Mount Sinai, inside the cloud that symbolizes God's presence. It uses this mention to present itself as the revelation of what was given to Moses during that time through God's angel of the presence (Jub. 1:27–29).⁴³ In this type of rewritten Scriptures, Moses is less a character in the story than a visionary who participates in the receiving and transmitting of the story. He is inserted into the chain of transmission composed by God → Angel of the Presence → Visionary (in Jubilees, Moses) → People and thus contributes to the authority of the book itself.⁴⁴ Consequently, the figure of Moses is modified. His status as last prophet is colored with apocalypticism and opens the possibility for expanded revelations given to the Moses of Jubilees, even in a time when prophetic transmission is understood to have ended.

Fourth Ezra and 1 Enoch give authority to their own apocalyptic revelations through allusions to Moses as well. Fourth Ezra 14:1–9 models Ezra like a new Moses, receiving a revelation like Moses in the burning bush. The parallel insists

---

41. Nilsen, "Memories of Moses," 290.
42. Nilsen, "Memories of Moses," 292.
43. See, e.g., Orval S. Wintermute's introduction to Jubilees in *OTP* 2:38; Cana Werman, "'The תורה and תעודה' on the Tablets," *DSD* 9, no. 1 (2002): 75–103; van Ruiten, *Abraham in the Book of Jubilees*, 8.
44. A construction also found in Revelation (Rev 1:1).

on hidden knowledge given both to Moses—adding an apocalyptic dimension to Moses absent from the canonical account—and Ezra (4 Ezra 14:8).[45] This lends legitimacy to Ezra's writing (4 Ezra 14:26) that similarly includes secret and public things and builds Ezra's revelations as transmitting a new law. First Enoch 85–89 presents an elaborate retelling of the story of Israel from the creation of Adam to the Persian domination, using animals.[46] Moses is described as a sheep in 1 En. 89:16. The treatment of Moses, where he is recognized as leader of the sheep (1 En. 89:22, 26, 38) but not as a "snow-white cow" or even as a "ram," might indicate that the apocalyptic revelation disclosed through visionary experiences and recorded in 1 Enoch is complementary to the divine revelation through the law.[47]

Moses and Egypt

Moses's early education and his relationship with Egyptian knowledge are the topic of two Jewish writers. Both Artapanus (third to second century BCE) and Ezekiel the Tragedian (second century BCE) associate Moses with Egyptian-acquired knowledge.[48] In Ezekiel the Tragedian (1:36–38), Moses receives a princely education in the royal court.[49] For Artapanus, Moses teaches important things to the Egyptians (3:4).[50] Artapanus mixes Moses with polytheistic traditions and is interested in showing the possible appeal of Moses to non-Jews.

---

45. See Christophe Nihan, "'Un prophète comme Moïse' (Deutéronome 18:15): Genèse et relectures d'une construction deutéronomiste," in Römer, *La construction de la figure de Moïse*, 70.

46. The Animal Apocalypse continues in 1 En. 90 until the revolt of the Maccabees (1 En. 90:13), leaving the "canon" of the Hebrew Bible. The narrative then moves onto the eschatological intervention of God and the final judgment (1 En. 90:14–42), which would indicate that the author of 1 Enoch was not aware of the limited victory of Judas Maccabeus in 164 BCE, when the temple was reconsecrated. See André Caquot, "1 Hénoch," in *La Bible: Écrits Intertestamentaires*, ed. André Dupont-Sommer and Marc Philonenko (Paris: Gallimard, 1987), 592.

47. For discussions of an alternative Judaism represented by Enochic literature, see, e.g., Gabriele Boccaccini, *Beyond the Essene Hypothesis: The Parting of the Ways between Qumran and Enochic Judaism* (Grand Rapids: Eerdmans, 1998); and John J. Collins, "How Distinctive Was Enochic Judaism," *Meghillot* 5–6 (2007): 17*–34*. See also Paul Heger, "*1 Enoch*: Complementary or Alternative to Mosaic Torah," *JSJ* 41, no. 1 (2010): 60.

48. For Artapanus, see the introduction by John J. Collins in *OTP* 2:889–96. For Ezekiel the Tragedian, see the introduction by R. G. Robertson in *OTP* 2:803–6.

49. The tradition of Moses being educated in Egyptian wisdom is also found in Josephus (*Ant.* 2.236) and Philo (*Mos.* 1.19–24). See Simon Butticaz, "Moïse, 'Le vagabond de Dieu,' Actes 7, 20–43," *Foi et Vie* 118, no. 3 (2018): 81. René Bloch, "Moses and Greek Myth in Hellenistic Judaism," in Römer, *La construction de la figure de Moïse*, 206, indicates that Ezekiel the Tragedian proposes a hybrid education for Moses since Moses is also presented as being educated by his mother.

50. Artapanus also constructs Moses as the ancestor of Greek culture by claiming that he

Often, the murder of the Egyptian by Moses is left out of the retelling of Moses's story (e.g., Liber Antiquitatum Biblicarum; Sirach; Hebrews), but Ezekiel the Tragedian includes it. In Ezekiel (as in Exod 2:15), the murder of the Egyptian is reported to pharaoh and provokes Moses's fleeing, even though Moses acts in self-defense (contra Exod 2:12).[51] In Artapanus, the killing (3:18) occurs at a different moment in Moses's story (he is fleeing into Arabia) and does not provoke his leaving Egypt.[52]

Moses as the Beloved of God

In Sirach's Praise of Famous Men (Sir 44:1), Moses is presented as "beloved by God" (Sir 45:1), a godly man.[53] Sirach highlights Moses's accomplishments: the greatness of Moses's military achievements (Sir 45:2), the miracles (45:3b), and the gift of the commandments (45:3c). Perhaps the longest development (45:5) details Moses's special relationship with God, which allows him to hear God's voice and to receive the commandments face to face. This relationship is explicitly presented as having the teaching of the people of God as its purpose (Sir 45:5).

Moses at Qumran

George Brooke has shown that the evidence found in the Dead Sea Scrolls proposes a dilemma about Moses.[54] Brooke writes that, in the sectarian texts, the "majority of references to Moses indicates his status as Lawgiver or at the very

---

should be identified with Hermes and with the Mousaeus whom Artapanus claims taught Orpheus. See Cana Werman, "*Jubilees* in the Hellenistic Context," in *The Heavenly Tablets: Interpretation, Identity and Tradition in Ancient Judaism*, ed. Lynn LiDonnici and Andrea Lieber, JSJSup 119 (Leiden: Brill, 2007), 145. Aristobulus also associates Moses with Orpheus (10:4 and 13:4).

51. See Collins, "Artapanus," 893.

52. There is a peculiar reference to the events following the murder of the Egyptian in 4 Macc 2:15–18. Fourth Maccabees mentions that Moses became angry with Dathan and Abiram, who are sometimes associated with the two quarreling Israelites who criticize Moses about the murder of the Egyptian. The passage in 4 Maccabees is preoccupied with praising reason. As a model of reason, Moses restrains himself and does not express his anger against Dathan and Abiram.

53. This description of Moses as being in a special relationship with God is also found in a text difficult to analyze and date, the Sibylline Oracles. In Sib. Or. 2:245, Moses is "the great friend of the Most High." Even if book 2 of the Sibylline Oracles was reworked by a later Christian hand (see Valentin Nikiprowetzky, in Dupont-Sommer and Philonenko, *La Bible*, 1037), it is still an interesting witness to the description of Moses as the friend of the Lord.

54. George Brooke, "Moses in the Dead Sea Scrolls: Looking at Mount Nebo from Qumran," in Römer, *La construction de la figure de Moïse*, 209–21.

least as the mediator of the Law to Israel."[55] Yet, compositions at Qumran are also interested in Moses's "prophetic status."[56] For example, 4Q175, a collection "of messianic proof-texts," talks about an eschatological prophet. Brooke indicates that most scholars identify the eschatological prophet with Elijah or the Teacher of Righteousness, but some see in the figure a *Moses redivivus*, based on 11Q13 (11QMelch).[57] For Brooke these are positive association with Moses, confirmed in two compositions that discuss a possible deification of Moses (4Q374) and an apotheosis (4Q377).[58] The first impression of Moses in the scrolls is positive, and Moses could even be a holy figure.[59]

Yet, as Brooke remarks, the portrayal of Moses in the scrolls is also lacking. Brooke indicates that the scrolls insist on Moses's importance for the law, the covenant, the cult, and prophecy but do very little with Moses's life.[60] Even concerning Moses's law, the scrolls insist that it must be correctly interpreted by the community.[61] Quite a few writings at Qumran supplement Moses's law. Jubilees is part of this effort, as are the Rule of the Community or the Temple Scroll, a "rewritten form of the Law" without reference to Moses.[62] Finally, copies of texts associated with Enoch at Qumran indicate another path for constructing the identity of Jewish communities than the one proposed by the Mosaic tradition. While Brooke insists that these elements are insufficient to construct "a persistent anti-Mosaic faction within the sect," it demonstrates that Moses was not sufficient to respond to all the needs of the community.[63] For Brooke, this ambiguous portrayal of Moses is influenced by the conviction that Moses is only a worthy example: a prototype for what every member of the community can hope to achieve through respect of the rules of the community.[64]

---

55. Brooke, "Moses in the Dead Sea Scrolls," 210.
56. Brooke, "Moses in the Dead Sea Scrolls," 212.
57. See for a fuller discussion, Brooke, "Moses in the Dead Sea Scrolls," 212–13.
58. For the reading of 4Q377 as an apotheosis, see Crispin H. T. Fletcher-Louis, *All the Glory of Adam: Liturgical Anthropology in the Dead Sea Scrolls*, STDJ 42 (Leiden: Brill, 2002); and Jan Willem van Henten, "Moses as Heavenly Messenger in *Assumptio Mosis* 10:2 and Qumran Passages," *JJS* 54, no. 2 (2003): 216–27.
59. Brooke, "Moses in the Dead Sea Scrolls," 215.
60. See Brooke, "Moses in the Dead Sea Scrolls," 216. One exception is a mention in CD V, 18, where Moses and Aaron are described as defending the side of the Prince of Lights against Yannes, on the side of Belial, a hint referring to Moses's abilities as a magician. This allusion to the Egyptian magicians is also found in 2 Tim 3:8, where Moses is presented as standing on the side of truth. Aaron is not included in 2 Timothy.
61. Brooke, "Moses in the Dead Sea Scrolls," 218.
62. Brooke, "Moses in the Dead Sea Scrolls," 219.
63. Brooke, "Moses in the Dead Sea Scrolls," 219.
64. Brooke, "Moses in the Dead Sea Scrolls," 220–21.

Moses in Liber Antiquitatum Biblicarum

Moses as a character plays a particularly important role in Liber Antiquitatum Biblicarum. His story covers chapters 9-19, but he is mentioned often in the other chapters as well. Several aspects of Moses are put forward. He is the one through whom the respect of the cult and commandments can preserve God's covenant with the people; he is the perfect leader and God's special friend. Moses's special status is seen in the way his story is embellished, particularly his birth and death.

Before Moses's birth, God announces that Moses will be a faithful servant and a wonder worker (LAB 9:7). In addition, Moses is the one who will access what no one has seen before and who will receive the gift of the revelation of the law (LAB 9:8). Liber Antiquitatum Biblicarum clarifies Moses's origin and describes a respectable family, well established in the Levites tribe.[65] Moses's birth is preceded by Miriam's dream, something unique to Liber Antiquitatum Biblicarum (9:10). It emphasizes three aspects of Moses: Moses will work signs, he will save God's people, and his leadership will be eternal. Finally, LAB 9:13 notes that Moses is born already circumcised. Thus, Liber Antiquitatum Biblicarum solves the problem created by Moses's lack of circumcision on the eighth day in the Scriptures of Israel, even though the commandment to circumcise has already been given to Abraham in Gen 17:12.

Liber Antiquitatum Biblicarum also expands the story surrounding Moses's death in order to highlight God's special relationship with Moses (LAB 19). Before Moses dies, he is the beneficiary of a few final divine revelations (LAB 19:10). After God's revelations, Moses's appearance changes and he dies in glory (LAB 19:16). Liber Antiquitatum Biblicarum also insists that, out of love, the Lord buries him with his own hand, "in the light of all the world" (LAB 19:16), repeating that fact, and emphasizing that this was done according to God's promise. Moses's death also interrupts "the heavenly liturgy ... an event that never happened before and will never be repeated."[66] After his death, Moses is recalled by several characters and presented as God's friend.[67] Moses is furthermore presented as God's servant (20:2), one of "a very select group" in Liber Antiquitatum Biblicarum.[68]

---

65. Thomas Römer, *Moïse "Lui que Yahvé a connu face à face"* (Paris: Gallimard, 2002), 28, indicates that the verb *lqḥ* in Exod 2:1 can indicate an illicit sexual relationship or even rape.

66. Frederick J. Murphy, *Pseudo-Philo: Rewriting the Bible* (New York: Oxford University Press, 1993), 94-95.

67. By God in LAB 23:9, by Joshua (24:3) and Kenaz (25:3, 5). Deborah calls Moses God's beloved (LAB 32:8).

68. Murphy, *Pseudo-Philo*, 85. It includes Abraham (6:11), the resisters to Jair's idolatry

Finally, Liber Antiquitatum Biblicarum insists on the importance of the cult established by Moses at God's command. It is the way to redeem humanity's previous sins.[69] Respect of the cult also means that idolatry is condemned severely. Unique to Liber Antiquitatum Biblicarum is the reason given for Moses being barred from entering the promised land: Moses should not be confronted with idols (LAB 19:7), which possibly erases Moses's failure at Meribah.

Major Figures of Israel in the New Testament

Abraham and Moses are the two figures most quoted in the New Testament, similar to what we find in early Jewish texts. Compared to early Jewish literature, the use of Abraham in New Testament literature is less varied. Overall, the New Testament focuses on the question of Abraham's faithfulness, a theme present in other early Jewish texts (Sir 44:19–21; Jub. 17:15–18; CD III, 2; XVI, 6).[70] In two cases (Jas 2:21 and Heb 11:17), Abraham's faithfulness is associated explicitly with the sacrifice of Isaac, an episode also discussed by other Jewish texts of the period (Jub. 18:16; Wis 10:5). In the New Testament, there is no interest in Abraham's turn away from idolatry (Jdt 5:7–8; Jub. 11–12; Apoc. Ab. 1:7–9; 2:4; 5; 7:9–12).

For Moses, New Testament texts reflect several preoccupations of early Jewish texts. They consider how a new law can be related to Moses (particularly in Matthew; cf. 4 Ezra 14:1–9; but also 1 En. 85–89; Jub. 1:27–29). In Acts 7, Moses's relationship to Egypt is also discussed (just like in Artapanus and Ezekiel the Tragedian). However, in the New Testament, none of these aspects are as important as presenting Moses as a rejected prophet, misunderstood by his own people. This use of Moses helps to understand the destiny of Jesus as crucified Messiah but also of Jesus's first disciples. Finally, if like early Jewish texts (Sir 45:1; Sib. Or. 2:245; LAB 19; 23:9; 25:3, 5; 32:8), the New Testament transmits the idea of Moses's special bond with God, this aspect is subordinated to the goal of showing that Jesus is even more special (John 3:14; 5:39–46; 6:31–33; 2 Cor 3:7–8, 12–13; Heb 11:25–26). The New Testament does not discuss the idea that Moses guarantees the cult, an idea important in some early Jewish texts (LAB 13:1; 21:7; 30:1; Jub. 49:22; Eup. 2:16; Sir 45:15).

(38:4), and the patriarchs (15:5), as well as Balaam, who attributes the title to himself a bit too generously (18:4).

69. E.g., obeying the prescriptions of Moses reverses the curse of Adam and transforms the threat initially contained in rain into a blessing (LAB 13:10). See C. T. Robert Hayward, "The Figure of Adam in Pseudo-Philo's Biblical Antiquities," *JSJ* 23, no. 1 (1992): 6.

70. There is a trace of Abraham's past in Acts 7:2–4, where one can assume that the theophany is sufficient to lead Abraham out of idolatry, but the theme is not problematized explicitly.

In contrast to other early Jewish texts, David and Elijah are used particularly often in the New Testament. This is related to David and Elijah's association with messianic expectations, something also present in some texts from Qumran (4Q174 I, 10; 4Q252 V, 2; 4Q285 7; possibly 4Q558 51 for Elijah).

Abraham in the New Testament

In comparison with early Jewish literature, one notes several aspects of the New Testament use of Abraham. The New Testament, just like LAB 6–7 but in contrast to Jdt 5, Jub. 11–12, or Apocalypse of Abraham (1:7–9; 2:4; 5; 7:6–12; 8:1–5), is not interested in Abraham's idolatrous past. However, the New Testament does reflect another preoccupation of early Jewish literature, namely the emphasis on Abraham's faithfulness, which makes him the recipient of an eternal covenant, associated with the promises of land and descendants. This covenant promise of descendants is the focus of the New Testament's use of Abraham. In several texts, the promise of descendants is related to the question of membership in the people of God.[71] In the Gospels, two remarkable uses of Abraham (Luke 16:19–31 and John 8:31–59) highlight that to be a descendant of Abraham one needs to display faithfulness and good moral behavior.[72] For Rom 4 and Gal 3:6–18; 4:21–31, as well as Jas 2:21–26, the question of membership in the people of God is at the center of the discussion of Abraham. Only two mentions in the New Testament (Heb 11:17 and Jas 2:21) highlight the connection between Abraham's faithfulness and the sacrifice of Isaac, a link that plays an important role in early Jewish literature (Sir 44:20; Jub. 17:15–18; 18; Wis 10:5; possibly CD III, 2–3). Finally, Heb 7:1–10 mentions Abraham as a foil for Melchizedek, building on Gen 14:17–20. This is a unique use in early Jewish literature.

Abraham in Luke 16:19–31 and John 8:31–59

In Luke 16:19–31, Abraham appears as a figure in a narrative about the destiny of two different men after death. There is the poor man Lazarus, who led a miserable life and receives his reward in the afterlife, being welcomed by Father Abraham. On the other side, there is the rich man, who, upon his death, observes Lazarus's closeness to Abraham from afar, separated by a great chasm, and suffering in Hades. Perhaps one can see in Abraham's association with the realm of death something like the Testament of Abraham, where Abraham visits the

---

71. See William Baird, "Abraham in the New Testament: Tradition and the New Identity," *Int* 42, no. 4 (1988): 367–79.

72. E.g., see Baird, "Abraham in the New Testament," 370.

afterlife (T. Ab. 11–14). It could also be explained by the tradition of those who will feast with Abraham, Isaac, and Jacob in the kingdom of heaven (Matt 8:11). Feasting does play an important role in the Lukan story since the rich man is described as feasting every day while Lazarus despairs of receiving the leftovers from the rich man's table.

The rich man begs Abraham to intervene in favor of his brothers who are still alive. Here too, one might hear an echo of Abraham's behavior in the Testament of Abraham where Abraham can condemn or save souls (T. Ab. 10:4–11).[73] Yet, in Luke 16, Abraham refuses to get involved and insists that the rich man's brothers have everything they need to escape torment after death since they can simply follow Moses (i.e., the law) and the prophets. As William Baird indicates, the conduct of the rich man excludes him from being counted among Abraham's children.[74]

What Luke shows through a story, John 8:31–59 discusses in a controversy about who can claim to be the children of Abraham. Both parties, the Jews and Jesus, affirm that they are the true heirs of Abraham. While the Jews claim Abraham for themselves, Jesus goes further: he asserts that Abraham saw Jesus's day and got joy from it (John 8:56), but he also says that he preexists Abraham (John 8:58).[75] In a revelatory formula typical of John and reminiscent of God's own revelation (Exod 3:14), Jesus declares his superiority over Abraham. Those who follow Jesus can trust that they are on Abraham's side but also that they receive an identity more valuable than the one claimed by Jesus's adversaries in the Gospel of John. The Jews' appeal to Abraham as ancestor is denied by Jesus when he accuses them of not acting like Abraham (John 8:39). Two of Paul's letters will also discuss the contest surrounding Abraham and who is worthy of belonging to the lineage of Abraham.

Abraham in Paul and James

In Galatians and Romans, Paul enlists Abraham to defend his understanding of the way non-Jews should be integrated in the people of the God of Israel. The question is the same (Who can claim Abraham as their ancestor?), as is the answer (both Jews and nations can), yet the uses of Abraham are different in Romans and Galatians. Both Romans and Galatians quote Gen 15:6, which Paul

---

73. This could also be an allusion to Abraham's bargaining with the Lord about Sodom in Gen 18:23–33.
74. Baird, "Abraham in the New Testament," 370.
75. As Baird, "Abraham in the New Testament," 371, points out, 4 Ezra 3:13–14 transmits a tradition about Abraham knowing the end times.

uses to show that Abraham put his faithfulness in God and it was counted toward righteousness. In Romans, the quotation challenges the necessity of circumcision for righteousness. Since Abraham trusts God and it is counted toward righteousness before his circumcision, he can be the ancestor of both circumcised and uncircumcised (Rom 4:11–12). In Gal 3:6, Gen 15:6 is similarly used to affirm that those who believe are descendants of Abraham. The promise made to Abraham in Gen 12:3 about the blessings of all nations prefigures the gospel that Paul has received, namely that the good news is also for the nations (Gal 3:8).

Romans then focuses on Abraham's faithfulness or obedience (πίστις) to emphasize that the promise is for all descendants of Abraham, not just those who practice the law but also those who display the same faithfulness as the one found in Abraham. The promise of becoming the father of many nations is used to signal Abraham's trust in God's promise and to present him as a model of faithfulness, a model that the Christ believers can emulate (Rom 4:24–25). Abraham as a model of faithful obedience is common in early Jewish literature and allows Paul to insert his non-Jewish Christ believers in the promises made to Abraham.[76] This is summarized in the first part of Galatians as well (Gal 3:6–9), but then Paul takes his discussion of Abraham in a different direction, insisting more on the promise made to Abraham and the necessary mediation of Christ to bring this promise to the nations (Gal 3:14). Galatians 3:16 uses Gen 13:15; 17:8; and 24:7 to highlight that the promise is made to Abraham and his single offspring, namely, Christ. Paul does not pick up the content of the promise mentioned in Genesis, the land, but associates the promise with the notion of heritage and adoption (Gal 4:1, 7). Thus, in his final use of Abraham (Gal 4:21–31), which retells the double lineage of Abraham through Hagar's son (4:24) and Isaac (4:28), Paul achieves his goal, which is to counterintuitively associate the non-Jews with the lineage of Isaac and thus of Sarah (even though she remains unnamed). Abraham is the ancestor to whom the non-Jews should turn, not through circumcision but through faithfulness and obedience. Paul's use of Abraham and Isaac as ancestors of the non-Jews, while it relies on Jewish interpretative techniques, is original and directly connected to his goal in Galatians, namely to downplay circumcision as the path to inclusion in the people of God.

While Paul does not refer to the sacrifice of Isaac as an example of Abraham's obedient trust, both James (Jas 2:21) and Hebrews (Heb 11:17) use it as an example of Abraham's faithfulness. James's discussion (2:21–26) explicitly interprets Abraham's πίστις as faithful obedience, translated into active behavior.

---

76. See Sir 44:19–21; 1 Macc 2:52; Jub. 17:15, 17; 18:16; 19:8; 4Q226 frag. 7 for explicit descriptions of Abraham as faithful. Abraham is presented as righteous and blameless in Wis 10:5 and as a friend of God in CD III, 2.

Abraham in the Epistle to the Hebrews

Hebrews's use of Abraham stands out. In the list of heroes found in Heb 11:4–39, the usual aspects of the figure are mentioned; they all characterize Abraham's faithfulness. Yet Heb 7:1–10 presents a unique perspective on Abraham. It is subordinated to the role and importance of Melchizedek.[77] The use of Melchizedek in Hebrews could come from extrabiblical traditions, such as the one behind 11Q13 and 2 Enoch that portray him as semidivine, but could also be related to Hebrews' own hermeneutical strategies, in particular the strategy of filling gaps in the biblical text.[78] In Heb 7, the importance of Melchizedek is connected to the understanding of Christ as "a high priest who once for all sacrificed himself (Heb 9,26) and who 'always lives to make intercession.'"[79] Hebrews wants to show that Jesus's office as eternal high priest is prefigured in Melchizedek, who is superior to the patriarch.[80] Jesus thus stands in Abraham's and Melchizedek's continuity but is superior to both.

Moses in the New Testament

Moses's reception in the New Testament reflects some uses in early Jewish texts, as well as the diversity of aspects of the figure. I will discuss three aspects here, starting with the association between Moses and the law. Second, in contrast to early Jewish texts that insist on Moses as God's beloved (Sir 45:1; LAB 32:8), the New Testament elaborates on Moses as a rejected prophet. This is prevalent in the only extensive retelling of Moses's life somewhat comparable to what is found in early

---

77. Melchizedek is never mentioned in the New Testament outside of Hebrews. In the Scriptures of Israel, he is similarly mysterious, appearing only in Gen 14:18–20, as priest of the Most High who blesses Abram and to whom Abram gives one tenth of everything. He is also mentioned in Ps 109:4 LXX (Ps 110:4 MT). He remains a minor figure in early Jewish literature: no mention in the Apocrypha, almost none in the Pseudepigrapha. The exception is 2 En. 71–72, which discusses his mysterious birth and might contribute to his status as semidivine. There is also one mention in Pseudo-Eupolemus (17:6). In Qumran, there is no use of him except for 11Q13 (See Gard Granerød, "Melchisedek in Hebrews 7," *Bib* 90 [2009]: 197, who adds 4Q401 and 4Q543–548 to 11Q13). He reappears in a gnostic treatise associated with Sethian Gnosticism (NHC IX, 1). On NHC IX, 1, see the introduction by Birger A. Pearson, "Melchizedek" in *The Nag Hammadi Scriptures: The Revised and Updated Translation of Sacred Gnostic Texts in One Volume*, ed. Marvin Meyer (New York: Harper, 2009), 595–98.
78. See Granerød, "Melchisedek in Hebrews 7," 201.
79. Granerød, "Melchisedek in Hebrews 7," 189.
80. See Baird, "Abraham in the New Testament," 372. Melchizedek is also a prototype for Jesus in Heb 7. This use is seen three times in Hebrews before Heb 7: Heb 5:6, 10; 6:20. See Granerød, "Melchisedek in Hebrews 7," 192–93.

Jewish literature (LAB 9–19), Acts 7:20–44. Finally, New Testament texts negotiate Moses's position in relationship to the messiah.[81] In contrast to other early Jewish texts, the New Testament downplays Moses's role as guaranteeing the cult.[82]

Moses and the Law

Like other early Jewish texts, the New Testament texts identify Moses with the law.[83] There are several examples of New Testament texts referring to what "Moses commanded" when quoting the Pentateuch. One such example is Matt 8:4 (// Mark 1:44; Luke 5:14), where the healed leper must "offer the gift that Moses commanded," a reference to the instructions given by YHWH to Moses about leprosy in Lev 14:2–32. Another famous example is the controversy surrounding divorce reported in Mark 10:3 (// Matt 19:7). Here Jesus asks what Moses commands about divorce and the Pharisees answer with a reference to Deut 24:1–4. Mark 7:10 shows that Moses could be perceived as the author of the Ten Commandments: "For Moses said, 'Honor your father and your mother.'" The identification between Moses and the law is seen in the transfiguration episode found in the Synoptic Gospels (Mark 9:2–8 // Matt 17:1–8; Luke 9:28–36). In this story, the figure of Moses has come to stand in for the law. His character simply is the law.[84] The same is true of Luke 16:29–31; 24:27; Acts 15:21; and 2 Cor 3:15. Moses becomes a name for the five first books of the Torah and no longer refers to the figure of Moses.

---

81. Perhaps a similar concern is found at Qumran to clarify the relationship between Moses and the Teacher of Righteousness or the coming messiahs. See Brooke, "Moses in the Dead Sea Scrolls," 213, 217. Brooke mentions 4Q504 6 12; 4Q505 122 1 where Moses is simply one of the prophets.

82. For Moses as guaranteeing the cult in early Jewish literature: LAB 13:1; 21:7; 30:1 (in Liber Antiquitatum Biblicarum, this is also seen in the way Phinehas is presented as the successor of Moses); Jub. 49:22 for the proper respect of the feast of Passover; Eup. 2:16 presents the lampstand that Moses fashioned as a model for the ones in the temple. In Sir 45:15, it is Moses who ordains and anoints Aaron. The notion of priesthood as an attribute of the messiah is found in Acts 3:13, but the notion of a messiah-priest is generally less important in the New Testament (except in Hebrews, evidently) than in other Second Temple texts. Jesus's priestly function is found behind the title "servant of God" (τὸν παῖδα αὐτοῦ," Acts 3:13, 26; 4:27, 30). The title is used for Jesus and David (Acts 4:25) in Acts and recalls the expression "Moses the servant of YHWH," found eighteen times in the MT.

83. See 1 Esd 1:11; 5:49; 7:6, 9; 8:3; 9:39; Tob 1:8; 6:13; 7:11, 12, 13; Sus 3 and 62; Bar 2:28; Test. Zeb. 3:4; CD XV, 9; 1QS V, 8; VIII, 22; 1QM X, 1–4. For the New Testament: Mark 1:44 // Matt 8:4 and Luke 5:14; Mark 10:3, 4 // Matt 19:7, 8; Mark 12:19 // Matt 22:24 and Luke 20:28; Mark 7:10; Luke 2:22; 16:29, 31; 24:27, 44; John 1:17, 45; 5:46; 7:19; 8:5; Acts 3:22; 6:14; 13:39; 15:1, 5, 21; 26:22; 28:23; Rom 10:5, 19; 1 Cor 9:9; 2 Cor 3:15; Heb 10:28.

84. See also François Bovon, "Moses in Luke Acts," in *New Testament and Christian Apocrypha*, ed. Glenn E. Snyder (Grand Rapids: Baker Academic, 2011), 130.

Moses as Rejected Prophet in Acts 7:20–44

Acts 7:2–53 evokes several figures of Israel, but none is developed quite in the manner of Moses. Moses's story covers verses 20–44 and features two aspects unique to Acts. First, and this is true in a smaller fashion of the figure of Joseph (7:9–16), Acts emphasizes the sufferings of Moses and the rejections he faced when dealing with the people of Israel. Consequently, and this is the second aspect, it is Moses who is constructed in terms of the figure of Jesus in Acts.[85] In this "Jesusification" of Moses, the author of Acts finds support for the destiny of his heroes, Jesus of course, but also Stephen, Paul, and the other apostles who suffer on behalf of God. Acts' insistence on the people's rejection of Moses is unique among early Jewish texts, and Stephen's speech does not mention Moses's own hesitations or doubts about his mission.[86] Because this angle in retelling the story of Moses is unique, it will be the focus of the analysis of Acts 7.[87]

Already when recounting Moses's early years, Acts introduces the motif of the threatened newborn. The use of ἀναιρέω to describe the action of pharaoh's daughter (Acts 7:21) might be a play on the meaning of ἀναιρέω, which can be both "to remove, to take away" but also "to destroy, to kill."[88] In Acts, the use of ἀναιρέω additionally highlights the parallels between the perils that threaten Moses and Stephen's imminent martyrdom.[89] This is confirmed by the next episode retold in Acts 7:23–29: the murder of the Egyptian and the fight with the two Israelites the next day.[90]

---

85. See Simon Butticaz and Daniel Marguerat, "La figure de Moïse en Actes 7: Entre la christologie et l'exil," in Römer, *La construction de la figure de Moïse*, 223–47.

86. See Bovon, "Moses in Luke Acts," 141–42.

87. Acts 7 also talks about Moses's beauty. Acts 7:20 presents Moses as pleasing (ἀστεῖος, Exod 2:2 LXX; the only other use of the word in the New Testament is in Heb 11:23, also to describe Moses) before God. With the underlying Hebrew for LXX, this physical beauty can relate to inner moral orientation. In the LXX, this use is confirmed by 2 Macc 6:23, where the term is used to refer to Eleazar's λογισμὸν ἀστεῖον. Judith 11:23 and Sus 7 also use ἀστεῖος to refer to beautiful women. In Judith, it is explicitly stated that Judith is not only beautiful in her appearance but also ἀγαθὴ ἐν τοῖς λόγοις σου ("wise in speech"). Acts furthermore mentions that Moses is pleasing *before God*. Beyond possible New Testament echoes (Luke 3:22; 12:32), this might parallel traditions encountered in Liber Antiquitatum Biblicarum, where Moses is presented as "glorious" (LAB 9:16) or as God's beloved (LAB 32:8; Sir 45:1; Sib. Or. 2:245). Additionally, Acts 7:22 associates Moses positively with Egyptian wisdom, like other early Jewish texts (Artapanus and Ezekiel the Tragedian).

88. A similar play on the meaning of ἀναιρέω is possible in Exod 2:5 LXX and 2:10 LXX.

89. See Butticaz, "Moïse, 'le vagabond de Dieu,'" 82.

90. This episode is related in Ezekiel the Tragedian but absent from Artapanus. Pseudo-Philo, Sirach, and Heb 11 leave this episode out when retelling the story of Moses. Jude 9 alludes to it when it mentions the burial of Moses and the tradition according to which the devil argued with the archangel Michael about Moses's right to be buried since he was a murderer.

Acts underscores Moses's intention when killing the Egyptian in a unique way: "He supposed that his kinsfolk would understand that God through him was giving them salvation [σωτηρίαν] but they did not understand" (Acts 7:25). Acts explains that already Moses, who is God's intermediary to offer salvation, just as Jesus and the apostles are, is rejected by his kin.[91] For Acts, this is part of an apologetic enterprise that explains why Jesus and his most important emissaries (Stephen, Peter, and Paul) are consistently rejected by their Jewish peers. They had already misunderstood Moses's true intention as mediator of salvation. This theme reappears in the next episodes of Moses's life recalled by Acts, forty years later. The burning bush episode (Acts 7:30–34) focuses on God's discourse to Moses (7:32, 33–34) and serves to introduce the more important next section (Acts 7:35–41).[92]

In this section, it is Moses who announces the messiah (Acts 7:37), using Deut 18:15.[93] The quotation of Deut 18:15 in Acts 7:37 includes the use of the verb ἀνίστημι ("to raise") to speak of the prophet raised by God.[94] This could function as an allusion to Jesus's resurrection. More importantly, though, Acts 7:35–41 emphasizes Moses's rejection by his kin (7:35 and 39).[95] These multiple rejections are a sign of election. Just as Moses was chosen by God to be God's prophet and was then rejected by his own, in the same way Jesus was chosen to be God's beloved and has been rejected by his own. This also indicates how one should interpret the destiny of the first martyrs in Acts and their rejection by their own: they follow Moses's and Jesus's path, and this path reveals that they are chosen by God.[96]

---

91. See Butticaz, "Moïse, 'le vagabond de Dieu,'" 82.

92. Several elements indicate that Acts 7:30–34 directly uses Exod 3:1–10 LXX (Exod 3:6 in Acts 7:32; Exod 3:5 in Acts 7:33; Exod 3:7 in Acts 7:34; Exod 3:8 and 3:10 in Acts 7:34b), but there are modifications. Acts 7:30–34 inverts the order of God's words to Moses: God's revelation comes before the command that Moses remove his sandals. Absent from Acts is God's first direct discourse to Moses in Exodus, which forbids Moses to get closer (Exod 3:4–5). In Acts, after God's revelation (7:32), Moses realizes he should not look. All of Moses's reactions show that Moses is aware that he is witnessing a theophany, thus Moses's question in Exod 3:4 is not needed. Compared to the use of the episode of the burning bush in the Pseudepigrapha and the Apocrypha, Acts highlights continuity with the past story of Israel through the title "God of your fathers, God of Abraham, Isaac, and Jacob."

93. For the use of Deut 18:15–20 in Acts 7 (and Acts 3), see Nihan, "'Un prophète comme Moïse,'" esp. 75. Acts 3:22 is the only other passage in the New Testament that explicitly establishes Jesus as the new Moses using Deut 18:15 LXX.

94. See Butticaz and Marguerat, "La figure de Moïse en Actes 7," 240.

95. There is a link between the rejection of Jesus in Acts 3:12–26 and the rejection of Moses in Acts 7. See also Paul S. Minear, *To Heal and to Reveal: The Prophetic Vocation according to Luke* (New York: Seabury, 1976).

96. See Bovon, "Moses in Luke Acts," 139. For David P. Moessner, the construction of Moses in Deuteronomy, with Moses being called by God and then rejected by the people, could even be the pattern of the construction of the figure of Jesus. See Moessner, "Luke 9:1–50: Luke's Pre-

The episode of the golden calf, mentioned in Acts 7:39–41, might be the climax of the people's repeated refusal to trust Moses. Yet it is not exploited in the Pseudepigrapha or the Apocrypha, which rely on Moses's importance for early Jewish communities to shape the identity of their communities.[97] When Jubilees recalls the life of Moses in Jub. 47–50, it very briefly mentions the hostility of the children of Israel against Moses after the killing of the Egyptian (Jub. 47:12), but in the retelling of the events of the exodus, Jubilees does not mention Israel's resistance to Moses. Similarly, in Artapanus's retelling of the exodus, no mention is made of hostility toward Moses from the part of the Israelites (Artapanus 3:34–37). Acts uses both episodes (the killing of the Egyptian and the golden calf) and insists on the rejection motif.

Consequently, it is no longer the figure of Jesus that is constructed using Moses, but it is Moses who is shaped by what happens to Jesus.[98] This is also seen in the use of characteristics of Jesus being applied to Moses. At the end of the section on Moses's childhood, Moses is presented as "powerful in his words and deeds" (Acts 7:22). This is in contradiction with the portrayal of Moses in Exodus, which insists that Moses was slow in speech and weak tongued (Exod 4:10 LXX), but is very close to the way in which the pilgrims of Emmaus describe Jesus (Luke 24:19).[99] Like Jesus, Moses performs signs and miracles (Acts 7:36), a formula that is found in the Exodus account of Moses (Exod 11:9–10) and that Acts uses for the actions of God, Jesus, and the apostles.[100] Like Jesus, Moses comes for salvation (7:25), and like Jesus he is denied. When the people reject Moses, they turn toward idolatry (7:40–41), and so if one now rejects Jesus, one similarly turns to idolatry. As a figure from the past, Moses helps to justify Jesus's role as messiah.

Jesus and Moses

Other New Testament texts are also preoccupied with negotiating the relationship between Jesus and Moses, recognizing Moses's importance but insisting on Jesus's superiority.

---

view of the Journey of the Prophet like Moses of Deuteronomy," *JBL* 102, no. 4 (1983): 575–605, quoted here in Butticaz and Marguerat, "La figure de Moïse en Actes 7," 225–26.

97. Second Esdras 1:32 uses the tradition of the prophets rejected by the people, as well as the image of God gathering God's children like a hen (2 Esd 1:30), which is understandable since 2 Esd 1–2 are later Christian (second or third century CE) additions to 4 Ezra.

98. This point is made by Butticaz and Marguerat, "La figure de Moïse en Actes 7."

99. See Butticaz and Marguerat, "La figure de Moïse en Actes 7," 237.

100. As Butticaz and Marguerat, "La figure de Moïse en Actes 7," 238, indicate, Exod 11 has deuteronomistic origins (LXX Deut 4:34; 6:22; 7:19; 11:3; 13:1–2; 26:8; 28:46; 29:3; 34:11). For Acts' use, see Butticaz and Marguerat, "La figure de Moïse en Actes 7," 238: God: Acts 2:19; Jesus: Acts 2:22; apostles: Acts 2:43; 4:30; 5:12; Stephen: Acts 6:8; Paul and Barnabas: Acts 14:3; 15:12.

Matthew models Jesus on the figure of Moses. Two aspects are usually identified by scholars. First, the opening chapters of Matthew (Matt 1:18–2:23) use Moses's birth story to shape the narrative, with two motifs in particular being used: the newborn being threatened by a powerful king (Matt 2:13–16), and the ambiguous paternal origin of the newborn (Matt 1:18–19).[101] According to Arland Hultgren, the parallel between Moses and Jesus goes beyond the shaping of the Matthean Jesus, it allows constructing the beginnings of the Christ-believing community in terms similar to those of the constitutive epic of the identity of Israel.[102] Second, Benjamin Bacon already noticed that the five discourses found in Matthew are introduced by a narrative and conclude with a stereotyped formula, just like the five books of the Pentateuch are each introduced by long narratives.[103] While this does not mean that Matthew aimed his gospel as a new Pentateuch, it does reinforce his presentation of Jesus as a Moses-like figure, both in his teachings and his miracles.[104] The setting of the Sermon on the Mount (Matt 5:1–7:29) encourages comparison between the mount of Jesus and Sinai, creating what Dale Allison calls a "Mosaic preface" that prepares delivery of a new law.[105] Jesus is presented as a mediator of the divine law, but he also adds to the gift of the law in much the same way as Jub. 1:27–29 and 4 Ezra 14:1–9 present their own reading of the Torah. The discourse on the mount concludes with an affirmation of the authority of Jesus (Matt 7:29). His descent from the mountain (Matt 8:1) is presented in terms echoing those used in Exod 34:29 LXX about the descent of Moses.[106] After talking about the law, Jesus, like Moses, *enacts* the law in a series of miracles.[107]

---

101. See, e.g., David M. Hay, "Moses through New Testament Spectacles," *Int* 44, no. 3 (1990): 243. One sees allusions to Exod 2:15 in Matt 2:13–14 and to Exod 4:19 in Matt 2:20. Also Élian Cuvillier, "Références, allusions et citations: Réflexions sur l'utilisation de l'Ancien Testament en Matthieu 1–2," in *Écritures et réécritures: La reprise interprétative des traditions fondatrices par la littérature biblique et extra-biblique; Cinquième colloque international du RRENAB; Universités de Genève et Lausanne, 10–12 juin 2010*, ed. Claire Clivaz et al., BETL 248 (Leuven: Peeters, 2012), 229–42. For Dale C. Allison, *The New Moses: A Matthean Typology* (London: T&T Clark, 1993), this use of Moses goes back to the traditions used by Matthew. For a detailed list of parallels, see Arland J. Hultgren, "Matthew's Infancy Narrative and the Nativity of an Emerging Community," *HBT* 19, no. 1 (1997): 94–95.

102. See Hultgren, "Matthew's Infancy Narrative," 100.

103. Bacon, *Studies in Matthew* (New York: Holt, 1930), 81.

104. See, e.g., François P. Viljoen, "The Superior Authority of Jesus in Matthew to Interpret the *Torah*," *In die Skriflig* 50, no. 2 (2016): a2062, DOI: 10.4102/ids.v50i2.2062. Allison, *New Moses*, 194, rightly discredits Bacon's thesis.

105. Allison, *New Moses*, 180.

106. Viljoen, "Superior Authority of Jesus," 4.

107. See Patricia Sharbaugh, "The Light Burden of Discipleship: Embodying the New Moses and Personified Wisdom in the Gospel of Matthew," *JMT* 2, no. 1 (2013): 56. This presentation

Jesus's superiority over Moses is also clear, for example, in John 3:14 and 6:31–33. Two miracles attributed to Moses, the lifting of the serpent (Num 21:4–9) and the gift of manna (Exod 16:4–36), are superseded by showing that Jesus is the one being lifted up to provide eternal life (John 3:14–15) and that he is the bread of life (John 6:32–33, 35). The gifts that take place in Jesus surpass the ones that Moses facilitated.[108] In John 5:39–46, Moses is presented as the one who wrote about Jesus (presumably in the Torah, but for the Johannine Jesus, Scripture in general testifies to him) and is now not trusted by the Jews.[109] The Johannine community argues that Moses is on their side and that one cannot use Moses against Jesus. Those who do miss the point of God's action entirely.

Finally, Paul also negotiates the Christ believers' relationship with Moses. Galatians 3:19 classically alludes to Moses as the mediator of the law. First Corinthians 10 and 2 Cor 3 make more original uses of the exodus and wilderness traditions.[110] In 1 Cor 10:2, Paul indicates that all who crossed the sea were baptized εἰς τὸν Μωϋσῆν ("into Moses").[111] This use suggests a typology that establishes a correspondence between Moses and Christ and presents a positive image of Moses.[112] Moses's role is erased later, when the rock at Massah and Meribah is identified with Christ (1 Cor 10:4) or when Paul exhorts the Corinthians not to tempt Christ in the manner that the Israelites had put him to test (1 Cor 10:9). Paul constructs an analogy between the destiny of the wilderness generation and the Corinthians' possible future if they do not heed Paul's warnings, but his posi-

---

of Jesus as the new Moses is confirmed in Matt 11:25–30, where at least two passages from the Scriptures of Israel contribute to this construction, according to Sharbaugh, "The Light Burden of Discipleship," 48, 49–56. Echoes of God's gift of rest in Exod 33:14 are found in Matt 11:28–29. They show that Jesus does more than take on Mosaic features, he also partakes in actions reserved to God in the Scriptures of Israel by offering eschatological rest. Jesus's self-description as meek (πραΰς) in Matt 11:29 recalls Moses, the meekest person according to Num 12:3 LXX, as well as Sir 45:4, which indicates that meekness is one of the reasons why God chooses Moses.

108. See also Dorothy A. Lee, "The Significance of Moses in the Gospel of John," *ABR* 63 (2015): 59–60.

109. As Lee indicates, Nathaniel already makes this claim in John 1:45 ("Significance of Moses in the Gospel of John," 57).

110. In 1 Cor 10:1–13, references are found to Exod 13:21 (the pillar of cloud); Exod 14:22 (crossing of the sea); Exod 16:4–36 (manna); Exod 17:6–7 and Num 20:7–13 (waters of Massah and Meribah); Num 14:29–30 (no one from the wilderness generation will enter the promised land, save for Caleb); Exod 32:4–6 (golden calf, with the only explicit quotation in the passage); Num 25:1–9 (the Israelites sleeping with the Moabites and the plague stopped by Phinehas); Num 21:5–6 (the poisonous serpents); Exod 16:2 and Num 14:2 (the grumbling against Aaron and Moses).

111. Cf. for this expression 1 Cor 1:13, 15; Rom 6:3.

112. See Michel Quesnel, *La première épître aux Corinthiens*, Commentaire biblique: Nouveau Testament 7 (Paris: Cerf, 2018), 234.

tion toward Moses is not negative. Second Corinthians 3 is more directly critical. The use of Moses in 2 Cor 3:7, 12–13 is original since the idea of a fading glory of Moses's face is not found in Exod 34:29–35 or in other extrabiblical traditions.[113] For David Litwa, Paul walks the line between maintaining the importance of Moses and at the same time not wanting to present him as "a hero too high to be imitated."[114] Moses is an eminent predecessor, but the Christ believers can have access to the same glory and revelation given to Moses through their experience in Christ.[115]

David in the New Testament

In view of the multifaceted aspects of David's story and of the legendary episodes that surround his life in the Scriptures of Israel, one might expect diverse reappearances of the figure in New Testament texts.[116] This is not the case. The overwhelming majority of the mentions highlight that Jesus is the Davidic messiah. This is found quite regularly in the Synoptic Gospels, where Matthew especially and Luke to some degree expound on Mark's seven mentions of the name to insist on Jesus's identity as son of David.[117] For Matthew, where the name is most used, David's importance to construct Jesus as the messiah is clear already in Jesus's genealogy (Matt 1:1) and serves as proof that Jesus is "*a* son of David in the genealogical sense."[118] Even Abraham's importance is connected to his role as ancestor of David in Matthew's genealogy. In addition, the genealogy itself, which mentions King David in verse 6, is divided in three periods where David plays a central role as the hinge that articulates the first twenty-eight generations. This importance of David for the Gospel of Matthew is also seen in the way Matthew adapts the episode of Jesus's triumphal entrance in Jerusalem (Matt 21:1–9 // Mark 11:1–10 // Luke 19:28–38 // John 12:12–16). All four gospels quote the first

---

113. See M. David Litwa, "Transformation through a Mirror: Moses in 2 Cor. 3.18," *JSNT* 34, no. 3 (2012): 289. See LAB 19:16; also Philo, *Mos.* 2.69–70.

114. Litwa, "Transformation through a Mirror," 294.

115. Hebrews 11:25–26 is a last example of a reflection on the relationship between Moses and Jesus. Moses is enduring ill-treatment (Heb 11:25) in solidarity with the people of God. This abuse is for Christ (τὸν ὀνειδισμὸν τοῦ Χριστοῦ). Moses prefers this ill treatment to the treasures of the Egyptians because Moses is aware of a future reward.

116. The Dead Sea Scrolls allude to the multifaceted aspects of David: CD V, 1–6, which excuses David for his many wives and for the murder of Uriah. For a presentation of David in the New Testament, see Jouette M. Bassler, "A Man for All Seasons: David in Rabbinic and New Testament Literature," *Int* 40, no. 2 (1986): 163.

117. Matt 9:27; 12:23; 15:22; 20:30, 31; 21:9, 15; 22:42–45; Luke 3:31; 18:38; 20:41–44.

118. Bassler, "Man for All Seasons," 163. Emphasis in the original.

part of Ps 117:26 LXX, but only Matthew precedes the quote with the exclamation "Hosanna to the son of David!" emphasizing Jesus as the Davidic messiah.[119]

Luke also refers to a Davidic understanding of Jesus's messiahship. This appears mostly in the infancy section of his gospel (Luke 1–2) and in the genealogy (Luke 3:23–38). Luke focuses on the concepts of the house of David (Luke 1:27, 69; 2:4), of the town of David (Luke 2:4, 11), and of the family (πατριά) of David (Luke 2:4). To this, one can add the mention of the throne of David in Luke 1:32. Here Jesus is presented as the Son of the Most High, and as the one who will inherit the throne of his ancestor David. Luke both recuperates attributes associated with King David for Jesus and shows the superiority of the Davidic messiah. This debate about the relationship between the messiah and David is explicitly discussed in a passage found in all three synoptics (Mark 12:35–37 // Matt 22:41–46 // Luke 20:41–44) and alluded to in John 7:42. The gospel writers are concerned with establishing a continuity with David and affirming the superiority of Jesus, the son of God.[120] The relationship between the messiah and David is also discussed in Acts. David is both ancestor (Acts 13:22–25) and prophet (Acts 1:16; 2:25; 4:25), but he, in contrast to Jesus, has died (Acts 2:29).[121] In Acts 2:29–32, Peter proposes an explanation of Ps 15:8–11 LXX and explains that the holy one who has not experienced corruption (Ps 15:10 LXX) is not David himself, but one of his descendants. Acts 13:36, quoting this same psalm, reaffirms that David had indeed known decay of the flesh after death. This might be in response to some speculations about David, later attested in rabbinic literature, according to which David might participate in the world to come or might come back as another David.[122] Jesus comes from the Davidic lineage but surpasses David, as God's son.[123]

Finally, three occurrences highlight other aspects of the figure of David. In Mark 2:23–28 (// Matt 12:1–8 // Luke 6:1–5), Jesus loosely recalls an episode of the story of David to justify his disciples' behavior. Just as David considers that it is acceptable to demand the bread of the presence for his soldiers (1 Sam 21:1–6), so Jesus explains that his disciples can pluck heads of grain on the Sabbath, affirming that "the Son of Man is lord even of the Sabbath" (Mark 2:28). Once more, Jesus is presented in continuity with David and yet going further than David.

---

119. Mark 11:9–10 does mention the "coming kingdom of our father David," and Luke 19:38 and John 12:13 mention the king (of Israel for John), which could recall David as well.

120. See also Bassler, "Man for All Seasons," 167.

121. Bassler, "Man for All Seasons," 160, indicates that the rabbis also present David as prophesying the future.

122. For a discussion of rabbinic traditions about the death of David, see Bassler, "Man for All Seasons," particularly 158.

123. This is also found in Rom 1:3; 2 Tim 2:8; Rev 5:5; 22:16.

David asks the high priest for the bread and assures him that he and his companions are pure. Jesus simply affirms his lordship over the Sabbath. Revelation 3:7 indicates that "the holy one, the true one" holds the "key of David." This might be an allusion to Isa 22:22, which mentions giving the key of the house of David to Eliakim, the Lord's servant. In Isaiah, the key controls access to Jerusalem and the house of David and symbolizes lordship. Revelation might appropriate authority over David's house as a means of showing that the messiah controls access to the people of God. Finally, Heb 11:32 mentions David among other heroes of faith: Gideon, Barak, Samson, Jephthah, Samuel, and the prophets.[124] For these characters, faith is demonstrated through warrior-like actions, the unique occurrence in the New Testament where David is presented as something else than the psalmist or the ancestor of the messiah, and where there is an explicit reference to his past as fighter and conqueror.[125] This image of David is unique in the New Testament and also rare in early Jewish texts. It resurfaces in rabbinic literature, especially in the legends forming out of the combat between David and Goliath. For the rabbis, as Jouette Bassler indicates, David's successes are representative of God's involvement on his side and not of David's own exploits.[126] This is like Hebrews' interpretations of military and heroic exploits as displays of faith.

None of the unsavory episodes of David's life are discussed in the New Testament, although one might perceive an allusion to David's problematic lineage in Matthew's genealogy of Jesus (Matt 1:6), the only place where David's involvement with Bathsheba is mentioned.

Elijah in the New Testament

Inclusion of Elijah in the present discussion is related to one specific question, which concerns the role of Elijah in the eschatological scenario and specifically Elijah's relationship to the coming of the messiah. As is well known, Elijah does not die but is carried into heavens on a chariot of fire, drawn by fire horses (2 Kgs 2:11). This episode opens space for speculations about Elijah's return at the

---

124. The list is unparalleled in the New Testament or other early Jewish literature, but it mentions judges discussed uniquely in Liber Antiquitatum Biblicarum: Gideon in LAB 35–36; Barak in LAB 31–32; Samson in LAB 42–43; Jephthah in LAB 39–40; Samuel in LAB 51–59 and 64–65. Gideon is mentioned outside of Liber Antiquitatum Biblicarum once in Jdt 8:1, the genealogy of Judith.

125. There might be an allusion to this soldiering aspect in Rev 5:5, where the root of David is the origin for the lion of Judah. Hebrews 11:32–34 is filled with allusions to heroic actions, variously traced back to Gideon, Barak, Samson, Jephthah, and David. David can be associated directly with the administration of justice (2 Sam 8:15), shutting the mouths of lions (1 Sam 17:35), winning strength out of weakness (1 Sam 17:42–51), and with putting foreign armies to flight (1 Sam 17:52).

126. See Bassler, "Man for All Seasons," 157–58.

end times, speculations that build on the end of Mal 3:22–24 LXX. As Markus Öhler notes, in early Jewish literature, Elijah's return is associated with the day of judgment, where he comes to call for repentance and spare the earth.[127] The Synoptic Gospels (but not the Gospel of John) add to Elijah's role as forerunner of the final judgment the notion that Elijah's coming must precede the coming of the messiah, something not found in other early Jewish texts.[128]

Mark and Matthew's use of Elijah is sufficiently similar that they can be treated together. Both answer the question whether Elijah is John the Baptist or Jesus, and both introduce Elijah as a character in the narrative during the episode of Jesus's transfiguration (Mark 9:2–8 // Matt 17:1–8) and at the crucifixion (Mark 15:34–36 // Matt 27:46–49). Luke's use is distinctive and amounts to constructing the figure of Jesus in terms of the Elijah-Elisha pair. The figure is thus particularly important for Luke's work. Outside the use of Elijah in the Gospels and Acts, there are only two other mentions of Elijah in the New Testament, Rom 11:2 and Jas 5:17–18. This should remind one that despite abundant secondary literature, Elijah is a lesser figure in the New Testament. In Rom 11:2, Elijah is used to illustrate the notion of a remnant that proves God's faithfulness despite the betrayals of the people.[129] Finally, in Jas 5:17–18, another aspect of Elijah is brought out, the power of his prayer.[130]

---

127. Öhler, "The Expectation of Elijah and the Presence of the Kingdom of God," *JBL* 118, no. 3 (1999): 461–76. Öhler lists the following witnesses to early Jewish speculations about Elijah: Sirach 48:10 indicates that Elijah will calm the wrath of the Lord and restore the tribes of Jacob; LAB 48:1 identifies Phinehas with Elijah and discusses his role in the end times; Sib. Or. 2:187–89 speaks of Elijah's return. Apocalypse of Elijah (third century CE) has two accounts of the coming of Elijah with Enoch (5:32–35 and 4:7–23). Öhler sees the first one as possibly transmitting Jewish traditions, while 4:7–20 is influenced by Christian expectations, notably Rev 11:3–13.

128. There are only two mentions of Elijah in the Gospel of John (1:21 and 25) to indicate that John the Baptist should not be identified with Elijah. John does not know or chooses not to transmit the episode of the transfiguration or Jesus's misunderstood cry on the cross. John's understanding of Jesus as the incarnate *logos* and his downplaying of John the Baptist also means reducing Elijah's importance. See Öhler, "Expectation of Elijah," 463, 468. Sirach 48:10 does not mention the messiah in relationship with Elijah's return. First Enoch 90:31 has a reference to Elijah in an eschatological context, but it is not associated with the messiah.

129. Paul uses a shortened quotation of 1 Kgs 19:10, 14 to recall Elijah's despair (for a discussion of the form of the quotation, see Michael G. Vanlaningham, "Paul's Use of Elijah's Mount Horeb Experience in Rom 11:2–6: An Exegetical Note," *MSJ* 6, no. 2 [1995]: 224–27). Paul leaves out the beginning of Elijah's speech in 1 Kgs 19:10, 14 which insists on Elijah's abundant zeal. This is a bit surprising since zeal is an important notion in Paul. Galatians 1:14 and Phil 3:6 both mention Paul's own zeal, perhaps in reappropriations of the zeal of Elijah and Phinehas (Num 25:11).

130. Reference to the fervent prayer of Elijah is also found in 4 Ezra 7:109. Compared to uses in other early Jewish texts and in the Gospels, James downplays the status of Elijah by insisting that he is "a human being . . . like us" so that anyone can relate to the great prophet and imitate his fervent

Elijah in Mark and Matthew

Several narrative elements in Mark and Matthew indicate that John the Baptist should be identified with Elijah. Mark 1:6 and Matt 3:4 present John the Baptist as wearing a leather belt, something reminiscent of Elijah's description in 2 Kgs 1:8. John the Baptist's ministry in the desert, where he proclaims a baptism of repentance for the forgiveness of sins (Mark 1:4) and insists on repentance since the kingdom has drawn near (Matt 3:1–2), also corresponds to the role of Elijah as forerunner of the final judgment (Mal 3:22–24 LXX). The reference to the Baptist's death in Mark 6:17–29 // Matt 14:1–12 is also reminiscent of Elijah's sufferings at the hands of Jezebel through Ahab (1 Kgs 19:1–14).[131]

Furthermore, Mark and Matthew both reject the identification of Jesus with Elijah. In Mark, Jesus is identified as Elijah twice (Mark 6:15; 8:28; once in Matt 16:14). Jesus corrects this identification in a dialogue with his disciples (Mark 8:29). Mark 9:11–13 picks up the motif of Elijah's return to "restore all things." Jesus affirms that Elijah has already come, presumably in the person of John the Baptist. Jesus also indicates that Elijah has been the object of sufferings that prefigure what will happen to the messiah, another allusion to John the Baptist's fate. In the parallel passages to Mark 9:11–13, Matthew explicitly identifies John the Baptist with Elijah in Matt 11:14 and 17:13, also insisting on the sufferings that he experienced. In their presentation of John the Baptist as Elijah, Mark and Matthew indicate that Mal 3:22–24 LXX has been fulfilled.

Elijah is also present in the transfiguration story (Mark 9:2–8 // Matt 17:1–8 // Luke 9:28–36). In this episode, Elijah appears briefly along with Moses while Jesus is transformed into a theophanic being. Traditionally, Moses and Elijah are seen to represent the law and the prophets.[132] Elijah's presence could again be related to the expectation of the return of Elijah before judgment (Mal 3:22–24 LXX), which can be connected to the expectation of the return of a prophet like Moses (Deut 18:15–18). Moses and Elijah could also be there because they represent two of the righteous who now live in heaven.[133] According to Angela

---

prayer. Here, Elijah illustrates the conviction that prayer can be "powerful and effective" (Jas 5:16). For James, any believer is capable of the same. For Elijah in Jas 5, see Mariam Kamell Kovalishyn, "The Prayer of Elijah in James 5: An Example of Intertextuality," *JBL* 137, no. 4 (2018): 1027–45.

131. See Jean-Daniel Dubois, "La figure d'Élie dans la perspective lucanienne," *RHPR* 53, no. 2 (1973): 160.

132. This interpretation is ancient; it is recalled by Angela Standhartinger, "Jesus, Elija und Mose auf dem Berg: Traditionsgeschichtliche Überlegungen zur Verklärungsgeschichte (Mark 9,2–8)," *BZ* 47, no. 1 (2003): 67. In Luke's version, Moses and Elijah's presence is explained through the conversation they have with Jesus about his departure to Jerusalem (Luke 9:31).

133. See Standhartinger, "Jesus, Elija und Moses auf dem Berg," 68, 70–71.

Standhartinger, the transfiguration in the oldest Markan version can be read through the theophanies experienced by Moses and Elijah on the mountain. In Sirach's praise of the ancestors, Elijah and Moses are the only ones who hear God's word directly (Sir 45:5; 48:7) or who perform miracles through a word of God (Sir 45:3; 48:5).[134] The transfiguration would be Jesus's own Sinai, his shining clothes, a reflection of God's glory that appears to Jesus. Confirmation of this comes from the apparition of Elijah and Moses and from the clouds and voice from heaven. Moses's apparition would indicate Jesus's status as new lawgiver, while Elijah's presence helps to construct the call for discipleship.[135]

One last occurrence specific to Mark and Matthew deserves to be discussed, namely the confusion around the calling of Elijah while Jesus agonizes on the cross (Mark 15:34–36 // Matt 27:46–49). Jesus exclaims "Eloi, Eloi, lema sabachthani," a quotation from Ps 22:1, which could build a rapprochement with David. Yet the ones standing there (mis)interpret it and declare: "Look, he is calling Elijah" (Mark 15:35 // Matt 27:47). The bystanders are in the wrong temporality. They have not grasped that it is no longer the time for Elijah to come.[136]

Elijah in Luke

Luke takes his own perspective on the figure of Elijah and does not focus on Elijah's role in the end times.[137] Rather, he chooses to present Jesus as inheriting aspects both of Elijah and Elisha.

Luke is careful to avoid the identification of John the Baptist with Elijah.[138] He does not have parallels for the statements in Mark and Matthew that identify John the Baptist with Elijah. In the infancy narratives, he does connect John the Baptist with Elijah, claiming that he will go "with the spirit and power of Elijah" (Luke 1:17). If John the Baptist receives the spirit and power of Elijah (just like Elisha did) and does function in a way that is reminiscent of Elijah as evoked in Mal 3:22–24 LXX, Luke is much more willing to construct the figure of Jesus

---

134. See Standhartinger, "Jesus, Elija und Moses auf dem Berg," 72. She also discusses Josephus's presentation of Elijah, which conforms to Moses. Allison, *New Moses*, 39–45, also shows how 1 Kgs 17–19 and 2 Kgs 1–2 are presenting Elijah as a second Moses.

135. Standhartinger, "Jesus, Elija und Moses auf dem Berg," 78–79, 81.

136. See Mark Whitters, "Why Did the Bystanders Think Jesus Called upon Elijah before He Died (Mark 15:34–36)? The Markan Position," *HTR* 95, no. 1 (2002): 119–24.

137. This also explains Luke's modification of Jesus's cry on the cross. As Dubois writes ("La figure d'Élie dans la perspective lucanienne," 172), in Luke, one does not expect an Elijah that functions as a savior but as a sacerdotal messiah. As the new Elijah, Jesus cannot call upon himself.

138. See, e.g., Dubois, "La figure d'Élie dans la perspective lucanienne," 159.

in terms of Elijah.[139] Jesus's ascension (Luke 24:51 and Acts 1:9) contains parallels to the traditions about Elijah. For example, the same verb in the passive (ἀναλαμβάνω: "to lift up, take up") is used to speak of the ascension of Elijah (2 Kgs 2:9; Sir 48:9) and Jesus (Acts 1:2).[140]

In addition, Luke sets up several clues to understand Jesus in terms of the Elijah-Elisha pair. Both Jesus and Elijah promise the spirit, to the disciples and to Elisha respectively (Luke 24:49; 2 Kgs 2:9–10).[141] Elijah's special relationship to Elisha is also recalled in Jesus's call to discipleship in Luke 9:61–62, where Elisha's reason for delaying his following are repeated (Luke 9:61; 1 Kgs 19:19–20). Jesus himself recalls Elijah (and Elisha) after his opening preaching in Nazareth to explain why he is rejected there. He affirms that Elijah was not sent to the widows of Israel, but to a widow in Sidon (Luke 4:26; 1 Kgs 17:9) and that Elisha did not go to the lepers of Israel, but to Naaman the Syrian (Luke 4:27; 2 Kgs 5:8–14). In Luke, the Elijah-Elisha pair contributes to make the figure of Jesus understandable, as prophet, miracle worker (Luke 7:11–17 is paradigmatic in that regard and unique to Luke), and as one who gets taken into heaven with God.[142] This influence of Elijah on the portrayal of Jesus in Luke also impacts the presentation of Peter and Paul in Acts. They are pursuing the work of Jesus, and they also acquire Elijah-like traits, as seen in two resurrection stories attributed respectively to Peter (Acts 9:36–43) and to Paul (Acts 20:9–12).[143]

Minor Figures of Israel in the New Testament

The preceding sections focused on male figures of the Scriptures of Israel. This part redresses this bias somewhat by looking at lesser-used female figures who play sporadic, important roles in the New Testament. I will treat Eve, Sarah, Hagar, Tamar, Rahab, Ruth, and Bathsheba.

In the Pseudepigrapha, they appear mostly in rewritten Scriptures, such as Sarah or Rebecca in Jubilees, but are otherwise used very little. The exception is

---

139. See Dubois, "La figure d'Élie dans la perspective lucanienne." Dubois mentions two others passages where Luke makes use of the traditions identifying John the Baptist with Elijah, Luke 1:76 and 7:27.

140. For a list of all parallels, see Dubois, "La figure d'Élie dans la perspective lucanienne", 170.

141. See Dubois, "La figure d'Élie dans la perspective lucanienne," 170. Raymond E. Brown, "Jesus and Elisha," *Pers* 12, no. 1 (1971): 85–104, underscores the importance of Elisha to construct Jesus in Luke.

142. For a detailed discussion, see Dubois, "La figure d'Élie dans la perspective lucanienne," 168.

143. For a detailed discussion of the parallels, see Dubois, "La figure d'Élie dans la perspective lucanienne," 174.

Eve, mentioned in several texts (and repeatedly in the Life of Adam and Eve). Tamar is mentioned in retellings of the story of Israel (Jubilees; Liber Antiquitatum Biblicarum; the Testament of Judah). Ruth is mentioned briefly in LAB 4:11. Rahab is never mentioned. Hagar appears once in Baruch (3:23) and in the Apocalypse of Daniel (a late text, from the ninth century CE; 1:2–3; 2:11), next to the mentions in Jubilees and Liber Antiquitatum Biblicarum. The New Testament is thus particular in its appropriations of female figures for theological arguments. As has been argued elsewhere, Liber Antiquitatum Biblicarum also presents certain important women (LAB 31–32: Deborah, but also Jephthah's daughter [LAB 39:10–40:9]), and Jubilees insists on the role of Rebecca.[144] This practice is different from the New Testament texts, which use several feminine characters for presenting specific arguments. In other early Jewish texts, this occurs only for Eve, although narrative elaboration on some characters, such as Tamar in Liber Antiquitatum Biblicarum or Rebecca in Jubilees also lend to theological constructions. New Testament usages and the discussion surrounding Eve in other early Jewish texts are more explicit in their theological orientation.

Eve

Eve is mentioned explicitly twice in the New Testament (2 Cor 11:3 and 1 Tim 2:13), and she contributes to constructing the "I" behind the speech of Rom 7. New Testament uses crystallize around Eve's responsibility in transgressing God's command in the garden of Eden. Pseudepigraphic texts discuss Eve in the same manner and show an interest in the serpent or in the adversary symbolized by the serpent. This is the case for the occurrences of Eve in Enochic literature.[145] Second Baruch 48:42 bemoans the depravity of the ancestors and describes Eve as obeying the serpent. Although unnamed, Eve is accused of being at the origin of sin in Sir 25:24 and of having led humanity to death.[146] In the Testament of Adam (second to fifth century CE), Eve is identified as the one through whom sin was created (T. Adam 3:5). The limits imposed on humanity because of Eve (and

---

144. For women in Liber Antiquitatum Biblicarum, see Pieter Willem van der Horst, "Portraits of Biblical Women in Pseudo-Philo's *Liber Antiquitatum Biblicarum*," *JSP* 3, no. 5 (1989): 29–46; Mary Therese DesCamp, *Metaphor and Ideology:* Liber Antiquitatum Biblicarum *and Literary Methods through a Cognitive Lens*, BibInt 87 (Leiden: Brill, 2007), esp. ch. 10.

145. E.g., 1 En. 69:6 mentions Eve amid the names of the condemned angels. Among those, Gader'el is responsible for giving instruments of death to humanity. He is also the one who misled Eve since, through her transgression, humanity lost access to the tree of life and tasted death.

146. See Nicholas Elder, "'Wretch I Am!' Eve's Tragic Speech-in-Character in Romans 7:7–25," *JBL* 137, no. 3 (2018): 749.

sometimes Adam) are also discussed in the Apocalypse of Adam (first to fourth century CE) and the Testament of Abraham (see, e.g., T. Ab. A 8:9). Finally, the Life of Adam and Eve (first century CE) elaborates on what happens to the first humans after their expulsion from Eden. The Latin and Greek recensions are dissimilar and Eve's role in each differs.[147] In the Greek version, Eve recalls the story of the transgression in detail, elaborating on the role of the devil in it and lamenting her responsibility. Eve's sin as the origin of human transgressions and death is a repeated motif.[148] Adam and Eve's repentance opens the Latin text. During Eve's repentance, she is tempted a second time by the devil, and she interrupts her penance early. When she realizes she has been deceived, she laments (Latin LAE 11:1–3), with elements that echo motifs of Rom 7:7–25.

If one understands Rom 7:7–25 as "speech-in-character," various characters stand behind the "I" of Rom 7: Adam, the people of Israel, possibly Medea, but also Eve.[149] The treatment of Eve in Life of Adam and Eve suggests that an interpretation of Eve as "wretched" (Rom 7:24) is possible. For Nicholas Elder, both Life of Adam and Eve and Rom 7 use "the themes of sin, desire, commandment, and Eve because these were traditional tropes about Eve in Second Temple Judaism."[150] Furthermore, Rom 7:11 (ἐξαπατάω: "to deceive, cheat") uses the same verbal root found in the LXX when Eve explains to God she was deceived by the serpent (Gen 3:13; ἀπατάω: "to deceive, mislead"). The situation of the "I" in Rom 7:11 corresponds to Eve's position in Gen 3:1–6, 13: the serpent seizes the opportunity given by God's command to Adam in Gen 2:16–17 to seduce Eve, and this trick leads to the death of Eve (and Adam).[151]

Second Corinthians 11:3 confirms that Paul sees Eve foremost as the one who has been deceived. The verb ἐξαπατάω is explicitly associated with Eve in 2 Cor 11:3. In this section, Eve functions as Hagar will in Galatians (Gal 4:24–25, 30). Both are counterexamples that Paul uses to convince his addressees to follow his instructions. In Galatians, Paul uses Hagar to discourage circumcision. In 2 Corinthians, Eve is a warning for the Corinthians not to be deceived by the

---

147. See the introduction by M. D. Johnson to Life of Adam and Eve, *OTP* 2:249–57. It is also disputed whether Life of Adam and Eve is a Christian or Jewish text.

148. Greek LAE 7:1; 9:2; 10:2; 14:2; 32:1–2. See Elder, "'Wretch I Am!,'" 753–54.

149. For speech-in-character, see. e.g., Stanley K. Stowers, "Romans 7.7-25 as a Speech-in-Character (Προσωποποιία)," in *Paul in His Hellenistic Context*, ed. Troels Engberg-Pedersen (Minneapolis: Fortress, 1995), 180–202; Jean-Baptiste Édart, "De la nécessité d'un sauveur: Rhétorique et théologie de Rm 7:7–25," *RB* 105, no. 3 (1998): 359–96.

150. For a discussion of the relationship between Rom 7 and Life of Adam and Eve, see Elder, "'Wretch I Am!,'" 753–54. Elder sees Rom 7:7–25 as Eve's lament, particularly about the fact that she is a captive of the law.

151. See also Austin Busch, "The Figure of Eve in Romans 7:5–25," *BibInt* 12 (2004): 1–36; and Nicholas Elder, "'Wretch I Am!'"

super-apostles. Just like the serpent who deceived Eve hid behind God's command, the super-apostles (2 Cor 11:5) are behind the thoughts that could lead the Corinthians astray. If the Corinthians listen to the super-apostles, as Eve listened to the serpent, they will deviate from what is ordered by God.[152] But the Corinthians, in contrast to Eve, are not abandoned. Paul is looking out for them. If the Corinthians listen to him, they will avoid being corrupted and will not know Eve's fate. The reference to Eve in the argument highlights the seriousness of the matter. Paul wants to show that this is not simply about choosing Paul over the super-apostles. It is about identifying the deceiver behind the super-apostles' preaching (2 Cor 11:14), and following God's command by obeying Paul's preaching. Here Paul uses the story of Eve's deception by the serpent as an illustration of the perilous situation in which the Corinthians find themselves. If they follow the deceptive super-apostles, they will be like Eve. Paul invites them to avoid this situation by following him.

With 1 Timothy, we return to a use of Eve that corresponds to other pseudepigraphic usages. In 1 Tim 2:8–15, the author of the letter seeks justifications for controlling the women who are active in his community. Two arguments aim to show Eve's primordial inferiority, which all women inherit: she was created second (1 Tim 2:13), and she "was deceived and became a transgressor" (1 Tim 2:14). When the author of 1 Timothy speaks of the transgression, he also uses the verb ἐξαπατάω (see Rom 7:11 and 2 Cor 11:3), but he no longer names Eve, calling her "the woman." This universalizes his argument, so that he can control the position of women in his community. He also shifts the blame onto Eve and exonerates Adam, something found in other early Jewish texts.[153] The argument concludes with the affirmation that childbearing brings salvation to women (1 Tim 2:15). In 1 Timothy, Eve can no longer be understood without her saintly counterpart, Mary. As the Protevangelium of James shows, Mary herself is presented as immaculately conceived. She then conceives without the stain of sin and delivers without suffering, remaining a virgin even after birth.[154] Mary reverses the curse of Eve for women and replaces Eve as a better mother of humanity. A similar alternative between Eve and a model mother is found in 4 Macc 18:7–8 (first century CE).[155] The mother of the seven soon-to-be-martyred sons describes herself as different than Eve in insisting she protected "the rib built into woman's body" and that the "destroyer, the deceitful serpent" did not "defile the purity

---

152. See also Stefan Krauter, "Eva in Röm 7," *ZNW* 99, no. 1 (2008): 6 and 7.
153. Sir 25:24; GLAE 9:2; 10:2; 14:2; 25:1, 3; 32:1–2; as well as Philo, *Opif.* 155–170. See Elder, "'Wretch I Am!,'" 748, 749–54.
154. See Prot. Jas. 4:2, 4; 11:2–3; 16:2; 19:1–20:4.
155. See Krauter, "Eva in Röm 7," 8.

of [her] virginity." Here, too, chaste and pious motherhood is presented as an alternative to Eve's corruption.

Hagar and Sarah

While Paul, like other early Jewish texts, uses Abraham as a model of faith for his communities, in Gal 4:21–5:1, he focuses on Abraham's offspring through Sarah and Hagar. The well-known allegory names Hagar explicitly and associates her with several negative characteristics: she is a slave woman (Gal 4:22); her child is born according to the flesh (Gal 4:23), for slavery (Gal 4:24); she corresponds to the present Jerusalem (Gal 4:25); she will eventually be driven out, along with her child, and will not inherit the promise (Gal 4:30). Paul rehearses elements associated with the story of Hagar from Gen 16 and 21:9–21, leaving out Hagar's encounters with the angel of the Lord in Gen 16:9–14 and 21:17–19. Indeed, Paul makes Hagar into a foil for those among the Galatians who are intent on circumcision as the way for joining the people of God. Counterintuitively, Paul associates the circumcised Jews with the figure of Ishmael, usually understood as the ancestor of the nations (Gen 25:12–18), hoping to discourage the Christ believers in Galatia from circumcision. In this effort, he discards any elements of the Hagar story that could be read positively and insists on the exclusion of Hagar and her descendants.

Sarah, although unnamed in Galatians, stands in contrast to Hagar, the slave woman. Sarah is free, her child is born through the promise (Gal 4:23). She corresponds to the Jerusalem from above (Gal 4:26), and she will rejoice (Gal 4:27). Her son, explicitly named in Gal 4:28, allows the Christ believers to understand themselves as sons of the promise, heirs to the covenant made to Abraham. In the corresponding counterintuitive identification of the circumcised Jews with Hagar and her children, Paul associates his uncircumcised Christ believers with the unnamed Sarah and her (circumcised on the eighth day) son, Isaac. The story of Hagar and Sarah and their sons reinforces Paul's point, namely that non-Jews no longer need to be circumcised to be included in the people of God. The two women do not matter in the story. Their sons, and how each represents different paths of access to the God of Israel, are what matters.

Three other uses of Sarah in the New Testament consider her simply as accessory, either to demonstrate Abraham's faithfulness or to insist on God's sovereignty.[156] First Peter 3:6 is the only mention of Sarah where her own qualities are explicitly recognized, yet even there, the text highlights her obedience to

---

156. Romans 4:19 and Heb 11:11 both mention Sarah's barrenness and insist that this did not deter Abraham from being faithful. Romans 9:9 uses the story of Sarah as an indication

Abraham. This obedience is exemplary in a household code destined to discipline wives in the first communities by encouraging them to accept the authority of their husbands (1 Pet 3:1–6). The women addressed by Peter can become children of Sarah provided they do good works and do not fear anything frightful (1 Pet 3:6). This lack of fear is difficult to relate to Sarah directly. The background for the use of Sarah could be Gen 12:11–13 and 20:1–5, where Sarah obeys Abraham in pretending to be his sister in foreign and dangerous contexts.[157]

Tamar, Rahab, Ruth, and the Wife of Uriah

Tamar, Rahab, Ruth, and the wife of Uriah appear in the first part of the genealogy of Matthew as ancestors for David and Solomon (Matt 1:3–6). Tamar, Rahab, and Bathsheba might shed some light on Mary's unusual pregnancy and the accusations it elicited. Adversaries of Christianity criticize the pregnancy as being the product of an illicit relationship with a Roman soldier, and the Protevangelium of James devotes considerable space to preserving the purity of Mary (Prot. Jas. 13:1–16:3).[158] David's relationship with Bathsheba, identified as Uriah's wife in Matt 1:6, begins with a rape and a murder. The only thing known about Rahab is that she is a prostitute (Josh 2:1; 6:17). Tamar's mothering of Perez and Zerah (Matt 1:3) takes place through a ruse (Gen 38:13–30), in which Tamar poses as a prostitute. Possibly, the references to these three women can suggest that even if the origins of Jesus were marred by a suspicious pregnancy, it would not prevent Jesus's claim to Davidic origin.

All the women are also outsiders. Tamar might be a Canaanite, Rahab is a prostitute in Jericho, and Ruth is a Moabite. Bathsheba is described solely as the wife of Uriah, a Hittite (2 Sam 11:3). In the Scriptures of Israel, they are also praised for their faithfulness.[159] Finally, all share a relationship with Jewish males

---

that God can choose his true descendants (Rom 9:8) among Abraham's children, here only the descendants of Isaac.

157. It could perhaps also be a reference to her laughing in Gen 18:12 or to the harsh way she deals with Hagar in Gen 16:6. Or, as Mark Kiley suggests, Sarah functions for the author of 1 Peter as a model of "submissive obedience even in the midst of an unjust situation" that might also be frightening. See Kiley, "Like Sara: The Tale of Terror behind 1 Peter 3:6," *JBL* 106, no. 4 (1989): 689–92. Aída Besançon Spencer, "Peter's Pedagogical Method in 1 Peter 3:6," *BBR* 10, no. 1 (2000): 107–19, similarly sees Gen 12:11–13 as the background to 1 Pet 3:6.

158. For Mary's pregnancy as the result of a Roman soldier, see famously Origen, *Cels.* 1.69. For a discussion of Jesus "ben Pantera," see Christopher B. Zeichmann, "Jesus 'ben Pantera': An Epigraphic and Military-Historical Note," *JSHJ* 18, no. 2 (2020): 141–55.

159. Judah says of Tamar that she is more "in the right" than he (Gen 38:26); Rahab is spared following her actions toward the Jewish spies (Josh 6:17); Ruth is faithful to the God of the Israelites (Ruth 1:16).

and are early examples of outsiders who respond faithfully to the God of Israel, just as outsiders from the nations will respond faithfully to Jesus later.[160] Richard Bauckham adds that all four women are gentiles and are "included in order to show that the Messiah, whose male ancestors in his direct descent from Abraham could not, by definition, be Gentiles, nevertheless had Gentile ancestors, thereby suggesting his suitability to be the Messiah for Gentiles as well as for Jews."[161]

In the Scriptures of Israel, Tamar and Ruth mother sons related to David. Rahab, however, is nowhere mentioned as mother in Scripture and does not reappear in early Jewish literature to my knowledge.[162] However, Rahab returns in the New Testament, in addition to the mention in Matt 1:5. She is a model of faithfulness in Heb 11:31, and she is praised for her good works in Jas 2:25.[163] Several questions arise in relationship with the mention of Rahab in Matthew: Is Rahab the same as the one mentioned in Hebrews and James (unmistakably the Rahab of Josh 2 and 6), especially since Matthew is the only one who spells her name as Ῥαχάβ? Where does Matthew find the tradition of Rahab as mother of Boaz, and why does he use it?

If the tradition that Rahab's son was Ruth's husband is not found elsewhere in early Jewish literature, one should note that it is possible to assume a temporal proximity (in the narrative world, evidently) between Rahab and Ruth. Rahab lived at the time of Joshua, while Ruth's story is presented as happening during the days of the judges (Ruth 1:1).[164] Thus, the Rahab of Josh 2 and 6, were she to appear in Matthew's genealogy, would be mentioned more or less at this point in the genealogy or at least corresponds to this generation of the genealogy.[165] If one admits that the Ῥαχάβ of Matt 1:5 is the Rahab of Josh 2 and 6 (and the one of Heb 11 and Jas 5), one needs to ask why Matthew would include Rahab in his

---

160. See for this argument E. Ann Clements, *Mothers on the Margin? The Significance of the Women in the Gospel of Matthew* (Cambridge: Clarke & Co, 2014).

161. Bauckham, "Tamar's Ancestry and Rahab's Marriage: Two Problems in the Matthean Genealogy," *NovT* 37, no. 4 (1995): 313–29.

162. Yair Zakowitch, "Rahab als Mutter des Boas in der Jesus-Genealogie (Matth. I, 5)," *NovT* 17, no. 1 (1975): 1, indicates that there is not "even the most hidden hint" that Rahab could be the mother of Boaz.

163. Zakowitch, "Rahab als Mutter des Boas," 1–5.

164. Zakowitch, "Rahab als Mutter des Boas," 2; Raymond E. Brown, "*Rachab* in Matt 1,5 Probably Is Rahab of Jericho," *Bib* 63, no. 1 (1982): 79–80, makes the same argument in response to Jerome D. Quinn, "Is ΡΑΧΑΒ in Mt 1,5 Rahab of Jericho?," *Bib* 62, no. 2 (1981): 225–28.

165. Bauckham, "Tamar's Ancestry and Rahab's Marriage," 320–29, adds the evidence of 1 Chr 2:54–55, which, according to Jewish hermeneutical practices of the time, allows one to understand Rechab = Rahab as the wife of Salma, especially since Rahab needed a husband. Bauckham also mentions the rabbinic tradition that has Joshua marry Rahab (b. Meg. 14b–15a).

list of feminine ancestors for Jesus. In Matthew, Rahab occupies a space between Tamar and Ruth and is inserted in a genealogy that associates Tamar with Ruth, as is already the case in Ruth 4:12, which affirms that Boaz's house, through Ruth, will be like "the house of Perez, whom Tamar bore to Judah."[166] Matthew's choice of Rahab is not arbitrary.[167] Rahab comprises everything needed to be part of the genealogy: she is a foreigner, a prostitute, who acts with courage and self-denial to ensure the safety and future of the people of Israel. She is only missing an Israelite husband and child. Matthew could rely on connections between Tamar, Ruth, and Rahab to bring Rahab in as a mother. Although Matthew was not in want of other illustrious women he could have included in the genealogy, he prefers another foreigner, famous for her devotion to the Israelites and their God. She is the only one of the four women in Matthew's genealogy to reappear in the New Testament.

Hebrews 11:31 and Jas 2:25 both present Rahab as a prostitute without commenting on this fact and assuming it is well known.[168] James and Hebrews make the same point about Rahab: her welcome and protection of the spies reveal faithfulness (Heb 11:31), which motivates actions that will justify her (Jas 2:25). In Hebrews, Rahab is part of a list of heroes of faithfulness, while in James she is associated with Abraham as an example of a righteous and obedient individual. James insists on the similarity between Abraham and Rahab, but Rahab acts, welcoming the strangers and sending them out. Rahab's actions interpret Abraham's faith. Rahab does not need to believe God to be justified; she only needs to act faithfully. In that way, she is the equivalent of Abraham, presented as friend of God in Jas 2:23. This use of Rahab is unique to the New Testament. In other early Jewish texts, she is not mentioned.[169]

Conclusion

At the end of this incomplete presentation of a few important figures in early Jewish texts, it is possible to make three concluding remarks.

First, a striking aspect of the use of figures in all early Jewish texts is the focus on exemplarity, as Annette Yoshiko Reed also notes.[170] Texts emphasize aspects

---

166. Rahab is associated to both Ruth and Tamar in midrashic traditions; see Zakowitch, "Rahab als Mutter des Boas," 2, 4, 5.

167. Against this identification, see Quinn, "Is 'PAXAB in Mt 1,5 Rahab of Jericho?"

168. Codex Sinaiticus in its original reading of Heb 11:31 indicates that Rahab is the one *called* prostitute, possibly pointing to some discomfort.

169. Josephus also recognizes her value, *Ant.* 5.11–14.

170. Reed, "Construction and Subversion of Patriarchal Perfection."

that are "most apt for emulation" by addressees.[171] For Reed, this is connected both to Hellenistic insistence on imitation for education and to the use of *exempla* in Roman historiography. She indicates that *exempla* are usually found in speeches made by characters rather than in the narrative itself.[172] This corresponds to the context of one of the most important reinterpretations of a figure of Israel in Acts 7. Moses's role as *exemplum* is elaborated in a speech attributed to Stephen. Early Jewish literature, including the New Testament, also presents figures as examples that need to be imitated, even though it emphasizes different figures (Jacob is more important for other Jewish texts than for New Testament texts, which can emphasize Elijah, for example). The purpose is to shape the identity and *ethos* of the communities. Readers "should pattern themselves" after these figures.[173] As a result, the less palatable features of some figures are carefully downplayed. While contemporary interpretations of ancient figures make much of their downfalls, ancient texts will erase Abraham's cowardice when it comes to Hagar, David's rape of Bathsheba and murder of Uriah, or Noah's drunkenness.

Even Adam, whom I did not have space to discuss here, can be excused for his transgression. In Jub. 3:23, for example, God expresses his anger for the serpent and for Eve but not for Adam. Second Baruch 4:3 recognizes the transgression of Adam and develops a reflection about the responsibility of human beings in sin. In 2 Bar. 54:15, 19, Adam, while his initial relationship with sin is recognized, is exonerated from responsibility in the sin of those who come after him. In 2 Bar. 54:19, each individual becomes their "own Adam." In contrast, 4 Ezra is harsher toward Adam and blames him for both his own transgression and for provoking the fall of his descendants (4 Ezra 3:21, 26; 7:116, 118). This discussion resembles 1 Cor 15:21–22, which links death to Adam and contrasts it to life in Christ. Romans 5:12–21 also makes Adam the origin of sin, even though the discussion that follows admits that not all human beings sin in the manner of Adam (Rom 5:14). Eve is one of the rare characters that is systematically treated in a negative manner despite her role as ancestor of humanity. She joins Cain—a much more evidently bad figure than Eve—in this group of figures consistently treated as a bad example (1 John 3:12 and Jude 11). Her fault, in contrast to Adam's, is neither diminished nor excused. In the New Testament, the refusal to exonerate Eve contributes to controlling the role of women in early communities through marriage and motherhood.

---

171. Reed, "Construction and Subversion of Patriarchal Perfection," 196.
172. Reed, "Construction and Subversion of Patriarchal Perfection," 197.
173. Reed, "Construction and Subversion of Patriarchal Perfection," 201.

Second, if one excludes Moses and Abraham, the choice of figures among various early Jewish texts varies greatly. Enoch is practically absent from the New Testament but is at the origin of a rich literature elsewhere.[174] Phinehas, Aaron, and Melchizedek, as well as the twelve patriarchs, the sons of Jacob (particularly Levi and Judah), and Jacob's wives, are much more important in early Jewish literature outside the New Testament. The New Testament is also not interested in extending the stories of ancient figures, possibly because it sees the story of Jesus and the communities as the necessary continuation of past narratives.[175]

Finally, in using various figures as models, each community also reinforces their claim to legitimacy. In appropriating various figures, the communities behind texts as diverse as the canonical Gospels, Jubilees, 4 Ezra, 1 Enoch, or the Damascus Document affirm that their own members are imitators of the revered ancient figures. This is seen clearly in the use of Moses in the Dead Sea Scrolls and in Jubilees, but one also sees it in the list of heroes in Heb 11 or in the way James treats Elijah. The ancient heroes become models that can be imitated, appropriated, and even surpassed by members of these relatively new communities. This use is particularly important in the New Testament, which frequently shows Jesus's superiority over important figures of Israel. These uses all contribute to constructing Jesus as the legitimate messiah and the communities of the Christ believers as the authentic heirs to the traditions and figures gathered in the Scriptures of Israel.

Bibliography

Adams, Sean A., and Zanne Domoney-Lyttle, eds. *Abraham in Jewish and Early Christian Literature*. LSTS 93. London: T&T Clark, 2019.
Allison, Dale C. *The New Moses: A Matthean Typology*. Edinburgh: T&T Clark, 1993.
Bacon, Benjamin W. *Studies in Matthew*. New York: Holt, 1930.
Baird, William. "Abraham in the New Testament: Tradition and the New Identity." *Int* 42, no. 4 (1988): 367–79.

---

174. Three mentions of Enoch are found in the New Testament: Luke 3:37 includes Enoch in the genealogy of Jesus; Heb 11:5 presents Enoch as an example of faith; and Jude 14 quotes from 1 En. 1:9. There are probably other allusions to 1 Enoch in the letter. John 3:13 might be a correction of the idea that Enoch was taken into heaven (but it could also be an allusion to Elijah).

175. There is evidence of extending the stories in Christian literature outside of the New Testament canon: e.g., Martyrdom of Isaiah or Apocalypse of Elijah, which have traces of Christian interventions and extend the stories of Isaiah and Elijah.

Bassler, Jouette M. "A Man for All Seasons: David in Rabbinic and New Testament Literature." *Int* 40, no. 2 (1986): 156–69.

Bauckham, Richard. "Tamar's Ancestry and Rahab's Marriage: Two Problems in the Matthean Genealogy." *NovT* 37, no. 4 (1995): 313–29.

Bloch, René. "Moses and Greek Myth in Hellenistic Judaism." Pages 195–208 in *La construction de la figure de Moïse/The Construction of the Figure of Moses*. Edited by Thomas Römer. TranseuSup 13. Paris: Gabalda, 2007.

Boccaccini, Gabriele. *Beyond the Essene Hypothesis: The Parting of the Ways between Qumran and Enochic Judaism*. Grand Rapids: Eerdmans, 1998.

Bovon, François. "Moses in Luke Acts." Pages 129–45 in *New Testament and Christian Apocrypha*. Edited by Glenn E. Snyder. Grand Rapids: Baker Academic, 2011.

Brooke, George J. "Genre Theory, Rewritten Bible and Pesher." *DSD* 17, no. 3 (2010): 361–86.

———. "Moses in the Dead Sea Scrolls: Looking at Mount Nebo from Qumran." Pages 209–21 in *La construction de la figure de Moïse/The Construction of the Figure of Moses*. Edited by Thomas Römer. TranseuSup 13. Paris: Gabalda, 2007.

Brown, Raymond E. "Jesus and Elisha." *Per* 12, no. 1 (1971): 85–104.

———. "*Rachab* in Mt 1,5 Probably Is Rahab of Jericho." *Bib* 63, no. 1 (1982): 79–80.

Busch, Austin. "The Figure of Eve in Romans 7:5–25." *BibInt* 12 (2004): 1–36.

Butticaz, Simon. "Moïse, 'Le vagabond de Dieu,' Actes 7, 20–43." *Foi et Vie* 118, no. 3 (2018): 80–85.

Butticaz, Simon, and Daniel Marguerat. "La figure de Moïse en Actes 7: Entre la christologie et l'exil." Pages 223–47 in *La construction de la figure de Moïse / The Construction of the Figure of Moses*. Edited by Thomas Römer. TranseuSup 13. Paris: Gabalda, 2007.

Caquot, André. "1 Hénoch." Pages 463–625 in *La Bible: Écrits Intertestamentaires*. Edited by André Dupont-Sommer and Marc Philonenko. Paris: Gallimard, 1987.

Clements, E. Ann. *Mothers on the Margin? The Significance of the Women in the Gospel of Matthew*. Cambridge: Clarke & Co, 2014.

Collins, John J. "Artapanus (Third to Second Century B.C.)." *OTP* 2:889–903.

———. "How Distinctive Was Enochic Judaism?" *Meghillot* 5–6 (2007): 17*–34*.

Cuvillier, Élian. "Références, allusions et citations: Réflexions sur l'utilisation de l'Ancien Testament en Matthieu 1–2." Pages 229–42 in *Écritures et réécritures: La reprise interprétative des traditions fondatrices par la littérature biblique et extra-biblique; Cinquième colloque international du RRENAB; Universités de Genève et Lausanne, 10–12 juin 2010*. Edited by Claire Clivaz, Corina Combet-Galland, Jean-Daniel Macchi, and Christophe Nihan. BETL 248. Leuven: Peeters, 2012.

Daly-Denton, Margaret. "David the Psalmist, Inspired Prophet: Jewish Antecedents of a New Testament *Datum*." *ABR* 52 (2004): 32–47.

DesCamp, Mary Therese. *Metaphor and Ideology:* Liber Antiquitatum Biblicarum *and Literary Methods through a Cognitive Lens*. BibInt 87. Leiden: Brill, 2007.

Doran, R. "Pseudo-Eupolemus (prior to First Century B.C.)." *OTP* 2:873–82.

Dubois, Jean-Daniel. "La figure d'Élie dans la perspective lucanienne." *RHPR* 53, no. 2 (1973): 155–76.

Édart, Jean-Baptiste. "De la nécessité d'un sauveur: Rhétorique et théologie de Rm 7:7–25." *RB* 105, no. 3 (1998): 359–96.

Eisenbaum, Pamela. "Heroes and History in Hebrews 11." Pages 380–96 in *Early Christian Interpretation of the Scriptures of Israel*. Edited by Craig A. Evans and James A. Sanders. JSNTSup 148. Sheffield: Sheffield Academic, 1997.

Elder, Nicholas. "'Wretch I Am!' Eve's Tragic Speech-in-Character in Romans 7:7–25." *JBL* 137, no. 3 (2018): 743–63.

Fletcher-Louis, Crispin H. T. *All the Glory of Adam: Liturgical Anthropology in the Dead Sea Scrolls*. STDJ 42. Leiden: Brill, 2002.

Gil, Roger, and Eberhard Bons. "Judith 5:5–21 ou le récit d'Akhior: Les mémoires dans la construction de l'identité narrative du peuple d'Israël." *VT* 64, no. 4 (2014): 573–87.

Granerød, Gard. "Melchisedek in Hebrews 7." *Bib* 90 (2009): 188–202.

Hay, David M. "Moses through New Testament Spectacles." *Int* 44, no. 3 (1990): 240–52.

Hayward, C. T. Robert. "The Figure of Adam in Pseudo-Philo's Biblical Antiquities." *JSJ* 23, no. 1 (1992): 1–20.

Heger, Paul. "*1 Enoch*: Complementary or Alternative to Mosaic Torah." *JSJ* 41, no. 1 (2010): 29–62.

Henten, Jan Willem van. "Moses as Heavenly Messenger in *Assumptio Mosis* 10:2 and Qumran Passages." *JJS* 54, no. 2 (2003): 216–27.

Horst, Pieter Willem van der. "Portraits of Biblical Women in Pseudo-Philo's *Liber Antiquitatum Biblicarum*." *JSP* 3, no. 5 (1989): 29–46.

Hultgren, Arland J. "Matthew's Infancy Narrative and the Nativity of an Emerging Community." *HBT* 19, no. 1 (1997): 91–108.

Johnson, M. D. "Lives of Adam and Eve (First Century A.D.)." *OTP* 2:249–95.

Kaestli, Jean-Daniel. "Moïse et les institutions chez Hécatée d'Abdère." Pages 131–43 in *La construction de la figure de Moïse/The Construction of the Figure of Moses*. Edited by Thomas Römer. TranseuSup 13. Paris: Gabalda, 2007.

Kamell Kovalishyn, Miriam. "The Prayer of Elijah in James 5: An Example of Intertextuality." *JBL* 137, no. 4 (2018): 1027–45.

Kiley, Mark. "Like Sara: The Tale of Terror behind 1 Peter 3:6." *JBL* 106, no. 4 (1987): 689–92.
Krauter, Stefan. "Eva in Röm 7." *ZNW* 99, no. 1 (2008): 1–17.
Kugel, James. *A Walk through Jubilees: Studies in the Book of Jubilees and the World of Its Creation*. JSJSup 156. Leiden: Brill, 2012.
Lee, Dorothy A. "The Significance of Moses in the Gospel of John." *ABR* 63 (2015): 52–66.
Litwa, M. David. "Transformation through a Mirror: Moses in 2 Cor. 3.18." *JSNT* 34, no. 3 (2012): 286–97.
Minear, Paul S. *To Heal and to Reveal: The Prophetic Vocation according to Luke*. New York: Seabury, 1976.
Moessner, David P. "Luke 9:1–50: Luke's Preview of the Journey of the Prophet like Moses of Deuteronomy." *JBL* 102, no. 4 (1983): 575–605.
Murphy, Frederick J. *Pseudo-Philo: Rewriting the Bible*. New York: Oxford University Press, 1993.
Nihan, Christophe. "'Un prophète comme Moïse' (Deutéronome 18,15): Genèse et relectures d'une construction deutéronomiste." Pages 43–76 in *La construction de la figure de Moïse/The Construction of the Figure of Moses*. Edited by Thomas Römer. TranseuSup 13. Paris: Gabalda, 2007.
Nikiprowetzky, Valentin. "Sibylline Oracles." Pages 1041–1140 in *La Bible: Écrits Intertestamentaires*. Edited by André Dupont-Sommer and Marc Philonenko. Paris: Gallimard, 1987.
Nilsen, Tina Dykesteen. "Memories of Moses: A Survey through Genres." *JSOT* 41, no. 3 (2017): 287–312.
Öhler, Markus. "The Expectation of Elijah and the Presence of the Kingdom of God." *JBL* 118, no. 3 (1999): 461–76.
Pearson, Birger A. "Melchizedek." Pages 595–606 in *The Nag Hammadi Scriptures: The Revised and Updated Translation of Sacred Gnostic Texts in One Volume*. Edited by Marvin Meyer. New York: Harper, 2009.
Piovanelli, Pierluigi. "'Rewritten Bible' ou 'Bible in Progress'? La réécriture des traditions mémoriales bibliques dans le judaïsme et le christianisme anciens." *RTP* 139, no. 4 (2007): 295–310.
Quesnel, Michel. *La première épître aux Corinthiens*. Commentaire biblique: Nouveau Testament 7. Paris: Cerf, 2018.
Quinn, Jerome D. "Is 'PAXAB in Mt 1,5 Rahab of Jericho?" *Bib* 62, no. 2 (1981): 225–28.
Reed, Annette Yoshiko. "The Construction and Subversion of Patriarchal Perfection: Abraham and Exemplarity in Philo, Josephus, and the *Testament of Abraham*." *JSJ* 40, no. 2 (2009): 185–212.
Robertson, R. G. "Ezekiel the Tragedian (Second Century B.C.)." *OTP* 2:803–19.

Roitman, Adolfo. "The Traditions about Abraham's Early Life in the Book of Judith." Pages 73–87 in *Things Revealed: Studies in Early Jewish and Christian Literature in Honor of Michael E. Stone*. Edited by Esther G. Chazon, David Satran, and Ruth Clements. JSJSup 89. Leiden: Brill, 2004.

Römer, Thomas. *Moïse "Lui que Yahvé a connu face à face."* Paris: Gallimard, 2002.

———. "Qui est Abraham? Les différentes figures du patriarche dans la Bible hébraïque." Pages 13–33 in *Abraham: Nouvelle jeunesse d'un ancêtre*. Edited by T. Römer. Essais bibliques 28. Geneva: Labor et Fides, 1997.

Ruiten, Jacques T. A. G. M. van. *Abraham in the Book of Jubilees: The Rewriting of Genesis 11:26–25:10 in the Book of "Jubilees" 11:14–23:8*. JSJSup 161. Leiden: Brill, 2012.

Sanders, E. P. "Testament of Abraham (First to Second Century A.D.)." OTP 1:871–902.

Sharbaugh, Patricia. "The Light Burden of Discipleship: Embodying the New Moses and Personified Wisdom in the Gospel of Matthew." *JMT* 2, no. 1 (2013): 46–63.

Spencer, Aída Besançon. "Peter's Pedagogical Method in 1 Peter 3:6." *BBR* 10, no. 1 (2000): 107–19.

Standhartinger, Angela. "Jesus, Elija und Mose auf dem Berg: Traditionsgeschichtliche Überlegungen zur Verklärungsgeschichte (Mark 9,2–8)." *BZ* 47, no. 1 (2003): 66–85.

Stowers, Stanley K. "Romans 7.7–25 as a Speech-in-Character (Προσωποποιία)." Pages 180–202 in *Paul in His Hellenistic Context*. Edited by Troels Engberg-Pedersen. Minneapolis: Fortress, 1995.

Uhlenbruch, Frauke, and Sonja Ammann. "Fan Fiction and Ancient Scribal Cultures." *Transformative Works and Cultures* 31 (2019). DOI: 10.3983/twc.2019.1887.

VanderKam, James C. "Moses Trumping Moses: Making the Book of *Jubilees*." Pages 25–44 in *Dead Sea Scrolls: Transmission of Traditions and Production of Texts*. Edited by Sarianna Metso, Hindy Najman, and Eileen Schuller. STDJ 92. Leiden: Brill, 2010.

Vanlaningham, Michael G. "Paul's Use of Elijah's Mount Horeb Experience in Rom 11:2–6: An Exegetical Note." *MSJ* 6, no. 2 (1995): 223–32.

Vermes, Geza. *The Complete Dead Sea Scrolls*. London: Penguin, 2004.

———. *Scripture and Tradition in Judaism: Haggadic Studies*. 2nd ed. StPB4. Leiden: Brill, 1973.

Viljoen, François P. "The Superior Authority of Jesus in Matthew to Interpret the Torah." *In die Skriflig* 50, no. 2 (2016): a2062. DOI: 10.4102/ids.v50i2.2062.

Werman, Cana. "*Jubilees* in the Hellenistic Context." Pages 133–58 in *The Heavenly Tablets: Interpretation, Identity and Tradition in Ancient Judaism*. Edited by Lynn LiDonnici and Andrea Lieber. JSJSup 119. Leiden: Brill 2007.

———. "'The תורה and תעודה' Engraved on the Tablets." *DSD* 9, no. 1 (2002): 75–103.
Whitters, Mark. "Why Did the Bystanders Think Jesus Called upon Elijah before He Died (Mark 15:34–36)? The Markan Position." *HTR* 95, no. 1 (2002): 119–24.
Wintermute, O. S. "Jubilees (Second Century B.C.)." *OTP* 2:35–142.
Wise, Michael O., Martin G. Abegg Jr., and Edward M. Cook, eds. *The Dead Sea Scrolls: A New Translation*. Rev. ed. New York: Harper Collins, 2005.
Zakowitch, Yair. "Rahab als Mutter des Boas in der Jesus–Genealogie (Matth. I, 5)." *NovT* 17, no. 1 (1975): 1–5.
Zeichmann, Christopher B. "Jesus 'ben Pantera': An Epigraphic and Military-Historical Note." *JSHJ* 18, no. 2 (2020): 141–55.

PART 5

ISRAEL'S SCRIPTURES IN EARLY CHRISTIANITY OUTSIDE THE NEW TESTAMENT

This final section of the book, "Israel's Scriptures in Early Christianity Outside the New Testament," offers one of the most distinctive features of this collection. Mindful of the growing emphasis on the question of reception in the field of biblical studies, the five chapters in this section move beyond the first century CE and investigate the early impact of the New Testament authors' use of Scripture on early Christian writers. How does their engagement with Israel's Scriptures compare with that in the New Testament? The chapters investigate how the authors of the New Testament supplied a hermeneutical precedent for subsequent Christian writers or, conversely, how these later writers might have ignored the precedent set by the New Testament in order to strike out on their own.

Much like in the treatment of Jewish interpretations of scriptural books and characters in the previous section, it would be impossible to be exhaustive given the broad scope of early Christian interpretative activity. Instead, these chapters are illustrative probes that consider specifically how several sets of texts or media—apocryphal gospels, apocryphal apocalypses, the *adversus Judaeos* tradition, the critical tradition associated with Marcion and his heirs, and early Christian pictorial art—take up and interpret the Scriptures of Israel. The final chapter of this section acknowledges that early

Christian art constitutes an important form of scriptural interpretation that can be profitably interpreted in tandem with, and often reflects, the theological writings of the day.

∽

38

Israel's Scriptures in the Apocryphal Gospels

TOBIAS NICKLAS

How many gospels do we have? This question sounds easy—and many Christians would answer: "four." However, nobody can give a fully adequate answer. This has to do with several different problems. First, the number of texts that we may call "gospel" increases with every new finding. It was just a bit more than ten years ago that the discovery of the Gospel of Judas was made public.[1] In the meantime, we may mention the edition of Papyrus Oxyrhynchus 5072, an old fragment of very gospel-like Jesus sayings in the Greek language.[2] And in her recent work on the Armenian Infancy Gospel, the Armenian scholar Mari Mamyan discovered that this text survives in more than one recension, one of which has been completely unknown to the scholarly world.[3]

Second, this series of findings may make us aware of a second problem: What is a gospel? Shall we call the Gospel of Judas a gospel if it shows almost no interest in the life of Jesus and at the same time takes a heavily critical stance toward all kinds of more traditional gospel materials and associated ideas? Are the few short passages of Jesus stories on Papyrus Oxyrhynchus 5072 (as well as other comparable fragments) the remains of what used to be a more or less

---

1. The first critical edition was by Rodolphe Kasser and Gregor Wurst, eds., *The Gospel of Judas Together with the Letter of Peter to Philip, James and a Book of Allogenes from Codex Tchacos: Critical Edition* (Washington, DC: National Geographic, 2007).

2. See Juan Chapa, "5072," in *The Oxyrhynchus Papyri: Volume LXXVI (No. 5072–5100)*, ed. Juan Chapa and Daniela Colomo, Graeco-Roman Memoirs 97 (London: Egypt Exploration Society, 2011), 1–19.

3. Mamyan's edition of the Armenian Infancy Gospel is planned to appear 2023.

complete gospel, or should we think of them as the surviving remnants of a paraphrase, an excerpt, or a passage from a homily? In some cases—like the so-called Coptic Unknown Berlin Gospel (P.Berol. 22220)—we have learned that this text (like many others) should not be labeled a gospel, at least not in a narrower sense of the word. Instead, it belongs to a group of writings that can be called "Apostolic memoirs."[4] These texts remind us of gospels—they tell stories related to Jesus, Mary, or the disciples—but they form a distinct group of writings that were produced (probably) since the sixth century CE to trace important elements of the Egyptian miaphysite church's "identity" to the origins of the Christian movement.

Perhaps we should add a third problem: in some cases, which are in several ways very interesting, we know that certain texts must have existed and may even have been quite influential, but the remaining traces of these writings are too small to offer a fuller overview of their use of Israel's Scriptures. We may, for example, think about the Gospel of Marcion. This text is usually understood as a revised version of Luke's Gospel, while at least some scholars see it as a key for the development of the Synoptic Gospels.[5] It would, of course, be fascinating to give a description of Marcion's use of Israel's Scriptures in his gospel—when, in fact, we only have traces of this text in writings produced to refute Marcion and his ideas. A reliable examination of this text's remains is thus almost impossible. Other cases offer different problems: the Paidika, often labeled the Infancy Gospel of Thomas, for example, is transmitted in so many different forms that it is probably wise not to talk about an original version of this text and its possible relation to Israel's Scriptures. Instead, we have to concentrate on one certain witness (or a well-defined group of witnesses) of this text and investigate its (or their) special use of the Scriptures.

All this means that it is impossible to give a full overview of the use of Scripture in "the" apocryphal gospels. All that I can do is to offer a few more or less well-chosen examples. It also does not make sense to offer any statistical or quasi-statistical overview of quotations, allusions, and echoes to certain passages of Israel's Scriptures. Instead, I am interested in different ways of using Scripture in some examples of well-known apocryphal gospels. As the use of Scripture in so-called gnostic writings is an (important and difficult) issue on its own, here I

---

4. See Alin Suciu, *The Berlin-Strasbourg Apocryphon: A Coptic Apostolic Memoir*, WUNT 370 (Tübingen: Mohr Siebeck, 2017).

5. For a recent overview of the discussion, see Daniel A. Smith, "Marcion's Gospel and the Synoptics: Proposals and Problems," in *Gospels and Gospel Traditions in the Second Century: Experiments in Reception*, ed. Jens Schröter, Tobias Nicklas, and Joseph Verheyden, BZNW 235 (Berlin: de Gruyter, 2019), 129–74.

exclude the material from Nag Hammadi and related writings.[6] In the following overview I start with the Gospel of Peter, a (fragmentary) account of Jesus's passion and resurrection that in parts resembles the canonical gospels and their use of the Scriptures of Israel but, compared to them, shows a few interesting developments. The two following examples come from two fragmentary writings that cannot be attributed to an otherwise known gospel. At least one of these, the Unknown Gospel on Papyrus Egerton 2, is very old, while the date of the second, the gospel on P.Oxy. 840, is disputed. Both of them may show that developments we find in the canonical gospels could go on in the second and later centuries. It would be highly fascinating to have better evidence for the question of how far Jewish followers of Jesus—usually labeled "Jewish Christians"—tried to relate Jesus and his deeds to the Scriptures of Israel. Unfortunately, their gospels are only preserved in a highly fragmentary form, that is, in quotations by later Christian authors of the majority church. I will choose the fragments of the Gospel of the Ebionites that allow at least a few important insights.

The final step will lead us to look into one of the most successful extracanonical writings of all, the Protevangelium of James. This text, which is often labeled an infancy gospel but also speaks of Mary's birth and childhood, tells us a lot about the use of scriptural motifs to create new narratives. One may be surprised that a few quite well-known texts are missing, but both the Gospel of Thomas, mainly a collection of Jesus logia, and the Gospel of Mary offer only very limited material for our purpose. The same is true for the Infancy Gospel of Thomas mentioned above, a text that tries to evoke the Jewish world of Jesus's childhood but only does so in a highly artificial manner. The boy Jesus behaves like a "little creator" who, on a Sabbath, forms sparrows out of mud and brings them to life (ch. 2); he deals with scribes and provokes his teachers; he performs miracles and is in trouble with "the Jews." Topics of proper scriptural interpretation seem not to be important for this writing. Dozens of other "gospels" and gospel-related texts could be mentioned here—on the whole, however, the examples offered here supply a representative overview of second- and third-century extracanonical gospels.[7]

---

6. But see Christopher M. Tuckett, "Principles of Gnostic Exegesis," in Schröter et al., *Gospels and Gospel Traditions*, 277–310; and, somewhat more specific on creation accounts, Pierre Létourneau, "Creation in Gnostic Christian Texts, or: What Happens to the Cosmos When Its Maker Is Not the Highest God," in *Theologies of Creation in Early Judaism and Ancient Christianity: In Honour of Hans Klein*, ed. Tobias Nicklas and Korinna Zamfir, DCLS 6 (Berlin: de Gruyter, 2010), 415–34.

7. As this would open a completely different field, I exclude texts that offer (or presuppose) something like a "gnostic" myth of creation (see above n. 6). In addition, most of the later literature, like the Gospel of Gamaliel, the Apostolic Memoirs, texts and traditions about

The Gospel of Peter

If we talk about the Gospel of Peter, we usually refer to a fragment of a Greek passion and resurrection account that was discovered in the so-called Akhmim-Codex from the sixth or seventh century. Even if the substance of this writing can be dated around the middle of the second century CE, it is by no means certain that it is identical to the Gospel of Peter mentioned by some ancient Christian authors like Serapion of Antioch (quoted by Eusebius of Caesarea, *Hist. eccl.* 6.12.1–6) or Origen (*Comm. Matt.* 10.17). Although this text does not seem very concerned with Israel's Scriptures, it is especially interesting for our purposes. First, in only two, partially parallel passages do we find something like a marked citation from Scriptures. According to verse 5, Herod, whom the text understands as Jesus's judge, tells Pilate that "the Jews" would bury Jesus's body before the Sabbath, "for it is written in the law that the sun should not set on one that had been put to death."[8] Somewhat later, in verse 15, we read that "the Jews," who, according to the Gospel of Peter, had crucified Jesus, become anxious because of the darkness covering Judea during midday. The text goes on: "It is written that the sun should not set on one who had been put to death." Interestingly, the Torah does not exactly include this command. Very probably these two passages refer to Deut 21:22–23, according to which the body of a person who had been executed should not be openly displayed overnight but be buried the same day. Neither Gos. Pet. 5 nor 15 seem to be interested in an exact quotation of Deuteronomy. Instead, the apocryphal writing offers something like a very free paraphrase that makes the text more fitting to the gospel's context, according to which it was midday when "darkness covered all Judea" (v. 15):

> Deut 21:23 LXX
> οὐκ ἐπικοιμηθήσεται τὸ σῶμα αὐτοῦ ἐπὶ τοῦ ξύλου,
> ἀλλὰ ταφῇ θάψετε αὐτὸν ἐν τῇ ἡμέρᾳ ἐκείνῃ
> "his [dead] body shall not remain [during the night] upon the tree,
> but bury him at the same day"

> Gos. Pet. 5 (cf. 15)
> ἥλιον μὴ δῦναι ἐπὶ πεφονευμένῳ
> "that the sun should not set upon one that had been murdered"

Bartholomew, Lives of the Virgin, etc., are still completely under researched. This is partly due to the fact that many of them are transmitted in very different text forms and languages.

8. Texts and translations from Thomas J. Kraus and Tobias Nicklas, eds., *Das Petrusevangelium und die Petrusapokalypse: Die griechischen Fragmente mit deutscher und englischer Übersetzung*, GCS NS 11 (Berlin: de Gruyter, 2004). All Scripture translations, unless otherwise noted, are by the author.

There is, however, also a second interesting shift. While Deut 21:23 LXX speaks of someone who is executed because of a crime, both Gos. Pet. 5 and 15 speak about someone who had been murdered (ἐπὶ πεφονευμένῳ). This is, of course, a crucial statement: in this way, the Gospel of Peter's "Jews" call themselves "murderers of Jesus" by using this passage. This first observation corresponds to others. The Gospel of Peter tells a story full of motifs that were originally developed from the Scriptures or allude to them. Within the Gospel of Peter, however, this is not always visible any longer. This can be shown by many examples. Both in the Gospel of Mark and in the Gospel of Matthew, Jesus dies with the words of Ps 21 LXX on his lips (Mark 15:34: ὁ θεός μου ὁ θεός μου, εἰς τί ἐγκατέλιπές με; Matt 27:46: θεέ μου θεέ μου, ἱνατί με ἐγκατέλιπες; both cases translatable as "My God, my God, why have you forsaken me?"), a passage whose context abounds in verbal allusions to other passages in Ps 21 LXX. The Gospel of Peter, however, has these words: "My power, power, you have forsaken me" (v. 19: ἡ δύναμίς μου, ἡ δύναμις, κατέλειψάς με). Even though verse 12 includes the motif of dividing Jesus's garments and casting lots over them (developed from Ps 21:19 LXX), Jesus's last words do not sound like Ps 21 LXX anymore. One could, of course, consider the idea that the Gospel of Peter tries to avoid the word God and replaces it by "power." But this does not make much sense. After all, the (quite brief!) Gospel of Peter uses the word "God" otherwise five times (vv. 6, 9, 45, 46, 48). It is thus probable that the author of the Gospel of Peter was no longer concerned with the scriptural background of Jesus's last words. He may, however, have been concerned with the question of why Jesus, the "Lord," was not able to show his supernatural powers (which had led to so many miracles) and had to suffer and die on the cross.

Other cases are comparable. According to verse 14, "the Jews" decide not to break "his" (probably Jesus's) legs "so that he might die in torment." Of course, this motif reminds one of John 19:31, 33 where we read that the soldiers who come to break Jesus's legs discover that he has already died. A bit later John connects the fact that Jesus's legs are not broken to a (somewhat mysterious) marked scriptural citation: "None of his bones shall be broken." Even if we cannot be fully sure whether these words refer to Exod 12:46 or Ps 34:21, the motif seems to show that John understands Jesus as the true paschal lamb. The Gospel of Peter uses the same motif. Its connection to Scripture, however, is lost. The passage obviously just wants to show how cruelly "the Jews" treat Jesus.

Other cases are more difficult. According to verse 16, Jesus's Jewish executioners offer him "gall with vinegar to drink," which in this context is obviously understood as a poisonous drink to kill him more quickly. Of course, the motif finds its roots in Ps 68:22 LXX. Interestingly, the Gospel of Peter's combination of "gall" and "vinegar" fits better with the psalm than the synoptic parallels do, where either "gall" (Matt 27:34) or "vinegar" (Mark 15:36; Matt 27:48; Luke 23:36;

John 19:28–30) is mentioned. Gospel of Peter 16 is thus closer to the psalm than at least Mark, Luke, and John, while in Matthew two verses have to be combined to reach the same effect. Even this does not yet mean that the Gospel of Peter is aware of the scriptural background of this combination. After all, the same combination can be found in a group of second-century writings related to Jesus's passion (see Barn. 7:3–5; Syr. Didascalia 19; Sib. Or. 8:303; Irenaeus of Lyons, *Haer.* 3.19.2; Tatian's *Diatessaron*, and many others).[9] The decisive point, however, is perhaps verse 17, where we read: "And they fulfilled everything and filled the measure of sins upon their head." At least in this case the story is understood as a "fulfillment" (probably) of the Scriptures of Israel, which at least here are interpreted as prophecies of Jesus's fate.

A final example may show an additional aspect. Gospel of Peter 18, certainly one of the strangest passages of the entire text, does not have any parallels in the canonical gospels. During the darkness at midday (v. 15: μεσημβρία), some people (obviously "Jews") "went about with lamps, because they thought it was night, and fell down." This motif does not show any relevance for the overall plot, but if we follow Martin Meiser, it can be understood as result of an otherwise unknown narrative interpretation of Isa 59:9–10 LXX ("Therefore, judgment departed from them . . . while they expected light, darkness came upon them; while they waited for dawn, they walked in untimeliness. They shall feel for the wall like blind men. . . . They shall fall at midday as at midnight"), where we find the judgment (κρίσις; for the judgment of Jerusalem, see also Gos. Pet. 25), the combination of "darkness" (σκότος) and "midday" (μεσημβρία; both Gos. Pet. 15), the idea of "walking around" (Gos. Pet. 18; here περιέρχομαι instead of περιπατέω), and the idea of "falling down" (Gos. Pet. 18).[10] This combination of motifs (partly changing the *Vorlage* found in the gospels that came to be canonical), which is necessary to create this allusion, is so sophisticated that we have to consider the author of our text to be consciously alluding to Scripture.

The result of all this is quite intriguing: Scripture is called "the law" (νόμος), and what is written down is binding for "the Jews" (see vv. 5 and 15). At the same time, Scripture can also be understood as a prophecy that is to be fulfilled (v. 17). While the Gospel of Peter does not seem very interested in actual citations of Scripture, whether marked or unmarked, or even in its correct wording, it represents a stage of the transmission of Jesus material after the canonical gospels.

---

9. It is thus possible that the Gospel of Peter took over the motif not from a scriptural background but only from "collective memory" about what kind of ideas have to be part of a story of Jesus's passion.

10. On these observations, see Martin Meiser, "Das Petrusevangelium und die spätere großkirchliche Literatur," in *Das Evangelium nach Petrus: Text, Kontexte, Intertexte*, ed. Thomas J. Kraus and Tobias Nicklas, TUGAL 158 (Berlin: de Gruyter, 2007), 188.

As we have seen with two examples, the Gospel of Peter seems to take over motifs that were developed as narrative interpretations of scriptural passages but in places revises them such that their scriptural background is no longer recognizable. At the same time, it still seems to develop new motifs from other scriptural passages, as we have seen in the case of Isa 59:9–10 and its relation to verses 12, 15, and 18: the reenactment of Jesus's passion with the help of scriptural reasoning continues!

Fragments of Otherwise Unknown Jesus Material

The Unknown Gospel (UG) on Papyrus Egerton 2 (and Papyrus Cologne 255)

During the last century, a number of fragmentary Jesus stories, or collections of Jesus sayings, on papyrus or parchment were discovered in the deserts of Egypt. The most spectacular of these is the so-called Unknown Gospel on Papyrus Egerton 2, sometimes simply labeled the Egerton Gospel. Its text is preserved on two fragments of a codex plus a few tiny additional pieces, which seem to go back to the late second or early third century CE and thus belong to the oldest witnesses of Christian material culture. As far as we see from its remains, the Unknown Gospel offered a mixture of scenes that partly show close parallels to the Gospel of John and partly seem to be (less closely) related to the synoptic material, while other scenes are completely independent. Israel's Scriptures play an important role for this text on several levels.

Fragment 1 verso (+ Papyrus Cologne 255 verso) describes Jesus in a debate with a group of νομικοί, that is, "experts in (very obviously, Jewish) law" and (later) the "leaders of the people" (line 6). A heated debate arises: in several sentences closely paralleled to a combination of John 5:39 and 45, Jesus prompts the leaders to "search the scriptures in which you think you have life" (lines 8–9). These Scriptures "bear witness about me."[11] A hermeneutical problem is addressed. While the "we-group" behind the Unknown Gospel's Jesus understands the Scriptures of Israel as prophesying (and thus witnessing to) Jesus, their Jewish opponents still do not know "where he comes from" (adapted from line 17; cf. John 9:29). That is why Jesus (and with him, the "we group") has Moses on

---

11. If not indicated otherwise, texts and translations are taken (or slightly adapted) from Tobias Nicklas, "The 'Unknown Gospel' on *Papyrus Egerton 2*," in *Gospel Fragments*, ed. Thomas J. Kraus, Michael J. Kruger, Tobias Nicklas, Oxford Early Christian Gospel Texts (Oxford: Oxford University Press, 2009), 9–120.

his side: Moses has "written about me to your/our[12] forefathers" (line 22; cf. John 5:46). Of course, this passage does not offer a citation of, or even verbal allusion to, Israel's Scriptures. Instead, the Scriptures per se and the correct way of understanding them are central for this debate. The Jewish leaders *may* have the Scriptures; they even should study them intensely. But as long as they do not find Jesus in these Scriptures, it is Moses himself who accuses them. In this way it seems impossible to still "have life" (line 9) in them. Even though the passage does not mean that every part of Scripture refers to Jesus, a reading that excludes the idea that they speak about Jesus means to fall victim to a dangerous misunderstanding.[13]

After a brief and fragmentary passage, according to which "the leaders" want to arrest Jesus (frag. 1 recto, P. Cologne 255 recto), the text offers a brief story of the healing of a leper (recalling freely Mark 1:40–45 par.). Again, this passage neither cites Scripture nor offers any verbal allusion to it. It is, however, not understandable without the scriptural concept of purity and, more specifically, of leprosy. While Leviticus demands that the healing of a leper has to be witnessed by *one* priest and describes a complex series of rituals to be performed before a former leper can be reintegrated to society (Lev 14:2–31), the Unknown Gospel's Jesus orders the leper to show himself "to the *priests* [pl.] and offer for your purification as Moses commanded" (lines 20–22). Is this a sign that the author of the Unknown Gospel is not aware of the concrete scriptural background regarding this problem? We should be cautious, as the whole passage is lacunose and the plural reading "priests" depends on the remains of an *iota* in the article. After all, the same scene describes a Jesus who, contrary to the synoptic parallels, avoids touching the leper. Does the text want to show that Jesus tries to avoid becoming unclean via contact with the leper? This is a plausible interpretation, in which case the question of purity may play an even broader role than in the synoptic parallels.

In fragment 2 recto we find Unknown Gospel's only remaining marked citation. Jesus is asked whether it is "allowed to hand over to the kings what belongs to their government" (lines 7–8), a clear variation of the question about the payment of taxes to be found in the Synoptic Gospels (see Mark 12:14b par.; Matt 22:17; and Luke 20:22; cf. also Justin, *1 Apol.* 17.64). Jesus does not reflect on this question, at least not in the remaining text, but refers to Scripture: "Well

---

12. The exact text is a matter of debate.

13. For comparable tendencies in other early Christian literature, see Tobias Nicklas, "Frühchristliche Ansprüche auf die Schriften Israels," in *Scriptural Authority in Early Judaism and Ancient Christianity*, ed. Geza G. Xeravits, Tobias Nicklas, and Isaac Kalimi, DCLS 16 (Berlin: de Gruyter, 2013), 347–68.

did Isaiah prophesy about you: this people honors me with their lips but their heart is far away from me—in vain do they worship me" (lines 13–17). Even the introduction of this quotation is interesting: Jesus not only marks the following passage as coming from Isaiah, he also understands it as a prophecy, in this case not referring to Jesus, but to his contemporaries, the people of Israel. The passage itself corresponds exactly to Isa 29:13 LXX, a passage that is also quoted in Mark 7:6 and Matt 15:8, but in a different context: just the word δέ after μάτην seems to be missing.

Probably the most fascinating passage, however, is fragment 2 verso. The remaining text is so fragmentary that for a long time it seemed impossible to offer a full and more or less reliable reconstruction of the scene. This has been changed only recently by Lorne Zelyck, who offers a text that is heavily influenced by scriptural parallels that had not been discovered yet:

> Then Jesus, as he walked, stood on the bank of the Jordan River; and reaching on the right hand, he took salt and scattered it upon the river. Then he poured out much water over the ground. He prayed, and it was filled before them. Then it brought forth a crop of great abundance, produced by an everlasting gift for all these people.[14]

Fragment 2 verso demonstrates a special problem: the text of Zelyck's reconstruction shows verbal parallels to 2 Kgs 2:13 and 6:7; it is influenced by 2 Kgs 2:19–22, the episode about "healing" the water of a source with the help of salt (and Josephus's retelling of the same passage in *J.W.* 4.459–464). The reconstructed text thus can be understood as both alluding to 2 Kgs 2:19–22 (plus other passages) and using an otherwise unknown Elisha typology for its description of Jesus's deeds. All this is made even more probable by some passages in both the sixth century Topography of the Holy Land by a certain Theodosius (§§1 and 18) and the Itinerary of the so-called Piacenza Pilgrim (§§13–14). Theodosius relates Elisha's spring in Gilgal (close to Jericho) to a "Lord's field" that, according to both writers, can be connected to memories about Jesus's sowing, planting, and/or plowing a furrow.[15]

At the same time, Zelyck's ingenious reconstruction remains a reconstruction, and as long as we do not have further evidence from new witnesses of the Unknown Gospel, we will never be certain whether he is correct. The important point is this: the passage on fragment 2 verso may have been an interesting witness for a narrative rewriting of a scriptural passage that creates an Elisha-Jesus

---

14. Translation by Zelyck, *The Egerton Gospel (Egerton Papyrus 2 + Papyrus Köln VI 255): Introduction, Critical Edition, and Commentary*, TENTS 13 (Leiden: Brill, 2019), 143.

15. For more details, see Zelyck, *Egerton Gospel*, 152–53.

typology. At the same time, this is based on a somewhat circular argument: the reconstruction was only made possible because the editor, Zelyck, considered this possibility, and only the idea that there *could be* a scriptural parallel (or a parallel influenced by Scripture) led to his reconstruction of a text that finally shows this parallel.

The Unknown Gospel on Papyrus Egerton 2 thus offers evidence for the use of Scripture on several levels. Similar to the canonical gospels, we find a marked citation plus several allusions to Scripture and scriptural concepts. Isaiah 29:13 LXX is quoted in the Synoptic Gospels as well (Mark 7:6 par.; Matt 15:8), but we cannot be sure whether the author of the Unknown Gospel was aware of this; the contexts of the quotation are too different. Both the Unknown Gospel and the synoptics, however, have in common that they describe Jesus quoting Scripture. Fragment 2 verso may be a witness of an otherwise unknown Elisha-Jesus typology, but it also points to the problems related to the reconstruction of ancient writings. In addition, the Unknown Gospel can be understood as part of an early discourse *about* Scripture more generally. Like the Gospel of John, it is an early example of the idea that Scripture (and even its "author," Moses) prophesies Jesus. According to the Unknown Gospel, Scripture, or at least parts of it, have to be read with a Christ-focused hermeneutic. As a result, Jewish nonchristological readings of the same passage are understood as deficient (and not "life-giving" anymore).

Papyrus Oxyrhynchus 840

Papyrus Oxyrhynchus 840 is a parchment page of a miniature codex that was produced in the fourth or fifth century CE. It offers a story of Jesus, who enters a temple, probably the temple in Jerusalem, together with his disciples. There they meet a certain Pharisaic high priest called Levi (recto, line 10), who confronts them with the question of how he and his disciples can feel themselves permitted "to trample this place of purification and see these holy vessels" without having taken a bath of purification (recto, lines 12–15).[16] Jesus asks the priest whether he is clean, and the priest responds: "I am clean, for I bathed in the Pool of David, and went down by one staircase and came up by another, and then I came and looked upon these holy vessels" (verso, lines 24–30). Jesus's response is harsh. According to him, natural water can clean only the outer skin but never the inside of a person. This is first shown by the case of dogs and pigs that may lie in the water "day and night" but do not become clean and then illustrated by prostitutes and pipe girls whose inside, even if they wash themselves, remains

---

16. Text and translations taken (or adapted) from Kraus, Kruger, and Nicklas, *Gospel Fragments*.

"full of scorpions and all wickedness" (verso, lines 40–41). The fragment breaks off with the idea that Jesus and his disciples have bathed in "living waters from heaven which come from the Father above" (verso, lines 41–45).

This short text does not offer any citation of Scripture. But, of course, the use of names like Levi and David relates to figures from the Scriptures of Israel. Besides this, the motif of "living waters," which recalls John 4:14; 7:37–38; or even Rev 22:17, may also be developed from passages like Jer 2:13 or Zech 14:8. The most interesting point, however, is the text's discussion of the question of purity. The debate whether this fragment contains a possibly old, perhaps even authentic Jesus story that was preserved by Jewish Christ followers started already with the text's first edition in 1908.[17] It seems clear that P.Oxy. 840 is concerned with the role of the Jerusalem temple and its priesthood but, even more, with questions of cultic purity related to Scripture. But to what degree is this the text's real concern? I think that already the quite artificial figure of a Pharisaic high priest called Levi should warn us. A somewhat closer look reveals that our text is not very specific regarding special aspects of ritual purity. That is why some years ago, Harald Buchinger and Elisabeth Hernitscheck, building on a suggestion by François Bovon, demonstrated that the language of the text shows a clear awareness of special terminology and developments related to fourth-century Christian rituals of baptism.[18] If we follow Buchinger and Hernitscheck, the text is not primarily interested in aspects of Jewish ritual purity but makes most sense as a cult-critical voice related to late antique debates about Christian baptism. Even if superficially, the story seems to relate to debates about ritual purity with roots in Israel's Scriptures, mainly in the book of Leviticus; it is probably best understood as already being far removed from these thoughts. The "place of purity" in the Jerusalem temple reminds one much more of a late antique church, and the idea of purification is mainly related to the question of whether baptism with water can free one from sins. This text, which looks very much like a part of a Synoptic Gospel and which seems closely related to the narrative and discourse worlds of Israel's Scriptures, is thus probably much more distanced from them than a first view may suggest.

---

17. Bernard P. Grenfell and Arthur S. Hunt, "Fragment of an Uncanonical Gospel," in *The Oxyrhynchus Papyri*, vol. 5 (Oxford: Egypt Exploration Fund, 1908), 1–10. For an overview of later research on the fragment, see Michael J. Kruger, *The Gospel of the Savior: An Analysis of P.Oxy. 840 and Its Place in the Gospel Traditions of Early Christianity*, TENTS 1 (Leiden: Brill, 2005), 1–13.

18. Buchinger and Hernitscheck, "P.Oxy. 840 and the Rites of Christian Initiation: Dating a Piece of Alleged Anti-sacramentalistic Polemics," *EC* 5, no. 1 (2014): 117–24; following Bovon, "Fragment Oxyrhynchus 840, Fragment of a Lost Gospel, Witness of an Early Christian Controversy over Purity," *JBL* 119, no. 4 (2000): 705–28.

Fragments of So-Called Jewish-Christian Gospels: The Gospel of the Ebionites

Unfortunately, we do not have manuscript evidence of any of the so-called Jewish-Christian gospels, that is, the Gospel of the Hebrews, the Gospel of the Nazarenes, and the Gospel of the Ebionites, known from ancient Christian literature.[19] Instead, I will focus on one of these writings that can be more or less clearly distinguished from the others, the Gospel of the Ebionites, of which only a few quotations in Epiphanius of Salamis's *Panarion* are preserved. The sparse evidence we have about this writing makes any statement about its possible date of origin quite difficult. The time around the middle of the second century CE (perhaps even a bit later), however, may be at least a good guess.[20] If we follow Ps.-Hippolytus's *Elenchus*, the Ebionites lived "comfortably to Jewish customs, saying that they are justified according to the law, and saying that Jesus was justified by practicing the law" (*Haer.* 7.34.2).[21] That is why we can imagine that halakic questions must also have played a role in their gospel.[22] This is indeed the case in at least some of the fragments preserved by Epiphanius. A very illuminating passage can be found in fragment 3 (*Pan.* 30.13.4–5), where the text deals with John the Baptist. While the part about John's garments follows the parallels in Mark 1:6 and Matt 3:4 very closely, the text offers a slightly different statement about John's diet, which, according to the Gospel of the Ebionites, does not include locusts. Instead, we read: "And his food . . . was wild honey, the taste of which was manna, like a cake in oil" (καὶ τὸ βρῶμα αὐτοῦ . . . μέλι ἄγριον, οὗ ἡ γεῦσις ἡ τοῦ μάννα, ὡς ἐγκρὶς ἐν ἐλαίῳ). This passage can be understood as alluding verbally to both Num 11:8 and Exod 16:31 LXX. Like Israel in the desert, John receives heavenly food. At the same time, the text avoids the idea that John ate locusts. This has sometimes been seen as a matter of *kashrut* regarding the question of which kinds of locusts are allowed to be eaten and which are not,

---

19. I do not want to enter the debate about the question whether the ancient church knew of two or three of these gospels, but see Jörg Frey, "Die Fragmente judenchristlicher Evangelien," in *Antike christliche Apokryphen in deutscher Übersetzung*, vol. 1, *Evangelien und Verwandtes*, ed. Christoph Markschies and Jens Schröter, 7th ed. (Tübingen: Mohr Siebeck, 2012), 560–92.

20. Text, translations, and the numbering of the fragments follow Andrew F. Gregory, *The Gospel according to the Hebrews and the Gospel of the Ebionites*, Oxford Early Christian Gospel Texts (Oxford: Oxford University Press, 2017). On introductory questions, see Gregory's book and Jörg Frey, "Die Fragmente des Ebionäerevangeliums," in Markschies and Schröter, *Antike christliche Apokryphen in deutscher Übersetzung*, 1:607–16.

21. Translation by Albertus F. J. Klijn and Gerrit J. Reinink, *Patristic Evidence for Jewish-Christian Sects*, NovTSup 36 (Leiden: Brill, 1973), 112.

22. This may have been even more the case than in the Gospel of Matthew, but we cannot, of course, be completely certain.

but it may also and more simply mirror the Ebionites' own vegetarian lifestyle, a halakic rigidity that could perhaps be explained by the semipagan environment in which the Ebionites lived.[23] The fact that fragment 7 (*Pan.* 30.22.4–5) describes a Jesus who does not want to eat meat at Passover seems to be explicable along the same lines. But perhaps there is even an additional link to another saying preserved in fragment 6 (*Pan.* 30.16.5), according to which Jesus rejects all sacrifice (*Pan.* 30.16.5: "I came to abolish the sacrifices"), an idea without any clear parallel in the synoptic accounts but probably a radicalization of prophetic criticism of Israel's cult to be found in many parts of Israel's Scriptures.

Andrew Gregory writes: "Whether or not John's diet is to be considered vegetarian, there can be no doubt that these words of Jesus [in fragment 7] make clear his own rejection of meat of every kind, not just the Passover lamb. However, the fact that in the ancient Mediterranean world there was a strong link between meat and sacrifice, even if not all meat was sacrificed, makes it difficult not to associate Jesus's rejection of meat with his rejection of the Temple cult, especially in the light of his rejection of sacrifice in excerpt 6."[24] In other words, even if none of these fragments offers citations or verbal allusions to clearly identifiable passages of Israel's Scriptures, they participate in early Jewish and ancient Christian discourses on important scriptural topics, like kosher food and proper cult.

While the few remains of the Gospel of the Ebionites do not offer any example of a marked citation of Scripture, fragment 4 (*Pan.* 30.13.7) on John's baptism of Jesus makes the connection between the heavenly voice and Ps 2 more explicit than the synoptic parallels do (but see Luke 3:22; Justin, *Dial.* 88.8; and others). It appends the words ἐγὼ σήμερον γεγέννηκά σε ("Today I have begotten you"; see Ps 2:7). Of course, this is not an insignificant addition to the sentence "You are my son, the beloved one, in you I am well pleased" (see also the allusions to Ps 2:7; Isa 42:1; and possibly Gen 22:2), but it makes clear that the Ebionites understand Jesus as God's *adopted* son.

Other fragments show a special interest in Israel or figures of the history of Israel, even if, according to *Pan.* 30.14.3, the Gospel of the Ebionites had "removed the genealogies according to Matthew." This seems, however, not due to a disinterest in Jesus's background in Israel but has to do with the idea that only his life *after baptism* mattered (see also *Pan.* 30.13.6, according to which the Gospel of the Ebionites started with the appearance of John the Baptist). While fragment 2 (*Pan.* 30.13.6 and 30.14.3) stresses that John the Baptist "is said to be

---

23. For an overview of the Jewish discussion, see James A. Kelhoffer, *The Diet of John the Baptist: "Locusts and Wild Honey" in Synoptic and Patristic Interpretation*, WUNT 176 (Tübingen: Mohr Siebeck, 2005), 40–59.

24. Gregory, *Gospel according to the Hebrews*, 253–54.

out of the family of Aaron the priest," fragment 1 ("Jesus's call of the Twelve"; see *Pan.* 30.13.2–3) emphasizes that the apostles' mission is εἰς μαρτύριον τοῦ Ἰσραήλ ("as a witness of Israel"). This is probably a conceptual allusion to the idea that the Twelve in some way represent the original twelve tribes of Israel, a conception that can be found both in Scripture (like Exod 24:4; 28:21; 36:21; Josh 4:5; Ezek 47:13; and others) and in early Jewish writings (including New Testament texts like Acts 7:58). The closest parallel, however, may be found in Barn. 8:3, which explicitly calls the Twelve "a witness to the tribes—as there are twelve tribes of Israel."

Of course, we have only small bits and pieces of what seems to have been a full gospel, which used all synoptics as its sources (but seems not to have known or used John). But even now, a certain tendency seems to be recognizable: in its own description of a Jesus who is adopted as "Son of God" because of his proper Torah observance, the Gospel of the Ebionites seems to be interested in discourses and debates that have their roots in the Scriptures of Israel. At the same time, the use of Scripture is not only related to the interpretation of Torah for a proper ordering of one's life; Scripture is also understood as prophesying Jesus and what happened to him, an observation that can be made best in the baptism scene where the heavenly voice not only offers something of a mixed citation of Scripture but also finishes with Jesus's words to the Baptist: ἄφες, ὅτι οὕτως ἐστὶ πρέπον πληρωθῆναι πάντα ("Let things be, for in this way it is fitting *that all things be fulfilled*").

Infancy Gospels: The Protevangelium of James

The so-called Protevangelium of James may be one of the most successful Christian apocryphal writings of all. Its text is not only extant in around 150 manuscripts; it was also translated into Syriac, Georgian, Latin, Arabic, Coptic, and other languages and even formed the basis for other, later apocryphal writings, like the Gospel of Pseudo-Matthew.[25] At the same time, its focus on Mary and the idea that this focus corresponds to a certain "people's religion" may have been the reason why this writing has been far less studied than, for example, a text like the Gospel of Thomas and probably even the Gospel of Peter. The text is usually dated to the second half or, perhaps better, the end of the second century

---

25. On introductory questions and the Greek text, see, e.g., Gerhard Schneider, ed., *Evangelia Infantiae Apocrypha = Apocryphe Kindheitsevangelien*, FC 18 (Freiburg im Breisgau: Herder, 1995); the translation follows, or is adapted from, J. K. Elliott, *A Synopsis of the Apocryphal Nativity and Infancy Narratives*, NTTS 34 (Leiden: Brill, 2006).

CE. While many authors have considered the Protevangelium's provenance to be in Syria, Jan N. Bremmer has offered new arguments for a possible origin in Alexandria.[26] The question of the Protevangelium's use of Scripture can be answered only with the use of examples.

First and foremost, the Septuagint—or probably better, some form of the Old Greek version of the Scriptures—formed an important part of the author's literary universe. His collection of books must have contained even some of the lesser-known parts of the LXX, like Tobit, Judith, and even Susanna. His acquaintance with the LXX goes so far that he used typical LXX vocabulary and phraseology, something that we may also observe in the Gospel of Luke. Referring to the still valid results of Harm R. Smid's 1965 dissertation, Bremmer writes:

> Smid actually lists all the words that occur in Prot. Jas. and the Septuagint, which is only helpful to a certain degree, as he does not distinguish between words generally known and used in the Greek of the time and words specific to the Septuagint, such as ἁγίασμα (6:3, 8:2 etc.), ἁγιαστήριον (6:1), ἔντρομος (11:1), θυσιαστήριον (5:1), καταπέτασμα (10:1), πατριάρχης (1:3), ὕψωμα (6:2) and φονευτής (22:1) or nearly exclusive to the Septuagint at the time of composition, such as ἱλασμός (1:1). In addition, we have to notice phrases such as "As the Lord God lives" (4:2, 6:3 etc.), which occurs frequently in the Septuagint (Judg 8:19; Ruth 3:13, etc.). It is obvious from this list that the author knew a number of books of the Septuagint and regularly used typically Jewish words to describe his fictional Jewish world.[27]

At the same time, the Protevangelium's story does much to connect itself to figures and related stories found in Israel's Scriptures. Joachim's childlessness, for example, is compared to the situation of Abraham, who only in his old days became father of Isaac (Prot. Jas. 1:4; but see also Anna's prayer in 2:4, referring to Sarah; cf. Gen 18:1–15; 21:1–3). In this context we also read about an "angel of the Lord" (Prot. Jas. 7:1; see also 7:2) who prophesies that Anna will bear a child (by using words resembling Luke 1:13; Gen 16:11; Judg 13:3–7; and 1 Sam 1:20). When somewhat later the lot chooses Joseph as Mary's future husband, who, as an old man, hesitates to marry her, the high priest reminds Joseph of the fate of Dathan, Abiram, and Korah after they rejected God's will (Prot. Jas. 9:2; cf.

---

26. Bremmer, "Date and Provenance of the *Protevangelium of James*," in *The Protevangelium of James*, ed. Jan N. Bremmer et al., Studies on Early Christian Apocrypha 16 (Leuven: Peeters, 2020), 49–70.

27. Bremmer, "Date and Provenance," 52, referring to Harm R. Smid, "Protevangelium Jacobi" (PhD diss., Rijksuniversiteit te Groningen, 1965).

Num 16:31–33). When Joseph, finally, discovers Mary to be pregnant, he laments the situation: "Who has deceived me? Who has done this evil in my house and defiled the virgin? For as Adam was absent in the hour of prayer and the serpent came and found Eve alone and deceived her, so also has it happened to me" (Prot. Jas. 13:1; see not only Gen 3:13 but also early Jewish parallels like LAE 33:2 and Apoc. Mos. 7:2). After Jesus's birth, Salome calls herself "seed of Abraham, Isaac, and Jacob" (Prot. Jas. 20:2, but not in the short reading of P.Bodm. V).

In addition to that, the Protevangelium of James is full of conceptual allusions to important topics of Israel's Scriptures. The motif of the "great day of the Lord" (mentioned in Prot. Jas. 1:2; 2:2) may be very unspecific, but it probably relates vaguely to the celebration of the Day of Atonement (Yom Kippur). Several passages show a clear interest in questions of ritual, menstrual, and sexual purity.[28] Mary, for example, does not grow up like other children. Instead, Anna prepares a "sanctuary in her bedroom and did not permit anything common or unclean to pass through it" (Prot. Jas. 6:1; see also 6:2–3). At the age of three, Mary is given as a temple virgin to the "temple of the Lord" (Prot. Jas. 7), but when she is twelve, the priests consider the problem of her possible menstrual impurity. Throughout the story, Mary is developed into a kind of pure dwelling place of God's son to be born from her. Lily Vuong goes so far to describe her as "a symbolic Temple replacement" and "a sacred Temple suitable for the Son of God."[29] This does not come by accident. Instead, a whole subplot is concerned with the "temple of the Lord" (Prot. Jas. 6:1; 7:1–2; and others), which is first understood as a place of sacrifice for justification (Prot. Jas. 5:1), the place where the pure child Mary grows up until she is twelve (Prot. Jas. 6–8), and with which she remains in contact even afterwards (Prot. Jas. 10:1).[30] Even later, important decisions take place at or in relation to the temple (Prot. Jas. 15:2; 16:1–2), which, however, fades somewhat out of the focus of the story. Quite surprisingly, however, after the stories of Jesus's birth, the adoration of the magi and the slaying of the infants, the Protevangelium closes with an event in the temple. The priest Zechariah, the father of John the Baptist (Prot. Jas. 23:3), is murdered; his blood turns into stone (Prot. Jas. 24:1) and remains and defiles the temple forever (see Prot. Jas. 24:2). If we understand the Protevangelium of James as being concerned with the important scriptural topic of God's proper dwelling place on earth, one can understand

---

28. For an overall overview, see Lily C. Vuong, *Gender and Purity in the Protevangelium of James*, WUNT 2/358 (Tübingen: Mohr Siebeck, 2013), 60–192.

29. Both quotations from Vuong, *Gender and Purity*, 191.

30. See also Tobias Nicklas, "Israel, der Tempel und der theologische Ort des Protevangeliums Jacobi," in Bremmer, *Protevangelium of James*, 133–58.

this storyline as a statement regarding an important scriptural topic. It tries to show that the temple in Jerusalem had fulfilled its function throughout Israel's history but had lost it with the birth of Jesus, the savior of Israel, and the (almost simultaneous) murder of Zechariah.

As already mentioned, the Protevangelium of James not only imitates the language of the Septuagint but is full of both verbal and conceptual allusions to the Scriptures of Israel (see, e.g., Prot. Jas. 1:4 // Exod 24:18; 34:28; 1 Kgs 19:8; Prot. Jas. 2:3 // 1 Sam 1:6; Prot. Jas. 4:4 // Isa 54:1; Prot. Jas. 9:3 // 2 Sam 6:14; Prot. Jas. 14:1 // Deut 22:22–27; and many others). Besides that, Anna's prayers (Prot. Jas. 3 and 6:3) remind one of the Psalms (even if they do not only use typical biblical imagery). At the same time, one does not find clearly marked (or even unmarked) citations in this text. This goes along with the observation that the Protevangelium omits some of the important fulfillment quotations found in the Gospel of Matthew's infancy narrative, certainly a *Vorlage* of the Protevangelium.[31] While the text seems to be very interested in Matt 1:21, which expresses the idea that Jesus will save his people from their sins, it does not take over Matt 1:23 with the fulfillment quotation of Isa 7:14 LXX. While this alone could be pure accident, it becomes even more striking when we look into the text's story about the magi. According to Matt 2:6, the high priests and scribes respond to Herod that the Messiah is born "in Bethlehem of Judea, as this is written by the prophet," after which a marked citation of Micah 5:2 mixed with 2 Sam 5:2 follows. The Protevangelium only has the words "in Bethlehem of Judea, for thus it is written" (Prot. Jas. 21:2). This is even more interesting, as the parallel scene in the later Ps.-Matt 16:1 (which certainly uses the Protoevangelium of James as its *Vorlage*) *inserts* this quote again. The same can be said about the Matthean quotation related to Herod's slaying of the infants (Matt 2:18; but see Prot. Jas. 22:1). One can only speculate about the reasons.[32]

All this makes the Protevangelium a story that "sounds" scriptural in many ways. Its use of language tries to imitate the Septuagint. Its story is placed in a world that sounds very biblical: the text mentions figures from the Scriptures, uses scriptural motifs, and is concerned with important scriptural topics. While it does not offer marked citations, it not only alludes to scriptural passages and concepts but develops a storyline interested in the scriptural question of God's

---

31. On the Protevangelium's relation to the New Testament gospels, see Jens Schröter, "Fortschreibung und Adaption früher Traditionen über die Geburt Jesu im *Protevangelium Jacobi*," in Bremmer, *Protevangelium of James*, 71–95.

32. The Protevangelium does not mention the holy family's flight to Egypt (Matt 2:15, but see Prot. Jas. 22:2).

proper dwelling place in this world. While the temple loses this role during the narrative, Mary develops into a kind of pure temple, wherein the Son of God who will be the savior of Israel can dwell and, finally, be born.

Conclusion

This overview of a few extracanonical gospels is, of course, somewhat distorted. I did not discuss some of the most prominent examples of early Christian gospels, like the Gospel of Thomas or the Gospel of Mary. The reason for this is that neither of these writings offers any quotations of Israel's Scriptures or shows clear verbal allusions.[33] Moreover, only a very few passages could be discussed that allude to concepts that are first and foremost related to the Scriptures of Israel. Together with these two writings, the examples introduced above show a broad range of early approaches to Scripture.

1. In several instances we have recognized that the creative development of stories and/or motifs via a narrative interpretation of Scriptural passages did not stop with the production of the New Testament gospels. Examples of newly developed motifs could, for example, be discovered in the Gospel of Peter and the Unknown Gospel on Papyrus Egerton 2, which, perhaps, even developed a completely new Jesus miracle story out of Elisha traditions. At the same time, we find examples of motifs that were originally developed from Scripture, or at least connected to it in New Testament writings, the scriptural background of which, however, became less clear during the tradition (see, e.g., the idea that Jesus's legs were not broken in the Gospels of John and Peter).
2. As in the canonical gospels, many passages in apocryphal writings presuppose concepts from Scripture and are interested in matters of halakah. We can observe this, for example, in the Unknown Gospel on Papyrus Egerton and P.Oxy. 840, while the Gospel of the Ebionites perhaps even mirrors aspects of the Ebionites' strange food halakah, and the Protevangelium of James is interested in matters of Mary's (sexual) purity.
3. As we have seen, the degrees of scriptural influence in different apocryphal gospels varies. The Protevangelium of James is perhaps the gospel that goes furthest: like the Gospel of Luke, it uses a language influenced by the Septuagint, and perhaps even more than all canonical writings it creates something

---

33. See, e.g., the indexes of major commentaries on these books like Simon J. Gathercole, *The Gospel of Thomas: Introduction and Commentary*, TENTS 11 (Leiden: Brill, 2014); and Christopher M. Tuckett, *The Gospel of Mary*, Oxford Early Christian Gospel Texts (Oxford: Oxford University Press, 2007).

like a "biblical story world," wherein biblical characters, motifs, places, and the rest play a role, even though the text does not offer a single marked quotation from Scripture.

4. Of course, we also discover quotations from Scripture. The most interesting passage perhaps is a quotation of Isa 29:3 in the mouth of Jesus in Papyrus Egerton 2. The fact that the same passage is also quoted in the canonical gospels, but in a quite different context, may show us that certain scriptural quotations were prominent enough among early Christians that they could wander between different narratives.

Bibliography

Bovon, François. "Fragment Oxyrhynchus 840, Fragment of a Lost Gospel, Witness of an Early Christian Controversy over Purity." *JBL* 119, no. 4 (2000): 705–28.

Bremmer, Jan N. "Date and Provenance of the *Protevangelium of James*." Pages 49–70 in *The Protevangelium of James*. Edited by Jan N. Bremmer, J. Andrew Doole, Thomas R. Karmann, Tobias Nicklas, and Boris Repschinski. Studies on Early Christian Apocrypha 16. Leuven: Peeters, 2020.

Buchinger, Harald, and Elisabeth Hernitscheck. "P.Oxy. 840 and the Rites of Christian Initiation: Dating a Piece of Alleged Anti-sacramentalistic Polemics." *EC* 5, no. 1 (2014): 117–24.

Chapa, Juan. "5072." Pages 1–19 in *The Oxyrhynchus Papyri: Volume LXXVI (No. 5072–5100)*. Edited by Juan Chapa and Daniela Colomo. Graeco-Roman Memoirs 97. London: Egypt Exploration Society, 2011.

Elliott, J. K. *A Synopsis of the Apocryphal Nativity and Infancy Narratives*. NTTS 34. Leiden: Brill, 2006.

Frey, Jörg. "Die Fragmente des Ebionäerevangeliums." Pages 607–20 in *Antike christliche Apokryphen in deutscher Übersetzung*. Vol. 1, *Evangelien und Verwandtes*. Edited by Christoph Markschies and Jens Schröter. 7th ed. Tübingen: Mohr Siebeck, 2012.

———. "Die Fragmente judenchristlicher Evangelien." Pages 560–92 in *Antike christliche Apokryphen in deutscher Übersetzung*. Vol. 1, *Evangelien und Verwandtes*. Edited by Christoph Markschies and Jens Schröter. 7th ed. Tübingen: Mohr Siebeck, 2012.

Gathercole, Simon J. *The Gospel of Thomas: Introduction and Commentary*. TENTS 11. Leiden: Brill, 2014.

Gregory, Andrew F. *The Gospel according to the Hebrews and the Gospel of the Ebionites*. Oxford Early Christian Gospel Texts. Oxford: Oxford University Press, 2017.

Grenfell, Bernard P., and Arthur S. Hunt. "Fragment of an Uncanonical Gospel."

Pages 1–10 in *The Oxyrhynchus Papyri*. Vol. 5. Oxford: Egypt Exploration Fund, 1908.

Hieke, Thomas. "Das Petrusevangelium vom Alten Testament her gelesen: Gewinnbringende Lektüre eines nicht-kanonischen Textes vom christlichen Kanon her." Pages 91–116 in *Das Evangelium nach Petrus: Text, Kontexte, Intertexte*. Edited by Thomas J. Kraus and Tobias Nicklas. TUGAL 158. Berlin: de Gruyter, 2007.

Kasser, Rodolphe, and Gregor Wurst, eds. *The Gospel of Judas Together with the Letter of Peter to Philip, James and a Book of Allogenes from Codex Tchacos: Critical Edition*. Washington, DC: National Geographic, 2007.

Kelhoffer, James A. *The Diet of John the Baptist: "Locusts and Wild Honey" in Synoptic and Patristic Interpretation*. WUNT 176. Tübingen: Mohr Siebeck, 2005.

Klijn, Albertus F. J., and Gerrit J. Reinink. *Patristic Evidence for Jewish-Christian Sects*. NovTSup 36. Leiden: Brill, 1973.

Kraus, Thomas J., Michael J. Kruger, and Tobias Nicklas. *Gospel Fragments*. Oxford Early Christian Gospel Texts. Oxford: Oxford University Press, 2009.

Kruger, Michael J. *The Gospel of the Savior: An Analysis of P.Oxy. 840 and Its Place in the Gospel Traditions of Early Christianity*. TENTS 1. Leiden: Brill, 2005.

Létourneau, Pierre. "Creation in Gnostic Christian Texts, or: What Happens to the Cosmos When Its Maker Is Not the Highest God." Pages 415–34 in *Theologies of Creation in Early Judaism and Ancient Christianity: In Honour of Hans Klein*. Edited by Tobias Nicklas and Korinna Zamfir. DCLS 6. Berlin: de Gruyter, 2010.

Meiser, Martin. "Das Petrusevangelium und die spätere großkirchliche Literatur." Pages 183–96 in *Das Evangelium nach Petrus: Text, Kontexte, Intertexte*. Edited by Thomas J. Kraus and Tobias Nicklas. TUGAL 158. Berlin: de Gruyter, 2007.

Nicklas, Tobias. "Das unbekannte Evangelium auf P.Egerton 2 und die Schrift." *SNTSU* 33 (2008): 41–65.

———. "Die Gottverlassenheit des Gottessohns: Funktionen von Psalm 22/21 LXX in frühchristlichen Auseinandersetzungen mit der Passion Jesu." Pages 395–415 in *Aneignung durch Transformation: Beiträge zur Analyse von Überlieferungsprozessen im frühen Christentum; Festschrift für Michael Theobald*. Edited by Wilfried Eisele, Christoph Schäfer, and Hans-Ulrich Weidemann. HBS 74. Freiburg im Breisgau: Herder, 2013.

———. "Frühchristliche Ansprüche auf die Schriften Israels." Pages 347–68 in *Scriptural Authority in Early Judaism and Ancient Christianity*. Edited by Geza G. Xeravits, Tobias Nicklas, and Isaac Kalimi. DCLS 16. Berlin: de Gruyter, 2013.

———. "The Influence of Jewish Scriptures on Early Christian Apocrypha." Pages 141–52 in *The Oxford Handbook of Early Christian Apocrypha*. Edited by Andrew Gregory, Christopher Tuckett, Tobias Nicklas, and Joseph Verheyden. Oxford: Oxford University Press, 2015.

———. "Israel, der Tempel und der theologische Ort des Protevangeliums Jacobi." Pages 133–58 in *The Protevangelium of James*. Edited by Jan N. Bremmer, J. Andrew Doole, Thomas R. Karmann, Tobias Nicklas, and Boris Repschinski. Studies on Early Christian Apocrypha 16. Leuven: Peeters, 2020.

———. *Jews and Christians? Second Century "Christian" Perspectives on the "Parting of the Ways" (Annual Deichmann Lectures 2013)*. Tübingen: Mohr Siebeck, 2014.

———. "The 'Unknown Gospel' on *Papyrus Egerton 2*." Pages 9–120 in *Gospel Fragments*. Edited by Thomas J. Kraus, Michael J. Kruger, and Tobias Nicklas. Oxford Early Christian Gospel Texts. Oxford: Oxford University Press, 2009.

Schneider, Gerhard, ed. *Evangelia Infantiae Apocrypha = Apocryphe Kindheitsevangelien*. FC 18. Freiburg im Breisgau: Herder, 1995.

Schröter, Jens. "Fortschreibung und Adaption früher Traditionen über die Geburt Jesu im *Protevangelium Jacobi*." Pages 71–95 in *The Protevangelium of James*. Edited by Jan N. Bremmer, J. Andrew Doole, Thomas R. Karmann, Tobias Nicklas, and Baris Repschinski. Studies on Early Christian Apocrypha 16. Leuven: Peeters, 2020.

Smid, Harm R. "Protevangelium Jacobi." PhD diss., Rijksuniversiteit te Groningen, 1965.

Smith, Daniel A. "Marcion's Gospel and the Synoptics: Proposals and Problems." Pages 129–74 in *Gospels and Gospel Traditions in the Second Century: Experiments in Reception*. Edited by Jens Schröter, Tobias Nicklas, and Joseph Verheyden. BZNW 235. Berlin: de Gruyter, 2019.

Suciu, Alin. *The Berlin-Strasbourg Apocryphon: A Coptic Apostolic Memoir*. WUNT 370. Tübingen: Mohr Siebeck, 2017.

Toepel, Alexander. *Das Protevangelium des Jakobus: Ein Beitrag zur neueren Diskussion um Herkunft, Auslegung und theologische Einordnung*. FTS 71. Münster: Aschendorff, 2014.

Tuckett, Christopher M. *The Gospel of Mary*. Oxford Early Christian Gospel Texts. Oxford: Oxford University Press, 2007.

———. "Principles of Gnostic Exegesis." Pages 277–310 in *Gospels and Gospel Traditions in the Second Century: Experiments in Reception*. Edited by Jens Schröter, Tobias Nicklas, and Joseph Verheyden. BZNW 235. Berlin: de Gruyter, 2019.

Vuong, Lily C. *Gender and Purity in the Protevangelium of James*. WUNT 2/358. Tübingen: Mohr Siebeck, 2013.

Zelyck, Lorne R. *The Egerton Gospel (Egerton Papyrus 2 + Papyrus Köln VI 255): Introduction, Critical Edition, and Commentary*. TENTS 13. Leiden: Brill, 2019.

39

Israel's Scriptures in the Apocryphal Apocalypses

MICHAEL KARL-HEINZ SOMMER

Asking about Scripture in apocryphal apocalypses confronts researchers with a variety of problems. One has to cope with an almost unmanageable range of methodological controversies and a multifaceted culture of discussion. The research landscape on ancient apocalypses is currently changing, which makes the attempt at analyzing the use of Scripture in apocryphal apocalypses difficult. On the one hand, at the moment it is very hard to tell which texts count as apocalypses and which do not. Controversies about the definition of the genre have raised doubts that "apocalypticism" as a literary genre can be defined precisely. Researchers doubt that categories such as "apocalypse" and "prophecy," which have been clearly distinguished since the middle of the nineteenth century, existed separately from each other in antiquity.[1] On the other hand, it is nearly impossible to conclude how "apocryphal" apocalypses read and interpret Scriptures because the theological and literary characteristics of these texts differ enormously from each other. The project "Ancient Christian Apocrypha in German Translation" (ACA) by Christoph Markschies and Jens Schröter repeatedly emphasized that it is hardly possible to speak of a closed "canon" of "apocryphal apocalypses."[2] Markschies made it clear that a large number of sources is still not edited and

---

1. See Jörg Frey, "Die Apokalyptik als Herausforderung der neutestamentlichen Wissenschaft: Zum Problem; Jesus und die Apokalyptik," in *Apokalyptik als Herausforderung neutestamentlicher Theologie*, ed. Michael Becker and Markus Öhler, WUNT 2/214 (Tübingen: Mohr Siebeck, 2006), 23–94. See also Frey, "Editorial: Apokalyptik und das Neue Testament," *EC* 4, no. 1 (2013): 1–6.

2. Christoph Markschies, Jens Schröter, and Andreas Heiser, eds., *Antike christliche Apokry-*

translated.³ Further, the textual history of many apocryphal apocalypses is very complex. Although many of them were read and copied widely at the end of late antiquity and during the Middle Ages, the text forms differ substantially. Because they never reached canonical status, translators and scribes could copy them with great freedom. In short, apocryphal apocalypses are "living texts."[4]

"Apocryphal apocalypses" should therefore not be used as an umbrella term; at least, one should avoid describing collectively a closed library of source material so as not to commit the fallacy of suggesting that research has already given a complete overview of ancient apocalypses and has come to a viable generic definition.

In addition, handbook categories about the provenience of apocalyptic literature have changed radically in recent decades. Key terms like "crisis phenomenon," "marginalized literature," or "political counter-transcripts" have been heavily criticized in recent years.[5] Researchers assigned apocalyptic literature a very important role in the narrative of early Christianity. It was pointed out that these texts cannot be detached from other ancient Christian discourses. Researchers meanwhile no longer treat apocalypses as marginal texts that were read only by "Christian" minorities or "religious" outsiders. Rather, their research contributes to the understanding of early Judaism and ancient Christianity across the board.[6] Of course, new theses about the political, social, and theological significance of apocalyptic literature and its sociocultural location within early Christianity also concern ideas about how they read Israel's Scriptures.

Instead of systematizing lines of how apocryphal apocalypses interpret Scriptures, I read a selection of texts and assess them as theologically independent sources that have grown and developed readings of Scripture in the broader context of the Greco-Roman society at large. In my opinion, it also does not make sense to separate apocalypses from the rest of early Christian discourses about Israel's Scriptures because at least some of them have parallels with ideas that can be found in the apostolic fathers and the early Christian apologists.[7]

---

phen in deutscher Übersetzung, vol. 1, *Evangelien und Verwandtes*, 7th ed. (Tübingen: Mohr Siebeck, 2012). The project of Markschies and Schröter will continue the ACA.

3. Christoph Markschies, "Editorial," *ZAC* 20 (2016): 1–20.

4. This means that often their form and content changed when they were handed down. The reception history of the texts had influence on their content.

5. Frey, "Editorial," 2–3.

6. See Frey, "Die Apokalyptik," 92–94.

7. Especially when one compares early Christianity as a kind of "scene," in an exchange of ideas between loosely, openly organized groups, it becomes clear that apocalypses are not marginalized phenomena, but have been firmly networked with the discourse universe of early Christianity.

I especially draw attention to five texts: 5 Ezra, the Greek/Ethiopian Apocalypse of Peter, the Apocalypse of Zephaniah, the Ascension of Isaiah, and the Apocalypse of Paul. All of these texts come from different times and cultures; they spread different ideas, ethics, and theologies, some of which are related to each other, but some are completely disparate. My primary concern is not to find connecting and separating elements in these texts but to show how apocalyptic literature can be located in the broad horizon of early Christianity in the social context of the Mediterranean world.

Fifth Ezra and the Use of Scripture by the Apostolic Fathers and Early Christian Apologists

Fifth Ezra is a short apocalypse that survives in two recensions in Latin manuscripts of the Bible.[8] The story of the text portrays God's rejection and replacement of Israel by the followers of Christ. Thus, in some of the manuscripts, 5 Ezra is placed directly before 4 Ezra in order to provide a "Christian" reading of this text. The origins of 5 Ezra are unclear, but there are good reasons to date 5 Ezra back to the second century CE. One of the most important arguments for that is that 5 Ezra reads the Scriptures in the same way as many church fathers. Fifth Ezra clearly demonstrates that the development of Christian understandings of Scripture in apocalyptic narratives did not take place without any connections to other Christian discourses.

The Use of Prophetic Cult Criticism in the Early Church and in Fifth Ezra

From a purely technical point of view, the use of Scriptures in this text is comparable to the Revelation of John. Both texts seem to live out of the writings of Israel without directly quoting Israel's Scriptures. However, in contrast to Revelation, 5 Ezra shows parallels to Christian writers of the second century, trying to establish borderlines between Christian and Jewish identity.[9] Although 5 Ezra differs literarily from the Epistle of Barnabas and Justin Martyr, it shares many ideas with them. Fifth Ezra takes up the writings of Israel (in particular, 1 Baruch; Isa 1; Jer 7; and Zech 7–8, as well as the great narrative of Exodus)

---

8. The French recension is from the ninth, and the handwritings of the Spanish recension stem from the eleventh and twelfth centuries.

9. See Hugo Duensing and Aurelio de Santos Otero, "Das fünfte und sechste Buch Esra," in *Neutestamentliche Apokryphen in deutscher Übersetzung*, vol. 2, *Apostolisches Apokalypsen und Verwandtes*, ed. Wilhelm Schneemelcher, 6th ed. (Tübingen: Mohr Siebeck, 1997), 581.

and rewrites these texts in such a way that they support a kind of substitution theology.[10] Therefore, 5 Ezra even uses similar word clusters from the prophets as Justin Martyr, Irenaeus of Lyon, and Clement of Alexandria. Since the 1960s, works on the sources of the Epistle of Barnabas (Robert A. Kraft, Pierre Prigent, James Carlton Paget, and James N. Rhodes) and on the use of Scripture by Justin Martyr (above all, Oskar Skarsaune and Charles Munier) have noted that Barnabas, Justin, Irenaeus, and Clement of Alexandria received a similar cluster of prophetic texts.[11] These scholars commented that the early Christian authors directly quote verbal phrases from Isa 1; 58; Jer 6–7; Zech 7–8; and Ps 50. They play with these texts in discourses about God's rejection of Israel. If we look a little closer, we also find traces of these intertexts in the *Apologia* of Aristides (*Apol.* 14–15; Ignatius of Antioch, *Smyrn.* 7.2; Tertullian, *Marc.* 2.18–19), and perhaps even in the Shepherd of Hermas (Herm. Mand. 8). Also in the third and fourth centuries, traces of Isa 1; Jer 7; and Zech 7–8 are encountered on a regular basis (e.g., in Cyprian, *Eleem.* 4; and Ps.-Gregorius, *Test.* 12; somewhat further in the Apos. Con. 2.17).

Reminiscences of these text clusters were very prominent in texts that wanted to prove that Christian ethics have their origins in Israel's Scriptures; that God introduced Christian sacraments like baptism, the Eucharist, and confession in the history of Israel; and that the prophets announced the Christ event. At the same time, authors read these texts in such a way that they appear as if God would deny and discard specific Jewish worldviews. These texts served as proof texts in discourses against Jewish identities as well as in discussions against dualistic theologies, Valentinians or Marcionites, and against lines of Roman-Hellenistic philosophy.

Fifth Ezra belongs to all these texts because it reads Jer 7; and Isa 1; 58 in a similar manner to Barnabas, Justin, and Irenaeus.[12] As Veronika Hirschberger has

---

10. See Michael Wolter, *5. Esra-Buch, 6. Esra-Buch*, JSHRZ 3.7 (Gütersloh: Gütersloher Verlagshaus, 2001), 790–93.

11. Robert A. Kraft, "The Epistle of Barnabas: Its Quotations and Their Sources" (PhD diss., Harvard University, 1961), 95; Pierre Prigent, *Les Testimonia dans le Christianisme primitif: L'Épitre de Barnabé I–XVI et ses sources*, EBib (Paris: Gabalda, 1961), 29; James Carlton Paget, *The Epistle of Barnabas: Outlook and Background*, WUNT 2/64 (Tübingen: Mohr Siebeck, 1994), 104 n.13; James M. Rhodes, *The Epistle of Barnabas and the Deuteronomic Tradition: Polemics, Paraenesis, and Legacy of the Golden-Calf Incident*, WUNT 2/188 (Tübingen: Mohr Siebeck, 2004), 42 n. 25; Oskar Skarsaune, *The Proof from Prophecy: A Study in Justin Martyr's Proof-Text Tradition; Text-Type, Provenance, Theological Profile*, NovTSup 56 (Leiden: Brill, 1987), 296; Charles Munier, *L'Aplogie de Saint Justin Philosophe et Martyr*, Paradosis 38 (Fribourg: Editions Universitaires, 1994), 78.

12. Against Veronika Hirschberger, *Ringen um Israel: Intertextuelle Perspektiven auf das 5. Buch Esra*, SECA 14 (Leuven: Peeters, 2018).

shown, Jer 7 is one of the most important intertexts for understanding 5 Ezra. The author of 5 Ezra used Jer 7 as a kind of role model to structure his own literary outline. Thus, traces of Jer 7 appear in 5 Ezra 1 as well as in 5 Ezra 2. Like the Epistle of Barnabas, Justin, Irenaeus of Lyon, Clement of Alexandria, and Tertullian, 5 Ezra only uses excerpts from Jer 7 that create a negative image of the biblical Israel. In Jer 7:22–23, God criticizes Israel's cult practice. He claims that Israel offered him burnt and slaughtered victims in the desert although he did not enact any cult laws on the day he led Israel out of Egypt. In the next verse (Jer 7:23), God commands keeping the covenant and the commandments. Jeremiah 7:22–23 simply follows the great narrative of the Torah. Indeed, according to the storyline of Exodus, God did not reveal the cult law to Israel on the day of the exodus itself. Only as Israel reached Mount Sinai did God reveal a legal framework for his people, consisting of social as well as cultic laws. Jeremiah 7:22–23 thus recalls that the sacrificial law as a whole is part of the larger framework of the covenant. Sacrifices are only valid if Israel follows the values and norms of the entire Torah.

Fifth Ezra interprets Jer 7 differently. The text takes out single phrases of Jer 7:22–23 and puts them together with a different meaning. Fifth Ezra 1:31 (Spanish rec.) leaves out the phrase "in the day that I brought them out of the land of Egypt" from Jer 7:22. Thus, 5 Ezra portrays God as if he did not reveal the cult law to Israel (*non mandavi vobis*, "I have not given you a commandment").[13] At the same time, 5 Ezra 1:31 changes the content of Jer 7:22 in order to create very broad borderlines against Jewish forms of worshiping. Whereas God criticizes only burnt offerings and sacrifices in Jer 7:22, the God of 5 Ezra rejects several cultic identity markers representing an ideal biblical Israel (sacrifice, festival calendar, Rosh Khodesh, Sabbath, and circumcision).

Fifth Ezra 1 reads Jer 7 as if God had not enacted the cult law. From this perspective, Israel's cult appears as if Israel did not understand God's revelation correctly. According to 5 Ezra 1:31, Israel's cult practices demonstrate that Israel disregarded God's commandments.

In this regard, 5 Ezra goes a little further than Barnabas, Justin, Irenaeus, and Clement. They all quote Jer 7 to relativize the cult law and to criticize a portrayal of a biblical Israel. However, none of them goes as far as to let God say that he never commanded the cult.

The Use of Prophetic Texts as a Lens for the Torah

Fifth Ezra uses Jer 7 as a key to read the Torah in such a way that it simply appears as an ethical guideline without any commandments about Jewish cult

---

13. Unless otherwise noted, all translations are by the author.

practices. Hirschberger convincingly emphasizes that God's commandments are fundamentally important for 5 Ezra (5 Ezra 1:7, 8, 24, 34; 2:1, 33, 44) but only in an ethical sense: "Die Gebote sind für 5 Esra von zentraler Bedeutung.... Sie werden in 5 Esra 1,7.8.24.34; 2,1.33.40 in verschiedenen Begrifflichkeiten genannt und auf das Übernehmen sozialer Verantwortung hin gedeutet (2:20–23)."[14]

Barnabas, Justin, Clement, and Irenaeus regularly quote Isa 1; 58; and Zech 7–8 in order to prove that social laws replace the cult law of the Torah. Thus, it is not surprising that these texts also appear in 5 Ezra. Allusions to those texts appear when 5 Ezra outlines his understanding of God's commandments in greater detail (5 Ezra 2:20–23). Many researchers have noted that 5 Ezra 2 receives cult-critical prophetical texts to describe how God's commandments look.[15] Fifth Ezra 1–2 not only refers to Isa 1; Jer 7; and Zech 7–8 in order to diminish the role of the cult laws of the Torah; these texts also serve as a template for 5 Ezra to define God's commandments as a collection of exclusively ethical laws.

Table 39.1. The List of God's Commandments in 5 Ezra 2:20–23

The list of God's commandments in 5 Ezra 2:20–23 (CMNEVL)			Parallels in the Scriptures
2:20ab	Justification of widows and orphans	*Viduam iustificate; pupillum iudica*	Isa 1:17, 23; Jer 5:28 LXX; Sir 35:14–15; Isa 10:2; Jer 7:6; Ezek 22:7; Zech 7:9–10; Mal 3:5
2:20c	Care for the needy	*egentibus subministra*	Tob 1:17
2:20d	Protection of the orphan	*Orfanum tuere*	Isa 1:17, 23; 10:2; Jer 5:28; 7:6; Ezek 22:7; Zech 7:9–10; Mal 3:5
2:20e	Clothing of the naked	*nudum vesti*	Isa 58:6; Tob 1:17
2:21a	Care for the broken and the weak	*Confractum ac debilem cura*	Isa 1:17
2:21bc	Protection of the lame	*claudum inridere noli, sed tutare*	

---

14. Hirschberger, *Israel*, 83 [ET: "The commandments are central to 5 Ezra.... They are in 5 Ezra 1:7, 8, 24, 34; 2:1, 33, 40 in various terms and referred to assuming social responsibility (2:20–23)"].

15. Duensing and Santos Otero, "Esra," 585 n. 11; Wolter, *5. Esra*, 812; Hirschberger, *Israel*, 63–64.

2:21d	Helping the blind to see the clarity of God	Luscum ad visionem claritatis meae admitte	Isa 58:8
2:22a	Care for the old and the young	Senem et iuvenem intra muros tuoscollige	
2:22b	Protection of children	Infantes tuos custodi	
2:22c	Care for slaves and manumitted slaves	Servi et liberitui laetentur	Isa 58:6
2:23a	Burying the dead	Mortuostuosuti invenero suscitabo	Tob 1:17

Fifth Ezra not only uses the Scriptures to create borderlines between Jews and Christians or to declare the cult law of the Torah invalid; it also uses especially the Prophets to express an idea of Christian ethics.

The Greek/Ethiopian Apocalypse of Peter

The Greek/Ethiopian Apocalypse of Peter is one of the earliest Christian tours of hell. Whereas the Greek Akhmim-Codex (Papyrus Cairensis 10759) witnesses only the tour of hell, the longer Ethiopian version of the apocalypse puts the vision of hell into a narrative framework. Jesus gives his disciples a revelation of the coming of God's great day where God is going to punish all evildoers in hell. The origin and date of the text are debated, although one can see a trend among scholars to read the apocalypse as a text from Egypt that was written in the first quarter of the second century.

The Use of Scripture in the Greek/Ethiopian Apocalypse of Peter

As in 5 Ezra, the use of Scripture in the Greek/Ethiopian Apocalypse of Peter cannot be studied in isolation from the broader context of early Christian discourses about Scriptures.[16] Nevertheless, both texts differ in many ways. Tobias

---

16. See Richard Bauckham, *The Fate of the Dead: Studies on Jewish and Christian Apoc-*

Nicklas pointed out the Jewish character of the Apocalypse of Peter in several studies.[17] Both the theology and the eschatology of the text are based on the prophetic writings of Israel.[18] In addition, the text also includes gospel traditions related to Matthew. The Christology of the text itself is not very pronounced compared to the strong monotheistic image of God. Christ himself is clearly subordinate to God. The Apocalypse of Peter highlights that the God of Israel is the creator of the world who also has the power to destroy his creation. He will judge his creation at the end of time. Apocalypse of Peter 1–6 uses the language of the creation texts of Genesis and the Psalms as well as the day of the Lord traditions of the writings of Israel (Isa 1:13; Amos 5; Mal 3; Zeph 1; Zech 14) to construct these ideas. Further, the Apocalypse of Peter employs freely parts of Ezek 37:1–14 to portray the resurrection of the dead on the last day. Although Israel's writings influenced the text's depiction of God and concept of history, interpreters have not yet analyzed the Jewish roots of the apocalypse's ethics. In my view, Nicklas's observation that "questions of proper Torah observance do not play any role in this text" is correct.[19] He is certainly right that the Apocalypse of Peter shows no interest in the cultic law of the Torah. Indeed, the Apocalypse of Peter does not deal with Jewish identity markers or with the cult. However, I believe that the text has a different understanding of the Torah. In my view, the Apocalypse of Peter values the Torah as a collection of ethical commandments

---

alypses, NovTSup 93 (Leiden: Brill 1998), 160–258; Enrico Norelli, "Situation des apocryphes pétriniens," *Apocrypha* 2 (1991): 34–62; Norelli, "Pertinence théologique et canonicité: Les premières apocalypses chrétiennes," *Apocrypha* 8 (1997): 157–58; Jan N. Bremmer, "The Apocalypse of Peter: Greek or Jewish?," in *The Apocalypse of Peter*, ed. Jan N. Bremmer and Istvan Czachesz, SECA 7 (Leuven: Peeters, 2003), 1–14; Bremmer, "Orphic, Roman, Jewish and Christian Tours of Hell: Observations on the Apocalypse of Peter," in *Other Worlds and Their Relation to This World: Early Jewish and Ancient Christian Traditions*, ed. Tobias Nicklas et al., JSJSup 143 (Leiden: Brill, 2010), 305–21; Tobias Nicklas, "Resurrection – Judgment – Punishment: Apocalypse of Peter 4," in *Resurrection from the Dead: Biblical Traditions in Dialogue; Resurrection des mortis; Traditions bibliques en dialogue*, ed. Geert van Oyen and Tom Shepherd, BETL 249 (Leuven: Peeters 2012), 461–74; Nicklas, "'Insider' und 'Outsider': Überlegungen zum historischen Kontext der Darstellung 'jenseitiger Orte' in der Offenbarung des Petrus," in *Topographie des Jenseits: Studien zur Geschichte des Todes in Kaiserzeit und Spätantike*, ed. Walter Ameling, Altertumswissenschaftliches Kolloquium 21 (Stuttgart: Steiner 2011), 35–48.

17. E.g., Tobias Nicklas, "Jewish, Christian, Greek? The Apocalypse of Peter as a Witness of Second Century Christianity in Alexandria," in *Beyond Conflicts: Cultural and Religious Cohabitations in Alexandria and in Egypt between the 1st and the 6th century CE*, ed. Luca Arcari, STAC 103 (Tübingen: Mohr Siebeck, 2017), 27–46.

18. See Martha Himmelfarb, *Tours of Hell: An Apocalyptic Form in Jewish and Christian Literature* (Philadelphia: University of Pennsylvania Press, 1983).

19. Nicklas, "Jewish," 28.

that show ways to become righteous. The text distinguishes between ethical and cultic Torah. The Apocalypse of Peter is committed to the former without actively fighting the cultic law.

Righteousness and the Scriptures of Israel

Like 5 Ezra, the Apocalypse of Peter uses allusions to Scripture to express the idea of righteousness. The vision of hell (Apoc. Pet. 7–13, Ethiopic) explains in detail the concept of righteousness by putting together catalogs of vices and virtues. In the tour of hell, the reader sees clearly what happens to unrighteous people and gets an idea of what righteousness really means. By pointing out negative consequences of unjust behavior, the text expresses a notion of ethics.

In the following table, one can see a profile of the apocalypse's catalog of vices. It is obvious that the text brings together references to the Scriptures to draw a list of sins and merits.

Table 39.2. Vices in the Apocalypse of Peter

Akhmim Codex (Akh)	Ethiopic Text	Parallels in the Torah
Decalogue		
Falling away from God (frag. 10r)	Blasphemy (Apoc. Pet. 9)	Exod 20:7
Idolatry (frag. 10r)	Idolatry (Apoc. Pet. 10)	Exod 20:3; Deut 5:7; 6:14; 7:14; 8:19; 11:16, 28; 13:14; 28:14, 36; 29:25; 30:17
	Honoring of mother and father (Apoc. Pet. 11)	Exod 20:12; 21:17; Lev 20:9; Deut 5:16
Murder (frag. 9v)	Murder (Apoc. Pet. 7)	Exod 20:13; Deut 5:17
Neglecting God's commandments (frag. 10v)	Neglecting God's commandments (Apoc. Pet. 8)	Exod 20:7; Deut 5:10
	Fraud (Apoc. Pet. 9)	Exod 20:15, 17; Deut 5:19, 21
Lies (frag. 10v)/Gossiping against righteousness (frag. 8r; frag. 9r)	Gossiping against righteousness (Apoc. Pet. 7; 9)	
Adultery (frag. 9v)		Exod 20:14; Deut 5:18

Ethics of the Scriptures

Usury (frag. 10v)	Usury (Apoc. Pet. 10)	Lev 25:36
Fornication and homosexuality (frag. 10v)	Homosexuality (Apoc. Pet. 10)	Lev 18:22
	Prostitution and fornication (Apoc. Pet. 7; 8)	Deut 23:18–19
	Magic (Apoc. Pet. 12)	Lev 19:26; Deut 18:10
Neglecting widows and orphans (frag. 10r)	Neglecting widows and orphans (Apoc. Pet. 9)	Exod 22:21; Deut 10:18; 24:17; 27:19

Other Traditions

Abortion (frag. 9r)	Abortion (Apoc. Pet. 8)	
Persecution of righteous people (frag. 9r)	Persecution of righteous people (Apoc. Pet. 9)/ Killing of witnesses (Apoc. Pet. 9)	
	Premarital sex (Apoc. Pet. 11)	
	Disobedient slaves	

The Apocalypse of Peter uses catalogs of vices from Christian traditions, revealing an ethical and noncultic understanding of the Torah. If you take a look at the ethics of the tour of hell from a wider angle, you notice that the core of the catalog is strongly influenced by the Decalogue, enriched with allusions to at least some social commandments of the Scriptures.

Theophilus of Antioch and the Apocalypse of Peter

If you compare the ethical profile of the Apocalypse of Peter with Theophilus of Antioch, you will notice clear parallels.[20] Both texts come from different cultures and are, of course, not directly related to each other. But both work with similar traditions.[21] Particularly, the ethics of Theophilus *Autol.* 3.9–12 are very close to

---

20. For more details, see Ferdinand R. Prostmeier, "Die Jesusüberlieferung bei Theophilos von Antiochia 'An Autolykos,'" in *Ein neues Geschlecht: Entwicklung des frühchristlichen Selbstbewusstseins*, ed. Manfred Lang, NTOA, SUNT 105 (Göttingen: Vandenhoeck & Ruprecht, 2014), 179–214; Robert M. Grant, *Theophilus of Antioch: Ad Autolycum* (Oxford: Claredon, 1970).

21. Oskar Skarsaune, "The Development of Scriptural Interpretation in the Second and Third Centuries—except Clement and Origen," in *Hebrew Bible/Old Testament: The History of Its Interpretation* (Göttingen: Vandenhoeck & Ruprecht, 1996), 1.1:377.

those of the tour of hell, although the apocalypse, unlike Theophilus, does not indicate which Scriptures it receives or use the Scriptures to create borderlines to pagan philosophy. However, both texts share a comparable idea of ethics, consisting of social laws of the Torah and the Prophets. Both also emphasize that they interpret the Torah ethically, but they do not actively reject the cultic law. Theophilus quotes Isa 1:58; Jer 6–7; and Zech 7–8. The author works with traditions that 5 Ezra also uses, but without using them to create discourse against Jewish identities. The Apocalypse of Peter does not quote the Scriptures, but it uses distinctive attributes and motif clusters.

Table 39.3. Theophilus of Antioch and the Apocalypse of Peter

Theophilos		**Apocalypse of Peter**
Fear of God	*Theophilus quotes the Decalogue*	
	Worshiping other gods	Blasphemy (Apoc. Pet. 9); falling away from god (frag. 10r [Akh])
	Idolatry	Idolatry (Apoc. Pet. 10)
Good Works	Honoring father and mother	Honoring father and mother (Apoc. Pet. 11)
Righteousness	Adultery	Adultery (frag. 9v [Akh])
	Murder	Murder (Apoc. Pet. 7)
	Stealing	Fraud (Apoc. Pet. 9)
	Lies	Lies (frag. 10v [Akh])
	Adultery	Adultery (frag. 9v [Akh])
	Theophilus quotes the Torah	
	Caring for the right of the poor	
	Killing righteous people	Persecution of righteous people // killing of witnesses (Apoc. Pet. 9)
	Not to justify godless people	
	Rejection of Gifts	
	Theophilus quotes Isaiah 1 and Isaiah 58	
	Ensuring the compliance with the law of God	Spreading gossip (Apoc. Pet. 7; 9)
	Neglecting widows and orphans	Neglecting widows and orphans (Apoc. Pet. 9)
	Help for imprisoned	
	Clothing of the naked	
	Theophilus quotes Joel 2	

> Prayer of the community
> Forgiveness
> *Theophilus quotes Zechariah 7*
> Charity
> Neglecting widows and orphans   Neglecting widows and orphans (Apoc. Pet. 9)

Theophilus's catalog is a little longer than the one of the Apocalypse of Peter. It is also obvious that the apocalypse does not interpret Joel 2. In addition, some virtues that Theophilus adopted from Isa 58 and from Zech 7 (caring for prisoners, clothing the naked, charity) do not appear in the tour of hell. On the other side, neither text hides the fact that their ethics strongly rely on the Scriptures. Even the prohibition against persecuting and killing the righteous ones, which scholars have used in discussions about the provenance of the apocalypse, appears in the context of Theophilus as a value anchored in the Scriptures. Theophilus extensively reflects on his understanding of Scripture. In his view, these ethics demonstrate the unity of Israel's Scriptures with the Gospels. Although the Apocalypse of Peter does not show any such reflections, it is very clear that the text values Israel's Scriptures as a fountain of Christian ethics, theology, and messianism.

The Apocalypse of Zephaniah

At the end of the nineteenth century, the National Library in Paris and the Royal Museums in Berlin each bought parts of a bundle of loose papyri from Sohag Abbey that contained fragments of two Coptic codices. Both contain different text fragments that can be associated with the tradition of the Apocalypse of Zephaniah. The largest surviving part of the apocalypse is attested on nine pages of the Ahkmim Codex. This is the main witness for the Apocalypse of Zephaniah, which I am going to use in this chapter. Although the Ahkmim Codex contains large parts of the Apocalypse of Zephaniah, it is not possible to arrange the pages of the codex without any problems. There is some leeway in how to put together the parts of the codex into a storyline. Depending on how one reconstructs the storyline of the Apocalypse of Zephaniah and evaluates the way in which its parts relate to each other, different ideas of the use of Scriptures arise.[22]

---

22. Cf. Georg Steindorff, *Die Apokalypse des Elias: Eine unbekannte Apokalypse und Bruchstücke der Zephaniah-Apokalypse*, TUGAL 17.3a (Leipzig: Hinrichs, 1899), esp. 1–4. Further,

The Apocalypse of Zephaniah (Akh) is a perfect example of the fact that apocryphal apocalypses are living traditions. It is obvious that the text changed during its reception history. The role of Scripture changes dramatically in the different parts of the text.

The literary character of the storyline of the text is not coherent. If one follows the narrative process of the text reconstructed by Georg Steindorff and the translation of Bernd J. Diebner, the Apocalypse of Zephaniah (Akh) reports the journey of a seer to the afterlife that ends with a vision of the great day of the Lord. The first-person perspectives of the text and the day of the Lord sections do not fit together seamlessly. Both passages seem to use the Scriptures differently. In the last chapters of the text, allusions to the Scriptures of Israel play a large role. The text portrays God's last judgment and refers therefore to the prophetic writings. The role of Scripture in the main part of the apocalypse is different from the ending but nonetheless interesting. In my view, the text tries to convey Jewish ideas about God and the fundamental story of the exodus to a broader cultural context. The text retells Greco-Egyptian narratives about life after death and connects them with Jewish ideas of God.

The Writings in the Seer's Journey

The Scriptures of Israel only play a role in a few parts of the main section.[23] The Jewish provenance of the text is not recognizable in many parts of the narrative. The text only uses names that are known from Jewish traditions. The text calls God "Adonai Sabaoth" and uses the title of Pantocrator of the Minor Prophets. In addition, it uses motifs from Ezek 1–3 and Dan 7 when it describes the *angelus interpres* (Apoc. Zeph. [Akh] 9; folio 4 [Paris]).[24]

In two passages of the text (Apoc. Zeph. [Akh] 8 and 9; folio 4 [Paris]), the narrator prays to Adonai. He begs for his help because he is afraid on his journey through the hereafter. In these short prayers, the text refers in a summarizing manner to the exodus narrative (Exod 1–12), the central narrative of the history of Israel, and alludes to the LXX of Daniel (Dan 13).

Albrecht Dietrich, *Nekyia: Beiträge zur Erklärung der neuentdeckten Petrusapokalypse* (Leipzig: Teubner, 1893).

23. See Michael Sommer, "The Apocalypse of Zephaniah and the Tombs of the Egyptian Chora: An Archaeological Contribution to B. J. Diebner's Opinion about the Relation between Clement of Alexandria and the Coptic Tradition of the Apocalypse of Zephaniah," in *Alexandria: Hub of the Hellenistic World*, ed. Benjamin Schliesser et al., WUNT 460 (Tübingen: Mohr Siebeck, 2021), 207–28.

24. Similar motifs of Ezek 1–3 and Dan 7 appear in many apocalyptic traditions (e.g., Rev 1).

Apoc. Zeph. 9 [folio 4 (Paris)]
You will save me from this tribulation. You, who saved Israel from the hand of the pharaoh, the king of Egypt (Exod 1–12). You saved Susanna from the hand of the sinful elders (Dan 13 LXX).

The text also recalls core elements of Israel's history. However, these intercessions are not essential for the main narrative. They contribute nothing to the storyline itself. Nevertheless, they are enormously important for the idea of Scripture in the text. The main storyline of the text retells a widespread narrative about the afterlife, which stems from Egypt's cultural memories. This narrative should be interpreted in a Jewish way.

If we look at archaeological excavations from Tuna-El-Gebel, Dakhla, Akhmim, and Thebes, we see similar narratives as in the Apocalypse of Zephaniah (Akh).[25] Grave chambers portray a similar journey to the land of the dead on their walls. On tomb paintings, we find narratives that are based on reminiscences of the Egyptian Book of the Dead.[26] In many tombs, the journey to the afterlife begins with a funeral scene and leads to the hall of weighing of the heart. The deeds of the deceased are measured on scales. If they have proven themselves in life, they can travel to the place of justice. If they are unworthy, they are eaten by the soul-eater Ammit. The deceased travels through the hereafter on a ship-bark and has to cross guarded gates, in front of which guard figures determine if they are clean.

The Apocalypse of Zephaniah recounts a comparable story about the journey to the afterlife, combining references to the writings of Israel and Jewish traditions at crucial points. The apocalypse's afterlife journey begins with a funeral scene (Apoc. Zeph [Akh] 1; folio 1 recto [Paris]). The seer recognizes parts of his own burial. While psalmodizing, people stare at his body as his soul travels to the realm of the dead. The netherworld itself is spatially structured and coexists with the immanent world. Guardian figures stand in front of dangerous gates to the underworld. They grant entry only to clean people. The guardian angel Eremiel guides the seer through the afterlife to the court hall named Amente. The seer experiences his own trial (Apoc. Zeph. [Akh] 9–12; folios 5–6 [Paris]).

---

25. See Marjorie S. Venit, *Visualizing the Afterlife in the Tombs of Graeco-Roman Egypt* (Cambridge: Cambridge University Press, 2016); Katja Lembke, Cäcilia Fluck, Günter Vittmann, *Ägyptens späte Blüte: Die Römer am Nil*, Sonderbände der Antiken Welt (Mainz: von Zabern, 2004); Sommer, "Tombs."

26. For further information, see John H. Taylor, *Death and the Afterlife in Ancient Egypt* (London: British Museum, 2001); Taylor, *Journey through the Afterlife: Ancient Egyptian Book of the Dead* (London: British Museum, 2010); Erik Hornung, *Die Unterweltsbücher der Ägypter* (Düsseldorf: Artemis, 2002).

A hybrid-type accuser—half cat, half reptile—leads the process in which God does not appear to be involved. Instead, the accuser weighs two scrolls with the good and the bad deeds of the seer on a weighing scale. Furthermore, the seer recognizes a soul-eating creature, which devours the souls of the accused who are found unworthy. The seer passes the weighing process and the *angelus interpres* guides him to a port, from where the seer is led to the place of righteousness. He travels over the sea of the netherworld on a ship-bark (Apoc. Zeph. [Akh] 13–16; P. 1862 [Berlin]).

The only difference between the Apocalypse of Zephaniah and the grave paintings is that the Egyptian narrative is combined with Jewish traditions. Adonai Sabaoth replaces Osiris, and Eremiel fulfills the function of Thoth. The few echoes of the traditions of Israel are supposed to present the writings of Israel in such a way that they form a symbiosis with ideas from the cultural memory of the Egyptian Chora.

The use of Scripture in the main part of the Apocalypse of Zephaniah can be characterized as culture assimilation. Through the short reminiscences of the central motif elements of the Jewish founding narrative in Exod 1–12 and the book of Daniel (Dan 13 LXX) in Zephaniah's prayer (Apoc. Zeph. [Akh] 8 and 9 [folio 4 (Paris)]), the Apocalypse of Zephaniah demonstrates that Greco-Egyptian narratives could also be combined with Jewish thinking. A popular narrative is expressed using vocabulary found in Israel's Scriptures.

The Scriptures of Israel in the Last Chapters of the Apocalypse of Zephaniah

The intertextual character of Apocalypse of Zephaniah changes drastically at the end of the text. The number of reminiscences of the Scriptures increases significantly. As soon as the seer enters the ship-bark, the text mentions Abraham, Isaac, and Jacob, as well as Enoch and David. They are introduced as archetypes of righteousness.

In the very last chapter, the text uses the tradition of the day of the Lord from the prophets (Apoc. Zeph. [Akh] 17–18; folio 7 [Paris]). Certainly, texts like Isa 2; 13; Joel 2; Amos 5; and Zeph 1, which portray God's intervention in history on his great day, are found in many apocalypses (and esp. in Rev 6:12–17) and have influenced Jewish cultural memory in a broad way. It is therefore not entirely clear whether Apocalypse of Zephaniah reads Israel's Scriptures directly or simply took over traditions that are inspired by the prophetic literature. In any case, the motifs of Apocalypse of Zephaniah recall strongly motifs that can be found in Isa 1; 13; Amos 5; Zeph 1; and Joel 2. Apocalypse of Zephaniah 18 (Akh); folio 7 (Paris) portrays the day of the Lord. As in Isa 13:6 and Rev 6:17, God shows his wrath, and as in Joel 2:1, the Apocalypse of Zephaniah mentions that the sound of trumpets will introduce the day of the Lord. Like Joel 1:15 and Rev 6:17, the Apocalypse of Zephaniah asks:

> **Apoc. Zeph. 18 (Akh); folio 7 (Paris)**
> Who will be able to stand before him when he rises in his anger?

The Lord will rise and pour out his wrath on all creation. The apocalypse also alludes at least implicitly to creation texts in Genesis and the Psalms. Apocalypse of Zephaniah mixes the image of God as Pantocrator and creator with the notion that he also has the power over time and history. The apocalypse reveals that God will act in history at the end of time. In the main part of the apocalypse, the relation between God and his creation is not so closely linked as it is in the last chapters of the text. The text underlines God's transcendence and employs angelic beings who mediate between the sphere of God and the immanent world. The depiction of God as well as the intertextuality of the text's ending differ from its main part.

If one only looks at Apoc. Zeph. 18, the Apocalypse of Zephaniah seems to be a typical Jewish apocalypse that uses language of the day of the Lord tradition from Scripture. Although the text does not quote from Scripture, its motifs remind us of Joel 1:15; 2:1; Isa 13:6; and Zeph 1:14–18. Comparable allusions to the day of the Lord tradition appear also in Christian apocalypses, like in Rev 6:12–17 and in Apoc. Pet. 4.

The Relationship between the Two Parts

The two parts of the Apocalypse of Zephaniah use Scripture differently. The ending of the Apocalypse of Zephaniah heavily relies on the day of the Lord tradition and alludes frequently to the prophets, whereas in the main part of the Apocalypse of Zephaniah, Israel's Scriptures do not play a major role. It is obvious that the two parts use Israel's Scriptures differently. In my view, these parts were not originally connected to each other. Rather, these parts were combined to form a single text in the fifth century. When one reads the two parts isolated from each other, one encounters two different perspectives on Israel's traditions. However, when one reads these two parts as a coherent story, then the question arises how the different ideas of Scriptures relate to each other. If one reads the text as a whole (like in the Akhmimic Codex), one encounters a story that brings together a non-Jewish model of the afterlife and the judgment over the soul with the biblical idea of the day of the Lord and God's judgment at the end of history. With this in mind, I doubt that the text should be assessed as coherent. In my view, both parts do not belong together.

If one wants to read the main part of the Apocalypse of Zephaniah as a document of the second century—and there are a number of reasons for that—the idea of eschatology that is given by the whole text does not fit the discourses of that period. The narrative promotes the idea of two court trials: one directly after death over the soul, the other one on the day of the Lord over all creation. The first court presentation is expressed with reminiscences of the Egyptian Book of the Dead. The second uses echoes of scriptural prophecy.

The notion of the coexistence between a universal and a particular judgment is encountered in the Christian traditions of late antiquity only in the post-Augustinian period.[27]

The Apocalypse of Zephaniah proves that apocryphal apocalypses are living texts. Two different apocalypses grew together into one text in later times in order to adapt new eschatological ideas. At the same time, the hermeneutics of Scripture of the entire text changed.

The Ascension of Isaiah

Like the Apocalypse of Zephaniah, the Ascension of Isaiah is a "living text."[28] This means that the text changed its form and meaning through a vivid reception history. The text was edited and enriched with extensions that changed the whole character of the storyline as well as the text's use of Scripture. The ascension itself has two parts.[29] The first part narrates the martyrdom of the prophet (Ascen. Isa. 1–5), whereas the second part unfolds Isaiah's ascension to heaven (Ascen. Isa. 6–11). Both parts were expanded by interpolations (Ascen. Isa. 3:13–5.1 // Ascen. Isa. 11:2–22). Each of them has the intention to Christianize a genuinely Jewish version of the text.[30] Unlike in the Apocalypse of Zephaniah, the idea of Scripture that resulted from the textual additions has strong parallels with second-century discourses about the relation between the prophets of Israel and the Christ event.

---

27. Michael Sommer, "Between Jewish and Egyptian Thinking: The Apocalypse of Zephaniah as a Bridge between Two Worlds?," in *Dreams, Visions, Imaginations: Jewish, Christian and Gnostic Views of the World to Come*, ed. Jens Schröter, Tobias Nicklas, and Armand Puig i Tàrrech, BZNW 247 (Berlin: de Gruyter, 2021), 319–42.

28. Enrico Norelli, *Ascensio Isaiae: Commentarius*, 2 vols., Corpus Christianorum Series Apocryphorum 7–8 (Turnhout: Brepols, 1995); Jonathan Knight, *The Ascension of Isaiah*, Guides to the Apocrypha and Pseudepigrapha (Sheffield: Sheffield Academic, 1995).

29. Only the Ethiopian tradition has preserved both parts in a coherent manner.

30. See Detlef G. Müller, "Die Himmelfahrt des Jesaja," in *Neutestamentliche Apokryphen in deutscher Übersetzung*, vol. 2, *Apostolisches, Apokalypsen und Verwandtes*, ed. Edgar Hennecke and Wilhelm Schneemelcher, 5th ed. (Tübingen: Mohr Siebeck, 1989), 547–62.

The Scriptures in the Martyrdom of Isaiah (Ascen. Isa. 1–5)

The text uses the first part of the book of Isaiah to characterize its protagonist. Ascension of Isaiah receives information about Isaiah's family relation and life data from Isa 1:6–7 in order to relate its portrayal of the prophet with the biblical Isaiah. The narrative is a kind of rewriting of the biblical story of Isaiah based on the biographical information given in the first chapters of Isaiah. Further, the text also employs 1 and 2 Kings and 2 Chr 33. In addition, the text plays with the biblical image prohibition, especially with Exod 33:20. The text wants to explain that Isaiah's vision of God does not violate the prohibition of making images of God.

> **Ascen. Isa 3:9**
> But Moses said: No man can see God and live; and Isaiah said: I have seen God and I live. (translation based on Charles)[31]

The Christian interpolation, starting from Ascen. Isa. 3:13, sheds a different light on the use of Scripture. This passage stylizes Isaiah's visions as a prophecy of the Christ event. Through the Christian interpolations, the reminiscences of the biblical texts have a different function. The Christian parts of the text not only intervene in the storyline of Ascension of Isaiah but also serve as a lens that conveys a new meaning to the biblical Isaiah. If one reads the biblical book with Ascension of Isaiah in mind, the biblical prophets appear to be solely messengers of the coming of Christ. Through the interpolation, the words of the prophet should appear as Christ prophecy. In the eyes of the Christian Ascension of Isaiah, the prophet Isaiah had already announced the arrival of Christ, his passion, his death, his descent into the realm of the dead, and his resurrection. He also predicted that Israel would execute God's beloved Son and that the church would triumph after a period of persecution. Ascension of Isaiah 4 points out further that all of this is foreshadowed in the Psalms; the Wisdom of Solomon; Proverbs; and in the books of the prophets Isaiah, Amos, Hosea, Micah, Joel, Nahum, Jonah, Obadiah, Habakkuk, Haggai, Zephaniah, Zechariah, Malachi, and Daniel. Variants of this hermeneutic, which interprets Israel's writings as Christ prophecies, emerged and spread throughout the second century.

Scriptures in the Vision of Isaiah (Ascen. Isa. 6–11)

The use of the Scriptures in the Ascension of Isaiah is a little more complex than in that of the martyrdom. Ascension of Isaiah 6–11 have been expanded and interpolated two times, which had an enormous effect on the text's understanding

---

31. Robert H. Charles, *The Ascension of Isaiah* (London: Black, 1900).

of Scripture. As in Ascen. Isa. 1–5, the Christian interpolators had the intention of Christianizing Israel's prophetic literature. The Jewish parts of the ascension do not directly quote the writings of Israel but presuppose that its readers have knowledge of at least the Torah and the Prophets. The interpolations adopt this perspective on the Scriptures and interpret them in a christological sense. The text itself narrates the prophet's ascent to the seventh heaven. His journey is spiritual, and he meets the righteous ones of Israel in the seventh heaven. One recognizes a text that not only presupposes the history of the book of Isaiah but also recognizes Israel's founding narrative as authoritative.

Then, in chapter 9, the Christian interpolation portrays Isaiah as a prophet foretelling the Christ event. In Ascen. Isa. 9, Isaiah learns from an angel that in the end of times the Son of God will descend to the world, be crucified, and resurrect. This is the beginning of a period of salvation. Ascension of Isaiah 11 goes a little further and expands the vision of Ascen. Isa. 9. According to the second expansion, Isaiah has a vision in the seventh heaven. He sees the Virgin Mary giving birth to Christ. Ascension of Isaiah 11 comments on the gospel narratives and shares common ideas with the interpretation of Isa 7 by Justin Martyr (*1 Apol.* 1.33).

The Apocalypse of Paul (*Visio Pauli*)

The Apocalypse of Paul was probably written in the fourth or fifth century CE. The Latin text is possibly the oldest of the many different, sometimes fragmentary strands of textual traditions (Greek, Armenian, Syriac, Slavic, Coptic, Ethiopian). The Latin version preserves the full text of the apocalypse.[32] The narrative itself is relecture/rereading of 2 Cor 12. It expands on this text and reports about Paul's ascension to heaven. Paul gets insight into paradise and hell and recognizes the fate of souls after death.[33]

To create this story, Vision of Paul uses older apocalyptic traditions. It uses the Apocalypse of Elijah and Slavonic Enoch, as well as the Apocalypse of Zephaniah, the Greek/Ethiopian Apocalypse of Peter, and the Revelation of John. In addition, it refers to Greco-Roman images of the afterlife, such as the Archerusian Lake and Tartarus. However, its use of Scripture differs significantly from those in the texts we have analyzed above.[34]

---

32. See Lenka Jiroušková, *Die Visio Pauli: Wege und Wandlungen einer orientalischen Apokryphe im lateinischen Mittelalter unter Einschluß der alttsechischen und deutschsprachigen Textzeugen*, Mittellateinische Studien und Texte 34 (Leiden: Brill, 2006).

33. Further, Jan N. Bremmer and Istvan Czachesz, eds., *The Visio Pauli and the Gnostic Apocalypse of Paul*, SECA 9 (Leuven: Peeters, 2007).

34. Hugo Duensing and Aurelio de Santos Otero, "Apokalypse des Paulus," in Hennecke and Schneemelcher, *Neutestamentliche Apokryphen in deutscher Übersetzung*, 2:644–75.

On the one hand, the text has a dualistic idea of the body. Body and soul are strictly separated from each other. However, Vision of Paul wants to present both parts of human nature—the body and the immortal soul—as parts of God's creation. For this purpose, the text interprets the creation texts of Israel's Scriptures. On the other hand, the text unfolds a twofold vision of salvation. Its idea of paradise and of a messianic empire not only relies heavily on Scripture but appears as a fulfillment of the promises of the Torah.

Creation in the Apocalypse of Paul

Before the text develops its cosmology, it emphasizes that it is rooted in Scripture. The text creatively adopts the story of Gen 1–2. At the beginning of the narrative, the Apocalypse of Paul underlines that the text understands God as the creator of the cosmos (Vis. Paul 3.7). The text also underlines that the human race consists of children of Abraham. Further, Paul applies the language of creation to demonstrate the world's demise. According to Vis. Paul 4–6, the sun, moon, stars, and sea witness how corrupted the people of the earth are. However, for the Apocalypse of Paul, humanity is an image of God (Vis. Paul 7). The text refers several times to Gen 1:26 (Vis. Paul 14.16). In Vis. Paul 16, Paul realizes that the souls have to give an account of their deeds to God. This text refers to Gen 1:26 twice in order to highlight that all souls were created by God who shaped them in his image.[35] Although the Vision of Paul has a dualistic anthropology, by referring to the biblical story of Genesis, it emphasizes that both parts of the human being are created, even if the soul is immortal. It is striking that the text links its own Christian account of a narrative about salvation to the history of Israel. In this regard, Vision of Paul uses biblical figures from Genesis as well as from the wisdom literature to create archetypes of righteous ones. The text goes so far as to rewrite biblical narratives like Job in order to give them happy endings. Vision of Paul reports that the righteous Job gets rewarded in heaven, which gives the book of Job a different ending.

Exodus and Genesis, Paradise, and the Messianic Kingdom

The text's vision of paradise refers not only to the biblical narrative of creation but also takes up the promise of the holy land from Exodus. It also alludes to Exod 19–20 and the covenant. When Paul enters paradise, he meets Enoch and Elijah (Vis. Paul 20). An angel guides Paul further down from the third to the second heaven to the gates of heaven. From there, Paul sees the land of promise.

---

35. Albert L. A. Hogeterp, "The Relation between Body and Soul in the Apocalypse of Paul," in Bremmer and Czachesz, *Visio Pauli*, 105–29.

Vision of Paul employs one of the central promises that God made to his people in the Torah in order to Christianize it (Vis. Paul 44 seems to do the same with the covenant). Paradise itself is described in more detail at the end of the apocalypse. The text strongly alludes to Gen 2–3 (Vis. Paul 45). Furthermore, the description of paradise also draws on the childhood stories of the Synoptic Gospels. Paul meets Mary in paradise, whereby Vision of Paul tells the story of the virgin birth. In addition, Paul encounters the patriarchs, Lot, Adam, Cain, and Noah in paradise, where the Joseph story (Gen 36–37) and Gen 2:1–3:4, 6; and Gen 19 appear behind Vis. Paul 48–49. A little different, but in some ways connected to the text's account of paradise, is its description of the messianic kingdom (Vis. Paul 22.1–23.31). Paradise is described similarly, where Vision of Paul also refers to Exodus and Genesis. Vision of Paul announces that after the first earth has passed, the promised land will be revealed. Then Christ will reign as king in the promised land for one thousand years, which the text presents as a reward for the faithful. The text describes the messianic kingdom by using Exod 3:8 and Gen 2:11–12. It is called the land of milk and honey in which four rivers flow (Gen 2:11), and trees provide food for the residents.[36] Vision of Paul uses the promises God made to Israel and interprets it in an anti-Jewish way. The text uses the promise of the land, that is, one of the core elements of the Torah's idea of the covenant, to express a Christian vision of salvation. It is obvious that, in the eyes of the Vision of Paul, the Christ event and the Christian idea of salvation is the fulfillment of the promises God addressed to Israel in the Torah.

Conclusion

It is nearly impossible to provide a systematic summary of the use of Scripture in the apocryphal apocalypses. The literary and theological characteristics of the apocryphal texts differ too much from each other. However, I offer five theses about 5 Ezra, the Greek/Ethiopian Apocalypse of Peter, the Apocalypse of Zephaniah, the Ascension of Isaiah, the Apocalypse of Paul.

1. Many texts show that they are part of the early Christian culture of discussion about adequate use of Scripture. The anti-Jewish reading of Scripture in 5 Ezra has similarities with the Epistle of Barnabas, Justin Martyr, and Irenaeus of

---

36. Further Jacques van Ruiten, "The Four Rivers of Eden in the Apocalypse of Paul (*Visio Pauli*): The Intertextual Relationship of Gen 2:10–14 and the *Apocalypse of Paul* 23:4," in *Jerusalem, Alexandria, Rome: Studies in Ancient Cultural Interaction in Honour of A. Hilhorst*, ed. Florentino García Martínez and Gerard P. Luttikhuizen, JSJSup 82 (Leiden: Brill, 2003).

Lyon. Further, like Theophilus of Antioch, the Apocalypse of Peter uses Scripture to express an idea of Christian ethics that is rooted in the Torah.
2. Fifth Ezra, the Ascension of Isaiah, and the Vision of Paul have in common that they read Scripture in an anti-Jewish way that is comparable with the substitution theology of the church fathers. The Ascension of Isaiah reads the book of Isaiah as if the biblical prophet had foreshadowed the Christ event. The Vision of Paul uses God's promise of the land to express an idea of Christian salvation. And 5 Ezra declares the cultic law of the Torah invalid by rearranging the cult-critical texts of the prophets.
3. At least some apocryphal apocalypses try to translate Israel's tradition into the cultural discourses of their own social environment. It is obvious that the Apocalypse of Zephaniah uses an Egyptian folk narrative to portray the seer's journey to the land of the dead. The text integrates allusions to Israel's Scriptures to assimilate Jewish and Greco-Egyptian discourses.
4. Like the biblical Apocalypse of John, many apocryphal apocalypses show great interest in the prophetic day of the Lord tradition. Texts like Isa 2; 13; Joel 2; or Zeph 1 usually serve as models for the coming of God on the last day that many apocalypses portray.
5. Many apocryphal apocalypses are living texts. Their history of tradition and translation is not as stable as the biblical Apocalypse of John. On the contrary, many apocryphal apocalypses were reworked as they were handed down. Examples like the Ascension of Isaiah or the Apocalypse of Zephaniah show that these also influenced their scriptural hermeneutics.

Bibliography

Bauckham, Richard. *The Fate of the Dead: Studies on Jewish and Christian Apocalypses*. NovTSup 93. Leiden: Brill, 1998.

Bremmer, Jan N. "The Apocalypse of Peter: Greek or Jewish?" Pages 1–14 in *The Apocalypse of Peter*. Edited by Jan N. Bremmer and Istvan Czachesz. SECA 7. Leuven: Peeters, 2003.

———. "Orphic, Roman, Jewish and Christian Tours of Hell: Observations on the Apocalypse of Peter." Pages 305–21 in *Other Worlds and Their Relation to This World: Early Jewish and Ancient Christian Traditions*. Edited by Tobias Nicklas, Joseph Verheyden, Erik Eynikel, and Florentino García Martínez. JSJSup 143. Leiden: Brill, 2010.

Bremmer, Jan N., and Istvan Czachesz, eds. *The Visio Pauli and the Gnostic Apocalypse of Paul*. SECA 9. Leuven: Peeters, 2007.

Carleton Paget, James. *The Epistle of Barnabas: Outlook and Background.* WUNT 2/64. Tübingen: Mohr Siebeck, 1994.

Charles, R. H. *The Ascension of Isaiah.* London: Black, 1900.

Dietrich, Albrecht. *Nekyia: Beiträge zur Erklärung der neuentdeckten Petrusapokalypse.* Leipzig: Teubner, 1893.

Duensing, Hugo, and Aurelio de Santos Otero. "Apokalypse des Paulus." Pages 644–75 in *Neutestamentliche Apokryphen in deutscher Übersetzung.* Vol. 2, *Apostolisches, Apokalypsen und Verwandtes.* Edited by Edgar Hennecke and Wilhelm Schneemelcher. 5th ed. Tübingen: Mohr Siebeck, 1989.

———. "Das fünfte und sechste Buch Esra." Pages 581–90 in *Neutestamentliche Apokryphen in deutscher Übersetzung.* Vol. 2, *Apostolisches, Apokalypsen und Verwandtes.* Edited by Wilhelm Schneemelcher. 6th ed. Tübingen: Mohr Siebeck, 1997.

Frey, Jörg. "Die Apokalyptik als Herausforderung der neutestamentlichen Wissenschaft: Zum Problem; Jesus und die Apokalyptik." Pages 23–94 in *Apokalyptik als Herausforderung neutestamentlicher Theologie.* Edited by Michael Becker and Markus Öhler. WUNT 2/214. Tübingen: Mohr Siebeck, 2006.

———. "Editorial: Apokalyptik und das Neue Testament." *EC* 4, no. 1 (2013): 1–6.

Grant, Robert M. *Theophilus of Antioch: Ad Autolycum.* Oxford: Clarendon, 1970.

Himmelfarb, Martha. *Tours of Hell: An Apocalyptic Form in Jewish and Christian Literature.* Philadelphia: University of Pennsylvania Press, 1983.

Hirschberger, Veronika. *Ringen um Israel: Intertextuelle Perspektiven auf das 5. Buch Esra.* SECA 14. Leuven: Peeters, 2018.

Hogeterp, Albert L. A. "The Relation between Body and Soul in the Apocalypse of Paul." Pages 105–29 in *The Visio Pauli and the Gnostic Apocalypse of Paul.* Edited by Jan N. Bremmer and Istvan Czachesz. SECA 9. Leuven: Peeters 2007.

Hornung, Erik. *Die Unterweltsbücher der Ägypter.* Düsseldorf: Artemis 2002.

James, Montague R. *The Apocryphal New Testament.* Oxford: Clarendon, 1924.

Jiroušková, Lenka. *Die Visio Pauli: Wege und Wandlungen einer orientalischen Apokryphe im lateinischen Mittelalter; Unter Einschluß der alttsechischen und deutschsprachigen Textzeugen.* Mittellateinische Studien und Texte 34. Leiden: Brill, 2006.

Knight, Jonathan. *The Ascension of Isaiah.* Guides to the Apocrypha and Pseudepigrapha. Sheffield: Sheffield Academic, 1995.

Kraft, Robert A. "The Epistle of Barnabas: Its Quotations and Their Sources." PhD diss., Harvard University, 1961.

Lembke, Katja, Cäcilia Fluck, and Günter Vittmann. *Ägyptens späte Blüte: Die Römer am Nil.* Sonderbände der Antiken Welt. Mainz: von Zabern, 2004.

Markschies, Christoph. "Editorial." *ZAC* 20 (2016): 1–20.

Markschies, Christoph, Jens Schröter, and Andreas Heiser, eds. *Antike christliche*

Apokryphen in deutscher Übersetzung. Vol. 1, *Evangelien und Verwandtes*. 7th ed. Tübingen: Mohr Siebeck, 2012.

Müller, Detlef G. "Die Himmelfahrt des Jesaja." Pages 547–62 in *Neutestamentliche Apokryphen in deutscher Übersetzung*. Vol. 2, *Apostolisches. Apokalypsen und Verwandtes*. Edited by Edgar Hennecke and Wilhelm Schneemelcher. 5th ed. Tübingen: Mohr Siebeck, 1989.

Munier, Charles. *L'Apologie de Saint Justin Philosophe et Martyr*. Paradosis 38. Fribourg: Editions Universitaires, 1994.

Nicklas, Tobias. "Christliche Apokalypsen in Ägypten vor Konstantin: Kanon, Autorität, kontextuelle Funktion." Pages 95–117 in *Book of Seven Seals: The Peculiarity of Revelation, Its Manuscripts, Attestation and Transmission*. Edited by Thomas J. Kraus and Michael Sommer. WUNT 363. Tübingen: Mohr Siebeck, 2016.

———. "'Insider' und 'Outsider': Überlegungen zum historischen Kontext der Darstellung 'jenseitiger Orte' in der Offenbarung des Petrus." Pages 35–48 in *Topographie des Jenseits: Studien zur Geschichte des Todes in Kaiserzeit und Spätantike*. Edited by Walter Ameling. Altertumswissenschaftliches Kolloquium 21. Stuttgart: Steiner, 2011.

———. "Jewish, Christian, Greek? The Apocalypse of Peter as a Witness of Second Century Christianity in Alexandria." Pages 27–46 in *Beyond Conflicts: Cultural and Religious Cohabitations in Alexandria and in Egypt between the 1st and the 6th century CE*. Edited by Luca Arcari. STAC 103. Tübingen: Mohr Siebeck, 2017.

———. "Resurrection – Judgment – Punishment: Apocalypse of Peter 4." Pages 461–74 in *Resurrection from the Dead: Biblical Traditions in Dialogue; Resurrection des mortis; Traditions bibliques en dialogue*. Edited by Geert van Oyen and Tom Shepherd. BETL 249. Leuven: Peeters, 2012.

Norelli, Enrico. *Ascensio Isaiae: Commentarius*. 2 vols. Corpus Christianorum Series Apocryphorum 7–8. Turnhout: Brepols, 1995.

———. "Pertinence théologique et canonicité: Les premières apocalypses chrétiennes." *Apocrypha* 8 (1997): 147–64.

———. "Situation des apocryphes pétriniens." *Apocrypha* 2 (1991): 31–84.

Prigent, Pierre. *Les Testimonia dans le Christianisme primitif: L'Épitre de Barnabé I–XVI et ses sources*. EBib. Paris: Gabalda, 1961.

Prostmeier, Ferdinand R. "Die Jesusüberlieferung bei Theophilos von Antiochia 'An Autolykos.'" Pages 179–214 in *Ein neues Geschlecht: Entwicklung des frühchristlichen Selbstbewusstseins*. Edited by Manfred Lang. NTOA. SUNT 105. Göttingen: Vandenhoeck & Ruprecht, 2014.

Rhodes, James M. *The Epistle of Barnabas and the Deuteronomic Tradition: Polemics,*

Paraenesis, and the Legacy of the Golden-Calf Incident. WUNT 2/188. Tübingen: Mohr Siebeck, 2004.

Ruiten, Jacques van. "The Four Rivers of Eden in the Apocalypse of Paul (Visio Pauli): The Intertextual Relationship of Gen 2:10–14 and the Apocalypse of Paul 23." Pages 263–83 in *Jerusalem, Alexandria, Rome: Studies in Ancient Cultural Interaction in Honour of A. Hilhorst*. Edited by Florentino García Martínez and Gerard P. Luttikhuizen. JSJSup 82. Leiden: Brill, 2003.

Skarsaune, Oskar. "The Development of Scriptural Interpretation in the Second and Third Centuries—except Clement and Origen." Pages 373–442 in vol. 1, part 1 of *Hebrew Bible/Old Testament: The History of Its Interpretation*. Edited by Magne Sæbø. Göttingen: Vandenhoeck & Ruprecht, 1996.

———. *The Proof from Prophecy: A Study in Justin Martyr's Proof-Text Tradition; Text-Type, Provenance, Theological Profile*. NovTSup 56. Leiden: Brill, 1987.

Sommer, Michael. "The Apocalypse of Zephaniah and the Tombs of the Egyptian Chora: An Archaeological Contribution to B. J. Diebner's Opinion about the Relation between Clement of Alexandria and the Coptic Tradition of the Apocalypse of Zephaniah." Pages 207–28 in *Alexandria: Hub of the Hellenistic World*. Edited by Benjamin Schliesser, Jan Rüggemeier, Thomas J. Kraus, and Jörg Frey. WUNT 460. Tübingen: Mohr Siebeck, 2021.

———. "Between Jewish and Egyptian Thinking: The Apocalypse of Sophonias as a Bridge between Two Worlds?" Pages 319–42 in *Dreams, Visions, Imaginations: Jewish, Christian and Gnostic Views of the World to Come*. Edited by Jens Schröter, Tobias Nicklas, and Armand Puig i Tàrrech. BZNW 247. Berlin: de Gruyter, 2021.

Steindorff, Georg. *Die Apokalypse des Elias: Eine unbekannte Apokalypse und Bruchstücke der Zephaniah-Apokalypse*. TUGAL 17.3a. Leipzig: Hinrichs 1899.

Taylor, John H. *Death and the Afterlife in Ancient Egypt*. London: British Museum, 2001.

———. *Journey through the Afterlife: Ancient Egyptian Book of the Dead*. London: British Museum, 2010.

Venit, Marjorie S. *Visualizing the Afterlife in the Tombs of Graeco-Roman Egypt*. Cambridge: Cambridge University Press, 2016.

Wolter, Michael. *5. Esra-Buch, 6. Esra-Buch*. JSHRZ 3.7. Gütersloh: Gütersloher Verlagshaus, 2001.

40

Israel's Scriptures in the Adversus Judaeos *Literature*

DAVID LINCICUM

In the early seventh century, Isidore of Seville could pronounce summarily, "The Old Testament is so called because it ceased when the New came."[1] From the vantage point of the first two centuries of the Christian church's existence, Isidore's certainty looks like a position that required years of argumentation and interpretation to achieve. The subordination of the Old Testament to the New had to be systematically undertaken by a comprehensive rereading of the former in light of the latter. But even before the boundaries of either testamentary collection were clear, there flourished hermeneutical impulses to seek an accordance between authoritative predecessor texts in Israel's Scriptures and the novelty of the Christian message. These impulses first gave rise to debates within early Judaism as followers of Jesus argued with their coreligionists about the truth and meaning of the Jesus followers' claims in an intra-Jewish interpretative dispute. But as the Jesus movement took on more gentile members and its center of gravity slowly shifted away from the Palestinian Judaism that gave the movement its first impulse, a hermeneutical divide opened up between the early Christians (sometimes of Jewish, sometimes of gentile stock) and their non-Christ-believing Jewish peers. It is impossible to characterize that hermeneutical

---

1. *Etymologies* 6.1.1: *Vetus Testamentum ideo dicitur, quia ueniente Nouo cessauit.* ET from *The "Etymologies" of Isidore of Seville*, trans. Stephen A. Barney et al. (Cambridge: Cambridge University Press, 2006), 135.

divide with essentializing descriptions of what was always and everywhere the case, but certain lines are broadly clear.

From the first decades of the second century, at roughly the time when the last texts that would make up the New Testament were being composed, we see the emergence of a literary movement that scholarship has come to characterize as the *adversus Judaeos* tradition. This literature, written, as the name suggests, "against the Jews," is usually seen to include three major genres: thematic treatises or homilies, dialogues between a Christian and his Jewish interlocutor, and collections of *testimonia*, that is, scriptural passages taken from the Old Testament and arranged to "prove" the truth of the Christian message. The tradition begins in the second century but continues, in various guises, throughout late antiquity and the medieval period and well into the early modern world.[2]

Central to each of these genres is the interpretation of Israel's Scriptures. This is for an obvious reason: they are the common source of authority to which each side in these (usually artificial, almost always one-sided) debates can appeal. Jews and Christians become, in this tradition, divided by a common book as Christians attempt to demonstrate that the scriptural inheritance overwhelmingly points to Jesus as the Messiah and to the church as the true people of God. Scholars since Adolf von Harnack have debated whether this literature offers us a window onto real contact between Jews and Christians "on the ground" or whether in the end it simply amounts to an act of Christian self-definition against the foil of a merely "symbolic Judaism."[3] We need not settle the dispute

---

2. For useful broader accounts, see A. Lukyn Williams, Adversus Judaeos: *A Bird's Eye View of Christian Apologiae until the Renaissance* (Cambridge: Cambridge University Press, 1935); Marcel Simon, *"Verus Israel": A Study of the Relations between Christians and Jews in the Roman Empire AD 135–425*, trans. Henry McKeating (Oxford: Oxford University Press, 1986); Heinz Schreckenberg, *Die christlichen Adversus-Judaeos-Texte und ihr literarisches und historisches Umfeld*, 3 vols., EHS.T 172 (Frankfurt am Main: Lang, 1982–1994); Samuel Krauss, *The Jewish-Christian Controversy from the Earliest Times to 1789*, vol. 1, *History*, ed. and rev. William Horbury, TSAJ 56 (Tübingen: Mohr Siebeck, 1996); Ora Limor and Guy G. Stroumsa, ed., *"Contra Iudaeos": Ancient and Medieval Polemics between Christians and Jews*, TSMJ 10 (Tübingen: Mohr Siebeck, 1996); Andreas Külzer, *"Disputationes graecae contra Iudaeos": Untersuchungen zur byzantinischen antijüdischen Dialogliteratur und ihrem Judenbild*, Byzantinisches Archiv 19 (Leipzig: Teubner, 1999); Sébastien Morlet, Olivier Munnich, and Bernard Pouderon, eds., *Les dialogues* adversus Iudaeos: *Permanences et mutations d'une tradition polémique*, CEAug 196 (Paris: Institut d'Études Augustiniennes, 2013).

3. For the term "symbolic Judaism," see Miriam S. Taylor, *Anti-Judaism and Early Christian Identity: A Critique of the Scholarly Consensus*, StPB 46 (Leiden: Brill, 1995); for nuancing of this view, see James Carleton Paget, "Anti-Judaism and Early Christian Identity," ZAC 1, no. 2 (1997): 195–225.

in order to appreciate the interpretative strategies of the texts in play, but it is not improbable that such considerations would vary across texts and contexts.[4]

This chapter will consider only some of the earliest examples of the *adversus Judaeos* tradition: the so-called Epistle of Barnabas, Justin Martyr's *Dialogue with Trypho*, the fragmentary Dialogue of Jason and Papiscus, and some early Latin examples in Tertullian's treatise *Adversus Judaeos* and in the anonymous tractate *De duobus montibus Sina et Sion* before briefly considering some later trajectories in Cyprian's *Ad Quirinum* and Ps.-Gregory of Nyssa's *Testimonia*. Our concern throughout is not to offer a comprehensive treatment of the use of Scripture in these texts, which would be an impossibly large task, but to characterize their basic hermeneutical stances and text selections and to compare these with what we find in the New Testament, asking to what extent the New Testament served as a predecessor, even unwittingly, for the *adversus Judaeos* tradition.

Epistle of Barnabas

The Epistle of Barnabas is a treatise with epistolary characteristics that stems from the first decades of the second century and takes as one of its major purposes the demonstration that the Jewish Scriptures when rightly read prefigure Jesus Christ and the major institutions of the early church.[5] Barnabas usually presents marked citations and overwhelmingly favors verbs of speaking in introducing those scriptural citations, particularly in the present tense.[6] This seems to convey a sense of the immediacy of the scriptural address, directed to the present of Barnabas's readers or hearers. Intriguingly, in those few times when the term "it is written" (γέγραπται) occurs as an introductory formula, there is often some

---

4. Consult Guy G. Stroumsa, "From Anti-Judaism to Antisemitism in Early Christianity?," in Limor and Stroumsa, *"Contra Ioudaeos,"* 1–26.

5. For a critical survey of the introductory issues and the various positions in play, see James Carleton Paget, *The Epistle of Barnabas: Outlook and Background*, WUNT 2/64 (Tübingen: Mohr Siebeck, 1994).

6. Note verbs of speaking: saying (λέγει/λέγων/λέγοντι): 2.4–5, 7, 10; 3.1, 3; 4.4, 5, 7, 8, 11; 5.2, 4, 12, 13, 14; 6.1, 2, 3, 4, 6, 7, 9, 10, 12, 13, 14, 16; 7.4; 9.1, 2, 3, 5, 8; 10.2, 10, 11; 11.2, 4, 6, 8, 9, 10; 12.1, 2, 4, 9, 11; 13.2, 4, 5, 7; 14.2, 7, 8, 9; 15.2, 3, 4, 5, 6, 8; 16.2, 3, 5. Εἶπεν: 5.5; 6.12; 10.1; 12.7; 14.3; cf. 10.11. Φησίν: 7.7, 11; 10.4, 5; 12.7. Other related terms occur: "proclaimed" (ἐκήρυξεν), 6.13; or "prophesies" (προφητεύει) in 12.10. Note also the resumptive "we have previously said" (προειρήκαμεν), 6.18, looking back to 6.12; "Hear how the priests of the temple have revealed something about this" (7.3); "Pay attention to what he commanded" (7.6; cf. 7.7, 9); "The Spirit of the Lord prophesies" (9.2); "Take this again" (9.5); "Moses had commanded" (12.6); "Observe how David calls him Lord" (12.11). Sometimes we find simply ἀλλά (10.6, 7) or καί (11.5).

question about the provenance of the citation: it occurs in 4.3, with reference to Enoch; in 4.14, perhaps with reference to Matt 22:14 or a similar tradition; and in 16.6, citing an uncertain source (Enochic? Cf. 1 En. 89.56, 66).[7]

Barnabas wants to demonstrate the clear fulfillment or realization of Jewish Scripture in the events of its author's recent past. To that end, it reads Jewish Scripture as a vast field of types, all pointing forward to consummation in Jesus. The characteristic mode of conceptualizing Scripture is, therefore, prophetic. Barnabas takes a particular interest in the prophets and even ascribes a substantial quotation of Ps 1:3–6 to "another prophet" (ἐν ἄλλῳ προφήτῃ) in 11.6–7. One might extend what Barnabas says about the Christian community to his interpretation of Scripture: "those who long to be saved look not to the human person but to the one who dwells and speaks in that person" (16.10). Barnabas does not, like Matthew, use the language of fulfillment, but presents its scriptural interpretation as a "gnosis" that offers its hearers true insight into the deep structure of Israel's Scripture.

Table 40.1. Scriptural Citations in the Epistle of Barnabas and New Testament Parallel Citations

Epistle of Barnabas	Scriptural Citation	New Testament Parallel Citation
Barn. 2.5	Isa 1:11–13	
Barn. 2.7	Jer 7:22–23	
Barn. 2.8	Zech 8:17	
Barn. 2.10	Ps 51:17 (50:19 LXX)	
Barn. 2.10	a possible citation from a nonextant Apocalypse of Adam(?)[8]	
Barn. 3.1–5	Isa 58:4–10	Luke 4:18 (for Isa 58:6)
Barn. 4.3	Enoch	
Barn. 4.4	Dan 7:24	
Barn. 4.5	Dan 7:7–8	
Barn. 4.7	Exod 34:28 (cf. 31:18)	
Barn. 4.8	Exod 32:7	
Barn. 4.11	Isa 5:21	
Barn. 5.2	Isa 53:5, 7	1 Pet 2:24
Barn. 5.4	Prov 1:17	

7. It also occurs in 5.2, but not as part of an introductory formula, and in 15.1, in a citation of the Decalogue.

8. A marginal note in H (Codex Taphou 54) suggests this identification.

Israel's Scriptures in the Adversus Judaeos Literature

Barn. 5.5	Gen 1:26	
Barn. 5.12	Zech 13:7	Matt 26:31; Mark 14:27
Barn. 5.13	Ps 22:20 (21:21 LXX)	
Barn. 5.13	Ps 119:120 (118:120 LXX); with 22:16 (21:17 LXX)	
Barn. 5.14–6.2	Isa 50:6–9	
Barn. 6.2–3	Isa 28:16	Rom 9:33; 10:11; 1 Pet 2:6
Barn. 6.3	Isa 50:7	
Barn. 6.4	Ps 118:22, 24 (117:22, 24 LXX)	Matt 21:42; Mark 12:10; Luke 20:17
Barn. 6.6	Ps 22:16 (21:17 LXX); and 118:12 (117:12 LXX)	
Barn. 6.7	Isa 3:9–10	
Barn. 6.8 (cf. 6.13)	Exod 33:1, 3	
Barn. 6.12 (cf. 6.18)	Gen 1:26, 28	
Barn. 6.13	an unknown source	
Barn. 6.14	Ezek 11:19	
Barn. 6.16	Ps 42:2 (41:3 LXX); and 22:22 (21:23 LXX)	Heb 2:12 (Ps 22:22)
Barn. 7.3	Lev 23:29	Acts 3:23
Barn. 7.6–7 (cf. also 7.4)	Lev 16:7, 9, 8	
Barn. 7.8	an unknown source	
Barn. 9.1	Ps 18:44 (17:45 LXX)	
Barn. 9.1	Isa 33:13	
Barn. 9.1	Jer 4:4	
Barn. 9.2	Jer 7:2–3	
Barn. 9.2	Ps 34:12 (33:13 LXX) (inter alia)	
Barn. 9.3	Isa 1:2, 10	
Barn. 9.3	Isa 40:3	Matt 3:3; Mark 1:3; John 1:23; Luke 3:4
Barn. 9.5	Jer 4:3–4	
Barn. 9.5	Deut 10:16	
Barn. 9.5	Jer 9:25 LXX	
Barn. 9.8	Gen 14:14; 17:23	
Barn. 10.1 (cf. 10.4–7)	Lev 11:7–15	
Barn. 10.2	Deut 4:10, 13	
Barn. 10.10	Ps 1:1	

Barn. 10.11	Lev 11:3	
Barn. 11.2	Jer 2:12–13	
Barn. 11.3	Isa 16:1–2	
Barn. 11.4	Isa 45:2–3	
Barn. 11.4–5	Isa 33:16–18	
Barn. 11.6–7	Ps 1:3–6	
Barn. 11.9	Zeph 3:19(?)	
Barn. 11.10	a possible allusion to Ezek 47:1–12?	
Barn. 12.1	a tradition in common with 4 Ezra 4:33; 5:5	
Barn. 12.2	an allusion to Exod 17:8–13	
Barn. 12.4	Isa 65:2	Rom 10:21
Barn. 12.6	Lev 26:21	
Barn. 12.7	Num 21:4–9	Cf. John 3:14
Barn. 12.9	Exod 17:14	
Barn. 12.10	Ps 110:1 (109:1 LXX)	Matt 22:44; Mark 12:36; Luke 20:42; Acts 2:34; 1 Cor 15:25; Heb 3:13
Barn. 12.11	Isa 45:1	
Barn. 13.2	Gen 25:21–23	Rom 9:12 (Gen 25:23)
Barn. 13.4	Gen 48:9, 11	
Barn. 13.6	Gen 48:14, 18, 19	
Barn. 13.7	Gen 15:6	Rom 4:3; Gal 3:6; James 2:23
Barn. 14.2	Exod 24:18; 31:18	
Barn. 14.3	Exod 32:7–8, 19	
Barn. 14.7	Isa 42:6–7	
Barn. 14.8	Isa 49:6–7	Acts 13:47 (for Isa 49:6)
Barn. 14.9	Isa 61:1–2	Luke 4:18–19
Barn. 15.1	Exod 20:8 // Deut 5:12	
Barn. 15.2	Exod 31:13–17, etc.	
Barn. 15.3	Gen 2:2–3	Heb 4:4
Barn. 15.8	Isa 1:13	
Barn. 16.2	Isa 40:12; 66:1	Acts 7:49 (Isa 66:1)
Barn. 16.3, 5, 6	unknown sources	

Table 40.1 summarizes Barnabas's use of Scripture and notes instances in which the same text is cited in the New Testament. The sheer number of citations indicates the importance of scriptural interpretation for the author. Barnabas draws on prior tradition, probably including both the use of secondary cita-

tion, that is, scriptural texts lifted from the New Testament and repurposed, and traditional collections of *testimonia* assembled thematically.[9] One can see that, although there are some significant overlaps with the New Testament's use of Scripture, there are also a high number of new texts introduced. Over sixty of these citations find no parallel in the New Testament. Broadly speaking, Barnabas prefers to cite the prophets (roughly thirty-four times), the Pentateuch (roughly twenty times) and the Psalms (roughly eleven times). In this sense, Barnabas's functional canon seems similar to what we find in the New Testament. Even in some instances where the same text is deployed in both Barnabas and the New Testament, the interpretation often differs.[10] For example, in Barn. 12.4, Isa 65:2 is cited—though unlike Paul's use of this text in Rom 10:21 to indicate Jewish resistance to his message, Barnabas takes this as a symbol of the cross.[11] This is in keeping with Barnabas's typological interests. The treatise seems to operate with a kind of evacuating hermeneutic that denies the reality of the institution or literal force of the commandment in the original and focuses everything on the Christian referent to which everything before is a shadowy prefiguration that can only be understood if one has the sort of insight that Barnabas itself divulges. Also notable is the relatively high number of quotations from unknown sources occurring in 2.10 (Apocalypse of Adam?); 4.3 (Enoch?); 4.4 (Danielic?); 7.8 (Day of Atonement); 7.11; 10.5 (one should not eat sea eel or octopus or cuttlefish); 11.9, 10; 12.1. All this suggests that Barnabas might be something like the product of early Christian school activity.

Justin Martyr, *Dialogue with Trypho*

Justin Martyr's *Dialogue with Trypho* comes from a few decades after Barnabas and reflects an even more extensive engagement with both scriptural tradition

---

9. See Klaus Wengst, *Tradition und Theologie des Barnabasbriefes*, AKG 42 (Berlin: de Gruyter, 1971); Ferdinand R. Prostmeier, *Epistola Barnabae/Barnabasbrief: Eingeleitet, kritisch ediert und übersetzt*, FC 72 (Freiburg im Breisgau: Herder, 2018), 51–54.

10. For an analysis, see Maarten J. J. Menken, "Old Testament Quotations in the *Epistle of Barnabas* with Parallels in the New Testament," in *Textual History and the Reception of Scripture in Early Christianity*, ed. Johannes de Vries and Martin Karrer, SCS 60 (Atlanta: Society of Biblical Literature, 2013), 295–321.

11. For the question of whether Barnabas knows the Pauline writings, see Andreas Lindemann, *Paulus im ältesten Christentum: Das Bild des Apostels und die Rezeption der paulinischen Theologie in der frühchristlichen Literatur bis Marcion*, BHT 58 (Tübingen: Mohr Siebeck, 1979), 272–82; James Carleton Paget, "Paul and the Epistle of Barnabas," *NovT* 38, no. 4 (1996): 359–81; Carleton Paget, "Paul and the *Epistle of Barnabas*," in *The Apostolic Fathers and Paul*, ed. Todd D. Still and David E. Whilhite, Pauline and Patristic Scholars in Debate 2 (London: Bloomsbury, 2017), 79–100.

and with Justin's New Testament (and other) predecessors in their use of that tradition.¹² The *Dialogue* purports to be a written account of a debate that happened in Ephesus some years previously (*Dial.* 1.1; cf. Eusebius, *Hist. eccl.* 4.18.6) between a Jew, Trypho, and Justin, the Christian philosopher. The *Dialogue* takes as its theme the establishment of the truth of Christianity over against Judaism, but there are a number of more complex aims being prosecuted as well, including positioning the right kind of Christianity over against various "heretical" alternatives.¹³ That Trypho has been literarily crafted in at least some sense is clear, though opinions vary as to whether and to what degree historical events may lie behind the *Dialogue*.¹⁴ But it seems that Justin is reacting to actual Jewish concerns and objections to the early Christian interpretation of Scripture.¹⁵

Trypho says to Justin that Christians "scorn this covenant, spurn the commands that come afterward, and then you try to convince us that you know God, when you fail to do those things that every God-fearing person would do" (10.3). In response, Justin marshals a large number of scriptural citations in the course of the *Dialogue*, sometimes citing them at great length. Justin strives to prove that Christians are the rightful heirs of the Scriptures of Israel. God merely ordained circumcision, ritual law, and sacrifices as punitive or remedial measures for an intransigent people. Their true telos, however, was always to point to the Messiah in his two comings, first in humility and then in glory. Among the numerous scriptural texts that are discussed, there are some whose accuracy or legitimacy is disputed by Trypho. In a remarkable discussion in *Dial.* 71–73, Justin alleges that the Jews have falsified or deleted pro-Christian passages from the Septuagint: Jewish teachers "have deleted entire passage from the version composed by those elders at the court of Ptolemy [i.e., the Septuagint], in which it is clearly indicated that the Crucified One was foretold as God and man, and

---

12. English translation: Thomas B. Falls, *St. Justin Martyr: "Dialogue with Trypho,"* rev. Thomas P. Halton (Washington, DC: Catholic University of America Press, 2003); Greek text: Philippe Bobichon, *Justin Martyr, "Dialogue avec Tryphon": Édition critique, traduction, commentaire*, 2 vols., Paradosis 47 (Fribourg: Academic Press, 2003); and Miroslav Marcovich, ed., *Iustini Martyris "Dialogus cum Tryphone,"* Patristische Texte und Studien 47 (Berlin: de Gruyter, 1997).

13. See Matthijs den Dulk, *Between Jews and Heretics: Refiguring Justin Martyr's "Dialogue with Trypho,"* Routledge Studies in the Early Christian World (London: Routledge, 2018).

14. For a survey of opinions about Trypho, see Timothy J. Horner, *Listening to Trypho: Justin Martyr's "Dialogue" Reconsidered*, CBET 28 (Leuven: Peeters, 2001), 15–32 (though his quest for an original "Trypho text" is fraught with difficulties).

15. For the argument that Justin derives his understanding of Jewish exegesis from firsthand contact with Jewish teachers (or from Jewish-Christians who had such first-hand contact), see Philippe Bobichon, "Comment Justin a-t-il acquis sa connaissance exceptionnelle des exégèses juives?," *RTP* 139, no. 2 (2007): 101–26.

as about to suffer death on the cross." Justin goes on to mention a dispute about the translation of Isa 7:14 and cites a spurious text ascribed to Ezra; Jer 11:19; a text ascribed to Jeremiah that is also mentioned in Irenaeus (*Haer.* 3.20; 4.22; and *Dem.* 78); and a version of Ps 96:10 (95:10 LXX), "The Lord reigned from the tree," that probably reflects a Christian interpolation.[16] The last of these citations recurs throughout the *adversus Judaeos* literature.

We also find Justin making implicit work of his predecessors' scriptural selections and citations. He made use of at least Paul, Matthew, Luke, and perhaps 1 Clement or Barnabas, together with a number of *testimonia* that probably circulated independently before the composition of his work.[17] One particularly striking example of Justin's reliance on prior scriptural work is found in *Dial.* 95-96. There, without citing or mentioning Paul, Justin brings together the two Deuteronomy citations that form the centerpiece of Pauline argument in Gal 3:10-13, almost certainly indicating his dependence on the unmentioned Pauline letter.[18] But in so doing, Justin has inevitably transformed Paul's argument for his own context. He has, as Rodney Werline notes, "transformed Paul's argument that Jesus' death removes the curse of Torah, nullifies it, and unites Jew and Gentile in Christ, into a prophecy about the tensions between Jews and Christians in the second century CE."[19] From a detailed investigation of the textual character

---

16. See William Adler, "The Jews as Falsifiers: Charges of Tendentious Emendation in Anti-Jewish Christian Polemic," in *Translation of Scripture: Proceedings of a Conference at the Annenberg Research Institute, May 15-16, 1989*, ed. David M. Goldenberg, JQRSupp (Philadelphia: Annenberg Research Institute, 1990), 1-27, who also notes how this criticism was resisted subsequently by Origen, Jerome, and Augustine.

17. See the magisterial treatment, still unsurpassed, in Oskar Skarsaune, *The Proof from Prophecy: A Study in Justin Martyr's Proof-Text Tradition; Text-Type, Provenance, Theological Profile*, NovTSup 56 (Leiden: Brill, 1987).

18. See, e.g., Charles H. Cosgrove, "Justin Martyr and the Emerging Christian Canon: Observations on the Purpose and Destination of the Dialogue with Trypho," *VC* 36, no. 3 (1982): 225; and esp. Dietrich-Alex Koch, *Die Schrift als Zeuge des Evangeliums: Untersuchungen zur Verwendung und zum Verständnis der Schrift bei Paulus*, BHT 69 (Tübingen: Mohr Siebeck, 1986), 250-51; contra, e.g., Philipp Vielhauer, "Paulus und das Alte Testament," in *Studien zur Geschichte und Theologie der Reformation: Festschrift für Ernst Bizer*, ed. L. Abramowski and J. F. G. Goeters (Neukirchen-Vluyn: Neukirchener Verlag, 1969), 39 n. 28. Note the discussion of options in Lindemann, *Paulus im ältesten Christentum*, 353-55.

19. Rodney Werline, "The Transformation of Pauline Arguments in Justin Martyr's Dialogue with Trypho," *HTR* 92, no. 1 (1999): 91. Werline also provides a convincing argument that Justin has used and transformed Paul's picture of Abraham. See also the attention paid to the connections between Paul's arguments and Justin's in David Rokéah, *Justin Martyr and the Jews*, JCPS 5 (Leiden: Brill, 2002), 43-80, 130-32 (although Rokéah seems to me to present Paul in a contestable manner and to overstate the hostility of both Justin and Paul to Jewish tradition).

of Justin's citations, Oskar Skarsaune concludes that "Justin seems in most cases to be directly drawing on Romans when he has OT quotations in common with Romans."[20] He goes on to note that Galatians also provides key texts for Justin, while the evidence from 1 Corinthians is less conclusive.[21]

Table 40.2. Shared Citations in Justin's Dialogue *and Paul*

Justin	Scriptural citation	Paul
Dial. 11.5; 23.4; 92.3; 119.5–6	Gen 15:6	Rom 4:3, 9
Dial. 11.5; 119.4	Gen 17:5	Rom 4:17
Dial. 17.2	Isa 52:5	Rom 2:24
Dial. 20.1	Exod 32:6	1 Cor 10:7
Dial. 27.3 (= esp. Rom 3:12–17)	Pss 14:1–3; 5:9; 140:3; 10:7; Isa 59:7–8; Ps 36:1	Rom 3:10–18
Dial. 32.5; 123.4	Isa 29:14	1 Cor 1:19
Dial. 36.3–4	Ps 24:1	1 Cor 10:26
Dial. 39.1	1 Kgs 19:10, 14, 18	Rom 11:3–4
Dial. 39.4; 87.6	Ps 68:18	Eph 4:8
Dial. 42.1	Ps 19:5	Rom 10:18
Dial. 42.2; 114.2	Isa 53:1	Rom 10:16
Dial. 78.11	Isa 29:13–14	1 Cor 1:19
Dial. 95.1	Deut 27:26	Gal 3:10
Dial. 96.1	Deut 21:23	Gal 3:13
Dial. 118.4 (Isa 52:15–53:1)	Isa 52:15	Rom 15:21
Dial. 119.2 (includes Deut 32:16–23)	Deut 32:21	Rom 10:19
Dial. 119.4	Isa 65:1–2	Rom 10:20–21
Dial. 130.1, 4	Deut 32:43	Rom 15:10
Dial. 140.3; cf. *Dial.* 32.2; 55.3; *1 Apol.* 53.7	Isa 1:9	Rom 9:29
Dial. 141.2	Ps 32:1–2	Rom 4:7–8

One could repeat this exercise for Matthew, Luke, and other of Justin's predecessor texts. Table 40.2 offers a striking indication of the ways in which a New Testament author's selection of texts can set the agenda for subsequent authors even if Paul's particular interpretation of a scriptural text was not always

---

20. Skarsaune, *Proof from Prophecy*, 96.
21. Skarsaune, *Proof from Prophecy*, 99–100. Table 40.2 is adapted from the tables in Skarsaune, 93–100. Note also Isa 54:1 in *1 Apol.* 53.5 and Gal 4:27.

preserved or respected. If Justin is writing from Rome, it may be unsurprising that he knows and relies on the letter Paul sent there and that was presumably preserved by its Roman recipients. The fact that Justin differs in notable instances in the use to which he puts these texts suggests that he may have treated Paul and the other authors on whom he relies as "finding aids" for locating hermeneutically significant passages in the Scriptures. Justin's overriding aim of demonstrating that the Scriptures fundamentally prefigure a turn away from Israel toward the gentiles differs at a basic level from Paul's own hermeneutical priorities since Paul remains within the realm of Judaism.

Dialogue of Jason and Papiscus

Next we turn to a minor text preserved only in a handful of quotations, the *Dialogue of Jason and Papiscus*, traditionally though not certainly ascribed to Aristo of Pella.[22] The second-century physician and critic of the Christian movement, Celsus, derided the dialogue in his anti-Christian treatise, the *True Doctrine* (Ἀληθής λόγος), as a work that "does not deserve laughter, but rather pity and hatred."[23] Origen, in reply, asserts to the contrary that "if one reads it impartially, one will discover that the book does not even arouse laughter, in a writing in which a Christian discusses with a Jew by means of Jewish Scripture and teaches that the messianic prophecies suit Jesus, and yet in a manner not ignoble nor unbecoming the character of a Jew, the other man opposes his argument with his reply."[24] This remark offers us a sense of the contents of the *Dialogue*, and casts it as in certain ways similar to Justin's *Dialogue with Trypho*. Most notable for our purposes is the assertion that the exchange takes place "by means of Jewish scripture" (ἀπὸ τῶν Ἰουδαϊκῶν γραφῶν). In contrast to the *Dialogue with Trypho*, however, the Jewish interlocutor, Papiscus, converts and asks to be baptized in the end.[25]

---

22. On this dialogue, see Lawrence Lahey, "Evidence for Jewish Believers in Christian-Jewish Dialogues through the Sixth Century (Excluding Justin)," in *Jewish Believers in Jesus: The Early Centuries*, ed. Oskar Skarsaune and Reidar Hvalvik (Peabody, MA: Hendrickson, 2007), 585–91. Texts and translations of the fragments are conveniently collected in Harry Tolley, "The Jewish-Christian Dialogue *Jason and Papiscus* in Light of the Sinaiticus Fragment," *HTR* 114, no. 1 (2021): 1–26. I draw on Tolley's article for the sources that follow.

23. Preserved in Origen, *Cels.* 4.52 = Tolley, "Jewish-Christian Dialogue *Jason and Papiscus*," 21.

24. Origen, *Cels.* 4.52 = Tolley, "Jewish-Christian Dialogue *Jason and Papiscus*," 21.

25. Celsus Africanus, *Ad Vigilium Episcopum de Iudaica Incredulitate* = Tolley, "Jewish-Christian Dialogue *Jason and Papiscus*," 22–23.

Jerome twice mentions the *Dialogue* (as the *Altercatio Jasonis et Papisci*). In his commentary on Paul's letter to the Galatians, he refers to the alternative Greek text for Deut 21:23 found in the dialogue: λοιδορία θεοῦ ὁ κρεμάμενος ("the one who hangs is a curse of God"), as opposed to Paul's ἐπικατάρατος πᾶς ὁ κρεμάμενος (ἐπὶ ξύλου) ("every one hanging [on a tree] is cursed").[26] From this brief reference, we can infer that the *Dialogue* probably engaged in secondary citation through Paul but did so with some knowledge of alternative renderings. In his *Hebrew Questions on Genesis*, Jerome also criticizes the *Dialogue*, together with Tertullian and Hilary, for suggesting that the Hebrew of Gen 1:1 is "In the son, God made heaven and earth."[27]

In the recently discovered *Homily on the Feast of the Circumcision* by Sophronius of Jerusalem (ca. 625 CE), we find the most substantial quotation to date of the *Dialogue*.[28] The conversation centers on the Christian shift from Sabbath to Lord's day. When asked by his Jewish interlocutor about the rationale for this shift, the (Jewish-)Christian Jason replies, "In this way, God commanded this through Moses, saying: 'Behold, I am making the last things just as the first! The last [day of the week] is the Sabbath, but day one after the Sabbath is first.'"[29] Here the Dialogue cites the same agraphon that we find also cited in Barn. 6.13 as a Mosaic authority.[30] Not unlike some of the "fuzzier" citations in the New Testament, so also here we see an authority invoked whose status as such may have been disputed, or at least an authority that failed to be received in the eventual canon, a phenomenon that is not uncommon in the second century.[31] The fragment also cites a christological reading of Gen 1:1, like the one Jerome complains about, a reading that might owe something to John 1:1.

---

26. Jerome, *Ad Galatas* 2.3.13b–14 = Tolley, "Jewish-Christian Dialogue *Jason and Papiscus*," 22.

27. *Qu. hebr. Gen.* 1:1 = Tolley, "Jewish-Christian Dialogue *Jason and Papiscus*," 22.

28. John M. Duffy, "New Fragments of Sophronius of Jerusalem and Aristo of Pella?," in *Bibel, Byzanz und Christlicher Orient: Festschrift für Stephen Gerö zum 65. Geburtstag*, ed. Dmitrij Bumazhnov et al., OLA 187 (Leuven: Peeters, 2011), 15–28; François Bovon and John M. Duffy, "A New Greek Fragment from Ariston of Pella's *Dialogue of Jason and Papiscus*," *HTR* 105, no. 4 (2012): 457–65; Tolley, "Jewish-Christian Dialogue *Jason and Papiscus*."

29. See Tolley, 24–25.

30. See Alfred Resch, *Agrapha: Ausserkanonische Schriftfragmente gesammelt und untersucht*, 2nd ed. (Leipzig: Hinrichs, 1906), 167–68; Ferdinand R. Prostmeier, *Der Barnabasbrief: Übersetzt und erklärt*, KAV 8 (Göttingen: Vandenhoeck & Ruprecht, 1999), 275–76. Also, note the very fragmentary papyrus PSI XI 1200 bis, which seems to contain similar text; Antonio Carlini, "Amicus Plato . . . : A proposito di PSI XI 1200, Gorg. 447B ss.," in *Miscellanea Papyrologica*, ed. Rosario Pintaudi, Papyrologica florentina 7 (Florence: Gonnelli, 1980), 41–45.

31. For "fuzzier" citations, see Greg Lanier, "'As It Is Written' . . . Where? Examining Generic Citations of Scripture in the New Testament," *JSNT* 43, no. 4 (2021): 570–604.

Early Latin Examples: Tertullian, *Adversus Judaeos* and Ps.-Cyprian, *De duobus montibus Sina et Sion*

The beginnings of our evidence for the Latin-speaking anti-Jewish tradition take us to North Africa and to Tertullian's treatise *Adversus Judaeos*. The authorship and integrity of the tractate have been disputed, not least in light of its rough character and the overlap in book three of Tertullian's *Adversus Marcionem*. Geoffrey Dunn has mounted a case for its authorship by Tertullian and its integrity as a treatise.[32] Our interest in the use of Scripture is not materially affected by these considerations. The treatise begins by recalling a debate between a Christian and a proselyte Jew. Since everyone was clamoring to be heard at once, "it was decided to settle the questions that have been reconsidered in writing, after a more careful examination of the texts" (1.1). This tractate is the written reconsideration of such texts. Although Tertullian does not clarify whether he was involved in the debate personally or whether this is simply a literary device, at points he uses the direct address to speak to an interlocutor (e.g., 7.1). The interpretation of the Scriptures is central to the argument; as Tertullian summarizes later in the work: "from that accord of the Scriptures, by prior authority of the majority of instances, we have spoken out against the Jews" (11.11).

Broadly one might say that the first half of the treatise is involved in demonstrating the temporality and limited validity of Jewish institutions, while the second half takes a christological turn and demonstrates that Christ's coming, in two stages, was foretold in Scripture. Old favorites recur, such as reflection on Isa 7 and the virgin birth, but we also find a lengthy reflection on Dan 9's seventy weeks (see 8.3–16). Much of the substance of the argumentation harkens back to Tertullian's predecessors, Irenaeus and Justin, and Tertullian also makes ready use of the New Testament's own deployment of Jewish Scripture to prove his case—taking, for example, the citations and allusions to the Psalms in the passion narratives as demonstrating that Jesus's death was predicted (and so ordained) by God.[33]

If Tertullian deploys several traditional strategies to make his case, he also occasionally introduces new tactics. One novel argument is an appeal to a "law of paradise" more ancient than the law of Moses:

---

32. Geoffrey Dunn, *Tertullian's "Aduersus Iudaeos": A Rhetorical Analysis*, PatMS 19 (Washington, DC: Catholic University of America Press, 2008).

33. For Tertullian's predecessors, see Geoffrey Dunn, *Tertullian*, ECF (London: Routledge, 2004), 66–67.

the law of God was already in existence before Moses, as [it had been given] first at a more ancient time—in paradise—then afterward to the patriarchs. And thus also, it has been given to the Jews at certain times when [God] wanted, and has been reformed at certain times. The result is that now we do not pay attention to the law of Moses in such a way as though it were the first law, but as a subsequent one. At a certain time, God both produced this law for the gentiles, as had been promised through the prophets, and that has improved it, as [God] foretold would happen, with the result that, just as the law has been given through Moses at a certain time (*certo tempore*), so it may be believed to have been observed and kept for a limited time (*temporaliter*).[34]

This strategy enables Tertullian to conceive of the Mosaic law as in some real sense ordained by God but, at the same time, not as a permanent or binding legislation but rather one subject to "reformation" at given periods (cf. also 4.11). Many of the Mosaic injunctions, such as circumcision, come to be seen as punitive ("a sign for a stubborn people" in 3.7), and like Barnabas, Tertullian emphasizes the role of the golden calf episode in turning God's favor away from Israel (3.13).

We find the familiar critique of Levitical sacrifices by means of appeal to the prophets' anti-cultic rhetoric. According to Tertullian, this rhetoric demonstrates that "carnal sacrifices are understood as having been rejected" (5.6). In part this is due to the fact that, on Tertullian's understanding, the Jews "were marked out indelibly as answerable for the crime of idolatry" (1.7). Throughout his treatise, he operates with an allegorical understanding that displaces literal observance: "It is clear that both a temporal sabbath has been shown and an eternal sabbath has been foretold. A circumcision of the flesh has been foretold and a circumcision of the spirit foretold beforehand. A temporal law and an eternal law have been announced. Carnal sacrifices and spiritual sacrifices have been foreshown" (6.1). In all this it is clear that, as Dunn characterizes him, "Tertullian was an out-and-out supersessionist; for him, the Christians had replaced the Jews."[35]

Another early treatise in the Latin *adversus Judaeos* tradition is the Pseudo-Cyprianic *De duobus montibus Sina et Sion*, which probably belongs to the third century.[36] This anonymous tractate considers the "two mountains," Sinai and

---

34. *Adv. Jud.* 2.9; see Sabrina Inowlocki, "Tertullian's Law of Paradise (*Adversus Judaeos* 2): Reflections on a Shared Motif in Jewish and Christian Literature," in *Paradise in Antiquity: Jewish and Christian Views*, ed. Markus Bockmuehl and Guy G. Stroumsa (Cambridge: Cambridge University Press, 2010), 106. Latin text from Hermann Tränkle, *Q. S. F. Tertulliani Adversus Iudaeos* (Wiesbaden: Steiner, 1964).

35. Dunn, *Tertullian*, 65.

36. Anni Maria Laato, *Jews and Christians in "De duobus montibus Sina et Sion": An Ap-

Zion, and offers a thoroughly typological interpretation of Israel's Scripture: "That which was written figuratively in the Old Testament," the treatise begins, "must be understood spiritually through the New Testament, since it has been fulfilled in reality through Christ."[37] Like Paul in Gal 4:21–31, the author uses Mt. Sinai to stand in for the Mosaic covenant but speaks of Zion instead of Paul's "Jerusalem above." The structure and argument are not entirely lucid, but a binary hermeneutic operates throughout: Sinai, and by extension the Jews, are earthly (2.2), carnal and hard (3.2), and "turned away from God in hatred" (7.1), while Zion, and Christians, are heavenly and spiritual (2.2), holy (3.1), and those whose resurrected flesh will be "spiritual and immortal" (11.1).[38] Jerusalem is a "prophet-killing city" that is "accursed and abandoned, and not undeserved, by the prophet Isaiah's spiritual word" (3.1). In the end, according to the author, the treatise has demonstrated "that the two mountains Sinai on earth and Zion in heaven, are images of the two covenants: the old, Sinai, and the new, Zion. These two mountains, that is, covenants, have in later times been proven and revealed to be two peoples: the earlier and preceding Jewish people and the later and subsequent Christian people" (11.1). The text is brief enough that we can supply a list of its principal citations (table 40.3).[39]

Table 40.3. Scriptural Citations in De duobus montibus Sina et Sion

4.1	Gen 2:7
3.3	Gen 25:23
6.2	Gen 25:25
6.1	Exod 16:4
9.6	Ps 1:3
2.1; 9.1	Ps 2:6–7a
9.3–5	Ps 24:3–5 (23:3–5 LXX)[40]
9.6	Ps 37:9 (36:9 LXX)
9.1	Ps 96:10 (95:10 LXX)

---

proach to Early Latin Adversus Iudaeos Literature (Åbo: Åbo Akademi University Press, 1998); critical edition: Clara Burini, ed., *Pseudo Cipriano, I due monti Sinai e Sion: De duobus montibus*, BPat (Fiesole: Nardini, 1994).

37. 1.1, cited according to Laato's translation.

38. For the lack of lucidity, note that, e.g., the etymological section in 3.4–5.2, in which we find a particular emphasis on the putative etymologies of Hebrew names as foreshadowing what was to come, does not obviously advance the argument of the treatise.

39. This table draws on Laato, *Jews and Christians*, 182–87, where she also supplies a helpful list of introductory formulas.

40. The Latin translation of the Psalms follows the Septuagint numbering.

7.2	Ps 106:14 (105:14 LXX)
8.3	Ps 137:3–4 (136:3–4 LXX)
7.2; 14.1	Song 1:6
7.1	Wis 2:17–22
1.2; 9.5, 6; 10.1	Isa 2:3
4.1	Isa 40:12
8.3	Amos 8:10
6.2	Mal 1:2–3
15.2	Matt 12:18–20
10.1	Matt 27:46
1.1	John 1:17
4.3	John 2:19–21
9.6	John 7:37–38
9.2	1 Cor 1:18
9.2	1 Cor 1:23–24

Although this perspective could be expanded by including allusions and unmarked citations, we see a clear emphasis on Psalms, Genesis, and Isaiah, together with the clear work that New Testament citations also perform for the author. There are some surprises here, though, including the use of the Song of Songs twice. We also find alongside the scriptural citations some apocryphal traditions. We find a discussion of the apocryphal account of Adam's origin reflecting the four points of the compass in 4.2 and a New Testament agraphon: "He himself guides and advises us in his disciple John's letter to Paul: 'See me in yourselves like any of you sees himself in the water or a mirror'" (13.1).[41] The textually dubious citation of Ps 96:10 (95:10 LXX) also appears here (9.1).

Later Trajectories: Cyprian, *Ad Quirinum*, and Ps.-Gregory of Nyssa, *Testimonia*

In the constraints of this chapter, we can do no more than offer a brief look at succeeding developments. In addition to the ongoing production of dialogues and treatises, we see the emergence of works that consist of long chains of citations of the scriptural text, arranged under thematic headings.[42] The snowballing

---

41. On this see J. E. Bruns, "Biblical Citations and the Agraphon in Pseudo-Cyprian's Liber de montibus Sina et Sion," *VC* 26, no. 2 (1972): 112–16.

42. Further on the development of the *testimonia* hypothesis, note the foundational work (excessive in certain regards but amassing a huge amount of detail) by J. Rendel Harris with

tradition of selecting scriptural passages for their apologetic value comes to full fruition in these collections.

Cyprian describes his *Ad Quirinum* this way: "this treatise has been ordered in an abridged compendium, so that I should not scatter what was written in too diffuse an abundance, but, as far as my poor memory suggested, might collect all that was necessary in selected and connected heads, under which I may seem, not so much to have treated the subject, as to have afforded materials for others to treat it."[43] The headings include such topics as "That the Jews could understand nothing of the Scriptures unless they first believed in Christ"—a proposition proved by citing Isa 7:9, John 8:24, Hab 2:4, Gen 15:6, and Gal 3:6–9. That the New Testament supplies at least some of the precedents in selecting the scriptural passages is demonstrated here by the inclusion of Gal 3:6–9, together with Gen 15:6, which Galatians cites. Book 1 is particularly anti-Jewish, while book 2 is taken up with christological matters, and book 3 contains practical advice.[44] Typically, passages are strung together with only brief introductory phrases ("In Isaiah" or "In like manner, Paul to the Galatians"), although there are occasionally more substantial interventions made (e.g., at the end of 2.16 on the "stone").

The *Testimonies against the Jews* that survive under the name of Gregory of Nyssa similarly collects scriptural citations under twenty-two headings: the Trinity, the incarnation, the virgin birth, Jesus's miracles, his betrayal and passion, the cross and the darkness that attended it, the resurrection, the ascension, the glory of the church, circumcision, sacrifices, the Sabbath, sealing with the sign of the cross, the gospel, the unbelief of the Jews and the church of the gentiles (ch. 16, one of the longest in the work), the parousia, the name "Christians," that Herod

---

Vacher Burch, *Testimonies*, 2 vols. (Cambridge: Cambridge University Press, 1916–1920). On Harris's work, see esp. the excellent and sympathetic treatment of Alessandro Falcetta, "The Testimony Research of James Rendel Harris," *NovT* 45, no. 3 (2003): 280–99. Cf. also Martin C. Albl, *"And Scripture Cannot Be Broken": The Form and Function of the Early Christian Testimonia Collections*, NovTSup 96 (Leiden: Brill, 1999).

43. Book 1, Praef., cited according to the ANF translation. On this treatise, see Edwina Murphy, "'As Far as My Poor Memory Suggested': Cyprian's Compilation of *Ad Quirinum*," *VC* 68, no. 5 (2014): 533–50, arguing for the authenticity of this against Charles A. Bobertz, "An Analysis of *Vita Cyprian* 3.6–10 and the Attribution of *Ad Quirinum* to Cyprian of Carthage," *VC* 46, no. 2 (1992): 112–28; cf. Bobertz, "'For the Vineyard of the Lord of Hosts Was the House of Israel': Cyprian of Carthage and the Jews," *JQR* 82, no. 1–2 (1991): 1–15, esp. 3–5. The latter article argues that Cyprian's Jews are almost entirely biblical rather than contemporary; contrast William Horbury, *Jews and Christians in Contact and Controversy* (Edinburgh: T&T Clark, 1998), ch. 7, who sees an actual dialogue with Jews envisaged by the treatise.

44. For another collection of testimonia related particularly to Christology, see Robert V. Hotchkiss, ed. and trans., *A Pseudo-Epiphanius Testimony Book*, SBLTT 4 (Missoula, MT: Scholars Press, 1974).

will be troubled, baptism, the flight into Egypt, and the Holy Spirit.[45] Broadly the testimonies emphasize the failings of Israel, the obsolescence of the Jewish law, and God's foreshadowing of the Christian church as Israel's replacement. A wide range of texts is quoted, with particularly strong representation from the Psalms and Isaiah. We find occasional allusions or summaries rather than full citations, and also several false attributions: Isaiah 49:6–9 is ascribed to Jeremiah (4); Jer 7:22 is ascribed to Isaiah (12); Num 11:16 is ascribed to Exodus (22); and Hag 2:4–5 is ascribed to Zechariah.[46] A number of the cited scriptural texts seem to be lifted from the New Testament, as their variant textual form indicates, although there are also a number of unknown or uncertain citations.[47]

Conclusion

The majority of the authors of the New Testament were Jews, citing their ancestral Scripture to make sense of and communicate the significance of what had happened in the life and death of Jesus. If at times they cite Scripture polemically, this is often an intra-Jewish dispute, and so not foreign to the broader scriptural discourse of the Second Temple period. But arguments born in intra-Jewish discussion look very different when they take root in the soil of a gentile church, particularly when that church gains political power. In the development of the *adversus Judaeos* tradition, we witness an increasing distance between the social contexts of earliest Christian interpretation and those of the subsequent church.

---

45. See the excellent edition, translation, and study by Martin C. Albl: *Pseudo-Gregory of Nyssa, "Testimonies against the Jews,"* WGRW 5 (Atlanta: Society of Biblical Literature, 2004). A list of all the texts cited in the work can be found on pp. xxiii–xxx.

46. See further Albl, *Pseudo-Gregory of Nyssa*, 138.

47. Albl, *Pseudo-Gregory of Nyssa*, 138–40. Note the following: "You complete the years, O God, by your power" (Ἔτη τελεῖς, ὁ Θεός, τῇ δυνάμει σου, 1.4); "You will see the great king" (Καὶ βασιλέα μέγαν ὄψεσθε, 2.4); "Look! The heifer has given birth, and has not given birth" (Ἰδοὺ ἡ δάμαλις τέτοκε, καὶ οὐ τέτοκε, 3); "'And then these things will be accomplished,' says the Lord, 'when the tree of trees is bent, and rises, and when blood drips from the tree'" (καὶ τότε ταῦτα συντελεσθήσεται, λέγει Κύριος, ὅταν ξύλον ξύλων κλιθῇ, καὶ ἀναστῇ, καὶ ὅταν ἐκ ξύλου αἷμα στάξει, 7); "Circumcise your heart, and not the flesh of your foreskin" (Περιτέμνεσθε τὴν καρδίαν ὑμῶν, καὶ μὴ τὴν σάρκα τῆς ἀκροβυστίας ὑμῶν, 11); "Let me destroy this people, and I will give you a nation that is great, and much more so than this one" (Ἔασόν με ἐξαλεῖψαι τὸν λαὸν τοῦτον, καὶ δώσω σοι ἔθνος μέγα, καὶ πολὺ μᾶλλον τούτου, 16); "And in the end his name will be manifest in all the earth, and many peoples will be called by his name, and those going along his ways will live in them" (καὶ ἔσται ἐπ᾽ ἐσχάτου τὸ ὄνομα αὐτοῦ ἐπιφανὲς ἐν πάσῃ τῇ γῇ, καὶ τῷ ὀνόματι αὐτοῦ ἐπικληθήσονται λαοὶ πολλοί, καὶ κατὰ τὰς ὁδοὺς αὐτοῦ πορευθέντες, ζήσονται ἐν αὐταῖς, 18, ascribed to Hosea).

Nevertheless, we find certain commonalities. In the New Testament and in the texts surveyed here, the Scriptures of Israel are the unquestioned fund of authority that resource thought and discourse. Naturally there are significant and fraught differences in the interpretative starting points and hermeneutical sensibilities of the Christians of the second and third centuries and their Jewish interlocutors, but both agreed on the need to justify their stances from Scripture. We lack extant contemporary Jewish anti-Christian literature, but the earliest works of the *adversus Judaeos* tradition do offer us a plausible window onto this facet of the debate.[48] We also find a certain fuzziness to the interpretative practices employed throughout the tradition. Citations are regularly ascribed to the wrong author, a relatively high number of unknown or apocryphal texts are cited, and we find the perdurance of textually dubious citations, like Ps 96:10 (95:10 LXX).

To differing degrees in these texts, we find that the selection of passages by the authors of the New Testament has had an impact on subsequent interpretation of them. Particularly as time passes, we find a de facto setting of the hermeneutical agenda by the ways in which the New Testament authors point to important texts or "text-plots" to which subsequent authors return, whether directly or by means of secondary citations via the New Testament.[49] Sometimes the interpretations are radically different, but even when the interpretative moves seem similar, the different contexts speak to the consequential shifts in import. In a certain sense, the *adversus Judaeos* tradition demonstrates that, viewed from the standpoint of their reception, the authors of the New Testament lent hostages to fortune in selecting the scriptural passages on which they constructed their arguments.

Bibliography

Adler, William. "The Jews as Falsifiers: Charges of Tendentious Emendation in Anti-Jewish Christian Polemic." Pages 1–27 in *Translation of Scripture: Proceedings of a Conference at the Annenberg Research Institute, May 15–16, 1989*. Edited by David M. Goldenberg. JQRSupp. Philadelphia: Annenberg Research Institute, 1990.

---

48. One might, however, note the surprising lack of scriptural citation in the material derived from "Celsus's Jew," as he is referred to, in the *Contra Celsum*; see James Carleton Paget, "The Jew of Celsus and *adversus Judaeos* Literature," *ZAC* 21, no. 2 (2017): 232.

49. The language of "text-plots" is drawn from C. H. Dodd, *According to the Scriptures: The Sub-structure of New Testament Theology* (New York: Scribners, 1953).

Albl, Martin C. *"And Scripture Cannot Be Broken": The Form and Function of the Early Christian* Testimonia *Collections*. NovTSup 96. Leiden: Brill, 1999.

———. *Pseudo-Gregory of Nyssa, "Testimonies against the Jews."* WGRW 5. Atlanta: Society of Biblical Literature, 2004.

Bobertz, Charles A. "An Analysis of *Vita Cyprian* 3.6-10 and the Attribution of *Ad Quirinum* to Cyprian of Carthage." *VC* 46, no. 2 (1992): 112-28.

———. "'For the Vineyard of the Lord of Hosts Was the House of Israel': Cyprian of Carthage and the Jews." *JQR* 82, no. 1-2 (1991): 1-15.

Bobichon, Philippe. "Comment Justin a-t-il acquis sa connaissance exceptionnelle des exégèses juives?" *RTP* 139, no. 2 (2007): 101-26.

———. *Justin Martyr, "Dialogue avec Tryphon": Édition critique, traduction, commentaire*. 2 vols. Paradosis 47. Fribourg: Academic Press, 2003.

Bovon, François, and John M. Duffy. "A New Greek Fragment from Ariston of Pella's *Dialogue of Jason and Papiscus*." *HTR* 105, no. 4 (2012): 457-65.

Bruns, J. E. "Biblical Citations and the Agraphon in Pseudo-Cyprian's Liber de montibus Sina et Sion." *VC* 26, no. 2 (1972): 112-16.

Burini, Clara, ed. *Pseudo Cipriano, I due monti Sinai e Sion: De duobus montibus*. BPat. Fiesole: Nardini, 1994.

Carleton Paget, James. "Anti-Judaism and Early Christian Identity." *ZAC* 1, no. 2 (1997): 195-225.

———. *The Epistle of Barnabas: Outlook and Background*. WUNT 2/64. Tübingen: Mohr Siebeck, 1994.

———. "The Jew of Celsus and *adversus Judaeos* Literature." *ZAC* 21, no. 2 (2017): 201-42.

———. "Paul and the Epistle of Barnabas." *NovT* 38, no. 4 (1996): 359-81.

———. "Paul and the *Epistle of Barnabas*." Pages 79-100 in *The Apostolic Fathers and Paul*. Edited by Todd D. Still and David E. Whilhite. Pauline and Patristic Scholars in Debate 2. London: Bloomsbury, 2017.

Carlini, Antonio. "Amicus Plato . . . : A proposito di PSI XI 1200, Gorg. 447B ss." Pages 41-45 in *Miscellanea Papyrologica*. Edited by Rosario Pintaudi. Papyrologica florentina 7. Florence: Gonnelli, 1980.

Cosgrove, Charles H. "Justin Martyr and the Emerging Christian Canon: Observations on the Purpose and Destination of the Dialogue with Trypho." *VC* 36, no. 3 (1982): 209-32.

Dodd, C. H. *According to the Scriptures: The Sub-structure of New Testament Theology*. New York: Scribners, 1953.

Duffy, John M. "New Fragments of Sophronius of Jerusalem and Aristo of Pella?" Pages 15-28 in *Bibel, Byzanz und Christlicher Orient: Festschrift für Stephen Gerö zum 65. Geburtstag*. Edited by Dmitrij Bumazhnov, Emmanouela

Grypeou, Timothy B. Sailors, and Alexander Toepel. OLA 187. Leuven: Peeters, 2011.

Dulk, Matthijs den. *Between Jews and Heretics: Refiguring Justin Martyr's "Dialogue with Trypho."* Routledge Studies in the Early Christian World. London: Routledge, 2018.

Dunn, Geoffrey. *Tertullian*. ECF. London: Routledge, 2004.

———. *Tertullian's "Aduersus Iudaeos": A Rhetorical Analysis.* PatMS 19. Washington, DC: Catholic University of America Press, 2008.

Falcetta, Alessandro. "The Testimony Research of James Rendel Harris." *NovT* 45, no. 3 (2003): 280–99.

Falls, Thomas B. *St. Justin Martyr: "Dialogue with Trypho."* Revised by Thomas P. Halton. Washington, DC: Catholic University of America Press, 2003.

Harris, J. Rendel, with Vacher Burch. *Testimonies*. 2 vols. Cambridge: Cambridge University Press, 1916–1920.

Horbury, William. *Jews and Christians in Contact and Controversy.* Edinburgh: T&T Clark, 1998.

Horner, Timothy J. *Listening to Trypho: Justin Martyr's "Dialogue" Reconsidered.* CBET 28. Leuven: Peeters, 2001.

Hotchkiss, Robert V., ed. and trans. *A Pseudo-Epiphanius Testimony Book.* SBLTT 4. Missoula, MT: Scholars Press, 1974.

Inowlocki, Sabrina. "Tertullian's Law of Paradise (*Adversus Judaeos* 2): Reflections on a Shared Motif in Jewish and Christian Literature." Pages 103–19 in *Paradise in Antiquity: Jewish and Christian Views.* Edited by Markus Bockmuehl and Guy G. Stroumsa. Cambridge: Cambridge University Press, 2010.

Isodore of Seville. *The "Etymologies" of Isidore of Seville.* Translated by Stephen A. Barney, W. J. Lewis, J. A. Beach, and Oliver Berghof. Cambridge: Cambridge University Press, 2006.

Koch, Dietrich-Alex. *Die Schrift als Zeuge des Evangeliums: Untersuchungen zur Verwendung und zum Verständnis der Schrift bei Paulus.* BHT 69. Tübingen: Mohr Siebeck, 1986.

Krauss, Samuel. *The Jewish-Christian Controversy from the Earliest Times to 1789.* Vol. 1, *History.* Edited and revised by William Horbury. TSAJ 56. Tübingen: Mohr Siebeck, 1996.

Külzer, Andres. *"Disputationes graecae contra Iudaeos": Untersuchungen zur byzantinischen antijüdischen Dialogliteratur und ihrem Judenbild.* Byzantinisches Archiv 19. Leipzig: Teubner, 1999.

Laato, Anni Maria. *Jews and Christians in "De duobus montibus Sina et Sion": An Approach to Early Latin Adversus Iudaeos Literature.* Åbo: Åbo Akademi University Press, 1998.

Lahey, Lawrence. "Evidence for Jewish Believers in Christian-Jewish Dialogues through the Sixth Century (Excluding Justin)." Pages 581–639 in *Jewish Believers in Jesus: The Early Centuries*. Edited by Oskar Skarsaune and Reidar Hvalvik. Peabody, MA: Hendrickson, 2007.

Lanier, Greg. "'As It Is Written'... Where? Examining Generic Citations of Scripture in the New Testament." *JSNT* 43, no. 4 (2021): 570–604.

Limor, Ora, and Guy G. Stroumsa, eds. *"Contra Iudaeos": Ancient and Medieval Polemics between Christians and Jews*. TSMJ 10. Tübingen: Mohr Siebeck, 1996.

Lindemann, Andreas. *Paulus im ältesten Christentum: Das Bild des Apostels und die Rezeption der paulinischen Theologie in der frühchristlichen Literatur bis Marcion*. BHT 58. Tübingen: Mohr Siebeck, 1979.

Marcovich, Miroslav, ed. *Iustini Martyris "Dialogus cum Tryphone."* Patristische Texte und Studien 47. Berlin: de Gruyter, 1997.

Menken, Maarten J. J. "Old Testament Quotations in the *Epistle of Barnabas* with Parallels in the New Testament." Pages 295–321 in *Textual History and the Reception of Scripture in Early Christianity*. Edited by Johannes de Vries and Martin Karrer. SCS 60. Atlanta: Society of Biblical Literature, 2013.

Morlet, Sébastien, Olivier Munnich, and Bernard Pouderon, eds. *Les dialogues adversus Iudaeos: Permanences et mutations d'une tradition polémique*. CEAug 196. Paris: Institut d'Études Augustiniennes, 2013.

Murphy, Edwina. "'As Far as My Poor Memory Suggested': Cyprian's Compilation of *Ad Quirinum*." *VC* 68, no. 5 (2014): 533–50.

Prostmeier, Ferdinand R. *Der Barnabasbrief: Übersetzt und erklärt*. KAV 8. Göttingen: Vandenhoeck & Ruprecht, 1999.

———. *Epistola Barnabae/Barnabasbrief: Eingeleitet, kritisch ediert und übersetzt*. FC 72. Freiburg im Breisgau: Herder, 2018.

Resch, Alfred. *Agrapha: Ausserkanonische Schriftfragmente gesammelt und untersucht*. 2nd ed. Leipzig: Hinrichs, 1906.

Rokéah, David. *Justin Martyr and the Jews*. JCPS 5. Leiden: Brill, 2002.

Schreckenberg, Heinz. *Die christlichen Adversus-Judaeos-Texte und ihr literarisches und historisches Umfeld*. 3 vols. EHS.T 172. Frankfurt am Main: Lang, 1982–1994.

Simon, Marcel. *"Verus Israel": A Study of the Relations between Christians and Jews in the Roman Empire AD 135–425*. Translated by Henry McKeating. Oxford: Oxford University Press, 1986.

Skarsaune, Oskar. *The Proof from Prophecy: A Study in Justin Martyr's Proof-Text Tradition; Text-Type, Provenance, Theological Profile*. NovTSup 56. Leiden: Brill 1987.

Stroumsa, Guy G. "From Anti-Judaism to Antisemitism in Early Christianity?" Pages 1–26 in *"Contra Iudaeos": Ancient and Medieval Polemics between Christians* and Jews. Edited by Ora Limor and Guy G. Stroumsa. TSMJ 10. Tübingen: Mohr Siebeck, 1996.

Taylor, Miriam S. *Anti-Judaism and Early Christian Identity: A Critique of the Scholarly Consensus*. StPB 46. Leiden: Brill, 1995.

Tolley, Harry. "The Jewish-Christian Dialogue *Jason and Papiscus* in Light of the Sinaiticus Fragment." *HTR* 114, no. 1 (2021): 1–26.

Tränkle, Hermann. *Q. S. F. Tertulliani Adversus Iudaeos*. Wiesbaden: Steiner, 1964.

Vielhauer, Philipp. "Paulus und das Alte Testament." Pages 33–62 in *Studien zur Geschichte und Theologie der Reformation: Festschrift für Ernst Bizer*. Edited by Luise Abramowski and J. F. Gerhard Goeters. Neukirchen-Vluyn: Neukirchener Verlag, 1969.

Wengst, Klaus. *Tradition und Theologie des Barnabasbriefes*. AKG 42. Berlin: de Gruyter, 1971.

Werline, Rodney. "The Transformation of Pauline Arguments in Justin Martyr's *Dialogue with Trypho*." *HTR* 92, no. 1 (1999): 79–93.

Williams, A. Lukyn. *"Adversus Judaeos": A Bird's Eye View of Christian Apologiae until the Renaissance*. Cambridge: Cambridge University Press, 1935.

41

Israel's Scriptures in Marcion and the Critical Tradition

DIETER T. ROTH

It is widely recognized that the second century CE is a vitally important era for the study of early Christian history and for numerous issues related to scholarship on Christian origins. The debates and discussions surrounding Israel's Scriptures that took place during this time only underscore the validity of this general observation, as evidenced by heated disputes concerning, for example, the place of these texts within early Christianity, their proper interpretation, and whether or not they were "divinely inspired" (and if so, by which deity?). Of particular significance in these discussions are three individuals whose views of Israel's Scriptures diverged rather significantly from those of protoorthodox groups and who, in part for this reason, were branded as heretics by their opponents.[1] These three figures are Marcion, Apelles, and Ptolemy, and though their views also entail important differences, they all embraced critical views of Israel's Scriptures. Though the ensuing discussion certainly cannot be exhaustive, the first part of this chapter contains three sections considering each of their views regarding Israel's Scriptures and the reasons why these views were held. The second part contains three further sections considering select gospel texts and the

---

1. For "protoorthodox" as a designation for the trajectory in early Christianity that led to the later views defined as "orthodoxy," see Bart Ehrman, *The Orthodox Corruption of Scripture: The Effect of Early Christological Controversies on the Text of the New Testament* (Oxford: Oxford University Press, 1993), 12–13.

readings of them arising out of or related to Marcion's, Apelles's, and Ptolemy's particular views of Israel's Scripture. Ultimately, this chapter seeks to highlight the manner in which these "heretical" movements can offer important insight into and shed light upon a sometimes overlooked critical tradition concerning Israel's Scriptures in early Christianity.

Marcion's View of Israel's Scriptures

Any attempt to understand the place and use of Israel's Scriptures in Marcion's thought, at least as it is presented to us in the sources,[2] must begin by recognizing the fundamental significance of Marcion's conviction that the deity revealed as the Father of Jesus Christ is not the same deity revealed in Israel's Scriptures. Though the various comments concerning the specifics of Marcion's views at this point are not entirely consistent, leading E. C. Blackman to observe that "concerning the precise nature of Marcion's contrasted gods or principles there has been some dispute," the fact that Marcion distinguished between the Father of Jesus Christ and the Creator God is not a matter of dispute.[3] For instance, Justin Martyr stated that "there is a certain Marcion of Pontus, who even now is teaching his disciples to believe that there is some other god greater than the Demiurge [i.e., the Creator]" (1 Apol. 26.5).[4] Furthermore, Irenaeus of Lyon, in Haer. 3.12.12, indicated that followers of Marcion say that there are two gods, one being "good," but the other being "evil,"[5] though in Haer. 3.25.3, Irenaeus reported that Marcion divided God

---

2. As noted near the outset of my monograph, Dieter T. Roth, *The Text of Marcion's Gospel*, NTTSD 49 (Leiden: Brill, 2015), 7: "it is important to note that there are no extant manuscripts of any of Marcion's works and all that is known . . . is found in the writings of his adversaries." See also Judith M. Lieu, *Marcion and the Making of a Heretic: God and Scripture in the Second Century* (Cambridge: Cambridge University Press, 2015), 7: "the sources for Marcion and his teaching come almost exclusively from those who opposed him."

3. E. C. Blackman, *Marcion and His Influence* (London: SPCK, 1948), 66. Elements of the following are drawn from and overlap with my more extensive discussion in Dieter T. Roth, "Evil in Marcion's Conception of the Old Testament God," in *Evil in Second Temple Judaism and Early Christianity*, ed. Chris Keith and Loren T. Stuckenbruck, WUNT 2/417 (Tübingen: Mohr Siebeck, 2016), 340–56.

4. Μαρκίωνα δέ τινα Ποντικόν, ὃς καὶ νῦν ἔτι ἐστὶ διδάσκων τοὺς πειθομένους, ἄλλον τινὰ νομίζειν μείζονα τοῦ δημιουργοῦ θεόν· (text of the Charles Munier edition *Justin, Apologie pour les chrétiens*, SC 507 [Paris: Cerf, 2006]). Unless otherwise noted, translations here and throughout are by the author.

5. *Et quidem hi qui a Marcione sunt statim blasphemant Fabricatorem, dicentes eum malorum factorem, propositum initii sui intolerabiliorem habentes, duos naturaliter dicentes Deos distantes ab inuicem, alterum quidem bonum, alterum autem malum* (text of the Adelin Rous-

in two, considering one to be "good" and the other to be "judicial."[6] In addition, Clement of Alexandria, in *Strom.* 2.39.1, commented that Marcionites do not view the law as "evil," but rather as "just" because they distinguish "the good" from "the just,"[7] and in *Strom.* 3.12.1, he referred to Marcion's followers viewing natural processes as evil because they derived from evil matter and a just Creator. Finally, in his five-volume work *Adversus Marcionem*, Tertullian made several explicit references to Marcion considering the Creator as "inferior"[8] and indicated that Marcion became afflicted with the idea of there being two gods on the basis of Luke 6:43: "No good tree bears bad fruit, nor again does a bad tree bear good fruit" (NRSV).[9] By combining this verse with the Creator God's words in Isa 45:7, "I create evil" ("cited" as *Ego sum qui condo mala* in *Marc.* 1.2.2),[10] Marcion interpreted the evil tree creating evil fruit as referring to the Creator and believed that there must be another God to correspond with the good tree creating good fruit.[11]

The dualism set forth by Marcion had several significant implications for his perception of and interaction with Israel's Scriptures. First, it is important to note that Marcion viewed an antithetical relationship between the Father of Jesus Christ and the Creator God as having been revealed in their respective Scriptures. That is to say, Marcion believed that the Father of Jesus had been revealed in the one gospel and ten letters of Paul used in Marcion's church and that the Creator God had been revealed in Israel's Scripture.[12] Thus, even though

---

seau and Louis Doutreleau edition *Irénée de Lyon, Contre les hérésies, Livre III: Tome II, texte et traduction*, SC 211 [Paris: Cerf, 1974]).

6. *dividens Deum in duo, alterum quidem bonum et alterum iudicialem dicens* (Rousseau/Doutreleau).

7. Τί τοίνυν τὸν νόμον βούλονται; Κακὸν μὲν οὖν οὐ φήσουσι, δίκαιον δέ, διαστέλλοντες τὸ ἀγαθὸν τοῦ δικαίου (text of the Claude Mondésert edition *Clément d'Alexandrie, Les stromates: Stromate II*, SC 38 [Paris: Cerf, 1954]).

8. See *Marc.* 1.6.4 (*deterior*); 1.11.9 (*inferiorus*); 2.2.3 (*inferiorus*); and 5.18.10, where there is an explicit juxtaposition of a "superior" and an "inferior" god.

9. *Passus, infelix, huius praesumptionis instinctum de simplici capitulo dominicae pronuntiationis, in homines non in deos disponentis exempla illa bonae et malae arboris, quod neque bona malos neque mala bonos proferat fructus* (*Marc.* 1.2.1; text of the Claudio Moreschini edition in *Tertullien, Contre Marcion, Tome I*, SC 365 [Paris: Cerf, 1990]). See also the references to Marcion and Luke 6:43 in Hippolytus, *Haer.* 10.15; Pseudo-Tertullian, *Adversus omnes haereses* 6; and Origen, *Princ.* 2.5.4.

10. See also the reference in *Marc.* 2.14.1 to Marcionites arguing that, on the basis of Isa 45:7, the Creator himself claims to be the creator of evil: *Ecce, enim inquiunt, ipse se conditorem profitetur malorum dicens: Ego sum qui condo mala* (text of the Claudio Moreschini edition in *Tertullien, Contre Marcion, Tome II*, SC 368 [Paris: Cerf, 1991]).

11. *In creatorem interpretatus malam arborem malos fructus condentem . . . alium deum praesumpsit esse debere in partem bonae arboris bonos fructus* (Moreschini, *Marc.* 1.2.2).

12. For a discussion and reconstruction of Marcion's Gospel, see Roth, *Text of Marcion's*

Israel's Scriptures in Marcion and the Critical Tradition

Marcion rejected the deity found in Israel's Scriptures and denied the authority of Israel's Scriptures for his movement, the texts constituting Israel's Scriptures were viewed as correct and accurate in their portrayals of the Creator. Thus, they are important for underscoring Marcion's belief concerning a basic incompatibility between the Creator and both the Father of Christ and Christ himself.[13] In fact, one of the writings attributed to Marcion was a work entitled *Antitheses*, and though it has been debated whether it also contained commentary on Marcion's Scriptures and/or a summary of Marcionite theology, it is clear that the *Antitheses* did, at the very least, juxtapose texts found in Israel's and in Marcion's Scriptures.[14] The purpose of this juxtaposition was to highlight the antithetical character of the deity in Israel's Scriptures and the deity or that deity's Christ presented in Marcion's Scriptures.[15] For example, the Creator God revealed his ignorance by having to ask Adam where he was, whereas Jesus knew the thoughts of men.[16] The Creator God required eye for eye and tooth for tooth, whereas Je-

---

Gospel; and for Marcion's Pauline letter collection, see Ulrich Schmid, *Marcion und sein Apostolos: Rekonstruktion und historische Einordnung der marcionitischen Paulusbriefausgabe*, ANTF 25 (Berlin: de Gruyter, 1995).

13. Andrew McGowan's statement that Marcion's "two gods and rejection of the Hebrew Bible" are "among the few things most people are agreed upon about Marcion's doctrine" is true as far as it goes, though there are important nuances to the precise nature of the "rejection of the Hebrew Bible" (see McGowan, "Marcion's Love of Creation," *JECS* 9, no. 3 [2001]: 295-96).

14. For a helpful overview of these issues, see Sebastian Moll, *The Arch-Heretic Marcion*, WUNT 250 (Tübingen: Mohr Siebeck, 2010), 107-14. See also the discussion in Eric W. Scherbenske, "Marcion's *Antitheses* and the Isagogic Genre," *VC* 64, no. 3 (2010): 255-79. Though Adolf von Harnack admitted that a reconstruction of the *Antitheses* was ultimately impossible, he provided what he saw as citations from and references to it in appendix 5 of his monograph (*Marcion: Das Evangelium vom fremden Gott; Eine Monographie zur Geschichte der Grundlegung der katholischen Kirche*, 2nd ed., TUGAL 45 [Leipzig: Hinrichs, 1924], 256*-313*; the impossibility of reconstructing the *Antitheses* is admitted on p. 84).

15. Tertullian stated, *Nam hae sunt Antithesis Marcionis, id est contrariae oppositiones, quae conantur discordiam evangelii cum lege committere, ut ex diversitate sententiarum utriusque instrumenti diversitatem quoque argumententur deorum* (Moreschini, *Marc.* 1.19.4). Lieu's observations concerning the role that the Scriptures play here is also worth noting: "the 'Antitheses' do assume that the scriptural accounts offer an appropriate foundation for investigating the character of God," and "it was from Scripture that the Creator could be characterised as loving war, inconsistent, responsible for evil, and so on" (*Marcion and the Making of a Heretic*, 286, 357).

16. See *Adamantius Dialogue*, 36, lines 13-14 (1.17). References to the *Adamantius Dialogue* provide both the page and line number from the W. H. van de Sande Bakhuyzen edition of the Greek text in Pseudo-Origen, *Der Dialog des Adamantius: ΠΕΡΙ ΤΗΣ ΕΙΣ ΘΕΟΝ ΟΡΘΗΣ ΠΙΣΤΕΩΣ*, GCS 4 (Leipzig: Hinrichs, 1901), followed by the divisions in C. P. Caspari's edition of Rufinus's Latin translation of the text in *Kirchenhistorische Anecdote: Nebst neuen Ausgaben patristischer und kirchlich-mittelaltlicher Schriften*, vol. 1, *Lateinische Schriften: Die Texte und die Anmerkungen* (Oslo: Malling, 1883), 1-129.

sus taught that one must turn the other cheek.[17] The prophet of the Creator God called on a bear to devour children, whereas Jesus loved little children and had them come to him.[18] The Creator God brought his people out of Egypt carrying the spoils of gold, silver, and possessions, whereas Jesus, when he sent out his disciples, told them not to carry two tunics, bags, gold, or a staff.[19]

Though Israel's Scriptures were therefore, in a certain sense, important for Marcion's thought as the negative pole in his antithetical constructions and for the demonstration of the inferior character of the Creator,[20] when it came to Marcion's own Scriptures, the church fathers believed that they had been created through an editorial process. For instance, Tertullian stated that Marcion viewed the gospel text as having been falsified or interpolated by defenders of Judaism (*a protectoribus Iudaismi, Marc.* 4.4.4) and that Marcion thus sought to expunge these corruptions from his gospel.[21] Though one may question some elements of the polemic of Marcion's opponents accusing him of being a mutilator of the Gospel of Luke,[22] many scholars continue to view Marcion as having edited at least some sections of his gospel text.[23] This editing activity appears to have been driven, at least in part, by the desire to sever connections between Jesus and

---

17. See Tertullian, *Marc.* 4.16.2; and *Adamantius Dialogue*, 32, lines 3–6 (1.15).
18. See Tertullian, *Marc.* 4.23.4; and *Adamantius Dialogue*, 32, lines 24–27 (1.16).
19. See Tertullian, *Marc.* 4.24.1; and *Adamantius Dialogue*, 22, lines 1–9 (1.10).
20. See also Lieu, *Marcion and the Making of a Heretic*, 285–88.
21. For discussions of the meaning of this disputed passage, see Dieter T. Roth, "Prophets, Priests, and Kings: Old Testament Figures in Marcion's Gospel and Luke," in *Connecting Gospels: Beyond the Canonical/Non-Canonical Divide*, ed. Francis Watson and Sarah Parkhouse (Oxford: Oxford University Press, 2018), 44–45 n. 21; and Enrico Norelli, "Marcion et les disciples de Jésus," *Apocrypha* 19 (2008): 11–12; contra Matthias Klinghardt, *Das älteste Evangelium und die Entstehung der kanonischen Evangelien*, 2 vols., TANZ 60 (Tübingen: Francke, 2015), 1:138; and Klinghardt, "Markion vs. Lukas: Plädoyer für die Wiederaufnahme eines alten Falles," *NTS* 52, no. 4 (2006): 495. See also Christopher M. Hays, "Marcion vs. Luke: A Response to the *Plädoyer* of Matthias Klinghardt," *ZNW* 99, no. 2 (2008): 218–19; and Lieu, *Marcion and the Making of a Heretic*, 415–16.
22. See, e.g., Tertullian's question, "What Pontic mouse is more ravenous [*comisor*] than he who has gnawed away the Gospels?" (*Marc.* 1.1.5; see also *Marc.* 4.2–6). Epiphanius contended that Marcion "did not cut just the beginning [of Luke] off. He also cut off many words of the truth both at the end and in the middle" (*Pan.* 42.9.2) and in twenty-three of seventy-eight scholia referenced passages or words that Marcion οὐκ εἶχεν or that he removed (using verbs such as παρακόπτω). The English translation here and throughout is that found in *The Panarion of Epiphanius of Salamis*, trans. Frank Williams, 2nd ed., 2 vols., NHS 35, 36 (Leiden: Brill, 2009).
23. See, e.g., Lieu's nuanced conclusion: "At the end of these investigations it remains certain that the Gospel that Marcion used as his core text followed the same structure and sequence of textual units as canonical Luke, but that it may have lacked some of the passages and verses now part of the latter.... Marcion did edit the version of the written Gospel that he received, although arguably not to such an extent as his opponents believed, and as might appear from

the Creator God or the Scriptures of the Creator God. For this reason, it is not surprising to find opponents of Marcion, and Epiphanius in particular, indicating that passages connecting Jesus to the fulfillment of Israel's Scriptures, such as Jesus's self-identification as a prophet who must be killed in Jerusalem and the subsequent lament over Jerusalem (Luke 13:33–34) or Jesus's statement that everything written about the Son of Man by the prophets will be accomplished (Luke 18:31–33), were not found in Marcion's Gospel.[24] The same can be said for some passages found in Luke involving characters found in Israel's Scriptures.[25] Passages referring to and employing such figures that are attested as not being present in Marcion's text include the entirety of Luke 1–2; Jesus's genealogy in Luke 3:23–38; Jonah being a sign to the Ninevites along with the references to the Queen of the South and Solomon in Luke 11:30–32; the references to Abel, Zechariah, and the prophets in Luke 11:49–51; and Moses and the burning bush in Luke 20:37–38a.[26] Though the final section of this chapter will highlight that rejecting or redacting does not fully capture Marcion's interaction with Israel's Scriptures, such responses form a central aspect of Marcion's legacy.

Apelles's View of Israel's Scripture

In addition to interacting with Marcion himself, several sources discuss followers or disciples of Marcion, among whom the most prominent appears to have been Apelles.[27] Though the descriptions of Apelles and his views are at

---

a comparison between a reconstruction of his 'Gospel' and canonical Luke" (Lieu, *Marcion and the Making of a Heretic*, 209).

24. In addition to the twenty-three scholia in which Epiphanius discussed "excised" elements (see n. 22), in fourteen scholia he made explicit reference to variant readings (see Roth, *Text of Marcion's Gospel*, 272). For Luke 13:33–34, see *Pan.* 42.11.6(41), discussed in Roth, *Text of Marcion's Gospel*, 75, 319–20. For Luke 18:31–33, see *Pan.* 42.11.6(52), discussed in Roth, *Text of Marcion's Gospel*, 75, 326–27.

25. The following examples are taken from my longer discussion in Roth, "Prophets, Priests, and Kings," 45–46. In that discussion I also note that not *every* reference to figures from Israel's Scriptures is attested as absent from Marcion's Gospel.

26. For Luke 1–2, see Tertullian, *Marc.* 4.7.11; Epiphanius, *Pan.* 42.9.1 and 42.11.4–5; Origen, *Ex libro Origenis in Epistolam ad Titum*; Hippolytus, *Haer.* 7.31.5; and Jerome, *Jo. hier.* 34. For the references and brief discussion, see Roth, *Text of Marcion's Gospel*, 75, 285–86, 396–97. For Luke 3:23–38, see Epiphanius, *Pan.* 42.11.4–5, discussed in Roth, *Text of Marcion's Gospel*, 75, 285–86. For Luke 11:30–32, see Epiphanius, *Pan.* 42.11.6 (σχ. 25), discussed in Roth, *Text of Marcion's Gospel*, 75, 310. For Luke 11:49–51, see Epiphanius, *Pan.* 42.11.6 (σχ. 28), discussed in Roth, *Text of Marcion's Gospel*, 75, 312. For Luke 20:37–38a, see Epiphanius, *Pan.* 42.11.6 (σχ. 56), discussed in Roth, *Text of Marcion's Gospel*, 76, 329–30.

27. See, e.g., Eusebius, *Hist. eccl.* 5.13. As noted above concerning Marcion (see n. 2), it is

times conflicting, the report by Eusebius of Rhodo's description of Apelles having formed a school within the Marcionite movement is generally accepted (*Hist. eccl.* 5.13.1–2).²⁸ At the same time, Apelles appears to have modified Marcion's teaching in several significant ways, including the rejection of Marcion's dualism (Epiphanius, *Pan.* 42.1.4–6; Eusebius, *Hist. eccl.* 5.13.2).²⁹ He also posited that Christ either took a true body from the substance of the stars as he descended to the earth or from the four elements once he was on the earth (Tertullian, *Carn. Chr.* 6.3; Epiphanius *Pan.* 42.2.3).³⁰ Most significantly for present purposes and as discussed below, he formulated his conception of Israel's Scriptures in a rather different way than did Marcion. The works attested as having been written by Apelles include the *Syllogisms* (*Syllogismoi*) and the *Revelations* or *Manifestations* (*Phaneroseis*).³¹ The latter work was apparently based on revelations given through a prophetess named Philoumene (Tertullian, *Praescr.* 30.6), and the former work was dedicated to demonstrating that Israel's Scriptures did not contain, as Marcion believed, true teachings concerning an inferior God, but rather that these texts themselves were inferior and untrue.³²

Though the entire work is no longer extant, several fragments of the contents of the *Syllogisms* have been preserved.³³ For instance, Ambrose presented a syllogism that Sebastian Moll rightly considered "ideal for a demonstration of Apelles' method."³⁴ In *Parad.* 8.38, Ambrose wrote, "Did God know Adam would transgress his commandments or did he not? If he did not know, there is no

---

once again important to bear in mind that the information we have concerning Apelles derives from his opponents, a point rightly emphasized by Katharina Greschat, *Apelles und Hermogenes: Zwei theologische Lehrer des zweiten Jahrhunderts*, VCSup 48 (Leiden: Brill, 2000), 2, 18.

28. See the discussion in Gerhard May, "Apelles und die Entwicklung der markionitischen Theologie," in *Gerhard May: Markion; Gesammelte Aufsätze*, ed. Katharina Greschat and Martin Meiser, VIEG.B 68 (Mainz: von Zabern, 2005), 94–97.

29. Tertullian reported that Apelles understood the creator to be a "renowned angel" who, apparently due to the sinfulness of his actions, had to repent for his creation of the world (*Carn. Chr.* 8.2; see also *Praescr.* 34.4). See further, May, "Apelles," 100–102. Epiphanius refers to the creator in Apelles's system as "not good" and his creatures as "not well made" due to his "inferior intelligence" (*Pan.* 44.1.6).

30. For additional references, see Roman Hanig, "Der Beitrag der Philumene zur Theologie der Apelleianer," *ZAC* 3, no. 2 (1999): 251 n. 43.

31. See Pseudo-Tertullian, *Adversus omnes haereses* 6.6; and Tertullian, *Praescr.* 30.6.

32. Concerning Philoumene, see Hanig, "Der Beitrag der Philumene," 241–65.

33. The text appears to have been of considerable length as Ambrose, *Parad.* 5.28, comments on statements found in volume 38 (!) of the work.

34. Moll, *Arch-Heretic*, 153. For the arguments that the ensuing syllogism was authored by Apelles, see Greschat, *Apelles und Hermogenes*, 60; and Adolf von Harnack, "Sieben neue Bruchstücke der Syllogismen des Apelles," in *Die gnostischen Quellen Hippolyts in seiner Hauptschrift gegen die Häretiker*, ed. Hans Stählin, TUGAL 6.3 (Leipzig: Hinrichs, 1890), 118.

assertion of divine power. But if he did know and yet gave orders that inevitably were neglected, it is not godlike to give a superfluous precept. But he gave an order to that first-formed Adam which he knew he would in no way keep. God does nothing superfluous; therefore the writing is not of God."[35] Apelles argued that regardless of whether God knew or did not know that his commandment to Adam would be transgressed, in either scenario, the God presented in Genesis reveals an attribute that is not consistent with divine attributes. In other words, Genesis reveals a God who is either not omniscient or a God who commanded something superfluous, neither of which is consistent with what Apelles claimed it means to be God. Therefore, it follows that a text setting forth God in this manner is not a text that has its origin in God. A further example of Apelles's reasoning can be found in Origen, who recounted that Apelles disputed the veracity of the account concerning Noah's ark by arguing that there would not even have been room for four elephants, let alone all the animals that were supposedly on the ark. For this reason, Apelles is reported to have concluded, "it is evident, therefore, that the story has been fabricated: if this is so, it is evident that this writing is not of God" (Origen, *Hom. Gen.* 2.2).[36] Though the discussion of additional fragments could reveal further nuances of Apelles's views,[37] these two examples provide adequate grounds for understanding the basis for Hippolytus's report that Apelles "slanders the Law and the Prophets, claiming that the Scriptures are merely human and false" (*Haer.* 7.38.2)[38] or Pseudo-Tertullian's statement that Apelles wrote the *Syllogisms* in order to prove that "everything which Moses has written about God is not true, but is false" (*Adversus omnes haereses* 6.6).[39] It is not surprising,

---

35. The translation is that of Robert M. Grant, *Heresy and Criticism: The Search for Authenticity in Early Christian Literature* (Louisville: Westminster John Knox, 1993), 82. Jerome, *Pelag.* 3.6, attributes this same line of thought to "Marcion" and all the "heretics who mutilate the Old Testament." Harnack, *Marcion*, 274*, ascribed the passage in Jerome to Marcion's *Antitheses*; however, Greschat, *Apelles und Hermogenes*, 65–66, contends that it should be viewed as coming from Apelles's *Syllogisms*.

36. *Constat ergo fictam esse fabulam; quod si est, constat non esse hanc a Deo scripturam* (text of the Peter Habermehl edition of Rufinus's translation in *Die Homilien zum Buch Genesis*, Origenes Werke mit deutscher Übersetzung 1.2 [Berlin: de Gruyter, 2011]). For the Greek text as found in the catena, see Louis Doutreleau, "Le fragment grec de l'homélie II d'Origène sur la Genèse: Critique du texte," *RHT* 5 (1975): 36, 38.

37. Harnack, *Marcion*, 404*–20*, provides excerpts from the sources for Apelles, and Greschat, *Apelles und Hermogenes*, 50–68, analyzes sixteen extant fragments from Apelles's *Syllogisms*. See also the discussion in Grant, *Heresy and Criticism*, 79–86.

38. νόμον δὲ καὶ προφήτας δυσφημεῖ, ἀνθρώπινα καὶ ψευδῆ φάσκων εἶναι τὰ γεγραμμένα· (text of the Miroslav Marcovich edition in *Hippolytus: Refutatio Omnium Haeresium*, PTS 25 [Berlin: de Gruyter, 1986]). See also Hippolytus, *Haer.* 10.20.2.

39. *Omnia, quaecumque Moyses de deo scripserit, vera non sint, sed falsa sint* (text of the

therefore, to find Hans von Campenhausen concluding that, differently from Marcion and other "heretics," it was only Apelles who, "so far as we know, dared to dismiss the Old Testament as nothing more than an untrustworthy collection of lies and fables."[40]

At the outset of this section, however, it was noted that the descriptions of Apelles's views are not entirely consistent. Thus, on the one hand, and in line with the discussion of the *Syllogisms* above, we can read Origen's claim that Apelles considered "the Scriptures of the Jews to be myths" (*Cels.* 5.54).[41] On the other hand, Pamphilus of Caesarea referred to a remark by Origen that Apelles "did not in every way deny the Law and the Prophets to be of God."[42] Furthermore, Epiphanius cites Apelles referring to an agraphon and stating, "he [i.e., Jesus] said in the Gospel, Be ye able money-changers. For from all of scripture I select what is helpful and make use of it" (*Pan.* 44.2.6).[43] The application of this statement from "the Gospel" is, according to Apelles, that just as able money changers distinguish between a real and counterfeit coin, one must distinguish between the real and the counterfeit in "all of scripture." As Moll points out, such statements do not seem to "portray Apelles" as a "radical Old Testament critic" in quite the same way as is apparently set forth elsewhere.[44] The conflicting testimony is not easy to reconcile, and various explanations have been presented in the scholarly literature: Apelles changed his mind and attitude toward Israel's Scriptures later in life, or he "learned a lesson" from too radical of a rationalist approach to Israel's Scriptures and thus softened his views, or he levied his negative evaluations against the "Mosaic" texts in particular.[45] Yet, regardless of whether Apelles

---

Emil Kroymann edition in *Quinti Septimi Florentis Tertulliani Opera*, vol. 2, *Opera Montanistica*, CCSL 2 [Turnhout: Brepols, 1954]).

40. Hans von Campenhausen, *The Formation of the Christian Bible*, trans. J. A. Baker (Philadelphia: Fortress, 1972), 77.

41. μῦθον ἡγούμενος εἶναι τὰ Ἰουδαίων γράμματα (text of the Paul Koetschau edition in *Origenes Werke*, vol. 2, *Buch 5–8 gegen Celsus; Die Schrift vom Gebet*, GCS 3 [Leipzig: Hinrich, 1899]).

42. *Licet non omnibus modis Dei esse deneget Legem vel prophetas* (text of the Georg Röwekamp edition *Pamphilus von Caesarea: Apologia pro Origine/Apologie für Origenes*, FC 80 [Turnhout: Brepols, 2005]).

43. Concerning this agraphon, "Be ye able money-changers," see the discussion in Giovanni Battista Bazzana, "Apelles and the Pseudo-Clementine Doctrine of the False Pericopes," in *"Soyez des changeurs avisés": Controverses exégétiques dans la littérature apocryphe chrétienne*, ed. Gabriella Aragione and Rémi Gounelle, CBiPa 12 (Strasbourg: Université de Strasbourg, 2012), 11–32.

44. Moll, *Arch-Heretic*, 156. See also May, "Apelles," 98. Harnack, *Marcion*, 192 n. 1, stated that given the general testimony of the sources, one is "unprepared" for or "caught off guard" by these statements attributed to Origen and found in Epiphanius.

45. For changing his mind, see Éric Junod, "Les attitude d'Apelles, disciple de Marcion, à l'égard de l'Ancien Testament," *Aug* 22 (1982): 113–33. Junod posits that in the later *Phanero-*

rejected Israel's Scriptures as a "false" revelation in part or in toto, the significant point remains that he did not agree with Marcion's view of these Scriptures being a "true" revelation concerning an "inferior" God.

Ptolemy's View of Israel's Scriptures

A final "heretic" often brought into contact with both Marcion and Valentinus is Ptolemy, a figure perhaps best known for his *Letter to Flora*.[46] When considering this individual, one should begin by noting that there has been significant scholarly debate concerning whether this Ptolemy is the same Ptolemy that Justin Martyr records as having been martyred under the Roman prefect Lollius Urbicus (mid-second century CE; *2 Apol.* 1–2) and whether the female convert mentioned by Justin is Flora. Though one can understand why scholars have been "tempted" to make this association, it is not certain, and despite remaining an "intriguing possibility," will not be assumed here.[47]

Ptolemy's *Letter to Flora* has been preserved in Epiphanius, *Pan.* 33.3–7, and for several reasons, it is this text that will be the primary focus of the ensuing

---

seis Apelles altered his earlier position set forth in *Syllogismoi*. A century earlier, Adolf von Harnack argued that Apelles initially rejected Israel's Scriptures, later distinguished between that which is true and that which is false in them, but ultimately returned to the position of rejecting them (*De Apellis gnosi monarchica* [Leipzig: Bidder, 1874], 66–67, 69–71). For softening his views, see Moll, *Arch-Heretic*, 157. For Mosaic texts, see Greschat, *Apelles und Hermogenes*, 68–69.

46. A helpful outline of the letter highlighting the rhetorical structure of the work can be found in Ismo Dunderberg, *Beyond Gnosticism: Myth, Lifestyle, and Society in the School of Valentinus* (New York: Columbia University Press, 2008), 80. Although the caveats in my ensuing discussion in the main text should be kept in mind, still important to consult is the introduction to the edition by Gilles Quispel, *Ptolémée, Lettre à Flora: Texte, Traduction et Introduction*, 2nd ed., SC 24 (Paris: Cerf, 1966).

47. Note the observation by Winrich Löhr, "La doctrine de Dieu dans la Lettre à Flora de Ptolémée," *RHPR* 75, no. 2 (1995): 179: "on est *tenté* d'avancer l'hypothèse (*assez douteuse, il faut l'admettre*) qu'elle est bel et bien cette même Flora à qui Ptolémée avait adressé sa Lettre justement fameuse" [ET: "one is *tempted* to put forward the hypothesis (*quite dubious, it must be admitted*) that she is indeed this same Flora to whom Ptolemy had addressed his justly famous letter"] (emphasis added). The "intriguing possibility" quotation is from Ismo Dunderberg, "The School of Valentinus," in *A Companion to Second-Century Christian "Heretics,"* ed. Antti Marjanen and Petri Luomanen, VCSup 76 (Leiden: Brill, 2005), 76. The rationale for this identification is helpfully summarized in Gerd Lüdemann, "Zur Geschichte des ältesten Christentums in Rom: I. Valentin und Marcion II. Ptolemäus und Justin," *ZNW* 70, no. 1–2 (1979): 101–2; as are the grounds for questioning the identification in Christoph Markschies, "New Research on Ptolemaeus Gnosticus," *ZAC* 4, no. 2 (2000): 247–49. A particularly balanced discussion of the question can be found in Dunderberg, *Beyond Gnosticism*, 90–93.

discussion. First, though several sources present Ptolemy as a Valentinian, including Epiphanius, the writing we have from Ptolemy's own hand offers rather different types of allegorical interpretations than those ascribed to the Valentinians in Irenaeus, *Haer.* 1.1–9, a point to which I will return below.[48] Second, though Ptolemy concluded his letter with comments that Flora will learn, "God willing," the "origin and generation" of "the natures" that "arose from the first principle of all" (*Pan.* 33.7.8–9), it is uncertain whether Ptolemy ever ended up offering this teaching or whether he would have presented it along the lines of the Valentinian cosmogenic myth presented elsewhere. The *Letter to Flora* itself, however, contains few elements, if any, of this myth, and importing it into the reading of the letter may end up perpetuating "old prejudices derived from the early anti-Valentinian polemicists such as Tertullian."[49] For these reasons, even if there were some type of historical connection between Ptolemy and Valentinus, there is value in following Ismo Dunderberg's suggestion that it is "advisable to interpret Ptolemaeus's *Letter to Flora* without trying to read too much developed Valentinian mythology into it."[50]

In the introduction to his letter, Ptolemy included a statement that identifies two positions concerning the law given through Moses: "For some say it was given by our God and Father but others, taking the direction opposite to theirs, insist that it was given by our adversary the devil, the author of corruption—as, indeed, they ascribe the creation of the world to him, calling him the father and maker of this universe" (*Pan.* 33.3.2). Though there is widespread agreement that the "some" group consists of protoorthodox Christians, the identity of the "others" has been debated. Werner Foerster and Bentley Layton, for instance, ascribed the view to certain "gnostics," whereas Winrich Löhr entertained the idea that the view may have been an invention by Ptolemy.[51] Though Adolf von

---

48. See Epiphanius, *Pan.* 33.1.1; along with, e.g., Irenaeus, *Haer.* 1 prologue; Hippolytus, *Haer.* 6.35.6; and Tertullian, *Val.* 4.2.

49. Dunderberg, *Beyond Gnosticism*, 78. Dunderberg refers to Tertullian, *Val.* 1.16–18, and cites: "They do not even reveal their secrets to their own disciples before they make them of their own, but instead they have a trick by which they persuade them before they teach."

50. Dunderberg, *Beyond Gnosticism*, 79.

51. See Werner Foerster, *Von Valentin zu Herakleon: Untersuchungen über die Quellen und die Entwicklung der valentinianischen Gnosis*, BZNW 7 (Giessen: Töpelmann, 1928), 81–82; and Bentley Layton, *The Gnostic Scriptures: A New Translation with Annotations and Introductions* (New York: Doubleday, 1987), 307. See Winrich A. Löhr, "Die Auslegung des Gesetzes bei Markion, den Gnostikern und den Manichäern," in *Stimuli: Exegese und ihre Hermeneutik in Antike und Christentum; Festschrift für Ernst Dassmann*, ed. Georg Schöllgen and Clemens Scholten, Jahrbuch für antikes Christentum Ergänzungsband 23 (Münster: Aschendorff, 1996), 80 n. 11.

Harnack was of the opinion that the identification of this view with Marcion was "not certain," this identification has often been posited in the scholarly literature.[52] One can read, on the one hand, the claim of Elaine Pagels that "both Justin and Ptolemy, in their respective writings, actively opposed the teaching of Marcion,"[53] and on the other hand the claim of Lieu that "there is no reason to suppose that [in their interpretations of the law] Justin and Ptolemaeus specifically have Marcion in view, or even that they develop their own ideas under the pressure of the challenges he provoked."[54] Even among those understanding Marcionites to be one of the groups in view in the *Letter to Flora*, the extent to which the expressed view is a caricature or an accurate portrayal of Marcion's thought is disputed.[55] Once again, however, Dunderberg has helpfully observed that he believes "a more nuanced assessment of his [Ptolemy's] relationship to Marcionite theology is needed. Ptolemaeus's own position that the Creator-God is neither the supreme God (as some people claim) nor the devil (as other people claim), and the arguments he offers in support of this position, are, in fact, very close to those of Marcion."[56] At the very least, all can likely agree on the facts that Ptolemy is aware of various contemporary views on the law and presents his own thought, at least in part, over and against other perspectives, and that even if one understands Ptolemy as having adopted a position similar to Marcion's, Ptolemy has certainly modified it.[57]

---

52. Harnack, *Marcion*, 315* n. 1.

53. Elaine Pagels, "Irenaeus, the 'Canon of Truth,' and the 'Gospel of John': 'Making a Difference' through Hermeneutics and Ritual," *VC* 56 (2002): 346 n. 28. Similarly, e.g., Christoph Markschies, "Die valentinianische Gnosis und Marcion—einige neue Perspektiven," in *Marcion und seine kirchengeschichtliche Wirkung / Marcion and His Impact on Church History*, ed. Gerhard May, Katharina Greschat, and Martin Meiser, TUGAL 150 (Berlin: de Gruyter, 2002), 166; and Almut Rütten, "Der Brief des Ptolemäus an Flora: Ein Beispiel altkirchlicher Gesetzesauslegung in Auseinandersetzung mit Marcion," in *Christlicher Glaube und religiöse Bildung: Frau Prof. Dr. Friedel Kriechbaum zum 60. Geburtstag am 13. August 1995*, ed. Hermann Deuser and Gerhard Schmalenberg, GSTR 11 (Gießen: Selbstverlag des Fachbereichs Evangelische Theologie und Katholische Theologie und deren Didaktik, 1995), 53–74.

54. Lieu, *Marcion and the Making of a Heretic*, 412.

55. See, e.g., Quispel's comments on the passage in *Ptolémée, Lettre à Flora*, 76; and von Campenhausen, *Formation of the Christian Bible*, 86 n. 133, for the view that a caricature of Marcion's teaching is being presented. Moll, *Arch-Heretic*, 48–49, however, contends that Ptolemy is accurately depicting Marcion's teaching. For a few critical remarks on Moll's reading, some of which are drawn upon in the preceding discussion above, see Roth, "Evil in Marcion's Conception," 346–47.

56. Dunderberg, *Beyond Gnosticism*, 78. See also his longer discussion of the issue on pp. 87–90.

57. See, e.g., Löhr, "La doctrine de Dieu," 191.

The crucial aspects of Ptolemy's reflections upon the law in Israel's Scriptures center on two sets of threefold divisions.[58] The first set of divisions divides the law along the lines of the idea that the law "which is contained in the five books of Moses has not been made by one legislator" in that "it has not been made by God alone, but some of its provisions have been made by men" (*Pan.* 33.4.1). Thus, the divisions are (1) the words of "God himself and his legislation," (2) the words of "Moses" as he "made certain provisions of his own notion," and (3) the words of "the elders of the people" who "have inserted certain commandments of their own" (*Pan.* 33.4.2). The second set of divisions arises from Ptolemy's belief that the first component of the first set of divisions, "the Law of God himself," is "again divided into some three parts" (*Pan.* 33.5.1). Here the divisions are (1) the "pure legislation with no admixture of evil," which is "the Decalogue itself"; (2) the "law intermingled with injustice," which is the law "which regards retribution" (i.e., the *lex talionis*); and (3) "the typical and allegorical legislation in the image of things that are spiritual and excellent" (*Pan.* 33.5.1–2).[59]

Though I will consider Ptolemy's hermeneutical justification for these divisions in the final section of this chapter, one additional point needs to be made here. As Ptolemy began to conclude his letter, he recognized that an important component to his argument still needed to be addressed, namely, for him "to say who this God is who has made the Law" (*Pan.* 33.7.2). The position advocated by Ptolemy is that the lawgiver is neither the "perfect God" and "Father" of the Savior, who is "good"; nor the "devil," who is "evil or unjust"; but rather a God "who stands between them . . . and may properly be called just" (*Pan.* 33.7.3–5). It is important to note that Ptolemy clearly viewed "just" as superior to "evil" but inferior to "good" and that he viewed the law in Israel's Scriptures as having been made by the "God" located in this intermediary position. Thus, Ptolemy concluded his discussion of the law by invoking ideas already found in his introduction to the letter. As noted above, the idea "that Ptolemy's notion of inauthentic portions of Scripture is, at least in part, an attempt to appropriate Marcion's hermeneutic" is debatable.[60] It is once again worth underscoring, however, that

---

58. Though Philo did not denigrate any part of the law and regarded it as perfect, Francis T. Fallon, "The Law in Philo and Ptolemy: A Note on the Letter to Flora," *VC* 30, no. 1 (1976): 45–51, has pointed out similarities between Philo and Ptolemy in their respective divisions of the law. Though the nature of the divisions is once again different, it is worth noting that Justin, *Dial.* 44, also set forth the division of the law into three parts.

59. Additional, helpful overviews of these divisions can be found in, e.g., Grant, *Heresy and Criticism*, 50–51; Lieu, *Marcion and the Making of a Heretic*, 411–12; and Löhr, "La doctrine de Dieu," 185.

60. Kevin M. Vaccarella, "Shaping Christian Identity: The False Scripture Argument in Early Christian Literature" (PhD diss., Florida State University, 2007), 43.

Israel's Scriptures in Marcion and the Critical Tradition

at the very least it seems that Ptolemy, whether in reaction to or appropriation of Marcion or not,[61] was reflecting upon the law in Israel's Scriptures within a wider stream of second century thought and was explicitly distinguishing his view from the views of others.

The Interpretation of Gospel Passages Related to Israel's Scriptures in Marcion

Though it has been argued that Marcion's view of Israel's Scriptures likely resulted in some redactional changes to his gospel text, Judith Lieu rightly observes that when one reads Tertullian's work against Marcion, this "heretic" is presented not simply as "an emender, or mutilator, of the Gospel text" but also as "a persistent reader and interpreter of it."[62] In other words, Marcion's conviction that Israel's Scriptures had nothing to do with the Father of Jesus Christ or Jesus Christ himself resulted not only in alterations to his gospel text but also in interpretations informed by this belief. For instance, Tertullian indicated that the rebuke of the blind man by those going before Jesus as he approached Jericho (Luke 18:35, 39) was understood by Marcion to have been motivated by the blind man wrongly calling Jesus "Son of David" (Luke 18:38). Thus, according to Marcion, the man was not scolded because his calling out was disruptive but rather because what he was saying was erroneous (*Marc.* 4.36.9). Similarly, when discussing Luke 20:41, 44, Tertullian's insistence that Jesus was not "correcting a mistake" of the scribes (*Marc.* 4.38.10) would appear to indicate that Marcion understood Jesus's words as revealing that the designation "David's son" for the Christ was erroneous.[63] Jesus, according to Marcion, was claiming that the Christ should not be identified as "David's son" but instead as "Lord."[64] A further example of note can be found in the attestation of Marcion's understanding of the transfiguration account in Luke 9:28–36. A lengthy discussion of this passage and the manner in which Marcionites understood it can be found in the fourth-century work *Prose Refu-*

---

61. Note Lieu's striking observation: "it has proved possible to identify Ptolemaeus both as arguing against Marcion, and, conversely, as adopting a fundamentally Marcionite position" (!) (*Marcion and the Making of a Heretic*, 412).

62. Lieu, *Marcion and the Making of a Heretic*, 192. The following comments concerning Marcion's interpretations of his gospel text are drawn from my more extensive discussion in Roth, "Prophets, Priests, and Kings," 50–51, 52–55.

63. Luke 20:42–43 are unattested for Marcion's Gospel.

64. As I noted in Roth, "Prophets, Priests, and Kings," 51, whereas Luke presumably intends to *supplement* the designation "David's son" with "Lord," Marcion intends to *supplant* "David's son" with "Lord."

tations of Mani, Marcion, and Bardaisan, by Ephrem. In his discussion, Ephrem queried, "But concerning Moses and Elijah who were found on the mountain in company with Isu [i.e., Jesus], what do the Marcionites say that they were doing in his presence?" and, "Was it in order to fight that he went up thither?"[65] H. J. W. Drijvers has offered a summary of the account that "according to Marcionite exegesis Moses and Elijah were guarding the mountain . . . against the Stranger [i.e., the Father of Jesus]" and concluded that "the confrontation between the two parties, Moses and Elijah on one side, Jesus on the other, may have had the character of a struggle."[66] Though there are several elements to this "struggle" in Ephrem's account, the adversarial understanding of Jesus's encounter with these characters in Israel's Scriptures is also underscored by Tertullian.[67] Near the conclusion of this pericope, God's voice says that one should listen to Jesus (Luke 9:35), and for Marcion, the clear implication is that one should therefore *not* listen to Moses and Elijah (*Marc.* 4.22.1). Lieu thus points out, "for Marcion the divine words 'listen to him' carried as a corollary, 'and not to them,'" and Moll rightly concludes that "it is not enough that Christ was heard, but it was imperative that he was heard *instead of* the Old Testament prophets" (emphasis original).[68] It would appear, therefore, that Marcion's approach to Israel's Scriptures was not only one of rejection by exclusion or excision but, at times, also by interpretation.

The Interpretation of Gospel Passages Related to Israel's Scriptures in Apelles

A complicating factor when considering Apelles is the question concerning whether he utilized Marcion's Gospel or rather had his own gospel. Though Jerome refers to a Gospel of Apelles in a lengthy list of "heretical Gospels" found in the preface to his *Commentariorum in Matthaeum*, leading some to consider that

---

65. The English translation is that found in *S. Ephraim's Prose Refutations of Mani, Marcion, and Bardaisan*, ed. and trans. C. W. Mitchell, A. A. Bevan, and F. C. Burkitt, 2 vols. (London: Williams & Norgate, 1912–1921), 2:xxxix, xl.

66. H. J. W. Drijvers, "Christ as Warrior and Merchant: Aspects of Marcion's Christology," in *Papers Presented to the Tenth International Conference on Patristic Studies Held in Oxford 1987: Second Century, Tertullian to Nicaea in the West, Clement of Alexandria and Origen, Athanasius*, ed. Elizabeth A. Livingstone, StPatr 21 (Leuven: Peeters, 1989), 77.

67. See my longer discussion of Ephrem in Roth, "Prophets, Priests, and Kings," 52–54.

68. Lieu, *Marcion and the Making of a Heretic*, 230. Moll, *Arch-Heretic*, 69. For further discussion of Marcion's interpretation of Luke 9:35 and the unfortunate manner in which his view has continued to appear in scholarship, see Dieter T. Roth, "Transfiguring the Transfiguration: Reading Luke 9:35 *Adversus Marcionem*," *CBQ* (forthcoming).

Israel's Scriptures in Marcion and the Critical Tradition

Apelles produced a unique gospel, it seems more likely that Apelles employed Marcion's scriptural texts.[69] Nevertheless, it could very well be that Apelles redacted and edited these texts further, a practice also attested for other successors of Marcion.[70] Regardless of the precise shape and content of the gospel text utilized by Apelles, it is quite unfortunate that almost nothing concerning Apelles's use and understanding of it has been transmitted. Only three references to the role of gospel texts in Apelles's thought exist, namely, an appeal to Luke 8:21 in order to reject the birth of Christ (Tertullian, *Carn. Chr.* 7.1), an indication that the (angelic) creator of the world is the "lost sheep" in Luke 15, and the citation by Epiphanius of the agraphon noted above. At the same time, it is worth noting that two out of the three references have to do either with Israel's Scriptures or the being associated with the act of creation recounted in them.

The Interpretation of Gospel Passages Related to Israel's Scriptures in Ptolemy

When considering Ptolemy's interpretation of gospel passages, the question of the extent to which anti-Valentianian writings are included in the understanding of Ptolemy plays an important role. For instance, if one considers that which Irenaeus stated after indicating that he wished to speak of "those surrounding Ptolemy,"[71] one encounters allegorical readings shaped by what Irenaeus presents as the Valentinian cosmogenic myth. In fact, right at the outset of his work, Irenaeus contended that these disciples of Valentinus saw the thirty aeons of their system represented by the thirty years of the private life of "the Savior" (see Luke 3:23) and that these aeons are presented in the parable of the Laborers in the Vineyard (Matt 20:1–16).[72] These types of allegorical interpretations,

---

69. For Apelles producing his own gospel, see, e.g., Junod, "Les attitudes d'Apelles," 114. For Apelles using Marcion's Gospel, see Harnack, *Marcion*, 190 n. 1; and Greschat, *Apelles und Hermogenes*, 31–33. Pseudo-Tertullian, *Adversus omnes haereses* 6.6 indicates that Apelles utilized Marcion's collection of Pauline letters: *solo utitur apostolo, sed Marcionis, id est non toto* (Kroymann).

70. Such activity by Apelles appears to be attested in Hippolytus, *Haer.* 7.38.2: τῶν δὲ εὐαγγελίων καὶ τοῦ ἀποστόλου τὰ ἀρέσκοντα αὐτῷ αἱρεῖται (Marcovich). Tertullian, *Marc.* 4.5.6 ascribed ongoing alterations to the texts at the hands of Marcion's followers.

71. *Dico autem eorum qui sunt circa Ptolomaeum*; λέγω δὴ τῶν περὶ Πτολεμαῖον (text of the Adelin Rousseau and Louis Doutreleau edition *Irénée de Lyon, Contre les hérésies, Livre I: Tome II, texte et traduction*, SC 264 [Paris: Cerf, 1979]).

72. The "thirty aeons" are revealed in the parable by adding together the hours at which the laborers were hired: 1 + 3 + 6 + 9 + 11 = 30. Grant, *Heresy and Criticism*, 51–56, provides a helpful summary of the numerous passages discussed by Irenaeus.

however, are not found in the *Letter to Flora*. In fact, as Dunderberg noted, the ethical element of the instruction in the *Letter to Flora* "makes the allegorical interpretation in Ptolemaeus's treatise strikingly different from the sample of Valentinian allegorical exegesis in Irenaeus."[73] Once again, the focus here will be upon the manner in which Ptolemy understands gospel texts as informing his view of the law in Israel's Scriptures in the *Letter to Flora*.

In order to explain the first set of threefold divisions presented above, Ptolemy claimed that "the truth of this can be proved from the words of the Savior" (*Pan.* 33.4.3).[74] One must simply consider the dispute concerning divorce and note that the Savior argued that from the beginning God did not intend divorce to occur but that Moses permitted it due to a hardness of hearts (*Pan.* 33.4.4).[75] Thus, the "law of God" forbids the separation of a married couple whereas the "law of Moses" permits it. Commenting on this passage, Moll may be correct in observing that Ptolemy does not seem "interested in discrediting Moses. On the contrary, he is very much concerned with saving Moses's reputation by stressing that he did not teach contradictory to God's Law because of personal ambition or vanity, but simply because of the circumstances, that is, because of the hard-hearted people."[76] At the same time, the use of the Savior's words to set what Moses taught over and against what God taught is evident. Furthermore, the Savior also made it plain that "certain traditions of the elders have been intermingled with the Law" (*Pan.* 33.4.11). Ptolemy here cited verses from Matt 15:4–9, where God's law to honor one's father and mother is said to have been nullified by "the tradition of you [sic] elders" (*Pan.* 33.4.12). Ptolemy then concludes that on the basis of these passages, he has shown that the law is divided into "Moses' own legislation, the legislation of the elders, and the legislation of God himself" (*Pan.* 33.4.14).

As Ptolemy transitioned to the second set of divisions within the law of God, he continued to appeal to that which was done and taught by the Savior. First, the pure law "unmixed with inferior matter, is the Decalogue itself," though Ptolemy also claimed that the Ten Commandments were "in need of fulfillment by the Savior, for though they contained the legislation in its pure form they were incomplete" (*Pan.* 33.5.3). Second, however, there is "law intermingled with injustice" for there is the law "which regards retribution" (*Pan.* 33.5.4). Ptolemy argued that if one takes an eye

---

73. Dunderberg, *Beyond Gnosticism*, 78. See also Löhr, "La doctrine de Dieu," 189–90.

74. For a response to the rather unlikely suggestion by Christoph Markschies, "New Research," 239–42, that the "Savior" and the "Demiurge" are the same figure, see Herbert Schmid, "Ist der Soter in Ptolemäus' *Epistula ad Floram* der Demiurg? Zu einer These von Christoph Markschies," *ZAC* 15, no. 2 (2011): 249–71.

75. Ptolemy explicitly cited Matt 19:8 and Matt 19:6 in making this argument. Grant has pointed out that almost without exception, "Ptolemaeus cites the Savior's words exclusively from Matthew, without naming him" (Grant, *Heresy and Criticism*, 50).

76. Moll, *Arch-Heretic*, 144.

for an eye or a tooth for a tooth, "the second offender does no less of an injustice and commits the same act, changing it merely in its order" (*Pan.* 33.5.4). Though again, this law came about through the frailty of its recipients, "the Son ... has abolished this portion of the Law."[77] Finally, there are "the laws of sacrifices, circumcision, the Sabbath, fasting, the Passover, the Feast of Unleavened Bread and the like" that were "outwardly ... abrogated" but "spiritually ... adopted" (*Pan.* 33.5.8–9). Here again the Savior taught that spiritual, and not animal, sacrifices are to be offered; that a circumcision of the heart, and not of the foreskin, is desired; that keeping the Sabbath means desisting from evil works; and that keeping a spiritual, and not bodily, fast includes abstaining from evil (*Pan.* 33.5.10–13).

In sum, therefore, concerning this second set of divisions, "according to Ptolemaeus, the Savior fulfilled the Ten Commandments (by making them perfect) and abolished the laws based upon retaliation. Moreover, the Savior showed that the cultic laws should no longer be understood literally but 'spiritually'—as moral guidance of conduct intended for Christians."[78] These persistent appeals to the Savior's teaching led von Campenhausen to draw the following conclusion concerning the underlying hermeneutical assumption in Ptolemy's approach to the law: "The law is to be assessed by the words of Jesus. It is binding for Christians only in so far as it is acknowledged by Jesus and confirmed by his perfect teaching."[79] It is important to note, however, that Ptolemy actually claimed a bit more than this, for in *Pan.* 33.6.6 the assertion is made that "the Savior's disciples have given proof of these divisions, and so has the apostle Paul."[80] Thus, Ptolemy has actually argued that it is on the basis of the teachings of the Savior, his disciples, and Paul that he has set forth his views of the law in Israel's Scriptures.

Conclusion

Controversies concerning Israel's Scriptures have accompanied Christianity throughout its history, from antiquity to modernity. After all, near the conclusion

---

77. Interestingly, Ptolemy stated that "this commandment was and is just," but it is "not in accord with the nature and goodness of the Father of all" (*Pan.* 33.5.5). In this context, one also finds what appears to be a fascinating admission that in Matt 15:4, the Son adapted his teaching and agreed with "the old school" (*Pan.* 33.5.7). Though some have viewed Ptolemy here speaking of the Christ of the Creator God (see Quispel, *Ptolémée, Lettre à Flora*, 36), it is more likely that he saw the Son of the Supreme God making a concession (so also Dunderberg, *Beyond Gnosticism*, 84).

78. Dunderberg, *Beyond Gnosticism*, 82.

79. Von Campenhausen, *Formation of the Christian Bible*, 84.

80. Moll, *Arch-Heretic*, 152, refers to Ptolemy using "the New Testament as the *hermeneutical key* to understand the Old" (emphasis original).

of his work on Marcion, Harnack infamously set forth the thesis: "The repudiation of the Old Testament in the second century was an error which the great church rightly rejected; to retain it in the sixteenth century was a fate from which the Reformation was not yet able to escape; but still to preserve it as a canonical document in Protestantism since the nineteenth century is the consequence of a religious and ecclesiastical paralysis."[81]

One may rightly dispute vehemently the conclusion of this thesis, but it should also be pointed out that the supposed "repudiation" of Israel's Scriptures by some in the second century to which Harnack referred was not a monolithic rejection. Marcion took Israel's Scriptures "seriously, as direct and reliable evidence of the Creator's character and behavior," which, in turn, led Marcion to view the Creator as "morally distinct and inferior."[82] Apelles appeared decidedly unsatisfied with this solution and seemed to pursue a far more radical critique of Israel's Scriptures. These Scriptures were anything but reliable, and therefore they themselves were inferior and false. Ptolemy embraced a view that set forth two sets of distinctions with the law as found in Israel's Scriptures, ascribing this understanding to the teaching of the Savior, his disciples, and Paul, while also contending that the God behind this law was neither the "good" God nor the "evil" devil. Not surprisingly, it is not merely New Testament authors and the church fathers whose interpretations of both gospel traditions and Israel's Scriptures were influenced by their views of Israel's Scriptures themselves. The same is also true for numerous "heretics." As such, any discussion of Israel's Scripture in early Christianity, and especially in the second century, must continue to both recognize and wrestle with figures such as Marcion, Apelles, and Ptolomy and the critical tradition concerning Israel's Scriptures that they embodied.

Bibliography

Bazzana, Giovanni Battista. "Apelles and the Pseudo-Clementine Doctrine of the False Pericopes." Pages 11–32 in *"Soyez des changeurs avisés": Controverses exégétiques dans la littérature apocryphe chrétienne*. Edited by Gabriella Aragione and Rémi Gounelle. CBiPa 12. Strasbourg: Université de Strasbourg, 2012.

Blackman, E. C. *Marcion and His Influence*. London: SPCK, 1948.

Campenhausen, Hans von. *The Formation of the Christian Bible*. Translated by John A. Baker. Philadelphia: Fortress, 1972. Original: *Die Entstehung der christlichen Bibel*. BHT 39. Tübingen: Mohr, 1968.

---

81. Harnack, *Marcion*, 217.
82. Lieu, *Marcion and the Making of a Heretic*, 366.

Caspari, C. P. *Kirchenhistorische Anecdote: Nebst neuen Ausgaben patristischer und kirchlich-mittelaltlicher Schriften*. Vol. 1, *Lateinische Schriften: Die Texte und die Anmerkungen*. Oslo: Malling, 1883.

Doutreleau, Louis. "Le fragment grec de l'homélie II d'Origène sur la Genèse: Critique du texte." *RHT* 5 (1975): 13–44.

Drijvers, H. J. W. "Christ as Warrior and Merchant: Aspects of Marcion's Christology." Pages 73–85 in *Papers Presented to the Tenth International Conference on Patristic Studies Held in Oxford 1987: Second Century, Tertullian to Nicaea in the West, Clement of Alexandria and Origen, Athanasius*. Edited by Elizabeth A. Livingstone. StPatr 21. Leuven: Peeters, 1989.

Dunderberg, Ismo. *Beyond Gnosticism: Myth, Lifestyle, and Society in the School of Valentinus*. New York: Columbia University Press, 2008.

———. "The School of Valentinus." Pages 62–99 in *A Companion to Second-Century Christian "Heretics."* Edited by Antti Marjanen and Petri Luomanen. VCSup 76. Leiden: Brill, 2005.

Ehrman, Bart. *The Orthodox Corruption of Scripture: The Effect of Early Christological Controversies on the Text of the New Testament*. Oxford: Oxford University Press, 1993.

Ephrem the Syrian. *S. Ephraim's Prose Refutations of Mani, Marcion, and Bardaisan*. Edited and translated by C. W. Mitchell, A. A. Bevan, and F. C. Burkitt. 2 vols. London: Williams & Norgate, 1912–1921.

Fallon, Francis T. "The Law in Philo and Ptolemy: A Note on the Letter to Flora." *VC* 30, no. 1 (1976): 45–51.

Foerster, Werner. *Von Valentin zu Herakleon: Untersuchungen über die Quellen und die Entwicklung der valentinianischen Gnosis*. BZNW 7. Giessen: Töpelmann, 1928.

Grant, Robert M. *Heresy and Criticism: The Search for Authenticity in Early Christian Literature*. Louisville: Westminster John Knox, 1993.

Greschat, Katharina. *Apelles und Hermogenes: Zwei theologische Lehrer des zweiten Jahrhunderts*. VCSup 48. Leiden: Brill, 2000.

Habermehl, Peter. *Die Homilien zum Buch Genesis*. Origenes Werke mit deutscher Übersetzung 1.2. Berlin: de Gruyter, 2011.

Hanig, Roman. "Der Beitrag der Philumene zur Theologie der Apelleianer." *ZAC* 3, no. 2 (1999): 241–77.

Harnack, Adolf von. *De Apellis gnosi monarchica*. Leipzig: Bidder, 1874.

———. *Marcion: Das Evangelium vom fremden Gott; Eine Monographie zur Geschichte der Grundlegung der katholischen Kirche*. 2nd ed. TUGAL 45. Leipzig: Hinrichs, 1924.

———. "Sieben neue Bruchstücke der Syllogismen des Apelles." Pages 111–20 in *Die gnostischen Quellen Hippolyts in seiner Hauptschrift gegen die Häretiker*. Edited by Hans Stählin. TUGAL 6.3. Leipzig: Hinrichs, 1890.

Hays, Christopher M. "Marcion vs. Luke: A Response to the *Plädoyer* of Matthias Klinghardt." *ZNW* 99, no. 2 (2008): 213–32.

Junod, Éric. "Les attitudes d'Apelles, disciple de Marcion, à l'égard de l'Ancien Testament." *Aug* 22, no. 1/2 (1982): 113–33.

Klinghardt, Matthias. *Das älteste Evangelium und die Entstehung der kanonischen Evangelien*. 2 vols. TANZ 60. Tübingen: Francke, 2015.

———. "Markion vs. Lukas: Plädoyer für die Wiederaufnahme eines alten Falles." *NTS* 52, no. 4 (2006): 484–513.

Koetschau, Paul. *Origenes Werke*. Vol. 2, *Buch 5–8 gegen Celsus; Die Schrift vom Gebet*. GCS 3. Leipzig: Hinrich, 1899.

Kroymann, Emil. *Quinti Septimi Florentis Tertulliani Opera*. Vol. 2, *Opera Montanistica*. CCSL 2. Turnhout: Brepols, 1954.

Layton, Bentley. *The Gnostic Scriptures: A New Translation with Annotations and Introductions*. New York: Doubleday, 1987.

Lieu, Judith M. *Marcion and the Making of a Heretic: God and Scripture in the Second Century*. Cambridge: Cambridge University Press, 2015.

Löhr, Winrich A. "Die Auslegung des Gesetzes bei Markion, den Gnostikern und den Manichäern." Pages 77–95 in *Stimuli: Exegese und ihre Hermeneutik in Antike und Christentum; Festschrift für Ernst Dassmann*. Edited by Georg Schöllgen and Clemens Scholten. Jahrbuch für antikes Christentum Ergänzungsband 23. Münster: Aschendorff, 1996.

———. "La doctrine de Dieu dans la Lettre à Flora de Ptolémée." *RHPR* 75, no. 2 (1995): 177–91.

Lüdemann, Gerd. "Zur Geschichte des ältesten Christentums in Rom: I. Valentin und Marcion II. Ptolemäus und Justin." *ZNW* 70, no. 1–2 (1979): 86–114.

Marcovich, Miroslav. *Hippolytus: Refutatio Omnium Haeresium*. PTS 25. Berlin: de Gruyter, 1986.

Markschies, Christoph. "Die valentinianische Gnosis und Marcion: Einige neue Perspektiven." Pages 159–75 in *Marcion und seine kirchengeschichtliche Wirkung/ Marcion and His Impact on Church History: Vorträge der Internationalen Fachkonferenz zu Marcion, gehalten vom 15.–18. August 2001 in Mainz*. Edited by Gerhard May, Katharina Greschat, and Martin Meiser. TUGAL 150. Berlin: de Gruyter, 2002.

———. "New Research on Ptolemaeus Gnosticus." *ZAC* 4, no. 2 (2000): 225–54.

May, Gerhard. "Apelles und die Entwicklung der markionitischen Theologie." Pages 93–110 in *Gerhard May: Markion; Gesammelte Aufsätze*. Edited by Katharina Greschaft and Martin Meiser. VIEG.B 68. Mainz: von Zabern, 2005.

McGowan, Andrew. "Marcion's Love of Creation." *JECS* 9, no. 3 (2001): 295–311.

Moll, Sebastian. *The Arch-Heretic Marcion*. WUNT 250. Tübingen: Mohr Siebeck, 2010.

Mondésert, Claude. *Clément d'Alexandrie, Les stromates: Stromate II*. SC 38. Paris: Cerf, 1954.

Moreschini, Claudio. *Tertullien, Contre Marcion: Tome I*. SC 365. Paris: Cerf, 1990.

———. *Tertullien, Contre Marcion: Tome II*. SC 368. Paris: Cerf, 1991.

Munier, Charles. *Justin, Apologie pour les chrétiens*. SC 507. Paris: Cerf, 2006.

Norelli, Enrico. "Marcion et les disciples de Jésus." *Apocrypha* 19 (2008): 9–42.

Pagels, Elaine. "Irenaeus, the 'Canon of Truth,' and the 'Gospel of John': 'Making a Difference' through Hermeneutics and Ritual." *VC* 56, no. 4 (2002): 339–71.

Quispel, Gilles. *Ptolémée, Lettre à Flora: Texte, Traduction et Introduction*. 2nd ed. SC 24. Paris: Cerf, 1966.

Roth, Dieter T. "Evil in Marcion's Conception of the Old Testament God." Pages 340–56 in *Evil in Second Temple Judaism and Early Christianity*. Edited by Chris Keith and Loren T. Stuckenbruck. WUNT 2/417. Tübingen: Mohr Siebeck, 2016.

———. "Prophets, Priests, and Kings: Old Testament Figures in Marcion's Gospel and Luke." Pages 41–56 in *Connecting Gospels: Beyond the Canonical/Non-Canonical Divide*. Edited by Francis Watson and Sarah Parkhouse. Oxford: Oxford University Press, 2018.

———. *The Text of Marcion's Gospel*. NTTSD 49. Leiden: Brill, 2015.

———. "Transfiguring the Transfiguration: Reading Luke 9:35 *Adversus Marcionem*." *CBQ* (forthcoming).

Rousseau, Adelin, and Louis Doutreleau. *Irénée de Lyon, Contre les hérésies, Livre I: Tome II, texte et traduction*. SC 264. Paris: Cerf, 1979.

———. *Irénée de Lyon, Contre les hérésies, Livre III: Tome II, texte et traduction*. SC 211. Paris: Cerf, 1974.

Röwekamp, Georg. *Pamphilus von Caesarea: Apologia pro Origine / Apologie für Origenes*. FC 80. Turnhout: Brepols, 2005.

Rütten, Almut. "Der Brief des Ptolemäus an Flora: Ein Beispiel altkirchlicher Gesetzesauslegung in Auseinandersetzung mit Marcion." Pages 53–74 in *Christlicher Glaube und religiöse Bildung: Frau Prof. Dr. Friedel Kriechbaum zum 60. Geburtstag am 13. August 1995*. Edited by Hermann Deuser and Gerhard Schmalenberg. GSTR 11. Giessen: Selbstverlag des Fachbereichs Evangelische Theologie und Katholische Theologie und deren Didaktik, 1995.

Sande Bakhuyzen, W. H. van de. *Pseudo-Origen, Der Dialog des Adamantius: ΠΕΡΙ ΤΗΣ ΕΙΣ ΘΕΟΝ ΟΡΘΗΣ ΠΙΣΤΕΩΣ*. GCS 4. Leipzig: Hinrichs, 1901.

Scherbenske, Eric W. "Marcion's *Antitheses* and the Isagogic Genre." *VC* 64, no. 3 (2010): 255–79.

Schmid, Herbert. "Ist der Soter in Ptolemäus' *Epistula ad Floram* der Demiurg? Zu einer These von Christoph Markschies." *ZAC* 15, no. 2 (2011): 249–71.

Schmid, Ulrich. *Marcion und sein Apostolos: Rekonstruktion und historische Einordnung der marcionitischen Paulusbriefausgabe*. ANTF 25. Berlin: de Gruyter, 1995.

Vaccarella, Kevin M. "Shaping Christian Identity: The False Scripture Argument in Early Christian Literature." PhD diss., Florida State University, 2007.

Williams, Frank, trans. *The Panarion of Epiphanius of Salamis*. 2nd ed. 2 vols. NHS 63, 79. Leiden: Brill, 2009.

42

Israel's Scriptures in Early Christian Pictorial Art

ROBIN M. JENSEN

The history of Christian pictorial art begins in the early third century. Art historians and archaeologists have identified few distinctively Christian physical remains that date prior to that time.[1] One plausible explanation for the seemingly late emergence of Christian art is that self-identified adherents to the Christian movement only slowly emerged as a viable market for Roman artisans' workshops. In the meantime, Christian clients likely repurposed neutral decorative images and the mythological scenes of traditional Greco-Roman polytheism to express their religious beliefs.[2] This explanation, that Christians had and used artifacts decorated with religious subjects before they made their own in the early third century, contradicts an older, but no longer widely held argument that first- and second-century Christians did not make or use visual art because they were more faithfully obedient to the Second Commandment's prohibition of idol making (i.e., "graven images") than later generations and therefore eschewed all types of figurative art.[3]

---

1. Jeffrey Spier, "The Earliest Christian Art: From Personal Salvation to Imperial Power," in *Picturing the Bible: The Earliest Christian Art*, ed. Jeffrey Spier (New Haven: Yale University Press, 2007), 1; also, Paul Corby Finney, *The Invisible God: The Earliest Christians on Art* (Oxford: Oxford University Press, 1994), 110.

2. Jaś Elsner, "Archaeologies and Agendas: Reflections on Late Ancient Jewish Art and Early Christian Art," JRS 93 (2003): 114–15; and Leonard Rutgers, *The Jews in Late Ancient Rome: Evidence of Cultural Interaction in the Roman Diaspora*, RGRW 126 (Leiden: Brill, 2000), 75–76 and 92–93.

3. On this, see the seminal article by Mary Charles Murray, "Art and the Early Church,"

The main problem with this latter argument is that while early Christian writers consistently denounced idols and idolatry, they rarely condemned pictorial images in general. Moreover, their critique of pagan idols only occasionally cited the biblical commandment against the making of graven images. Instead, Christian critics more often echoed traditional philosophical arguments that depictions of the gods were merely insensate, human-made artifacts and should not be confused with the deities they represented.[4] Thus, Christian condemnation of idols was mainly directed against polytheists' cult images (and not pictorial art as such) and primarily attacked pagans for imputing power to lifeless objects. Essentially, Christian denunciation of idolatry at best only tangentially applies to the question of why Christians had no discernable art of their own for the first two hundred years, a lack that is probably better explained simply by their gradual development of a distinct material culture than by adherence to biblical condemnation of figurative images.

The Emergence and Content of Early Christian Iconography

Whatever the reasons for its initial absence, by the early third century, a recognizably Christian iconographic repertoire had begun to emerge in wall painting and relief sculpture. Extant examples have come dominantly from western burial contexts: decorating the burial chambers of the Roman catacombs, inscribed onto grave slabs, and adorning the fronts, sides, and lids of stone sarcophagi. Having been preserved in underground spaces and cemeteries allowed the survival of most of the extant specimens. Christian-themed motifs also featured on small objects like lamps, rings, pottery plates and bowls, and glass vessels, and also were typically discovered in burial chambers. By contrast, artifacts that would have been made for nonfunereal contexts were likely lost to natural causes (e.g., earthquakes, erosion, and fires) or human destruction (e.g., wars, neglect, urban renovation, and iconoclasm).

One important exception to the burial context of early Christian art is the cycle of paintings discovered on the walls of a baptismal chamber attached to

---

JTS 28, no. 2 (1977): 303–6; followed by Finney, *Invisible God*. Their work challenges articles by prominent earlier historians, including Gerhard B. Ladner, "The Concept of the Image in the Greek Fathers and the Byzantine Iconoclastic Controversy," *DOP* 7 (1953): 5; and Ernst Kitzinger, "The Cult of Images before Iconoclasm," *DOP* 8 (1954): 85. For a brief summary of the scholarship, see Robin M. Jensen, "Introduction: Early Christian Art," in *The Routledge Handbook of Early Christian Art*, ed. Robin M. Jensen and Mark D. Ellison (London: Routledge, 2018), 1–3.

4. The primary literature on this subject is extensive and includes Tertullian, *Idol.*; Minucius Felix, *Oct.*; and Clement of Alexandria, *Protrep*. For an overview analysis of early Christian texts against idols, see Robin M. Jensen, "Aniconism in the First Centuries of Christianity," *Religion* 47, no. 3 (2017): 408–24.

the mid-third-century renovated house church in the Syrian outpost of Dura Europos, which survived because Roman defenders of the city filled it in to make a defensive wall. Its fortunate discovery allows historians to surmise that this was not a unique instance of church decoration, and other places of Christian worship were similarly adorned with pictorial art. The surviving subjects depicted in this place included images of Adam and Eve, the Good Shepherd with his flock, Jesus healing the paralytic, Jesus walking on water, David slaying Goliath, and the five wise brides coming to the tent of the bridegroom.[5]

Although popular decorative elements like garlands, bowls of fruit, vines, birds, and floral motifs probably had little specifically Christian significance, other common symbols like fish, anchors, grape harvesting, and boats could have alluded to certain teachings, affirmations of adherence to the community, or hopeful expectations about the afterlife.[6] Some figures probably also alluded to details found in one or more biblical stories. For example, in some settings, a dove might allude to the descent of the Holy Spirit at Jesus's baptism. When it appears with an olive branch in its beak, the dove might refer to the story of Noah. The dove also might signify the state of the deceased's soul in the afterlife, especially when joined by the legend, *"in pace."* A boat could be a reference to Noah's ark but also to the church as the ark of faith in which the faithful are baptized and hence delivered from the grave.

Maritime scenes featuring fish and fishermen were universally popular but had a particular resonance in Christian funerary iconography. The fish by itself could symbolize Christ, especially when joined by an acrostic based on the letters of the Greek word *ichthys* ("fish"), which reveals the title *Iēsous Christos Theou Huios Sotēr* ("Jesus Christ, Son of God, Savior").[7] Used for a Christian epitaph, one or two fish joined by an anchor might signify the followers of Christ, hooked by the anchor of faith. Yet, because fish also appear frequently in New Testament narratives—the calling of the disciples from their nets to become fishers of men, the miracle of the multiplication of loaves and fish, or the miraculous

---

5. For a good resource for bibliography and some excellent essays on the history of the discovery and finds at Dura Europos, see Lisa Brody and Gail Hoffman, eds., *Dura-Europos: Crossroads of Antiquity* (Boston: McMullen Museum of Art, Boston College, 2011). For discussion of the iconography, see Michael Peppard, *The World's Oldest Church: Bible, Art, and Ritual at Dura-Europos, Syria* (New Haven: Yale University Press, 2016).

6. On these motifs see the work of Paul Zanker and Björn Ewald, *Living with Myths: The Imagery of Roman Sarcophagi*, trans. Julia Slater, Oxford Studies in Ancient Culture and Representation (Oxford: Oxford University Press, 2012), 28–29, 127–29.

7. On this acrostic see Tertullian, *Bapt.* 1; Sib. Or. 8:217–50; and Optatus of Milevis, *Against Parmenian* 3.2.1. For more on the fish symbol and with bibliography, see Robin M. Jensen, "The Fish: An Early Christian Symbol for Christ," in *The Reception of Jesus in the First Three Centuries*, ed. Chris Keith et al., 3 vols. (London: Bloomsbury, 2019), 3:271–90.

Fig. 42.1. *Adam and Eve, from the Catacomb of Peter and Marcellinus, Rome, third century*

catch of fish at the end of John's Gospel—fishing scenes or platters of fish may also allude to those stories.

Similarly, the image of a shepherd with a ram over his shoulders might have been intended to represent the biblical "Good Shepherd" (cf. Ps 23; John 10:1–9). However, the figure of a shepherd shouldering a ram also has an ancient pre-Christian precedent. Because Hermes, the gods' messenger and caretaking guide to the underworld, was often shown in this guise, this popular motif could be adapted to express the belief the Christian Shepherd would safely conduct the deceased from this life into the next.[8] Yet, as it also appeared in decoration of the Dura Europos baptistery and, eventually, in a variety of ecclesial settings, the figure clearly projected other valences than divine care for the dead.[9]

All of these symbols, therefore, had many possible meanings, and because they belonged to Roman decorative art broadly, they were not definitively or necessarily Christian. Soon, however, certain images emerged with no obvious

---

8. For a summary of this image in Christian and pre-Christian iconography, see Johannes Quasten, "Der Gute Hirte in frühchristlicher Totenliturgie und Grabeskunst," in *Miscellanea Giovanni Mercati*, 6 vols., Studi e testi 121 (Vatican City: Biblioteca Apostolica Vaticana, 1946), 1:373–406; Nicholas Cachia, *The Image of the Good Shepherd as a Source for the Spirituality of the Ministerial Priesthood: I Am the Good Shepherd; The Good Shepherd Lays Down His Life for the Sheep (John 10.11)*, Tesi Gregoriana Serie Spiritualità 4 (Rome: Gregorian University Press, 1997); and Jennifer Awes Freeman, *The Good Shepherd: Image, Meaning, and Power* (Waco, TX: Baylor University Press, 2021), 79–120; and Freeman, "The Good Shepherd and the Enthroned Ruler: A Reconsideration of Imperial Iconography in the Early Church," in *The Art of Empire: Christian Art in Its Imperial Context*, ed. Robin M. Jensen and Lee M. Jefferson (Minneapolis: Fortress, 2015), 159–96.

9. See Johannes Quasten, "The Painting of the Good Shepherd at Dura Europos," *Medieval Studies* 9 (1947): 1–18; Robin M. Jensen, *Baptismal Imagery in Early Christianity* (Grand Rapids: Baker Academic, 2012), 75–82.

Fig. 42.2. Noah with Adam and Eve and Moses striking the rock, from the Catacomb of Peter and Marcellinus

Fig. 42.3. Daniel with lions and Habbakuk, detail of an early Christian sarcophagus now in the Vatican, Museo Pio Cristiano, early fourth century

or direct antecedents in Greco-Roman art, and that depicted episodes from the Bible. Series of popular Scripture-based figures decorated the walls of wealthier families' burial chambers or the fronts, ends, and lids of large and costly stone coffins (sarcophagi). An emerging repertoire of Christian pictorial art comprised these images, frequently in crowded compositions that mixed Old and New Testament figures in a seemingly jumbled collection. The result is a clearly expanding pattern of incorporating biblical narrative imagery in funerary decor. In addition, based on the frequency of their application, some stories evidently were favored over others.

Fig. 42.4. Daniel in the center surrounded with scenes from the Jonah story and Noah in the ark, vault painting, from the Catacomb of Peter and Marcellinus

Fig. 42.5. Three Hebrew youths, from the Catacomb of Priscilla, Rome, third century

Israel's Scriptures in Early Christian Pictorial Art

Many, if not most, among the earliest of these biblical narrative images were drawn from stories in the Hebrew Bible and, less frequently, from the Apocrypha (e.g., Tobit and Susanna). These included depictions of Adam and Eve (shown flanking the tree with the forbidden fruit), Noah in his ark, Abraham offering his son Isaac for sacrifice, Moses receiving the Law, Moses striking the rock in the wilderness, Daniel in the lions' den, the three Hebrew youths in the fiery furnace, Jonah being swallowed and then spit up by the sea creature, Balaam pointing to the star, and Susanna with the elders. In the early to mid-fourth century, additional types appeared, including the creation of Adam and Eve, Adam and Eve's expulsion from Eden, Cain and Abel presenting their offerings to God, Abraham entertaining his three angelic visitors, Pharaoh's daughter finding the baby Moses, Moses and the Israelites crossing the Red Sea, Jacob's dream of the ladder, scenes from the Joseph cycle, Daniel with the Babylonian dragon, Elijah's ascent to heaven, and a dejected-looking Job with his wife.

Although no two images are completely identical, they are very similar and easily identified. For example, Adam and Eve are usually depicted as standing to either side of the tree bearing the forbidden fruit. In some examples, they hang their heads, look dejectedly downwards, and cover their genitals with their hands (fig. 42.1). Other times they gaze at one another and Adam gestures toward Eve as if deflecting blame (cf. fig. 42.2). Depictions of Noah in the ark are noticeably different from later pictorial renderings of the story. In early Christian art, Noah stands with his hands lifted in the posture of prayer, alone in his box-like ark, without animals, wife, or sons (figs. 42.2, 42.4, and 42.6). Daniel is represented simply as a front-facing heroic nude, standing in prayer, flanked by two lions, and usually receiving a gift of food from the prophet Habakkuk (fig. 42.3). The three Hebrew youths are portrayed in two scenes: as rejecting Nebuchadnezzar's idol and in the fiery furnace, their hands raised in prayer (fig. 42.5). Moses is most frequently shown striking the rock in the wilderness to give water to the wandering Hebrews (cf. fig. 42.2). Without question, the most popular of all of the Old Testament figures was Jonah, who appears in an unparalleled sequence of three or four scenes (being thrown overboard and swallowed by the fish, being cast up on dry land, and reclining beneath his gourd vine; figs. 42.6 and 42.4).[10] If one counts all these episodes individually, Jonah is by far the most popular biblical character in Christian art.

The formal composition and context of these images almost certainly contributed to their perceived meaning. Notably, the compositions are abbreviated

---

10. Given the chronological scope of this chapter, I use the language of "Old Testament" to denote the Christian collection of scriptural texts that are elsewhere in this volume referred to as the Scriptures of Israel.

Fig. 42.6. Jonah being swallowed by the sea monster and spit up on dry land with Noah (left), detail of the lid of an early Christian sarcophagus, now in the Cathedral of Osimo, Italy

rather than elaborated. Unlike the Roman mythological murals or sarcophagus reliefs, which often render events in complex and often sequential fashion, Christian examples typically display only one or two characters and a single representative moment in the story. Little is added in the way of background or context, and the images are rendered more as allusions than as illustrations and, as such, require a trained viewer to recognize them. Rather like a synecdoche, one specifically identified narrative detail represents or evokes a whole narrative. In addition, most of the Christian images are sketchily or crudely rendered. Proportions are often awkward, spacing is cramped, depth of field is shallow, the characters' relative scale is frequently distorted, and individual figures are usually combined in what seems a jumbled or even haphazard fashion.

Although the exact numbers of the various surviving images are difficult to precisely calculate, in general, Old Testament scenes outnumber New Testament ones about four to one in the third century. While some New Testament scenes also appear in third-century Christian art, they became far more frequent in the fourth century, when the balance is a little more even. Depictions of Christ raising Lazarus and John baptizing Christ are probably the earliest, but other New Testament stories gradually emerged, including Jesus multiplying loaves; changing water to wine; meeting with the Samaritan woman at the well; and as healing the paralytic, the blind man, and the hemorrhaging woman. Extrabiblical scenes joining them include Peter's arrest and Peter in the guise of Moses striking the rock and healing his jailers. As with the Old Testament images, certain expected New Testament stories are evidently missing. Depictions of the transfiguration, the Last Supper, and the crucifixion are missing from the extant catalog of earliest Christian iconography.

Israel's Scriptures in Early Christian Pictorial Art

Various Explanations for the Dominance of the Old Testament in Early Christian Art

The remarkable dominance of Old Testament stories in early Christian art has caused historians to offer theories about why early Christians chose to decorate their burial places with these rather than with images from the New Testament, which to some minds seem more specifically Christian (and presumably more logical). Any argument that these decorations were made mainly for Jewish rather than Christian patrons is undermined immediately by the combination of New Testament with Old Testament scenes.

Nevertheless, the theory that these images were first produced for Jews has been suggested by a number of historians. Among them was Josef Stryzgowski, whose highly polemical book, *Orient oder Rom*, was published in 1901. Stryzgowski's work was largely a reaction to the earlier work of Franz Wickhoff, who had argued that the style and content of early Christian iconography was influenced by contemporary Roman art.[11] Stryzgowski particularly noted the high ratio of Old Testament to New Testament images in the Roman catacombs and attributed this to the presumed influence of hypothetical Jewish artworks originating in the east, especially among Jews of Parthia, Mesopotamia, or Asia Minor. The analysis of modern historians over Stryzowski's work continues to be polemical, including characterizations of his work as reflecting orientalism, racism, and extreme nationalism.[12]

Several later scholars adopted Stryzgowski's theory and presumed either an earlier or synchronous hellenized Jewish pictorial art from which artisans drew their models when serving Christian clients. The discovery and excavation of the extensively decorated mid-third-century synagogue in Syria's site of Dura Europos in the 1930s, with its rich cycle of biblically themed frescos, provided additional support. The find overturned all assumptions that Jews, obedient to the Mosaic prohibition of graven images, were strictly aniconic and consequently

---

11. Josef Strzygowski, *Orient oder Rom: Beiträge zur Geschichte der spätantiken und frühchristlichen Kunst* (Leipzig: Hinrich, 1901); Franz Wickhoff's work, *Die Wiener Genesis* (Vienna: Tempsky, 1895), was republished as *Römische Kunst (Die Wiener Genesis)* in 1912 (Berlin: Meyer & Jessen).

12. For modern analyses of this debate, see Annabel Wharton, *Refiguring the Post-Classical City: Dura Europos, Jerash, Jerusalem, and Ravenna* (Cambridge: Cambridge University Press, 1995), 1–12; Elżbieta Jastrzębowska, "Josef Strzygowski und Josef Wilpert : Zwei Gesichter derselben Wissenschaft," in *Von Biala nach Wien: Josef Strzygowski und die Kunstwissenschaften*, ed. Piotr O. Scholz and Magdalena A. Dlugosz (Vienna: European University Press, 2015), 43–54; Ivan Foletti and Francesco Lovino, "Introduction: Orient oder Rom, and Joseph Strzygowski in 2018," in *Orient oder Rom? History and Reception of a Historiographical Myth (1901–1970)*, ed. Ivan Foletti and Francesco Lovino (Prague: Institute of Art History, Czech Academy of Sciences, 2018), 7–14.

made no figurative art. It demonstrated that at least some Jews not only included pictorial art in their places of worship but, furthermore, such art might include scenes and characters from biblical narratives.

The American archeologist James Henry Breasted, the first scholar to publish any of the Dura paintings, arrived at the site shortly after its discovery in 1920 and photographed the wall paintings found in the Temple of Bel. Although he arrived before the synagogue's subsequent discovery (1932), his 1924 book, *The Oriental Forerunners of Byzantine Painting: First-Century Wall Paintings from the Fortress of Dura,* proposed that the art of Dura represented a missing link between the art of the East and West.[13] This work drew upon Strzygowski's theories, which now seemed to be validated by the paintings in the temple. Once the synagogue came to the attention of art historians, links between Jewish and Christian pictorial art seemed more obvious to those seeking sources for the Roman catacomb paintings.

In subsequent decades, more early Jewish art came to light, especially synagogue mosaics in the Galilee region. The existence of figurative and scriptural imagery and even figures from the zodiac and the pagan god Helios allowed a new chapter to be added to the history of Jewish art in late antiquity, resulting in extensive studies by such luminaries as Lee Levine, Steven Fine, Rachel Hachlili, and Ze'ev Weiss.[14] From the first, these discoveries prompted more theories, including those of the provocative scholar Erwin Goodenough, who published a thirteen-volume, encyclopedic study of Jewish symbols from 1953 to 1968.[15] In addition to proposing a mystical form of Judaism as the source for many of the newly discovered figures, Goodenough believed he identified overlaps with Greco-Roman mystery cults and Christian iconography. In a briefer essay, he strenuously argued for a Jewish influence on early Christian art, in particular claiming to discern similarities between the wall paintings found in the mid-third-century Dura Europos synagogue and the paintings in Christian catacombs.[16] Goodenough maintained that while Christians had no difficulty in

---

13. Breasted, *The Oriental Forerunners of Byzantine Painting: First-Century Wall Paintings from the Fortress of Dura on the Middle Euphrates,* OIP 1 (Chicago: University of Chicago Press, 1924). Breasted was the founder of the Oriental Institute at the University of Chicago.

14. Levine, *Visual Judaism in Late Antiquity: Historical Contexts of Jewish Art* (New Haven: Yale University Press, 2013); Fine, *Art and Judaism in the Greco-Roman World: Toward a New Jewish Archaeology* (Cambridge: Cambridge University Press, 2010); Hachlili, *Ancient Synagogues—Archaeology and Art: New Discoveries and Current Research,* HdO 105 (Leiden: Brill, 2013); and Weiss and Levine, eds., *From Dura to Sepphoris: Studies in Jewish Art and Society in Late Antiquity,* JRSSup 40 (Portsmouth, RI: Journal of Roman Archaeology, 2000).

15. Goodenough, *Jewish Symbols in the Greco-Roman Period,* 13 vols. (New York: Pantheon, 1953–1968).

16. Erwin R. Goodenough, "Catacomb Art," *JBL* 81, no. 2 (1962): 112–42.

developing scenes from the New Testament, he asserted, "Dura shows that at this time Jews, or at least some Jews, had done much better at expressing their hopes in art." He added, "from the Christian representations alone we should presume that OT characters appear so often because Christians inherited a considerable body of OT illustrations from Jews."[17]

In the mid 1960s, the historian of early Christian art Pierre du Bourguet's widely read and accessible handbook, *Early Christian Painting*, claimed the Christian catacomb frescoes were directly influenced by artworks produced by Jews living in Rome. He referred to the Jewish catacombs along the Via Appia as exemplary, but because of the lack of biblical motifs in those catacombs, not to mention figurative art in general, du Bourguet turned to the Dura synagogue as evidence for his hypothesis.[18] While both Goodenough's and du Bourguet's work were being cautiously assessed by art historians, they were often accepted as definitive by church historians, including the distinguished historian of early Christianity Henry Chadwick, who took it for granted that early Christian images were modeled after existing Jewish art. Chadwick believed the higher frequency of Old Testament scenes to New Testament images in Christian art was due to the existence of Jewish models, in particular the paintings of the Dura Synagogue.[19]

Although the Dura synagogue paintings demonstrate the emergence of Jewish pictorial art around the same time as Christian iconography, neither the content nor the style of the Dura synagogue paintings is in any way like those of the catacomb paintings. For example, one of the fourth-century catacomb paintings that Goodenough cites, a scene of Pharaoh's daughter finding the infant Moses (fig. 42.7), differs from the earlier version in the Dura Synagogue in almost every conceivable sense (fig. 42.8). For example, the dress and posture of the women in the Dura painting clearly reflect an eastern style and echoes Palmyrene portraiture. Moreover, the nudity of the princess is not only surprising in the synagogue context but is far from similar to her completely covered and veiled appearance in Rome. The striking contrast between these two paintings makes it difficult to understand how any art historian could argue that the one from Rome was modeled after—much less shared a common source with—the one from Syria.

Nevertheless, the claim that the Dura synagogue paintings are important evidence for understanding the content and style of early Christian art persisted

---

17. Goodenough, "Catacomb Art," 133.
18. Du Bourguet, *Early Christian Painting* (New York: Viking, 1965), 11–12.
19. Chadwick, *The Early Church*, Pelican History of the Church 1 (London: Penguin, 1967), 279–80.

Fig. 42.7. Pharaoh's daughter finding Moses, Via Latina Catacomb, Rome, fourth century

Fig. 42.8. Pharaoh's daughter finding Moses, Dura Europos Synagogue, mid-third century

in the subsequent analysis of other highly respected art historians. In an article written in the 1950s, Kurt Weitzmann hypothesized that (now lost) illuminated manuscripts of the Hebrew Scriptures, most likely the full Septuagint but possibly the Pentateuch or Octateuch, were produced by Jews living in Antioch or Alexandria—regions in which Jews and Christians were known to have had mutually positive relationships or connections. He then proposed that these circulated among ateliers across the Mediterranean region and ultimately served as models adapted by artisans working for Christian patrons.[20] Thus, the iconography in the Dura paintings, the Christian catacomb frescoes, and in a number of surviving Byzantine illuminated manuscripts had a common source.

Weitzmann's lost illuminated Bible theory was widely accepted by other art historians, including John Beckwith, who, along with Bezalel Narkiss, suggested that these "possibly illuminated" Bible manuscripts could even be reconstructed by reference to the Dura synagogue paintings.[21] Taking this a step further, Narkiss identified occasional midrashic elements found in the Christian catacomb paintings, like the portrayal of the dreaming Joseph resting his head on three stones. The appearance of certain Jewish elements in Christian art, he proposed, could be explained by an earlier Jewish source although he acknowledges that no such source has been found.[22]

Similarly, in their collaboratively authored work, *The Frescoes of the Dura Synagogue and Christian Art*, Kurt Weitzmann and Herbert Kessler argued for the importance of studying the Dura synagogue paintings as a link or possible source for the early Christian iconography in Rome.[23] These two historians discussed each of the synagogue frescoes in order to identify parallel compositions in Christian pictorial imagery. Each author took on one part of the project. Weitzmann, expanding on his earlier thesis, linked specific sections of the Dura panels with related scenes in the Byzantine manuscripts. His aim was not only this, however, since he wished to confirm his theory that these two

---

20. See Kurt Weitzmann, "Die Illustration der Septuaginta," *Münchner Jahrbuch der bildenden Kunst* 3/4 (1952–1953): 96–120; trans. and repr. as "The Illustration of the Septuagint," in *No Graven Images: Studies in Art and the Hebrew Bible*, ed. Joseph Gutmann (New York: Ktav, 1971), 201–31. Also, Kurt Weitzmann, "The Illustration of the Septuagint," in *Studies in Classical and Byzantine Illumination*, ed. Herbert Kessler (Chicago: University of Chicago Press, 1971), 45–75.

21. Beckwith, *Early Christian and Byzantine Art*, Pelican History of Art 33 (Harmondsworth: Penguin, 1970), 39; Narkiss, "Representational Art," in *The Age of Spirituality: Late Antique and Early Christian Art, Third to Seventh Century; A Catalogue of the Exhibition at the Metropolitan Museum of Art, November 19, 1977–February 23, 1978*, ed. Kurt Weitzmann (New York: Metropolitan Museum of Art, 1979), 367.

22. Narkiss, "Representational Art," 369.

23. Weitzmann and Kessler, *The Frescoes of the Dura Synagogue and Christian Art*, Dumbarton Oaks Studies 28 (Washington, DC: Dumbarton Oaks, 1990).

corpora, widely separated by time and space, had a shared archetype. For his part, Kessler concentrated more on finding some coherent program in the synagogue paintings themselves and sought to uncover an element of competition as well as collaboration between Jews and Christians in Dura that initially had implications for compositional details of later Christian artworks, including some of the mosaics at Ravenna.[24] Finding a number of convincing examples in Byzantine-era illuminated manuscripts, they sought to find the missing link between them. Weitzmann in particular, by identifying the similarities in the manuscript miniature, posited that the Dura paintings most likely were based on an early Jewish illuminated Bible or Book of the Prophets.[25] Weitzmann, then considering the Dura context in particular, proposed that Jews and Christians likely shared artistic models or even workshops, which would explain some of the similarities in styles between the Christian baptistery paintings and the Dura synagogue frescoes.[26]

As reasonable as it might seem, the difficulty with this thesis is that, to date, no such lost model or common archetype—or anything like it—has been discovered. Additionally, as noted above, while the content of some Dura frescoes appears to have parallels in later Byzantine illuminated manuscripts, the rare, surviving examples of Jewish pictorial art from the third century (e.g., the Dura synagogue paintings) differ both stylistically and thematically with the Old Testament narrative scenes in Christian catacomb art. Furthermore, most of the Old Testament figures found in the Christian catacombs and on early sarcophagus reliefs are not portrayed in the Dura synagogue (e.g., the temptation of Adam and Eve, Noah in the ark, Moses striking the rock in the wilderness, Daniel in the lions' den, the three Hebrew youths, Jonah swallowed by the sea creature, and Susannah with the elders). Conversely, most of the Dura synagogue images have not been found in early Christian art (e.g., Samuel anointing David, Elijah raising the widow's son, the ark destroying the idols of Dagon, Elijah defeating the priests of Baal, the miraculous well, the consecration of the temple, Ezekiel with the raising of dry bones, and the episodes from the story of Esther). The only overlapping narratives are Pharaoh's daughter finding the baby Moses (a rare scene in early Christian art), Moses and the Israelites crossing the Red Sea, and the binding of Isaac, which appear entirely different from one another. Unlike the Dura synagogue paintings, which display narrative images rendered in complex and often sequential fashion, Christian examples are abbreviated and sketchy. They are very different from the skillfully executed scenes, each set off by

---

24. Weitzmann and Kessler, *Frescoes*, 169–83.
25. Weitzmann and Kessler, *Frescoes*, 5.
26. Weitzmann and Kessler, *Frescoes*, 6–13.

painted frames, that appear in the ascending registers of the Dura-Europos synagogue. Consequently, although some later examples of Christian art, including a cycle of mosaics in the fifth-century Roman basilica of Santa Maria Maggiore, and illuminated manuscripts from the sixth century and into the Middle Ages show some interesting connections, perceiving significant similarities between this Jewish and Christian iconography is difficult.

Positing a connection between early Jewish and Christian iconography is problematic for another reason. Superficially, the dominance of Old Testament themes in early Christian art might be surprising to those who assume early Christian visual imagery would have favored New Testament narratives and, further, that the evident popularity of Old Testament subjects logically drew from some Jewish source. Implied in this assumption is a problematic tendency to divide the two testaments and overlook the importance and role of the Hebrew Scriptures for early Christian teaching and tradition. With the notable exception of certain gnostic groups and the famous heretic Marcion, early Christians consistently regarded the Old Testament writings as holy Scripture and read them in their communal worship along with the Gospels and apostolic epistles.

Because the Old Testament was always considered Christian Scripture, assuming a Jewish source for these motifs in early Christian art is unwarranted. Surviving early Christian sermons, catechetical lectures, poetry, exegetical works, liturgical texts, and theological treatises frequently cite stories from the Pentateuch and Octateuch. Most importantly, Christian writers and preachers do not simply treat these stories as literal, historical narratives, but allow them a variety of interpretative and theological purposes. Moreover, as much as these purposes are evident in the literary record, they were likely also circulating in the oral tradition.

Some scholars have suggested that one of these roles might belong to rituals surrounding the care for and burial of the Christian dead. Arguably, certain early prayers offered for the souls of the dead, the *commendatio animae*, assured the bereaved of God's faithful deliverance from death and danger, by giving such examples as the Isaac's deliverance, the rescue of Daniel from the lions' den, or the three Hebrew youths from the fiery furnace.[27] Although the oldest surviving

---

27. This theory was proposed in the late nineteenth century but still has strong support. See Alfred Stuiber, *Refrigerium Interim: Die Vorstellungen vom Zwischenzustand und die frühchristliche Grabeskunst*, Theophaneia 11 (Bonn: Hanstein, 1957), 169–74; but more recently summarized (with helpful bibliography) by Catherine Brown Tkacz, *The Key to the Brescia Casket: Typology and the Early Christian Imagination*, Christianity and Judaism in Antiquity 14 (Notre Dame: University of Notre Dame Press, 2002), 109–37. A similar type of prayer is noted in Cyprian of Antioch, *Oratorio ad Graecos* 2; and in the Apos. Con. 7.35, which praises God's providential care for the faithful.

examples date to the turn of the fifth century, the possibility that they reflect earlier practices is a reasonable assumption. Furthermore, their funerary association fits well with the context of most surviving examples of early Christian art. Yet, the earliest known example of one of these prayers for the commendation of the dying dates comes from the *Ordo Romanus* 49 (ca. 800 CE) and the overlap of cited Old Testament figures with early Christian iconography is weak, particularly as it relies on the existence of yet another hypothetical source.

A different approach seeks to explain the popularity of these Old Testament figures as a response to Christian physical and social vulnerability in the third and early fourth century. Visual references to God's deliverance of the faithful from danger or death during times of persecution would have inspired courage and offered comfort. This view is especially evident in the work of Graydon Snyder, whose popular study of Christian art in the centuries before Constantine proposed that most of the Old Testament images in the Christian catacombs were symbols of peace and safety at times when Christians were imperiled by political persecution. Snyder particularly singles out the figures of Noah, Jonah, Daniel, Susannah, and the three Hebrew youths as examples of divine rescue from threatening earthly forces. Emphasizing the pre-Constantinian social matrix and discounting any mystical, liturgical, or doctrinal meanings, Snyder further discounts a specific funerary relevance for the images, claiming that many were included in the Christian baptistery at Dura Europos as well as other "non-sepulchral locations."[28] Snyder specifically resists "supposing a theological meaning that can be adduced from contemporary or even later theological literature" in contrast to what he describes as a pictorial response by a disenfranchised group living in a hostile surrounding.[29]

One objection to Snyder's thesis is that since few non-sepulchral examples of early Christian art have survived apart from the Dura Europos baptistery murals, drawing comparisons is almost impossible. In addition, modern scholars have tended to correct the exaggerated perception of Christians facing constant persecution. Rather, even during the Great Persecution at the beginning of the fourth century, overt hostility and threat were sporadic and local rather than recurrent and widespread. In fact, Christians mostly lived in relative security and harmony with their non-Christian neighbors. Finally, as Snyder himself recognized, death itself was something from which Christians believed they were delivered, if not immediately, then at least in the final resurrection at Christ's second coming.

A further problem with identifying the Old Testament figures in early Christian art as examples of God's promised deliverance from death or danger is that, in early Christian literature, these figures are regarded as foreshadowing elements

---

28. Snyder, *Ante Pacem: Archeological Evidence of Church Life before Constantine*, rev. ed. (Macon, GA: Mercer University Press, 2003), generally, but see pp. 25, 38.

29. Snyder, *Ante Pacem*, 24.

Fig. 42.9. The Israelites crossing the Red Sea, sarcophagus front panel from the Cathedral of St. Trophime, Arles (France), fourth century

of the Christian salvation story. This occurs already in the New Testament, as Paul's First Epistle to the Corinthians, in which the Israelites' crossing the Red Sea is given as a type of baptism and the rock that Moses struck to provide water for the thirsty escapees becomes a figure of Christ (1 Cor 10:2–4). Paul's christological application of these episodes from Exodus could be one of the reasons for the popularity of their depiction in early Christian catacomb paintings and sarcophagus reliefs (fig. 42.9). Later Christian preachers and exegetes also saw these stories as prefiguring the passage from death to new life in baptism.[30] Similarly, Abraham's offering of Isaac was understood to be a prophetic figure of Christ's—God's beloved Son's—voluntary sacrifice on the cross.[31] Abraham's three visitors at Mamre were seen as indicative of the Holy Trinity. Other biblical characters, like the three Hebrew youths, Daniel, and Susanna were regarded as types of Christian martyrs, falsely accused and steadfast to their faith.[32]

Visual depictions of these stories thereby illuminated a providential continuity between the first and second testaments and allowed the narratives and the

---

30. E.g., see Tertullian, *Bapt.* 9.1; Cyprian, *Ep.* 69.15.1–2; Gregory of Nyssa, *Diem lum.*; Basil of Caesarea, *Bapt.* 1; Cyril of Jerusalem, *Myst.* 1.1–2; and Augustine, *Enarrat. Ps.* 106.3; among many others. For the role of Old Testament stories in baptismal catecheses and related liturgical documents, see Jensen, *Baptismal Imagery*, which considers a wide range of narrative episodes as symbolizing different aspects of Christian initiation.

31. Among these are Melito of Sardis, *Pasch.*; Irenaeus, *Haer.* 4.5.4; Tertullian, *Adv. Jud.* 10.6 and 13.20–22; Ambrose, *Abr.* 1.8; and Augustine, *Civ.* 16.32. For a summary of how these writers interpreted Old Testament stories in this way, see Robin M. Jensen, "Early Christian Images and Exegesis," in Spier, *Picturing the Bible*, 65–85.

32. Daniel as a type of the Christian martyr is discussed below.

characters to represent that connection. Christian viewers would have regarded them as not only witnesses to the truth of their faith but evidence that it had an ancient and venerable legacy. The rich and multifaceted typological and allegorical interpretation of Old Testament stories in Christian exegesis also allowed viewers to arrive at a variety of different interpretations of these biblical scenes, depending on how the sermons, prayers, or catechetical lectures they had received prompted them to see. Finally, the figures' placement in a composition, their physical setting or context (e.g., a tomb or a church wall), and even the style, composition, and technique in which they are fashioned affected how spectators viewed and drew meaning from them.

Illustrative Cases

The final part of this chapter presents three examples of early Christian depictions of Old Testament stories (Noah's ark, Daniel in the lions' den, and Jonah) and explores some of the possible meanings that their viewers may have seen in them as well as exegetical strategies of those stories employed by early Christian writers.

Noah in the Ark

The first example, the scene of Noah in the ark (cf. figs. 42.2, 42.4, and 42.6), omits most of the story recounted in the book of Genesis (Gen 6). The more than fifty examples in catacomb painting and the dozen or so carvings found on early Christian sarcophagi show no evidence of drowning humanity, nor do they include figures of Noah's wife, sons, sons' wives, or animals.[33] These details were evidently superfluous to the image's intended message. The ark is depicted as a simple box, with an open lid, just large enough to hold Noah alone. Noah stands in the posture of prayer, perhaps noting the dove flying overhead, bearing an olive branch in its beak. Clearly, the image reduces the story to this particular moment, when Noah realizes that he has been delivered from death. While this reference to God's deliverance from death makes sense for a tomb, the image may have more than one valence.

In a rare exception, a sarcophagus relief from Trier, dated to the early fourth century, depicts Noah and his seven family members in an ark that includes

---

33. For a brief study see Jutta Dresken-Weiland, *Bild, Grab, und Wort: Untersuchungen zu Jenseitsvorstellungen von Christen des 3. und 4. Jahrhunderts* (Regensburg: Schnell & Steiner, 2010), 287–94.

Fig. 42.10. Opening of Noah's ark (above) and Noah's sacrifice (below), from the Ashburnham Pentateuch, Spain or Italy, now in the Bibliothèque Nationale de France, fifth to sixth centuries

various animals (a lion, deer, cow, and dog). The fact that this unusual example survives suggests that the full narrative and its echoes in the epistles of 1 and 2 Peter were well known, although rarely illuminated in full. The contrast between the usual, abbreviated Christian iconography with later compositions is all the more striking when one compares them with the illuminations from early Christian manuscripts, like the Ashburnham Pentateuch, which features two full-page illustrations, one with the ark floating amidst the flood waters filled with drowned humans and animals and the second depicting Noah and his family with animals departing after the ark came to rest on dry land (fig. 42.10).

In the New Testament, the story of Noah is cited in both Epistles of Peter (1 Pet 3:20 and 2 Pet 2:5). In the first instance, the author remarks that Noah, his wife, his sons, and their wives made up a symbolic number of eight righteous souls saved through water. This water, he says, prefigured baptism, a bath that is not for "a removal of dirt from the body, but an appeal to God for a good conscience, through the resurrection of Jesus Christ." This idea is reinforced in the text of 2 Peter, where Noah is identified as a "herald of righteousness" along with the seven others.[34] While these passages emphasize the number of eight, saved through the baptism-prefiguring flood, the early Christian images show only Noah.

For early Christians, baptism was the essential sacrament for salvation, and Noah's story is often given as its sign. For example, Justin Martyr argues that the story of the flood prefigures Christian baptism, adding that only those saved through water, faith, and wood are spared God's judgment. He explains that the floodwaters represent baptism, Noah's righteousness symbolizes the faith, and the wood of the ark signifies the wood of the cross (*Dial.* 138.2–3). Similarly, in his treatise *On the Unity of the Catholic Church*, Cyprian of Carthage insists no one can have God for Father if they do not have the church as mother and adds that since there was no escape for anyone outside the ark, there is no escape for someone outside the church (*Unit. eccl.* 6).[35]

Seeing Noah's ark as a figure of the church continued in the writings of fourth-century exegetes, including John Chrysostom (*Laz.* 6.7), Ambrose of Milan, and Augustine of Hippo (*Catech.* 20.32, 34). John Chrysostom's interpretation especially elaborates on a few more of the story's details by identifying the raven as a symbol of sin and the dove as the sign both of God's forgiveness and the gift of the Holy Spirit at baptism (Ambrose, *Myst.* 3.10–11; and *Sacr.* 1.23 and 2.1).

In early Christian iconography, Noah appears to be protected from the deluge by a small wooden box (sometimes with little feet) rather than a substantial boat. This might indicate a conflation of Noah's ark with the ark of the covenant but in a later historical period is similar in appearance to portable Christian altars and early medieval reliquaries. As Jennifer Freeman has noted, this iconographic blurring of ark and ark of the covenant, and in later iconography with altars and caskets containing the holy relics of saints, expresses a visual conflation of

---

34. On the symbolism of the number eight, at least as interpreted by later Christian authors, see Clement of Alexandria, *Strom.* 5; Augustine, *Ep.* 55.13.23; and *Serm.* 260a.4. Discussion and additional examples are found in Reinhart Staats, "Ogdoas als ein Symbol für die Auferstehung," *VC* 26, no. 1 (1972): 29–52; and Jensen, *Baptismal Imagery*, 204–6.

35. See also Cyprian, *Ep.* 67.2; 73; and 75. Other examples are found in Tertullian, *Idol.* 24 and *Bapt.* 8.4.

instruments, each signifying physical, sacramental, and spiritual deliverance.[36] The dove in the image both refers to the bird in the Genesis story and the Holy Spirit at Jesus's baptism. Thus, Noah in early Christian art is not simply a figure of deliverance from death but also a reference to baptism, the essential ritual for assuring one's hope for afterlife resurrection.

Daniel with the Lions

A second example is the way that early Christian pictorial art rendered the story of Daniel in the lions' den. The prophet Daniel appears in several images in early Christian art, including the Greek Septuagint additions to the Hebrew book of Daniel, which contains the stories of Susanna and the elders and of Daniel exposing the priests of Bel and slaying the dragon. Far more popular, however, are scenes of Daniel with the lions.[37] The simple composition typically shows Daniel as a youthful, beardless, heroic nude, with the two lions flanking him (cf. figs. 42.3 and 42.4). While in the numerous catacomb paintings he is alone, in many of the sarcophagus reliefs he is joined by the prophet Habakkuk, as described in Bel 33–39. In a few rare examples he is clothed in a Babylonian-styled costume: a short, decorated tunic over trousers, a cape fastened at his shoulder, and a Phrygian-styled cap (fig. 42.11). In almost all instances, he is presented frontally, with his arms raised in the prayer (*orans*) position, often with his weight shifted to one leg in a traditional *contrapposto* stance. Ordinarily two lions approach him, sometimes with mouths open and front paws raised aggressively, but in instances the lions appear to be quite docile.

The usual presentation of Daniel as a nude, especially found in the Roman examples, requires some explanation, since this is not part of the biblical narrative. Like the representation of Noah, this appears to be an allusion to Christian baptism, a ritual that was administered to nude, primarily adult recipients in the first centuries of Christianity.

Daniel's nudity might also be a reference to resurrection from death and perhaps a type of Christ, rising from the tomb and leaving his grave clothes behind. This link is strengthened by the narrative itself. Daniel was imprisoned in the

---

36. Jennifer Freeman, "Altar-ed Arks: Form as (Theological) Function in Late Antique and Early Medieval Reliquaries," in *Death and Rebirth in Late Antiquity*, ed. Lee Jefferson (Lanham, MD: Lexington Books, 2022). Here Freeman disputes an older theory by Mary Charles Murray that the ark was based upon the chest in the Greco-Roman myth of Perseus and Danae; see Charles Murray, *Rebirth and Afterlife: A Study of the Transmutation of Some Pagan Imagery in Early Christian Funerary Art*, BARIS 100 (Oxford: BAR, 1981), 103–5.

37. See again Dresken-Weiland, *Bild, Grab, und Wort*, 235–47.

lions' den, a stone was rolled across the opening, and he was left there to die, only to be found the next morning alive in his tomb-like prison (Dan 6:16–19). While the scriptural story lacks any overt reference to resurrection, at least one surviving textual source makes the link. Hippolytus of Rome's *Commentary on Daniel* imagines that the prophet's words as he emerges from the tomb proclaimed that Christ himself stretched out his hand to raise him as one of the living from among the dead and into the resurrection of new life (*Comm. Dan.* 10.16).

Early Christian texts also present Daniel as a type of the early Christian martyr. In some of the early iconography, one might see Daniel in the guise of a Christian martyr facing the beasts. In a mosaic from Roman Africa, Daniel is confronted by four lions standing on angled platforms, which recalls the *bestiarii* fights in the Roman arena (fig. 42.12). Both the African fathers Tertullian and Cyprian describe Daniel as the model martyr, especially as he is imprisoned for his refusal to obey a wicked ruler's edict to offer worship only to himself (Dan 6:7–9). Darius thereby becomes the representative archetype of the Roman emperor, ordering Christians to pay homage to his own image, as well as to those of the pagan gods. The story of Daniel thereby becomes a story of encouragement and consolation to Christians suffering persecution for resisting idolatry. That some of those Christians were also thrown to lions makes the story all the more relevant to that context. In his treatise *On Idolatry*, Tertullian specifically describes Daniel as one who was in all other ways submissive to Darius until it put him into danger of apostasy. This Daniel had no fear of the royal lions but did fear the fires of hell (*Idol.* 15.10). While Daniel's story ends happily and many of the martyrs died, elsewhere Tertullian contends that he fits the perfect profile of the martyr. In fact, he adds, if Daniel had died by being devoured by lions, God's purpose to reveal his divine power would not have been accomplished (*Apol.* 40).

Cyprian, writing in the aftermath of the Decian persecution in the mid-third century, similarly describes Daniel as a courageous, faithful, and glorious example for Christian martyrs. He too insists that Daniel's witness was true and his heroism absolute, although he did not die but was rescued by God. Therefore, Cyprian proclaims neither death nor survival constitutes the martyrs' victory, but their crown lies in their refusal to yield to the demands of an earthly tyrant (*Laps.* 19; *Ep.* 61.2.1). The martyr's reward is not only her crown but also immediate entrance to paradise upon death, which makes this also a hopeful reminder even for those who died a natural death and so also appropriate for funerary settings (e.g., catacomb chambers, mausolea, and sarcophagi). However, depictions of Daniel also show up in non-sepulchral contexts, including pottery lamps, ceramic bowls and platters, and terra-cotta ceiling tiles. In early Christian art,

Daniel could be interpreted as a polyvalent figure, signifying one who is baptized and thereby rescued from death, as a Christ figure insofar as he emerges at dawn from his tomb, and as typifying the courageous Christian martyr who steadfastly confesses faith in the face of persecution by earthly authorities.

Jonah Swallowed and Cast Up

Our final example, early Christian depictions of the tale of Jonah, appears in an entirely different format from other Old Testament narrative scenes. Shown in a unique sequence of three or, sometimes, four episodes, this exceptionally popular subject features only the middle of the scriptural narrative, in which Jonah is thrown overboard, swallowed by the sea creature, regurgitated from the creature's

Fig. 42.11. Mosaic of Daniel from Thyna, now in the Archeological Museum of Sfax (Tunisia), fifth to sixth centuries

mouth, and (finally) reclines beneath a trellis shaded by a leafy gourd vine (figs. 42.4 and 42.6). The biblical episode describing Jonah's attempts to avoid the Lord's command to go and preach to the Ninevites is not depicted, nor is the conclusion, in which the Ninevites repent and the sulking Jonah nearly dies from exposure. Thus, while the text of the biblical narrative focuses on the inhabitants of Nineveh, their sinful behavior, their conversion, and Jonah's resentment at God's mercy, the images of the cycle illuminate a secondary theme. Here, instead of teaching a lesson about obedience to God's will, the message indicating the hope for resurrection from death was undoubtedly more meaningful in a funerary context.

These motifs are found in all media of early Christian art, from catacomb paintings (cf. fig. 42.4) to sarcophagus reliefs (cf. fig. 42.6), pottery lamps, gems, gold glasses (fig. 42.13), and church pavement mosaics (fig. 42.14). Most of these show Jonah being fed, headfirst, into the mouth of the creature. Many also include Jonah's emergence from the creature's mouth and finally his reclining under his shady vine. Most early Christian depictions of this scene present Jonah as a nude, and his nakedness, especially in repose, suggests the innocence of the prelapsarian Adam, the bliss of the righteous dead in the interim state between

Fig. 42.12. Daniel mosaic from Memoria of the Blossi, from Furnos Minus, now in the Bardo Museum, Tunis, fifth century

Fig. 42.13. Jonah swallowed by the whale, bottom of a gilded glass cup, from Rome, now in the Louvre, fourth century

Fig. 42.14. Jonah being fed to the sea monster, pavement mosaic from the Basilica Patriarcale, Aquileia (Italy), fourth century

death, and, finally, the hoped-for resurrection into a paradisiacal garden. His posture is also notably similar to that of the Roman hero Endymion, beloved of the goddess Selene, who appears often on pagan sarcophagi in a similar pose and also nude (or nearly so) as he wakes each night from a perpetual sleep to receive his nocturnal lover.[38]

The iconographic suggestion of Jonah's blissful posthumous reward corresponds to some extent with early Christian textual exegesis of the Jonah story.[39]

---

38. See Marion Lawrence, "Three Pagan Themes in Christian Art," in *De Artibus Opuscula XL: Essays in Honor of Erwin Panofsky* (New York: New York University Press, 1961), 323–34.

39. For a detailed summary of the typological application of Jonah by early Christian

While Justin Martyr appears to follow the Lukan version of the "sign of Jonah" as an admonition against wickedness and assurance of God's mercy to repentant sinners (Luke 11:29–32; *Dial.* 107), Irenaeus employs the story as an instance of bodily resurrection against his gnostic adversaries (*Haer.* 5.5.2).[40] As Irenaeus explains, if Jonah could stay in the creature's belly for three days and be regurgitated whole, certainly God could raise dead bodies from their graves. Tertullian similarly cites the example of Jonah as proof of the bodily resurrection (*Res.* 58). Yet, the pictorial image is not only one of eventual bodily resurrection but seems also to suggest the righteous soul's untroubled sleep in the interim period.

Further significance might be given to the depiction of Jonah as nude. As in the case of Daniel in early Christian art, Jonah is nearly always represented as naked, perhaps, as with Daniel, alluding to Christ's resurrection, as well as the promised resurrection of the Christian believer. This promised resurrection is, however, obtained initially through the sacrament of Christian initiation, a ritual undertaken by adult converts who were stripped and plunged into a watery font while completely nude. As depicted, the three episodes from the Jonah story could be understood as symbolizing that ritualized death and rebirth and its heavenly reward.[41] Basil of Caesarea, in fact, attested to this symbolism, when he interpreted Jonah's three days in the monster's belly as a figure of the triple immersion in the baptismal rite (*Spir. Sanc.* 14.32). Jonah is then a type both of Christ's first resurrection and the Christian's anticipated sharing in it through the rebirth of baptism.

Conclusion

Old Testament narratives were a predominant source for the earliest Christian pictorial art. This may be explained by the fact that Christians regarded the Hebrew Scriptures not only as their Bible but as testimony to the coming of Christ along with the church and its rituals. They featured the stories of Abraham and Isaac, Noah, Jonah, Moses, Daniel, and the three Hebrew youths in their iconography in part because they witnessed to God's ancient and abiding care for his chosen people, of which they now counted themselves, but also because

---

writers, see Yves-Marie Duval, *Le Livre de Jonas dans la littérature chrétienne grecque et latine: Sources et influence du Commentaire sur Jonas de saint Jérôme*, 2 vols. (Paris: Études Augustinennes, 1973).

40. Irenaeus here also refers to the three Hebrew youths who survived the fiery furnace and came out whole in body.

41. Jensen, *Baptismal Imagery*, 153–56.

they regarded them as witnesses to the truth of the Gospels. While their religious beliefs might have seemed novel to Romans and even to Jews, the perceived coherence of both testaments was proof of Christianity's legacy, validity, and continuity. After the Constantinian "peace of the church," many of the popular Old Testament figures were no longer subjects for Christian pictorial art. The Good Shepherd never entirely vanished, but along with Abraham, Noah, Daniel, the three youths, and Jonah, he became a minor character, while images of Christ, the Virgin Mary, and the saints came to dominate the decoration of church apses and walls.[42] Life cycles of Christ and the Virgin Mary on ivory book covers and large-scale mosaics were the favored narrative images. Depictions of Jesus transferring the scroll of the law to Peter and Paul became particularly prominent in Rome, where the two holy apostles were especially venerated as founders of the church.

Some exceptions exist, including the programmatic mosaics showing episodes from Genesis and Exodus adorning the nave of Rome's early fifth-century Basilica of Santa Maria Maggiore and unprecedented scenes from Genesis discovered among the fourth-century wall paintings of the Via Latina catacomb (e.g., Abraham with the three visitors, Jacob's ladder, and Moses with Pharaoh's daughter). Textual evidence from the early fifth century, such as a poem of Paulinus of Nola (*Carm.* 27.511–42) or an epistle from Abbot Nilus of Sinai (*Epistle to Olympiodorus*), indicates that their church decoration included Old Testament imagery. Such exceptions arguably prove the rule: that Old Testament scenes, once so popular, slowly but surely were overtaken, first by images of Christ teaching, healing, and working wonders and, by the end of the fourth century, by portraits of holy men and women along with scenes of Jesus's transfiguration, passion, resurrection, and ascension. The rare Old Testament narratives showing Abraham's sacrifice of Isaac or Melchizedek's and Abel's offerings that appear in the sixth-century sanctuary of Ravenna's Basilica of San Vitale were clearly intended as typological allusions to the eucharistic sacrifice at the altar directly below.

Reasons for this gradual disappearance of Old Testament scenes in monumental Christian art are unclear, but it appears to be circumstantially linked with the radical shift in the church's political, social, and economic status. However, it is not simply that Christians were no longer threatened by hostile authorities or even that many more of them belonged to the elite, aristocratic, and wealthy classes. Christians did not cease to love their Old Testament stories or find them

---

42. See Boniface Ramsay, "A Note on the Disappearance of the Good Shepherd from Early Christian Art," *HTR* 76, no. 3 (1983): 375–78.

to be reassuring in times of personal danger or stress. They did not stop finding prophetic and typological figures in the Hebrew Scriptures. Many sermons preached from fifth- and sixth-century pulpits testify to the inspirational, didactic, and dogmatic value of the Hebrew Scripture narratives that emphasized the continuity between the testaments and Christian inclusion in the covenant. It seems more likely that, as Christianity began to be an imperially patronized institution, supportive donors sponsored monumental works of art to be displayed in places designed for increasingly elaborate public liturgies. For this they clearly tended to favor triumphant representations of Christ enthroned or saints receiving their crowns of glory. Funds once dedicated to decorating private burial spaces were diverted to adorning imposing public ecclesial structures. The large mosaic programs that suited apses and nave walls were less conducive to displaying the intimate and edifying biblical narrative scenes favored by earlier generations. These remained, but in smaller formats, such as illuminated manuscripts like the early sixth-century Ashburnham Pentateuch or the Vienna Genesis, which allowed a close link between word and image and were the primary context in which Christians after the mid-fourth century would have encountered scenes from Old Testament narratives.

Bibliography

Beckwith, John. *Early Christian and Byzantine Art*. Pelican History of Art 33. Harmondsworth: Penguin, 1970.

Bourguet, Pierre du. *Early Christian Painting*. New York: Viking, 1965.

Breasted, James Henry. *The Oriental Forerunners of Byzantine Painting: First-Century Wall Paintings from the Fortress of Dura on the Middle Euphrates*. OIP 1. Chicago: University of Chicago Press, 1924.

Brody, Lisa, and Gail Hoffman, eds. *Dura-Europos: Crossroads of Antiquity*. Boston: McMullen Museum of Art, Boston College, 2011.

Cachia, Nicholas. *The Image of the Good Shepherd as a Source for the Spirituality of the Ministerial Priesthood: I Am the Good Shepherd; The Good Shepherd Lays Down His Life for the Sheep (John 10.11)*. Tesi Gregoriana Serie Spiritualità 4. Rome: Gregorian University Press, 1997.

Chadwick, Henry. *The Early Church*. Pelican History of the Church 1. London: Penguin, 1967.

Dresken-Weiland, Jutta. *Bild, Grab, und Wort: Untersuchungen zu Jenseitsvorstellungen von Christen des 3. und 4. Jahrhunderts*. Regensburg: Schnell & Steiner, 2010.

Duval, Yves-Marie. *Le Livre de Jonas dans la littérature chrétienne grecque et latine: Sources et influence du Commentaire sur Jonas de saint Jérôme*. 2 vols. Paris: Études Augustinennes, 1973.

Elsner, Jaś. "Archaeologies and Agendas: Reflections on Late Ancient Jewish Art and Early Christian Art." *JRS* 93 (2003): 114–28.

Fine, Steven. *Art and Judaism in the Greco-Roman World: Toward a New Jewish Archaeology*. Cambridge: Cambridge University Press, 2010.

———. "Jewish Art and Biblical Exegesis in the Greco-Roman World." Pages 25–50 in *Picturing the Bible: The Earliest Christian Art*. Edited by Jeffrey Spier. New Haven: Yale University Press, 2007.

Finney, Paul Corby. *The Invisible God: The Earliest Christians on Art*. Oxford: Oxford University Press, 1994.

Foletti, Ivan, and Francesco Lovino. "Introduction: *Orient oder Rom*, and Josef Strzygowski in 2018." Pages 7–14 in *Orient oder Rom? History and Reception of a Historiographical Myth (1901–1970)*. Edited by Ivan Foletti and Francesco Lovino. Prague: Institute of Art History, Czech Academy of Sciences, 2018.

Freeman, Jennifer Awes. "Altar-ed Arks: Form as (Theological) Function in Late Antique and Early Medieval Reliquaries." In *Death and Rebirth in Late Antiquity*. Edited by Lee Jefferson. Lanham, MD: Lexington Books, 2022.

———. *The Good Shepherd: Image, Meaning, and Power*. Waco, TX: Baylor University Press, 2021.

———. "The Good Shepherd and the Enthroned Ruler: A Reconsideration of Imperial Iconography in the Early Church." Pages 159–96 in *The Art of Empire: Christian Art in Its Imperial Context*. Edited by Robin M. Jensen and Lee M. Jefferson. Minneapolis: Fortress, 2015.

Goodenough, Erwin R. "Catacomb Art." *JBL* 81, no. 2 (1962): 112–42.

———. *Jewish Symbols in the Greco-Roman Period*. 13 vols. New York: Pantheon, 1953–1968.

Hachlili, Rachel. *Ancient Synagogues—Archaeology and Art: New Discoveries and Current Research*. HdO 105. Leiden: Brill, 2013.

Jastrzębowska, Elżbieta. "Josef Strzygowski und Joseph Wilpert: Zwei Gesichter derselben Wissenschaft." Pages 43–54 in *Von Biala nach Wien: Josef Strzygowski und die Kunstwissenschaften*. Edited by Piotr O. Scholz and Magdalena A. Dlugosz. Vienna: European University Press, 2015.

Jensen, Robin M. "Aniconism in the First Centuries of Christianity." *Religion* 47, no. 3 (2017): 408–24.

———. *Baptismal Imagery in Early Christianity*. Grand Rapids: Baker Academic, 2012.

———. "The Dura Europos Synagogue and Christian Baptistery: Early Christian Art and Religious Life in Dura Europos." Pages 174–89 in *Jews, Christians, and*

Polytheists in the Ancient Synagogue. Edited by Steven Fine. London: Routledge, 1999.

———. "Early Christian Images and Exegesis." Pages 65–86 in *Picturing the Bible: The Earliest Christian Art*. Edited by Jeffrey Spier. New Haven: Yale University Press, 2007.

———. "The Fish: An Early Christian Symbol for Christ." Pages 271–90 in vol. 3 of *The Reception of Jesus in the First Three Centuries*. Edited by Chris Keith, Helen Bond, Christine Jacobi, and Jens Schröter. 3 vols. London: Bloomsbury, 2019.

———. "Introduction: Early Christian Art." Pages 1–17 in *The Routledge Handbook of Early Christian Art*. Edited by Robin M. Jensen and Mark D. Ellison. London: Routledge, 2018.

———. *Understanding Early Christian Art*. London: Routledge, 2000.

Kitzinger, Ernst. "The Cult of Images before Iconoclasm." *DOP* 8 (1954): 83–150.

Ladner, Gerhard B. "The Concept of the Image in the Greek Fathers and the Byzantine Iconoclastic Controversy." *DOP* 7 (1953): 1–34.

Lawrence, Marion. "Three Pagan Themes in Christian Art." Pages 323–34 in *De Artibus Opuscula XL: Essays in Honor of Erwin Panofsky*. New York: New York University Press, 1961.

Levine, Lee. *Visual Judaism in Late Antiquity: Historical Contexts of Jewish Art*. New Haven: Yale University Press, 2013.

Murray, Mary Charles. "Art and the Early Church." *JTS* 28, no. 2 (1977): 303–45.

———. *Rebirth and Afterlife: A Study of the Transmutation of Some Pagan Imagery in Early Christian Funerary Art*. BARIS 100. Oxford: BAR, 1981.

Narkiss, Bezalel. "Representational Art." Pages 366–71 in *The Age of Spirituality: Late Antique and Early Christian Art, Third to Seventh Century; A Catalogue of the Exhibition at the Metropolitan Museum of Art, November 19, 1977–February 23, 1978*. Edited by Kurt Weitzmann. New York: Metropolitan Museum of Art, 1979.

Peppard, Michael. *The World's Oldest Church: Bible, Art, and Ritual at Dura-Europos, Syria*. New Haven: Yale University Press, 2016.

Quasten, Johannes. "Der Gute Hirte in frühchristlicher Totenliturgie und Grabeskunst." Pages 373–406 in vol. 1 of *Miscellanea Giovanni Mercati*. 6 vols. Studi e testi 121. Vatican City: Biblioteca Apostolica Vaticana, 1946.

———. "The Painting of the Good Shepherd at Dura Europos." *Medieval Studies* 9 (1947): 1–18.

Ramsay, Boniface. "A Note on the Disappearance of the Good Shepherd from Early Christian Art." *HTR* 76, no. 3 (1983): 375–78.

Rutgers, Leonard. *The Jews in Late Ancient Rome: Evidence of Cultural Interaction in the Roman Diaspora*. RGRW 126. Leiden: Brill, 2000.

Snyder, Graydon. *Ante Pacem: Archeological Evidence of Church Life before Constantine*. Rev. ed. Macon, GA: Mercer University Press, 2003.

Spier, Jeffrey. "The Earliest Christian Art: From Personal Salvation to Imperial Power." Pages 1–24 in *Picturing the Bible: The Earliest Christian Art*. Edited by Jeffrey Spier. New Haven: Yale University Press, 2007.

Staats, Reinhart. "Ogdoas als ein Symbol für die Auferstehung." *VC* 26, no. 1 (1972): 29–52.

Strzygowski, Josef. *Orient oder Rom: Beiträge zur Geschichte der spätantiken und frühchristlichen Kunst*. Leipzig: Hinrich, 1901.

Stuiber, Alfred. *Refrigerium Interim: Die Vorstellungen vom Zwischenzustand und die frühchristliche Grabeskunst*. Theophaneia 11. Bonn: Hanstein, 1957.

Tkacz, Catherine Brown. *The Key to the Brescia Casket: Typology and the Early Christian Imagination*. Christianity and Judaism in Antiquity 14. Notre Dame: University of Notre Dame Press, 2002.

Weiss, Ze'ev, and Lee Levine, eds. *From Dura to Sepphoris: Studies in Jewish Art and Society in Late Antiquity*. JRASup 40. Portsmouth, RI: Journal of Roman Archaeology, 2000.

Weitzmann, Kurt. "Die Illustration der Septuaginta." *Münchner Jahrbuch der bildenden Kunst* 3/4 (1952–1953): 96–120. Trans. and repr., "The Illustration of the Septuagint." Pages 201–31 in *No Graven Images: Studies in Art and the Hebrew Bible*. Edited by Joseph Gutmann. New York: Ktav, 1971.

———. "The Illustration of the Septuagint." Pages 45–75 in *Studies in Classical and Byzantine Illumination*. Edited by Herbert Kessler. Chicago: University of Chicago Press, 1971.

Weitzmann, Kurt, and Herbert Kessler. *The Frescoes of the Dura Synagogue and Christian Art*. Dumbarton Oak Studies 28. Washington, DC: Dumbarton Oaks, 1990.

Wharton, Annabel. *Refiguring the Post-Classical City: Dura Europos, Jerash, Jerusalem, and Ravenna*. Cambridge: Cambridge University Press, 1995.

Wickhoff, Franz. *Die Wiener Genesis*. Vienna: Tempsky, 1895. Repr., *Römische Kunst (Die Wiener Genesis)*. Berlin: Meyer & Jenssen, 1912.

Zanker, Paul, and Björn Ewald. *Living with Myths: The Imagery of Roman Sarcophagi*. Translated by Julia Slater. Oxford Studies in Ancient Culture and Representation. Oxford: Oxford University Press, 2012.

Zimmermann, Norbert. "Catacomb Painting and the Rise of Christian Iconography in Funerary Art." Pages 21–38 in *The Routledge Handbook of Early Christian Art*. Edited by Robin M. Jensen and Mark D. Ellison. London: Routledge, 2018.

Contributors

Garrick V. Allen, senior lecturer in New Testament Studies, University of Glasgow, United Kingdom

Michael Avioz, professor of Bible, Bar-Ilan University, Ramat Gan, Israel

Martin Bauspiess, Privatdozent in New Testament, Eberhard Karls Universität Tübingen, Germany

Richard J. Bautch, professor of humanities, associate dean in the School of Arts and Humanities, St. Edward's University, Austin, Texas

Ian K. Boxall, associate professor of New Testament, The Catholic University of America, Washington, DC

Marc Zvi Brettler, Bernice and Morton Lerner Distinguished Professor in Judaic Studies, Duke University, Durham, North Carolina

Jaime Clark-Soles, professor of New Testament, Altshuler Distinguished Teaching Professor, director of the Baptist House of Studies, Perkins School of Theology, Southern Methodist University, Dallas, Texas

Michael B. Cover, associate professor, Judaism and Christianity in Antiquity, Department of Theology, Marquette University, Milwaukee, Wisconsin

A. Andrew Das, professor of religious studies, assistant dean of the faculty for assessment and accreditation, Elmhurst University, Elmhurst, Illinois

CONTRIBUTORS

Susan Docherty, professor of New Testament and early Judaism, head of theology and philosophy, Newman University, Birmingham, United Kingdom

Paul Foster, professor of New Testament and early Christianity, School of Divinity, The University of Edinburgh, United Kingdom

Jörg Frey, professor of New Testament, Judaism of antiquity, and hermeneutics, Universität Zürich, Switzerland

Alexandria Frisch, assistant professor of Jewish Studies, George Mason University, Fairfax, Virginia

Edmon L. Gallagher, professor of Christian Scripture, Heritage Christian University, Florence, Alabama

Gabriella Gelardini, professor of Christianity, religion, worldview, and ethics (KRLE), Nord University, Bodø, Norway

Jennie Grillo, Tisch Family Associate Professor of Theology, University of Notre Dame, Notre Dame, Indiana

Gerd Häfner, professor of biblical studies, Ludwig-Maximilians-Universität München, Germany

Matthias Henze, Isla Carroll and Percy E. Turner Professor of Hebrew Bible and Early Judaism, Rice University, Houston, Texas

J. Thomas Hewitt, lecturer in early Judaism and Christian origins, School of Divinity, History, Philosophy and Art History, University of Aberdeen, United Kingdom

Robin M. Jensen, Patrick O'Brien Professor of Theology, University of Notre Dame, Notre Dame, Indiana

Martin Karrer, professor emeritus of the New Testament and its environment, Kirchliche Hochschule Wuppertal, Wuppertal, Germany

Matthias Konradt, professor of New Testament, Universität Heidelberg, Germany

Katja Kujanpää, postdoctoral researcher, biblical studies, University of Helsinki, Helsinki, Finland

Contributors

John R. Levison, W. J. A. Power Professor of Old Testament Interpretation and Biblical Hebrew, Perkins School of Theology, Southern Methodist University, Dallas, Texas

David Lincicum, associate professor of Christianity and Judaism in antiquity, University of Notre Dame, Notre Dame, Indiana

Grant Macaskill, Kirby Laing Chair of New Testament Exegesis, The School of Divinity, History, Philosophy and Art History, University of Aberdeen, United Kingdom

Tobias Nicklas, professor of exegesis and hermeneutics of the New Testament, Universität Regensburg, Germany; Centre for Advanced Studies "Beyond the Canon," Universität Regensburg, Germany; research associate, University of the Free State, Bloemfontein, South Africa

Valérie Nicolet, associate professor of New Testament, Institut protestant de théologie, faculté de Paris, France

Karl-Wilhelm Niebuhr, professor of New Testament, Friedrich-Schiller-Universität Jena, Germany

George Parsenios, dean and professor of New Testament, Holy Cross Greek Orthodox School of Theology, Brookline, Massachusetts

Benjamin E. Reynolds, professor of New Testament, Tyndale University, Toronto, Canada

Dieter T. Roth, associate professor of New Testament, Boston College, Chestnut Hill, Massachusetts

Dietrich Rusam, Privatdozent in New Testament, Rheinische Friedrich-Wilhelms-University Bonn, Germany; lecturer in Old and New Testament, Otto-Friedrich-Universität, Bamberg, Germany

Jens Schröter, professor of exegesis and theology of the New Testament and the ancient Christian Apocrypha, Humboldt-Universität zu Berlin, Germany

Claudia Setzer, professor of religious studies, Manhattan College, Riverdale, New York

CONTRIBUTORS

Elizabeth Evans Shively, senior lecturer in New Testament Studies, School of Divinity, University of St Andrews, St Andrews, United Kingdom

Michael Karl-Heinz Sommer, Privatdozent of exegesis and hermeneutics of the New Testament, Universität Regensburg, Germany

Angela Standhartinger, professor of New Testament studies, Philipps-Universität Marburg, Germany

Gert J. Steyn, professor of New Testament exegesis and theology, Theologische Hochschule Ewersbach, Germany; emeritus professor of New Testament studies, University of Pretoria, South Africa

Todd D. Still, Charles J. and Eleanor McLerran DeLancey Dean, William M. Hinson Chair of Christian Scriptures, Baylor University, George W. Truett Theological Seminary, Waco, Texas

Rodney A. Werline, Leman and Marie Barnhill Endowed Chair in Religious Studies, Barton College, Wilson, North Carolina

Benjamin Wold, associate professor of early Judaism and Christianity, Trinity College Dublin, the University of Dublin, Ireland

Archie T. Wright, executive director, The Catholic Biblical Association of America, Washington, DC; visiting lecturer, The Catholic University of America, Washington, DC

Index of Modern Authors

Abegg, Martin, 623, 772, 881
Achenbach, Reinhard, 769
Achtemeier, Paul J., 525–26, 528
Adams, Samuel L., 706
Adams, Sean A., 7, 146, 172, 288, 885
Adler, William, 985
Aejmelaeus, Anneli, 83, 97, 367–68, 379–80
Aejmelaeus, Lars, 375
Ahearne-Kroll, Patricia, 585
Ahearne-Kroll, Stephen P., 258, 729–31, 839
Ahn, Sanghee M., 301
Aitken, James K., 88
Albl, Martin C., 146, 308, 343, 993–94
Albrecht, Felix, 83, 100
Alexander, Philip S., 26, 146, 155
Allen, David M., 6, 435, 480, 486, 777
Allen, Garrick V., 197, 557, 559, 570, 734, 757, 758–59
Allen, Leslie C., 734
Allison, Dale C., Jr., 47–48, 59–60, 69–71, 74–75, 215, 231–32, 503, 509, 708, 829–30, 835, 838, 841, 906, 913
Aly, Zaki, 768
Ammann, Sonja, 884
Andersen, Francis I., 73
Anderson, Bernhard W., 72
Anderson, Gary A., 582, 586
Anderson, Janice Capel, 197
Argall, Randall A., 128
Assis, Elie, 744

Attridge, Harold W., 167, 486, 584, 665, 826, 832–33
Aucher, Johann Baptist, 168
Aune, David E., 560, 583, 745
Aus, Roger D., 448
Auwers, Jean-Marie, 95
Avioz, Michael, 188, 190, 192–93, 195–96, 198

Bacon, Benjamin, 906
Baird, William, 898–901
Balla, Peter, 377–78
Ballentine, Deborah Scoggins, 580
Barclay, John, 37–38, 184, 866
Bar-Cohn, David, 62
Barr, David L., 569
Barr, James, 130
Barthélemy, Dominique, 5, 97
Barton, John, 15, 26–27, 30, 32–33, 35, 563
Basser, Herbert W., 188
Bassler, Jouette M., 449, 908–10
Bauckham, Richard, 116, 523–24, 532–33, 535–37, 562, 565, 615, 920, 958–59
Baumgarten, Albert, 688
Baumgarten, Joseph M., 705
Bauspieß, Martin, 265, 267, 270–73, 277
Bautch, Richard J., 645, 647–48, 650, 653, 670
Baxter, Wayne, 220
Bazzana, Giovanni Battista, 1008
Beale, G. K., 7, 124, 410–12, 552, 556–57, 562, 564–66, 569, 776, 871–72

INDEX OF MODERN AUTHORS

Beare, Francis W., 435
Beaton, Richard, 209–10, 216, 219, 231, 803, 808
Becker, Adam H., 112
Becker, Joachim, 669
Becker, Jürgen, 175
Beckwith, Roger T., 30–32, 772, 1035
Beers, Holly, 800, 810
Beetham, Christopher A., 198, 410–13
Begg, Christopher T., 199
Belleville, Linda L., 374
Bendavid, Abba, 61
Bendemann, Reinhard, 350
Berlin, Adele, 61, 73, 818
Bernstein, Moshe J., 151–52, 154–55
Berrin, Shani, 149
Best, Ernest, 424, 444
Betz, Hans Dieter, 662
Bieringer, Reimund, 375
Bigg, Charles, 524
Black, Matthew, 612
Blackman, E. C., 1001
Blenkinsopp, Joseph, 702, 861
Blischke, Folker, 35
Bloch, René, 893
Blomberg, Craig L., 807–8
Blowers, Paul M., 14
Bobertz, Charles A., 993
Bobichon, Philippe, 984
Boccaccini, Gabriele, 109, 121, 893
Bock, Darrell L., 267, 324, 326, 330, 333
Bockmuehl, Markus, 435, 582, 586
Boda, Mark J., 723
Boer, Martinus C. de, 399
Bøgh, Birgitte Secher, 658
Böhl, Eduard, 3
Böhler, Dieter, 94
Böhm, Christiane, 827, 842–43
Bokedal, Tomas, 25–26, 38
Bond, Helen, 197
Bons, Eberhard, 87, 94, 886
Bonsirven, Joseph, 3, 5
Booth, Wayne C., 316
Borchardt, Francis, 93
Borgen, Pedar, 8, 172, 181, 291, 294, 307
Boring, M. Eugene, 437
Bormann, Lukas, 429

Bornkamm, Günther, 338
Bosshard-Nepustil, Erich, 95
Botner, Max, 245, 254
Böttrich, Christfried, 4, 263–64, 268, 275–76, 280, 490
Bovon, François, 270, 273, 278–81, 902–4, 941, 988
Boxall, Ian K., 567–68
Boyarin, Daniel, 493, 495, 715
Bratcher, Robert G., 240, 559
Brawley, Robert L., 318
Breasted, James H., 1032
Breed, Brennan W., 59, 674, 868
Bremmer, Jan, 945–47, 959, 970–71
Brettler, Marc Zvi, 48, 59, 67, 69, 71–72, 818
Brodie, Thomas L., 248, 265, 277
Brody, Lisa, 1025
Brooke, George J., 35, 50, 113, 142, 144, 148–50, 751, 761, 796–97, 819, 823, 826, 884, 894–95, 902
Brown, Catherine, 871
Brown, Raymond, 548, 551, 716, 726, 871, 914, 920
Brownlee, William, 796
Brox, Norbert, 525
Bruce, F. F., 444
Bruns, J. E., 992
Buchinger, Harald, 941
Bultmann, Rudolf, 840
Bunta, Silviu N., 73
Burch, Vacher, 993
Burchard, Christoph, 509
Burini, Clara, 991
Burney, C. F., 53
Busch, Austin, 916
Butticaz, Simon, 893, 903–5
Bynum, Wm. Randolph, 756
Byrne, Máire, 580
Byron, John, 549

Cachia, Nicholas, 1026
Cadbury, Henry J., 237
Caird, George B., 562
Cameron, Michael, 827
Campbell, Anthony F., 51–52, 54
Campbell, Jonathan G., 141, 196, 238, 240, 752
Campenhausen, Hans von, 1008, 1011, 1017

Index of Modern Authors

Caneday, Ardel, 784
Cappellus, Louis, 2
Caquot, Andre, 893
Caragounis, Chrys C., 874
Carey, Holly J., 258, 839
Cargill, Robert, 138
Carlini, Antonio, 988
Carmignac, Jean, 148
Carpzov, Johann Gottlob, 2
Carr, David M., 31, 651
Carras, George P., 189, 445
Carroll, John T., 656, 660
Carson, D. A., 7–8
Casey, Maurice, 874
Chadwick, Henry, 1033
Chae, Young S., 219
Chambers, Nathan J., 582, 586
Chapa, Juan, 931
Chapman, Stephen B., 26, 29, 33, 40
Charles, R. H., 4, 371, 557, 561, 572, 969
Charlesworth, James, 4
Cheung, Luke L., 775
Chibici-Revneanu, Nicole, 614
Childs, Brevard S., 26, 68, 264
Christensen, Duane L., 769, 772
Ciampa, Roy E., 363, 370–71, 373, 389, 401–2, 785
Clark, Herbert, 7
Clark-Soles, Jaime, 292, 296–98, 300
Clemen, August, 3
Clements, E. Ann, 920
Cohen, Naomi G., 175
Cohen, Shaye J. D., 191
Cohick, Lynn H., 421
Collins, Adela Yarbro, 172, 255–56, 566, 609, 730, 744, 839–40, 871, 873, 875
Collins, John J., 33, 68, 118, 121, 126, 129–30, 184, 239, 255, 605, 608–9, 701, 705, 744, 751, 757–58, 860, 867–69, 873, 893–94
Colson, Francis H., 770
Compton, Jared, 495
Cook, Edward, 623, 881
Cook, John Granger, 372
Cosgrove, Charles H., 319, 985
Couser, Gregory A., 461
Cover, Michael, 164, 167–70, 172–76, 180, 182, 373

Cowey, James M. S., 85
Cranfield, C. E. B., 341
Crawford, Sidnie White, 141, 143, 152, 768, 770
Cross, Frank Moore, 54
Crossley, James G., 151
Crowe, Brandon D., 209, 215, 280
Cuvillier, Élian, 906

Dafni, Evangelia G., 89
Dahl, Nils, 291, 603, 608, 610
Daly-Denton, Margaret, 819, 831, 883
Danby, Herbert, 604
Darnell, D. R., 863
Das, A. Andrew, 388–89, 401–4
Daube, David, 865
Davids, Peter H., 513–14, 524
Davidson, Samuel, 3–4
Davies, W. D., 231–32
Davila, James R., 112–13, 773
Day, Adam W., 809
Deissmann, Adolf, 345, 350
Dell, Katharine, 65
Derrett, J. Duncan M., 200
DesCamp, Mary Therese, 915
DeSilva, David A., 701
De Troyer, Kristin, 91, 94, 97–98
Deutsch, Celia M., 693–94, 713
Dibelius, Martin, 707
Diebner, Bernd Jörg, 863, 964
Dietrich, Albrecht, 964
Díez Merino, Luis, 420
Di Lella, Alexander A., 862
Dimant, Devorah, 149
Dines, Jennifer M., 380
Dittmar, Wilhelm, 4, 437–38, 774
Docherty, Susan E., 60, 196, 479, 493, 777
Dodd, C. H., 307, 544, 995
Dodson, Joseph R., 119
Doering, Lutz, 130, 151, 436, 508, 525, 592, 681
Dogniez, Cécile, 89
Domaradzki, Mikolaj, 171
Dömer, Michael, 323
Domoney-Lyttle, Zanne, 885
Donfried, Karl P., 338, 449
Döpke, Johann C. C., 3, 5
Dorival, Gilles, 25–26, 30, 87, 822

Doutreleau, Louis, 1002, 1007, 1015
Dowd, Sharyn E., 240
Dragutinovic, Predrag, 464
Dresken-Weiland, Jutta, 1040, 1043
Drijvers, H. J. W., 1014
Driver, Daniel, 130
Drury, John, 201
Drusius, Joannes, 2
Dubois, Jean-Daniel, 912–13
Du Bourguet, Pierre, 1033
Duensing, Hugo, 954, 957, 970
Duffy, John M., 988
Duling, Dennis C., 604, 612
Dulk, Matthijs den, 984
Dunderberg, Ismo, 1009–11, 1016–17
Dunn, Geoffrey, 989–90
Dunn, James D. G., 73, 710, 714
Duval, Yves-Marie, 1048
Dyer, Bryan R., 468

Earp, J. W., 770
Eberhart, Christian, 96
Eck, Werner, 89
Eco, Umberto, 245
Édart, Jean-Baptiste, 916
Edenburg, Cynthia, 72
Edsall, Benjamin, 733
Ego, Beate, 94, 99
Ehorn, Seth M., 7, 146, 288
Ehrenkrook, Jason von, 192
Ehrman, Bart, 1000
Eisenbaum, Pamela M., 488, 680, 691
Eissfeldt, Otto, 68
Elder, Nicholas, 915–16
Elliott, J. K., 944
Ellis, E. Earle, 200, 422, 441
Ellis, Nicholas J., 513
Elon, Menachem, 687
Elsner, Jaś, 1023
Emadi, Samuel, 6, 66
Engberg-Pedersen, Troels, 349–50
Epstein, Isidore, 606
Erho, Ted M., 459
Euler, Alida C., 221
Evans, Craig A., 75, 142, 196, 445–46, 654, 838
Ewald, Björn, 1025

Fabry, Hans-Josef, 839
Falk, Daniel K., 8, 787
Fallon, Francis T., 1012
Falls, Thomas B., 984
Farrer, Austin, 573
Farris, Stephen, 153
Feder, Frank, 94
Fee, Gordon D., 410
Fekkes, Jan, III, 557, 569, 801–2, 805, 812
Feldman, Louis H., 8, 188, 190, 192–94, 198, 200, 582, 685
Feldmeier, Reinhard, 89, 524–26
Ferda, Tucker S., 752, 754–55
Ferguson, Everett, 773, 780
Fernández Marcos, Natalio, 97–98
Fine, Steven, 1032
Finnegan, Ruth, 49
Finney, Paul Corby, 1023–24
Fishbane, Michael, 49, 57, 59, 61, 63, 65, 69, 237, 819
Fisk, Bruce N., 196
Fitzmyer, Joseph A., 141, 263–64, 266, 268, 277, 341–42, 347, 604, 615, 727, 755, 844
Fletcher, Michelle, 557, 569
Fletcher-Louis, Crispin H. T., 895
Flint, Peter W., 35, 138, 143–44, 150, 788, 796, 823–25, 847, 864
Fluck, Cäcilia, 965
Flusser, David, 868–69
Foerster, Werner, 1010
Foletti, Ivan, 1031
Foster, Paul, 210, 408–10, 412–13, 780, 842
Foster, Robert J., 513, 515
Fowl, Stephen, 429, 432, 434–35
Fraade, Steven D., 151
Francis, Frederick, 708
Fredriksen, Paula, 661, 679, 683, 684, 690–91
Freedman, David Noel, 73
Freeman, Jennifer Awes, 1026, 1042–43
Frend, W. H. C., 864
Fretheim, Terrence E., 581
Frey, Jörg, 523–24, 530, 533, 536, 540, 834, 942, 952–53
Friedman, Richard Elliott, 71
Friis, Martin, 188
Frisch, Alexandria, 875
Füglister, Notker, 317

Index of Modern Authors

Furnish, Victor Paul, 374
Furstenberg, Yair, 679

Gabbay, Uri, 169
Gadamer, Hans-Georg, 15
Gager, John, 691
Gallagher, Edmon L., 28–30, 35, 38, 40, 42, 828
Galor, Katharina, 138
García Martínez, Florentino, 142, 704, 798
Gathercole, Simon J., 948
Gaventa, Beverly Roberts, 661
Gelardini, Gabriella, 470, 473, 480–81, 485–86, 488, 492–93, 822
Gempf, Conrad, 450
Gentry, Peter, 5
Gerrig, Richard, 7
Gese, Hartmut, 264, 840
Gil, Roger, 886
Gilbertson, Jen, 256
Gillingham, Susan E., 826
Gleason, Randall C., 492
Glöckner, Michael, 517–18
Goff, Matthew, 702, 704–5, 707
Goldingay, John, 747
Goodacre, Mark, 58
Goodenough, Erwin, 1032–33
Goodman, Martin, 40, 188
Goodwin, Charles, 309
Gordley, Matthew J., 715
Gosse, Bernard, 652
Götte, Monika E., 533
Gough, Henry, 3
Goulder, Michael D., 200, 567
Gräbe, Peter, 664–65
Gradwohl, Roland, 479, 484–86
Granerød, Gard, 901
Grant, Robert M., 965, 1007, 1012, 1015–16
Grässer, Erich, 470
Gray, John, 51
Green, William Scott, 598
Greenberg, Moshe, 687
Greer, Rowan A., 774
Gregory, Andrew F., 942–43
Grenfell, Bernard P., 941
Greschat, Katharina, 1006–7, 1009, 1015
Grinfield, Edward W., 3
Grossman, Jonathan, 73
Grossman, Maxine, 653–54
Gruen, Erich, 166
Grünstäudl, Wolfgang, 524
Grypeou, Emmanouela, 606
Gundry, Robert H., 216, 231, 871
Gussmann, Oliver, 37
Gzella, Holger, 96

Haacker, Klaus, 341–42, 348
Hachlili, Rachel, 1032
Haenchen, Ernst, 715
Häfner, Gerd, 454
Ham, Clay Alan, 210
Hamerton-Kelly, Robert G., 164
Hamilton, Catherine Sider, 221, 694
Hanegraaff, Wouter J., 788
Hanig, Roman, 1006
Hannah, Darrell D., 748, 799–800
Hanson, Anthony T., 454
Harlow, Daniel C., 138–39, 141, 143–44
Harmon, Matthew S., 809
Harnack, Adolf von, 388, 1003, 1006–11, 1015, 1018
Harrington, D. J., 625, 704, 738
Harris, J. Rendel, 307, 992–93
Hartman, Lars, 131
Hatina, Thomas, 236–37
Hausherr, Jamie N., 772
Hay, David, 168, 600, 607–8, 616, 906
Hays, Christopher M., 1004
Hays, Richard B., 6, 11, 48, 59, 125, 128, 218, 222, 228, 236–37, 239, 366, 370, 372, 389, 410, 412, 429, 432, 443, 557, 559, 812, 830, 835, 839, 841, 843
Hayward, Robert, 549, 897
Heger, Paul, 893
Heil, John Paul, 219
Heiser, Andreas, 952–53
Hengel, Martin, 238–39, 845
Henry, W. Benjamin, 459
Henten, Jan Willem van, 94–95, 864, 873, 895
Henze, Matthias, 8, 110, 866–67
Hermann, Markus-Liborius, 476
Hernández, Juan, 91–92
Hernitscheck, Elisabeth, 941
Hertog, Cornelis G. den, 84
Herzer, Jens, 525

INDEX OF MODERN AUTHORS

Hewitt, J. Thomas, 598, 603, 606, 610–11, 613
Himmelfarb, Martha, 959
Hing, Lau Chi, 432
Hirschberger, Veronika, 955, 957
Hirschi, Vincent, 515, 518
Hoehner, Harold W., 423
Höffken, Peter, 37
Hoffman, Gail, 1025
Hofius, Otfried, 266, 279, 431
Høgenhaven, Jesper, 752–53, 825
Hogeterp, Albert L. A., 753, 971
Holladay, Carl R., 166–67, 169
Holladay, William L., 650
Holloway, Paul A., 435
Holtz, Gudrun, 175, 468
Holtz, Traugott, 326
Honigman, Sylvie, 85
Hooker, Morna, 237, 747
Horbury, William, 701, 993
Horgan, Maurya P., 147, 149
Horne, Thomas H., 3
Horner, Timothy J., 984
Hornung, Erik, 965
Horst, Pieter Willem van der, 915
Hossfeld, Frank-Lothar, 829
Hotchkiss, Robert V., 993
Hübner, Hans, 378, 432, 438
Huffman, Douglas S., 772
Hughes, Julie A., 153
Hühn, Eugen, 4
Huizenga, Leroy A., 213
Hultgren, Arland J., 906
Human, Dirk J., 833
Hunt, Arthur S., 941
Huotari, Paavo, 380–81
Hurtado, Larry W., 593–94, 614

Inowlocki, Sabina S., 194, 990
Isaac, E., 636
Isidore of Seville, 977

Jacob, Benno, 489
Jacobson, Howard, 167, 190
Jain, Eva, 824
Janowski, Bernd, 839
Japhet, Sara, 51, 57, 61–62, 72
Jastrzębowska, Elżbieta, 1031
Jauhiainen, Marko, 557

Jean-Baptiste, Humbert, 138
Jensen, Robin M., 862–63, 1024–26, 1039, 1042, 1048
Jeremias, Joachim, 434
Jewett, Robert, 198, 342, 349, 734
Jiroušková, Lenka, 970
Johnson, Franklin, 3
Johnson, Luke Timothy, 871
Johnson, M. D., 916
Johnson, Nathan C., 734
Jones, Donald Lee, 324
Jonge, Henk Jan de, 95
Jonge, Marinus de, 599
Jonker, Louis, 62
Jordaan, Gert J. C., 495
Joüon, Paul, 52
Juel, Donald, 600, 607, 615
Junius, Franciscus, 2
Junod, Éric, 26, 1008, 1015

Kaestli, Jean-Daniel, 38, 882
Kalmin, Richard, 694
Kamell, Mariam J., 508
Kamell Kovalishyn, Mariam, 508, 912
Kamesar, Adam, 8
Kampen, John, 702
Kaplan, Jonathan, 69
Karner, Gerhard, 93
Karrer, Martin, 87, 92, 98, 100, 481, 494, 776, 782
Käsemann, Ernst, 57, 341, 347
Kasser, Rodolphe, 931
Katz, Peter, 788
Kaufmann, Yehezkel, 57
Kauhanen, Tuukka, 97, 378
Kautzsch, Emil Friedrich, 3–4
Kazen, Thomas, 151
Keefer, Arthur, 7
Keener, Craig S., 775
Keesmaat, Sylvia C., 640, 842
Kelber, Werner H., 730
Kelhoffer, James A., 943
Kellermann, Ulrich, 863
Kelly, J. N. D., 524
Kennedy, Joel, 214
Kessler, Herbert, 1035–36
Kiley, Mark, 919

Index of Modern Authors

Kilgallen, John J., 326–27
Kim, Keunjoo, 90
King, Justin D., 445
Kinzig, Wolfram, 1
Kirby, Diana Jill, 197
Kistemaker, Simon J., 832
Kitzinger, Ernst, 1024
Klausner, Joseph, 600
Klawans, Jonathan, 167, 299, 310
Klein, Anja, 819
Klijn, A. F. J., 604, 942
Klinghardt, Matthias, 1004
Kloppenborg, John S., 268, 276
Knight, George A. F., 788
Knight, Jonathan, 968
Knoppers, Gary, 40, 61, 648, 653
Knowles, Michael, 210, 232
Koch, Dietrich-Alex, 5, 10, 165, 266, 342–43, 353, 365–67, 372–73, 378, 381–83, 437, 843, 985
Koch, Klaus, 129–30
Koenen, Ludwig, 768
Koester, Craig, 306, 558, 870
Koetschau, Paul, 1008
Kolarcik, Michael, 706
Konkel, Michael, 91
Konradt, Matthias, 213, 225
Kooij, Arie van der, 89, 92
Köstenberger, Andreas J., 286, 308–9
Kowalski, Beate, 454, 567
Koyfman, Shlomo A., 151, 155
Kraft, Robert A., 5, 194, 231, 955
Kratz, Reinhard, 862
Kraus, Hans-Joachim, 490
Kraus, Thomas J., 536, 934, 940
Kraus, Wolfgang, 278, 327, 495–96, 768
Krause, Joachim, 648
Krauss, Samuel, 978
Krauter, Stefan, 917
Kreuzer, Siegfried, 84, 98
Kristeva, Julia, 123
Kroymann, Emil, 1008, 1015
Kruger, H. A. J., 773
Kruger, Michael J., 940–41
Kubiś, Adam, 295
Kugel, James L., 131, 188–89, 193, 549, 582–83, 590, 592, 774, 825

Kujanpää, Katja, 7, 365, 375, 378–82, 385
Külzer, Andreas, 978
Kynes, Will, 65, 699

Laato, Anni Maria, 990–91
Labendz, Jenny R., 39
Ladner, Gerhard B., 1024
Lahey, Lawrence, 987
Lambrecht, Jan, 349
Lanfranchi, Pierluigi, 167
Lang, Markus, 458, 464
Lange, Armin, 9, 27, 39–41, 75, 140, 771, 782, 817, 823–24, 827
Lanier, Gregory A., 7, 988
Lawrence, Marion, 1047
Layton, Bentley, 1010
Le Donne, Anthony, 310
Lee, Dorothy A., 907
Lee, John A. L., 83, 88
Leiman, Sid Z., 26, 31, 39
Leipziger, Jonas, 99
Lembi, Gaia, 188
Lembke, Katja, 965
Le Moigne, Philippe, 89
Leo, Friedrich, 172
Léonas, Alexis, 97
Létourneau, Pierre, 933
Levenson, Jon D., 602, 610, 616–17
Levey, Samson H., 605
Levin, Christoph, 72
Levine, Amy-Jill, 48, 71, 681
Levine, Lee I., 863, 1032
Levinskaya, Irina, 690
Levinson, Bernard M., 49, 61, 64
Levison, John R., 622–25, 633–36, 638–40, 664
Levy, Ian Christopher, 23
Lewis, Jack P., 31
Leyisraël, Mikra, 51
Lichtenberger, Hermann, 350
Lierman, John, 486
Lieu, Judith, 544, 551–52, 847, 1001, 1003–5, 1011–14, 1018
Lilly, Ingrid E., 91
Lim, Timothy, 5, 9, 28, 30–31, 34–35, 41, 143–46, 149–50, 156, 189, 769
Limor, Ora, 978–79

INDEX OF MODERN AUTHORS

Lincicum, David, 3, 59, 366, 435, 610, 770, 783–85, 829, 843
Lincoln, Andrew T., 414, 418, 420–22
Lindblom, Johannes, 624
Lindemann, Andreas, 983, 985
Linebaugh, Jonathan A., 119
Litwa, M. David, 908
Litwak, Kenneth D., 153
Loader, William R. G., 778
Löhr, Winrich A., 1009–12, 1016
Lohse, Eduard, 338, 341
Lona, Horacio E., 95–96
Long, Fredrick J., 375
Long, Phillip J., 200
Longenecker, Bruce, 123
Longenecker, Richard N., 420
Louw, Theo A. W. van der, 83
Lovino, Francesco, 1031
Lüdemann, Gerd, 1009
Lundbom, Jack R., 775
Luz, Ulrich, 760
Lyons, Michael A., 238–39, 257

Macaskill, Grant, 60, 116, 119, 134, 713
Mack, Burton L., 702
Mackie, Scott, 183
MacLachlan, Helen, 3–4
Magness, Jodi, 138
Maier, Harry O., 572
Malbon, Elizabeth Struthers, 247
Malherbe, Abraham J., 444
Mallen, Peter, 811
Mambelli, Anna, 100
Mamyan, Mari, 931
Mann, Joshua L., 275
Marcovich, Miroslav, 984, 1007, 1015
Marcus, Joel, 48, 52, 74, 249, 254–56, 617, 838–39, 870
Maresch, Klaus, 85
Marguerat, Daniel, 903–5
Markschies, Christoph, 952–53, 1009, 1011, 1016
Marmur, Michael, 49
Martens, Peter W., 14
Martin, Francis, 589
Marttila, Marko, 749
Martyn, J. Louis, 402, 683

Mason, Rex, 757
Mason, Steve, 41, 188, 865
Mathewson, David, 567
Matson, Joshua M., 770
Matthewson, David, 802
May, Gerhard, 1006, 1008
McAuley, David, 435
McCarthy, Carmel, 52
McDonald, Lee Martin, 32
McGowan, Andrew, 1003
McLean, Bradley H., 771, 817, 827
McNamara, Martin, 572, 770
McWhirter, Jocelyn, 245
Meade, John D., 29–30, 38, 40, 42
Meeks, Wayne A., 302
Meer, Michaël van der, 85, 89
Meier, John, 676, 685–87, 692
Meier, Samuel A., 50, 53
Meiser, Martin, 101, 936
Mele, Salvatore, 332
Menken, Maarten J. J., 5, 7–8, 146, 211, 216–18, 220, 224, 230–31, 309, 416, 795, 801, 827, 829, 836, 983
Menn, Esther M., 837
Merkle, Benjamin L., 457
Metso, Sarianna, 751, 799–800
Metzger, Bruce M., 25, 604
Michel, Otto, 3
Miler, Jean, 231
Milikowsky, Chaim, 193
Miller, Cynthia L., 50
Miller, Dale, 201
Miller, Geoffrey D., 66
Miller, Lulu, 700
Miller, Patricia, 201
Minear, Paul S., 904
Mirguet, Françoise, 194
Mitchell, Margaret M., 178
Mittmann-Richert, Ulrike, 266, 268
Mobley, Gregory, 580
Moessner, David P., 904–5
Moffitt, David M., 612, 614, 680
Moll, Sebastian, 1003, 1006, 1008–9, 1011, 1014, 1016–17
Mondésert, Claude, 1002
Moo, Douglas J., 256, 341–42, 348, 350–51
Moore, Carey A., 749

Index of Modern Authors

Moore, Nicholas J., 36
Morales, Rodrigo, 639–40
Moreschini, Claudio, 1002–3
Morgan, Donn F., 772
Moritz, Thorsten, 409, 415–16
Morlet, Sébastien, 978
Morray-Jones, Christopher R. A., 563
Moss, Charlene McAfee, 210, 216
Motyer, J. Alec, 779
Moule, C. F. D., 75
Mounce, Robert H., 872
Mowinckel, Sigmund, 601–2
Moyise, Steve, 15, 66, 240, 555–57, 560, 562, 567, 572, 787, 795, 801, 827, 842
Mroczek, Eva, 32, 41, 311, 674–75, 828
Müller, Darius, 559
Müller, Detlef G., 968
Munier, Charles, 955, 1001
Munnich, Olivier, 978
Murphy, Edwina, 993
Murphy, Frederick J., 737, 896
Murphy-O'Connor, Jerome, 664
Murray, Mary Charles, 1023–24, 1043
Myers, Alicia D., 302, 307

Nahkola, Aulikki, 195
Nanos, Mark D., 198
Narkiss, Bezalel, 1035
Nathan, Emmanuel, 663
Nel, Pieter, 495
Neubrand, Maria, 348
Neusner, Jacob, 598–99
New, David S., 780
Newman, Judith, 654, 662, 723–24, 731–33, 741
Newsom, Carol A., 59, 629, 654, 836
Nickelsburg, George, 115–16, 126–27, 131, 532, 606, 731, 734, 758, 798
Nicklas, Tobias, 934, 937–38, 946, 959
Nicolet, Valérie, 831
Niebuhr, Karl-Wilhelm, 501–2, 504, 506, 508, 510
Niehoff, Maren R., 8, 168–69, 172
Nigosian, Solomon, 773
Nihan, Christophe, 893, 904
Nikiprowetzky, Valentin, 8, 163, 182, 894
Nilsen, Tina Dykesteen, 891–92

Nolland, John, 602
Nordheim-Diehl, Miriam von, 490
Norelli, Enrico, 958, 968, 1004
Norton, Jonathan D. H., 141, 147, 241, 379
Novenson, Matthew V., 68, 600–601, 604, 606

O'Brien, Kelli, 237
O'Brien, Mark A., 51–52, 54
Oegema, Gerbern S., 605
Öhler, Markus, 434, 437, 911
Ophir, Adi, 87
Osburn, Carroll D., 532
Ossandón Widow, Juan Carlos, 38
Ostmeyer, Karl-Heinrich, 214
Otto, Eckart, 666, 769
Owen, Henry, 2
Owen, Paul L., 614

Paffenroth, Kim, 265
Pagels, Elaine, 1011
Paget, James Carleton, 955, 978–79, 983, 995
Pajunen, Mika S., 824
Pakkala, Juha, 64
Pao, David W., 800, 803, 807
Parker, Henry M. D., 867
Parry, Donald W., 824
Parsons, P. J., 5, 231
Patmore, Hector M., 759
Paulien, Jon, 556–57, 569
Paulsen, Henning, 524
Pearce, Sarah J. K., 188, 769
Pearson, Birger A., 901
Penner, Jeremy, 723
Peppard, Michael, 1025
Perdue, Leo G., 580–81
Person, Raymond, 769
Pervo, Richard I., 657, 659
Peters, Melvin K. H., 768–69
Petit, Françoise, 170
Pevarello, Daniele, 706
Pfeiffer, Rudolf, 25
Phinney, D. Nathan, 141
Pietersma, Albert, 459, 822
Pinter, Dean L., 188
Piotrkowski, Meron M., 89,
Piotrowski, Nicholas G., 214, 216
Piovanelli, Pierluigi, 884

Plümacher, Eckart, 267-68
Popkes, Enno Edzard, 844
Porter, Stanley E., 10, 48, 66, 389, 432
Porton, Gary, 200
Pouchelle, Patrick, 100
Pouderon, Bernard, 978
Priest, John, 773-74
Prieur, Alexander, 271
Prigent, Pierre, 955
Prostmeier, Ferdinand R., 961, 983, 988
Pulkkinen, Marika, 369, 372
Pummer, Reinhard, 40
Punt, Jeremy, 59

Quasten, Johannes, 1026
Quesnel, Michel, 907
Quinn, Jerome D., 920-21
Quispel, Gilles, 1009, 1011, 1017

Rad, Gerhard von, 55, 57, 723, 773
Rahlfs, Alfred, 343, 604
Rajak, Tessa, 188, 864
Ramsay, Boniface, 1049
Rappaport, Solomon, 200
Rayburn, Robert G., II, 481
Reardon, Timothy W., 784
Reddish, Mitchell G., 668
Reed, Annette Yoshiko, 112, 194, 311, 583, 886, 921-22
Reim, Günter, 833
Reinhartz, Adele, 283, 286, 296, 682
Reinink, Gerrit J., 942
Resch, Alfred, 988
Rese, Martin, 320, 322, 329
Resseguie, James L., 569
Reumann, John, 435
Reymond, Eric D., 701
Reynolds, Benjamin E., 110, 874
Rhodes, James M., 955
Ribbens, Benjamin J., 833
Richter, Amy E., 142
Richter, Karl Ernst, 162
Riesner, Rainer, 268
Ringgren, Helmer, 267, 326
Ritter, Christine, 231
Roberts, J. J. M., 602
Robinson, J. Armitage, 382
Rodgers, Zuleika, 196-97

Roitman, Adolfo, 886
Rokéah, David, 985
Roloff, Jürgen, 320, 326, 328-29
Römer, Thomas, 51-52, 54, 880, 885, 890, 893, 896, 903
Roncace, Mark, 199
Ronis, Sara, 678
Rösel, Martin, 83, 88, 90
Rosen-Zvi, Ishay, 87, 695
Roskam, Gert, 173
Rosner, Brian S., 370-71, 373
Roth, Dieter, 1001-5, 1011, 1013-14
Rothfuchs, Wilhelm, 212
Rothschild, Clare, 788
Rousseau, Adelin, 1001-2, 1015
Rowëkamp, Georg, 1008
Rowland, Christopher, 562-63
Royse, James R., 169-70
Rückl, Jan, 54
Ruf, Martin G., 537
Ruhnken, David, 25
Ruiten, Jacques T. A. G. M. van, 889, 892, 972
Ruiz, Jean-Pierre, 567
Runesson, Anders, 693
Runia, David T., 163, 182, 827
Rusam, Dietrich, 263-64, 266-67, 270-71, 275-76, 281-82, 321-22, 330
Rutgers, Leonard, 1023
Rütten, Almut, 1011
Ruzer, Serge, 151-52, 156
Ryle, Herbert Edward, 29-30

Sacchi, Paolo, 121
Salvesen, Alison, 5
Sanders, E. P., 691, 885
Sanders, Jack, 701, 706, 824
Sanders, James A., 26, 133
Sänger, Dieter, 839
Sänger, Patrick, 85
Santos Otero, Aurelio de, 954, 957, 970
Sarna, Nahum M., 818
Satran, David, 864-66
Savran, George W., 50, 70
Schäfer, Peter, 608
Schalit, Abraham, 194
Schaller, Berndt, 177, 356, 383

Index of Modern Authors

Schaper, Joachim, 822
Schelkle, Karl-Hermann, 524
Schenker, Adrian, 86, 91
Scherbenske, Eric W., 1003
Schifferdecker, Kathryn, 580
Schiffman, Lawrence H., 150–51, 753, 869
Schiffner, Kerstin, 268
Schironi, Francesca, 169–70
Schliesser, Benjamin, 347
Schmelz, Georg, 459
Schmid, Herbert, 1016
Schmid, Konrad, 265, 748, 769
Schmid, Ulrich, 98, 1003
Schneider, Gerhard, 319, 321, 328, 774, 944
Schneiders, Sandra S., 285, 304
Schniedewind, William M., 54
Scholem, Gershom, 600
Schorch, Stefan, 90, 118
Schreckenberg, Heinz, 978
Schreiber, Stefan, 332, 344
Schröter, Jens, 265, 350, 373, 843, 947, 952
Schuchard, Bruce G., 286, 309
Schuller, Eileen, 629, 823
Schürer, Emil, 40, 821
Schürmann, Heinz, 270, 273
Schüssler Fiorenza, Elisabeth, 556, 562, 735, 737
Scott, James, 639
Screnock, John, 190
Seeligmann, Isaac Leo, 89
Segal, Michael, 756–57
Seifrid, Mark A., 339
Seitz, Christopher R., 513, 797
Senior, Donald, 209
Setzer, Claudia, 693
Sharbaugh, Patricia, 906–7
Shaw, David A., 6
Shepherd, Michael B., 238, 251
Sheridan, Ruth, 296
Shinall, Myrick C., Jr., 677
Shires, Henry M., 781
Shively, Elizabeth E., 239, 246, 248, 252, 839
Siegel, Michal Bar-Asher, 113
Siegert, Folker, 88, 168, 380
Sievers, Joseph, 188
Sigismund, Marcus, 98
Silva, Moisés, 154, 198, 429, 434, 810

Simon, Marcel, 978
Simon, Uriel, 73
Skarsaune, Oskar, 955, 961, 985–86
Slenczka, Notger, 264
Sloan, Paul T., 254
Smith, Daniel A., 932
Smith, W. Andrew, 165
Sneed, Mark R., 699
Snyder, Graydon, 1038
Soards, Marion L., 523
Sommer, Benjamin D., 47–48, 65–66, 69
Sommer, Michael, 964–65, 968
Spawn, Kevin L., 50, 54–55, 57, 60
Spencer, Aída Besançon, 919
Spencer, F. Scott, 328
Sperber, Alexander, 758–59
Spieckermann, Hermann, 89
Spier, Jeffrey, 1023, 1039
Spilsbury, Paul, 192, 195, 199
Staats, Reinhart, 1042
Stackert, Jeffrey, 61, 64
Standhartinger, Angela, 436, 912–13
Stanley, Christopher D., 7, 10, 366–67, 369, 373, 376–77, 382, 389, 394, 418, 752, 785
Stanton, Graham N., 220, 232
Steck, Odil Hannes, 748
Steinberg, Julius, 32
Steindorff, Georg, 963–64
Stemberger, Günter, 29, 41, 821–22
Stendahl, Krister, 6, 146, 216, 231, 690–91, 754
Sterling, Gregory E., 166, 170, 172, 176–77, 191–92, 195
Stern, Sacha, 34
Sternberg, Meir, 7
Steyn, Gert J., 145, 322, 330, 469, 473, 492, 494, 767, 773, 777–78, 781, 833
Still, Todd D., 441, 444
Stipp, Hermann-Josef, 91
Stokes, Ryan E., 116
Stone, Michael E., 110, 365, 606–7, 867
Stone, Timothy J., 32
Stowers, Stanley K., 916
Strack, H. L., 29, 41
Strauss, Mark L., 320–21, 329
Strawn, Brent A., 816
Streeter, B. H., 265

INDEX OF MODERN AUTHORS

Streett, Daniel R., 785
Stromberg, Jacob, 238–39
Stroumsa, Guy G., 978–79
Strugnell, John, 365
Strzygowski, Josef, 1031
Stuart, Douglas, 774
Stuckenbruck, Loren T., 110, 599–600, 608, 613, 862, 865
Stuhlmacher, Pete, 124, 747
Stuiber, Alfred, 1037
Suciu, Alin, 932
Suggs, Jack, 713
Sundberg, Albert C., 30, 32, 39
Surenhusius, Willem, 2
Svebakken, Hans, 183
Swanson, Dwight, 797
Swartley, William M., 248
Sweet, John, 559, 572
Swete, Henry Barclay, 555, 558, 564, 571, 822

Taft, Robert E., 827
Talbert, Charles H., 668
Talmon, Shemaryahu, 140
Tannehill, Robert C., 316, 318
Tasker, David R., 587
Tatum, Gregory, 663
Taylor, John H., 965
Taylor, Miriam S., 978
Teeter, D. Andrew, 132
Thackeray, Henry St. John, 5, 91, 420
Thatcher, Tom, 310
Theobald, Michael, 338
Theophilos, Michael, 873
Thielman, Frank S., 419, 422, 425
Thiessen, Matthew, 678, 685–86, 693
Tholuck, F. August, 3
Thompson, Marianne Meye, 589–91
Thrall, Margaret E., 375
Tigay, Jeffrey, 658, 769
Tigchelaar, Eibert J. C., 128, 139–40, 142, 798
Tilly, Michael, 339
Tkacz, Catherine Brown, 1037
Tobin, Thomas H., 661
Tolley, Harry, 987–88
Tooman, William A., 123, 237–38, 240, 244, 259
Toorn, Karel van der, 31
Torrance, T. F., 130, 589

Tov, Emanuel, 5, 42, 52, 91, 140, 143–44, 231, 824
Toy, Crawford Howell, 3
Tränkle, Hermann, 990
Tripaldi, Daniele, 759
Tromp, Johannes, 549–50
Tropper, Amram, 190
Troxel, Ronald L., 89–90
Trudinger, L. Paul, 560
Tuckett, Christopher M., 933, 948
Turpie, David, 3–4
Twersky, Isadore, 676

Ueberschaer, Frank, 93
Uhlenbruch, Frauke, 884
Ulfgard, Håkan, 155
Ulrich, Eugene, 34, 41, 140, 144, 826, 829, 861
Unnik, Willem C. van, 508
Utzschneider, Helmut, 84
Uusimäki, Elisa, 705, 751

Vaccarella, Kevin M., 1012
VanderKam, James C., 27, 34–35, 138, 140, 144, 150, 152, 154–55, 758, 798, 847
Vanhoye, Albert, 560, 567, 569
Vanlaningham, Michael G., 911
Van Leeuwen, Raymond C., 65
Vaux, Roland de, 772–73
Venard, Louis, 3
Venit, Marjorie S., 965
Verheyden, Joseph, 268, 276, 365
Vermes, Geza, 141, 189, 195, 534, 865, 874, 881, 884, 889
Vielhauer, Philipp, 985
Viljoen, François P., 906
Vittmann, Günter, 965
Vogelgesang, Jeffrey M., 567
Vögtle, Anton, 524, 532
Vollenweider, Samuel, 434
Vollmer, Hans, 3
Vorster, W. S., 237
Vortisch, Johannes, 221
Vos, J. Cornelis de, 90, 511
Vos, Louis Arthur, 559
Vuong, Lily C., 946

Waaler, Erik, 779
Waard, Jan de, 146, 327

Wagner, J. Ross, 63, 323, 368, 612, 802, 804, 806, 811
Wakefield, Andrew H., 784
Wallace, Howard N., 62
Walton, John H., 580
Ware, James Patrick, 434
Warner, Megan, 72
Washburn, David L., 770
Wasserberg, Günter, 322
Wasserman, Tommy, 245
Waters, Guy Prentiss, 434
Watson, Francis, 370, 374–75, 426, 785
Watts, Rikk E., 240, 245, 249, 255, 416, 795, 838
Weber, Beat, 774
Webster, Brian, 140
Wedderburn, A. J. M., 680
Weeks, Stuart, 700
Weigold, Matthias, 9, 27, 75, 771, 782, 817, 827
Weima, Jeffrey A. D., 441–42, 444–46, 450–51
Weiser, Alfons, 774
Weiß, Alexander, 344–45
Weiss, Hans-Friedrich, 467
Weiss, Wolfgang, 325
Weiss, Ze'ev, 1032
Weissenberg, Hanne von, 751
Weitzmann, Kurt, 1035–36
Wells, L. S., 550
Wengst, Klaus, 438, 983
Weren, Wim J. C., 324, 330
Werline, Rodney A., 722–23, 725, 732, 739, 985
Werman, Cana, 892, 894
Wevers, John William, 90
Wharton, Annabel, 1031
Whiston, William, 770
Whitters, Mark, 913
Wieringen, Archibald van, 646, 649
Wilckens, Ulrich, 341, 348
Wilcox, Max, 420, 612
Wiles, Gordon, 731–32
Wilk, Florian, 101, 381–82, 431, 433, 748, 806, 809
Williams, A. Lukyn, 978

Williams, Catrin H., 288, 301, 303–4
Williamson, H. G. M., 747, 797
Willitts, Joel, 219–20
Wills, Lawrence M., 700, 864
Wilson, Walter, 167
Winn, Adam, 248
Winston, David, 117
Wintermute, O. S., 634, 863, 892
Wise, Michael O., 623, 772, 881
Witherington, Ben, III, 119, 713
Witmer, Stephen E., 445
Witte, Markus, 93
Woan, Sue, 834
Wold, Benjamin, 122, 704, 706, 709
Wolfe, Benjamin P., 456
Wolff, Hans Walter, 67
Wolter, Michael, 265, 268, 270, 273, 277–81, 341, 348, 355, 955, 957
Wooden, R. Glenn, 94
Wright, Benjamin G., III, 84, 89, 164–65, 700, 706
Wright, N. T., 123–24, 639
Wright, Robert B., 604, 750
Wurst, Gregor, 931

Yadin, Yigal, 870
Yonge, C. D., 712
Yoon, David, 6
Young, Robb Andrew, 71

Zacharias, H. Daniel, 213, 221
Zahn, Molly M., 152, 195–96, 237–39
Zakovitch, Yair, 71–72
Zakowitch, Yair, 920–21
Zangenberg, Jürgen K., 138
Zanker, Paul, 1025
Zapff, Burkhard M., 93
Zeelander, Susan, 195
Zeichmann, Christopher B., 919
Zelyck, Lorne, 939–40
Zenger, Erich, 475, 982
Zevit, Ziony, 66, 68
Ziegert, Carsten, 84
Ziegler, Joseph, 431
Ziethe, Carolin, 228

Index of Subjects

Abraham, 129, 131–32, 152–54, 163, 192–94, 213–14, 228, 281, 301, 303–4, 322, 339–40, 346–49, 358, 390–92, 396–97, 400, 471–72, 476–77, 482–83, 488–91, 493, 495, 502–3, 509, 513–14, 583–84, 590, 592, 602n16, 606n34, 610–11, 615, 617, 652, 657–60, 662–63, 668, 726–27, 784, 880n1, 881–82, 884–90, 892, 896–901, 904n92, 908, 918–21, 923, 945, 966, 985n19, 1029, 1039, 1048–49; descendant(s)/offspring/seed of, 62, 303, 351–52, 354, 391, 395–96, 398, 484, 602n16, 606n34, 611, 615, 648, 657, 660, 726, 784–85, 885, 887–88, 898–900, 918–20, 946, 971. *See also* Akedah; covenant: Abrahamic

Adam, 72–74, 115, 124, 176–78, 339, 349–50, 371, 413, 456–57, 532, 549, 550, 581, 734, 893, 897n69, 916–17, 922, 946, 972, 992, 1003, 1006–7, 1025–27, 1029, 1036, 1045

adultery, 510, 686, 690, 692, 705, 771, 778, 960, 962. *See also* marriage

adversus Judaeos, 14, 977–95

Akedah, 193, 392, 403–4, 511, 513–14, 610, 617, 884, 888, 897–98, 900, 1029, 1036–37, 1039, 1049

Alexandria, 39–40, 82–85, 113, 118, 162–84, 945, 1035

Alexandrian interpretation, 9, 164–69, 174–76, 178. *See also* allegorical interpretation

allegorical interpretation, 9, 27, 64, 66, 75, 163, 165, 169–72, 174–83, 339, 396–97, 491, 493n42, 617, 686, 688, 810, 918, 990, 1010, 1012, 1015–16, 1040

allusion. *See* conceptual allusion; verbal allusion

Ancient of Days, 97, 247, 255, 565, 607, 613n57, 736, 756, 758, 868–69

angels, 116, 121, 254, 291, 293, 304, 442, 444, 470, 476, 482, 484–85, 529–35, 537, 539, 567, 624–25, 640, 642, 659, 669, 703, 709, 717, 737, 756, 758, 798, 802, 805, 863, 866, 869, 871–72, 874, 915n145, 918, 945, 964–67, 970–71, 1029; angelic warfare, 869–70, 872; angel of God's presence, 638–39, 888, 892; seraphim, 736, 802–3

Anna, mother of Mary, 945–47

antichrist, 552, 553, 873

Antioch (Syrian), 98, 113, 117, 120, 122, 130, 166n9, 175–76, 316, 330, 627, 1035

Antiochus IV Epiphanes, 31, 403, 449, 553, 724, 757, 861, 867, 873

Apelles, 1005–9, 1014–15, 1018

Apocalypse of Paul, 970–73

Apocalypse of Peter, 523–24, 532n19, 537, 954, 958–63, 970, 972–73

Apocalypse of Zephaniah, 863, 954, 963–68, 970, 972

apocalyptic(ism), 14, 110, 126, 128–30, 152, 155, 167, 530, 535–36, 552, 563–64, 573, 669, 684, 686–89, 700n2, 703–4, 706, 707n2, 709, 717, 734–35, 755–60, 812, 866, 869–71, 876, 884–85, 892–93, 952–73; and Daniel,

Index of Subjects

755–70, 839, 861, 867–76; in Mark, 246, 255, 759–60, 839, 874; in Pauline Epistles, 124, 163, 175, 178, 349, 430, 436, 683, 690, 710
Apocrypha. *See* deuterocanonical books
apocryphal gospels, 14, 931–49
Aquila, 5, 82, 97, 342, 380–82, 434
Aristobulus of Alexandria, 9, 86n23, 100n86, 164, 167n14, 169, 894n50
Artapanus of Alexandria, 166, 893–94, 897, 903n87, 905
Ascension of Isaiah, 954, 968–70, 972–73
Assumption of Moses, 530–31, 535–36
Athanasius of Alexandria, 25, 28

Balaam, 115, 131, 531, 533–35, 537–40, 558, 570–71, 574, 624–26, 897n68, 1029
baptism, 219, 258, 317, 326, 328–29, 528, 626, 634, 637, 677, 683, 735, 754–55, 807, 907, 912, 941, 955, 987, 994, 1025, 1039, 1042–43, 1045, 1048; baptisteries, 1024–26, 1036, 1038; of Jesus, 246, 251, 273, 324, 547, 610n47, 637, 943–44, 994, 1025, 1030, 1043
Bathsheba, 602n16, 910, 914, 919–20, 922
beasts, 805, 862–64, 870–71, 874, 876, 910n125, 1027, 1029, 1036–37, 1040, 1043–45; opponents of martyrs, 737, 1044–45; representing empires, 756, 867–68, 871–73, 875; representing figures, 606–8, 616, 757, 872–73
beatitudes, 116n14, 155, 703, 705, 707, 831–32
blindness, 272, 637, 682, 771, 799, 807, 811, 958, 1013, 1030; metaphorical use of, 247, 249, 259, 552, 689, 694, 936
Booths. *See* Sukkot
burial, 890n35, 903n90, 965, 1024, 1027, 1031, 1037, 1050; catacombs, 1024, 1031–36, 1038–40, 1043–45, 1049; sarcophagi, 1024, 1026–28, 1030, 1036, 1039–41, 1043–45, 1047

Cain, 115, 531, 533–34, 539, 544–45, 548–50, 922, 972, 1029
canon, 12, 25–42, 50, 67, 81, 95, 101, 114–20, 133–34, 139–43, 264–65, 282, 310–11, 340, 453, 468, 475, 500–501, 523, 535–36, 555–57, 674–75, 825–26, 828n30, 844, 860, 881, 952–53, 983, 988, 1018; Alexandrian, 39–41, 92

catena, 146, 173–74, 375–79, 435, 473, 559, 740, 799, 812, 821n11, 831n41, 832, 843–44, 846, 1007n36. *See also* composite citation
Christology, 163–64, 183, 212–22, 280, 285, 288, 293, 296–99, 301–4, 306, 325–26, 330, 357, 426, 429, 433, 436, 529, 538, 547, 550, 560, 564–66, 569, 573, 587, 610, 613n57, 617–18, 657–58, 663, 682, 767, 778, 783, 786, 788–89, 813, 817–18, 828, 835, 841, 844–47, 940, 959, 970, 988–89, 993, 1039; wisdom Christology, 119, 693, 705, 707, 710–17
church fathers. *See* patristic authors
circumcision, 87, 181, 331, 338–39, 347–48, 358, 388–89, 391, 396, 399, 401, 606n31, 652, 658–59, 663, 675, 683–84, 690, 695, 885, 888–89, 896, 900, 916, 918, 984, 990, 993, 1017; of the heart, 347–48, 623, 659, 1017
citation. *See* marked citation; unmarked citation
citational mashup. *See* composite citation
Codex Alexandrinus, 100–101, 165, 345n24, 352n47, 400, 631n12, 665, 778
Codex Sinaiticus, 4, 101, 345n24, 352n47, 359, 631n12, 921n168
Codex Vaticanus, 101, 352n47, 359, 400, 631n12, 778
collective memory. *See* social memory
Community Rule, 24, 138, 141, 584, 633, 739, 774, 799, 882, 895
composite citation, 7, 57–58, 63, 87n31, 146, 224, 232, 245–46, 257, 270, 288, 295, 322, 329, 354–55, 359, 373, 375–79, 418, 421–22, 468, 525, 561–62, 564–66, 615n65, 754n25, 780, 782–83, 804, 944, 947. *See also* catena
conceptual allusion, 11–13, 49, 66–69, 74, 478–79, 705, 707, 710–16, 777, 834–37, 871, 881, 884, 944, 946–47; in Acts, 316, 318–23, 325; in Catholic Epistles, 504–6, 511–15, 520, 528, 544–46, 548, 552–53; to Isaiah, 798–99, 802–5, 809, 812; in John, 285, 288, 291–92, 294, 296, 300, 302, 304, 306, 308, 310; in Luke, 267, 276; in Mark, 239, 243–44, 246, 248–49, 252, 256, 258; in Matthew, 209, 212–13, 221–24, 229–30; in Pauline Epistles, 363, 389, 403–4, 415, 417, 429–30, 436–38, 441, 449–51, 453–54; in

INDEX OF SUBJECTS

Revelation of John, 562, 564, 569–70. *See also* verbal allusion
Council of Jerusalem, 317, 627, 679, 683–86
Council of Yavneh, 29–31
covenant, 11, 13, 66–67, 91, 96, 127, 129, 141, 153, 196, 238, 322, 351, 355, 396, 401–2, 449, 479–87, 492, 495–96, 507, 531, 645–71, 695, 722, 724, 739, 774–75, 787, 956, 972, 984, 1050; Abrahamic, 327, 348, 352, 392, 396, 402, 482–85, 489, 495, 531, 558, 611, 645, 648, 651–52, 656–60, 662–63, 668, 726–27, 884–85, 887–89, 898, 900, 918; Davidic, 27, 53, 68, 330–31, 645, 648, 652n13, 656, 668, 727, 810; eternal covenant, 651, 653–54, 662, 810, 885, 898; Mosaic, 71, 126, 179, 245, 255, 373–74, 402, 495, 645, 648–53, 656, 658, 660, 662–63, 666, 668, 882, 895–96, 971–72, 991; new, 156, 245–46, 255, 373–74, 384, 479–80, 492–93, 645–46, 649–53, 660, 663–67, 671, 806, 991

Damascus Document, 34, 141, 148, 151, 153, 155, 599, 653, 667n49, 688, 819n8, 882, 888–89, 923
Daniel, book of, 31–32, 35, 38, 48, 58–59, 97, 117, 140, 143, 149, 166, 238, 601n14, 628–29, 724, 755–60, 839, 964, 966, 969, 1027–29, 1036–37, 1038–40, 1043–45, 1048–49; in the New Testament, 209, 211, 229–30, 239, 252, 441, 478, 557, 561, 565–68, 571, 573, 607n36, 613–15, 670, 735–36, 758–60, 860–76. *See also* Son of Man
David, 62–63, 69, 72, 98, 145, 191–92, 213–14, 220, 229, 231, 244, 256, 278, 292, 296, 299, 319–20, 329–30, 378, 470, 488, 490, 572, 589–90, 607, 625, 645, 648, 659, 727, 731, 757, 804, 898, 902n82, 908–10, 913, 919–20, 922, 941, 966, 1025, 1036; as author of Psalms, 148, 211, 214, 221, 241, 317, 320, 324, 340, 355, 471, 475, 477, 489, 492, 615, 816–17, 824–26, 828–32, 836–37, 842–43, 846, 882–83, 910. *See also* covenant: Davidic; messiah: Davidic
Day of Atonement, 168, 345, 486, 490–91, 496, 551, 680n14, 787, 823, 946, 983
Day of the Lord, 442, 450, 569, 743–44, 805, 807, 946, 959, 964, 966–68, 973

Dead Sea Scrolls, 5–6, 8–9, 27, 32–35, 41, 65, 68, 75, 110–11, 138–57, 238, 311, 397, 399–400, 494, 527, 529, 552, 584, 591–93, 622–23, 633–34, 636–37, 641, 653–54, 657, 659, 686, 688, 723, 730–31, 751–52, 768, 770, 772, 787, 797–801, 819n8, 823–26, 829n34, 868, 881–84, 889n35, 894–95, 908n116, 923
Decalogue, 183, 191, 212, 226, 232, 340, 357, 423, 426, 510, 553n15, 690, 770–71, 775, 777–79, 788, 902, 960–61, 962, 1012, 1016–17
Demetrius of Alexandria, 166, 888n31
deuterocanonical books, 34, 39–40, 101, 110–12, 129, 200, 310–11, 468, 475, 478, 500, 536, 622, 699, 701–2, 706, 711, 732, 882–85, 901n77, 904n92, 905, 992, 1029
Deuteronomistic History, 57, 71, 166, 259, 769, 818
Deuteronomy, 8, 11, 35, 51–52, 56–57, 61–64, 66, 71, 83–86, 140–42, 183, 209, 215, 263, 354–55, 363, 366, 392–95, 430, 474, 478, 487, 559, 590, 658–59, 767–89, 844, 861, 891–92, 904n96, 985; eschatology, 775, 778, 780–85, 789; influence on cult and liturgy, 769, 772–74, 778, 786–89. *See also* Shema; Song of Moses
diaspora, 88, 163, 174, 467, 469, 509, 524, 583–84, 682–84, 690, 876, 885
divorce, 23, 64, 151, 686–88, 695, 902, 1016. *See also* marriage
Docetism, 305, 547
dreams, 149, 304, 625, 628–29, 866, 868, 891, 896, 1029, 1035

ecstasy, 623–27, 630–32, 635, 641; ecstatic prophecy, 623–27, 630
Eden, 558, 704, 748, 750, 915–16, 1029
election, 228, 320–21, 329, 334, 341n8, 352, 442, 449, 590, 592, 594, 615, 635, 654, 758, 769, 798–800, 808, 812, 844, 884–88, 891, 904, 1048
Elijah, 70–71, 73, 93n59, 152, 193, 196, 230, 246, 251, 276–77, 279–80, 302, 318, 354, 503, 507–8, 512–13, 515, 570–71, 624, 726, 865, 880, 895, 898, 910–14, 922–23, 971, 1014, 1029, 1036
Elijah-Elisha narrative, 248, 267, 276–77, 280

Index of Subjects

Elisha, 276–77, 726, 911, 913–14, 939–40, 948
Enoch: as alternative to Torah, 121–22; literary figure, 318, 636, 884n17, 911n127, 966, 971; literature, 34, 36, 94, 115–17, 125–29, 131, 138, 140, 142, 165, 530–33, 535, 537, 539, 541, 555, 563, 599, 636, 675, 678, 711, 761, 876, 884n17, 892–93, 895, 911n128, 915, 923, 970, 980, 983; second book of, 116, 129, 490–91, 901; Similitudes of Enoch, 598, 605–6, 716, 758, 798–800, 869
Epistle of Jeremiah, 34, 89n40, 125, 140, 553n15
eschatology, 13, 59, 118, 120, 126, 433, 491, 502, 506–7, 510, 515–17, 519, 527, 536–37, 539–40, 586, 599n5, 695, 706, 708–9, 743–61, 807, 813, 862, 864, 868–70, 876, 888n30, 893n46, 910, 958–59, 967–68, 970; in Dead Sea Scrolls, 5–6, 142, 148–49, 156–57, 592, 654, 662, 703–4, 706, 709, 751–53, 798, 806, 811, 869–70, 895; in Gospels, 228, 236, 245–46, 255, 277–78, 730, 753–55, 759–60, 780–83, 805–7, 811, 832, 873–74, 907n107, 911–14; in Pauline Epistles, 177n55, 179, 340, 366, 371, 373, 384, 397, 407, 431–32, 435–36, 445, 450–51, 660–61, 743–44, 783–85, 789, 813, 845
Essenes, 121
Esther, book of, 24–25, 29, 34–35, 38–39, 42, 73, 94–95, 140, 1036
Eucharist. *See* Lord's Supper
Eve, 456–57, 549–50, 914–18, 922, 946, 1025–27, 1029, 1036
exile, 54, 109, 124, 126, 214, 243, 327, 404, 479–80, 507–8, 557, 566, 570–71, 574, 588, 628, 636, 645, 648–52, 655, 670, 724, 727, 732, 741, 743–44, 747–55, 758, 761, 861, 864–65, 885. *See also* diaspora
exodus from Egypt, 64, 67, 71–72, 74, 84, 86n23, 120, 167, 215, 248, 251, 259, 268, 299, 369–70, 384, 403–4, 479–87, 558, 569–70, 574, 588–89, 634, 637–40, 642, 650, 724, 729, 736–38, 749, 782, 818–20, 891, 905, 907, 954, 956, 964, 1004
Ezekiel, 29, 38–39, 61, 91, 140–41, 155, 209, 223, 251, 487, 518, 624, 632–33, 670, 694, 723, 745, 769, 802, 865, 1036; in Revelation of John, 557–59, 562, 564, 566–69, 572–73

Ezekiel the Tragedian, 167, 893–94, 897, 903n87
Ezra, literary figure, 563, 586, 623, 867, 892–93, 985. *See also* Fifth Ezra

fasting, 230, 563n25, 688, 866, 1017
Fifth Ezra, 954–58, 972–73
food laws, 87, 99, 248, 338, 357, 457–59, 679, 683–86, 942–43, 948
fulfillment, 55, 57–59, 75, 124, 146, 237, 239, 245–46, 253, 257–58, 270n25, 271, 289, 296, 304–6, 318, 320, 322, 325, 329–30, 340, 357, 426, 527, 624–26, 636, 641, 652, 658n28, 662n36, 668, 722, 725, 727, 729, 733, 748, 751, 753, 755, 783, 803, 807, 810–11, 813, 816–17, 821n11, 830–31, 835–38, 841, 846, 912, 936, 944, 971–72, 980, 991, 1005, 1016–17; in Matthew, 57–59, 146, 209, 211–12, 215–20, 223, 226–28, 692, 695, 804, 808, 810, 828, 947

Gabriel, 59, 229, 724
Galilee, 85, 88, 217, 248, 258, 324, 739, 804, 1032
Genesis Apocryphon, 152, 196n32, 884n17
gentiles, 11, 87–88, 198, 217, 250, 257, 282, 316, 322, 324, 326, 328, 330–32, 334, 337n1, 338–39, 341n8, 347–49, 354–55, 358, 389, 391–92, 398, 403–4, 407, 435, 442, 444–45, 451, 518, 524, 528–29, 601n14, 602n16, 615, 618, 634, 679–80, 682–83, 726, 728–29, 733, 740, 780, 783, 808, 813, 840, 890, 900, 919–20, 977, 987, 993; salvation of, 227–28, 271, 322, 330–32, 338–39, 351, 358–59, 606n31, 611, 626, 639, 660–62, 679–80, 686, 689–91, 695, 727, 733, 784, 802, 808–9, 813; and Torah, 156, 175, 331, 388, 394, 514n24, 662, 675, 676n5, 679–80, 683–85, 689–91, 695, 784, 990
gezerah shevah, 154, 346n28, 783–84
Gnosticism, 491, 584, 901n77, 932–33, 955, 1009–10, 1015–16, 1037, 1048
golden calf, 191, 370, 484, 495, 905, 907n110, 990
"golden rule," 779–80, 789
gospel, 117, 236, 254–55, 316, 338–42, 344, 346, 348, 351–54, 358–59, 388, 391, 433, 448,

451, 461, 634, 637, 679, 709, 809, 811, 841, 900, 993
Gospel of Judas, 931
Gospel of Mary, 933, 948
Gospel of Peter, 532n19, 933–37, 944, 948
Gospel of Pseudo-Matthew, 944
Gospel of the Ebionites, 942–44, 948
Gospel of the Hebrews, 942
Gospel of the Nazarenes, 942
Gospel of Thomas, 933, 944, 948
Greco-Roman culture, 1, 9, 166, 172, 194, 199, 307, 401–2, 404, 407, 423, 438, 556, 625, 630, 693, 717, 731, 864, 953, 970, 1023, 1027, 1032, 1043n36

Hades, 281, 373, 535, 564, 898, 958, 960–63, 970, 1044
Hagar, 175, 178, 195, 810, 881, 885, 900, 914–16, 918, 919n157, 922
halakah, 99, 112, 128, 150–51, 155n50, 189, 197, 511, 520, 682, 688, 692–93, 695, 942–43, 948
Hasmoneans, 31, 90
Hebrew Bible. *See* Tanak
Hebrew Scriptures. *See* Tanak
hell. *See* Hades
Hellenistic Judaism, 4, 82–83, 85–86, 89, 118, 129–30, 162–69, 454, 537, 624, 863
Hodayot, 141, 153–54, 591, 629, 633, 654–55, 659, 661–62, 688, 731, 836n57, 847–53
Holy Spirit, 13, 33, 119, 122, 246, 324, 581, 583–86, 594–95, 606, 622–42, 654–55, 710, 712, 798, 800, 808, 824, 990, 994, 1025, 1042; in Acts, 315, 319–20, 324–26, 331–32, 623, 626–27, 630–32, 635–37, 641, 659, 828–29, 832, 836; in Catholic Epistles, 527, 538, 541; in Hebrews, 476–77, 635, 667, 833; in John, 631, 641; in Luke, 267, 272, 630–31, 637, 641, 660, 811, 913–14; in Mark, 241, 246–47, 254–55, 258, 638; in Matthew, 211, 213–14, 216, 218; in the Pauline Epistles, 120, 179–80, 359, 371, 373n37, 374, 399, 443, 445, 450, 623, 625–28, 631–32, 634–35, 639–42, 661–64, 671, 712, 784n58, 785, 789, 811; in Revelation of John, 736
Homer, 163, 167, 169–70, 173, 175
household code, 407, 422–23, 919

idols and idolatry, 88, 118, 120, 131, 155, 191, 297, 303, 369–70, 378, 389, 391, 451, 472, 480–81, 484, 490, 492, 495, 534–35, 546, 552–53, 588, 677, 680, 683, 690, 771, 885–88, 896, 898, 905, 960, 962, 969, 990, 1023–24, 1029, 1031–32, 1036, 1044. *See also* golden calf
inspiration, 27, 32, 34, 36–38, 149, 157, 169, 173–74, 355, 453, 527, 541, 572, 623–32, 637, 641, 828–29, 836, 846, 1000
intertextuality, 6, 14–15, 66n68, 123, 210, 237–38, 259, 297, 307–8, 311, 368, 389, 403, 410–16, 429, 435, 555–57, 564, 568–69, 573, 699, 716, 757, 770–71, 774, 786–87, 821, 835, 955–56, 966–67
introductory formula, 7, 10, 13, 27–28, 49–59, 147–49, 210–12, 215–16, 220, 223–24, 226–27, 240–41, 243–44, 263, 269–70, 289–90, 295, 318, 324, 328, 469, 475–78, 502–4, 558–63, 750, 752, 754, 782, 786, 827–28, 830–31, 883n10, 939, 979–80, 991n39, 993; in Pauline Epistles, 341, 343, 350, 352, 354–55, 357–58, 364–66, 376, 379, 384, 390, 396, 400–401, 404, 455–56, 784, 843
Isaac, 173, 193, 196, 228, 267, 321, 351–52, 396–98, 404, 472, 482–83, 485, 602n16, 648, 652, 654–55, 658, 881–82, 899, 890n35, 900, 904n92, 918–19, 945–46, 966, 1048. *See also* Akedah
Isaiah, book of, 29, 35, 38, 47–48, 58, 61, 63, 65, 68, 74, 89–90, 117, 165, 570, 606, 628, 650–51, 694, 732, 768–69, 783, 795–813, 865, 968–70; in Gospels and Acts, 209, 211–12, 216–18, 236–40, 243, 245–47, 249, 251–53, 255–59, 264, 267–73, 282, 286–90, 293, 298, 300–304, 332, 616–17, 630, 634, 659–60, 726–27, 729–30, 753–55, 761, 801–11, 813, 838–39, 938–40; in Hebrews and Catholic Epistles, 474–75, 478, 517–18, 525, 801, 803–4, 808, 810, 813; judgment and eschatology, 747–55, 798–802, 804–8, 811–13; messianism, 798–804, 806, 809–13; in Pauline Epistles, 340, 341n8, 352–54, 358, 363, 372–73, 376n47, 379–83, 396–97, 418–19, 423–26, 430, 433, 441, 446–48, 450, 661–62, 732–34, 801–2, 804–13, 844; at Qumran, 140–42, 148, 153, 155–56, 797–801; in Revelation of John, 557–59, 566, 569–70, 573, 801–7, 809, 812–13; servant songs, 116, 218, 221, 238–39, 246,

Index of Subjects

249, 251–53, 255–57, 259, 280, 292, 321, 324, 404, 430, 434, 444, 505–6, 637, 734, 747, 800–801, 807–10, 813, 837, 839, 861; Song of the Vineyard, 617, 798, 802

Jacob, 84, 173, 193–94, 217, 228, 291–93, 301, 303–4, 321, 340, 352, 396, 472, 483, 507–8, 558, 570, 590, 592, 648, 652, 751, 808, 881–82, 884, 889–92, 899, 904n92, 922–23, 946, 966, 1029, 1049

Jeremiah, book of, 29, 38, 41, 57–59, 61, 64, 91–92, 140, 143, 173, 209, 211, 223–25, 363, 368, 450, 474, 478–81, 508, 557, 559, 647n6, 648–52, 665–67, 671, 689, 724, 769, 861, 865; at Qumran, 140, 143. See also covenant: new; Epistle of Jeremiah

Jerome, 28–29, 61, 98, 523n2, 862, 985n16, 988, 1014–15

Jewish Bible. See Tanak

Job, 29, 38, 41, 65, 69, 73, 95n68, 96, 140, 363, 383, 429–30, 432–33, 437, 502–3, 512–13, 515, 580–81, 583, 595, 628–29, 700, 705, 707, 710, 971, 1029

John the Baptist, 212, 217, 256, 270, 278–79, 281, 288, 293–94, 302, 305, 551, 626, 634, 647n5, 656, 660, 677, 725, 753–55, 761, 806–7, 880, 911–13, 914n139, 942–44, 946

Jonah, 72–73, 247n33, 863, 969, 1005, 1028–30, 1036, 1038, 1040, 1045–49

Josephus, 9, 110, 188–201, 341n7, 486–87, 490–92, 496n50, 506, 513n21, 549, 590, 622, 625, 627, 686, 688, 693, 770–71, 773, 864–66, 887n28, 893n49, 913n134, 939; and Jewish canon, 24, 26, 28, 30, 32–33, 36–42, 95, 674

Joshua, 69–71, 74, 482, 507, 533, 628, 648, 650, 786, 920

Joshua, book of, 29, 38, 41, 61, 73, 85, 86n23, 140, 152, 243, 478, 528, 769, 891–92

Josiah, 69, 71, 74, 769

Jubilees, book of, 24, 33–34, 94, 121–22, 129, 131–32, 138, 140–42, 152, 196n32, 311, 513n21, 582–83, 590, 592, 595, 634, 639, 675, 678, 773, 882, 884, 887–90, 892, 895, 905, 914–15, 923

Judith, 94, 99, 886, 903n87, 910n124, 945

Justin Martyr, 846–47, 954–57, 970, 972, 983–87, 989, 1001, 1009, 1011, 1042, 1048

kaige, 82, 85, 96–97. See also Theodotion

Ketuvim. See Writings (division of canon)

kingdom of God, 180, 226, 247–48, 250, 254, 259, 316, 449, 475, 510, 613, 616, 668, 687, 708, 735–36, 744, 756–57, 801, 807, 834, 845, 869, 871, 874n54, 875, 889, 912, 971–72, 985

Korah, 115, 370, 461, 531, 534–35, 539, 945

laments, 236, 256–57, 351, 433, 585n16, 638–40, 642, 714–15, 722, 730, 732, 738, 831–32, 837, 839–40, 916, 946, 1005

law, 10, 13, 52, 60n44, 66–67, 70–71, 74, 85–86, 281, 296, 299, 340, 342, 348–51, 353, 357–58, 388–89, 391, 393–95, 397–402, 501–2, 510–11, 530, 623, 649–51, 653, 659–60, 662–63, 665–67, 674–95, 701–2, 704–6, 709–11, 733, 739–40, 751–52, 769–72, 774, 777–80, 784–85, 788–89, 799, 807, 811–12, 830, 885, 889, 892–93, 895–96, 900, 902, 906–7, 913, 916n150, 936–37, 944, 956–62, 971–73, 984–85, 989–90, 994, 1002, 1010, 1012–13, 1016–18, 1029, 1049. See also covenant: Mosaic; food laws; gentiles: and Torah; halakah; "the law and the prophets"; purity; Torah (division of canon)

"the law and the prophets," 1, 30, 32–33, 225, 236, 264–65, 270, 274, 279–81, 317, 339, 342, 348, 358, 659, 674–75, 692, 701, 740, 818, 826, 828, 899, 912, 962, 970, 1007–8. See also Prophets (division of canon); Torah (division of canon)

Letter of Aristeas, 9, 83, 85–86, 164, 772

lex talionis, 771, 779, 788, 1012, 1016–17

Liber Antiquitatum Biblicarum. See Pseudo-Philo

lions. See beasts

liturgy, 13, 142, 351, 356, 475, 557, 588, 591–93, 623, 626, 631, 650, 654, 665, 687, 721–41, 752, 769, 772–74, 778, 786–89, 818–20, 827–30, 832, 837, 840, 846, 861, 863, 866, 873, 886, 947, 1029, 1037–38, 1040, 1043; heavenly worship, 734–37, 860, 896; Israelite and Jewish cult, 151, 593, 811, 818, 821–23, 832, 883n11, 895, 897, 902, 956; penitential prayer, 632, 652, 722–25, 739–40; praise of God or Jesus, 580, 588, 626–27, 661, 723, 725–29, 731–33, 735–39, 800, 839–40. See also sacrifice

INDEX OF SUBJECTS

Logos, 174, 491, 581, 583, 595, 682n17, 710, 712–13, 715, 911n128
Lord's Supper, 274, 594, 660, 664, 786, 829, 955, 1030, 1049
Lot, 193, 471, 488–89, 495, 534n25, 537–39, 972
Lucianic recension, 54n27, 98, 377n51
LXX. *See* Septuagint

manna, 294, 304, 369, 818–19, 907, 942
Manual of Discipline. *See* Community Rule
Marcion, 14, 932, 955, 1001–6, 1008–9, 1011–15, 1018, 1037
marked citation, 10, 13, 48–60, 74, 777, 934, 938, 940, 943, 947, 979; in Acts, 317–18, 324–25, 328–34; in Catholic Epistles, 504, 509–11, 520, 525–28, 530–31, 537, 548; of Daniel, 867, 873; in Hebrews, 468–77, 488, 491; of Isaiah, 798–800, 802–5, 807, 809–10, 812; in John, 285–90, 293–95, 300, 306, 308–10; in Luke, 263–64, 268–70; in Mark, 239–41, 256; in Matthew, 209–12, 218–20, 222; in Pauline Epistles, 339, 341, 343, 346–47, 350–58, 363–64, 366–67, 372, 389–98, 402, 415, 419–20, 422–23, 426, 429, 437, 441, 443, 454–55, 460–62, 842–43; of Psalms, 330, 819–20, 821n11, 830–31, 842–43; in Revelation of John, 555, 558, 562. *See also* unmarked citation
marriage, 363, 457–58, 591, 652–53, 666, 686–87, 704, 771, 889–90, 922. *See also* adultery; divorce
martyrdom, 280, 345n25, 566, 614, 623, 629, 694, 731, 759, 863–64, 884, 903–4, 917, 968–69, 1009, 1039, 1044–45
Mary, 267, 273, 588, 630, 677, 725–28, 917, 919, 932–33, 944–46, 948, 970, 972, 1049; Song of, 153, 267
Masoretic text, 2, 41–42, 98, 130, 140, 143, 191, 197–98, 230–32, 258, 265, 289, 293–96, 309–10, 380–82, 390, 400, 414n12, 419, 422, 493–94, 758–59, 768–69, 788, 805, 808–9, 811–12, 822, 824–25, 862
Melchizedek, 126, 183, 471, 482, 488–95, 612, 614–15, 898, 901, 923, 1049
messiah, 13, 148, 156, 217–18, 249–50, 253–54, 259, 274–75, 295, 297, 302, 306, 320, 324, 351, 388, 400–401, 413, 598–618, 637, 754, 756, 759, 803–4, 808, 813, 902, 904–5, 911–12, 913n137, 914, 920, 923, 947, 963, 984, 987, 1005; Davidic, 23, 67–68, 156, 213–14, 216, 220–21, 223, 229, 246, 254, 257, 259, 295, 320–21, 401, 488, 491–92, 565, 592, 604–9, 611n50, 614–15, 648–49, 652n13, 723, 727, 734, 798, 800, 804, 810, 813, 883, 898, 908–9, 919, 1013; as judge, 756, 758–61, 798, 804, 807–8, 832, 874; priestly, 488, 491–93, 601–2, 611–12, 614, 664–65, 667, 675, 680, 798, 833, 901, 902n82; resurrection of, 334, 611–14, 616, 810, 813, 817, 828n33, 834, 840–41, 875, 904. *See also* covenant: Davidic; sonship
Michael, 115, 531, 535–36, 539, 583, 869, 872, 886, 903n90
midrash, 57n35, 125, 128, 153, 190, 200–201, 291, 294, 307, 312, 339, 346n26, 359, 420, 421n24, 485, 487–88, 493, 525, 566, 675, 681, 692, 695, 781, 870, 921n166, 1035. *See also* rabbinic literature
Mishnah, 29, 310, 394, 535, 603–4, 675, 679n11, 689, 695, 770
mixed quotations. *See* composite citation
monotheism, 90, 710, 774, 959
Moses, 47, 69–71, 74–75, 84, 86, 115, 120–21, 126, 131, 152, 194–96, 317, 321, 327, 476–77, 480, 482–88, 495–96, 570–71, 589, 625, 628, 634, 659–60, 666, 702, 737, 882, 884–85, 891–97, 901–8, 922–23, 1014, 1016, 1027, 1029–30, 1034, 1036, 1038–39, 1049; in the Gospels, 214–15, 223, 230, 241, 251, 255, 279, 295, 299, 301–4, 692, 902, 906–7, 912–13, 937–38, 1005; in Pauline Epistles, 340, 345, 349, 354, 370, 373–75, 384, 403, 420n21, 434–35, 454, 459–60, 462, 663–64, 907–8; in Philo, 167, 169, 172–75, 179–83, 630, 712; a prophet like, 230, 251, 278, 280, 292, 302, 322, 658, 775, 782–83, 789, 895, 912. *See also* covenant: Mosaic; Song of Moses
MT. *See* Masoretic text

Nag Hammadi. *See* Gnosticism
Nazareth, 216, 245, 272–74, 276, 324, 637, 726, 811, 914
Neviim. *See* Prophets (division of canon)

Index of Subjects

Noah, 125, 152, 229, 527, 537–39, 583, 647–48, 702, 881, 922, 972, 1007, 1025, 1027–30, 1036, 1038, 1040–43, 1048–49

Odes, 100–101
oral culture, 286, 301, 308, 310–11
Oral Torah, 40, 308, 310, 480, 486, 689, 695. *See also* law; Torah (division of canon)
Origen, 5, 40, 163–64, 365, 380, 382, 934, 987, 1007–8
Oxyrhynchus Papyri, 840, 931–33, 940–41, 948

parables, 219, 223, 243, 247–48, 253–55, 266n14, 616–17, 657, 680–81, 802–3, 828, 1015
parousia, 222, 322, 433, 445, 450, 532, 536–38, 661, 683–84, 708, 743, 746, 759–60, 806, 984, 993, 1038
Passover, 70, 255–56, 292, 305–6, 551, 610n48, 660, 684, 772, 786, 821n11, 829, 902n82, 943, 1017
patristic authors, 39–40, 163, 491, 557, 954, 973, 1004, 1018
Pentateuch. *See* Torah (division of canon)
Pesaḥ. *See* Passover
pesher, 9, 65n66, 139, 141, 143n17, 145, 147–51, 154, 173, 307, 312, 342n12, 420–21, 493n42, 688, 695, 729, 796–97, 812, 825n23, 829n34
Peter, 249, 263n1, 276, 296, 315–31, 333–34, 523–25, 536, 610, 612n55, 626–27, 630–31, 636–37, 641, 657–58, 681, 685–86, 728, 819–20, 832, 836, 904, 909, 914, 1030, 1049; Petrine Epistles, 353, 523–41, 611, 615, 635, 735, 745–46, 776, 803–4, 808, 810, 813, 827, 834, 846, 1041–42
Pharisees, 23, 41, 120, 212, 214, 218–19, 223, 226–27, 232, 248–49, 281, 302, 614–15, 675, 679–82, 685, 688–89, 693–95, 808, 902, 940–41
Philo of Alexandria, 9, 24, 39, 86, 110, 118, 125, 162–84, 189, 475, 486–87, 490–92, 493n42, 494, 496, 506, 513n21, 534, 539–40, 549, 585–87, 622, 624–25, 627, 629–30, 686, 688, 711–12, 770–71, 773, 775, 777, 784, 1012n58; and Pauline Epistles, 174–81, 341n7, 345, 370n22, 374, 391, 438, 457

prayer. *See* liturgy
promised land, 483, 486–87, 507, 518, 649, 666, 781, 885, 887, 891–92, 897–98, 900, 907n110, 971–73. *See also* covenant: Abrahamic
prophetic books, 24, 30, 148, 556–58, 565, 573, 865–66, 955, 968, 973
Prophets (division of canon), 28–30, 32, 35, 64, 91–93, 95, 173–75, 225, 227, 232, 236, 259, 264–65, 275, 289, 317, 340, 358, 441, 468, 474, 495, 500, 517–18, 525, 527, 531, 537, 557, 624, 657, 659, 687, 692, 783, 818, 826, 828, 899, 912, 958, 962, 964, 970, 983, 1007–8, 1014, 1036. *See also* canon; "the law and the prophets"; Torah (division of canon); Writings (division of canon)
Psalms, book of, 8, 13, 29, 32, 41, 61–62, 82, 91–92, 95, 98, 192, 209, 236, 240, 256–57, 259, 264, 288, 293–95, 299, 317, 340, 358, 363, 369, 372, 399, 418, 420, 426, 430, 448, 473–75, 478, 487, 525, 537, 557, 559, 565, 573, 614–17, 705, 707, 722–23, 726–33, 737–39, 786, 797, 816–53, 861, 909, 935–36, 947, 959, 967, 983, 989, 992, 994; with law and prophets, 30, 173, 265, 275, 299, 317, 342n13, 473, 475, 828; as prophetic, 64–66, 219, 816–17, 824–25, 828–31, 835–38, 841, 846, 969; at Qumran, 113n8, 140–43, 148, 153. *See also* David: as author of Psalms; laments; liturgy
Psalms of Solomon, 99–101, 311, 555, 605–6, 608, 750–51, 755, 798, 867
pseudepigrapha, 4, 34, 110–14, 117, 125, 128–29, 167, 311, 453n1, 468, 475, 478, 556, 622, 881–85, 889n35, 901n77, 904n92, 905, 914–15, 917
Pseudo-Philo, 9, 168, 190, 196, 365, 370n22, 374, 513n21, 534, 625, 627, 771, 882, 885, 887–88, 892, 894, 896–97, 903n87, 903n90, 910n124, 915
Ptolemy, early Christian theologian, 1009–13, 1015–18
purity, 99, 150–51, 248, 331, 445, 632–35, 641–42, 662, 675–81, 684–85, 694–95, 778, 870, 886–87, 890, 910, 917–19, 938, 940–41, 946, 948. *See also* food laws; law

INDEX OF SUBJECTS

Q, 212, 230, 265–66, 676, 686, 693, 707n28, 717, 776–77, 875
Qumran. *See* Dead Sea Scrolls

rabbinic literature, 4, 24, 31, 39, 111, 125, 128, 153, 199, 200, 237, 310, 394, 398, 420, 491, 503, 606–7, 610n48, 612, 675, 678, 681, 686–87, 689, 692–93, 695, 825n23, 909–10, 920n165
Rachel, 304, 732
Rahab, 228, 503, 512–14, 602n16, 881, 914–15, 919–21
Rebecca, 339, 592, 889–90, 914–15
resurrection: of the dead, 23, 41n67, 96, 154, 156, 176–79, 229, 321, 349n36, 371–73, 384, 435, 462, 614, 662n35, 688–89, 805–6, 834, 840, 860, 914, 959, 991, 1038, 1043–48; of Jesus, 59, 178, 218–19, 222–23, 236, 253, 256, 258, 280–82, 296, 315, 319, 322–23, 329–30, 332, 334, 349, 353, 384, 611–12, 614, 618, 664, 729, 734, 834, 840–41, 904, 933–34, 969–70, 993, 1042–44, 1048–49. *See also* messiah: resurrection of
rewritten scripture, 9, 33, 91, 110, 143, 152, 166, 172, 190–91, 194–97, 199, 201, 245, 311, 365, 371–73, 383, 493n42, 704, 884, 892, 895, 914
Rome and Roman(s), 171, 198n45, 218, 316, 332, 337–38, 356, 523, 525, 570–71, 574, 684, 738, 783, 841, 865–68, 871–73, 875, 919, 922, 987, 1024–27, 1030–31, 1033, 1035, 1037, 1043–44, 1047, 1049
Rule of the Community. *See* Community Rule
Ruth, 29, 38, 94, 140, 228, 602n16, 881, 914–15, 919–21

Sabbath, 57–58, 87, 151, 155, 229, 243–44, 246–47, 483, 487, 594, 652–53, 675, 681–83, 695, 771–73, 808, 874n52, 909–10, 933–34, 956, 988, 990, 993, 1017
sacrifice, 88n35, 151, 255–56, 345, 482, 485, 492, 508, 529, 548, 551, 566, 633, 650, 664–67, 677, 680, 684–85, 702, 802, 833, 863, 943, 956, 984, 990, 993, 1017, 1041; Jesus as, 147, 305, 345, 496, 545–46, 550–51, 610, 666–67, 679–80, 736, 820, 833, 901, 935, 946, 990, 1039; offering, 634, 679, 683–84, 821, 823, 833, 956, 1029, 1049. *See also* Akedah; liturgy
Sadducees, 23, 40–42, 121, 154, 211, 612n55, 688–89, 728
Samaritan Pentateuch, 4, 41, 143, 782
Samaritans, 30, 40, 90–91, 95, 328, 787
Sarah, 163, 175, 178, 180, 195, 340, 352, 397–98, 527, 810, 881, 900, 914, 918–19, 945
Satan, 115, 246–47, 531, 535–36, 539, 553, 569, 678, 737, 781, 873; devil, 680, 903n90, 916, 1010–12, 1018
scribes, 23, 144, 169n20, 219, 223, 226, 246–50, 254, 323, 530, 563, 629, 649, 651, 659, 693–95, 714, 724, 796, 827, 862, 933, 947, 953, 1013
second coming. *See* parousia
Septuagint, 2, 4–5, 27, 39–42, 55–56, 81–102, 140, 143, 163–65, 191, 197–98, 230–32, 266–69, 272–73, 289, 293–96, 309–11, 318, 320–21, 323, 330–33, 493–94, 500n1, 501, 506, 510n18, 513, 519, 558, 571–72, 665, 674, 699, 768–69, 782, 805, 808, 816, 822, 862, 945, 947–48, 984–85, 1035, 1043; and Pauline Epistles, 342–45, 352–53, 356–57, 359, 364, 367–68, 379–83, 390, 392–95, 397, 399–400, 414n12, 419, 422, 431, 433, 463, 809, 811
servant songs. *See* Isaiah, book of: servant songs
Shema, 254, 610, 687, 770, 772, 774–75, 777–82, 788–89
Sheol. *See* Hades
shepherd image, 156, 219–20, 222–24, 256, 292, 296–97, 299, 638, 748, 835, 1025–26, 1049
Shepherd of Hermas, 25, 28, 955
Sinai. *See* covenant: Mosaic; exodus from Egypt
Sirach, 30, 34, 39, 42, 93, 99, 128–29, 140, 165, 311, 457, 478, 507–8, 537, 582, 591, 629, 701–2, 706, 710, 714, 724, 823, 882, 888, 894, 913; Greek preface to, 30–32, 93, 165, 265, 828n30
social memory, 301–4, 310–11, 936n9
Song of Moses, 250, 435, 470, 472, 473n10, 559, 561, 565, 569, 737, 773–75, 783, 787–89, 820–21
Songs of the Sabbath Sacrifice, 141, 734

Index of Subjects

Son of Man, 97, 116–17, 222, 247, 249–52, 254–55, 257, 259, 281, 291, 293, 304, 445, 556, 560, 564–65, 567, 569, 607–8, 611, 613–14, 616, 682n17, 713, 716, 756–60, 761, 860, 868–69, 873–76, 909, 1005

sonship, 156, 213, 215–16, 218, 221, 223, 273, 298, 351, 391, 592, 594, 744

Spirit. *See* Holy Spirit

Spirit of YHWH. *See* Holy Spirit

Stephen, 152, 276, 315, 326–29, 331, 333, 614, 623, 630–31, 658–59, 731, 903–4, 922

Sukkot, 56–57, 62–63, 197, 294, 772–73, 786, 889n33

supersession, 435, 646n4, 680, 833, 946, 954–57, 978, 987, 990, 993–94. *See also adversus Judaeos*

Symmachus, 5, 82, 97, 258, 342, 353, 380–82

synagogue, 27, 167–68, 181, 232, 329, 389, 401, 467, 469–70, 473, 495, 637, 681–82, 684, 690, 714, 726, 740, 811, 863, 1031–37

Talmud, 28–29, 310, 606, 694. *See also* Mishnah

Tanak, 12, 24, 28–33, 35–36, 38–39, 94, 99, 101, 133, 173–74, 265n10, 474, 488. *See also* canon; Prophets (division of canon); Torah (division of canon); Writings (division of canon)

targum, 4, 140, 200, 245n29, 374, 420, 459, 488, 491, 534, 572, 695, 758–59

temple in Jerusalem, 41, 62, 87–88, 126, 151, 214, 221, 229, 253–54, 292, 294, 298, 323, 326–27, 447, 475, 491, 508, 529, 551, 568, 573, 630, 657, 664, 675, 677, 679, 684–85, 692–93, 695, 702, 722, 727, 736, 772, 787, 805, 810–11, 818, 821–23, 832, 867, 871, 873, 883, 940–41, 943, 946–48, 1032, 1036; destruction by Babylonians, 57, 68, 224, 480; destruction by Romans, 40, 224–25, 254, 328, 496, 571, 692, 871, 875; heavenly, 253, 557, 568, 668–69, 675, 735, 745; humans as, 375, 615, 634, 680; Jesus as, 297, 300; Mary as, 946, 948. *See also* liturgy; sacrifice

temple in Leontopolis, 89

Temple Scroll, 33, 143, 151, 154, 770, 895

Ten Commandments. *See* Decalogue

Tertullian, 1n1, 36, 550, 956, 988–90, 1002, 1010, 1013–14, 1044, 1048

textual pluriformity, 42, 144–47, 572

Theodotion, 5, 82, 91, 97, 258, 342, 380–82, 566–67, 571–73, 862, 865n19, 870–71. *See also* kaige

Tobit, 24, 34, 42, 94, 99, 140, 558, 678, 945, 1029

torah. *See* law

Torah (division of canon), 24, 28–30, 32–33, 35, 38, 40–41, 52–53, 61, 63–64, 67, 82–85, 88, 90, 92–93, 95–96, 99, 101, 111, 120–22, 125–26, 133, 151, 173–75, 209, 212, 225–27, 232, 264–65, 289, 295, 299, 308, 310, 317, 326, 330, 340, 357–58, 454, 468–69, 473–74, 479, 481, 486–87, 495, 500, 503, 508, 510–11, 518, 525, 527, 537, 556, 559, 565, 629–30, 640, 648, 674–75, 681, 683, 686–95, 704, 706, 733, 771–72, 786, 818, 844, 882, 902, 906–7, 934, 956–59, 962, 1012. *See also* canon; halakah; law; "the law and the prophets"; covenant: Mosaic; Oral Torah; Prophets (division of canon); Writings (division of canon)

typology, 66, 69–75, 215, 219, 301–2, 339, 349, 369, 435, 528, 533n22, 540, 558, 562, 570–71, 663, 667, 840, 907, 939–40, 980, 983, 991, 1040, 1049–50

unmarked citation, 11, 13, 49, 60–66, 73, 525n10, 745, 947, 992; in Acts, 317, 321, 326–27, 329, 333; in Catholic Epistles, 504, 506, 515–19, 526–28, 531, 537–38, 541, 548; in Hebrews, 470–75, 477–78, 488, 492; of Isaiah, 798–800, 802–3, 805–8; in John, 285, 287–88, 291, 293, 295, 306, 308, 310; in Mark, 219, 239–41; in Matthew, 209, 222; in Pauline Epistles, 353–54, 356, 364–65, 367, 372, 384, 398–401, 415–17, 422, 426, 429–32, 436–37, 441, 443, 842–43; of Psalms, 831–34, 842–43; in Revelation of John, 558–62, 567. *See also* marked citation

verbal allusion, 11–13, 49, 66, 68–74, 132, 209, 212, 214–15, 475, 478–79, 707n27, 777, 783–84, 798, 800, 802–7, 812, 834–35, 881, 935, 938–39, 942–43, 947–48; in Acts, 316, 318, 320–21, 323–25, 331, 333–34; in Catholic Epistles, 504, 506, 515–20, 526–27, 531, 536–38, 540, 544–46, 548–53; to Daniel, 867, 869, 871, 873–74; in John, 285, 288, 291–92, 294, 300–301, 304–6, 308, 310; in Mark, 239–43, 244n26, 246–47, 249–53, 257–58; in Pauline Epistles, 344–45, 363–65, 401–3, 407, 409–19, 424–26, 429–30, 432–35, 437, 441–49, 451, 453–60, 463, 842–43; in Revelation of John, 555–56, 560, 562, 564–66, 568, 570, 573–74

Vision of Amram, 152, 536n33

visions, 11, 71, 131, 149, 229–30, 303–4, 316, 332, 371, 373, 445, 538, 556–57, 562–68, 570, 573–74, 607, 614, 624, 629, 685–86, 735–36, 756–57, 798, 801–3, 805, 809, 812, 839, 866–67, 870–73, 875–76, 892–93, 958, 960, 964, 969–70

wisdom, 13, 86, 99–100, 118–20, 122, 126, 130, 138, 155, 168, 175, 199, 300, 356, 366–69, 411, 436, 582, 606, 625, 632, 641, 699–717, 733, 798, 864, 893n49, 903n87; personified, 119, 299–300, 436, 580–81, 693–94, 705, 710–16, 888–89n31; and Spirit, 122, 581, 627–32, 635, 641; and Torah, 86, 122, 693, 701–2, 704–5, 709, 733. *See also* Christology: wisdom Christology

wisdom literature, 82, 91–92, 94–95, 101, 140, 153, 155, 167, 436, 528, 580, 595, 628, 649, 699–709, 711, 717, 971

Wisdom of Ben Sira. *See* Sirach

Wisdom of Solomon, 28, 35–36, 42, 94, 99, 117–20, 122, 127, 129, 166, 238, 311, 370, 425, 537, 558, 566, 573, 582, 590, 630, 701–2, 706, 969; and Paul, 119–20, 425

worship. *See* liturgy

Writings (division of canon), 28–32, 35, 92, 95, 173–74, 265, 441, 468, 474–75, 478, 500, 517n31, 525, 527, 531, 687, 826. *See also* canon; Prophets (division of canon); Psalms, book of: with law and prophets; Torah (division of canon)

Yom Kippur. *See* Day of Atonement

Index of Scripture and Other Ancient Sources

Hebrew Bible

Genesis

Ref	Pages
1	317, 389, 458, 540, 580
1–2	323, 569
1–3	371, 580
1:1	11, 292–93, 411, 544, 579–80, 988
1:1–2	582
1:1–2:3	581
1:2	581, 585
1:3	365
1:5	144
1:21	580
1:26	411, 971, 981
1:26–27	412
1:27	151, 176–79, 222, 240, 411–13, 415, 586
1:28	389, 409, 411, 584, 981
1:29	455, 458
1:31	455, 458
2	455–57
2–3	972
2:1–3:4	972
2:2	155, 471, 474, 477, 483
2:2–3	982
2:3	580
2:4	209
2:4–28:9	170
2:7	176–79, 364, 371, 585, 991
2:9–10	558
2:11–12	972
2:16–17	916
2:24	23, 211, 222, 240, 364, 384, 415, 422
3	118, 349, 455–57
3:1	558
3:1–6	916
3:3	558
3:6	972
3:7–21	411
3:13	916, 946
3:14–19	558
3:20	293
3:22	558
3:23	581
3:24	558
4	229, 291, 531, 534, 548–50
4:1	550
4:1–16	548
4:8	534, 545
4:14–15	534
4:24	229
5:1	209
5:2	240
5:24	318
6	540, 1040
6–8	229
6–9	117
6:1–4	530–31, 537
6:7	484
6:9	539
7–9	538
7:12	195
7:13–23	527
7:24	195
8:18	539
8:21	432
9:1	647
9:3	458
9:9	647
9:11	647
11:1–9	319, 888
11:7	319
11:26	888
11:31	886
12	193, 195
12:1	327
12:1–3	329, 887
12:2	250
12:3	213, 322, 391–92, 558, 561, 726, 900
12:6	390
12:7	154
12:10–20	72
12:11–13	919
12:17	72
13:15	390, 395, 900
14	173, 192, 488–89
14:14	981

14:17–20	155, 471, 474, 482, 488, 492, 898	21:9–10	175	38:13–30	919
		21:9–21	918	38:15	180
14:18–20	901	21:10	390, 397–98	38:25–26	180
14:20	493	21:12	351, 472, 475, 477, 482	39:6	891
15	132			40:8–19	149
15:3	148	21:17–19	918	41	132, 550
15:5	483, 624	22	192–93, 213, 403, 513	41:8–16	149
15:6	346–47, 359, 390, 514, 899–900, 982, 986, 993	22:2	396, 511, 943	41:38–39	628
		22:7–8	616	41:45	890
		22:7–18	154	44:34	73
15:7	624	22:9	511	47	132
15:12	624	22:12	396, 610	47:31	472, 483
15:13–14	327	22:16	610	48:9	982
15:16	358, 442, 483	22:16–17	396	48:11	982
15:16–21	648	22:17	471, 482	48:14	982
15:18	396, 483, 558	22:18	213, 317, 322, 328, 334, 392, 611	48:18	982
16	195, 918			48:19	982
16–18	396	22:28	87	49	192, 606–7
16:6	919	23:4	526	49:3–4	148
16:9–14	918	24	309, 484	49:8–12	84
16:11	945	24:7	396, 900	49:9	558, 565, 606, 616
17	391, 401	25–31	484	49:10	604–5, 608, 611, 615
17:1	174	25–36	506	49:11	558
17:4	96	25–50	504	49:26	751
17:5	348, 986	25:9	890	50:24–25	891
17:6	180	25:12–18	918	50:26	84
17:7	396, 651	25:21–23	982		
17:8	900	25:23	982, 991	**Exodus**	
17:10–14	658	25:25	991	1–12	964, 966
17:10–27	396, 411	25:28	592	1:7	84, 483
17:11–14	87	26:4	213, 322, 611	1:8	84, 891
17:12	896	26:4–5	392	1:9	87
17:23	981	26:5	86	1:20	87
18–19	67, 193	26:24	209	2	214, 304
18:1–15	267, 945	27:46–28:5	889	2:2	903
18:10	352	28:12	287, 291, 293, 304	2:5–10	84, 903
18:12	527, 919	28:14	304, 558, 561, 611	2:12	894
18:14	352	28:15	109	2:14	327
18:18	213, 392	28:17	304	2:15	894
18:23–33	899	29	304	2:24	483
19	193, 531, 538, 972	31:44	432	3	737
19:5	533	32:1–6	484	3:1	70, 299
19:8	534	32:7–10	484	3:1–10	904
20	195	32:28	889	3:3	170
20:1–5	919	35:9–12	889	3:5	70
21	173, 195	36–37	972	3:5–10	327
21:1	945	38:8	211, 264		

3:6	23, 41, 154, 180, 211, 222, 241, 264, 317, 321, 325	14:19	639	20:11	317, 323, 820, 853
		14:22	907	20:12	211, 226, 240, 415, 422–23, 426, 771, 779, 960
3:8	483, 972	14:31	251, 483		
3:12	209, 327	15	192		
3:14	92, 299, 899	15:1–18	737	20:12–16	222, 240, 264, 771, 778
3:15	317, 321, 325	15:1–19	100, 559, 565, 569		
3:17	483	15:2	250	20:12–17	258
4:4	483	15:11	565	20:13	226, 960
4:10	905	15:22–17:7	484	20:13–14	510
4:19	215	15:24	430, 434	20:14	226, 960
4:22	215, 588, 592, 724	15:26	849	20:15	960
6:5	483	16	302, 819	20:17	771, 960
6:8	483	16:2	434, 907	21:2–6	772
7–9	455, 459	16:4	182, 286, 819, 991	21:2–11	63
7–12	191	16:4–15	294	21:7–11	64
7–15	484	16:4–36	570, 907	21:12	226
7:1	287, 295	16:7–8	434	21:17	211, 240, 960
7:3	319	16:15	182, 286, 819	21:24	771, 779
7:11–12	460	16:18	364	21:24–25	226
7:14–24	571	16:31	942	21:32	229
7:14–11:10	570	16:35	215	22	994
7:22	460	17:1–7	195	22:9–11	687
8:3	460	17:6–7	907	22:21	517, 961
9:11	460	17:8–13	982	22:25	527
9:12	224, 232	17:14	982	22:27	86
9:16	352	17:15	88	22:28	86
10:1–20	569	19–20	971	23:10–19	772
11:1	72	19–23	484	23:13	197
11:9–10	905	19:1	480	23:20	58, 240, 245, 258, 270, 754
12	569	19:4	570		
12:2–28:34	170	19:5–6	449, 648	23:20–21	484
12:10	287, 821, 849	19:6	430, 438, 526, 529, 572, 735–36	23:20–24	638–39
12:14	660			23:22	90, 526
12:21	616	19:16	570	23:24	484
12:23	370	19:16–25	650	24:1	244
12:43	86	19:22–23:33	63	24:3	650
12:46	305, 821, 849, 935	20	174, 226, 778	24:3–8	507, 650
12:49	86	20:2–6	546, 553	24:4	505, 650, 944
13:1–10	774	20:3	960	24:5–8	666
13:2	264	20:4	88	24:6	255
13:11	483	20:4–6	771	24:7	650
13:11–16	774	20:5–6	648	24:7–8	526, 648
13:15	264	20:6	775	24:8	242, 255–56, 471, 477, 480, 650, 664
13:18	479	20:7	771, 960		
13:21	907	20:8	982	24:9	230, 244
13:21–22	639	20:8–11	681, 771–72	24:12–15	230
14	569	20:9–11	243	24:13	244

24:15	244	34:18–24	772	18:5	10, 353, 390, 393–94, 401, 681
24:18	892, 947, 982	34:27	486	18:8	690
25:1–31:11	628	34:28	70, 230, 947, 980	18:22	961
25:8	300	34:29	906	18:24–25	680
25:17–22	345	34:29–35	179–80, 230, 663, 908	18:29	782
25:40	477, 480	34:30–35	373–74	19:2	438, 449, 525–26
28:3	628	34:33–35	180	19:12	226
28:21	505, 507, 944	34:34	373	19:13	229, 456
29:18	432	35:40	487	19:15	295
30:33	782	35:1–3	483, 487	19:17	545
31:1–6	628	35:2–3	681	19:18	222, 226, 241, 254, 258, 264, 288, 357, 390, 398, 503, 509–10, 675–76, 775, 779–80
31:3	411	35:3	681		
31:7	345	35:4–33	628		
31:12–17	483, 487	35:12	345		
31:13–17	982	35:30–36:3	628		
31:17	483	35:31–32	411	19:26	961
31:18	980, 982	36:21	505, 507, 944	20:7	449
32	191, 480	38:5–8	345	20:9	960
32–34	471–72, 480, 483, 487, 495–96	40:29	487	20:26	449
		40:34	242, 244, 251	21:7	686
32:1	327			21:13	686
32:1–13	485			22:32	449
32:4–6	907			23	57
32:6	364, 369, 986	**Leviticus**		23:29	317, 322, 782, 981
32:7	980	1–16	677	23:33–43	197
32:7–8	982	1:9	432	23:40–42	56–57
32:8	403	1:13	432	24:5–9	229
32:12–17	486	4:3	601	24:16	403
32:14	485	5:11	264	24:17	226
32:15–29	485	6:15	601	24:18–20	779
32:19	982	10:10	677	24:19–20	226
32:30–33:6	486	11	458	24:20	771, 779
33	174, 472	11:3	982	25	772
33:1	981	11:7–15	981	25:9	545–46, 551
33:1–3	486	11:44–45	449, 526	25:36	961
33:3	981	12	677	25:39–40	430, 438
33:7	487	12:3	401, 683	25:39–46	64
33:7–23	486	12:6–8	264	25:43–53	411
33:10	352	13–14	243–44	26	651
33:11	485	14:2–31	938	26:11–12	364, 375–76
33:14	486, 639	14:2–32	677, 902	26:12	155
33:14–15	638–39	14:3–7	666	26:15	652
33:19–33	244	16:2	345	26:21	982
34:1	486	16:16	545–46, 551	26:34–35	57
34:6	244, 343, 545, 654	17–18	684	26:40	655–57, 665
34:6–7	480, 722	17–26	677	26:42	506, 652
34:10	322, 447, 480, 486	17:7	678	26:45	485, 658
34:15	88				

Index of Scripture and Other Ancient Sources

Numbers

5:11–28	687
6:3–4	648
6:26	448–49
7:89	345
10:9	154
10:10	487, 822
11:4–34	369
11:8	294, 942
11:16	994
11:24–29	88
12	182–83
12–14	487
12:3	907
12:6	556
12:7	182–83, 251, 471, 482
12:8	546
13–14	471
13:26	480
14	182, 530
14:1–25	182
14:2	434, 907
14:22	487
14:22–24	533
14:23	182
14:27	434
14:28	357
14:29–30	907
14:33–34	215
15:32–36	681
16	531
16:5	454–55, 461–63
16:30	579
16:31–33	946
16:32–35	535
17:6–15	370
18:15–16	677
19:6–18	666
20:1–13	195, 892
20:7–13	907
21:4–9	982
21:5–6	907
21:6	370
21:8	148, 151
21:49	907
22–24	531, 534, 538
22:18	540
22:28–38	540
22:35	624
23:7	506
24:2–4	534
24:13	148, 580
24:15–17	131, 534, 570
24:17	154, 217, 537, 605, 612
25:1–9	370, 570, 907
25:11	911
27:17	222, 242
27:20	70, 374
28:9–10	229
29:12–38	197
30:3	226
31:8	570
31:16	570
33:15	480
33:37	480
35	197
35:30	297, 479

Deuteronomy

1:8	506
1:27	435
1:31	329, 589
1:38	70
3:21	70
3:28	70
4:2	556
4:4–41	197
4:5–8	86
4:10	981
4:11–12	777
4:13	648, 981
4:24	472, 481, 776–77
4:27–31	722
4:34	724
4:35	776
5	778
5:1	774
5:6–21	553, 770
5:7	960
5:8–10	771
5:10	775, 960
5:11	771
5:12	155, 982
5:12–15	681, 771–72
5:15	72
5:16	211, 240, 415, 422, 771, 776, 779, 960
5:16–20	240, 258, 264, 776, 778
5:16–21	771
5:17	226, 776, 960
5:17–18	510
5:17–20	776
5:17–21	357
5:18	222, 776, 960
5:19	960
5:21	771, 960
6	780
6–8	781
6:4	247, 610, 711, 772, 776
6:4–5	87, 241, 254, 258, 676, 779–80
6:4–6	770
6:5	71, 222, 264, 287, 775–76, 780
6:5–9	774–75, 782
6:6–9	774
6:8–9	774
6:10–16	781
6:10–25	781
6:12	781
6:13	215, 222, 264, 777, 781
6:14	960
6:16	215, 222, 264, 331, 333, 777, 781
6:22	319
7:6–8	411
7:9	343
7:14	960
7:19	319
7:21	154
8	780
8:2	781
8:2–4	215
8:2–20	781
8:3	215, 222, 230, 264, 777, 781
8:4	781
8:5	781
8:7–10	781
8:11–14	781
8:17	777
8:17–20	781

8:19	960	18	333, 775, 783, 789		454–56, 460–61, 463,
9:3	472, 777, 788	18:10	961		776
9:4	777, 788	18:15	230, 242, 244, 251,	25:5	241
9:9	70, 230		278, 280, 317, 322,	25:5–6	211, 264
9:12	403		327, 334, 612, 658,	26:8	319, 724
9:16	403		775–76, 782, 904	26:18–19	449
9:18	230	18:15–18	302, 912	27:4	90
9:19	472, 477, 480,	18:15–20	782	27:5–6	56
	484–85, 777	18:15–22	658, 783	27:19	961
9:20	495	18:18	322	27:26	783, 986
10–33	768	18:19	782	28	724
10:2	777	18:20	553	28:10	724
10:12–13	659, 774–75	19:1–12	197	28:14	960
10:12–21	659	19:5	364	28:21	739
10:16	659, 981	19:15	222, 230, 287, 290,	28:26	390, 392, 394–95,
10:18	517, 961		297, 321, 461, 546,		401, 404
10:18–19	659		776	28:36	960
10:20	215, 222	19:19	11	28:46	319
11:4	768	19:21	222, 771, 776, 779	28:58	390, 392, 404
11:13–21	774	20:2–5	154	29:3	354, 776, 788
11:14	516, 518	21:6–8	210	29:13	96
11:16	960	21:13	776	29:16	88
11:19–21	774	21:21	11	29:17	472, 475, 481, 776,
11:22	775	21:22	325–26		788
11:25	430	21:22–23	785, 934	29:17–20	768
11:28	960	21:23	306, 390, 394–95,	29:25	960
13:2–6	553		783–85, 789, 935,	30–32	787
13:14	960		986, 988	30:1–4	722
14:1	588	22:21	11	30:1–10	775
14:1–2	151, 590	22:22–27	947	30:4	242
14:29	517	22:24	11	30:6	411
15:1–18	772	23:4	784	30:10	390, 392, 404
15:7	546	23:5	534	30:11	546
15:11	546	23:16–17	430, 438	30:11–14	149
15:12	63	23:18	88	30:12	776, 787
15:12–18	63–64	23:18–19	961	30:12–14	353, 711
15:13–15	64	23:22	226	30:14	777, 787
16:1–17	772	23:25	243	30:15	244
16:13	62	24	64	30:17	960
16:13–16	197	24:1–4	64, 75, 226, 240, 242,	31	786
16:15	62		686, 902	31–33	788
16:18–19	295	24:6	52	31–34	773
17–33	768	24:7	11	31:5–7	768
17:1–7	403	24:14–15	229, 456	31:6	472, 477, 482, 777, 786
17:6	287, 290, 297, 472,	24:16	51, 56	31:8	472, 477, 482, 777, 786
	481, 776–77	24:17	961	31:9–13	772, 786
17:7	11, 364, 776	25:4	364, 366, 384,	31:10–12	786

Index of Scripture and Other Ancient Sources

31:29	775
32	435, 774, 783, 787, 820–21
32:1–7	768
32:1–43	559, 565, 773, 788
32:4	343, 545, 562, 565, 738, 777, 787
32:4–6	589
32:5	430, 435, 588
32:5–6	589
32:8	589
32:16–23	986
32:17	678
32:21	353, 777, 787, 986
32:25	821
32:35	97, 356, 443, 472, 475, 477, 481, 777, 787
32:36	472, 477, 481, 777, 787, 820, 852
32:39–43	768
32:40	768
32:40–43	773
32:43	470, 475–76, 482, 733, 769, 777, 787–88, 821, 851, 986
32:43–45	768
32:47	435
32:51	892
33	775
33:1	131
33:12	447
34	192
34:5	251, 892
34:7	374
34:9	70, 628
34:10	775, 891
34:10–12	33, 485
34:11	319
34:15	251
35:21	435

Joshua

1:1	251
1:2	70
1:5	69–70, 209
1:7	251
1:12	251
1:13	251
1:15	251
2	920
2:1	919
2:1–16	512, 514
4:5	505, 507, 944
5:6–7	507
5:10–12	773
5:15	70
6	920
6:17	919
6:22–25	512, 514
8:30–31	56
8:31	52
9:2	83, 92
9:24	251
11:15	251
22:4	251
22:5	251
24:2–3	391, 886
24:4	506
24:9–10	534
24:15	650
24:24	650
24:25	648
24:32	506

Judges

2:4	323
2:17	403
3:9–10	625
5	192
5:19	571
6–8	132
6:12	448–49
6:13	72
7:3–6	132
7:25	132
8:19	945
9:7	323
10:1–2	191
13:3–7	945
13:5	216, 321
13:7	216
16:17	231

Ruth

1:1	920
1:9	323
1:14	323
1:16	919
2:4	448–49
4:12	921

1 Samuel

1:1–2:11	267
1:5–6	267
1:6	947
1:20	945
1:22	146
2	192
2:1	726
2:1–10	153, 267
2:8	267
2:11	726
2:10	364, 601
2:27–36	57
2:35	601
4:19	450
7:12–14	605
8:2	588
10:6–11	624
11:4	323
12:3	601
12:5	601
12:22	842–43, 851
13:14	317, 329
15	73
16:6	601
16:7	191, 295
16:14–16	584
17	192
17:35	910
17:40	193
17:42–51	910
17:52	910
19:5	221
20:5	773
20:24–27	773
21:1–6	155, 909
21:1–7	229, 244
24:7	601
24:17	323

25:3	193	6:5	88	22:19	564, 568
26:9	601	6:20	568	22:39	92
26:23	601	8:25	723		
		8:56	251	**2 Kings**	
2 Samuel		8:65–66	62	1–2	513, 913
1:14	601	9:5	320	1:8	246, 912
1:16	601	10:1–13	229	2:4	60
3:32	323	11:41	92	2:4–11	246
5:2	220, 296, 299, 947	12:8	506	2:9–10	914
5:8	229	15:3	72	2:11	910
6:14	947	15:29	55	2:11–12	318
7	54, 155, 648	15:34	69	2:11–14	276
7:8	364	16:31	570	2:13	939
7:11–14	213, 592	17–19	513, 913	2:19–22	939
7:12	287, 295, 612	17–24	244	4:17–37	244, 248
7:12–13	320	17:1–7	571	4:31–37	248, 277
7:12–14	810	17:3	246	5:1–14	276, 726
7:12–16	53, 411	17:7–17	276	5:8–14	914
7:12–18	411	17:8–16	726	6:7	939
7:14	156, 213, 364, 411, 470, 473n8, 475–76, 482, 588, 590, 592	17:9	914	9:27	571
		17:17–24	248, 277	9:36	251
		18	507	10:10	251
7:14–15	648	18–19	246	14:3	52
7:14–16	723	18:1	571	14:3–4	69
7:23	438	18:1–45	512	14:6	51, 54, 56
8:16	588	18:21	193	15:28	69
8:17	588	18:28	624	16:2	69
11:3	919	18:31	505, 507	18:3	69
13:36	323	18:41–46	571	18:12	251
17:6–7	229	19	70, 196	19:15	820, 853
17:23	229	19:1–8	570	21:8	251
19:22	601	19:1–14	912	22–23	52, 71, 769
21:19	191	19:2	244	22:2	69
22	192	19:3–18	246	23:21–23	773
22:3	471	19:4	73	23:25	71
22:50	843, 848	19:8	230, 947	23:29	571
22:51	601	19:10	196, 354, 911, 986		
23:1	601, 605	19:12	70	**1 Chronicles**	
23:5	648	19:14	196, 911, 986	2:7	403
24:16	370	19:18	98, 196, 986	2:54–55	920
		19:19–20	914	3:10–16	214
1 Kings		20:11	92	15:15	93
2	53	21	246, 513	16:8–9	62
2:3	52–53	21:23–24	570	16:8–36	61
2:4	53–54	22	553	16:10–11	62
2:5	221	22:3	727	16:13	62, 449
2:10	319	22:13–28	584	16:22	601–2
2:27	57	22:17	222, 556	16:27–28	737

17:13	470, 473, 588, 590	6:19–22	773	5:12	364
19:11	737	9	739	5:12–13	710
22:10	588, 590	9–10	653, 666	5:13	367, 383
25:2	219	10:3	653, 656, 666–67	7	69
28:6	588, 590			7:12	580
28:20	472	**Nehemiah**		9:8	244, 580
29	736	1	739	9:13	580
29:10	588, 590	1:5	775	9:22	399
29:11	735–36	1:7	251	11:6–7	716
29:15	849	8	91	11:16	774
		8:14–18	773	13:13	433
2 Chronicles		8:15	56, 60	13:15–16	432
1:3	251	9	67, 723, 739	13:16	429–30, 433
4:13	93	9:6	820, 853	13:18	430, 433
6:9–10	320	9:10	319, 724	13:27	430, 433
6:36	545	9:13	68	15:8	733
6:42	601	9:14	251, 771	18:21	442, 445–46
7:8–10	62	9:20	655, 664	19:25	430
8:12–13	772	9:26	221	19:25–26	429, 433
9:1–2	229	9:30	623	22:29	709
11:15	678	10	653	26:12–13	580
18:16	222	10:29	251	27:2–5	628
20:7	503, 514	10:30	653, 667	27:21	774
21	513	10:30–33	656	28	710
23:18	52	10:31	772	31:33	73
24:9	251	10:33	653	32:6–9	628
24:20–22	229	10:35	52	38–41	581
25:4	52	10:37	52	38:8	321
29:26–28	821	13:2	534	38:8–11	580
29:30	219	13:22	771–72	38:12–41:34	580
30:5	772			39:30	713
31:3	52, 56	**Esther**		41:3	356
33	969	5:3	35	42:17	96
35–36	91	5:6	35		
35:12	52, 95	7:2	35	**Psalms**	
35:13	772	8:6	73	1–2	98
35:26	52			1:1	705, 826, 981
36:15–16	221	**Job**		1:2	826
36:19–21	224	1:1	443, 446	1:3	826, 991
36:21	57–58	1:6	553	1:3–6	980–81
37:21	59	1:7	527	1:4	826
		1:8	443, 446	1:5	96, 826
Ezra		1:21	321	2	155, 246, 590, 729, 734, 737
1	72	2:3	443	2:1–2	317, 324, 329, 333–34, 560, 729, 847
3:1–6	773	3:8	580		
3:2	52	3:16	774	2:1–3	98
3:12	68	5:9	773	2:2	608, 610
6:18	653, 667				

INDEX OF SCRIPTURE AND OTHER ANCIENT SOURCES

2:6–7	991	14	845	22:9	223, 838, 848
2:7	27, 213, 240, 242, 246,	14:1–3	399	22:10–16	848
	253, 258, 317, 330, 333,	14:2	515	22:11	321
	470–71, 473, 475–77,	14:2–3	842, 844, 848,	22:14	223, 525, 527, 848
	482, 492, 560, 608,		850	22:15–18	848
	610, 637, 832, 847, 943	14:4	740	22:16	981
2:7–12	847	15:3	705	22:17–19	848
2:8–9	560–61, 847	15:8–11	909	22:18	241, 287–88, 305
2:9	608	15:10	848, 909	22:19	241, 838, 848
2:11–12	430, 434	16:8–11	317, 319–20, 332,	22:20	981
3	837		334, 848	22:22	155, 981
3:8	774	16:8–22	61	22:22–32	833, 839
4:4	415, 421	16:10	319, 333	22:23	832, 848
4:5	842, 847	16:23–33	61	22:24	838, 840
4:6	346	16:34–36	61	22:26	840
5	845	17:7	518	22:27	331
5:9	740	17:50	732	22:28–29	838–40
5:10	344, 842, 844, 847	18	845	22:30	840
6	739	18:5	353	22:32	840
6:2–3	730, 831, 883	18:22–24	399	23	299, 835, 1026
6:4	287, 847	18:31–32	633	23:1	244
6:9	222, 847	18:44	981	23:2	835, 848
7:8–9	831	18:50	733, 843–44, 848	24	580, 822, 845
7:18	732	19	580, 845	24:1	364, 843, 848, 986
8	69, 372, 580, 616, 845	19:1–7	848	24:3–5	991
8:3	222, 230–31, 847	19:3	355	25:5	631
8:4	616	19:3–6	848	26:6	210
8:5	65	19:5	842, 844, 848, 986	27:7	732
8:5–7	471, 475–76, 482, 831,	20:10	516, 518	27:12	221, 242, 838, 848
	847	21	935	29:13	732
8:6	10, 616	21:1–2	81	31:1–2	346
8:6–9	65	21:2	288	31:2	346
8:7	364, 372, 415, 417–18,	21:8–9	257	31:6	848
	430, 436, 841, 843,	21:19	935	32	739, 845
	845, 848	21:23	471, 476, 482	32:1–2	842, 849, 986
8:8	581	22	81, 221, 236, 238–39, 257,	32:4	343
8:24	581		288, 730, 832–33, 837,	32:6	448
9:9	565		839–40, 848	33:3	736
10	845	22:1	730, 913	33:9	525–26
10:7	740, 842, 844, 848	22:1–22	833	33:19	432
11:17–20	633	22:2	81n2, 222, 241, 257,	34:3	726
12:1	799		831, 838, 848	34:9	528, 834, 849
13	98	22:5	838	34:12	981
13:1–3	344	22:5–7	848	34:12–18	849
13:2	346	22:7	244	34:13–17	525, 527, 849
13:3	343	22:7–8	838, 848	34:16	849
13:7	355	22:8	242	34:18	732

34:19	287, 295, 883	43:22	350	68	236, 749
34:20	205, 823	44	845	68:5	287, 294, 588
34:21	821, 849, 935	44:2–3	842	68:10	286, 294, 309, 357
35:2	344	44:3	724	68:17	411
35:9	726	44:7–8	470, 476, 482	68:18	415, 986
35:11	242, 838, 849	44:23	849	68:19	831, 841, 850
35:11–12	221	45:1–18	849	68:21	242
35:19	299, 849–50	45:7–8	832, 849	68:22	287, 290, 935
36	845	45:7–13	849	68:23–24	355
36:1	740, 986	45:11–12	849	68:29	432
36:2	842, 844, 849	46:6	445	69	238–39, 730, 835, 837, 845
36:24–28	633	47:7	450		
37:9	991	48	822	69:1	837
37:11	849	48:3	222	69:4	299
37:29	65	49:2	355	69:5	830, 835, 850
37:32	221	49:8	242	69:9	294, 298
38	739	50	955	69:10	843, 845, 850
38:8–11	835	50:6	343	69:15	256
38:12	838, 849	51	632, 634, 739, 837, 845	69:18	837
38:14–15	838			69:21	305
39:7	98	51:1–2	740	69:22	221, 242, 837–38, 850
39:13	525–26, 849	51:3–19	850		
40	833	51:4	740	69:23–24	842, 844–45, 850
40:3	736	51:6	842, 850	69:26	225, 317–18, 827, 850
40:6	146	51:10–12	632, 634		
40:7–9	472, 477, 482, 833, 849	51:11	732	69:29	850
		51:12	579	69:30–36	837
40:9	399, 833	51:17	980	70:1	433
41	730	52:2–4	344	71:6	321
41:2	589	53	845	72:2	565
41:3	733	53:3–4	842, 848, 850	72:10–11	228
41:6	732	53:8	732	73:13	210
41:9	287	54	837	74	580
41:10	242, 827, 830, 835–36, 838, 849	55:23	525, 527, 850	75:9	850
		56–57	837	76:3	489
41:12	732	56:10	732	77:8	434–35
42–43	236, 730	56:14	849	77:24	181–82, 286, 294, 818
42:2	981	58	774	78	818
42:4–5	732	59–60	837	78:2	219, 232, 828, 850
42:5	242, 256, 730	61:13	343	78:6	442, 445–46
42:6	222, 241, 730, 831, 838, 849	62	845	78:18	331
		62:13	222, 834, 842, 850	78:24	181–82, 286, 294, 818, 850
42:11	242, 256	63:1	305		
42:12	222, 241, 730, 838, 849	65:2	399	78:41	331
		67:6	517	78:56	331
43:5	222, 241–42, 256, 730, 838, 849	67:19	419–20, 426	78:70–72	296
		67:36	447–48	79:1–6	737

79:10–11	737	95:8–11	832	107:31	722
79:13	737	95:11	471, 473, 477, 832, 851	107:43	722, 836
80:8–9	243	96:1	736	107:136	722
81	822	96:1–13	61	109	173
81:6	287, 295	96:7	470	109:1	264, 414, 416–18, 471, 475–76, 482
82	822, 828	96:10	985, 991–92, 995		
82:1	831, 883	96:11	737	109:2	355
82:1–8	850	97:7	821, 832, 851	109:2–3	221
82:2	831	98:1	736	109:8	317, 334, 827–28, 852
82:2–4	774	100:5	722	109:25	838, 848
82:6	295, 298, 830, 850	101:26–28	471, 476, 482	109:81	318
86:3	849	101:27	98	110	236, 371–72, 489, 492, 614, 817, 827, 832, 834, 841, 845
86:8–10	560, 565	102	238, 739		
86:9	562, 850	102:26–28	832, 851		
88:8	448	103:4	98, 470, 476, 482	110:1	154, 211, 214, 222, 241–42, 254, 257, 317, 320, 325, 333–34, 371, 411–12, 415, 607, 614, 616, 838, 841, 842–45, 852, 982
88:23	447–48	103:17	851		
89:3–4	449	103:13	588, 591		
89:4	537	104	580, 832		
89:4–5	320	104:4	851		
89:9	835	104:24	711		
89:13	724	105	67, 818	110:1–4	852
89:21	317, 329, 850	105:1–2	62	110:1–7	852
89:26	588	105:1–15	61	110:4	155, 471, 473–74, 477, 482, 488, 492–93, 614, 852, 901
89:26–27	590	105:3–4	62		
89:27	411	105:5	62		
89:27–28	213	105:6	62, 391, 449	111:2	562
89:28	560	105:9–11	68	112	845
89:51	525, 527	105:10	68	112:7–8	506
89:51–52	846	105:15	602	112:9	364, 843, 852
89:52	603–4	105:42	68	113–118	829, 852
90:4	541, 746, 850	106	67, 818, 845	114	67
90:11–12	264, 781	106:1	61	114:1	382
91:11–12	851	106:8–12	835	114:4	852
92	823	106:14	331, 369, 992	115:1	379
93	823	106:47–48	61	115:2	343
93:1	443, 445	107	738–39, 835	116	845
93:11	367	107:1	722, 835	116:10	364, 843, 845, 852
94	822, 845	107:3	851	116:11	842, 845, 852
94:7–11	181–82	107:4–9	835	117	845
94:11	182–83, 364, 843, 845, 851	107:8	722	117:1	733, 843–44, 852
		107:9	851	117:6	472, 477, 482, 786
94:14	821, 842, 845, 851	107:10	217	117:22	264
95	482, 833	107:15	722	117:26	287, 295, 909
95:7–8	471, 473, 477, 851	107:17–22	835	118	236, 258, 333, 786
95:7–11	150, 154–55, 471, 473, 476, 481, 492, 833, 851	107:21	722	118:6	852
		107:23–32	835, 851	118:14	250
		107:25	835	118:19	251

Index of Scripture and Other Ancient Sources

118:22	242, 244, 249–51, 317, 323–24, 333–34, 525–26, 529, 631, 803, 832, 852, 981	145:6	820	24:21	526
		145:9	517	24:22	287
		145:17	562	25:21	710
		145:21	399	25:21–22	356
118:22–23	222–23, 241, 323, 617, 852	146:6	317, 323, 728, 832, 853	26:11	537–38
		148	580	27:1	708
118:24	981	149	580	28:5	331
118:25–26	240, 253, 832, 852	149:1	736	28:13	545
118:26	222, 831	151	34, 98	31:17	526
119	143	151:6	98	33:34	709
119:1	399				
119:20	981	**Proverbs**		**Ecclesiastes**	
121:2	324	1–9	703, 705	1:2	35
124:8	324	1:16	740, 844	2:14	545
126:1	444	1:17	980	5:1–6	687
130	739	1:20–21	300	5:7	411
130:4	545–46, 551	1:20–33	300	8:2	687
130:5–6	730	1:29–31	300		
132:11	320, 852	2:3–6	411	**Song of Songs**	
132:22	333	3:11	710	1:6	992
134	821	3:11–12	472, 477, 481, 590		
134:3	324	3:12	588	**Isaiah**	
134:14	472, 820	3:19	711	1	954–55, 957
135	67, 818	3:25	526–27	1–5	807
135:4	68	3:34	509–10, 519, 525, 527	1–12	799
135:9	724	7	705	1–33	796
135:14	852	8	119, 733	1–39	747
136	67, 823	8:2–31	710	1:1	556, 795
136:11–12	771–72	8:15	708	1:2	981
136:25	399	8:22	580	1:4	796
137:3–4	992	8:22–23	715	1:9	352, 795, 801–2, 986
138:3	442	8:22–27	712	1:9–11	802
139:4	344	8:22–31	300, 411, 580	1:10	981
139:5	319	8:30	581	1:11–13	980
139:7	712	8:32–36	300	1:13	959, 982
139:8	214	9:3	715	1:13–14	773
139:14	562	10:12	525, 527, 709	1:17	515, 517, 957
140	845	10:19	708	1:23	515, 517, 957
140:3	740	11:2	708	1:24	563, 796
140:4	842, 844, 853	11:31	525, 527, 746	2	61, 448, 966, 973
142:2	344	13:2	432	2:1	556
143	739, 845	14:24	708	2:2–5	228
143:2	399, 842, 846, 853	17:3	442, 526	2:3	992
143:8	399	17:27	708	2:5	545
143:10	631	20:9	545	2:10	446, 448
144:9	736	24:12	222, 343, 710, 834, 842, 850	2:10–12	744
144:18	432				

2:19	446, 448	8:12–13	525, 527	13:10	222, 241, 255, 760, 805, 807
2:21	446, 448	8:14	352–53, 525–26, 615, 801, 803–4, 808	13:20	805
2:60	228	8:16	861	13:21–22	805
3:9–10	981	8:17	471	14:3–23	799
3:11	343	8:17–18	155, 476, 482	14:11	222, 799
4:4	634	8:18	471	14:13	222, 799
4:5	579	8:23–9:1	216, 228, 231, 804	14:15	222, 799
5	247, 798	9	970	14:28	796
5:1–2	222	9:1	217, 365, 727	15:1	796
5:1–4	244	9:1–2	146	16:1–2	982
5:1–7	253, 363, 617, 802	9:2	451	16:5	295
5:2	617	9:6	804	17:1	796
5:7	798	10–11	798	17:12	796
5:8	796	10:1	796	18:1	796
5:9	518	10:2	957	18:4	796
5:11	796	10:3	525–26	19:1	796
5:20	451, 796	10:5	796	19:18–20	89
5:21	796, 980	10:22–23	352, 801	19:24–25	89
5:22	796	10:33–11:5	798	21:1	796
6	290, 564, 736, 798, 801	10:33–11:16	798	21:3	450
6–33	807	10:34–11:1	799	21:9	805
6:1	303, 556, 795	11	801, 804	21:11	796
6:1–3	809	11:1	216, 231, 317, 565, 795, 798, 804	21:13	796
6:1–6	803			22	372
6:1–13	303	11:1–4	808	22:1	796
6:2–3	802	11:1–16	747	22:13	364, 372, 384, 795, 799
6:3	561, 565, 736, 798, 802	11:2	411, 525, 572, 606, 628, 798	22:22	572, 910
6:9	211, 803	11:2–4	605	23–24	558
6:9–10	219, 222, 230, 240, 242, 247, 249, 258, 266, 271, 317, 332–34, 795, 803, 809	11:3	606	23:1	796
		11:3–4	295	23:1–18	805
		11:4	447, 449, 565, 572, 608, 798–800, 804, 809	23:17	805
				24–27	805
6:10	287, 298, 303, 552, 803	11:6–10	799	24:16	131
7	803, 970	11:9	411	24:17	148
7:1	795	11:10	565, 606, 612, 733	25:6–8	228
7:4	89	11:11–16	749	25:8	364, 373, 380, 805
7:9	993	12	994	25:18	812
7:10	803	12:2	471	26	806
7:14	90, 147, 215–16, 232, 267, 795, 803, 947, 985, 989	13	738, 966, 973	26:17	450
		13–23	805	26:19	217, 806–7
		13–27	806, 813	26:20	472, 481
		13–33	804, 806	26:21	131
7:17	154	13:1	796	27:9	355, 661, 801, 811
8:8	803	13:6	450, 966–67	28–33	806
8:11	796, 798	13:9	450, 805	28:1	796

Index of Scripture and Other Ancient Sources

28:7	382	35:10	807	40:28	68
28:11	809	36:1	795	41–55	813
28:11–12	364, 381–82	37:6	796	41:1	796
28:16	156, 352–53, 525–26, 529, 615, 801–4, 806, 808, 981	37:16	820, 853	41:4	803
		37:21	796	41:8	391, 503, 514, 800
		37:30	799	41:8–9	506, 734
28:22	352	37:33	796	41:8–10	752
29:1	796	38:1	795–96	41:9	808
29:3	949	38:5	796	41:10	209
29:10	354–55, 801, 806	39:1–4	748	41:14	252
29:11	861	39:5	796	41:26	796
29:13	211, 219, 222, 240, 248, 411–13, 939–40, 986	39:6	748	41:27	748
		39:7	748	42	246, 637
		39:8	748	42–61	801
29:14	364, 367, 806, 986	40	744, 748, 753	42:1	213, 240, 242, 246, 253, 258, 449, 506, 637, 734, 736, 800, 808, 943
29:15	796	40–53	238		
29:16	806	40–55	72, 238–39, 252, 630, 727, 747, 749		
29:18	807				
29:18–19	217	40–66	47, 61, 66–68, 257, 747	42:1–4	146, 218–19, 221, 228, 231–32, 747, 807–8
29:22	796	40:1	748	42:3	218
30:1	796	40:1–2	732, 749, 807	42:4	808
30:6	796	40:1–5	752, 799–800	42:6	430, 435, 630
30:20–21	443, 445	40:3	58, 148, 156, 240, 245–46, 249, 258, 269–70, 279, 286, 288, 293, 302, 570, 727, 752, 754, 795, 799, 807, 981	42:6–7	982
31:1	796			42:7	217
31:4	796			42:9	748
31:8	799			42:10	736
31:21	807			42:10–13	257
32:7	799			42:15–16	749
32:9–20	636	40:3–5	264, 268–69, 293, 748–50, 751, 753–55, 800, 807	42:16	242, 249, 451
33:1	796			42:18	796
33:13	981			42:19	734
33:16–18	982	40:4	269, 751, 761	42:22	243
33:19	382	40:4–8	754	43:1	404, 724, 796, 808
34–35	807	40:5	269–71, 517, 727, 751	43:1–7	752
34–48	796	40:6	506, 525	43:3	752
34–66	796	40:6–7	515, 517	43:4–7	748
34:4	222, 241, 255, 760, 807	40:6–8	525–26	43:6	378
		40:6–9	528	43:10	800
34:8–15	807	40:8	545	43:14	252, 748, 796
34:10	807	40:8–9	525	43:14–21	570
34:11–15	807	40:10	243, 246	43:16	796
34:13	805	40:10–11	748	43:16–17	748
35	807	40:11	797	43:19	569, 748–49
35:5	795	40:12	982, 992	43:20	449
35:5–6	156, 217, 799	40:13	356, 364, 367, 733, 801	43:20–21	808
35:5–7	249	40:23	245	43:21	525–26, 529
35:8	449				

43:22	808	49:3	403, 506, 800, 808	52:7–10	748
43:25	243, 247	49:4	430, 433, 442, 444, 809	52:10	257, 451, 727, 809
44:1	734, 796, 800			52:10–15	809
44:1–5	636	49:6	330, 333, 430, 435, 630, 727, 734, 800, 808–9, 982	52:11	364, 375, 377
44:2	734, 796, 800			52:12	253, 256
44:3	636			52:13	251, 253, 257, 334, 434, 734, 800, 837, 861
44:6	803	49:6–7	257, 982		
44:8	796	49:6–9	994		
44:21	734, 748	49:7	752, 796	52:13–53:12	221, 321, 430, 434, 734, 747, 810, 839
44:22	253	49:8	257, 364, 384, 403, 796		
44:23	253, 737			52:15	631, 986
44:24	252	49:9–12	749	52:15–53:1	986
44:26	734, 748	49:13	727, 737	53	242, 251–52, 322, 324, 358, 526, 528, 810
44:28	242, 317, 329, 748	49:13–17	752, 800		
45:1	601–2, 796, 982	49:18	357, 795	53:1	239, 287, 298, 795, 800–801, 803, 809, 812, 986
45:2–3	982	49:24	242		
45:3	411, 795	49:24–25	243		
45:4	449, 734	49:25	796	53:2	434
45:7	584, 1002	49:26	748	53:3	239, 244, 257
45:9	796	50	238, 251	53:4	217, 231, 256, 525, 527–28, 810
45:10	796	50:1	796		
45:11	588, 796	50:4	242, 251	53:4–6	239
45:12	588	50:4–9	747	53:5	525, 527–28, 980
45:14	796	50:6	221, 242, 250, 257	53:6	242, 254, 256, 525, 810
45:16–17	433	50:6–9	981		
45:18	796	50:7	981	53:7	221, 242, 257, 616, 839, 980
45:18–26	429–30	50:7–9	257		
45:21–22	433	50:10	251, 734, 849	53:7–8	239, 282, 317, 321, 328, 333–34, 810
45:22–24	257	51:1	796		
45:23	357, 429–33, 437	51:3	748	53:9	525–26, 528, 545, 810
45:24	431	51:5	257	53:10	241, 252, 256
46:13	630, 748	51:9–11	835	53:10–12	242, 244, 252, 257
47	558, 570	51:10	253	53:11	321–22, 434
47:1–15	748	51:11	748	53:11–12	221, 256
48:1	796	51:17	256, 810	53:12	239, 242–44, 250, 252–54, 434, 537–38, 810, 839
48:1–9	799–800	51:21–52:2	748		
48:12	803	51:22	730		
48:14	748	51:22–23	752	54	173, 239
48:17	796	52	809	54–66	238–39
48:20	257	52–53	238–39	54:1	175, 390, 396–97, 810, 947, 986
48:21	748	52:1–2	810		
49	800, 808–9	52:1–3	752, 800	54:1–3	810
49–66	796, 800	52:3	506, 525–26, 796	54:4–10	752, 800
49:1	403–4, 796, 808	52:4–6	748	54:5–7	810
49:1–6	505, 747, 800	52:5	986	54:6	250
49:2	564–65, 800, 804, 809	52:7	257, 353, 416, 419, 424, 799–801, 809	54:11–12	397, 797, 810

Index of Scripture and Other Ancient Sources

54:13	286, 289, 294, 443, 445, 795	62:10	245	66:22	540, 569, 812
55:1–5	68	62:11	217, 232	66:24	240, 256
55:3	27, 317, 322, 330, 334, 810	62:12	253		
		63	638, 649	**Jeremiah**	
56–66	570, 747, 812	63:1–6	566	1:1–3	270
56:1	796	63:7–14	639–40, 642	1:5	321, 403
56:4	796	63:7–64:11	650	1:6	9
56:7	222, 241–42, 253, 294, 684, 811	63:8	67	2:12–13	982
		63:9	253, 638	2:13	941
57:3–4	447, 449	63:9–14	638–39	2:30	221
57:4	287	63:10	655, 664	3	65
57:14	245	63:11	655, 664	3:1	64
57:19	89, 415, 419	63:12	724	3:1–5	64, 75
58	955, 957, 963	63:14	638–39, 644, 664	3:4–5	588
58:4–10	980	63:16	588–89, 640	3:7–8	588
58:6	264, 273, 324, 637, 726, 811, 957–58, 980	63:19	246, 650, 655	3:19	589
		64:1	242	4:3–4	981
58:8	958	64:2	650, 655	4:10	91
58:10	451	64:3	365, 631	5:9	356
58:13	155	64:3–6	655, 657, 665	5:16	365
59:2–21	399	64:8	588–89	5:21	240, 242, 249, 258
59:7–8	344, 740, 844, 986	65	811–12	5:24	516, 518
59:8	727	65:1–2	353–54, 801, 812, 986	5:25	651
59:9–10	936–37	65:1–5	812	5:28	957
59:10	242, 249	65:2	982–83	6–7	955, 962
59:15–21	659	65:6–7	812	6:16	222, 231
59:17	416, 424, 443, 446	65:8	796	6:24	450
59:20	654, 811	65:9	449	7	954–57
59:20–21	355, 655, 661, 801	65:13	254	7:2–3	981
59:21	655, 657, 659, 661–62, 665	65:16	343, 365, 631	7:6	221, 517, 957
		65:17	537–38, 540, 569	7:11	222, 225, 241–42, 253, 294, 684, 810
60:1	727	65:17–18	89		
60:1–2	68	65:18	579	7:22–23	956, 980–81, 984
60:3–11	569	65:23	430, 442, 444	7:25	723
60:6	228	66	448	8:23	430, 436
60:21	65	66:1	222, 324, 796, 982	9	368
61	811	66:1–2	327, 795	9:1	430, 436
61–66	238	66:4	446, 448	9:22–23	364, 367–68
61:1	156, 217, 795, 799, 811	66:5	447–48	9:25	981
61:1–2	264, 272–73, 726, 811, 982	66:6	446, 448	10:6–7	565
		66:7	450	10:7	91, 562
61:1–4	637	66:10–11	438	10:25	442, 445–46, 724
61:4	811	66:12	796	11:19	985
61:7	811	66:13	447	11:20	97, 442, 444
62–64	812	66:15	446, 448	12:3	442, 506, 518
62:8	724	66:18	228	13:16	451
		66:18–21	89	13:21	450

14:13	91	39:41	343	22:7	515, 517, 957
14:19	724	44:4	723	22:26	677
15:7	505, 508	46:10	450	23	568
15:11	728	49:11	209	23:45	518
17:19	442	50–51	558	26–27	558
18:1–2	224	50:6	222	26–28	568
19	224			26:21	560
19:1–13	224	**Lamentations**		27:30	560
19:4	221, 224	2:15	838	28:2	447
19:11	224	3:64	343	29	568
21:12	295	4:13	225	29:3	569
22:3	515, 517	4:20	601	30:3	450
22:24	357			32	568
23:1–6	223	**Ezekiel**		33:24	68
23:5	216, 287, 295, 605, 608, 798	1	568, 798	34	223
		1–3	964	34:4	222
23:5–6	223	1:1–28	564	34:5–6	242
23:7–8	71	1:10	564	34:16	222
25:12	724	1:24	564	34:23	223
25:30	131	1:26–28	736	34:25	256
27:6	222	2	568	36–39	91
29:10	724	3:3	560–61, 567	36:17	724
30–31	479	3:12	624	36:23	449
31:2	479–80, 483, 485	3:14	624	36:26	725
31:9	588–89	5–7	568	36:27	443
31:10	589	5:11	357	37	738
31:15	231–32, 732	6:11	568	37:1–14	959
31:22	579	7:2–3	568	37:3	560
31:31	75, 256	7:8	724	37:5	567, 572
31:31–34	154, 156, 471–73, 477, 479–81, 649–50, 660, 665	7:15	568	37:7	221
		9–10	568	37:10	560, 567, 572
		9:8	724	37:12–13	221
31:32	91	9:11	564	37:14	443, 445
31:33	655	11:5	624	37:24	223
31:34	443, 445, 651, 655, 657	11:9–20	634	37:26	256, 322
		11:19	725, 981	37:27	155, 376
31:35	231	11:20	567	38–39	568
32	224	12:2	240, 242, 258	38–48	568
32:4	546	12:2–5	249	39:17–20	568
32:36–41	651	12:25	568	39:17–29	636
33:15	216, 608, 798	13:5	450	40–48	568
33:21–22	656	14:3–11	568	40:1–42:20	569
33:22	611, 652, 656	16	568	43:2	560–61, 567, 572
33:26	648	16:38	518	44:24	295
35:15	723	20:33–38	377	47:1–2	745
38:32	91	20:34	364, 375, 377	47:1–12	982
39:17	91	20:41	432	47:7	745

Index of Scripture and Other Ancient Sources

47:12	572, 745	6:21–22	871	8:23	442, 444
47:13	505, 944	6:23	870	8:23–25	861
47:13–23	507	6:25	737	8:26	861
		6:26–27	735	9	60, 724–25, 739, 866, 989
Daniel		6:28	867	9:2	58
1	865	7	116, 567–68, 607–8, 613,	9:4	722
1–5	867		616, 744, 756–58,	9:6	512, 516, 723
1–6	866, 871		760, 866–67, 874–75,	9:8	728
1:12–14	567		964	9:10	723
2	411, 868–69, 872	7–12	867, 871, 876–77	9:13	724, 740
2–4	567	7:1–8	567	9:14	723
2:4	222	7:2	874	9:14–19	143, 652
2:4–7	149	7:2–14	11	9:15	728
2:8	411	7:3	607	9:17	728
2:9	222	7:7	608, 867, 872	9:19	728
2:24–45	756	7:7–8	980	9:21	723
2:27	866	7:8	861	9:24	59, 861
2:28	222	7:9	564–65, 607, 613	9:24–27	861
2:28–29	566	7:9–10	736	9:25	800
2:32–33	868	7:9–14	798	9:25–26	68, 601
2:35	869	7:10	567	9:27	211, 244, 254, 805,
2:45	869	7:11	872		873
3	871, 873	7:12–14	605	10	567, 869
3:4	737	7:13	97, 222, 229, 241–42,	10:5–6	564
3:6	222, 564		244, 255, 257, 443,	10:6	565
3:7	737		445, 558, 561, 564–65,	10:14	45, 552
3:29	737		607–8, 613–14, 616,	10:20–21	869
3:32–33	861		756, 758–61, 832, 838,	10:21	872
3:38–40	861		873	11	869
3:49–50	870	7:13–14	222, 247, 249, 252,	11:21–45	861
4	866		567, 737	11:30	869
4:2–3	724, 735	7:14	222, 735, 874	11:31	211, 244, 254, 873
4:4	866	7:15	229	11:32	865
4:6–9	149	7:15–27	567	11:32–33	238
4:14	242	7:16	149	11:33	861
4:19	149	7:20–22	861	11:34	869
4:34	736	7:21	872	11:36–39	447, 449
4:34–35	735	7:22	363	11:40	545, 552
5:7	866	7:24	980	11:40–12:3	869
5:11–12	629	7:25	872	11:41	869
5:12–16	149	7:35	567	12	567, 869
5:19	737	8	567, 872	12:1	242, 872
5:26	149	8:9–14	861	12:1–2	238
5:31	867	8:10	872	12:2	41, 806
6:7–9	1044	8:16–18	229	12:3	430, 435–36
6:10	723	8:17–19	552	12:4	566, 861
6:16–19	1044	8:19	545	12:7	567

12:10	865
12:11	211, 241, 244, 254, 861, 873
13	964–66
14	871
14:38	870

Hosea

1:1	270
1:6	526, 529
1:9	526, 529
1:10	802
2:1	352
2:22	343
2:23	802
2:25	352
3:1	515, 518
4:2	648
5:8	148
6:2	242, 250–51
6:3	516, 518
6:6	155, 212, 222, 227, 685
6:7	73
9:7	624
10:8	561
11	215
11:1	97, 215, 219, 230–31
11:1–5	85
12:6	89
13:14	364, 373, 384

Joel

1–2	569, 774
1:15	450, 743–44, 967
2	963, 966, 973
2:1	450, 967
2:10–11	255
2:11	450
2:31	450
2:32	809
3	319, 636
3:1	636
3:1–4	635, 641
3:1–5	317, 319, 321, 325, 334
3:2	97
3:3	319, 331
3:4	356
3:5	55, 321, 333, 353
3:14	450
3:18	286, 295

Amos

1:6	563
2:12	648
3:13	561–62, 565
4:11	67
4:13	89, 562
5	959, 966
5:7–20	506
5:8	451
5:18	450
5:18–20	744
5:20	450–51
5:25	154
5:25–27	327
5:26–27	148
6:9–10	317
6:12	432
8:5	773
8:10	992
9:1	556
9:11	145, 151, 154, 605, 883
9:11–12	317, 331–32, 334

Obadiah

1	556, 563
15	450

Jonah

1–2	835
1:5–16	247
2:1	222
3	229
4:2	722
4:3	72, 728
4:6	3

Micah

1:1	270
1:21	947
2:1	774
2:3	563
2:10–11	799
3:1–8	624
3:6	451
4	61
4:1–5	228
4:9	450
4:10	727
5:1	220, 232, 274
5:2	287, 295
5:3	605
6:8	227
7:6	222, 230, 242
7:8	451
7:18–20	545

Nahum

1:1	556
1:2	356
1:7	589

Habakkuk

1:1	556
1:5	317, 330, 334
1:12	147
1:17	145
2:3	537–38
2:3–4	97, 472, 481
2:4	151, 156, 341, 358, 394, 399–400, 475, 478, 993
2:5–10	149
2:6	147
2:8	148
2:15	145
2:16	145
2:20	147
3:13	601

Zephaniah

1	959, 966, 973
1:7	450
1:14	450
1:14–16	744
1:14–18	967
3:15	287, 295
3:19	982

Index of Scripture and Other Ancient Sources

Haggai

1:3	209
2:4	209
2:4–5	994
2:6	472, 477, 481

Zechariah

1:12	58
2:10	242
3:1	553
3:1–5	536
3:2	531, 536
3:8	216, 798
4:2	564
4:2–3	736
6:12	216
7	963
7–8	954–55, 957, 962
7:9	295
7:9–10	957
7:12	33, 623
8:16	295, 415, 421
8:17	226, 980
9:9	217, 231–32, 287
9:11	242
10:2	242
10:10	287
11:12	229
11:13	224, 232, 636
12	757–60
12:1	757
12:3	757
12:4–5	757
12:6	757
12:7	757
12:8	757
12:9–13:1	238
12:10	287, 306, 558, 561, 636, 756–61
12:11–14	757
12:14	561
13	239, 258
13:7	148, 156, 220, 222, 241, 256, 258, 981
13:9	752
14	959
14:4	244
14:4–5	221
14:5	442, 444–45, 447
14:8	286, 295, 941
14:9	772
14:16–19	773

Malachi

1:2–3	352, 992
1:6	588, 771
1:14	669
2:1	670
2:4–9	670
2:10	588–89
3	513, 959
3:1	58, 222, 240, 245–46, 249, 258, 264, 270, 727, 749, 754, 807
3:4–6	727
3:5	518, 670, 957
3:15	331
3:16	670
3:18	774
3:22–23	279
3:22–24	33, 911–13
4:4	251
4:5	450
4:5–6	244, 246
4:6	242

Deuterocanonical Books

Tobit

1:6	772
1:17	957–58
3:2	723
3:14	728
4:3	771
4:15	398
13:4	590, 592

Judith

5	898
5:5–21	886
5:7–8	886, 897
5:20	728
5:24	728
7:11	728
8:1	910
8:25–27	391
9:12	728
9:14	589
11:10	728
11:16–17	886
11:19	222
11:23	903
14:19	847
16:1	736
16:13	736
16:17	516, 518

Wisdom of Solomon

1:6	432
1:7–8	630
1:14	573
1:14–16	118
1:16	120
2	223
2:10–20	221
2:12	702, 706
2:13	506
2:17–22	992
2:18	591, 848
2:23	120
2:24	118
3:1–9	238
3:5–6	528
3:16	445
4:7–5:16	223
5:14	826
5:17–20	425
6–9	430, 436
6:1–21	436
6:4	702, 706
6:12–11:1	710
6:16	436
6:22	715
7:1	321
7:7	630
7:7–9	436
7:10	715
7:22	581
7:24	712

7:24–26	702	4:4–6	713	44:1	894
7:25–26	715	4:10	708	44:18	96
7:26	712	4:12	716	44:19–20	391, 888, 897, 900
7:29	715	6:18–27	436	44:20	391, 898
8:4	716	6:27–28	436	44:23	505, 508
8:4–6	711	6:37	701	45:1	897, 901, 903
8:17–21	436	7:17	848	45:1–3	894
8:19	436	7:27	771	45:3	913
9:2–3	584	10:12	591	45:4	907
9:9–10	716	14:1	775	45:5	894, 913
9:10	436, 715	14:7	851	45:11	505, 507
9:16–17	716	15:1	701	45:15	897, 902
9:16–18	716	15:2	436	47:8	591
9:17	436, 630	15:19	535	48:1–11	513
10	99	16:7–10	533	48:5	913
10–19	120	16:12	343	48:7	913
10:1–11:1	889	17:12–13	402	48:9	914
10:3	534	22–26	165	48:21	370
10:5	889, 897–98, 900	23:1	591	48:24	749
10:6	539, 889	23:4	591	49:6–7	224
10:7	534	23:9	687	49:15	891
10:15–11:14	702	24	733	50:1–24	823
11–19	570	24:1–9	300, 712	50:18	823
11:10	590	24:7–12	715	51:1	732
13:1	92	24:8	701, 715	51:12	732
15:1	343	24:9	715	51:13–30	430, 436
16:6	702, 706	24:23	402, 701	51:21	436
16:9	569, 573	25:24	457, 915, 917	51:23–26	714
16:20	850	28:7	402	51:23–30	436
17:1	733	32:13	591		
17:7	367	33:13	591	**Baruch**	
18:4	702	33:14–15	584	1:15–3:8	723
18:14	573	34:22	456	1:20	251, 739
18:14–16	566, 573	35:14–15	957	2:20	723
18:16	573	36	724, 729	2:24	723
18:25	370	36:1	728	2:28	251, 902
19:4	444	36:1–22	724	3:4	739
19:17	539	38:3	447	3:9	772
		38:6	447	3:9–4:4	710, 733
Sirach		38:6–8	724	3:23	915
1:1	173	38:24–39:3	173	3:29	711, 716
1:10	365	39:1–11	724	3:29–37	733
1:15	715	39:6	629	3:33	715
1:24–25	411	39:8	402, 629	3:37	715
2:15	775	43:24	851	4:1	716, 733
3:1–16	771	43:26	712	4:5	732
3:17–24	708	44–50	99, 702	4:5–5:9	749

4:12	397
4:21	732
4:27	732
4:30	732
4:31–35	749
4:37	751, 851
5:6–9	800
5:7	749–51, 800
5:8	751
5:9	749

1 Maccabees

1:33	883
1:52	391
1:60–62	391
2	863
2:31	883
2:52	391, 900
2:53	891
2:60	863
4:24	823
7:32	883
12:9	341
13:51	737
14:36	883

2 Maccabees

1:27	505, 508
2:13–14	31
2:13–15	828
6:14	442, 444
6:19	863
6:23	86, 903
7	238
7:23	584
7:28	582, 585
7:37–38	345
10:7	737
14:4	737
15:2	728
15:3–4	771–72
15:9	265, 342

1 Esdras

1:5	883
1:6	882
1:11	882, 902
5:5	883
5:48	882
5:49	902
7:6	882, 902
8:3	95, 882, 902
8:82	723
9:39	882, 902
9:45	95
9:48	506

3 Maccabees

2:1–20	728
2:2–3	728
2:4–7	533
2:21	590
5:7	590
6:3	391
6:6–7	863
6:32	823
7:6	590

2 Esdras

1:30	905
6:6–18	507
6:17	505
19:6	820

4 Maccabees

2:2	891
2:5	771
2:8	772
2:15–18	894
6:28–29	345
7:11	370
13:9	864
15:25	438
16:19–20	391
16:20	888
16:21–22	864
16:22	438
16:24	864
17:21–22	345
18:7–8	917
18:10	265, 342, 829
18:15	823, 831, 883
18:18–19	773

PSEUDEPIGRAPHA

Apocalypse of Abraham

1–8	391
1:4–9	887
1:7–9	897–98
2:4	887, 897–98
2:5	898
3:7	887
5	887
7:1–7	887
7:6–12	898
7:9–12	897
7:10	887
7:12	887
8:1–5	887, 898
17–19	798
18	564
27:7	391
31:4–8	391

Apocalypse of Daniel

1:23	915
2:11	915
14:11	828, 883

Apocalypse of Elijah

4:7–23	911
5:32–35	911

Apocalypse of Ezra

2:16	457

Apocalypse of Moses

7:2	946

Apocalypse of Peter

1–6	959
4	967
6	759
7–13	960–61
9	963

Apocalypse of Sedrach

14:4	828, 883

Apocalypse of Zephaniah

4:2	758
6:10	863
8	964, 966
9	964–66
9–12	965
13–16	966
17–18	966
18	967
19	966

Ascension of Isaiah

1–5	694, 968–70
1:6–7	969
3:9	969
3:13–5:1	968
4:21	828, 883
4:22	890
6–11	968–69
9	970
11	970
11:2	883
11:2–22	968

2 Baruch

4:1–7	745
4:3	799
14:18	584
17:2–3	349
36–40	799
36:7	868
40:1–3	607
48:8	851
48:42	349, 915
49:2	371
51:11	436
54:15	349, 922
54:19	922
56:5	349
57:1–2	888
57:13	391
70–74	799
73:2	217

1 Enoch

1–36	734
1:6	800
1:9	35, 115, 142, 530–31, 923
2:1–5:4	535
3:9–4:4	710
5:4	556
6–12	530–31, 533, 537
9:3	556
10:4–5	533
10:12	530, 533
10:14	533
12:4	530, 533
14	564
14:8–23	798
14:13	432
15:3	530, 533
17:1	851
25:4–5	750
39:6	800
39:12	798, 802
42	733
42:1–2	713
42:1–3	710, 715
42:2	716
45	758
45:3–4	758, 800
46	758
46:1	758, 869
46:3	411
46:3–4	758
46:4	869
46:6	799
47:12	745
48	809
48:10	606, 847
49	798
49:2	800
49:2–4	606
49:3–4	798
49:4	800
51:1	371
51:3	800
51:4	852
51:5	800
54:5	533
56:6	758
60:3	432
60:6	771
60:8	532
60:12–22	582
62:2	798
62:3–5	116
62:13–16	436, 430
62:14–16	371
69:6	915
80	531, 535
80:6	535
81:5	399, 853
82:6	535
85–90	126, 893, 897
89:16	893
89:22	893
89:23	893
89:29–35	126
89:56	980
89:65–72	868
89:66	980
89:72–90:1	868
90	893
90:2–5	868
90:6–19	868
90:13	893
90:14–42	893
90:20	758
90:31	911
90:33–36	745
91:1	636
91:11–17	126
91:16	540, 812
92–105	128
93:1–10	126
94–96	430
95:1	436
96:4–5	436
96:8	436
99:2	126, 128
104:2	430, 435–36
104:4	430, 436
104:6	430, 436
108:3	850

2 Enoch

12	129
22	798
33:1–2	541

Index of Scripture and Other Ancient Sources

42	116	13:37–38	799	7:20–39	539
49	117	13:37–40	607	10:23	131
50	117	14:1–9	897, 906	11	129, 131–32, 887
51	117	14:8	893	11–12	897–98
71–72	490–91, 901	14:44–46	95	11–23	513
		14:45–46	674	11:11	132
Ezekiel the Tragedian				11:12	132
1:36–38	893	**5 Ezra**		11:16–17	391
		1	956	12:1–15	887
4 Ezra		1–2	957	12:2–8	391
3:7	349	1:7	957	12:16–24	391, 887
3:13–14	899	1:8	957	12:17	887
3:13–15	888	1:24	957	12:20	887
3:21	349, 922	1:31	956	12:22–23	888
3:26	922	1:34	957	12:22–24	887
3:32	402	2	956–57	12:25–27	97
4:23	402	2:1	957	15:1	889
4:33	982	2:20–23	957	15:1–2	773
5:5	982	2:21	958	15:9–35	391
5:29	402	2:22	958	15:11–34	889
6:1–6	586	2:23	958	16:17–18	396
6:54	584	2:33	957	16:20–31	773, 889
7:32	608	2:44	957	17:15	900
7:37	608			17:15–18	888, 897–98
7:46	402	**Joseph and Aseneth**		17:15–18:16	536
7:109	911	4:8	890	17:17	900
7:116	922	8:9	851, 890	17:17–18	888
7:118	349, 922	12:1–2	585	18:16	897, 900
8:27	402			19:8	900
11–12	867–68	**Jubilees**		19:9	514
11–13	607, 734	1:20	556	19:15–31	890
11:35	872	1:20–21	634	19:18	592
11:37	607	1:22–25	634	19:21	890
11:39	608	1:24	592	19:29	590, 592
12:1	608	1:24–25	590	20:8	771
12:3	872	1:27	639, 888	22:1–9	773
12:11–12	867	1:27–29	892, 897, 906	22:10–23	890
12:31–32	606	1:29	540, 639	22:16–18	890
12:32	604, 607–8, 883	2:1–2	639	22:20	890
13	804	2:2	582–83	22:26–23:2	281
13:3	607–8, 869	2:14	584	23:1–3	890
13:10–11	799	2:26	771–72, 851	23:10	391
13:12	869	3:23	922	23:31	771
13:32	609	4:30	541	24:11	391
13:35–36	869	6:17–31	773	25:1–10	889
13:37	609, 869	7:20	771	25:5	890
				25:8	890

32:4–9	773	9:16	903	35:2	592
32:17	889	10:7	850	37:4	592
32:27–29	773	11:9–10	771	42	541
34:18–19	773	12:1	230, 374	61:5–10	550
35:12–13	771	12:2–3	370		
35:29	890	13:1	897, 902	**Lives of the**	
44:1–4	774	15:5	897	**Twelve Prophets**	
44:49	773	18:4	897	4:3–4	866
46:9	194	18:13	534	4:9	866
47–50	905	19	896–97	21	513
47:12	905	19:7	897		
48:4	800	19:10	896	**Odes of Solomon**	
48:6	800	19:16	896, 908	2	769
49:22	897, 902	20:2	896	2:35	97
		21:7	897, 902	9	101
Ladder of Jacob		23:5	391	9:11	850
7:35	851	23:9	896–97	11–14	101
		25:3	897		
Letter of Aristeas		25:5	897	**Prayer of Manasseh**	
9–11	83	26:13	365	10	850
10	86	28:2	541		
30	164	28:6	625	**Psalms of Solomon**	
39	88	30:1	897, 902	2:16	346
46–50	88	31–32	910, 915	2:25	867
47–50	164	31:9	625	2:34	346
160	772	32:8	896–97, 901, 903	6	730
228	771	35–36	910	6:6	365
301–311	83, 96	38:4	897	7:1	287, 849
307	164	39–40	910	8:17	749
		39:10–40:9	915	9:9	391
Liber antiquitatum bibli-		42–43	910	11	751
carum (Pseudo-Philo)		48:1	911	11:4	749–50
3:10	540	51–59	910	11:5	750–51
4:11	915	57:2	535	14:1–2	775
4:15	888	64–65	910	14:3	745
4:16	887			16:5	732
6–7	898	**Life of Adam and Eve**		17	798, 804, 809
6–8	513	3:3	457	17:4	320
6:1	888	9:2	917	17:8	346
6:4	391	10:2	917	17:21	604
6:11	888	11:1–3	916	17:21–25	217, 605
7:4	888	14:2	917	17:23–24	560, 608, 847
9–19	902	21:3	550	17:24	798, 800
9:7	896	25:1	917	17:29	798
9:8	896	25:3	917	17:31	228
9:10	625, 896	32:1–2	917	17:32	604–5
9:13	896	32:2	592	17:37	798
		33:2	946		

18:5	604	*Testament of Benjamin*		*Testament of Reuben*	
18:7	798	3:1	890	4:5–6	553
		4:1–7:2	584	4:8	891
Questions of Ezra		5:4	890	*Testament of Simeon*	
A35	828, 883	10:4	391	2:6	891
		10:6–8	371	4:4	890
Sibylline Oracles		*Testament of Dan*		5:1	890–91
1:42–45	457	1:4	890	*Testament of Solomon*	
1:148–98	539	1:5	891	22:6–8	852
1:280–81	539			23:1–4	852
2:187–89	911	*Testament of Gad*			
2:245	894, 897, 903	1:4	891	*Testament of Zebulun*	
3:324	867	1:5	891	3:4	882, 902
3:329	867	1:9	891	8:4	890
3:397	867	*Testament of Issachar*			
3:593–94	771	7:3	771	**Dead Sea Scrolls**	
3:616–17	431				
4:49–101	868	*Testament of Job*		**ALD (Aramaic Levi Document)**	
6:16	883	4:10	433	10:12–13	850
6:25	850	12:3	456	13:3	852
7:31	883	26:1	433		
8:217–50	1025	33:3	614	**CD**	
8:303	850, 936	39:12	583	**(Damascus Document)**	
		Testament of Joseph		I, 18	688
Susanna		1:2	890	II, 12	654
3	882, 902	6:5	553	II, 14–III, 2	153
7	903	18:4	891	II, 17–III, 13	533
46	871			III, 2	514, 889, 897, 900
62	863, 882, 902	*Testament of Judah*		III, 2–3	391, 898
		20:1	552	III, 4	882
Testaments of the Twelve Patriarchs		20:1–4	584	III, 10–20	156
		25:4	371	III, 13	653, 656
Testament of Abraham		*Testament of Levi*		IV, 13–19	148
8:9	916	2–5	798	IV, 19–V, 2	151
10:4–11	899	9:1–14	391	V, 1–6	908
10:13	391	13:9	890	V, 17–19	459
10:14	583	16:2	342	V, 21–VI, 1	342
11–14	899			VI, 3–7	151
14:6–8	886	*Testament of Moses*		VI, 3–11	148
14:14	886	8:2–4	866	VI, 18	771–72
				VII, 9–21	154
Testament of Adam		*Testament of Naphtali*		VII, 16	146, 883
3:5	915	3:4–5	533–34	VII, 19	882
4:3	828, 883	4:1	340	VII, 19–21	148
		5:8	340	VIII–X	249
Testament of Asher		8:6	97	IX–XVI	151
1:3–9	584				

INDEX OF SCRIPTURE AND OTHER ANCIENT SOURCES

IX, 2	398	XII, 12	850	I, 2–3	142
IX, 7–8	398	XII, 23	238	I, 3	265, 342
X, 14–19	155	XIII, 12–13	848	I, 21–26	652
X, 16–17	772	XIII, 20	851	I, 21–III, 12	634
XII, 23–XIII, 1	604	XIII, 22–41	836	II, 11–12	609
XIV, 19	604	XIII, 25–26	836, 849	II, 15	774, 787
XV, 1–8	687	XV, 5–6	238	III–IV	584
XV, 9	882, 902	XV, 25	848	III, 6–9	634
XVI, 1–3	34	XVI, 26–27	238	III, 13–IV, 26	584
XVI, 1–12	687	XVII, 35	591	III, 17–18	584
XVI, 6	885, 889, 897	XVIII, 27–28	826	III, 17–19	552
XIX, 5–13	148	XX, 14–16	629	V, 8	882, 902
XIX, 7–10	156			V, 21	344
XIX, 33–34	156	**1QM (War Scroll)**		V, 24–29	217
XX, 17	882	I, 1–2	869	VI, 6	826
XX, 21–22	771	I, 4	869	VI, 6–8	147
		VII, 6	869	VI, 18	344
1Q28B		X, 1–4	882, 902	VIII	807
(Rule of Benedictions)		X, 1–8	154	VIII, 5	798, 802
V, 20–29	798	X, 17	849	VIII, 7	156
V, 23–27	153	XI, 6	882	VIII, 7–8	804
		XI, 10	758	VIII, 11–12	149
1Q33 (War Scroll)		XI, 11–12	799	VIII, 13–15	148
See 1QM (War Scroll)		XIII, 6–7	869	VIII, 13–16	156
				VIII, 14	751, 799
1Q34		**1QpHab**		VIII, 15–16	342
(Liturgical Prayers)		**(Pesher Habakkuk)**		VIII, 16	623
II 3	584	V, 1	147	VIII, 22	882, 902
		V, 6	147	IX, 3–4	634
1QHᵃ		VI, 8–10	145	IX, 11	775
(Thanksgiving Psalm)		VII, 1–5	149, 527	IX, 19–20	752
II, 14	688	VII, 5–VIII, 3	400	IX, 19–21	751
III, 14–15	851	VII, 6–13	552	IX, 26–X, 7	730
IV, 11	850	VII, 8	149	X	723
V, 10–11	848	VII, 14–19	148	X, 10	774
V, 18	851	VIII, 1	151		
V, 23–24	849	VIII, 1–3	156	**4Q161 (Pesher Isaiah A)**	
VII, 38	848	VIII, 6–9	147	8–10 III, 1–25	798
VIII, 20	662	IX, 2–7	148	8–10 III, 20–21	798
VIII, 26–37	654	XI, 2–8	145		
VIII, 29–30	633	XI, 3–4	148	**4Q164 (Pesher Isaiah D)**	
VIII, 34	655, 657, 665	XII, 6–9	148	I, 1–5	797, 800
IX–XI	731	XII, 16–XIII, 3	147		
IX, 10–17	758			**4Q165 (Pesher Isaiah E)**	
X, 25–26	826	**1QS (Community Rule)**		1–2	797
XI, 15–16	851	I, 1–5	654, 656	2–3	797

Index of Scripture and Other Ancient Sources

4Q169 (Pesher Nahum)
3–4	688

4Q174 (Florilegium)
I, 1–2	529
I, 7–9	148
I, 10	898
I, 10–11	156
I, 10–12	148
I, 10–13	734
I, 11	798
I, 11–12	151
I, 12	146
I, 14	826
I, 15	865
I, 15–17	148
I, 16	865
I, 18–19	847
I, 19	148
I, 21	592
II, 3	865
IV, 2–5	148

4Q176 (4QTanḥumim)
I, 1–11	800
I, 4–9	799
I, 15–20	752
I, 20–II, 2	752
II, 3–11	752
II, 4–9	800
II, 8–11	800
II, 11–13	752
II, 20–III, 1	752
III, 2–4	752
III, 5–12	752

4Q177 (Catena A)
I, 1–4	799
I, 2–3	148
I, 2–5	799
I, 3	847
I, 6–7	799
I, 8	148
I, 8–9	148
II, 3–7	148
II, 9	148
II, 9–10	148
II, 11–13	148
III, 6	148
III, 13–14	148
Frags. 12–13	831

4Q185 (Sapiential Admonitions)
II, 8–11	706

4Q226 (Pseudo-Jubilees)
Frag. 7	900

4Q242 (Prayer of Nabonidus)
1–3 I, 5	866

4Q246 (Aramaic Apocalypse)
II, 1	592, 869
II, 5	869
II, 9	869

4Q252 (Peshar Genesis)
IV, 3–6	148
V, 2	898
V, 2–3	883
V, 2–4	608
V, 3	604

4Q271 (Self-Glorification Hymn)
4 II, 7	885

4Q285 (Sefer ha-Milḥamah)
5	798

4Q327 (The Calendar)
1 16	591

4Q374 (Exodus/Conquest Tradition)
2 II, 9	851

4Q378 (Apocryphon of Joshua)
I, 8	591

4Q379 (Apocryphon of Joshua b)
18 4	591

4Q381 (Non-Canonical Psalms B)
31 8	850

4Q392 (Works of God)
IX, 6	591

4Q393 (4Q Communal Confession)
1 II, 2–4	850
3 3–4	851

4Q397 (Miqsat Ma'ase ha-Torah)
IV, 9–10	142
IV, 10–11	825
IV, 15	342

4Q416 (Instruction)
III–IV	704

4Q418 (Instruction)
43–45 I, 9	826
86 1	591

4Q418b (Quotation from Psalm 107)
1 3	851

4Q423 (Instruction)
7 3	591

4Q427 (Hodayot)
II, 7–9	238

4Q429 (Hodayot)
1 II, 5	851

4Q432 (Hodayot)			**4Q525 (Beatitudes Scroll)**		**ANCIENT JEWISH WRITERS**
5 1–2	851	II, 1	155		
		II, 3–4	705–6		
4Q436 (Barkhi Nafshi)		II, 5–6	155	Philo	
I, 7	800				
		4QMMT (Halakhic Letter)		*De Abrahamo*	
4Q437 (Barkhi Nafshi)		13–15	552	1–6	172
I, 8–9	800	117	391	9	585
				60–88	391
4Q448 (Apocryphal Song and Prayer)		**11Q5 (The Great Psalms Scroll)**		61	341
				121	341
I, 2	591			157	341
		XVIII, 3–4	714	235	491
4Q460 (Narrative Work and Prayer)		XVIII, 7	882	273	514
		XVIII, 16	882	275–276	391
I, 5	591	XXI, 11–XXII, 1	825		
		XXIV, 7	853	*De cherubim*	
4Q464 (Exposition on the Patriarchs)		XXVII, 2–11	824	25	345
		XXVII, 3–11	32	27–29	630
III, 7	148	XXVII, 11	65, 148, 824	49	173, 590
				124	341
4Q502 (Ritual or Marriage)		**11Q11 (Apocryphal Psalms)**		*De confusione linguarum*	
39 3	591	VI, 5–6	715	39	173
		VI, 10–11	851	166	777
4Q504 (Words of the Luminaries)				*De congressu eruditionis gratia*	
		11Q13 (Melchizedek Document)			
III, 6–7	592			11–12	175
III, 10–11	739	II, 9–10	828, 883	34	341
III, 12–14	342	II, 9–12	831	90	341
VI, 12	902	II, 12	148	99	491
XVIII, 15–16	636	II, 15–16	800	147	171
		II, 17	148		
4Q505 (Words of the Luminaries)		II, 17–18	800	*De decalogo*	
		II, 23–24	800	8	341
122 1	902	II, 24	148	17.84	687
				37	341
4Q511 (Songs of the Sage)		**11Q14 (Sefer ha-Milhamah)**		51	590
		1 I	798	154	341
127 1	591				
		11Q19–21 (The Temple Scroll)		*De ebrietate*	
4Q521 (Messianic Apocalypse)				95–96	370
		XXIX, 7–8	155	208	341
II, 1–13	156	XLVIII, 7–10	151		
II, 5–8	637			*De fuga et invention*	
II, 7	799			100–101	345
II, 11–13	637			*De gigantibus*	
II, 12	799			23	630
				27	712

Index of Scripture and Other Ancient Sources

De migratione Abrahami	
6	713
44–45	514
86–93	688
91	585, 587
113	534
157	585
192	585

De mutatione nominum	
2–10	174
7	92
11	92
12–13	506
14	92
24	173
29	590
81–83	506
125	173
134–136	180
139	173
203	534

De opificio mundi	
74	590
76	590
77	341, 590
155–170	917

De plantatione	
59	773

De posteritate Caini	
26	784
38–39	534
158	341

De praemiis et poenis	
53–54	486
162–171	661

De somniis	
1.135	585
1.168–172	506
1.230–231	92
2.245	173
2.252	630

De specialibus legibus	
1–4	172
1.9	391
1.65	624
1.79	370
1.295	849
2.197	590
2.261	771
3.1	171
3.1–6	630
4.49	624
4.78	183

De virtutibus	
124	430, 438
212–216	391, 513

De vita contemplativa	
1	171
25	828
90	585

De vita Moises	
1.19–24	893
1.148	486
1.155–158	486–87
1.264–314	570
1.274	624, 630
1.277	625
2.1	172
2.25–44	165
2.27–44	86
2.37	165
2.40	165
2.58	539
2.69–70	908
2.70	374
2.95	345
2.97	345
2.161–166	370
2.191	630

Legum allegoriae	
1.31	177–79
1.43	712
1.65	775
2.54–56	486
2.59	506
3.79–82	491
3.105	773

Quaestiones et solutiones in Genesin	
2.43	175
3.9	624
4.97	712
33	457

Quis rerum divinarum heres sit	
106	341
159	341
166	345
199	711
265	624
286	341

Quod deterius potiori insidari soleat	
52	771
54	711
114	773
161	341

Quod Deus sit immutabilis	
77	850
87–90	180
182	851

Josephus

Against Apion	
1.1	26
1.37–40	674
1.37–41	95
1.37–42	30
1.37–43	24, 828
1.42–43	674
1.54	26
1.91	26
1.127	26
1.217	26
2.45	26, 341
2.174	26
2.175	829
2.178	829
2.190–219	189
2.206	771

Jewish Antiquities	
1–11	195

1.17	194	5.93	590	*Jewish Wars*		
1.20	590	5.213	194	1.61		320
1.26	341	5.257	194	1.68–69		37
1.52–62	549	5.276	194	3.352		26
1.61	534	5.318–337	38	4.184		693
1.74	539	6.162	191	4.193–208		688
1.82	26, 341	6.189	193	4.235		506
1.89–90	195	6.296	193	4.348		693
1.139	26, 341	7.243	489	4.355–357		688
1.154–157	391	7.367	821	4.381–382		693
1.154–256	513	7.369	192	4.388		693
1.156	887	7.380	590	4.459–464		939
1.157	193	7.392–94	320	5.556		535
1.162–164	195	8.109–119	148	6.438		491
1.180	491	8.337	193	7.426–429		89
1.183	489	9.20–28	513	*The Life*		
1.186–190	195	9.28	26	12		41
1.215–219	195	9.46	26	418		26
1.224	192	9.208	194			
1.227	193	9.214	194	**NEW TESTAMENT**		
1.230	590	9.242	192			
1.258	506	10.49	26	Matthew		
1.272	728	10.78	38	1		213
2.152	590	10.79–80	225	1:1	209, 213, 228, 804	
2.176	192	10.89–96	225	1:2–3		232
2.199	194	10.112–130	225	1:2–16		228
2.205–237	214	10.156–158	225	1:2–17		214
2.236	893	10.176–180	225	1:2–4:16		213
2.238–253	194	10.186–281	864	1:3–6		919
2.347	26, 194, 341	10.210	26	1:5		514
3	487	10.218	194	1:15–16		882
3.33–38	195	10.267	865	1:17–18		804
3.81	26	11.152	192	1:18–19		906
3.105	26	11.158	38	1:18–2:23		906
3.244–247	197	11.159–183	38	1:20		213
3.318	486	11.184–296	38	1:21	218, 803, 947	
3.320	486	11.337	864	1:22	211, 215, 220, 226	
4.40	728	12.113	26	1:22–23	216, 692	
4.46	728	12.322	864	1:23	90, 147, 149, 209, 218,	
4.62	590	13.167	26		232, 267, 803	
4.76–78	195	13.249	320	2	210, 215, 223,	
4.119	625	13.297	40		224–25, 233	
4.172–173	197	13.299	37	2–4		214
4.196	194	13.316–362	513	2:2	217, 228	
4.278	771	16.182	344	2:5		211
5.1–15	513	18.16	40	2:5–6		803
5.11–14	921	20.44–45	391	2:6	216, 220, 232, 947	
5.41	728					

Index of Scripture and Other Ancient Sources

2:9	217	5:17	74, 225, 227, 236, 265, 342	9:27	217
2:11	228			9:36	218, 222
2:12–20	152	5:17–20	692–93	10:1	678
2:13–16	906	5:17–48	692	10:6	218, 222
2:15	97, 149, 209, 211, 215, 219, 231, 692, 803, 947	5:18	264, 281	10:23	604, 611
		5:20	226, 693	10:29–32	593
		5:21	211, 226, 776	10:32–33	875
2:16	224	5:21–48	225, 675–76	10:35–36	222, 230
2:17	211, 692	5:23–24	88	11:2	217
2:17–18	223, 225, 803	5:27	211, 226, 776	11:2–6	156
2:18	209, 224, 231–32, 947	5:31	211, 226	11:4–6	217
2:20	214	5:32	686	11:5	806
2:23	146, 209, 216, 231, 692, 804	5:33	211, 226	11:5–6	807
		5:33–37	117	11:10	211–12, 222
3:1–2	912	5:34–35	222	11:13	211, 227, 236, 265, 342
3:1–4	880	5:34–37	687	11:14	912
3:3	156, 211–12, 754, 803, 807, 981	5:35	849	11:19	216, 714
		5:38	211, 776	11:21	228
3:4	912, 942	5:38–42	117, 779	11:23	217, 222, 805
3:9	228	5:43	211, 226, 398, 593	11:25–30	714
3:13–17	677	5:48	693	11:28–29	907
3:16–17	218	6:2–4	117	11:29	222, 231
3:17	212, 729, 847	6:9	591–93	12:1–8	155, 227, 909
4:1–11	215, 780	6:13	736	12:1–14	226
4:2	229	6:26	593	12:3	212, 227
4:3	729	7:12	30, 225, 227, 236, 265, 342	12:3–4	229
4:4	211, 215, 222, 230, 777			12:4	229
4:6	211, 803, 830, 851	7:23	222, 847	12:5	212, 227
4:7	215, 222, 777	7:28–29	225	12:7	212, 222, 227, 231
4:10	211, 215, 222, 777, 787	7:29	906	12:9–14	808
4:12–17	149	8:1	906	12:15	218
4:13	804	8:4	902	12:15–17	808
4:14	211	8:5	217	12:17	211
4:14–16	692, 803	8:11	228, 899	12:17–21	692
4:15	228	8:13	657	12:18	219, 258
4:15–16	146, 209, 219, 231, 804	8:14–15	681	12:18–20	992
		8:14–17	149	12:18–21	146, 209, 218, 221, 228, 231–32, 807
4:16–17	215	8:17	209, 211, 217, 231, 239, 692, 810		
4:23	682			12:19–20	218–19
4:25–5:1	225	8:20	713	12:21	218–19, 808
5	74	8:23–27	738, 835, 851	12:23	217
5:1–7:29	70–71, 152, 906	9:1	217	12:40	222
5:3–12	116–17	9:9–13	226–27	12:41–42	229
5:5	849	9:13	212, 222, 227, 231	12:42	713
5:8	155	9:18–19	277	12:50	593
5:10–12	155	9:18–26	677	13:13	219
5:11	875	9:20–22	677	13:14	803
		9:23–27	277		

13:14–15	211, 219, 222, 230–31, 803	21:4–5	692	24:3	759
		21:5	209, 217, 229, 231–32	24:3–25:46	760
13:35	209, 211, 219, 231, 692, 828, 830, 850	21:6	212	24:8	450
		21:9	217, 832, 852, 908	24:15	32, 211, 861, 873
13:42	222	21:11	221	24:15–16	230
13:49	826	21:12–13	684	24:21	587
13:50	222	21:13	211, 222, 810	24:27	760
13:54	682	21:14	229	24:28	713
14:1–12	912	21:16	222, 227, 230–31, 831, 847	24:29	222, 760, 805, 807
15:1–20	226			24:29–31	760
15:4	211, 776, 778–79, 1017	21:33	222, 802	24:30	222, 229, 561, 756, 759–60, 873–74
15:4–9	1016	21:33–46	223, 616		
15:7	211	21:42	212, 222, 830–31, 852, 981	24:37–44	153
15:7–9	219, 222			24:43	556
15:8	939–40	21:46	227	25:31	116, 787
15:19	226, 232	22:13	414	25:31–32	607
15:21	218, 228	22:14	980	25:31–46	116
15:21–28	228	22:17	938	25:46	759
15:22	217, 228	22:23–33	154	26:3	693
15:24	222	22:24	211	26:6–13	229
16:1	947	22:29	222	26:15	229
16:14	225, 912	22:31	211–12, 227	26:24	616
16:27	222, 845, 850	22:32	222, 882	26:29	593
17:1–8	71, 902, 911–12	22:34–40	226–27, 676	26:30	829, 852
17:1–9	229–30	22:36–40	779	26:31	156, 211, 220, 222, 981
17:5	230, 729, 782	22:37	776	26:38	222, 730, 831, 849
17:13	912	22:37–39	212, 222	26:52–54	220
17:24	217	22:40	30, 227, 236, 265	26:54	222, 692
18:16	222, 230, 776	22:41–45	154	26:56	216, 220, 692
18:22	229	22:41–46	214, 909	26:63	221
19:3–9	151, 226, 686	22:42	214	26:64	222, 229, 832, 852
19:4	212, 227, 586	22:43	829, 831, 835	26:67–68	221
19:4–5	211, 222	22:43–44	222	27	225
19:6	1016	22:44	852, 982	27:3–8	224
19:7	902	23	681	27:3–10	210, 225, 233
19:7–8	211	23:2–3	694–95	27:9	146, 211, 692
19:8	1016	23:8–10	226	27:9–10	58, 209, 221, 223–25, 232
19:16–22	227	23:16–26	226		
19:18	226, 232, 776	23:23	227, 694	27:24	210, 871
19:18–19	212, 222, 778	23:29–36	694	27:25	224
19:19	226, 398, 776	23:34	714	27:30	221
19:28	875	23:34–36	714	27:34	221, 935
20:1–6	1015	23:35	229	27:35	221, 848
20:8	229	23:36	694	27:39	221, 848
20:28	252	23:37	221	27:43	221, 223, 833, 848
20:30–31	217	23:37–39	714	27:46	81, 221–22, 731, 831, 833, 848, 935, 992
21:4	211, 220	23:39	222, 852		

Index of Scripture and Other Ancient Sources

27:46–49	911, 913	2:17	657	6:17–29	912		
27:47	913	2:18–20	688	6:23	35		
27:48	221, 837, 850, 935	2:23–28	151, 681, 909	6:30–44	248		
27:51–53	221	2:24	243	6:32–52	248		
28	222	2:25	227	6:34	242		
28:16–20	217	2:25–26	244	6:39	834		
28:18	222	2:28	247, 839	6:41	243		
28:18–20	225, 229	3:1–6	675, 682	6:48	244		
28:19	219	3:2–4	247	6:52	248		
		3:4	244	6:53–56	248		
Mark		3:11	678	7:1	248		
1–10	236	3:14	248	7:1–3	675		
1:1	245	3:14–15	247–48, 255	7:1–5	685		
1:1–13	245	3:15	678	7:1–14	151		
1:2	52, 58, 212, 245, 249, 270	3:20–21	247	7:1–23	675, 778		
1:2–3	236, 240, 258, 270, 754	3:22	247–48, 678	7:3	675, 695		
		3:22–30	248	7:5	689		
1:2–4	156	3:24	681	7:6	249, 939–40		
1:3	58, 249, 807, 981	3:27	242–43, 247–48	7:6–7	240		
1:4	912	3:28	247, 253, 255	7:10	211, 240, 248, 776, 778–79, 902		
1:4–8	243, 246	3:30	678				
1:4–13	246	3:31–35	247, 255	7:14–16	248		
1:6	880, 912, 942	3:35	593	7:15	679, 685		
1:7	243, 246–47, 253	4:10–12	248	7:19	248, 675		
1:8	258	4:11	258	7:21–23	248–49		
1:9	245	4:11–12	552	7:24	228		
1:9–11	677	4:12	219, 240, 249, 803	7:24–30	244, 248		
1:10	242, 246	4:17	256	8:1–10	248		
1:10–11	253	4:32	242	8:18	240, 242, 258		
1:11	240, 242, 246, 258, 637, 729, 847	4:35–41	738, 835, 851	8:22–10:52	249		
		4:37	835	8:27	242, 249		
1:12–13	246, 248, 678, 780	4:38–41	247, 835	8:28	912		
		4:41	247	8:29	912		
1:13	230, 870	5:1–13	678	8:31	242, 249–51, 253, 255–57, 875
1:14	254	5:7	678				
1:14–15	246–48	5:18–20	248	8:32–33	251		
1:21–28	247	5:19–20	254	8:34–37	251		
1:21–29	682	5:21–24	244, 248	8:34–9:1	255		
1:21–31	681	5:25–34	677	8:35	254		
1:23–24	678	5:35–43	244, 248, 677	8:37	242		
1:34	678	6:1–6	273	8:38	254, 532		
1:38–39	247	6:1–12	248	9:2–8	71, 244, 248, 902, 911–12		
1:40–45	677, 938	6:3	501, 506				
1:44	243–44, 882, 902	6:3–4	273	9:4	782		
2:1–3:6	246, 248, 253	6:7	678	9:7	242, 251, 729, 782, 847		
2:7	243, 246, 254	6:14–29	246				
2:10	247	6:15	880, 912	9:9–13	246		

9:11–12	242	11:15–19	253, 684	13:34	255
9:11–13	912	11:17	241–42, 294, 810	13:62	613
9:12	239, 244, 257	12:1	255	14–15	839
9:13	244	12:1–9	244, 247, 253	14:9	256
9:14–29	248	12:1–11	802	14:18	242, 836, 838, 849
9:31	242, 249–50, 253, 255, 257, 875	12:1–12	616	14:21	239, 244, 257, 838, 875
9:32	251	12:5	253	14:22–25	255
9:33	242, 249	12:7–8	253	14:24	242, 256
9:33–37	251	12:10	212, 227, 830, 981	14:25	593
9:42	256	12:10–11	253, 852	14:26–28	839
9:43	256	12:14	938	14:27	156, 220, 241, 256, 258, 981
9:45	256	12:18	258		
9:47	256	12:18–23	689	14:27–28	258
9:48	240	12:18–27	154	14:29	239
10:1–10	151	12:19	241	14:32	532
10:2–12	151	12:23	831	14:32–34	256
10:3	902	12:24	23, 421	14:33–34	730
10:3–4	242	12:24–27	689	14:34	241–42, 256–57, 831, 838, 849
10:3–9	23	12:26	41, 211, 227, 241, 882		
10:6	586	12:28	254	14:36	256
10:6–8	240	12:28–31	675–76	14:41	224, 257, 875
10:9	686	12:28–34	151, 254, 779	14:49	220, 241, 684, 838
10:11–12	686	12:29	258, 776	14:56	242
10:17	242, 249	12:29–30	87, 241	14:57	838, 848–49
10:18	254	12:30	776	14:61	242, 257, 838–39
10:19	212, 240, 258, 511, 776, 778	12:31	258, 398, 511	14:62	241–42, 616, 838–39, 852, 875
		12:32	776		
10:28–31	255	12:33	776	14:65	242, 257
10:32	242, 249	12:35–37	23, 154, 214, 254, 320, 614, 909	15:2	602
10:32–34	249			15:5	838
10:33	255, 257, 281	12:36	211, 241, 414, 729, 829–30, 852, 982	15:19	241
10:33–34	242, 250, 875			15:23	242, 838
10:34	253, 257	13	759	15:24	241, 257, 833, 838, 840, 848
10:35	257	13:3–4	244		
10:35–41	251	13:5–23	254	15:29	838, 840, 848
10:42–45	251	13:8	450	15:29–30	242, 257
10:43	251	13:9	254–55	15:30–31	838
10:45	242, 244, 251–53, 256, 839	13:9–13	255, 258	15:31–32	223
		13:11	258	15:32	602, 838, 840, 848
10:46	249	13:12	242	15:34	81, 241, 731, 831, 833, 838, 840, 848, 935
10:52	242, 249	13:14	244, 254, 873		
11–13	236	13:19	242, 587	15:34–36	911, 913
11:1–10	908	13:24	805	15:35	913
11:1–11	839	13:24–25	241	15:36	242, 837–38, 850, 935
11:9–10	240, 253, 832, 852	13:24–27	254–55, 839	15:37	838, 840
11:11	253	13:25	807	15:38	221
		13:26–27	242, 874		

15:38–39	258	2:1–20	273	4:4–6	266
15:39	838–40	2:4	273, 883, 909	4:5–6	781
15:40	838, 840, 849	2:10	329	4:7	781
15:43	833	2:11	100, 321, 605, 909	4:8	264, 777, 781
16:1–8	258	2:11–12	274	4:9	781
16:6–7	258	2:16–20	274	4:10	830
16:8	432	2:17–18	155	4:10–11	264, 851
16:19	852	2:20	156, 727	4:12	264, 333, 777, 781
		2:21	683	4:14–30	263, 272
Luke		2:21–38	727	4:16–20	682
1–2	101, 909, 1005	2:22	264	4:16–30	273, 329
1:1	265, 318	2:23	264, 266	4:18	324, 333, 980
1:1–4	282	2:24	266	4:18–19	264, 272, 637, 811, 982
1:1–2:52	754	2:25	727		
1:10	822	2:25–35	630	4:18–21	156
1:13	945	2:27	264, 677	4:20	273
1:13–17	270	2:27–40	154	4:21	264, 273, 279, 811
1:16–17	754	2:29–32	727	4:22	273
1:17	913	2:29–35	153	4:24	273, 322, 602
1:26–38	274	2:30–31	275	4:24–27	152
1:27	267, 883, 909	2:31	324, 727	4:25–26	276
1:32	329, 909	2:32	727	4:26	914
1:32–33	275, 320, 331, 333	2:34	727	4:27	275, 318, 914
1:32–35	592	2:38	252	4:28–29	276, 330
1:33	882	2:39	264, 677	4:31–37	682
1:34	267	2:41–44	154	4:33–34	277
1:35	267	2:44	142	4:41	602
1:43	321	3:1–2	268	5:8	321
1:46–55	101, 153, 267	3:2	270	5:14	264, 902
1:48	726	3:2–7	156	5:17–26	321
1:50	851	3:3–20	755	5:21–24	277
1:52	267, 728	3:4	270, 279, 754, 981	5:24	875
1:52–53	267	3:4–6	268–70, 807	5:26	273
1:53	851	3:6	271, 279	5:32	657
1:55	726	3:21	677	5:35–43	277
1:67–79	726	3:21–22	273, 324	6:1–5	909
1:68	252, 278	3:22	729, 811, 847, 903, 943	6:17–7:1	71
1:68–71	727			6:35	593
1:68–79	101, 153, 331, 656	3:23	214, 1015	6:43	1002
1:69	883, 909	3:23–38	909, 1005	6:46	321
1:72	647, 656	3:31	329	7:6	321
1:73	687	4:1	781, 811	7:11–17	152, 276, 278–79, 677, 914
1:76	279, 807, 914	4:1–13	780–81		
1:76–79	270	4:2	230, 781	7:13	277, 279
1:78	278–79	4:2–4	781	7:16	273, 278, 322
2	327	4:3	781	7:18–22	156
2:1–2	268	4:4	230, 264, 777, 781	7:18–23	279

7:18–28	278	12:32	903	20:9–18	802
7:19	273	12:39	556	20:9–19	616
7:22	279, 321, 806–7	12:42	277	20:17	264, 323, 333, 830–31, 852, 981
7:22–23	155	13:5	657		
7:26	279	13:6–9	802	20:17–18	323
7:27	212, 264, 914	13:10–16	681	20:22	938
7:34	875	13:10–17	682	20:28	264
7:35	714	13:15	277	20:37	264, 321, 325, 882
7:36	679	13:27	847	20:37–38	1005
7:39	322, 782	13:29	851	20:41	1013
8:10	803	13:33–34	1005	20:41–44	320, 329, 333, 909
8:19–21	328	13:34	714	20:42	414, 828, 830–31, 982
8:21	1015	13:35	832, 852		
8:21–22	875	14:1	679	20:42–43	264, 852
8:22–25	738, 835, 851	14:1–5	681	20:44	1013
8:40–42	277	15	1015	21	759
8:40–56	677	15:9	657	21:22	318
8:42–48	677	15:17–24	657	21:25	805
8:49–56	277	16	899	22:17–20	660, 664
9:28–34	71	16:7	264	22:20	647
9:28–36	279, 902, 912, 1013	16:14–31	281	22:37	239, 244, 810
		16:16	236, 265, 270, 273, 279, 281, 342	22:61	321
9:30	279			22:63–71	324
9:30–31	281	16:18	686	22:69	616
9:31	912	16:19–31	281, 898	23:1–25	324
9:35	280, 782, 1014	16:29	342	23:11	323
9:44	875	16:29–31	902	23:12	324
9:59–62	152	16:30	281, 657	23:19	322
9:61–62	914	16:31	342	23:34	833, 848
10:1	273	17:5–6	277	23:35	848
10:7	456	17:24–25	875	23:36	837, 850, 935
10:21	805	17:26–36	153	23:42	321
10:21–22	714	18:14	323	23:43	657
10:25–28	676	18:20	264, 281, 776, 778	23:46	848
10:26	264	18:28	1013	23:47	276, 657
10:27	264, 281, 776	18:31	264, 275, 328	23:49	849
10:39	277	18:31–33	275, 281, 334, 1005	24:6–8	275
10:41	277			24:6–12	324
11:1	321	18:35	1013	24:13–15	272
11:29–32	1048	18:38–39	329	24:13–25	274
11:30–32	1005	18:39	1013	24:17	275
11:37	679	19:28–38	908	24:19	276, 280, 322, 905
11:39	277	19:38	832, 852	24:21	252, 280
11:49–51	714, 1005	19:45–48	684	24:22–24	280
12:6–8	593	19:45–21:38	327	24:25	275, 782
12:8–9	874	19:46	264, 810–11	24:25–27	263, 272, 274, 280, 334, 782
12:24	593	19:47	684		

Index of Scripture and Other Ancient Sources

24:26	275, 317, 322, 324	1:72–73	727	6:31–33	897, 907		
24:27	173, 236, 264, 328, 342, 902	1:76–77	727	6:31–58	181, 291		
24:31	274	1:78–79	727	6:32	301		
24:32	264, 272	2:13–16	684	6:32–33	907		
24:35	274	2:13–25	292, 298	6:35	292, 907		
24:36–39	275	2:14–22	149	6:38	294		
24:44	30–32, 173, 236, 265, 275, 317–18, 342, 828	2:16	294	6:40	552		
		2:17	286, 290, 293–95, 298, 831, 845, 850	6:42	294		
24:44–47	334			6:45	286, 289, 294		
24:44–49	263, 326, 329, 331	2:19–21	992	6:45–59	149		
24:45	264	2:21	297	7:1–8:59	296		
24:46	324, 605, 611	2:22	149	7:2	292		
24:46–47	322	3:7	754	7:19–23	301		
24:46–49	320	3:9	754	7:22	292		
24:48	329	3:10–14	754	7:24	294–95		
24:49	914	3:13	923	7:37–38	941, 992		
24:51	276, 914	3:14	301, 897, 907, 982	7:38	286, 288–89, 295		
24:53	327	3:14–15	907	7:42	287, 295, 883, 909		
		3:15	754	8	303		
John		3:17	754	8:12	292, 297, 715		
1–12	296	3:23	754	8:17	287, 289–90, 296		
1:1	11, 293, 715, 988	4	304	8:24	292, 300, 993		
1:1–9	587	4:5	891	8:28	292, 300		
1:1–18	300, 715	4:12	303–4	8:31–59	898–99		
1:3	583, 715	4:13–14	304	8:39	899		
1:4	293	4:14	941	8:44	291		
1:4–5	715	4:21–23	593	8:50	715		
1:8–10	739	4:22	95	8:53	304		
1:14	297, 300, 715	4:26	292, 300	8:56	899		
1:17	301, 992	5:1–18	682	8:58	292, 300, 303, 899		
1:18	716	5:17	594	9:1–40	682		
1:19	302	5:18	301, 547, 682	9:28–29	301		
1:21	782, 911	5:19–23	594	9:29	937		
1:22	807	5:25	552	10:1–9	1026		
1:23	156, 286, 288–89, 293, 302, 309, 754, 981	5:28–29	806	10:1–18	292		
		5:39	302, 937	10:9	292		
1:25	911	5:39–46	897, 907	10:11	292, 297, 299		
1:29	292, 305, 551	5:45	937	10:14	292, 299		
1:34	847	5:45–47	301–2	10:31–39	298		
1:36	305	5:46	782, 938	10:33	547		
1:41	292	6	181–82, 291, 294, 304	10:34	287, 289–90, 295, 298, 309, 830, 850		
1:45	265, 292, 301, 342, 907	6:20	292, 300				
1:47	292	6:22–59	294, 302	10:36	298		
1:49	729, 847	6:25–65	594	11:4	715		
1:51	287, 291, 293, 295, 304	6:31	286, 288, 294, 309, 818–19, 830, 850	11:5	715		
				11:27	297		
		6:31–32	302	12:12–16	908		

1121

INDEX OF SCRIPTURE AND OTHER ANCIENT SOURCES

12:13	287–88, 291, 295, 832, 852	19:8	292	2	319, 330–31, 333, 626, 636
12:14–15	287	19:24	287, 304, 309–10, 833, 848	2–3	329
12:15	288, 309	19:28	287, 289, 304–5	2:1–4:1	315
12:27	287, 291, 847	19:28–29	837, 850	2:3–4	326
12:36	290, 298	19:28–30	936	2:14–36	152
12:36–43	149	19:31	551, 935	2:16	317
12:37–41	298	19:31–37	821	2:16–21	333, 636
12:38	239, 287, 289, 304, 309–10, 809	19:33	305, 935	2:17	322
		19:36	287–88, 304–5, 821, 849	2:17–18	326
12:39	289			2:17–21	321, 325, 334
12:39–40	287, 803	19:36–37	756	2:18	97
12:40	288, 303, 309, 552, 803	19:37	287–88, 304, 306, 309	2:19	321, 325, 331
				2:21	321, 331
12:40–41	809	20:17	594, 716	2:22	325
12:41	289–90, 304	20:28	297	2:22–36	149
12:43	303	20:30–31	292, 297, 306	2:24	450
13	836	21:16	296	2:25	831, 909
13:3	716	21:22	611	2:25–26	319
13:18	287–89, 298, 309, 836, 849	21:23	611	2:25–28	317, 332–33, 810, 848
		21:25	297		
13:19	292, 300			2:25–32	324
13:34–35	676	**Acts**		2:27	320, 330, 333
14–17	299	1–5	316	2:29	324
14:6	293, 305	1:1–14	316	2:29–31	330, 828
14:16	631	1:2	914	2:29–32	909
14:26	631	1:4	320	2:29–35	687
15:1	292, 297	1:4–11	315	2:29–39	328
15:1–4	802	1:5	754	2:30	148, 265, 320, 333, 852
15:18	835	1:8	315–16, 320, 326, 328, 332, 334	2:31	320, 333, 831, 848
15:25	287, 289, 295, 298–99, 830, 845, 849–50	1:9	914	2:32	329, 605, 611
		1:9–11	276	2:33–36	320, 333
16:7–11	631	1:13–14	315	2:34	414, 829–31, 852, 982
16:13–15	631	1:14	827	2:34–35	333–34
16:28	716	1:15–26	149, 315, 827	2:36	320, 330, 334, 610
16:32	156	1:16	264, 324, 828, 830, 836, 849, 909	2:38	326, 328, 330, 334
17	835			2:39	321, 333
17:5	715	1:16–20	225	2:40	328, 330
17:12	287	1:17	149	2:41	319, 328
17:14	835	1:18	225	2:46	327
17:22	715	1:20	318, 331, 828, 830, 850, 852	3:1	822
17:24	300, 715			3:1–10	657
18:5–6	292, 300	1:21–22	326	3:1–11	323–24
18:8	300	1:22	329	3:6	323, 325
18:20	684	1:24	827	3:10	323
19:7	547	1:42–47	315	3:11	327
				3:11–4:4	657

Index of Scripture and Other Ancient Sources

Ref	Pages	Ref	Pages	Ref	Pages
3:12–26	323, 904	5	326, 331	7:51	659
3:13	324–25, 334, 882, 902	5:12	325	7:51–52	623
3:13–19	319	5:20	327	7:51–53	152
3:13–26	325	5:29–32	325	7:52	276
3:14	333	5:31	326, 333–34	7:53	659
3:15	329	6:5	328	7:55–56	325, 614, 616
3:16	325	6:10	630	7:58	276, 944
3:17	329	6:13	326	8	328
3:18	142, 317–18, 322, 602, 782	7	328, 331, 333, 658–59, 731, 891, 897, 903, 922	8:1	315–16
				8:1–3	315, 328
3:18–26	149	7:2–4	897	8:5	328
3:21	317, 322, 782	7:2–53	9, 152, 883, 903	8:12	328
3:21–24	658, 782	7:3	327	8:14–17	328
3:22	317, 327, 329, 602, 612, 776–77, 783, 904	7:6–7	327	8:25	328
		7:8	647, 658	8:26–40	328, 332
3:22–23	322, 334, 782–83	7:9–10	891	8:27–33	810
3:22–25	146	7:9–11	327	8:32	264
3:23	331, 981	7:9–16	903	8:32–33	317, 321, 328, 331, 333–34, 810
3:23–24	278	7:9–19	891		
3:24	317, 322	7:18	891	8:32–35	239
3:25	328, 331, 334, 647, 658	7:20–44	902–3	8:34	334
3:25–26	657	7:21	903	8:34–35	810
3:26	324	7:22	905	8:35	264, 282, 328
4	322, 331, 728, 832	7:23–29	903	8:36	328
4:1	728	7:24–29	327	9:36–42	276–77
4:1–22	323	7:25	904–5	9:36–43	914
4:3	728	7:27–28	327	10	330
4:7	325	7:30	659	10:1–48	316, 332
4:8	832	7:30–34	904	10:9–16	99
4:8–12	631	7:32	325, 904	10:9–35	151
4:10	325, 329	7:32–34	327	10:11–16	685
4:11	323, 333–34, 832, 852	7:33–34	904	10:17	686
4:12	325	7:35	252, 659	10:19	686
4:12–16	334	7:35–41	327, 904	10:34–35	686
4:13	325	7:36	905	10:40–41	329
4:15	728	7:37	278, 317, 329, 776–77, 782, 904	10:44–46	626
4:17	325			10:45	686
4:24	323, 728, 819–20, 832, 853	7:38	659	10:47	686
		7:39–40	327	11:1–2	686
4:24–28	324	7:39–41	905	11:5–10	685
4:24–30	728	7:40–41	905	11:17	627
4:25	729, 831, 909	7:42–43	327	11:18	316
4:25–26	329, 334, 829, 847	7:44	88	11:26	282, 316
4:27	333	7:46	882	11:27–28	627
4:27–28	328	7:48	328	11:28	685
4:29–30	325	7:49	982	12:1	315
4:31	326	7:49–50	327	12:17	331, 506

1123

13	316–17, 330, 333	17:2–3	451	1:9–13	337
13–14	331	17:4–5	330	1:16	338, 344, 689
13:5	682	17:6	682	1:16–17	341, 348, 740
13:6–41	9	17:10	682	1:16–5:21	349
13:13–49	329	17:11	264, 829	1:16–8:39	349
13:15	236, 342	17:28	28	1:17	156, 342, 400
13:16–22	333–34	18:4	682	1:17–15:21	339
13:20	317	18:6	754	1:18	731
13:22	329, 850	18:19	682	1:20	587
13:22–25	909	18:24	176, 264, 829	2:1	352
13:23	317, 329	18:26	682	2:1–11	833
13:27	329	18:28	264	2:6	342, 710, 834, 842–45, 850
13:30	329	19:6	626		
13:32	329	19:8	682	2:9–10	689
13:32–34	27	20:7–12	277	2:17	309
13:33	333, 729, 828, 847	20:9–12	914	2:19	450
13:33–35	331	20:24	316	2:24	377, 986
13:34	330, 810	21:13	316	2:29	347
13:35	333, 810, 828, 848	21:18–26	506	3:1–2	689
13:36	330, 909	21:20–25	683	3:2	358
13:38	329–30, 334	21:25	683	3:4	710, 830, 842–45, 850, 852
13:38–39	330	21:26	327		
13:41	330, 334	22:3	675	3:10	710, 830
13:44–47	330	22:17	327	3:10–11	343–44
13:47	334, 809, 813, 982	24:5	826	3:10–12	842, 848, 850
14:1–2	682	24:14	236, 342	3:10–17	98, 740
14:3	331	24:18	327	3:10–18	146, 339, 359, 843–44, 986
14:15	819, 832, 853	26:22	342		
15	331	28	331	3:12–17	986
15:1–21	683	28:8	754	3:13	842, 847, 853
15:1–28	332	28:20	282	3:13–18	343
15:7–11	331	28:23	95, 236, 342	3:14	842, 848
15:11	333	28:25–28	334	3:18	842, 849
15:13–21	501, 506	28:26	333	3:20	344, 399, 842, 844, 853
15:16	145–46, 883	28:26–27	266, 271, 282, 317, 331, 803		
15:16–18	317, 331–32, 334			3:21	339, 342, 344
15:16–28	331	28:28	271, 332	3:21–24	740
15:17	331	28:31	271	3:24–25	344
15:21	684, 902			3:25	345, 351, 679
15:22	627	**Romans**		3:28	344
15:25	684	1–3	740	3:28–31	142
15:27	627	1–8	339, 342	3:29–30	349
15:32	627	1–15	339	4	346, 898
16:3	683	1:2	93, 339–40	4:1–12	391
16:13	682	1:3	909	4:3	341, 346, 390, 982, 986
17:1	682	1:3–4	612, 733–34, 841		
17:2	264	1:9	687	4:3–8	146, 346

4:6	829–31, 843	9:1–5	351	10:18–20		844
4:7	830	9:3–5	401	10:19	351, 777, 787, 986
4:7–8	842–44, 849, 986	9:4	86, 96, 675, 689	10:20–21		986
4:9	346, 986	9:4–5	66–67	10:21		982–3
4:10–12	347–48	9:5	733	11	354, 661–62, 671
4:11–12	900	9:6	351, 358	11:1		352
4:13–16	348	9:6–29	351–52	11:1–10		354
4:17	585–86, 986	9:6–33	142	11:2	341, 821, 830, 842–45,
4:19	918	9:8	352, 919		851, 911
4:23–24	346, 349	9:10–13	339, 352	11:2–5		196
4:24–25	900	9:12	982	11:3		196
4:25	747	9:15	352	11:3–4		986
5	72, 349	9:15–19	806	11:4		98, 196
5:6–10	351	9:17	341, 352	11:7		351
5:12	120, 349	9:20	806	11:8	776, 788, 806, 840
5:12–21	339, 349–50, 922	9:20–24	806	11:8–10		844
5:14	349, 922	9:24–29	352, 358	11:9		831, 843
6:5	407	9:25	52	11:9–10	842–45, 850
6:8	407	9:25–33	146	11:11–12		615
7	350, 690, 915	9:26	592	11:11–24		354
7:7	691, 776	9:27	351	11:17		671
7:7–25	349, 916	9:29	376, 802, 986	11:17–19		671
7:11	916–17	9:30	615	11:23		671
7:12	690–91	9:30–10:21	352	11:25		355
7:13	691	9:31	351	11:26		351, 882
7:16	691	9:32	352	11:26–27		671, 811
7:16–17	675	9:33	359, 381, 615, 804,	11:27		647, 662
7:22	350, 691		806, 981	11:29		675
7:25	691	9:36	340	11:30–32		811
8:2	634	10–15	787	11:33–36		356, 733
8:11	662	10:5	394	11:34–35		733
8:14–17	640	10:5–8	783	11:35		359
8:15	592, 662	10:5–13	353	12–15		339
8:15–16	594	10:6	776, 787–88	12:1–15:13		356
8:18–30	587	10:6–10	149, 711	12:19	97, 377, 382,
8:20	35	10:8	777, 787		777, 787
8:24	350	10:9	353	12:19–21		356
8:29	594	10:11	341, 353, 615, 809, 981	12:20		340, 710
8:34	602, 614, 842,	10:13	809	13:8		676
	844–45, 852	10:14–15	809	13:8–10		357
8:36	350, 840,	10:14–21	353, 359	13:9	183, 398, 511, 690,
	842–44, 849	10:15	377, 381, 419		776, 778
8:38–39	350, 529	10:15–16	813	13:14		184
9	351, 671	10:16	812, 986	14–15		357
9–11	339, 348, 351, 691,	10:16–17	239	14:10–12		431
	732, 783, 801, 809,	10:18	830, 842–44,	14:11		357, 430
	811, 813		848, 986	14:19		357

15:2	357–58	4:5	450	14:27	623
15:3	357, 840, 843, 845, 850	5:5	450	15	72, 176, 363, 371, 841
15:4	341	5:13	11, 364	15:2–5	747
15:8	358	6:2	363	15:3	341
15:8–9	606	6:3	530	15:4	841
15:8–12	146, 358	6:16	364, 384	15:7	501, 506
15:9	840, 843–44, 848	6:18–19	634	15:20–28	845
15:9–11	844	7	363	15:21–22	349
15:9–12	733, 844	7:10–16	151	15:22	371
15:10	777, 787–88, 986	8:1	357	15:23–28	614
15:11	843–44, 852	8:6	610	15:24	530, 613
15:12	612, 804	9:4–11	366	15:24–27	418, 616
15:13	733	9:9	384, 460–61, 463, 776	15:25	365, 371, 414, 834, 843, 852, 982
15:15–16	679	9:9–11	64, 364	15:25–27	371, 614
15:16	634	9:10	365–66	15:26	845
15:19	627	9:14	460	15:27	10, 364, 417, 418, 430, 436, 841, 842–43, 848
15:21	377, 813, 986	10	363, 369, 384	15:32	364
15:22–25	337	10:1–5	369	15:32–33	372
15:22–29	337	10:1–13	434	15:33	363–64
16:1	407	10:2	907	15:42–54	120
16:4	407	10:2–4	1039	15:44	179
16:25–26	149	10:4	907	15:45	177–79, 349, 364, 371
		10:6	369	15:45–49	176
1 Corinthians		10:7	364, 986	15:47	177–78
1:12	176	10:9	370, 907	15:47–49	177, 179
1:18	366, 992	10:11	149, 369, 527	15:54	364, 380, 805
1:19	364, 367, 806, 986	10:11–13	435	15:54–55	373, 384
1:21	445	10:14–33	370	15:55	364
1:23	306	10:23	357		
1:23–24	986	10:26	364, 830, 843–44, 848, 986	**2 Corinthians**	
1:26	368	11:8–9	457	1–2	363, 711
1:27–31	367	11:24–25	664	1:3–8	732
1:31	364, 367–38, 384	11:25	647, 664	1:14	450
2:1–5	627	11:26	611	1:24	711
2:2	628	12	363	1:25	712
2:4	631	12–14	623	1:30	711–12
2:8–11	628	12:4–11	625	2:7	711
2:9	364–65, 367	13	357, 676	2:14–7:4	373
2:9–10	631	14	626	3	384, 907–8
2:10–14	120	14:3–5	357	3–5	120
2:16	364, 367	14:21	364, 377, 381–82, 384, 830	3:4–6	663
3:5–9	363			3:4–18	373
3:9–17	529	14:23	623	3:6	156
3:13	528	14:25	414	3:6–13	374
3:19	364, 367, 383, 830	14:26	827	3:6–14	647
3:20	364, 367, 843, 848				
4:1	149				

Index of Scripture and Other Ancient Sources

3:7	180, 230, 374, 908	12	970	3:10–13	985
3:7–8	897	12:19	357	3:10–14	403–4
3:7–11	180	13:1	364, 776	3:11	156, 341, 394, 399–400
3:7–18	179, 181, 664	13:10	357		
3:10	179–80, 663			3:12	10, 353, 390, 393, 401, 784
3:12–13	897, 908	**Galatians**			
3:12–18	71, 180	1–2	402, 808, 813	3:13	306, 390, 393, 395, 397, 401, 776, 783–84, 789, 986
3:13	180, 374	1:1	403		
3:14	181	1:1–2	401		
3:14–16	373	1:6	392, 403	3:14	392, 611, 662, 900
3:15	902	1:7	403	3:15–17	398
3:16	180	1:11–12	403	3:16	154, 390, 606, 611, 842, 846
3:16–17	680	1:14	690, 829		
3:19	710	1:15	404	3:17	402
3:20	845	1:15–16	403, 689, 808	3:17–18	682
4:2–3	375	1:19	501, 506	3:19	604, 606, 615
4:6	450	1:20	687	3:22	341
4:13	364, 379, 830, 843–45, 852	1:24	403, 808	3:23–36	403–4
		2:1–9	683	3:24	175, 662
5:1	690	2:1–10	403	3:26	592
5:1–8	680	2:1–13	506	3:29	391
5:17	587	2:2	392, 403, 809	4:1	900
5:21	395, 679	2:4	683	4:1–7	403–4, 639
6	690	2:7–9	338	4:3–5	403–4
6:2	364, 384, 403	2:8	392	4:6–7	594
6:12–20	680	2:9	331, 392	4:7	900
6:14–16	378	2:11–13	686	4:8	389
6:14–7:1	375, 379	2:12	392, 690	4:8–9	445
6:16	375–76, 384, 680	2:14	392	4:11	403
6:16–18	146, 364	2:15	689	4:19	388
6:17	377	2:15–16	388	4:21	830
6:18	378, 384	2:16	344, 399, 846	4:21–31	173, 175, 352, 388, 396, 402, 810, 898, 900
7	690	3:1	400		
7:1	378	3:1–3	389		
7:4	375	3:1–5	662	4:21–5:1	397, 918, 991
7:10–11	686	3:2	344	4:24	900
7:18–20	683	3:5	344	4:24–25	388, 916
7:19	690	3:6	390–91, 514, 900, 982	4:27	390, 396–97, 404
8:6	711–12, 715	3:6–7	395	4:28	900
8:15	364	3:6–9	142, 900, 993	4:30	341, 390, 397, 916
9:5	340	3:6–14	784	5:6	87
9:9	364, 830, 843–44, 852	3:6–18	898	5:7	400
10:8	357	3:8	341, 390–91	5:13	397, 776
10:17	364, 368	3:10	344, 390, 395, 397, 401, 776, 783, 986	5:14	288, 357, 390, 398, 511
11:3	915–17			6:12–13	389
11:5	917	3:10–12	662	6:16–7:1	155
11:14–12:21	363–64				

1127

Ephesians

1:7	408
1:7–8	407
1:15–23	409
1:17	631
1:20	415–17, 841, 852
1:20–22	418, 616
1:22	407, 415, 417–18, 841, 842–43, 848
2:5	408
2:6	407
2:11–18	409
2:13	419
2:14	419
2:17	415, 418–19
2:21–22	419
3:10	407
3:21	407
4:8	415, 419–20, 426, 831, 841, 850, 986
4:8–10	409
4:25–26	415, 421
4:25–5:2	409
4:26	842, 847
5:5	602
5:13–20	409
5:19	827
5:22–33	422
5:22–6:9	407
5:23–32	407
5:31	415
6:1	423
6:1–4	409
6:2	776
6:2–3	415, 422, 426
6:4	423
6:10–17	425
6:11	425
6:14	416, 424–25
6:14–17	424
6:15	416, 424–25
6:17	416, 424–25
6:21–22	408

Philippians

1:3	731
1:8	432
1:11	432
1:19	429–30, 432–33, 437
1:20	433
1:27–2:18	429–30, 433
1:28	433
2:5–11	239, 733
2:6	434, 733
2:6–11	429, 431, 434
2:7	430, 434, 734
2:10	433
2:10–11	357, 429–31
2:11	431
2:12	432, 434
2:12–13	433
2:12–18	435–36
2:14	434
2:14–16	430
2:15	433–35
2:16	433, 435
2:17–18	435
3	430
3:2–21	436–37
3:4–5	690
3:5	683, 829
3:5–6	689
3:5–17	436
3:6	675, 911
3:7–8	436
3:8–14	436
3:10–11	430
3:17	436
3:18	436
3:21	430, 436
4:3	432, 850
4:5	432
4:18	432

Colossians

1:3–27	409
1:6	411
1:9–10	411
1:10	411
1:12–14	411
1:13	409, 411
1:14	408
1:15	411
1:15–17	411, 587
1:15–18	713, 715
1:15–20	411, 711–12, 733
1:18	407
1:23–33	119
1:24–25	407
1:26–27	411, 712
2:2–3	411
2:3	411, 712
2:9–14	409
2:11	411
2:12–14	407
2:13	408, 411
2:15	409
2:15–18	530
2:22	411–13
3:1	411–12, 414, 416–17, 423
3:1–3	407
3:5–12	409
3:6–11	413
3:9–10	411–12
3:10	409, 411, 413, 415
3:12	411
3:16	409, 827
3:18–19	409, 422
3:18–41	407
3:20–21	423
4:1	411
4:5	411, 712
4:7–8	408

1 Thessalonians

1:1	449
1:4	449
1:5–6	450
1:9	444, 451, 680
1:10	450
2	444
2:1–12	444
2:4	442, 444
2:12	449
2:13–16	444
2:16	442, 444
3:5	442
3:13	442, 444, 450, 532
4	441, 445
4:1–8	451

Index of Scripture and Other Ancient Sources

4:3–4	449	2:14	457, 917	1:1–3	713
4:3–7	680	2:15	456, 458, 917	1:1–6:20	470
4:5	442, 445	3:4	407	1:3	680, 852
4:6	443	3:15	407	1:5	155–56, 470, 476, 482, 729, 832, 847
4:7	449	4:3	457		
4:8	443, 450, 634	4:3–4	453, 458, 463	1:5–13	146
4:9	443	4:4	587	1:6	470, 476, 482, 777, 787–88, 821, 832, 851
4:13	445	4:7	129		
4:13–15	743	4:13	455	1:7	98, 470, 476, 482, 484, 832, 851
4:17	443, 445, 450	5:3–16	461		
5	450–51	5:17	460–61	1:8–9	470, 476, 482, 832, 849
5:1–11	743	5:18	454–55, 460, 463, 776		
5:2	556, 743	5:19	461	1:10–12	471, 476, 482, 832, 851
5:4	556	5:23	458		
5:4–8	450			1:12	98
5:8	424–25, 443, 446	**2 Timothy**		1:13	471, 476, 482, 832, 851
5:11	357	2:2	464		
5:23	443, 450	2:8	883, 909	2	483
5:24	449	2:17–18	462	2:2	479, 484
5:26	450	2:19	454–55, 461–63, 534	2:3	485
		2:24–25	464	2:5	486
2 Thessalonians		3:1–5	459	2:6–8	471, 476, 482, 831, 847
1	448	3:8–9	454–55, 459, 462–63		
1:6	446, 448	3:13	462	2:7	486
1:7	532	3:15	341, 829	2:10	485
1:8	445–46, 448	3:15–17	462–64	2:11	680
1:9	446, 448	3:16	453, 454	2:12	832, 848, 981
1:9–10	450	4:16–18	871	2:12–13	155, 471, 476, 482
1:10	447–48			2:14	680
1:12	447	**Titus**		2:17	486, 680
2	441, 449	1:9	464	3–4	181–83, 484, 487
2:2	450	1:14	129	3–6	473
2:4	447, 449	2:2–10	407	3:1	680
2:8	447	2:14	252	3:1–6	182–83, 482–83
2:13	447, 449, 635	3:9	464	3:5	182, 471, 482
3:13	450			3:7	833
3:16	448–49	**Philemon**		3:7–11	471, 476, 481, 833, 851
		4	731	3:7–4:7	833
1 Timothy		5	430, 438	3:7–4:10	153–54
1:4	129	7	438	3:7–4:13	181
1:7	464			3:11	182–83
2:8–15	917	**Hebrews**		3:12	482, 484
2:11–12	456–57	1	98, 486	3:12–4:10	150
2:13	915	1–2	485	3:13	485, 982
2:13–14	453–54, 456, 458–59, 463	1–6	473	3:15	471, 477
		1:1–2	149, 486, 587	4:3	183, 471, 477, 832, 851
				4:4	471, 477, 487, 831, 982

4:5	471, 477	8:6–13	142	10:19–13:25	470
4:7	471, 477, 831–32	8:7	485	10:22	183
4:12	565	8:7–13	647, 665	10:26–31	487, 820
4:12–13	485	8:7–10:10	156	10:28	481, 776–77
4:14	183	8:8–12	471, 477, 479–80	10:30	97, 356, 472, 477, 481, 777, 787, 820–21, 852
4:14–16	680	8:12	480		
4:14–5:10	492	8:13	154, 485	10:37	472, 481
4:14–6:12	492	9	88, 666	10:37–39	156
4:16	183, 480, 486	9–10	183	10:38	342, 400, 472, 478, 481
5:1–10	680	9:1	485		
5:5	471, 477, 482, 492, 729, 847	9:1–10:17	487	11	9, 891, 903, 920, 923
		9:5	345	11:4	549
5:6	471, 477, 482, 492–93, 852	9:7	486	11:4–38	152–53
		9:11	602	11:4–39	901
5:7–10	484	9:11–14	680	11:4–40	883
5:10	852	9:12	252	11:10	584
5:11–6:12	492	9:13–14	635	11:11	918
6:4–8	487	9:15	485–86	11:13	849
6:5	479	9:15–22	665, 647	11:17	897–98, 900
6:6	484	9:15–10:18	485	11:18	472, 477, 482
6:13–18	484	9:18	485	11:21	472
6:14	471, 477, 482	9:18–22	484	11:22	891
6:19–20	484, 486	9:19	479, 666–67	11:23	903
6:20	852	9:20	471, 477, 480, 666	11:25	908
7	183, 488, 493–95, 901	9:22	666–67, 680	11:25–26	897, 908
7:1–3	471, 482, 492	9:23	486	11:31	514, 920–21
7:1–10	898, 901	9:24	528	11:32	910
7:1–21	173	9:25	486	11:32–34	910
7:1–10:18	470, 492	9:25–28	680	11:33	870
7:4	471, 482	9:26	901	12	777
7:11	852	9:28	484, 747	12:2	306
7:15	612	10:1	675	12:4–11	486
7:15–16	605, 611	10:1–13	680	12:5	710
7:15–22	142	10:5	98, 183	12:5–6	472, 477, 481
7:17	471, 477, 482, 852	10:5–7	472, 477, 482, 833, 849	12:15	472, 481, 776, 788
7:21	471, 477, 482, 852			12:15–17	153
7:21–28	687	10:5–10	147	12:18–21	481, 484
7:25	496	10:7	479	12:21	472, 477, 480, 484, 777
7:26–28	680	10:11–12	680		
8:1	852	10:11–18	665, 667	12:22–29	487
8:1–2	486	10:12	852	12:26	472, 477, 481
8:1–6	665	10:16	486, 667	12:29	472, 481, 776–77, 788
8:1–10:18	664, 667	10:16–17	472, 477, 480	13	481, 786
8:2	665	10:17–18	667	13:2	786
8:5	471, 477, 480, 484	10:19–22	680	13:5	472, 477, 482, 777, 786
8:6	664–65, 680	10:19–23	486	13:6	472, 477, 482, 852
8:6–12	486	10:19–39	484	13:7–8	483

Index of Scripture and Other Ancient Sources

13:7–17	486	5:3	516–17, 708	2:11	502, 525, 849		
13:9–16	486	5:7	516, 518	2:12	525–26, 615		
13:10–12	786	5:7–11	153	2:17	526		
13:11–12	680	5:7–20	509	2:18	525		
13:17	483	5:8–9	708	2:20	525		
13:22	469, 485	5:10	512–13, 516–17	2:21	528		
		5:11	433, 502, 513	2:21–23	358		
James		5:12	687	2:21–25	239, 528		
1:1	503, 509, 511	5:13	827	2:22	525–26, 810		
1:2–27	509	5:13–18	153	2:22–25	747, 810		
1:5	709	5:16	912	2:24	525–26, 810, 980		
1:10–11	506, 515, 517, 708	5:17	512	2:25	525, 527, 810		
1:12	708	5:17–18	507, 513, 911	3:1–6	919		
1:19	708	5:20	708–9	3:5–6	527		
1:21	708			3:6	526, 918–19		
1:22	708	**1 Peter**		3:10–12	525, 527, 849		
1:25	510	1:1	524, 808	3:14–15	525, 527		
1:27	515, 517–18, 708	1:2	526, 635	3:19	115, 117		
2:1	503, 511	1:4	528	3:20	1042		
2:1–3:12	509–10	1:6	525	3:20–21	527		
2:5	506	1:6–7	528	3:22	616, 845, 852		
2:8	398, 500–503, 509, 519, 676	1:7	525–26, 602	4:3	615		
		1:10	526–27	4:7	149, 745		
2:8–11	510	1:11	527	4:8	525, 527		
2:10	511	1:13	524–26	4:12	745		
2:11	500, 519, 776	1:14	808	4:12–14	525		
2:14–26	513	1:16	525–26	4:13	745		
2:18–26	153	1:18	252, 525–26	4:14	525, 527		
2:19	711	1:23	528	4:17	745		
2:21	511, 897–98, 900	1:24	525, 528	4:18	525, 527, 709, 745–46		
2:21–24	509	1:24–25	525	4:19	587		
2:21–26	514, 898, 900	1:25	525	5:1	525		
2:23	500, 502–3, 509, 519, 921, 982	2:2	528	5:5	510, 519, 525, 527		
		2:3	525, 834, 849	5:7	525, 527, 850		
2:25	512, 920–21	2:4	525, 852	5:8	525, 527, 848		
3:8	708	2:4–6	156	5:13	523, 525		
3:13–5:6	509	2:4–8	525				
3:14	708	2:4–10	529	**2 Peter**			
4:4	510, 515, 518	2:5	529, 804	1:11	602		
4:5	500, 502, 510	2:6	525, 615, 803, 981	1:12–15	536		
4:6	500, 502, 509, 519, 708–9	2:6–8	155, 252–53, 525–26, 808	1:19	537		
				1:19–21	538		
4:10	708	2:7	852	1:20–21	623		
4:11	708	2:7–8	59, 803	2	537		
4:14	708	2:8	615, 803	2:1–3:4	524		
5	920	2:9	525, 735, 808	2:4	537		
5:1–6	506, 518	2:9–10	87, 526	2:4–7	538		

2:4-10	537, 539	3:17	546	1:7	97, 558, 561, 567, 573
2:5	538-39, 1042	3:23	676	1:8	92, 559
2:6	538-39	4:1-2	553	1:9	560
2:7	538-39	4:2	547	1:9-20	565
2:8	539	4:6	552	1:10	556
2:9	539	4:10	546, 550	1:11	559
2:10	539	4:21	775	1:12	556
2:11	539	5:2	775	1:12-20	564
2:14-16	570	5:2-3	676	1:13	567
2:15-16	534, 538-39	5:3	546	1:13-14	97, 567, 613
2:22	537-38	5:7	546	1:14	565
3:3	536, 746	5:21	546, 552-53	1:15	559-60, 572
3:4	536, 746			1:16	565, 809
3:5	537, 586	**2 John**		1:17	559, 567
3:5-7	540, 746	6	676	1:18	564
3:6	537-38	7	547	1:19	566-67, 573
3:8	537-38, 746, 850	12	546	1:20	563
3:9	537-38, 541			2-3	556
3:10	450	**Jude**		2:1	559, 563
3:13	537-38, 812	1	506, 529	2:1-22:5	149
3:13-14	537-38	3-18	524	2:4	556
3:15-16	536	4	530	2:7	558
3:17	537-38	5	529, 531	2:8	563
3:20	539	5-7	530	2:10	567
		6	529, 531	2:12	563, 565, 573
1 John		7	531	2:14	534-35, 570
1:1	544, 553	8	530	2:16	565
1:3	547	9	116, 531, 535, 903	2:17	812
1:5	715	10	530	2:18	560, 563
1:6-7	552	10-11	548	2:20	563, 570
1:7	545, 551	11	530-31, 534-35, 570, 922	2:23	97, 845, 850
1:8	545	12	529-30	2:25	604, 611
1:8-10	739	12-13	521, 535	2:26-27	560-61, 847
1:9	545	14	531-32, 923	2:27	560
2:2	545, 550-51	14-15	35, 115, 142, 165, 530	3:1	563
2:7-11	676	16	530	3:3	556
2:9-10	545	18	529	3:5	850
2:11	552			3:7	563, 572, 910
2:17	545	**Revelation**		3:10	556
2:18	545, 551, 553	1	568, 613	3:14	563, 812
2:19	547	1:1	566-67, 573, 892	3:18	528
2:23	547	1:2	556	4-5	567-68
3	548	1:3	149, 556, 563, 569	4:1	556, 566, 573
3:5	545	1:4	583, 735	4:1-8	736
3:12	534, 544-55, 548-50, 922	1:5	560, 569, 737	4:1-11	155
3:14	545	1:6	560, 572	4:5	570
				4:7	564

Index of Scripture and Other Ancient Sources

4:8	561, 572, 802	11:8	571	16:7	567		
4:9	573, 736	11:11	560, 567	16:9	561		
4:11	557, 567, 573, 587	11:15	560	16:15	556		
5	568, 616	11:17	572	16:16	571		
5:1–2	556	11:17–18	557	16:18	570		
5:5	558, 565, 616, 804, 883, 910	11:18	560	17	568, 872		
		11:18–19	668–69	17:1–2	805		
5:6	556, 565, 569, 873	11:19	570, 647, 668	17:1–22:25	570		
5:8	736	12	872	17:2	805		
5:8–10	827	12:1–6	556	17:4	873		
5:9	736–37	12:1–17	668	17:9–10	563, 872		
5:9–10	557	12:3	567, 871	17:12	561, 563, 567		
5:11	567	12:5	560, 847	17:15	737		
5:13	556	12:6	558, 567, 569	17:16	872		
6	568	12:9	558, 873	18	558, 568, 570		
6:1	569	12:10	556, 561	18:1	560–61, 572		
6:1–17	556	12:12	787	18:1–8	738		
6:8	561	12:13	569	18:2	805		
6:10	787	12:14	558, 567	18:2–3	807		
6:12–17	966–67	12:17	558, 570	18:3	805		
6:16	561	13	873	18:4	566, 570		
6:17	966–67	13:1	11, 871–72	18:9–24	738		
7–8	568	13:1–10	567	18:19	560		
7:8	891	13:2	561, 871–72	18:21	560, 872		
7:9	373	13:4	873	19	804		
7:13	559	13:5	567, 872	19–20	568		
7:14	558, 560	13:7	737, 872	19:2	567, 787		
7:17	805–6, 812, 848	13:11–18	568	19:3	807		
8–9	570	13:12	873	19:9	559		
8:1	573	13:15	567, 873	19:11	572, 804		
8:3	556	13:18	873	19:11–16	565, 573		
8:5	570	14:3	736	19:13	566		
9:1–11	569	14:6	737	19:15	560, 565, 804, 809, 847		
9:3	561, 573	14:6–7	669				
9:11	571	14:10	850	19:17–21	568		
9:14	558–59	14:11	567, 807	19:21	565, 804		
9:19	561	14:14	567	20:4	573		
10	561, 568	14:18	561	20:4–6	560		
10:4	559, 573	15	737	20:6	561		
10:6	567–68, 853	15:2–4	558, 569	20:11	573		
10:8–11	556	15:3	559, 777, 787	21–22	558, 568, 573		
10:10	560	15:3–4	91, 560–61, 565	21:1	540, 812		
10:11	563	15:4	562, 669, 850	21:1–5	569		
11:5	602	16	570	21:2	574		
11:5–6	571	16:1–21	558	21:4	806, 812		
11:6	561	16:4–7	738	21:7	567		
11:7	567	16:5	572	21:16	568–69		

21:22	568	b. Soṭah		Lamentations Rabbah	
21:24–26	569	9:15	603	24	193
22:1–2	558, 569, 745	22a	689		
22:2	572	48b	32	Mekilta	
22:6	566–67			31:13	681
22:7	556, 563	m. 'Abot			
22:9	556, 563	1:1	687, 689	Numbers Rabbah	
22:10	556	2:5	689	22:5	534
22:14	561	3:11	391		
22:16	804	5:10	689	Pirque Rabbi Eliezer	
22:17	941	5:19	535	21	550
22:18–19	556	6:7	394		

Rabbinic Works

		m. Giṭṭin		Sipre Numbers	
		9:10	686	157	534
b. Baba Batra					
14b	28	m. Makkot		Tanḥuma Vayera	
		1:10	689	23	193
b. Baba Meṣi'a				42	193
59	688	m. Qiddušin			
		4:14	391	Targum Isaiah	
b. Baba Qamma				54:1	397
38a	394	m. Sanhedrin			
		10:2	535	Targum of the Prophets	
b. Berakot				*Micah*	
1.1	687	m. Soṭah		5:1	605
47	689	9:15	603–4, 612, 634	5:3	605
b. Makkot		m. Tamid		Yalqut Rubeni	
24a	400	1:1–4	821	43:3	536
		3:2–5	821		
b. Megillah		5:1	770	## Early Christian Writings	
14–15	920	6–7	823		
		7:4	822		
b. Pesaḥ					
116b	829	m. Yadayim		Acts of Peter	
117a	317	3:5	30–31	24	852
b. Šabbat		y. Berakot		Adamantius	
31a	398, 676	9:5	694	*Dialogue*	
b. Sanhedrin		y. Soṭah		1.10	1004
38b	607	3:4	694	1.15	1004
59a	394			1.16	1004
98b	606	y. Sukkah		1.17	1003
106a	534	55b	168		

Index of Scripture and Other Ancient Sources

Ambrose

De Abraham
1.8	1039

De mysteriis
3.10–11	1042

De paradiso
5.28	1006
8.38	1006

De sacramentis
1.23	1042
2.1	1042

Apostolic Constitutions
2.17	955
7.35	1037
7.35.7	863

Aristides

Apologia
14–15	955

Athanasius

De decritis
18.3	25, 28

Augustine

De cathechizandis rudibus
20.32	1042
20.34	1042

De civitate Dei
16.32	1039
18.42–44	82

Enarrationes in Psalmos
106.3	1039

Epistulae
55.13.23	1042

Sermon 289
1–3	656

Basil of Caesarea

De baptismo
1	1039

De Spiritu Sancto
14.32	1048

1 Clement
4:12	535
11:9	539
12:1–8	514
13:1	369
16:5–6	848
18	850
22:1–8	849
30:2	519
34:3	850
34:8	365
36:3	851
36:4	847
36:5	852
41:7	534
50:6	849
51:3–4	534
51:4	535
53:1	829
54:3	848

2 Clement
11:7	365
14:5	365

Clement of Alexandria

Stromata
1.15.4	169
1.44.3	1
2.39.1	1002
3.12.1	1002
3.71.3	1
4.134.4	1
5	1042

Cyprian

De catholicae ecclesiae unitate
6	1042

De lapsis
19	1044

De opere et eleemosynis
4	955

Epistulae
61.2.1	1044
67.2	1042
69.15.1–2	1039
73	1042
75	1042

Oratorio ad Graecos
2	1037

Cyril of Jerusalem

Mystagogic Catecheses
1.1–2	1039

De Duobus montibus Sina et Sion
1.1	992
1.2	992
2.1	991
2.2	991
3.1	991
3.2	991
3.3	991
4.1	991–92
4.3	992
6.1	991
6.2	991–92
7.1	991–92
7.2	992
8.3	992
9.1	991
9.2	992
9.3–5	991
9.5	992
9.6	991–92
10.1	992
11.1	991
14.2	992
15.2	992

Didache
1:2	398, 780

3:7	849	4.3	980	11.10	982		
12:1	852	4.4	980	12.1	982		
		4.5	980	12.2	982		
Epiphanius of Salamis		4.7	980	12.4	983		
		4.8	980	12.10	852		
Panarion		4.11	980	12.11	982		
30.13.2–3	944	4.14	980	13.2	982		
30.13.4–5	942	5.2	980	13.4	982		
30.13.7	943	5.4	980	13.6	982		
30.14.3	943	5.5	981	13.7	982		
30.16.5	943	5.12	981	14.2	982		
30.16.6	943	5.13	981	14.3	982		
30.22.4–5	943	5.14–6.2	981	14.7	982		
33.1.1	1010	6.2–3	981	14.8	982		
33.3–7	1009	6.3	981	14.9	982		
33.3.2	1010	6.4	852, 981	15.1	982		
33.4.1	1012	6.6	848, 981	15.2	982		
33.4.2	1012	6.7	981	15.3	982		
33.4.3	1016	6.8	981	15.3–4	541		
33.4.4	1016	6.12	981	15.8	982		
33.4.11	1016	6.13	981, 988	16.2	982		
33.4.12	1016	6.14	981	16.3	982		
33.4.14	1016	6.16	848, 981	16.5	982		
33.5.1–2	1012	7.3	981	16.6	980, 982		
33.5.3	1016	7.3–5	936	16.10	980		
33.5.4	1016–17	7.4	981				
33.5.5	1017	7.6–7	981	**Epistle to Diognetus**			
33.5.7	1017	7.8	981	3:4	853		
33.5.8–9	1017	8.3	944				
33.5.10–13	1017	9.1	981	**Eusebius**			
33.7.2	1012	9.2	849, 981				
33.7.3–5	1012	9.3	981	*Demonstratio evangelica*			
33.7.8–9	1010	9.5	981	6.14	97		
42.1.4–6	1006	9.8	981				
42.2.3	1006	10.1	981	*Historia ecclesiastica*			
42.9.1	1005	10.2	981	2.1.13	328		
42.9.2	1004	10.4–7	981	4.18.6	984		
42.11.4–5	1005	10.10	981	4.26	100		
42.11.6	1005	10.11	982	4.26.13–14	1		
44.1.6	1006	11.2	982	5.13	1005		
44.2.6	1008	11.3	982	5.13.1–2	1006		
		11.4	982	6.12.1–6	934		
Epistle of Barnabas		11.4–5	982				
2.7	980	11.5–6	982	*Praeparatio evangelica*			
2.8	980	11.6–7	980	9.19.4	888		
2.10	980	11.9	982	9.34.11	93		
3.1–5	980			13.12.1	86, 100		

Index of Scripture and Other Ancient Sources

Gospel of Peter

5	934–36
6	935
9	935
15	934–36
17	936
18	936
25	936
45	935
46	935
48	935

Gospel of the Hebrews

Frag. 2	847

Gospel of Thomas

17	365

Hippolytus of Rome

Commentary on Daniel

10.16	1044

Ignatius

To the Ephesians

5.3	519

To the Smyrnaeans

7.2	955

To the Trallians

9–10	547

Irenaeus

Adversus haereses

1.1–9	1010
1.14.8	847
1.19.1	848
1.26.1	547
2.20.3	850
2.28.8	852
3.6.1	849, 852
3.6.2	850
3.9.2	852
3.10.5	852
3.12.1	850, 852
3.12.12	1001
3.16.2	852
3.16.3	852
3.19.1	850
3.19.2	936
3.20	985
3.21.2	82
3.25.3	1001
3.33.12	848
4.3.1	851
4.5.4	1039
4.9.3	847
4.17.1	849
4.17.3	849
4.21.3	847
4.22	985
4.28.1	849
4.33.11	849, 852
4.33.12	847, 850
4.36.2	849
4.36.6	848
4.38	850
5.5.2	1048
5.17.3	849
5.21.2	851
5.23.2	541

Demonstration of the Apostolic Preaching

78	985

Jerome

Ad Galatas

2.3.13–14	988

Adversus Joannem Hierosolymitanum liber

34	1005

Adversus Pelagionos dialogi III

3.6	1007

De viris illustribus

1	523

Epistulae

106.2.2	98

Questionum hebraicarum liber in Genesim

1:1	988

John Cassian

Collationes

12	625

John Chrysostom

De Lazaro

6.7	1042

Justin Martyr

1 Apology

17.64	938
26.5	1001
35	848
38	848
40	847–48, 1044
45	852
53.5	986
53.7	986

2 Apology

1–2	1009

Dialogue with Trypho

1.1	984
10.3	984
10.3–4	391
11.5	986
17.2	986
20.1	986
23.4	986
27.3	343, 848, 850, 986
32.2	986
32.5	986
32.6	852
33.1–2	852
36.3	848
36.3–4	986
38.3–5	849
39.1	986
39.4	986
42.1	848, 852, 986

42.2	986	**Optatus of Milevis**		10:1	946	
44	1012	*Against Parmenian*		11:2–3	917	
55.3	986	3.2.1	1025	13:1	946	
56.14	852			13:1–16:3	919	
63.3	852			14:1	947	
64.8	848	**Origen**		15:2	946	
68.5	852	*Against Celsus*		16:2	917, 946	
71–73	984	1.49	40	19:1–20:4	917	
78.11	986	1.69	919	20:2	946	
81.3	850	4.52	987	21:2	947	
81.8	541	5.54	1008	22:1	947	
83.2	852			22:2	947	
87.6	850, 986	*Commentarium in evangelium Matthaei*		23:3	946	
88.8	847, 943			24:1–2	946	
92.3	986	10.17	934			
95–96	985	*De principiis (Peri archōn)*		**Pseudo-Gregory**		
95.1	986	2.5.4	1002	*Testimonies against the Jews*		
96.1	986	*Homilies on Genesis*		12	955	
97.3	848	2.2	1007			
98	848					
99.1	848			**Pseudo-Hippolytus**		
101.1–3	848	**Paulinus of Nola**		*Refutatio omnium haeresium (Philosophoumena)*		
102.1	848	*Carmina*				
103.1	848	27.511–542	1049	6.35.6	1010	
103.6	847			7.31.5	1005	
105.5	848	**Polycarp**		7.34.2	942	
107	1048	*Epistle to the Philippians*		7.38.2	1007, 1015	
113.5	852			10.15	1002	
114.2	986	12:1	829, 847	10.20.2	1007	
118.1	852					
118.4	986	**Protoevangelium of James**		**Pseudo-Justin**		
119.2	986	1:2	946	*Cohortatio ad Graecos*		
119.4	986	1:4	945, 947	37.2–3	625	
119.5–6	986	2:2	946			
122.6	847	2:3	947	**Pseudo-Tertullian**		
123.4	986	2:4	945	*Adversus omnes haereses*		
124.2	850	3	947			
127.5	852	4:2	917	6	1002	
130.1	986	4:4	917, 947	6.6	1007	
130.4	986	5:1	946			
138.2–3	1042	6–8	946	**Shepherd of Hermas**		
140.3	986	6:1–3	946	8	955	
141.2	849, 986	6:3	947			
		7	946	**Syriac Didascalia Apostolorum**		
Melito		7:1–2	945–46			
Peri pascha		9:2	535, 945			
62	847	9:3	947	19	936	

Index of Scripture and Other Ancient Sources

Tatian

Oratio ad Graecos
15	847

Tertullian

Adversus Judaeos
1.1	989
1.7	990
2.2	991
2.9	990
3.1	991
3.2	990
3.7	990
3.13	990
4.11	990
5.6	990
6.1	990
7.1	989, 991
8.3–16	989
10.6	1039
11.1	989, 991
13.20–22	1039

Adversus Marcionem
1.1.2	1002
1.1.5	1004
1.2.2	1002
1.6.4	1002
1.11.9	1002
1.19.4	1003
2.2.3	1002
2.14.1	1002
2.18–19	955
4.1.1	1
4.2–6	1004
4.4.4	1004
4.5.6	1015
4.7.11	1005
4.16.2	1004
4.22.11	1014
4.23.4	1004
4.24.1	1004
4.36.9	1013
4.38.10	1013
5.18.10	1002

Adversus omnes haereses
6.6	1006

Adversus Praxean
15.1	1
31.1	1

De baptismo
1	1025
8.4	1042
9.1	1039

De carne Christi
6.3	1006
7.1	1015
8.2	1006

De idololatria
15.10	1044
24	1042

De patientia
5.15	550

De praescriptione haereticorum
30.6	1006
34.4	1006

De resurrectione carnis
58	1048

Theophilus of Antioch

Apologia ad Autolycum
3.9–12	961

Visions of Paul
3.7	971
4–6	971
7	971
14.16	971
16	971
20	971
22.1–23.31	972
44	972
45	972
48–49	972

GRECO-ROMAN LITERATURE

Aelius Aristides

In Defense of the Oratory
43	625

Aeschylus

Prometheus vinctus
480	601

Apollodorus

Bibliotheca
3.5.1–2	318

Aristotle

Politica
1.3.1	407

Artapanus of Alexandria
3:18	894
3:34–37	905

Chrysippus

On Mixture
216.14–17	630

Diodorus Siculus

Bibliotheca historica
2.1–34	868
13.2–3	318

Euripides

Hippolytus
516	601

Herodotus

Histories
1.95	868
1.130	868
4.205	318

INDEX OF SCRIPTURE AND OTHER ANCIENT SOURCES

Homer

Iliad

2.784	169

Lucian

Alexander (Pseudomantis)

59	318

Pausanias

9.36.2–3	318

Polybius

The Histories

1.1.4	171

Plato

Apologia

22C	625

Plutarch

De liberis educandis

10	407

Sulla

36.2	318

Pseudo-Longinus

On the Sublime

9.9	389

Seneca

Epistulae morales

94.1	407